PRAISE FOR THE INVISIBLE BRIDGE

New York Times Book Review 100 Notable Books of 2014
NPR.org Best Books of 2014
Los Angeles Times Best Books of 2014
San Francisco Chronicle 100 Recommended Books: The Best of 2014
Kansas City Star 100 Best Books of 2014
Publishers Weekly Favorite Books We Read in 2014
WashingtonPost.com Best Political Books of 2014

"A Rosetta stone for reading America and its politics today . . . A book that is both enjoyable as kaleidoscopic popular history and telling about our own historical moment . . . Epic work."
—*The New York Times Book Review*

"It takes something like a miracle worker to synthesize history—especially recent history—in a way that's coherent, intelligent and compelling. . . . That's what [Perlstein] does in *The Invisible Bridge*, his best work yet. He's written something like a national biography, a deep exploration of both the politics and the culture of the late 20th century. Somehow, you don't want it to end. As a single volume, it's one of the most remarkable literary achievements of the year. As the third book in a series, it makes clear that Perlstein, like Robert A. Caro and H. W. Brands, is one of the most impressive, accomplished writers of history in the country."
—NPR.org

"Rick Perlstein has established himself as one of our foremost chroniclers of the modern conservative movement. . . . Much of *The Invisible Bridge* is not about politics per se but about American society in all its weird, amusing, and disturbing permutations. He seems to have read every word of every newspaper and magazine published in the 1970s and has mined them for delightful anecdotes. . . . It would be hard to top it for entertainment value."
—*The Wall Street Journal*

"Enthralling, entertaining . . . oddly charming and ultimately irresistible."
—*The Boston Globe*

"For Americans younger than fifty-five, the story of conservatism has been the dominant political factor in their lives, and Rick Perlstein has become its chief chronicler, across three erudite, entertaining, and increasingly meaty books. . . . *The Invisible Bridge: The Fall of Nixon and the Rise of Reagan* . . . finally brings into focus the saga's leading character, Ronald Reagan. . . . What gives *The Invisible Bridge* its originality is the way Perlstein embeds Reagan's familiar biography in the disillusionments of the seventies."
—*The New Yorker*

"*The Invisible Bridge* is a magnificent and nuanced work because of Perlstein's mastery of context, his ability to highlight not just the major players but more important, a broader sense of national narrative."

—*Los Angeles Times*

"Engrossing . . . Invaluable to readers aching to find answers to why the country is so deeply polarized today."

—*The New York Times*

"A mixture of scholarly precision, outrage and wry humor."

—*Pittsburgh Post-Gazette*

"This is gripping material. . . . Perlstein's gift lies in illustrating broad political trends through surprising snapshots of American culture and media."

—*Chicago Reader*

"Rick Perlstein is becoming an American institution . . . a superb researcher and writer."

—*The New Republic*

"[A] magisterial survey of America during the mid-1970s . . . In many ways, *The Invisible Bridge* is Perlstein's biggest accomplishment. . . . Through the accumulation of divergent storylines, a knack for finding telling anecdotes, and a frenzied pace that magnetizes Perlstein's writing, he manages to create a vivid portrayal of this turbulent epoch. . . . Perlstein's true genius lies in his ability to dig out, synthesize, and convey a jagged, multi-layered episode of history in a compelling prose. . . . Perlstein has again delivered a superb portrayal of American conservatism, crowning him as one of the leading popular historians of our time."

—*Forbes.com*

"Perlstein has an eye for telling detail, understands the potency of American regionalism, and is shrewd about electoral technique and rhetoric. He vividly captures personalities, and his biographical chapter on Reagan is an especially masterful distillation. He is empathetic in entering into his subjects' perspectives, gifted at recounting the sheer bizarreness of history's twists and turns."

—*Financial Times*

"Invaluable . . . Perlstein is among the best young historians working today. . . . His rich, deeply knowledgeable books . . . tell us almost as much about 21st century developments like the birth of the Tea Party and the current Congress' intractable gridlock as they do about the politics of the 1960s and '70s."

—*San Francisco Chronicle*

"Perlstein ranges far beyond political history, in his case touching on just about everything interesting that happened in the United States between 1973 and 1976. . . . The narrative bounces entertainingly and revealingly from high policy to low humor."

— *The Washington Post*

"This is an ambitious, wide-ranging, and superbly written account filled with wonderful insights into key players. . . . Perlstein views the rise of Reagan, with his celebration of America's 'special destiny' and moral superiority, as a rejection of a more honest and practical view of our role in the world after the traumas of Vietnam and Watergate. This is a masterful interpretation of years critical to the formation of our current political culture."

— *Booklist* (starred review)

"To call this book rich in anecdotes is an understatement. Perlstein adopts a you-are-there narrative that gives the reader a sense of what average Americans took in during the turbulent period from Watergate to the 1976 elections. . . . The mini-biography of Reagan nestled in the pages is a page-turner, as is Perlstein's climactic account of the nail-biter presidential nominating convention in 1976."

— Associated Press

"He tells a great tale, in every sense. . . . It says a lot about the quality of Rick Perlstein's material and storytelling that more than 700 pages into his latest cinder block of ink and tree, I could still keenly relish yet another tasty fact, another aside. . . . Also extraordinary is the writer's herculean research and the many relevant or just colorful items he uses to fill in the edges and corners and form the frame of this sprawling portrait. . . . There's much to enjoy here."

— *Newsday*

"Full of the tragic, the infuriating, and the darkly funny . . . Outstanding work."

— *Publishers Weekly* (starred review)

"Sweeping, insightful and richly rewarding. . . . His riveting narrative continues the author's efforts to chronicle the ascendancy of conservatism in American political life. . . . This is a fascinating, extremely readable account of an important decade in America's political history."

— *BookPage*

"A compelling, astute chronicle of the politics and culture of late-20th-century America . . . Perlstein once again delivers a terrific hybrid biography of a Republican leader and the culture he shaped. . . . Perlstein examines the skeletons in the Reagan, Ford and Carter closets, finds remarkable overlooked details and perfectly captures the dead-heat drama of the Republican convention. Just as deftly, he taps into the consciousness of bicentennial America. He sees this world with fresh eyes."

— *Kirkus Reviews* (starred review)

"This is certainly one of the most thorough political investigations of this time frame and an important read for scholars of this period. Recommended."

—*Library Journal*

"A rip-roaring chronicle . . . An exhaustive and kaleidoscopic picture of what it felt like to be an American from early 1973 when the prisoners of war began coming home from Vietnam to Ronald Reagan's failed effort to capture the Republican presidential nomination in August 1976."

—*The American Prospect*

"A volume on the Reagan presidency surely beckons. If it is as crammed with historical gems as this one, readers will be well served."

—*The Economist*

"The author of *Nixonland* is certain to generate new debates among conservatives and liberals about Reagan's legacy."

—*USA Today*

"Perlstein knows so very much about American politics, some of it profoundly evocative of lost worlds and pregnant with understanding of our own. . . . What places Perlstein among the indispensable historians of our time is his empathy, his ability to see that the roles of hero and goat, underdog and favorite, oppressor and oppressed are not permanently conferred. . . . It requires such an empathy to reimagine the mid-'70s as a time, rather like our own, when almost nobody looking at the surface of day-to-day life was able to take the full measure of the resentment boiling just underneath it."

—*Bookforum*

"The twists and turns along the way are more than worth the ride by anyone interested in high-level politics and intrigue as well as those with a bent toward the cultural side of the dreary—and violent—seventies. And let's face it: anyone who can keep a reader's attention in a tome that covers only three years (1973 to 1976) in over 800 pages deserves some kudos."

—*Origins*

"Witty look at the high-voltage politics and culture of the early '70s."

—*The Kansas City Star*

"*The Invisible Bridge* is even more compulsively readable than the previous two volumes in the series."

—*Washington Monthly*

"A painstakingly crafted illustration of the political landscape that made the improbable inevitable."

—*Entertainment Weekly*

"One of America's greatest chroniclers of the origins of the modern American right wing."

"Perlstein's energetic style and omnivorous curiosity about his subject make him a winning narrator. . . . Perlstein deftly captures the wellspring of Reagan's nature."

"A fascinating look at how the GOP was transformed in the Ford and Rockefeller years into the party it is today."

"Perlstein's achievement, both in this volume and the series as a whole, is impressive. The research is prodigious, the prose vivid, and one can only imagine what his treatment of Reagan's presidency will bring. . . . Perlstein covers a great deal of ground masterfully."

"A lovely book that I paged through hungrily."

"Rick Perlstein skillfully recounts the era that was shaped by the scandal and the way in which the sordid activities of the Nixon administration unfolded on a day-by-day basis."

"Perlstein has an unmatched ability to convey the sense of an era. Even readers who didn't live through 1970s America will feel as if they did after reading this book."

"Perlstein's narrative gift allows him to take Reagan's seeming simplicity and dissect the layers of complexity that went into crafting it."

"Magisterial."

"Magnificent . . . An extraordinary book, massive in scope and detail, and essential to a complete understanding of our nation's politics. There are two contemporary historians who must be read by anyone hoping to understand American politics. One is Robert Caro, and the other is Rick Perlstein."

ALSO BY RICK PERLSTEIN

Before the Storm:
Barry Goldwater and the Unmaking of the American Consensus

Nixonland:
The Rise of a President and the Fracturing of America

THE
INVISIBLE BRIDGE

THE FALL
OF NIXON
AND
THE RISE
OF REAGAN

RICK PERLSTEIN

SIMON & SCHUSTER PAPERBACKS

NEW YORK LONDON TORONTO SYDNEY NEW DELHI

To the memory of my father, Jerry Perlstein

Simon & Schuster Paperbacks
An Imprint of Simon & Schuster, Inc.
1230 Avenue of the Americas
New York, NY 10020

First Simon & Schuster trade paperback edition August 2015

SIMON & SCHUSTER PAPERBACKS and colophon are registered trademarks
of Simon & Schuster, Inc.

For information about special discounts for bulk purchases,
please contact Simon & Schuster Special Sales at
1-866-506-1949 or business@simonandschuster.com.

The Simon & Schuster Speakers Bureau can bring authors to
your live event. For more information or to book an event,
contact the Simon & Schuster Speakers Bureau at 1-866-248-3049
or visit our website at www.simonspeakers.com.

Manufactured in the United States of America

10 9 8 7 6 5 4 3 2 1

Library of Congress Control Number: 2014381509

ISBN 978-1-4767-8241-6
ISBN 978-1-4767-8242-3 (pbk)
ISBN 978-1-4767-8243-0 (ebook)

If the people believe there's an imaginary river out there,
you don't tell them there's no river there.
You build an imaginary bridge over the imaginary river.

—ADVICE TO RICHARD NIXON FROM NIKITA KHRUSHCHEV

CONTENTS

PREFACE

THIS IS A BOOK ABOUT HOW RONALD REAGAN CAME WITHIN A HAIRS-breadth of becoming the 1976 Republican nominee for president. But it is also about much more. In the years between 1973 and 1976, America suffered more wounds to its ideal of itself than at just about any other time in its history. First in January 1973, when Richard Nixon declared America's role in the Vietnam War over after some eight years (if you count it from the first major air strikes and Marine landings in 1965) or nine years (if you count it from the congressional authorization that fol-lowed the Gulf of Tonkin incident in 1964) or twelve years (if you count the first major infusion of fifteen thousand U.S. military "advisors" in 1961) of fighting. Some 58,000 Americans dead, $699 billion expended in American treasure: Nixon called this "peace with honor," but that just obscured the fact that America had lost its first war. Then, almost immediately, televised hearings on the complex of presidential abuses known as Watergate revealed the men entrusted with the White House as little better, or possibly worse, than common criminals, in what a sen-ator called "a national funeral that just goes on day after day." Then in October came the Arab oil embargo—and suddenly Americans learned overnight that the commodity that underpinned their lifestyle was vul-nerable to "shocks," and the world's mightiest economy could be held hostage by some mysterious cabal of Third World sheikhs.

This list omits a dozen smaller traumas in between. (One of my favorites, lost to everyday historical memory, was the near doubling of meat prices in the spring of 1973, when the president's consumer advisor went on TV and informed viewers that "liver, kidney, brains, and heart can be made into gourmet meals with seasoning, imagination, and more cooking time.") In the next few years the traumas continued, compounding: The end of a presidency, accompanied by fears Richard Nixon might seek to hold on to his office by force of arms. Inflation such as America had never known during peacetime. A recession that saw hundreds of thousands of blue-collar workers idled during Christmastime; crime at a volume and ghastliness greater, according to one ob-server, "than at any time since the fifteenth century." Senate and House hearings on the Central Intelligence Agency that accused American presidents since Dwight Eisenhower of commanding squads of lawless assassins.

With these traumas emerged a new sort of American politics—a stark discourse of reckoning. What kind of nation were we to suffer such hu-miliations, so suddenly, so unceasingly, so unexpectedly? A few pages hence, you will read these words from one expert: "For the first time, Americans have had at least a partial loss in the fundamental belief in ourselves. We've always believed we were the new men, the new people, the new society. The 'last best hope on earth,' in Lincoln's terms. For the first time, we've really begun to doubt it." And that was only February 1973. By 1976, a presidential year, such observations would become so routine that when the nation geared up for a massive celebration of its Bicentennial, it was common for editorialists and columnists to question whether America deserved to hold a birthday party at all—and whether the party could come off without massive bloodshed, given that there had been eighty-nine bombings attributed to terrorism in 1975. The lib-erals at the *New Republic* reflected upon the occasion of the most har-rowing 1975 trauma—the military collapse of our ally South Vietnam, the nation on behalf of which we had expended those thousands of lives and billions of dollars—that "[i]f the Bicentennial helps us focus on the contrast between our idealism and our crimes, so much the better."

The most ambitious politicians endeavored to speak to this new na-tional mood. An entire class of them—"Watergate babies"—were swept into Congress in 1975, pledging thoroughgoing reform of America's broken institutions. And nearly alone among ambitious politicians, Ronald Reagan took a different road.

RETURNING TO THE NATION'S ATTENTION TOWARD THE END OF HIS SEC-ond term as California governor, as pundits began speculating about which Republican might succeed Richard Nixon (and then which ones might succeed his replacement, Gerald Ford), Reagan, whenever he was asked about Watergate, insisted it said nothing important about the American character at all. Asked about Vietnam, he'd say the only dis-honor was that America had not expended *enough* violence—that "the greatest immorality is to ask young men to fight or die for my country if it's not a cause we are willing to win." One of the quotes he liked to repeat in those years came from Pope Pius XII, writing in *Collier's* magazine in 1945, when the United States was on top of the world: "The

American people have a genius for great and unselfish deeds. Into the hands of America, God has placed the destiny of an afflicted mankind."

When Reagan began getting attention for talking this way, in America's season of melancholy, Washington's touts cited him only to dismiss him. No one who called the Watergate burglars "well-meaning individuals committed to the reelection of the President . . . not criminals at heart," as Reagan had in the spring of 1973, could be taken seriously as a political comer. But a central theme of my previous two books chronicling conservatism's ascendency in American politics has been the myopia of pundits, who so frequently fail to notice the very cultural ground shifting beneath their feet. In fact, at every turn in America's reckoning with its apparent decline, there were always dissenting voices.

They said things like: Richard Nixon just *couldn't* be a bad guy. And that America just *couldn't* be surrendering its role as God's chosen nation: not possible. At first such voices sounded mainly in the interstices of America's political discourse—in letters to the editor; among right-wing institution builders whose industriousness exploiting the cultural confusions of the 1970s was being largely ignored by the guardians of polite opinion; in conservative churches whose pews grew more crowded even as experts insisted religious belief was in radical decline. ("Christians must accept being a definite minority for the time being," one professor told a reporter for a widely republished wire story in 1976.) But these voices were moving from the margins to the center.

This was related to what Ronald Reagan was accomplishing politically. But things shifted independently of him, too. "Nation's Hunger to Feel Good Erupts in Fever of Patriotism," ran one wire service headline about the Bicentennial celebration on July 4, 1976. The keynote of articles like this, which were common, was *surprise*—surprise that it wasn't so hard to unapologetically celebrate America, after all. "The feeling of the day sort of crept up on many of us, took us by surprise," as Elizabeth Drew, Washington's most sure-footed chronicler of the passing political scene and certainly no conservative herself, wrote in her own article about that special day. "There was a spirit to it that could not have been anticipated. For those of us who had been in despair about this Bicentennial Fourth of July, who feared the worst, the surprise was a very pleasing one."

This book is about how that shift in national sentiment took place.

THIS BOOK IS ALSO A SORT OF BIOGRAPHY OF RONALD REAGAN—OF RONald Reagan, rescuer. He had been a sullen little kid from a chaotic, alcoholic home, whose mother's passion for saving fallen souls could never save her own husband. It also seemed to have kept her out of the house almost constantly. But by the time of Ronald Reagan's adolescence, the boy who told his friends to call him "Dutch" had cultivated an extraordinary gift in the act of rescuing himself: the ability to radiate blithe optimism in the face of what others called chaos—to reimagine the morass in front of him as a tableau of simple moral clarity. He did the same thing as a politician: skillfully reframing situations that those of a more critical temper saw as irresolvable muddles (like, say, the Vietnam War) as crystalline black-or-white melodramas. This was a key to what made others feel so good in his presence, what made them so eager and willing to follow him—what made him a leader.

But it was why, simultaneously, he was such a *controversial* leader. Others witnessing precisely this quality saw him as a phony and a hustler. In this book, Ronald Reagan is not a uniter. He is in essence a divider. And understanding the precise *ways* that opinions about him divided Americans—as in my earlier book that focused on the national divisions revolving around Richard Nixon—better helps us understand our political order of battle today: how Americans divide themselves from each other.

The pattern emerged extraordinarily early. In 1966, when Reagan, the TV host and former actor in B movies, shocked the political universe by winning the Republican nomination for California governor, a young aspiring journalist named Ralph Keyes began researching a profile of him (it never got published). Industriously, Keyes tracked down acquaintances who had attended tiny Eureka College in central Illinois with Reagan, or taught him there, between 1928 and 1932. The divergent recollections of Reagan map precisely onto how they would sound if you corralled a random sample of politically attuned citizens today. Half remembered him as a hero, a figure of destiny:

> *"Always articulate, always had an idea, always moving, always had a program, always with action and words. My sister is a class-mate of his and what she and others thought was that he had a future."*
>
> *"He was a respected leader of campus life. He was a first-class gentleman . . . a conscientious, dedicated fellow. He was always committed to principles and big ideals."*

And half judged him precisely the opposite, shallow at best, a manipulative fraud at worst:

"Dutch was the cautious big man on a small campus. He'd run a mile to avoid a controversy . . . if this is governor of California material I don't know what I am. . . . Very immature, strictly rah-rah . . . He was a very personable guy but I never felt he was really a human being, that he ever did anything spontaneously."

"[A] whale of a good cheerleader . . . Reagan made his biggest impression on me in leading yells."

"Ronald Reagan was a man who was spending a great deal of time impressing the populace with little evidence of depth. . . . I don't think he is intelligent enough to be cynical."

Before Reagan had served a single day in any political office, a polarity of opinion was set—and it endured forevermore. On one side: those who saw him as the rescuer, hero, redeemer. Read a handwritten get-well note he received after the 1981 assassination attempt against him. It referred to his first job, as a youthful lifeguard: "I met you in the 20s in Lowell Park, Illinois. Do you remember the good times we had in the 20s. You were 17 years old then and everyone called you Duch [*sic*]. Please get well soon. We need you to save this country—remember all the lives you saved in Lowell Park." The letter appears in a religious biography of Reagan that argues that his coming into the world, culminating with his single-handed defeat of the Soviet empire, was literally providential, the working out of God's plan.

On the other side: those who found Reagan a phony, a fraud, or a toady. The first time such an opinion of Reagan shows up in the historical record is in his high school yearbook. He's depicted fishing a suicide out of the water, who begs, "Don't rescue me. I want to die." Reagan responds, "Well, you'll have to postpone that: I want a medal." Like the Reagan-worship, the Reagan-hate lives on. I think of a friend who grew up in California in the 1960s and '70s. I'd wanted to share this manuscript with her, thinking it would benefit from her brilliance. She told me that I'd best not send it; she couldn't think straight about Reagan for her rage. Her beef, and that of millions of others, was simple: that all that turbulence in the 1960s and '70s had given the nation a chance to finally reflect critically on its power, to shed its arrogance, to become a more humble and better citizen of the world—to *grow up*—but Reagan's rise nipped that imperative in the bud. Immanuel Kant defined the Enlightenment, the sweeping eighteenth-century intellectual-cum-political movement that saw all settled conceptions of society thrown up in the air, which introduced radical new notions of liberty and dignity, dethroned God, and made human reason the new measure of moral worth—a little like the 1960s and '70s—as "man's emergence from his self-incurred immaturity." For these citizens what Reagan achieved foreclosed that imperative: that Americans might learn to question leaders ruthlessly, throw aside the silly notion that American power was always innocent, and think like grown-ups. They had been proposing a new definition of patriotism, one built upon questioning authority and unsettling ossified norms. Then along came Ronald Reagan, encouraging citizens to think like children, waiting for a man on horseback to rescue them: a tragedy.

The division was there even among his own offspring. Maureen, for instance, his eldest, who became a Republican activist, wrote of the time her father as governor missed one more in a train of important milestones in her life (he was away representing President Nixon at an international meeting in Denmark). She cast it in the most optimistic possible way: "I think dad always regretted times like these, at least a little bit, the way the tug and pull of his public life kept him from enjoying firsthand the successes of his children. Oh, he enjoyed them with us in spirit, and he was always there for us emotionally." She wrote in a similar way of both her and her brother Michael missing their father's wedding to his second wife because they were both stashed away by their self-absorbed parents at boarding schools: it was for the best—"because my folks wanted only the smallest of ceremonies." She was her father's daughter. In this book you will read how Ronald Reagan framed even the most traumatic events in his life—even his father's funeral—as always working out gloriously in the end, evidence that the universe was just.

At the other pole there was his other daughter, Patti, a rock-and-rolling liberal. She wrote, "I had been taught to keep secrets, to keep our image intact for the world. . . . Under our family's definition of 'loyalty,' the public should never see that under a carefully preserved surface was a group of people who knew how to inflict wounds, and then convincingly say those wounds never existed." She wrote of how her mother, Nancy, beat her, was addicted to pills, and used their house's state-of-the-art intercom system (installed by General Electric, their corporate benefactor) as a tool for Orwellian surveillance. (Maureen described that same intercom system as a providential gift, writing of the time it broadcast the sound of little Ron, the youngest, crashing to the floor in the nursery, allowing them to save his life.)

Call Maureen's version "denial"—liberals are always accusing conservatives of a politics of being in denial. Call Patti a cynic, always seeing everything in a negative light—and God knows conservatives are always accusing liberals of doing *that*. Optimism, pessimism; America the innocent, America the compromised: these incommensurate polarities have come to be part of the very structure of the left-versus-right order of battle in American political life—as much as the debate over the role of government led by Barry Goldwater that I described in my first book, *Before the Storm;* and the culture war between mutually recriminating cultural sophisticates on the one hand and the plain, earnest "Silent Majority" on the other that I wrote about my second, *Nixonland*.

NOTE WELL, THOUGH, THAT REAGAN'S SIDE IN THIS BATTLE OF POLITICAL affect, which is carried out far above the everyday minutiae of policy debates and electoral tallies, has prevailed. Listen to Liz Cheney in 2009, speaking for Republican multitudes: "I believe unequivocally, unapologetically, America is the best nation that ever existed in history, and clearly that exists today." And here is Mitt Romney, accepting the Republican nomination in 2012, speaking of the day he watched Neil Armstrong land on the moon: "Like all Americans we went to bed that night knowing we lived in the greatest country in the world." He'd been saying the same sort of thing on the campaign trail all year, in nearly every speech: a Google search for "Mitt Romney" and "greatest nation in the history of the earth" just yielded me 114,000 hits.

Such utterances, of course, are meant to be an ideological reproach to Democrats, supposedly always "apologizing for America." As if. Here was San Antonio mayor Julian Castro's keynote address at the Democratic National Convention in 2012: "Ours is a nation like no other. . . . No matter who you are or where you come from, the path is always forward." The first lady, Michelle Obama, spoke of her campaign journeys to meet Americans around the country: "Every day they make me proud. Every day they remind me how blessed we are to live in the greatest nation on earth." Then her husband, accepting the Democratic nomination: "We keep our eyes fixed on that distant horizon knowing that Providence is with us and that we are surely blessed to be citizens of the greatest nation on earth." And here is Samantha Power, the president's choice as ambassador to the United Nations, at her confirmation hearings, early in 2013, questioned about a magazine article she published a decade earlier in which she wrote that American foreign policy needed "a historical reckoning with crimes committed, sponsored, or permitted by the United States." Senator Marco Rubio, Republican of Florida, demanded to know what crimes she was referring to. She would only respond, "America is the greatest country in the world and we have nothing to apologize for."

This is a book about how such rhetoric came into being, and how such hubris comes now to define us. In certain ways we live in some of the darkest times in our history: global warming threatens to engulf us; political polarization threatens to paralyze us; the economy nearly collapsed because of the failure of the banking regulatory regime; competition from China threatens to overwhelm us; social mobility is at its lowest point in generations—to name only a few versions of the national apocalypse that may yet come. But at the same time, somehow, something almost like a cult of official optimism—*the greatest nation in the history of the earth*—saturates the land. How did it happen? That is one of the questions *The Invisible Bridge* poses.

Here is another: What does it mean to *truly* believe in America? To wave a flag? Or to struggle toward a more searching alternative to the shallowness of the flag-wavers—to criticize, to interrogate, to analyze, to *dissent*? During the years covered in these pages Americans debated that question with an intensity unmatched before or since—even if they didn't always know that this was what they were doing. I hope this volume might become a spur to renewing that debate in *these* years—a time that cries for reckoning once more, in a nation that has ever so adored its own innocence, and so dearly wishes to see itself as an exception to history.

CHAPTER ONE

"Small and Suspicious Circles"

ONCE UPON A TIME WE HAD A CIVIL WAR. MORE THAN SIX HUNDRED thousand Americans were slaughtered or wounded. Soon afterward, the two sides began carrying out sentimental rituals of reconciliation. Confederate soldiers paraded through the streets of Boston to the cheers of welcoming Yankee throngs, and John Quincy Adams II, orating from the podium, said, "You are come so that once more we may pledge ourselves to a new union, not a union merely of law, or simply of the lips: not . . . of the sword, but gentlemen, the only true union, the union of hearts." Dissenters from the new postbellum comity—like the abolitionist William Lloyd Garrison, who argued that the new system of agricultural labor taking root in the South and enforced by Ku Klux Klan terror hardly differed from slavery—were shouted down. "Does he really imagine," the *New York Times* indignantly asked, "that outside of small and suspicious circles any real interest attaches to the old forms of the Southern question?"

America the Innocent, always searching for totems of a unity it can never quite achieve—even, or especially, when its crises of disunity are most pressing: it is one of the structuring stories of our nation. The "return to normalcy" enjoined by Warren Harding after the Great War; the cult of suburban home and hearth after World War II; the union of hearts declaimed by Adams on Boston's Bunker Hill parade ground after the War Between the States.

And in 1973, after ten or so years of war in Vietnam, America tried to do it again.

On January 23, four days into his second term, which he had won with the most commanding landslide in U.S. history, President Richard Nixon went on TV to announce, "We have concluded an agreement to end the war and bring peace with honor in Vietnam and South Asia." The Vietnam War was over—"peace with honor," in the phrase the president repeated six more times.

But "it wasn't like 1945, when the end of the war brought a million people downtown to cheer," Mike Royko, the *Chicago Daily News'* regular-guy columnist, wrote. "Now the president comes on TV, reads his speech, and without a sound the country sets the clock and goes to bed." He was grateful for it. "There is nothing to cheer about this time. Except that it is over. . . . Mr. Nixon's efforts to inject glory into our involvement were hollow. All he had to say was that it is finally over."

Royko continued, "It is hard to see the honor. . . . Why kid ourselves? They didn't die for anyone's freedom. They died because we made a mistake. And we can't justify it with slogans and phrases from other times.

"It was a war that made the sixties the most terrible decade our history. . . . If we insist on looking for something of value in this war then maybe it is this:

"Maybe we finally have the painful knowledge that we can never again believe everything our leaders tell us."

Others, though, longed for the old patriotic rituals of reconciliation. And their vehicle became the prisoners of war held in Hanoi by our Communist enemies. "The returning POWs," Secretary of Defense Elliot Richardson told the president, "have dramatically launched what DOD is trying to do to restore the military to its proper position." The president, pleased, agreed: "We now have an invaluable opportunity to revise the history of this war."

It began twenty days after the president's speech, at the airport in Hanoi. What the Pentagon dubbed "Operation Homecoming" turned the network news into a nightly patriotic spectacle. Battered camouflage buses conveyed the first sixty men to the planes that would take them to Clark Air Base in the Philippines; a Navy captain named Galand Kramer unfurled a homemade sign out the window, scrawled on a scrap of cloth: GOD BLESS AMERICA & NIXON. The buses emptied; officers shouted out commands in loud American voices to free American men, who marched forth in smart formation, slowing to accommodate comrades on crutches. On the planes, and on TV, they kissed nurses, smoked too many American cigarettes, circulated news magazines with their wives and children on the cover, and drank a pasty white nutrient shake whose taste they didn't mind, a newsman explained, because it was the first cold drink some of them had had in eight years. On one of the three planes they passed a wriggling puppy from lap to lap. "He was a Communist dog," explained the Navy commander who smuggled him to freedom in his flight bag, "but not anymore!"

At Clark, the tarmac was thronged by kids in baseball and Boy Scout uniforms, women in lawn chairs with babes in arms, airmen with movie cameras, all jostling one another for a better view of a red carpet that had been borrowed at the last minute from Manila's InterContinental Hotel because the one Clark used for the usual round of VIPs wasn't sumptuous enough. In a crisp brocaded dress uniform with captain stripes newly affixed, Navy flier Jeremiah Denton, the first to descend, stood erect before the microphone and pronounced in a slowly swelling voice:

"We are honored to have the opportunity to serve our country —"
(A stately echo: *"country–country — country . . ."*)
"We are profoundly grateful to our Commander in Chief and our nation for this day."
(*"Day — day — day . . ."*)
"God —"
(*"God — God — God . . ."*)
"Bless —"
(*"Bless — bless — bless . . ."*)
"America!"
(*"America — America — America . . ."*)

In days to come cameras lingered on cafeteria trays laden with strawberry pie, steak, corn on the cob, Cornish game hens, ice cream, and eggs. ("Beautiful!" sighed a man in a hospital gown on TV to a fry cook whipping up eggs.) When the men were in Hawaii for refueling on Valentine's Day, the cameras luxuriated over the nurses who defied orders and broke through the security line to bestow leis on their heroes. Then the cameras followed the men to the base exchange, where a boom mike overheard Captain Kramer gingerly trying on a pair of bell-bottomed pants: "I must say, they're a little different from what I would normally wear!"

The next stop was Travis Air Force Base in California, where for twelve long years the flag-draped coffins had come home. Now it was the setting for Times Square 1945 images: wives leaping into husbands' arms; teenagers unabashedly knocking daddies off their feet; seven-year-olds bringing up the rear, sheepish, shuffling — they had never met their fathers before. From there the men shipped out to service hospitals around the country, especially prepared for their return with color TVs and bright yellow bedspreads to mask the metallic hospital tone; once more words like *"God — God — God"* and *"duty — duty — duty"* and *"honor — honor — honor"* and *"country — country — country"* echoed across airport tarmacs. The first men to touch ground had been given expedited discharge to comfort terminally ill relatives. Press accounts credited at least one mother with a miraculous recovery. Miracles, according to the press, were thick on the ground.

> *"The first thing she did when she raced to embrace her husband . . . was slip his wedding ring on his finger. The ring, she told reporters, had been sent to her, along with her husband's wallet. . . ."*
>
> *" 'By all rights he should have come out on a stretcher. But he refused and was determined he was going to come out walking.'"*
>
> *"When Captain John Nasmyth Jr. landed after years of captivity, a dozen strangers rushed up to him and thrust into his hand metal bracelets bearing his name. The strangers had been wearing the bracelets for as long as two years or more, as amulets of their concern and their faith in his safe return."*

Those bracelets: invented by a right-wing Orange County, California, radio host named Bob Dornan, they became a pop culture phenomena in 1970 after being introduced at a "Salute to the Armed Forces" rally in Los Angeles hosted by Governor Ronald Reagan. By the summer of 1972, they were selling at the rate of some ten thousand per day. Wearers vowed never to remove them until the name stamped on the metal came home. Some, the *New York Times* reported, believed them to "possess medicinal powers"—and not just the children who displayed them two, ten, a dozen to an arm. A Wimbledon champ said one cured his tennis elbow. The pop singers Sonny and Cher wore them on their hit TV variety show. Lee Trevino insisted his bracelet saved his golf game. And now that they were no longer needed, there was talk of melting them down for a national monument on the Mall in Washington, D.C.

When Captain Nasmyth arrived in his hometown, he was led to a billboard that read HANOI FREE JOHN NASMYTH. He chopped it down with a ceremonial ax, his entire community gathered round as a fifty-three-piece band blared "When Johnny Comes Marching Home." A black POW addressed a undergraduate classroom at a black university in Tennessee. The students examined him as if they had unearthed, a newspaper said, a "member of a nearly extinct sociological species: American Negro, circa 1966." He told them, "We have the greatest country in the world." That made front-page news, too.

One of the most quoted returning warriors was a colonel who

noted all the signs reading "We Love You." "In a deeper sense," he said, "I think what people are saying is 'We Love America.'" Another announced the greatest Vietnam miracle of all: that the POWs had *won the Vietnam War*. "I want you all to remember that we walked out of Hanoi as winners. We're not coming home with our tails between our legs. We returned with honor."

NBC broadcast from a high school in a tiny burg in Iowa—John Wayne's hometown—where wood shop students fashioned a giant key to the city for a POW native son; then the anchorman threw to his correspondent in the Philippines, who filled five full minutes of airtime calling the names, ranks, service branch, and hometowns of twenty exuberant Americans as they bounded, limped, or, occasionally, were borne upon stretchers, down the red carpet, to their next stop, the base cafeteria. ("Scrambled eggs!" "How many?" "How many can you handle?") The screen filled with red-white-and-blue banner. NBC's Jack Perkins signed off: "The prisoners' coming back seems the one thing about Vietnam that has finally made all Americans finally, indisputably, *feel good.*"

Not all Americans. Columnist Pete Hamill, on Valentine's Day in the liberal *New York Post,* pointed out that the vast majority of the prisoners were bomber pilots, and thus were "prisoners because they had committed unlawful acts"—killing civilians in an undeclared war. He compared waiting for the POWs to come home to his "waiting for a guy up at Sing Sing one time, who had done hard time for armed robbery."

There was the *New York Times,* which in one of its first dispatches from the Philippines reported, "Few military people here felt the return of the prisoners marked the end of the fighting. 'They're sending out just as many as come back,' said a young Air Force corporal who works at the airport. 'They're all going to Thailand, they're just moving the boundaries of the war back.'"

Not even all POWs agreed they were heroes. When the first Marine to be repatriated arrived at Camp Pendleton, every jarhead and civilian employee on base stood at attention to receive him. After the burst of applause stopped, Edison Miller held up a clenched fist in the manner favored by left-wing revolutionaries, then turned his back to the crowd.

In fact nothing about the return of the POWs was indisputable; the defensiveness of the president's rhetoric demonstrated that. At a meeting of the executive council of the AFL-CIO in Florida on February 19, Nixon spoke of the "way that our POWs could come off those planes with their heads high, knowing that they had not fought in vain." The next day, before a joint session of the South Carolina legislature, he answered a Gold Star Mother who wrote to him questioning the meaning of her son's sacrifice: "I say to the members of this assembly gathered here that James did not die in vain, that the men who went to Vietnam and have served there with honor did not serve in vain, and that our POWs, as they return, did not make the sacrifices they made in vain."

With honor, not in vain: a whole lot of people must have been worrying otherwise. Or else it wouldn't have been repeated so much.

"The nation begins again to feel itself whole," proclaimed *Newsweek. Time* speculated how "these impressive men who had become symbols of America's sacrifice in Indochina might help the country heal the lingering wounds of war." However, some stubbornly refused to be healed. It would take more than a "Pentagon pin-up picture," a *Newsweek* reader wrote, to make her forget "that these professional fighting men were trained in the calculated destruction of property and human life." A *Time* reader spoke up for his fellow "ex-grunts," who had received no welcoming parades: "Why were we sneaked back into our society? So our country could more easily forget the crimes we committed in its name?"

TURN ON THE TV, OPEN A NEWSPAPER OR A DENTIST-OFFICE MAGAZINE, and a new journalistic genre was now impossible to avoid: features that affected to explain to these Rip van Winkles all they had missed while incommunicado in prison camps at a time when, as NBC's gruff senior commentator David Brinkley put it, "a decade now is about equal to what a century used to be, because change is so fast."

On February 22 the *Today* show devoted both its hours to the exercise. "Generally, they've been years of crisis," the anchorman began.

A DEMAND EQUALITY sign:

"They walked in picket lines, they badgered congressmen, they formed pressure groups"—Who? The attractive blond newscaster (there weren't any of those in 1965), whose name was Barbara Walters, was speaking of women, only ordinary women. "They strived for 'lib,'" she continued—"as in liberation."

A mob of long-haired young men:

"Protest, demonstrations, disorders, riots, even death flared" on elite college campuses, where students "didn't trust anyone over thirty" and contested "the whole fabric of Western Judeo-Christian morality."

Gene Shalit, *Today*'s bushy-haired entertainment critic, reported how "federal legislation brought the vote to two million more blacks," and that "in 1964, when the first POWs were taken in Vietnam, most of us thought that was what was wanted. The phrase most often used was 'equal opportunity.' . . . Then came 1967 and a riot in Detroit. . . . There was Malcolm X, a failure in every way according to the 'white' code; he became a folk hero among blacks."

Nineteen new nations, from Bangladesh to Botswana; a war in Israel won in six days—"but terrorism followed": cue picture of a man in a ski mask on a balcony in Munich, at the 1972 Olympics.

Bonnie and Clyde, the hit movie from 1967, made the criminal life "look like fun and games" and changed Hollywood; *The Godfather,* from 1972, "the biggest moneymaker since 1965's *Sound of Music*," "at once glorified and sentimentalized the mafia." *Last Tango in Paris,* in theaters now, featured "clear depictions of the most elemental sexual acts, and perhaps some aberrations as well, but what it shows most is that here in New York at five dollars a ticket the film is a sellout, and that ordinary respectable folks like you are all going to see it."

Finally there came a familiar Hollywood image: a tall, handsome man in a Stetson. But the still was from *Midnight Cowboy,* and the camera pulled back to show that the titular cowboy was hugging a shrunken and disheveled Jewish man, and Barbara Walters explained it signified the new Hollywood trend "toward dealing openly with homosexuality."

Assassinations and attempted assassinations: Malcolm X. Martin Luther King. Robert F. Kennedy. George Wallace.

Fashion: "*Unisex*—remember that word. . . ."

Some ninety minutes later, two chin-stroking *penseurs* were asked by the stern-voiced anchorman what was the most profound change the POWs faced. Answered the editor of *Intellectual Digest:* "For the first time Americans have had at least a partial loss in the fundamental belief in ourselves. We've always believed we were the new men, the new people, the new society. The 'last best hope on earth,' in Lincoln's terms. For the first time, we've really begun to doubt it."

THIS PRETENSE THAT SOME SIX HUNDRED POWS NEWLY RETURNED TO their families would want to waste two hours of their lives learning about the latest slang from Gene Shalit felt a little bit fantastic. But the ritual was not for them. It was for us—all those Americans doubting for the first time that America might just not be the last best hope on earth. "Having missed much of the destructiveness of these past few years," one letter writer to the *Washington Post* exulted, they had "preserved a vision of the way America ought to be." As if these men might somehow be able to mystically deliver us across the bridge of years—to the time before the storm. It was their gift to us.

On the *CBS Evening News* the same day as that *Today* show, a lovely bride was seen with a man in officer's dress, a wedding march pealing forth from the organ. Walter Cronkite narrated:

"Dorothy said her husband's return was like a resurrection, and that for her it was like a new life beginning. So she went out and bought an all-new white wedding gown. And Dorothy and Johnny Ray reaffirmed the marriage vow they first made four and a half years ago."

(Cut to ten seconds on the long white train of her gown, then the cross above the altar; fifteen seconds of him slipping on the wedding ring.)

"It was a short, simple ceremony."

(Kiss, organ, recessional.)

"Captain and Mrs. Johnny Ray will soon be home to their three children in Pauls Valley, Oklahoma. David Dick, CBS News at the post chapel, Fort Sam Houston, San Antonio, Texas."

That was one sort of homecoming story. Here was another: at Balboa Naval hospital, where many POWs convalesced, a wife later told an oral historian, "It was like the Spanish Inquisition. Everyone asked how the wives had behaved. I could hear beatings in some rooms. A lot of women had been swinging."

Certain outlets told many similar stories—like the "newspaper of record," the *New York Times,* which in 1878 had scolded the "small and suspicious circles" who dared suggest the Civil War had not ended America's racial ordeal. The *Times* was a very different institution almost a century later. Most American institutions were very different from what they had been even a decade before. For the small and suspicious circles had expanded exponentially.

On its front page on February 5 you could meet Alice Cronin, dressed in faded hip-hugging bell-bottomed jeans and no shoes, smoking cigarettes, hair flopping loose, posing outside her San Diego home as movers unloaded the fashionable puffy white leather couch she bought "for the return of her husband, a Navy pilot held by Hanoi for six years." She was worried: "Mike married a very traditional wife.... Now my ideas and values have changed.... I can't sit home and cook and clean house. I'm very career oriented, and I just hope he goes along and agrees with that ... he's missed out on a lot—liking a more casual lifestyle, being nonmaterialistic." She hoped he understood why she didn't trust a single thing the administration said about Vietnam. She also hoped he would go along with something else: "shifting sexual mores, the whole thing about relationships not necessarily being wrong outside of marriage. I know myself really well sexually, and he's missed out on a good deal of that."

She was contrasted to Sybil Stockdale, a classic by-the-book officer's wife, who spoke from "her sunny kitchen," where she was busy mending the rug left over when her husband, James Stockdale, the highest-ranking Navy POW, took off for his first bombing mission over the Gulf of Tonkin in 1964. For his return, she explained, "I want the living room to look the same."

There were two groups of POW wives, Alice Cronin explained. "I'm definitely in the second group." There were, by 1973, two groups of just about everything. Two kinds of POW reports, for instance. Some played up the sentimental rituals of reconciliation. An example of the other kind ran on NBC—cutting from Operation Homecoming footage at Travis Air Force Base to the hospital bed of a sad-eyed, fidgety Marine private, paralyzed from the waist down, complaining, "We were kind of snuck in the back door."

Newspapers in small towns like Bend, Oregon; Reading, Pennsylvania; and Lewiston, Maine, ran with the Navy's press release about the poetry written in captivity by a Navy commander in tribute to the "women who wait at home" (*"Are not these women, of men gone to war / The unsung heroes, today as before. . . ."*). But in the *New York Times,* columnists like Tom Wicker rued "the warped sense of priorities on the home front" that allotted so much more attention to "these relatively few POW's than the 50,000 dead boys who came home in body bags, some of them with smuggled heroin obscenely concealed in their mangled flesh," and "for whom the only bracelet is a band of needle marks." He noted that the administration had frozen funding for treatment for drug-addicted veterans and in its fiscal 1974 budget proposed to arbitrarily limit the allowable number of patients in veterans hospitals. Meanwhile the *Times* editorialized that in the "succession of hand salutes, stiffly prepared statements, medical bulletins, and canned handouts concerning the joys of steak and ice cream" of Operation Homecoming, the "hard-won lessons of Vietnam are in danger of being lost." Which, on the merits, was sound editorial judgment. For that had been Richard Nixon's intention for the POW issue from the start.

When American pilots were first taken prisoner in North Vietnam, U.S. policy had been pretty much to ignore them—part and parcel of President Lyndon B. Johnson's determination to keep the costs of his increasingly futile escalation from the public. The enemy, though, preferred publicity—which was why, in June 1966, they announced to the world these pilots would be put on trial as "air pirates," and paraded them through Hanoi past jeering crowds for the cameras on the Fourth of July. In 1967 the first American flier was tortured into appearing on film to say he was being treated humanely. Also in 1967, the first American peace activists visited North Vietnam, documented widespread civilian carnage, and returned with a devastating argument: The Pentagon claimed its laser-guided bombs were the most accurate in the history of warfare. But if that was true, pilots had to know they were targeting civilian areas—and if that was false, then who knew what else the Pentagon was lying about?

A war of position emerged, peaceniks versus the Pentagon, with the POWs tossed about like political footballs. Communist officials began releasing to antiwar activists small numbers of prisoners who had arrived at doubts about the war. The Pentagon worked to silence them. Meanwhile, Sybil Stockdale organized, against the Pentagon's wishes, a "League of Wives of American Prisoners of War" (later the National League of Families of Prisoners of War), which agitated for attention to the prisoners' plight. From two directions at once, Johnson's attempt to play down the existence of hundreds of American prisoners came a cropper. And in 1969, the new Republican president had spied in the dilemma a political opportunity.

One day in the first spring of Richard Nixon's presidency, reporters at a routine Pentagon briefing perked up when the Secretary of Defense himself, Melvin Laird, took the podium. He confirmed the existence of from 500 to 1,300 of what he termed "POW/MIAs." This was new phraseology, partly cynical and strategic: downed fliers not confirmed as actual prisoners used to be classified not as "Missing in Action" but "Body Unrecovered." Soon the administration began referring to these 1,300 *as if* they were, every one of them, actually prisoners. "The North Vietnamese claimed they were treated humanely," Secretary Laird intoned gravely. "I am distressed by the fact that there is clear evidence that this is not the case."

It was the American public's introduction to these men. Laird demanded that the enemy reveal their names, send home the sick and wounded, and allow impartial inspections and free exchange of mail— the Geneva Conventions, he announced, required no less. "Most importantly, we seek the prompt release of all American prisoners," he said, before launching into an emotional peroration about the enemy's cruelty: "Hundreds of American wives, children, and parents continue to live in a tragic state of uncertainty caused by the lack of information concerning the fate of their loved ones."

The North Vietnamese officials' astonishment was like that of the British officer after the Great War who, witnessing the way America trampled on logic and good military order to get its troops home first, remarked, "How odd it is that only American boys have mothers." These Vietnamese men had lost children themselves—to American bombers that by their lights flew in plain defiance of the most basic Geneva Convention requirements: that wars be declared, that civilians be spared. They had seen schools, hospitals, farmers' fields obliterated. They had lined streets with mile after mile of underground concrete cylinders in which Hanoi residents cowered every time they heard the approaching airborne hum. They answered Secretary Laird that they would not so much as give out prisoners' names "as long as the United States does not cease its war of aggression and withdraw its troops from Vietnam."

For Nixon, this was a political boon. A *Washington Post* editorial enshrined the bomber pilots as pluperfect victims: "It is hard to see how so retrograde a response advances the interests of any government that seeks to present itself to the world as fair and humane." The Pentagon and State Department sent forth public relations cadres and co-opted Sybil Stockdale's embryonic League of Wives of American Prisoners of War, sometimes inventing chapters outright. When Hanoi announced on July 4—a favorite day for Communist propaganda aimed at international opinion—that North Vietnam would be releasing more prisoners to antiwar activists, the Pentagon reversed its ban on its members speaking to the press. Images of families without fathers began showing up in the weekly picture magazines—martyrs to an enemy so devious, as the *Armed Forces Journal* put it, they denied hundreds of little boys and girls "a right to know if their fathers were dead or alive." Their North Vietnamese captors, yet more astonished, reflected on the *tens of thousands* of prisoners whom America's South Vietnamese allies kept likewise incommunicado, and redoubled their defiance.

On Labor Day, 1969, the campaign intensified: the Pentagon put two freed prisoners behind a press conference podium, where they described solitary confinement in dark stone rooms, beatings, bodies bound in cruel contortions for hours with straps and ropes. They added cinematic embellishments: that POW Fred Cherry had been hung from the ceiling by his broken arm, which became so infected he almost lost it (on the tarmac at Andrews Air Force Base four years later, it became plain Cherry's arm was in fact perfectly intact); that Navy flier Richard Stratton had had his fingernails pried loose (they weren't). The timing was strategic: a peace group had just reported back on the treatment of prisoners by our South Vietnamese allies, in prison camps designed and built by us; they were manacled to the floor in crippling underground bamboo "tiger cages," many merely for the crime of advocating peace, but the American military's advisor had described these prisons as being like "a Boy Scout recreation camp."

At the peace talks in Paris, the "POW issue" became the cornerstone of Nixon's stalling tactics to settle the war on his preferred terms—another astonishment for the North Vietnamese: in previous wars, the disposition of prisoners had been something settled *following* the cessation of hostilities. Meanwhile, stateside, a dialectic unfolded: whenever the public showed signs of turning away en masse in disgust from the war, the martyrs in the Hanoi Hilton were symbolically marched to the foreground, their suffering families walking point.

At Christmastime, precisely one month after investigative reporter Seymour Hersh revealed the My Lai Massacre, POW wives were invited to stand mute beside the president in the Oval Office while he lied that "this government will do everything that it possibly can to separate out the prison issue and have it handled as it should be, as a separate issue on a humanitarian basis." On Christmas Eve, three airliners leased by Texas billionaire H. Ross Perot lifted off. One, christened "The Spirit of Christmas," bore fifty-eight POW wives and ninety-four of their children to demand a meeting with Communist negotiators in Paris. The others, christened "Peace on Earth" and "Goodwill Toward Men," tried to deliver thirty tons of Christmas dinners, holiday gifts, clothing, and medical supplies directly to the prisoners in Hanoi. (In Paris, the wives were lectured on truths stern-faced North Vietnamese diplomats considered self-evident: that the way to free their husbands was to prevail upon their government to stop the futile and sadistic terror bombing of North Vietnam, for which there was no sanction in international law. A wife asked: "What should I tell my son, age nine, when he asks where is my father and when is he coming home?" An apparatchik responded: "Tell him his father is a murderer of North Vietnamese children and that he is being punished." The wives emerged too shattered to speak to the press.)

In spring 1970, which bloomed in the shadow of the expansion of the ground war into Cambodia and the martyrdom of four college students at Kent State University in Ohio, seven hundred POW/MIA relatives were flown to Washington at taxpayer expense for a rally hosted by the Daughters of the American Revolution and funded by defense contractors. Ross Perot testified before Congress of the North Vietnamese's incredulity at all this concern over "just 1,400 men." (Americans were plainly more morally sensitive than Communists.) He then relayed how, when they told him of hospital wards shattered by American bombs, he promised to pay to rebuild them himself, as if that solved the problem. The first POW bracelets were unveiled at that spring's annual "Salute to the Military" ball in Los Angeles. Governor Ronald Wilson Reagan presided, and Hollywood choreographer LeRoy Prinz, who had worked with Reagan on the 1944 film *Hollywood Canteen,* directed the grand cavalcade.

By then, Jonathan Schell of the *New Yorker* observed, the American people were acting "as though the North Vietnamese had kidnapped 400 Americans and the United States had gone to war to retrieve them." Matchbooks, lapel pins, billboards, T-shirts, and bumper stickers ("POWs NEVER HAVE A NICE DAY!") proliferated; fighter jets made thunderous football stadium fly-bys; full-page ads blossomed in every newspaper, urging Hanoi to have a heart and release the prisoners for the sake of the children. "They just dig holes in the ground and drop them in," one wife explained to a magazine of her understanding of the Hanoi Hilton. "They throw food down to them, and let them live there in their waste." She was confused. In fact she was precisely describing how prisoners were treated in *South Vietnam,* as revealed in a stunning photo essay from the American-built prison camp at Con Son Island in a July 1970 issue of *Life.*

Here was how the Vietnam War had deformed America: by making such intellectual distortion systematic—a "lunatic semiology," as a wise historian later described it, where "sign and referent have scarcely any proportionate relation at all." It was one of the reasons the suspicious circles began expanding exponentially, even into the ranks of POW families themselves—who reasoned that if Nixon said there would be war so long as there were prisoners, and the Communists said there would be prisoners so long as there was war, as Tom Wicker wrote, "we may keep both troops and prisoners there forever."

In 1971, the summer the *Times* published the Pentagon Papers, revealing in the government's own hand that most of what the American people had been told about Vietnam for twenty-five years had been lies, a rump group of antiwar wives broke off from Sybil Stockdale's League of Families, demanding the White House stop treating their husbands as "political hostages." They appeared on platforms with Jane Fonda and John Kerry, wrote letters to the president demanding "a complete troop withdrawal NOW!" and seconded the nomination of 1972 Democratic presidential candidate George McGovern, who pledged to remove all American forces from Vietnam within sixty days of his inauguration.

But Richard Nixon said that this would be surrender, and that Americans did not surrender. He won his reelection mandate, 61 percent and forty-nine states. Seventy-eight days later he triumphantly announced "peace with honor." His critics argued there had been no honor: that the terms he had arrived at were the same ones on the table when Lyndon Johnson began peace negotiations in 1968—purchased at the expense of 15,183 more American dead and four million more tons of American ordnance over North and South Vietnam. The evening news, meanwhile, showed skirmishes still breaking out in all three Southeast Asian nations, and American bombing runs continuing into Cambodia, where the government had almost ceased to function despite hundreds of millions of dollars in U.S. aid—it sounded a little like South Vietnam ten years earlier. The story the administration was telling about prisoners of war was instrumental to how it was attempting to occlude these facts.

The POWs returned. God bless America. Let the healing begin.

FOUR HUNDRED PHOTOGRAPHERS, CAMERAMEN, JOURNALISTS, AND SUP-port staff encamped at Clark Air Base in the Philippines to cover the return. Then they learned their contact with the heroes would be third-hand and censored—the better to preserve the men's health, the Pentagon insisted, though according to the telegram the *New York Times* fired off to the secretary of defense "they were healthy enough to eat anything, horse around in the hospital, go shopping, see movies, and talk to virtually everyone else who runs into them." So why couldn't they speak with reporters? The *Los Angeles Times* printed the concerns of a sociology professor: "The last thing the Pentagon wants is the inevitable necessity of the public—via its surrogate, the press—confronting these men and discussing, in however imperfect form, the war they wasted their years upon." Then, the explanation shifted: access to POWs would be limited to protect their privacy. The *New York Times* responded to *that* on the news pages: "They did not say, however, why the prisoners would be placed under orders forbidding public statements if they wanted to make them." Then the *Times* reported a Pentagon policy that civilian POWs would be given medical treatment only if they agreed not to talk to the press.

On February 21 the newspaper of record, noting how the POWs' praise for Richard Nixon sounded suspiciously close to the administration's own catchphrases, reported that "the military's repatriation effort was carefully programmed and controlled" by a team of nearly eighty military public relations men. The *Washington Post*'s ombudsman, Robert C. Maynard, echoed the argument the next morning in an essay headlined "Return of the Prisoners: Script by the Military." "Not surprisingly," he concluded, "we received a number of paeans to 'honorable peace' and could only wonder how that phrase happened to be among the first to pop out of the mouths of men in captivity for such long periods of time." He also said, "They return to a society more surely programmed in 'them-against-us' terms than the one they left."

That was true enough. The *Post,* led by its investigative reporting team of Carl Bernstein and Bob Woodward, had led all other media in foregrounding the scandal that ensued after men tied to Nixon's White House and reelection campaign were caught breaking into the Watergate hotel and office complex back in June. The White House had made excoriating the *Post*'s alleged vendetta against it—and characterizing the *Post* as a pillar of the "liberal establishment"—central to its campaign rhetoric. And in March 1973, Nixon's opinion of the *Post* was echoed when the entire letters page was given over to readers' responses to the ombudsman's report. Many defended the president. The POWs' "feel gratitude toward [Nixon] for sticking out the war and making their own sacrifice meaningful," a Henry T. Simmons of Washington wrote. "This has got to be intolerable to the *Washington Post*." A retired Air Force officer wrote: "The media . . . must be embarrassed and galled. . . . Most Americans were thrilled. . . . You can be sure that I am not following a military script when I say, as I now do, 'God bless America!'" A housewife from Staunton, Virginia, signing her letter "Mrs. Frank J. McDonough," noted, "Imagine Maynard's reaction . . . if the men had returned bitter at their country and praising Hanoi the way he wanted them to. No mention would have been made of Hanoi propaganda, or the one-sided views of America presented in newspapers like yours that they were undoubtedly permitted to read. We would have heard nothing but praise for their 'courage' and 'forthrightness' in presenting 'the truth.' As a matter of fact, if even one POW does attack America, I'm sure it will be all over your front page."

Others, however, spoke for the suspicious circles: "You really told it like it is," a Dorothy Woodell of Sacramento, California, wrote, noting she had made Xerox copies of the article to send "to everyone I know." She was certain "there is more to be said on the issue," but added "I'm sure that if you had said it, it never would have been printed anyhow."

THE POW STORY TOOK SHAPE AS A DOMESTIC CIVIL WAR. A *NEW YORK Times* dispatch from the Philippines recorded, "When one man deplaned here, his wife rushed toward him—but he warned her off with a stern whisper: 'I have to salute the flag, don't bother me.'" A February 23 front-page story by Seymour Hersh reported that "camp life included occasional fist fights, a few near-suicides, and many cliques. . . . One pilot reportedly pulled a knife on another prisoner during an argument." It ran the day of returnees' first stateside press conferences, where they insisted that with most of their comrades still in the hands of the enemy, they wouldn't comment on what had happened in captivity. Aggressive network correspondents pushed and pushed, as if to break them. Rattled, Captain James Mulligan (who had recently learned his own wife had been an antiwar leader) grabbed a microphone. "I feel very strongly that it's about time the American people started pulling together. It's about time we all realize where we're going! It's about time we start raising the flag instead of burning it. I know people have strong feelings! . . . But we are all Americans. And it's about time we all get back to, to—the main thing!"

The follow-up questions grew sharper. ("Are you 100 percent satisfied with the way the Nixon administration handled the war?") The answers became more defensive. One POW said he was "fantastically impressed with the courage that President Nixon displayed in an election year"; Robinson Risner, one of the most famous of the POWs, who had been on the cover of *Time* in 1965 as "the classic example of the kind of dedicated military professional who was leading the American effort in Vietnam," felt "beyond any doubt" that war protesters "kept us in prison an extra year or two." "What do you think of the divisiveness?" an airman was asked. He responded, "Once a week we would get up and say the Pledge of Allegiance; we could not understand how people could be so unpatriotic as to *condemn the Government in time of war* and like Captain Mulligan said—and I think it's a beautiful phrase—I think it's time we start *raising flags instead of burning them.*" (The president underlined those words in his briefing on the press conferences.)

The *New York Times* kept rolling out exposés—for instance, reporting that the California-based organization known as VIVA, or "Voices in Vital America" (originally formed, with the intention of harassing campus antiwar activists, as the "Victory in Vietnam Association"), had earned $3,693,661 in 1972, "almost entirely" from sales of POW bracelets, which it marked up for a 400 percent profit, and that it hoped "sales of the bracelets with the names of those still missing may pick up now." NBC ran an exposé from the South Vietnamese prison island of Con Son. Anchorman John Chancellor began by reminding viewers that North Vietnam had always offered to release American prisoners in exchange for prisoners held by South Vietnam, and that still, a month after the peace settlement, "the South Vietnamese are holding about 100,000 political prisoners." He appeared stricken by the cruel absurdity of the facts he was forced to relate. The reporter in the field, who had long hair, interviewed two American hospital workers in South Vietnam who said that if prisoners didn't give the right answers to interrogators they "reached under the ribs and cracked the rib," and presented before the cameras a feeble old woman, a former Con Son prisoner, her eyes swollen shut, being hand-fed like a baby because she could not eat by herself. *Time*'s correspondent described the released prisoners he had seen as "grotesque sculptures of scarred flesh and gnarled limbs. They move like crabs, skittering across the floor on buttocks and palms."

On Wednesday, February 28, a shouting match broke out on the floor of the New York State Assembly. One assemblyman offered a resolution honoring Vietnam Veterans Week—"in support of liberty and freedom of all men" and in "rededication to the precepts that have made America such a tower of strength among the nations of the world."

"This is a lot of bunk!" exploded Assemblyman Franz S. Leichter, Democrat of Manhattan. "We were fighting for Thieu and bamboo cages for his political opponents!"

A Republican from Brooklyn: "Your opposing this resolution is a disgrace as far as I'm concerned!"

A conservative Democrat: "I have stood this nonsense long enough. For three years I've listened to him and his peace movement. I ask you all in the spirit of America and the spirit of the American flag to vote in favor, and God bless America."

A liberal: "There's a lot of difference between blessing America and blessing Richard Milhous Nixon." He added that it was "a credit to a nonwhite race who'd been invaded and pillaged that they did treat the prisoners the way they did."

That Thursday, newspapers ran a United Press International interview with a Minnesota POW who reported that his darkest day in captivity came when he heard of the reelection of the president. On Friday the Nixon administration worked furiously on political damage control after its controversial announcement that North Vietnam would enjoy reconstruction aid as part of the postwar settlement. Routine in the case of previous wars, this time the proposal brought down a rain of political vituperation. After all, hadn't the president himself said these Communists were merciless torturers?

On Sunday the next batch of 106 POWs left Hanoi, their cult more insistent, more pious, more defensively reactionary: "We wanted to come home, but we wanted to come home with honor," a colonel boomed from the tarmac microphone at Clark. "President Nixon has brought us home with honor. God bless those Americans who supported our President during our long ordeal." On Monday the *Post* featured a profile headlined "Free Navy POW Sure U.S. Right in Asia," whose subject said he was "glad to put my wife back in skirts. I think a woman should be a woman and not whatever they're trying to be with all these movements."

The skeptics were growing more insistent, too. "These people had their feet on the ground while in prison," a Pentagon source told the *Times'* Seymour Hersh for his article "POWs Planned Business Venture." "They heard enough and knew enough . . . 'to realize that there would be demands for books, speeches, and endorsements. . . . There's really nothing sinful in taking advantage of what's left,' the officer said. 'That's the way to play the game.'" "The POWs: Focus of Division," the *Times* reported the next morning in a summary of Operation Homecoming so far. "It scares me in a way," they quoted an official of the National League of Families as saying. "If the prisoners are not careful they will destroy their credibility. They've been away so long, they don't realize the depth of division in this country."

That depth of division: the same afternoon CBS announced a program it would be featuring in prime time, two nights later, an adapted version of a surreal off-Broadway drama that would soon win the Tony Award for best play, *Sticks and Bones,* by Vietnam veteran David Rabe. It opened on a bucolic suburban sitcom family. A sergeant shows up at the door to return their son, blinded in Vietnam. He can't stay for coffee: "I've got trucks out there backed up for blocks. . . . And when I get back they'll be layin' all over the grass; layin' there all over the grass, their backs been broken, their brains jellied, their insides turned into garbage. No-legged boys and one-legged boys. I'm due in Harlem; I got to get to the Bronx and Queens, Cincinnati, St. Louis, Reading. I don't have time for coffee. I've got deliveries all over this country." The father is named "Ozzie." The mother is "Harriet." They are so horrified that their son has fallen in love with a Vietnamese woman that they manipulate him into killing himself, then throw out his body with the trash.

Newsweek's reviewer, a fellow traveler of the New Left who wrote under the pen name "Cyclops," rhapsodized of the playwright: "Like a wounded Dreiser or a young O'Neill, he blunders into deep terrors and thrashes there. Such is his strength that he pulls us in after him. We are back among primal things, evil ceremonies, the sacrifice of the blind seer, the scapegoat become garbage, the rites claustrophobic. The final image on the TV screen is so perfect and so perfectly appalling that your mind will want to throw up." The *Times*' critic thought the production "not very good," though he said it went without saying that it had to be broadcast nonetheless.

Local CBS affiliates disagreed. "We did not feel it was appropriate for TV in Detroit, where our working-class audience would be offended," said one station manager. An executive in Mississippi said, "They can't sanitize it enough to what suits me." After only two minutes of commercials were sold for the two-hour block, CBS's president released a statement: "In light of recent developments, many of us both at the network and among the stations are now convinced that its presentation on the air at this time might be unnecessarily abrasive to the feelings of millions of Americans whose lives or attention are at the moment emotionally dominated by the returning POWs and other veterans who have suffered the ravages of war."

The producer, Joseph Papp, said CBS was obligated to put on the show no matter who objected; it was a First Amendment issue. The American Civil Liberties Union got involved. A Syracuse, New York, station manager begged to be allowed to carry the feed: "Dammit, it's real. Life isn't just a bowl of cherries." But when the network broadcast was canceled, he was forced to show a Steve McQueen movie just like every other affiliate. "Only a society with a great deal more self-confidence than ours could stand the disruptiveness of high art on TV," wrote a liberal columnist for the *Chicago Tribune*.

On March 28, the last POW shot down over North Vietnam landed at Clark Air Base. His last name, coincidentally, was "Agnew," just like the jingoistic vice president. But this Agnew brazenly told the press there was neither honor nor peace in the Paris settlement. It was a cover-up, he said, predicting that as soon as the last American troops left, Communist troops would overrun South Vietnam. That same day, the Yale psychology professor Robert J. Lifton, who a decade and a half earlier had helped explain how Communist captors had "brainwashed" American POWs during the Korea War, argued in the *New York Times* that it was the American people who now were being brainwashed—in the very act of sanctifying men whose job was "saturation bombing of civilian areas with minimal military targets," but who were now held up as vessels of "pure virtue," propaganda tools for the "official mythology of peace with honor," in order to prevent the possibility of "extracting from this war its one potential benefit: political and ethical illumination arising from hard appraisals of what we did and why we did it."

And also on that same day, CBS president William Paley gave word on *Sticks and Bones:* "We will run the show when things have calmed down." *When things have calmed down:* that had been what Operation Homecoming was supposed to have done.

There were two tribes of Americans now.

One comprised the suspicious circles, which had once been small, but now were exceptionally broad, who considered the self-evident lesson of the 1960s and the low, dishonest war that defined the decade to be the imperative to question authority, unsettle ossified norms, and expose dissembling leaders—a new, higher patriotism for the 1970s. They lived, for example, in the sleepy suburb in Northern California visited by a *New York Times* writer who reported back that "people think and feel differently from what they once did. They ask questions, they reject assumptions, they doubt what they are told." They said things like, "Now I'd rather not say the pledge; it has such little meaning to me. The things that are in it just aren't true." They even included, among their numbers, career military men, like the returned POW who told NBC how much he appreciated returning to a country finally willing to reconsider its prejudices—"shedding its Linus blankets, starting to think for itself." They included officials of the big, "mainline" Protestant churches, who took out a full-page ad in the *New York Times,* on the day the last POW came home, criticizing Nixon for hosting South Vietnam's torture-master president, for whose preservation the nation had sacrificed some fifty-eight thousand soldiers and billions of dollars of treasure, as a "spiritual disaster for America"; and the American Psychological Association which proclaimed that the POWs had "been assigned the role of heroes in a war that has no heroes, the central role in an elaborate drama staged to provide justification for the President's policy, to create the illusion of victory and to arouse a sense of patriotic fervor."

And they included Lyndon Johnson's former press secretary, Bill Moyers, whose job had once been to sell America on the nobility of the Vietnam cause, and who now was an avuncular commentator for the Public Broadcasting Service. On TV he grilled General Maxwell Taylor about whether the recent "unworthy and unwinnable war" had made it harder to recruit forces for the new all-volunteer force, now that the draft had ended with the beginning of 1973. The general responded that those who had fought in Vietnam would refuse that characterization. Moyers asked why, if that were so, record numbers of them had deserted. The general insisted that was only because they had been poisoned by the liberal media. Moyers then asked why, if *that* was the case, so many of our allied European governments opposed the Vietnam War, too. Taylor responded that this was because they read the U.S. press— which, he said, should have been subject to wartime censorship.

General Taylor had once been a favorite general of Kennedy-era liberals. Robert F. Kennedy had called him "relentless in his determination to get at the truth," and named one of his sons after him. Now Maxwell Taylor was a tribune of the other tribe, the one that found another lesson to be self-evident: never break faith with God's chosen nation, especially in time of war—truth be damned.

This was Richard Nixon's tribe. The one that, by Election Day 1980, would end up prevailing in the presidential election. Though Richard Nixon, like Moses, would not be the one who led them to that promised land.

THE LAST FREEDOM BIRD ARRIVED AT TRAVIS AIR FORCE BASE IN CALIFORnia to a spontaneous chorus of "God Bless America" from the crowd of 6,500 who had waited hours through typhoon-like rains that tore chunks off nearby buildings. A new round of celebrations blossomed: local boys throwing out first pitches for opening day; drum and bugle corps; ice cream, steak, endless proud patriotic bluster from bunting-draped platforms. The ceremonial bestowing of gifts: Free use of a brand-new Ford LTD for a year. Free admission to Walt Disney World. Free passes, plated in gold, to every major-league baseball game—forever. Captain John Nasmyth appeared, impromptu, on *The Sonny & Cher Comedy Hour.*

And on the first of April, VIVA held a grand ball at the Beverly Wilshire Hotel hosted by Governor Reagan. Lorne Greene, who played the frontier patriarch on TV's *Bonanza,* introduced the distinguished personages on the dais, including John Wayne and astronaut Buzz Aldrin. All wore POW bracelets. Singer Martha Raye, a veteran of USO tours, was escorted by a Green Beret, and wore a green beret, too. Pat O'Brien, who costarred as Knute Rockne with Ronald Reagan in *Knute Rockne, All-American,* announced the color guard, and led the singing of "The Star-Spangled Banner." The president of Pepperdine University quoted Kipling.

Lorne Greene gestured for silence. The guests of honor marched forth in grand procession, two by two with their consorts, as the band struck up the anthem "Stout-Hearted Men": *"Start me with ten who are stout-hearted men, and I'll soon give you ten thousand more."*

The man held longest in Hanoi finally took the stage. "Let it loose!" Greene commanded. The crowd rose as one. Their ovation lasted eight minutes.

The evening's host took to the podium. Governor Reagan's final peroration was addressed to the men: "You gave America back its soul.

God bless a country that can produce men like you." He soon would sign a bill exempting them from state taxes on their earnings while they were in captivity—which could run, with combat pay and family allowances and retroactive promotions, to a lump sum, in 2010 figures, amounting to half a million dollars per POW. "It Won't Be Enough," read a headline in the *Los Angeles Sentinel.*

Then Reagan flew east—"back on the sawdust trail," he told the cloud of reporters who had started following him everywhere, because it looked like he might be running for president. To an ecstatic reception at a luncheon of Young Republicans in Washington, he said this business about the Watergate bugging caper was not relevant to their party's future: the presidential election of 1972 was "the most clear-cut choice in the last forty years," a "head-on confrontation between two opposing philosophies that have polarized this nation." Conservatism won, and would continue to win, he said—a curious argument given that the candidate who won had proposed programs of such dubiously conservative provenance as wage and price controls, a guaranteed minimum income, and the federal Environmental Protection Agency.

Reagan traveled to New Orleans, where he extolled the virtues of free enterprise, cajoled his partisan audience to elect more Republicans to lesser offices, boasted of his recent welfare reform in California, and plugged his new tax limitation proposal. Then he brought up the stout-hearted men—and nearly couldn't continue. He apologized afterward to reporters backstage: "I guess I'm going to have to quit talking about those fellows. I can't do it without choking up."

The reporters followed up a bit rabidly—asking whether he wrote his own speeches; about the recent appearance on TV of the last movie he made, *The Killers,* the only one in which he played a villain ("I wish they would stop showing it"); about whether he was running for president. (They always asked that; he always demurred, insisting, "The office seeks the man.")

Next, in Atlanta, he called Watergate a partisan witch hunt. The president already had his own Justice Department prosecuting the burglars, he said—"What more can you ask?"

He struck reporters as foolishly blithe. One of the Watergate burglars had just told the nation that the White House had pressured him to lie, in a cover-up he suspected went straight to the Oval Office, and that "members of my family have expressed fear for my life if I disclose the facts in this matter." Barry Goldwater said, "It's beginning to be like Teapot Dome." Republican officials reported fund-raising was near a standstill.

Only Reagan was calm. "This man has just been elected," he had reassured the anxious Young Republicans in Washington. Republicans possessed a "2-to-1 majority philosophically." Watergate did not matter—except if the liberals obsessively pursuing what he privately called the president's "lynching" were allowed to let it matter. At his weekly press conference in Sacramento, he called the president "a truthful man." In Atlanta he praised Nixon for refusing to allow his aides to testify before the Senate investigating committee. A reporter promptly pointed out that, no, the president had recently reversed course and ordered his aides to cooperate. Blithely indifferent to the contradiction, Reagan said he supported that, too, then promptly dismissed the whole matter with a quip. Democrats were in hysterics about someone bugging their office? "It seems to me that they should have been happy that somebody was willing to listen to them." Then he excused himself to meet with twenty-five top party contributors.

Let some cry havoc. Just this sort of performance of blitheness in the face of what others called chaos was fundamental to who Ronald Reagan was. It was fundamental to why he made so many others feel so good. Which was fundamental to what he was to become, and the way he changed the world.

CHAPTER TWO

Stories

PEOPLE TOLD STORIES ABOUT RONALD REAGAN—LEGENDS OF A MAN who was larger than life.

Stories about the day of his birth, in 1911. A snowstorm had made the roads of Tampico, Illinois, nearly impassable just as his tiny mother began a long and difficult labor. Of a mother's agony, a child was born. The doctor told her she would never bear another. The blustering Irish Catholic father swept in: "For such a little bit of a Dutchman," he cried, "he makes a hell of a lot of noise, doesn't he!" The mother replied, "I think he's perfectly wonderful. *Ronald Wilson Reagan.*"

There are other versions of the story, too—and they clash with the first. In one, after saying he "looks like a fat little Dutchman," Jack Reagan adds, "But who knows, he might grow up to be president someday." In another, Ronald Reagan was given the nickname "Dutch" not when he was an infant, and not by his father, but after he and his older brother, Neil, were marched off to the barber after growing their hair defiantly long. Neil ended up with a style Ronald said made him look like the cartoon character Moon Mullins; his lifelong nickname became "Moon." Neil snapped back that his little brother's made him look "Dutch." And then there is someone who claimed to know the Reagans when they were young, who did not recall Ronald ever being referred to as "Dutch" at all. Which may, or may not, square with the story as Ronald Reagan set it down in his memoir *An American Life,* in which he named *himself:* "I never thought 'Ronald' was rugged enough for a young red-blooded American boy and as soon as I could, I asked people to call me 'Dutch.'" It's hard to make stories about Ronald Reagan match up. Even, or perhaps especially, the stories Ronald Reagan told about himself—which are where most of the stories originated.

Stories about his first memory: a hot summer day in Galesburg, Illinois, a train depot, an ice wagon, two mischievous boys scurrying beneath a freight train to liberate some refreshing shards of ice—and a blast of steam as the train chuffs to life and nearly finishes them off. *An*

American Life adds the fillip: "Our mother, who had come out on the porch in time to see the escapade, met us in the middle of the park and inflicted the appropriate punishment." However, as president he once offered another "first memory" to admirers in Chicago, where he lived when he was four: Jack rushed in with the news of the tragedy of the capsizing of the SS *Eastland* in the Chicago River, killing more than 840, and sought to impress on his two boys the epochal nature of the event by fetching them downtown to view the scene.

The family lived in an apartment in Chicago for a year, after his father received an exceptionally promising department store job; it was one of more than a dozen rented homes in which Ronald Reagan would spend his childhood. In his first memoir, 1965's *Where's the Rest of Me,* he remembered teeming Chicago sidewalks lit by coin-operated gaslights; clanging horse-drawn fire trucks trailing clouds of steam (thus his first ambition, to be a firefighter); a beer truck that Neil tried to grab hold of that ran him over with its steel-rimmed wheels (the leg healed without complications, goes the story: a miracle). There was the time their mother was off on an endless errand, their father nowhere to be found. The boys wandered off from their apartment to find them, but not before blowing out what they thought were oil lamps. Since the lights they had blown out were fueled by gas, not oil, his parents returned to a house full of deadly methane. Meanwhile the boys crossed the University of Chicago's Midway—terra incognita—and got lost. A friendly drunk came upon them and returned them home. "Jack clobbered us," the story ends.

The family soon moved to a tiny town called Galesburg, where the tales are of a "Huck Finn–Tom Sawyer" idyll: swimming in clear-bottomed creeks and treacherous canals (Dutch was always the best swimmer), meadows to roam, caves to explore, trees to climb. Over-the-river-and-through-the-woods holidays at his mother's people's farm in the country. A magical vacant lot crawling with emerald-green snakes. Chaotic neighborhood football scrums: no real field, no yard lines, no goal, just a mob of excited youngsters chasing a lopsided ball one of the richer kids was able to buy. A story that was etched in strikingly specific detail: The five-year-old lay on the floor with the evening paper. Jack asked him what he was doing, and the little boy said he was reading. His skeptical father asked him to prove it; the little boy recited the details of an explosion in Jersey City, New Jersey, in which German saboteurs blew up an ammunition depot. He remembered, "The next thing I knew he was flying out the door and from the porch inviting all our neighbors to come over and hear his five-year old son read"—and he also remembered that these formative experiences as a news consumer produced in him "an uneasy feeling of a world outside my own."

Two years later, and Monmouth, Illinois, the family's next little town: the awful flu epidemic of 1918, quarantined neighborhoods, shuttered churches, masked townspeople, wreaths with black ribbons guarding doorways. His mother almost died. "The house grew quiet," he recalled, "and I sat watching for the guy with the black bag, and when he came down Jack went outside with him and I waited with a lurking terror for him to come back. . . . I went to bed and woke up with a weight digging at the pit of my stomach until one day Jack said 'she's going to be all right,' and his face looked like the sun was out." Then came the eleventh day of the eleventh month of 1918—Armistice Day. Glorious parades where "the streets suddenly filled up with people, bonfires were lighted, and grown-ups and children paraded down the street signing and carrying torches in the air." Then Ronald Reagan came down with bronchial pneumonia—he was so close to death, he says, the entire neighborhood came by to keep vigil. One boy brought him a collection of lead soldiers to play with: "the sun shone through the window," he recalled, "and I felt like a king with an army of 500."

Many stories index an unmistakable loneliness. In one, wandering on his own, he discovered in an unused hayloft a collection of artfully preserved birds' nests and eggs and glass-encased butterflies. He began scampering up trees, collecting eggs, punching tiny holes in both ends and blowing out the inside. The story ends in a family communion: his father scavenged an old display case from the shoe store where he worked, then hauled it up to the hayloft, his boy's new playpen. Reagan, too, found kindly old benefactors: a childless couple who lent the boy the use of their overstuffed gargoyle of a parlor chair, from whence he contemplated a "mystic atmosphere" of fragrant leather tomes and shawls and antimacassars and glass globes encasing exotic birds and flowers, and read all the latest grown-up magazines. "Aunt Emma and Uncle Jim" kept a jewelry shop next door to his father's shoe store; their basement seduced him with its clanging and ticking and shining treasures. They gave him cookies and chocolate and a ten-cent weekly allowance.

THE STORIES HE TOLD TELL A STORY IN THEMSELVES. THEY FREQUENTLY feature great, melodramatic traumas: the sinking of a great ship, a saboteur's explosion, a near explosion in the family flat. Almost always, they end in some sort of redemption—even if redemption is a paternal "licking," justly administered. Even those stories from the cruel winter of

1918 resolve into glorious celestial images: "the sun shone through the window"; "his face looked like the sun was out"—as if his mother's almost dying and himself almost dying were the best things that could have happened to him.

When he was ten the family moved to Dixon, Illinois—the river town where, though the family lived in five separate rented houses there, he finally began to feel at home. Dixon stories fixate about how he was the smallest kid in his age group—which sets the stage for his redemptions. Ice-skating on the frozen Rock River, he would turn his too-big overcoat, handed down from his big brother, into a sail, letting the wind carry his tiny body for miles. Playing football as a kid, "a scrawny, undersized, underweight nuisance," he frequently found himself on the bottom of a "mass of writhing, shouting bodies." That "gave me my first taste of claustrophobia. I got frightened to the point of hysteria." He taught himself to "time my charges so that I was in one of the upper layers of bodies." Toughened up, "I had a collection of the largest purplish bruises possible. More than once, I must have been a walking coagulation. . . . Those were the happiest times of my life."

Panic attacks, a mass of scar tissue: the happiest time of his life.

A downtown merchant displayed mannequins wearing the uniforms of the high school football team the Dixon Dukes, whom Dutch watched practice every day. "Filling one of those purple and white jerseys became the noblest and most glamorous goal in my life." He was too small to make the team. But that, too, was opportunity for redemption. He was spurred to take his first job, digging foundations for houses, which, he said, was the way he built up enough muscle to finally win a place on the squad.

A good thing he was scrawny, or he would never have acquired the character it took to be strong.

Everything always works out in the end, gloriously.

Why?

"WE TELL OURSELVES STORIES," A WISE WOMAN NAMED JOAN DIDION once said, "in order to live." It is how we organize the chaos of experience into the order we require just to carry on. And in the life of the young Ronald Wilson Reagan, there was more than the usual ration of chaos to organize. One biographer recites the catalogue: "Between the ages of six and ten he attended a different school every year. . . . As a baby he lived in his first house for four months and his second for eight. He lived in five different places in Dixon, four different ones in Tampico, two in Galesburg—all rented. Sometimes they subleased to pay their own rent." Another biographer reasonably points out, "At any given spot, he could have easily forgotten his address."

Much later, Ronald Reagan had an explanation—a story—that let him find comfort in the itinerancy: that his father, uneducated but street-smart, a natural-born salesman "endowed with the gift of blarney and the charm of a leprechaun," was searching out upward mobility for his family. It was a token of his Americanism, even a sort of cowboy heroism: "Like a lot of Americans whose roots were on the nineteenth-century frontier, he was restless, always ready to pull up stakes and move on in search of a better life for himself and his family."

In fact most of Jack Reagan's moves were lateral—and few if any, evidence suggests, were voluntary. Jack Reagan was an alcoholic. When the family left Chicago, it was after an arrest for public drunkenness. "Details of the incident are unknown," Jack's grandson Ron Reagan discovered, "but it resulted in his losing his new job." With the passage of Prohibition five years later, it wasn't just public drunkenness that might result in arrest; possessing alcohol was a federal crime. Jack Reagan would nonetheless disappear for days at a time, apparently going back to Chicago—where deaths due to alcohol increased by 200 percent in the first three years of the Volstead Act, and "psychosis has supplanted the old delirium tremens," the Associated Press reported, owing to the proliferation of unfermented liquor cut with fuel oil. Jack's older brother was committed to the Dixon State Hospital for the Feeble Minded for just such alcoholic psychosis in 1920.

Jack Reagan was also something of a dandy, specializing in the somewhat disreputable trade of selling women's shoes (what kind of man handled women's feet for a living?). He was glad-handing and blarneyful ("Jesus walked barefoot, but then he didn't have to deal with our Illinois winters, now did he?" "I'm glad you chose that pair, they can walk to church and dance a jig on the way home"), and claimed expertise in the made-up science of "proctipedics"—which he learned from a correspondence course advertised in the newspapers. His wife, however, was a teetotaler—a pillar of the Disciples of Christ church in every town in which they alighted. Her calling card was her devotion to fixing others, as she wrote in a sonnet she presented to her adult Sunday school class:

> To higher, nobler things my mind is bent
> Thus giving of my strength, which God has lent.
> I strive some needy souls' unrest to soothe
> Lest they the path of righteousness shall lose
> Through fault of mine, my Maker to present.

If I should fail to show them of their need,
How could I hope to meet Him, face to face.

Needy souls were everywhere. Nelle Reagan considered it her duty to rescue each and every one of them. She was forever leaving the family hearth to pray with the families of sick children, to visit tuberculosis patients (though the disease, communicable through the air, took both Jack's parents within a week of each other when Jack was sick). She visited the local jail, entertaining prisoners with dramatic readings and hymns, accompanying herself on banjo or mandolin, preaching from the Bible, feeding them apples and cookies while bringing a modest lunch of soda crackers for herself. She developed a reputation for literal miracles. "Many of us," a contemporary recalled, "believed Nelle Reagan had the gift to heal. . . . It was the way she prayed, down on her knees, eyes raised up and speaking like she knew God personally, like she had had lots of dealings with him before." One local mother went to church to pray for her four-year-old daughter after doctors pronounced her case hopeless. Christians must accept death, the pastor told her. Mrs. Reagan, though, spent the afternoon with the family praying for a miracle. Moments later, the mother testified, "the abscess burst. . . . the next morning the doctor said, 'I don't need to lance this.' God had heard Nelle Reagan's prayer and answered it."

But there was one person she never could heal: her own alcoholic husband.

In Dixon, the family became relatively more settled, moving less often. But if anything the household was apparently more chaotic. Nelle began taking custody of released prisoners, housing them in her sewing room, calling them "her boys." (Her own boys, meanwhile, slept two to a bed.) One hagiographic biography of Ronald Reagan calls her "an extraordinary woman who appears to have possessed only positive traits." A more skeptical observer described the constantly absent Nelle's household as "a surreal Norman Rockwell painting with his alcoholic Catholic father, devout Christian mother, Catholic brother, and ever-changing boarders the family took in."

Nelle also loved to perform. Small-town newspapers like the *Dixon Telegraph* being organs for busybodies, we can follow her progress. In 1922, at Dixon State Hospital, she "entertained the patients with a short and enjoyable program"; in 1924 she played two roles in *The Pill Bottle*, "a delightful portrayal of missionary work"; in 1926 she was a guest at a Baptist church for a recitation titled "Ship of Faith"; in 1927 at the American Legion for a "splendid talk" on George Washington's boyhood. "FELLOWS HOME SCENE OF HAPPY MEETING," Dixonians learned of an April 27, 1927, party she hosted on the status of Christianity in Japan; "MRS. J. E. REAGAN IS HOSTESS TO SOCIETY," they read four months later of her presentation on "The Large World—My Neighborhood," where she entertained "questions regarding the newspapers, moving pictures, radio, steamship and airplane, and how they tie the world together."

Another sort of item, however, frequently appeared cheek by jowl with the social notes in small-town newspapers: shaming accounts of men arrested for drunkenness. "DIPSOMANIAC AND KLEPTOMANIAC IS THE DOUBLE AFFLICTION OF POOR FRED WEST." "MAN WHO VIOLATED PAROLE WILL HAVE TO TAKE TREATMENT FOR BOOZE APPETITE." "SON APPEARS BEFORE JUSTICE ASKING FOR PARENT'S COMMITMENT TO HOSPITAL." Jack Reagan apparently never showed up in such hometown newspaper accounts, by what miracle we do not know. Maybe it had something to do with the peripatetic manner in which he practiced his affliction. Perhaps it helped that he was a regular pinochle partner of Dixon's police chief. Maybe editors exercised deference to his teetotaling church lady wife; one of the distinguishing features of Prohibition was its selective local enforcement as a way to exert social control against disreputable outsiders. Or maybe it was just luck. Either way, the anxious uncertainty of life in the Reagan household had to have been awful. Fulton, Tampico, Chicago, Galesburg, Tampico again, Dixon: the next town over the horizon just might bring the family redemption. Or it might bring burning shame. Disorder, futility, and alienation were keynotes of Ronald Reagan's formative years. It is hardly a wonder that a bright and frightened child might organize his recollections otherwise.

Take the story of the "oatmeal meat." His older brother, who grew up an unsentimental man, once told a historian of his Saturday chore when the family lived in Chicago: he was sent to the butcher with instructions to buy a ten-cent soup bone to last the week. He was also to ask for a free chunk of liver for the cat. The punch line: "We didn't have a cat." The liver was the family's big Sabbath meal. When Ronald Reagan recollected his family's mealtimes, however, he told the story rather differently. "Our main meal," he wrote in An American Life, "frequently consisted of a dish my mother called 'oatmeal meat.' She'd cook a batch of oatmeal and mix it with hamburger. . . . It was moist and meaty, the most wonderful thing I'd ever eaten."

Maybe it was. Probably it wasn't. As an adult, when asked to name his favorite food, Ronald Reagan always said steak. In his speeches, a juicy T-bone always stood for the height of sensual delight—as well as the ill-gotten gains of welfare cheats. In a 1985 private letter to his former boss he fondly remembered the day when he was a lifeguard and they devoured four pounds of spareribs at the beach; another time he lovingly recalled getting a "rib facial" at his favorite restaurant when he was a radio personality in Des Moines, Iowa; indeed, what little primary evidence we have from his childhood suggests an obsession with meat. "I have 12 rabbits and am going to kill 3 and eat them," he wrote in his earliest surviving letter, which continues in a chatty stream of consciousness until something sensual seems to monopolize his attention in mid-thought:

"well I will have to close,
"now Ronald Reagan
"PS.
"Smell that meat
"Ain't it good."

Ronald Reagan was an athlete of the imagination, a master at turning complexity and confusion and doubt into simplicity and stout-hearted certainty. Transforming his life, first in his own and then in others' eyes, into a model of frictionless ease—and fashioning the world outside him into a stage on which to display it—was how he managed to fly.

THE PROCESS SEEMED TO HAPPEN WITH A SUDDENNESS, IN THE TWO INtense years after the family moved to Dixon when he was ten, in 1921. An inner transformation appeared to have taken place—the act of will that turned Ronald Reagan into what he was to become. The evidence is recorded in the photographs.

There is a picture of Ronald Reagan from the summer when he was ten, a group shot of the caddies for a ladies' golf tournament in Dixon. Moon Reagan is front and center, posed jauntily with a golf bag beside him, looking confidently into the camera. Dutch is awkwardly off to one side as if eager to escape the frame. Most of the boys are hatless, though some wear those sporty 1920s newsboy caps. Ronald, alone, is covered by a dweebish beanie. He looks distant, hardly present. He looks like the kind of boy he actually was: lonely and a little bit scared, the figure described by one writer on chaotic families as the "Boy Who Disappears." She writes of quiet and withdrawn children like these, "Because they try so hard to stay invisible, they are often overlooked by people who might be able to help them." The photograph fitted others' recollections of him: that he was "subdued," "shy and retiring"; that he would "sit for hours . . . looking at those glass-encased collections"; that "he was very quiet and he could go for hours all by himself playing with lead soldiers."

There is another group photo including Ronald Reagan taken perhaps a year later. Again he is off to one side—but this time it is because the other boys serve as his retinue. Neil and Dutch have joined the new boys' marching band organized by the Dixon YMCA. All alone in his room he had been practicing baton twirling, just like what he had seen in the Armistice Day parade in Monmouth, with a broomstick or an old brass bedpost. And so the formerly timid boy was chosen drum major. Here he is the photograph's star—and he knows it. He proudly displays his gold-tipped staff and nifty striped tie—he's the only boy wearing one. His feet are precisely splayed, hip proudly forward; alone among the boys, he seems to understand that if you cock your elbow in just the right way, the cape that is part of their uniform juts out with jaunty flair instead of lying flat. And then there is the face: It is alive. It is the face of *Ronald Reagan*. He would never appear lost, forlorn, or empty-eyed in a photograph again. Try to find one.

There is a picture from when he is about twelve. Again he is with a group of fellow caddies—only this time, he sits, proudly, front row center. His eyes look almost steely. He seems to have carefully posed himself: legs splayed, fashionable basketball sneakers out front, fist out in his chin. He seems, in fact, as aware of the lines his body presents before the viewer as a dancer.

He had just started wearing spectacles. He told that story, like all the others, in tones of melodramatic redemption. He had been the last boy picked for baseball games: "The whole world was made up of colored blobs that became distinct when I got closer—and I was sure it appeared the same way to everyone else." (Being the Boy Who Disappears, he made no demand on his parents' attention by pointing out something was wrong.) Then, once upon a time, the family was out for a drive in the country and he put on his mother's spectacles as a lark and let out a "yelp that almost caused Jack to run off the road." He had healed himself; he could see.

But he is not wearing his glasses in that second golf course photo—even though you would think glasses are a tool that would come in handy for a caddy. Until the day Ronald Reagan died, in fact, he was almost never photographed wearing glasses. Here was a constant: if a camera was present, or an audience, he was aware of it—aware, always, of the gaze of others: reflecting on it, adjusting himself to it, inviting it. Modeling himself, in his mind's eye, according to how he presented himself physically to others. Adjusting himself to be seen as he wished others to see him—until the figure he cut became unmistakable. So unmistakable that in a caricature he drew of himself in his high school yearbook, he presents himself in silhouette—and yet he is immediately recognizable to us, even now, as *Ronald Reagan.*

What happened, in those few years between the two pictures of himself as a caddy: the one of a distant, shy boy, the other of a boy presenting himself with the confidence of a hero? Here the evidence is suggested in a story that Reagan recalled in a moment of rare vulnerability—for which he slipped into a distancing third person address. Up until about that age of ten, he said, he used to make up plays in his head and act them out to himself, out loud—until people started making fun of him: "What are you doing, kid? Talking to yourself?" He wrote: "Enough cracks like that, and a sensitive boy . . . begins to feel a little silly. . . . So from then on he doesn't pretend openly."

Instead, he started to pretend inside—a decision that coincides with a singular event he also recalled with striking specificity: being issued, on December 20, 1921, three weeks before his tenth birthday, Card No. 3695 the Dixon Public Library. He began checking out an average of two books a week, books of a very definite description.

Boys' adventure books of the late nineteenth and early twentieth centuries hewed to rigid genre conventions. They almost always began in the same way: they introduce a boy or man who will soon be revealed as the story's hero, but outwardly does not appear heroic at all. The boys are fatherless or family-less, itinerant or otherwise without a place in the world. In one of young Reagan's favorites, the protagonist is the son of a man named Lord Greystoke, who is sent to deepest, darkest Africa to make an official investigation for the Crown. The elder Greystoke's ship wrecks, and he finds himself and his wife thrown "upon an unknown shore to be left to the mercies of savage beasts, and, possibly, still more savage men." His wife bears him a son, both the baby's parents pass away—and our hero has been introduced, as alienated from his circumstances as a human can possibly be: a man among beasts.

Tarzan of the Apes unfolds the essential lesson embodied in every adventure tale of the sort so assiduously devoured by this Boy Who Disappears: that some souls are born under the sign of grace, and that though it might not look so at first, this grace will always eventually show itself in the fullness of time, whatever temporarily chaotic and isolating accidents of circumstances into which the hero finds himself thrown.

Young Tarzan, at the age of ten—around the age Ronald Reagan was when he first encountered this story—is described to be as strong as a normal man of thirty. Belonging to neither the world of beasts nor that of men, he takes on the best qualities of both: a "quickness of mental action far beyond the power of the apes," yet able "to spring twenty feet across space at the dizzy heights of the forest tops." Deploying these gifts with the "indifferent ease that was habitual to him," he dispatches one by one the ignoble tyrant-apes who delight in rampaging against their weak and helpless subjects; protecting the weak, strong yet never flaunting strength, selflessly sacrificing—these are the qualities proper to a hero. Boy Tarzan, lonely and apart, turns out not to be inferior to those around him but, simply, to be *better*. Indeed, it turns out that the very circumstances of his alienation—"the training of his short lifetime among the fierce brutes of the jungle"—is the *superior* crucible for the shaping of heroes. This was a moral that a boy who hoped to escape degraded circumstances by wishing himself into heroism was exquisitely primed to appreciate. Here was a satisfying story of how the world worked. Or could be made to work in the mind of a lonely ten-year-old boy.

He read every Tarzan story he could get his hands on. When he found an adventure story he liked, he always read as many sequels as he could get his hands on. Stories by the former Unitarian minister Horatio Alger, for example, were even more useful—because in these the gift of grace was revealed not by dint of aristocratic blood but by its absence: unearned, aristocratic privilege is what villains use to lord over the weak, and the nobility of the *true* aristocrats—simple, stout-hearted boys of modest circumstance who rise by dint of honest hard work (and the sponsorship of a rich deus ex machina who always arrives in the nick of time when your heart is pure and you love your mother and protect her from the world's cruel imprecations)—reveals itself by turns via adventure after adventure, overcoming all setbacks, unto the very last page, when the final algebraic equation is magnificently, gloriously solved: "As for Frank, all goes smoothly with him. He is diligent in business, and is likely to become a rich man." Everything always works out in the end, gloriously.

We know exactly what kind of books Ronald Reagan loved as a boy because he told us, in details verifiable to anyone with a Dixon map: "I would make what to me was a long trek on foot in the evening after dinner—we called it supper then—down Hennepin Avenue past South Central School, up the hill and across the street to the library. I would usually take out two books. I made those trips at least once a week and sometimes more often . . . the Rover Boys; Frank Merriwell at Yale; Horatio Alger . . . all the Tarzan books . . . the other books that he wrote about John Carter and his frequent trips to the strange kingdoms to be found on the planet of Mars."

We also know a book he hated: *Brown of Harvard*. Its "hero" is an indolent Don Juan from "one of the oldest and best families in Cambridge," who aspires to be a poet and has "a handsome, almost careless countenance, and a wealth of curly hair which cropped up round about the edges of a woefully unsizeable cap." (That's a giveaway: a real hero, the sort Dutch Reagan preferred, carried himself exquisitely. Lord Greystoke has "features regular and strong; his carriage that of perfect, robust health"; Alger's Ragged Dick "had a frank, straight-forward manner"; another Alger hero "had a pleasant expression, and a bright, resolute look, a warm heart, and a clear intellect, and was probably, in spite of his poverty, the most popular boy in Groveton.") Reagan liked to contrast *Brown of Harvard* to *Frank Merriwell at Yale,* his hands-down favorite. It begins with Merriwell, a freshman of modest family background, finding himself challenged to a fight in which he accidentally shows up some entitled cad's actual ignobility. ("Barely had the words left the little referee's lips when—tap, tap, tap!—Merriwell had struck Diamond with three light blows with his open hand. . . . Never had they seen three blows delivered with such lightning-like rapidity.") It ends with a baseball game between Yale and the hated rival Harvard. The umpire hands the game ball "to the freshman pitcher Yale had so audaciously stacked up against Harvard," who skillfully holds Harvard to only two runs—then wins the game with two outs in the bottom of the ninth by cracking a soaring home run.

IN 1972, A LONG ISLAND ENTREPRENEUR ANNOUNCED A PLAN TO REPUB-lish the Merriwell books as an antidote to what ailed America. "We need renewal and affirmation," he said, "and Frank offers it to us, for he is the democratic ethic in action." *Life* magazine ran a patronizing feature on the development, mocking this foolish man who "feels that the U.S.A. jumped the track and lost direction after the era of gaslight and cable car" and who held up a storybook hero as "the country's guide and measuring stick as national singularity is restored." Frank Merriwell, the suspicious circles agreed—master football player, tennis player, fencer, wrestler, sharpshooter, horseman, boxer, and oarsman, who once won the Congressional Medal of Honor by lifting his chaste sweetheart to the saddle of his galloping horse just before a speeding locomotive would have smashed her to smithereens—was ridiculous. So was this "shrewd enough fellow in other fields of endeavor" who was "willing to say he patterned himself after Merriwell when he was growing up, a poor boy."

Ronald Reagan would have disagreed. As a child, he had aspired to Merriwell's world—where virtue and villainy are always visible, revealed plainly in everyday performances (at least to those who also are virtuous; that is how good people recognize each other). Where good and evil are absolutes. Where the point of the story was that, though it might not look that way at the start, these truths became self-evident by the end—with plenty of adventure along the way. As an adult, Reagan unashamedly spoke of Frank Merriwell as a role model. Through Merriwell's world, he rehearsed what he wished to become, and began searching out ways to display it in the *real* world.

ONCE, WHEN RONALD REAGAN RAN FOR GOVERNOR OF CALIFORNIA, A political reporter asked him about his upbringing. He talked nonstop about his mother. He never even mentioned his father.

It could not have been difficult to cast Nelle Reagan within his emergent moral worldview: sweet but tough, stalwart but saintly, she was like all those mothers in his stories unto whom every sacrifice was due. Her philosophy fitted, too: she had, as Ronald Reagan put it, "a sense of optimism that ran as deep as the cosmos."

Shortly before he was born she was baptized into the Disciples of Christ, a Presbyterian splinter with elements of both liberalism and fundamentalism: a disdain for liquor but also an expansive role for women and reverence for education. Its rituals became a chaotic family's bedrock: Sunday school, then services, then "Christian Endeavor" club and a second evening service on the Sabbath; prayer meetings every Wednesday night; all manner of volunteer work through the week. Nelle became president of its Missionary Society. She was also always reading and rereading a book called *That Printer of Udell's: A Story of the Middle West,* a novel by a Disciples of Christ minister named Harold Wright Bell.

Out of curiosity, her eleven-year-old son picked it up himself. He found in it the same moral matrix of all his favorite books: indolent and hypocritical "gentlemen," a virtuous drifter whom they despise for his mean circumstances but who turns out to be far more noble than they, a chaste damsel to be rescued from defilement just in the nick of time—and, in the end, virtue rewarded, when the fatherless hero ends up as the town's first citizen. The only difference is the religious tincture: in this novel the strutting hypocrites are pillars of the church—until, that is, the hero melodramatically exposes their hypocrisy, introduces the community to the true meaning of faith, eliminates drunkenness and other species of loose morality from the town, and is rewarded by election as their representative in the United States Congress. All this for practicing the biblical injunction that is the volume's last words: "Inasmuch as you have done it unto one of the least of these, my brethren, ye have done it unto Me."

It taught Dutch an important life lesson: Christians could be heroes, too, just like Frank Merriwell and Ragged Dick. A few days after reading it, Ronald Reagan went to his mother and told her he wanted to declare his faith and be baptized, too.

Church offered another attraction: an opportunity to perform. His mother was a ham. A neighbor described her voice, when calling her boys in for dinner, as "theatrical." The family never missed a "Chautauqua," the itinerant speaker series that toured Middle America; in Tampico, Jack and Nelle played in amateur theatricals at the opera house. She had changed her name from the apparently more prosaic "Nellie" to "Nelle"—what a friend called her "professional poetry-writing name"; in Dixon, she became one of the town's favorite "readers"—dramatic reciters of sentimental literature, a favorite parlor diversion of the time. Soon her second son started tagging along on her rounds (perhaps, since she was always off somewhere performing, and ministering, it started just as a way to spend time with her). In 1924 he acted in a Christmas play called *The King's Birthday*. Three weeks later, at the church annual meeting, he "convulsed the audience," the *Telegraph* reported, "with his one-act dramatic reading." That summer he traveled with his mother to Tampico. "Each number Mrs. Reagan gave was enthusiastically encored," a *Telegraph* reporter they apparently brought in tow recorded; "Ronald Reagan was encored several times." He was fourteen. The following Easter he led the entire packed sanctuary in the annual sunrise prayer. He began, a biographer wrote, to emulate Nelle's "mellow, distinctive voice, tinged with a hopeful cadence. When trying to be persuasive, he would lower the volume, speaking 'barely above a whisper' to win a confidential intimacy, and he instinctively knew just the right moments to raise that volume and lower the pitch for intensity."

The stories Ronald Reagan told about his father, meanwhile, are few, abbreviated, and cryptic. They suggest a mercurial, unpredictable presence, rushing, rushing, rushing, appearing out of nowhere to fill a space with his aggression: dashing in at the tail end of his wife's difficult labor; hurtling forth with news of the *Eastland* sinking. In one story Dutch is working at his job digging foundations when his father appears as the noon whistle blows. His son has just hoisted a pick in the air: "Without moving the pick another inch, I relaxed my wrists, opened my hands, walked out from under the pick, and headed toward Jack. The pick plunged to earth and stuck in the ground an inch or two from one of my bosses' toes. As Jack and I walked away together, he said: 'That was the damnedest exhibition of laziness I've ever seen in my life.'"

And there the tale ends—in admiration? Consternation? It's hard to tell.

In another, Jack catches Dutch fighting in the schoolyard, "surrounded by a circle of eggers-on. He stopped the fight, tongue-lashed the crowd—then lifted me a foot in the air with the flat side of his boot. 'Not because you were fighting,' he said, 'but because you weren't winning.'"

And there *that* story ends—though with an admixture of resentment: "That was my first sample of adult injustice. I *had* been winning."

The resentment resurfaces again in the curious tale of the rotten potatoes: "My father bought a carload of second-hand potatoes for personal speculation. My brother and I were ordered to the siding to sort the good potatoes from the bad." They spent days in that sweltering boxcar, "gingerly gripping tubers that dissolved in the fingers with a dripping squish, emitting an odor worse than that of a decaying corpse." Here Jack resembles nothing so much as the evil stepfather in the Horatio Alger book *Silas Snobden's Office Boy*, who shows up out of nowhere and barks, "I'm your father now, and I mean that you shall treat me as such. When do you get your pay?"

Her mother's beloved pastor died suddenly. Dutch made his replacement practically his surrogate father. He assures us that his actual father could occasionally show "great sensitivity"—like the time Moon's senior class decided to wear tuxedos for graduation, and Moon decided not to show up because the family could not afford one. Then Jack invites him on a walk. They end up at Mr. O'Malley's clothing store, where the haberdasher is waiting to fit him for a tux. It is telling that Moon, the family cynic, did not interpret the gesture as sensitive. He remembered it as Jack trying to save face in public. There is also the fact that sudden, extravagant acts of generosity are a frequent mark of alcoholic patriarchs, making up for equally extravagant failures.

There was little place for his father in Reagan's heroic scripts, except as a figure to be pitied. In fact, the most famous story he tells of his father feels like a scene straight out of a novel by Harold Wright Bell—whose own father had been an itinerant drunk, too. One day, Reagan related in the opening pages of the memoir he published in 1965, he "came home to find my father flat on his back on the front porch and no one there to lend a hand but me. He was drunk, dead to the world. I stood over him for a minute or two. I wanted to let myself into the house and go to bed and pretend he wasn't there. Oh, I wasn't ignorant of his weakness. I don't know at what age I knew what the occasional absences or the loud voices in the night meant, but up until now my mother, Nelle, or my brother handled the situation and I was a child in bed with the privilege of pretending to sleep."

There follows the redemption:

"But sometime along the line to each of us, I suppose, must come the first moment of accepting responsibility. If we don't accept it (and some don't), then we must just grow older without quite growing up. . . . I bent over him, smelling the sharp odor of whiskey from the speakeasy. I got a fistful of his overcoat. Opening the door, I managed to drag him inside and get him to bed."

Then, the happily-ever-after:

"In a few days he was the bluff-hearted man I knew and loved and will always remember."

A good thing his father was passed out drunk, or else Ronald Reagan would not have had the opportunity to come of age.

WHAT HAD LURED JACK TO DIXON IN THE FIRST PLACE WAS THE PROMISE of a partnership in a fancy new shoe store. "Mr. Reagan, who will act as manager, is an experienced shoe man and also a graduate practipedist," the *Telegraph* reported, adding an untruth no doubt provided by the story's subject, who "had years of experience in many of the larger cities throughout the state." (Galesburg, Monmouth, and Tampico were all smaller cities.) A historian who studied the terms of the partnership learned that the deal looked more like indentured servitude, in which he was to pay back his ownership share in commissions that always fell short of expectations.

Ronald Reagan would have to find his masculine role models elsewhere. Luckily, as adolescence dawned, a new mass medium was providing any number of real-life Frank Merriwells to emulate. Historians would call it the "Golden Age of Sport"—a time, as its bard, sportswriter Grantland Rice, put it, of "the greatest collection of stars that sport has ever known since the first cave man tackled the mammoth and the aurochs bull." In the 1920s, the number of people who paid to see college football games doubled (the stadium at Frank Merriwell's Yale held 75,000 fans). The biggest boxing matches were held in stadiums, including the grandest of them all: the "House That Ruth Built," Yankee Stadium, which opened with an audience of 74,217 when Dutch was twelve.

George Herman Ruth, he of the proliferating nicknames—"Babe," the "Bambino, "the "Sultan of Swat," the "Maharaja of Mash"—was a prototype for a new kind of cultural hero: hymned as so larger than life that the year he hit fifty-four home runs, one press-box Aeschylus called the feat "as incredible as the first heavier-than-air flying machine." Sports poetry became a regular feature in new magazines of mass circulation like *Collier's*, where Dutch could have read Grantland Rice's lyric about a farm boy who played for the nearby University of Illinois—

> *. . . which of them to tackle*
> *Each rival must decide;*
> *They shift with spectral swiftness*
> *Across the swarded range,*
> *And one of them's a shadow,*
> *And one of them is Grange.*

Writing like that was how the nation learned that what it was observing were not merely boys' games played by men but world-historic moral clashes revealing the moral secrets of the universe.

Boxing had been an outlaw sport until World War I, when the Army began using it for infantry training. Then the American Legion led a movement to lift state boxing bans as a patriotic duty and a young man who had grown up in hardscrabble mining camps (Babe Ruth had grown up in an orphanage, raised by monks) became champion by beating a fighter fifty-four pounds heavier than he in a fight the *New York Tribune* called the greatest bout "dating back to days beyond all memory." Jack Dempsey had hardly lost before 1926, when Gene Tunney felled him before eighty thousand fans at Yankee Stadium. "Honey, I forgot to duck," Dempsey told his wife—absurdly modest, just like a hero was supposed to be. The *Dixon Telegraph* had found the contest important enough to run three features on it in one day, not including a wire photograph rushed into the paper before press time captioned, "Tunney Starts Aggressive Attacks in the First Round." Ronald Reagan, who made the exact same quip about not ducking to *his* wife after a 1981 assassination attempt, was plainly paying attention.

Sports stars were intimations that actual fleshly human beings, not just storybook heroes, could become superhuman, too. Sportswriting encapsulated a moral vision—the same one Dutch imbided in his adventure stories. The actual Babe Ruth once unloaded a sack of letters on a rookie with the instructions to "put the letters from the broads in one pile and the ones with the checks in the other. Throw the other junk away, especially the sappy stuff from fans." The mythic Babe Ruth "spent innumerable hours going out of his way to help youngsters singly and in groups, to take them autographed balls, to help pay their doctors' bills"—at least in the writing of Grantland Rice, who also wrote, "The true democracy in the United States is not to be found among politicians, our so-called statesmen, our labor union leaders or our capitalists. It is only to be found in sport. . . . Here you are measured by what you are and what you can do. Nothing else counts." It was sports, he said, more than war, "that help build up clean living, cool heads, stout hearts, and sound judgement under fire." The heroes it raised up proved it.

There were suspicious circles even then. Scolds at the *Saturday Evening Post* carped that in the reckoning of a writer like Rice, Babe Ruth could not just show up for a game in St. Louis but instead "arrived after the manner of a human avalanche hurtling on its downward way from the blue Missouri heavens." They argued that the reason for the hyperbole was commerce: "the sporting news must be played up as glorious and magnificent; the dull, the shoddy, the second-rate in sports must be left unsaid"; to write otherwise "might quench the inherent idealism in sports which is born and bred in every youngster in the United States. But most of all, it would discourage a potential customer." Hagiography was part of the hustle, wrote W. O. McGeehan of the *New York Herald Tribune,* who called boxing "the manly art of modified murder": "they raise false idols. They make heroes of brutes, they make demigods of inconsequential young men without character or true courage, they make saintly characters out of the vicious." And, said the young liberal theologian Reinhold Niebuhr in the *Nation,* it could not last: "Heroes can thrive only where ignorance reduces history to mythology. They cannot survive the coldly critical temper of modern thought when it is functioning normally, nor can they be worshipped by a generation which has every facility for determining their foibles and analyzing their limitations."

The scolds lost the contest. Radio came; the first heavyweight championship was broadcast in 1921, the first World Series in 1922. And when Dempsey and Tunney fought their rematch in 1927, *Radio Digest* claimed Graham McNamee's broadcast caused 127 radio listeners to have heart attacks. The United Press tripled the size of its sports bureau; the average metropolitan newspaper carried two thousand inches of

sports copy a week, twice the amount carried a decade earlier; and the
Chicago Tribune, which circulated across the Midwest, ran a column
called "My Most Thrilling Moment in Football"—every day.

More important, for a young man in Dixon, local newspapers described contests fought by local "nines" (baseball teams), "gridders"
(football players), and "grapplers" (wrestlers) in the exact same melodramatic way—frequently on the front page. Small-town Midwestern
boys could become terrestrial gods, too: Dutch learned that from the
newspaper every single day.

His first surviving letter ("Smell that meat. Aint it good") is also the
first surviving piece of his sportswriting: "Dixon High school has played
10 games won 8 tied 1 and lost 1 they tied sterling." He turned the discussion to Sunday School: "our class took the banners for attendance
and collection"—"*took the banners*" is Golden Age sportswriting to
a T—before turning back to football again, to a game that was canceled
because "there captain got yellow" (sports even then for him was a test
of character and mettle), and to a local boy named Garland Waggoner,
son of his mother's beloved, recently deceased, pastor: "monday mom
got a letter from Mrs. Waggoner and she said Garland has made the team
at Eureka they played Illinois this week." Garland Waggoner became a
football star at Eureka. And, at that, Dutch Reagan's hero.

Heroes were everywhere, every day, in a small-town Midwestern
paper like the *Telegraph.* It was part of the culture of the 1920s—
headlines like ROUND WORLD FLIERS RESUME FLIGHT TOMORROW; UN-
SUNG HEROES OF U.S. / BOYS IN POSTAL SERVICE FACE UNTOLD HARDSHIPS
/ BUT ARE NEVER RECOGNIZED IN HONORS; "HUMAN FLY" TO SCALE BANK
BUILDING. Charles Lindbergh dipped a wing when he flew over town on
the way to an appearance in Peoria.

Such news in the *Dixon Telegraph* ran beside evidence of a modern
world that was becoming increasingly chaotic, confusing, unmoored:
"PONZI LEAVES JAIL WITH ONE IDEA—TO ACCUMULATE ANOTHER FOR-
TUNE." "GIRL BRANDED YOUTH WITH 'KKK' HE SAYS." "GEN. DAWES
CONDEMNED LA FOLLETTE / 'UNTRIED AND DANGEROUS RADICALISM'—
MAMMOTH CROWD." "FIENDISH SLAYER IS HEADING FOR CANADIAN BOR-
DER." "Swooping down upon the East Davenport Turner Hall Tuesday,
prohibition officers and a squad of local police seized more than 4,000
pints of beer, which was dumped."

Thank God for the glory of sport. How deeply did the canons of
sports heroics inform Ronald Reagan's inner transformation? His son
Ron once told a story about his father's last days, when he could look
back at a life in which he had become, by any reasonable reckoning,

precisely the kind of man he had dreamed of: first a movie star adored by millions; then the most powerful man in the world, the slayer of evil empires. Weakened by Alzheimer's disease, his mind reduced to its most primal constituents, he would wake with a start and cry that there was somewhere he needed to be: not a movie set where Bette Davis or George Cukor was waiting for him, nor the White House Situation Room, but a locker room. "There's a game," he would murmur; "they're waiting for me."

He was always a strong swimmer, and in the spring of 1926 he and Jack talked the operators of the local beach on the Rock River into hiring him as a lifeguard, even though he was only fifteen. He told the stories again and again: how he was hired at Lowell Park at eighteen dollars a week (fifteen in other tellings) and all the hamburgers he could eat; how he selflessly guarded the treacherous waters twelve hours a day, seven days a week, for the next seven summers; how his exploits soon proved so heroic that his boss (or in other versions, his father) provided him with an old tree stump in which to carve notches memorializing each life he saved—"the notches multiplied, and the log soon began to look like a flock of woodpeckers had chipped away at it." "I guess you were notches one, two, and three on my log," he wrote to a Dixon friend decades later. In 1986, at an Oval Office photo opportunity with the president of the U.S. Lifesaving Association, he told how, one time during college when he went back to the beach to visit with his replacement, he was asked to watch the water while the other man went to the bathroom: "Would you believe I had to go in and make a rescue while he was gone?" He also loosed himself from his religious obligations— beach, not church, was his Sunday duty now.

F. Scott Fitzgerald, right around this time, defined "personality" as "an unbroken series of successful gestures." This named the accomplishment Dutch Reagan began displaying once summer was over, in high school. A new English teacher came to town, J. B. Frazer, who graded compositions not just for spelling and grammar but for imaginative liveliness. "Before long," Reagan wrote, "he was asking me to read some of my essays to the class, and when I started getting a few laughs, I began writing with the intention of entertaining the class. I got more laughs and realized I enjoyed it as much as I had those readings at church. For a teenager still carrying around some old feelings of insecurity, the reaction of my classmates was more music to my ears." Frazer also turned their lowly school into a theater powerhouse. And with his newfound confidence, Ronald Reagan discovered another avocation. By his senior year he never missed the chance to perform—usually star—in the productions. He had a way, a classmate remembered, of "sauntering across the stage," drawing attention to himself "even when he was not speaking."

Frazer saw in Dutch a natural leader, "endowed with a curious, keen, and retentive mind." He also admired Reagan's "very unusual mother," who "had that rare ability to make the ideal and fine seem quite practical to others," and noticed Dutch revealing the same talent. Frazer, who soon became the latest in a series of Reagan's surrogate fathers, also noticed another emerging trait: the intensity of his longing to be someone else. "He wanted to live the character. He didn't just want to parrot the lines."

Then summer, and his next season at the lifeguard stand. "You know why I had so much fun at it?" he said in one of his first big Hollywood fan magazine features. "It was like a stage. A lot of people had to look at me." He brought his windup Victrola to work and imitated the play-by-play calls of exciting recent sports matches, recalled with photographic memory. The lifeguard stand was also his director's chair. When he wanted to clear the water before closing time to leave for a date, he'd wait until no one was looking—always aware of others' gaze—and skip a rock across the water: "Oh, that's just an old river rat," he would say loudly, and watch the swimmers clear out. When action was lulled he might demonstrate one of his famous swan dives, or offer comic relief by waddling like a chimp. He took a shine to a local beauty, and when she spurned him, he landed the pretty daughter of the new preacher instead. (There's a photograph of him in his dashing lifeguard singlet, goofing with Margaret "Mugs" Cleaver, his hand resting dangerously low on her hip.)

Then, a thrashing in the distance—and lo, there was Dutch, flinging off his glasses, making another save.

He later expressed resentment of swimmers who downgraded his heroics, particularly the strapping young farm boys who "rarely encounter water deeper than an irrigation canal and would invariably underestimate the river's power." He recalled them saying, "Y'know, I was just fine out there—didn't really need your help." "I'd just nod," he reported himself responding, "and keeping carving my notch.'" (The hero must always be modest.)

He crafted a sort of prose poem on his own heroics for his high school annual. "Meditations of a Lifeguard" is a token of how effortlessly his mind swirled fiction and fantasy into soul-satisfying confections with himself at the center of the world. He sets the scene—"A mob of water-seeking humans intent on giving the beach guard something to worry about"—then grants the lifeguard-narrator the power to author reality itself: he is the one who "paints the ether a hazy blue, by the use of lurid, vivid, flaming adjectives." He offers a taxonomy of the lesser beings in his charge: a "big hippopotamus with a sandwich in each hand, and some firewater tanked away"; a " 'frail and forty' maiden"; boys distractedly enacting adventure stories. He saves them, one by one—and concludes with the effortless wooing of a passing lovely: "She speaks and the sound of her voice is like balm to a wounded soul, the worried expression fades in the glow of a joyous realization, the birdies strike up in chorus, and somewhere celestial music plays the haunting strains recognizable as 'The End of a Perfect Day.'"

A perfect day: it revolved around himself, the rescuer, surrounded by those just waiting to be rescued, a grateful public he could superintend with perfect command.

His rescues became a staple in the *Telegraph:* the daring nighttime save in which Dutch arrived just in the nick of time after "[o]ne of the members of the party who was said to have attempted to rescue him was forced to abandon the attempt when he too was in danger of being taken down"; the arrogant stranger who was "warned repeatedly against entering deep water and responded by cursing the guard. He sank in the deep water and after a struggle Reagan succeeded in rescuing him." The accounts, however, read as suspiciously tidy to at least one historian, who wonders whether Reagan didn't also have a hand in drafting them. Some in his community were suspicious, too—how convenient that people always managed to almost drown themselves whenever young Reagan was around, and how annoying that he never seemed to shut up about it. His senior yearbook featured a comic dialogue on the subject:

"Drowning Youth—Don't rescue me. I want to die.

"Dutch Reagan—Well, you'll have to postpone that: I want a medal."

Football, however, not swimming, was the Golden Age's sacred sport. The year Reagan entered high school, Grantland Rice enumerated the qualities it inculcated: "Condition, courage, stamina, loyalty, service, team play, fortitude, and skill. There has been no finer game yet devised for the youth of any country." It was also Ronald Reagan's favorite sport. When he was president, he called it "a kind of clean hatred," a downright necessary invention: "the last thing left in civilization where two men can literally fling themselves bodily at one another in combat and not be at war." He described spending countless afternoons looking out on the high school playing field from an earthen ledge in his family's yard, "watching and hearing the clash of padded bodies butting up against one another and dreaming of the day when I could put on a uniform and join the combat." When that day came, he was so tiny the coach could hardly find a practice uniform for him—and he couldn't make the team.

What would a boy in an adventure story do?

Pull himself up by his own bootstraps—for anything was possible for he who was born under the sign of grace, grace that will always eventually reveal itself in the fullness of time, whatever temporarily degraded accident of circumstance into which he finds himself thrown. Degraded circumstance, after all, is the superior crucible for the shaping of heroes. That was the summer he took the job digging foundations for houses. "It was midseason of that third year when it happened," as he spun the tale. "I found myself learning plays at guard among my heroes. All week long I figured it was being used to discipline or scare the regular guard into more effort. I can never describe the feeling on the following Saturday when I heard the coach in that impressive pre-game locker room hush come to right guard in the starting lineup. His next word was 'Reagan.'

"I had a good day—particularly on defense—and there I was at last, and for the rest of the season, a 'regular.'" (Reagan's youngest son recalls his father once telling him, "It's funny, whenever I think of playing football back then, it's always a gray, cloudy day"—more melodramatic that way.)

Sport, that manly testing ground of character—where, "R.R. '28" wrote in another prose poem in his senior high school annual, "all the soul is laid bare." This particular piece began with a reference from Scripture: "To every man comes Gethsemane!" Gethsemane was the garden where Jesus prayed alongside his disciples for the courage to face his greatest test, crucifixion; where Christ taught that though the spirit was willing, the flesh might be weak. Such tests could also come, Dutch Reagan insisted, "on the level sward in the shadow of a deserted grandstand." He told the story of a high school football star, "a storybook type, tall, good looking, and very popular," who selfishly stopped trying after his team stopped winning games. In one contest he faked an injury rather than come back for the second half and "risk his brilliant reputation by being flopped for losses." The team lost a game it should have won. And so, on the sixth day, he revisited the scene of his shame. "An early harvest moon made ghostly figures of the milky mist tendrils that hung over the deserted gridiron like spirits of long dead heroes." Those spirits were "pointing ghostly scornful fingers at him. The quitter cringed before the visions his tortured mind brought up." He "saw for the first time how cheap he really was. Great sobs shook him and he writhed before the pitiless conscience that drove him on in his agony of self-punishment."

Then, from temporarily degraded circumstances, redemption: "his sobs ceased and he stood up, his face to the sky, and the ghosts of honored warriors urged him and drew him from the low shadows. A love and loyalty took the place of egoism. His hand strayed to the purple monogram he wore"—purple and white were the Dixon school colors— "and as he looked at the curving track, at the level field, he realized he loved them." The next game, his team once again behind at the half, our hero "rose and spoke." (*Christ has died. Christ has risen.*) "In three minutes the team trotted out to warm up, and eleven boys were wiping tears from their eyes as the quitter took his place by the full-back."

The tale closely resembled something by Grantland Rice—whom the author honors in the story's final line, quoting Rice's most famous poem: "It matters not that you won or lost, but how you played the game." Like the Galloping Ghost, Red Grange, our hero soared "in a ground-gaining stride that made the coach want to recite poetry"; "he sailed, and as he side-stepped a man . . . his bird-like flight changed to a ripping, tearing smash." He scored two touchdowns and was borne off the field on his teammates' shoulders.

In the story, for a brief and unbearable moment, the hero is racked by a complex moral ambivalence (ordinary mortals, after all, sometimes selfishly take time off when they're having a tough day). Then his soul is restored to coherence by the plain act of deciding simple grace resides within reach of his own simple decision—just as R.R. '28 says you're supposed to in another of his yearbook texts, a poem titled "Life": "I wonder what it's all about, and why / We suffer so, when little things go wrong? / We make our life a struggle, / When life should be a song." It revealed his personal liturgy of willed self-confidence. He had become a virtuoso of self-confidence, a maestro at *staging ways to display* his self-confidence. The performances gave him an outward glow. People began to follow him, envy him: they doubted, hesitated, feared; he did not. He graduated from high school transformed: thirty notches carved in his lifeguard log; beau of the town's prettiest girl (he won her away from the quarterback); dashing leading man; yearbook art director (perhaps it was he who came up with the idea to give the book a Hollywood theme, listing the editorial staff as "PRODUCERS"); fashion trendsetter (among the school year's highlights, the *Dixonian* includes December 19: "Derbies appear. Ronald Reagan enters with corduroy and high cuts"; in his picture he sports an ascot where the rest of the seniors wear long ties); vice president of the new Hi-Y club (chartered "to create, maintain, and extend throughout the school and community, the highest standards of Christian character"); "Heap Big Chief" of the junior-senior banquet (it featured an Indian theme); senior class president. "Life is just one grand sweet song, so start the music," he published as his yearbook quote.

"He always left people with a way of saying 'God bless you,'" a classmate recalled, "that made them feel—just maybe—he had an inside track." Some began seeing him as a figure of destiny.

IN RONALD REAGAN'S CHAOTIC CHILDHOOD THE IMAGINATION WAS armor. There is nothing unusual about that; transcending the doubts, hesitations, and fears swirling around you by casting yourself internally as the hero of your own adventure story is a characteristic psychic defense mechanism of the Boy Who Disappears. He pushes doubt and confusion from the forefront of his consciousness with the furious energy of a boy who fears that if he does not do so he might somehow be consumed.

The strategy can backfire, however, when the boy becomes a man and must finally face the austere everyday ambivalence and incoherence of the adult world. The long-delayed realization that one's fantasies do not actually map reality can leave behind a wrecked grown-up more alienated, helpless, and terrified than he ever was before. Which is why most people, with greater or lesser degrees of success, simply grow out of it.

But Ronald Reagan was not like the rest of us. He was, in this particular sense, a much, much stronger man. Perhaps it was that he worked out in the psychic gymnasium of boyhood fantasy with ten times the furious determination of an ordinary boy. Perhaps it was a more mysterious gift. However the outcome was achieved, it's not a controversial point to make: at turning complexity and confusion and doubt into simplicity and stout-heartedness and certainty, Ronald Reagan's power was simply awesome. As an athlete of the imagination, he was a Babe Ruth, a Jack Dempsey, a Red Grange.

The real-world consequences of his chaotic upbringing hardly ever went away; he was presented with them constantly. And yet that awful reckoning the world forces upon those who retreat into fantasy, in order to deny complexity, never seemed to have forced itself upon him; his armor was just that strong. "There's a wall around him," as his wife Nancy put it. "He lets me come closer than anyone else, but there are times when even I feel that barrier."

It was the stories: the ones he told himself, the ones he told others, the ones born of heroic situations that he always was scanning the horizon to put himself at the center of, to prove to himself the world was always in actuality the way he preferred it to be. It was his greatest political skill. *"Looking back my memory is very vivid"*; *"I shall always remember"*; *"fresh in my memory"*: phrases like these saturate his recollections. They seem to do so in inverse proportion to the actual power of his recall. The gap between the one and the other was the measure of how he made himself, and others, feel good.

And by 1973, beginning his seventh year as governor of California, with two years to go in his term, in the season of Operation Homecoming, he had hardly changed in his essential being. And he was thinking about running for president.

CHAPTER THREE

Let Them Eat Brains

PRESIDENTS ARE ALWAYS ALSO STORYTELLERS, PURVEYORS OF USEFUL NA-
tional mythologies. And surprisingly enough, Richard Nixon, this awkward man who didn't even really like people, had not been so bad at the
duty—at least in the first four years of his presidency.

At his inauguration he promised to "bring us together"; pundits
swooned. A little more than nine months later he delivered one of the
most politically successful addresses in the history of the presidency: the
"Silent Majority" speech, which in a single evening increased the number of Americans who approved of his handling of the Vietnam War by
19 percentage points. In August 1971, at the lowest political ebb of his
term, against a backdrop of some of the darkest economic portents since
the Great Depression, he told a story about how he would protect the
plain people from economic marauders menacing America from abroad,
and sang out the dry economic details of Executive Order No. 11615,
"Providing for the Stabilization of Prices, Rents, Wages, and Salaries,"
like a celestial chorus: "Today we hear echoes of those voices preaching
a gospel of doom and defeat. . . . I say let Americans reply: 'Our best
days lie ahead.'" A pollster said of the approval that followed, "I've
never seen anything this unanimous, unless it was Pearl Harbor."

Storied diplomatic triumphs followed: the opening to China, agreements with the Soviet Union to beat nuclear missiles into plowshares, an
apparent endgame in Vietnam at the Paris peace negotiations. A grateful
nation granted him reelection against the Democrat George McGovern with forty-nine of fifty states and a record 61 percent of the vote,
including millions who had never voted Republican before: Southern
good ol' boys, hard-hat-wearing union members, Jews.

There had been speed bumps. On June 17, 1972, four Cuban burglars
were caught breaking into Democratic headquarters at the Watergate
office complex in Washington, D.C. One of their accomplices, James
McCord, had headed security for the president's reelection office. The
Washington Post discovered that two accomplices—E. Howard Hunt,

late of the CIA, and G. Gordon Liddy, of the FBI and Bureau of Alcohol, Tobacco and Firearms—had worked in Nixon's White House and reelection campaign, respectively. But the political damage was deftly neutralized. "I'm not going to comment from the White House on a third-rate burglary attempt," the president's spokesman, Ron Ziegler, said, even as Carl Bernstein and Bob Woodward of the *Washington Post* kept up a steady stream of scoops tying the conspirators to the Nixon reelection campaign, and reported that squads of dirty tricksters had circulated the country sabotaging the Democratic contenders' campaigns. But the "third-rate burglary" explanation held. The *Chicago Tribune* did not run a front-page story on Watergate until late in August. A Watergate inquiry by the fiercely independent chairman of the House Banking and Currency Committee, Wright Patman of Texas, could not win enough votes to go forward. Before the 1972 election, Gallup asked the public, "Which candidate—Mr. Nixon or Mr. McGovern—do you think is more sincere, believable?" Nixon won, 59 percent to 20. "Now," he wrote in his memoirs of his reelection landslide, "I planned to give expression to the more conservative values and beliefs of the New Majority throughout the country, and use my power to put some teeth into my New American Revolution."

In the weeks before his re-inauguration, during the Christmas season, no less, he had risked international opprobrium by carpet bombing North Vietnam for almost a fortnight. He weathered the political storm. He was weathering all the storms—and then, on January 27, 1973, he signed the Paris Peace Accords. The gross national product grew 8.7 percent in the first quarter. The Dow was high, unemployment low, inflation predicted to fall below the previous year's 3.5 percent—and, his economists told him, with no worry about more inflation in the long term. At the news of advance work for a summit in June with Soviet leader Leonid Brezhnev at Camp David, a twenty-three-year-old wrote to his hometown newspaper about how all his life it had been his "duty to hate two things: (1) Monday mornings and (2) Communists. I am no longer supposed to hate Communists, and now I fear that Monday mornings are in jeopardy. Is nothing sacred anymore?" In New York a group of supporters began researching a constitutional amendment to allow Nixon to serve a third term.

And so he took bold steps to remake Washington in his image. Chief of Staff H. R. "Bob" Haldeman sent a curt letter to hundreds of presidential appointees demanding their resignations; they were replaced with more loyal men. Nixon announced a radical reorganization of the executive branch to give the new loyalists more power. He announced a labor leader as his new labor secretary, a historic first. That held out the promise of consummating one of his dearest dreams: to peel off the white working class from its historic attachment to the Democratic Party. "I think we're going to keep them split," his consigliere on the project, Charles Colson, enthused, "and I'm awful bullish about what we can do in this country."

The four burglars and their supervisor, Howard Hunt, pleaded guilty. The zealous G. Gordon Liddy refused to testify in the trial. Only James McCord appeared in the courtroom. The indictment was extraordinarily narrow—making the claims of Ted Kennedy or Woodward and Bernstein that this strange crime stood at the center of a matrix of Nixonian corruption sound fantastical. The trial began, ten days before the inauguration, in the gilded ceremonial courtroom of John J. Sirica, an obscure federal judge whose badgering of witnesses about matters beyond his brief—"Did they get any money to go in there? Was it purely for political espionage? What was the purpose?"—made him look like a fool. For example a handsome and smooth young treasurer in the Nixon campaign, Hugh Sloan, was asked about the time in the spring of 1972 he was authorized by his boss, an even smoother deputy campaign manager named Jeb Stuart Magruder, to pass over an enormous wad of cash:

"What was the purpose of turning over $199,000 to Liddy?"

"I have no idea."

"You have no idea?" the judge chuffed incredulously—and started pressing even more intently. Why, he wondered, every time cross-examination led to Nixon headquarters, or to questions regarding the hundreds of thousands of dollars other investigations had already established had been laundered through Mexico before passing through the malefactors' hands, did memories grow vague?

Timorous prosecutors did not follow his lead. On January 29, 1973, they closed their argument, noting that the defendants were "off on an enterprise of their own," apparently at the sole instigation of G. Gordon Liddy. At a cocktail party, the judge was asked only half jokingly if "the McGovern people have hired you to try to reverse what happened in November." The jury convicted McCord after only ninety minutes of deliberation. Judge Sirica complained, "I am still not satisfied that all the pertinent facts that might be available—I say *might* be available—have been produced before an American jury." He set bond at one hundred thousand dollars. Then he ran to the media to spread more imprecation. It got little coverage. The *New York Times* dismissed the judge's "dignified clamor." On February 7, the Senate set up a special subcommittee

under Senator Sam Ervin of North Carolina—not a nationally prominent name—to investigate 1972 Nixon campaign abuses. The resolution
to establish it passed 77–0, and hardly would have been unanimous had
anyone in Washington imagined it would amount to much. Senator
Ervin himself considered it "simply inconceivable that Nixon might
have been involved."

Operation Homecoming dawned. Borne aloft by its political capital,
the president announced a budget that slashed his predecessor's Great
Society programs. *Newsweek* called it "one of the most significant
American political documents since the dawning of the New Deal."
He also announced an unprecedented plan to simply refuse to spend—
"impound"—$12 billion in funds already authorized by Congress. The
Constitution said the legislative branch decided how tax dollars got
spent. So Senator Ervin labeled him "King Richard," and opened a hearing on "whether the Congress of the United States shall remain a viable
institution." Congressman Wright Patman, the day before Valentine's
Day, said, "I have been in Congress under seven presidents . . . and
never during this 44-year-old period have we been closer to one-man
rule." Arkansas senator J. William Fulbright said Nixon might literally
be committing an act of treason. Let them bray. Fulbright's hometown
paper editorialized that he sounded like "an arcane and vaguely academic version of Joe McCarthy."

In March, in a speech flaying "soft-headed judges," Nixon proposed stern new anticrime measures. Then he vetoed a bill to help the
handicapped. Exhilarated liberals, certain the president had overstepped,
brought patients in wheelchairs to cheer the veto override vote. That
vote, however, failed. Richard Nixon's approval rating was a staggering
65 percent. He looked forward to a spectacular second term.

THEN THINGS BEGAN TO GO OFF THE RAILS.

Saturday, March 17, the day Pat Nixon had observed her birthday
for as long as her husband had been a politician—because that was
St. Patrick's Day; she was actually born on March 16—the White House
staged a concert starring Merle Haggard. Country music fans and Irish
Catholics: both were among the traditionally Democratic blocs Nixon
was trying to cement for the Republicans for all time—with some apparent success.

Guests wearing tuxedos arrived to a serenade of violin and harps.
Haggard wore boots, an open-throated shirt, and a cowboy hat. The
president toasted him: "We can't offer you moonshine, we can't offer
you Irish whisky. But there's California champagne—watch out!"

A bluegrass band took the stage. Guests appeared to be embarrassed at the cultural mismatch.

Merle Haggard took the stage. He later said it felt like performing to mannequins. Came the dramatic highlight: a giant American flag rose from the back of the stage. Haggard swung into his law-and-order hit, "Okie from Muskogee."

The *New York Times* observed an incongruity: the president had three days earlier sent his message asking Congress to attack crime "without pity," but Haggard was a felon, convicted for robbery. The next week the *Chicago Tribune* ran a query from a reader: "Do you know whether he's the first ex-convict to perform in the White House?"

It spoke to an emerging dilemma: when people thought of the White House, crime was the image coming to mind. Watergate news stories had been accelerating. The Committee to Re-elect the President, mysteriously still in operation, kept on returning campaign contributions made by shady characters: $305,000 to a "reclusive Texas land dealer"; $100,000 to a Gulf Oil executive that "found its way through a Mexican bank to the leader of the bugging raid"; $250,000 to Robert L. Vesco, the "principal defendant in a Securities and Exchange Commission suit against the alleged looting of $224 million from Investors Overseas Services, Ltd." The General Accounting Office referred the cases to the Justice Department. The *Times* asked, "WHAT WAS THE MONEY FOR?" And: "Why, long after the election was over and the giant surplus was well-known, did an additional $246,000 dribble into the Nixon treasury in January and February?"

In hearings to permanently confirm L. Patrick Gray, acting FBI chief since the death of J. Edgar Hoover, Democrats accused Gray of coaching witnesses appearing before the Watergate grand jury. It arrived that an obscure White House aide named John Dean might be able to clear up the question of whether and why this had happened. But the president, citing an unfamiliar constitutional doctrine called "executive privilege," said Dean could not testify before any investigating body. A political cartoonist depicted Pat with a rolling pin as the president tried to sneak into bed after midnight: "And don't give me any of that 'executive privilege' nonsense!"

On March 23, in the ceremonial courtroom at the D.C. criminal courts building, Judge Sirica convened the apparently routine sentencing hearing of the "Watergate 7"—the four burglars, Howard Hunt, G. Gordon Liddy, and James McCord. Boredom was written in the sketch artists' faces. Then the judge announced he had received a letter from one of the defendants, McCord, and asked for a sealed envelope.

Faces perked up. This was not ordinary procedure.

The judge began reading aloud McCord's letter. It began by explaining why he hadn't responded frankly to the judge's questions about details of the case: "Several members of my family have expressed fear for my life if I disclose knowledge of the facts in this matter either publicly or to any government representatives. Whereas I do not share their concerns to the same degree, nevertheless, I do believe retaliatory measures will be taken against me, my family, and my friends should I disclose such facts. Such retaliation could destroy careers, income and reputation of persons who are innocent of any guilt whatever."

If he had answered those questions frankly at the time they were asked, the defendant said, the answer would have been, "There was political pressure applied to the defendants to plead guilty and remain silent.

"Perjury occurred during the trial of matters highly material to the very structure, orientation, and impact of the government's case and to the motivation of and intent of the defendants.

"Others involved in the Watergate operation were not identified during the trial when they could have been by those testifying.

"I would appreciate the opportunity to talk with you privately in chambers," the letter concluded. "Since I cannot feel confident in talking with an FBI agent, in testifying before a grand jury whose U.S. Attorneys work for the Department of Justice, or in talking with other government representatives, such a discussion with you would be of assistance to me."

"What all this means," wrote columnist Joseph Kraft—the kind of pundit editors around the country consulted to know exactly how much criticism of sacred cows was advisable—"is that the issue is obstruction of justice by a coverup at the highest levels." Watergate was about to be blown wide open.

Sirica's hunger for truth was displayed in the sentences he pronounced. Forty years for the four Cuban burglars, thirty-five years for Hunt, and forty-five years for McCord. These were terms more appropriate to unrepentant murderers than to the perpetrators of a "third-rate burglary." The judge then explained why he had issued them: the sentences were "provisional." If the defendants explained what they knew to the soon-to-be reconvened grand jury or the forthcoming Senate hearings, they would be reduced. That explained the shorter, six-year, eight-month sentence G. Gordon Liddy got: his lawyers had told Sirica that no matter what his sentence was, he would never, ever talk.

• • •

AT HIS WEEKLY MEETING WITH THE REPUBLICAN CONGRESSIONAL LEAD-
ership, the president with the 65 percent approval rating was unexpectedly forced into a defensive crouch: "Hugh, I have nothing to hide," he
told the Senate minority leader, Hugh Scott of Pennsylvania.

He repeated it: "The White House has nothing to hide."

Then, he said it a third time: "I repeat, we have nothing to hide and
you are authorized to make that statement in my name."

He also repeated that he could not permit any members of his White
House staff to appear before any grand jury or committee of Congress
whatsoever: executive privilege. The senators, the papers reported, were
"disturbed by the White House attitude." That was obvious enough,
simply from the fact they'd leaked the meeting in such detail.

Kraft wrote that a "flurry of developments has transformed the
Watergate affair from a sideshow into a political bomb that could blow
the Nixon administration apart." Woodward and Bernstein got space
on page A1 to remind readers of McCord's connection to all the most
Godfather-like incidents, like the time the previous summer when
former Nixon attorney general and campaign manager John Mitchell's unhinged wife, Martha, called UPI reporter Helen Thomas to say
that she was being held in California as a "political prisoner." It had
been McCord's arrest in the Watergate burglary, Bernstein and Woodward explained, that originally set Martha Mitchell off. "McCord also
leased an office in downtown Washington last spring next to Senator
Edmund S. Muskie's presidential campaign headquarters," they pointed
out. "Muskie was the chief target of an elaborate campaign of political
espionage and sabotage conceived in the White House and conducted
against the Democratic presidential candidates in 1971–1972, according
to federal sources."

Patterns were beginning to add up.

Patrick Gray admitted at his confirmation hearings that White
House counsel John Dean had been present at FBI interrogations of
Watergate witnesses. International Telephone & Telegraph Corporation,
the company suspected of bribing the Nixon campaign in exchange for
the dropping of an antitrust suit, was revealed to have hired a former
CIA chief to influence a presidential election in Chile. Robert Vesco
was reported to have allegedly delivered $200,000 in cash-filled suitcases
to the Nixon campaign three days after a new campaign disclosure act
made it illegal to do so. The Sunday *New York Times'* Week in Review
section, which ran its Watergate roundup under a graphic of the roof of
the White House blowing off, reported that the FBI had spied on hard-
hitting reporter Daniel Schorr of CBS under the pretext of considering

him for a fictitious White House job. *Time* gingerly wondered how "persistent allegations . . . about safes full of secret campaign cash" comported with a White House "that has so strongly denounced the permissiveness and the decaying morality of modern life." Senator James Buckley of New York, brother of William F., likewise gingerly said the "reports indicate less than wholehearted cooperation by the administration." Lowell Weicker, the Connecticut Republican who would sit on the subcommittee investigating Watergate, was more blunt: he said that "somebody still in the White House" had to have directed political espionage in the 1972 Nixon reelection campaign.

The president could hardly take comfort in the fact that for the moment, the public's attention was still mostly elsewhere—on food prices, which had jumped more in January than any other month in twenty-five years. He promised they would drop soon. Instead, the Consumer Price Index for February rose at the highest rate since 1951. The price of meat was on a course to doubling within the year. In political cartoons, housewives asked butchers for steak on the layaway plan. Johnny Carson said meat prices were so high that "Oscar Mayer had his wiener appraised."

NO ONE WAS SURE WHERE THE IDEA OF A NATIONAL BOYCOTT OF MEAT IN the first week in April came from. Perhaps Connecticut, where a housewife saw a cartoon about the butcher selling beef on the installment plan, and explained to newspapers about the day she persuaded the junior members of the Connecticut Federation of Women's Clubs, then got her congressman to back them: "The more I laughed, the more I wanted to cry." Perhaps in Southern California's San Fernando Valley, where another housewife returned from her neighborhood market, telephoned her friend, and simply said: "It's time." Each telephoned five others, asking them to boycott on Tuesdays and Thursdays. ("We are focusing on particular days so they can see we have clout," the organizer said, like a Chicago ward heeler. "The American mother feels her family is threatened, you see. And you threaten a mother bear's cubs and watch out.") They distributed eighteen thousand leaflets, whose recipients mimeographed them in turn; by the middle of March they started getting calls from around the country—including one from a panicked executive of the South Dakota Stock Growers Association, who suggested they find cheaper cuts for their "family servings of protein."

President Nixon's consumer advisor, Virginia Knauer, made a presentation for the press, suggesting "liver, kidney, brains, and heart can be made into gourmet meals with seasoning, imagination, and more cooking time." She then trilled, "From my own experience I have found a shopper can generally trim as much as ten percent off her food budget." An aide demonstrated a cost-per-serving slide rule for the cameras. On NBC that night, Knauer's lesson in home economy was the lead story. It was followed by a field report on a schoolteacher's wife who surreptitiously slipped horse meat into her husband's sandwiches (a similar story made it onto an episode that fall of *All in the Family*).

Cut to an ad for Bayer pain reliever.

The president repeated Mrs. Knauer's let-them-eat-liver advice from his news conference podium; the mail in response, the Week in Review reported, was "unprintable." At the Merle Haggard concert the White House served broiled chicken as a national example. Fishmongers started profiteering: a pound of striped bass went for fifty cents on Monday, and ninety cents at week's end. "It makes me literally sick to go into the grocery store," a suburban Washington mother told the *Post*.

The White House begged the boycotters to have patience, saying price controls would only compound the problem. Instead, the movement snowballed. Housewives in Manhattan marched behind a cow marked "WE WANT MEAT NOT PROMISES," demanding prices be rolled back to December 1972 levels. In Chicago activists passed out peanut butter and jelly sandwiches to pedestrians at the Dirksen Senate Office Building—demanding *1967* prices. "I don't know what Nixon is eating for lunch today," said one of them, a housewife named Jan Schakowsky, a leader in the burgeoning consumers' movement, "but I bet there's meat on the table." San Francisco demonstrators mailed yard-long sticks of bologna—a pound of which having gone up forty cents in price in two years—to President Nixon and Governor Reagan.

RONALD REAGAN AT HIS SACRAMENTO PRESS CONFERENCE THAT WEEK was remarkably blithe about the whole thing, as if the government shouldn't be concerned about popular outrage at all. This price rise, he said, was caused by bad weather, that's all—and "I'm not in favor of picketing Him." He said he knew what he was talking about, as a cattle rancher himself. The press gaggle thought that was a curious thing to bring up, for it only reminded people of his biggest controversy as governor so far.

In 1971, a student-operated radio station at Sacramento State College reported that Reagan's 1970 tax return claimed he owed precisely zero dollars and zero cents. Reagan was befuddled when confronted with the news at a press conference; then he offered a recollection that he might have got a *refund* on his federal taxes. The governor's office released a statement saying the reason was unspecified "business reverses." He refused to say anything more—with a vengeance: "We fought a war about that! I say all men have a right to be safe in their books and records. That's what the Revolution was about."

One month later, the *Sacramento Bee* broke the story of what these "business reverses" entailed, and it was a doozy: the governor had contracted with a company that advertised to clients with a net worth of at least $500,000 that "tax laws favor cattle. . . . When you buy them, you become a farmer and can keep your books on a cash basis. You put in dollars that depreciate or are deductible. You take out capital gains." Voilà: newly minted cowboys, whose ranks included Jack Benny, Alfred Hitchcock, and Arnold Palmer, "lose" enough money, in the company's boast, "to avoid or postpone payment of any income tax." The inquiries compounded, sending Reagan's wife Nancy into a rage. She said she hoped her husband would never run for office again, because "I'd always believed that people are basically good, and I'm trying very hard to hold on to that," but politics, she now realized, was "dirty." The *New York Times* discovered steers with "Reagan Cattle Company" brands in states hundreds of miles away—a "Trident Bar" mark in Wyoming, a "Gunsight R" in Montana, and a "Gunsight Rocking R" in Nevada. They also tracked down a copy of Reagan's contract with the company, signed by his personal attorney and close friend William French Smith. This, apparently, was what he meant two years later when he called himself a "rancher."

But the story had quickly faded: of the networks, only ABC paid attention, giving it all of twenty seconds; Democrats were too high-minded in their attacks to be effectual; and only one politician proved palpitatingly ambitious enough to leverage the story for publicity and release his own taxes (Georgia governor Jimmy Carter, who had paid $13,339.31 on $46,542.66 in income). But here Reagan was now, raising the issue again, of his own volition—and reporters pounced:

"Governor, a few years ago there was a revelation of your investment in beef cattle. Do you still have an investment in that area?"

Firmly, confidently, he returned: "They were bulls. Breeding bulls. A small herd of breeding bulls. And I have been disposing of those." Then he deftly changed the subject with a blizzard of authoritative-sounding gibberish about two-year-old weather statistics and the role of corn in determining cattle prices in the marketing stage. His inquisitors gave up. Once he got wrapped into one of his stories, they knew further questioning was futile. The way he managed to convey simple innocence in the face of a complex morass: it was almost preternatural. How could you make anything stick to someone who radiated confidence like that? He was like that stuff pots and pans were covered with—Teflon. Some reporters had given up attempting to interview him altogether: "It's just like hearing the same record over and over again. I don't think he knows how to be candid." Sacramento novices who scored interviews nonetheless would emerge thrilled with the wonderful material they unearthed—only to look at old Reagan speeches, and find out the words were identical.

THE DAY BEFORE JAMES MCCORD'S LETTER, THE UNITED AUTO WORKERS endorsed the April meat boycott. Representative William Cotter introduced into the *Congressional Record* the culinary sensation sweeping the nation: the Virginia Citizens Consumer Council's "one week meatless menu," starring lentil soup, macaroni, tuna fish casserole, and, for Sunday dinner, "lasagna without meat." Fast-food executives discussed selling "soybean burgers." A Cleveland judge set bond at three thousand dollars for a man accused of stealing seventy-seven pounds of sirloin from a restaurant, and lectured that "this should be a warning to the public generally that society will not countenance the stealing of meat, which is more precious than jewels."

Like this was the Soviet Union or something.

The White House, growing desperate, sent word through the first lady's press secretary that the Nixons were eating more leftovers and fresh vegetables: "They like zucchini a lot." A chain of thirteen stores in the Washington area announced they would shut down for a day in solidarity against Nixon's glib inaction. Three days later, a thirty-six-store Massachusetts chain joined them. The prices for cattle and pork belly futures started plummeting. A Dubuque, Iowa, packing company curtailed operations.

The president tried a televised speech, turning to a rhetorical formula that used to work: self-pity and patriotic bromides:

"Good evening: Four years and two months ago, when I first came into this office as president, by far the most difficult problem confronting the nation was the seemingly endless war in Vietnam." He ended it. "Hundreds were being held as prisoners of war." He brought them home. He then quoted one of them, Colonel George McKnight, who had told him, "Thank you for bringing us home on our feet instead of our knees." Only then did he bring up inflation—as "one of the most terrible costs of war," framing a logic that those who did not patriotically endure it dishonored warriors' heroic sacrifices. He mentioned a policy intervention—a price ceiling on beef, pork, and lamb—then concluded, as he had every big TV speech since "Checkers" in 1952, with a sentimental allegory: "A few days ago, in this room, I talked to a man who had spent almost eight years in a Communist prison camp in North Vietnam. For over four years he was in solitary confinement. In that four-year-period he never saw and never talked to another human being except his Communist captors. He lived on two meals a day, usually just a piece of bread."

You could stop eating meat for two days. But wouldn't you be dishonoring *him*?

It didn't work. More people boycotted than the organizers dared dream. The *Chicago Tribune* found 85 percent support, and 50 percent fewer meat sales—and 25 percent more business at a place called the "Green Planet Health Food Restaurant" on Lincoln Avenue. Sales were down 80 percent in some parts of New York City. Another new movement the American people learned about that week was the "Gray Panthers": old people were "ready to be radicalized," their leader insisted. "I'm just serving warning." She singled out the high cost of food as one of the reasons. A frustrated, defiant Nixon served roast prime tenderloin of beef—"selling in San Clemente markets,'" Walter Cronkite reported, "for upwards of three dollars a pound"—at a dinner for South Vietnamese strongman Nguyen Van Thieu.

Time put "Food Prices: The Big Beef" on the cover April 2; it hadn't yet run a cover on Watergate. Seventeen percent of the country hadn't even heard yet of the scandal; of those who had, only a third thought it was a serious thing.

The Silent Majority might be ignoring Watergate. The sense that something was rotten in Washington spread nonetheless. "I've never protested anything before," a new insurgent told the *Tribune*. But now that the price of bologna had risen 40 percent, she was ready to start. Rumor had it that the summer might bring gas rationing. In Atlanta, a witness in a prostitution case complained to the federal Price Control Board that the fee for sexual services had leaped from $25 to $35. The price of onions started soaring, too. Horse meat, slide rules, a world in which anything that reliably had cost one dollar might soon suddenly cost two: it did something to people.

Crime, meanwhile, was becoming a national obsession—the upcoming TV season would have ten cops-and-robbers shows, a record—and crime had begun getting stranger. On New Year's Eve, a twenty-three-year-old black veteran named Mark James Essex, who lived in a New Orleans shack spray-painted with slogans like "My *Destiny* lies in the BLOODY *DEATH* of Racist PIGS," shot three policemen. Two weeks later—to kick off the revolution, he said—he began massacring white guests at a downtown Howard Johnson's. Two dozen policemen opened fire on someone they believed to be the perpetrator. They actually were shooting at each other. They didn't know that Essex had already been machine-gunned to shreds by a Marine combat helicopter—also live on TV.

Toward the end of January what the *New York Times* described as "a two-day ordeal of blazing gunfights, death, and terror at a Brooklyn sporting goods store" ended in a daring roof escape of nine people held hostage by four gunmen identifying themselves as "servants of Allah": "O Muslims!" went their manifesto. "Unite against the oppressive infidels whose aim is the destruction of Islam." At the end of February, activists of the American Indian Movement seized the town of Wounded Knee, South Dakota, site of the last massacre of the nineteenth-century Indian wars. Set upon by federal marshals, they staged an armed standoff that lasted nine weeks. Two Indians died from sniper fire. A marshal was paralyzed from a gunshot wound. (At the Academy Awards ceremony, in solidarity, Marlon Brando sent a Native American woman named Sacheen Littlefeather to accept the Best Actor award on his behalf.) Black September, the terrorists responsible for the massacre of Israeli athletes at the 1972 Munich Olympics, stormed the Saudi Arabian embassy in Khartoum, Sudan, demanding the release of Sirhan Sirhan, the Palestinian assassin of Robert F. Kennedy, and murdered two U.S. diplomats.

Two days later, a massive *New York Times* front-page story featured someone named Ted Patrick, who made a living "deprogramming" young people snatched from religious communes and cults. "They are worse than the Manson sect because he had only a small number of followers," Patrick claimed. "If authorities don't do something about this, our nation is going to be controlled by a handful of people." They were groups like the "Children of God," whose members "regard all existing social structures as corrupt and show their '100 percent discipleship' by surrendering their worldly goods to the organization." The liberal National Council of Churches, the umbrella organization for mainstream denominations like the Methodists, said it found "nothing bizarre, coercive, or secretive" about such "high-demand religious groups, of which there are hundreds." The ACLU called what Patrick did "criminal acts of abduction." A defiant parent replied he would stick with Patrick and kidnap his kid back nonetheless: "if they want to put me in jail, I'll go to jail." A deprogrammed disciple said if it hadn't been for Patrick, "I'd still be under the mental control of these people."

March was also the month when it seemed as if every other local official was headed to jail. Miami's mayor was indicted for conspiracy to bribe a judge to free a convicted drug offender. The circuit court judge who had dismissed the case was indicted, too. Another Miami judge was indicted for taking a bribe to free a child molester. New York State released a report on "systematic and organized burglaries, larcenies, and thefts" by Albany police. New Orleans's district attorney, Kennedy assassination conspiracy theorist Jim Garrison, was about to go on trial for playing footsie with pinball companies. In Maryland's lower legislative chamber, a delegate was arrested for conspiring to distribute forty pounds of heroin. A Queens assistant district attorney was indicted for shutting down the investigation of a Ponzi scheme whose victims included his own son-in-law, and was under suspicion for ignoring two gruesome gangland slayings. A former Philadelphia city commissioner got six years for contract kickbacks; a former chairman of the city planning board was sentenced for selling bank stock below market value to political pals. That capped off a three-year period in the City of Brotherly Love in which a judge went to jail for check fraud, the housing authority advisory board chairman went down for bribery, the stadium construction coordinator went to jail for extortion, and a former chief court clerk got two-to-ten for robbery. Former Illinois governor Otto Kerner was on his way to jail for kickbacks from a racetrack owner, and one of Chicago mayor Richard Daley's right-hand men cut a deal for the provisioning of voting machines that profited him $187,000—and then a three-year jail term. A Republican alderman was on the way to a bribery conviction that could earn him eighty-six years in jail. "Over the past three years in New Jersey alone," observed *Time,* "sixty-seven officials have been indicted and thirty-five convicted"—mayors, legislators, judges, highway officials, postmasters, and a congressman.

And then there was Washington, D.C., where on April 4 came the next turn of the Watergate screw.

CHAPTER FOUR

Executive Privilege

OFFICIAL WASHINGTON HAD ALWAYS BEEN A LITTLE NERVOUS AT THE president's appointment of L. Patrick Gray as acting director of the Federal Bureau of Investigation: he was a Nixon loyalist in a position that was supposed to be nonpolitical. In his Judiciary Committee confirmation hearings, Democrats began grilling him on an even more worrisome matter: allegations that he had cooperated with White House attempts to interfere with the Watergate investigation. Nixon tried to put the matter to rest by giving senators a chance to look at the investigation's records—but only for a half hour each day. John Dean had received unlimited access to those selfsame records; Donald Segretti, the young prankster who had traveled the country in 1972 sabotaging Democratic campaigns, had been shown records of the investigation on him by Gray, too. What was supposed to have been a routine hearing turned into the Senate's first Watergate inquisition.

The name of the president's personal lawyer and the campaign's chief fund-raiser, Herbert Kalmbach, came up: he had been ordered to pay Segretti's salary by presidential appointment secretary Dwight Chapin. John Dean's name kept coming up, too: what did it mean that he had apparently been the one to hire G. Gordon Liddy in the first place?

Meanwhile, what the *New York Times* called "a little-understood and seemingly mundane issue called 'executive privilege'"—by which the president claimed that the Constitution's doctrine of separation of powers kept him or his staff from providing any information requested by Congress involving his conduct of office—was sending Sam Ervin through the roof: "Divine right went out with the American Revolution and doesn't belong to White House aides," he said. "That is not executive privilege. It is executive poppycock." He added that if the president would not allow aides to testify under oath voluntarily, he himself would force them to do so under pain of arrest.

On April 4, Pat Gray withdrew from consideration as acting FBI chief. WOR radio in New York called it the "first blood Congress has drawn in the Watergate affair." *Time* called it the president's biggest set-back since 1970. The magazine also featured a fawning profile of "Watergate Prober Sam Ervin," whose impending inquiry "could easily lead to the most fascinating Capitol Hill TV drama since the Army-McCarthy hearings of 1954." Not quite what the president wanted to hear.

AT LEAST ALL THE POWS NOW WERE HOME. THAT MEANT ANOTHER round of patriotic festivities. In Washington, Captain Jeremiah Denton and soon-to-be-admiral James Stockdale were awarded the Navy's John Paul Jones Award for Inspirational Leadership; Denton sobbed openly. Portsmouth, Virginia, only recently the site of a bloody desegregation brawl, honored native son Fred Cherry, who not incidentally was black, with a parade featuring eight brass bands. He told the assembly, "I do not regret one moment in North Vietnam."

Because all the prisoners were released, the stricture that had prevented them from describing their captivity was lifted. They began sitting at press conferences to describe their awful ordeal. The front pages of conservative heartland newspapers from Fredericksburg, Virginia, to Spokane, Washington, featured a serialized Associated Press interview with Jeremiah Denton—the POW, editors reminded readers, who had "stepped to the microphones and, in a moment the nation will long remember . . . said, 'God bless America'"—under headlines such as "I WAS LIKE A CRIPPLED ROACH" and "PRAYERS HELPED DENTON ENDURE TORTURE." The UPI ran a competing series from Air Force Major Charles Boyd. The right-leaning weekly *U.S. News & World Report* gave thirteen pages to an account from Lieutenant Commander John S. McCain, son of the former chief of naval operations in the Pacific. He said, "I admire President Nixon's courage . . . he had to take the most unpopular decisions that I could imagine—the mining, the blockade, the bombing." (Actually, according to polls, these actions were popular.) He added, "In the context of history, Watergate will be a very minor item as compared with the other achievements of this administration." And he enthused, "I see more of an appreciation of our way of life. There is more patriotism. The flag is all over the place."

Their stories: downed fliers with cracked vertebrae and shattered ankle sockets, facing villagers seeking to tear them limb from limb, led to prison camps with overflowing toilet buckets, maggot-ridden rice, bones set without anesthesia, and solitary confinement in cold cement rooms for months at a time. They did not know whether they would ever see another American again. Then men furtively glimpsed shadows through cracks in walls, found notes marked on toilet paper

with matchsticks, read legends like GOD WILL FIND STRENGTH. ROBIN-
SON RISNER, SEPTEMBER 18, 1965 scrawled upon bare stone walls—and
eventually someone remembered the "tap code" used by Korean War
POWs ("Joan Baez Sucks" was one of the first successful messages).
Through such glancing communication they were able to reestablish
a full-fledged military chain of command—the "4th Combined POW
Wing," they called it—to enforce the code of conduct the military established for prisoners of war after several Korean War prisoners defected
to the Communists. Its central tenets included: "If I am captured I will
make every effort to escape and aid others to escape. . . . I will accept
neither parole nor special favors from the enemy. . . . I will make no oral
or written statements disloyal to my country or harmful to their cause."

Out of suffering, Americans learned, they devised a miraculous sort
of makeshift civilization. Then their captors, cruel Oriental despots with
names like "The Bug" ("a psychotic torturer, one of the worst fiends
that we had to deal with") and "Zorba" (a hideously incompetent doctor) and "The Cat" ("a dapper and effeminate intellectual"), sought to
crush it, punishing with torture captives who maintained their status as
proud American fighting men. So these stout-hearted men fought back
by taking actions that invited *more* torture. "We now began to lie on the
railroad tracks," Denton explained at his April 1 press conference. "We
forced them to be brutal to us." Welcoming torture, enduring it, absorb-
ing it, was how they proved their mettle as warriors.

Camp griots memorized the name of every prisoner they heard of,
passing on stories of valor from cell to cell and camp to camp: legends
upon which to build a resistance. "Everybody says we had nothing to
do," one of the returnees explained. "But we did have something to
do . . . resist the North Vietnamese attempts to exploit us . . . the only
weapons were our bodies and our pain." Resistance, the more futile the
better, became the way they gave meaning to their lives.

"How the POWs Fought Back," *U.S. News* headlined McCain's
essay. "Fighting back" was the way, as Captain James Mulligan said, "we
walked out of Hanoi as winners." In time the "we" became collective,
expanding out to encompass the nation—which hadn't really lost the
war at all. The POWs' survival proved it.

Nixon spent more and more time working on Operation Homecoming, precisely in proportion to his mounting Watergate troubles.
He fiddled with the prose of a presidential proclamation and the design
for a POW medal; he micromanaged the sending of corsages to all the
POWs' wives (he specified the name and the address of the florist in Hawaii) and the planning for a White House gala on May 24. "They could

have a great impact on the destiny of this country," he explained to an aide on April 11, the day the *Washington Post*'s lead story was "Mitchell Aide Got $70,000 of Bug Fund," and an arrest of twenty-one youths went down in Cincinnati "when a policeman noticed marijuana smoke 'hanging over the neighborhood like a cloud. . . . There was marijuana fudge in the oven. They were boiling marijuana on the stove in tea bags and they had some burning in the fireplace. It was going up the chimney and we could smell it all over the neighborhood.'"

It was also baseball's opening day. A POW named Charlie Plumb threw out the first pitch at the new Royals Stadium in Kansas City. He had prayed silently from the pitcher's mound: "Dear God, help me put this one down the chute." He fired a strike, and felt as if the ovation that followed lifted the stadium three feet off the ground. Here was the sort of veneration reserved for saviors: men whose suffering might wash away a nation's sins.

THE SUSPICIOUS CIRCLES REMAINED APPALLED BY OPERATION HOME-coming. The American Psychological Association on April 11 put out a statement complaining that the POWs had been exploited "in an elaborate drama staged to provide justification for the President's policy, to create the illusion of victory and to arouse a sense of patriotic fervor." The *New York Times* reported on a citizen's inquiry into Vietnam war crimes in which a witness recalled seeing an Army major gun down thirty-three women, children, and old men from his helicopter. Jane Fonda went on the news in Los Angeles: "The condition of the returning prisoners should speak for itself to prove the men have not been tortured," she said. "I think the only way that we are going to redeem ourselves as a country for what we have done there is not to hail the pilots as heroes, because they are hypocrites and liars." And wasn't it suspicious that the prisoners who most vociferously claimed torture were the ones with the highest military rank? "We have no reason to believe that U.S. Air Force officers tell the truth," she said. "They are professional killers." It made her persona non grata in places like Georgia, where the showing of her movies was outlawed. In 1973, the Maryland Legislature proposed what would have been the first bill of attainder in its history to ban Fonda from the state and grant the government power to seize all money made from her films. "I wouldn't go so far as to execute her, but I think we should cut her tongue off," one legislator argued.

But plenty of ordinary Americans thought what she said made sense. They could point to the constant affirmations of Pentagon spokesmen all through February and March of the "obvious good physical health" of the returnees, that they evinced only "a few instances of mild situation adjustment problems which required family counseling." They could point out the absurdity of Nixon and his supporters' justification for the "Christmas bombings": if it had been done to free the prisoners, what to make, then, of the fact that the bombings themselves *created* more POWs than had been captured in the years 1969, 1970, and 1971 combined?

And they could point out, in the face of the orgy of jingoistic discourse about an enemy whose cruelty knew no bounds, that however ugly the treatment of American POWs might have been, the treatment of prisoners by our South Vietnamese allies was exponentially worse. "The contrast . . . between our happy and apparently healthy POWs and the 'grotesque sculptures of scarred flesh and gnarled limbs' who have been 'politically reeducated' by Mr. Thieu," a *Time* letter writer said, "might make one more prayer of thanksgiving in order: 'Dear God, thank you for allowing me to be captured by the enemy, and not by the friends I was sent to fight for.'"

BEHIND THE DEBATE LAY EXTRAORDINARY COMPLEXITY. THE PHILOSO-pher Alistair Horne has written, "It is one of the most difficult things in this world to establish the truth about torture; whether it did or did not take place, and the nature and scale of it." No torturer, in the centuries-long annals of the practice, ever admits that what he is doing is torture, and the North Vietnamese were no exception: they saw the way they treated their prisoners as a quasi-juridical attempt to prosecute criminals—"air pirates"—violating the Geneva Conventions. At the same time, "The plaintiff is as unlikely to tell the unadorned truth as his oppressor; for [to credibly claim torture] is so superlative a propaganda weapon given into his hands."

That weapon was deployed by the U.S. government constantly, in its claim that the enemy's torture was world-historically cruel. It was not. The tormenters themselves had learned their techniques from the French, as captives in the very prisons they now commanded. Jeremiah Denton demonstrated them in photographs that accompanied his series of AP interviews: suspension upside down for hours at a time; solitary confinement lasting months or even years—and what the POWs called the "rope trick," which in the Spanish Inquisition was known as the *corda* and celebrated as "the queen of torments," and which reappeared in the twenty-first century in the American prison at Guantánamo Bay, Cuba.

The complexity was compounded by conflicts within the POW community itself. North Vietnam was a war-ravaged nation struggling to throw off what it saw as a barbarian invasion, to heal the humiliation of death from the skies, to rouse its collective will to defeat a much more powerful adversary (which, by all accounts, North Vietnam did extraordinarily well). That required a tool of modern statecraft: propaganda. A surrendered, humiliated enemy saying exactly what the regime wanted him to say was the most powerful propaganda tool they possessed. Reason enough for any loyal, self-respecting American flier to resist, and to understand his own resistance as a contribution to military victory. But the queen of torments could not be resisted for long—even the most macho top gun soon learned that. Which introduced complications.

As soon as the enemy's enhanced interrogation methods became systematic, the ranking POWs devised ways to adjust the draconian strictures of their Code of Conduct and still be able to live with themselves. The first loosening, put out by tap code by Denton late in 1965, allowed soldiers to give the minimum of cooperation required to make it stop once they couldn't stand it anymore. In time the allowances became more elaborate—a bizarre efflorescence of high military bureaucracy in dank concrete cells, complete with a Pentagon-style acronym, "BACK US." One bright line: prisoners were never allowed to confess to crimes. This was war. The torture room was an extension of the battlefield. Americans would walk out of Hanoi as winners—so long as they mustered the heroic will never, ever, to confess crimes.

And within the camps, that doctrine set off an American civil war.

A flier named Richard Stratton reasoned that making up some harmless confession was preferable to making a substantive confession after passing out from pain. So he let himself be filmed making one so absurd the North Vietnamese were humiliated around the world when they released the film. Stratton considered that a victory. His "commanding officers" called it treason—defiance of a direct military order. So they issued another: ostracize Stratton. Some prisoners judged that too nonsensical to take seriously. So two camps evolved, pragmatists and hard-liners. The pragmatists called the hard-liners zombies and masochists. Some became friends with their guards. But such indiscipline shook the very foundation of the hard-liners' self-esteem, built under the most trying circumstances imaginable. And by 1968, a place that was represented five years later as an example of simple, stout-hearted American patriotism began displaying the same recriminatory divisions as the society from which it emerged.

Then a new generation of prisoners began arriving in the camps, ones who agreed with the new arguments back home about the war's illegality and futility. "There's no glory or honor in Vietnam," a crusty old colonel told one of them, Edison Miller, a promising young flier being groomed for general and shot down in 1967. "Don't go over there and get your ass killed because that's a lousy stinking war." Some were not fliers at all: they were grunts. And while fliers wore clean socks and punched buttons at thirty thousand feet, and were career officers whose military honor (or simple career ambition) protected them from doubt, ground pounders knew enough to consider the war a shameful waste from their personal experience alone.

And then, in 1969, for reasons never quite understood, something else occurred to unmoor the hard-liners' carefully wrought identity as warriors: torture inexplicably stopped, never to return. Solitary confinement ended, too. Prisoners now inhabited a single communal jail, and its exercise yard included a basketball hoop, Ping-Pong table, pool, and communal barbecue pit—one reason the POWs returned looking so hale and hearty. For the hard-liners, there was no more war to give meaning to their suffering. So they invented superfluous occasions for conflict. When their captors limited church services to eight men at a time, for example, they went on a two-day hunger strike, bellowing choruses of "The Star Spangled Banner" all the while. For the anti–hard-liners—especially the Army GIs who'd been captured by the Vietcong and held in Spartan camps in the South Vietnamese jungle, and considered the "Hanoi Hilton" a comparative paradise—the John Wayne sound-alikes attempting to instill military discipline became outright enemies. Some declared loyalty to the antiwar movement. On Mother's Day 1970, Edison Miller released a statement to the world: "Today America's mothers must face the fact that their sons are killing fellow human beings and destroying foreign countries for an unjust cause, making our actions not only illegal but immoral." Then he made a tape with another antiwar POW, Navy Commander Robert Schweitzer, arguing there was no need to follow the Code of Conduct because it didn't apply in an illegal war. They began organizing their fellows into a "Peace Committee." The gossamer simulacrum of good military order assembled by a valorous band of brothers disintegrated into an undisciplined chaos. Their "Battle of Hanoi" was being lost—by the enemy within. They themselves had said unpatriotic things over North Vietnamese radio, but only under torture. People like Miller (who argued that one of the reasons he was so hated was that he had stood up to torture *better* than they) did so voluntarily. His adversaries were men who had been racked by years of guilty sleepless nights for the simple act of giving their torturers more than their name, rank, and serial number—and feared they would be court-martialed upon their return for doing only that. At that thought, some ambitious spit-and-polish career officers seemed to snap.

Jim Stockdale had been flying his fighter-bomber over the Gulf of Tonkin on August 2, 1964, when he witnessed the fact that the attack by which Lyndon Johnson created the pretext to begin the Vietnam War had not actually taken place at all. After he was shot down he came to understand this knowledge as enforcing upon him an overwhelming and awesome patriotic duty: to stand up to torture so manfully that the enemy could never extract from him the secret that would shame the United States in the eyes of the world. As his Congressional Medal of Honor citation explained, "He deliberately inflicted a near-mortal wound to his person in order to convince his captors of his willingness to give up his life rather than capitulate"—the first and only Medal of Honor awarded for a suicide attempt. He drew up new "Command Goals" that put constructing a coherent, heroic story upon their return—and debunking the stories told by the traitors—at its center. (They still sent their messages in code, which now concluded, "RWHSWDGBU!"—"Release with honor, stick with Dick, God bless you!")

After the Christmas bombings, the Peace Committee released a New Year's statement: "We strongly appeal to the members of Congress to exercise all your legal and moral power to bring about peace.... This statement is made by those who know that more delay can only increase the suffering, lengthen our confinement, and aggravate the well-being of the country which we serve."

At that, a hard-liner named Theodore Guy, calling their message "insubordination on the battlefield," drew up a military plan to "liquidate them."

Then they finally all arrived home. That freed hard-liners like John McCain and Jeremiah Denton to tell their stories. And Peace Committee members like Walter Wilber to tell theirs. He went on *60 Minutes* and asked what was wrong about saying the same things about the Vietnam War that senators like Ted Kennedy and Majority Leader Mike Mansfield did. He called it a matter of patriotism: "Because I'm a military officer doesn't reduce my citizenship rights a bit; in fact it just *emphasizes* them.... I *do* believe the First Amendment—the right to free speech—applies wherever I am in the world." A twenty-seven-year-old POW named John Young said, "I was an American first, and I decided it was my duty to speak out."

But two of the hard-liners believed it was *their* duty to put men like this American in jail. One of the accusers was Ted Guy, the one who had to be talked down from shooting them "on the battlefield." The other was James Bond Stockdale. He had been shocked at his inability to find anyone at the Pentagon who thought the Code of Conduct was even a legally enforceable document. How, he asked incredulously, had the government abandoned its own military code? Since the military brass wouldn't be doing any courts-martial, Guy and Stockdale took advantage of a provision that let them initiate proceedings themselves.

For a White House worried about military recruitment now that the draft had ended, desperate to put the divisions of Vietnam behind it, this new outbreak of the old civil wars over Vietnam was a headache indeed. In fact, on the same day the *Post* headlined "Mitchell Aide Got $70,000 of Bug Fund," the political dilemma of POW against POW became the subject of an intense Oval Office meeting—alongside another Vietnam issue that threatened to become even worse.

A SCENE FOR A FLY—OR A BUG—ON THE WALL OF THE OVAL OFFICE ON April 11.

Roger Shields, the Pentagon official running Operation Homecoming, listened patiently as the president unfurled his idea to deploy POW "superstars" like John McCain in an "indoctrination program" to sell the new all-volunteer armed forces: "It's like a producer putting on a great play or a great movie. You have a hell of a bunch of stars in this one. It's an all-star cast—even the bit players. . . . Oh, I know the service line is, well, you gotta treat the Admiral's son just like, ah, the son of the enlisted man. That's crap . . . they must be used in an effective way."

A starry-eyed thirty-three-year-old in the Oval Office for the first time, Shields gingerly attempted to change the subject.

"Mr. President, I, I—"

Mr. President interrupted him, riffing on.

"It's particularly important because the euphoria doesn't last forever . . . we can't let the, the fervent, uh, feeling that these men have, that there are things for them to do, ah, be dissipated . . . we've got to use them correctly."

Shields abandoned the attempt, going with the flow of his commander in chief. People tended to do that in the Oval Office. The president was going on about the "pitiful left-wing and media" people accusing Operation Homecoming of being staged when Shields ventured a second attempt: "We knew that there were, ah, some problems, a few problems with regard to misconduct."

"Sure."

Shields then explained why the landings of the Freedom Birds had been staged the way they had, with one senior officer on each plane as tarmac spokesman: because frank exchanges between reporters and prisoners might reveal the civil war that had transpired in the camps. But the president did not seem to have the stomach for the discussion. It had been a difficult day. He recollected, fondly, Galan Kramer's homemade banner reading GOD BLESS AMERICA & NIXON. Then, finally, he changed the subject to a politically sensitive press conference Shields was giving the next day, the topic Shields had been trying discuss in the first place.

"You, ah, incidentally, you are working on the MIA, talking to our—"

"That's correct."

"To the extent you can."

"That's correct."

"The, ah, the main thing there, of course, is to just—let it be known that these bastards probably aren't going to come out with anything. Ah, we have got to make an enormous effort in the public relations sense as well as to what we do, ah, as I'm sure you know."

He was referring, in his awkward, vague way, to a bill come due from an extraordinary act of official deception. Operation Homecoming had returned 587 American prisoners of war—but for years Nixon had referred to 1,600 Americans being held in North Vietnam. That number folded in more than one thousand personnel, mostly pilots, who crashed in the dense Vietnamese brush and in previous wars would have been classed as "Killed in Action/Body Not Recovered"—but had been reclassified as "MIA" so the president could make the North Vietnamese look bad for his Paris negotiations. Now the families of those other 1,013 were making insistent noises: what was the government going to do about *them*?

The Operation Homecoming statements by the Secretary of Defense and the Joint Chiefs of Staff included the promise that "we will not rest until all those still known captive are safe and until we have achieved the best possible accounting for those missing in action." Holding the government to that pledge had now become the raison d'être of the National League of Families of American Prisoners of War and Missing in Southeast Asia, the organization that had taken off as a White House front group. VIVA was still selling bracelets hand over fist—now bearing the names of MIAs. It had even come up with a new flag honoring them: a forlorn, gaunt, hangdog flat-topped silhouette, barbed wire and a guard tower in the background, a military laurel, and the legend POW-MIA: YOU ARE NOT FORGOTTEN. Soon it adorned Veterans of Foreign Wars and American Legion posts across the land. On March 30 the brigadier general who supervised the release announced he "did not rule out the possibility that some Americans may still be held in Laos." The commander of the "4th Combined POW Wing," in a spirit of political hardball, told the press, "I am gratified that our nation appears prepared to follow through on comprehensive plans to account for those who are still missing in action." Chicago MIA families were now saying that the administration was "abandoning" men "seen in photos coming out of Indochina or who have been reported alive by returning POWs." It was one more aspect of the Americans' lunatic semiology that baffled hapless Communist officials. "We have not come this far," one declared in exasperation at being once more enjoined to "prove" they held no more prisoners, "to hold on to a handful of Americans, after all what would that prove?" The issue was a godforsaken mess.

And there was another Southeast Asia mess: Cambodia. As late as 1970 Nixon's excuse for dropping bombs on the neutral nation had been that it was necessary to protect the retreat of American ground forces from South Vietnam. But now it was April 1973, the boys were back home, and B-52s were still dropping 24,000 tons a month. Secretary of State William Rogers told Congress it "was justified because the continued presence of North Vietnamese troops in Cambodia threatened the right of self-determination in Vietnam." That was surreal, considering that the Paris Peace Accords we had just signed allowed 145,000 North Vietnamese troops to garrison *inside* South Vietnam. Another excuse arose: Communist communications lines in the countryside had to be intercepted. So why, the suspicious circles asked, were bombs falling on the country's most heavily populated areas?

Another mess was domestic. As part of his plan to dismantle as much of Lyndon Johnson's Great Society as he could, Nixon had hired a thirty-two-year-old right-wing activist named Howard Phillips, ostensibly to "run" the Office of Economic Opportunity—but actually to take the agency apart piece by piece. And on April 11, a federal judge ruled on what the *Washington Post* called "the most brazen usurpation of the powers of Congress and as crass an assault on its prerogatives as we can imagine": that if the president let Howard Phillips continue to dismember OEO, he "would be clothing the President with a power entirely to control the legislation of Congress, and paralyze the administration of justice."

And then there was Watergate—of which Attorney General Richard Kleindienst had just testified before Congress, defending Richard

Nixon's novel doctrine of executive privilege in a way that drove senators insane.

"The Congress has no power at all to command testimony from the executive departments?" asked Senator Edmund Muskie, the object of the worst Watergate dirty tricks during the 1972 presidential campaign season.

Replied Kleindienst, "If the President of the United States so directs."

"Do we have the right to command you to testify against the will of the President?"

"If the President directs me not to appear, I am not going to appear."

"Does that apply to every appointee of the Executive Branch?"

"I'd have to say that is correct." And if Congress did not like that, Kleindienst continued, it could "cut off our funds, abolish most of what we can do, or impeach the president."

Senator Ervin, startled, followed up: how could an impeachment take place if none of the president's men could be compelled to supply facts? Kleindienst's answer was chilling and strange: "You don't need facts to impeach a president."

Republicans and Democrats both fumed that they had never heard senators addressed like that in their chamber. A Harvard constitutional law expert called Kleindienst's claims "utterly ridiculous." A Yale professor said they "can't hold water." Democratic senator Lawton Chiles of Florida said it sounded "so unreal that I wondered if it was really me—if I hadn't parted from my senses." The chair of the House Republican Conference, John Anderson of Illinois, said it "borders on contempt for the established law of the land." A Pennsylvania Democrat called it "monarchical or totalitarian."

King Richard: just like Senator Ervin said. And now Ervin, with his investigatory committee already meeting in closed session, was in a position to do something about it, threatening subpoenas: "I don't like the surgeon's knife, but sometimes a cancer comes—a cancer that has to be eradicated the same way."

THE WATERGATE GRAND JURY RE-IMPANELED, SUPPOSEDLY IN SECRET, but leaking like a sieve: that James McCord had testified that E. Howard Hunt's wife (who had died in a plane crash the previous December with $10,000 in crisp hundred-dollar bills in her purse) was a conduit for bribes to the Watergate defendants; that John Mitchell had received the transcripts from the bugs at Democratic headquarters; that Mitchell, Dean, Colson, and Magruder were active participants in obstructing the

Watergate investigation; that G. Gordon Liddy had made a detailed presentation in Attorney General Mitchell's office, including charts, graphs, and a multimillion-dollar budget, about how the Nixon reelection campaign could spy on and sabotage Democratic presidential campaigns.

John Mitchell was spotted at the White House—perhaps strategizing about how to handle the rumored indictment?

On April 17, the president, looking haggard and tense, read three minutes' worth of lawyerly words on TV from a sheaf of typescript in the White House briefing room. He claimed that a month earlier, on March 21, "as a result of serious charges which came to my attention," he "began intensive new inquiries" into Watergate. He claimed "major developments . . . concerning which it would be improper to be more specific now, except to say that real progress has been made in finding the truth." He expected "all government employees and especially White House staff employees" to cooperate "in this matter." He concluded, "I condemn any attempts to cover up in this case, no matter who was involved."

Then he absented the room. Young Ronald Ziegler, his spokesman, took over. The former skipper on the "Jungle Cruise" attraction at Disneyland was pressed about all the contradictions between the president's new statement and his previous ones.

There was no contradiction, Ziegler said, because the previous ones had been based on "investigations prior to the president's action."

The reporters kept pressing him, question after question after question. On the eighteenth query, he uttered the immortal words: "This is the operative statement. The others are inoperative."

Time magazine helpfully catalogued what statements were now "inoperative":

The White House's claim that what had happened at the Watergate on June 17, 1972, was merely "a third-rate burglary attempt"; the claim of Attorney General Kleindienst on August 28, 1972, of "the most extensive, thorough, and comprehensive investigation since the assassination of President Kennedy"; the president's reassurances the next day that his counsel John Dean had carried out an investigation on his behalf, such that he could now "say categorically . . . that no one in this administration, presently employed, was involved in this very bizarre incident"; his statement the next day that while "overzealous people in campaigns do things that are wrong," "what really hurts is if you try to cover it up," and that he himself wanted the guilty to be prosecuted "as soon as possible"; his campaign manager's October 16 avowal that the *Washington Post* had "maliciously sought to give the appearance of a direct connection between the White House and the Watergate, a charge which the *Post* knows—and a half-dozen investigations have found—to be false"; three days later, the promise of the campaign's deputy director Jeb Magruder that "when this is all over, you'll know that there were only seven people who knew about the Watergate, and they are the seven who were indicted by the grand jury"; then the president's statement that he had "absolute and total confidence" in John Dean's 1972 investigation; and John Mitchell's statement on March 29 that claims he had known about the burglary beforehand were "slanderous and false."

All, apparently, inoperative.

The president went into seclusion for the next thirteen days. On the fifth day a Gallup poll was released. It found that 41 percent of Americans believed Richard Nixon knew about the bugging plans before they were carried out. The next issue of *Time* summarized the state of knowledge: that the June 1972 burglary "has been revealed as clearly part of a far broader campaign of political espionage designed to give Nixon an unfair, illegal—and unnecessary—advantage in his reelection drive. It was financed with secret campaign funds, contributed in cash by anonymous donors and never fully accounted for, in violation of the law. Then, after the arrests in the Watergate break-in, the same funds were used to persuade most of them to plead guilty and keep quiet about any higher involvement." *Time* concluded that the "scandal was rapidly emerging as probably the most pervasive instance of top-level misconduct in history." A high official at 1600 Pennsylvania Avenue reported the mood in the West Wing: "It's like the last days in a Berlin bunker in 1945. They're all sitting there waiting for the bombs to drop."

Word was there would be another presidential announcement, this one the evening before May Day. Perhaps the bombs would drop then.

CHAPTER FIVE

"A Whale of a Good Cheerleader"

IT SEEMED THAT BY APRIL 30 RICHARD NIXON HAD NO CHOICE BUT TO say something about Watergate: six Republican senators said they would not run for reelection unless he did. Young men who last month bestrode Washington like colossi were hiring lawyers under threat of indictment, leaking accusations against colleagues, writing messages on legal pads rather than speaking them aloud—who knew whether their offices, too, were bugged?

New outrages compounded daily. John Mitchell contradicted his own previous sworn testimony. Deputy campaign manager Jeb Stuart Magruder told investigators he had passed transcripts from Democratic National Committee phone bugs to the Oval Office. Chief of staff H. R. "Bob" Haldeman and domestic affairs counselor John Ehrlichman, the president's two closest advisors, had hired criminal representation. A young staffer named Kenneth Reitz had quit his job running the 1974 congressional campaigns after it was revealed he'd run a spy shop within the Youth Division of the Committee to Re-elect the President. Pat Gray resigned from the FBI altogether after the shocking admission that he had mishandled Watergate evidence from the safe of E. Howard Hunt, which ended up in an FBI "burn bag"—containers in which sensitive materials were destroyed. The evidence, allegedly, included forged cables meant to frame John F. Kennedy for the assassination of South Vietnam's president Ngo Dinh Diem; a spy dossier on Ted Kennedy; and a memo on Hunt's meetings with a lobbyist linked to bribes paid to Nixon by International Telephone & Telegraph. Reporters unearthed a new private treasury of $600,000 to finance dirty tricks—like the thousands of copies of the *Washington Post* the White House bought, then shredded, to fake votes in a poll on whether or not the president was doing the right thing in Vietnam. "I don't know why any citizen should ever again believe anything a government official says," one White House staffer told *Time.*

Then, the staggering news at the Los Angeles trial of Daniel Ellsberg, the defense intellectual who leaked the Pentagon Papers, that on September 3, 1971, Hunt and Liddy had overseen a break-in at the office of Ellsberg's psychiatrist. The burglars spoke "Cuban-style Spanish." They worked for a unit of the White House, America now learned, referred to internally as the "Plumbers."

A newsweekly quoted a White House staffer: "Don't let your incredulity factor get too high—there's more to come." A distinguished British journalist published an op-ed in the *Times* calling the United States a "banana republic." Theodore White announced he was extending his deadline for *Making of the President 1972;* he needed to add a new chapter on Watergate. It grew harder to entertain the notion that the president had simply been above it all.

And so he left his seclusion and, American flag peeking from behind his right shoulder, American flag pin ornamenting his lapel, a bust of Abraham Lincoln and a picture of his family beside him, explained how he was cleansing the rot.

He began, as he always did, on a maudlin note: "I want to talk to you tonight"—*pause*—"from my heart." He outlined the problem: several of his closest aides, including "some of my most trusted friends," had been accused of illegal activity in the 1972 presidential election. "The inevitable result of these charges has been to raise serious questions about the integrity of the White House itself."

He claimed he himself had learned about the break-in: from news reports while "in Florida trying to get a few days' rest after my visit to Moscow." (A bid for pity: he had been working hard, making peace.) He said he had been appalled, ordering an internal investigation about whether members of his administration were involved, and "received repeated assurances that they were not." And it was only because of those assurances from people he trusted, he said, that "I discounted stories in the press that *appeared*"—he emphasized the word—"to implicate members of my administration and other members of the campaign committee."

Then he elaborated on what he had claimed two weeks earlier: that on March 21 new information convinced him he had been deceived. He addressed the audience directly: "There had been an effort to conceal the facts both from the public—from *you*—and from me." So he ordered a new investigation, reporting "directly to me, *right here in this office.*" Those not cooperating would be forced to resign.

Then came the lead for the next day's news stories: "Today, in one of the most difficult decisions of my presidency, I accepted the resignation of two of my closest associates in the White House, Bob Haldeman, John Ehrlichman—two of the finest public servants it has been my privilege to know." Not, he hastened to assure his audience, out of any "implication whatever of personal wrongdoing on their part. . . . But in matters as sensitive as guarding the integrity of our democratic process, it is essential not only that rigorous legal and ethical standards be observed but also that the public—*you*—have total confidence that they are both being observed and enforced by those in authority and particularly by the President of the United States."

He also announced that he had let loose his attorney general, Richard Kleindienst—again, not because the individual had done anything wrong but because he was "a close personal and professional associate of some of those who are involved in the case"; and, in passing, that John Dean had resigned also. He explained nothing whatsoever about that.

There came a sort of apology. Nixon had "decided, as the 1972 campaign approached, that the presidency come first and politics second." So "the easiest course would be for me to blame those to whom I delegated the responsibility to run the campaign." He shook his head histrionically: "But that would be a *cowardly* thing to do."

He, instead, would fight for the truth—but not let that distract him from pressing tasks like "reducing the danger of a nuclear war that would destroy civilization as we know it."

That introduced the Checkers-style sanctimony. He listed the goals he had written on Christmas Eve for his second term. They included "to make it possible for our children, and for our children's children, to live in a world of peace." And: "To make this country be more than ever a land of opportunity—of *equal* opportunity, *full* opportunity, for every American." And to "establish a climate of decency and civility."

"There can be no whitewash at the White House," he concluded, and asked for the nation's prayers.

And then he absented himself from the nation's TV screens, left to the mercy of the reviews.

THE MARQUEE EDITORIALISTS GRANTED NIXON THE BENEFIT OF THE doubt. The Associated Press found only two prominent critics of the speech, both Democratic governors: the left-wing John J. Gilligan of Ohio, and the Georgia moderate, Jimmy Carter. Be that as it may, just about every commentator and official of any significance united in a new consensus: Watergate was something historically awful—and the men responsible, whoever they turned out to be, were louts.

Everyone, that is, except Governor Ronald Wilson Reagan of California.

He offered his thoughts after greeting a group of high school visitors in his Sacramento reception room. Reporters asked him about speculation from Barry Goldwater that Reagan might be called to Washington to help reorganize the White House. "That's very kind of the senator," he answered in the third person, "but Ronald Reagan has got his hands full right here." Then he minimized Watergate. It all was part of the usual "atmosphere of campaigning," where pranks were just part of the game. "They did something that was stupid and foolish and was criminal"— then corrected himself: "It was illegal. Illegal is a better word than criminal because I think criminal has a different connotation." He said, "The tragedy of this is that men who are not criminals at heart" had to suffer. It saddened him "that now there is going to have to be punishment."

That Reagan thought the Watergate conspirators were not "criminals at heart" was the headline—"Political Spies Not 'Criminals,'" as the *Los Angeles Times* put it—and a laugh line. NBC's John Chancellor smirked, "Reagan, who talks a lot about 'law and order,' described the burglars as 'well-meaning individuals committed to the reelection of the president.'" Tom Wicker used Reagan, "that exponent of law and order," as Exhibit A in a sermon about what happens in a world run according to the Gospel of Richard Nixon, where good guys were always good no matter what they actually did, bad guys were always and everywhere ontologically evil, and no one will be safe until " 'we' crack down on 'them,' occasionally adopting their tactics."

Ronald Reagan divided the world into good guys and bad guys. Richard Nixon and his team were good guys. So they could not have done evil at all.

Time ran a digest on which prospects to replace Nixon in 1977 were "up" and which were "down." John Connally, the tough former Texas governor, JFK and LBJ intimate, and Nixon treasury secretary, was looking good—he had magnanimously chosen Nixon's difficult week to officially announce he was switching to the Republican Party. The dashing Illinois senator Charles Percy was in great shape after introducing a Senate resolution for an independent Watergate prosecutor. Governor Nelson Rockefeller of New York was in good shape for his remoteness from the scandal. Ronald Reagan, however, who "put his foot in his mouth by saying that the Watergate conspirators were not 'criminals at heart,'" was down, down, down. He had just announced that he would not be running for reelection next year, which was interpreted as a move to position himself for a presidential run. Excusing Watergate sure seemed a funny way to begin.

· · ·

THE NOTION OF REAGAN RUNNING FOR PRESIDENT HAD BEEN IN THE AIR for years. In 1968 he made a surprise last-minute entrance into the nomination fight at the Republican National Convention in Miami—and with heavy initial support from Southern delegates—had come shockingly close to the prize. He had emerged as the hottest politician in the country. For a new issue had arisen in the second half of the 1960s, and Ronald Reagan owned it.

The issue was campus militancy. When he first starting running for governor in 1966, advisors armed with the most sophisticated public opinion research that money could buy told him not to touch it. The last thing they wanted for the candidate who costarred beside a chimp in the film *Bedtime for Bonzo* only fifteen years earlier was for him to associate himself with anti-intellectualism by attacking higher education. In fact, they wanted him to announce his candidacy standing beside two Nobel laureates. What's more, they explained, the student uprising in Berkeley didn't even show up in their polling as a public concern.

He told his experts to go climb a tree. "Look," he lectured them, "I don't care if I'm in the mountains, the desert, the biggest cities of the state, the first question is: 'What are you going to do about Berkeley?' And each time the question itself would get applause.'"

Ronald Reagan knew audiences. It was a key element of his political genius. One of the things at which brilliant politicians are better than mediocre ones is smelling new public concerns over the horizon *before* they are picked up by polls—before the public even knows to call them "issues" at all. "This is how it became an issue," he told interviewers later. "You knew that this was the number one thing on the people's minds."

Berkeley: late in 1964 a police car had rolled onto the middle of the University of California's flagship campus to dislodge a student signing up students for the Mississippi civil rights movement. Thousands gathered around the police car, trapping it, and turning it into a makeshift dais for inspiring, idealistic oratory. The "Free Speech Movement" began, and it soon became the seedbed for a nationwide antiwar movement of unprecedented breadth and intensity. In fashionable circles, the youthful energy represented by the rise of civic activism among college students was judged a tonic. Even aging Republicans got in on the act. "I think the people of your age have a function right now," Dwight D. Eisenhower told the 1966 graduates at Kansas State University. "My generation and even those who are younger have grown pessimistic and lethargic. You people can do much for your elders." NBC's David Brinkley praised "a new generation of students who demand to find their own way in a society filled with social crisis."

Reagan, on the other hand, quipped, "I'd like to harness their youthful energy with a strap." And said he wished Congress would declare war in Vietnam, so "the anti-Vietnam demonstrations and the act of burning draft cards would be treasonable"—which is to say, punishable by death. (His own opinion on ending the war, expressed in October 1965, was "It's silly talking about how many years we will have to spend in the jungles of Vietnam when we could pave the whole country and put parking stripes on it and still be home by Christmas.")

Excoriating student protest came naturally to him. College was at the heart of his sentimental imagination—Frank Merriwell and all that—but it was also where he learned once and for all that heroes were not just for storybooks. "As far as I'm concerned everything good that has happened to me—everything—started on this campus," he put it at a 1980 campaign appearance at his alma mater, Eureka College, decked out in a vintage football jersey in the school colors of maroon and gold.

Eureka: "Sounds like the name of a college in a movie," a Hollywood columnist wrote in a 1949 profile. Dutch became aware of the little campus operated by the Disciples of Christ when his hometown hero Garland Waggoner became a football star there. He said that upon his first visit to its few modest redbrick, ivy-covered buildings, he "wanted to get into that school so badly it hurt when I thought about it." Getting there and staying there had been no easy thing: rural America was in an agricultural depression even before the Great Crash of 1929. Then the Depression put Jack Reagan's Fashion Boot Shop out of business. Overselling his football prowess, downplaying his B average, Reagan talked his way into a $180 athletic scholarship, paying the rest of his way washing dishes, lifeguarding, and coaching the swim team he himself helped establish. (He had never swum in a real pool before.) That made quite a contrast to the entitled brats tearing down Berkeley. Part of what made Berkeley such a powerful issue for traditionally Democratic voters was class resentment— something Ronald Reagan understood in his bones.

College to him meant something specific—an arena of knights-errant and blushing damsels; contests of manly derring-do; and, yes, even intellectual exploration. (Disdain for learning was one of the things that made the foppish *Brown of Harvard* so contemptible.) Immediately, he pledged a fraternity. (He never seemed more apoplectic during the Berkeley crisis than when he announced he had learned a left-wing professor was biased against boys wearing fraternity caps.) He scored a room in the fraternity house's converted attic with a panoramic view of his new proving ground. (Henceforth whenever he moved into a new home it was almost always one with a panoramic view; life was more dramatic that way). And soon an opportunity to cast himself as Frank Merriwell arrived—when, three months into his freshman year, nearly the entire student body went on strike to demand the resignation of the school's unpopular president.

No one either then or now—no attentive eyewitnesses, no diligent historians, no reporters who covered the exciting events for the *Chicago Tribune,* not the Associated Press, not even the *New York Times*—has ever been able to come up with a coherent explanation of precisely why the strike happened. Some blamed flapper-besotted students frustrated with President Bert Wilson's refusal to lift a ban against dancing. Another theory held the opposite: the instigators were moralists annoyed at Wilson's indifference to campus dissipation. Or that, following a trip to New York, he tried to force fancy new administrative theories on the college, which alienated his colleagues. Others note a professional rivalry with a popular professor who had been passed over for Wilson's job (and who, according to some accounts, orchestrated the entire affair from behind the scenes, from fanning fears of staff cuts to spreading rumors that Wilson's daughter was a sex fiend). Or maybe it was just that students were bored.

A fog of crosscutting motives and narratives, a complexity that defies storybook simplicity: that is usually the way history happens.

But not, however, in the mind of Ronald Reagan.

He made the strike the centerpiece of his 1965 memoir, writing just as Berkeley was becoming an epicenter for the national campus revolt. In Reagan's morality tale, President Bert Wilson, Scrooge-like, had decided to impose "such a drastic cutback academically that many juniors and seniors would have been cut off without the courses needed for graduation in their chosen majors"—"cutting the heart out of the college." Wilson then rammed the plan through the board of trustees "[w]ithout a thought of consulting students or faculty," who both responded "with a roar of fury."

But not, Reagan insisted, with *too* much fury: students responded with "no riotous burning in effigy but a serious, well-planned program, engineered from the ground up by students but with the full support and approval of almost every professor on the campus." ("I get a bit smug when I contrast that college strike to some of the . . . fevered picketing of these more modern times," he later told a correspondent; the contrast was surely in his mind when an effigy at Berkeley bearing a sign reading REDUCE REAGAN BY 10% was hung the first month of his governorship by students protesting *his* budget cuts.)

In his telling, students then devised a counterplan that reorganized the university according to all of President Wilson's stated aims, which Wilson then rejected. So they raised up a petition to present to the board of directors, demanding his resignation. "The board met on the last Saturday before Thanksgiving vacation," Reagan wrote—a dirty trick, by which they might sign off on the president's foul deed before the students had a chance to fight it, the cuts presented as a fait accompli when they helplessly returned from vacation.

Then . . .

Every great adventure story needs a suspenseful turning point—a moment of high drama upon which everything stands or falls. And in the imagination of Ronald Reagan, nothing heightens drama better than a football game.

"The football team met Illinois College that afternoon," he wrote. But the crowd, he said, was distracted. He presents a striking visual image: "In the second half, newsboys hit the stands with extras headlining the fact that our petition to the board had been denied. Looking back from the bench was like looking at a card stunt"—that stadium ritual where spectators hold up coordinated color cards to trace out images. "Everyone was hidden by a newspaper." Afterward no one left for Thanksgiving. "We all remained on campus, waiting until midnight for the summit to break up." The college bell tolled; "as prearranged as Paul Revere's ride," the school chapel filled with students and faculty.

Dramatically, just in the nick of time, evil was foiled

Enters our star—a lowly freshman, just like his favorite Yale hero: "it was my turn to come off the bench. It had been decided that the motion for putting our plan into effect should be presented by a freshman." He took the stage. He gave a brilliant speech. "When I came to actually present the motion there was no need for parliamentary procedure: they came to their feet with a roar—even the faculty members present voted by acclamation. It was heady wine. Hell, with two more lines I could have had them riding through 'every Middlesex village and farm'— without horses yet.' . . . In the end it was our policy of polite resistance that brought victory. After a week, the new president resigned." And so they received "an education in human nature and the rights of man to universal education that nothing could erase from our psyches. . . . The four classes on campus became the most tightly knit groups ever to graduate from Eureka. . . . Campus spirit bloomed. A remarkably close bond to the faculty developed."

HERE IS THE PROBLEM: MANY OF THESE EVENTS ARE MATTERS OF record—which contradicts Reagan's story at almost every point. The showdown meeting took place on a Tuesday, for instance, not a football Saturday. Nobody else remembered Ronald Reagan saving the day; he appears in no contemporary newspaper account. "You know, I read that part of his autobiography on Eureka College," a classmate told a writer decades later, "and I wondered whether he and I went to the same school. This thing is pretty dreamy."

But it is true he did emerge shortly after the strike as an incipient Big Man on Campus. Maybe he was being honored for his ability *after* the event to present the fog of bureaucratic war as a simple morality tale to a confused student body, giving students the clarity they needed to bind themselves together in the wake of an acrimonious conflict. We do, after all, tell stories in order to live.

In February the freshman made his first appearance in the school paper's gossip column: "Dutch Reagan's debut as cheer leader in the Normal cage"—that is, at the basketball auditorium at Illinois State Normal University—"was very much in his favor . . . He was full of spirit and the Normal rooters followed him almost perfectly." He began playing the lead in school plays; the word that reappears in reviews is "presence." He also began wearing dark horn-rimmed glasses, like Harold Lloyd's in *The Freshman,* eagerly stitching himself into the elaborate rituals of 1920s varsity life—"'E' Tribe"; a seventy-fifth anniversary pageant set in the "Forest Primeval"; pep rallies, in whose defense he wrote an impassioned jeremiad, signed "Dutch Reagan," imagining sports as savior of his school's floundering Depression-era fortunes:

> *"Eureka Spirit"—it is advertised and upheld as something superior to that of other schools. But is it? . . . Let's live basketball and Eureka till Mac's Red Devils take Illinois College in the last game of the season. It's our year in at least three major sports. Now let's get a freshman class in here of over one hundred and let's go home and wake up the Christian churches to the fact that this is their school and they owe it their support. "Let's get in there and pitch"!*

In sports where he wasn't skilled enough for conference competition, he found other ways to make himself indispensable. For instance, a classmate remembered him as the basketball team's regular yell leader— "one of the best we've ever had. He turned that crowd upside down . . . a whale of a good cheerleader." He became the football team's tackling dummy: "Although 'Dutch' failed to get much competition this season he has the determination and fight to finally win out, if he sticks to football throughout his college career," his sophomore yearbook read. "He never gives up when the odds are against him." Maybe he wrote that; he was on the yearbook staff. Or maybe he didn't: "He never quit," Coach McKenzie—another new surrogate father—remembered. "Others did." (He scored his only touchdown in a game at Illinois State Normal College, he told reporters in 1982—"lowering himself to the Oval Office floor, showing how he picked up an ISNU fumble, then lurched up to recreate a frantic romp to the end zone.") His coach even figured into his story about why his grades weren't impressive. Dutch claimed he flubbed them on purpose—a happy ending. "I was afraid if my grades were good I might end up an athletic teacher at some small school. I wanted more than [Coach] Mac had."

In his junior year he added the Booster Club, and displayed an interest in international politics: on March 22, 1931, a "lively discussion over world peace and the chances of another war" was led by "Ronald Reagan, better known as Dutch . . . and as the saying goes, 'he needs no introduction.'" By the next school year he was senior class president.

THERE WAS ONE COLLEGE DETAIL THAT ONLY HIS CLASSMATES REMEMbered; Reagan never spoke of it himself. They recalled how the Reagan brothers staged the school's first homecoming dance—"the biggest thing seen here in years"—charging their classmates a premium to attend, and splitting the proceeds. Another recollection of a classmate that never found its way into Reagan's self-representations: in 1932, he bet five of his fraternity brothers that within five years he would be making five thousand dollars a year. His girlfriend recalled that he told them if he didn't make that much, "I'll consider these four years here wasted."

The stories he chose to tell, tell a story in themselves, as do those he chose not to.

"We had a special spirit at Eureka," he wrote, "that bound us all together, much as a poverty-stricken family is bound": tuition fees "made no pretense of covering the actual cost of an education," and many students couldn't pay the tuition anyway; the endowment was inadequate, so professors would "go for months without pay"; part of the endowment was a farm, from whose produce the school sometimes paid its debts. "Oh, it was a small town, a small school, with small doings. It was in a poor time without money, without ceremony, with pleasant thoughts of the past to balance fears of the uncertain future. But it somehow provided the charm and enchantment which alone can make a memory of a school something to cherish." In Ronald Reagan's recollections of Eureka there could never be anything venal (except in the person of President Bert Wilson, because he was a villain).

That made quite a contrast with the "multiversity"—as Chancellor

Clark Kerr termed the sprawling campuses of the University of California system. Reagan traversed the state in 1966 offering an image yoking protesters who believed themselves the moral equivalent of the Founding Fathers to that varsity culture of the 1920s: "I'm sorry they did away with paddles in fraternities." He isolated the villains: Chancellor Kerr, for entertaining the students' grievances, and Governor Pat Brown, ex officio member of the Board of Regents, for not having immediately taken the ringleaders "by the scruff of the neck and thrown them off campus— personally." That would "put the rest of them back to work doing their homework." When *he* was governor, Reagan said, the watchword would be "obey the rules or get out." The tactics of what they called the "New Left," he said, better resembled that of the "Old Right," which his generation had fought so hard to defeat—the Nazi Party.

Such perorations would get a rousing ovation every time. And that, even more than singling out alleged abuses of California's welfare system by "able-bodied malingerers," or his fulminations against the violation of economic liberty represented by the state's new statute outlawing racial discrimination in housing, or high taxes and runaway government spending generally, was how he won his stunning upset victory.

Then, when it became Governor Reagan's job to superintend the university upon his inauguration in 1967, he wrangled control of the Board of Regents in order to have Clark Kerr fired, wrested from the nine campus chancellors their final authority to appoint faculty, and instituted tuition for the first time in the system's history. It was *not* the business of the state, he said, "to subsidize intellectual curiosity"—the intellectual curiosity of students whom he sometimes labeled "brats," "freaks," and "cowardly fascists," but whose "academic freedom" he insisted he himself guarded as zealously as a crusading knight. Except, however, when he did not: "Academic freedom does *not* include attacks on other faculty members or on the administration of the university," the former student striker once scowled on TV, "or seeking to incite incidents on other campuses." When one of the founders of the New Left group Students for a Democratic Society was recruited to the faculty at the campus in Santa Barbara, Reagan said that was like hiring an arsonist to work at a fireworks factory.

It made him a national political star. Of the sixty-seven times Reagan was featured on the three network newscasts between 1967 and 1970, more than half concerned his stance on campus militancy. For instance, in the fall of 1968, a Berkeley faculty member recruited Black Panther Minister of Information Eldridge Cleaver as guest lecturer for Social Analysis 139X—Dehumanization and Regeneration in the American

Social Order. Reagan said if it happened he would investigate the school from "top to bottom"—for "if Eldridge Cleaver is allowed to teach our children, they may come home one night and slit our throats." Cleaver taught anyway, proclaiming in one lecture, "Ronald Reagan is a punk, a sissy, and a coward, and I challenge him to a duel to the death or until he says Uncle Eldridge. I give him a choice of weapons—a gun, a knife, a baseball bat, or marshmallows."

After the Reagan-controlled Board of Regents rebuked Cleaver, a 1,500-student march culminated in the holding of a dean hostage. Reagan, on ABC, scowled: "The calls and the letters make it pretty clear that the people have reached the end of the line, and I don't blame them." When school opened the next semester, San Francisco State College students demanding a new ethnic studies program blockaded campus buildings. Reagan answered with soldiers bearing fixed bayonets. Tear gas flew back and forth, and bonfires illuminated the streets. On NBC Reagan said that the "small group of criminal anarchist and latter-day fascists" whom he held responsible—those who "seek to close down the campuses, our universities, and even our high schools," a goal which was "not in any way to be confused with the traditional and generally acceptable activities of students who always seek change through proper and constructive channels"—would soon receive their comeuppance: "Those who want to get an education and those who want to teach should be protected at the point of a bayonet if necessary."

The next month, the same movement surfaced at Berkeley. He visited the campus for an inspection; a throng started chanting "Fuck Reagan"; the governor responded with an outstretched middle finger. Students shattered the glass door of the building where he was meeting.

It was then that a CBS reporter confronted him with an apparently irrefutable argument: every time he escalated such deployments, conflict only escalated. Reagan responded with the logic of Frank Merriwell at Yale: he was rescuing damsels in distress. "When you see a coed, a girl trying to make her way to class, and she is pushed around, and physically abused for trying to go through the picket line and go to class," he said, "this girl is entitled to have the forces of law and order to defend her right to go to class."

The reporter stood silent, incredulous. He had no idea what this strange man was talking about. Though this strange man, it had to be said, was then enjoying the highest approval ratings of his term.

Later that spring, when Berkeley students forcefully seized a spit of vacant campus land and declared it a "People's Park," Reagan dispatched not just National Guard troops but a Sikorsky helicopter that spewed tear gas at students cornered into a crowded campus square. A student was shot observing events from a rooftop. Reagan said, "The police didn't kill the young man. He was killed by the first college administrator who said some time ago it was all right to break the laws in the name of dissent." His address at the Commonwealth Club in San Francisco defending the military deployment—he was beating back, he said, "a revolutionary movement involving a tiny minority of faculty and students finding concealment and shelter in an entire college generation. . . . Stand firm and the university can dispose of this revolution within the week"—made all three networks.

The following year, as bomb scares swept the nation following the conviction of seven New Left activists for conspiring to disrupt the 1968 Democratic National Convention in Chicago, UC Santa Barbara students burned down a Bank of America branch. Marx-minded student leaders welcomed such incidents as "heightening the contradictions"—a necessary precursor to the longed-for revolution. Reagan barked back, four days before the shootings at Kent State: "If it's to be a bloodbath, let it be now. No more appeasement."

Hard to know how a politician could bounce back from *that* in an election year. Or so said his detractors. Instead, he won reelection overwhelmingly. *Life* profiled him that fall as "The Hottest Candidate in Either Party," noting, however, that Reagan had "failed almost completely to keep his campaign promises of 1966—the cost of higher education and welfare has risen hideously, California campuses have remained battlegrounds, and his 'tax reform' has been turned down in the legislature." *Life*'s quotation marks signified skepticism about how a tax plan that delivered most benefit to upper incomes counted as reform at all. And yet, even more than in 1966, he attracted thousands of Democrats who'd never imagined voting for a Republican before in their lives. "His most effective campaigners," *Life* explained, "have been those college-based Reagan haters who rioted over People's Park in Berkeley and set fire to the Bank of America's branch in Isla Vista last spring."

A fat lot of good that would do him in 1973, went conventional wisdom, now that the Paris peace settlement had put Reagan's most effective campaigners out of business. A political cartoon told the story: an archaic-looking hippie, like something from another age, held up his picket sign with a peace symbol in one hand and a placard reading UNEMPLOYED in the other. Reagan couldn't even count on the loyalty of Republican conservatives, either: their hearts belonged, as their bumper stickers proclaimed, to "Spiro of '76." And there was this: Vice President Spiro Agnew would be fifty-six at convention time. John Connally would be fifty-nine. Chuck Percy would be fifty-six—and Reagan, at sixty-five, would be eligible for Social Security. "Around the mouth and neck," George Will of *National Review* wrote, "he looks like an old man."

Ronald Reagan's closest political advisors had been meeting for weekly breakfasts, racking their brains on how to move him into the front ranks of presidential contenders. The plan they arrived at was announced the week after the end of the Vietnam War. Bad accounting and an improving economy had left California with a nearly $1 billion budget surplus. Reagan said he intended to "return the money to taxpayers"— novel language at the time. His method would be unprecedented: the state's first ballot initiative sponsored by a sitting governor. The state made a tactical decision the pundits called ill-advised: to put it on the ballot for November 1973, instead of in 1974. It set off an apparently impossible scramble to get six hundred thousand signatures by June to get it on the ballot. The plan baffled the pundits. George McGovern had made middle-class tax relief a centerpiece of his presidential campaign only a few months earlier; that, obviously, had gone nowhere. The details of the plan devised by four right-wing Reagan advisors—economist Milton Friedman, Martin Anderson, a lawyer named Anthony Kennedy, and Chief of Staff Edwin Meese—were confusing. The aim was to put a ceiling on state taxes and spending. But it seemed to bestow most of its favors on those who were already well-off—and what sort of political sense did a giveaway to the rich make for Ronald Reagan? sneered the *Los Angeles Times* in a May 16 article about allegations that state employees were gathering signatures while on the job. It pointed out revelations that the governor had paid no state income tax in 1970, because of "so-called business losses," and noted his decision to lift a moratorium on offshore drilling in effect since a disastrous 1969 Santa Barbara Channel oil spill. The Democratic state assembly leader Bob Moretti pounced, calling the proposal "economic war on the interests of people in California."

Reagan had a response for that: he was defending an innocent maiden called "the taxpayer" against a devouring beast called "government." He asked, "Are we automatically destined to tax and spend, spend and tax indefinitely, until the people have nothing left of their earnings for themselves? Have we abandoned or forgotten the interests and well-being of the taxpayer whose toil makes government possible in the first place? Or is he to become a pawn in a deadly game of government monopoly whose only purpose is to serve the confiscatory appetites of runaway government spending?"

His opponents scratched their heads at that, too. If Sacramento housed such profligate spenders, why did the state budget have a surplus in the first place? If confiscatory taxes were the aim, why were there no tax increases on the table in the legislature?

Be that as it may, Ronald Reagan was back on the national news once more.

A CBS reporter addressed the camera from the front porch of a clearly gobsmacked housewife, her luxurious home surrounded by perhaps two dozen newsmen and camera operators: "No, it wasn't the Fuller Brush Man making the rounds in Los Angeles this morning. . . ."

"Hello, how are you, it's Ronald Reagan!"

"What a surprise! Wonderful!"

The reporter broke in: "Reagan's problem is that the California legislature has refused to buy his plan for cutting taxes, so the governor was out ringing doorbells getting signatures to bypass the legislature. . . ."

"All right! I'll sign!"

Then next door: *"Hello, Mrs. Marshman."*

Mrs. Marshman literally swooned: the advantage of a matinée idol in politics.

"Reagan wants to roll back California's present personal income tax and ease the future tax bite with a constitutional ceiling on state spending. But his critics are already charging that the stakes are more personal, that the California tax reduction is simply Reagan's first move in an all-out campaign for the Republican presidential nomination. Bill Walker, CBS News, Los Angeles."

Nationally, however, the electorate's attention was elsewhere.

NIGHTCLUB COMICS, LAPEL BUTTONS, AND BUMPER STICKERS TOLD THE story: "Four more years? Maybe ten to twenty." "Don't Blame Me. I voted for McGovern." "Free the Watergate 500." Nixon's approval ratings plunged below 50 percent for the first time. Ministers frantically rewrote their Sunday sermons on "Watergate morality" to keep up with cascading revelations: the indictments of John Mitchell and campaign fund-raiser and former Commerce Secretary Maurice Stans; news that the judge in the Ellsberg case had been offered the FBI directorship as a bribe; White House ties to the forged Diem cables—and the imminent debut of live coverage on May 17 on all three networks and PBS of Senator Ervin's Watergate hearings.

Yet here was Ronald Reagan on May 15 releasing a statement to reporters awaiting his appearance at his regular press conference: "Now that the Watergate controversy is under federal investigation, and is before a grand jury, the courts, and the Senate, I will make no further statement regarding any of the individuals involved." Because, he said, they were "none of my business." And not much of theirs, either—for Watergate was being "blown out of proportion."

The reporters were astonished. There was something comical about this genial ostrich standing before them, peddling fairy tales in a time when serious moral reckoning with the failings of America's governing institutions was entering the national political conversation as never before.

What they did not recognize was that maybe he was onto something. The previous year, when that entrepreneur in New York announced he would be republishing Frank Merriwell novels as "the country's guide and measuring stick as national singularity is restored," the national media mocked him. Things proved different that spring when a major paperback publisher brought out a long-buried Horatio Alger novel called *Silas Snobden's Office Boy*. The *New York Times* featured it in not one but two decidedly nonpatronizing articles: one found its invitation to an "Eden before Eve" "filled with startling relevances"; the other said, "If it has never been your good fortune to experience pure innocence, then reading an Alger novel is as good a substitute as you will find." A seller's market in innocence was emerging. What the jacket copy advertised as a "LOST TREASURE CHEST OF CHARM AND NOSTALGIA" was just the thing "to rouse the memories of the old, the wonder of the young, the ire of the cynics, and the conscience of post-Watergate America." The *Los Angeles Times* welcomed, at long last, a novel with "no subtle characterizations, no crises of identity, no dark nights of the soul, no whining about fate." *Publishers Weekly* pronounced it "a delight."

It was around then, three days after the Ervin hearings began broadcasting live, that the Democratic electoral analysts Richard Scammon and Benjamin Wattenberg asked in the *Washington Post*, "Does Watergate have coattails?" Possibly not, they concluded. According to the Harris Poll, by a margin of 73 to 15 percent, voters agreed, "Dirty campaign tactics exist among both the Republicans and Democrats. And the Nixon campaign people were no worse than the Democrats, except they got caught at it." Maybe they were satisfied with what Nixon had told them two weeks earlier. Maybe they preferred ostrichlike innocence. The Senate hearings would tell.

CHAPTER SIX

Sam Ervin

THE DAY BEFORE YESTERDAY SENATOR SAM ERVIN HAD BEEN A BACK-bencher. Now, he was a household name.

White-haired and jiggly-jowled, his long, bushy eyebrows as tangled as a line of Arabic script, with a forehead that all but broke out in spasms in the midst of his high-flown orations, he was almost a caricature of a Dixie courthouse pol. As a senator, he had had no particular accomplishments to his name, in part because his ideology was so idiosyncratic it was hard to imagine him pulling together any sort of legislative coalition. On the one hand, he was a conservative, even a reactionary: deriding federal school integration and the Civil Rights Act, mocking the Equal Rights Amendment (which he hated so much he put his franking privileges at anti-ERA crusader Phyllis Schlafly's disposal), saying the Vietnam War ought to be ended by bombing North Vietnam until it was a parking lot. On the other, he made his first mark as a state legislator in the year of the Scopes Trial, 1925, by speaking out against a ban on the teaching of evolution. ("Monkeys in the jungle," he quipped, "will be pleased to know that the North Carolina legislature has absolved them from any responsibility for humanity in general and for the North Carolina legislature in particular.") As a justice on his state's supreme court he sprung a black man convicted of raping a white woman by carrying out the radical act of actually reading the lower court transcript. ("Boss, we never get off death row," the grateful defendant told him. "We on death row from the day we be here until the day we die.") His maiden speech in the Senate denounced Joseph McCarthy. The majority leader, Lyndon Johnson, was impressed: "You don't scare easily." Sam Ervin most certainly did not.

A simple thread, the senator always claimed, tied everything he believed together: plain devotion to the Constitution as it was written. A *Time* profile explained: "For more than a dozen years, he has chaired hearing after hearing on Constitutional rights and the erosion of the separation of power in all but empty committee rooms." Now, Congress "has decided that it needs a constitutionalist—a man of great legal knowledge and judicial temperament—and in discovering that fact, it has discovered Sam Ervin."

Now the nation discovered him—in an opening statement that displayed the sort of hammy melodrama with which the American public would soon become so familiar: "If the many allegations made to this date are true, then the burglars . . . were in effect breaking into the home of every citizen of the United States." So these proceedings would be "a test of whether the democratic process under which we operate in a nation that still is the last, best hope of man on earth in his eternal struggle to govern himself decently and effectively" could even survive.

Ervin called the first man, though he looked practically like a boy, to the committee's green witness table: Robert C. Odle, twenty-nine, former office manager of the Committee to Re-elect the President—which some newspapers had taken to calling by the onomatopoeic acronym "CREEP." But what took place next, after all that hype, was a sleep-inducing anticlimax.

Dreary Odle delved into an interminable explanation, as dry as dust, of how the committee apportioned and accounted for funds, using the example of briefcases purchased for every state chairman and vice chairman. The 550 spectators, including Daniel Ellsberg and actress Lee Remick, who had been lining up since 5 A.M. to ensure good seats in the overflowing hearing room, where Teapot Dome had been investigated fifty years before and Joseph McCarthy had terrorized witnesses thirty years after that, stifled yawns—as did Chairman Ervin, in a picture that went out over the UPI wires.

A columnist said it was like "watching grass grow." In New York City this soporific show ran on all six TV channels at once. In Chicago, the three network affiliates received more than two thousand phone calls from housewives angry at the preemption of their favorite game shows and soap operas. "The word of the day was 'crap,' as in, 'Why are you showing that Watergate crap?'" the *Tribune* quoted a station employee. "I've never heard that word so many times in a single day."

Then, the next day, the show started getting interesting. The witness was James McCord, and his description of a meeting with a former official of the White House counsel's office and current deputy director for criminal enforcement at the Bureau of Alcohol, Tobacco and Firearms sounded for all the world like a scene from *The Godfather*.

"Sometime in July 1972, shortly after I got out of jail, which was in June 1972, about midday there was a note in my mailbox at my residence and when I opened the letter, which had not been stamped nor sent through the mails, it was a note from Jack Caulfield signed 'Jack' which said, 'Go to the phone booth on Route 355 near your home,' and he gave three alternate times at which I could appear at the phone booth for a telephone call from him."

McCord did as he was told. The voice on the telephone had a New York accent and informed him, "I am a friend of Jack's. . . . He will be in touch with you soon."

The story continued, increasingly labyrinthine, like *The Maltese Falcon* or *North by Northwest.* In October 1972 the message was conveyed to McCord that the defendants were to plead guilty and go to prison, and that their families would be provided for financially, and they would be given executive clemency after serving a portion of their term, followed by a guarantee of a job. McCord said he categorically refused to play ball. Then he said he had evidence the White House had tapped the phone at his home.

He spoke of the time, during the burglary trial, when he was finally asked to meet his contact, Jack Caulfield, in person, at "the second overlook on the George Washington Parkway." There, leaning out of his automobile, Caulfield revealed that he had just attended a "law enforcement meeting in San Clemente, California."

Which, everyone in the hearing room and watching TV at home knew, happened to be the location of President Nixon's "Western White House."

His next utterance electrified the room. "Caulfield stated that he was carrying the message of executive clemency to me 'from the very highest levels of the White House.' He said that the President of the United States . . . had been told of the results."

Two or three times, McCord said, he refused the offer. Each time it was repeated—soon, as a threat: "The president's ability to govern is at stake. Another Teapot Dome scandal is possible, and the government may fall. Everybody else is on track but you."

Another meeting with Caulfield. "He stated that I was 'fouling up the game plan.'"

("Game plan": Nixon buffs knew that to be a favorite presidential phrase.)

"Get closer to your attorney," he was told.

(His attorney had been furnished and paid for by the reelection committee.)

"'Do not talk if called before a grand jury, keep silent, and do the same if called before a congressional committee.'"

(The congressional committee was rapt.)

"'You know that if the administration gets its back to the wall, it will have to take steps to defend itself.'"

He then said that on the night before his sentencing, "Jack called me and said that the administration would provide . . . $100,000 in cash if I could tell him how to get it funded through an intermediary. I said that if we ever needed it I would let him know. I never contacted him thereafter, neither have I heard from him."

The panel members began their questioning, incredulous. They asked for clarification: Had he actually said operations to spy on Democrats had been planned . . . *in the attorney general's office*? That Liddy had proposed a budget of $450,000 in that meeting, and had spent $7,000 just on the charts to lay it out? And then held up typed plans for entry into DNC headquarters while claiming the superior who had approved them was . . . Charles Colson, *the president's closest political aide*? That the June 17, 1972, burglary was actually a *second* break-in, to fix malfunctioning bugs installed weeks earlier?

All this James McCord blandly affirmed.

Senator Daniel Inouye of Hawaii quizzed him about the concept of "deniability"—a new concept for much of the public. Was it true that the operation was designed in conjunction with John Mitchell, but set up so that if it were discovered, the former attorney general could plausibly lie that he had had nothing with it?

Yes, McCord replied, that was true, too.

Then Senator Howard Baker of Tennessee diverted the direction of the questioning to a theme the panelists would return to over and over that summer. They never could quite believe the answers they were receiving.

"Mr. McCord," asked Senator Baker, "please tell me whether or not you knew that this sort of activity was illegal? . . . What was your motivation? Why did you do this?"

Because, McCord responded, he believed he was following orders that had come from the attorney general of the United States. And because he was daily receiving intelligence reports that antiwar groups associated with George McGovern were planning violence "that would endanger the lives of people at the Republican National Convention."

Concerning the question of executive clemency: why, he was asked by one of the panel's Republicans, Senator Edward Gurney of Florida, had he testified about it only reluctantly? "Because," he said, "it involved directly, in my opinion, the President of the United States."

At that, Gurney, Nixon's most dyed-in-the-wool loyalist on the committee, abruptly changed the subject. But now the awful question was out there: was the President of the United States the one behind it all? And what retaliation did witnesses fear if they revealed it?

THE COMMITTEE RECONVENED TUESDAY AFTERNOON, MAY 22, WITH McCord still at the witness table. A man burst into the hearing room, waved his arms in the president's trademark Churchillian "V for victory" salute, and cried at the top of his lungs, "My name is Ed Kelley and I'm announcing for the President of the United States!" His companion was wrestled from the hearing room before she had a chance to bellow her own intervention: to demand that President Nixon be brought to the witness table—to be asked, she said, "Richard Milhous Nixon, are you guilty?" In fact, she told reporters gathered around her outside the hearing room, "We are all guilty. We all have to come of age and realize where we have been when all this happened." Even soap opera addicts could plainly see that daytime television did not get much more dramatic than this.

A housewife wrote to the *Louisville Courier-Journal:* "I've served notice to my family. I do not intend to sauté an onion, dust a tabletop, nor darn a sock while these hearings are on. I wouldn't miss a word for the world." Volume at the New York Stock Exchange plummeted; brokers preferred to crowd around portable television sets (Watergate got more coverage than the fact that inflation was at its highest level in twenty-two years). On the funny pages a woman cast a glance over to her husband stretched out on his La-Z-Boy: "During the Watergate hearings, he got hooked on daytime TV and hasn't done a lick of work since." Some high schools suspended classes, set up TVs in the cafeteria, and turned the hearings into a makeshift all-day civics lesson. The *Boston Globe* reported sixty students crowded around the set in "the main corner of one of the great universities," and that across campus "a faculty group kept another set going all morning and afternoon." Washington was at a standstill. "A lot of people didn't show up yesterday," the maître d' at the legendary Capitol Hill expense account restaurant Sans Souci complained. "I guess they were home watching television."

A Maryland congressman named William O. Mills had been watching. He was found shot to death with a twelve-gauge shotgun the day after it was disclosed that he had failed to report a $25,000 contribution to his congressional campaign from the Committee to Re-elect the President, in violation of Maryland law. In one of his seven suicide notes he said he had done nothing wrong, but since he could not prove his innocence he saw death as the only solution.

And they were watching at the White House, where a young staffer told an AP reporter, "I sit in constant fear that somehow my name will come up." But no one was watching, claimed Ronald Ziegler, who *Time* magazine's Hugh Sidey wrote now "presides in front of his pale blue backdrop every morning with a large, uncomprehending sadness behind his eyes." Said Ziegler: "The president had been much too busy to tune in." Though not too busy, apparently, to release a four-thousand-word statement the day the hearings opened. The *New York Times* bannered it across the entire front page: *"NIXON CONCEDES WIDE WHITE HOUSE EFFORT TO CONCEAL SOME ASPECTS OF WATERGATE; CITES HIS CONCERN OVER NATIONAL SECURITY."*

The statement read like a forest ranger seeking to contain wildfires. He copped to authorizing a program of wiretaps between 1969 and 1971; to a 1970 "intelligence plan" that included "authorization for surreptitious entry . . . on specified situations related to national security"; and the establishment in 1971 "of a Special Investigations Unit in the White House," operating "under extremely tight security rules," to "plug leaks of vital national security information." He later claimed calamities would have befallen the nation had he done anything different. But each action, he insisted, had been legal and justified.

The wiretaps had been revealed in a Seymour Hersh *Times* story ten days earlier. Nixon said they were "legal under the authorities then existing" and necessary to save secret negotiations to end the war and limit nuclear arms. The 1970 intelligence plan story had been broken on May 21 by Senator Stuart Symington: it revealed that a document by a young White House staffer named Tom Charles Huston recommended lawbreaking to collect intelligence on U.S. citizens. The president said that plan had been a response to "gun battles between guerrillas and police," and the bomb threats sweeping the nation, but had been rejected five days after its submission. As for the "Special Investigations Unit"—that was the group colloquially known as the "Plumbers"—it was necessary to plug leaks that had grown so grave, "other governments no longer knew whether they could deal with the United States in confidence." About their side activities breaking into offices: well, he said he had known nothing about that. Nor the subsequent coverups, clemency offers, "illegal or improper campaign tactics," bribery of Watergate defendants, offers of executive clemency, nor attempts to implicate the CIA.

"With hindsight," he concluded, "it is apparent that I should have given more heed to the warning signals I received along the way about a Watergate coverup and less to the reassurances" he'd been getting from others. But everything *he* had done, he reassured the nation, was legal. And it had been done only to protect us from enemies foreign and domestic—for reasons of "national security": the document repeated the phrase twenty-two times.

This time, the reviews were dreadful. The *Times* said the statement had "the quality of a lawyer's brief on behalf of a client trying to defend himself." A political cartoonist showed Nixon wrapped in an American flag, simpering, "Help! My name is National Security and I'm being threatened!" Another depicted a flag emblazoned across Nixon's chest covered with hundred-dollar bills and "Mexico" stickers. In a third, the president pulled a giant American flag curtain across a theater proscenium marked "Watergate investigations" and announced, "That's all, folks!"

On May 19 the new attorney general nominee, whom the president had introduced in his April 30 speech, Elliot Richardson, appointed Archibald Cox, his former professor at the Harvard Law School, as Watergate independent prosecutor. In Richardson's confirmation hearings he had pledged Cox would have "full authority" to investigate the scandal. But Richardson's stipulation that as attorney general he would retain "ultimate power of removal over the special prosecutor" introduced a note of controversy into the proceedings—how independent would the independent prosecutor truly be? So Richardson, a suave Brahmin of the Eastern elite, gave his personal pledge he would not "countermand or interfere with the special prosecutor's decisions or actions." Cox stood next to Richardson at a press conference and pronounced himself satisfied he had all the independence and authority he required to bring the guilty to justice even if the evidentiary trail should take him straight to the Oval Office. On May 24, the Senate confirmed Richardson, 82 votes to 3. Ronald Reagan still wondered what all the fuss was about. He said Watergate was "not criminal, just illegal."

THANK GOD, NIXON HAD TO THINK, A PRESIDENT HAD THE POWER TO stage useful distractions. The week before the hearings began, he announced Soviet leader Leonid Brezhnev would visit the United States in the middle of June, for the first time since 1967 (which surely would consume some of the oxygen that might otherwise be devoted to the first anniversary of the Watergate break-in, on June 17). And then, on the day of Richardson's confirmation, the Vietnam POWs descended on Washington, D.C., for their most rousing patriotic spectacle yet.

The festivities began with a presidential speech (officially a "briefing") to more than five hundred POWS decked out in blinding dress whites at the State Department amphitheater. The subject was his tormenters in the media and on Capitol Hill who accused him of excessive secrecy. "Had we not had . . . that kind of secrecy," he said, "you men would still be in Hanoi rather than in Washington today." He added, pumping the words out with rhythmic intensity, "I think it is time to stop making heroes out of those who steal secrets and publish them in newspapers." At the reference to the Pentagon Papers, the standing ovation lasted for over a minute.

The heroes moved out to a mammoth red-and-yellow circus-style tent, two by two with their dates, more than a thousand guests flown in for the occasion at government expense—the biggest dinner in White House history, the press was informed. There, the president toasted the Christmas bombings to another standing ovation. He praised the POW wives as the "First Ladies of America." Then—the same day a *Chicago Tribune* cartoon depicted a gaggle of housewives worshipping a golden calf and an anthropologist observing, "I think it started when steak went to three dollars a pound"—they settled down to a sirloin steak banquet.

The president seemed almost giddy. He shook hands with every single one of the more than six hundred men, some for a minute at a time, as if their energy might rub off on him. He led a rousing chorus of the "POW Hymn," composed by Air Force Colonel Quincy Collins in the Hanoi facility known as the "Zoo" in 1969. He went to bed looking forward to the next day's blanket coverage. But the utterances from the green witness table sucked up all the media oxygen instead.

The former FBI agent who had monitored the DNC bugging from a listening post in a Howard Johnson's hotel room across the street explained how he'd been dispatched to spy on congressional offices. Cuban burglar Bernard Barker was asked why he'd been willing to participate in burglaries. He replied that the operation had been presented to him as "a matter of national security" ordered by a level "above FBI and CIA." Senator Baker wondered what would motivate a World War II hero, a successful businessman, "to do something that you knew to be illegal." At that things got downright surreal: "Senator," Barker replied, "E. Howard Hunt, under the name of Eduardo, represents to the Cuban people their liberation." Herman Talmadge of Georgia asked who he thought backed the operation. He answered, Nuremberg-style, "Sir, I was there to follow orders, not to think."

The gallery laughed. Barker, however, choked up. "I am part of a team with which I am very proud to be associated. We'll have to live with the term 'burglar.' But we resent, very emotionally, the words that we were 'hired.' There was no need to buy our silence. We were not for sale. . . . We're just plain people who very truthfully believed that Cuba has a right to live."

With material like that, who cared about Richard Nixon's little garden party for POWs? ABC gave nine minutes to Watergate and forty seconds to the gala—concluding, over footage of the cheering men at the State Department auditorium, with the latest Watergate revelation: that John Dean had surreptitiously removed incriminating Watergate documents from the White House. The most widely distributed UPI story about the party concerned the unfortunate tale of POW Michael Branch. He had initially turned down his invitation because of dental work scheduled at Fort Knox, then traveled to Washington to attend when that work finished ahead of schedule. He was turned away at the door—almost certainly because he'd been a member of the Peace Committee in Hanoi.

A titillating AP wirephoto from the party, captioned "WHITE HOUSE GUESTS: *Playboy* magazine model Miki Garcia, who has a 38-22-36 figure on a 5-foot-4, 108-pound frame, arrives for gala dinner with her date, ex-POW Galand Kramer," might have been the most damaging PR all. For it obliterated the very political purpose of Operation Homecoming—to reassure Americans they had returned to the innocence they had supposedly once known.

Pointing up the POWs' solid, stand-up American families had been key to the day's choreography. To many Americans that was what the POWs were *for*. Evangelical Christians had practically adopted them as mascots: signing them up to fill stadiums at "Youth for Christ" rallies; turning their memoirs into TV movies; recruiting them for spiritual retreats in the Colorado Rockies hosted by astronaut-cum-evangelist Jim Irwin. A *Playboy* bunny at the White House on the arm of a recently divorced POW queered the sale. It served as a reminder of how badly out of joint the nation had become, and how little anyone, whether evangelist or president, could do about the revolution in sexual mores.

A dominant narrative in newspapers about POWs now was that their families were disintegrating just as quickly as everyone else's—including Vietnam veterans, 38 percent of whom, according to one study, separated from their wives within six months of returning to the States. One could read of how Fred Cherry sued his wife for divorce on grounds of adultery, then filed a lawsuit to get the back pay she had spent while he had been in captivity; or how the fifth-longest-held POW, Ray Vohden, returned home to learn his marriage was over and was amazed to find that his wife, and his comrades' wives, now openly "admit to relationships with other men that we regard as misconduct";

or that the first captured flier, Lieutenant Everett Alvarez Jr., returned to divorced parents and a wife pregnant by a new husband—a situation, he told the press, that felt like being "back in torture." At the gala, POWs had been wary of greeting any comrade's female companion by name for fear she was not the wife their comrade had spoken of so lovingly and longingly in their cells.

Broken marriages were everywhere now—especially in California, where Ronald Reagan, in 1970, had signed the nation's most liberal "no-fault" divorce law. Its most avid lobbyists had been not libertines but lawyers, sick of a system that required one-half of every miserably incompatible couple to invent some trumped-up offense upon which to "sue" the partner, making attorneys a party to fraud. Since a stringent honesty in family matters was now seen as a necessity for social health, thirteen other states followed by 1973. A divorce deluge followed. "The Broken Family," the cover of the March 12, 1973, *Newsweek* read—the same issue where, on the letters page, readers responded to the *Newsweek* cover two weeks earlier featuring POW "Lt. Comdr. Paul Galanti and Wife," he in dress khakis and she in Jackie Kennedy white gloves, "the most wonderful cover I have ever seen on any magazine!" according to one letter writer. "It is they who are whole and the rest of us are the ones who are fragmented," wrote another.

Then, flipping the pages further, readers learned that at the current rate, four out of ten couples who married in 1973 would end their union in divorce.

In *Newsweek*, an Atlanta marriage counselor wondered what the point of matrimony was in the first place: "People get married because they have a fantasy of exclusive possession that duplicates the parent-child relationship." In a book published the next year, *The Courage to Divorce*, Susan Gettleman and Janet Markowitz argued that divorced women "almost without exception look and feel better than ever before," and that their children would gain "greater insight and freedom as adults." But a juvenile court judge quoted in *Newsweek* worried about the increasing number of couples in which neither wanted custody of the children. "It's a critical problem," he said. "We are having a wholesale abdication of parental responsibility."

Upon one thing, however, all the experts could agree: nowadays, as one said, "getting divorced is not much different from taking a bath." *It's Not the End of the World*, insisted the title of a novel for preteen girls by an author named Judy Blume. The plot begins with a young adolescent, whose parents are getting divorced, rhapsodizing about a story she has seen on television about two separated parents whose little boy was kidnapped, then found by the FBI: "The mother and father were so glad to see him they decided to make up and everyone lived happily ever after. It was a nice show." She hatches a similar scheme to reunite her parents. She then learns to accept her parents' separation by reading a volume titled *The Boys and Girls Book About Divorce*. This was an actual book, by a faculty member at the Columbia University College of Physicians and Surgeons, reviewed glowingly in *Time* magazine. It confidently asserted, in a line quoted in the novel, "Fathers who live close by but do not visit and fathers who live far away and hardly ever call or write either do not love their children at all, or they love them very little." Her story ended with an epiphany: "I'm through fooling myself." The cover tagline read, "A novel about love and real life."

"Real life": even kids were expected to join the suspicious circles now.

That summer, in the small town of Pekin, Illinois, a local physician started an advice column. He wrote in his inaugural article, "I would not give 'the pill' to a teenage girl just because she asked for it"—yet he added that it went without saying that he might if the circumstances were right. Advice to teenagers used to be different. A decade earlier Pat Boone sold several hundred thousand copies of *Between You, Me, and the Gatepost* dispensing wisdom like "KISSING is something that belongs to the One-And-Only, that one you hope to love some day . . . and you'd better start right now taking care of yourself for that ONE."

The previous year a divorced father in the ABC TV movie *That Certain Summer* explained his "homosexual lifestyle" to his fourteen-year-old son. The sitcom *Maude* featured an arc of episodes concerning abortion. The ancient Anglo-Saxonism *fuck* was introduced for the first time into the *Oxford English Dictionary.* Johnny Carson was no longer required to have his *Tonight Show* monologues prescreened by network censors. In January 1973 the Supreme Court, in *Roe v. Wade,* made "abortion on demand"—in the words of its vociferous detractors, who were not many, were not well organized, and were most of them Catholic—legal in all fifty states. In 1969, 68 percent of respondents had told Gallup that premarital sex was wrong; only 48 percent said so now.

"'Masters and Johnson' are two names you'll be hearing a lot about, and their book *Human Sexual Response,*" bushy-mustached Gene Shalit had explained in the February *Today* show roundup for the returning POWs; in the book, the married scholars concluded from observations of humans coupling in their laboratory that during sex any woman could have, and should demand, an orgasm. Later, Masters and Johnson and their imitators opened clinics in which husbands and wives received hands-on instruction on how to proceed. The aim of their work, they explained in an interview that summer in the *Los Angeles Times*, was to disassociate sex from sin; sexual pleasure, they said, was simply "natural."

America went orgasm crazy—a development, it turned out, quite salubrious to the publishing industry. Dr. David Reuben's *Everything You Always Wanted to Know About Sex but Were Afraid to Ask* was only the first pedagogical bestseller of many. (Its areas of instruction included something called "69": "She feels the insistent throbbing of the organ against her lips and experiences a slightly salty taste, as well as the characteristic but not unpleasant odor of the sudoriferous glands of the area. . . . By simultaneous cunnilingus and fellatio every possible sense is brought to a fever pitch and a mutual orgasm occurs rapidly.") Other volumes littering the bedside tables of suburban couples: *The Sensuous Woman*, by "J." (it was parodied in newsweekly ads for the Japanese automobile manufacturer Datsun: "*The Sensuous Car*, by 'D.'"), "the first *how*-to book for the female who yearns to be *all* woman." *My Secret Garden: Women's Sexual Fantasies*, which consisted of the answers its author, Nancy Friday, had received from an advertisement she took out reading "FEMALE SEXUAL FANTASIES wanted by serious female researcher. Anonymity guaranteed." Chapter titles included "Insatiability," "Pain and Masochism, or, 'Ouch, Don't Stop!'" and "The Zoo."

Couples flocked to films like *Deep Throat* (it made $25 million showing in seventy-three cities, despite or perhaps because of the criminal court judge in New York City who proclaimed its four episodes of cunnilingus and seven of fellatio—he counted—a "feast of carrion and squalor"), and *Behind the Green Door*, which began its run as the highest-grossing sex film ever at a gala Manhattan premiere, the social event of the season (the projectionist showed the reels out of order; no one noticed). The cover of a book called *Loving Free* advertised, "For the first time a real couple tells how they broke through their inhibitions to develop sexual excitement and joy in marriage." Not to learn to do so, men discovered, was to risk being drummed clear out of the marital bed, perhaps via a no-fault divorce. The authors had first published *Loving Free* anonymously, the preface explained, "because of the effect this frankness might have on the lives of their children" ("Making love standing up kills your arches!" . . . "Now that we've mentioned vibrators . . ."). Then they changed their minds, surprised to learn that none of their children's friends cared—the younger generation had already relieved itself of its sexual innocence by sneaking copies of *Loving*

Free from the nooks that parents believed were perfect hiding places. The authors undertook a publicity tour, beginning in their conservative hometown, Milwaukee.

For some POWs it was agonizing. Women, sex, the family: who could have imagined such verities could *change*? The POW who chopped down the hometown billboard reading HANOI RELEASE JOHN NASMYTH and appeared on *Sonny & Cher* published an op-ed for the *Los Angeles Times:* he claimed to have been neither surprised nor disconcerted by the long-haired men, the new slang, the short skirts ("indeed, I hoped the mini wasn't just a fad"), but said he was flummoxed by "women's lib," which he described by telling the story of revisiting his old favorite cocktail lounge one Friday afternoon. "The couple at the next table were having a heated discussion which ended abruptly when the woman shouted an obscenity and commanded, 'Buster, get out of my life.' The red-faced dude left and the attractive, though somewhat foul-mouthed, young lady turned to me. . . . almost without pausing for breath, she said, 'You look like a nice guy. Want to come over to my apartment for a little while?'

"'I've got a date in an hour,' I said.

"'Hell, that's plenty of time.'"

Captain Nasmyth was out of step. Researchers at the Kinsey Institute had carried out a massive new survey in 1972, learning that four-fifths of men surveyed—and no less than 100 percent of women— thought the idea of the woman initiating sex was just fine. They also found that 75 percent of men and even more women thought schools should teach sexual education, and that only 8 percent abjured masturbation, 85 percent approved of cunnilingus, and only 5 percent of men over the age of twenty-four were virgins. But not all POWs were out of step. Many were glad to join the revolution.

"I've been visiting friends in Los Angeles," Mormon POW Jay Jensen said early on after his release, "and most everybody is divorced." He was astonished, but not for long. "I feel that I have spent six years in hell and that I have been resurrected and I'm going to start a new life," he decided, before choosing a new mate of his own using a "Prospective Wife Analysis Chart." He then squired her on an extended honeymoon, made up of the free vacations a grateful nation had given him for his sacrifice. Another POW blew his stack when he saw the way his seventeen-year-old son dressed. "Well, six months later, *I* had red pants, a white shirt, and a blue jacket."

Then there was Captain Galand Kramer of Tulsa, Oklahoma, last seen on the news holding up his hand-lettered scrawl GOD BLESS AMER-

ICA & NIXON and gingerly trying on a pair of bell-bottoms at the PX. He soon found himself divorced by a woman's liberationist who explained to the *New York Times,* "I could either exist or live. Life has too many facets to dwell on one." So Galand Kramer decided to live as well. On the Freedom Birds the men had passed around stacks of *Playboy* magazines, gifts from the Clark Air Base medical officers. That was where he met Miss January 1973, she of the diaphanously backlit amber halo of hair, glistening lips, extravagant eyelashes, and green glass beads playing peekaboo with her ample left breast—and also a patch of pubic hair, an innovation *Playboy* had introduced one year earlier to compete with raunchier upstart *Penthouse,* to the delight of the surprised POWs.

And now Miss January was Captain Kramer's girl.

Gay Talese, the legendary New York journalist, was writing a book on how the sexual revolution had come about. He was a nice Catholic boy who was a sophomore in college the first time he masturbated. Talese began his research in 1971 by canvassing the "massage parlors" of Manhattan, where one could order up a "girl" from a photo album, then disappear with her into a back room.

"Do you want anything special?" said the girl to the journalist.

"Can we have sex?"

"I don't do that. I don't French, either. I only give locals."

"Locals?"

"Hand jobs."

"Okay. I'll have a local."

He enjoyed himself so much, the married Talese wrote in the book that ensued, *Thy Neighbor's Wife,* that he spent "the remainder of that year and into 1972" visiting massage parlors so often that he became "socially acquainted not only with the masseuses but also the young managers and owners."

Richard Nixon's most frequent Oval Office rants had long since consisted of perorations of how the sickening sexual excesses of liberal elites were bringing Western civilization to its knees (his recent obsession was the simultaneous appearance of *Last Tango in Paris* on the covers of *Time* and *Newsweek*). In moral matters, Gay Talese seemed more in touch with the electorate than the president. Nixon had tried sweeping America's moral confusion under a red-and-yellow tent. He was met with citizens wondering in letters to the editor why the president had to insult "families of those killed in Vietnam" just "to get an audience responsive to his views and ego needs." One wrote, "How many spectacular extravaganzas has he held for the permanently injured Vietnam veterans who go through living death each day in the veterans hospitals throughout this land?" A new Gallup poll had his approval rating 23 points lower than it had been only three months earlier. The suspicious circles were expanding.

JUDGE SIRICA'S COURTROOM BECAME A STOP ON WASHINGTON TOURIST itineraries. And new Watergate stories popped up every day: about rich backers who had appointed the president's "Western" and "Southern" White Houses—in San Clemente, California, and Key Biscayne, Florida—with guesthouses, swimming pools, and elaborate gazebos, and built him a little bowling alley beneath the north portico of the White House. But Nixon had also spent hundreds of thousands from *public* funds to improve the properties—first the White House said only $39,525 had been spent on "Casa Pacifica," then $354,252, a figure ultimately revised to $1.8 million, but only for "security purposes." ("Nixon is absolutely right," a liberal wrote the *Detroit News* in response to a Nixon economic speech. "He told us that we are the best-housed people on earth . . . he is the first President in our history with three houses.")

G. Bradford Cook, chairman of the Securities and Exchange Commission, resigned after being on the job for less than three months, caught up in the emerging scandal involving financier Robert L. Vesco that would lead to the indictment of, among others, Nixon fund-raiser Maurice Stans and Attorney General John Mitchell. Elliot Richardson, the new attorney general designate, one of few Nixon hands still held to be above reproach, was accused of hiding his knowledge of John Ehrlichman's responsibility for ordering the Ellsberg break-in.

More fake letter-writing campaign accusations. More revelations on scandals long thought buried: bribes from the dairy industry to the reelection campaign in exchange for favorable price support decisions; Howard Hunt sent to California to harass a lobbyist named Dita Beard who had information implicating CREEP for taking bribes from the conglomerate International Telephone & Telegraph, in exchange for the dismissal of an antitrust suit; American Airlines confessing to an illegal $75,000 cash donation to the reelection campaign at the personal insistence of presidential fund-raiser Herb Kalmbach. Revelations that Howard Hunt had been ordered to raid the apartment of the assassin of George Wallace to plant Democratic literature there. Accusations that Hunt "had a contract" from "low-level White House officials" to murder the president of Panama for not obeying American Bureau of Narcotics directives. And on and on.

A typical network newscast might have five or more Watergate segments. A *New York Times* "The Watergate Web" chart included sixty-four names. A May 28 Harris poll found 81 percent of Americans agreed that corruption in Washington was "serious"; only 27 percent said they respected the federal government. Plain-speaking Midwesterners feared fascism: "Don't say 'it can't happen here.' It can and it could," a *Chicago Tribune* reader wrote. "General Haig, in full uniform, is Nixon's chief assistant. (Alexander Haig had replaced Haldeman as White House chief of staff.) A former CIA man is Secretary of Defense."

On Memorial Day, Senator Edmund Muskie stood at the grave of FDR and decried how "'national security' became the excuse for systematic deception"; in Milwaukee, Representative Clement J. Zablocki cited as his contribution to Memorial Day the unprecedented vote in his House Foreign Affairs Subcommittee authorizing by a tally of 8 to 1 a "War Powers" bill cutting off the president's extralegal bombing in Cambodia within 120 days of passage. It was the first time in history a congressional panel had voted to undercut a military action the president insisted was necessary.

THE NEXT DAY FRONT-PAGE HEADLINES REPORTED COLONEL THEODORE Guy had filed accusations of treason against eight fellow prisoners. A Peace Committee member countersued Colonel Guy for defamation, saying the hard-liners' entire story of creating a military command under trying circumstances had been a lie made up to salve their guilty consciences for cooperating with their captors.

The civil war within the POW community exploded into view at the worst possible time for the president. "A decision to go on trial could open up a Pandora's box," that Sunday's *Times* Week in Review observed. There was "enough in that box for a renewed debate about a war that seemed at one point on the verge of slipping mercifully into history." The next day a Canadian diplomat sent to observe what was supposed to be a cease-fire in Cambodia told the press he had spent his time dodging American bombs: "In fact, what we have been doing is observing a war."

Next, a POW named Edward A. Brudno was found with his head in a plastic bag. In captivity, Brudno spent seven years composing an epic 127-verse ode to his wife. He came home, his rabbi told the media, to discover the "wife he had known in her youth and immaturity ... had developed into a very strong person ... he couldn't stand it." He was also despondent about America's reconciliation with China: for hadn't

containing the Maoists' imperial lust been one of the major reasons for
his sacrifice in the first place? His suicide note, written in French, read,
"There is no reason for my existence . . . my life is valueless."

Still, the POWs were heroes: that was all the right cared to know.
James J. Kilpatrick, editor of the conservative daily the *Richmond News-
Leader,* who appeared weekly on CBS's *60 Minutes* holding down the
right side of the weekly "Point/Counterpoint" debate segment, portrayed Brudno as a martyr to the Communists' cunning perfidy: "The
Pentagon tried, but the North Vietnamese won." And on the day of
Nixon's POW gala, Ronald Reagan posted a friendly letter to his childhood minister in Dixon, Illinois. On Watergate, he said, "we are witness
to a lynching . . . to watch the 'night riders' ignore the harm they are
doing to our nation in these troubled times makes me a little sick." So he
was so very grateful for his beloved POWs. "These men without exception became stronger, kinder, gentler, and more sensitive men because of
their experiences." (*Without exception.*) "Many who had no particular
faith before are deeply religious. Man after man told us very simply he
lived to come home only because of faith in God. I try to think of them
when I see the daily headlines."

And, from the other side: the POWs were villains. That was all many
on the left cared to know. The week of Brudno's suicide, Jane Fonda
published a long letter on the POWs in the *Los Angeles Times* accusing the POWs of "trying to pose as the heroic victims when they are
responsible for killing countless Vietnamese."

The full House Foreign Affairs Committee approved the War Powers bill 31 to 4. Clem Zablocki, meanwhile, opened hearings on the Vietnam "Missing in Action" issue. The point was to debunk a spreading
fantasy. It failed. That 1,300 men were still counted as MIA was just an
artifact of misleading statistics, he said: from the testimony both of the
returnees and of the North Vietnamese, we know "there are no missing
in action or prisoners of war in Southeast Asia at this time that they believe are alive." Which only meant, to many POW-MIA families whom
the White House had politically organized for cynical reasons in the
first place, that Congress was part of the cover-up. "Why are you willing to believe the enemy on this subject when they do not tell the truth
on any other subject?" the Corpus Christi, Texas, chapter of the National League of Families soon raged in a letter to the Pentagon. "The
fact is, *you have no proof our men are dead.*"

AT LEAST NEARLY ALL AMERICANS AGREED ON ONE THING: THE COUNTRY
was in the midst of an "energy crisis." In January, Senator Henry

"Scoop" Jackson of Washington had called it "the most critical problem—domestic or international—facing the nation today." *Newsweek* spoke of "doomsday implications." Des Moines almost ran out of heating oil in a record cold winter; Denver high schools went on three-day weeks to conserve fuel. Then came spring, and panic. Utility officials in San Antonio cut gas allotments by 67 percent and the eleventh-largest city in the nation nearly went dark for the foreseeable future, but for a mercy mission of borrowed out-of-state fuel trucks, like the United Nations rescuing some tropical banana republic. Factories closed in West Virginia, Illinois, and Mississippi. Grain shipments were stranded on barges, and flights from New York's JFK Airport scheduled as "nonstop" had to make landings to refuel.

White House aide Peter Flanigan promised that "the United States is not going to go back to the cold, the dark, and the bicycle." That just sounded like another government lie. In June, two thousand independent service stations simply shut down. Thousands of others began imposing ten-gallon limits per purchase. The "Skylab" space station, just launched into orbit, was meant to pave the way for a permanent human presence in space. Soaring temperatures within the spacecraft almost scuttled the launch. An editorial cartoon parked the astronauts at a gas station: "Don't worry," a NASA official told them, "you guys can't go anyway. He can let us have only 10 more gallons of gas."

The most traumatic thing about the shortages was that nobody had heretofore dreamed such a thing possible. "Popeye is running out of cheap spinach," the commerce secretary said. But the idea that energy was a commodity subject to scarcity was a new concept. It was just *there*, like the birds in the air, like the air itself, an American birthright like milkshakes and spring rains and Opening Day. In 1955 the chairman of the U.S. Atomic Energy Commission had said electricity would soon be so cheap it would no longer be metered. In 1966 a government report predicted, "The nation's total energy resources seem adequate to satisfy expected requirements through the remainder of the century at costs near present levels." Now that abundance had become scarcity as if overnight, conspiracy theories multiplied. The Nixon administration "was acting in concert with the major companies to produce a shortage" in order to kneecap the independent oil producers, Senator Adlai Stevenson III rumbled; Senator Walter Mondale said energy companies were faking the shortage to spur construction of the controversial oil pipeline to Prudhoe Bay, Alaska, where oil had been discovered in 1968.

But Americans also blamed themselves. It was part and parcel of a new vernacular ideology: civilization was destroying the earth. The evidence seemed to be everywhere. In Los Angeles, beaches were closed after five million to six million tons of raw sewage flowed into the Pacific when the pumping system failed. In New Jersey, thick, frightening patches of "red tide" choked the beaches—harmlessly, authorities insisted, though they were contradicted by newspaper warnings that "a toxic variety can irritate the ears, eyes, nose and skin." Annually, millions of pounds of smelly dead alewife fish washed up on Lake Michigan's shores; record earthquakes hit Nicaragua, Mexico, Peru, China, and Italy; dormant volcanoes mysteriously erupted in Iceland; Jerusalem suffered a snowstorm; 1,500 birds suddenly died in England; massive fish kills appeared in Lake Erie; floating islands of decaying vegetable matter emerged in the middle of the Caribbean; this spring, 1973, the Mississippi River spilled over flood protection gates in Louisiana for the first time in decades. "A growing, man-made dead sea of waste matter has seemingly come to life off the Atlantic Coast"—this was a *Los Angeles Times* editorial—"and is moving to rejoin the civilization that created it. At the center of this water contamination, no ocean creatures survive. On its fringes, diseased and rotted fish have been found. Within, chloroform bacteria and the viruses of encephalitis and hepatitis thrive, waiting for targets to attack." Two years earlier there had been a biblical infestation of gypsy moths on the East Coast. Who could deny the planet was in full-bore rebellion?

The Club of Rome, a gathering of wizards from the Massachusetts Institute of Technology supported by seventeen top scientists from six nations, published *Limits to Growth,* a report based on computer simulations that concluded the most benign possible outcome of current trends was the complete collapse of civilization by the year 2100—unless, that is, the world resolved to immediately shift to a "no-growth" economy. The book version sold four million copies. Another perennial bestseller, Paul Ehrlich's *The Population Bomb,* predicted "hundreds of millions of people are going to starve to death." The *New York Times'* new "environmental reporter" explained, "The industrial society is getting dangerously crowded, complex, and putrid. . . . We urgently need a change in social values," and "the shift can occur only if we have what the MIT group correctly calls a Copernican Revolution of the mind."

With that new household phrase, *energy crisis,* a new ideology arose: a sort of hair shirt patriotism. Young marrieds proudly announced their intention never to reproduce: "We've messed up this earth so badly it's going to come to an inglorious end in another generation or so," one couple told a researcher, "and so I don't want to be responsible for creating someone who has to live with the mess we've made." *Christianity Today* suggested readers walk more and ride bikes, the better, in the words of the Eighth Psalm, to "consider thy heavens, the work of thy fingers, the moon and the stars." In Burlington, Vermont, which announced its intention to become "Energy Conservation City USA," families signed a pledge to return to 1950 levels of energy use. A *Chicago Tribune* reader wondered, "It is hard to understand how, in the face of a gasoline shortage, we can continue to encourage stock car racing, the Indianapolis 500, and pleasure boating. . . . Better to go slow on gasoline than to be cold next winter."

Actually the synthetic methyl-based alcohol used to fuel Indy cars contained no petroleum. But people weren't getting hung up on details. Fuel companies started advertising for people *not* to use their product (Mobil: "Smart drivers make gasoline last"). Senators urged states to lower their speed limits. A citizen from rural Carpentersville, Illinois, wrote to the *Chicago Tribune* to chime in: "The oversized, overpowered, and status-styled car is no longer needed in modern living. Nor can we afford the waste of fuel to propel it. Its size also makes extrawide highways essential." A new movie came out, about a future New York City grown to 40 million, homeless people lining the streets, the inhabitants rioting for the scarce "high-energy vegetable concentrates" they survive upon. Strawberry jam costs $150 a jar. The authorities encourage suicide to cull the herd, gifting those who choose death with access to video clips of all the animal and plant life the earth used to enjoy. In the movie's shock ending, it turns out food processors—the fictional doppelgängers of the rapacious energy companies—secretly harvested these human bodies to produce food. *Soylent Green* become one of the summer's hits.

The Los Angeles mayoral election the Tuesday after Memorial Day was watched as a national bellwether. Tom Bradley, the city's first black city council member, had lost his race for the office four years earlier, even though opinion polls predicted he would win. Political scientists interpreted the results as suggesting white voters either lied to pollsters so as not to sound racist, or simply could not bring themselves to pull the lever for a black man on Election Day. The same opponent, Sam Yorty, ran the same sort of scare campaign—only this time, Bradley *did* win. Perhaps Angelenos had become less racist—but the main reason for Bradley's success in a city that was only 20 percent black was his unprecedented "antigrowth" platform. In Los Angeles, planners had long boasted of having the most freeways of any city in the world and looked forward to the day when L.A. would have 10 million residents. Bradley pledged public transportation instead. He also promised no more new housing would be built in open spaces. The day before yesterday, such ideas would have seemed downright un-American.

The statewide electorate had already approved a ban on all construction along the Pacific Coast and almost half of California's incumbent county supervisors had been voted out that year by amateur politicians promising curbs on their communities' growth. At the spring convention of the California League of Cities, 70 percent of the assembled mayors and councilmen attributed their election to their antigrowth positions. Selling austerity was the new political imperative. Richard Nixon's new Environmental Protection Agency proposed controls to contain smog, intended to reduce auto traffic by 60 percent in New Jersey by 1977. In Georgia, Governor Carter ordered state police to use slower patrol speeds and state workers to use stairs instead of the elevators for trips of two floors or less.

But some conservatives called the idea of an energy crisis a liberal conspiracy. One *Chicago Tribune* reader complained that our new "can't-do nation" had "followed the Nader flag into a forest of empty gas tanks." And Ronald Reagan said that if California ran short of energy that summer it would be the fault of environmentalists who wouldn't let nuclear power plants be built. And "there wouldn't be an awful lot" government could do about a fuel shortage anyway. The head of the state government's resources agency countered that there were plenty of things government could do—and that the reason nuclear facilities weren't being built was that their sites were on earthquake faults.

The 1970s were throwing up so many new ways for Americans to disagree.

IN A CURIOUS DEVELOPMENT, THE PRESIDENTIAL ASPIRANT WHO SAID WE shouldn't do anything about Watergate or the energy crisis was enjoying a political boom.

Nixon administration aide Kevin Phillips, author of *The Emerging Republican Majority,* published a feature in the June issue of *Harper's* called "Conservative Chic"—*Harper's* headline writers were ironic; the author was not—predicting the Nixon administration would "cement its coalition by creating a new managerial and communications establishment that merchandises the values that Middle Americans hold dear," and that "the liberal establishment of the Sixties will begin to wither." The nationally syndicated columnist Reg Murphy called that "the most ludicrous political analysis of our time." Most conservatives agreed with Murphy: all the ascendant ideological forces came from the left. The *Wall Street Journal*'s editorialists agonized over an 85–10 vote on Senator Henry "Scoop" Jackson's bill to develop a mandatory national fuel-allocation formula: "The way the mood was out there today," they quoted a Democratic Senate source as saying, "they would have voted to nationalize the oil companies." Which, indeed, Scoop Jackson would soon be proposing.

Republicans were on the ropes, their titular leader an embarrassment: the press reported that the Richard M. Nixon Foundation, H. R. "Bob" Haldeman, chairman of the board, was putting plans for Nixon's presidential library "on the back burner"; the Week in Review reported, "In private, some Congressional Republicans are beginning to consider the political benefits that might flow from a Nixon resignation and the resultant ascent of Spiro T. Agnew." A big Republican National Committee fund-raising dinner in Washington, meanwhile, had been only half subscribed.

But a dinner for the state GOP in California headlined by Ronald Reagan was standing room only.

NBC News did a report on the curiosity. The governor, his head tilted to the side, his evening wear exquisite, was soon to head out for another turn on what he called the "mashed potato circuit." He said he was "itching" to sell his conservative beliefs. Asked whether the Watergate scandal helped his presidential chances, he replied charmingly, practically blushing, "Ahhhh, um—maybe distance lends enchantment!" His most prominent "kitchen cabinet" backer, Henry Salvatori (an oilman, which made him popular culture's new villain, though the Reagan camp apparently had no compunctions about putting him out front), said his man was in clover: "Because—I'll ask you a question: have we had one little ounce of scandal in California on anything in this administration? I'll answer for you—none at all!"

"So Governor Reagan as a national figure within the Republican Party has been strengthened by this Watergate?"

"Oh, he has been and will be. He stands twenty feet tall!"

"Or at least tall enough to keep his head above Watergate. Tom Brokaw, NBC News, Los Angeles."

CHAPTER SEVEN

John Dean

IN WASHINGTON, WATERGATE WAS NOW ALL BUT THE FOURTH BRANCH OF government. Some days it threatened to supersede the other three. Which was why the day before the hearings were set to resume on June 5, Clark Clifford, a towering figure among Washington's bipartisan "Wise Men," who had served all the Democratic presidents since Harry S. Truman, published an op-ed in the *New York Times.* "[T]he executive branch virtually has ceased to function," he lamented. "The public's loss of confidence is widespread and increasing. The credibility of Mr. Nixon has been seriously affected by four public statements he has made which are sharply contradictory." Foreign policy crises were being ignored; talented people had stopped applying for government jobs; the stock market was crippled, and it all would only get worse "as additional witnesses tell their stories and as men faced with the forbidding prospect of lengthy prison sentences decide to tell the truth."

Clifford proposed a solution. Under the Twenty-fifth Amendment to "that noblest of all documents, the Constitution of the United States," Vice President Agnew could resign; Congress, working in healthful bipartisan fashion, could propose three replacements from both parties of "outstanding ability and the highest character"; Congress would confirm a new vice president who would promise not to run for president in 1976; then the president could resign, an act that "would assure him a place in history for his unselfish dedication to the nation's good." The new chief executive would usher "into the Government the ablest individuals in the country," make "decisions based solely upon merit," and govern in concert with Congress just as the Founders intended.

The graphic accompanying the piece was Nixon removing the crown from his own head. If he did so, Clifford triumphantly concluded, a "government of national unity" could "transform the next three and a half years from years of bitterness, divisiveness, and deterioration to years of healing, unity, and progress." Civilization: saved. Who could disagree?

Conservatives, it turned out. Pat Buchanan, Nixon's right-wing speechwriter, took to the pages of the *New York Times* to howl that "the President's traditional adversaries are happily drawing up surrender terms." His conspiracy theory claimed that Clifford, Joe Kraft, and an unnamed political reporter had combined to force the president to "betray the mandate of 1972," not as nonpartisan patriots but as de facto operatives for George McGovern, who, Buchanan gloated, had won no more than "nine percent of the Florida and Wisconsin primaries." A former Republican congressman wrote to the *Chicago Tribune* that the "Watergate hullaballoo" was a "cover-up for an unconscionable attempt by Nixon foes to seize the presidency." Senator Jesse Helms of North Carolina said the "emphatic rejection of liberalism" at the ballot box in 1972 "was a bitter pill for some to swallow. Through a process of selective indignation, Watergate became the lever to reverse the judgment of the people"—even though Democratic improprieties "make Watergate look like a Sunday school picnic."

Opinions like these accounted for perhaps a third of the Watergate letters to the editor published by newspapers that spring and summer. Richard Nixon's aggrieved defenders insisted that his Javerts were "sabotaging our country here and abroad"; that a hysterical press "has made us appear to be a nation of adolescents" (this came from conservative publisher Henry Regnery); that they were "making an irresponsible attempt to destroy confidence in government itself just because of the admitted stupidity of a handful of people." It was, wrote a woman from Richmond, Virginia, "a disgrace to downgrade our President as some have." They did so, a City University of New York math professor argued, in order to deny President Nixon a nomination for the Nobel Peace Prize.

Many tied their critique to the POWs—those "magnificent Americans who understand honor, duty, sacrifice, and love of country as few of the rest of us do," who "know they can trust our President because his words and deeds have been proven by the passage of time and events. I for one join with these great patriots in backing Mr. Nixon and his policies." Ronald Reagan, for his part, still nearly broke up during the part of his speeches when he described meeting POWs: "Holding out was the only thing we could do, they told me, the only thing we could still do for our country. . . . Where did we find men like these, just ordinary guys. . . . American guys from the farms, from the small towns, from the cities . . ." Then he would launch into his peroration about why Republicans must not feel defensive: "The Republican Party has traditionally been the victim of shenanigans worse than Watergate. There is documentary proof." Or he would say that politicians should stop making statements about Watergate altogether: "It's time for us to shut up and let the law take its course," he barked from the national governors' conference, during an interview in which he said he wasn't even thinking about the 1976 presidential race.

And most of all, the Watergate defenders agreed with their president when he said his quest for national security explained everything the public needed to know about his administration's alleged wrongdoing—and that, a doctor in Bethesda, Maryland, wrote, "sure as hell is good enough for me."

The liberal media—the "pack of howling wolves" (Mrs. Robert Brauham of Peoria, Illinois)—had "been trying to discredit the Nixon Admin since it took office in 1969" (Richard Riggs of Corona del Mar, California), "printing every sleazy rumor that comes out of Washington before it is declared fact or fiction." Now they just operated under the color of Watergate. Where "nobody was murdered, nobody bodily maimed," complained C. A. Nolan Sr., Rural Route 4, Madison, Indiana—adding, "It been over 20 years since I have read or heard a word about the 'lost $81 million' that disappeared during the New Deal–Fair Deal years." No one talked about the Pearl Harbor conspiracy, either, a Morton Grove, Illinois, man pointed out—when, while "the President [was] examining his stamp collection, the chief of staff out riding, the fleet [was] maneuvered into Pearl Harbor as sitting ducks."

They made high-minded appeals to due process and Anglo-Saxon common law, attacked the very notion of congressional investigatory hearings (where "innuendo may pass for fact, rumor for reason"), and deployed liberal clichés to grind liberal noses in what they said was rank liberal hypocrisy. After all, one wrote, "The liberal politicians, who are most indignant, and the news media, which scream the loudest about Watergate, are the same ones yelling 'witching' and 'McCarthyism' when one of their group is caught with his hands in the cookie jar." In actual fact the committee was obsessed to a fault with non-incrimination; sometimes an hour of witness testimony would be gobbled up with excruciatingly boring circumlocution to avoid placing any individual in legal jeopardy. Senator Ervin had been one of the most loyal votes for Nixon in the Senate. The toughest questioner on the committee was Lowell Weicker, a Republican. No matter. To the diehards the hearings were an obvious Democratic congressional coup. The editorialists of the *Burlington Free Press* provided the context: "Certain people can never forgive President Nixon for (1) successfully concluding the war in Vietnam and (2) winning reelection in a landslide of historic proportions. So if the Nixon haters cannot embarrass the President on substantive things, perhaps the Watergate caper can raise a little dust." Besides, "In Red China and Russia there are hundreds of 'Watergates' and worse, but nobody could call attention to official misconduct, even if they dared to."

Then there was the way the liberal media worshipped the Kennedys. Protected them. Even though everyone knew they were more corrupt than Richard Nixon could possibly imagine—"wire tapping at the Watergate" being "childish pranksterism compared to the massive fraud perpetrated upon the American public in the election of John F. Kennedy by a small margin achieved by the massive vote fraud in Illinois and Texas." Hadn't Attorney General Robert F. Kennedy—liberal hypocrite!—been a champion of wiretapping? And what about Ted Kennedy? "I keep being reminded," a Louisville newspaper reader wrote, "of a girl named Mary Jo Kopechne." A bumper sticker emerged: NOBODY DIED AT WATERGATE.

Administration defenders in the mainstream media that spring and summer included syndicated columnists William F. Buckley and Nick Thimmesch, *National Review*'s Jeffrey Hart, and editorialists at right-leaning papers like the *Chicago Tribune,* the *Detroit News,* and the *Richmond News Leader,* which thought that Nixon's four-thousand-word statement "moves him toward the sunlight of restored public confidence," and that "the assignment given to various 'plumbers' . . . was a prudent, proper, and indeed indispensable assignment." In the media, they were decidedly in the minority. Most of his defenders were just ordinary letter-writing citizens.

One of them was Baruch Korff, a rabbi from Taunton, Massachusetts. After the *New York Times* turned down his letter to the editor denouncing the Ervin Committee's "noisy claque," which "resembles nothing more than the Parisian mob cheering and shouting as the tumbrels deposit their victims before the guillotine," Korff published it himself as an ad with his own money, and in just three days harvested three thousand letters of support, hundreds of phone calls, and thirty thousand dollars in donations.

The defenders could be quite funny. It could be a Communist plot, a *Chicago Tribune* reader argued, and maybe Sam Ervin was in on it, too: was he not one of the hounders of Joseph McCarthy? And "if Senator McCarthy had not been censured," this correspondent wrote, "we would not be in the mess we're in now."

But they could be frightening, too.

"Watching Watergate in Archie Bunker Country," said the cover of the June 18 issue of *New York* magazine. It began with the author, top-drawer trend journalist Gail Sheehy, recording what happened when the proprietor of Terry's Bar in Astoria, Queens, asked his patrons if he might tune the bar's TV to the hearings. Nine men cried "Forget it!" "The majority called for Popeye cartoons. But Terry couldn't find a channel that wasn't polluted with the 'search for unvarnished truth.' They had no choice. Television was suppressing their freedom not to know."

These ironworkers, sandhogs, elevator operators, and beer truck drivers said things like this: that Ted Kennedy "killed a broad" ("Now *there* was a mountain, and they made a molehill out of it"); that the Democrats "couldn't get themselves elected if they tried, so they're picking on the number-one man"; that George McGovern was the man behind the coup. (What about the fact that McGovern kept on defending Nixon? A man named Bernie responded: "That's the tip-off!") Terry, the proprietor, was building a house in the mountains: "When the revolution comes, I got it built like a bomb shelter." None of them voted—so they wouldn't show up on jury rolls. They treated a copy of the *New York Times,* slid across the bar by the reporter, like a hunk of plutonium: "No! I'm not interested in it!"

But they had opinions all the same.

On Daniel Ellsberg: "That guy, listen, if I were in charge of the country I would've found some way of shooting him." (Someone added, "If I was Nixon that's what I'd do—I'd shoot every one of them.")

On freedom: "My opinion, there's too much freedom in this country."

On political philosophy: "I'd take a police state over an anarchistic state. I'm not so sure a police state wouldn't be so bad in this country."

Besides, concluded Terry: "If there's any guilt on Nixon's part, it's only in the men he picked."

AS IT HAPPENED, ANOTHER, VERY DIFFERENT TRIBE OF WATERGATE OB-servers made a similar case: Clark Clifford's sort of people. Washington insiders treated D.C. as their village. They found the idea that Watergate was all the fault of the bad seeds the president kept around him, rather than the president himself, a comforting thought.

These were the sort of people Nixon himself had always identified as his tormentors—the "Eastern liberal elite." By now they had more or less made their peace with him. They protected him—or protected something they grandiloquently referred to as "the presidency." And as the scandal gathered steam they began addressing Dick Nixon as one of their own, a fellow gentleman of honor. Like Nixon's grassroots defenders, they shared a taste for kings.

Elliott Roosevelt, son of the thirty-second president, spoke for them from Lisbon, where Europeans were incredulous about Watergate: "The most frequent comment I hear is that 'America is destroying itself in the eyes of the world.' . . . Why does our leadership and our press seem intent on self-immolation for suddenly discovering moral beliefs when [spying] has been a way of life in our system since the start? . . . Why don't we just throw the inept offenders to the wolves and don't ruin the presidency?" Of the absurd, exculpatory stratagems issuing from the White House, they opined that the President of the United States could not possibly have had anything to do with them. "Only he can sweep aside preposterous claims of 'executive privilege' and order Mr. Dean and other White House aides to testify," the *New York Times* editorialized April 1. Which was not likely, given that Nixon was the one who had ordered the preposterous claims in the first place.

They labeled their scapegoats the "Orange County Boys": "Ehrlichman, Haldeman, and their assistants," *Time* wrote, "often regarded by veteran politicians as arrogant, inexperienced, and selfishly protective of the President." *Outsiders,* unschooled in their Village's ways; the "wrong sort"—attempting, Stewart Alsop sniffed in *Newsweek*, "to alter the very nature of the ancient American political system. Politicians have played tricks on each other since politics was invented. But this is not politics, this is war." If only the czar knew.

Syndicated columnist Bill Anderson mocked Bob Haldeman's déclassé interior decoration of the White House and said the underlying problem was that he had been an advertising man. *Time*'s mandarin in chief Hugh Sidey wrote, "the energies of these men were directed not at solving the problems but ignoring or minimizing them." The guiding metaphor was telling: they were *dirty*—like pollution. It pointed to the Village's preferred advice to the president: get rid of them, and you thus get rid of Watergate. "Nixon has a staff infection," their in-house comedian, Mark Russell, joked. If only more White House denizens could be like that nice Henry Kissinger, whom all of the pundits worshipped: "It is of considerable interest," Sidey wrote, "that the administration's leading humorist and bon-vivant—its most accessible major official—is Henry Kissinger, untouched by scandal and clearly the man who has achieved the most."

Remove the infection, went the argument, and Watergate went away; Washington could function again. And all the right people—people like Henry Kissinger—could finally get back to work setting the world right.

Soviet officials preparing for Leonid Brezhnev's upcoming visit to Washington, columnist Peter Lisagor's sources were telling him, saw the inquisition against the president as an impediment to their ongoing attempts to establish a more stable entente between East and West: "They appeared to understand a truth about a nation's foreign policy that some"—the accursed *some*—"Americans have ignored, namely that it cannot be compartmentalized. Uncertainty, confusion, rot at a country's core has a debilitating effect along all its extremities. . . . A machine clogged at its center will function feebly, if at all."

Then Kissinger turned out to be tainted, too. The latest news was that he, not Nixon, had overseen the 1969 wiretappings—spying on his very own staff, some of the most distinguished young gentlemen in Washington. Joseph Kraft, one of Kissinger's best friends, had recently filed a column about the national security advisor's birthday party, titled "HENRY KISSINGER, THE VIRTUOSO AT 50." Maybe it would not have been so fulsome if Kraft had known at the time of its writing that Kissinger had tapped his phone, too, and that the bash, at Manhattan's tony Colony Club, included two men whose family phones had been bugged. "How Kissinger Fooled Us All," a *New York* magazine article proclaimed the next week. It was a mess. No one in all the right circles knew what to think.

Which suggests why Clark Clifford went out on a limb proposing the president's resignation. Clifford proceeded on the presumption that it wasn't really the president's fault, but he should fall on his sword nonetheless—as a "magnanimous action."

THE PRESIDENT'S CONNECTION WITH THE CONSPIRACY MIGHT SOON BE better understood. John Wesley Dean III, it was said, was working out some kind of deal to testify before the Ervin Committee.

Dean was the man who knew all the Watergate secrets. The president said so himself—ever since August 29, 1972, ten weeks after the break-in, when he announced that he had assigned his young counsel the task of investigating the scandal. The president explained Dean came back with a report that no one employed by the White House or his reelection committee had been involved in "this very bizarre incident." Dean then showed up in the news again early in March when it was revealed he had coerced the director of the FBI into sharing its files with the White House, sat in on FBI interviews of Watergate witnesses then lied about it, and was perhaps involved in the destruction of evidence from E. Howard Hunt's safe in the days following the DNC break-in.

And then the news came: he was ready to testify under oath that he had been doing it all at the behest of the Oval Office. That was when Washington discourse about Dean started shifting. Reports began surfacing that he was in fact the *instigator* of the Watergate cover-up—perhaps even of the Watergate break-in itself.

And now he would probably be testifying on TV—telling tales, a June 3 *Washington Post* story revealed, of the thirty-five meetings with the president since 1972 in which they discussed the cover-up together. If true, that would make Nixon a notorious liar—since he said he hadn't even known of any cover-up until the middle of March 1973. "We categorically deny the assertions and implications of this story," came the response from the White House. Then, reporters asked, would the White House give the Ervin Committee the logs that had been kept of all the president's meetings, to prove the assertions untrue? *Never*, the president's spokesman replied. Until two days later the White House reversed itself, and said it would do exactly that.

In the matter of Dean versus the president, most Villagers knew exactly where they stood. Joseph Alsop spoke for them. "A general judgment of his character has been reached," he wrote: Dean was "a smooth-faced young man who is reportedly obsessed by fear of going to jail because of his consciousness of his own good looks." The very idea that the affairs of state of the greatest nation in the world, Alsop wrote the day Dean was granted limited immunity by the Ervin Committee, should be held up by "the self-serving allegations of a bottom-dwelling slug like Dean," a proven liar, was enough "to make all common sensible Americans exclaim, 'This can't go on!'"

It went on. The hearings would reopen June 5, with the three networks rotating gavel-to-gavel coverage. At night, PBS ran the whole thing again as a repeat. This was despite the request of special prosecutor Archibald Cox that televised hearings be suspended for three months to better preserve due process. The committee refused: "The American people are entitled to find out what actually happened without having to wait while justice travels on leaden feet," Sam Ervin responded in his usual orotund style. Editorial boards agreed. The *Louisville Courier-Journal* compared the TV proceedings to the Nuremberg and Eichmann trials—the public needed such public rituals to grasp "the point at which obedience to orders becomes a denial of higher and universal laws of civilized behavior"—and also the Army-McCarthy hearings, where "the people finally grasped the essence of a kind of tyranny, rooted in public fear, that was as evil as anything it purported to expose."

THE NEXT DAY CAME BEFORE THE COMMITTEE A SOBER YOUNG MAN named Hugh Sloan. The discussion turned to questions of money, and things began to perk up.

Sloan had testified in the trial of the Watergate burglars about being instructed to pay massive sums in cash to G. Gordon Liddy in the summer of 1972, with no idea why. This was the very thing Judge Sirica had been most adamant about in his frustration over what the prosecutors had refused to pursue. Now the details were voluminously forthcoming.

The treasurer had been instructed by the campaign's deputy director, Jeb Stuart Magruder, to disburse $83,000 to Liddy in cash. Being a responsible young man, Magruder promptly reported this most unusual request to his superior, Maurice Stans, who had once been the secretary of commerce. What was the money for, he asked, and why did it have to be cash? "I do not want to know and you don't want to know," returned Stans.

Murmurs.

Legal tender had circulated like snowflakes in the offices of the Committee to Re-elect the President. April 6, 1972, the day before a new campaign finance law began requiring public disclosure of all donations, almost $1.8 million in cash had flooded the office. A number of key campaign figures, like Liddy and Herb Kalmbach, the president's personal lawyer, had authority to draw cash whenever they liked— entering the office with empty trunks, leaving with ones filled with hundred-dollar bills. His concerns, Sloan related, became more pressing after the arrests at the Watergate on June 17. He had by this point disbursed $199,000 in cash to G. Gordon Liddy. He approached John Mitchell for guidance.

"He told me, 'When the going gets tough, the tough get going.'" The hearing room erupted in laughter.

The melodramatic turns continued. Jeb Stuart Magruder explained to him that the FBI was going to be sniffing around the committee. He was not to respond with the truth. He was to say the amount disbursed to Liddy was not $199,000 but $80,000.

"He must have been insistent because I remember making to him on that occasion a statement, 'I have no intention of perjuring myself.'"

"What did he say to you when you said that?"

"He said, 'You may have to.'"

Sloan was directed to meet with the appointment secretary to the President of the United States, Dwight Chapin, a man in close contact with the president in the Oval Office every single day of the week. Chapin told him it was time for him to take a vacation. "He suggested that the important thing is that the president be protected."

He met later that same afternoon with Bob Haldeman, once more outlining his ethical concerns, which the chief of staff did not quite comprehend. "I believe he interpreted my being there as personal fear and he indicated to me that I had a special relationship with the White House, if I needed help getting a lawyer, he would be glad to do that."

Two weeks after that, Magruder took him to a bar and told him that he should tell federal investigators that the amount he gave G. Gordon Liddy was not $80,000, but $40,000. He refused. "Their reaction was incensed."

"Did they suggest you might take a little trip?"

"Yes, sir."

He got a phone call later that evening from another top campaign official, Fred LaRue, who "impressed on me the urgency of departure, to the extent of suggesting that I had a reservation on, I believe, a 6 A.M. flight at Dulles. He urged me to take a room at the Dulles Marriott that evening and to leave my home immediately."

Conveniently timed vacations, it seemed, were as common a currency at the Committee to Re-elect the President as trunks stuffed with hundred-dollar bills. Conveniently timed vacations; and also, it seemed, mafia-style threats. After Sloan returned, Fred LaRue told him to take the Fifth Amendment with the grand jury "to stay in the good graces of the campaign organization."

That same day, California liberal Republican congressman Paul Mc-Closkey, who was known as "Pete," demanded an impeachment inquiry. A fascinating figure, he was a decorated Marine-turned-peace-crusader who'd mounted a quixotic presidential primary campaign against Nixon in New Hampshire in 1972 and wrote a book called *Truth and Untruth: Political Deceit in America.* He spoke on the floor for only six minutes before being silenced by a parliamentary trick by Earl F. Landgrebe of Indiana, a far-right congressman best known for his efforts to smuggle Bibles into the Soviet Union.

The next morning the *New York Times* printed a leak of Tom Charles Huston's 1970 security plan—which had included within its text a warning that the break-ins it was recommending to the president were "clearly illegal."

• • •

SLOAN WAS FOLLOWED BY ANOTHER FRESH-FACED YOUNG PRESIDENT'S man, Herbert Porter, the campaign scheduler. He described the same sorts of furtive meetings with Jeb Stuart Magruder, but whereas Sloan had responded with fits of conscience, Porter had cooperated. All this pricked the ears of Senator Howard Baker of Tennessee, one of the seven-member panel's three Republicans. Baker's 1966 ascension to the Senate in Democratic Tennessee had been in no small part due to his personal friend Vice President Nixon's campaigning on his behalf. The White House had hoped for him as an ally, but he never felt quite comfortable in the role. Instead he kept on turning the hearings' sessions to incredulous inquisitions about how the White House had managed to become such an ethical sewer. *Time* called him "The Man Who Keeps Asking Why." He was young, handsome, and eloquent (he soon won a place on *Women's Wear Daily*'s "stud list" alongside Robert Redford and Mick Jagger), and these interventions became an evening news staple.

"Did you ever have any qualms about what you were doing? I am probing into your state of mind, Mr. Porter."

"I understand. I think the thought crossed my mind, senator, that I really could not see what effect it had on reelecting a President of the United States. On the other hand, in all fairness, I was not the one to stand up in a meeting and say this should be stopped, either, so I do not—I mean there is space in between. I kind of drifted along."

Drifted along.

"At any time, did you ever think of saying, 'I do not think this is quite right, this is not quite the way it ought to be?' Did you ever think of that?"

"Yes, I did."

"What did you do about it?

"I did not do anything. . . . In all honesty, probably because of the fear of group pressure that would ensue, of not being a team player."

"What caused you to abdicate your own conscience and disapproval, if you did disapprove, of the practices or dirty tricks operation?"

"Well, Senator Baker, my loyalty to this man, Richard Nixon . . . I felt as if I had known this man all my life—not personally, perhaps, but in spirit. I was appealed to on this basis."

THE LIBERALS FOR WHOM THE HEARINGS WERE A NEW RELIGIOUS RITE settled in pleasantly for the long haul. A twenty-three-year-old in Cincinnati found himself perversely glad he was laid up the entire summer with a back injury; it let him sit home and watch every day on TV. A kid in Worthington, Ohio, began taking a transistor radio with him everywhere he went. A boy subbing on a friend's *Washington Post* paper route was late delivering the papers every day because he read the whole front section on somebody's porch before starting his day. An eleven-year-old who couldn't get enough of it wrote a fan letter to Sam Ervin, and two months later was thrilled to find a giant box filled with the entire transcript of the hearings on his parents' porch. A ten-year-old from Hawaii traveled with his grandma and mother and sister on his first visit to the mainland, including Disneyland, the Grand Canyon, his grandparents' home in Kansas, and Yellowstone, watching the PBS reruns at Howard Johnson's motels every night before bed. He later became the forty-fourth president of the United States.

Liberals wrote sanctimonious letters to editors. A *Washington Post* reader wrote regarding those frustrated at the preemption of daytime TV that they'd better pay attention or "you might find 'The Dating Game' preempted again in 1984." A man from Chicago mocked Nixon's supporters, who said, "Whatever he did, he did it for the good of his country." Another leader, he thrusted, had followers who said the same thing. "His name was Adolf Hitler."

Two hundred of them packed the House gallery on June 12 when New York City's Bella Abzug, who had introduced a resolution for Nixon's impeachment on her first day as a new congresswoman in 1971, and Berkeley's Ron Dellums, a self-described socialist, held the lower chamber's first impeachment hearing. Abzug mocked the pundits who implored the president to put the matter to a rest by telling the "whole truth": "clearly if telling the 'whole truth' would exonerate the President [he] would have done so long ago." They were voices in the congressional wilderness. Joseph Alsop wrote that no more than fifty members had any interest in impeachment, and approvingly quoted "one of the House's most influential Democrats" about John Dean: "You'd have to be crazy to want to impeach the President of the United States on the evidence of a man like that."

ON JUNE 12, HERB PORTER TESTIFIED ONCE MORE, ABOUT HOW HE SET UP fake demonstrations and organized the infiltration of Democratic campaigns, how he delivered memos stolen from Edmund Muskie's presidential campaign to John Mitchell. Then it was Maurice Stans's turn to answer why $1.777 million in mostly corporate donations had been given in cash in the frantic moments before the April 7 donation disclosure deadline. Why had records for these cash receipts and disbursements been destroyed? And why was not Stans's dear old friend the president informed of this most unusual manner of handling campaign accounts?

"They were destroyed," Stans said, "because there was no require-ment they be kept, and insofar as contributors were concerned we wanted to respect the anonymity that they had sought and that they were entitled to under the law—"

Ervin: "Were they destroyed before or after the break-in?"

"They were destroyed after the break-in and I would insist, Mr. Chairman, that there is no relevance between the two."

"You swear, you are stating upon your oath that there is no connec-tion between the destruction of the records and the break-in of the Wa-tergate or any fear that the press or the public might find out from these records what the truth was about these matters?"

There was, Stans insisted, absolutely none.

So why do it?

"Very simply, for the reason—"

"It's too simple for me to understand, really."

Stans tried again, offering that it was so every candidate and charity in town wouldn't be harassing the contributors for donations—which didn't make sense. The question wasn't why the campaign had kept contributions from the public; it was why it hadn't even kept a record for itself. Stans replied that there was nothing illegal in doing so. At that, Sam Ervin stuck in the shiv: "Mr. Stans, do you not think that men who have been honored by the American people as you have ought to have their course of action guided by ethical principles which are superior to the minimum requirements of criminal law?"

That was Sam Ervin all over. A fat old Southerner who looked like one of the bad guys from *In the Heat of the Night,* he was, once upon a time, the go-to strategist for anti–civil rights filibusters. He had opposed Medicare and called the feminists pushing the Equal Rights Amendment "blame fools." Now he was a liberal hero. Ballantine published a mass-market paperback of *Quotations from Chairman Sam,* featuring thirteen pages of photographs. In September he recorded an album of his favor-ite stories, right in the parlor of the modest little house where he'd been living with his wife for fifty years, in the same little town where he'd been born, where he began "reading law" in his dad's one-room office by the county courthouse when he was fifteen, like he was Abraham Lincoln or something. At the hearings he banged a rainbow-hued gavel carved for him by a local Cherokee Indian. "Just a country lawyer," he called himself—again and again and again.

He was, of course, much more than that: the law school from which he had graduated, with honors, was Harvard, and he had been a legislator since 1925—taking a break only to serve on North Carolina's supreme court. Critics quickly tired of the country-dumb act. The *Chicago Tribune*'s cartoonist drew him as a talking doll: "Pull mah string and watch me do mah thing!" They mocked his pretensions to impartiality and moral seriousness: to him, wrote a Cincinnati man, "all witnesses are guilty, all witnesses are covering up, and all witnesses are liars. It's become an inquisition, not a hearing." A *Los Angeles Times* reader from Thousand Oaks said he "resembles my grandfather a whole lot, and my grandpa is a fine old chap, if I may say so." What he was not, however, was a suitable judge of presidents: "This man has become a national folk hero, and for what? For clobbering the President? For twitching his eyebrows and quoting the Bible?"

CONSERVATIVES HAD THEIR OWN HERO ON THE COMMITTEE TO CHEER, liberals a villain to hiss: Senator Edward Gurney of Florida, who like Howard Baker became in 1967 the first Republican senator in his state since Reconstruction—but who, unlike Baker, showed abject loyalty to Nixon, who had helped both win their elections in 1966. He dismissed Watergate as "one of those political wing-dings that happen every political year," and said that the very investigation he was a part of was having a "catastrophic effect on the institution of the presidency."

Ervin and Gurney butted heads when Maurice Stans took the stand. Ervin kept needling Stans about a payment of $50,000 from the Committee to Re-elect the President to Maryland Republicans to pad the take on an undersubscribed dinner in honor of Vice President Agnew. "They wanted it to look more successful than it apparently was," Ervin forced Stans to finally admit.

Ervin didn't let up: "Yes. In other words, they wanted to practice a deception on the general public as to the amount of honor that was paid to the Vice President."

"Mr. Chairman, I am not sure this is the first time that has happened in American politics."

"You know, there has been murder and larceny in every generation, but that hasn't made murder meritorious or larceny legal. . . ."

At that, Edward Gurney finally interjected like a defense attorney: "Mr. Chairman! I for one have not appreciated the harassment of this witness by the chairman!"

He did not prevail in his attempt to save Maury Stans, who was taking it upon himself to defend the poor millionaires whose names were being dragged through the mud for the patriotic act of donating to Dick Nixon. "It is very unfair," he whined in an unfortunately aristocratic accent. "Somebody has got to speak up for these people." Ray Kroc, for example, the McDonald's hamburger magnate: he hadn't been interested *at all* in influencing the minimum wage law, nor the decisions of the president's price commission concerning the cost of beef. Stans offered himself as another example. "I volunteered or was drafted, whatever the case may be, because I believed in my president. You know by now from what you have heard, but I know you cannot feel, the abuse to which I have been subjected because of the associations I fell into. All I ask, Mr. Chairman and members of the committee, is that when you publish your report you give me back my good name."

That was not very likely. "Maurice Stans, President Nixon's top political fundraiser," a wire report on his appearance began, "was grilled Wednesday by an incredulous panel of Democratic senators as he testified about his ignorance of the financial dealings involved in the Watergate scandal."

And then, directly below that, in at least one Midwestern paper: "The Senate Watergate committee has secret sworn testimony indicating that Maurice Stans was told by John Mitchell the full story of the bugging of Democratic Party headquarters a week after the break-in, it was learned Wednesday."

Mafia stuff. And it seemed to go to the top. The nineteenth witness, Jeb Stuart Magruder, testified beginning June 14, under "use immunity," a recent innovation in the criminal law (ironically written by a young White House counsel named John Dean) that stipulated a witness could not be convicted on evidence introduced in the testimony for which he received immunity. Magruder copped to everything he knew. The schemes to infiltrate the Democratic presidential campaigns. The infamous meeting in the attorney general's office in which G. Gordon Liddy unveiled "professionally done" full-color charts outlining "Operation Gemstone," his million-dollar plan to, among other things, kidnap and spirit Democratic conventioneers "to a place like Mexico" to "be returned to this country at the end of the convention," and to outfit a yacht anchored just off the convention site with surveillance equipment and hookers to "obtain information from them." (Senator Ervin: "I am going to ask the audience to please refrain from laughter or any kind of demonstration.") John Mitchell's receipt of the Watergate bug transcripts (the attorney general's only response: this material was "not worth the money . . . paid for it"). And Magruder's work covering up the crime: destroying incriminating evidence; devising the lies about how much money Liddy received and for what; scapegoating Liddy as the operation's architect; and perjuring himself before the grand jury and suborning Hugh Sloan to do the same.

Then, the questions from the panelist. The Man Who Keeps Asking Why homed in on how indifferent, even casual, the conspirators seemed about lawbreaking on behalf the chief constitutional officer of the United States. "I knew you were going to get into this line of questioning," Magruder said, then launched into what sounded like a prepared speech. He spoke of his days attending Williams College, the tony liberal arts school on the Eastern Seaboard, and taking a course in ethics from its chaplain, the Reverend William Sloane Coffin. ("Remember," he used to tell his students, "even if you win the rat race, you're still a rat.") Magruder flashed forward to his work in the White House, as the Vietnam War raged. The antiwar movement was calling the president a warmonger, even a war criminal. But the president, he said, "was trying very diligently to settle the war issue, and we were all against the war—I think this is a primary issue!" He took on a strident tone. "We saw continual violations of the law done by men like William Sloane Coffin!"

It was a very Nixonian moment. Rev. Coffin was precisely the sort of elite WASP liberal against which Nixonites had been defining themselves since Nixon beat Jerry Voorhis for Congress in California in 1946: a scion of New York wealth; a Skull and Bones member recruited by the son of Connecticut senator Prescott Bush; a CIA agent back when that organization was basically a gentlemen's club, who went on to become a minister who occupied one distinguished pulpit after another advocating left-wing social crusades—including, starting in 1967, draft resistance, for which he went on trial.

"Now he tells me my ethics are bad, and yet he was indicted for criminal charges"—

The camera cut to Senator Ervin, looking shocked.

—"and I believe as firmly as they did that the President was correct in this issue. So consequently—and let me just say, when these subjects came up, and I knew that they were illegal and I'm sure that the others did—we had become somewhat inured in using some activities in helping us in accomplishing this in this cause, in what we thought was a legitimate cause."

The response was intense and immediate—a cynosure of the debate over Watergate. Bill Moyers, the former preacher who had been Lyndon Johnson's aide, now a pundit with PBS, pointed out, "Coffin's higher law was God. What was Magruder's? Well, it was clearly Nixon. And I think therein lay the seeds to the entire problem." Rev. Coffin was reached for comment: "Jesus and Jimmy Hoffa broke the law," he said, "but there's a world of difference between what they did. Whatever *we* did, we did in the open to oppose an illegal war in Vietnam. What he and the others did they did behind closed doors." The *New York Times* op-ed page extended Rev. Coffin its welcome; on that page he recollected, "I used to say to him, 'You're a nice guy, Jeb, but not yet a good man. You have a lot of charm but little inner strength. And if you don't stand for something you're apt to fall for anything.'" Magruder was, he said, a very 1950s kind of fellow—"agreeing his way through life." He argued that the 1960s had given America the gift of skepticism, that people no longer need to agree their way through life to succeed—and that through Magruder "we have the opportunity to learn . . . the ancient lesson that to do evil in this world you don't have to be evil."

QUESTIONS LIKE THESE WERE HOW WATERGATE TRULY BECAME A NATIONAL conversation—water-cooler fodder for people who didn't know Haldeman from Ehrlichman from Adam. Moments like that were how the crystal-chandeliered hearing room, flanked by fifty-foot Corinthian columns and faced with marble, became as familiar a TV setting as Fred Sanford's junkyard in *Sanford and Son* or Mary Richards's bachelorette apartment in *The Mary Tyler Moore Show*. Watergate was now everywhere—for instance, on the Minneapolis street where CBS filmed the establishing shot for the exterior of Mary Tyler Moore's character's apartment. The building had become an attraction for tourist buses, which was why the owner hung a large banner outside reading "IMPEACH NIXON." It could be agonizing—"like a national funeral that just goes on day after day," Senator J. Bennett Johnston Jr. of Louisiana said. But in a sense it also could be fun.

Father's Day, June 17, dads received gag gifts: A "fine heavy-quality towel with 'Watergate Hotel' embroidered upon it. Let your friends think there was more than one burglary." "A jigsaw puzzle that will bug you." The "Watergate Scandal" card game. ("No one wins, there are just losers.") The *Watergate Comedy Hour* LP (released on the "Hidden Records" label), and Mort Sahl's latest, *Sing a Song of Watergate*. "DON'T BUG ME!" sweatshirts. (Images of ladybugs became ubiquitous, code that its wearer was a Watergate buff.) "Candles for those burned up about Watergate. In red, white, or blue."

Unfamiliar with how criminal defendants talked when trained by criminal lawyers, Americans found the exotic language from the witness table fascinating. Harry Reasoner of ABC did a humor piece on a married couple on vacation arguing about who was responsible for forgetting the toothpaste: "'Since there was no cap on it, I hesitated to place it in my shaving kit, where it might compromise my razor. I assume, in fact my recollection is that I was told, that you would seek out the cap and complete the packing of the toothpaste while I was eating break-fast.'" Such phrases as "at this point in time" and "at that point in time" (legalese for "now" and "then") became the nation's favorite inside joke: On *Sesame Street,* Cookie Monster stood accused of stealing, what else, cookies—an offense, after whispered consultation with his lawyer, he happened not to recollect at this point in time. Then he started eating the microphone.

It was everywhere, and soon it would be even more so. One thing Magruder insisted on throughout his five hours of self-incriminating testimony was that Richard M. Nixon had nothing to do with any of it. That was why John Dean was so intensely anticipated: he was the one who insisted the president had something to do with it all. Dean was scheduled to begin on June 19. Viewers bated their breath.

And then they released their breath, when the committee announced hearings would be postponed for a week while the president hosted Leonid Brezhnev.

THE PRESIDENT WHO NEVER HAD TIME TO WATCH WATERGATE HEARINGS did have time to dash first to a tiny town in the middle of Illinois where Watergate was an "unknown word," the *Chicago Tribune* explained. The *Trib* was incorrect concerning Pekin, Illinois, where Nixon unveiled the cornerstone of a research center dedicated to the late Illinois Republican senator Everett McKinley Dirksen: actually, the crowd was lousy with signs protesting both Watergate and the bombing of Cambodia, though just before the presidential motorcade passed through, Secret Service men confiscated those placards for destruction. In his speech there, the president said, "We live in a time when many people are cynical about politics and politicians," and "it would be a tragedy" to "let our disappointment with some aspects of the system turn into despair with the system as a whole." It would take a cynic, apparently, to point out that Dirksen was the father-in-law of Ervin Committee panelist Howard Baker, and that this might have had *something* to do with why the president chose this particular cornerstone to dedicate following a period in which he made fewer public appearances than in any other month in his presidency.

In Washington on June 18 government employees were excused early from work. They waved Soviet flags before Brezhnev's arriving motorcade. ("How disheartening," a *Washington Post* reader wrote, "so soon after our returning POWs have been tortured by the Communists!") The global chessboard had been the scene of Nixon's greatest triumphs ever since the freshman congressman had won a berth on a fact-finding commission inquiring into the success of the Marshall Plan in 1947, and once more Nixon scored points: a parley with the premier at Camp David brought agreement on guidelines for restarting arms limitation talks in Geneva and an accord on joint cooperation on peaceful uses for atomic energy. Those meetings were followed by a reception at Nixon's Western White House in San Clemente, where the Soviet leader met Bob Hope, Frank Sinatra, and Gene Autry—and one of the only politicians present: Governor Ronald Reagan, who emerged to once more dismiss Watergate before the press: "I just think it's too bad that it is taking people's attention from what I think is the most brilliant accomplishment of any president of this century, and that is the steady progress towards peace and the easing of tensions."

The distraction didn't work. Monday's *Time* magazine featured a picture of a nebbishy blond man and the cover slug "Dean Talks," reporting the latest leaks: that he would testify that the president discussed granting executive clemency to Howard Hunt ("if true, this is an outright admission of the President's willingness to consider cover-up activity"); that he knew of the cover-up as early as September 15, 1972; that after the Sirica letter the president "discussed with Dean the possibility of his own impeachment—a damaging indication of how seriously Nixon took his own involvement." And also the latest on Dean: that he had "borrowed" four thousand dollars from the secret campaign fund to finance his honeymoon. Senate Minority Leader Hugh Scott was quoted concerning that: "Nothing is so incredible that this turncoat will not be willing to testify it in exchange for a reward. . . . A man who can embezzle can easily tell lies." *Time* also reported that the White House had hired its own private detectives to dig up that particular piece of dirt.

A government lawyer who the *Wall Street Journal* said "had distinguished himself at practically nothing before being admitted to the White House inner sanctum" was about to accuse the President of the United States of criminality. Nothing like it had ever happened before. In Central Park, a busking folksinger tried to make his way through Bob Dylan's "Like a Rolling Stone." But he just couldn't concentrate; he was quivering with joyful anticipation of what beans the young White House counsel might spill to hasten the undoing of Tricky Dick. In suburban D.C., meanwhile, the counsel was prisoner in the home he shared with both his beautiful new wife and, now, a complement of

U.S. marshals; his lawyers took seriously the rumors that he might be rubbed out.

He'd noticed from his only TV interview that his eyelids flickered in a squirrelly twitch. So he dug up a pair of old glasses to wear. Then he went to the barber because his hair was too long. The president, in fact, had once chosen him to sit in on an Oval Office meeting with college newspaper editors because he was the one who looked most like a "hippie."

The barber made polite conversation on the one subject every last customer was interested in: "What do you think of these Watergate hearings?"

"They're pretty interesting, but I haven't been able to see much of them."

"I'll say they're interesting. I'm bringing my TV set to the shop next week. I want to see this guy Dean get his butt kicked."

"Yeah, that's going to be something. We'll find out what the squealer has to say for himself."

"Right. You know, I can't imagine a guy lying that way about President Nixon. The guy is crazy, maybe."

"Could be," John Dean said, with all sincerity.

ABC'S VOLUBLE CAPITOL HILL REPORTER SAM DONALDSON AND ANCHOR-man Frank Reynolds bantered back and forth like football announcers before the big game. Donaldson explained that the room was always standing room only for these hearings. "But today the *staff* members, and they can be pretty blasé here on Capitol Hill, have a line outside, and that line stretched all the way down the hall this morning." A sprig of curled wire sprouted from his ear, he fanned a sheath of paper: "The word is that the Xerox broke down! So they could only get out 98 pages!" Dean's full statement was 245 pages. That made it all the more suspenseful. No one knew what he was going to say.

How, Reynolds wondered, with all the imprecations flying around that John Dean was a self-serving prevaricator, could viewers know whether he was making all this up?

Answered Donaldson: "Well, many of the lawyers on this committee say you just look at him the same way you'd look at any witness: Does he look credible? Does he sound credible? You test his story against the stories of others. Where are there discrepancies? How many people buttress him?"

Reynolds: "But on the question of conversations Dean has while *with the President,* how does the committee go about getting corroborating or discrediting testimony on that?"

Now there was a question: *could you* call the president before a Senate panel to ask whether or not he was a liar?

At which, with perfect dramatic timing, the doughy-faced chairman in a cream-colored summer suit and yellow tie stirred into action.

"There's the gavel! Sam Ervin, the chairman, and the session is under way!"

HE LOOKED HARDLY MORE THAN A BOY. BEHIND HIM SAT HIS BEAUTIFUL wife, Maureen, her hair piled tight in a blond bun, eyes green, eyebrows gorgeously shaped. There was another contrast, too, with all the other witnesses: they all had had lawyers beside them to whisper in their ears. Dean was alone.

He began reading the statement he had been working on in isolation since April. It would take him all day. He got a ninety-minute break for lunch—which he spent lying on his back, exhausted.

The voice belied the baby face: deep, even, intense, a monotone. As a rhetorical strategy, for five days John Dean would fight every urge to emote, even to smile. "Laughter," he had told himself, "sounds insincere." Photographers crouched before the table pointing their cannons at him, elbowing each other for angles, and he reacted not at all. For minutes at a time, hunched, he did not even look up. From time to time he took birdlike sips of water. His text was unliterary, unadorned; it simply reconstructed everything relevant he could remember about his White House experience. The most astonishing revelations, and he read them like a grocery list.

First he explained what he had learned immediately upon his ascension to White House counsel: the abiding obsession of the President of the United States was not foreign policy, nor getting his program through Congress, nor even his reelection. It was protesters—any protester, no matter how innocuous: even the lone man, one day, who stretched out a ten-foot banner in Lafayette Park across from the White House. The word came straight from Dwight Chapin, the president's personal assistant: "get some 'thugs' to remove that man from Lafayette Park." (The gallery murmured. Ervin admonished them: "The audience is here by the consent of the committee, and I am going to request the audience to refrain from giving expression of their feelings by laughter or otherwise.") Dean described his role in that incident as the one, he claimed, to which he would become most accustomed: talking down

White House janissaries from insane acts. He got the Secret Service to talk to the man instead. Orders also constantly came demanding he task the FBI and CIA with figuring out whether protests were being run by Democratic Party saboteurs. "We never found a scintilla of viable evidence," Dean said. "This was explained to Mr. Haldeman, but the President believed the opposite was, in fact, true." A madman, it seemed, lived in the White House.

Leaks were an obsession. Dean elaborated on a story that had percolated in the media for months: the White House plan to firebomb the Brookings Institution, to uncover alleged damning information about the Kennedy administration. Dean said presidential confidant Charles Colson personally ordered him to arrange it. Dean then flew to San Clemente at the earliest possible moment to stop it.

Then there was the proposed twenty-four-hour surveillance of Senator Ted Kennedy. Dean said he had sought to turn that off, too, by arguing that stalking a man whose two brothers had been murdered by mysterious gunmen might prove an unwise proposition. Surveillance continued nonetheless. One of the documents Dean introduced into evidence was a 1971 spy report on Kennedy's stay at a private estate in Honolulu: "Discreet inquiry determined that Kennedy used the estate solely for sleeping purposes."

Illegal spying operations, Dean said, had been continuous. "Operation Sandwedge": an attempt to create a dummy security corporation ("Security Consulting Group") to support "the capacity to provide 'bag men' to carry money and engage in electronic surveillance." "Operation Gemstone": Dean described what it was like in the attorney general's office at that infamous January 24, 1972, meeting in which Gordon Liddy proposed hiring prostitutes to entrap Democrats at their national convention, and docking a boat offshore to incarcerate protest leaders. "I recall Liddy saying that the girls would be high class and the best in the business."

Guffaws.

He remembered Liddy's excuse after his men were caught at the Watergate: that it was Magruder's fault for cutting his spying budget. And that Liddy "told me that he was a soldier and would never talk." Then he told the mind-blowing story of cleaning out Howard Hunt's safe. The General Services Administration was summoned to open it using drills. Dean took custody of a briefcase inside the safe that "contained loose wires; Chapsticks—for your lips—with wires coming out of them; and instruction sheets for walkie-talkies"; and the forged cables meant to frame John F. Kennedy in the assassination of South Vietnam's President Diem. He then said Chief of Staff Haldeman had been the one who ordered the destruction of it all:

"I remember well his instructions. He told me to shred the documents and 'deep six' the briefcase. I asked him what he meant by 'deep six.' He leaned back in his chair and said: 'You drive across the river on your way home at night—don't you?' I said, 'yes.' He said, 'Well, when you cross over the bridge on your way home, just toss the briefcase into the river.'"

Murmurs.

He methodically described his attempts to influence the CIA to shut down the FBI's Watergate investigation, his arrangements with Herbert Kalmbach (at the instruction of John Mitchell and with the approval of Haldeman and Ehrlichman) to finance the payoff to the defendants to perjure themselves. Then the proceedings recessed for lunch.

Frank Reynolds, lips pursed, looked haunted. "Very difficult to summarize what Dean said," the anchorman uttered. "Every paragraph contains some sort of a bombshell." But "if you found this morning's testimony startling, I can only say that you will find this afternoon's testimony equally startling." And as he previewed the extraordinary things they would hear about the conduct of the President of the United States, innocence seemed to drain from his face.

FOR MORE THAN A YEAR RICHARD NIXON HAD BEEN CONSISTENT: NOT just that he hadn't known anything about plans to burglarize any buildings, but that in the aftermath he had cordoned himself off from any knowledge of it so as not to influence the course of justice. Alleged promises of executive clemency, money offered to defendants to testify in a certain way, even the lawsuits the Republican National Committee had taken out against the Democratic National Committee for defamation: he had learned about all of that in the newspapers—until, he always adamantly insisted, March 21, when, as he had explained while looking the American people in the eye back on April 17, John Dean schooled him on the cover-up, and he turned all the power at his disposal toward making sure justice was served.

Methodically, Dean led the panel through his personal meetings with the president that he said showed each of these claims were lies.

On September 15, 1972: the president called Dean in for a stroking session to congratulate him on his work keeping the suspicion limited to Liddy—Nixon expressing special delight when Dean volunteered that he had made ex parte contacts with the judge handling the DNC's civil case, to influence him. "I left the meeting with the impression that the President was well aware of what had been going on," he concluded.

Then, after his re-inauguration, in February: Nixon called Dean into the Oval Office and said that from now on he would be reporting directly to the president with Watergate updates. It was a reward for having helped shut down a House Watergate inquiry; distracting the media from the Oval Office's direct ties to campaign dirty trickster Donald Segretti; working to launder donations left over from the 1968 campaign into a bribery slush fund; and plotting strategy on how to deal with the Ervin Committee. Dean said he kept trying to warn Nixon: that the cover-up since June 17 had been criminal; that he, Dean, shared culpability; and that perhaps the president did not want a liaison in the Oval Office who was guilty of obstruction of justice. "He would not accept my analysis and did not want me to go into detail."

March 13: "I told the President that there was no money to pay these individuals to meet their demands. He asked me how much it would cost. I told him that I could only estimate, that it might be as high as a million dollars or more. He told me that was no problem and he also looked over at Haldeman and repeated the statement."

The President of the United States, talking like a mafia don.

March 21: "I began by telling the President that there was a cancer growing on the presidency, and if the cancer was not removed, that the President himself would be killed by it." He related how, in a panic, he reviewed for the president the whole story: the Gemstone meetings in Mitchell's office; Haldeman's and Mitchell's receipt of wiretap transcripts; Kalmbach raising and distributing hush money; Magruder's perjury. "I concluded by saying that it is going to take continued perjury and continued support of these individuals to perpetuate the cover-up and that I did not believe that it was possible to continue it."

The bizarre meeting of April 15: "The President recalled the fact that at one point we had discussed the difficulty in raising money and that he had said that $1 million was nothing to raise to pay to maintain the silence of the defendants. He said that he had, of course, only been joking when he made that comment." Dean then described the curious moment when the president got out of his chair, went to a corner of his office, "and in a nearly inaudible tone said to me he was probably foolish to have discussed Hunt's clemency with Colson." As they took their leave, Dean said he "told the President that I hoped that my going to the prosecutors and telling the truth would not result in the impeachment of the president. He jokingly said, 'I certainly hope so also,' and he said it would be handled properly."

At that, anchorman Reynolds looked like a balloon relieved of its air. "Well. Lotsa laughs," he said. "Huh," he added, practically under his breath.

DEAN'S WEEK AT THE GREEN TABLE STOPPED BUSINESS IN THE OFFICES OF high White House officials. House Republicans skipped debates on the floor, glued to a TV set installed in their cloakroom. Evans and Novak reported that most "reluctantly gave Dean high marks as a witness," and that his testimony "may have finally broken the self-confidence of the Nixon administration. If that has happened, the President's painful choice lies between resignation or a presidency crippled far into the future."

The second day commenced with his grilling by the panel. The committee's brilliant majority counsel, Sam Dash, author of the standard legal study on the subject of wiretapping, asked if the president had known of the illegality of the cover-up. Dean, heart-stoppingly, said that was obviously the case. The minority counsel, Fred Thompson, a young sideburned and dandyish former assistant U.S. attorney only recently responsible for putting away bank robbers and moonshiners back in Tennessee, tried with considerably less sharpness to impeach Dean's motives. And when Senator Eugene Talmadge, Democrat of Georgia, took his turn, he displayed a list Dean had submitted of all the people in the White House and on the reelection committee who Dean believed had violated laws. He asked Dean the significance of the asterisks beside most of names. They all were lawyers, Dean explained.

Laughter.

Lunch break.

Frank Reynolds summarized the day so far: "He seemed to retain his composure and so far as we can tell right now was not caught in any contradictions."

Donaldson described the passing scene: senators and journalists milling about, spectators buzzing excitedly, Dean pulling himself into a tight circle with "with some lawyers," "some aides," and "some bodyguards."

Reynolds, with a start: "He has bodyguards?"

He did. Woodward and Bernstein had picked up what they thought were credible rumors that there might be attempts to assassinate him. Innocence was melting all over.

Commercials for Clairol Naturally Blond Colors ("I'm mist... I'm fawn... I'm surf... I'm buttercup!") and Final Net ("So you *finally got* little Janie married!'). Senator Lowell Weicker, Republican of Connecticut, took over. He cut an imposing enough figure: six foot

six, 250 pounds, gruff-voiced, born in Paris, Yale '53, heir to an industrial fortune—an East Coast aristocrat with the confidence proper to
the class. When he had been named to the Ervin Committee, he hired
his own private investigative staff. In his May 17 opening statement he
called Watergate "the acts of men who almost stole America." Now he
developed a line of questioning running through a mind-numbingly
diverse array of *other* Nixon-related thefts of America: another blizzard
of names, dates, organizations, activities for those who couldn't keep
track of it all already.

It was when Weicker began inquiring into the details of Dean's filing
system that people abruptly woke up.

"Just briefly—and this will end my questioning, and I apologize to
the committee for taking so much time, but it is a subject that I confess I
don't have every last bit of information on. It is a difficult thing to piece
together, but I think it is a very important part of the story—"

Most people had long ago lost the thread of what precisely the story
at that point was supposed to be about. It involved something called
the "Intelligence Evaluation Committee," which turned out not to have
been involved in anything improper: "As I say," Dean said wearily, "I
don't know of the IEC itself preparing political material." He appeared
to be taking pity on his overeager interrogator, determined to lead him
toward a more promising scent.

"Of course," he then said, "as I have submitted in documents, other
agencies were involved in seeking politically embarrassing information
on individuals who were thought to be enemies of the White House. I
might also add that in my possession is a rather, very much down the
line to what you are talking about, is a memorandum that was requested
by me to prepare a means to attack the enemies of the White House.
There was also maintained what was called an 'enemies list,' which was
rather extensive and continually being updated."

Now the murmuring lasted a full five seconds. Maureen "Mo" Dean
broke into a smile. Some reporters broke out in giggles. A boring afternoon had been electrified. And Richard Nixon's "enemies list" became
the new national obsession.

Carol Channing, it appeared from the documents soon entered into
committee records, was on the Enemies List. So were Paul Newman
and Steve McQueen. And Barbra Streisand, and composer-conductor
Leonard Bernstein. And the general secretary of the World Council of
Churches. Ten Democratic senators and the twelve black members of
the House. Newspapers like the *New York Times,* the *St. Louis Post-
Dispatch,* and, of course, the *Washington Post.* Andy Warhol made the

cut (the result of an accounting fluke: he donated 350 posters of Richard Nixon reading "Vote McGovern" to the Democrat's presidential campaign, and they were reported as being worth $350,000, making him one of McGovern's biggest donors). The head of United Artists, the film studio. ("Success here could be both debilitating and very embarrassing to the Muskie Machine.") A principal in "[t]he top Democratic advertising firm—they destroyed Goldwater in '64. They should be hit hard." Morton Halperin, a former Kissinger staffer, now an executive in the open-government group Common Cause. ("A Scandal would be most helpful here.") Mary McGrory of the *Post*. New York Jets quarterback Joe Namath, whose inclusion was exceedingly curious: the long-haired, mustache-and-fur-coat-wearing Casanova avoided politics except for his ostentatious patriotism. (A proposal was offered after the 1972 Olympics to revivify their cosmopolitan spirit by removing national anthems from medal ceremonies; Namath vociferously complained.) At least one "enemy," an aide to the hawkish Democratic senator Scoop Jackson, was a fervent Nixon supporter. "Heaven help us," he reacted, "if this is the slipshod way they do their intelligence work." Another, a *Baltimore Sun* reporter, had been dead for three months when his name was added.

Many considered inclusion an honor; Daniel Schorr said he prized it "more highly than my Emmy award." A *Wall Street Journal* reporter wrote of his suspicion about what acts might have got him listed: maybe the time he wrote of "the Madison Avenue fuzziness Mr. Ziegler brings to the English language," or when his wife announced at a party thrown by a White House speechwriter that they used an ashtray embossed with the presidential seal as a dog dish. Administration critics who were left off complained of the oversight. A fashionable bar in Manhattan held a party with the Enemies List as guest list. A gag book, *White House Enemies; Or, How We Made the Dean's List,* printed the names (more than two hundred, all told), the relevant memos, wacky political cartoons, a word search, and an Art Buchwald column, all wrapped in a cover depicting Nixon as a Nazi matron guarding twenty "enemies" in striped prison suits behind barbed wire. Others did not find it funny. William F. Buckley Jr. said the Enemies List was "fascist in its reliance on the state as the instrument of harassment."

So what did the "enemies list" really signify? Charles Colson, its primary author, claimed a benign purpose: to "keep the social office, the personnel office, the press office, the counsel's office, and other offices in the White House advised of persons who had been particularly supportive of the President or persons who had been particularly critical of the President." A document introduced into the record written by Dean and dated August 16, 1971, suggested differently. It asked: "How can we use the available federal machinery to screw our political enemies?"

It wouldn't be easy, the memo allowed; the Internal Revenue Service was "dominated and controlled by Democrats." Where there had been a will, however, there had been a way: presently, "enemies" from Andy Warhol to Walter Mondale to the author of an investigative series in *Newsday* on Nixon's friend Bebe Rebozo stepped forward to report that they had seen their tax returns aggressively audited during precisely the period in question.

SENATOR DANIEL INOUYE, THE JAPANESE-AMERICAN MEDAL OF HONOR winner whose right arm had been amputated during World War II, took his turn questioning Dean. At a February meeting in California in which the Watergate principals strategized about the just-announced members of the Ervin Committee, Ehrlichman punned on his name as "Ain't-no-way," as in "ain't no way he's going to give us anything but problems." But there is an old joke that defines a liberal as someone who can't even take his own side in an argument. Perhaps that was why this liberal used his time on Dean's third day by reading thirty-nine questions White House counsel Fred Buzhardt had prepared with the help of a young White House aide named Diane Sawyer to challenge Dean's testimony. This, since Nixon was refusing to testify, Inouye said in his aristocratic voice, would "give the President his day in court."

"There is no reason to doubt," the document read, "that John Dean was the principal actor in the Watergate cover-up," with "a great interest in covering up for himself." It went on to portray Dean as the instigator, on behalf of his patron John Mitchell, of the Watergate burglary itself. For more than an hour and a half, Dean punched through the inquisition effortlessly. The next day the White House backtracked, sending out a deputy press secretary to claim the questions hadn't come from the White House at all, but from Buzhardt acting in his capacity as an independent citizen. Reporters joked they had been rendered "inoperative."

The third day the Man Who Keeps Asking Why had his turn. "The net sum of your testimony is fairly mind-boggling," Senator Baker began. He said he had no desire to impeach it. He was interested, however, in context. He stated the central question in a way that would be repeated again and again in the months to come. "What did the President know and when did he know it?" It reverberated. It named the stakes.

At which, at Baker's prompting, Dean went through his recollections once more—demonstrating that the president knew quite a lot, quite early in the game. At least if you trusted John Dean. That was the bottom line: it was his word against the president's. "The record is essentially incomplete if we don't have the testimony of all those present," Baker pointed out at adjournment. "The man who can tell us what was in the President's mind is the President." He said he hoped his old friend might testify. A White House spokesman quickly announced that for Nixon to do so would do "irreparable damage" to the Constitution.

CHAPTER EIGHT

Nostalgia

THE SUSPICIOUS CIRCLES FOUND THE PRESIDENT'S RETREAT BEHIND THE Constitution excruciating. The man he had made his attorney general, John Mitchell, after all, had arrogated for himself such extraordinary powers to surveil without a warrant that the Supreme Court had smacked him down unanimously. John Mitchell was the man who had allowed G. Gordon Liddy to drone on in the sacred citadel of justice about plans to kidnap, spy on, and entrap Democrats with prostitutes. Who was under indictment for arranging an illegal quid pro quo donation of $200,000 in cash passed over in a suitcase. And on July 10, this paragon of constitutionalism would have his day at the witness table to defend himself before the American people.

The Ervin Committee had adjourned for a long Independence Day holiday. In the interim, American morality seemed all but to disintegrate. In Atlantic City, boxer Ernie Terrell lost to Chuck Wepner in a decision so fishy it touched off a near riot. Terrell, asked if he could believe what had just happened, said, "I didn't believe Watergate could happen. I didn't believe John F. Kennedy and Malcolm X could have been assassinated." In Texas, an industrial poultry farm drowned forty-three thousand baby chicks, claiming it was cheaper than feeding them grain. In New Orleans an arsonist torched a gay bar, killing twenty-nine. In Illinois, a former governor, Otto Kerner Jr., faced a jail term. Democratic senator Jim Abourezk of South Dakota accused Big Oil of an "artificially contrived" shortage "to force the independent sector of the industry out of business and to get a price increase."

You could read several stories a day now about the new postdraft, post-Vietnam military careening between disciplinary breakdown and disciplinary overreach, a supposedly bedrock institution in utter identity confusion. The U.S. Air Force Academy tossed out two professors for criticizing the Pentagon—while simultaneously boasting of new, post-Vietnam "progressive" and "enlightened" disciplinary latitude, even while suffering a 40 percent attrition rate after three major cheating scandals in a row. Then came news that fifteen Air Force cadets had been hospitalized after "survival, evasion, resistance, and escape" (SERE) training in an exercise simulating a mock POW camp, in which they were forced to squat on their haunches for hours at a time, were slapped and switched with tree branches, and were stuck all night in isolation boxes in which they could neither stand nor lie down.

Pentagon studies disclosed nearly half of low-ranking Navy and Army personnel suffered an "exceptionally high rate of binge drinking, belligerence while drinking, and job, police, and financial problems relating to alcohol." At West Point, nineteen cadets were under investigation for participating in a cheating ring, just as a cadet named James Pelosi was found guilty by his peers of an honor violation—not putting down his pencil the instant the order to cease work was given on an examination—and was exonerated on a technicality by a board of officers. His resentful classmates then submitted him to "silence," a grotesque underground torment in which no cadet would make even eye contact with him until he resigned. He refused for more than a year and a half, losing twenty-six pounds from the stress. "The whole academy class should be tested psychologically to detect dormant sadism that might result in future Vietnams," wrote a reader in *Time*.

Admiral Stockdale filed treason charges against two more members of the POW Peace Committee. One of them committed suicide.

This was the United States, the week of its 197th birthday. "The Roman Empire crumbled from within," wrote a Chicagoan in the *Tribune*. "Isn't that what is happening to us?"

So when the sixty-seventh attorney general of the United States denied outright what six previous witnesses had attested to in sworn statements before Congress, it just seemed like the way of the world. Mitchell offered no quarter, either growling, glowering, or sitting in stony silence in the face of questions he did not prefer, cracking sadistic one-liners at the ones he deigned to answer. He knew nothing. The panel reacted with incredulity. He had frequently cruised along the Potomac with Nixon on the presidential yacht *Sequoia*, they pointed out, and yet the president had never bothered to ask him what he knew about Watergate? (No—and if he had, "I would have spelled it out chapter and verse.") Why, they asked, hadn't Mitchell told him the truth of his own accord? Because, he answered, then the president would "lower the boom," turn Watergate into a huge national story, and threaten his own reelection.

The brazenness of his answers astonished them. Why hadn't he thrown Liddy out of his office, with all his talk of kidnapping and call girls? "I should have thrown him out the window." Why hadn't he done more to hasten justice for the burglars? He replied, "It would have been simpler to take them out on the White House lawn and shoot them all." When they grilled him about why he continued to do nothing as the scandal mounted, with breathtaking cynicism he replied that they had an election coming up, and coming clean would only lead investigators to even more offensive "White House horror stories"—horror stories he glibly acknowledged: the ITT scandal, the Diem cable forgery, other "alleged extracurricular activities in the bugging area," the Brookings firebombing rumbling, "miscellaneous matters" concerning Senator Kennedy; "this, that, and the other thing."

Senator Talmadge pressed: "Am I to understand from your response that you place the expediency of the next election above your responsibilities as an intimate to advise the President of the peril that surrounded him? . . . *Did you state* that the expedience of the election was more important than that?"

"Senator, I think you have put it exactly correct. In my mind, the re-election of Richard Nixon, compared to what was available on the other side, was so much more important that I put it in just that context."

Then why not, Senator Inouye asked later, lower the boom *after* Election Day? Because, Mitchell replied, that would be "a detriment" to a successful second term.

He said he had never approved any bugging operations; Magruder's claim that he had was a "palpable, damnable lie." And since Mitchell wouldn't acknowledge the truth of a single thing any other witness said—and the president could never be cross-examined—an awful, awesome dread settled upon anyone who wished this particular horror might somehow, someday, *end:* "Watergate" could only ever resolve to a bog of crosscutting claims. A waste of time. A civic catastrophe.

Then Mitchell dropped his cool.

If he had known about the burglary at Ellsberg's psychiatrist's office, Senator Weicker asked, why didn't he honor his oath as attorney general and tell the Ellsberg trial judge about it?

Mitchell pulled away from the green table in rage; stood up, face flushed; and exclaimed: "It's a great trial being conducted here, isn't it!"

Senator Ervin pointed out that the Constitution said the president had an obligation, not to win reelection or even carry out a successful second term, but to "faithfully execute the laws." What about that? For a brief moment Mitchell dropped his amoral front. "I think," the former attorney general admitted, "that is a reasonable interpretation of the subject matter and, of course, in reflection it is a serious one."

• • •

PERHAPS THE PRESIDENT, IF UNCONSCIOUSLY, AGREED. HIS PERSONAL physician claimed he had never been sick while he was president, and recalled only once prescribing him medicine—for a sore throat, in 1959, in Moscow. And then, at 5:30 on the morning of Mitchell's third day in the hot seat, the president called for his doctor, complaining of discomfort on the right side of his chest. The symptoms receded; then, at midday, he took a call from Senator Ervin informing him of the committee's unanimous resolution to access every federal government document "relevant to or proving or disproving any matters the committee is authorized to investigate," specifically every piece of paper prepared or received by John W. Dean.

Shortly thereafter, the symptoms returned.

At the elevator to a suite at Bethesda Naval Hospital the Secret Service set up a command post containing a white telephone with several push-button lines. White House crews moved in half a dozen heavy metal boxes of the sort used to carry papers on presidential trips, and two attaché cases, one black and one brown—the nuclear "football." At eight thirty that night the president checked in. He'd be there, doctors said, possibly a week. Suspicious circles were not the only ones to suspect the illness was psychosomatic. One constituent from North Carolina wrote to his senator blaming him for "bugging the Pres. of the U.S. until you caused him to get sick."

FRIDAY THE THIRTEENTH, AND THE BAD LUCK WAS ALL THE PRESIDENT'S. At a closed-door interview with committee staff, a young bureaucrat with a comb-over offered a clue about the curious moment Dean described on April 15 when the president got out of his chair, went to a corner of his office, and uttered unexpected words of contrition. Sitting before the television cameras that Monday, he introduced himself as Alexander Butterfield, "the Administrator of the Federal Aviation Administration," explaining his job had once been the "smooth running of the President's official day." Sam Dash explained that the reason this witness was appearing voluntarily and without counsel on only three hours' notice was that "at a staff interview with Mr. Butterfield on Friday some very significant information was elicited."

Hardly any preliminaries. Fred Thompson, in an officious tone of voice, hurriedly asked him, "Mr. Butterfield, are you aware of the installation of any listening devices in the Oval Office of the President?"

On the TV feed, a reporter who had been nodding off—these colloquies were becoming awfully routine—whipped his head around with a start.

"I was aware of listening devices; yes, sir."

Another reporter looked up. His mouth was agape. Of an instant the bottom had dropped out of everything anyone thought they knew about Watergate.

The moment was sublime, uncanny. An awe at recording technology, and the suffusing dread it produced in an increasingly paranoid culture, had been a fixture of the political culture long before Butterfield spoke. The *Washington Post*'s first editorial on the Watergate burglars quoted *Mission: Impossible:* "This tape will self-destruct in five seconds . . . good luck." A *Time* cover in April, 1973, featured Nixon, Dean, Haldeman, Ehrlichman, et al. entangled in audiotape; a *New York Times* Week in Review graphic a month later featured a man being stabbed in the back while operating a reel-to-reel tape recorder, to illustrate the unlovely tendency of Watergate principals to tape their phone conversations. One day, a boring stretch of hearing was broken when it was revealed that Nixon taped phone calls with his own brother Donald. Senator Lowell Weicker read aloud a transcript of a conversation between Ehrlichman and Richard Kleindienst about how to screw . . . Senator Lowell Weicker. On the funny pages a character in *Boner's Arc* swore to keep a piece of gossip in confidence—then grabbed her reel-to-reel to record it. Francis Ford Coppola's "thriller about privacy," *The Conversation,* was in production; it starred Gene Hackman as a surveillance technician consumed by paranoia following his efforts to get to the bottom of a murder he has accidentally recorded with a powerful long-distance microphone. It was as if the zeitgeist could predict what was coming.

The facts, Butterfield explained, were these: In 1970 the president installed listening devices in the Oval Office, his Old Executive Office Building "hideaway" office, and the White House Cabinet Room—"of course for historical purposes," he meekly clarified, as if to shield himself from the awful burden of having just changed the course of history himself. The system was voice activated, and operated continuously. It was sensitive to the point of a whisper. Besides Butterfield, two other of Nixon's lowly personal aides, and three Secret Service agents, no other official except Bob Haldeman knew about the system. ("No kidding," the former attorney general Richard Kleindienst exhaled in astonishment upon hearing the news on a business trip in London.)

Sam Dash teased out implications. Did the president ever *turn off* this silent witness to his every utterance? "No, sir. As a matter of fact, the President seemed to be totally, really oblivious, or certainly uninhibited by this fact."

"The tapes you mentioned were stored, are they stored by a particular date?"

"Yes, sir, they are."

For anyone for whom it was not yet clear, Dash clarified the awesome import:

"If either Mr. Dean, Mr. Haldeman, Mr. Ehrlichman, or Mr. Colson had particular meetings in the Oval Office with the President on any particular dates that have been testified before this committee, there would be a tape recording with the President of that full conversation, would there not?"

There would be indeed. Dash had only one more question—the only one now that mattered: "What would be the best way to reconstruct those conversations, Mr. Butterfield, in the President's Oval Office?"

"Well, in the obvious manner," Butterfield responded: "to obtain the tape and play it."

That meant it would not just be Dean's word against the president's—if only the committee could subpoena those tapes.

THE FIRST SCENE IN THAT THRILLER UNFOLDED AT THE WHITE HOUSE West Gate, where two young staffers of the special prosecutor's office arrived with a subpoena for tapes of nine key conversations—the first subpoena of a president since Aaron Burr's treason trial in 1805.

The president, amazed that anyone as close to him as Butterfield would not have understood that the correct answer to questions he'd been asked was "executive privilege," from his hospital bed, addressed a letter to Judge Sirica, who would be deciding this Watergate case, too: "With the utmost respect for the court of which you are chief judge, and for the branch of government of which it is a part, I must decline to obey the command of that subpoena. In doing so I follow the example of a long line of my predecessors as President of the United States who have consistently adhered to the position that the President is not subject to compulsory process from the courts." Two other letters he addressed to the Watergate committee concerning their own subpoena. In one, the president asserted that the "special nature of tape recordings of private conversations" made them even more privileged than paper documents, because they "contain comments that persons with different perspectives would inevitably interpret in different ways." The other letter indicated he refused to meet to discuss the matter.

Ervin read both letters aloud in the caucus room, drawling out a response in indubitably Ervinian fashion: The president was not "immune from all the duties and responsibilities which devolve upon all the other mortals who dwell in this land." He said the crisis was worse than the Civil War—was, in fact, "the greatest tragedy this country has ever suffered." And, live on national TV, his committee voted unanimously to sue the President of the United States. That was unprecedented, too.

Judge Sirica set arguments for August 7. President Nixon announced he would listen only to the opinion of the Supreme Court—four of whose nine members, cynics pointed out, he had appointed. A showdown between the Constitution's three branches was set. It would unspool for months—while the TV melodrama rolled on, audiences more riveted than ever.

Herbert Kalmbach sat down at the great green table after Butterfield was dismissed. He described his consternation with the "James Bond scenario" he had been drafted into: passing wads of hundred-dollar bills in hotel rooms to a man he knew only under aliases. The man was Anthony Ulasewicz, the Runyonesque former New York City cop on call whenever the White House needed a man in the shadows. Kalmbach had barreled into John Ehrlichman's office in July 1972, imploring reassurance: "John, I am looking right into your eyes," he recollected saying. "I know Jeanne and your family, you know Barbara and my family. You know that my family and my reputation mean everything to me, and it is just absolutely necessary, John, that you tell me, first that John Dean has the authority to direct me in this assignment"—in other words, that John Dean was not acting on his own but that he had the approval of a higher-up—"that it is a proper assignment, and that I am to go forward with it."

"And did he look you in the eyes?" Sam Dash asked.

"Yes, he did."

"What did he say to you?"

"He said, 'Herb, John Dean does have the authority, it is proper, and you are to go forward.'"

THE REVELATION OF TAPES RAISED ANTICIPATION THAT THE SLUICE GATES of truth might finally open. Then John Ehrlichman and Bob Haldeman testified for eight days between them through early August, and dashed those hopes. Ehrlichman, who claimed "no recollection" of any such conversation with Kalmbach, was supposed to be the nice guy of the team. Not this week. Senator Ervin sanctimoniously recited the parable of the Good Samaritan. Ehrlichman snapped back, "I read the

Bible, I don't quote it." He used mocking nicknames for the principals; Sam Dash was "the Professor"; John Dean was "the star witness"—and Watergate's true villain. Which didn't make sense, considering that Ehrlichman didn't seem to consider any of the actions the Watergate committee was looking into villainous. The president, he insisted, was only fighting for peace on earth and goodwill toward all men. The people opposing him (who were "favorable to the North Vietnamese and their allies") were enemies of same. He couldn't find anything "seriously embarrassing" in operations like the burglarization of the office of Daniel Ellsberg's psychiatrist—an operation he himself had approved "if it is not traceable," according to a August 1971 memo the committee offered into evidence. It was, he insisted, "a vital national security inquiry," "well within the President's inherent Constitutional powers."

Senator Talmadge: "If the President could authorize a covert break-in, [and] you don't know exactly where that power would be limited, you don't think it could include murder or other crimes *beyond* covert break-in, do you?"

Coolly, with an accent that made him sound like a working-class white ethnic from Milwaukee, the bald witness responded: "I don't know where that line is, Senator."

The Georgian pressed.

"Do you remember when we were in law school, we studied a famous principle of law that came from England and also is well known in this country, that no matter how humble a man's cottage is, that even the King of England cannot enter without his consent?"

The witness set his jaw and furrowed his brow. "I am afraid," he said, "that has been considerably eroded over the years."

No pause from Talmadge: "Down in my country we still think it a pretty legitimate principle of law."

The chamber exploded in cheers. You could read the shock on the bald man's face.

IT WAS THE MOST INTENSE OUTBURST FROM THE GALLERIES SINCE A MAN named Gordon Strachan, a Haldeman aide, preceded him on the stand. Strachan was one of those sad young White House men the hearings had thrown up in such profusion. Senator Joseph Montoya of New Mexico, who liked to give each witness a chance to expiate his sins, asked him, "Because of Watergate, many young people are writing to us expressing great consternation about our country and also saying that public service is not as attractive as before Watergate. . . . What advice do you have for those people?"

An innocent-looking blond young man, twenty-nine years old, his face still pockmarked by acne like a teenager's, his lip trembling, sitting next to a lawyer in pinstripes, replied: "My advice would be to stay away." The hearing room erupted in laughter.

But nervous laughter. The kind that bespeaks a radical discomfort—like when you really want to cry. The moment immediately became one of Watergate's great conversation pieces. And when it was his turn to make his closing statement, that was what Ehrlichman chose to address.

"Your gallery laughed," he noted. "But I don't think many Americans laughed. Nor do I agree with Gordon's advice. . . . Our government and our politics are only as idealistic as the people in those buildings."

Ehrlichman was arguing that he was one of those idealists. "If you go to work for the President and the executive branch there are very few in Congress or the media that are going to throw rosebuds at you. . . .

"You will encounter a local culture which scoffs at family life and morality just as it adulates the opposite and you will find some people who have fallen for that line.

"But you will also find in politics and government many great people who know that a pearl of great price is not had for the asking and who feel that this country and its heritage are worth the work, the abuse, the struggle, and the sacrifices. Don't stay away. Come and join them and do it better."

He meant "better than his inquisitors on the Ervin Committee." The editors of the conservative *Chicago Tribune* found that peroration so moving they printed it in full. It was a profoundly Nixonian moment. Staging the rhetorical distinction between the uprightly patriotic and the degenerate aliens who sought to subvert patriotism was what Nixonism was all about. The masterpiece had been his speech of November 3, 1969: two million Americans had just protested his failure to end the Vietnam War, a veritable outpouring from Middle America, and Nixon managed to turn them into loud-mouthed hippies calling for "the first defeat in our nation's history." He had continued: "It might not be fashionable to speak of our national destiny these days." But he would do so nonetheless—coining the phrase the "great silent majority" to identify those who supported him in Vietnam, because they were patriots. The approval rating of his handling of the war had gone up from 58 to 77 percent overnight after that speech.

On July 24, Ehrlichman's crew-cut right-hand man, Bob Haldeman, began testifying. He was uncharacteristically accommodating—until Senator Weicker pulled out a memo to Haldeman dated October 14, 1971, and Haldeman exposed the other side of the Silent Majority rhetorical coin: it welcomed division. It welcomed hate. For if the world was divided between good and evil, hating evil was the appropriate response. And what violations of procedural nicety weren't permissible in order to *vanquish evil*?

The memo consisted of advance instructions for a presidential appearance in Charlotte, North Carolina, with the Reverend Billy Graham. Demonstrators would be "violent," it explained. "They will have extremely obscene signs." The senator held up the document and pointed to the margin: "Is that your writing there where it says, 'good'?"

Haldeman acknowledged it was.

The senator continued reading: "It will not only be directed toward the President, *but also toward Billy Graham.*" He pointed out that, also in Haldeman's handwriting, the words "also toward Billy Graham" had been underlined, and beside them had been penciled in "great." The administration *welcomed* violence and obscenity directed at the president and a beloved divine.

Once more the hearing room erupted in that odd nervous laughter.

Weicker had revealed something ugly and untoward about how the White House thought and worked. The attitude showed up in the writings of Watergate conspirators. E. Howard Hunt wrote pseudonymous thrillers as a hobby. They were being brought back into print under his own name by opportunistic publishers. In one of them one of his heroes intoned, "We became lawless in a struggle for the rule of law—semi-outlaws who risk their lives to put down the savagery of others." And G. Gordon Liddy wrote in his memoir, "To permit the thought, spirit, life-style of the '60s movement to achieve power . . . was a thought as offensive to me as was the thought of surrender to a career Japanese soldier in 1945."

It was precisely such reaction to the insurgencies of the 1960s that led to Nixon's reelection in 1972, with an unprecedented forty-nine-state landslide. Not in spite of the paranoia and dread that was its unseemly underside—the same paranoia and dread that helped produce Watergate—but in some sense because of it. It was Richard Nixon's unique contribution to all the conservative Republican electoral successes to come over the next few decades. But it had rarely been articulated, held up to the light, as Senator Weicker did now.

There had always been another political consequence of the "thought, spirit, life-style of the '60s" that the Liddys and Hunts and Haldemans didn't quite grasp. It was a new vision of patriotism produced in the 1960s—a perfect passion for the rule of law, of the fairest possible proceduralism, a longing for political innocence that pundits referred to as the "New Politics." It was Sam Ervin's sort of patriotism. It was the patriotism confronted by George McGovern in his acceptance speech at the 1972 Democratic convention: "We reject the view of those who say, 'America—love it or leave it.' We reply, 'Let us change it so we may love it the more.'" It was the spirit that helped explain why law school applications were increasing by almost 50 percent among young people: young idealists wanted to be like Sam Dash—or like the staff assistants who lurked in the background of the TV shots, whose hair and sideburns were frequently as long as any hippie's. (The real threats to law and order—the hearing witnesses—wore crew cuts.)

Here was a moment that framed what Watergate meant: a battle over the meaning of America.

Two visions of patriotism clashed that summer in the letters pages. Why, a man from Indiana asked, was Ted Kennedy "always finding fault with our good, hard-working President? Our country needs Richard Nixon. We need more men like him. Many people prayed for his re-election. I am one of them." They believed the Ervin Committee was "so intent on putting a noose around Nixon's neck that they are blindly acting as pallbearers for the nation."

The other side critiqued—decorously, usually, for they were liberals—the "alarmingly high percentage of Americans more than willing to tolerate lawlessness as long as it is conducted in the name of 'Americanism' or even 'law and order.'" They addressed Sam Ervin as a man who "holds the future of the right of free citizenship in your hand as fully as have only a few others in history"; quoted the *Federalist Papers;* complained "that the most thoroughgoing effort to convert the United States into a police state came from the most publicly pious, God-Fearing President of modern times." One boasted in a letter to the *Washington Post* of his son's ambition to be a public servant—even though "he possesses two qualities that 'at this point in time' appear to be definitely undesirable . . . he is scrupulously honest and he has a very good memory." Their appeal to the word *patriotism* was just as explicit as the conservatives' appeal to it: "Any President's true patriotism would show in his own rejection of unlimited power," one of them wrote.

In recent years the first group's version of patriotism had ruled public opinion. In April 1970, for instance, on the eve of the Kent State shootings and in the wake of the frightening disorder of the late 1960s, 76 percent in a Gallup poll maintained that the First Amendment should be suspended if that meant no more disruptive protests in the streets. These were the people who had elected Richard Nixon in 1968, in a tangle of rage and piety. Who believed, with Richard Nixon, that our neighbors might be our enemies, and our enemies might destroy us.

But now a shift was afoot. The suspicious circles were expanding into places like the Worcester, Massachusetts, living room of a conservative blue-collar worker whose son happened to be Abbie Hoffman, the Chicago Seven defendant and hippie savant. Now John Hoffman sat in front of his tiny black-and-white TV and told himself that, yes, "Abbie had been right all along": American decency was indeed a sham.

They expanded, too, into a Republican county thirty miles down the road from Pekin, Illinois, that a liberal college professor visited late in July and wrote about for the *Chicago Tribune*. The first person he visited was the state's attorney, who showed his visitor the little plastic bug he had placed atop a framed letter from Richard Nixon thanking him for running the local reelection effort. "Sometimes I can just sense what people are thinking when I pass them on the street. They're saying to themselves: 'If that's what goes on in Washington, I wonder what Paul's got to hide up in his office.'"

Down the hall, the local circuit court judge said regretfully that if John Dean's testimony had been given in his courtroom he would have had to find it credible.

A young farmer's wife told the visitor: "It's just so stupid. Why didn't the man"—Nixon—"just have more trust in the American public?"

And down the highway, in the men's grill room at Bloomington Country Club, the guys shooting the bull after the first round of a golf tournament started in about Watergate.

"You know," one exclaimed, "this thing is just like cheating on your wife. I mean, if you were cheating on your wife, you wouldn't stand up and tell everyone the truth about it. Would you?"

When most of the golfers chortled their agreement, another told them all to shut up: "Cut it out. You know darn well that this thing isn't like that at all." The liberal college professor reported that the consort finally agreed: "Cheating on your wife is just not the same thing as cheating on your country."

In a new poll, the majority of the American people said they wished they'd voted for George S. McGovern. Nixon's approval rating fell to 31 percent, the lowest of any president since Hoover. The favorability ratings of the Ervin Committee members ranged from 69 to 84 percent. Howard Baker was mentioned for the 1976 Republican nomination. Only 17 percent believed the press was out "to get President Nixon on Watergate," and only 40 percent now thought there was too much coverage. Americans did tell the Harris poll they found the president more believable than John Dean—but only by 38 to 37 percent. "Apparently," one dry wit wrote to his local newspaper, the "President of the United of States is one percent more believable than a confessed felon."

THEN AN ENTIRELY NEW WHITE HOUSE CRISIS PRESENTED ITSELF: VICE President Spiro Agnew, that pathetic man a heartbeat away from the presidency, was in legal trouble.

A virtually unknown figure nationally in 1968, with only a year's experience as Maryland governor and four years as Baltimore County's chief executive before that, he had become Nixon's running mate for the most craven of political reasons: he had caught Nixon's eye after putting down urban riots with unmatched ruthlessness. He was a veritable freak for conformity and order. One of his county employees told a journalist the story of how he once returned from a two-week camping trip unshaven, eager to get back to work; Agnew sent him home with orders not to return until he shaved. Agnew had accepted the nomination, intoning, "I stand here with a deep sense of the improbability of this moment." In office he was reduced to attending ribbon cuttings and attending to a policy portfolio of fifth-tier issues like maritime affairs and Native American rights—until, in October 1969, Pat Buchanan, practically his only West Wing fan, came up with the idea of drafting him as the administration's attack dog against the radicals, and the liberal media elites the White House believed to be cosseting radicals. Or, in Agnew's memorable words, "the cacophony of seditious drivel emanating from the best-publicized clowns in our society and their fans in the Fourth Estate."

He was still sticking to that script—blasting the Ervin Committee for using "McCarthy tactics," and for exploiting "the misguided zeal of a few individuals" in order to "wash our dirty linen in public." He said he'd "never been more proud of my party" than during Watergate, and called Ervin's hearings a "rain dance" that could "hardly fail to muddy the waters of justice beyond repair." On August 6 he said he agreed with his president that Watergate was not an issue for Congress but belonged in the courts instead—because he had "confidence in the criminal justice system of the United States." Which had to be a bit embarrassing when it was announced on August 7 that the criminal justice system was investigating *him*—for accepting bags full of cash from construction companies from his years as Baltimore County executive and Maryland governor.

"I am innocent of any wrongdoing," Agnew declared, pinning the hubbub on "masochistic persons looking for all that is wrong." His lawyer, writing to the presiding judge, mimicked the arguments of the president: "I do not acknowledge that you or any Grand Jury have any right to the records of the Vice President. Nor do I acknowledge the propriety of any Grand Jury investigation of possible wrongdoing on the part of the Vice President so long as he occupies that office."

Investigators, undaunted, kept investigating.

Nixon gave his next speech to the public on August 15. For this one, unlike every other speech from the Oval Office, the picture of his family, the bust of Abraham Lincoln, and the American flag were out of view. The previous evening, at 11:45 P.M., bombing strikes over Cambodia ended fifteen minutes before the War Powers Act, passed over the president's veto, would have rendered their continuation a violation of federal law. But those who thought the president might finally be humbled heard him say instead, "Not only was I unaware of any cover-up, I was unaware there was anything to cover up." He said those who kept vigil over their "backward-looking obsession with Watergate" might "destroy our hopes for the future," and keep the government from "matters of greater importance." (The phone-tapped Joseph Kraft responded mercilessly: "Like, for instance, what? . . . No business before the American people is anywhere near as important as achieving honest government—which is what the Watergate affair is all about.") Nixon pointed to his predecessors: "Every President since World War II has believed that in internal security matters, the President has the power to authorize wiretaps without first obtaining a search warrant."

Bottom line: releasing tapes "would set a precedent that would cripple all future Presidents." So he would refuse to do it. (Barry Goldwater Jr., a congressman from Los Angeles, answered curtly: "He asks for the trust of the American people, but he doesn't trust them enough to let them hear the tapes.") The reason, Nixon concluded, was that the relationship between a president and his aides was like that "between a lawyer and his client, between a priest and a penitent, and between a husband and wife": it required confidentiality. (A letter writer wondered if it was accidental that he omitted the relation between a psychiatrist and his patient.)

Only a little over a quarter of the 77 percent of the country who heard the speech believed it. Fifty-four percent found it "not at all convincing." A habitual presidential defender, columnist William S. White, called it "extraordinarily weak." Barry Jr.'s dad, the 1964 Republican nominee, said Nixon "did not add anything to his other speeches that would tend to divert suspicion from him."

He stepped into the box again a week later for his first press conference in fourteen months to announce the appointment of Henry Kissinger as secretary of state in addition to his current post as national security advisor. But eighteen of the twenty-one questions hounded him on Watergate. Of the three exceptions, two were on Spiro Agnew, and the third was on whether Nixon would apologize to the American people for ordering some 3,700 bombing raids over Cambodia, hiding the fact even from the top military brass via, the public had just learned, a falsified set of ledgers, while publicly claiming to "have scrupulously observed the neutrality of Cambodia." Clark Mollenhoff, the toughest old bastard in the Washington press corps, all but accused the president of being a dictator: "Where is the check on authoritarianism by the executive if the president is the sole judge of what the executive branch makes available and suppresses?"

AT LEAST NIXON STILL HAD RONALD REAGAN.

On August 2, 1973, returning from a monthlong vacation, the California governor called the Ervin Committee a "lynching" and a "witch hunt"—even as the *Washington Post* reported Nixon had spied on *him*, spreading stories about him behaving oddly at a party. He managed to excuse the president even for that. "I don't know what they're referring to," he told the *Post*. "I was a perfect picture of decorum. You've really caught me here with mixed emotions because I don't know whether to get a sort of glint in my eye and let you think there's a side of me that no one knows."

But what about Nixon taping him when he visited the Oval Office? What did he think about that? No big deal. "Matter of fact," Reagan said, the tapes probably "made me sound good." (They did not. In one 1971 conversation, Nixon called him "pretty shallow" and of "limited mental capacity." Kissinger called the notion of Reagan as president "inconceivable.")

When the news came out that Vice President Spiro Agnew was under federal investigation for taking bribes not just as county executive in Maryland, but in his vice presidential office, David Broder quoted Republican after Republican not daring to defend him. "After the Watergate experience, no one is eager to be the first to rush into print with a denial," a state chairman said. Ronald Reagan, however, was plenty eager. "I have known Ted Agnew to be an honest and honorable man," he told Broder. "He, like any other citizen of high character, should be considered innocent until proven otherwise." (The same week he said an alleged cop killer, not yet tried, deserved the electric chair.)

Came next the president's August 15 speech, and another Reagan encomium: "His message was the voice of reason which went a long way toward putting the whole situation in better perspective." It came as Agnew's legal trouble, as one wag had recently put it, became "the best news to reach second-string Presidential candidates since Edward Kennedy's car went off that bridge." The second-string presidential candidate named Ronald Reagan seemed determined to sabotage that opportunity. It drove his advisors to distraction.

Rowland Evans and Robert Novak had published a column about the Reagan aides positioning their boss as a presidential prospect. They cited his record as "the successful architect of clean, frugal government, free of scandal and geared to lower taxes," and his distance from an irretrievably corrupted White House. Problem was, his backers complained, Reagan kept defending Watergate conspirators "as no worse than double parkers." His aides were quoted rejoicing that Reagan *finally* seemed to get it—that he had ceased his defense of the president and was concentrating instead on his new bid for national attention: Proposition 1, the tax-limitation initiative for which he had won a spot on the November 6 California ballot. "He believes the appeal of lower taxes, limited spending, and reduced government is universal."

He was about the only one who believed it. At the annual June governors' conference at the Sahara Tahoe Hotel, everything he said seemed calculated to remove him from serious consideration as an important voice in the national conversation. A columnist surveyed the governors about what they thought should be the top national priority. Democrat Reuben Askew of Florida said "learning to live with nature." Tom McCall, Republican of Oregon, listed "strong land-use planning." Republican governor Otis Bowen of Indiana said "improved transportation services." Almost everyone mentioned inflation, the environment, and restoring the integrity of government. Governor Reagan alone, as if from a different political planet, said, "Our highest national priority should be to halt the trend toward bigger, more expensive government at all levels before it is too late." He added an apocalyptic fillip: "We as citizens will either master government as our servant or ultimately it will master us."

He called a press conference on the ballot initiative. Reporters asked only about Watergate. ("About 90 percent of everything said so far is unfounded rumor, accusations, and so forth," he answered.) He explained the tax-limitation idea at a session of fellow governors. With a single exception (Governor Meldrim Thomson Jr. of New Hampshire, who was such an extremist he'd once proposed issuing atomic weapons to members of the National Guard), they called it foolhardy—"a political ploy and an insult to the legislative branch," said one Democrat. A Republican called it "superfluous, unwise, and unnecessary."

Reagan, unfazed, said the governors simply hadn't understood it. Then he got to work selling it back home. He was nothing if not a salesman.

He also had an ace in the hole. Wealthy backers pumped out $436,452 (including a $110,000 loan guaranteed by thirteen of them, including car dealer Holmes Tuttle, oil scion William H. Doheny, and construction magnate J. Robert Fluor) to collect the 520,806 signatures needed to get it for the ballot—the most spent to qualify a ballot initiative since these same men spent $396,000 on a 1972 drive to cut state workers' salaries.

The 5,700 words of the complicated measure included a rollback of the personal income tax rate from 8.3 to 7 percent and a provision that if the state collected more than an allotted amount in any year the surplus would be refunded to taxpayers. It established an emergency fund of not more than 0.2 percent of taxpayer income to maintain government functions—but only the governor could declare the emergency. It also set tax limits for cities, counties, and special districts. Finally, it exempted the wealthy from California tax law's $10,000 mandatory minimum assessment, and included a rebate for lower-income taxpayers. At the end of August the state government's official nonpartisan fiscal legislative analyst, a highly respected bureaucrat of thirty years' standing named A. Alan Post, whom Reagan had once offered a job as his administration's finance director, weighed in with his assessment: Proposition 1 would force an immediate $620 million reduction in next year's state budget. Reagan roared back that Post was serving as a "cat's paw" for Democratic Assembly Speaker Robert Moretti. He said he only wished Post's were "honest mistakes—they were not. They were deliberate distortions."

Post had just been profiled as a model of objectivity and rectitude on the front page of the *Wall Street Journal.* He had once been, in fact, a registered Republican—then changed his status to "declined to state," to foreground his nonpartisan scrupulousness. The chairman of the California senate Republican caucus rose to defend him: "Alan Post doesn't slant figures." So did the Republican floor leader in the California assembly: "I have never personally been of the opinion he is partisan." Post appeared before the assembly Ways and Means Committee to patiently explain his statistics-laden seventy-five-page conclusions that over a four-year period Prop 1 would require budget cuts totaling $3.5 billion, and would merely shift the tax burden to localities and property taxes. The governor's chief deputy director of finance called that "misleading, distorted, and biased." A shouting match nearly broke out.

Post appeared a second time, offering five ways the governor could shrink state government without forcing a fiscal crisis, including privatizing the Department of Consumer Affairs, increasing tuition and student fees, and reducing tax relief for senior citizens. Moretti listed all the nonpartisan organizations that called Proposition 1 irresponsible, including the League of Women voters. Michael Deaver, one of six top gubernatorial aides who'd taken a leave of absence to work for the referendum campaign, promptly declared that the League "has lost its right to be regarded as a non-partisan, fact-finding organization." Complained Moretti, "Apparently anybody who disagrees with him is just 'bad people.'" Indeed, Reagan had first attempted to pass his tax reform via statute, but a state senate committee bottled it up. He had labeled that partisan "sabotage"—even though it lost a vote in plain daylight, by a margin of 80 percent, including a majority of his fellow Republicans.

THE DEBATE UNFOLDED WITH WHOLESALE PRICES UP 60 PERCENT SINCE the beginning of the year. The University of Michigan's Survey Research Center reported consumer confidence was at the lowest point in its twenty-five years of measuring. Only 30 percent expected "good times" in 1974. Meat prices spiked again. A cartoonist depicted a grocer frantically stamping items that were still in a housewife's cart: "Hold it—prices just went up again!" Another had a newsman grimly reading a report from the White House: "The wholesale price index soared—with honor, of course." A *Washington Post* letter writer suggested that "meatless Mondays" was too timid a response, and proposed foodless Mondays instead. Perhaps this was dry humor. But he offered no indication he didn't mean it.

It was an inauspicious time to make an argument that government was too active; most took for granted that government bore direct responsibility for controlling prices. That was why, on September 7, the president's Cost of Living Council set a new ceiling for domestic crude oil prices, at $4.25 a barrel, about a dollar below the prevailing world price. And it was an inauspicious time, one of economic crisis, to press the notion of handcuffing the government with tax cuts and expenditure ceilings. So Bob Moretti challenged Reagan to a televised debate. Reagan called that a "campaign gimmick" and refused. Moretti said Reagan refused because "he cannot answer the questions we raise as to which programs will be cut." So he challenged the governor again. And again and again. Five times Reagan said no. He was playing an entirely different game. And playing it very well.

It was true that his statistics did not add up. In fact they contradicted each other—a circumstance he dispatched with the casual blitheness that drove his opponents insane. They claimed his plan would create deficits. He responded it would produce $41.5 billion in *new* revenue over the next decade and a half. But at that, he also stated that the plan's intention was to give the state *less* money to spend.

To those who said it would force cuts in popular programs, he pointed out that it included an emergency fund that would protect them. But then he would say he didn't want to protect government bureaucracies anyway. His critics would scratch their heads—and unveil another brace of statistics. Reagan in turn would respond with moralistic perorations: "When the advocates of bigger and bigger government manage to get their hands on an extra tax dollar or two they hang on like a gila monster until they find some way to spend it." At which his opponents would respond, yes, with many more statistics. But they only ended up looking like pedantic asses. Which was just the game Reagan was playing.

ON ONE THING ALL PARTIES AGREED: PROPOSITION I WAS A VEHICLE FOR the governor's national ambitions. Wrote the *National Review* contributor and syndicated columnist John Chamberlain, "If the tax revolt is as real as Reagan thinks, and if individuals are alive to their opportunity to keep special interest politicians from raiding their bank accounts, November 6 in California could mark a genuine turn in history." Said Edmund G. "Jerry" Brown Jr., who was California's secretary of state and son of the man Reagan beat to become governor in 1966, and who hoped to succeed him in 1974, Proposition 1 was "just a vehicle to use to run for President," and "a hoax, pure and simple." Indeed Reagan said he'd like to see constitutional tax limitation at the federal level, and proposed an amendment "requiring that no congressman can introduce a spending measure without at the same time introducing a revenue measure to pay for it."

Reagan's national profile was raised further on September 13 when he was roasted on *The Dean Martin Comedy Hour*. That he hadn't been much of a movie star was the standing joke of the affair. Don Rickles, the bald-headed master of insults, joked about how people couldn't remember how to pronounce his name. "The greatest thing I can say about Governor *Reagan*, or Governor *Ree*-gan, or whatever they call you . . ." Quipped roast master Dean Martin, "He never made an X-rated movie. All his movies were rated 'M.' You couldn't get in unless you were accompanied by a moron." They were also "so bad they were shown at drive-outs."

The Man of the Hour, crinkle-eyed and square-shouldered, chortled genially. "He laughs at anything!" Rickles thrusted—

"My brother died!"

Rickles mimicked guffaws.

Cut to Reagan—guffawing.

Rickles turned serious: "Black, white, Jew, gentile, we're all working for the same cause."

Thoughtful pause.

"To figure out how you became governor!"

Rickles mocked the guest of honor's national ambitions: "I'll never forget the story about you standing on the White House lawn throwing rocks at the president's window, yelling, 'Dick! Dick!'" Paternally, he turned to him: "Don't beg!" Jack Benny collapsed in convulsions on Reagan's shoulder—and Reagan, amiably, laughed.

Dean Martin pretended to read a congratulatory telegram from *Playgirl* that invited Reagan to pose as a centerfold: "We feel the American public would like to see a politician who has nothing to hide." An older comedian took the podium. He made quite a contrast to comics like George Carlin, Cheech and Chong, and Richard Pryor, who were revolutionizing the field with sewer-mouthed sex-and-drug stuff, who could never abide the evening's formal dress. "How can you aspire to such a high office?" he mock-asked. "You've never even had a good scandal attached to your name. No cheating, no lying, no bugging . . . Who's going to trust a politician like that?"

It got a pretty good laugh, even though it was not true. In 1967 his administration was thrown on its heals when one of Reagan's (male) top aides was caught having sex with a younger (male) aide, and another aide leaked the "homosexuality ring" scandal to a columnist. But that had been forgotten, or perhaps forgiven, now that men having sex with each other was not so scandalous. But the leak itself fit Watergate to a T: it came about because Reagan's press secretary Lyn Nofziger spied on the aide's hotel room to get the incriminating evidence to crush a bureaucratic rival. But no one watching TV knew that. The viewers just saw a genial man on the dais laughing along with Jack Benny and Phyllis Diller.

He took the podium for the traditional final riposte, giving as good as he got.

To Jack Benny: "He's not a tightwad. That's just an act. On my last birthday he gave me a set of encyclopedias." (Pause, perfect timing.) "Paperback."

To Dean Martin: he really was a lot like Reagan. "We both like horses and golf. We both made a lot of movies. The only difference is—"

Pause.

"I knew how to quit!"

On Watergate: "I've sat here watching this whole show, and the best thing I can do for you all is invoke executive privilege."

Perfect pause.

"I refuse to release the tape."

Dean Martin himself didn't get any laughs bigger than that. Reagan then concluded to a standing ovation.

It must have been quite a spectacle for liberals—for instance the state senator in California, George Moscone, who said the governor's recent veto of a bill to increase aid to a half million elderly, blind, and crippled welfare recipients would cause "mass starvation and suicide among those who could no longer afford to live." Reagan was also about to sign a bill restoring the death penalty in California, making capital punishment mandatory for eleven different categories of murders. You might, if you happened to follow the news out of California, have considered him a heartless man. But here he just seemed like a great guy.

THE SHOW PLAYED TO A CORE OF HIS APPEAL. DEAN MARTIN'S TV ROASTS were new that year, and at the same time very old-fashioned. They danced to the music of classic Hollywood, as it was once depicted in magazines with names like *Photoplay* and *Modern Screen*, which shaped the notion of the "movie colony" as an intimate little village of folks who were, yes, glamorous, but also, it just so happened, a lot like you and me. Sure, the jokes could be a little racy ("Mark Spitz wasn't always Jewish. But he was swimming in the ocean when he had a run-in with a swordfish"), but that was a part of the fun, too: the thrill of being let in (or seeming to be let in) on these slightly dangerous lives, their inside jokes, their peccadillos. That old Hollywood was gone now—killed by the death of the studio system and the rise of arty directors like Francis Ford Coppola and Martin Scorsese and outlaw stars like Marlon Brando and Jane Fonda, enraptured by authenticity and left-wing political engagement and disdainful of mere "entertainment." (Sending up an Indian to accept your Academy Award: hard to imagine Jimmy Stewart doing that.) But fans of the former Hollywood now got to enjoy the good old days in comforting visits: in disaster movies cast to the gills with all the old familiar stars; in TV variety shows hosted by has-beens like Jackie Gleason—and in the political career of Ronald Reagan, whose appearances beside the likes of Bob Hope and Jimmy Stewart and Martha Raye were part of what made him so pleasant. It was part of what made Reagan's national prospects seem grand. Because nostalgia was becoming a national cult.

Late that summer an unusual film became a surprise hit. Whereas the cool movies these days were rather depressing, *American Graffiti* was light and buoyant. It was set in 1962, and nothing much happened—high school kids in a small California town cruising up and down the local strip, listening to rock and roll, hanging out at Mel's Diner. No sex, hardly even hints, remarkable for a movie about high school kids in summertime; the men were more interested in their eroticized cars. The contrast could not have been stronger to a quintessential New Hollywood picture from two years earlier set in a similar period and milieu: *The Last Picture Show,* which displayed high school students in explicit poolside orgies.

The ads, which explicitly invited the viewer into his own nostalgic reverie, helped: "Where were you in '62?" they asked. A postscript explained what the characters were doing in the present day. One was killed by a drunk driver. Another was missing in action in Vietnam. *American Graffiti* promised to deliver us across the bridge of years to the time before the 1960s storm. So did the new nostalgia magazines, obsessively focused on trivia like Tarzan's costars and the Lone Ranger's wardrobe—and a revived *Saturday Evening Post,* complete with recycled Norman Rockwell covers. *Life* magazine had been out of business since December, but a fat photo compendium *The Best of Life* had a 800,000-copy first printing. Heavy on pictures from the 1930s, '40s, and '50s, it excluded *Life*'s most famous photo: a Vietnamese girl running naked down the street after her school was napalmed by U.S. warplanes.

A restaurant chain called "Shakey's Pizza Parlor and Ye Old Public House" booked Dixieland combos in candy-striped vests and handed out ersatz straw hats made of Styrofoam; another, the Ground Round ("the robust eating & drinking emporium"), promised diners "a happy atmosphere filled with checkered tablecloths . . . stone fire-place, nostalgia-filled jukebox, and free peanuts in the shell for everyone." (You could throw the peanut shells on the floor. There seemed something welcomingly old-fashioned in that.) Comic books were big; at the "Nostalgia '73" convention in Chicago you could buy a copy of the first Superman comic for a thousand dollars, like it was a Picasso or something. "It's a form of escape," one collector told the *Tribune.* "It's just like you want to recapture the past." (This gentleman so obsessed with recapturing the past was nineteen years old.) Buster Keaton festivals were in, and *Grease,* a Broadway musical about high school in the 1950s.

Fashion was all shaped suits for men and long skirts for women, hats for both—and, of all things, saddle shoes. Bette Midler had a hit with the Andrews Sisters' "Boogie-Woogie Bugle Boy," and Herman Wouk's sprawling World War II novel *The Winds of War* was on the fiction best-seller list, as was *The Class of '44.* Another hit movie, *The Sting,* was set in the 1930s—and scored with Scott Joplin rags from the 1890s. Later it was shown in double features with *American Graffiti,* and was still running a year after its release. The patriotic belter Kate Smith was hauled out of mothballs to sing "God Bless America" for the white working-class fans flocking to see the "Broad Street Bullies"—the Philadelphia Flyers hockey club. A Canadian broadcaster named Gordon Sinclair recorded himself reading an editorial praising the United States as "the most generous and least appreciated nation on earth" over the strains of a band playing "America the Beautiful." It became a bestselling record. Some disc jockeys played it every hour on the hour, and columnist David Broder called him "the fellow who's probably had the greatest impact on American opinion these past couple of months," other than Judge John Sirica. The preternaturally warm and supportive Walton clan scrapped through the Great Depression together every week on TV. Everyone wanted to be somewhere else. A somewhere else with clear-cut heroes and villains. Anywhere but the 1970s, which just kept getting less innocent each day.

Late in August, at the annual Soap Box Derby in Akron, Ohio, a fourteen-year-old was stripped of first prize after officials X-rayed his car and discovered an electromagnet in the nose to pull him out of the starting gate more quickly. Immediately, special pleaders argued he had done no wrong. A publicist at the University of California, Los Angeles reminisced in an op-ed on all the ways he and his buddies used to cheat, and said he couldn't wait to help his son do the same: "Grownups should put their expectations of youngsters in line with reality."

PROXIMATELY, THAT REALITY INCLUDED: IN CHICAGO, THE RESIGNATION of the police superintendent after thirty-five of his officers were convicted of shakedowns; and in Boston, the collapse of the shabbily constructed Tobin Bridge, where a single strike by an errant truck caused two hundred feet of the upper roadway to collapse into the Mystic River. In Florida, a jury acquitted eight activists from Vietnam Veterans Against the War indicted by the Nixon Justice Department for planning violence at the Republican National Convention in 1972—for the same reason a similar indictment against alleged conspirators in Camden, New Jersey, had been rejected by a jury in May: both plots had been instigated by FBI agent provocateurs. The acquittal was quietly devastating to the moral excuses of Watergate malefactors like James McCord, who claimed in his Ervin Committee testimony that reports of planned violence at that convention were the reason they'd been willing to break the law for Richard Nixon.

A reader wrote to the *Los Angeles Times:* "Tell the students that on their way home they should be exceptionally careful about strangers sitting around in cars. Students should be told not to accept money, rides, or presents from strangers." That same day, elsewhere in the paper, you could learn about plans to cut the municipal workweek to four days to help unclog the city's dystopian traffic congestion, and that in Sacramento lawmen pondered whether to abandon the state capitol after a study revealed the building might collapse in the event of even a minor earthquake or fire. It was easy to feel that civilization was falling apart.

Meanwhile in Sacramento, the governor was fighting for Proposition 1 so hard he even managed to find a way to acknowledge something bad might have happened at the White House: the way his opponents distorted statistics, he said, was "a little bit like Watergate." At utterances like these, opponents were still throwing up their hands. If Reagan wanted to cut taxes and spending, Jerry Brown pointed out, why had he raised both in his previous seven years as governor, despite having a line-item veto? (He had even authorized a surprise tax increase for the Los Angeles school district two weeks after his initiative made the ballot.) "How can a magic formula, written by invisible lawyers, do what Ronald Reagan has been unwilling or unable to do?"

And indeed, if government employees were such money-sucking monsters, why did the state budget have a surplus in the first place?

Reagan would say something like "The real issue is that these people believe the government should be taking more taxes from the people." Then his aides would have to concede the point that actually no tax increases were expected for years. Their boss would point to "some of this country's most distinguished economists," who'd signed off on the plan because they believed spiraling taxes would create "the biggest economic bellyache America has ever known unless we do something about it." Critics would point out that the only economists saying this were right-wing ones who despised taxes as such. And that writing intricate tax policy into a constitutional amendment that could not be adjusted without further constitutional amendments turned the state's governing charter into a laboratory experiment, straitjacketing its flexibility to respond to crises.

He told a cheering crowd at the Disneyland Hotel: "What they mean by 'flexibility' is the unlimited ability to get into your pockets." And made yet more moralistic perorations: "Have we really forgotten what the Constitution is for? It is not designed to protect government from the people; it is to protect the people against government. It is not a document in which government tells the people what they can do. It is a contract by which the people tell the government what we, the people, will permit government to do."

The only consistency in his story was the casting. There were the good guys: anyone fighting to cut taxes. And the bad: the government bureaucrats after your hard-earned cash. As a morality tale, it was compelling. The public opinion expert Samuel Lubell had a new book out in which he reported his interviews around the country with middle-class Americans. "Every use of government was becoming a tax issue," he observed. "Welfare brought protests that 'people on relief are crushing the middle class.'"

But whether Reagan could convince people that Proposition 1 wouldn't also crush the middle class was still an open question. Moretti said that if Proposition 1 passed, "by the time the walls come crashing down around whoever the next governor of this state is," Reagan would "be campaigning in Mississippi someplace, saying, 'I don't understand the problems they're having out there; when I was in charge, things ran smoothly.'" He published an op-ed eviscerating Reagan's key claims—especially his favorite claim, that state, federal, and local taxes ate up 44.7 percent of the average person's income and would increase to a whopping 54 and maybe even 67 percent. That was "sheer deception," Moretti said, citing the estimate of the Tax Foundation—another respected outfit no one had thought to call ideological before—that the tax burden was actually 32.7 percent, and to reach the more extravagant figures "the governor included receipts to government which are not taxes," like private donations to the University of California, college bookstore revenues, U.S. postal receipts, sale of agricultural products by the federal government, and admissions to college athletic events. He also double-counted many of the government's receipts.

On the merits, it was a devastating rebuttal. But perhaps not devastating enough. As the fall weather turned crisp, the Las Vegas oddsmaker Jimmy the Greek concluded that, all in all, Proposition 1 had a 3-to-1 chance of passage.

. . .

ON SEPTEMBER 26 THE ERVIN COMMITTEE SQUEEZED IN ITS LAST WITNESS whose testimony was televised live before folding up its green table. In the *Pittsburgh Post-Gazette*, the headline introducing him read "NIXON WRITER BACKS POLITICAL SPYING TACTICS." The Nixon writer in question was Patrick J. Buchanan, and in addition to writing speeches, his job had been preparing Nixon's summaries each morning of what was in the papers and newscasts—an angry daily soupçon of liberal perfidy, media bias, and, wherever possible, news from the heartland of ordinary Americans who loved the person Buchanan affectionately called the "Old Man" as much as he did. Later, the American people would learn that Pat Buchanan had advised the president to build a bonfire on the White House lawn and burn the tapes. His testimony was the first time a witness provided a thoroughgoing strategic overview of what all the 1972 dirty tricks that had become known as "Watergate" were intended to accomplish: sabotaging all the other Democratic candidates in order to leave George McGovern, the field's weakest link, as the last man standing, and in the process to turn the Democratic Party into a nest of recrimination and distrust.

But first, leading up to Buchanan's appearance, candid memos he had written were leaked: for instance, advice to "cut the Democratic Party and country in half," as he put it in 1971, to end up with "by far the larger half." And his question, also in 1971, not long before Edmund Muskie's presidential run collapsed following his emotional reaction to attacks on his wife, "Who should we get to poke the sharp stick into his cage to bring Muskie howling forth?" And his gloating, in April 1972, that "[o]ur primary objective, to prevent Senator Muskie from sweeping the early primaries, locking up the convention in April and uniting the Democratic party behind him for the fall, has been achieved. The likelihood—great three months ago—that the Democratic Convention could become a dignified coronation ceremony for a centrist candidate who could lead a united party into the election—is now remote." Watergate buffs insisted this proved that Nixon had stolen the 1972 election.

In his opening statement, Buchanan went on the offensive. He accused the leakers of a "covert campaign of vilification" against him, and claimed he had never recommended "that the reelection committee infiltrate the campaigns of our opposition." And that he had known nothing of "any ongoing campaign of political sabotage."

"The election of 1972 was not stolen!" he concluded. It had been won on "the quality and character of our candidate."

Then he spent the next hours boasting of how the Nixon team had infiltrated the campaigns of the opposition and carried out an ongoing campaign of political sabotage. It was an extraordinary performance.

He proudly admitted to arranging fake demonstrations against Democratic candidates; setting up fake Democratic campaign committees; drumming up fake enthusiasm for the black female candidate Shirley Chisholm; sending insulting letters to Democratic candidates, ostensibly from other Democratic candidates; personally writing ads ostensibly written by independent groups; planting letters to editors ostensibly written by private citizens. ("When will you people realize that he was elected President and he is entitled to the respect of that office no matter what you people think of him?" read one.) Then he would ask what all the fuss was about: "I've ghosted speeches for Presidents, for Vice Presidents, senators, Republican chairman. I have ghosted letters to editors. . . . What is illicit about ghosting an ad in which individuals are going to put their names on them?"

Documents pointed to a note from Colson to Haldeman to organize a White House public relations campaign attacking CBS; one from Magruder to "get independent station owners to write NBC saying they should remove [anchorman Chet] Huntley now"; others on how to create "an inhibiting effect on the networks" by exploiting "their professed concern with achieving balance"—for instance by having the Republican National Committee chair charge "that there is a political conspiracy in the media to attack this Administration. . . . Utilize the antitrust division to investigate various media. . . . Utilize the Internal Revenue Service . . . Just the threat of an IRS investigation will turn their approach." All the sorts of things Buchanan was defending as normal politics—somehow simultaneously with a smile and a sneer, even admitting to turning down the assignment to run the Plumbers, not because it was "something that was illicit or unethical or wrong," but because he thought it was bad strategy.

The gobsmacked committee began the grilling. "Turn to tab 16 of your July 28, 1971, memo," Sam Dash asked.

"Yes, sir."

"Turn to page five."

Dash read: "We would like to utilize Ron Walker's resources where possible to handle some close-in operations, pickets and the like, and candidate visits to various cities." He asked Buchanan what that meant. The speechwriter with the slicked-back hair answered, "If you have at the airport a group of individuals with a sign that they throw up at the right moment, 'This is Nixon country,' for example, you are liable to get an Associated Press photograph with Senator Muskie with the sign, which is, we feel, advantageous."

Dash came back: "This would be to give the appearance of a demonstration against the candidate."

Which was where the witness was supposed to get defensive. That was what every other witness had done. Instead, Buchanan took it as an opportunity to boast some more, musing that "if Senator Muskie were having difficulty with some particular questions, something like that, you could draft the questions and get the local Republicans there to put them on the press bus, or to hand out their fliers at the Muskie rally, put them on the seats of chairs."

Dash followed up by reading a memo in which Buchanan recommended joining a club for top-dollar Democratic donors: "This would give us many advantages in keeping track of Democratic contenders and their strategy."

Dash didn't even have time to ask a question.

"Yes, sir, that idea is taken out of Larry O'Brien's campaign book that it is a good thing for Democrats to get on the mailing list for all Republican materials they find." Spying on the opposing camp was "a common thing done in American campaigns."

Young Pat Buchanan could turn the proposition that two wrongs made a right—especially if the second wrong was triple the size of the first—into a sublime sort of political poetry. The *New York Times* quoted a White House insider who said it was "the only day of hearings I've really enjoyed." The Nixon-friendly newspaper *Sun* of Durham, North Carolina, hosannaed "A NEW KIND OF WATERGATE WITNESS": "Billed as an expert on 'dirty tricks,' Mr. Buchanan played the dirtiest trick of them all on the committee members by taking the wind out of their inquisitorial sails and making them and their counsel look like a bunch of confused nitpickers."

The committee's caucus of suspicion did tear into Buchanan's recommendations for defeating the influence of liberal tax-exempt foundations like the Ford Foundation, which was promoting allegedly nefarious activities like registering voters in Negro areas. The foundations, Buchanan returned, affected to be serving some neutral public good but were actually "quasi-political operations"—which was why he promoted right-wing quasi-political foundations to take them on. He called the left-wing think tank the Institute for Policy Studies an "arm" of Ford, and claimed it funded one of the most scabrous underground newspapers, the *Quicksilver Times,* in its plans to disrupt the 1972 Republican convention. The *New York Times,* in an editorial called

"Anatomy of a Smear," pointed out that the Institute for Policy Studies had never given a penny to the *Quicksilver Times*.

But by the time Buchanan said that, the mood of the proceedings had shifted: he charmed the panel to his side, and most of the panelists ended up praising him as the best witness they had called. Senator Weicker even, meekly, thanked him. The *Times* was amazed to find the senators "too enthralled by Mr. Buchanan's joviality to question his arrogant insistence that even the most outrageous election abuses perpetrated by the President's surrogates were nothing more than politics as usual."

But then again, maybe the *Times* was guilty of the same thing. The next week it gave him space to respond, in an op-ed titled "Anatomy of a Lynching Syndrome." And in fact, within media circles, the brazen way Buchanan played the game had been enjoyed as a guilty pleasure. Columnist Jules Witcover, for instance, penned a fulsome profile dubbing him a "man of spirit." We were now "in a kind of movie-set society," a correspondent from the suspicious circles wrote the *Times* about the embrace of Buchanan. "In considering the damage Watergate has done to so many of our accepted values, perhaps the one that has been most dangerously undermined is face value—that reality is what we perceive it to be." Maybe this young man had a future.

CHAPTER NINE

The Year Without Christmas Lights

ON SEPTEMBER 11, 1973, THE EVENING NEWS REMINDED AMERICANS THAT their country was still so much saner and safer than most of the rest of the world. In the South American nation of Chile, warplanes began strafing radio stations and newspapers. Images arrived of people scattering in fear ahead of tanks in the streets. Fearsome generals in coats with starred epaulets ordered President Salvador Allende, the world's only elected Marxist leader, to step down. A military communiqué: "The armed forces and the body of carabineros are united in their historic and responsible mission of fighting to liberate Chile from the Marxist yoke. Signed, General Augusto Pinochet Ugarte, Commander-in-Chief of the Army."

Pinochet's coup came the day before a planned national referendum scheduled by Allende, a man as fastidiously obsessed with his nation's constitution as Sam Ervin was about his, to ratify or reject his government. But the military chose not to chance democracy. Instead they rounded up thousands and deposited them in the national stadium, some marked for execution. In the streets of Santiago, loudspeakers barked out commands: "All people resisting the new government will pay the price." For at least seventy-five people, in the first three weeks, the price was execution by Pinochet's Caravana de la Muerte—the "Caravan of Death." One bullet-riddled body, belonging to the popular, pacifist singer Víctor Jara, was found dumped in a Santiago backstreet, his hands broken and his wrists cracked.

The ousted president, refusing to yield, made his way to the parliament for one last speech. Then he fell back to the presidential palace, now strafed by planes and pummeled by tanks, forty civil servants still pinned inside. The majestic building nearly burned to the ground. "Oh, baby!" a CBS Radio correspondent intoned on the air with an intake of breath as machine-gun volleys sounded. "We're in the wrong place. . . . We are pinned down on a corner . . . looking at a policeman with an automatic rifle. . . . What the hell am I doing *here*?"

And then, three weeks later, the evening news had once more re-minded Americans of how terrifying the world so blessedly far beyond our borders could be. With canny savagery, Egypt and Syria launched a simultaneous attack on Israel at the one time the entire nation shut down: Yom Kippur, the holiest day on the Jewish calendar. Eight hun-dred tanks of Soviet manufacture rolled over the Suez Canal on pontoon bridges. Seventy thousand troops, some paddling rubber boats, attacked in wave after wave. High-tech Soviet surface-to-air missiles crushed the supposedly unbeatable Israeli air defenses, which in 1967 had wiped out the Egyptian Air Force before they could leave the ground in only two hours, leaving ground troops naked and exposed. New missiles, manned by highly trained infantry, not the hapless amateurs Israel had faced in the 1956 and 1967 wars, began crushing the Israeli tank corps, also sup-posedly undefeatable. Israel's defense minister declared it "the start of all-out war again"—the fourth in the land of Abraham, Isaac, and Jacob since the modern state of Israel was declared twenty-five years earlier. Sheikh Amid Fahan, Egypt's highest religious authority, declared it a "jihad"—a holy war—and called on every Muslim to join the battle against "the enemies of Allah." Iraq and Tunisia immediately promised to do so. Egypt's foreign minister said there could be no peace while Is-rael occupied Palestinian lands; Israel's foreign minister said occupation would continue until there was peace.

BACK HOME, A UFO SCARE WAS AFOOT: TWO MEN FROM PASCAGOULA, MIS-sissippi, reported a cigar-shaped vessel with flashing blue lights pulled them up in its tractor beam; there claw-handed beasts paralyzed them and performed a medical examination. Within weeks Gallup reported 51 percent of Americans thought extraterrestrial visitations were real. Fifteen million said they'd seen one themselves. The Pascagoula witness showed up on *The Dick Cavett Show*.

It was around this time that *Time* put drug mystic Carlos Castaneda on the cover, and three books battled it out on the paperback bestseller list: *The Gods from Outer Space* and *Chariots of the Gods,* both by Erich von Däniken, which proposed "ancient aliens" had built monu-ments like the Pyramids, Stonehenge, and the sculptures on Easter Is-land; and *Bermuda Triangle*, which wondered whether the lost city of Atlantis was responsible for the supposedly mysterious disappearances there. You could learn about such theories at an exhibit in Montreal, at the municipal fairgrounds that once hosted Expo '67—or at the down-town branch of State Savings Mutual Bank on Wilshire Boulevard in Los Angeles, where before opening an account you could "talk to experts on ESP, hypnosis, bio-feedback, shape energy, plant sensitivity, and acupuncture, hosted by Leah Caverhill of the National Academy of Applied Awareness," the "lady who predicted the Watergate scandal a year before it happened. Enter a room-size energy pyramid for an actual demonstration." Learn "extraordinary facts about UFO's, astrology, numerology, graphology, palmistry, tarot, and the comet Kohoutek. . . . Come with an open mind." It was advertised alongside the bank's seminars on tax law.

In that same city, a neuropsychologist named Thelma Moss claimed that a technique known as "Kirlian photography," which captured the electrical coronal discharges around objects, could reflect the physical and emotional states of living subjects, perhaps to diagnose illnesses. Perhaps that sounded absurd. But if it were all merely hokum, why would UCLA have let Dr. Moss open a laboratory that studied extra-sensory perception, poltergeists, and telepathy under the auspices of the great university's Neuropsychiatric Institute, and why would the journal *Behavioral Neuropsychiatry* (vol. 6, nos. 1–12, pp. 71–80) have published a paper of which she was a coauthor: "A Laboratory Investigation of Telepathy: The Study of a Psychic"?

On *The Tonight Show,* an Israeli "paranormalist" named Uri Geller tried and failed to demonstrate his signature claim—that he could bend metal spoons with his mind—but then, as he explained to host Johnny Carson, he had simply not felt "strong" that particular night; and after all in the prestigious British scientific journal *Nature,* two physicists claimed results affirming that Geller may indeed "have the ability to receive and send information in a way other than by the known normal senses." The editors did acknowledge that several referees found the experiment "weak in design and presentation"—but then again, might not those reviewers be entrapped within the same sort of limited "linear" paradigms of thinking it was the work of savants like Geller and Moss to transcend? Once upon a time "the occult" had been the redoubt of rubes. Now, in a world where the usual sources of authority no longer had answers for anything, the weird stuff was getting more serious consideration.

A cheap paperback soon came to market. *Predictions for 1974* starred a panoply of psychics with names like "Countess Amy" and "Aquarius." It featured, alongside news-to-come about traffic accidents ("A submarine and a UFO will collide off the Aleutian Islands"), the occult ("reincarnation will be espoused by more and more young people as a valid explanation for the dislocations in modern society"), celebrities ("Dean Martin may have a health problem and definitely should be careful of his nose"), and celebrities and the occult ("A youthful female actress of sudden fame will publicly announce that she used witchcraft to obtain her current level of success and happiness"), prediction after prediction about how the world would collapse. That was what the future looked like now. Deaths from record bitter cold. Deaths from a "nerve gas leak" off the coast of Florida. A 1929-style stock market collapse. A declaration of bankruptcy by New York City—"the first tangible sign of the collapse of our entire civilization." Single people banned from buying big cars. Locusts and floods, "like the plagues of Egypt," worldwide droughts, rising sea levels "inundating all coastal areas throughout the world." Rationing of every staple, urban blackouts, riots, martial law. "Disaster will hit one of New York's skyscraper landmark buildings." "Man is an endangered species," as one soothsayer put it—and he wasn't even the most morose of the lot.

A map of the dreads of a nation—just when, as the autumn leaves began to fall, America's imagined safe distance from the chaos abroad crumbled, and the sort of things that seemed once to happen only in banana republics visited us here at home.

OCTOBER WAS RUNG IN WITH BIBLICAL PROPHECIES FROM AN ASSISTANT secretary of the interior. "With anything less than the best of luck," Stephen Wakefield announced, "we shall probably face shortages of heating oil, propane, and diesel fuel this winter. . . . I am talking about men without jobs, homes without heat, children without schools."

In Los Angeles the Department of Water and Power predicted a 35 percent energy shortage by April. This forecast came the day after the president's Cost of Living Council set a new ceiling on the price of domestic crude; the major oil companies responded by raising the prices they charged their affiliate service stations by about a penny a gallon. In San Francisco three thousand service stations shut down for three days in protest: street corners become ghost towns in the beautiful City by the Bay.

Warnings that such things might soon come to pass had been frequent that summer. They were ignored. No one trusted government warnings. No one trusted much of anything. On October 2, a committee choosing an Episcopalian bishop used slips of paper rather than voting aloud: "With Watergate," a bishop explained, "our committee was so concerned that our meeting place might be bugged that we never mentioned any of the candidates' names."

That same week Vice President Spiro Agnew spoke before the annual conclave of the National Federation of Republican Women in Los

Angeles. He proclaimed his innocence, promising, "I will not resign if indicted."

Two weeks later, on October 10, he resigned, after being indicted.

He had pleaded nolo contendere—"the full equivalent to a guilty plea," the judge explained—to a single reduced charge of income tax evasion. He received a three-year suspended sentence and a ten-thousand-dollar fine, less than what the prosecution said he owed the IRS in taxes for his graft, and less than what he had taken in an envelope from a single Maryland building contractor. Pursuant to his deal with prosecutors, he resigned effective immediately. Then he gave a speech blaming his fall on the "new post-Watergate morality"—referring to the sins of the prosecutors, not his own.

There followed the usual liberal protestations that this was just to be expected from the "law-and-order" hustlers in Richard Nixon's employ, and the usual right-wing ones that since Agnew was a conservative the Establishment hated, he had to have been framed. More interesting, however, was a new note: scales falling from eyes. In Palm Springs, where Agnew golfed with Sinatra, a wealthy resident explained how Agnew had "commanded our respect and trust as no one in government has for so many years." With "the Watergate incident, we would not believe the news media and closed our eyes to the truth." Now, however, he realized "it would be catastrophic if all the politicians in Washington were thoroughly investigated. For, we may not have a government."

Agnew's plea deal opened the floodgates of a corrosive cynicism. The president had refused to entertain the idea of amnesty for draft resisters; but Agnew had been afforded amnesty all but automatically. So Gordon Strachan, the young Haldeman aide who earned laughs for warning young idealists away from Washington, had been proved wrong; as one *Los Angeles Times* letter writer put it: young people *should* go into public service. Then they would have "the privilege of committing felonies." An inmate wrote from Los Angeles County Jail: "My horrendous crime of plain drunk has drawn me 120 days"; if only his crime was political he'd be free to walk the streets. Another wrote that the sixty days he got for breaking a window during a strike was "a clear reminder that, as Thrasymachus says in Plato's *Republic,* justice is whatever those in power say it is, and whatever is to their advantage." Someone nominated the "Theme from *Shaft*" as the new national anthem.

On October 14 the *New York Times* reported a poll demonstrating a 12 percentage point increase in public cynicism regarding government. Two professors reported on their annual canvass of graduate students entering the University of Michigan's Institute for Public Policy Studies.

A year earlier, 12 percent had agreed that "often those who enter politics think more about their own welfare or that of their party than about the welfare of the citizens." This year the figure had jumped to 94 percent.

Children were cynical, too: whereas kids used to collect images of sports heroes they now hoarded "Wacky Packages," a twelve-year-old middle finger collectively extended at consumer capitalism. The product had bombed when the Topps Chewing Gum company tried it out in 1967. Now, though, the time was ripe. "Cap'n Crunch" became "Cap'n Crud." "Ultra Bright" was "Ultra Blight." "Post Alphabits" became "Pest Awful Bits" ("FREE 24 Vol. Set Encyclopedia Britannica in Every Box!"). "Rice A Phony." "Blunder Bread." They were subversive in form, too, not just content: not cards, but stickers—the adolescent equivalent of subway graffiti. A fifth-grade teacher told *New York* magazine it had taken half a day to pry them off desks at the end of the school year.

New York also noted the increasingly political turn of *Mad* magazine—2.4 million copies sold a month, and no ads or branded merchandising: kids' one redoubt of purity in a cruddy, overcommercialized world. In one recent gag, the "Corporate Ecologist of the Year" explained how his company was spending million of dollars responding to pollution: "on advertising—to clean up the corporate image." "Starchie Bunker" got a visit from an "old World War II buddy," Adolf Hitler, then CBS gave Hitler a spin-off sitcom. *New York*'s distinguished political correspondent Richard Reeves wrote that *Mad* was turning his son into a smart-ass. It did him proud: "The kid can spot the sham piling up all around him." Another parent told Reeves, "I think it made her secure in being skeptical. . . . It's really a shortcut to a kind of sanity-preserving sophistication." *Mad*'s publisher chimed in: "We all need some cynicism." Reeves asked a seven-year-old what Wacky Packages' appeal was. He said, "I think they're bringing out the truth."

The brat named the spirit of the age. Everything was fraudulent. America making the world safe for democracy? CBS Radio now reported from Chile on suspicions that the United States had instigated the coup there. The anchor clarified: "Actually, no evidence has yet been uncovered that Washington had any direct responsibility for the events in Santiago"—though such was the national atmosphere of suspicion that they reported on the rumor anyway.

JUST TWO DAYS AFTER AGNEW'S RESIGNATION THE WHITE HOUSE HONored the new Twenty-fifth Amendment of Sam Ervin's favorite document, which sharpened the rules for presidential succession, and nominated a new vice president: Gerald Ford, the House minority leader. Nixon called it "a new beginning for America." The *Washington Post*'s cartoonist found the choice so unlikely he depicted the new veep as a stunned game show winner—"wait, that's not all—a complete set of Secret Service Men, plus three years, expenses paid in the second highest office in the land!" The *Chicago Daily News*' Mike Royko said it was like something out of a Woody Allen script—So you want to become vice president?

"First, find safe district and keep getting elected."

"Don't die, so you can pile up a lot of seniority."

"Stay in the mainstream of your party, even when it does something dumb."

And finally: "Don't make enemies."

Conservatives had wanted Reagan, and he seemed like a contender. But Reagan *had* made enemies. Nixon needed someone anodyne, who could quickly get confirmed by Congress, and Ford was a man of Congress—thirteen terms representing little Grand Rapids, Michigan, since his first election in 1948, which had also been his last competitive election. Apparently *because* he was mediocre, Ford was the one—the proverbial heartbeat away.

Or maybe an impeachment away. It had long been a Washington joke: the oafish Spiro Agnew was Nixon's "impeachment insurance." Nixon had joked about it himself in the Oval Office: "What the hell, you know. People say impeach the President. Well, then they get Agnew!" Now the insurance policy had expired. William Rusher, publisher of *National Review* and not a bad political operative himself, wrote, "We've demonstrated we can replace a Vice President, so I expect we could replace a President." Nixon named Ford on the same day the U.S. Court of Appeals for the District of Columbia Circuit ruled that the president "is not above the law's command" and would have to turn over the seven tapes Judge Sirica had asked for, unless he appealed to the Supreme Court, which the judge gave the president until October 19 to do.

The only question then was what he would do if the Supreme Court ruled against him. Which was an ominous question indeed. J. Anthony Lukas of the *New York Times* called it a potential "constitutional apocalypse."

On August 7 Sirica had demanded from the president's representatives an explanation as to why they refused to follow a court order. Nixon's lawyer Charles Alan Wright responded with a crystalline argument wrapped in the highest possible principle: the demand to X-ray the innards of Oval Office deliberation was "a serious threat to the nature of the presidency as it was created by the Constitution, as it has been sustained for 184 years, and as it exists today," and would alter "the total structure of the government." In an oral argument he raised the specter of judicial anarchy: there were more than four hundred federal district judges in the United States, each with a lifetime appointment. Could America maintain a democracy once each and every one of them was allowed to compel presidents to cough up private papers?

Then there was the problem of precedent: no president, and no department of the government, had ever been held in contempt by either the courts or Congress for "refusing to produce information" that "the President has determined must be withheld in the public interest"—and the public interest, the president had determined, would be eviscerated unless every future president could "expect candid and frank advice from his underlings." Thus the president was acting, Wright argued, to faithfully execute the laws—"ultimately to protect the right of the American people to informed and vigorous advice for their President."

Cue "The Star-Spangled Banner."

Then cue ominous clouds. Wright ended with a passively aggressive hint: "Whether a decision adverse to the President could be enforced is a question."

On August 29, Judge Sirica handed down his first decision regarding the tapes, establishing what he thought was a middle ground—the president could turn them over for Sirica's inspection; Sirica would vet them for privacy and national security concerns. He added a riposte to Wright's menacing threat: "That the court has not the physical power to enforce its order to the President is immaterial to a resolution of the issue." Then came an ominous rumble from San Clemente: the president was considering an appeal—but was also looking into "how otherwise to sustain" his legal position. At a September 5 press conference, asked what that meant, Nixon invoked President Lincoln—who "indicated several times during his Presidency that he would move in the national interest in a way that many thought was perhaps in violation of the law." Then Nixon insisted it would not be appropriate to explain further what he meant, "until we go through the appellate procedure."

That procedure was now almost completed. There was only the Supreme Court to go. And if the president defied the highest court in the land, Ted Kennedy said on the floor of the Senate, "It would be Chile, really, without the bloodshed." Pinochet, after all, knew enough to claim he was defending *his* nation's constitution, too.

But everyone knew that could not happen here.

• • •

ON OCTOBER 14, AMERICANS LEARNED THAT THE MIDDLE EAST WAR WAS
not so far away after all: an American airlift was on its way to Israel,
which exceeded in a couple of weeks the amount of supplies ferried to
Berlin in 1948 over eleven months.

The decision had been made five days earlier. The State Department
presumed Israel would regain its footing and quickly battle its way back
to the status quo ante, and a peace process could begin. Instead, Israeli
diplomats passed word to Henry Kissinger that Israel continued to suffer "staggering and totally unexpected" reverses—forty-nine downed
warplanes, five hundred disabled tanks. The Soviet Union was resupply-
ing Egypt and Syria by air. Prime Minister Golda Meir sent an emissary
to the White House, who warned the president that if the other Arab
nations smelled Israel's panic they would unite militarily to end the Jewish state once and for all. The decision: load American cargo planes to
the gills with the most modern tanks and planes in America's arsenal—
along with, Kissinger promised Israel's ambassador, "assurances that
you will have replacements."

Ronald Reagan helped make the decision. The California governor
received regular security briefings from Kissinger; the White House, it
turned out, was a little obsessed with Reagan. On one level it thought
him a clown: A gossip item in June about John Ehrlichman's empty
family home, up for sale Great Falls, Virginia (one house hunter caused
consternation when he picked up the phone line that still led directly to
1600 Pennsylvania Avenue), revealed a poster of Reagan in a cowboy
outfit in the house's rec room, covered over with a "Nixon's the One"
sign. And in that 1971 Oval Office conversation about Reagan, Nixon
worried, "With a Reagan in here, you could damn well almost get yourself in a nuclear war." Kissinger agreed: "He has no judgment." Be that
as it may, Kissinger still solicited him for advice on the extraordinarily
delicate matter of how to frame an Israeli resupply operation that if
handled incorrectly could lead to a military confrontation with the Soviet Union. Reagan suggested: "Why don't you say you will replace all
the aircraft the Arabs claim they have shot down?"

That was brilliant. Since the Arabs were wildly exaggerating their
success, presenting them with a Hobson's choice—saying nothing or
facing international humiliation—was perfect. Reagan's interpersonal
intelligence was something to behold. Which was why the White House
was obsessed with him in the first place. Kissinger found himself wishing he had Reagan on his State Department staff.

There was another motivation for America doing what it could to help Israel win: petroleum. Nixon and Kissinger hoped the Arabs would realize that the only way to obtain their strategic objectives was by cooperating with the United States. But the petroleum industry interpreted the situation in the opposite way. Aramco, the consortium of international petroleum companies operating in the Middle East, had written to the president on October 12 warning that the resupply would provoke a cutback from Saudi Arabia. So did the British ambassador to the United States, who asked Henry Kissinger, "What will be your posture when the Arabs start screaming 'oil' at you?"

"Defiance," the secretary of state replied.

Defiance, however, soon backfired, in the most terrifying way.

Nixon had never taken seriously the idea that Arab states could or would use oil as a weapon. In fact, Nixon had never taken the oil problem seriously at all. "Concentrate on the big game," he said to his treasury secretary, George Shultz, when warned about the geopolitical consequences of possible shortages the previous March; he called such worries "escapist." West German chancellor Willy Brandt warned him two months later of the potential for an oil embargo. Nixon poohpoohed him: There were "too many companies and nations fighting each other" for any embargo to work. Four weeks later it was French president Georges Pompidou's turn to sound the alarm. Nixon told him to stop worrying about irrelevant Third World nations: "The five fingers," he said—"a strong Europe, a strong U.S., Russia, China, and for the future, Japan"—were the world economy's fist. "The rest do not matter." National Security Council and State Department aides warned Kissinger, too. His response was downright hysterical: "Don't talk to me about barrels of oil. They might as well [be] bottles of Coca-Cola. I don't understand!"

Men like these did not see that the world was shifting beneath their feet. The astonishing cheapness of energy, the unacknowledged linchpin of America's extraordinary postwar growth, had been a function of a one-time world glut in production—from 8.7 million barrels a day in 1948 to 42 million in 1972. In a globalizing world America's share of those barrels, once 64 percent, was now 22 percent—even as Europe's postwar demand had increased fifteenfold, Japan's 137-fold. Regulatory bodies like the Texas Railroad Commission deliberately induced scarcity to keep prices up, even as environmental concerns introduced new bottlenecks in supply: a spectacular 1969 oil spill off Santa Barbara scotched offshore drilling; auto emissions standards added about 300,000 barrels a day to U.S. demand; refineries became harder to build; environmentalists stymied a planned pipeline to move oil discovered in Alaska's

Prudhoe Bay. Cities converted their dirty coal-burning power plants to cleaner ones burning oil, further squeezing supply; new synthetic fabrics and petrochemicals compounded the addiction. In just the short window between 1970 and 1973, America's oil imports, once all but nonexistent, doubled. Now 29 percent came from abroad—the lion's share from Middle East nations that mostly despised the United States.

Fifteen years earlier Nikita Khrushchev had called the divided city of Berlin "the testicles of the West," which he need only squeeze to make the United States scream. Now that pressure point was oil. "We are in a position to dictate prices," Saudi Arabia's oil minister, Sheikh Ahmed Zaki Yamani, informed the world in April, "and we are going to be very rich."

They were also, apparently, determined to dictate politics. "America's continued support of Zionism against the Arabs makes it extremely difficult for us to continue to supply the United States with oil," said Saudi Arabia's king. Fortunate that the Middle East producers seemed such a sad-sack sort of crew. Yes, the Arabs had their oil cartel, the Organization of Petroleum Exporting Countries, or OPEC. Together its eleven members produced more than 80 percent of the world's exported oil. They had tried to coordinate a boycott during the 1967 war. It failed miserably—for all it took to disintegrate any boycott was for one nation to seize a quick financial windfall as the region's only supplier of oil. The president was asked at his September 5 press conference about "threats from the Arab countries to use oil as a club to force a change in our Middle East policy"—and the pooh-poohing he'd privately given the likes of Shultz and Pompidou now was on the record: "Oil without a market," he said, "as Mr. Mossadegh learned many, many years ago, does not do a country much good." A mafia-style threat: Mohammad Mossadegh had been the left-wing president of Iran. When he'd expropriated British Petroleum's oil fields in 1953, he found himself the victim of a CIA-sponsored coup. And also Economics 101: a state whose economy was based on oil couldn't simply stop selling oil to the world's richest country—unless it wanted to stop having an economy.

He apparently had not noticed what Libya's charismatic, ambitious strongman Colonel Muammar Gadhafi, said when he'd expropriated the holdings of Occidental Petroleum in 1971: "People who have lived without oil for 5,000 years can live without it again for a few years in order to attain their legitimate rights." And what with the new War Powers Act, and America's anxiety about getting into "another Vietnam," American saber rattling did not resound like it used to.

In the Sinai Desert, on October 14 and 15, Israel's American tanks bulled past Egypt's Soviet ones, ferried across the Suez Canal to crush the surface-to-air missile batteries. On October 16, the first Israeli troops poured into Egyptian territory, President Anwar Sadat asked the Soviet Union to convene the United Nations to seek a cease-fire—and the Arab states in OPEC declared themselves the world economy's new fist, unilaterally raising their price for crude oil from $3.00 to $5.11 per barrel. The next day they announced they would sell no oil to the United States, and that until Israel withdrew from occupied Palestinian territories, they would reduce production altogether by 5 percent a month.

Nixon, unimpressed, asked Congress for $2.2 billion to pay for continued resupply of Israel. On Saturday, October 20, the fighting entered its fifteenth day and a CBS reporter asked Secretary of Defense James Schlesinger about the soldiers being sent to Israeli airports to help unload American matériel: "Could this become another Vietnam? . . . Mr. Secretary, isn't there a danger, in sending these dozens of American military personnel to Israel, that they for some reason might be captured and then it would be necessary to send more U.S. personnel to rescue them?"

Then the confrontation back home took an astonishing turn.

ARCHIBALD COX WAS EVERYTHING RICHARD NIXON HATED: A KNOW-it-all Kennedy-loving Harvard professor. At every opportunity in the tapes case, with moralistic hauteur, Cox described the president's obduracy as just the sort of thing one would expect from a crook with a guilty conscience. His argument was that the tapes should simply be turned over to himself and the grand jury, with no intervening review by any judge; his briefs dismissed "executive privilege" concerns as irrelevant "where there is reason to believe that the deliberations may have involved criminal conduct." He also kneecapped the argument that the president was protecting the effectiveness of future presidents; Cox pointed out that "the interest in free discussion by government officials cannot outweigh the interest in the integrity of the government itself." Indeed he eviscerated any notion that principle had anything to do with the president's arguments at all. Nixon claimed that what would collapse all future expectations of Oval Office privacy was the very act of anyone, ever, at any time listening to these conversations. But, noted Cox, hadn't Bob Haldeman, in his opening statement to the Ervin Committee, revealed that the president had loaned him tapes of Oval Office conversations? Haldeman had told the committee, claiming the tape recorder as his silent witness, that it was true that the president told Dean they could raise a million dollars to pay off the burglars—and that the president had added, "but that would be wrong." (TAPES CLEAR NIXON—HALDEMAN, the headlines had read.) Pointed out Cox: "Not even a President can be allowed to select some accounts of a conversation for public disclosure and then to frustrate further grand jury inquires [*sic*] by withholding the best evidence of what actually took place." The point was both devastating and humiliating.

After making that argument, Cox left Judge Sirica's chambers wondering why Nixon, if he wasn't involved, wouldn't just turn over the tapes to prove himself innocent. Publicly, he said, "There is no reason to believe that respondent"—that is, Richard Nixon—"would disregard a final binding order fixing legal responsibility." Even *Richard Nixon* would never summon men at arms to assert his authority over another branch of the government. That would be dictatorship. That would be unimaginable.

On the morning of Saturday, October 20, John Dean's appearance in Sirica's courtroom to plead guilty to one count of conspiracy to obstruct justice and of defrauding the United States was knocked off the front page by news that the president would be skipping his appointed showdown with the Supreme Court. In a late-night secret Oval Office meeting, said the news, Howard Baker and Sam Ervin had arrived at a compromise: instead of Judge Sirica getting to listen to tapes he would read a summary prepared by the president. "The authenticity of this summary," the president explained in a public statement, "would be assured by giving unlimited access to the tapes to a very distinguished man, highly respected by all elements in American life for his integrity, his fairness, and his patriotism, so that the man could satisfy himself that the statement prepared by me did indeed include fairly and accurately anything on the tapes that might be regarded as related to Watergate."

That "very distinguished man," Senator John Stennis of Mississippi, whom Nixon kept referring to as "Judge" Stennis, was nearly deaf and seventy-two years old. He had supported the president down the line on just about all his controversial decisions, and knew next to nothing about Watergate developments because he had spent most of summer recuperating from a mugging on a street outside the Capitol early in the year—a detail that granted the president the added maudlin advantage of sympathy: nobody in the polite little village that was Washington, D.C., would dare challenge a damned thing Stennis said.

In a statement published in the Saturday morning papers, written in the rueful tones of a man determined to protect the rights of a poor, pitiable, helpless victim from her traducer, Nixon explained, "The attorney general made what he regarded as a reasonable proposal for compromise

and one that goes beyond what any president in history has offered."
He said Archibald Cox had had it within his power to end this excruciating constitutional crisis all on his own, because if only he had accepted
this magnanimous offer "there would be no further attempt by the special prosecutor to subpoena still more tapes or other presidential papers
of a similar nature." But Cox, villainously, had refused. "Though I have
not wished to intrude upon the independence of the special prosecutor, I have felt it necessary to direct him, as an employe of the executive
branch, to make no further attempts by judicial process to obtain tapes,
notes, or memoranda of presidential conversations."

An "employe of the executive branch." What did that mean? Was it
a threat?

Yes, it was. The president had presumed that the backstopping of
Ervin and Baker would be enough to rid him of this meddlesome priest,
and this irksome tapes business, once and for all. Instead, on the evening
of Saturday, October 20, he had to order a massacre.

THE GRAY-HAIRED HARVARD PROFESSOR IN THE BUNCHED SUIT STEPPED
up to the press conference microphones. Networks broke into the
soap operas. This show was more melodramatic anyway. Arms folded,
Archibald Cox said that to comply with the president's orders "would
violate my solemn pledge to the Senate and the country." He then
explained that the president, in "refusing to comply with the court
decrees," was selling the nation a bill of goods: that a summary of tape
contents would probably not even be admissible in court—which may
have been Nixon's point in insisting on summaries. He promised to
continue court efforts to obtain the tapes themselves, and said that if
the president refused to comply with his orders, he would find him in
contempt of court.

In Syria, Israeli forces reached within ten miles of Damascus. In
Oslo, the announcement was made that Henry Kissinger (but not Richard Nixon) would share the Nobel Peace Price with his North Vietnamese negotiating partner, Le Duc Tho. And in Washington, Chief of
Staff Alexander Haig relayed to Attorney General Elliot Richardson a
direct order from the President of the United States. On D-day in 1944,
Richardson had been a twenty-three-year-old platoon leader who pulled
to safety a fellow officer shot in a minefield. He later recalled that the
decision he now faced felt equally stressful. He had been ordered by
the president to fire Archibald Cox. He decided to refuse it, and resign
instead.

Alexander Haig, who everyone remembered had shown up in his

general's uniform on his first day as chief of staff, like he was Pinochet or something, telephoned Deputy Attorney General William Ruckelshaus, now acting attorney general, with the same demand: "This is an order from your Commander-in-Chief." Ruckelshaus refused and resigned, too.

The acting attorney general was now a man named Robert Bork, who wore a funny little beard and was so far to the right he had opposed outlawing racial segregation. He followed orders. The word went forth: the office of special prosecutor had been abolished as an independent entity. The TV cameras then recorded an unbelievable scene: FBI agents, acting on a White House directive, sealed the prosecutor's office—thousands of pages of evidentiary documents, interview tapes, painstakingly prepared reconstructions of criminal and near-criminal events, the entire bureaucratic infrastructure of the investigation, all the prosecution's evidence for every last Watergate trial from lowly Bud Krogh to mighty John Mitchell: now it was impounded, off-limits to anyone.

Men at arms, summoned by the President of the United States asserting his authority over another coequal branch of the government; the most sensitive and crucial inquiry in the constitutional history of the republic—cut down, perhaps for good. To the suspicious circles it felt as though a fascist takeover was imminent.

NBC's ANCHORMAN: "THE COUNTRY TONIGHT IS IN THE MIDST OF WHAT may be the most serious constitutional crisis in its history." The head of the American Bar Association said Nixon was waging "an intolerable assault upon the courts, our first line of defense against tyranny and arbitrary power." A former ABA head, the prominent Houston lawyer Leon Jaworski, who had been considered friend enough to the president that his name was suggested to head his defense, said the FBI's actions "resembled those of the Gestapo." Senator Robert Byrd of West Virginia said that "this sounds like a Brown Shirt operation thirty years ago." Senator Robert Packwood of Oregon, a Republican, said that "the office of the Presidency does not carry with it a license to destroy justice in America." Edmund Muskie came out for impeachment. And Sam Ervin now revealed the president had deceived him into accepting the Stennis compromise—privately claiming to Ervin that the deal was for verbatim transcripts, then turning around and telling the public it was for summaries.

Archibald Cox, too, rushed out a statement: "Whether we shall continue to be a government of laws and not men is now for Congress and ultimately the American people to decide."

On Sunday, as Israeli forces encircled the Egyptian Third Army and pushed within forty miles of Cairo, and Henry Kissinger flew to Moscow for emergency discussions about the Middle East crisis, Western Union offices in Washington were flooded by more than a million telegrams. Senator James Buckley, William F. Buckley's brother, and three conservative Republican House members announced that 90 percent of their constituents wanted the president fired. HONK FOR IMPEACHMENT, read signs in Lafayette Park; the 1600 block of Pennsylvania Avenue became bedlam as motorists obliged them. "If he didn't hear," an observer said, "he had cotton in his ears." A thirty-four-year-old couple from Baltimore soon ran out of their supply of three thousand impeachment bumper stickers. "We both voted for Nixon because he had a secret plan to end the war," one told the AP. "Now he's got a secret plan to end the Justice Department."

The American Civil Liberties Union took out an ad explaining: "Why it is necessary to impeach President Nixon and how it can be done." Its membership rolls exploded. Ralph Nader announced a grassroots campaign for impeachment. Seventeen law school deans jointly demanded appointment of a new special prosecutor. At the AFL-CIO's annual convention, nine hundred delegates adopted a resolution demanding impeachment or resignation—a humiliation indeed: AFL-CIO chief George Meany had been a key recruit toward Nixon's dream of a post–New Deal "New Majority." The next day Meany released a statement averring, "The events of the last several days prove the dangerous emotional instability of the President," and that he should either resign or be impeached.

Since early in April, when then–attorney general Mitchell defiantly told senators if they wanted White House aides to testify before them, they would have to wait for the House to proceed, as the Constitution stipulated, toward impeachment, the "I" word had been the White House's ultimate tool to shut critics up. The presumption was that any such constitutional apocalypse was unthinkable. No longer. When the House returned to business on Monday, October 22, congressmen introduced forty-four Watergate-related bills. Twenty-two, sponsored by eighty-four separate members, called for impeachment or an investigation of a possible impeachment.

AT LEAST THE INTERNATIONAL CRISIS HAD BEEN STAYED. ON MONDAY, the superpowers jointly agreed to sponsor a United Nations cease-fire to go into effect two days later. On Tuesday Democrats voted for the Judiciary Committee to hold impeachment hearings; the din from Lafayette Park was still seeping through White House windows as Charles Wright and Alexander Haig attempted to assure reporters that tyranny had not befallen the land. But Haig did not help his case when he boasted with a grin that it had been his own idea to send the FBI to seal Cox's office, and that his actions had been entirely appropriate.

Tuesday was the day Judge Sirica set for the White House to answer his order to produce the tapes—a date set at a less dramatic time, but one Sirica still demanded the White House honor. It was also the day, at high noon, that Speaker of the House Carl Albert told a crowded press briefing that he had authorized the House Judiciary Committee to begin work on an impeachment inquiry. Sirica's ceremonial courtroom was jammed. Everyone in Washington wanted to be there to hear Nixon's lawyer turn the next screw, and to see what this courageous judge would do in response. It was as if the Constitution hung on a hinge.

Sirica read aloud his August 29 order to produce the tapes, so nervous that he accidentally read a part of the document twice.

Charles Wright stepped to the well of the courtroom: "Mr. Chief Judge, may it please the court. I am not prepared at this time to file a response. I am, however, authorized to say that the President of the United States would comply in all respects with the order of August 29. . . ."

Since Sirica could not believe what he had just heard, he asked the lawyer to repeat himself.

"He will comply in all respects with what Your Honor had just read. As the court is aware, the President yesterday filed with the clerk of the court a response along different lines, along the lines indicated in the statement to the country Friday. That statement, if it was ever officially filed with the court, is now withdrawn. . . .

"This President does not defy the law, and he has authorized me to say he will comply in full with the orders of the court."

"This President does not defy the law": people used to take that for granted. At least, though, the crisis had been averted. Crises were being averted all over—for a minute, at least.

THE SOVIETS SAID ISRAEL WAS THE FIRST TO BREAK THE CEASE-FIRE, BY preparing a move on Damascus. They issued an ultimatum to the president: stay Israel's hand, even if it takes American military force, or "we should be faced with the necessity urgently to consider taking appropriate steps unilaterally." Maybe that meant arming *all* the Arab states. Or pouring troops into the Middle East. American intelligence learned that seven Soviet airborne divisions—hundreds of thousands of personnel— had been mobilized, aircraft readied in Yugoslavia to move them, and forty thousand amphibian naval infantry prepared to sail the Mediter-ranean toward the battle zone. Nixon called it "the most serious threat to U.S.-Soviet relations since the Cuban Missile Crisis." Compounding the frustration, the United States had been pressing Israel to honor the cease-fire. But in a post-Vietnam strategic context, America had trouble getting even allies to do what it wished.

Alexander Haig, Schlesinger, and the CIA director met late into the night, without bothering to wake the Watergate-addled president. They decided to move the military from DEFCON 4 to DEFCON 3—all troops reporting to barracks for possible mobilization for battle. Soviet officials, who were bluffing, were amazed at the panic. "Who could have imagined the Americans would be so easily frightened," one said. A Johnson administration official told *Time* that the administration had received similar bluster at the end of the 1967 Arab-Israeli war and sim-ply ignored it.

The Middle East war ended to headlines that Union Oil's profits soared 62 percent in the third quarter and Exxon's were up 81 percent, and the conclusion was immediately drawn: DEFCON 3 had all been a Watergate-motivated hoax. KISSINGER: ALERT ISN'T A COVER-UP, read headlines for a press conference in which the exasperated national se-curity advisor said, "We are attempting to conduct the foreign policy of the United States with regard to future generations.... There has to be a minimum of confidence that the senior officials of the American govern-ment are not playing with the lives of the American people."

Around then Gail Sheehy returned to a bar she had visited in sum-mer, now for an October 24 issue of *New York* in which every feature article was about Watergate.

"'I believe in a dictatorship,'" one patron told her.

"'More strongly than you did before?'

"'Much more strongly. This whole thing is a black eye to the country.... I think the President should be above the law, definitely.'"

Three times as many protesters clogged Lafayette Park as when the Saturday Night Massacre went down a week earlier. But they weren't all protesting the president. Some were protesting the protesters. GOD BLESS NIXON, one of the signs read: "We're glad that we have a President who still has nerve. We're glad we have a President who isn't namby-pamby. He should have gotten rid of Cox a long time ago."

Ronald Reagan seemed to agree. The *Los Angeles Times* canvassed prominent California Republicans after the Saturday Night Massacre. The vice chairman of the state party was "appalled"; Houston Flournoy, the likely Republican nominee to replace Reagan as governor, was "dismayed and appalled." Reagan, on the other hand, released the statement: "I will not comment on the issue of Archibald Cox being discharged since it is relatively unimportant." Then, naturally, he commented. The dilemma Nixon faced in Cox's defiance was "the same problem that confronted President Truman during the Korean War." He referred to Truman firing Douglas MacArthur after the general made personal public statements advocating the invasion of China—apparently an offense of equal gravity to rejecting the Stennis compromise. "What is important," he said, "is that the President has agreed to make available the pertinent information contained in the tapes. Now we should have patience until the content of those tapes is known." Then, the next day, when the White House violated the Stennis compromise, Reagan announced he agreed with that, too: it "justifies our continued patience and confidence that our system of government is continuing to work. . . . Yesterday, I urged that all of us should be patient. The President's actions today avoids any appearance of defying the courts."

SOON, THOUGH, THE WHITE HOUSE ACTED IN A WAY THAT MADE ITS DEFI-ance of the courts unmistakable. Meeting with Judge Sirica in chambers to discuss procedures for handing over the subpoenaed tapes, White House Watergate lawyer Fred Buzhardt admitted that two of the tapes, including what was allegedly the very first recorded presidential discussion of the Watergate break-in, and a crucial April 15 meeting in which John Dean told the president he was meeting with Watergate prosecutors, did not exist.

The *Detroit News* had been among Nixon's most stalwart Watergate defenders. Now it editorialized, "Someone in the White House is guilty of either unbelievable stupidity or outright lies." Reporters called House Speaker Carl Albert for his reaction: "I am past the point of reacting," he said with a weary shake of the head. The cartoonist Herblock depicted Richard Nixon as a conjurer holding his magic wand over a puff of smoke marked "disappearing justice officials" and "disappearing tapes." A widely read Wall Street newsletter reported that the New York Stock Exchange had contingency plans in place, quietly announced to top traders, to cease trading immediately for as long as two days immediately upon Nixon's resignation. (Reportedly traders were angry; they expected a big rally when Nixon stepped down.) *Time* magazine published its first editorial in fifty years of publication. It called for Nixon's removal from office.

William F. Buckley Jr. sent around wires to prominent conservatives asking whether the *National Review* should do the same. The most prominent recipient: Ronald Reagan. He sent a two-word reply: "HELL NO."

Time's title legend read, "Nixon's Jury: The People." The jury was not leaning the president's way. The issue sold a record 350,000 copies on the newsstands. The next Gallup poll recorded a historic low in presidential approval ratings: 27 percent. A *Los Angeles Times* letter writer observed, "Please to remember the Fifth of November gunpowder treason and plot. I see no reason why gunpowder treason should ever be forgot."

A genuinely scary Halloween. In New Jersey a weeklong swamp fire threw up smog that produced a sixty-car pileup and nine deaths. In New York the *Times* editorialized on a subway accident in which "miraculously no one died": "According to passengers' testimony, it was nearly an hour before either instructions or help reached this dangerous and frightening scene."

In *Esquire* Tom Wolfe noted the fact that people who hijacked airplanes and took over buildings were becoming cultural heroes to an alienated populace—seen as men "at the end of their ropes" risking it all in a struggle against the "system." The terrorist, as his fan construed it, created "his own society, his own system: in the bank vault, in the Olympic quarters, in the prison courtyard . . . striking out against the endless exfoliations of American power. . . . I finally cut through the red tape. . . . *I am a celebrity!*"

Trick-or-treating was just about too frightening to contemplate. The Copley newspaper chain's advice columnist was asked how to "protect our small 'spooks.'" He replied he could do "five columns on this subject." His best advice: don't let children enter anyone's home; don't let them follow a stranger anywhere; and most of all—don't accept unwrapped items, or eat anything before it's been examined by an adult: "Sadists have been known to insert pins, razor blades, glass and even poison into food for the children." (This actually was just an urban legend.) The AP's advice columnist added "drugs hidden in malted milk balls." After a nine-year-old girl was murdered on Halloween in Fond du Lac, Wisconsin, the *Milwaukee Journal* questioned whether trick-or-treating itself just provided a time and place to make "children easy marks for sick minds."

Parents too scared to let their kids trick-or-treat alone would have missed a Bill Moyers special on PBS that was pretty scary in itself. He argued that the Cold War had drenched the nation in "something of the paranoia Germany had when Hitler came in." Grantland Rice's "it's how you play the game" had transmogrified into Vince Lombardi's "Winning isn't everything, it's the only thing." Watergate, then, was no less about Richard Nixon than it was about *us,* an emanation of our national soul: a nation that now believed "it's us against them, and the only goal is to win, with no quarter asked or given."

Moyers closed the show with a roundtable. One member was a political science professor. The other two were a former Republican official and the Washington editor of *National Review,* a bow-tied young gentleman named George Will. The Republican official was contrite: "We felt only Nixon could save the world." George Will was utterly scathing, granting Nixon no quarter. He blamed Watergate on hysterical Republican partisans insisting "that virtually every possible Democratic candidate was a garish sham who would destroy the country, *but* we couldn't trust the American people to choose that way in a fair fight." The panel suggested the near impossibility of finding any Republican who would defend the administration.

It thus revealed the political isolation of Governor Reagan, still maintaining that "when they calm down a bit," the American people would "take pride" in a system that so efficiently rooted out a few bad apples.

RONALD REAGAN WAS NOT JUST ISOLATED ON WATERGATE. HE WAS ISO-lated on the energy crisis, too. With thousands of San Francisco gas stations shuttered and Los Angeles officials projecting 35 percent energy deficits for 1974, and state demand for electricity increasing 8 percent annually, on October 3 he vetoed a bill to create a five-member commission with power to approve and site new power plants, devise and implement conservation plans (including invoking regulations controlling the sale of electrical devices like toasters and irons, amending building codes, and requiring fluorescent instead of incandescent lighting), and promote research and development of new energy sources— "independent," an aghast *Los Angeles Times* editorial pointed out, "from the kind of special interest influence that has helped retard sound energy policy planning for so many years." He also shocked observers by simultaneously vetoing a bill that he had previously supported to establish air pollution control districts in six California counties.

Democrats predicted "blackouts for years to come." Moretti said Reagan had just killed "the most important and far-reaching piece of legislation of the last ten years." Others pointed out "serious conflicts of interest": hadn't Reagan been a paid propagandist for General Electric? Reagan, with blithe confidence, just said the program hadn't been studied thoroughly enough and contained too many "unacceptable features." (The next month the pilot of his state-leased Cessna 500 announced he had cut the craft's cruising speed 25 knots and began flying higher to reduce air resistance, saving twenty-five to thirty gallons per round-trip between Sacramento and Los Angeles.)

Reagan defied the spirit of the age: Americans believed government could easily and harmlessly tell economies what to do—on meat prices, fuel prices, wages, whatever. Richard Nixon hardly hesitated to oblige them; his program of price controls announced in August 1971 was already in "Phase IV," extending governmental authority to dictate prices into the following spring. Administration skeptics like George Shultz called it intellectually bankrupt: "We have seen baby chicks drowned, pregnant sows, and cows bearing next year's food slaughtered," he told the president, all because of the hubristic refusal to let the free market allocate scarcity. That fell on the deafest of ears—as the president, on the day of Reagan's energy veto, used his discretionary authority to control the allocation of home heating oil and propane gas to dealers nationwide. He was only giving the people what they wanted.

Reagan had a different way of looking at things. He said the public was hoodwinked about the power of government to solve their economic problems by those same devouring Gila-monster bureaucrats he had cast as the enemy in the Proposition 1 fight, now in its home stretch.

Moretti campaigned in the homestretch with an anti–Proposition 1 op-ed that included the following inspiring passage: "The 1973–74 state revenues, as defined by the plan, are divided by 1973 estimated personal income to reach the starting point of 7.6 percent. In 1974–75, 0.1 percent is subtracted from this number (thus, 7.5 percent) which is then multiplied by estimated 1974 personal income. The resulting amount is what the state is permitted to spend in the next fiscal year. When this amount, roughly $9.3 billion, is compared to how much the state will have to spend next year simply to maintain existing programs and services, roughly $9.9 billion, the only option remaining is to cut more than $600 million from existing programs." Snooze. Reagan campaigned by spending four times more than the opposition on snazzy television commercials. The campaign also sent out a fusillade of automated recorded phone messages. The governor, meanwhile, made frantic rounds of the state on what critics pointed out was a jet plane partially paid for with taxpayer funds, as he bellowed forth about the Gila monsters: "When a government becomes powerful, it is destructive, extravagant, and *violent*."

The voters went to the polls, defied Jimmy the Greek, and sided with the Gila monsters—voting down Proposition 1 by 54 percent to 46.

Objectively speaking, it was hard to pry much of a message about the mood of the public from the results. Turnout was anemic. Voters were confused at the initiative's stupefying complexity. Be that as it may, pundits outside the state drew a simple conclusion: as a national political figure, they wouldn't have Ronald Reagan to kick around anymore.

"VOTERS SMARTER THAN REAGAN," editorialized the far-off *Milwaukee Journal.* "The proposition had the surface appeal of the politicians' favorite, but false homily," the *Journal* patiently explained, "that says government should 'live within its income' like everyone else.' Government in fact is not like everyone else, but uniquely different. It alone can, and must be able to, determine the level of its own income, through the taxing power. To equate its financial situation with that of a private household is utter illogic. To say the resources of a sovereign government shall be chained forever after to whatever the tax laws happen to yield at a given moment in the past is dangerous nonsense." A government, they said, was a vehicle for sorting out human priorities. "Reagan's demagogic ploy would have gone at them all backward, by starting with an arbitrary, pre-fixed revenue ceiling regardless of what had to be done and who would get hurt. And it's always the poor who get stuck worst under that kind of tax philosophy." This conventional wisdom did not look to be changing anytime soon.

A victory on Proposition 1 was supposed to propel Reagan on a nationwide tour to sell the concept to other states. Now he had lost—and promised to make the tour anyway. His janissaries promised to fight alongside him. "What if," the governor's director of consumer affairs sincerely asked, "Martin Luther King Jr. had said, 'I have no dream'?" Reagan himself proclaimed, "How can trying to reduce the people's taxes be a defeat?" Everything always works out in the end, gloriously.

THE DAY AFTER THAT CALIFORNIA VOTE, RICHARD NIXON WENT ON TV and announced "a very stark fact: we are heading into the most acute energy shortage since World War II." Americans, he said, would have to cut back: "less heat, less electricity, less gasoline"—almost stop being Americans at all.

There had been no panic up until then. Oil tankers loaded with Middle Eastern crude when the embargo was announced were not about to turn back; any practical decrease in supply would probably take at least six weeks to develop; the amount of oil at stake was only a small fraction of the supply anyway. The president, however, pushed urgency. Maybe he wanted to reassure Americans that they still actually *had* a president. Maybe he wanted to reassure himself.

He called for shorter school and factory hours. And the cancellation of 10 percent of jet flights. The federal government would provide an example by setting thermostats to 68 degrees or less, he said ("and that means in this room, too, as well as in every other room in the White House"); government vehicles would be limited to 50 miles an hour. He told governors to pass 50-mph speed limits in their states, Congress to pass an emergency statute returning to year-round daylight saving time, relaxing environmental regulations, hastening construction of nuclear plants and the Alaska pipeline. Start carpooling, he recommended: "How many times have you gone along the highway," he quizzed, "with only one individual in that car?"

Thousands of times, of course—for wasn't zooming alone across endless vistas of highways supposed to be the most American pastime of all?

Not anymore, apparently. What he was describing, Nixon allowed, sounded "like a way of life we left behind with Glenn Miller and the war of the forties." The president implored his hearers instead to make another comparison: that time, which seemed so long ago, when America first landed a man on the moon:

"Let us unite in committing the resources of this nation to another new endeavor, an endeavor that in this Bicentennial era we can appropriately call 'Project Independence.'

"Let us set as our national goal, in the spirit of Apollo, with the determination of the Manhattan Project, that by the end of this decade we will have developed the potential to meet our own energy needs without depending on any foreign energy sources.

"Let us pledge that by 1980, under Project Independence, we shall be able to meet America's energy needs from America's own energy resources."

Then the president went off script. Jutting out his chin, he said he would like "to close with a personal note." He began with a brag. "We have ended the longest war in America's history. All of our prisoners of war have returned home. We have made progress toward our goal of a real prosperity, a prosperity without war." And yet: "*some* publications have called on me to resign the office of President of the United States."

"I have no intention whatever of walking away from the job I was elected to do. As long as I am physically able, I am going to continue to work 16 to 18 hours a day for the cause of a real peace abroad, and for the cause of prosperity without inflation.... And I am confident that in those months ahead, the American people will come to realize that I have not violated the trust that they placed in me when they elected me as President of the United States in the past, and I pledge to you tonight that I shall always do everything that I can to be worthy of that trust in the future. Thank you and good night."

THE PUBLIC STILL TRUSTED HIM ENOUGH TO BEHAVE AS IF THE ENERGY equivalent of Pearl Harbor had already arrived. Honoring a nonbinding presidential request, gas stations began closing down from 9 P.M. Saturday through midnight on Sundays. So people began "topping off"—filling their tanks every time they passed a gas station, leading to hours-long lines in which idling cars . . . just wasted more gas. Everyone wanted to get to a pump before the last drop was gone and one of the ubiquitous SORRY, NO GAS TODAY signs was hoisted up. Then they would have to return tomorrow—when prices were usually two cents a gallon higher. Tempers flared, no architect having thought to design a corner gas station for the eventuality of dozens of angry motorists cutting fellow motorists off at street corners like drivers in the Indianapolis Motor Speedway.

Time called the energy crisis the "most serious economic threat to face the nation since the Depression." Schools in Massachusetts and Connecticut, states reliant on oil for heat, announced Christmas break for the entire months of December and January. At the New England School of Art, heated only to 65 degrees in the Boston chill, nude models were afforded the comfort of roasting in their own body heat in a clear plastic tent. A farmer in Muncie, Indiana, became famous for a Rube Goldberg contraption to convert manure into methane to power his lights, refrigerator, and Ford pickup; another in Leslie, Michigan, achieved his fifteen minutes of renown by doing the same with leaves, brush, and garbage. Children begged permission not to bathe; didn't heating water waste energy, too?

On the Watergate front, on November 13, Ronald Ziegler announced "Operation Candor": over the next weeks, the president would "fully and publicly" answer all charges. Joseph Kraft, in a column titled "Toward Impeachment," was not impressed: "President Nixon, in fact, is one of the least trustworthy witnesses on his own behalf." *Time* pointed out this was the thirteenth time since the scandal began to unfold that "Richard Nixon vowed to disclose all of the facts and put the story to rest."

The story, lately, was about finances. On November 17 the *Washing-*

ton Post front page trumpeted devastating new findings in the old saga of the "milk money," the hundreds of thousands donated to the Republican Party as early as August 1969 from dairy interests in exchange for price supports for their industry: the Associated Milk Producers' lawyer now revealed the donations came after a conversation with Attorney General John Mitchell about how to buy favor with the administration. Other stories concerned the president's personal finances: about how he had hidden profits from a Florida land sale by registering the deed in the name of his daughter Tricia; about how he claimed California as his voting residence even though he paid no state taxes there; about three previously undisclosed financial trusts benefiting Nixon controlled by Haldeman and Ehrlichman. The evening of the *Post*'s dairy story the president submitted himself on live TV to the questions of the nation's newspaper managing editors, who were meeting at Disney World. Before they could ask him about his financial dealings, he volunteered his own account—one uncannily similar to the first grand slam he hit on live TV: the 1952 "special fund" speech, which had saved his political life under circumstances at least as dire as the ones he faced now. His conclusion gave the water-cooler wags the most memorable catchphrase of the scandal so far.

"I have never profited, never profited from public service—I have earned every cent. And in all of my years of public life, I have never obstructed justice. And I think, too, that I could say that in my years of public life, that I welcome this kind of examination, because people have got to know whether or not their President is a crook. Well, *I am not a crook.*"

The President of the United States was not a crook. That was surely good to know.

The Operation Candor reviews were not kind. *Time* said "the list of . . . the distortions, innuendoes, and false assumptions is astonishing." And that was *before* the story of the Gap.

THE ANNOUNCEMENT CAME FROM FRED BUZHARDT, A WHITE HOUSE LAWyer: his review of the tapes to prepare them for the court subpoena revealed that for eighteen and a half minutes in the middle of a conversation between Nixon and Haldeman from June 20, 1972, all you could hear was a buzz.

A now-private citizen named Archibald Cox explained the import before Judge Sirica's bench: the June 20 meeting had been "the first opportunity for full discussion on how to handle the Watergate incident. The inference that they reported on Watergate and may well have received instructions is almost irresistible." Another inference flowed immediately from the revelation: No claim of Richard Nixon's had been more strenuous than that the tapes were under "my sole personal control." So didn't that make the gap his sole personal responsibility? The prosecution team, now under the direction of a new special prosecutor, Leon Jaworski, got to work investigating whether the president had *personally* destroyed evidence of criminal wrongdoing. Earthquake upon earthquake: this was Watergate now.

The prosecution put forward a female lawyer, Jill Wine Volner, to question the scandal's latest, unlikely, protagonist: Rose Mary Woods, Richard Nixon's personal secretary since 1951. On November 8, Judge Sirica asked her whether it was possible to accidentally erase a tape. She replied, "I don't think I'm so stupid as to erase what's on a tape." Now, under rapid-fire questioning from Volner, she offered a convoluted, contradictory tale of how she had done exactly that—one involving foot pedals, push buttons, an unexpected phone call, and a long bodily stretch. Investigators and news photographs then found themselves assembled in her White House office for a demonstration of the push-button-and-foot-pedal stretch in question. But during the demonstration, she *couldn't* push down the pedal and the button at the same time. She had to have been lying.

Newsweek's next cover: "Rose Mary's Boo Boo." You soon could buy the image on a souvenir silver ingot, comically embossed, "18 Minutes of Hum Along with Dick and Bob 1973," to add to your expanding collection of Watergate kitsch—which also now included an eight-track tape starring eighteen and a half minutes of silence, "Sealed in a 'perfectly clear' plastic case for all to see."

IN RHODE ISLAND, A PRIZE HIGH SCHOOL COMPOSITION WAS CUSTOMAR-ily chosen to be signed by the governor as the official state Thanksgiving proclamation. The governor refused to sign this year's winner, in which a seventeen-year-old wrote, "Thanksgiving seems to be pretended, a farce, little more than an outdated tradition no one has yet found time to discard." *Time*'s Thanksgiving cover had Archie Bunker in his trademark easy chair, stalactites of frost hanging from his cigar and winter cap—he couldn't afford home heating oil. *Newsweek*'s featured a freezing Uncle Sam holding an empty cornucopia and the legend "Running Out of Everything." Jesse Jackson said, "When the energy crisis is exposed as the hoax it is, it will be bigger than Watergate." Adding to the sticky precipitate of national dread was an issue that was supposed to be dead and buried: Vietnam. Governor Reagan, in Singapore as a special presidential representative for a trade deal, said North Vietnam must "return" the POWs and MIAs supposedly still being held, and that if it didn't, "bombing should be resumed." He accused liberals in Congress of taking away "the power to sway those monkeys over there to straighten up and follow through on the deal."

A coffee table book, *They Could Not Trust the King*, with text by William Shannon of the *New York Times* editorial board, went to press. It called Watergate "a complex and far-reaching political plan that could serve as dress rehearsal for an American fascist coup d'etat." In Memphis, Nixon addressed governors for an "Operation Candor" meeting where, one of the governors leaked, he had reassured them that no Watergate bombshells were imminent and that all seven extant subpoenaed tapes were "audible"—even as he knew about the eighteen-and-a-half-minute gap. A court-appointed scientific panel ruled with virtual certainty that the erasure had to have been deliberate.

Senator Jackson opened hearings investigating the energy crisis with an accusation: "For the major oil companies," he said, "the shortages were good business." He said the White House knew the crisis was coming and did nothing, in order to help his friends' bottom lines. Plastic bags, made with petroleum, became prohibitively expensive; petrochemicals were also ingredients in many lifesaving drugs—so pharmaceutical executives projected a shortage. Twenty-five New Hampshire towns suspended police, fire protection, garbage pickups, road repair, and school transportation. The mayor of Rensselaer, Indiana, turned off the city's 425 streetlights, until a rash of burglaries forced him to turn them on again. In an interview he revealed his motives as less than Christian: "If everyone in the country would make this kind of effort, we could tell the Arabs to go to hell."

Unchristian motives were everywhere. A gas station owner stopped letting drivers of big cars buy more than a dollar of gas at a time—"just enough to keep them off the road." People started driving with a full can of gas in the trunk, which turned their cars into inadvertent firebombs. The Senate came within eight votes of passing a law rationing gasoline.

Then December, and the presidentially mandated closing of service stations from Saturday evening until Monday morning. A Hanford, California, gas station owner shot up six of the pumps of a rival who stayed open across the street. A Miami man yelled to a gas station attendant who wouldn't sell to him on a Saturday night, "I am going to get some gas even if I have to kill somebody"—and then, waving a pistol, almost honored his pledge. Auto supply houses ran out of siphons, tools for the new street crime of choice, and locks for gas caps. Amid reports of gas going at some stations for 99.9 cents a gallon, more ambitious crooks started hijacking petroleum trucks. Brooklyn motorists filled up with "Gambinoil"—oil the Gambino crime family stole from industrial oil tanks and sold to area dealers at 70 percent more than legitimate distributors. But who were the real mafiosi? "I hear about organized crime," a citizen wrote to the *Berkshire Eagle* in Massachusetts, "but has anyone tried to find out why these same companies are responsible for organized famine, organized monopolies, organized profiteering? . . . I'm an avid supporter of free enterprise, but what the oil companies are doing isn't free enterprise; it's free back-stabbing aimed at the public." The newspapers reported oil tankers stacked twenty deep at U.S ports waiting—a kind of maritime arbitrage, the suspicious circles imagined, all the better to produce a false shortage, then make a killing once the price became high enough to unload them.

The Senate Subcommittee on Intergovernmental Relations released a poll indicating that 55 percent of Americans felt "alienated and disenchanted," compared with 29 percent in 1966. On the bright side: Gerald Ford replaced Spiro Agnew, and gave a stirring inaugural address. "In exactly eight weeks," he said, "we have demonstrated to the world that our great republic stands solid." In other good news, *Time* magazine pointed out that the gas crisis made it harder for people to abandon their families. And Ronald Reagan told reporters at the Southern Republican Conference in Atlanta that the "average citizen," by his own private initiative, could solve the energy crisis himself "by turning off the lights as he goes through different rooms to go into the den and watch television."

Outside, the protesters held up signs reading, for example, DIG UP THE BODIES IN THE WHITE HOUSE LAWN.

And then it was Christmastime, when darkness literally descended.

THE IDEA HAD BEEN PIONEERED BY NO LESS AN INSTITUTION THAN THE Norman Rockwellian Sears, Roebuck. Already, custodians in Sears's hometown, Chicago, were cleaning offices by flashlight. The public safety committee of the Milwaukee Common Council held an evening meeting by candlelight. New York banned outdoor store lighting after 9:30 P.M. So why not suspend energy-wasting yuletide illumination? It seemed only the patriotic thing to do.

A lead editorial in the *Los Angeles Times* proposed readers voluntarily forgo "decorative fountains, waterfalls, and related décor," "outdoor security lighting during daylight," and "outdoor Christmas decorations. . . . And even a small reduction in the number of lights on indoor Christmas trees would save some of our limited electricity." The city obliged, passing an ordinance surpassing even the restrictions during World War II. Officials said they had no choice—for the Department of Water and Power had contracted for 48 percent of the city's power supply from Arab nations: the sheikhs who stole Christmas. Across the country, the *New York Times* headlined "LOS ANGELES A SHADOW OF ITS USUAL RADIANT SELF."

A letter writer from Whittier, California, proposed a moratorium on energy-wasting Christmas cards. Reno, Nevada, decided to extinguish an "eternal flame" lit with fanfare back in March by a returned Vietnam prisoner of war to honor veterans. Others debated whether the eternal flame that burned at the grave of President Kennedy in Arlington National Cemetery ought to be doused. The 2,200 cubic feet of natural gas it used a month cost $37. "Wouldn't it seem logical," a newspaper letter writer asked, "to use that gas for a better use such as heating homes or office buildings rather than just burning it for no real purpose whatever?" However, another correspondent called that heresy: "In this time of widespread public distrust for many of our political leaders, it is common to hear the statement, 'all politicians are crooks.' But to this I answer, 'But that's not true. I remember John Kennedy.' He was loved and trusted by the nation he led. He set high ideals for that nation to live up to, and he gave it great challenges to face."

That seemed so very long ago. On the cover of *Time*, a flaxen-haired boy who looked as if the bogeyman had just stolen his teddy bear. The accompanying article, "A Child's Christmas in America," began with vignettes:

"In St. Louis, ten-year-olds suit up for karate class. . . . 'Gonna teach 'em not to rip me off,' murmurs a disciple. 'Like *A Clockwork Orange*.'

"In Brooklyn, a boy scarcely old enough to go to school composes a graffito with a spray can against a handball court. The word: NIXON— with the X in the form of a swastika.

"In Anaheim, Calif., a group of preschoolers ponder the wonders of Disneyland. 'I'm going to live here when I grow up,' one of them vows. Why? 'Not a pollution anywhere.'"

Hijackers from the Palestinian group Black September set fire to a Pan Am jetliner in Rome, killed thirty people, then threatened to crash another flight into the center of Athens. The POWs showed up in the news again around Christmastime, in a cavalcade of stories about their high divorce rate. One wife described her husband's homecoming in *McCall's*. He couldn't accept that she had voted for George McGovern.

By the end of March, she wrote, she was "on the verge of tears all the time" and "ready to can the whole thing." John McCain gave an interview in *U.S. News* debunking the emerging narrative of the inevitable breakdown of the POWs' marriages: "Let me emphasize that there were many, many fine women who supported what they knew their husbands believed in. My wife, Carol, was one of those, and I'm very proud of her."

Merle Haggard, the felonious White House guest from March, sang a new hit song: "If We Make It Through December." And on Christmas Eve, OPEC unilaterally raised the price of crude, this time by a factor of four. Gas went up to fifty-five cents a gallon, gas lines up to as long as four hours. Richard Nixon's new "energy czar," William Simon, announced a mandatory emergency fuel allocation program that would provide for 20 percent less gas than currently demanded.

And alone among prominent public officials, Ronald Reagan said such "redundant, unclear, and contradictory rules" were not necessary at all.

Four days following Richard Nixon's triumphant reinauguration in 1973, he announced "peace with honor" in Vietnam. Shortly thereafter, the nightly news became a patriotic spectacle with the return of some 587 prisoners of war who had been held there in cruel conditions for as long as eight years.

[2]

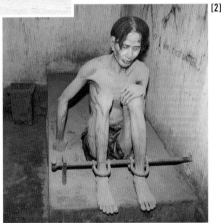

Suspicious circles, however, pointed to the even crueler treatment meted out by our ally South Vietnam to its *tens of thousands* of prisoners—seen here in a replica of a cell in the U.S.-built prison camp of Con Son. Critics called "Operation Homecoming" a propaganda campaign designed to short-circuit reckoning with the war's evils and a way to distract attention from America's ideological divisions, including among the POWs themselves.

[3]

In the last years of his second term as governor of California, Reagan emerged as the national tribune of the conservative side of those divisions. (Here, he welcomes home Air Force Lieutenant Colonel Lewis Shattuck, wearing an American flag eye patch.) "I guess I'm going to have to quit talking about these fellows," he said of the POWs. "I can't do it without choking up." In America's season of moral confusion, this stout certainty made him a presidential prospect.

4

Growing up in a chaotic home with an itinerant alcoholic father—between the ages of six and ten "Dutch" Reagan attended a different school every year—a lonely, frightened boy transformed himself in the confident image of his heroes from adventure stories and sports. Above, Reagan as a boy in Dixon, Illinois, the small city where he found his confidence. Below (first row, left), with brother Neil (far right), father Jack (middle row, left), and mother Nelle (last row, second from left), whom Reagan said bore "a sense of optimism that ran as deep as the cosmos." From the age of ten on, it's all but impossible to find a photograph in which Ronald Reagan does not appear aware of the camera.

It was around the time F. Scott Fitzgerald defined "personality" as "an unbroken series of successful gestures." The personality developed by the young Ronald Reagan— on stages from the YMCA boys band to a beachside lifeguard stand to college athletics to a regional radio station in Iowa—radiated blithe optimism in the face of what others called chaos. It was what made some so eager to follow him—and others to judge him a shallow fraud. (Above: Reagan at the job he worked during high school; below: the college footballer.)

7

Richard Nixon's second term took a sharp downward turn as the issue of alleged criminality in the White House, largely ignored by the press during the 1972 election, took center stage—as symbolized by an awkward appearance of country star Merle Haggard at the White House. "Do you know whether he's the first ex-convict to perform in the White House?" a reader asked a *Chicago Tribune* columnist.

Soon, Senate Watergate hearings led by North Carolina's colorful Sam Ervin (third from right, conferring with, from right, Senator Edward Gurney [R.-Fla.], Democratic counsel Sam Dash, unidentified female aide, Republican counsel Fred Thompson, and Senator Howard Baker [R.-Tenn.]) were revealing, live on TV, mafia-like behavior in Nixon's White House.

[10]

"During the Watergate hearings, he got hooked on daytime TV and hasn't done a lick of work since!"

[11]

"And don't give me any of that 'executive privilege' nonsense!"

TV viewers were riveted. Senators were shocked, meanwhile, by the defiance of the Nixon administration, which claimed that the novel constitutional doctrine of "executive privilege" kept the president from letting any of his aides testify before Congress on Watergate. Toward summer, Watergate came to dominate popular culture.

[12]

[13]

[14]

In spring, meat prices nearly doubled. After the president's consumer advisor Virginia Knauer (above, left) lectured that "liver, kidney, brains, and heart can be made into gourmet meals with seasoning, imagination, and more cooking time," the mail in response, according to a press report, was "unprintable." The earth seemed in rebellion: millions of tons of raw sewage dumped into the Pacific in Southern California, volcanoes erupting in Iceland, birds dying off mysteriously, thousands of dead fish washing up periodically on Midwestern beaches (above, right). Devastating energy shortages developed months before the October 1973 OPEC oil embargo quadrupled the price of a barrel of crude. "The Roman Empire crumbled from within," wrote a Chicagoan in the *Tribune*. "Isn't that what is happening to us?"

[15]

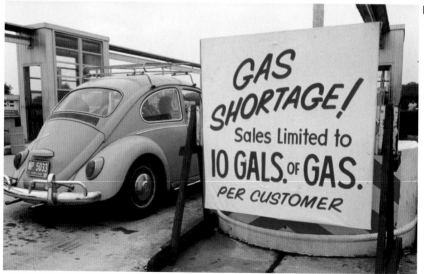

17

The president tried to heal the nation's blues by showcasing the POWs at the biggest dinner party in White House history. But the reputation of the POWs as patriotic, family-friendly tribunes had already attenuated with news of the civil war among them in the camps, a rash of suicides, and a wave of divorces. One newly divorced POW even brought *Playboy* magazine's Miss January as his date.

Sexual mores were shifting radically even among the suburban middle class, which was reading books like *Loving Free,* whose authors dropped their pseudonyms when it turned out none of their elementary school–age children's friends in suburban Milwaukee cared that their parents had written a sex manual.

Among the forty-three Nixon officials found guilty of Watergate-related crimes were John Erlichman (left) and John Mitchell, both seen testifying before the Ervin Committee.

John Dean, the president's White House counsel, had been given the job of coordinating the Watergate cover-up. Under limited immunity, he testified that the president's every public statement about the scandal had contained lies. Prior to his intensely anticipated appearance, he viewed himself on his only previous TV interview and noticed his eyes twitched. So he dug up an old pair of glasses to wear—the look for which he would become forever known.

It was Dean's word against the president's—until Nixon's personal aid Alexander Butterfield shocked the world when he revealed that Nixon kept a taped record of every word uttered in the Oval Office. Special prosecutor Archibald Cox, the bow-tied Harvard professor (left), argued before Watergate Judge John J. Sirica, whose courtroom became a D.C. tourist attraction, to make the tapes public. The showdown reached its dramatic high point when Nixon fired Cox in the Saturday Night Massacre, which critics decried as akin to a fascist coup. It reached its nadir when the White House revealed an eighteen and a half minute gap in the recording of a key meeting. Nixon's secretary Rose Mary Woods claimed she had *accidentally* erased it—but when she tried to show how, she actually revealed that was impossible.

23

December 10, 1973 / 50 cents

Newsweek

Rose Mary's Boo-Boo

Civilization continued its collapse. Mild-mannered heiress Patricia Hearst was kidnapped by a murderous far-left terrorist gang—then she announced she was joining them to fight for "the freedom of all oppressed people." Young people were abandoning promising lives to join weird religious cults, such as the one that followed the bizarre self-proclaimed messiah the Reverend Sun Myung Moon or (above, right) the Hare Krishnas. Parents hired "deprogrammers" to kidnap their children and reverse their "brainwashing." The anxieties over what two authors called "America's epidemic of sudden personality change" found expression in popular culture via *The Exorcist*, in which a twelve-year-old little girl was possessed by the devil, then, in the last reel, was restored to normalcy—which turned out to look a lot like America before the sixties happened.

Plain Speaking
an oral biography of
Harry S. Truman
by
Merle Miller

Americans longed to be anywhere but the 1970s; a wave of nostalgia ensued. The film *American Graffiti* (slogan: "Where were you in '62?") became a surprise hit. An oral biography of Harry Truman ("One's blood congeals at the thought of how far we have gone since those days," its author wrote) became a bestseller. Bette Midler scored a hit with the 1941 Andrews Sisters song "Boogie Woogie Bugle Boy."

Halloween was especially frightening in 1973. After General Augusto Pinochet staged a coup in Chile (aided, it was later learned, by the CIA), Senator Ted Kennedy predicted that if Nixon defied the courts and refused to turn over the tapes, "It would be Chile . . . without the bloodshed." After a surprise Arab attack on Israel, OPEC embargoed oil to the United States when Nixon sent weapons to save the Jewish state. The military was placed on higher alert—but Henry Kissinger then had to deny the alert was a hoax to distract attention from Watergate.

Scandal, War Link Shunned By Kissinger

[31]

WASHINGTON (AP) · Denying that the White House is "playing with the lives of the American people," Secretary of State Henry A. Kissinger icily rejected any suggestion that Thursday's Mideast developments were staged to obscure the still-boiling Watergate affair.

President Nixon postponed until Friday a news conference for questions about Watergate, even as new scandal disclosures surfaced and Republi-

was too busy with the Middle East to hold the news conference planned for Thursday night.

Kissinger, speaking at a State Department news conference, was asked whether domestic problems had prompted Nixon to call Thursday's early-morning military alert.

"We are attempting to conduct the foreign policy of the United States with regard for . future generations," he said,

The occult went mainstream. One Los Angeles bank advertised a presentation on "ESP, hypnosis, bio-feedback, shape energy, plant sensitivity . . . and the comet Kohoutek" alongside classes on income-tax preparation.

As major cities banned outdoor Christmas illumination to save electricity, a popular paperback, *Predictions for 1974*, provided a map of the dreads of a nation. Predictions included a 1929-style stock market collapse, locusts, floods "like the plagues of Egypt," and rising sea levels "inundating all coastal areas."

[34]

The public's longing for nostalgic release was a quiet weapon in Ronald Reagan's political arsenal when discussions began, following Vice President Spiro Agnew's resignation in the wake of a corruption investigation, about who might replace the wounded Richard Nixon. Here he is "roasted" in a fall 1973 episode of *The Dean Martin Comedy Hour.* The televised roasts were new that year, a kind of family reunion for all the beloved warhorses of the old Hollywood.

[35]

For instance, an NBC News report from Iowa on Reagan's presidential prospects featured a photograph from his days as a radio sportscaster, and depicted him enrapturing a political crowd with a tale about broadcasting a Cubs game according to a telegraphed play-by-play.

Sports nostalgia was preferable to sports reality—where, in 1974, Henry Aaron (seen here in an on-field celebration with Georgia's ambitious governor, Jimmy Carter) was receiving hate mail like "Dear Jungle Bunny, You may beat Ruth's record but there will always be one babe. Go back to the jungles." Note sparse crowd at Municipal Stadium in Atlanta, which proved indifferent to the hero in their midst.

As Watergate reached its endgame, Reagan's aides worried that their boss was sabotaging his presidential chances by refusing to distance himself from Nixon. He remained one of Nixon's few defenders, along with the Reverend Moon, the Jesuit priest and White House aide John McLaughlin (who said Nixon's taping system was "honorable" and that the president's profanity had "no moral meaning"), and Baruch Korff, a rabbi from Massachusetts (and "apologist for rampant immorality," said the president of the Union of American Hebrew Congregations) whose "Citizens Committee for Fairness to the Presidency" raised $30,000 in three days for ads like these.

38

The star of the House Judiciary Committee's impeachment hearings was the first-term Texas congresswoman Barbara Jordan, introduced to the nation live on TV: "My faith in the Constitution is *whole,* it is *complete,* it is *total,* and I am not going to sit here and be an idle spectator to the *diminution*—the *subversion*—the *destruction*—of the Constitution."

EXTRA	**DAILY ▣ NEWS**	EXTRA

NEW YORK'S PICTURE NEWSPAPER ©

Vol. 56. No. 39   New York, N.Y. 10017, Friday, August 9, 1974*   WEATHER Partly cloudy, windy and mild

NIXON QUITS

Washington, Aug. 8—President Nixon announced his resignation tonight in a TV address to the nation. Vice President Gerald R. Ford will become 38th President tomorrow.

Special 8-Page Pullout; Stories Start on Page 2

Nine days later, the president announced his resignation effective noon the next day, and he took off from the White House lawn and ceded the presidency to the vice president, Gerald Ford.

CHAPTER TEN

"That Thing Upstairs Isn't My Daughter"

THE NEW YORK CITY WINTER TURNED FIERCE FOR THE NEW YEAR, BUT people were still willing to wait in lines up to four hours long for tickets to a new hit movie—and then wait again to see it a second and third time. People started paying scalpers fifty bucks to get in. "It's like a cult," a theater manager said. "People must see it."

The Exorcist begins in the desert sands of the mysterious Middle East, where wicked oil sheikhs live. Cut to Georgetown, where wicked politicians live. There we meet Christine MacNeil, played by Ellen Burstyn. Christine is a liberal Hollywood movie actress, perhaps an atheist, perhaps based on George McGovern campaign volunteer Shirley MacLaine, who is starring in a movie about left-wing student radicals, and who may or may not be having an affair with her director. Her fascination is piqued by a liberal priest she accidentally encounters, Father Karras, who is also a psychiatrist, frequents singles bars, and suffers from an awful, soul-crushing alienation: "There's not a day in my life when I don't feel like a fraud," he says.

The condensation point for all the demonic energies circling around this broken society is a twelve-year-old girl, the actress's daughter, cute little Regan, played by a newcomer named Linda Blair. The devil is struggling to possess her, and wins. She shrieks and snarls, vomits—and murders a priest. Her head spins around 360 degrees. And, in a shot that might have been the most mind-blowing to yet appear in the entire history of cinema, she shouts like a deep, dark, guttural flamethrower, *"LET JESUS FUCK YOU! LICK ME! LICK ME!"* while shoving a crucifix between her twelve-year-old labia.

When scenes like these unspooled on the movie screen, unbelievable things started happening. At the first press screening in New York a woman in the sixth row started pacing the aisle, holding her head and murmuring, "Jesus, Jesus, Jesus, Jesus." When *The Exorcist* opened in Los Angeles, a theater manager counted an average of six vomiters and six fainters per showing. Exhibitors started stocking up on, of all things, kitty litter; it helped absorb the puke. A guard at the Manhattan theater told reporters about all the heart attacks and miscarriages he had witnessed.

Warner Bros. had thought the film's commercial prospects unpredictable at best—religious pictures didn't do well in these allegedly faithless times. *The Exorcist* opened in twenty-six theaters. As word of mouth spread, the studio struck new prints as quickly as possible—and in each new city, emergency room visits skyrocketed. In Boston the audience assaulted the image with rosary beads. In San Francisco a patron charged the screen. In Germany a boy shot himself in the head after a screening; in England a boy died of an epileptic seizure. In Chicago six people ended up in psychiatric wards, convinced demons had come to possess them, too; others showed up at rectories with their little ones in tow, begging for exorcisms.

Which of course only made people want to see it more. Within two months of its release *Variety* reported it was the fifth-highest-grossing film in history.

Why? What was the awesome appeal? Some of it was surely the shocking physicality of what showed up on the screen—like the arc of pea-green vomit Regan sends soaring into a startled priest's eye. Some of it was old-fashioned marketing genius. Publicists let it be known that director William Friedkin had seen five hundred aspirants for the role of the little girl who would be doing such awful things onscreen. They trumpeted the awful coincidences alleged to be haunting the production.

Beyond all that, the fact was this: within the relatively safe confines of a darkened, popcorn-scented hall, it is fun to be haunted. And yet, there were dozens of movies entering theaters that year that aimed to haunt. But only this one was sending patrons to the emergency room. Why?

Aristotle was the first writer to try to explain why it is pleasing to be horrified in a theater. A tragic story, he said, "has pain as its mother." Displaying that pain, containing it—"arousing these emotions through the representation of them"—storytelling thereby reduces it; viewers, he wrote, "settle down as if they have attained healing." The Greek word for this, *catharsis*, came from a medical term: "cleansing," "purification," or, more dramatically, *purgation.*

What was it that *The Exorcist* purged? What were the social pains that were its mother? Here was one: our actual little girls, our perfect symbols of innocence, had become alien and frightening. Take for example the real Linda Blair, the fourteen-year-old who beat out five hundred other aspirants to play the demon-filled Regan. The director had asked her if she knew what the movie was to be about. Because she had read the book, she reported, she did: "It's about a little girl who gets possessed by the devil and does a lot of bad things."

"What sort of bad things?"

"She pushes a guy out a window and masturbates with a crucifix—"

"What does that mean?"

"It's like jerking off, isn't it?"

"Yeah, do you know about jerking off?"

"Oh, sure."

"Do you do that?"

"Yeah, don't you?"

Here was another 1974 pain to be purged: the fear that someone you loved would disappear. A Missouri bank president and his wife disappeared, then were discovered shot to death, trussed to a tree, the banker with dynamite strapped to his chest. The editor of the *Atlanta Constitution* disappeared, kidnapped by individuals claiming to be members of an "American Revolutionary Army" seeking "to return the American government to the people." An IRS agent in Wisconsin was lured out to a farm, tied up, and threatened by right-wing extremists of the new "Posse Comitatus" movement, which pledged massive tax resistance against the United States.

Young people disappeared. A typical news report, from California: "The nude body of a young woman found in a desert wash near Blythe was tentatively identified as that of Laura Louise Escamillo, 20, of Idyllwild, sheriff's detectives reported. Officers said Miss Escamillo was last seen July 11 near Blythe attempting to hitch a ride home." In August, a pit full of decomposing corpses, most of them teenage runaways, was discovered outside Houston; the serial killer, Dean Arnold Corll, who had once owned a candy shop, lured them in with promises of drugs, food, and shelter. He piled up a final toll of twenty-seven corpses.

Sometimes, and even more frighteningly, children made *themselves* disappear. They ran away. They became willing captives to strange Svengalis and gurus, their personalities suddenly changed—or of a sudden it seemed they had no personalities at all. Like the onetime cheerleaders who joined the "Manson Family" and became obedient mass murderers. Or the bright college students discovered by their parents selling flowers on a street corner on behalf of the Reverend Sun Myung Moon (whose favorite movie was *The Exorcist*). Their parents, *Time* noted, "almost uniformly describe their children as having been well-rounded, industrious, and studious until they went off to college and became captured by drugs and radicalism." Steve Allen, the TV personality, discovered that his missing son had joined the "Love Israel" cult and now went by the name "Logic." In Houston in November 1973, a city traumatized by the Corll killings, tens of thousands gathered over three days in the Astrodome to celebrate the fifteen-year-old guru Maharaji Ji. As the scoreboard flashed HOLY BREATH WILL FILL THIS PLACE AND YOU WILL BE BAPTIZED IN HOLY BREATH, like some of the lines from the *Exorcist* script, his agents combed the aisles to recruit devotees willing to live a life of total regimentation on his ashrams, give up all their worldly goods, and never speak to their families again—in exchange for the promise of levitation and communion with extraterrestrials.

Then there were the children disappearing into lives of drug-filled dissolution, making of it some sort of moral rebuke to "the system." John Paul Getty III, heir to the great oil fortune, appeared to have done just that—then his mother started getting ransom notes for millions of dollars with the threat that unless they were paid "he will arrive in little pieces." Just before Christmas he turned up at a truck stop outside Naples, Italy, missing an ear. His grandfather refused to talk to him when his heir called to thank him for putting up the ransom; the elder Getty apparently believed he had got what he had deserved—one more child possessed by demons, unrecognizable to his family.

A national hotline opened, "Operation Peace of Mind," advertised with a poster of a scruffy-haired hitchhiking teenage boy. His sign said "Anywhere," and the caption read: *"Are you still alive? Let somebody know."* The massage parlors beloved by journalist Gay Talese were largely staffed by such runaways, as were the Times Square peep shows and whorehouses—like the one out of whose tenth-floor window a twelve-year-old named Veronica Brunson fell, or was pushed. "One wonders what a modern version of *The Adventures of Huckleberry Finn* would be like, or even if it would be permitted reading in our nation's high schools," Indiana senator Birch Bayh, whose son Evan was seventeen, reflected at a hearing on his proposed Runaway Youth Act.

THE NINETEEN-YEAR-OLD DAUGHTER OF RANDOLPH HEARST, SON OF THE founder of the newspaper empire fictionalized in *Citizen Kane,* disappeared February 4. She was sitting at home in her bathrobe in Berkeley, where she was a sophomore, in the apartment she shared with her boyfriend, a cohabitation unthinkable among respectable people only a few years before. Two armed men pushed in, struck her in the face with a rifle butt, and forced her into the trunk of a car. No news was forthcoming for a couple of days; and then a "military communique" arrived in the mail at the radical Bay Area radio station KPFA from the abductors, announcing they had served a "warrant" from the "Court of the People" to arrest the child of a "corporate enemy of the people," and that "all communications from this court must be published in full, in all newspapers, and all other forms of media. Failure to do so will endanger the safety of the prisoner," and in the event of a rescue attempt, "the prisoner is to be executed." The next communiqué promised future abductions, in order to finance "war against the establishment." It concluded: "Death to the fascist insect that preys upon the life of the people."

The kidnappers came from something called the "Symbionese Liberation Army"—which had recently claimed responsibility for the assassination of the black superintendent of the Oakland school system, whom they called the "black Judas of Oakland." Two SLA members were soon arrested—but others found easy shelter within Berkeley's radical underground.

A cassette tape arrived at KPFA on February 11 bearing Patricia Hearst's voice. Wearily, she informed "mom and dad" that she was "not being starved or beaten or unnecessarily frightened." She urged her parents to cooperate with the demands of what she called the "combat unit," assuring them, "They are not just a bunch of nuts and have been very honest with me." Officials pointed out that the recording appeared to have been stopped and started several times, suggesting she had been fed what to say; others, however, noting rumors that her boyfriend, Steven Weed, had been a member of Students for a Democratic Society, detected suspicious gestures of sympathy toward her captors. A man who identified himself as "Cinque," the SLA's "general field marshal," pronounced in a calm, clear voice, "I am not a savage killer and madman, we do hold a high moral value to life, but I am quite willing to carry out the execution of your daughter to save starving men, women, and children of every race." His "preliminary demands" were for Randolph Hearst to oversee the distribution of seventy dollars' worth of groceries to every Californian eligible for any form of public assistance and anyone who had ever been in prison or on parole—an outlay of $147 million by one estimate, $400 million by another. "If you do not meet these demands in good faith we will assume there is no basis for negotiations and we will no longer maintain in good health prisoners of war," the document concluded, demanding the SLA's emblem, a seven-headed snake, be printed in all the newspapers.

Placards of solidarity showed up on Bay Area lawns: GOD BLESS YOU, PATTY HEARST. Three mornings later, the fascist insect who preyed upon the life of the people, Patty's dad, stepped up to a bank of microphones and addressed his daughter directly—"Patty, I hope you're listening!"—and said that while meeting the SLA's demands as specified would be impossible, he was preparing "some kind of counteroffer that's acceptable." Randolph Hearst continued, struggling to compose himself: "Tell them not to worry. Nobody's going to bust in on them to start a shootout. You take care of yourself. We love you, Patty." He turned away, unable to continue. His wife, Catherine, a member of Ronald Reagan's conservative bloc on the University of California Board of Regents, sobbing beside him and clasping his hand, took over: "We love you, Patty, and we're all praying for you. I'm sorry I'm crying, but I'm happy you're safe and strong." She was sure, she said, that the captors had "good ideals," but "just went about it the wrong way."

"God bless you, honey. Take care of yourself."

British journalist Alistair Cooke, one of those European Tocquevilles who are better able to see us than we can see ourselves, begged his British readers' indulgence of the extreme indignity of parents negotiating with moral monsters over TV: "We were hearing a girl zombie apparently drained of all feeling except that of a beggar; and we were identifying, in a helpless way, with the sleepless anxiety of a mother and father at the end of their rope."

THOSE IMAGES ON THE NEWS HAD BECOME A NUMBINGLY FAMILIAR: EXhausted, gaunt, mystified parents, helpless against the demons who had stolen their child—a reason *The Exorcist* signified so heavily. And though it couldn't have been more different from the previous summer's surprise movie hit, *American Graffiti,* it also could not have been more the same. Both ended by strenuously maintaining that the world would have turned out just fine, had we just stayed in 1962.

The Exorcist's turning point came as the gaunt, frantic mother begs Father Karras, the faithless priest, to look into performing the ancient and mysterious rite of exorcism. Science, after all, has been helpless to explain her daughter's mysterious possession. Father Karras, a man of science, tells her that she is being ridiculous and that her daughter . . . but the mother interrupts:

"I'm telling you that thing upstairs isn't my daughter!"

Like the real-life middle-class Angelenos flocking to the downtown branch of State Savings Mutual Bank to embrace the healing powers of astrology, numerology, palmistry, tarot, and the comet Kohoutek, reason and progress having failed to deliver us from evil, why not embrace mystical solutions instead? And so, in the movie's dramatic final fifteen-minute set piece, ministrations of holy water, prayers declaimed in Latin, the simple profession that Satan is one and indivisible and perfectly, obviously evil, but that God is one and indivisible and perfectly good, together restore the innocent little girl to herself—and, incidentally, restore Father Karras's faith as well. Evil abated. Order restored.

The 1970s abated, too. In the last scene, the mother replaces the loose, flowing earth-toned slacks of earlier reels (*unisex: remember that word*) with a Jacqueline Kennedy–style tailored pink dress, long white gloves, and a fur hat and coat. Regan is presented in an old-fashioned coat of red, white, and blue. "She doesn't remember any of it," the mother tells a priest, and stares dreamily at his Roman collar, and then, as if instinctively, throws her arm around him in loving gratitude.

Just as in *American Graffiti* it was 1962 again, the time before the storm, before children disappeared.

AMERICANS NOW LONGED FOR INTIMATIONS OF INNOCENCE WHEREVER they could find them—even from that most degraded class of citizen: the politician.

The demon in the White House delivered his State of the Union address on January 30, 1974, pledging neither to resign nor to compromise the presidency by giving up more tapes and documents. (Once more the governor of California was about the only prominent figure to defend him: "Any President would resign if in his own mind he believed it would be for the good of the country to do so," he said on *Meet the Press*, then dismissed the latest news of more missing tape segments: "I certainly don't feel like I'm qualified to sit ... from 3,000 miles away and try to tell lawyers before a judge how to conduct that case.")

Nixon spoke nine days after his "energy czar" published plans for a nationwide "contingency rationing plan," variable from month to month according to available supplies. "Under the plan," the *New York Times* reported, "all licensed drivers at least 18 years old would receive coupons, which are being prepared by the Bureau of Printing and Engraving"; the White House had ordered more than 10 billion of them. Present projections were that "eligible drivers" in New York and its suburbs would be entitled to thirty-seven gallons a month. "There is nothing," an official admitted, "to keep anyone from going into the coupon buying-and-selling business": black-market America, like Casablanca during the war. Czar Simon then announced he might mandate a three-dollar minimum purchase—to prevent the very panic buying his previous announcements had engendered. Next, on February 4, Gulf Oil closed its terminal in Linden, New Jersey, for fear that picketing truckers would attack the employees or sabotage the facility— engendering more panic anew.

In Washington the harried president's lawyer James St. Clair argued that the prosecution of his client had become a persecution. Jaworski came back that this was nonsense—and that subpoenas of people at the White House might once more be forthcoming. A subpoena from another judge was already in the works, ordering Nixon's testimony in the trial of John Ehrlichman for ordering the burglary of Daniel Ellsberg's psychiatrist. ("Watergate West," the trial was nicknamed.) It was the first subpoena to a president by a state judge in the history of the United States. The White House said it would ignore it.

Then, on February 5, a forty-one-year-old Democratic state legislator named John Murtha won a special election to Congress in a rural district in Pennsylvania that had sent only Republicans to Washington for the last thirty years. Nearly the only Republican who didn't seem worried about the omen was Ronald Reagan—traveling the country so aggressively that an aide's memo plotting a potential presidential campaign strategy warned, "The Governor must look to the public as if he still cares about California." At a Lincoln Day dinner in Oklahoma City, Reagan roused the troops by insisting that it was the *Democrats* who should be under the microscope for corruption: "We in our party have too often been the victim of big city political machines voting tombstones, warehouses and county lots against us in every election." The ensuing ovation was ecstatic.

In a week, Michigan's Fifth District was to pick a replacement for Vice President Gerald Ford; he had been elected thirteen times with never less than 60 percent of the vote, and no Democrat had served in the Fifth District since 1910. The Democrat now running insisted Watergate was almost the only issue that mattered. "This country and this district cannot continue to survive so long as the moral and leadership vacuum exists in Washington," soft-spoken Richard Vander Veen said in announcing his candidacy. "Our constitution provides no equivalent to the British vote of no confidence," he said, "and my campaign could be just that—a referendum on Richard Nixon." He also said Nixon had to resign—and that if the president didn't, he would go to Washington to work for impeachment.

Vander Veen was a peculiar kind of Democrat—one apparently indifferent to being a Democrat at all. He spoke rarely if at all about the New Deal accomplishments upon which the party of Jefferson and Jackson had been winning elections for a generation. He took as his model instead George Romney, the Republican governor who had entered public life by fielding a nonpartisan citizens' commission to reform the Michigan constitution. He had imagined the previous year that a similar commission might help heal the entire mess in Washington itself. "We could style ourselves as Democrats or independents," he wrote; it didn't matter which; his and Ford's own Kent County had gone to ruin precisely because the only people allowed to run for office were those willing to "pledge their souls to the party store." Watergate, he thought, was caused by an excess of partisanship, and wasn't *really* the fault of Republicans at all: "Democrats can take an equal share of the blame for failing to present the country a candidate of sufficiently broad base in the presidential election of 1972."

The worst thing he would say about his Republican opponent, the head of the state senate, who had never lost an election in fifteen tries, was that he was a "career politician." (Vander Veen had never held elected office.) He had an ironclad policy of never speaking ill of a political foe; Gerald Ford, Vander Veen said in a hapless run against him in 1958, was "a fine fellow." For America needed politicians who were not politicians—who had "proven themselves to be successful in an honorable line of endeavor other than politics," one who "has a code of moral values and has demonstrated a capacity to adhere to . . . values." (Vander Veen was a corporate lawyer by trade, but his real passion was collecting rare books.) "I am a lifelong Democrat, and I have not always agreed with Gerald Ford on the issues," he said on the stump. But the vice president's integrity and reputation were beyond question, and that was the important thing: "We need Gerald Ford as President."

This was just the sort of antipolitician, it turned out, Americans longed for to effect their political deliverance.

The special election arrived on February 18—the same day as the start of the trial of John Mitchell and Maurice Stans for hoovering up $200,000 of Robert Vesco's cash, and the same day Richard Nixon engaged his own impassioned form of bipartisanship as a guest of Alabama governor George Wallace before forty thousand enthusiastic fans at "Honor America Day" in Huntsville, Alabama. "We in Alabama have always honored the office of the Presidency of the United States," the governor intoned from his wheelchair, a remarkable lie (he had made his political reputation by daring President Kennedy to send troops to Alabama to enforce federal law). The president said thanks to "you all" for "reminding all of us that here in the heart of Dixie, the heart of America is good and we are going to continue to be a great nation." Enthusiasts waved signs like the one with a picture of Abraham Lincoln and the legend, WHAT IF HE HAD QUIT? (once upon a time, Alabamans had dearly hoped he would), and another enjoining, REBELS SAY "HANG IN THERE" MR. P!

Energy czar William Simon was busy meting out fuel supplies state by state from Washington—more like a Soviet commissar: he dictated prices down to a penny, and when he announced that 90 percent of the nation's gas stations now had permission to raise prices an extra two cents a gallon, they dropped threats of a nationwide gas-station shutdown. But truckers barricaded freeways to protest skyrocketing operating costs: 350 rigs backed up traffic for twelve miles in the crucial Philadelphia-to-Wilmington corridor; the Ohio Turnpike was virtually motionless for twenty-four hours. Then independent carriers went on a wildcat strike, leaving the same arteries virtually deserted. Truckers who scabbed risked having bricks hurled down at them from overpasses; in Delaware, one was shot to death. "In no instance will we tolerate violence from those with grievances," the president said in a national radio address on that particular crisis, and pleaded for calm, adding that "despite the threat of violence from a handful of desperadoes, at least 80 percent of the nation's truckers stayed on the job."

Also on the highways, the "Honk for Impeachment" movement spread ("I even got a cop to honk," an enthusiast told a Michigan newspaper). Nixon's approval rating was a record-low 25 percent. And in Grand Rapids, the same citizens who had returned Gerald Ford to Congress thirteen times voted in their mild-mannered book collecting neighbor with 53,008 votes to 45,159. The sweating, celebrating crowds chanting "Nixon Must Go!" at Eastern Avenue Hall before the national and international news cameras stamped so hard, authorities feared the floor might collapse.

Maybe that flawed vessel the Democratic Party could save us after all. A book called *Plain Speaking*, composed of interviews a journalist named Merle Miller had done with the thirty-fourth president for an early 1960s TV special that never aired, was the year's runaway best-seller. Harry S. Truman, who had died in December 1972, was drafted from beyond the grave as the exorcist of the nation's Nixon demons. "There was not a duplicitous bone in his body," Miller wrote. He wore shirts "that could have come from J.C. Penney." "As nearly as he could remember," his "last act in the White House was returning a pencil or maybe it was a pen to the desk of the man he borrowed it from." (He was not a crook.) The first thing he did upon returning home after his presidential term, back at the old house at 219 North Delaware in Inde-pendence, Missouri? (His mother-in-law owned it, and "never stopped ruminating, aloud and whenever possible in the presence of her son-in-law, about all the people who would have made better Presidents than Harry. . . . And don't track up the kitchen with your muddy feet, Harry.") "I carried the grips up to the attic."

Here was a hero who said things like "I just never got to thinking I was anything *special*." And "I'm just an old Missouri farmer." And "Everything, all of it, belongs to the people. I was just privileged to *use* it for a while. That's all . . . it was only *lent* to me, and by that I'm includin' the power of the Presidency." There was the time, for instance, when his military aide presented him with some transcripts of FBI phone taps left over from Franklin Roosevelt's time. He recalled himself responding with vituperation: "I haven't time for any such foolishness as that. Tell them I don't authorize any such thing."

"One's blood congeals at the thought of how far we have gone since those days," Miller wrote. "And it's been downhill all the way."

The fact that Truman, like FDR and JFK and LBJ, had also secretly recorded White House conversations was not then known—but people should have known better than to buy the idea of Truman as a reluctant wielder of presidential power: Harry S. Truman had made the most extraordinary extensions of executive authority in the history of the office, an entire new national security state, licensing many of the practices later associated with Joseph McCarthy. This had been documented in a bestseller from the previous year, Harvard historian Arthur Schlesinger's *The Imperial Presidency*, but the public forgot about that—and the fact that this supposed unblemished scourge of corruption was nicknamed an "Office Boy" of Kansas City's crooked boss Tom Prendergast, or that his estimate of how many American lives he had saved by dropping atomic bombs kept ballooning as the decades went by (in 1946 he said that several thousand American men would have died in an invasion of Japan; by 1959, he claimed the number was upwards of a million). Then Garry Wills, one of the deans of American journalism's suspicious circles, documented in *Esquire* that many of the dramatic instances of "plain speaking" Truman presented to Miller, such as his supposed public dressing down of General MacArthur, actually did not happen—and also that Truman was driven by much the same ego-damaged defects of character associated with Richard Nixon. Never mind. A grateful citizenry was glad to look the other way and savor the myth. Suspicious circles were being cowed into abatement everywhere. Nostalgia, heroes, and myth was the flavor of the month.

Heroes like soft-spoken Richard Vander Veen. On the plane to Washington for Vander Veen's congressional swearing-in, the captain sent his party a flight of champagne. The congressman-elect gave his first news conference: "The silent majority has spoken and its message is clear: Richard Nixon has failed us. Richard Nixon cannot lead us." It was picked up on all three networks. In a Florida paper, the news brief below Vander Veen's words described the town of 1,200 in Washington State that had been without gasoline for a week, even for police cars; above that an AP wirephoto depicted motorists in an endless gas line looking on enviously as a family cruised by for their shopping trip in a horse and buggy. Things were still falling apart. That is why we needed heroes.

From Democrats Vander Veen got a standing ovation during his swearing-in ceremony for calling for impeachment. Republicans were simply shell-shocked. The new vice president, who found his coattails did not even extend to Grand Rapids, was reported to have muttered, "You can't mean that" at news of the election returns. Then, thinking fast, he told the press that the reason the Democrat won was "temporary turmoil" due to the energy crunch. RNC chair George H. W. Bush insisted Republicans still looked strong for 1974. At that, a conservative GOP congressman from Iowa literally leaped out of his sickbed and shouted at a reporter, "I'm damned sick and tired of the damned leadership of our party running around with their heads in the sand. They're a bunch of drunken optimists and if we don't face reality we'll lose fifty seats in November. We'll be having our Republican caucus in a phone booth."

The *Grand Rapids Press,* which endorsed the Republican as it always did, now editorialized, "As for our endorsement last week of Republican Robert VanderLann, the *Press* is eating crow . . . and it ain't that bad!"

And impeachment?

Once upon a time it had been the White House's favorite blunt instrument to shut people up about Watergate. As in: if you think Richard Nixon is so bad, then why don't you impeach him? It was such a drastic remedy, so historically discredited by the precedent of Andrew Johnson in 1868, that constitutional scholars dismissed it as unserious and unthinkable.

Not anymore.

The House had authorized $1.5 million to staff the Judiciary Committee inquiry. Late in 1973, the committee picked a lead investigator: John Doar, a Republican, because committee chairman Peter Rodino was obsessed with building a dispassionately nonpartisan inquiry. Doar had investigated civil rights crimes so thoroughly for Robert F. Kennedy's Justice Department that George Wallace once barked, "Someone should get a shotgun and blow Doar's head off." A week after the 1974 State of the Union address, the House voted 410 to 4 to give the Judiciary Committee broad power to subpoena anyone, including the president. And by spring Doar's staff of one hundred was working so thoroughly in their suite across the street from the Rayburn House Office Building that workmen had to reinforce the floor for all the extra file cabinets.

THEIR FIRST JOB WAS FIGURING OUT WHAT IMPEACHMENT WAS. A CONgressman had once argued on the floor of the House, concerning the attempt to unseat Supreme Court justice William O. Douglas, "The only honest answer is that an impeachable offense is whatever a majority of the House of Representatives considers to be at a given moment in history." But now that that congressman, Gerald Ford, had been chosen as Nixon's vice president, he apparently no longer believed this to be the case. Nixon said at a February 25 press conference, "You don't have to be a Constitutional lawyer to know that the Constitution is very precise in defining what is an impeachable offense." That definition, he said, was a serious criminal offense on the part of the president. In fact the Constitution could not be more vague. The Judiciary Committee's legal staff had just released a massively researched report arguing that the charter's reference to "high crimes and misdemeanors" was meant to encompass anything the House thought undermined the integrity of the office, disregarded constitutional duties, or violated the presidential oath of office—"a constitutional safety valve," as the report put it, which the Founders intended as "flexible enough to cope with exigencies" they couldn't have foreseen.

Many knowledgeable observers no longer thought even the lower standard would save Nixon. "Had he been a mafia associate," Joseph Kraft columnized, "he would have long since been tried and convicted and jailed just on the basis of the circumstantial evidence." There was also, as with the proverbial mafia prosecution, the question of *his* associates. The same day as the press conference, his personal attorney Herbert Kalmbach pleaded guilty to setting up fake political committees to launder Senate campaign contributions in 1970. (A *Los Angeles Times* cartoon: "I'd like to see my lawyer," Nixon says, to a jail guard, outside a cell marked "Kalmbach.") Four days later, the special prosecutor's office announced indictments including Haldeman, Ehrlichman, Mitchell, and Colson, on twenty-four counts of conspiracy, lying, and obstruction of justice. At Nixon's next live televised news conference, CBS's Dan Rather asked: "Would you consider the crimes returned in the indictments last week—those of perjury, obstruction of justice, and conspiracy—to be impeachable crimes if they did apply to you?" Taken aback at the harshest question in his career, the president fumbled a cliché. "Well, I have also quit beating my wife," he said, to nervous laughter.

No wonder he was nervous. A charge in Haldeman's indictment for lying to Congress fired up that old question of what the president knew and when did he know it. John Dean had claimed that the president in March 1973 had asserted it would be no problem raising the million dollars in hush money. In *his* Senate testimony, however, Haldeman said he'd been there, too, and told the panel he later reviewed the tape, and confirmed that the president had actually said that it wouldn't be a practical problem to raise a million dollars for hush money, but that it "would be wrong"—meaning, unethical. TAPES CLEAR NIXON— HALDEMAN, was what the slugs had read on July 31, 1973. But what the headlines now revealed was that the Watergate grand jury had been allowed to listen to those tapes, too—and it was indicting Haldeman because Nixon had never said anything of the kind. It was the first practical confirmation of just how stunning these tapes could be for the very future of the republic. And the Judiciary Committee had just requested forty-two more.

The whole thing now was political: was it imaginable, whatever the evidence, that Congress would impeach? And, because Nixon was a consummate politician, these were the terms on which he was now fighting. He hemmed around his latest refusals to turn over evidence with a campaign-like slogan—"One year of Watergate is enough"—and a pointed set of metaphors to match: his tormenters were off on "a fishing expedition requiring 42 tapes and a U-Haul truck." Then he got out on the old campaign trail, below what one editorial wag called the "Mason-Nixon Line," where he might find the fifty to sixty Democratic congressmen he would need to save his ass.

ON MARCH 16, A YEAR AFTER NIXON HAD HOSTED MERLE HAGGARD AT the White House, Air Force One pulled into a National Guard hangar in Nashville, Tennessee, where an invited crowd waved little American flags to lyrics urging people to "stand up and cheer for Richard Nixon," set to the tune of "Okie from Muskogee." Thereupon, the president motorcaded to opening night of the Grand Ole Opry's new theater, where he banged out "Happy Birthday" and "My Wild Irish Rose" to his wife on the piano with a big red ersatz barn in the background, then goofed about with a yo-yo presented to him by "King of Country" Roy Acuff, who was resplendent in a stage costume of brilliant blue with snazzy silver piping.

The president repeated his favorite corny old joke about the mystic powers of moonshine, which he'd been repeating on political sojourns in Dixie for years. Ignoring the man with the sign reading "He Ain't Country, He's Crooked," Nixon, looking clammy and awkward without a podium to protect him, pronounced, "Country music is America." Then, after a little yo-yo lesson from Acuff, he led the crowd in a booming rendition of "God Bless America."

Emboldened at a Houston question-and-answer session with the National Association of Broadcasters two days later, he made an extraordinary pledge of defiance to an impeachment inquiry he insisted was out of control: "I am suggesting the House follow the Constitution. If they do, I will."

The presidency, after all, was America. Richard Nixon was the president. The presidency must be preserved. So Richard Nixon had to be preserved. For the sake of America.

SENATOR JAMES BUCKLEY OF NEW YORK, THE NATION'S MOST PROMINENT conservative politician, did not agree. Two days after the president's return to Washington, Buckley gave a speech announcing, that Nixon's "credibility and moral authority" were "beyond repair," the presidency jeopardized "by a long, slow, agonizing, inch-by-inch process of attrition." So for the sake of the republic and the conservative mandate of 1972, he must voluntarily resign—as an "extraordinary act of statesmanship and courage."

Ronald Reagan answered Buckley an hour later at his regular Sacramento press conference. "I think all the evidence is to the contrary, including the fact that we are now going to get some oil from the Middle East." Impeachment had to be allowed to take its course, and would not disrupt the country: "I think there is something far more disruptive in establishing a precedent, if we ever do so, that by pressure alone the President can be forced to resign."

All winter Reagan had been framing the situation, as per usual, in terms maximally advantageous to the president. In Texas, Oklahoma, Kansas, and Utah, he lambasted the "Eastern press establishment" for harassing a president so committed to patriotically preserving the future integrity of the office by *not* handing over documents to his prosecutors. Reagan pioneered, too, a critique of the supposed integrity of the Judiciary Committee investigation. In actuality, Rodino had been proceeding as fairly as humanly possible—so much so that he no longer even spoke back home in his New Jersey district: "They want a bell-ringer of a speech against Mr. Nixon," he said, "and I just can't give it." John Doar refused to hire any staffers who had ever expressed an opinion about Watergate. Reagan's argument pressed the opposite case—that such labored deliberateness was corrupt: "I sometimes suspect the Rodino Committee," Reagan intimated darkly, "of trying to keep this thing going through this election year."

Soon the ranking minority member on the Judiciary Committee, Edward Hutchinson, was saying that, too. Then it became a right-wing refrain. But Reagan's newfound influence was not much boost for his national political prospects. Around the same time he began tongue-lashing the Judiciary Committee, he was also in the news as the first California governor in twenty-eight years to have a veto overridden. What he had vetoed was the legislature's attempts to block his plans to phase out the state's hospitals for the mentally ill and retarded. Oil, meanwhile, $2.70 a barrel in September 1973, was going for $13 now. The energy crisis flared with special intensity in California—where competitors in the Ontario 500 were granted just 200 gallons of fuel each for qualifying and 280 gallons for the race, and a plan went into effect restricting who could buy gas on what days based on whether their license plate ended with an odd or even number. Their governor blamed the problem on consumers—they were guilty of "panic buying."

Volunteers organized under the banner "People in Need" were hard at work fulfilling the SLA's demands to free Patty Hearst: distributing seventy dollars' worth of groceries to every Californian eligible for any form of public assistance and anyone who had ever been in prison or on parole. In some places, the distribution process descended into riots. Reagan, in Washington, D.C., for a governors' conference, was quoted by a reporter as saying at a fund-raising lunch, "Sometimes you wonder whether there shouldn't be an outbreak of botulism."

Baffling and bizarre, wishing botulism on poor people; reporters asked him to elaborate. He said it was a "joking remark"—much as he had said that his 1970 remark about student protesters, "If it's to be a bloodbath, let it be now," was a "figure of speech."

A *Los Angeles Times* reader noted, "Governor Reagan's remark about botulism will probably destroy him as a presidential candidate." But "even Republican governors must be allowed an occasional primal scream." Democrats in the state legislature piled on: "We have tried repeatedly to provide a program in which children could get through the school day without going hungry. Repeatedly the governor has vetoed these programs. . . . I hope the governor and his fat-cat Republican friends enjoyed their lunch." At that, Reagan blamed the newsman who reported his words for recklessly endangering Patty Hearst's life. "Frankly I think that he *was* as irresponsible as I have been *accused* of being."

• • •

THAT, FINALLY, WAS THE SMART PLAY. TO ATTACK THE MEDIA FROM THE right, and thereby to intimidate it into quiescence for fear of being accused of "liberal bias," was the new name of the game. One day in February, four of the erstwhile defendants from the notorious Chicago Seven trial, legendary 1960s radicals Jerry Rubin, Abbie Hoffman, Rennie Davis, and Tom Hayden, were scheduled to appear on Dick Cavett's talk show. The appointed evening arrived—and Cavett was replaced by a rerun, with no explanation. "ABC, as a broadcast licensee," a network spokesman eventually said, "has an obligation to insure fairness and balance in its programming in accordance with Federal Communications Commission requirements." This show as taped, the network said, had not been "balanced."

The cancellation was the fruit of a White House campaign of manipulation that began in 1969, when Nixon sent Spiro Agnew to attack news commentators as "a tiny and closed fraternity of privileged men, elected by no one." Behind the scenes, they assaulted the networks with threats—as revealed in several of the most revealing memos entered into evidence during the Ervin Committee hearings. In one, from September 1970, Charles Colson bragged of a meeting in which he warned network executives that unless the White House saw more "balanced coverage," TV stations would start losing broadcast licenses. "They are very much afraid of us," Colson reported, "and are trying hard to prove they are 'good guys.'"

Apparently they were even now—despite the president's maximal political weakness. Maybe having to report so many dastardly things about a Republican inspired network brass to proactively censor the left.

Of the Cavett episode, ABC singled out five areas in which the guests' opinions concerned it: on "the capitalist system, the administration, our system of justice and the courts, and U.S. foreign policy with regard to Vietnam and Cambodia." Cavett pronounced himself baffled. "If people eventually get to see the show," he said, "they won't be able to understand what the fuss was all about." They did eventually get to see it, heavily edited, five days after they got to see their president fondle a yo-yo at the Grand Ole Opry. They saw Jerry Rubin say that the real revolution lay in getting in touch with one's body and that when enough people did, capitalism would collapse. They saw Rennie Davis moon over his spiritual guru, the fifteen-year-old Maharaji Ji, and Abbie Hoffman say he'd been busy with "quiet things." Cavett, a little desperate to enliven the proceedings, asked what they would do if someone told them he or she was about to bomb a munitions plant. But only lip readers would have been able to discern that Abbie Hoffman thought it would be much more productive these days to monkey-wrench an oil refinery office—because ABC smudged out the sound. Then two conservatives spoke for half an hour, because "under the terms of his contract," a network spokesman explained, Dick Cavett had "to provide an opposing viewpoint."

Soon after, Pat Buchanan, the right-wing White House staffer, began a column in the nation's most widely read magazine, *TV Guide*, which reached a third of the adult U.S. population every week. Buchanan was one of five rotating columnists penning a new feature called "News Watch." The others were the former editor of the Republican National Committee's magazine; Edith Efron, the author of a 1971 book alleging liberal media bias that the White House (in another Ervin Committee revelation) had bumped onto the bestseller list by secretly purchasing thousands of copies; Kevin Phillips, a former Nixon Justice Department staffer and author of *The Emerging Republican Majority*, now working on a project to break up the networks on antitrust grounds; and John P. Roche, who had once been the Johnson administration's liaison to the liberal intellectual community but now fit the description of a "neoconservative"—a newly popular coinage for conservatives who used to be liberal. *TV Guide* was published by Walter Annenberg, Nixon's former ambassador to the United Kingdom and a social companion of Ronald and Nancy Reagan.

It all reminded the *New Yorker* of another Buchanan memo flushed out by Watergate investigators, this one proposing that scholars at the "private" foundation he had proposed the White House set up as a political front group "produce a book of papers on [the media's] lack of objectivity and need for reform." There was, too, the case of William Safire, the White House speechwriter and former public relations agent whose specialty had been coming up with terms of abuse for the media to put in the mouth of Spiro Agnew. The *New York Times* gave him an op-ed column, which debuted in April: clever pieces in the acceptable argot of the Georgetown villagers that somehow always also ended up letting Richard Nixon elegantly off the hook—like the one in which he recommended "a public bonfire of the tapes on the White House lawn," but only, mind you, to "re-establish the confidentiality of the presidency."

These apparent successes chipping away at the media's supposed anti-Nixon bias were cold comfort for Nixon. The day after the Cavett show the Judiciary Committee won a major procedural battle when John Doar, melodramatically guarded by police, picked up what the press called the "bulging briefcase"—a cache of evidence the special prosecutor insisted it would violate grand jury secrecy for Congress to see. Woodward and Bernstein of the *Post* reported it contained evidence that the president himself was involved in the cover-up. Judge Sirica ruled against Nixon after Rodino warned that without access to the documents, the impeachment inquiry would drag on for a year (and wasn't Nixon's latest slogan that "dragging out Watergate drags down America"?).

In April came the news that Nixon had paid $72,682.09 in taxes in 1969 but less than $800 in 1971—and got a $72,000 tax *refund* in 1970. The magic was due to a deduction received by donating his vice presidential papers to the government. Allegedly, he falsified the deed of gift to make it look like he donated them before the law under which he claimed the deduction expired. Now the IRS announced he owed the government $476,431, and that one year he had donated only $252 to charity. The *New York Times* banner on the subject was approximately as large as the one announcing the attack on Pearl Harbor. For the first time, a poll recorded a plurality, 43 to 41 percent, favoring impeachment.

On April 4, Judiciary Committee members reminded the White House they had waited thirty-eight days so far for a reply to their request for forty-two more tapes. One White House spokesman responded that the president was suffering under the yoke of a runaway prosecution seeking "carte blanche to rummage through every nook and cranny in the White House" and that this coequal branch of government was behaving "like a lot of children in homes all over the United States. When you are at meals and you want seconds, you have to clean your plate first." Another spokesman cried, "The mere fact of an impeachment inquiry does not give Congress the right to back up a truck and haul off White House files." Hotheads on the Judiciary Committee said that the White House was being criminally insolent, because the committee request had precisely designated which conversations they wanted and why, down to the minute. At that, Rodino made a public announcement: "We have been respectfully patient. The courts were patient. . . . The people have been patient for a long time. But the patience of this committee is wearing thin." He then granted the White House five more days, until April 9, to comply before this became the first House committee in history to subpoena a president.

The Saturday Night Massacre, with its visuals of agents of one branch of the government facing down another and its specter of a Strangelovian military takeover, had come last October 24. Now, a mere twenty-four weeks later, that same fear crept forth once more.

• • •

THEN THIS: AMID HEADLINES ABOUT THE NEW JUDICIARY COMMITTEE deadline and an announcement by the IRS that the president owed it almost a half million dollars, the SLA released a new tape featuring Patricia Hearst's voice.

"I would like to begin this statement by informing the public I wrote what I would like to say," she said. "I have never been forced to say anything on tape. Nor have I been brainwashed, drugged, tortured, hypnotized, or in any way confused." She went on to accuse her parents of being part of an FBI plot to assassinate both her and the people whom she now called her comrades. She had been given a choice, she said, of release or "joining the forces of the Symbionese Liberation Army and fighting for my freedom and the freedom of all oppressed people." She had chosen to join the SLA.

She ranted on and on: about how she learned that "the corporate ruling class will do anything in their power in order to maintain their position of control over the masses, even if this means the sacrifice of one of their own." That the food distribution had been "a sham"—this was obvious because "as members of the ruling class, I know for sure that yours and Mom's interests are never in the interests of the people." That if Randolph Hearst was interested in the people, he would have used his power to explain that the energy crisis was a conspiracy to reduce the labor force to "a small class of button pushers," and that "the law and order programs" of people like Richard Nixon and Ronald Reagan were "just a means to remove so-called violent (meaning aware) individuals from the community in order to facilitate the controlled removal of unneeded labor force from this country, in the same way that Hitler controlled the removal of Jews from Germany." She concluded, "I should have known that if you and the rest of the corporate state were willing to do this to millions of people to maintain power and to serve your needs you would also kill me if necessary to serve those same needs." This was why, she went on to explain, she had shed the name Patty and chosen "Tania" instead—"after a comrade who fought alongside Che Guevara in Bolivia for the people of Bolivia. . . . It is in the spirit of Tania that I say, 'PATRIA O MUERTE. VENCEREMOS.'"

In case anyone missed the point, they enclosed a photograph of Hearst in a beret and a guerrilla uniform, posed as if firing a machine gun at a running dog of the fascist imperialists, a dreamy look on her face and the SLA's seven-headed serpent emblem in the background. "HEARST QUITS FAMILY," a headline read. Demons had possessed her. Who could say it would not happen to your children, too?

CHAPTER ELEVEN

Hank Aaron

SPRINGTIME, AND YOUNG MEN'S FANCIES TURNED TO THOUGHTS OF BASE-ball. Surely, this of all years called for a good old-fashioned heroic saga straight out of the days of Grantland Rice—and, as if on cue, on Opening Day, on the very first swing of his twenty-first season, Henry Aaron of the Atlanta Braves cracked a sinker that did not sink right on over the left-center wall at Riverfront Stadium in Cincinnati for the 714th home run of his career, tying the "unbeatable" record Babe Ruth had held since 1935.

In that same fortnight members of the Symbionese Liberation Army, including Patty Hearst, were seen on security cameras robbing Hibernia Bank in San Francisco with machine guns; also in San Francisco, two hitchhiking teenagers became the tenth and eleventh victims of a spree of random murders of white citizens by black men in what police labeled the "Zebra" shootings. In a single two-hour period, at least six F5 tornadoes formed, the worst "Super Outbreak" of storms in U.S. history. One destroyed half of Xenia, Ohio, in a space of minutes, killing thirty-four. Nationwide the storms covered thirteen states and left a path of destruction 2,500 miles long, killing three hundred.

Women reporters marched with picket signs outside the National Press Club, demonstrating against their exclusion from its annual Gridiron Dinner. Ronald Reagan vetoed all but $1 million from a $5 million bill to help unemployed veterans get jobs. Henry Kissinger went, hat in hand, before the United Nations, in the wake of the OPEC oil humiliation, to plea for the world's resource-rich Third World nations to share their resources more fairly with the formerly mighty United States. Excerpts of the new book by Carl Bernstein and Bob Woodward about how they cracked Watergate, *All the President's Men,* ran in *Playboy,* where readers could also thumb through "The Devil Made Us Do It: A Ten Page Pictorial on the Occult." The Harris poll recorded that the public trusted the President of the United States less than the whistle-blower John Dean.

And in the age of John Dean and Patty Hearst, it seemed, even sports could not provide uncomplicated pleasure.

Hank Aaron's day soured before it began. He was already haunted by the news from Xenia, Ohio, when the Cincinnati Reds front office asked how they could accommodate him on his special day. It was April 4—the sixth anniversary of the assassination of Martin Luther King. A black man and a civil rights supporter, Aaron asked that there be a moment of silence before the game. They refused. "I should have known better," he later reflected: Cincinnati was one of the most reactionary cities in the North. And for millions of white Americans, "Hammerin' Hank" represented not something beautiful given to them but something taken: their secure sense of racial supremacy in a world gone dangerously mad.

For a year now he had been getting letters like these:

Dear Nigger,
   Everybody loved Babe Ruth. You will be the most hated man in this country if you break his career home run record.

Dear Jungle Bunny,
   You may beat Ruth's record but there will always be one Babe. Go back to the jungles.

   I hope you join brother Dr. Martin Luther King in that Heaven he spoke of.

His career had tracked the progress of integration in the major leagues: born poor near Mobile, Alabama (his dad found steady work for the first time thanks to President Roosevelt's executive order integrating war industries), inspired to become a major leaguer by Jackie Robinson, he was one of the last black stars to begin his career in the dying Negro Leagues. He was snapped up in 1952 by the Milwaukee Braves, and his first minor league stop was Eau Claire, Wisconsin, whose population included but seven blacks; he had never been inside a white person's home before. At his next, the Class A South Atlantic League, black players weren't allowed to argue the umpires' calls, and the best compliment Hank Aaron and his one black teammate ever got was "I just wanted to say that you niggers played a hell of a game." When he was in spring training the next year for the Braves, the Milwaukee papers nicknamed him "Stepin Fetchit."

But like in the words of the old Negro spiritual, he overcame—

leading the Braves to the 1957 World Series title, and winning individual titles for runs, RBIs, and home runs.

He did so quietly, modestly, an introvert in an extrovert's job. But he was also a rich black man—living, when the Braves moved to Atlanta the year Lester Maddox won the governorship after brandishing an ax handle to chase blacks from his restaurant, in the Deep South. By the time Aaron approached Babe Ruth's record, the heroic era of the civil rights movement, with its soaring images of melodramatic showdowns between vicious Southern sheriffs wielding clubs and humble warriors for justice wielding freedom songs, was over. It was replaced with something called "affirmative action": a bureaucratic, top-down attempt to compensate for past racial disadvantage by setting aside opportunities for blacks. Anger over that knew no regional bounds.

In Boston a cadre of liberals, including the congressman who was the former dean of the Boston College Law School, Father Robert Drinan, urged affirmative action for construction projects in their city, arguing, "If serious disorders break out in the near future, the Department of Labor can be cited as the proximate cause of such disorders." By 1974 a settlement was arrived at requiring 30 percent minority employment at sites in minority areas. The jobs were brokered through a "Third World Jobs Clearing House," supported by city funds, which soon was demanding a 50 percent share. Two thousand angry white Boston construction workers marched on City Hall. One told a reporter, "You been workin' ten to twelve years, some guy comes along from this Third World and grabs your job. What the hell?"

This noble attempt to redivide the economic pie, instituted by un-elected judges, guilt-ridden bureaucrats, and litigation-shy corporate personnel officers, happened to go forward at a time when that pie was shrinking: in 1974—a year, to take one affirmative action milestone as an example, when the federal government's Equal Employment Opportunity Commission handed down a consent decree to both the nation's nine largest steel manufacturers and the United Steelworkers of America union, ordering hiring quotas for women and minorities. But this same year, unemployment hit its highest level since 1961. Inflation had quadrupled, and for the first time in a generation real take-home pay dropped. In that context the attempt to redress past inequalities seemed to whites to come one-for-one out of their hides.

In the culture at large, Hank Aaron absorbed the brunt of that sort of anger. Stealing Babe's pride of place, to his new pen pals he was like one of those black construction and steel workers who'd stolen theirs— just another swaggering black man empowered to lord it over whites as if he owned the world. Soon, as one of them put it, "You boogies will think that you invented baseball or something."

In real life it didn't matter if Hank Aaron never swaggered. It was enough that he succeeded. On sports talk radio the argument was ubiquitous: he could not possibly have beaten a white man without sneaky unfair advantages, just like those affirmative-action hires: the baseballs he hit were more lively than the ones Ruth had to hit. He played in more games than Ruth. (The consensus seemed to be that Ruth would have hit 900 had the number of at-bats been equal, though the math became more creative in proportion to the racism: "Had Ruth played and been at bat as many times as you, old nigger, he would have hit just short of 1100 home runs.") Ballparks were smaller. ("Dear Nigger, you can hit all dem home runs over dem short fences, but you can't take dat black off your face.")

Were the claims of unfair advantage true? Not really. To cite another record, by the time his career ended in 1976 Aaron had hit for 722 more total bases than anyone else who had ever played the game—which had nothing to do with lively balls, tiny ballparks, or the number of games in a season. But stats were not driving this argument. The terror of racial displacement was. "I deplore the desecration of the memory and immortality of a great baseball player by extolling a modern pretender as 'the greatest,'" a Connecticut fan wrote as the death threats began coming daily, as if Jackie Robinson had never blazed the way at all. On days the FBI relayed to him a credible threat, Aaron politely informed his teammates not to stand too close to him in the dugout. One writer asked him to think of the children: Ruth "would do anything for a kid. . . . It is what is commonly known as a hero. Therefore, how could *you*, Mr. Aaron, ruin, destroy, and shatter to pieces the one record which separates Babe Ruth from any other man to play the great game of baseball?"

Aaron was certainly no hero in the city where Martin Luther King was buried. He drew ten thousand extra fans in any opposing ballpark he visited. He hit his 711th home run at home—and only 1,362 Atlantans showed up.

THE HOME RUN CHASE ALSO INDEXED AMERICA'S NEW PARANOIA, ITS wariness toward formerly trusted institutions, its new lack of respect for formerly taken-for-granted norms of decency. Before the 1973 season began, back when the POWs were coming home, the Braves' traveling secretary said publicly that the team hoped Aaron would break the record at home; then "we'll sell out every night." So every time Aaron struck out, fans accused him of doing it on purpose. Every time he sat on the bench, it was a scam. Then, as the 1974 season approached, when Braves owner Bill Bartholomay announced his intention to bench Aaron during the opening series in Cincinnati, the *New York Times* called it "a brazen defiance of baseball's integrity"—even though the practice was venerable and common. "Baseball's gone crooked," Dick Young of the *New York Daily News* wrote. "There is no delicate way of putting it. . . . I would feel slightly better, and so would the fans, if the Commissioner of Baseball had come out with a blistering order to the Braves that Hank Aaron must play the first three games, under threat of forfeit."

Came the big day in Cincinnati. Aaron blasted 714. He was, yes, promptly benched—and then, in the seventh inning, his moment in the sun was superseded when a young man ripped off his clothes and ran naked across the left-field upper deck for a full three minutes. He got two standing ovations, then signed a clutch of autographs as he was being taken away by police.

"Streaking" was the springtime's new fad: fifty Columbia University kids dashing nude through the streets of New York City; 2,500, a world record, through the campus of the University of Georgia; a female streaker at the University of Montana braving 30-degree temperatures— and, from the University of Pennsylvania, a "streak for impeachment" to encircle the White House was proposed. (A political cartoon showed a relieved President Nixon looking out a White House window: "Oh, it's only a streaker. For a moment there I thought you said leaker!") Right-wing North Carolina senator Jesse Helms seriously suggested "college authorities ought to take all the naked students into custody and herd them into a football stadium under guard and then require them to spend the night naked until their mothers come and request their release." He added, "It might be useful to hose down the streakers with cold water every 15 or 20 minutes." In Washington, the National Campaign to Impeach Nixon drew 6,500 for a raucous parade down Pennsylvania Avenue, five of them streaking through the line of march, past a Ford Edsel with the presidential seal on its side and an effigy of Nixon in a jail cell on the roof. And at the Academy Awards, just as David Niven was introducing Elizabeth Taylor to present the Best Picture award, to *The Sting,* a man named Robert Opel dashed across the stage to display what a quick-witted Niven called his "shortcomings." A streaker also raided the 1974 National Book Awards, crying "Read books! Read books!" (Then Adrienne Rich refused her poetry award— or rather, awarded it collectively to the two other female nominees,

Alice Walker and Audre Lorde, and to "all the women whose voices have gone and still go unheard in a patriarchal world." Allen Ginsberg sent up a friend who accepted his prize and shouted at the top of his lungs, "There is no longer any hope for the salvation of America!")

Later that season the Cleveland Indians offered beer for a dime a cup at a game against the Texas Rangers. There had already been a bench-clearing brawl between the two teams at a cheap-beer night in Arlington, Texas, a week earlier. Before this game, kids started setting off fireworks from their seats and the Texas manager Billy Martin tipped his cap and blew kisses to the booing crowd. In the second inning a hefty gal flashed her breasts on the on-deck circle and tried to kiss an umpire. In the fourth, a streaker slid into second base. In the fifth, a father and son mooned the outfield stands. By the sixth the fireworks were rocketing *into* the Texas dugout and fans started throwing golf balls, rocks, and batteries onto the field—and, following the seventh-inning stretch, they invaded the playing field, overwhelming security guards. In the ninth inning, when the home team tied the game at 5–5, a fan tried to celebrate by stealing the Rangers' star right fielder Jeff Burroughs's glove. The two got into a fistfight, and that was when the *real* riot began: Clevelanders armed with knives, chains, Chinese martial arts "nunchaku," and shards of seats they liberated from the stadium's concrete floor sent Texas players fleeing for their lives—but not before Martin, armed with a bat, led the rest of his team from the dugout to join the melee, crying "Let's get 'em boys!" like a demented Henry V recalling St. Crispin's Day.

Once upon a time, Grantland Rice said sports "help build up clean living, cool heads, stout hearts, and sound judgement under fire." Grantland Rice was long dead.

The night before Opening Day in Atlanta, the Braves' publicist was unable to sleep, terrified of what would happen if the off-duty cop who traveled everywhere with Aaron disguised as a fan, with a service revolver hidden away in a binocular case, plugged a streaker in the head. Aaron approached Los Angeles Dodgers pitcher Al Downing, the first black pitcher ever to start a Yankees World Series game, and handed him a note wishing him good luck. The encounter was soon the subject for racist conspiracy theories: two black men conspiring together to rob Babe Ruth of his glory.

Aaron's dad, seated for the game next to Governor Jimmy Carter, threw out the first ball. The second inning, the historic smack . . .

In New York, Frank Sinatra, opening a concert at Carnegie Hall: "To ease any tension in anybody's mind, Hank Aaron has hit the home run tonight." Sinatra had once been a man of the left. Now the former chairman of Democrats for Reagan in 1970 was much more a tribune of the sort of people who suspected any advance for blacks meant a reversal for whites. He said it without enthusiasm, to no more than polite applause. But Hank Aaron's response was anticlimactic as well: "Thank God it's over," he said when offered the microphone during the ceremony that interrupted the game. Then it started to rain, and for a moment it looked as if a cancellation would force the ordeal on him some other day. The ceremony ended. Half the crowd left. The president, too busy agonizing over his tapes to come to Atlanta, called only after Aaron had trotted out to right field. The call was accidentally disconnected before the hero made it back to the dugout.

THREE DAYS LATER, ON APRIL 11, THE HOUSE JUDICIARY COMMITTEE voted 33 to 3 to subpoena forty-two more taped conversations and gave the president two weeks to produce them. The next week Watergate special prosecutor Leon Jaworski requested a court order for sixty-four others—and then, the day after that, the Judiciary Committee asked for another 142. The president's lawyer James St. Clair requested one last extension to consider their response. By a vote of 34 to 4 the committee acceded to what Rodino called this "one *last* request"—that single word *last* veritably echoing across the marble walls.

Lawyer and president repaired to Camp David, and reached a historic decision. And night owls in Washington at 2:45 A.M. on April 29—about the hour when on a certain night in 1972 four Cubans were being arrested for burglary—could have spied several presidential employees rushing forth from 1600 Pennsylvania Avenue with typed manuscripts to the gloomy brick buildings where the 7,400 employees of the U.S. Government Printing Office impressed each day's *Congressional Record* into hot lead type on turn-of-the-century Linotype machines. They would soon be producing for the benefit of an eager nation a volume the size of a phone book with the portentous title *Submission of Recorded Presidential Conversations to the Committee on the Judiciary of the House of Representatives by President Nixon, April 30, 1974.* After that, the world would change.

It had been a year to the day since the president promised the nation, "There can be no whitewash in the White House." Now, his hair trimmed, his voice cool, his manner serene, he appeared on TV beside stack upon stack of blue volumes. "In these folders that you see over here on my left," he began, gesturing at the impressive array, "are more than twelve hundred pages of transcripts of private conversations I participated in between September 15, 1972 and April 27 of 1973. . . ."

(Skeptics soon pointed to the stagecraft: each book contained about twenty-five pages with wide margins and space between lines, making the release look much bigger than it actually was.)

"As far as what the President personally knew and did with regard to Watergate and the cover-up is concerned, these materials, together with those already made available, will tell it all. . . ."

(To those same skeptics that sounded like a hint he would resist further demands.)

"I have been reluctant to release these tapes, not just because they will embarrass me and those with whom I talked—which they will—and not just because they will become the object of speculation and even ridicule—and not just because certain parts of them will be seized upon by opportunistic opponents—which they will . . ."

(People just *had* to get their hands on these transcripts.)

"Because, in these and in all other conversations in this office, people have spoken their minds freely, never dreaming that specific sentences or even parts of sentences would be picked out as subjects of national attention and controversy."

He continued, to the point of tedium, with an elaborate and legalistic set of rationalizations, quoting the transcripts to explain why they precisely proved he had committed no crime, and no cover-up. For instance, he said the ones for March 21, the day concerning which John Dean had testified he had accepted the necessity of bribing defendants to perjure themselves, "show that I did not intend the further payment to Hunt or anyone else be made," that "by the end of the meeting, as the tape shows, my decision was to convene a new grand jury and to send everyone before the grand jury with instructions to testify."

He wound up after thirty-five minutes—the length of almost all his television speeches, the ideal length for a speech, he had long ago convinced himself—with sentimental bromides: that in an age when "peace may become possible in the Middle East for the first time in a generation," an age on the verge of "fulfilling the hope of mankind for a limitation on nuclear arms," there was "vital work to be done . . . so that Americans can enjoy what they have not had since 1956: full prosperity without war and without inflation. . . ."

(This was a retreat. He used to say the Americans already *had* full prosperity without war and without inflation.)

"[E]very day absorbed by Watergate is a day lost from the work that must be done by your President and by your Congress . . . the materials I make public tomorrow will provide all the additional evidence needed to get Watergate behind us and get it behind us now. Never before in the history of the presidency have records that are so private been made so public. In giving you these records—blemishes and all—I am placing my trust in the basic fairness of the American people ... no questions remaining about the fact that the President has nothing to hide in this matter."

Then he wrapped up by quoting Lincoln.

IN THE YEARS TO COME AMERICANS WOULD LEARN IN A BLIZZARD OF bestselling books precisely the strategy behind this unexpected capitulation: he thought it would help cool the fires. Instead it was like a bomb going off—the biggest blunder of Nixon's political career.

To Mike Doonesbury, the titular alter ego of Garry Trudeau's house comic strip of the suspicious circles, what came out of his TV sounded like this.

Panel one: "Of course, different people will no doubt have very different interpretations of what was said—particularly at the so-called hush money meeting."

Panel two: "In this meeting, we discussed the options with great candor. First, we could have paid the money in the interests of national security. But we might have bled dry."

Panel three: "Or, we could have taken everyone with knowledge of the case out and shot them. But as a lawyer, I knew that would be wrong. No, we wanted to get the whole thing out in the *open!*"

Panel four: Doonesbury buries his head in his hands.

The volume was the size and heft of a phone book, 1,308 pages of transcripts. It became available to the public the next day at the low, low price of $12.25. But you didn't even have to read it to get the drift. Just look at the magazine racks. *Newsweek,* announcing a special section of twenty-two pages of excerpts, from a "transcript team" of fifteen, part of "the most extensive treatment of a breaking story in the magazine's history," put this bit of dialogue from the crucial March 21 conversation on the cover:

> *"D That's why for your immediate things you have no choice but to come up with the $120,000 or whatever it is."*
>
> *"P Would you agree that that's the prime thing that you damn well better get done."*
>
> *"D Obviously ..."*
>
> *"P (Expletive deleted) ..."*

Time's cover, "Nixon's Gamble," featured the following excerpts:

"Nobody is a friend of yours."
"You could get a million dollars."
"You can say, I can't recall."
"I say (expletive removed) don't hold anything back."

That morning, lines at the printing office stretched around the block. Its three thousand copies sold out in three hours. Everyone turned first to March 21, on the page stamped "187," where John Wesley Dean ("D") explained why hush money posed a legal problem: "One, Bob is involved in that; two, John is involved in that; I am involved in that; Mitchell is involved in that. And that is an obstruction of justice." He added that "the blackmail is continuing." He detailed the problem of *keeping* it continuing: "You have to wash the money. . . . People around here are not pros at this sort of thing. . . . This is the sort of thing Mafia people can do: washing money, getting clean money, and things like that. We just don't know about these things, because we are not criminals and not used to dealing in that business."

The president, eagerly interested, replied: "How much money do you need?"

Dean answered, "I would say these people are going to cost a million dollars over the next two years."

And then came the president's astonishing boast that the mafia had nothing on *him:* "You could get a million dollars. You could get it in cash. I know where it could be gotten. It is not easy, but it could be done. But the question is who the hell would handle it? Any ideas on that?"

This was the conversation the president insisted proved he had not participated in a cover-up.

United Press International clogged its wires for four days transmitting the 350,000 words to member newspapers, many of which published the whole thing as supplements, sometimes for free. The *Chicago Tribune* published its forty-four-page section within hours of the official release—a herculean effort involving three hundred staffers and a budget of $250,000. (Congressman Dan Rostenkowski said their account of how they did it "would make a wonderful movie.") National Public Radio hit the air with a marathon reading of every last word; CBS's ninety minutes of key scenes starred correspondents Bob Schieffer as John Dean, Barry Serafin as the president, and Nelson Benton as Bob Haldeman. Bantam Books and Dell Paperbacks released a combined total of three million copies within a week; a bookstore owner called it his hottest-selling item since William Peter Blatty's *The Exorcist.* "We didn't realize the extent to which this book touched some kind of nerve in the American public," a publisher said. Neither did Richard Nixon.

Reporters soon realized how much of it was, simply, *off.* For example, 1,878 bits were designated as "inaudible" or "unintelligible"—and the president was inaudible twice as often as all other speakers combined, most often in conversations with Haldeman and Ehrlichman. Members of the public simply immersed themselves in the astonishing privilege of listening to these intimate moments of the powerful. To both, it soon became plain that the White House was a more sordid place than they had imagined. It wasn't the question of legal jeopardy that transfixed the country. It was the atmosphere the transcripts revealed.

The delight the participants took in what they got away with (infiltrating the Muskie campaign via an undercover secretary and chauffeur: "There is nothing illegal about that"). The endless intervals the president's men spent discussing how a principal might skillfully skirt perjury; the bizarre third-person grandiosity. A columnist for the *Hartford Courant* wrote: "They evince no concern for what might be the national interest, no idea of what might be right and what wrong. They just don't care. The only thing that bothered them was to keep secret as much as possible of the whole disaster." Speaking for multitudes, he concluded, "If the White House circle was innocent, why did they talk, over so many countless days and hours, just as though they were criminals?" The CEO of the United Presbyterian Church said it felt "almost as if the public had been admitted to the most private plotting within a felon's lair." Billy Graham literally vomited when he read it.

The sordidness emanated from the very language. The jock-macho talk ("game plan," "playing ball," "the big game"). The violence talk. ("Maybe someone will shoot him," followed by "Laughter." They were speaking of L. Patrick Gray, their nominee to head the FBI.) The martial talk, the enemies they saw as intent on seeing the president "bled to death." The new words, the mafia words: "absolute hang-out" (which meant telling the truth, which Nixon rejected); "modified hang-out" (which meant making it *look* as if you were telling the truth, which was the course they ultimately arrived at); the "stonewall" (a particularly favorite piece of jargon to the press, given how aptly it explained what reporters had been dealing with from Ron Ziegler for five years now).

And the fact that the president *swore* so damned much. That seemed to shock a blushing nation most of all.

The transcribers had left in some of the "hells" and "damns," though rarely from the president. With him, and where the language was saltier, the transcripts made an enduring contribution to American comic discourse: *expletive deleted*. This was the man who, during one of his debates with John F. Kennedy in 1960, soon after Harry Truman had said, "If you vote for Nixon you ought to go to hell," piously invoked "the tremendous number of children who come out to see the presidential candidates. It makes you realize that whoever is President is going to be a man that all the children of America will either look up to or will look down to, and I can only say that I am very proud that President Eisenhower restored dignity and decency and—frankly—good language to the conduct of the presidency." Now came the news that he swore worse than the little girl in *The Exorcist*. Then Seymour Hersh in the *New York Times* reported that in a Nixon-Dean conversation on February 28, 1973, the president made disparaging remarks about Jews and called Judge Sirica a "wop." The White House denied that any such language appeared on the tapes.

CBS's Eric Sevareid called the transcripts "a moral indictment without known precedent." Joseph Alsop recorded his "sheer flesh-crawling revulsion." At the annual Southern Baptist Convention, the pastor of a 4,300-member church in Columbia, South Carolina, told delegates that the transcripts were "one of the most pornographic, vulgar, and blasphemous documents" he'd ever read. (In his turn on the podium, Governor Carter of Georgia told his fellow Baptists they shared the blame: "There has never been an adequate role played by Christians in this nation . . . in shaping the standard and quality of public life.")

Republican officials were the most vituperative. Hugh Scott, the Senate minority leader, called it "deplorable, disgusting, shabby, immoral." Senator Robert Packwood lamented the lack of "even any token clichés about what is good for the people." A "Republican hierarch" told *Newsweek* he was "sickened" at having to "live with the fact that such a man is still in the White House." A Justice Department official pointed out that if this was the stuff Nixon was *forced* to release, in transcripts the White House provided, "Can you imagine what's in the stuff he's holding back?" William Safire wrote that the man who had rescued him from a public relations career and set him on a course as a *New York Times* columnist was "guilty of conduct unbecoming a president." However, Safire said he himself hoped the "personal humiliation" would save Nixon from those ravening for impeachment. This appeared unlikely, given that newspapers that had endorsed Nixon in 1968 and 1972 and now called for his removal included such Silent Majority standbys as the *Kansas City Times, Omaha World-Herald, Cleveland Plain Dealer,* and *Chicago Tribune,* and even his hometown *Los Angeles Times,* which said, "Justice for the President and the nation now requires his impeachment."

Then the Judiciary Committee, flooded with telegrams saying things like "Impeach the (expletive deleted)," ruled in a 20–18 party-line vote that the transcripts did not fulfill the subpoena. John Doar said, "Quite candidly, these transcriptions are not accurate." A grand jury concluded of the March 21 tape that "Mr. Nixon would be indictable for obstruction of justice if he were not president." Congressman William Steiger, Republican from Wisconsin, said running for Congress as a Nixon supporter was "a prescription for suicide."

WILLIAM HEARST, UNCLE OF PATTY AND EDITOR OF THE NATION'S LARGest newspaper chain, might have been excused for having other things on his mind. The U.S. attorney general, William Saxby, had just labeled the Symbionese Liberation Army part of an international criminal conspiracy, and stated that "based on her taped pronouncements Miss Hearst is part of it" and that the FBI would be willing to risk a shoot-out if it found where they were hiding—then he backed down, saying no action would be taken that would put Patty in jeopardy. (It indexed a debate that would rage for years: whether Patty Heart should be judged as responsible for her own actions. "Tania" herself weighed in without equivocation in the SLA's sixth taped communiqué, released on April 23, calling the idea she had been brainwashed "ridiculous to the point of being beyond belief.") Her uncle still found energy to speak of other taped voices—those of the president and aides, acting like a "gang of racketeers talking over strategy as they realize that the cops are closing in on them." He observed, "If any of the participants—ever—gave any consideration to what was right for the nation instead of themselves, then I must have missed it in the thousands of words I have waded through."

Which was not precisely true: they just spoke of the nation's interests as consubstantial with themselves. For instance, the time Haldeman told the president that Dean would never "sink low enough" to spill the beans, because "he's not anti-American and anti-Nixon."

In the middle of May, an SLA "combat unit" including Patty Hearst, resting in a motel near Disneyland after holding up a sporting goods store, watched live on TV as the FBI burned down a safe house holding six other SLA members, including their mysterious guru "Cinque." In other news, the president made plain he would not resign. Instead, as the "Honk for Impeachment" movement reinfested Lafayette Park, he mounted a public relations tour. In Phoenix, there were 16,000 people and five hundred pounds of confetti. In Spokane, the day the House Judiciary Committee, behind closed doors, began debating impeachment, he cut the ribbon for Expo '74 before a crowd of 55,000 on the banks of the Spokane River—where "IMPEACH NIXON" banners unfurled as he motorcaded to the dais with Governor Daniel J. Evans, and he made a Freudian slip and mispronounced his host's name as "Governor Evidence."

Then he promised "to develop the great resources in this country that will not pollute the atmosphere." A protester shrieked back: "Clean up the White House first."

HIS ENEMIES, YES, WERE VICIOUS AND AMORAL. AND SO HE SENT FORTH determined armies of citizens to slay them.

Syndicated humorist Art Buchwald put out a column in mock sympathy for that army, a list of talking points ranging from "Everyone does it" (no. 1) to "What about Chappaquiddick?" (nos. 2, 9, 19, and 32) to "A President can't keep track of everything his staff does" (no. 3)—all the way up to no. 36: "If you say one more word about Watergate I'll punch you in the nose." Nixonites didn't need the favor. They said those same things on their own. Letters poured into the White House. One, from a restaurant owner, included a check for ten thousand dollars with instructions to the president to apply it to his back taxes. Tom Charles Huston was introduced to enthusiastic applause for an address to a symposium on "Government Surveillance of Private Citizens: Necessary or Ominous?" It was convened by the conservative youth group Young Americans for Freedom, or "YAF," of which he used to be president. He offered the audience an extraordinary statement of contrition for trying to set up a private spy outfit in the White House: "The risk of the remedy was as great as the disease. There was a willingness to accept without challenge the Executive's claim to increased power. That's why we acted as we did, and it was a mistake."

A middle-aged woman responded that it was anything but a mistake: "When a kid has got a knife stuck in your back, you don't set up a commission and call in the professors." By way of illustration, she went on to tell a story about the time her son had been harassed by bullies the cops wouldn't do anything about. So she sent him to school with a baseball bat: "Here, you handle that punk!" The room rocked with delighted applause. She said the bully's mother came to complain. "So you know what I do? I go at *her* with a baseball bat!" Huston, incredulous, unable to get a word in edgewise, watched in horror from the podium as the cries went up: "Hooray for Liddy!" "Hooray for Watergate!"

A weekly White House "Defense Group" worked to amplify such voices. It was led by former Goldwater campaign official Dean Burch, a young communications staffer named Ken Clawson, and another young deputy assistant, Bruce Herschensohn, nicknamed "Dr. Happiness" for his relish for the job. Burch explained to the press, "What emerges from the transcripts is life as it is . . . in government and politics, life in industry and business—and yes, life in the editorial offices of every newspaper." Clawson riffed, "Those bastards can rip a single page out of the Bible and if they play it right they can make Jesus Christ sound like the devil," and called the impeachment drive "an attempted coup d'etat of the U.S. government."

Another defender was a grandiose and self-important Jesuit priest on the White House staff named John McLaughlin. The press office couldn't get any staffers to present the president's case before reporters. Father McLaughlin, though, volunteered. In a self-described "theological" analysis of the transcripts held for a gathering of reporters in Clawson's office, he said the tapes' foul language had "no moral meaning" but was instead a "form of emotional drainage" and "therapy"; he called claims of the conversations' amorality "erroneous, unjust" and described Nixon as "the greatest moral leader of the last third of this century." The priest was soon a celebrity, well-known for his luxurious pad at, of all places, the Watergate, and for the attractive young female aide from when he'd been an antiwar congressional candidate frequently seen on his arm. His religious superiors ordered him to leave the White House job for abusing his sacred calling. He left the priesthood instead.

Bruce Herschensohn was in charge of ringing up supporters—some of whom had sent literally cartons of supportive anti-impeachment petitions to the White House—and inviting them to the Oval Office. "I remember the tulips in bloom through the windows," gushed a housewife who personally delivered forty-eight thousand signatures to the commander in chief, paying her own way to Washington at Herschensohn's invitation on but a day's notice. And the president, she said, wore "one of the most direct 'I-don't-have-anything-to-hide' looks I've ever encountered."

The dean of the last-ditch supporters was a tiny retired Orthodox rabbi from Taunton, Massachusetts, named Baruch Korff. In the suspicious circles, he was fast becoming the tragedy's comic relief, rumbling in his borscht belt–comic Ukrainian accent that a great man's "blood has been sapped by vampires" and his body set upon by "vivisectionists . . .

unworthy of polishing his shoes." "This entire administration is being held captive by the *Washington Post*," he said. "I feel like I am in Hanoi and not in Washington." Full-page newspaper ads for his "National Citizens Committee for Fairness to the Presidency" denounced the "ASSASSINS" perpetrating this "RAPE OF AMERICA." He made endless rounds of media interviews: "If Nixon's guilty, then so were Johnson and Kennedy and Eisenhower and Truman. And, my God, could I tell you things about Roosevelt!" Fellow rabbis called him an embarrassment—"an apologist for rampant immorality," said the president of the Union of American Hebrew Congregations. So, according to *Time* magazine, did "some members of the President's inner circle." Not, though, the President of the United States. On May 13, he entertained Rabbi Korff in the Oval Office for a full ninety minutes.

CHAPTER TWELVE

"Here Comes the Pitch!"

RONALD REAGAN WAS ALSO A WATERGATE APOLOGIST—STILL. ASKED about the Oval Office tapes at his regular press conference, he replied, "I was struck by what appears to be a difference between some of the interpretation and the verbatim transcript"—which favored the president, he insisted—which "some commentators have left out."

He added, "I don't think anyone can make any judgment until they have read the entire 1,200 pages, the verbatim transcript, and not the interpretation of them"—which presupposed, since he was making a judgment, that he himself had read the thing (a week later he admitted he had read only two-thirds). So a reporter followed up, asking about the apparently incriminating things that *were* in the verbatim transcript. Reagan replied, cryptically, that commentators were ignoring "the flat statement by Dean to the President when he said, 'Mr. President, I know from my conversation that you were not aware of these things'"—a Reaganesque distortion of something rather different. What Dean actually said was "The reason I thought we ought to talk this morning is because in our conversations I have the impression that you don't know *everything* I know," upon which Dean told Nixon everything he knew—the precise evidence that Nixon was thereafter party to the cover-up. As usual, in those Reagan believed innocent, innocence was all he saw.

The governor was back in the network news on May 10 for the first time since the speculation over who would be Nixon's new vice president. He was introduced by NBC's weekend anchor Tom Brokaw as "one of the leading candidates for the Republican nomination." Brokaw then threw to reporter Tom Pettit at one of the sixty-three-year-old governor's old stomping grounds: the Drake Relays, which he used to cover for a sportscaster on the radio in Des Moines, in the state whose early nominating caucuses were newly influential in deciding presidential nominations.

"No other presidential prospect has his experience," Pettit narrated over a jaunty snapshot of a young self-dramatizing Ronald Reagan holding one of the pipes he liked to collect back then: "Reagan was in his early twenties when he broadcast over 600 Major League baseball games without ever going to the ballpark."

RETURN TO 1932. THE ADVENTURE OF RONALD REAGAN, SPORTSCASTER, had begun shortly after college graduation: another summer on his life-guard perch, then Labor Day and the close of the swimming season—and the harrowing possibility of Depression-era unemployment. There was an opening in the sporting goods department at Montgomery Ward. The position went instead to a high school basketball star. "If I'd got-ten the job I wanted at Montgomery Ward," related his postpresidential memoir *An American Life,* "I suppose I never would have left Illinois."

However, that story contradicted one told in his other memoir, in which he had said he had already determined to make himself a star.

The previous summer he succeeded in causing an older male men-tor to take a shine to him—one of his lifelong patterns. An out-of-town businessman named Sid Altschuler asked Dutch about his career plans. He said that he didn't know what he wanted to do, though he actually did: after winning an award for his performance at a theater festival at Northwestern University, Dutch had decided once and for all that he wanted to be an actor. But in 1932 in a small town back in the Midwest, you didn't say out loud to someone that you wanted to be an actor. "So I told him that I had thought about radio and being a sports announcer."

Reagan's account has Altschuler advising Dutch in Babbittish can-do argot: hit the road, cold-call radio stations one by one, pitch himself as a bright-eyed enthusiast so excited about the future of radio "I would take any kind of job simply to get inside the station." That pitch he would have been able to make quite sincerely. In Reagan's accounts of his childhood, his mentions of a passion for the movies are rare—but he was always a fanatic for radio.

There was the time his brother tried to build their own radio set and managed to blow out all the circuits in the house. There was the crystal set at his mother's family's farm: "I remember sitting with a dozen oth-ers in a little room with breathless attention, a pair of earphones attached tightly to my head, scratching a crystal wire. I was listening to raspy recorded music and faint voices saying, 'This is KDKA, Pittsburgh, KDKA, Pittsburgh.'" The brand-new medium, before the rise of the national networks, was an entertainment Wild West—a surreal farrago of fundamentalist preaching, gutbucket jazz, hog-calling contests, old-time fiddling, advertising jingles sung by groups with names like "the

Cornfield Canaries" and "the Seed House Girls," and political snake-oil peddlers like "Baker the Great Emancipator," who did battle with a sub-machine gun by his side lest the "financial octopi" come after him in his studio. One of the most popular radio acts of 1924 was an orchestra of jailbirds led by a convicted armed robber that performed weekly under guard in a studio beneath the capitol dome in Jefferson City, Missouri. Because the airwaves were so uncluttered, the most meager signal could reach nearly nationwide, much to the disgust of aesthetes like the man who wrote to Secretary of Commerce Herbert Hoover aghast that this "most thrilling achievement of modern science" was being "prostituted" to "bad English" and "cheap jazz" and "advertising of doubtful resorts and speakeasies to such an extent to be a source of common disgust."

Dutch loved it. It was one of the ways the Boy Who Disappears came into himself. The first time he heard that crystal radio set, he ventriloquized the announcer, to the delight of his family, who made him do it again and again; in high school he broadcast basketball games; in slow moments at the Lowell Park Beach he deployed a photographic memory to recount the weekend's football games in a rapid-fire staccato.

So he stuck out his thumb and hitchhiked to Chicago. He said he hid the plan from his father because of the daily announcements over the radio "urging people not to leave home looking for work because there was none." Historians of the New Deal say there were no such announcements. That detail, however, did set up a melodramatic tale of redemption.

On his first trip, after striking out at four radio stations, the story went, he was advised at the fifth to try out in the "sticks." He hitchhiked shamefacedly back to Dixon, accompanied, in his recollection, by a melodramatic thunderstorm. Jack offered him the dilapidated family Oldsmobile to scout the surrounding towns. The first station he alighted on was WOC in Davenport, Iowa, where an employee told him to go away, because the station had just hired someone else.

"How does anyone get a chance as a sports announcer if you can't even get a job in a radio station?"

"Not so fast, ye big bastard, didn't ye hear me callin' ye? Do ye perhaps know football?"

(The story's melodramatic turning point, when everything hung in suspense.)

It was the Scottish station manager, who rapped him on the shin with his picturesque cane and demanded, "Do ye think ye could tell me about a game and make me see it?"

He had been preparing all his life as if for exactly that. He described the last quarter of a game between Eureka and Western State in which the good guys won in the final twenty seconds with a sixty-five-yard touchdown run. There were "long, blue shadows settling over the field." There was a "chill wind coming in through the end of the stadium." There were—lots more details, unspooled for a full fifteen minutes with such sweaty aplomb that he was offered on the spot bus fare to Iowa City to share a tryout with a more experienced broadcaster at a real game. There, in the third quarter, his legend went, the station manager scrawled a message: "Let the kid finish the game."

Now he was a professional sportscaster—soon praised by a Davenport paper for "a crisp account of [a] muddy struggle [that] sounded like a carefully written story . . . his quick tongue . . . as fast as the plays."

Next he was transferred at a hundred dollars a week to the much bigger Des Moines affiliate, a 50,000-watt clear channel station audible in forty-four states and five Canadian provinces at night. It made "Dutch" Reagan—the only name by which anyone there ever knew him—a celebrity in farm towns across the Midwest.

More than ever, his very life became a performance. In descriptions from those who knew him, words recur like "dashing," and "blade." And "rakish": how he combed his hair, and wore his hats tipped to the left, and—after he took over announcement duties for a show sponsored by the Kentucky Club Pipe Tobacco Company—for the pipes that he was rarely photographed without, but which he never lit. He also, a friend recalls, had a way of "holding a slightly receding posture so that people often had to lean toward him to hear what he was saying (a manner that created an almost instant sense of intimacy)."

He became a frequent dinner speaker at events outside Des Moines (at father-son dinners, *Frank Merriwell at Yale*–style, he would exhort boys against "drink, cigarettes, and cheating"). And after his high school and college sweetheart Mugs Cleaver, the minister's daughter, decamped for a year in France, he became Des Moines's most eligible bachelor—at Club Belvedere, the town's one genuine night spot; and at Cy's Moonlight Inn, home of the city's first jukebox, and a dimly lit dance floor known as the "passion pit." "Next to spiked beer," someone said, "Reagan was the Moonlight's top attraction." When he was headed there after a broadcast shift he'd alert his entourage, which included much of the coaching staff at Drake (like Eureka, a Disciples of Christ school), in a special code. A light drinker, he was the designated driver; a hail-fellow-well-met, he also liked to buy beer for underage guys. He was ever alert to ways of placing others in the hero's debt.

Another stage setting was the public pool at Fort Dodge, a massive thing that supposedly held three thousand bathers; arriving, he would wave to admirers like a politician working a crowd. He bought his first car, a convertible two-seater Nash Lafayette, one of the first off the line, with a striking metallic brown finish. He loved to gun the motor and keep the top down, even in inclement weather—quite a show in the middle of a depression. But depressions could be occasions for demonstrative heroics, too. Thrilled by the way Franklin Roosevelt had sparked the nation back to life on the radio, Dutch developed an accomplished imitation, complete with dramatic waves of the imaginary cigarette holder.

He developed another stage for his performance of personality as well. He had, he admitted, "no particular desire to be an officer," holding to the fashionable opinion that America had already fought the "war to end all wars"—but he joined the cavalry regiment stationed at Fort Dodge nonetheless, because he was willing to do just about anything to get astride a horse. Luckily, the regiment didn't seem to notice that even after he matriculated in the equestrian course he kept on delaying the application process: it required an eye examination. (When the day for the eye test finally arrived, he cheated.) He especially liked his cavalry uniform's riding breeches. Sometimes he wore them to work, especially when interviewing celebrities. "All he ever wanted to talk about was horses," a professional gambler who owned stallions remembered of their conversations at Club Belvedere.

Just like in college, he was again master of all he surveyed—a perfectly calibrated persona. He somehow always managed to throw himself in the way of opportunities for demonstrative heroics—like the time when, his window open on a hot night, he heard a scream, saw a nurse in her white uniform fighting off an attacker, and grabbed a .45 automatic he kept on his mantel and aimed it out the window. The blade, as he himself told the story, for instance to the editors of *Sports Afield* in 1984, cried, "Leave her alone or I'll shoot you right between the shoulders!" Then he dashed down in pajamas and saw the damsel in distress to her destination. "He was so strong-sounding in his command," she recalled, "that the robber believed his gun was loaded—and so did I." He never invited anyone to his modest apartment in a run-down neighborhood— but did invite people when he moved into a ground-floor flat that used to be the sitting room of a sumptuous Victorian house, a more suitable stage.

Simultaneously acquiring the company of VIPs and maintaining an image as an ordinary guy, always making others feel good in his presence: here was the most exquisitely cultivated skill of the Boy Who

Disappears. The reviews were sterling—mostly. "He was always just one of the guys, never stuck up," a Drake football star and drinking buddy remembered. However, as ever, there were suspicious circles. Dutch bragged so often to a lifeguard at Camp Dodge about his heroics at Lowell Park that the lifeguard started searching for discrepancies. "Some just got a push," he came away concluding. "He had a good imagination." A girlfriend remembered, "I always had the feeling that I was with him but he wasn't with me. He was always looking over his shoulder, scanning the crowd. I'd say he was a born politician, courting important people, favoring good will—wanting it." Some found him a hero, and followed him; others thought him a ludicrous sham. It would ever be thus.

Back home the Depression had brought Jack Reagan to the direst of straits. The first job he could get when the Fashion Book Shop disappeared was at the Dixon State Hospital, where Nelle volunteered. The family sublet all but one room in their apartment. A succession of traveling sales jobs culminated at a seedy shoe store 170 miles away. Roosevelt's New Deal saved him: he got a job with the Works Progress Administration, distributing food and scrip to his fellow down-and-outers—many of them his former social superiors. He was happy. He stopped abusing alcohol. A Reagan biographer thinks these "days of government employment were, perhaps, the finest of his life, more exciting and fulfilling than any previous experience. The desperation and hope had helped him discover a capacity to fight for others as well as himself." His youngest son may well have agreed. Like his father, he had always been a Democrat.

At college, as college students tend to do, Reagan had planted his flag further to the left. Eureka had been founded by abolitionists. The grandchildren of abolitionists dominated it now, recruiting black students, pushing women's suffrage, dedicated to changing the world (even if dancing between the sexes was forbidden). Its faculty was full of radicals—including a teacher recruited from a Duluth, Minnesota, college run by the Industrial Workers of the World where the required texts included Marx's *Das Kapital* and Engels's *The Origins of the Family, Private Property, and the State,* and which an investigating committee of the New York legislature called the "mainstay of Finnish radicalism in this country."

Reagan was very much a part of this political culture—more than the school's Christian culture (one year he got a D in religion class). "He was a liberal," a religion professor remembered, "almost a socialist when he was here." His favorite professor, Alexander Charles Gray, was a former Disciples minister who became a socialist economist; Reagan called him "Daddy Gray" and took seven courses from him. One former student of Gray's founded the Southern Tenant Farmers Union in 1934, one of the few agricultural unions of the time and practically the only Southern institution that was racially integrated; another founded the Highlander Folk School, where the song "We Shall Overcome" was composed. In 1933, the year after Reagan's graduation, 877 showed up on campus to hear socialist leader Norman Thomas. There were 250 students at Eureka at the time; one-third of them belonged to the Intercollegiate Socialist Society.

Then, in Des Moines, he was exposed to other ways of seeing the world. His next surrogate father was the station's news director, H. R. "Charlie" Gross, the "fastest tongue in the business." Gross was a dyed-in-the-wool reactionary, gifted at depicting federal spending as a colorful theater of the absurd. Reagan boldly tried to sell him on the New Deal in lunch-counter debates—rigidly holding to positions, like Secretary of Agriculture Henry Wallace's program to pay farmers to kill pigs, that he privately considered absurd himself. What Gross's ripostes might have consisted of is suggested by the speeches he gave decades later as one of the most conservative members of the United States Congress: against Medicare ("I'm simply trying to save this country from bankruptcy"); against foreign aid ("I don't care whether you describe it in English, Latin, or Pig Latin"); against federal funding of rodent control in the slums ("How many children are bitten by squirrels that they feed and try to handle? On the basis of that, does anyone suggest a program to exterminate squirrels?"); the National Endowment for the Arts (grants "for the study of the tune Nero played as Rome burned")—and especially, that "Tower of Babel, the United Nations."

Dutch held Charlie Gross in awe, whatever their ideological differences. Gross was the only person he never swore around, the only colleague he consistently addressed as "Sir." "Somewhere around the last months of Dutch's employment at WHO," a colleague remembered, "I recall thinking that maybe Gross was winning him over."

Meanwhile, Reagan's regional fame grew apace. He wrote an "inside dope" sports column in the *Des Moines Dispatch*, aping Grantland Rice's purple prose (the Sugar Bowl was the "Saccharin Saucer") and soppy moralism: "Mr. and Mrs. Public shell out to see the Old College try," he wrote of a fight between Joe Louis and Bob Pastor he thought obviously fixed (no matter that the facts were not clear), not "sporting mud holes like the Black Sox Scandal." Most famously, he did play-by-play of the games of the Chicago Cubs. In an age before jet travel, the relevant technologies were a telegraph and a typewriter: a witness present at the game would relay the on-field goings-on to Des Moines in Morse code, and a clerk in the studio would type out the action on slips of paper and pass them through a slit in the soundproof wall to Ronald Reagan, who'd fill in the rest with his imagination while working a foot pedal to amplify and attenuate canned crowd applause. He got so good at it that he toured around delivering the show in person, including at the chapel at Eureka College and the Iowa State Fair.

Thus the skill that landed him, some four decades later, one spring day six weeks after Henry Aaron broke Babe Ruth's home run record, in a lavish feature on *NBC Nightly News*, calling the nation back to those simpler bygone days of Grantland Rice. In this sordid spring of 1974, it was just of the sort of nostalgia a traumatized nation was desperate to lap up.

NEWS CAME THAT THE HOMICIDAL GANG WHO HAD SWALLOWED UP PATTY Hearst included the former social chair of Chi Omega at Indiana University, a high school golfer and scion of an Episcopalian building supply family in Indianapolis, and a cute and perky former cheerleader and Sunday school teacher and Goldwater girl from Santa Rosa. In the sporting news, pitcher Dock Ellis of the Pittsburgh Pirates attempted to bean every batter in the Reds lineup in retaliation for a run-in two years earlier with a racist Cincinnati security guard. The May 10 newscast on NBC began with speculation on whether a rare face-to-face meeting between Vice President Ford and the president had included talk of presidential succession; it then segued to G. Gordon Liddy's conviction for contempt of Congress; then to the latest leak from the impeachment hearings that the president probably knew about the April 1972 meeting in the attorney general's office where Liddy proposed his "Operation Gemstone"—then to fears of a housing market collapse, news that a federal judge had ruled William Calley, the perpetrator of the My Lai Massacre, could remain free on bail, and a report on how colleges and universities across the country were running out of money.

Then came genial Ronald Reagan, regaling a giant Drake Relays audience with the story of how he did Cubs play-by-play:

"So you'd say, 'Here comes the pitch!' and . . ."

(*"He worked from very brief telegraphic descriptions which had to be typed up for every play of the game. . . ."*)

". . . now at this point you wait for the typewriter again and you say that 'there's a stall'—and if he doesn't start typing you say he's waved off the sign, wiped his hand on the rosin bag . . ."

(Pan to a sepia-toned shot of dashing Dutch at the microphone in trench coat, tie, and rakishly angled hat.)

And then, at jackrabbit speed, mounting in rhythm and intensity, his audience pulled in deeper and deeper—

". . . thereitgoesahardhitgroundballsecondbasemangoveroveraftertheballmakesaonehandstabgrabstheballalmostfallingdownthrowsit *just in time for the out*!!"

Then the country heard for the first of many times the tale about the time he had Dizzy Dean pitching against Billy Jurges (though in other tellings the batter was Augie Galan), and the telegraph machine malfunctioned: "I looked at Curly and Curly looked at me and I just *couldn't* say that to the audience, 'We've lost our service, we're going to have a brief interlude of transcribed music.'"

He laughed: "So I said, 'Diz Dean'—I slowed him down a lot, had him use the rosin bag, had him shake off signs, lengthy windup—'finally lets go with the other pitch.' And he fouled that one off to the right. Then he fouled one back to the stands! Then he fouled one off back of third base and I described two kids trying to get the ball. Then he fouled one off that just missed a home run by a foot—until *finally*, in the nick of time, Curly sat up, started typing, and I started another ball on the way to the plate, grabbed the wire, and said—'Jurges popped out on the first ball pitched.'"

As the laughter billowed he thanked his audience and stepped down. That old trouper's rule: always leave 'em laughing when you say goodbye.

THE IDEA OF A REAGAN PRESIDENTIAL BOOMLET, THOUGH, SEEMED hardly to last longer than a pop fly on the first ball pitched. "To the dismay of his political handlers," Washington dopesters Rowland Evans and Robert Novak wrote in their "Inside Report" column a few weeks later, "Ronald Reagan is no closer to a polite but clear break with President Nixon than he was a year ago and continues to resist that politically necessary rupture even as he prepares to run for President." The columnists were frankly astonished: "During a one-hour interview with us in his state capitol office, Reagan uttered not one discouraging word about Mr. Nixon." The political architects of his presidential run, they reported, "meeting secretly and regularly"—who having "watched plain, dull Jerry Ford in action, are confident their man can win"—were anguished at what they called their man's stubborn "Christian charity toward a fallen political comrade." In an interview, Reagan lectured Washington's most influential columnists, saying that he found no evidence of criminal activity—which was why, he said, Nixon's detractors were training their fire on "vague areas like morality and so forth." *Expletives deleted* did not dismay him; he made of them, in fact, a virtue: "I've had some meetings in this office when I've been enraged at the legislature that I would not have wanted my mother to hear!"

Evans and Novak concluded, "For such 'Christian charity' Reagan pays a price": in polls of California Republicans regarding a theoretical head-to-head matchup with Gerald Ford for the Republican nomination, in a state where Nixon's approval rating was but 18 percent, Reagan was down 7 points since November. Still he stuck to his guns: asked about Evans and Novak's column in his next press conference, he said that they may have "stretched it a little bit," but that he still presumed Nixon to be an unfairly harassed innocent.

No one seemed impressed with Ronald Reagan. At NBC News the reporter had signed off from Des Moines with the jape, "Sportscasting is clearly good training for politics. You learn the fine art of speaking with conviction—even when you don't know what you're talking about." Anchor Brokaw, unable to help himself, grinned from ear to ear. Reagan did not appear again on a national newscast until June 19, in a mocking CBS item on his success turning graffiti into a criminal offense carrying a five-hundred-dollar fine. He did not show up after that until October. Ronald Reagan might be charming, but Richard Milhous Nixon would require more credible defenders than this.

A STRIKE BY TEN THOUSAND MUNICIPAL WORKERS IN SAN FRANCISCO RE-duced hospital patients to two meals a day, served on paper plates, and diabetics got no special meals; transportation was paralyzed; hundreds of millions of tons of raw sewage surged into the world's most beautiful bay. A school strike in tiny Hortonville, Wisconsin, made *Time* magazine for the vociferousness of the passions it raised: a "teacher" hung in effigy from the local water tower by a gang of local toughs who designated themselves "The Vigilantes"; school board members finding *Playboy* magazine subscriptions they hadn't ordered showing up in their mailboxes and being woken up by harassing phone calls at 3 A.M.; a strike critic discovering his favorite hunting beagle hanged to death on his front porch on its own chain.

And meanwhile on the funny pages, Garry Trudeau followed a series of strips about oil barons reveling in the record profits with ones of congressmen agonizing in poker-game colloquies about how they might vote on impeachment.

Even conservative Republicans were on the fence—like Congressman Hamilton Fish Jr., a Judiciary Committee member from a New York district that was fifty-fifty for impeachment. What had tipped the scales for *him* toward impeachment was a constituent's letter reading, "Is Mr. Nixon utterly amoral? Or does he know the difference between right and wrong, but firmly believes that a lie repeated often and loudly enough *can* fool all of the people all of the time?"

Impeachment hearings had begun behind closed doors in the Rayburn Office Building. Twenty-one Democrats and seventeen Republicans sat earnestly on a two-tiered mahogany dais beneath stately portraits of illustrious predecessors from a Judiciary Committee that had only recently been a very different sort of body: a redoubt of backbench conservatives, a sleepy graveyard for progressive legislation. By the late 1960s, though, it suddenly found itself the white-hot center of all the most interesting issues, from open housing to criminal jurisprudence to privacy rights. Fresh-faced young liberals soon clamored to join; now more than half the membership was under fifty. Eleven were freshmen, and blacks and women were represented far out of proportion with their number in the rest of the House. "These aren't Southern gentlemen like Sam Ervin," a Republican member warned his caucus. "These guys are out for blood."

Chairman Rodino and his deputy John Doar determinedly refused to give it to them. Doar began his evidentiary presentation on May 9 in numbing chronological order, "with a level of precision," Jimmy Breslin wrote, "that approached life." His drone was interrupted by intervals in which members listened, using earphones clamped to their heads, to Oval Office conversations so contextless and of such poor audio quality that they often ended up more perplexed than when they began.

And since the hearings' very first vote had been to clear the room of both spectators and cameras, and had been accompanied by members' pledges to keep what happened behind those closed doors to themselves, reporters would lurk for hours on end in the marble corridors for those precious moments when a quorum call, lunch, or closing gavel sounded like a starting gun—when, as the *New York Times*' Anthony Lukas described the spectacle, "eighty to a hundred reporters thundered down the hallway after their favorites, begging for a scrap of data." One freshman Republican, New Jersey's Joseph Maraziti, dashed so quickly every evening in order to get on front pages proclaiming the president's innocence, he earned the nickname "Streaker." Liberals rushed to launder the opposite impression. What ended up running on the front page frequently revealed nothing useful at all. For instance, the day early in June when the *New York Times* headline NIXON TAPE IS SAID TO LINK

MILK PRICE TO POLITICAL GIFT faced off against the *Washington Post*'s
TAPE PROVIDES NO NIXON TIE TO MILK FUNDS: the future of the republic,
viewed through a glass darkly—in the hearing room, and everywhere
else.

On May 20 Judge Sirica upheld an appeal by the impeachment inquiry for sixty-four more taped conversations. The president refused,
filing an appeal refusing to comply with this or any "such further subpoenas as may hereafter be issued"—a position so uncompromising it
shook loose some die-hard supporters who had taken at face value what
had been his former public line that he could be forthcoming only in
the event of an impeachment inquiry. The committee voted 28–10, with
eight of seventeen Republicans voting with the majority, to dispatch a
public letter calling his refusal a "grave matter" that "might constitute a
ground for impeachment." Independent Prosecutor Jaworski asked the
Supreme Court to hear the case immediately. On May 31, the Supreme
Court agreed. The committee doubled down, subpoenaing forty-five
more conversations.

Bantam Books printed seventy thousand more copies of Philip
Roth's 1971 anti-Nixon satire *Our Gang* in a new "Pre-Impeachment
Edition." And Richard Nixon did what he always did when the politi-
cal going got most tough: he found a friendly audience to appeal to. In
March, it had been the Grand Ole Opry. In June, it was the rest of the
world, on a stature-enhancing foreign trip.

IN CAIRO, EXUBERANT STREETSIDE CROWDS CRUSHED TWENTY BODIES
deep for seven miles: Anwar Sadat, only recently armed to the teeth
with Soviet planes, tanks, and antiaircraft batteries, now stood beaming
beside Nixon in an open-topped limousine—a sight Americans hadn't
seen since November 22, 1963. Millions more lined Nixon's rail route to
Alexandria. In case of an assassination attempt, one of the train cars included a mobile operating room. It hardly seemed necessary: Egyptians
proved delirious Nixon fans, waving American flags, beating the air
with palm fronds, trilling ululations, even strewing rose petals across his
path. In Saudi Arabia, King Faisal embraced him, bestowed upon him
the Highest Order of King Abel Aziz al Saud, and implored the American people "to rally around you, Mr. President." Landing in Damascus
after Air Force One was escorted by four Soviet-built MiGs, Nixon announced reestablished diplomatic relations with Syria. In Jordan he and
King Hussein pledged "continued close friendship and cooperation."
Israel, his next stop, had reason to take offense at all of that; King Faisal,

after all, had said that peace would come in the Middle East only after Jerusalem was "liberated" from the Jews—but Nixon did pretty damned well there, too. After speeding at 75 mph from Ben Gurion Airport to Jerusalem in a forty-car procession that included thirty military vehicles, he promised enriched uranium and nuclear reactors to the Jewish state just as he had done for Egypt, proclaiming, "This is the cradle of civilization. We must make sure it is not its grave." Crowds went wild again—with help from the sixty thousand dollars the Israeli government spent on American flags.

It seemed that most rare and precious thing, a genuine advance toward Middle East peace. It buttressed the sturdiest defense the president's diehards could make, that he was a peacemaker. ("Pssst! China!" an offstage voice helpfully whispered to *Doonesbury*'s football-helmet-wearing Republican partisan B.D., as he haplessly attempted to defend the president in a June strip.) Politically, however, none of it mattered. Americans watched, Teddy White reflected, like voyeurs at a Judy Garland concert, seeing if the drug-addled old trouper could stagger her way through "Somewhere Over the Rainbow" one more time. Gallup revealed during Nixon's nine days in the Middle East that 52 percent of Americans favored impeachment or resignation. The Supreme Court agreed to rule on whether the grand jury was within its authority when it named him an "unindicted co-conspirator." The trip certainly hadn't relaxed him. In Egypt, amid glorious China-style photo opportunities at the Pyramids and the Sphinx, he endured a painful outbreak of an inflated vein—phlebitis, which caused his left leg to inflate to twice the size of his right.

Articles started appearing in the press demonstrating that, according to analyses done on the sophisticated audio equipment the Judiciary Committee was using, the White House's transcriptions of the subpoenaed conversations had been systematically distorted. Here was the president, in words entirely missing form the White House transcripts, telling John Mitchell, "I don't give a shit what happens, I want you to stonewall it, plead the Fifth . . . save the plan." There he was barking cover-up orders two months before he was even supposed to know a cover-up existed. The White House version had *John Dean* saying Hunt's blackmail demands were "worth buying time on" when actually those were the *president's* words. And it had the president *preferring* a "hang-out"—letting justice take its course, whereas he actually had *rejected* it. The White House said the discrepancies were honest mistakes. *Yeah, right*, answered the suspicious: honest mistakes like depicting the words "a phone call reporting the burglary" as "our phone calls. Bully!" Sure. The [expletive deleted] president's men talked like Teddy Roosevelt all the time.

THE PHLEBITIS-RACKED PRESIDENT INVOKED CHINA WHILE BOARDING the plane back home: "This journey, as that of two years ago, will contribute to peace not only in that area but throughout the world." Then he flew to the Soviet Union on five days' rest, the twenty-eighth country visit and 137,500th mile logged for peace during the course of his presidency. "He probably felt more at home now in the familiar walls of the Kremlin," Anthony Lukas reflected, "than he did on Capitol Hill." Nixon and Brezhnev, practically pals, loved exchanging extravagant gifts; this time around, the car-crazy Soviet leader got a Chevy Monte Carlo, which he had read was *Motor Trend*'s Car of the Year. But the old magic was gone. The Russians, who did not appreciate being cast as saviors for a political cripple, struck the words "close personal relationship" from *Pravda*'s text of the toast Nixon offered Brezhnev at the Grand Kremlin Palace.

That same day, Nixon's poor lawyer James St. Clair stood before the Judiciary Committee struggling through the impossible task of defending a client who would not tell him the truth. In California, Herb Kalmbach began a six-to-eighteen-month jail term. Then, the day before the Fourth of July, the president returned from Russia to his own virtual hermitage, Key Biscayne, where he hid out for a full four days.

This is not what Richard Nixon's Independence Day was supposed to look like. Presiding over the nation's July 4, 1976, Bicentennial had been a Nixonian obsession at least since he had rechristened Air Force One "Spirit of '76" for his 1972 trip to China. "The Spirit of '76" was also the theme for his January 20, 1973, inauguration ceremony. A federal Bicentennial commission had been established in 1966; he massively expanded it. Now his megalomania mocked him—as each Fourth of July became an occasion for ironists to hold forth on just how far from its patriotic ideals this nation and its leader had fallen.

The *New York Times* took up half its editorial page on July 4, 1973, to argue that never "has the nation been so shaken by doubt and uncertainty directly affecting its topmost leaderships, its most revered institutions, and the very structure of democratic government." Alongside that essay it featured one by Dr. Arnold Hutschnecker, who those in the know recalled had been Richard Nixon's psychotherapist, arguing that a board of psychiatrists should certify presidents for sanity. In November one Benjamin Levine of Brooklyn expressed a common sentiment in a letter to the *Chicago Tribune:* "It would be a sin and a shame if our President were still presiding over the affairs of our great nation when we celebrate the 200th anniversary of this country on July 4, 1976." In December, a corporate-sponsored reenactment of the Boston Tea Party, complete with National Guardsmen decked out in eighteenth-century period costume boarding a seventy-five-foot replica of the HMS *Beaver,* was humiliated by a "People's Bicentennial Commission" counterprotest, staged from a more impressive 150-foot ship, complete with museum displays on impeachment and explaining how the *actual* 1773 Tea Party was a protest against corrupt transnational capitalists like Richard Nixon's favorite ITT—whose Boston building, the protesters pointed out, had served as staging ground for the official commemoration.

This year, on July 4, 1974, Mike Royko compared presidential rhetoric: Jefferson said, "The whole of government consists of being honest." Nixon said, "Is it too late to go the hangout road?" *Esquire* published a full-page graphic, "On the Bicentennial of the United States of America," listing national "heroes"—including Benedict Arnold, Aaron Burr, Richard Speck, Leopold and Loeb, Charles Starkweather, Robert Vesco, Joe McCarthy, and G. Gordon Liddy. The *Today* show's Barbara Walters and Douglas Kiker needled the Bicentennial Commission director with questions about whether Watergate wouldn't "surely spoil" the celebration. Newspapers covered the "Boypower '76" scandal, revealing that a Boy Scouts of America drive to recruit one of every three eligible American lads by the Bicentennial had resulted in padding the rolls with fictitious names. Members of Congress spent their Fourth of July recess back home with, as one of them put it, "wet fingers sticking out of their heads": people like Senator Dole, up for reelection in Kansas, where in his home county Nixon's opponent had won but 25 percent in 1972; 25 percent was Nixon's approval rating now. Unfortunately, that quarter of the electorate comprised the very Republican diehards he needed to win. When asked dozens of times a day about Watergate, which it had been his job to minimize in 1972 as Republican National Committee chair, he was reduced to snapping back in that bizarre third-person Bob Dole way, ". . . but I'm running a campaign to re-elect Bob Dole!"

The scandal would completely rewire the off-year elections. That much now was plain.

THE PRESIDENT NEXT SPENT FOUR DAYS IN THE WHITE HOUSE, TAKING IN news of Supreme Court oral arguments in *United States v. Nixon* and of the release of the full Judiciary Transcripts and four thousand new pages of Watergate evidence. They included St. Clair's disastrously unpersuasive pleading; open-and-shut evidence that Nixon heard about the cover-up as early as June 30, 1972; top-level Oval Office memos ordering the establishment of "a political intelligence capacity" in 1971; evidence of the laundering of almost a million dollars officially earmarked for polling, but actually to be used for black operations—and the discovery of yet another nineteen-minute tape gap.

At that, the president decamped for a fortnight in the California ghost towns that once thrived by supporting his presidential retreat at San Clemente. The San Clemente Inn, disinclined to reserve blocks of rooms for a company about to go out of business, evicted White House staff and Secret Service agents from the quarters they had comfortably enjoyed since 1969; the Surf and Sand in Laguna Beach, whose brochures advertised "Our private meeting and banquet room is named the Press Corps Room in recognition of the members of the Fourth Estate," evicted the press. On July 13, John Ehrlichman was convicted of perjury and conspiring to violate Daniel Ellsberg's civil rights; on the fourteenth, new evidence emerged that at his Senate confirmation hearings to become secretary of state Henry Kissinger had lied about ordering phone taps and Senator Weicker said Nixon's personal role in editing the transcripts proved the Watergate cover-up was ongoing; on the fifteenth the Judiciary Committee released a devastating chapter-and-verse report on how the administration used the IRS to reward friends and punish enemies; on the sixteenth Judiciary Committee member Elizabeth Holtzman reported they were considering developing a bribery charge against the president in the milk money case; and on the seventeenth the panel released documents demonstrating that the Plumbers were intended for political, not "national security" purposes, and that the head of the Justice Department's Criminal Division testified under oath that the president told him to stop investigating the Ellsberg break-in—because he had known about it, and considered it "fully justified by the circumstances."

Surely now, the village of elite Washingtonians reasoned, the president in whom they had so unwisely invested their trust would take their advice and move to resign, sparing the nation the agonizing search for what was now being called a "smoking gun"—some still-elusive piece of evidence, preferably from the president's lips, proving he had absolutely, positively, committed a criminal act.

No such luck.

Instead, on July 18, James St. Clair gave an hour and a half of closing argument claiming that none of the indiscretions of the president's aides could be traced to Nixon in any "clear and convincing manner."

And at Washington's stately hilltop Shoreham Hotel, 1,500 of the president's staunchest supporters attended a dinner as guests of Rabbi Baruch Korff's National Citizens Committee for Fairness to the Presidency, eagerly dancing to the Lionel Hampton tune "We Need Nixon," patiently awaiting a promised phone call from the president from his hidey-hole in San Clemente. Several of his top officials were present, and also Julie Nixon Eisenhower, the president's lovely younger daughter, who had by then given 138 interviews and press conferences proclaiming her father's innocence. A journalist called her the de facto first lady. Her presence at this late date provided the president's remaining diehards further confidence for the fight—for surely he would not send out his own daughter to lie for him.

The defense case grew increasingly surreal and sordid. Judiciary members' switchboards were swamped by identically phrased phone calls concerning "the lynch-mob atmosphere created in this city by the *Washington Post* and other parts of the Nixon-hating media"; these were scripted by a George Mason University student named Karl Rove and his faux-grassroots group "Americans for the Presidency." In Richmond Hills, New York, the superannuated president of the Republican Club, which sported a gargantuan SUPPORT YOUR PRESIDENT across the entire face of the building, told *Newsweek* "they"—the presidents' persecutors—"were encouraging poor Negroes to come up here and endorsing fornication and supporting illegitimate children. And Patty Hearst! She's a product of a liberal environment." The Georgia state Republican chairman, for his part, maintained, "If the news media is attacking the President, he must be doing something right."

Then there were the glassy-eyed young people crowding the U.S. Capitol steps every morning bearing signs reading FORGIVE, LOVE, UNITE and chanting "God needs Nixon" in front of the Rayburn Office Building wearing sandwich-board images of Judiciary Committee members reading, "I am praying for ___." "This nation is God's nation," their leader explained. "The office of the President of the United States is, therefore, sacred." This leader was the Reverend Sun Myung Moon. Thousands of brainwashed "Moonies," it turned out, had been placed front and center at the White House Christmas tree lighting ceremony back in December in "Project Unity" armbands. They were the ones waving banners reading "God Loves the President" and "God Loves America" in time to "Deck the Halls." The president had come out to pay his respects; the Moonies literally knelt down to worship him.

Moon didn't actually believe God loved America—or at least its form of government, democracy, which he considered the work of

Satan; nor did he much love the deity whose birth Christmas celebrated, whom he considered decidedly inferior to himself. In fact his plan was to take over the country by 1977, lest Armageddon come. That was why the Moonies had been loaded into vans across the country, allowed five or four hours or even just three hours of sleep a night while chanting "Our Satan" incessantly to stay awake, all under the discipline of handlers who watched Hitler Youth films for their training in disciplinary techniques. Here they were: the president's people. And the president welcomed their devotion. In February, Moon had visited the Oval Office. Together, they bowed their heads for a prayer in which Moon proposed a national fast to preserve his presidency. The fast took place that July, kicked off in a ceremony attended by Bruce "Dr. Happiness" Herschensohn and Rabbi Baruch Korff.

This banquet was the president's chance to thank them. "Rabbi Korff's eloquence, his intelligence, his dedication," Nixon's disembodied voice boomed across the huge Shoreham banquet hall, "have been a great source of strength to me and all of us in these difficult times." The rabbi hung up the phone receiver, intoned, "We love you dearly," and brushed away a stubborn tear.

CHAPTER THIRTEEN

Judging

SHORTLY AFTER 11 A.M. ON JULY 24, A HOT, STICKY, OVERCAST WEDNES-day, the Supreme Court handed down its unanimous decision in Case 73-1766, *United States v. Nixon,* and cross petition 73-1834, *Nixon v. United States.* Reading its opening argument, a Nixon hater would have reason to worry. The Court affirmed, for the first time in its history, that something called "executive privilege" did in fact exist: the president had a right to keep his deliberations with subordinates from congressional scrutiny.

Next, though, came the thermonuclear explosion.

The man whom Nixon had appointed chief justice, reading out this next part in the courtroom, drew in a breath, then uttered: "The general-ized assertion of privilege must yield to the demonstrated specific need for the evidence in a pending criminal trial. . . . Accordingly, the judg-ment under review is affirmed."

Meaning, every subpoenaed conversation was now the property of the Congress of the United States.

From the Western White House, there was no immediate response.

AFTER WHAT SEEMED LIKE AN ETERNITY A STATEMENT FROM THE SURF and Sand Hotel was issued in the president's voice: "While I am disap-pointed in the result, I respect and accept the court decision, and I have instructed Mr. St. Clair to take whatever measures are necessary to com-ply with that decision in all respects."

"That's news?" a cameraman asked. It was: that this president now accepted the authority of the Supreme Court was a relatively surprising proposition.

The timing was remarkable. Only minutes later, Chairman Peter Rodino sat poised with his gavel in the air waiting for the signal from the TV cameraman to smack it down to open the Judiciary Committee's public impeachment hearings.

Nine impeachment counts were up for debate. The allegations

ranged from Nixon's role in accepting the ITT and dairy industry's bribes to his refusal of Congress's subpoenas: his secret, falsified bombing of Cambodia, his obstruction of justice in bribing defendants, his misuse of the CIA, his lying to investigators, his making up the story of John Dean's investigation, his misuse of federal funds to gussy up his private residences, and, finally, his violation of the oath to faithfully execute the laws by deploying the IRS, FBI, and Secret Service in "disregard of the constitutional rights of citizens."

The members got fifteen minutes each for opening statements. Rodino's counterpart in the Republican minority, Edward Hutchinson, said there wasn't sufficient evidence to go forward with hearings in the first place. Jack Brooks, Democrat of Texas, returned in thunder: "Never in our 198 years have we had evidence of such rampant corruption in government." Robert Kastenmeier of Wisconsin, one of the committee's liberal firebrand Democrats, started quietly, conversationally—and ended near to a bone-shattering shout: "Society, through its elected representatives, must condemn this conduct! Otherwise we will cease to be a government of laws. . . . I will, therefore, vote for the impeachment of Richard M. Nixon, and I do this with the belief that the House of Representatives will agree and that his trial in the Senate will result in his conviction and removal from office."

There followed a hush: he now was the first committee member to commit to the removal of the president.

That added fire to the presentation by Republican Charles Sandman of New Jersey, "his voice a snarl reminiscent of Joe McCarthy's twenty years before," Theodore White wrote. He called the inquiry "the joke of the century"—and said only the wickedness of the liberal media made anyone think differently.

Crowds overwhelmed the air-conditioning; on TV, congressmen's skin glistened, wet—much like another August day, in 1948, when the youngest member of the House Un-American Activities Committee turned himself overnight into a national figure while questioning the accused Communist Alger Hiss, the first time this strange, sweating man divided his country in two, catalyzing two separate and irreconcilable sets of apocalyptic fears about the state of the nation in the minds of two separate and irreconcilable groups of Americans, pro- and anti-Nixon.

Tom Railsback of Moline, Illinois, the last Republican to speak this first day, earnestly, desperately sought to cut through Nixonland's division. Railsback owed this president: he was one of Congress's dozens of fourth-term reps who might not have been elected had it not been for Nixon's campaign stops for them in 1966. Once there, Railsback had been tapped for the "Chowder and Marching Society," a social club for hot young Republican prospects, cofounded by Nixon in 1949. Now he spoke pensively, soberly, as if suppressing anguish. Richard Nixon had won the reelection vote in his district with nearly two-thirds of the vote. Richard Nixon "had only treated me kindly whenever I had occasion to be with him." He "has done many wonderful things for this country." Someday "historians are going to realize the contributions he had made."

But, Railsback offered, maybe it was time for him to go.

Not, Railsback said, for things like the ITT and dairy bribes, the bombing of Cambodia, or the income tax shenanigans—to impeach on those would be pettily partisan. He singled out instead areas "where a conservative or a moderate or a liberal should be more concerned about the state of our government"—what he called "the abuses of power." The president's knowledge that John Dean was ordering the IRS commissioner to audit McGovern's contributors. His knowledge, too, within a week of the break-in, of the plan to use the CIA to get the FBI to stop investigating the laundering of money through Mexico. Ordering Dean to falsify an exonerating Watergate report even while Dean was ordered to figure out how to bribe the burglars.

Railsback spoke of mail from constituents who said the country could not afford to impeach a president. He wondered if we could afford not to. For "if we're not going to really try to get to the truth, you're going to see the most frustrated people, the most turned off people, and it's going to make the period of LBJ in 1968, 1967—it's going to make it look tame. So I hope we just keep our eyes on trying to get to the truth."

That named a spirit of the age. Like the *New York Times* reporting on how the POWs' Operation Homecoming was a hustle. Like the Judy Blume novel that quoted a psychiatrist on how boys and girls needed to know that divorced fathers who did not visit them "do not love their children at all." Like *Life* magazine mocking Frank Merriwell, and Wacky Packages teaching kids that consumerism is a scam. Like Garry Wills in *Esquire* explaining the ways Harry Truman wasn't a plain speaker. Americans *had* to train their eyes on ugly truths. They had to abandon their heroes. They had to join the suspicious circles—to abandon blithe optimism. Did not the survival of the republic depend on it?

THE NEXT MORNING A REPUBLICAN NAMED CHARLIE WIGGINS, A GOOD lawyer, made the first effective case for the president. He began, like Rodino, booming out hosannas to equal justice under law. He spoke of how he had heard himself described on television as the president's "chief defender," and how he had winced: "In the context of the law, Mr. Chairman, personalities become irrelevant. . . . The law requires that we decide the case on evidence." He then unfurled a dazzling forensic presentation that picked up from Railsback's point about the CIA— allowing that the CIA's interference with the investigation was an obvious "wrongful act," but pointing out that in the committee's thirty-eight volumes of evidence there was "not a word, ladies and gentlemen, of presidential knowledge and awareness of that wrongful act."

No smoking gun: as simple as that.

The argument drove others to distraction. William Hungate, Democrat of Missouri, said that if an elephant walked into a room his Republican friends would ask for proof that it wasn't a mouse with a glandular problem. William S. Cohen, Republican of Maine, said if his colleagues woke up in the morning to a blanket of white they would demand proof that it had snowed the night before. Hamilton Fish Jr. said that of course "there was no smoking gun. The *whole room* was filled with smoke."

Smoke, magicians know, makes for a useful distraction. Just so, Wiley Mayne of Iowa called the president's accusers "extreme partisans" (though they came from both parties) and asked why there had never been a congressional investigation of how Lyndon Johnson became a millionaire. Trent Lott, whose Mississippi district voted 85.2 percent to reelect the president, recited a ledger full of statistics about how much the government had spent on the investigation—"Could any man withstand such scrutiny?"—without any "counterbalancing presentation of the other side of the story." (Maybe there would have been such counterbalancing presentations, had the president allowed his aides to testify before Congress.)

It took an unlikely woman in schoolmarmish glasses to call the proceedings back from the brink of silliness. A minister's daughter and freshman congresswoman from Houston, Barbara Jordan, got her fifteen minutes, though it took her only thirteen. She was black—she and Andrew Young of Georgia were the first two African Americans to be sent to Congress from the South since Reconstruction—and did not shy from foregrounding the fact: "Earlier today," she intoned solemnly, "we heard the beginning of the Preamble to the Constitution of the United States: 'We, the people.' It's a very eloquent beginning. But when that document was completed on the seventeenth of September in 1787, I was not included in that 'We, the people.'"

And then, because this young woman was one of the greatest orators the United States had ever produced, she did what great orators do: she loosened up her audience with a joke. "I felt somehow for many years that George Washington and Alexander Hamilton just left me out by mistake."

Now, however, we were a more perfect union. Now the Constitution made her an equal "*in-quis-i-tor.*" She pronounced with great rounded booming accents, "My faith in the Constitution is *whole,* it is *complete,* it is *total,* and I am not going to sit here and be an idle spectator to the *diminution*—the *subversion*—the *destruction*—of the Constitution."

And, from that majestic foundation, she scolded her seniors with such a severe power that even hard-bitten reporters were mesmerized.

She pointed to a basic constitutional fact these colleagues had been too obtuse to honor: that a vote for an article of impeachment was not a vote to remove the president, only a license for a Senate trial. (Stop insulting the Framers. "They did not make the accusers and the judges the same person.") She annihilated the argument that had been maintained for months about the standard for impeachment: the Founders were perfectly clear it was not a punishment for maladministration, nor for technical crimes, but—she quoted *The Federalist,* No. 65—"a method of national inquest into the conduct of public men," as a check on tyranny. She quoted the wise reminder of a former political scientist, Woodrow Wilson, that the Constitution's requirement of a two-thirds vote in the Senate guaranteed that "nothing short of the grossest offenses against the plain law of the land will suffice to give them speed and effectiveness. Indignation so great as to overgrow party interest may secure a conviction, but nothing else can." She turned to the evidence on record—that as of June 23, 1972, the president *knew* that money from his reelection committee had been found in the possession of one of the burglars, and that arrestee Howard Hunt had earlier committed illegal acts on the president's behalf, and that the president had been recorded discussing how to shelter him from prosecution. She quoted the opinion of James Madison, speaking at the Virginia ratification convention: "If the President be connected, in any suspicious manner, with any person and there be grounds to believe that he will shelter him, the House of Representatives can impeach." And Madison to the Constitutional Convention: that a president "is impeachable if he attempts to subvert the Constitution." She repeated that. She concluded, "If the impeachment provision in the Constitution of the United States will not reach the offenses charged here, then perhaps that 18th century Constitution should be abandoned to a 20th century paper shredder."

She yielded back the balance of her time, having efficiently laid out just what the president's defenders were demanding: specifics of what he did wrong. It was one of the greatest speeches an American politician had ever delivered, this from a politician no one had heard of—and live on TV. Though, this being politics, she hardly changed any minds. The next day, a Friday, debate began with Charles Sandman whining, "I want answers, and this is what I am entitled to! . . . This is a charge against the President of the United States, he is entitled to know specifically what he did wrong!"

SANDMAN WAS SHRIEKING AGAINST SOMETHING CALLED THE "SARBANES Substitute": a carefully worked out impeachment article accusing the president of violating his constitutional oath to "preserve, protect, and defend the Constitution," and his "duty to take care that the laws be faithfully executed," by obstructing justice and delaying and impeding the investigation of the events of June 17, 1972, and subsequently.

The article was the product of a motley caucus of seven Republicans and seven moderate Democrats, all natural allies of Nixon, half from districts where Nixon got more than 62 percent of the vote in 1972. It would have been the easiest thing in the world for members like this to vote to save the president for political reasons, no matter what. Instead, conscience had guided these fourteen to the conclusion that the president *did* deserve to be impeached—but that it had to happen in a bipartisan, passionless manner. Rodino asked Representative Walter Flowers of Mississippi, whose constituents had given George McGovern only 22.9 percent of their vote, to gather the fourteen into a working team to draft impeachment articles. They became known as the "Fragile Coalition."

It was by then plain that all but three of the committee's twenty-one Democrats would impeach the president on any charge that came to a vote—liberal hotheads like the "Mad Monk," colleagues' nickname for Father Drinan, who had introduced his first impeachment resolution in July 1973 over the secret bombing of Cambodia. Working to strike down Drinan's charge about Cambodia was the soul of the Fragile Coalition's reasoning: large majorities in both parties had voted funds to continue the bombardment, so how could they impeach over that?

Ten of the seventeen committee Republicans, meanwhile, seemed willing to go to their graves defending their president. Rabbi Korff's people—who now, in communiqués to a hard-core ten thousand culled from his volunteer list of 2.5 million, seemed on the verge of advocating violent revolution: "Don't be stalled. Don't be jived. Don't take 'no' for an answer. Your congressman and his staff are paid by your taxes, so make them listen to you. If they walk away, follow them. If they hang up the phone, call again. If they lock the doors, get their home addresses and meet them there. If they treat you with disdain or condescension, tell them what you think of them. And don't delete your expletives." They concluded, "One does not reason with lynch mobs."

This kind of recriminatory atmosphere strengthened the coalition's resolve: the House Judiciary Committee must not be a lynch mob. Any legitimate grounds for impeachment had to represent *continuing* offenses, had to be bipartisan, had to be a self-evident emanation from the Oval Office itself. Maybe, then, impeachment could become an *opportunity*—an opportunity to show, as the Fragiles liked to say among themselves, that "the system worked." That maybe extremism, the awful consequences of the cacophonous 1960s, could be excised from American life once and for all.

This was serious business. Fifty Capitol police now lined the Senate-side entrance when Vice President Ford was presiding, a platoon of their motorbikes forming a wedge around his car in addition to his regular Secret Service convoy—as if for someone who was about to be president.

And so, Saturday night, after a long day of parliamentary wrangling, came the slow, stately roll call on the Sarbanes Substitute: twenty-seven in favor, eleven opposed. A committee vote of 71 percent for impeachment. That meant it would probably happen.

Almost immediately after that vote, Peter Rodino hurriedly cleared the hearing room. Reports were that a plane had taken off from National Airport, with the intent of crashing into the Rayburn Office Building, or the Capitol, perhaps in coordination with military units loyal to the president. The reports seemed credible enough. These were death-haunted times. Back in February, a madman named Samuel Byck drove to Baltimore/Washington International Airport, shot an airport cop, stormed a DC-10 on the runway, and threatened to blow up the plane with the gasoline bomb he had strapped to his body unless the pilots flew it into the White House. Two weeks later, the media reported that had he chosen the less secure airport in his hometown of Philadelphia, Byck might have succeeded.

Inflation was up above 12 percent. The currency markets were on the verge of panic. Oil, $2.70 a barrel in September, now went for eleven bucks. The world seemed nigh unto apocalypse. ("Live today," a Pan American Airways commercial went. "Tomorrow will cost more.") Two weeks before the impeachment hearings, the perky hostess of the chat show *Suncoast Digest,* who incorporated homemade puppets into the program, was angry that the station owner had told the staff to concentrate on "blood and guts," and had cut away from her show to cover a shoot-out at a local restaurant. She began her broadcast with an uncharacteristic hard-news segment, with film from the restaurant shooting—which jammed in the projector, at which point she announced, "In keeping with Channel 40's policy of bringing the latest in blood and guts, and in living color, you are going to see another first—attempted suicide." She then shot herself in the head and died, leaving behind the script she had been reading from, which included a postscript: a third-person account of the breaking news story, to be read by whoever took over the news desk next. The *Sarasota Herald Tribune* ran a photo: "THIS Is the 38-Caliber Pistol Christine Chubbuck . . . used in her on-the-air suicide." The show *Gentle Ben*, about a little boy and the tame bear who was his pet, replaced *Suncoast Digest*.

The sane were a fragile coalition. "Many Americans are in the middle of a depression," ran an advertisement in the *Chicago Tribune* for the psychology columnist Dr. Joyce Brothers. "And a lot of people feel trapped and helpless to change things. If the state of the union has put you in an unhappy state of mind, take heart. . . . There *are* things you can do as an individual to attack the national problems and to fight your own depression. Find out 'How to Beat the Blahs' in this 3-part series starting Monday." Or maybe you could watch *Gentle Ben*.

THE NEXT WEEK OPENED WITH NEWS OF THE INDICTMENT OF JOHN CONnally, the man Nixon had hoped would succeed him, in the milk bribery case, and the sentencing of John Dean. There were votes passing the Fragile Coalition's impeachment Article II, on obstruction of justice, and Article III, on defying subpoenas; and votes striking down articles on the president's taxes and the Cambodia bombings. The ten Republicans who voted against every article were confident, just as Charlie Wiggins said, that "smoking gun" evidence simply wasn't there—evidence, say, that the president ordered the CIA to get the FBI not to investigate the laundering of money through Mexico. Ronald Reagan, too, said he was "not convinced that the evidence of an impeachable offense had been presented to the Congress or the people." Though he wasn't paying much attention. When Reagan was late to his press conference one morning, a reporter asked if it was because he had been watching the hearings on TV. "No, I was sound asleep," he responded. "As a matter of fact I was having a wonderful dream when they knocked on the door." And not, he denied with a chuckle, about becoming President of the United States.

That seemed unlikely. He was back in the national news—because his handpicked lieutenant governor, Ed Reinecke, whom he was grooming as his successor, had just been convicted in Washington, D.C., of lying to a Senate committee when he claimed he had never discussed with John Mitchell ITT's pledge to underwrite the Republican convention. Reagan said he had "no right" to ask Reinecke to resign until his appeals were exhausted.

The Nielsen ratings came out. Once again Ronald Reagan was an outlier. Only 10 percent of adults had not heard or watched any of the hearings. And a Harris poll taken August 2 found 66 percent of the country wanted to fire their president—up 13 points in a week.

Richard Nixon still would not budge. Nor Vice President Ford, who got a new nickname to describe his serpentine route around the country, fifty thousand miles in his first six months as vice president alone, delivering Agnew-style speeches in which he declaimed, "I can say from the bottom of my heart that the President of the United States is innocent!" That nickname was "Zigzag."

THE NEXT MONDAY THE WHITE HOUSE POSTPONED THE REGULAR 11 A.M. press briefing. The morning's *Washington Post* suggested a reason—a story by Woodward and Bernstein that something damning had emerged in new transcripts about to be released on the Supreme Court's order. The hearings had recessed; network correspondents went on vacation—and now they were called back by their bosses. Fragile Coalition members came back from vacations, too, though they hadn't quite been relaxing: Railsback reported that people left the room or turned their backs on him when he went home; others reported death threats; at least one was pelted with stones.

The White House postponed the briefing. And then did so again. Ron Ziegler finally appeared at lunchtime. He had tears in his eyes. He announced the president would go on TV that night, and in time for the evening newscasts, the nation learned why.

> Good evening. President Nixon stunned the country today by admitting that he had held back evidence from the House Judiciary Committee, keeping it secret from his lawyers, and not disclosing it in public statements. The news caused a storm in Washington, and some of Mr. Nixon's most loyal supporters are calling for his resignation.

They included Charlie Wiggins, choking back tears, who said "the magnificent public career of Richard Nixon must be terminated involuntarily." The new transcript bludgeoned Wiggins's soul. It recorded the president strategizing with Haldeman, on June 23, 1972, about how to use the CIA to get the FBI not to investigate the laundering of money through Mexico. "That's the way we are going to play it," the president exulted—exactly the smoking gun Wiggins had expended all his political capital and brilliant advocacy claiming didn't exist.

George Will called it a "smoking howitzer." Republican National Committee chairman George H. W. Bush posted an open letter: "Dear Mr. President, It is my considered judgement that you should now resign." Charles Sandman said he had to resign. The studiously apolitical Johnny Carson announced, "Tonight's monologue is dedicated to Richard Nixon. I've got a monologue that just won't quit." He got a standing ovation unlike any he had ever experienced. Surely, Nixon would resign now.

A REPORTER CALLED RONALD REAGAN "DEEPLY DISTURBED" BY THE NEW transcript. In a prepared statement, the governor passively voiced a most unusual conclusion: that "for the first time, it has been revealed that neither the Congress nor the American people have been told the entire truth about Watergate"—*for the first time*. He fell short of asking the president to resign. Instead, he said it was "absolutely imperative that he go before the Congress immediately and make a full disclosure of all information he has on this matter, answering any and all questions the members may have. The Constitutional process should then go forward in order to bring about the speedy resolution of this issue." He took questions for a half an hour—a strong man who seemed almost helpless, pitiably refusing conflict with a more powerful man, repeating over and over, "I think the process should go forward," suggesting Nixon step aside temporarily under the Twenty-fifth Amendment "during the Congressional investigation."

He seemed to be repeating White House talking points. For White House Deputy Press Secretary Gerald Warren insisted the president would not resign but instead "pursue the Constitutional process."

Warren went on to say that Nixon had only "great admiration and affection" for communications director Herb Klein. Of whom Nixon had said, on the newly released transcripts, that he "just doesn't have his head screwed on." And so the White House's perpetual mendacity machine ground on, as if it just didn't know how to stop. "If the current impeachment process were a boxing match," George Will wrote, "the referee would stop the fight." But there was no referee. And Richard Nixon would not throw in the towel.

Until, that is, a political man was presented by a group of political men with an unanswerable political argument.

The 1964 Republican presidential nominee had recently been the subject of a *New York Times Magazine* profile: "In 1964 He Was Bela Lugosi, but the Liberals Love Barry Goldwater Now." It confirmed Goldwater's new image as a comforting senior statesman, a refreshingly straightforward contrast to the monster occupying the Oval Office. Now he served as spokesman for the House and Senate Republican leaders who emerged from an Oval Office meeting. They had been "invited," he said. "The discussion was quite general in tone." They were just "four old friends talking over a very painful situation." They could report no decision on whether or not the president would resign. Hugh Scott, holding his pipe, looked disoriented, as if stuck in some surreal Buñuel scene, as he recited his lines: "The President is in entire control of himself. He was serene and he was most amiable." He was speaking to insistent rumors that the president was on the verge of a nervous breakdown and might stage a military coup.

Wednesday, August 7, the words "NIXON SAYS HE WON'T RESIGN" emblazoned atop the *Washington Post*, a mad insouciant team of French-led conspirators broke into the nearly completed construction site of the World Trade Center with more than half a ton of equipment, ascended the building's twin towers, and somehow rigged a high wire spanning the sixty yards in between. A spritely daredevil named Philippe Petit proceeded to dance in the sky for forty-five minutes for astonished and delighted pedestrians a quarter mile below. *This* was a first-rate burglary—though it took a Frenchman to achieve it. Americans couldn't do anything right.

Representative Earl Landgrebe, Republican of Indiana, showed up on the *Today* show the next morning and said, "I'm sticking with my president even if he and I have to be carried out of this building and shot." The NBC interviewer, incredulous, asked him about the new facts in evidence. He answered, earnestly, "Don't confuse me with the facts."

And on Thursday, August 8, Richard Nixon went on TV at nine for his thirty-seventh address to the nation as president, 852 days since the third-rate burglary at the Watergate. The public areas outside the White House were more crowded than on November 22, 1963—people honking for impeachment, shouting "Jail to the Chief," comparing rumors about how the military coup would go down. Then the airwaves crackled, the president spoke—and made a merely political argument, free of contrition, that although resignation was "abhorrent to every instinct in my body," it had become "evident to me that I no longer have a strong enough base in Congress to justify continuing the effort."

He was resigning. Effective noon the next day. The Goldwater delegation had sternly informed him he didn't have the one-third of senators' votes it would take to survive an impeachment trial, and he decided that he could no longer fight.

What thoughts were in this strange man's head, after he had risen so celestially high, then fallen so infernally low? He revealed them in an extraordinarily raw, intimate, improvised farewell address to his staff assembled in the White House—and to the Americans assembled, astonished, in front of their TVs. He suggested he didn't do all that much that was wrong: "Mistakes, yes. But for personal gain, never." That he was just a modest, plain, ordinary man, from a modest, plain, luckless family: "I remember my old man. I think that they would have called him sort of a little man, common man. He didn't consider himself that way. You know what he was? He was a streetcar motorman first, and then he was a farmer, and then he had a lemon ranch. It was the poorest lemon ranch in California, I can assure you. He sold it before they found oil on it." (His staff laughed; some might even have known the story was not true.) "And then he was a grocer. But he was a great man. . . ."

He choked back tears: "Nobody will ever write a book, probably, about my mother. Well, I guess all of you would say this about your mother—my mother was a saint. And I think of her, two boys dying of tuberculosis, nursing four others in order that she could take care of my older brother for three years in Arizona, and seeing each of them die, and when they died, it was like one of her own. Yes, she will have no books written about her. But she was a saint." (They only wrote books about *Kennedy's* mother, he was implying—the bastards.)

Then he almost suggested it really wasn't his fault—simply a natural response to enemies besieging him from all sides. Still, he regretted that he ever listened to them: "others may hate you, but those who hate you don't win unless you hate them, and then you destroy yourself."

And then he was gone—boarding the presidential helicopter with an incongruously wide grin and a V-for-victory salute.

And in Sacramento, Ronald Reagan read a statement from handwritten notes: "It is a tragedy for America that we have come to this, but it does mean that the agony of many months has come to an end." Concerning whether Nixon should be prosecuted for illegality, the man who the previous day had said he should go before Congress and tell the nation "the whole truth" now said his farewell speech had been disclosure enough: "I think the man has had a punishment beyond anything any of us could imagine." He was asked about speculation he might be tapped as vice president under President Gerald Ford. He demurred, suggesting Barry Goldwater instead, but added, "anyone who did receive such a call or was asked would have to consider it a call to duty." Then he traveled to Lake Tahoe as featured speaker at a national Young Republicans meeting, and blithely told them not to fear: "You can have faith in the Republican philosophy of fiscal common sense, limited government, and individual freedom."

He told the *Washington Post*'s Lou Cannon, "I don't believe the story has come out yet. I sure tried to read those transcripts and I think for myself mistakes were made but at the same time I think history [is] probably going to be far more kind to the administration with regard to accomplishments. When all this is going on our world leadership in times of trouble is far more effective than anything we've had for a great many years."

CHAPTER FOURTEEN

"There Used to Be a President Who Didn't Lie"

THE DIGNITARIES, STANDING AT CHAIRS STILL IN PLACE AFTER NIXON'S maudlin farewell speech to his staff, couldn't stop beaming, like people at a marriage ceremony where the bride looked exquisite. And after Chief Justice Warren Burger put forth the same words George Washington first intoned 185 years before, "preserve, protect and defend the Constitution"—he stopped there for the briefest moment, letting that glorious word sink in—"of the United States," the newly invested chief executive kissed beautiful Betty Ford upon both cheeks, and it was hard not to swell up inside.

The chief justice announced, "Ladies and gentlemen, the President of the United States"; and, hearing someone other than Richard Nixon introduced that way, and seeing the pride in the faces of his four handsome children—teenagers Steve and Susan; Jack, the college kid; and Mike, the mop-topped seminarian—it was hard not to swell up again.

He spoke for less than eight minutes: "not an inaugural address," he said, "not a fireside chat, not a campaign speech—just a little straight talk among friends." He addressed these friends directly. Since he was acutely aware that he hadn't been elected, he said, "I ask you to confirm me as your president with your prayers. And I hope that such prayers will also be the first of many." And he told them that since he had campaigned for neither the presidency nor the vice presidency, he was "not subscribed to any partisan platform," was "indebted to no man—and only one woman: my dear wife."

Nixon used his wife in speeches, too, most famously in the Checkers speech, when she gazed at him with an adoration so sanctimonious, humorist Mort Sahl said she ought to have been knitting an American flag. When Jerry did it, it sounded just right: sincere. As did his affirmation that those who confirmed him as vice president were "of both parties, elected by all the people, and acting under the Constitution in their name." He pledged to be president of all the people, unlike you-know-who, and said he believed "that truth is the glue that holds government together, not our government but civilization itself"—unlike, well, you-know-who.

Who was entirely gone now.

"In all my public and private acts as your president, I expect to follow my instincts of openness and candor with full confidence that honesty is always the best policy in the end. My fellow Americans, our long national nightmare is over. Our Constitution works; our great republic is a government of laws and not men. Here the people rule."

It was a masterpiece of American oratory, and seemed fully equal to its awesome historical moment. Its themes echoed the morning's *New York Times* front page, where Nixon's farewell address was praised as "conciliatory"; pundit R. W. Apple wrote of how the end of the "Watergate agony" presaged "an era of more open government"; a news article predicted a "honeymoon," even a permanent happy marriage, between Congress and the executive. Ford was described as a "pragmatic conservative" offering an "essentially unchanged foreign policy." Another article on foreign policy was headlined "Abroad, Officials and Citizens Call Outcome of the Crisis a Tribute to Democracy." There was a little profile of Frank Wills, the black security guard at the Watergate whose eagle eye in spotting an errant strip of tape that kept a door in the Watergate parking garage unlocked eventually brought a president down: "GUARD SAYS NO POSITION TOO HIGH," the headline ran—in America even the president was not above the law. The business page proclaimed "PSYCHOLOGICAL UPLIFT FOR ECONOMY SEEN IN SHIFT TO FORD." The op-ed page saw the *Times'* most respected columnist, James Reston, celebrating "A SENSE OF NATIONAL RECONCILIATION," and guest editorialists including James Madison—who wrote from beyond the grave ("Notes on Nullification," 1835) that "a political system which does not contain an effective provision for a peaceable decision of all controversies arising within itself, would be a Government in name only." Precisely two-thirds of that *Times* A-section's eighty-one articles concerned the nation's new transition of power. They all resounded with the very same theme: the resignation proved that no American was above the law, that the system worked, that the nation was united and at peace with itself.

OTHER PIECES, TELLING OTHER STORIES, WERE CONTAINED IN THAT DAY'S paper, too, of course. You just had to plunge well into the inside pages to find them.

From Philadelphia: three female Episcopalian deacons who had been ordained as priests were banned from performing their offices by their more conservative superiors in New York. From Texas: the sentencing, thanks to the Supreme Court's 1972 5–4 decision suspending the death penalty even though 60 percent of Americans supported it, of a serial killer to a term of nearly six hundred years in prison. From Jamaica, Queens: a criminal gang of police sergeants had extorted $250,000 from legitimate business owners. From Los Angeles: cops were buying bulletproof vests on their own dime because so many police officers were being cut down by remorseless perps, and the brass wouldn't do anything about it.

There were also the movie advertisements; they hardly spoke to a nation at peace with itself. Two masterpieces of Hollywood's new cinema of moral despair: Robert Altman's *California Split,* about a freakish netherworld of compulsive gamblers, which the *Chicago Sun-Times'* Roger Ebert called an allegory of the "American nightmare"; and Roman Polanski's *Chinatown,* a neo-noir tailor-made for the age of John Mitchell, in which a private eye played by Jack Nicholson finds hidden behind sunny Southern California's economic boom a depravity beyond all imagining, then accepts the rank futility of ever doing anything about it. Pornography ads: *Flesh Gordon* (in which Emperor Wang "the Perverted," leader of the planet Porno, conquered Earth with his mighty Sex Ray); *The Seduction of Lynn Carter* ("She was violated, again and again, in crude and unspeakable ways . . . and she loved every minute of it"); *Score* ("hilariously hits the bulls eye of bi-sexual chic"); *Craig from Frisco* (in which, in an ad next to the one for *Chinatown,* the titular star addressed the reader directly: "I'm appearing in a very unique new all male cast movie at the Park Miller. Casting for me, Helmut, and our four friends took months of research.").

Then there were ads for two extraordinary films drunk with the paranoia that had defined the long national nightmare. One came from the right—and made critics write like editorialists. *Playboy's* reviewer called its star a "folk-hero par excellence." The magazine *After Dark* called it a "time bomb of a movie, exploding at just the right moment in the glare of truth." Gene Shalit on the *Today* show called it "a rouser for everyone who wants safe cities." The picture was called *Death Wish,* and it starred Charles Bronson as a New York City architect who used to be liberal, until his daughter was raped and his wife murdered. His son-in-law pronounces defeat: "There's nothing we can do to stop it. Nothing but cut and run." The architect, by contrast, learns to shoot a gun—in an Old West ghost town—so he can start mowing down muggers at point-blank range. He soon cuts the city's murder rate in half, and wins a spot on the cover of *Time.*

Liberal reviewers recorded their disgust: The *Times*' Vincent Canby called it "a bird-brained movie to cheer the hearts of the far-right wing," then, ten days later, branded Bronson a "circus bear." *Time* called it "meretricious," "brazen," and "hysterical." Roger Ebert of the *Chicago Sun-Times* called it "fascist." But in the real-life New York City, where the murder rate had doubled in ten years, and where a psychiatrist published a *Times* op-ed bragging about all the violence he had prevented by leveling a pistol that he kept "never far from my reach while I attend to patients in my mid-Manhattan office," each vigilante act onscreen won ovations from grateful fans—sometimes standing ovations. It earned seven times its $3 million budget.

The other paranoid melodrama was *The Parallax View,* named after the optical illusion in which reality is distorted by the angle from which it is viewed. It starred the handsome, diffident, long-haired Warren Beatty as a new figure in the annals of lone-wolf Hollywood heroes: not a cowboy, nor a private eye, but, of all things, a newspaper reporter— just like the guys who, banging on typewriters, whispering into phones, and making mysterious assignations in underground Washington parking garages, had become the heroes of Watergate. (Woodward and Bernstein's book *All the President's Men* was enjoying its seventh of twenty-one weeks at the top of the *New York Times* bestseller list.) In selling the role, director Alan Pakula reportedly told Beatty, "If the picture works the audience will trust the person next to them a little less." The tagline on its advertising posters: "As American as apple pie."

Beatty's character watches a charismatic young senator speak at a Fourth of July event atop the Space Needle in Seattle: "Independence Day is very meaningful to me. I've been called too independent for my own good"—then shots ring out and the apparent shooter falls from the tower in a scuffle with security guards, and another mysterious figure slips away, unnoticed by anyone but our hero. A man who looks like Earl Warren sitting atop a Supreme Court–style bench announces the conclusion of a four-month official investigation proving the shooter acted alone, "motivated by a misguided sense of and a psychotic desire for wider recognition . . . no evidence of any conspiracy. No evidence whatsoever." The official announces that these findings must end "irresponsible speculation" for good.

Three years later, Beatty bangs out a story his crusty old editor has no intention of publishing, warning that his "creative irresponsibility" would destroy him. Disgusted, Beatty returns to his noirish rooming house, where he's visited by a frightened young woman who presents him with newspaper pictures of the scene at the Space Needle: "Since the assassination six of these people in these pictures have been killed in an accident."

Beatty was in one of the pictures, too—so when would they come after him?

Just like *Death Wish*, *The Parallax View* was ripped straight from the headlines—though this time from the headlines in the underground press, where Kennedy conspiracy theories thrived. The Warren Commission (which happened to include Gerald Ford), impaneled by President Johnson to investigate the assassination, was a *Rush to Judgment;* that 1966 book by the left-wing lawyer Mark Lane spent six months on the *New York Times* bestseller list after being rejected by fifteen publishers. In 1964, the year of the Warren Report's publication, the Gallup poll found that 75 percent of Americans, the highest proportion yet recorded, trusted the government "to do what is right most of the time." Of course that was also the same year, Americans now knew, that Lyndon Johnson got his blank check to make war in Vietnam by lying about what happened in the Gulf of Tonkin, then won his landslide reelection by promising he wouldn't send American boys thousands of miles away to do what Asian boys ought to do for themselves. Soon an irregular cadre of citizen investigators began working to prove the Warren Report was a "sleazy and insulting fantasy." And by 1974, when 62 percent *distrusted* their government to do the right thing most of the time, their conclusions were becoming mainstream. Coretta Scott King, for example, in an interview that spring in the women's magazine *McCall's,* said that the "same kind of people who were paid to do the dirty work in Watergate were paid to do the dirty work in the Kennedy and Martin Luther King assassinations."

Parallax hit all the tenets of the "assassination community" catechism: that mendacious elites exploited a nation's longing to trust in order to better control them (the hero cries, "Everyone was looking for an explanation! Every time you turned around someone was knocking off one of the best men in the country!"); that accessories to conspiracy were everywhere ("Face it," a coroner tells him in claiming his informant's death was obviously a suicide, "some people wanna die"); and that the powers that be got away with killing our truth-telling president by making the assassination look like the work of some miserable loner—a "patsy," as Lee Harvey Oswald himself had put it.

Another key tenet embodied in *The Parallax View* extended far beyond the conspiracists: that America, before Nixon, before Johnson, had had a truth-telling president—a president who had been innocent.

In pictures like *Klute* (1971, also directed by Pakula), *Alice Doesn't Live Here Anymore* (Martin Scorsese, 1974), and *Nashville* (Robert Altman, 1975), production designers used a certain visual shorthand to signify that characters whom liberal audiences might prejudge as reactionary—because they were working class, because they were Southerners, because they were cops—were meant to be perceived sympathetically: a picture of Jack and/or Robert Kennedy on their wall. "Kennedy" meant comfort, truth, trust, the calm before the storm. The collection of sentimental reminiscences by Kennedy family retainers, *Johnny, We Hardly Knew Ye*, stayed on the *New York Times* bestseller list for five months; the memoirs of eighty-two-year-old family matriarch Rose stayed there for six months. And the sentiment extended all the way down to schoolchildren. That spring, a kindergarten teacher in Long Beach, California, wrote in the *Los Angeles Times* about a lesson she was giving about presidents. One of the four-year-olds boldly pronounced, "The real President lies!" The teacher, taken aback, asked the child to elaborate. He responded, "There used to be a President who didn't lie, but he's dead!"

Among the assassinologists it was widely believed Kennedy had signed his own death warrant with a 1963 American University commencement address announcing unilateral suspension of all atmospheric testing of nuclear weapons and proclaiming that Americans had had "more than enough" of "war and hate and oppression": to the powers that be, that meant he had to go, and a patsy had to be readied to take the fall. Similarly, in the final reel of *The Parallax View*, depicted in quick-cut scenes of Hitchcockian vertiginous intensity, the reporter-hero infiltrates the shadowy corporation responsible for the assassinations by posing as one of those pathetic loners, is hired by it as a security guard, and is posted in the rafters at a campaign rally of another bold truth-telling politician. A professional sniper cuts down the target, drops his high-powered rifle, and steals away—at which point, as the authorities rush in to arrest the patsy, Beatty, Parallax agents cut him down, just like Jack Ruby did to Oswald. The last scene was identical to first, that same Earl Warren figure sternly pronouncing, "Although certain that this will do nothing to discourage the conspiracy peddlers, there is no evidence of conspiracy in the assassination. . . . There will be no questions."

The picture was fascinating, and might well have been a hit six months earlier. It did very little business now. Paranoia was out of fashion. The country had a president who didn't lie. Did anyone really imagine that outside the small and suspicious circles any real interest attached to the old forms of the executive-distrust question?

• • •

"THE COMMUTER AT 514 CROWN VIEW DRIVE IN ALEXANDRIA, VA., AWOKE shortly before 6 A.M. and, in baby blue summer pajamas, boiled water for his tea, cut the melon, and toasted the English muffin," began the Associated Press dispatch.

"Still in his pajamas, he popped his head out the front door looking for the morning paper. Not there yet.

"Thirty minutes later, he popped out again. Still no paper. The *Washington Post,* which had never charmed the 37th President of the United States, was now getting off on the wrong foot with the 38th."

Finally, an eager nation learned, Shelley Deming, fourteen, apologizing that the circulation man was late, delivered a newspaper to the Leader of the Free World and the new president traveled to the White House for his first day on the job. He met with his cabinet, "which until midday Friday was Richard Nixon's cabinet"; the chair where he used to sit in as vice president, and which he would now have to fill by appointment, was empty. He chatted easily with reporters who "no longer felt like uninvited guests who had to be watched near the silver. . . .

"It was a new day at 1600 Pennsylvania Avenue, zip code 20050. A new, new day."

No more parallax views. Just a balding, square-jawed, honest, straightforwardly pleasant man for a nation that could be honestly, straightforwardly pleasant once more—a man who smoked a pipe, like one of those kindly old dads in a 1950s television situation comedy. A pure pragmatist, they said, with no ideology to divide the nation. Indeed, it was reported, he took pleasure from compromise, hating no one (except, the profiles said, his biological father, who beat his mother, then abandoned the family; that was why his mother changed her son's name to Gerald Ford Jr., after her second husband, from Leslie King Jr., his original name). "A Ford, not a Lincoln," as he had charmingly described himself upon acceding to the vice presidency, winning a standing ovation in the Capitol Rotunda: "My addresses will never be as eloquent as Mr. Lincoln's. But I will do my very best to equal his brevity and plain speaking."

That business about the English muffin became the joyous keynote—a national talisman of normalcy restored. A *New Yorker* cartoon had a sleepy wife lecturing her irate husband: "The President of the United States of America makes his own breakfast." Which was appropriate, because the new first lady, née Betty Bloomer, was something of a feminist—and Jerry Ford was self-possessed enough not to feel unmanned by the fact. "We have carefully worked out the art of gentle compromise," she said in her first-day profile, in which, unlike Pat Nixon, who revealed a bitter, shrewish side when she revealed herself at all, Betty played as easygoing and funny. The former model and professional modern dancer gently mocked her husband's impatience. ("She whips out one of her husband's favorite T-shirts"—did Richard Nixon even own a T-shirt?—one reading, "Old Fords Never Die. They Just Move Faster.") She described, with breathtaking openness, how she solved a severe chronic pain problem: mild tranquilizers, and "therapy of tell-it-like-it-is conversations" with a psychiatrist. "A psychiatrist," she explained gently, "is nothing more than a sounding board, someone to talk to. I voiced a lot of entrenched feelings that were locked inside. But even more important, I got an honest reaction."

This was extraordinary. America had been a nation of shamefaced secrecy in so many of its intimate domestic affairs. The 1970s were when that began to change. Betty Ford was that transformation's Joan of Arc. "Free Spirit in the White House," read the cover of *Newsweek* for a profile of her the next year.

Meanwhile her husband modeled a new ethic of transparency in the White House. His press secretary, Jerry terHorst, chucked the menacing podium behind which Nixon blocked himself from the world and reversed the press room seating arrangement into something more like an encounter group, and sometimes had Ford give his news conferences in the White House Rose Garden. Introducing terHorst the first day of his term, Ford announced, "We will have a candid administration. I can't change my nature after sixty-one years." Soon so many Democrats had been invited to the White House that Art Buchwald joked that someone had mistaken an old Nixon Enemies List for the White House invitation list; a portrait of Harry Truman (Merle Miller's *Plain Speaking* was enjoying its ninth month on the bestseller lists) joined Eisenhower's and Lincoln's in the Oval Office; and the fight song of the University of Michigan (Jerry had been a football star there) replaced "Hail to the Chief." At the first state dinner, Jerry and Betty—who made no secret of how much they enjoyed sharing a bed—danced the night away to the Jim Croce hit "Bad, Bad Leroy Brown." *Newsweek,* after an extraordinary inside-cover photo essay ("Putting Watergate Behind Us") reprinting its thirty-eight covers on the subject, said, "The manner of his coming felt as cool and cleansing to a soiled capital as a fresh Lake Michigan Breeze." *Time* all but hymned a new plain-speaking Midwestern messiah, "a chief executive who worked in his shirtsleeves, who said what he meant and meant what he said, who by his honesty and

accessibility has swiftly exorcised the pinched ghosts of the Nixon era."
"Everywhere," Hugh Sidey wrote, "there was a feeling that the American presidency was back in the possession of the people."

Dependable, solid, uncontroversial—just like the cars Ford built. Though at that, wasn't it also the case that to partisans of Chevrolets, Fords were controversial indeed? And that Americans, being Americans, had always found things to passionately disagree about, to the point of violent rage—and that when American elites reached most insistently for talismans of national unity, it usually portended further civil wars?

ECONOMIC CRISES OBSCURED BY WATERGATE SHIVERED NAKED IN THE postresignation air. The *New York Times* listed them at the end of week two: "the worst inflation in the country's peacetime history" (the Wholesale Price Index, newspapers reported the day Ford became president, rose a staggering 3.7 in July), "the highest interest rates in a century, the consequent severe slump in housing, sinking and utterly demoralized securities markets, a stagnant economy with large-scale unemployment in prospect, and a worsening international trade and payments position."

Actually, it was worse than worsening. In 1948 America had made up about a quarter of the world's trade. Now it was less than 10 percent. In one year, 1970, the trade deficit with Japan, which manufactured cars at a rate of ten thousand a year in 1950 and now made more than a million, had risen from $3 billion to $8.5 billion. In 1971 America ran its first trade deficit since 1893. As for inflation, Nixon's price controls had been a thumb in the dike, whose end caused price hikes so overwhelming that newspaper editorialists called for a "Bureau of Shortages" to ration consumer goods. The economy was on the verge of recession— although in a poll a week after the inauguration, nearly half thought America was on the verge of a depression. By November, that proportion was 57 percent.

The new president promptly declared inflation "Public Enemy Number One." The markets didn't care. The Dow Jones Industrial Average, half of what it was in 1972, fell 12 percent more in its next eleven trading sessions—though at Ford's first news conference only five questions were on the economy and only three questions were on foreign policy. The others followed up on the insistent opening bark of the UPI's Helen Thomas:

"Do you agree with the Bar Association that the law applies equally to all men, or do you agree with Governor Rockefeller that former president Nixon should have immunity from prosecution? And would specifically, would you use your pardon authority, if necessary?"

The media obsession with the notion of Richard Nixon going to jail hastened Ford's determination to do something he believed would finally end the national nightmare once and for all. Things were still so very nasty. That week, former high-ranking Nixon officials leaked to the *Chicago Sun-Times* that Secretary of Defense James Schlesinger, worried that Nixon's evident "erratic behavior" during the Judiciary Committee hearings suggested he might launch a nuclear strike, "had kept a close watch during the last days of the Nixon administration to assure no orders were given to military units outside the chain of command." Someone firebombed Patricia Nixon's childhood home.

A president's resignation, noble speeches, and an open and transparent White House hadn't been enough; more healing plainly was called for.

On Day 11, President Ford ventured out of Washington for the first time, to the annual convention of the Veterans of Foreign Wars, in Chicago. He earned a huge, whistling standing ovation for stating his "strong conviction that unconditional blanket amnesty for anyone who illegally evaded or fled military service is wrong"—and then, citing precedents of Lincoln and Truman, and invoking the same biblical injunction to justice and mercy that graced his inaugural speech, he enraged his audience by saying draft dodgers and military deserters should get "a second chance" to earn their way back into United States without punishment. "I want your help and understanding," he concluded. "I ask all Americans who ever asked for goodness and mercy in their lives, who ever sought forgiveness for their trespasses, to join in rehabilitating all casualties of the tragic conflict of the past."

He believed himself to be accomplishing something profound. The issue of "amnesty" had been one of Richard Nixon's favorite hatchets in his strategy of governing by division. In Nixon's first news conference of his second term, a reporter asked why, with the Paris Peace Accords now sealed, he didn't offer amnesty to "help heal the wounds in this country." Nixon responded with a rant: he had just brokered "peace with honor"—"I know it gags some of you to write that phrase"—and though military service "had very little support among the so-called better people, in the media and the intellectual circles and the rest," it did have the support of "a majority of the American people, despite the fact that they were hammered night after night and day after day with the fact that this was an immoral war, that America should not be there, that they should not serve their country, that morally what they should do was desert their country." He concluded, "Amnesty means forgiveness. We cannot provide forgiveness for them." He then ordered Bob Haldeman to get an amnesty bill introduced in Congress and "make every dove vote on it"—to exploit a tender national wound in order to destroy his political enemies.

That was how wedge politics—Nixon politics—worked. Ford wished to model how the nation might transcend it.

The pundits found such gestures stupendous, crowning him a glorious statesman. But among millions of Americans who had long since stopped taking anything a powerful man said at face value, the reviews were quite different. Why had he kept saying, leading up to the resignation, "I can say from the bottom of my heart that the President of the United States is innocent?" Why was he speaking of "justice," "mercy," and "understanding" right now? Because he was greasing the skids for a con: amnesty for Richard M. Nixon. A letter writer to the *New York Times* predicted, a week before the Nixon presidency's end, "Before President Nixon will allow all of the dirty linen to be washed in the process of an impeachment and trial, he will resign. When Gerald Ford becomes President, he will grant Mr. Nixon executive clemency, and thus Mr. Nixon will avoid criminal prosecution. . . . And once again justice will have been debauched, as has happened so frequently with those lesser politicians who are guilty of gross sins against the body politics. Ah, well, such is the corruption of power."

And, the morning of Day 31, that was exactly what happened.

It was a Sunday, 11:05 A.M., when many Americans would have, like Ford, just returned from church—maybe in the mood for justice, mercy, and understanding. Their president appeared on TV. He began flatly:

"Ladies and gentlemen, I have taken a decision which I felt I should tell you and all my fellow American citizens as soon as I was certain in my own mind and in my own conscience that it is the right thing to do."

He had been advised, he said, that "years will have to pass before Richard Nixon could obtain a fair trial." He agreed with "equal justice for all Americans"—but "during this long period of delay and political litigation, ugly passions would again be aroused. And our people would again be polarized in their opinions. And the credibility of our free institutions of government would again be challenged at home and abroad"—and the courts might not yet believe Nixon had been accorded due process even then. "My conscience tells me clearly and certainly that I cannot prolong the bad dreams that continue to reopen a chapter that is closed. My conscience tells me that only I, as President, have the constitutional power to firmly shut and seal this book. My conscience tells me that it is my duty, not merely to proclaim domestic tranquility but to use every means that I have to ensure it."

He quoted Abraham Lincoln, just as Richard Nixon used to quote Abraham Lincoln: "I do believe that right makes might, and that if I am wrong, ten angels swearing I was right would make no difference." He said he also believed, "with all my heart and mind and spirit," "not as President but as a humble servant of God," that he failed the nation if he failed to show mercy. After all, he said, "I feel that Richard Nixon and his loved ones have suffered enough and will continue to suffer, no matter what I do, no matter what we, as a great nation, can do together to make his goal of peace come true."

He read a proclamation, then signed it, right there on TV:

"Now, therefore, I, Gerald Ford, President of the United States, pursuant to the pardon power conferred upon me by Article II, Section 2, of the Constitution, have granted and by these presents do grant a full, free, and absolute pardon unto Richard Nixon for all offenses against the United States which he, Richard Nixon, has committed, or may have committed or taken part in during the period from July 20, 1969—"

That's what he said: July 20, 1969. He meant January 20. He was nervous.

"—through August 9, 1974."

That evening the daredevil known as Evel Knievel was strapped into his custom-built, spike-tipped "X-2 Skycycle" rocket, with which he hoped to soar at 200 mph over the 1,600 feet between the banks of the Snake River Canyon, clad in his trademark red-white-and-blue jumpsuit. Knievel's loony jumps were television fixtures. Grown-ups watched, in these death-haunted times, in the half-unconscious wish to see someone snuffed out live on TV, Christine Chubbuck–style, as Knievel had almost been snuffed out live on TV in 1967 when attempting to jump the fountain at Caesar's Palace in Las Vegas, landing short, then flopping end over end like a rag doll (ABC showed it again and again, in slow motion). Little boys watched because Evel Knievel was the coolest human being in the world. Until that evening, when, having begged to stay up past their bedtimes, little boys saw his parachute deploy almost immediately after ignition, and kindergarten classrooms across the nation erupted into impassioned arguments over whether he had chickened out and done it on purpose—whether the hero was a hustler.

Charles Lindbergh had just died. *Time* said, "America lost not only one of its pioneers of the machine age but perhaps its last authentic hero." Everything was rotten. As Walter Cronkite had said, upon the resignation: "I think we ought to take Lysol and scrub out the Oval Office." Now the Lysol was needed again.

Ford would explain later—much to his surprise and chagrin, because he thought his country trusted him—that, with Nixon loudly claiming that the rest of the tapes and his presidential papers were his personal property, he, Ford, was spending a quarter of his time as president dealing with the legal issues surrounding Nixon. But the pardon was just more proof that everything about Washington was crooked.

Within moments, Western Union's lines were jammed by angry citizens eager to post telegrams of protest to the White House. Ford's press secretary, who had been kept in the dark on the decision though he was a friend going back twenty-five years, and who had told reporters his first day on the job that Ford wouldn't give Nixon a pardon, given that Ford had said so when asked about a pardon during his Senate confirmation hearings to become vice president, resigned immediately. By lunchtime, a throng descended upon Lafayette Park, calling for the president's head. During his next out-of-town trip, to Pittsburgh, Ford circulated among a crowd of students with a portable microphone—a symbol of the anti-Nixonian candor he had hoped would mark his presidency. The students shrieked "Jail Ford!" in his face. Congressmen fielded messages demanding his impeachment. Within the week, the president's approval rating dropped from 66 to 49 percent, the steepest decline in history. The *New York Times* discerned in his action the opposite of his intention: it was "unwise, divisive, unjust." *Newsweek* said he had "embraced the demon of Watergate." The previous weeks, these organs had lionized him.

Reflected Mary McGrory, the liberal syndicated columnist, "The Washington press corps lost its head over Gerald Ford. A thousand reporters turned overnight into flacks for Jerry Ford. They raved about his decency, his smile, his English muffins, his peachy dancing. . . . He perhaps did us all a favor by slapping us awake." Ordinary folks gave it to him worse. From a small town in Wisconsin called Slinger, whose ornaments were a ski hill called "Little Switzerland" and a dirt car racing track, a fellow wondered in the *Milwaukee Journal*, "How can a man be pardoned for crimes before he has been convicted of any? . . . I have always heard that a person was innocent until proven guilty and that all men are created equal, but now it appears that what I learned was all wrong. Perhaps in a week or two Mr. Ford will overrule the Ten Commandments."

Ronald Reagan disagreed. "I support him in the pardon," he told newsmen upon arriving for a speech in Louisville on overhauling the food stamp program. He was asked, too, about his future political plans. He said they would be "based on the record of the administration in the next two years."

CHAPTER FIFTEEN

New Right?

PRESIDENT FORD WASN'T THE ONLY MAN THAT SUMMER DECLARING A preliminary truce. In June, the *Washington Post*'s Joseph Kraft wrote a column about primary elections in the biggest state: "Reaganism has had it in California," he concluded. "Moreover, given California's record as political pacesetter for the nation, the primary here may be handwriting on the wall for right-wing populism everywhere."

He singled out specific results to make his argument. There was a good-government ballot proposition promoted by Ralph Nader, instituting the nation's strictest limits on campaign expenditures, which passed with 70 percent even though "all the big spenders in the Reagan camp" went to the mat against it. Second, "the triumph of Proposition 13, providing for the use of gasoline taxes for public transit." And finally there were the elections in which the two parties chose their gubernatorial candidate to succeed Reagan in the State House in 1975. The Democrats went with "just the kind of limousine liberal right-wing populists love to put down." He was Edmund G. "Jerry" Brown Jr., the Yale-educated son of the man Reagan beat in 1966, "identified with liberal causes from peace in Vietnam to racial harmony." And Republicans chose Houston Flournoy, "a political scientist from Princeton who takes the progressive stance in politics," who beat Reagan's hand-picked successor, Lieutenant Governor Ed Reinecke, by a margin of two to one.

The piece was called "The End of Backlash Politics"—which Kraft defined as "reaction against Lyndon Johnson's Great Society." And it was well and truly on the run—everywhere: "Recent developments in Detroit, Philadelphia, Minneapolis, and New York, as well as Los Angeles, suggest the decline of backlash mayors. At their conference in Seattle early last week, the governors were lining up to be seen in opposition to Mr. Reagan and the other leading right-wing populist, George Wallace." That heralded "the possibility of closing the parentheses on the era of backlash politics which has been so strong in the country since Ronald Reagan rode out of the TV movies back in 1966."

It took until the school year for those parentheses to jolt wide open.

IN BOSTON, A FURIOUS, IRRECONCILABLE DEBATE FOR MORE THAN A DE-cade had only recently appeared on the verge of tidy resolution.

In 1963, black militants organized school boycotts to protest the decrepit, overcrowded schoolhouses their children were forced to attend. The Massachusetts state legislature passed a Racial Imbalance Act, which required Boston to submit a desegregation plan. The city's school committee—what other cities call a school board—responded with a plan, according to a critic, "whose impact on racial balance it would take a theologian to discern." The state's Board of Education acted to suspend the city's school funding; the school committee sued the board to prevent the suspension, and lost in 1967. The charismatic lace-curtain Irish matron who led the school committee's backlash faction, Louise Day Hicks, promised she would fight for neighborhood schools "as long as I have breath left in my body" and almost won a Democratic primary for mayor.

The political war of position intensified; that was how Boston worked: as a city of fiefdoms, of parish boundaries, of "turf." No American municipality governed more purely according to the plural-ist principle of politically contending ethnic blocs—which, accord-ing to the settled wisdom of political science, was the best system yet devised to ensure urban peace. The Irish of South Boston, Dorchester, and Charlestown, and to a lesser extent the Italians of East Boston, saw themselves as political gangs—and the Brahmins who composed the lion's share of the city's population of do-gooders as just another rival gang. So were the blacks of Roxbury—who the Irish certainly did not see as victims of anything requiring legal redress. "Our children are innocent victims," Hicks insisted. An "open enrollment" compromise was supposed to be in effect, but the school committee sabotaged it. As a result, in 1971, the state board voted to end Boston schools funding. Cooler heads then worked out another compromise, which included enrolling a mixed student body at two spanking-new schools built with 25 percent state aid. Hicks, though, would have none of that: she lashed her people into a fury, boycotting the new schools, just as blacks had boycotted in 1963. They would outlast the rival gangs yet.

Brahmin do-gooders had their own tribal beliefs. These included the notion that insular, anachronistic fiefdoms like South Boston High, with its defiantly anticosmopolitan worldview, its defiant indifference to the game of upward mobility, its football and blood-soaked street fights, which produced the urban American version of Homeric epics, was—as the state commissioner of education put it—an "ugly institution" that "deserved to be changed." They got to work using their tribe's favorite tool: the federal judiciary, which had been nobly undoing the atavistic tribalism of the Southern states since *Brown v. Board of Education*. In March 1972, they sued the school committee in U.S. District Court. The case was assigned to Arthur Garrity, a formerly obscure federal judge appointed by President Johnson in 1966 at the recommendation of Senator Edward M. Kennedy.

At that spur, it seemed, politics started to work—just as a mandarin pundit would have predicted and preferred.

In April 1974, the state legislature repealed the divisive Racial Imbalance Act. That May, after an all-night vigil led by Hicks outside the State House, Governor Francis Sargent announced it would be replaced with a new, voluntary plan. Hicks spoke in favor. So did her antibusing comrades on the committee: like John Kerrigan, who once described a black reporter as "one generation away from swinging in the trees"; Ray Flynn, who compared school buses to the Soviet tanks that overran Budapest in 1956; and state senator William Bulger, who said that thanks to the Brahmin integregationists, his "constituents live under Orwellian conditions, saturated by an Orwellian media." But now the Brahmins were lying down with the brawlers, and as if according to Joe Kraft's script, peace seemed to have been achieved.

Then, on June 21, the last day of school in Boston, in between Nixon's trips to the Mideast and the Soviet Union, Judge Garrity handed down a decision that amounted to no less than a sociological blueprint for rewiring the entire Boston school system. Thus began the great battle of Boston's educational civil war.

The school committee majority called what they wanted "neighborhood schools." As Kerrigan put it: "Government has made continued concessions to convicted felons, homosexuals, abortionists, and others, yet persists in ignoring the pleas of parents who ask that they be accorded their rightful privilege of sending their children to their own neighborhood schools." But what Judge Garrity had exhaustively and indisputably demonstrated was that the school committee's district boundaries frequently required black children to travel greater distances from their homes in order to go to "neighborhood schools" than they would if schools were integrated.

Part of his remedy—the most controversial part—was "pairing"

South Boston High School with Roxbury High School, a school serving six all-black housing projects. Every South Boston sophomore was
ordered to attend Roxbury High, previously virtually all black. Every
Roxbury junior would go to South Boston High. But "Southie" was the
most tribal neighborhood in America's most tribal city. "We practice an-
cestor worship here," a forty-two-year-old factory worker explained to
a reporter visiting from New York; a button sported by many protesters
printed the title of a favorite tavern song, "Southie Is My Home Town."
It also had one of the highest unemployment rates in the country, during one of the worst recessions in history, in a city so decrepit that water
from decaying mains left over from the Victorian era regularly sent poisoned residents to the hospital. Memories of high school salad days were
what fueled these middle-aged men in dead-end jobs and dead marriages
and families with too many mouths to feed. It saved their souls—as
assuredly as the parish church down the street. And now some goddamned federal judge with a lifetime appointment was taking it all away.
"Why doesn't Governor Sargent just fire Judge Garrity?" one partisan
asked, not quite grasping that the world wasn't South Boston.

Six weeks after Garrity's decision, ten thousand rabid busing opponents walked from Boston Common to City Hall Plaza to raise hell.
They carried signs like "BOSTON FIREFIGHTERS LOCAL 718
DO NOT WANT THEIR CHILDREN FORCIBLY BUSED," and
"EQUAL JUSTICE FOR ALL." Their two United States senators
were scheduled to attend a meeting in the federal building in the plaza
that day. Men in chicken masks implored them to face the crowd. The
brother of America's first Catholic president, grandson of the man who
built Boston's first Irish political machine, decided to oblige them.

Senator Edward Moore Kennedy walked alone to the mall. Someone
shouted, "There he is! There he is! There he is!" and the mob joined in.

He approached the microphones, and a man intercepted him: "What
do you want to do, speak? You're not going to speak! You've taken
away our rights! We're going to take away your rights! How do you like
that?"

The crowd turned their backs on him and sang "God Bless America."

He approached the microphone once more. Someone spoke of
twelve-year-old Edward Kennedy Jr., a recent amputee from cancer:
"Your one-legged son! Send him over here!" Tomatoes and eggs started
flying. A woman punched him; a man tried to kick him.

"You're a disgrace to the Irish!"

"Let your daughter get bused there so she can be raped!"

"Why don't you let them shoot you like they shot your brothers!"

He finally made it back inside the federal building named for his brother. The crowd pressed so hard against the glass doors that one door shattered. "It was great," one of Hicks's aides reflected. "It's 'bout time the politicians felt the anger of the people. We've been good for too long."

Three days before school was set to begin, Mayor Kevin White gave a speech on all four Boston TV stations. Judge Garrity's ruling, he said, was now the law. He didn't like it. But "the traumatic events of the past several months in Washington have shown all of us we are a government of laws, and not men. No man, not even a president, stands above the law"—an argument lacking moral force, given that Ford's pardon of Nixon had just placed a former president above the law.

White went on to speak resentfully of "suburban liberals . . . who view busing as the solution to racial balance—as long as it stays inside the city." That referenced a landmark 5–4 Supreme Court decision a month and a half earlier, *Milliken v. Bradley*, which ruled that desegregation plans could not cross municipal lines. Justice Potter Stewart had reasoned that the emerging pattern of white suburbs and black inner cities was "caused by unknown and perhaps unknowable factors." Actually nothing could be more easily known: during the postwar years, federal subsidies flew in a torrent toward suburbs, in the form of interstate highways, mortgage deductions, and subsidies to banks that openly defied the letter and spirit of federal law by engaging in discriminatory lending patterns. That was why the suburbs in the Boston metropolitan area were 99 percent white. Now, however, the burden of rectifying the region's segregation was solely Boston's cross to bear. In the *Globe*, Harvard psychologist Robert Coles shocked liberals by calling Judge Garrity's decision "a scandal" for imposing integration "on working class people exclusively." But *Milliken* meant there was nothing anyone could do about that.

The mayor staffed a twenty-four-hour emergency communications center, planned more than a hundred coffee klatches between white and black citizens, and arranged for TV to be blanketed by sports heroes like Bobby Orr and Carl Yastrzemski smiling their way through commercials that ended with the tagline, "It won't be easy, but that never stopped Boston."

CAME THE FIRST DAY OF SCHOOL. IN SOUTHIE, HELICOPTERS *SWOFFED* overhead. Police squads swarmed, breaking up a mob, at which another mob took revenge, ripping out public phones, uprooting benches, terrorizing blacks at a nearby commuter train station. At Jamaica Plain

High School, shots were fired through the door. Street toughs stoned buses. Thugs enforced a white school boycott with fists and chains. That went on for weeks. So did the protest motorcades, blaring down the boulevards, with Irish matrons raised to be nothing but decorous in their public demeanor blasting their horns so aggressively that casings were separated from steering wheels. Marchers carried swastikas and KKK slogans, and—when they passed by unfortunate black bystanders—cries like "Bus the niggers back to Africa!" The third week ended with a menacing mob of three hundred in front of Garrity's house in bucolic Wellesley; for hours, a line of white-helmeted riot police was the only thing keeping them from storming his parlor. That was October 4, "National Boycott Day"—when a mob rushed from a bar to keep cops from arresting a stone thrower; the next night, a posse of tactical police crashed in and beat patrons at random.

THEY CALLED THEIR MAIN ORGANIZATION "ROAR": "RESTORE OUR Alienated Rights." Their grievances were rooted, in part, in class. ROAR leader Elvira "Pixie" Palladino memorably attested to that one afternoon when she heckled Ted Kennedy at a hearing on one of his signature issues, deregulation of airline fares: "We never took a plane in our lives. We're poor people. Why don't you talk about forced busing?" (Senator Kennedy, like Judge Garrity, sent his kids to private schools.) The people throwing rocks at school buses intersected with the vigilantes showing up at construction yards to harass the black activists seeking to close them down for not honoring the city's affirmative action settlement—"two groups of people," columnist Jimmy Breslin lamented, "who are poor and doomed and who have been thrown in the ring with each other."

Racialized fears of crime were a contributing factor. The previous fall, a white twenty-four-year-old Roxbury woman ran out of gas near her apartment and was set upon by six black kids who dragged her into a vacant lot, doused her with the fuel in the can she was carrying, and left her to die from her burns. Two days later, a white sixty-five-year-old man, fishing behind a black housing project, was stabbed to death with his own knife.

And the panic, finally, was not unrelated to sex—never far from fears about race. *Forced* busing: the very words suggested rape. One policeman guarding Southie was taunted by an old man who shouted he hoped the cop would find his wife "in bed with a nigger" when he got home. A flier distributed by the white "South Boston Liberation Army" instructed, "We do not expect you to hate blacks. We do not ask you to fight blacks." What was unacceptable, however, was *dating* blacks. "We seek revenge on anyone that violates this rule. Because of Forced Busing. Blacks are the enemy.... Don't be a white nigger."

Some days there were more police in schools than students. Rumors spread that armed black marauders would ride through their neighborhoods shooting whites at random; that blacks were carrying knives and razors to school to turn girls' rooms into rape rooms. So whites started carrying them first.

SEVEN HUNDRED AND FIFTY MILES TO THE SOUTHWEST, THE RIGHT-WING populists' weapon of choice was literally dynamite.

On June 27 in Charleston, West Virginia, three weeks after Joseph Kraft's column, the five members of the Kanawha County School Board heard arguments about whether to adopt a set of new language arts textbooks. The meeting room was packed to the rafters. More than a thousand protesters waited outside in a heavy rain. They were convinced the textbooks that education bureaucrats were forcing down their children's throats were satanic.

Inside, a preacher singled out a book on the curriculum's supplementary list for college-bound seniors, *Soul on Ice*. He made it sound as if the notorious memoir, in which the Black Panther Eldridge Cleaver called raping a white woman an "insurrectionary act" (then later in the book, no one mentioned, repented in shame), would have to be memorized by every kid in Kanawha County. "This is a people's battle!" he concluded, and the audience applauded ecstatically.

A school board member named Alice Moore, the Louise Day Hicks of Kanawha County, questioned her ally insistently. What did the minister think, she asked, about the textbook that featured the story of Androcles and the Lion? The one that, in the teacher's edition, suggested asking the children: "Do you think a real lion, if he hadn't eaten for three days, would remember Androcles and not eat him?" And which suggested, as an activity, discussing the similarities between "Androcles and the Lion" and the biblical story of Daniel in the lions' den?

The preacher responded that the equation of a fable by Aesop and the facts in Holy Scripture was the foulest sacrilege. The book of Daniel, he said, is "a true story.... I don't think many people would want to tear down those things and consider them as myths!"

"Yes," Moore responded. "In the Bible, the lions didn't kill Daniel because he was under the protection of the Lord." Liberal school bureaucrats' "intent was obvious ... attacking their religious convictions by compelling their children, by law, to be in that classrooms, and then undermining everything they believe in."

The board voted. Moore was the only member against adopting the textbooks. She emerged into the pouring rain, and was greeted by her throngs of admirers as a conquering hero and a Christian martyr. The Great Kanawha County Textbook War had begun.

THE STORY BEGAN A YEAR EARLIER, WHEN A TEXTBOOK SELECTION COM-mittee began reviewing books pursuant to a new state mandate requiring "multi-ethnic, multicultural balance" in local curricula. Four of the school board members applied themselves assiduously to whether the books the nation's biggest textbook companies tried to sell them satisfied that new standard. Moore, the board's only woman, applied herself contrariwise.

Moore was a transplant from Mississippi, and before that North Carolina, Alabama, and Tennessee, a beautiful woman with a regal Southern accent and impeccably curled hair—until the movement she captained took off, and she only had time to fix her hair into a fierce bun. It was her minister husband, she later said, who first turned her on to the moral catastrophe they had on their hands. He pointed to a line from *The Autobiography of Malcolm X*, one of the recommended textbooks: "All praise is due to Allah that I moved to Boston when I did. If I hadn't, I'd still be a brainwashed black Christian." She said her husband exclaimed, "Look what you just approved!"

That story as Moore told it did not quite add up; the chronology was all wrong. But then, Moore and her husband were deeply ensconced within an evangelical culture that prized above all else dramatic narratives of redemption—narratives that, for the sake of God's glory, might sometimes skirt the precise truth. Another of her redemption narratives was not quite right, either: in 1970, as she described it, a couple of years after her arrival in Kanawha, she was startled to discover that the district's comprehensive sexual education course, developed with the help of a grant from the U.S. Office of Education, "wasn't just a sexual education course. It dealt with every aspect of a child's life . . . how to think, how to feel, and to act . . . their relationship with their parents." The school superintendent told her there was nothing he could do about it. So, she always said, she decided to run for school board—entirely spontaneously, and with no help from anyone at all.

Regardless, Moore's campaign for the school board reflected the influence of the John Birch Society's anti–sex education front group the

Movement to Restore Decency (MOTOREDE). It was also fueled by the first campaign billboards a county school board race had ever seen, featuring the strikingly compelling slogan "Put a mother on the school board." Moore could soon claim her first political scalp: the superintendent who had offended her. This figure of the humble housewife, drafted against her will into public life by the awful, inexorable tides of liberal extremism, a reluctant lone prophet in the service of simple commonsense decency, would become a standard right-wing trope in the years to come in battles across the country.

Moore was already plugged into a national conservative network—the same network that began knitting itself together for the 1964 crusade to make Barry Goldwater president, which was supposed to have folded tent permanently after the electorate's landslide embrace of Lyndon Johnson's Great Society proved America was a liberal nation once and for all. And when the textbook question came down the pike, Moore knew just whom to call: the "Mel Gablers," as Norma Gabler insisted reporters refer to her and her husband, a conservative couple who ran a right-wing textbook evaluation shop out of their hometown—Hawkins, Texas, population 761—doing so, they always told reporters, from their modest kitchen table.

The Gablers were already infamous among the blindsided liberals of Texas—where their supporters would pack the public comment segments of State Board of Education meetings to unfurl their fifty-four-foot-long "scroll of shame" of unacceptable textbooks: any, that is, that exhibited warmth toward the United Nations or the New Deal, depicted the United States as anything less than God's chosen nation, disparaged Confederate generals as anything less than patriots, or identified the Founding Fathers as deists. They first won attention nationwide for their discovery that a high school history text from Macmillan, *Search for Freedom: America and Its People,* gave seven pages to Marilyn Monroe but only a few paragraphs to George Washington. "We're not quite ready for Marilyn Monroe as the mother of our country," Norma Gabler was quoted in papers around the country. "TEXAS COUPLE REVEAL FINDINGS—TEXTBOOKS DOMINATED BY FILTH," ran one 1973 headline.

By 1974, they won a requirement in their home state that any mention of evolution in biology books "should identify it as only one of several explanations of the origins of humankind," and "shall be edited, if necessary, to clarify that the treatment is theoretical rather than factually verifiable." They were spearheading a veritable textbook censorship movement—aided, unintentionally, by the U.S. Supreme Court's recent pornography decision in *Miller v. California* that municipalities had the right to ban expression that violated "contemporary community standards." In Richlands, Virginia, a hundred miles to Kanawha's south, the target was John Steinbeck's "pornographic, filthy, and dirty" *The Grapes of Wrath*. In the upscale bedroom community of Ridgefield, Connecticut, it was Mike Royko's lacerating biography of Richard J. Daley, *Boss,* because it "portrays politics in an un-American way and we don't want our kids to know about such things as corrupt politics." *Slaughterhouse Five,* Kurt Vonnegut's satire on the firebombing of Dresden, a particular Gabler bête noir, was being banned everywhere—and in a North Dakota town it was publicly incinerated, along with James Dickey's *Deliverance* and a short story anthology that included selections by Faulkner and Hemingway. The English teacher who had assigned them was thrown into jail.

The Gablers advised Alice Moore that liberal secularists' most dangerous weapon was books with a "morbid," "negative," or "depressing" tone. "Relativism" was another red flag. For instance Edgar Allan Poe's "The Cask of Amontillado": one Gabler report said the story's "gruesome, murderous, bizarre content," and the fact that "the murderer shows no signs of regret," made it unfit for schools. "To the vast majority of Americans," they argued, "the terms 'values' and 'morals' mean one thing, and one thing only; and that is the Christian-Judeo morals, values and standards as given to us by God through HIS Word written in the Ten Commandments and the Bible. . . . After all, according to history these ethics have prescribed the only code by which civilizations can effectively remain in existence!"

Thus armed, Alice Moore got to work to keep civilization in existence.

The six texts required for elementary school kids, the twenty-four required for secondary schools, and the more than three hundred optional supplementary texts, looked precisely how state-of-the-art language arts textbooks were supposed to look in 1974. An anthology intended for eleventh graders was called *The Human Condition.* Another was called *Monologue and Dialogue.* A huge, ungraded collection of 172 books from Houghton Mifflin, called *Interaction,* was edited by a rhetoric scholar from the Harvard School of Education named James Moffett, revered in his field, who wrote things like "For too long our schools have neglected the importance of oral language" and called for educators to attend to "the social and psychological forces which affect" how students learned. For members of the cosmopolitan professional classes of a capital city like Charleston, West Virginia, who hoped to get their children into schools like Harvard themselves, experts like Dr. Moffett were to be deferred to.

Alice Moore and her allies were informed by a different set of intellectual assumptions. They found just the title of a book like *The Human Condition* suspect: it suggested an affiliation with "secular humanism," what evangelical Christians described as the ideology that held up man as a higher authority than God, where human beings had the perfect power to determine their own fate. "Secular humanism," in turn, implied "situational ethics," which held that the only ground for moral judgment was experience—just like all that "experiential learning" of which liberal educators were so enamored.

It thus came as quite a shock to the four members of the board who fit just that cosmopolitan description, at their first meeting to rubber-stamp the books, to hear their colleague Alice Moore worry, with passively ladylike aggression, that in some of the volumes they were called on to approve "everything in America is denigrated."

An awkward silence followed. She broke through the unpleasantness with a charming apology. Then she launched into an objection to lessons on "dialectology" she had found in one of the books (*"For too long our schools have neglected the importance of oral language"*): she didn't want to see English being "watered down" by "ghetto dialect" and the "sloppy and vulgar" language of the streets.

The moment came and went. No one knew history was being made. The state required a decision by April 15. So the majority quickly voted the books through.

And in the hollers surrounding Charleston, West Virginia, the Joan of Arc they called "Sweet Alice" started girding for war.

Her troops called themselves "Creekers": rural folk, like the Reverend Avis Hill, who ran a combined church, school, and mission out of an abandoned rural store and service station—and who, like most fundamentalist preachers of the day, had only recently wanted nothing to do with worldly politics. That was Caesar's realm, inherently fallen. Then, according to *his* conversion narrative, somewhere on the road to Damascus he connected the foul textbooks to the failing grade his daughter had recently received for writing about how the Lord had created the heaven and the earth in six days. "Then it dawned on me . . . packing Johnny's lunch bucket, combing his hair, patting him on the head and saying, 'Honey, you go to school now. You mind what your teacher says'"—that no longer was possible. Teachers teaching evolution were agents of perdition. It was time get out from behind the pulpit. It was time to go to political war.

The teachers' adversaries, locally, were known as Hillers. One spokesman for the teachers was an Episcopalian rector, the Reverend James Lewis. He thought at one point that he might be killed. He wrote a newspaper article that was syndicated nationally: "The anti-textbook people of Kanawha County are confused and angry about everything from marijuana to Watergate. Feeling helpless and left out, they are looking for a scapegoat. They are eager to exorcise all that is evil and foul, cleanse or burn all that is strange and foreign. In this religious war, spiced with overtones of race and class, the books are an accessible target."

One such target was *Communicating,* a text published by D. C. Heath (whose founder, according to the Gablers, had supposedly said, "Let me publish the textbooks of a nation and I care not who writes its songs or makes its laws," though no one could ever quite point to when or where he had said it). One of its units taught "Jack and the Beanstalk." Teachers were encouraged to have "two or three students on a team debate such questions as whether Jack has a right to steal from the giant," and ask, "What difference there is between a rich man and a poor man stealing?" It thus put the Ten Commandments up for debate. Could a Christian stand for something like that?

Another argument concerned that book's cover. It pictured a little girl giving a bouquet to a little boy. The girl was white. The boy was black. "This is what it is all about," a protester patiently explained to a board member. Graffiti began showing up on Charleston walls reading, for instance, "GET THE NIGGER BOOKS OUT."

At the June 27 meeting, a black pastor took to the podium to testify in favor of adopting the textbooks. "Is it your feeling," Sweet Alice asked him, "that in order to represent minorities, specifically blacks, that we should present them with the Edridge Cleavers and George Jacksons"—George Jackson was a Black Panther who killed a prison guard, and published a bestselling book of prison letters, *Soledad Brother*—"and people of this type?"

"When you say 'people of this type,' it assumes that 'that type' is not representative or that there is some kind of defect in 'that type,' and—"

Sweet Alice interrupted: "You don't think that."

"I think they have a message from the other side of the American experience that ought be told," the black pastor returned. You could hardly hear him for the gasps from the Creekers in the gallery.

Through summer, in Kanawha as in Boston, passions intensified—for instance by means of a flyer purporting to reproduce a page of one of the textbooks featuring a giant erect penis and a demonstration of how to use a condom. (Board of education officials pointed out that the flyer's author, a self-ordained preacher named Ezra Graley, had actually made it all up, photocopying the pictures from an entirely unrelated book in the library.) On Labor Day eight thousand angry citizens heard an intense young preacher with a dimpled chin named Marvin Horan urge every family to boycott school when it opened in September. Another prayed aloud for God to smite down offending school board members.

The next day, the opening of school, about a fifth of the district's children stayed home—four-fifths of the county's Creekers. And in an extraordinary development, 3,500 coal miners walked out on the job. As did some Charleston city bus drivers. Honoring a picket line was a sacred principle in coal country—it was how, the previous year, miners in neighboring Brookside, Kentucky, forced their governor to back down from rationing gasoline. And so on September 11, the same day school opened in Boston, the Kanawha County school board backed down, officially closing the schools for three days while the books were removed for a thirty-day review—presuming that would make the irreconcilables stop. Instead, smelling the blood of a wounded opponent, they moved in for the kill.

At a rally that night, Alice Moore announced that the partial capitulation was "the best we can expect." She was jeered. Marvin Horan followed her and said it was time to double the boycott until the books were banned outright, forever. The next day a man was shot crossing a picket line at a trucking terminal, the crowd roughed up the *Charleston Daily Mail* photographer recording the violence, and mines shut across the three surrounding counties. The school superintendent said that "the county is bordering on lawlessness."

Monday, September 16, was a busy news day in Washington. Seymour Hersh of the *New York Times* reported the Nixon administration had spent $8 million to "destabilize" Salvador Allende of Chile; a senator recommended CIA chief Richard Helms and three other retired officials be cited for contempt for misleading Congress about the agency's role. President Ford announced the details of his program for military evaders: they would be granted clemency in return for at least eighteen months of alternative national service—and then at the press conference that followed, reporters badgered him about whether he'd been awarded the presidency in exchange for pardoning Nixon. "If your intention was to heal the wounds of nation, sir," he was asked accusingly, "why did you grant only a conditional amnesty to the Vietnam War draft evaders while granting a full pardon to President Nixon?" He was hammered, too, from the right, by the commander of the Veterans of Foreign Wars, who said Ford's mild feint toward conciliation of Vietnam War critics "does a gross injustice to those who served honorably, those who died and received wounds, and those who were so long imprisoned." Then the organization for draft resisters in exile told its members to boycott the deal because it was "too much to ask that we accept punishment for justified resistance to the illegal and immoral U.S. war in Indochina."

The president had received Alice Moore's lesson: conciliation often just whets opponents' appetite for blood.

Charleston schools reopened on Tuesday—except one junior high, which had received telephoned bomb threats. The "Vigilante Committee for Decency in Our Schools" circulated a letter lamenting that "as recently as 50 years ago" school board members "would have been lynched for less than their present activities"—though the vigilante committee did not actually "advocate anyone doing this, since these creeps are not worth going to jail for."

The hollers were now a mecca for reporters from as far away as London. Some handled the story with extraordinary sensitivity. Paul Cowan of the *Village Voice* became the protesters' most empathetic liberal chronicler. He won the trust of thoughtful interlocutors like Emmett Thompson, a fifty-nine-year-old riverboat engineer from Nitro, West Virginia, who explained, "You are making an insidious attempt to replace our periods with your question marks." Thompson, who sent his son to Lynchburg Bible College, a fundamentalist school founded and operated by the Virginia preacher and TV entrepreneur Jerry Falwell, longed for what he called a "return to the spirit of the Boston Tea Party," and explained to the Jewish, New Left veteran Cowan why he considered the books "moral genocide." For his part, Cowan, who did not entirely disagree, flushed out a 1970 document from the office of West Virginia's superintendent of schools promising to "induce changes . . . in the culturally lost of Appalachia. . . . The setting of the public school should be the testing ground, the diagnostic basis, the experimental center, and the core of this design." He read the conflict as, in part, a class war, between educated professionals eager to get their kids into the Ivy League, and plain folk who saw a traditional basic education as a route to upward mobility.

Other reporters were not so sensitive to the class nuances.

They just laughed—at claims that Admiral Farragut's line "Damn the torpedoes, full speed ahead" in a textbook taught children "cursing"; at the preachers waving in their faces a book called *The Late, Great Planet Earth,* which none of the reporters had heard of even though it had sold some five million copies since its publication in 1970; at people who argued that Israel's founding in 1948 foretold Christ's imminent second coming; and at their faux-learned disquisitions that "since humanism is now considered by the Court to be a religion" (the result of an ill-considered footnote in the 1961 case *Torcaso v. Watkins,* in which Justice Hugo Black innocently listed secular humanism among religions "which do not teach what would generally considered belief in the existence of God") they were being persecuted by an unofficial state religion. The protesters' best hope for banning the books was the U.S. Supreme Court, some decided, which could rule that they represented an illegal establishment of religion in public schools.

The media, meanwhile, became the enemy—like the CBS newsman who introduced himself at a protesters' meeting as a reporter for Walter Cronkite. His crew fortunately managed to flee ahead of the advancing mob. He, though, was stomped within an inch of his life by thugs as a crowd of hundreds looked on in approval.

NATIONALLY, PROTESTERS WERE NOT OUTLIERS. CONSERVATIVE-MINDED citizens everywhere felt ignored, patronized, dispossessed of the authority that was rightfully theirs. By the arrogant liberalism of unelected judges—like Arthur Garrity in Boston, or the judges in New York who unanimously raised the threshold for keeping juvenile delinquents in custody, after which a sixteen-year-old thereby released stabbed a kid to death on a Brooklyn subway platform. (A city official quoted in the *New York Times* blamed society: the stabbing was an example of our "failures to help troubled kids.") A Brooklyn trucker told a sociologist about the time five black kids pressed a knife to his neck in a stopped elevator and relieved him of a gold watch and two hundred dollars: "The judge gave them a fucking two-year probation."

Then there were the Supreme Court justices who, two days after the re-inauguration of Richard Nixon in 1973, ruled that no state could restrict any abortion performed in the first three months of pregnancy, and severely limited states' ability to regulate abortions performed after that. Here was a procedure so controversial that the archbishop of Los Angeles had pronounced in 1970, after California passed a law that let women terminate pregnancies with little more than a doctor's note claiming childbirth would cause emotional distress, that Catholics "excommunicate themselves from the church by cooperating in any way in abortion, even counseling one."

At first the *Roe v. Wade* backlash was mostly limited to Catholics. The attorney who represented the pro-choice side was a member in good standing of the Southern Baptists, a denomination that, at its 1974 convention, tabled an antiabortion resolution and reaffirmed one approving abortion in cases including "evidence of likely of damage to the emotional . . . health of the mother." The American Baptist Association, going further, endorsed what critics called "abortion on demand." But more fundamentalist Protestants were soon raising their voices, too. At the American Baptist convention a minister's wife from Arkansas thundered from the floor that abortion was "nothing less than legalized murder of masses of human lives." *Christianity Today*, Billy Graham's trade magazine for evangelical minsters, formerly ambivalent, even indifferent, on the issue, now editorialized that abortion "ought not to be regarded as a Catholic issue because Catholic leaders oppose it," and that since the fetus was a "human person," abortion was "manslaughter, if not murder." When the National Right to Life Committee organized in Detroit, the members chose a Methodist, Marjory Mecklenburg, as their first chair. In April of 1974, fifteen thousand activists, bearing signs reading DON'T MAKE THE WOMB A TOMB and ABORTION—HITLER'S FINAL SOLUTION, many of them young parents with sign-toting children in tow (I'M ADOPTED. I'M GLAD I WASN'T ABORTED), gathered for a silent vigil in downtown Cincinnati, the only sound a slow, mournful snare cadence. Silent, that is, until the speeches began. Congressman Lawrence Hogan, cosponsor of the constitutional "Human Life Amendment" to override *Roe*, boomed, "We as a nation have denied the most basic right of all—the right to life." Mecklenburg said that "seven arrogant and callous men"—the Supreme Court majority—had "brought America into the most destructive war in the history of mankind, . . . a war in which the toll of American lives will be many times greater than in World War II." And some people didn't even care!

For many it was the very antidemocratic nature of the Supreme Court that made its decision so galling. "Abortion is the monumental sort of issue over which wars are fought," a letter writer huffed angrily in the *Hartford Courant* that August, but it somehow had been disposed of once and for all in secret by unelected judges. "It is strange indeed that the major media and politicians have long tried to cover up discussion of this vital issue. I wonder why?"

That unthinking arrogance of liberals when it came to intruding into the formerly private realms of the family was starting to rankle more and more. For instance, that spring, in hearings on liberal Indiana senator Birch Bayh's proposed Runaway Youth Act, witness after witness from counterculture-rooted social service agencies spoke of "protecting minors' liberty interest," flatly opposed the idea of turning troubled kids over to police (avoiding involvement of police with runaways was indeed one of the stated principles of the bill), and believed in keeping parents out of the process as much as possible. These witnesses said things in the Senate hearing room like "Children represent the last vestige of slavery in this country." Meanwhile no representative of parents' interests was called to testify. That hadn't kept the $30 million bill from passing the Senate unanimously, then being folded into a Juvenile Justice Act, signed into law by President Ford on September 7.

It was just as Ronald Reagan had said in the greatest speech of his career, when he introduced himself to the nation as a political figure on October 27, 1964, speaking for the doomed presidential candidacy of Barry Goldwater, in a line that he repeated nearly verbatim in his gubernatorial inaugural speech in 1967: "This is the issue," he said—"Whether we believe in our capacity for self-government or whether we . . . confess that a little intellectual elite in a far-distant capitol can plan our lives for us better than we can plan them ourselves. . . . They say the world has become too complex for simple answers. They are wrong. There are no easy answers, but there are simple answers. We must have the courage to do what we know is morally right."

Hardly less eloquently, a Ford production worker outside Detroit named Dewey Burton told the *New York Times* much the same thing in October 1974. The *Times* had begun interviewing Burton for a regular series published just before every national election beginning in 1972— back when he identified himself as a committed Democrat. Now, he said sorrowfully, "More and more of us are sort of leaving all our hopes outside in the rain and coming into the house and just locking the door. . . .

"You can't blame it all on the politicians. But I wish just for once that one of them would say, 'No folks, I swear to God, if you'll elect me, I won't do a damn thing.' That's the fellow I'd vote for. Somebody who'd just leave us alone."

THAT WEARY, REACTIONARY DESPAIR: IT WAS AIMED, IN PART, AT THOSE liberal media gatekeepers who had made ordinary longings for simple order, tradition, and decorum suddenly seem so embarrassingly unfashionable. For instance, at CBS—which, once the furor died down, did eventually show *Sticks and Bones,* the scabrous satire in which the stand-in for the typical Ozzie-and-Harriet suburban family murders the blind-seer son for daring to demonstrate the evils of the Vietnam War. And, for instance, in the nation's newspaper of record—which editorialized that August against the Metropolitan Transportation Authority's plans to purchase subway cars that couldn't be covered with graffiti, which the *Times* found "always striking, sometimes cheerful." (But it wasn't against censorship entirely; another editorial was quite disturbed, for example, by "child-focused televised messages touting vitamins or other non-prescription drugs," which "should be legally impermissible.")

Patriotism—the old-fashioned kind—felt somehow forbidden. A liberal English teacher named Daniel Fader published a memoir about raising an adolescent in the 1970s, *Paul and I Discover America.* His son told him how he planned to sew a flag on the seat of his pants.

"Why would you want to do that, to sew the flag on the seat of your pants?"

"I don't know. Because that's where it belongs."

"Do what you like. If that's what you have to do, then do it. But if someone knocks you down because he doesn't like it, I won't be there to pick you up. And maybe I'll think you got what was coming to you."

The violence of his own sentiment shocked the author, and, gingerly, almost apologetically, he felt his way through where it had come from. "For the first time in our life together I was moved to speak to my son of my country, my flag, the immense weight of goodwill and affection that I bore it. I was moved to tell him of his grandfather who blessed the day my immigrant grandfather had removed his family from medieval Russia to twentieth-century America; of my uncle, his great-uncle . . . who cherished for a quarter of a century the knowledge that he had fought for his country; of a small, bandy-legged Cockney American who knew and loved his adopted country's flag so well that his devotion to it had cost him the clarity of his speech, the strength of his step, and too soon the full length of his life. I told him all this, as best I could . . . the reason why the crumpled flag in his hand and his intention to abuse it had aroused me to such violent denunciation."

You used to not have to explain this sort of thing. And to those of less liberal temperament than that memoirist, the new reality felt like it came out of nowhere—and they cast about for ways to make it all stop.

Perhaps they could do it by getting rid of those textbooks their children were bringing home. Like that history text *Search for Freedom,* the one starring Marilyn Monroe. Clad in fashionable earth tones, the book began in the key of suspicion: "It is said that on October 12, 1492, Christopher Columbus 'discovered' America." It ended, 418 pages later, with faint praise for Americans' traditional faith in the future, which, the authors concluded, "helps explain why Mexican-Americans who work in the fields of California or blacks and Puerto Ricans on the streets of Harlem still have reason to hope."

In between, in chapters with titles like "The Evil of Slavery" and "The Price of Plenty," figures ignored or derided in classrooms of past generations—Eugene Debs, Jane Addams, William Jennings Bryan ("He spoke of the wrongs done to the poor by America's rich men . . . who crushed the dreams of poor people"), and Chief Joseph (study question: "Do you think Chief Joseph was right to keep his promises when the white men did not keep theirs?")—occupied George Washington's and Andrew Carnegie's former pride of place. Chapters concluded with discussion questions that sounded open-ended, but pressed a thumb plainly on the scales. On Henry Ford: "Do you think it would be fun to work on an automobile assembly line? Why or why not?" On the Gilded Age: "The poor and weak . . . had difficulties defending themselves against the rich and powerful. Since there were so many more poor people, why do you think they usually were so helpless?" Descriptions of America's failings were blunt. *"Chicago, 1889 . . . The alleys running off Halsted Street, near Polk Street, smell like open sewers." "The United States really wanted to go to war. Spain just happened to be the enemy. . . . Perhaps it was not right, as some said, for the 'land of liberty' to be an imperial nation. But after the Spanish-American War there was no turning back."* A previous generation's patriotic triumphs were colored in faintly embarrassed tones. Of the Panama Canal, for instance, Teddy Roosevelt's Watergate-like boast was quoted: "I took the Canal Zone and let Congress debate." Black power leader H. Rap Brown— who at rallies in the 1960s would ask, "How many white folks did you kill today?"—was described neutrally, as one of the "new black leaders" who "disagreed with King." Martin Luther King himself, whom many conservatives still considered a Communist, was compared to Gandhi and Jesus Christ, "men of peace who gave their own lives to make the lives of others better." The Gablers, for their part, asked Macmillan whether, if it was going to compare MLK to Jesus, it couldn't at least mention Benjamin Franklin's invocation to Christ at the Continental Congress. According to the Gablers, Macmillan refused, saying, "That would be teaching religion."

Conservatives felt victimized by a sort of radicalism that, because it graced Middle American classrooms, did not seem radical to most Americans at all. They felt victimized by the TV shows invading their living rooms, too. Take the one that opened its third season that September with an extended metaphor comparing the Korean War to a cesspool. *M*A*S*H* had debuted in the fall of 1972, an obvious commentary on the war that was still going on, and spent its first season at the bottom in the ratings—and survived, legend had it, only because of the pillow talk of CBS honcho William Paley's wife, a fan. It was only in reruns in the summer of 1973 that ratings exploded. That was Watergate summer—and *M*A*S*H* fit the nation's new anti-institutional mood.

The villain was the guy who thought like John Wayne: Major Frank Burns, depicted as an oaf and hypocrite, his devotion to military discipline played for comic relief. ("I can't disobey an order. Unless someone gives me an order to do it.") The heroes, Hawkeye Pierce and Trapper John McIntyre, broke every rule, were constantly drunk on homemade moonshine, made incessant passes at nurses, and refused to recognize any moral distinction between the Communist North Koreans who were supposed to be the enemy and the South Koreans who were supposed to be America's allies. ("Throw away all the guns and invite all the jokers from the North and the South in here for a cocktail party. Last one standing on his feet at the end wins the war.") In one episode that fall, a Douglas MacArthur–type general dies in flagrante delicto. His aide-de-camp tries to get Hawkeye to falsify the paperwork to make it look like he fell leading troops into battle: "I appeal to your sense of decency. And your sense of fair play." Comes back Hawkeye: "Make up your mind!" Everything traditional patriots held sacred was a colossal joke on *M*A*S*H*, except when it was a colossal tragedy—as in the episode that ran on October 8, 1974, without a laugh track, and just showed scene after scene of horrifying combat surgery. There had never been a situation comedy like this.

For conservative parents who had had quite enough of all that, Kanawha County could be their Lexington and Concord. As Sweet Alice Moore put it to Paul Cowan of the *Village Voice*: "You just don't understand what you're doing to us. How can any school board force me to send my kids to a school that teaches that God is a myth, that justifies mothers who kill their young?"

KEVIN PHILLIPS, NOW A NATIONALLY SYNDICATED NEWSPAPER COLUMnist, called this burgeoning populist movement of which Moore was a part the "New Right." Soon, Charleston, West Virginia, became its mecca.

A fledgling right-wing Washington, D.C., think tank called the Heritage Foundation sent two staffers to West Virginia. James McKenna, a lawyer who had won a string of cases defending the rights of parents to "homeschool" their children, came to the defense of the alleged terrorists under indictment for violence. Connie Marshner, another Heritage Foundation emissary, was a young University of South Carolina graduate who in 1971 had accepted a job on Capitol Hill as a secretary for Young Americans for Freedom, which was where she quietly transformed herself into a power player, as an expert on Senator Walter Mondale's bill to establish a national system of federal child-care centers—the "therapeutic state invading the home," Marshner said. On her own, she started a letterhead organization to fight the bill. When Nixon vetoed it, calling it a threat to "the family in its rightful position as a keystone of our civilization," she claimed victory, and was hired as Heritage's first director of education. Soon she was hard at work finding "little clusters of Evangelical, fundamentalist Mom's groups" and transforming them into ground troops in the conservative movement army.

The Heritage Foundation had been incorporated in February 1973. Its two key principals, young congressional staffers named Edwin Feulner and Paul Weyrich, had conceived the idea while working on legislation to preserve funding for a supersonic transport plane. Washington's existing right-wing think tank, the American Enterprise Institute, came out with a paper favoring their position—after, however, Congress voted down the idea. Weyrich complained to AEI's president, William Baroody. Baroody defended his organization: "We didn't want to try to affect the outcome of the vote." It was then that these two conservative firebrands decided AEI had outlived its usefulness: the point of a think tank shouldn't be sobersided scholarship. It should be *political action*.

They approached an eager funder, the beer magnate Joseph Coors, who agreed. Within four months of Heritage's founding, Feulner and Weyrich were boasting of helping to kill a number of wage and price controls, cutting federal mass transit funding, keeping strikers from access to food stamps, and making progress toward a balanced-budget amendment to the Constitution. A year later, they saw the civil war in Kanawha as an opportunity to build their strategic capacity yet further. "If you pick the right fight at the right time," McKenna later reflected on this moment in Heritage's history, "it can be profitable. You can make your political points, you can help the people involved, and you can become a force in the political community."

A self-described "populist militant" named Robert Hoy came, too, aiming to link the activists in Massachusetts and West Virginia—to serve, he wrote, "as an introduction service among otherwise isolated groups around the country," to turn "the controversy from a local dispute over a few textbooks into a debate with national implications about basic questions of power and cultural destiny." The Gablers arrived. A group called Citizens for Decency Through Law, led by a Cincinnati banker named Charles Keating, sent Robert Dornan, the Orange

County TV host who had invented the POW bracelet and had recently hung Jane Fonda in effigy after a mock trial on the campus of the University of Southern California.

Conservatives used to call people like this "outsider agitators." They were supposed to be in retreat, Joseph Kraft had just informed the cognoscenti. And on October 6, they were the stars of a Sunday night rally before eight thousand people, right alongside the self-ordained Holy Roller preachers wearing combat fatigues and coonskin caps and buckskin boots, as things started getting insane.

"If we don't protect our children we'll have to account for it on the day of judgement!" Rev. Horan cried. The next day he was among the twenty militants arrested at a garage for sabotaging school buses. So was Rev. Graley, who was immediately sentenced to a sixty-day jail term. Twelve hours later, in protest, two elementary schools were firebombed.

Kanawha County, West Virginia, and Boston, Massachusetts: the same sort of politics of rage was coursing through both. In Boston that day a Haitian maintenance man stopped at a red light and was nearly beaten to death by a gang wielding hockey sticks. The next day 1,500 students poured out of Roxbury High after someone pulled a fire alarm. They rained stones on the adjacent Mission Hill neighborhood and overran riot-equipped police. The next day Judge Garrity refused the mayor's request to deploy federal marshals. President Ford was asked in that afternoon's news conference whether he would seek to change the judge's mind. Sandwiched between a boilerplate denunciation of violence and a shrugging apology that he had no power to intrude on another sovereign branch of government, Ford gratuitously offered the opinion that Judge Garrity's decision was "not the best solution to quality education in Boston."

White kids at Southie, as if in celebration, started a riot at lunch. Two weeks later, the White House made its first statement on Kanawha. Spokesmen pledged to do "whatever we can to help forestall additional violence in Charleston." This sounded neutral and conciliatory, but it actually followed a two-hour meeting between Ford's special assistant and anti-textbook activists, including the preacher who had circulated the flyer with the giant penis, Rev. Graley, who had just spent eleven days in jail for illegal picketing. From the jailhouse to the White House: Graley emerged to report to the media that a presidential assistant had assured him he had "read the books and said he was very shocked and depressed by what he had seen." Graley also announced that protesters had no intention of ceasing any of their activities. The next day a stick of dynamite was hurled through a window into an elementary school classroom containing hundreds of books and toys a teacher had spent a decade collecting for kids whose families could not afford them.

ONE OF THE THINGS RICHARD NIXON HAD BEEN MOST EXPERT AT AS PRESident was damping the ideological passions of his party's right wing. Now, with Nixon gone, those passions thrummed. And when Ford appointed Nelson Aldrich Rockefeller as his vice president, those passions exploded.

For Ford the choice was easy: Rockefeller was most qualified to be president. The *New York Times* had trilled how the appointment "reunited venerable symbols of Main Street and Wall Street in a balmy revival of Dwight D. Eisenhower's inclusive, middle-ground politics." But the conservatives for whom Kanawha was a debutante's ball were not having any of that. Barry Goldwater had become their hero in the 1950s precisely by savaging Dwight Eisenhower's centrism. Nelson Rockefeller was their villain for taking on Barry Goldwater. No matter that "Rocky" had moved far to the right since—for instance by passing the nation's most stringent drug law. No matter that Jerry Ford had sided with them on Boston and Kanawha. These were long-memoried elephants. They saw Ford's pick as his declaration of war against them. The American Conservative Union polled its members about what project they wished to see the group take on; they chose a movement to "discredit Rockefeller." Senator Helms, for his part, said the divorced and remarried Rockefeller "stole another man's wife" and advanced abortion legislation (he'd done neither); Helms testified before the Rules Committee that as a representative of "a dynasty of wealth and power unequaled in the history of the United States," Rockefeller could never place "the survival of the national interest" over "the survival of ingrained dynastic values." He added, "Needless to say Senator Goldwater is my choice for the vice presidency."

He didn't name Ronald Reagan. The California governor had been talked up as a possibility, first after Agnew's resignation, then with Ford's ascent. But it turned out he hadn't even been on Ford's list of top prospects. (Second place had been George Herbert Walker Bush, but Jules Witcover of the *Washington Star* noted, "Everyone knowledgeable in Republican politics considered Bush incompetent to be President.") Then Rockefeller told the press his new boss had "every intention" of seeking a full term in 1976. The UPI put out a story the next day quoting one of Reagan's political associates: "The chances of Gov. Ronald Reagan running for president or vice president in 1976 seemed to go out the window." Reagan, shrugging it off—he never admitted to seeking the presidency anyway—said it would have "no effect" on his plans to continue on the mashed potato circuit. The next week he humped it out to Maryland to speak at an event for Congressman Robert Bauman, the former chairman of Young Americans for Freedom, where he held that Ford dared not defy the "conservative mandate" of 1972—as if nothing at all had happened since Nixon won that mandate.

At Ford's first presidential news conference a reporter noted that "already some of your natural, conservative allies are grumbling that you are moving too far to the left. Does that trouble you?" He shrugged, indicating that it did not—and said that none of his decisions "fall in the political spectrum of left and right." Evans and Novak filed their next syndicated column in the autumn of 1974 dismissing the potential of a right-wing ideological rebellion against Ford—concluding it came from "a fringe of hardcore Reaganites . . . desperate to breath life into Reagan's expiring presidential hopes." In one paper that column was accompanied by a syndicated cartoon depicting two draft dodgers working off their crime with picks and shovels as Reagan walked by bearing an "AMNESTY FOR NIXON" picket sign. "Say," one asks the other. "Isn't that Ronald Reagan leading the new wave of permissiveness?"

This rattletrap "New Right" knew no compromise; its latest outrage was over conservative senators Barry Goldwater, John Tower, and Strom Thurmond not seeking to block Rockefeller's confirmation. Evans and Novak reported that these rightists were proposing a third-party presidential run by Reagan. Third parties being the last refuge of losers, "the Reagan rebellion," the duo concluded, "would soon be forgotten."

The president was not paying much attention. On September 23 he attended the Ninth World Energy Conference in Detroit, a conclave dominated by what used to be called the Third World, now known more respectfully as the "Lesser Developed Nations" since they had started using their natural resources to bid for superpower status. They seemed like the tail that wagged the First World dog. At the meeting, Ford all but threatened war against the next nation engaged in "rigging and distortion of world commodity markets." Henry Kissinger, speaking at the United Nations, offered similar threats: "The world cannot sustain even the present level of prices, much less continued increases." Unbowed, Kuwait's oil minister replied, "No one can wave a finger at us because we will wave a finger back."

FOUR DAYS LATER THE PRESIDENT LEARNED THAT A LUMP IN HIS WIFE'S right breast was malignant, and that even a full mastectomy might not contain the cancer. He had little time to worry, as he was putting the finishing touches on his speech introducing an unprecedented two-day open-door "conference on inflation." Eight hundred invited guests including the nation's top economists from both parties, and more than 1,200 onlookers and reporters jammed the International Ballroom at the Hilton Hotel in Washington as if Mick Jagger were about to give a graduate seminar. A certain degree of partisanship ensued. Right-wing economists recommended ending the U.S. Postal Service's monopoly on first-class mail, the Davis-Bacon Act mandating fair wages on government construction projects, and certain other federal regulations; labor-aligned economists asked Ford to keep wage and price controls. More extraordinary, however, was the thing on which the economists agreed. It was named by a brand-new word, one that would haunt the rest of the decade: *stagflation*.

Paul Samuelson, the 1970 winner of the Nobel Prize for economics and author of the field's definitive textbook, had twenty years earlier made a famous description of the triumphs of Keynesian economic science: "By the proper choice of monetary and fiscal policy we as the artists, mixing the colors of our palette, can have the capital formation and rate of current consumption that we desire." The formulation was translated into layman's terms by no less than Richard Nixon, in his 1969 inauguration speech: "We have learned at last to manage a modern economy to ensure its continued growth." It was one of those rare things in politics, a genuine consensus. It was, in fact, one of the reasons there existed a Nobel Prize for economics, first bestowed in 1969—the formerly dismal science's reward for devising an intellectual endeavor that seemed genuinely to maximize the public good for all.

Until, that is to say, these mid-1970s, when the economy stopped growing, and, as with a car thrown into neutral, furious application of all the old managerial tools brought no solution at all.

At his turn at the apex of the giant U-shaped table at the Hilton, Samuelson tried to explain why—though he wasn't too certain himself. It used to all be so simple: Economists knew that inflation and economic growth had a simple inverse relation. That if the economy stagnated, the Federal Reserve could loosen the money supply, or Congress could induce government spending, and the economy would speed back to health. Or if inflation was the problem, the economy could be cooled into balance by checks on government spending or by increased taxes—such as the income surtax Ford had proposed earlier that month. But that trade-off no longer worked, the bow-tied Democratic economist explained: "Our number one problem is 'stagflation'"—stagnation and inflation, simultaneously. Which, under the previously prevailing

Keynesian theories, could not possibly coexist. But there now was no consensus among economists, nor even any promising theory, about what to do.

Sure, Ford could increase taxes or cut spending to rein in inflation—and throw maybe a million American out of work in an election year. Or he could goose the economy, perhaps by releasing funds for public works—but then inflation might skyrocket out of control. This new presidency was evolving a theme: damned if he did, damned if he didn't.

There is a story that Franklin Delano Roosevelt was once asked what book he wished every Soviet could own. He answered, "The Sears, Roebuck catalogue." Indeed, since Roosevelt, Americans' inflation-adjusted incomes had doubled. Manufacturing wages had tripled. The specter haunting social criticism had been what human beings would do with all the free time American prosperity was producing. No more. Poor Gerald Ford, saddled with the blame. It was around this time that the new issue of *National Lampoon* hit the newsstands with the president shoving an ice-cream cone three inches north of his mouth.

POLITICIANS STARTED JOCKEYING FOR SPACE INSIDE THE PRESIDENT'S head before an economic speech scheduled for a joint session of Congress on October 7. Reagan sent him a telegram: "Dear Mr. President, I am concerned that the press reports indicate you will propose tax increases tomorrow in an effort to curb inflation. The 1972 election mandate was clear: no new taxes for four years, and reduce the size of the federal government. . . ." Congressman Wilbur Mills of Arkansas, who had amassed nearly biblical powers chairing the tax-writing Ways and Means Committee for a record eighteen years, gave a Democratic version of the same argument, releasing a statement pronouncing himself "unalterably opposed to an income tax surcharge which places its heaviest burden on the lower and middle-income classes."

The lame-duck right-wing governor could be ignored—but not, traditionally, someone like Mills. Here was the way Washington worked: long-serving congressmen and senators, almost always from the South, where elections were not quite democratic and incumbents had about as much chance of losing as they did of sprouting wings (Mills had been a congressman since 1939), leveraged their seniority into chairmanships of the committees that powered Congress like an engine room on a ship. And, like those engine rooms, the work they did was hidden from view, in backroom "markup" sessions in which power brokers from both parties drafted world-changing legislation via bonds of trust sealed with toasts of bourbon and branch water. When done right, in the old-fashioned way, the bills arrived on the floor "clean"—not amendable—and were passed by unrecorded vote, by obedient junior members directed by equally powerful "whips." Whips who left scars on those who dared disobey.

Wilbur Mills was at the apex of that system; his committee was invariably described in newspapers as the "powerful Ways and Means Committee," and he himself as "the most powerful man in Washington." But maybe now Mills could be defied. He was facing his first serious primary challenger, who was hitting him hard on the main issue that mattered this campaign season, that he'd accepted dirty money during his short-lived 1972 presidential run—"Wilbur's Watergate," the *New Republic* called it.

And then, in the same AP story announcing his displeasure with the surtax, came this: "Mills has been in seclusion since an incident early Monday when according to police his auto was stopped by police because it was traveling at a high speed with its lights off."

Washington insiders already knew it was quite more than that—and soon the rest of the world would know, too: that a not-so-young woman with Barbra Streisand curls by the name of Annabelle Battistella, Mills's next-door neighbor, had dashed out of the car in a bruised, drunken panic and leaped in apparent embarrassment into Washington, D.C.'s lovely Tidal Basin. And that her professional name, when she danced at the Silver Slipper topless lounge, was "Fanne Foxe, the Argentine Firecracker."

Jerry Ford tucked his surtax proposal, limited to Americans with incomes over fifteen thousand dollars, at the very end of his speech to the joint session of Congress that afternoon. He didn't like raising taxes; nor did he like the notion of liberals that all would be solved with $4 billion in new public works projects, nor their clamoring for new price controls. In fact, despite the honeymoon claims that this was a man beyond ideology, his economic conservatism was bone deep. As a congressman between 1970 and 1973 he followed the preferred course of Americans for Democratic Action, the liberal group, on only four votes. As president he chose as chairman of his Council of Economic Advisers free-market advocate Alan Greenspan—who was sworn in for the job standing next to his mentor, the hyper-free-market advocate Ayn Rand. And though Gerald Ford despised Ronald Reagan, when he went out to stump for Republican candidates later that month, you could hardly tell them apart: "We have to chop off these tentacles," he would say. "And as each of these tentacles withers, we have to return the power and the revenues they have grasped back to the states and localities where they belong."

That conservatism helped explain why he fell in love with an idea from economics columnist Sylvia Porter. She said that "consumers now are as eager to help combat inflation as we were eager to help fight Nazism." Wisconsin's Democratic senator Gaylord Nelson, founder of Earth Day, gave the notion a bipartisan tinge with similar language at the inflation summit.

What if inflation could be fought by individual citizen action? What if Ford could *jawbone* the nation out of its price funk?

His economics speech began with a banquet of bland policy proposals ("for the long range we must work harder on coal gasification"). He had been stumbling. Then the fun began. "My fellow Americans," he said, "ten days ago I asked you to get things started by making a list of ten things to fight inflation and exchange your list with neighbors, and to send me a copy."

He warmed to his subject.

"I have personally read scores of the thousands of letters received at the White House, and incidentally, I have made my economic experts read some of them too." They "showed me that a great deal of patriotic determination and unanimity already exists in this great land": cut kitchen waste by 5 percent, carpool, take the bus, ride bikes, walk; "share everything you can and a little bit more." He smiled folksily: "We can share burdens as we can share blessings."

The Nixon administration had suggested similar things during the food price explosion of the spring of 1973 (*"liver, kidney, brains, and heart can be made into gourmet meals with seasoning, imagination, and more cooking time"*). Nixon himself said them in his energy crisis speech in the fall (*"How many times have you gone along the highway or the freeway, whatever the case may be . . . cars with only one individual in that car?"*). They hadn't worked then. But, then, Richard Nixon hadn't had a nifty little prop.

The White House had approached a Madison Avenue advertising agency, which came up with the slogan: Whip Inflation Now. WIN. Forty-two minutes into the address, Ford explained how "a very simple enlistment form" would appear in the next day's newspapers. At that, the president pointed out in his lapel, next to his red-white-and-blue tie, the snazzy little button designed by the same guy who invented the yellow "smiley face."

"It bears the single word: WIN. I think that tells it all. I call upon every American to join in this massive mobilization and stick with it until we do win as a nation and a people."

He took the pin off and held it to the cameras. He got a standing ovation.

He promised to share more of the American people's suggestions the next week before the Future Farmers of America in Kansas City. In the interim came an earnest outpouring. He happily relayed examples in Kansas:

"Mrs. Laird Barber of Morris, Minnesota, wants to know if a national program can be organized to collect cans, glass, newspapers. . . . James Kincaid, of Belleville, Illinois, suggests a new type of government anti-inflation bond. . . . The Tennants report they do not use credit cards. They put something in their credit union each week and buy a government bond every month. . . . Robert Stewart writes from Waverly, Tennessee, that he has a heart condition, unfortunately, and draws a pension of only $251.27 a month. This allows him just two meals a day. . . . He asks me, and again I quote: 'Can we cut our government spending except for national defense?' . . . I think his example is a good one for all of us to observe. . . . From Hillsboro, Oregon, the Stevens family writes they are fixing up their bikes to do family errands."

Many of the ideas came from children. "Clean up your plate before you get up from the table"; "trash inventories"; dig school playgrounds up for "WIN vegetable gardens"; get your haircut at home. "Bob Cantrell, a 14-year-old in Pasadena, California, gave up his stereo to save energy."

WIN was a hit, for now. Golf legend Tom Watson wore his WIN button on the golf course: "It's not a joke. I put it on because I believe in it." (Governor George Wallace put one on, too, though his *was* a joke: "[It stands] for Wallace in November, doesn't it?" he said.) Capitalists did what capitalists do: soon came the WIN gardening tools, WIN paperweights, WIN mugs, pens, watches, hot plates. Meredith Willson, composer of *The Music Man*, wrote a WIN march, and the Marine and Navy bands added it to their repertoires. Two hundred thousand Americans sent in their WIN enlistment forms. Now that the campaign season was upon us, a reeling Republican Party had something to sell: collective obligation, in the key of homespun earnestness.

But a crop of unusual young Democratic candidates had a more salable post-Watergate product: suspicion, and redemption of that suspicion through a narrative of catharsis.

• • •

THE DAY AFTER FORD SPOKE IN KANSAS CITY, HE SPOKE AT A JUDICIARY subcommittee witness table, live on TV. The first president to testify before Congress since George Washington, coming so soon after Richard Nixon had so adamantly refused to do so, it was meant at once to display his openness, to empty out suspicions from the pardon—to end the national nightmare, again. Instead, he was set upon by a fusillade of paranoia.

Elizabeth Holtzman of New York, who had breathed fire at the Nixon impeachment hearings, treated the President of the United States like a criminal defendant. Ford had claimed in his opening statement that the subject of a pardon had never once been "raised by the former president or anyone representing him." Holtzman, after complaining that the short time allotted for grilling him was inadequate to examine the country's "dark suspicions," began listing those suspicions—though she barely got into the first one before the president interrupted:

"I want to assure you, the Congress, and the American people that there was no deal, period, under no circumstances."

He pounded the table. But he did acknowledge that he'd met with Alexander Haig before the resignation to discuss the various possible scenarios. Which only amplified suspicions more.

A Democrat asked how a high school teacher could explain to students how the pardon accorded with the principle of equal justice under law. A Republican, Edward Hutchinson, begged for the harassment to cease: "All reasonable questions," he said, "have been laid to rest." *Washington Post* columnist William Raspberry responded, "There is no way that last Thursday's namby-pamby session . . . could have eased anyone's doubts."

In other news from the paranoia front, the vice-president-designate Nelson Rockefeller fended off the most stringent confirmation process in the history of the republic, practically a Watergate-scale hearing in itself, over distrust that the billions in business interests he controlled would be put into a truly blind trust. Spokesmen for the disgraced former president, meanwhile, insisted Nixon couldn't testify in the Watergate cover-up trial beginning in Washington because of another outbreak of phlebitis. How convenient. A suspicious *Newsweek* cover asked, "How Sick Is Nixon?"

Sorry, Representative Hutchinson: the powers that be being perfectly rotten, the questions were only beginning.

"Establishment institutions in America are in deep trouble," pollster Lou Harris said in his September 30 newspaper column. Incumbent

Republicans were bearing the brunt. Hutchinson, whose Michigan district had been represented by a Democrat for precisely two years since 1884, faced the run of his political life. As did all his Republican Judiciary Committee colleagues. Wiley Mayne of Iowa, a congressman who sometimes had supported Nixon and sometimes had not, woke up to find his opponent braying that he'd acted "more like a defense lawyer for Nixon than like a representative of the people." Mayne's opponent promised to determine his votes in Congress through plebiscites taken in town halls in the district—and rocketed ahead in the polls. In New Jersey, where two-thirds of voters disapproved of the pardon, Charles Sandman, the congressman whose anti-impeachment ranting had reminded Teddy White of Joe McCarthy, desperately implored voters to accept that since he had switched his vote on articles of impeachment at the last minute, nothing he said before that should count.

A New Jersey lawmaker estimated that Republican candidates had gained 20,000 automatic votes when Nixon resigned—then lost 10,000 when he was pardoned. A Gallup poll said generic Democratic candidates beat generic Republicans by a margin of 54 to 35. The ratio of Democrats to Republicans in the 93rd Congress was already 235 to 182, and the Democratic National Committee was targeting an eye-popping one hundred seats more for turnover.

The *Time* magazine on the newsstands when Ford spoke on Capitol Hill predicted a Democratic landslide. But it also stressed something else: the people who'd won this year's Democratic nominations were an odd brand of Democrats. For many, this wasn't the just the first time they'd run in a campaign, but the first time they had worked in a campaign. They campaigned, almost, on their contempt for the body they sought to join. "I am running for Congress because I believe the Congress must be reformed," said thirty-four-year-old Tim Wirth of Colorado. And, like that fellow in Michigan, Vander Veen, they seemed almost militantly indifferent to partisanship. Thirty-six-year-old Gary Hart, running in Colorado for the Senate after managing George McGovern's 1972 presidential campaign, wrote an angry letter complaining that the article called him a liberal. "Traditional 'liberal' and 'conservative' slogans," he wrote, "are simply not adequate to cope."

Their economic ideologies were not traditionally liberal, either. "The best way out" of the energy crisis, Hart said, was not the nationalization of the energy companies, which Democrats like Scoop Jackson were calling for. It "is to work together. There will be a lot more cooperative ventures between the environmentalists and the energy developers." Snaking across Colorado's switchback mountain roads for the past eighteen months, he preached that America had to accept austerity—pledging, like Tom Bradley getting elected mayor in Los Angeles by promising no more freeways, *not* to develop Colorado's coal shale resources. "The party's over, the day of having it all is gone. . . . We're entering a period of history when conspicuous consumption and waste just must end."

Hart was the rock star of the 1974 Democratic candidates. He wore expensive cowboy boots with his silk suits. Not really a populist, he was, however, a reformer: his big campaign play was publishing the names of his opponent's contributors and the amounts they gave. Evans and Novak said Hart's "abandoning abrasive liberal ideology for a bland moderate facade" was actually subterfuge. Clearly they had not read the book he'd published the year before about the McGovern campaign, *Right from the Start*. "American liberalism," he had written in it, was "near bankruptcy." And George McGovern, while he brought into liberal politics the greatest organizers in a generation, "did not bring in a new generation of thinkers. He did not because it isn't there." Hart's billboards read, "They had their turn. Now it's our turn." His outmaneuvered opponent, the once-popular two-term conservative incumbent Peter Dominick, said Hart seemed to be "trying to get to the right of Attila the Hun."

Hart seemed almost angrier at other Democrats than at Republicans. His stock speech, "The End of the New Deal," argued that his party was hamstrung by the very ideology that was supposed to be its glory—that "if there is a problem, create an agency and throw money at the problem." It included lines like "The ballyhooed War on Poverty succeeded only in raising the expectations, but not the living conditions, of the poor." That was false: the poverty rate was 17.3 percent when LBJ's Economic Opportunity Act was passed in 1964 and 11.2 percent as Gary Hart spoke. But such claims did appeal to the preconceptions of people who Hart claimed must become the new base of the Democratic Party: those in the affluent suburbs, whose political power had been quietly expanding during the 1960s through redistricting and reapportionment. He called those who "clung to the Roosevelt model long after it had ceased to relate to reality," who still thought the workers, farmers, and blacks of the New Deal coalition were where the votes were, "Eleanor Roosevelt Democrats." He held them in open contempt.

The legacy of 1972 that Hart was proud of was the commission reforming the presidential nomination process, which McGovern had chaired. By incinerating the role of unions and urban machines, "the party redeemed its promise of access to the Democratic process for those outside the established center" and "regenerated itself with new leadership and new ideas." Like those of his own campaign, which he called "a contest Jefferson himself would welcome"—a purgation of a cynical old aristocracy, including a Democratic Party aristocracy.

This new kind of Democrat was said to care more about "lifestyle issues" like conservation, which blue-collar labor types viewed with distrust. (Hart's simpatico ticket mate for governor, Richard Lamm, came to prominence leading the movement to keep the 1976 Winter Olympics out of Denver, for the sake of the environment.) If anything, the new Democrats wanted smaller government. Michael Dukakis, the suburban Democrat running for governor in Massachusetts against a much more liberal Republican incumbent, was said by the UPI to want to "run the state like a bank." Jerry Brown would quote small-government nostrums he read in the magazines *Commentary* and *Public Interest*—house organs of the ascendant neoconservative movement. Though he came to the same conclusions quoting a bible of the environmental movement: E. F. Schumacher's *Small Is Beautiful: A Study of Economics as If People Mattered* (or, as the cover actually read, *small is beautiful: a study of economics as if people mattered*).

In their allergy to government activism they resembled Wisconsin's Democratic senator William Proxmire, chairman of the Joint Economic Committee, a former investment banker who in an interview in the *New Republic* "fondly allud[ed] to Ricardo, Marshall, and Pigou"—the grandfathers of neoclassical economics. Proxmire listed sixteen federal agencies he'd like to see go the way of all flesh—including the Small Business Administration, the Interstate Commerce Commission (because it "reduced competition" and protected "inefficient producers"), and, even though he was D.C.'s most famous jogger, the President's Council on Physical Fitness (its work "should be left to individuals and private institutions"). He complained of his fellow Democrats, "Say 'spend' and they salivated." "He seemed," the *New Republic*'s reporter Thomas Geoghegan marveled, "to invite a taxpayer revolt against government itself." His stock refrain was a Reaganite one: "If you want to get the government off your backs, get your hands out of the government's pockets."

THIS NEW BREED OF DEMOCRATIC CANDIDATE WAS SOON CHRISTENED with a nickname: the Watergate Babies. JFK was their first vote, an indelible touchstone. "I would guess everyone my age remembers 'Ask not what your country can do for you; ask what you can do for your country,'" David Broder quoted one of them, who was twenty-nine years old, as saying. Another, Norm Mineta, had devoted himself heart and soul to electing the first Catholic president as a rebuke to the prejudice he'd experienced as a Japanese-American who spent part of his childhood in a World War II internment camp. Joining the Kennedy campaign had steered Gary Hart away from a planned career as professor of philosophy and religion.

A remarkable number of Watergate Babies were professors: the thirty-two-year-old Ball State political science prof who ran against Judiciary Committee Republican David Dennis; the Purdue professor, Floyd Fithian, up against Earl "don't confuse me with the facts" Landgrebe; a chaplain on leave from Drexel University. Another of their formative political experiences was fighting against the Vietnam War. For example, an Iowa congressional candidate, Tom Harkin, was among the first to document the U.S.-built "tiger cages" in which our South Vietnamese allies tortured political prisoners. A candidate for the Democratic Senate nomination from New York, Texas-born Ramsey Clark, the son of Truman's right-leaning attorney general, then Supreme Court justice, had traveled to Hanoi in 1972 at the invitation of the Communist Party.

Clark chose as his campaign manager a radical journalist, Victor Navasky, whose last campaign experience was running for high school student government president. Clark limited donations to one hundred dollars a person and refused to hold a press conference to announce his candidacy. He wouldn't spend sixteen thousand dollars for a "benchmark poll" ("How am I to explain to a poor person in Harlem that I had to spend $16,000 for a 'benchmark'?"); he wouldn't rent a cheap campaign office in the Empire State Building because the art deco masterpiece was "a symbol of Rockefeller money"; he had Frank Serpico and one of the leaders of the Attica prison riots put his name in nomination at the state convention. A profile in the left-wing magazine *New Times* (entitled "The Anti-Politician") said it was as if campaign consultants had dreamed up "a candidate that would be positively unelectable": "He's lousy in crowds. Ignores his staff. Is bored by the press. Awkward shaking hands. Death on small talk. Wears suits out of the '50s (the top and bottom seldom match) and, are you ready, *hush puppies*." He shocked the New York Democratic establishment by winning. Then he called his Republican opponent Jacob Javits—who was nearly as liberal as he—a "Nixon thug."

Now, even reformers needed political machines. These couldn't be labor unions—they were part of the ossified aristocracy that got us into this mess in the first place. ("We are not a bunch of little Hubert

Humphreys," Gary Hart said about his young ideological fellow travelers, citing the politician most closely associated with the AFL-CIO.) Instead the reformers had Common Cause, the "citizen's lobby" founded in August 1970 by John Gardner, the Republican former college professor and LBJ's secretary of Health, Education, and Welfare. He said he'd started the group because Washington was "teeming with interest groups. Everybody is organized but the people."

The "people" were not, by this reckoning, blue-collar construction workers perfectly happy to see their twenty-term congressman scratch colleagues' backs in behalf of a project like the Supersonic Transport, the better to create union jobs. Common Cause was proud to have helped kill the SST. Instead, its several hundred thousand mailing-list members were well-educated, often suburban professionals whose most important political issues were reform of congressional processes, public financing of elections, and strict disclosure laws for both corporate and labor donations. Armed with this mailing list Common Cause had scored extraordinary successes both helping get the voting age lowered to eighteen and winning a lawsuit forcing the Committee to Re-elect the President to release the names of its donors—one of the things that had led to the Watergate investigation in the first place.

Their electoral crusade for 1974 was christened "Open Up the System." For it, they recruited six hundred volunteer "steering committee coordinators," 350 "publicity coordinators," and two hundred Washington-based full-time organizers, dedicated to training volunteers in classic campaign techniques. They were joined in their efforts by a media campaign sponsored by the Democratic Study Group, the liberal House caucus founded in 1959 by Eugene McCarthy to break the hold of the Jurassic seniority system, which had bottlenecked progressive legislation for generations. In the late 1960s they turned to fund-raising to elect like-minded colleagues, drafting Hollywood stars like Henry Fonda and Rod Serling as spokesmen. In 1974, they seized on Watergate as their opportunity to pack Congress with reformers to break the back of the seniority system once and for all. The Democratic National Committee kicked in with a surprisingly spirited coordinated effort, with the chairman of its campaign committee, the term-limited Georgia governor Jimmy Carter, surprising all and sundry with the Nixon-like intensity of his travel schedule in what in previous years had been a primarily ceremonial job.

It was working. In October the president added three more states to his homestretch campaign tour. "Whip Inflation Now" was soon seen as a joke and a colossal political failure (a *New York* magazine cover story titled "Ladies and Gentlemen, the President of the United States" depicted Bozo the Clown on the presidential podium with a giant red "WIN" button in his tweedy lapel). So Ford abandoned his homespun homilies and campaigned by means of right-wing hysteria instead. The "election of these extremists of the Democrats Party," he now said at campaign rallies, would threaten "the survival of the two-party system in the country."

THE WATERGATE BABIES, OVERWHELMINGLY, WON.

Enough Democrats were elected to the House of Representatives to outnumber Republicans in the 94th Congress by a ratio of more than two to one; thirty-one members were holding elective office for the first time. Three new Democratic senators increased the Democrats' margin in the upper chamber, 61 to 39. In a new survey on party identification by Republican pollster Robert Teeter, only 18 percent were willing to associate themselves with the GOP. States traditionally dominated by Republicans were now represented by Democrats: seven out of nine congressmen in Wisconsin, seventeen out of twenty-five in New England, five out of six in Iowa, nine out of eleven in Indiana. Gary Hart scored 23 percentage points more in Colorado than George McGovern had only twenty-four months earlier. Jerry Brown would be governor of California. He was thirty-seven years old. The man he replaced was sixty-four. (Ramsey Clark lost, after Jacob Javits exploited his trip to Hanoi.)

However, what kind of mandate Hart, Brown, and their Watergate Babies possessed was not entirely clear. The chairman of the Democratic National Committee said the victory revitalized "the old Democratic coalition" of FDR. The *New York Times* said Democrats in Congress were confident they could now enact that long-anticipated liberal holy grail: national health insurance. But few of the newly victorious Watergate Babies had even mentioned such New Deal–style legislation on the campaign trail. Vermont elected its first non-Republican senator since the founding of the Grand Old Party in the 1850s, though that senator-elect, Patrick Leahy, said there was "no place for partisanship" in celebrating his victory. A thirty-two-year-old congressman-elect from Michigan, James Blanchard, said, "I'm not entirely sure *what* my political philosophy is." Said Ronald Reagan of the Democratic speeches that fall, "Listening to them I had the eerie feeling we were hearing reruns of Goldwater speeches. I even thought I heard a few of my own."

Then there was the question of whether anyone was interested at all in following these new political leaders—or any sort of leader. Only a third of eligible Americans had bothered to cast a ballot. "Don't vote. It only encourages them," the bumper stickers said. Many of the bumpers that sported it still featured the sticker that popped up after Nixon was pardoned by Ford: "IMPEACH SOMEONE."

THE NEW RIGHT DIDN'T REGISTER IN THE ELECTORAL TALLIES. FOUR RE-turned prisoners of war had won Republican primaries; one, Leo Thorsness, challenging George McGovern, received backing from both the White House and RNC chairman George H. W. Bush and a warm profile as an up-and-comer in the *New York Times*. All lost in the general election.

The New Right registered in the streets and the hollers instead— where the electoral analysts in the media could safely ignore them, or dismiss them as crazies.

In West Virginia the Thursday before Election Day, someone exploded fifteen sticks of dynamite under the gas meter at the school board building just minutes after the superintendent left (he had just announced he would start enforcing truancy laws). Thousands of anti-textbook protesters rallied in the Charleston Civic Center, wearing huge stickers reading JESUS WOULDN'T HAVE READ THEM, singing "Amazing Grace" and "We Shall Not Be Moved" and "America the Beautiful," and cheering speeches about starting their own independent school system, given from a podium flanked by Old Glory on one side and a crucifix-emblazoned flag on the other. They shouted that it was time to shovel books into bonfires—a development that tested the limits of Paul Cowan's empathy: "Some of these protesters," he wrote, "were clearly capable of outright totalitarianism."

On November 8 the board voted 4–1 to return the most noncontroversial volumes to the curriculum and let the others be read only with special parental permission. Once more, compromise only poured gas on the flames. Dozens of white men patrolled Campbell Creek with shotguns, following rumors over citizens' band radio that carloads of blacks were on their way to burn churches. The next day school buses were shot at, and a car owned by parents who insisted on sending their kids back to school was blown up. A police cruiser escorting a school bus was punctured by a rifle shot.

In Boston, October ended with a tally of sixteen assaults against teachers. A two-thousand-car cavalcade snarled traffic from Quincy to South Boston. Then activists boycotted Election Day. On Thanksgiving Day, four thousand rallied at East Boston Stadium—replacing the annual Eastie-Southie football game, traditionally the greatest public event of the year, but not this year, because the football season had been canceled. On December 11, a white student was stabbed by a black student at South Boston High. A mob of white parents formed a blockade around the school to trap the black students and made ready to storm the building. Shattering glass; police horses charging. *"Kill the niggers! Kill the niggers!"* *"Niggers eat shit! Niggers eat shit!"* A chorus of mothers led that cheer. President Ford put the 82nd Airborne on alert.

THE ELECTION OF A CONGRESS IN WHICH DEMOCRATS OUTNUMBERED Republicans two to one obscured a simple underlying fact: right-wing culture was not in retreat. You could see it in the ongoing celebration of POW heroes like Jeremiah Denton, now commandant of the Armed Forces Staff College, who on November 19 was awarded the Navy's second-highest decoration, the Navy Cross, for blinking out the letters "T-O-R-T-U-R-E" in Morse code during a 1966 broadcast from North Vietnam he was forced to make. (He also said then to his captors, "I don't know what is happening, but whatever the position of my government is, I support it fully. Whatever the position of my government, I believe in it, yes sir. I am a member of that government, and it is my job to support it, and I will as long as I live"—at which they tortured him yet more brutally, but never tried to use him for propaganda purposes again.) You could see it on the bestseller lists—but only if you knew how to look. A nonfiction thriller called *Alive,* for instance, spent twenty weeks on the *New York Times* list. The yarn about how twenty-nine South American student rugby players survived a plane crash in the frozen remote Andes seemed simply a riveting tale to those trend-spotters, in D.C., in Manhattan, in Hollywood, who didn't understand the subculture that actually was driving the sales: evangelical Christians, enraptured by the fact that the students saw the most dramatic detail of their survival—cannibalism of their dead teammates' preserved, frozen flesh—as, in the words of one survivor, going "back to the source of Christianity." The continued explosion in sales of *The Late, Great Planet Earth* was invisible to those same cultural elites—because the Christian bookstores where many of its readers purchased it were not surveyed for bestseller lists.

The elites paid more attention to the new, second report from the Club of Rome, *Mankind at the Turning Point,* whose mass-market paperback edition announced, "Mankind today stands at the brink of a precipice." It argued that unless worldwide birth control was instituted in the next twenty years, starvation and disease would claim as many people as would be born and that the OPEC-driven explosion in energy prices was a blessing in disguise, because under previous prices fuel would have run out by the end of the century. *Science* magazine found the book's prescriptions "perhaps the only hope we have." *Time* found its plea for "a truly interwoven global economic system in which all nations helped one another for economic gain" a convincing alternative to "mankind's lemming-like rush toward disaster."

The 1968 book *The Population Bomb* was still selling (its worst-case scenario was the destruction of mankind in a nuclear holocaust by 1974; its best case was that America would be reduced to food rationing as most of the Third World fell to famine and anarchy). Paul Ehrlich, along with several other environmentalist writers, including Theodore Roszak, E. F. Schumacher, and Barry Commoner, published an anthology titled *Notes for the Future*. It proposed that precisely the things that were supposed to be the glory of our civilizations—technology, industry, the mastery of nature—were in fact "symptoms of a diseased society." Left-leaning apocalypticism had become a background hum within mainstream politics. Ehrlich himself had become a regular on *The Tonight Show*.

But both *Alive* and *The Late, Great Planet Earth* formed part of the background hum for their readers' politics, too: both books, and many others, argued that the militantly secular culture suppressing the "Christian worldview" foretold a far worse disaster than mere environmental collapse—it foretold the end of the world in fire and brimstone. Other such volumes were more explicitly political—like *The Politics of Pornography,* a selection that fall of the Conservative Book Club, which proposed that "streaking and similar crazes" were part and parcel of the conspiracy to "replace the dominion of God with one that makes man the measure of all things." Its author, Dr. Rousas J. Rushdoony, was a leader of a Christian Reconstructionist movement, which sought to "return" the United States government to biblical law. His 1972 book, *The Messianic Character of American Education,* which argued that "the nuclear family is the basic unit of God's covenant" and that this unit was being deliberately undermined by the education establishment, which worshiped the false messiah of the secular humanist state, was an inspiration for the professional conservatives organizing in Kanawha.

One place you could read about such books was *Christianity Today*—but not in the editorial content, which still took strikingly liberal positions. (The editors were so impressed with the arguments in *All We're Meant to Be: A Biblical Approach to Women's Liberation* that they came out in favor of the Equal Rights Amendment. In their survey of eighty-seven denominational leaders, eight of fourteen Baptist officials supported it, too.) Most of its ministerial readers still stayed away from social issues entirely, hewing to a theologically informed reluctance to get involved in "worldly" concerns, traditional in evangelical circles ever since the humiliations of the 1925 Scopes trial. Instead, the politics of the emerging "Christian right" was most visible in *Christianity Today*'s margins—its literal margins, in the ad columns.

"It is no longer expedient for Christians to be secluded from the mainstream of human events," read an advertisement in the September 13, 1974, issue from the Christian Freedom Foundation, a Buena Park, California, organization underwritten by the fantastically wealthy, right-wing DeVos family of Michigan. "Our country was established on a certain harmony of values preserved by our Christian heritage. As long as the majority of citizens were committed to these basic values, compliance with standards and national stability followed. But now this value consensus is disappearing. The tidal wave of defection from former standards is sweeping away good laws which once held firm. The decline of conscience renders the law ineffectual. The end of self-restraint is paving the way for a breakdown of order itself."

It concluded: "This is not the time for either panic or lethargy; it is time for critical thought, brave commitments and vigorous action motivated by the love of Jesus Christ. It is time for responsible Christians to take a hand in the affairs of state."

CHAPTER SIXTEEN

Watergate Babies

FISHBAIT WAS GONE.

William "Fishbait" Miller had been the official doorkeeper of the House of Representatives since 1949. Sixty-five years old, fat, his straight gray hair parted down the middle and his ties unfashionably thin, he was vaguely recognizable to the country for the magnolia drawl that announced presidents, prime ministers, generals, and queens before joint sessions of Congress. But his post was also an administrative one, for which he was paid $40,000 a year (House members made $42,500), and for which he controlled 340 patronage workers. He got and kept the job as reward for holding the coat of Mississippi reactionary William Colmer since the congressman's first campaign in 1932. He never was particularly good at his job, such as that job was; at one joint session he was supposed to announce a dignitary whose face he couldn't quite recall. A member from Texas whispered to him, "For God's sake, Fishbait, it's the Chief Justice!" He was, instead, the perfect symbol of the Dixiecrats' corrupt control of Capitol Hill. So in a move symbolic of their determination to break that power, the seventy-five new House freshmen voted in a bloc at the first Democratic caucus meeting on December 2, 1974, for his dismissal.

Wilbur Mills had managed to survive his reelection campaign. In December, the morning of the caucus meeting that cashiered Fishbait, the front pages reported that Fanne Foxe, the Argentine Firecracker, made her stripping debut in Boston. The event was newsworthy enough to draw a clutch of political reporters—whose astonishment was visible in the pictures that appeared on the nation's front pages of the eighteen-term solon leaping onstage and joining the show. Such was the image seared in Watergate Babies' retinas as they reported that morning for the first battle in what the *Washington Post* called a "revolution," and *U.S. News & World* Report labeled Washington's "biggest power shake-up in more than a century."

One vote was over who would chair the caucus. The establishment candidate was B. F. Sisk, a sixty-five-year-old eleventh-termer and loyal member of the Rules Committee—in whose back rooms, for decades, power brokers from both parties decided which bills would live and which would die, and how debate over those they granted the gift of life would be systematically limited. "Debate," in fact, was an overstatement; debates almost always took place under the notorious "closed rule," which made it all but impossible to amend a bill on the floor.

Sisk's opponent, Democratic Study Group fixture Phillip Burton, had led a fight to pressure the House Foreign Affairs Committee in 1973 to report out the first bill since the 1920s without a closed rule. The bill called for ending funding in Vietnam by a fixed date. "For the first time, we in DSG have broken through the parliamentary barricades erected by the Republican-Dixiecrat conservative coalition and forcefully condemned the Nixon administration's unnecessary prolongation of this bloody war," Burton gloated then. Now, the Republican-Dixiecrat coalition was in retreat, DSG was in the saddle, and with the votes of almost every one of the freshmen, Phil Burton became chair of the 94th Congress's mighty Democratic caucus.

Then, over the next few days, they got to work reinventing the House. First, they took away from Mills's Ways and Means Committee the power to pick who served on committees. Then, since Ways and Means was still powerful enough, they expanded its membership from 25 to 37, diluting the clout of its incumbent membership by adding reform-minded youngsters.

On December 10, 1974, Wilbur Mills retired. Promptly, House freshmen caucused and summoned all the other old committee chairs to audition, before what seventy-four-year-old Armed Services Committee chairman F. Edward Hébert of Louisiana called "a mob of crusading knights out to slay evil dragons." Hébert lied to their faces about his record approving nearly every request the Pentagon ever made. Then he said "we should have bombed the hell out of" North Vietnam.

One fresh feature of the 94th Congress was its six new women, bringing the total to eighteen, a record. One of them, thirty-five-year-old Pat Schroeder of Colorado, had seen her 1972 campaign as an antiwar housewife spied on by the FBI. At the meeting, she accused Hébert of having discriminated against her in the Armed Services Committee (he had once insisted she and the committee's black member, Ron Dellums, literally share a seat in the hearing room) because she was a woman. He responded that he would have treated her better if she had *acted* like a woman. The caucus fired him by a vote of 152–133. Afterward, to reporters waiting outside the hearing room, he called his inquisitors "boys and girls." He was not entirely wrong. One of them, freshman representative Tom Downey of New York, had attended his first peace march ten years earlier, at the age of fifteen.

Appropriations chair George Mahon (seventy-five years old) and the half-deaf chairman of the Agriculture Committee, W. R. Poage (seventy-six), who voted against the majority Democratic Party position more than he voted for it, were unhorsed for what a Common Cause report called "serious abuses" of procedural fairness and "arbitrary" treatment of colleagues. (Poage was replaced by the chairman of the Democratic Study Group.) Wright Patman lost his chairmanship of Currency and Banking, not for being a reactionary—he had been fighting concentrated power since the Progressive Era, and was the first congressman to undertake an investigation of Watergate—but solely for his age. "You can't have an 81-year-old chairman," even one who "was a hero to 90 percent of us," a young insurgent of the first Congress in history with an average age under fifty told the Associated Press. "Congress will never be the same," another new member told the press. "It's permanent.... I think the feeling is the sun is shining and now we really have a chance to do something."

One Old Bull, however, portentously survived. Wayne Hays of Ohio was known on Capitol Hill as the "meanest man in Congress." His Administration Committee enjoyed few powers outside the Capitol building but was a dictatorship within it. In charge of congressional staff allowances and benefits, he was known to cut them, and even to shut off members' air-conditioning, to settle personal scores—and to dock the pay of elevator operators and barbers who would not put up with his voluminous abuse. The *New York Times* called him "a disgrace to Ohio, the Democratic Party, and the House of Representatives." An Ohio paper pointed to his committee's one jurisdictional power of national import—federal election law—and claimed his work delaying implementation of the 1971 campaign finance law "made Watergate possible." But congressmen had a use for their very own sonofabitch: with his committee doling out perquisites like stationery allowances and government-paid trips home, they didn't have to vote for such appropriations themselves, on the House floor, on the public record. Such hustles seemed just the thing the Watergate Babies had in their sights. But after the Steering and Policy Committee voted 13–11 to strip his chairmanship, Hays began a furious overnight lobbying campaign promising to bestow on them more fringe benefits and a pay increase. Which his committee didn't have the jurisdiction to give—until, after the caucus voted to save him, they voted to newly give it to him.

"The clear inference," newspapers reported, "was that Congress expects Hays to give them a pay hike." Hays then confirmed the inference by telling reporters that "our take-home pay is like that of a peasant." (It was about four times America's median household income.) "The new idealists betrayed a small streak of venality," Howard Smith editorialized on ABC; the *Washington Post* said that "self-styled congressional reformers have tackled the establishment in order to establish themselves instead." Ralph Nader, whose Congress Watch had built much of the intellectual case for the House's decrepitude, cried sellout: "This is the type of political wheeling and dealing built on conflicts of interest that was widely rejected by voters in November. Surely the reform-minded members of the 94th Congress can do better than to perpetuate a man in office [in] response to the same old tradeoffs that have bred such cynicism about Congress in the public mind."

The Republican Party, it was true, seemed near to death. The *Washington Post*'s new conservative columnist George Will said visiting Republican National Committee headquarters was like visiting "the set for a political disaster flick, a political *Poseidon Adventure*." The bank holding the mortgage on the Capitol Hill Club, the private retreat where Republicans took their refreshment, was threatening to foreclose on the place. The party's pollster, Robert Teeter, explained that a majority of Americans considered Republicans "untrustworthy and incompetent." But here was a lesson Democrats would have all too much occasion to contemplate in the years ahead: to claim the mantle of purity is always a risky business. It just gives voters an excuse to be disillusioned once your ordinary humanity is exposed. How long did the new Congress's reputation for purity last? Two months, possibly. That was when a Maryland senator surveyed his constituents: "Do you have confidence in the ability of Congress to deal with today's problems?" They answered "no" by a margin of two to one. Commented a Baltimore couple: "We don't have enough confidence—or trust—in our congressmen to let them take out the garbage."

AMERICA STILL SEEMED ENTIRELY ROTTEN; NO WAVE OF BRIGHT-EYED reformers could change that. On Christmas morning a twenty-five-year-old model in Queens was beaten to death in her apartment, her neighbors ignoring the screams—in the same redbrick building where Kitty Genovese had lived. (Genovese had become a household name in 1964 after the *New York Times* reported that thirty-eight witnesses did nothing while she was knifed to death.) The new movie packing theaters was *The Godfather: Part II*. In a pivotal scene, a senator from Nevada wakes up from an alcoholic haze to see an unconscious prostitute—at which a consigliere assures the panicked politician that in exchange for his protecting the mobsters' criminality, no one need know that he murdered a hooker. In another, the heads of major American corporations sit around a table with mobsters, and President Batista of Cuba at the head; then a coven of mobsters conspires to divide Cuba as if divvying up a cake. "We're bigger than U.S. Steel," one says, and talks about putting a friendly president in the White House.

A banner headline in the December 22 edition of the *New York Times* read: "Huge C.I.A. Operation Reported in U.S. Against Antiwar Forces, Other Dissidents in Nixon Years." The article, by Seymour Hersh, reported that the spy agency had collected intelligence files on at least ten thousand American citizens in direct violation of its 1947 charter stipulating that it was allowed to work only outside the United States. The article also documented "dozens of other illegal activities by members of the C.I.A. in the United States, beginning in the nineteen-fifties, including break-ins, wiretapping, and the surreptitious inspection of mail." The jump took up nearly an entire inside page, with its tone of Orwellian menace suggested by the caption describing an image hovering above a photo of the CIA's Langley, Virginia, headquarters: "The agency's emblem symbolizes vigilance, directed to all points of the compass."

That long national nightmare that was supposed to be over: perhaps it was only beginning.

The *Times* ran thirty-two stories over the next two and a half weeks on a scandal that appeared to reach far deeper into "the system" than Watergate itself, reaching through the tenure of that supposed innocent, John F. Kennedy, all the way back to placid old Dwight D. Eisenhower. President Ford, caught unawares on the way to a ski vacation in Vail, Colorado, frantically backfilled to contain the damage. On January 5 he named a panel to be chaired by Vice President Rockefeller to investigate the allegations—like the panel in *The Parallax View*, you might say. One member, Douglas Dillon, a defense establishment überinsider and Rockefeller Foundation board member, had been privy himself to CIA secrets while serving under presidents Eisenhower, Kennedy, and Johnson. Another, General Lyman Lemnitzer, had as chairman of the Joint Chiefs of Staff deleted questions on the U-2 spy plane program for a 1962 House hearing. (According to one concerned congressman, it was "like the attempt of the totalitarian government described in George Orwell's book *1984* to rewrite history to suit the viewpoint of the government"; the congressman's name was Gerald Ford.) Another member, Lane Kirkland, was a top officer in the AFL-CIO, an organization so cooperative with hard-line Cold Warriors that its critics on the left dubbed it the "AFL-CIA." Rockefeller himself had been a member of Richard Nixon's Foreign Intelligence Advisory Board, the tiny top-secret civilian review panel that signed off on all covert activities. That meant that any genuine exposé of CIA abuses by this Rockefeller commission would . . . expose members of the Rockefeller commission. "Having the CIA investigated by such a group," the *Times* editorialized, "is like having the Mafia audited by its own accountants."

On January 19 came news of the publication in Britain of a shocking book-length exposé from an exiled former CIA agent, Philip Agee, called *Inside the Company: A CIA Diary*. That same day, the *Washington Post* confirmed rumors that J. Edgar Hoover had compiled files on the personal lives of congressmen—and, one week later, that the FBI had bugged Martin Luther King at the 1964 Democratic National Convention in Atlantic City, New Jersey. By February the new Congress planted its flag on the Sam Ervin model: both houses voted select committees to investigate both the FBI and the CIA—which, pace the injunction in Article I, Section 9 of the Constitution that "[n]o money shall be drawn from the Treasury, but in consequence of appropriations made by law; and a regular statement and account of the receipts and expenditures of all public money shall be published from time to time," had never had its budget reviewed by Congress, save for a tiny cadre of insiders who were given the tiniest little peek. One of them, John Stennis (Gerald Ford had been another), explained in 1971 how that system worked: "You make up your mind that you are going to have an intelligence agency and protect it as such, and shut your eyes some and take what is coming."

Not anymore. Between 1947 and 1974 some four hundred bills had been introduced to improve congressional oversight of intelligence agencies. All had come a cropper. But it took just two hours of debate for the Senate to pass this one, by a vote of 82–4; the world was different now. "In this year—so soon after Watergate—we cannot leave in doubt the operations and activities of agencies involved in such sensitive and secret endeavors," conservative Democrat Walter Huddleston of Kentucky said. Republicans were if anything harsher. Howard Baker, who had earlier tried and failed to charter an investigation on the CIA's role in Watergate, articulated a "shuddering fear" that the CIA was out of control. The Pennsylvania liberal Republican Richard Schweiker called it a "shadow government." Even Barry Goldwater, the security establishment's best friend, acceded to its investigation: "If surgery is required, let it be performed only after the most careful diagnosis." The suspicious circles, it seemed, were in the saddle.

THUS ARRIVED AN UNLIKELY DEVELOPMENT: CHASING SPOOKS BECAME A political opportunity. Frank Church, the liberal Democratic senator from Idaho, a longtime critic of the CIA ("I will do whatever I can, as one senator," he had said years earlier, "to bring about a full-scale congressional investigation of the CIA") and scourge of the Vietnam War ("a monstrous immorality")—and a presidential hopeful—maneuvered himself into the chairmanship of the new Senate Select Committee to Study Governmental Operations with Respect to Intelligence Activities. And for one of the members of the new Rockefeller commission, CBS reported, "the assignment could help keep presidential hopes alive."

That would be Governor Ronald Reagan, a surprise pick that had Washington insiders wondering if President Ford—approval rating: 42 percent—was more worried about a nomination challenge than anyone had previously thought. The *New York Times* did not approve. Reagan, it reported in a February article that read like an editorial, had "missed three of the four weekly meetings of the Presidential commission investigating the Central Intelligence Agency." He "reportedly told President Ford when he was asked to join the panel that his speaking engagements might conflict with the meetings." His secretary promised Reagan would "catch up by reading the transcripts of the missed sessions"—though, "according to the commission staff, Mr. Reagan has not yet visited the commission headquarters, where hundreds of pages of transcripts are kept in locked files." Instead, "During January, he gave seven 'major addresses' to such groups as the International Safari Club, in Los Angeles."

Who could take seriously a lightweight like that? Though CBS still spied a possible opening for a Reagan presidential bid: "If the economy overwhelms President Ford." Portents hinted at just that. In fact, that news was getting downright apocalyptic.

In December economists announced that the nation was officially in a recession. By January the projected annual growth rate was negative 5 percent. A Harris poll found only 11 percent of the country thought Ford was "keeping the economy healthy." Even the Godfather of Soul got into the act: "People! People! Got to get over, before we get under," growled James Brown in a new hit that was number four on the R&B charts: "There ain't no funky jobs to be found. Taxes going up . . . now I drink from a paper cup. Gettin' bad!"

On the heels of a Pentagon move to eliminate 11,600 civilian jobs at military bases, the auto industry announced 40,000 layoffs. Ford Motors cut production schedules at eleven of its twenty North American assembly plants and most of its forty-five manufacturing plants. Chrysler laid off almost 11,000 white-collar workers. American Motors idled 7,000 workers in one plant in Kenosha, Wisconsin, alone. In New Hampshire, a textile mill that had been in business since 1823 was scheduled to shutter. Maryland's largest private employer, the four-mile-long Sparrows Point steel complex, began laying off thousands; 100,000 steel workers lost their jobs nationwide between the previous summer and the upcoming fall; in December 1974—Christmastime—185,000 blue-collar workers found themselves without work. Businesses and consumers preferred products made elsewhere: foreign car sales were up 20 percent, American cars down almost 13. The *Economist* said, "Capitalism is being tested everywhere. Many people believe it is dying." It called the closing of 150 investment banks and securities dealers in the United States in recent weeks "some of the worst failures since the Great Depression." The National Association of Home Builders called the slump in its industry "far and away the worst since the Depression."

Since the Depression: a new household phrase.

It felt as if America did not even own itself. "Will Araby Bankrupt the World?" the January 25 *Saturday Review* cover asked. Rumor was that Saudis had bought up all the real estate in Beverly Hills. Arabs had bought us, yes, but they also hated us: in one page-turner selling out at airport book stores, *Black Sunday,* Palestinians had no trouble recruiting one of those sturdy patriotic heroes of 1973, a Vietnam prisoner of war, his brain too addled by torture to resist, to pilot an explosives-laden blimp into the Super Bowl; in another, *The Gargoyle Conspiracy*, Arabs assassinate the secretary of state. (*Time* noted jocularly that the Arab-bashing thrillers might someday no longer be published, if the Arabs bought all the publishing companies.) Meanwhile, the real-life secretary of state, in a Christmastime interview in *BusinessWeek,* hinted that a military strike to seize Middle East oil fields outright might be imminent. Then he left for a hat-in-hand tour of Arab capitals, as if making amends.

Gerald Ford, in his January 15 State of the Union address, was hardly more comforting: "I must say to you that the state of our Union is not good," he said. No president had ever told the citizenry anything like that.

But *Ronald Reagan* as the answer? His preferred solution to the crisis—turning management of the economy even more over to private interests—didn't sound right even to the conservative City of London gentlemen who edited the *Economist*. They opined that much of the blame for capitalism's tests lay with "a concentration of money into the hands of a few big banks, even more than these giants know what to do with."

In any event, with Ford tacking to the right, it was hard to see what room Reagan might have to maneuver. "FORD LAUDED BY WALL STREET ON INFLATION," read a headline about his speech to securities analysts who "generally applauded what they saw as President Ford's renewed determination to tackle inflation, rather than recession, as the nation's chief economic problem." He gave speeches in which he said things like "We face a critical choice. . . . Shall we slide headlong into an economy whose vital decisions are made by politicians while the private sector dries up and shrivels away?" The major economic idea in his State of the Union message was a tax rebate of around one hundred dollars for the average American, which was just the sort of thing a President Reagan would be likely to propose.

"President Reagan"—that inconceivable phrase. Ronald Reagan, who was still defending Richard Nixon, and who said two weeks before Gerald Ford's pardon that "the punishment of resignation is more than adequate for the crime."

Ronald Reagan, who told CBS "I hope to devote my time to hitting the sawdust trail and preaching the gospel of free enterprise"—"the gospel," like this was revealed truth or something.

This in a country where the most talked-about new bipartisan legislative proposal was soon to be Jacob Javits and Hubert Humphrey's "Balanced Growth and Economic Planning Act," which attempted to grow the country out of stagflation by setting up an Office of National Economic Planning to govern such heretofore unregulated parts of the economy as factory production, and which would submit six-year plans to Congress every twenty-four months. This might once have sounded like something out of the Soviet Union. But now—why not? One of Ford's aides, who would go on to become vice chairman of Goldman Sachs, thought Ford should co-opt the idea as his own, as "a highly constructive presidential initiative." Intellectuals devoured the arguments of sociologist Daniel Bell, in *The Coming of Post-Industrial Society: A Venture in Social Forecasting*, "that, today, we in America are moving away from a society based on a private-enterprise market system toward one in which the most important economic decisions will be made at the political level, in terms of consciously defined 'goals' and priorities.' . . . A turn to non-capitalist modes of social thought . . . is the long-run historical tendency in Western society."

Indeed the general public agreed. Free enterprise as "gospel"? When Gallup asked voters whether wage and price controls should be put back into effect—the most proximate example of the kind of thing Bell was talking about—66 percent said yes. When they asked how to deal with inflation, only 12 percent gave Reagan's answer: cut government spending. Only 6 percent of the public said that when unions asked for too much money it caused higher prices—Reagan's other favorite economic claim.

Columnist Colman McCarthy's year-in-review piece in the *Washington Post* announced, "We live in a time of collapse with expressions of hope . . . no brighter than Albert Camus' belief: 'The important thing is not to be cured but to live with one's ailments.'"

It wasn't the 1920s anymore. *Ronald Reagan?*

As it happened, there was a new biography out of Reagan's favorite author of boys' books, Horatio Alger. It advertised on its back cover its central Woodward-and-Bernstein-like investigatory find, an 1866 letter from the members of Alger's Unitarian congregation: "Horatio Alger. Jr., who has officiated as our minister for about 15 months past has recently been charged with gross immorality and a most heinous crime, a crime of no less magnitude than the abominable and revolting crime of unnatural familiarity with boys. . . ."

These were suspicious times. Heroes were what you were supposed to throw from pedestals. And yet here was gee-whiz, aw-shucks Ronald Reagan, acting like nothing had changed. Who when CBS inquired about his presidential ambitions demurred, like a Boy Scout, as always: "Anyone who is approached by his fellow citizens and is called to duty would have to give it serious consideration." But his fellow Republicans weren't interested; according to Gallup, 16 percent wanted him as their nominee—the same number as wanted to go back to Barry Goldwater.

Ronald Reagan. Who, now that he had ceded the governor's chair to Jerry Brown, was launching a new enterprise: a daily five-minute radio homily that his representatives claimed would soon be running on more than three hundred stations around the country.

LATE IN REAGAN'S SECOND TERM IN SACRAMENTO, AFTER HE ANNOUNCED he wouldn't run for a third, two top gubernatorial aides with backgrounds in public relations, Peter Hannaford (introspective, bespectacled, brainy) and Michael Deaver (intense, practical, a tough negotiator), created a firm that made launching Ronald Reagan's postgubernatorial career 60 percent of its business. What next, when he left Sacramento in January 1975? They entertained, then discarded, the notion of some sort of academic position at Pepperdine, the conservative Disciples of Christ university outside Malibu; likewise a job "as nominal head of a national organization, particularly one already known" (a conservative one like the U.S. Chamber of Commerce or the Freedoms Foundation, perhaps "even groups such as the Red Cross"), which might "provide 'instant' access and legitimacy for his opinions on a variety of topics." Maybe PBS specials documenting his visits to college campuses; or an offer, conceptualized by a magnate in the dehydrated onion and garlic industry named J. H. Hume, to be funded by the right-wing oil heir Richard Mellon Scaife, to take up a "Distinguished Public Affairs Fellowship" from the Hoover Institution at Stanford, with the aim of crafting an "opus magnus [sic] in the form of a book of essays on solutions to national and international problems."

That idea, too, went nowhere. A proposed condition of the Hoover fellowship was the hope that "he would restrict his speaking engagements and traveling insofar as possible to allow time for his own studies," which apparently did not entice. Another part of the offer that may have not have appealed to them was the stipend for the proposed half-time job: $25,000. One major goal for Deaver & Hannaford was to establish the governor as a viable presidential contender. Another was to make him a rich man. Memos larded with estimates of income and expenses flew around: speaking engagements estimated at an average fee of $5,000 per (soon he would be spending twelve to fourteen days a month on the road); freelance pieces under the governor's byline ("In addition to exploring interview opportunities [e.g. PLAYBOY] we should target for sales of six RR articles to major magazines at an average sale of $1,000"); talks with superagent Irving "Swifty" Lazar about a book deal with Knopf—for a "total estimated income" anticipated in one planning document at "Net: $134,440 . . . plus income from consulting, board memberships, personal investments, State retirement fund" (his actual earnings in 1975 were reportedly close to $800,000).

Like any corporate enterprise, the project had to be capitalized, and like any ambitious political enterprise—it was both—it needed to establish a reliable list of potential future supporters. Plans were laid for a direct mail campaign, the one stone to kill two birds: "To keep the nation following the conservative mandate of 1972 and to warn of the alternative—a neo-Socialist planned economy—we must speak out across America," ran the proposed pitch over Reagan's printed signature, to go out to the conservative mailing lists. "This takes time and money. I'm willing to invest the time, but I'm not a Rockefeller or a Kennedy, and I need your help to pay the costs."

A column was syndicated, with Hannaford, Pat Buchanan, and a young aide named Jeff Bell as ghostwriters, to be called "Viewpoint"; there was a full schedule of speeches, including, in April, one before the Pilgrim Society in London. ("RONALD REAGAN: A Program for the Future," a Deaver & Hannaford strategy memo dated November 4, 1974, noted at heading "I. Political Goals," subparagraph C: "Enhance foreign affairs credibility"). Possibly a syndicated radio program—though surely a more fertile field was television, for which a glamorous and lucrative proposal was on the table: a twice-weekly commentary spot on Walter Cronkite's marquee newscast.

Michael Deaver salivated at that one. Not the governor. As was frequently the case with his executive style, he was indifferent to details of his PR men's execution, showing up at the Deaver & Hannaford office only a couple of days a week—but he could be forcefully specific on things that mattered to him. Like that office's location: fifteen minutes from his Pacific Palisades home, he insisted, and fifteen minutes from the airport. And like the idea of a regular TV spot. "People will tire of me on television," he said. "They won't tire of me on the radio."

That Reagan constant: aware, always, of the gaze of others; reflecting on it, adjusting himself to it, inviting it; modeling himself, in his mind's eye, according to how he presented himself to others; adjusting himself to be perceived as he wished others to perceive him. Radio it would be. The first two stations to pick him up in syndication were WOC in Davenport and WHO in Des Moines—the stations, forty-two years earlier, where he had made his broadcasting debut.

> *"If you're under the impression that federal food stamps are only available to the elderly and the poor, you're in for a surprise. I'll be right back."*

> *"Why is the Consumer Protection Agency bill like a basket of kittens? It's more than a riddle. It's a fact of life. I'll be right back."*

> *"If you're charged with breaking the law, you're innocent until proven guilty. If you're charged with breaking some bureaucrat's regulation, it's the other way around. I'll be right back."*

> *"If you're not familiar with the term 'boondoggle,' consider the fact that our federal government recently underwrote the cost of a study dealing with Polish bisexual frogs. If that doesn't give you a hint, stand by. I'll be right back."*

Thus opened his first week's broadcasting efforts. After a commercial break, Reagan would satisfy the curiosity he'd stirred two minutes before with a simple, folksy story about a fundamentally sound, decent citizenry set upon by a government gone mad.

If you've had the experience of standing in the checkout line in the supermarket next to a strapping young fella with a big basket of groceries who pays for them in food stamps, and you're worrying how long you'll be able to find the cash to feed your family, and you've paid your taxes, you've probably worried about the food stamp program and how it works.

Not well, he went on to explain, telling the story of a father who made one hundred thousand dollars a year but whose college student son got food stamps in California, and another about a young woman in California who "took just enough college courses to avoid the food stamp work requirement who was studying to be a witch."

When you were young did you ever have the experience of trying to carry a basket of kittens? One would pop its head up and try to crawl up over the side of the basket and while you were trying to push him back down another would pop up on the other side of the basket, and it seemed there were more heads than you had hands?

That was what you needed to know about the Consumer Protection Agency bill, an innocuous-sounding law (despised, Reagan didn't say, by business lobbyists) that would create "a big new federal government bureaucracy that would have the power to supersede all other government agencies plus the power to take records and trade secrets from businesses and industries and make them public," which was "as big a threat to our free economy as anything that's been proposed." When senators filibustered, then defeated cloture three times, "in an unprecedented break with tradition they tried a fourth time and failed. But don't start a celebration. Like that basket of kittens, this one will pop again soon, maybe with a new title or maybe even as an amendment to some necessary piece of legislation that everyone supports."

It all went by fast, in a time before the casually suspicious could whip out laptop computers and google whether what he said was actually true—as, very often, it was not. Take the case of the Polish bisexual frogs: more than a year earlier, after an Idaho congressman introduced the "scandal" on the House floor, a columnist for an obscure little newspaper in Boca Raton, Florida, learned the research in question was of potential promise for understanding of how hybrids might improve the efficiency of agriculture—and had not been funded by American tax-payers at all.

It was hard to see what such tidy fabulism could accomplish po-litically. In his second week on the air, for instance, Reagan claimed that worries about high unemployment amounted to "a case of mass hysteria," an "artificially induced depression psychology," and were all the fault of how the Bureau of Labor Statistics incorporated into the un-employment numbers bored housewives looking for part-time work in households "where poppa's holding down a steady job," and fourteen-year-olds who wanted paper routes. But if the BLS started counting properly, he boldly proclaimed, the unemployment rate would be only 1 percent.

Two hundred thousand people had just been laid off in the automo-bile industry. Who was Ronald Reagan going to convince?

Sixty-six percent of the public surveyed had recently told Gallup they did not want to reduce spending for "social programs such as health, education, and welfare programs." RNC focus group research concluded, "The first thing that comes to people's mind about the Re-publican Party is that it's the party of big business."

And yet here was Ronald Reagan, blithely acting as if a mass elector-ate, incensed that "trade secrets from businesses and industries" would be made public, might rise as one against consumer protection and somehow turn the Republican Party into a fighting force in a nation that had just voted two to one for Democrats.

But then his, after all, was the zeal of the convert. He had left Iowa in 1937 a "hemophiliac, bleeding heart liberal." Then Hollywood, and a long, slow conversion. Let us pause to consider how it happened, and what that transformation might have meant for the future of the nation.

CHAPTER SEVENTEEN

Star

IN 1935 RONALD REAGAN PREVAILED UPON HIS RADIO EMPLOYERS TO PAY his travel expenses to a sumptuous resort off the coast of Orange County, California, Catalina Island, where the Chicago Cubs trained each February: the perfect opportunity, he convinced the boss, to store up a season's worth of color to fill in between the Cubs' telegraphed plays. In 1937, he made the trip for a third time, this time with an ulterior motive. Joy Hodges, a house vocalist at the station, had won a contract at RKO Studios; Hugh Hipple, a colleague from his previous station in Davenport, signed with Universal (Hollywood rechristened him as "Hugh Marlowe"); then WHO's country band, the Oklahoma Outlaws, was signed to appear in a Gene Autry singing cowboy picture.

Joy Hodges had showed up in Des Moines for a personal appearance and sat down with Dutch for an interview.

He asked, "Well, Miss Hodges, how does it feel to be a movie star?"

He was wearing his riding breeches. She thought he looked very handsome. Though he couldn't be quite sure how *she* looked. He never wore his glasses when he wished to impress.

She answered, "Well, Mr. Reagan, you may know one day."

That February, before checking in with the Cubs at Catalina, he checked into a hotel at Hollywood and Vine. His first stop was Republic Pictures, where the Oklahoma Outlaws were filming their cowboy picture. The Western mythos had always fascinated him: Monmouth, Illinois, where his family moved when he was six, boosted itself as the hometown of Sheriff Wyatt Earp; in Dixon a beloved teacher regaled her class with tales of her adventures as a waitress at the Harvey House restaurants at railway depots in remote frontier outposts; at the movie house he whiled away hours in awe at "the marvelous flickering antics of Tom Mix and William S. Hart as they foiled robbers and villains and escorted beautiful girls to safety, waving back from their horses"—his kind of guys. Republic, however, was not his kind of studio. The white linen suit he had carefully picked out for the trip wilted in the heat, a casting director handed him a stack of old scripts—cut-rate formula Westerns, Saturday serials, B pictures shown at the bottom half of double bills—and invited him to pick a scene for an audition the following week. His aspirations were higher than that. He never returned.

He retreated to Catalina, a more suitable setting for dreams: yachts, beach houses, a cocktail bar thirty yards long, a Moorish casino, an entire abandoned South Sea movie set left over from a Gloria Swanson picture. The Cubs' manager complained Reagan wasn't showing up to watch practice. Instead he spent his days daydreaming. He had already cast himself in his life's next role.

Joy Hodges was performing at the Biltmore Bowl, the ballroom where the Oscar ceremonies were held. He ambushed her backstage after the show, begging for a studio tour. She agreed—at which point he upped the stakes: an entry for a screen test. She agreed, introducing him to her agent, George Ward of the Meiklejohn Agency. Ward found Reagan just the type he preferred to sell: "likable, clean-cut all-American," with "good looks that appealed mostly to young girls and old women." And he knew just whom to approach. An up-and-coming contract player at Warner Bros. with just such all-American good looks, Ross Alexander, had just shot himself. Hollywood studios being factories, with Warners the most factory-like of them all, nothing could be allowed to slow down the assembly line; Warners would need someone to slot into Ross Alexander's roles. That was how George Ward got his prospect a screen test. However, Ronald Reagan would never tell the story this way himself. In his version, it happened just like a movie—and in 1937, movies did not feature handsome young studs shooting themselves in the head.

His version read like this:

"'Look, Joy told me that you would level with me. Should I go back to Des Moines and forget this, or what do I do?'"

(The melodramatic turning point, when all hung in suspense.)

"He didn't answer. He just picked up the phone, dialed a number which turned out to be Warners Brothers studio . . . and said, 'Max, I have another Taylor sitting in my office.'"

(From the other end of the line: "God made only one Robert Taylor!"—comic relief.)

Cue happy ending. He's led to the Warner Bros. lot, he aces the audition, and returns to Des Moines, where a telegram arrives:

WARNERS OFFERS CONTRACT SEVEN YEARS, ONE YEAR'S OPTION, STARTING AT $200 A WEEK. WHAT SHALL I DO?

He answered:

SIGN BEFORE THEY CHANGE THER MINDS. DUTCH REAGAN.

How could it have happened any other way?

SO IT WAS THAT ON JUNE 1, 1937, RONALD WILSON REAGAN WAS DELIV-
ered unto the doorstep of an American company town, its practices as
routinized as those of General Motors' Detroit, Kodak's Rochester, or
Goodyear's Akron. Its product was not even motion pictures, really. It
manufactured something called "stars." For when the Jewish immigrant
tycoons who had run nickelodeons in New York invented a mass entertainment industry of a scope never before seen in the world, one of the
first things they discovered was that the most efficient way to lure customers into an unfamiliar story was to put a familiar face on the poster.
People like Florence Lawrence, the "Biograph Girl." Or Rudolph Val-
entino. Or, when sound came in, a fast talker like James Cagney. Such
figures weren't merely actors: they were fully integrated personae. Their
ineffable essence—their "type"—lingered from one picture to the next.
Their skill as much as or more than their acting was in their ability to
project that type to the public offscreen as well: at Hollywood bistros,
in autograph sessions, in "candid" at-home shots in the fan magazines
that women devoured by the millions, at the beauty parlors, beside the
ironing board, between infant feedings, awash in reverie—an emotional
cathexis the studio wizards worked so desperately to produce. Souls simultaneously larger than life and yet somehow familiar.

Could "stars" be unearthed like precious gems? Could they be
made? No one ever figured that one out. And so the first step, "discovery," was a volume business, one that operated, as a book on the process
by the film historian Jeanine Basinger, *The Star Machine,* described it,
"on the principle that if it dropped a lot of nubile young blondes into its
star-making machine, at least one of them might come out looking like
a heartbreaker." Scouts fanned out everywhere, to vaudeville theaters,
nightclub acts, Miss Blossom of 1937 pageants—and radio stations. If
anything was remarkable about this chapter in Ronald Reagan's story, it
was that it took so long to get started.

Then came that screen test, which was divided in three parts: first,
acting a scene; second, trying on wardrobe; and finally, the test that
Basinger describes as "all-important"—the personality test. In it, the
"newcomer was photographed while off-screen 'testers' asked questions designed to relax the performer and reveal the natural personal-

ity." Then and only then might a provisional contract be conferred, and the real work begin: a "looking over" period in which the "talent" was weighed, measured, and prodded; studied under a literal magnifying glass (for skin blemishes . . .); glimpsed at every angle and under every condition of natural and studio light; and more—with "no parallel outside a tenth-century Arab slave-trading market."

The body thus revealed was then suitably transformed: platform shoes for the too-short; girdles for the too-fat; a hair color that showed up just right on black-and-white stock; plastic surgery. (The hairline of a prospect named Margarita Carmen Cansino sat too low, implying the fact that her father was Spanish; electrolysis took care of that, and turned her into "Rita Hayworth.") The "natural personality," as revealed in the personality test, was but raw material. James Stewart's, for example: in real life he attended a tony prep school, then Princeton, before MGM turned him into a scourge of the Ivy League swells.

Aspiring stars could be trained in just about everything: how to talk, how to walk (MGM starlets were recognizable for their "Metro walk": stomach tucked in, shoulders squared, right foot first), how to be interviewed. How to ride a horse, how to dance. How to be photographed, by both motion picture and still cameras. The latter were just as important—for instance, for those all-important movie fan magazine spreads, where the actor might be depicted in pursuit of some hobby invented out of whole cloth. Mickey Rooney allegedly raised his own chickens. He was featured in *Modern Screen* in 1940 gathering eggs. "I'd read stories about Alice Faye in the papers," one star, née Alice Leppert, recollected, "and I would wonder who that girl was."

Ronald Reagan arrived ahead of the game. He already came packaged inside a persona—one he'd been building himself since he was a boy.

He had chosen his movie star name (though the brass rejected it as too over-the-top, so his pals back in Iowa were shocked to see "Ronald" on marquees; they'd only ever known him as Dutch). He had fashioned his sumptuous voice ("Dear Mr. Reagan: You have the most wonderful voice in pictures," read one early fan letter), and had been studying himself being studied by the camera since he was a little boy. As in that group shot of the Dixon YMCA boys band where his elbow was cocked just so, his cape flared instead of lying just flat, and he handled his drum major scepter like a king.

Which was why the studio was able to shoot him off like a rocket, practically from the day he arrived.

Most first deals included a reassessment period after six months; Reagan landed a seven-year deal right away. The standard formula was to test newcomers in a series of walk-on roles before any real invest-ment began. But eleven days after his arrival in Hollywood, the *Chicago Tribune* headlined its regular Hollywood dispatch "SPORTS WRITER IS FEATURED IN FIRST MOVIE." In the dispatch, the "athletic looking, brown haired . . . former lifeguard" named his favorite role from Eureka College theatricals: Captain Stanhope in *Journey's End*—"same role at Pomona College which called Bob Taylor to the attention of movie scouts," Dutch, who'd clearly been paying attention to such things, later noted to an interviewer. He'd been preparing for this all his life.

That first movie, a B picture of about an hour's length, was *Love Is on the Air*. In the trailer, he introduced himself to the nation with an aw-shucks just-so story, leaning jauntily against the camera in a tweed three-piece suit, holding a fedora:

"My name is Ronald Reagan. A few months ago I was a sports an-nouncer on a radio station in Des Moines, Iowa. One day I ran into one of these movie talent scouts. I think I caught him off guard because the next thing I knew I was taking a screen test for Warner Brothers in Hollywood!"

(He cocked his head to the side earnestly, puppyish.)

"I guess it was OK. At least I liked Hollywood! So here I am."

He played a local radio announcer who in the nick of time and with the pretty girl at his side tricked the racketeers and leading citi-zens conspiring to defraud the town into exposing themselves before an open microphone. Then came the nifty fight sequence, which *Variety*'s reviewer singled out for praise. The *Prescott* (Arizona) *Evening Courier*'s review paraphrased the press release—and since Warners put out a fantastic press release ("a big, good-looking athletic lad named Ronald Reagan . . . going places in pictures"), it was a splendid review. Warners had him going places. The first fan magazine shoot came soon after: "New Answer to Maidens' Prayers" was illustrated with Dutch in a bathing costume, leaping out of a chair, eyes set stalwartly at the horizon, telling the same story ("Ronald 'Dutch' Reagan chalked up a record for himself of having saved seventy-seven lives in seven summers. But he declines to say how many of them were females") he'd managed to get told about him since his first appearance in the *Dixon Telegraph* in 1928.

He could only dream things would have jumped off this well.

Then, things promptly flatlined.

IN THE COMPLEX MULTIVARIATE ANALYSES OF THE STUDIO WIZARDS about which of the players they were throwing up against the wall were sticking, reviews played an outsize role: with so many pictures, some with a dozen or more billed actors, whether any given actor got mentioned was grounds for promotion. It wasn't happening for Reagan. When he was several spots down the bill from Humphrey Bogart in a cornpone comedy about pro wrestlers, *Swing Your Lady*, the *Chicago Tribune* didn't notice him; neither did the *Los Angeles Times* and the *New York Times* when he played in the goofy satire *Cowboy from Brooklyn*. In 1938 he got eight credits, each less memorable than the last. ("Doesn't add up to a masterpiece," *Variety* said of *Naughty but Nice*. "But it won't chase them out of the theaters.") The trailer for a particularly silly sequel in the "Tugboat Annie" series mispronounced his name. That happened again and again. Sometimes it was misspelled—"REGAN."

Maybe he had just chosen the wrong studio. Each had a personality, the lengthened shadow of a dictatorial czar—and at cheap Jack Warner's shop, famously averse to raising up too many swelled-headed stars, the signature product was the dark, brooding "social problems" picture, a genre uncongenial to the genial Dutch. "This fellow Reagan is a hard one to peg," a 1940 fan mag feature observed. "He's been in Hollywood for three years, so you'd think people would begin to have a fairly definite idea of what he's like. But all you're sure about is that everybody is fond of him." Not enough, apparently, for star billing.

Of course, a particularly charismatic player could single-handedly invent a type, often accidentally: Humphrey Bogart, as the hard-bitten, forlorn loner who opts for softhearted sacrifice in the last reel; Errol Flynn, the devil-may-care swashbuckler who made it all look so easy. Reagan did not reveal that sort of genius. When Warners finally did find a niche for him it was in the notoriously cheap "B unit" run by producer Bryan Foy. In his first picture as Secret Service Agent Brass Bancroft, *Variety* liked the "scrap scenes, one aboard a plane"; of the second, it opined, "Will be limited to bookings in lower half of duals as filler footage"; the third was so bad Reagan begged his bosses to keep it on the shelf. Now he had his type—and a humiliating nickname: the "Errol Flynn of the B's." It was as if he'd never left the Republic Pictures lot at all. As for Foy, the reason he said he liked working with Reagan was that "he showed up for work in the morning sober."

Sometimes he floated up to a "prestige" picture, as the star's amiable foil—almost as if his worth rested in his ability *not* to convey depth of emotion. (Nearly three decades later, when Jack Warner heard his former charge was running for governor, he protested: "No, no, Jimmy Stewart for governor; Ronald Reagan for best friend.") In a 1939 hit, he played pal to a dying Bette Davis; within Hollywood's unspoken codes, the nonromantic complement to the leading lady was, generally speaking, a homosexual—and there was Dutch, in *Dark Victory,* gallivanting around in a tuxedo, always on call with a cocktail shaker when she needed a shoulder to cry on at 5:30 A.M. At one point in the shoot he begged the director for a story change that would mark him as a romantic rival. The director shot back, "'Do you think you are playing the leading man?"

His self-worth had always come from being a star. He had brought an admiring crowd of Drake frat boys with him to Hollywood. His little brother, his parents—with whom, for a time, he lived—came, too. They were supposed to be witnessing his triumph. Instead they watched him become a face in the crowd.

And then, light broke through the clouds.

After an ill-fated engagement to marry his costar in *Secret Service of the Air,* Ila Rhodes (he never talked about it, and decades later was dismayed when an enterprising interviewer dug up her name), he married a button-nosed starlet named Jane Wyman, who played ditzy blond chorus girls in pictures like *Gold Diggers of 1937* and *George White's 1935 Scandals.* One of the gifts of his marriage, then of the birth of his first daughter, Maureen, in 1941, was the emergence of a marketable offscreen persona: now he was patriarch of a "perfect" young family. It was a role within which he could not have felt more comfortable. It made sense: his marriage had almost been produced like something out of the Bryan Foy unit. Their flirtation had begun on a nationwide vaudeville-style tour sponsored by a Hollywood power broker, columnist Louella Parsons, a fellow native of Dixon; they announced their engagement from her stage, then her column announced the romance to the world. The wedding reception took place in "Lolly's" home, and she henceforth featured the "great personality . . . being rapidly groomed by Warners for stardom" on a regular basis. (Perhaps it was Parsons who advised him that his original fiancée was miscast. "EXOTIC STAR IS PART INDIAN," ran one early feature on Ila Rhodes; "BLOND INDIAN PITCHES TEPEE AT STUDIO," headlined another—no fit partner for a clean-cut all-American.)

He found increasing representation in gossip columns and fan magazines.

RONALD REAGAN and Jane Wyman have often been called "Hollywood's nicest young couple." They have successfully managed to combine two active careers with maintaining a happy home and being parents. Jane attributes a great deal of their success to the fact that Ronald makes the decisions in the family. Another factor is that Ronnie has the disposition of an angel, according to Jane, who should know. They've never had a quarrel. And he never forgets an anniversary or a birthday. What a guy!

He would henceforth be featured far out of proportion to his box-office success—one of only three male stars to appear on the cover of *Photoplay* more than once. Then he got his breakthrough picture, one that blurred actor and role in just the way studio publicists liked best. In the storybook world of Grantland Rice, the only hero who loomed larger than Babe Ruth was Knute Rockne, the legendary Notre Dame football coach. Studebaker named a car after him. When he died in a plane crash in 1931 the king of Norway knighted him posthumously. Ten thousand were in attendance at Dearborn Station when his funeral train arrived in Chicago. And—to pick a certain Midwestern newspaper as an example—the *Dixon Evening Telegraph* ran nine stories about his passing over four days, upstaging news of one of the most catastrophic earthquakes in the history of the world. "KNUTE, SPINDLY BOY IN CHICAGO, SAW IN 'ECKIE,' HIGH SCHOOL QUARTERBACK, HIS IDEAL": the real world was trading places with legend, in just the way Reagan adored.

He wasn't long at Warners before he suggested they make a Rockne picture. Unsurprisingly, the studio ignored him. Also unsurprisingly, when a Rockne biopic was finally put on the schedule, with Pat O'Brien as star, it ignored him again, testing ten other young blades for George Gipp, the role Dutch burned to play. He got that audition only upon the intervention of a man whose appearance in his life marked another turning point in his fortunes: Lew Wasserman. In 1940, his agent's firm was acquired by the entertainment conglomerate MCA, whose chief executive, Wasserman, would soon become the closest thing Hollywood ever had to a king. He had already taken a shine to young Reagan—they'd socialized together, frequently in the company of Sidney Korshak, the colorful attorney of Chicago's organized crime syndicate. Wasserman decided to take Reagan on personally as his client. Their first coup was the Gipp audition—which Reagan won after telling the producer he had studied the story in Rockne's diaries so closely he practically wouldn't have to learn lines.

Knute Rockne never published a diary.

He did, however, publish a book. *Coaching: The Way of a Winner* argued that "the history or traditions of the school are a great thing to recite to your team, and to keep before them. Exaggerate these as much as you can." Such cynicism was not displayed in *Knute Rockne, All-American*—even as its plot turned on one of Rockne's most cynical acts, which became in the telling his most pure.

In real life George Gipp had been an inveterate gambler who cared for neither discipline nor corny school spirit, and who died a fortuitously storybook death. As he sat on the bench with a cold during a losing game against Northwestern, the crowd clamored for Gipp to be put in; the ailing hero single-handedly won the game with two glorious touchdowns, then died from pneumonia. And, eight years later, it is verifiably true, a player did cry something like "That's one for the Gipper" while scoring a game-winning touchdown against Army.

According to a story Grantland Rice told that was not verifiably true, this was because at halftime Knute Rockne tearfully regaled the team with the story of how George Gipp on his deathbed had begged him to stir them to victory by invoking his martyrdom—just the kind of story the cynical Rockne thought it was the coach's prerogative to invent. It was like the time in 1922 when he read his faltering team a "telegram" from his sick child Billy, who actually was in the pink of health. Or one of the five times he pretended he was about to quit, when he had no intention of quitting at all.

For Hollywood such details need not matter. Nor did they matter to Ronald Reagan, who had been telling such stories—"*To every man comes Gethsemane!*"—about how the world worked his entire life. He played the climactic scene of Gipp's spiritual rebirth from selfish playboy to stout-hearted man to within an inch of his life: "*Rock, sometime when the team is up against it and the breaks are beating the boys, tell them to go out there with all they've got and win just one for the Gipper. I don't know where I'll be then, Rock, but I'll know about it and I'll be happy.*" When he lived again in its last reel, his ghost inspiring a bedraggled team to victory, teary-eyed audiences left the theaters with a new star in mind—Ronald Reagan.

He brought his parents to the gala debut in South Bend, Indiana, the thrill of his Catholic father's life. Jack, many years on the wagon, enjoyed one last spree with his fellow Irish Catholic rogue, Pat O'Brien, and died shortly after. (Dutch told the story of Jack's funeral to his daughter Maureen: "My soul was just desolate, that's the only word I can use . . . all of a sudden I heard somebody talking to me, and I knew that it was Jack, and he was saying, 'I'm OK, and where I am it's very nice. Please don't be unhappy.' And I turned to my mother . . . and I said, 'Jack is OK, and where he is he's very happy' . . . the desolation wasn't there any more, the emptiness was all gone." Everything always works out in the end, gloriously.)

His next picture, *Santa Fe Trail,* was an honest-to-goodness Western. For his next he was "loaned out" to MGM—the sign of a suddenly hot property. Hollywood's preeminent columnist brought Reagan and Wyman along for "Louella Parsons Day" in Dixon, and he was received as a fellow superstar alongside Bob Hope and Ann Rutherford by a parade crowd estimated at fifty thousand. There he promoted *International Squadron*—his first leading role in a prestige picture (he "carries the starring burden," the *New York Times* said, "and proves he can carry it"). In August 1941 he came in fifth in the "rising star" section of the *Motion Picture Herald*'s annual poll of 13,900 exhibitors. And when Warners needed a young player for a key role in a major melodrama, *King's Row,* Reagan was one of the only actors it considered—as a young playboy victimized by a cruel physician who maliciously amputated his legs, who matures from the hardship into a hero. Reagan was so pleased with his performance he started screening the picture at his dinner parties.

By playing the character of the young blade traveling the journey from diffidence to stout-hearted manhood, in *Knute Rockne,* in *King's Row,* at last Ronald Reagan had a "type." By the unwritten rules of Hollywood, that meant he could now be a star. Warners tripled his salary (it was Lew Wasserman's first million-dollar deal). *King's Row* was nominated for a best picture Oscar. On December 3, 1941, Warners announced that Ronald Reagan got more fan mail that year than James Cagney, and that only Errol Flynn had received more. The world was his oyster. Life was again just one grand sweet song.

Then came December 7, 1941: a day that would live in infamy, and a day when his life began falling apart.

Other stars went overseas after Pearl Harbor and came back heroes—after enlisting as a private, James Stewart flew twenty dangerous missions in a B-17 Flying Fortress, and rose to colonel. Reagan's poor vision meant he couldn't see combat. Lew Wasserman was determined he stay home entirely. Wasserman himself, though twice classified as 1A, had managed to defer his own service for the duration. Doing the same for investments like Reagan was a specialty of both MCA and Warner Bros.

The first deferment came before Pearl Harbor, with the birth of Maureen. Then Warners, advised by Wasserman to make the case to the Pentagon that Reagan's absence would "represent serious financial loss to the studio," asked for him to be placed in the reserve pool. When that request was denied, Warners deployed a secret weapon: the studio's crooked military liaison, who kept a stack of pilfered blank U.S. Army commissions to steer Warners favorites into the safe assignments the studio preferred. Jack Warner himself had been instrumental in inventing one such assignment: the Army Air Corps' "First Motion Picture Unit," set up to produce training pictures and headquartered at a mothballed studio in Culver City where Hal Roach had once made the *Our Gang* shorts. This was where Reagan ended up. Though he himself told the story of his deployment a little differently. "I've just been told, here at the studio, of two very important parts that were to be mine," ran an article under his byline in *Photoplay*. "But I won't be doing these pictures. Uncle Sam has called me, a Reserve officer in the Cavalry, and I'm off to the war."

"Fort Roach," "Fort Wacky," and the "Culver City Commandos" were the nicknames Hollywood wags coined for the faintly ridiculous outfit, whose base commander was a stunt pilot who described their job as "putting a square peg in a square hole." Reagan alone took to the posting with utmost seriousness: the military breeches, the shiny leather boots, the jeeps, the "troops" he got to lead in formation like the toy soldiers he so adored in 1919. However, these soldiers talked back. "Knock it off with the marching around!" one of the hacks serving under him—producers, directors, and the like, many of them, unlike him, not fighting because they were simply too old—demanded. He was just a contract player who'd barely broken into the prestige ranks; these guys might later be his bosses. He had no choice but to comply.

He turned his attention to diversions like memorizing each issue of *Reader's Digest*, which he somehow managed to obtain before anyone else ("When we finally got our own copies," the writer Irving Wallace complained, "we'd already heard the whole damn issue from Reagan"); playing basketball on the base recreation league team; devouring a book by a mystic named Manly P. Hall, *The Secret Destiny of America*, whose rhetoric about Providence's great plan for the land between the oceans would recur often in Reagan's speeches in decades to come; and, as the post's director of administration, sending out disciplinary notes about the overflowing ashtrays in the script clerk's and assistant manager's offices. He didn't even get to shine in the training films: in *Jap Zero*, he played the schlemiel who accidentally shot at one of his own planes; in *The Rear Gunner*, in which he had only five lines, he played the officer who talked the hero into taking the job. He did star in one picture at Fort Roach: in an in-house gag as a general briefing a squadron before a vital mission, stabbing the wall map, barking "This is our target!"—at which the map rolled up like a window blind to reveal a naked girl.

Late in 1942 the Allies invaded North Africa and a movie was rushed into theaters. The *New York Times* called it "a picture which makes the spine tingle and the heart to take a leap." *Variety* called it a genuine contribution to the war effort. Made by the same producer as *Knute Rockne, All American,* it was the seventh-highest-grossing film of 1943; in March 1944 it won three Academy Awards. And, the *Hollywood Reporter* had reported a month after the war began, Ronald Reagan was supposed to play *Casablanca*'s lead instead of Humphrey Bogart. So close, and yet so far.

He looked dashing in his captain's uniform on the October 1944 cover of *Modern Screen;* meanwhile, the humiliations compounded. The star system was in churning transformation, as studios replaced actors sent to war with a different brand of leading man: younger, leaner, brooding—sensitive types, to match the tastes of young men and women thrown into serious adult responsibilities at younger and younger ages. Reagan overheard their names from the mouths of the swooning secretaries in Fort Roach's stenography pool—names like Van Johnson. Johnson had a plate in his head that saved his life after a car crash and rendered him ineligible for military service. He had been released from his contract at Warner Bros. just as the studio was tripling the value of Reagan's; then, in 1945, Johnson scored second place in the *Motion Picture Herald* poll of top Hollywood stars. Reagan never cracked the top ten.

He overheard the name "Jane Wyman" around town more frequently, too. A fan magazine began a new series letting its women readers imagine themselves in the lives of female stars; "Let's Pretend You're Mrs. Ronald Reagan" depicted her positively thriving in a husband's absence—"from being Jane Wyman, supporting player, to Jane Wyman, star." The former light-comic ingenue gave an Oscar-worthy performance in 1945 as the girlfriend of a desperate alcoholic in *The Lost Weekend.* "Our Child Must Not Hate," a magazine primer on how to raise children during a war, featured Jane Wyman's byline, and a subhead that made her husband the afterthought: "A new 'mother' code—one every man will support as strongly as Ronald Reagan." Another piece framed Jane as a feminist heroine ("The assumption that the place of every woman is in the home is obsolete"), and ran a family picture with Dutch barely even in the background. "Oh, Janie, dear, you're doing so well now," movie colony gossip recorded a friend of hers gushing. "Is it true that when you went to a restaurant the other night the waiter said, 'What does Captain Wyman want?'"

And then, one night, Reagan left the exclusive Hollywood bistro Ciro's an hour before Jane Wyman, at which she danced with Van Johnson. According to the gossip item the next morning, she was seen "looking into Van's eyes."

And then, one day, passing a radio, he overheard an announcement: "Ladies and gentlemen, the war in Europe is over." His response, as he remembered it for a 1985 interview, was curious: "I felt a chill, as if a gust of cold wind had just swept past." The rest of the nation was jubilant. But it was almost as if he felt afraid to face the rest of his life.

MODERN SCREEN: "HE'S BACK IN TWEEDS AGAIN, IS EX-CAPT. RONALD Reagan, and still tops with fans after three years in service." Which was how fan magazines worked: in close consultation with studio publicists, they told the stories Hollywood wanted told about itself. Even if they were not true. Warner Bros. didn't call Reagan back to the set to shoot a picture for another six months. The picture, a melodrama slated for Bogart and Bacall, *Stallion Road,* had been downgraded to a low-budget black-and-white. And it wasn't released for two years.

The motion picture business was changing. The Justice Department went after a source of Hollywood's monopoly power: the chains of theaters each studio owned, which had to show all the pictures the studio shoveled at them whether local audiences wanted to see those pictures or not. In 1940 the two sides agreed to the "Paramount Decree," meant to break that system up, driving picture volume down; that same year Warners shut down the Foy Unit. By the end of the war Warners was making but twenty movies a year where it used to make sixty—which amplified the value of "superstars," who could earn their keep making but two "prestige" pictures a year. Reagan's dazzling seven-year contract, $3,500 a week for five pictures a year, was now a relic—and Henry Fonda, after returning from hard service overseas in the Navy ("I don't want to be in a fake war in a studio," he had insisted), won a contract worth $6,000 a week to make only one movie a year. Reliable stock players who showed up sober and on time no longer counted for much.

Joy Hodges had advised Reagan that a key to success in the movie colony was playing the political game. He had played it like an obedient boy. More and more actors had complained of the unceasing indignities of star manufacture: the poking, the prodding, the flacking, the twenty-four-hour nature of the job, from the shooting days that "started" at seven (actually six, for you had to show up on set looking perfect) to the "breaks" taken standing against ironing boards to keep costumes from wrinkling (you "relaxed" on set only for staged photo shoots) to the fake "dates." Then there were the contracts themselves, in which refusal to take an assigned roll was punished by a six-month penalty tacked onto the end of a contract. *Gone With the Wind* star Olivia de Havilland filed suit against the practice in 1943, under California's indentured servitude law, and won.

But Reagan never complained. He worked earnestly and doggedly at building relations with fans—a free gift to the studio and its bottom line. He gave his mother—"Moms Nelle" in the argot of the fan club—a full-time job handling mail. A Reagan fan newsletter began publication in 1940; typical article: "I have met Ronald and his dear mother several times. They are both the most thoughtful and sweetest persons a body could ever meet . . . a 'regular guy'!" One enthusiastic correspondent, Lorraine Makler, started writing to him in 1943. He wrote to her as if she were a friend—and, soon, with her husband, Elwood Wagner, she indeed became one of his best friends.

The devotion he was inspiring was epic. So was his own devotion to the Hollywood grind. He was perfect star material. So *why wouldn't they let him be a star?*

Errol Flynn was a star. Errol Flynn, who rarely showed up for work sober, or free of bruises from fights—a severe frustration for the cinematographers seeking angles for close-ups. Errol Flynn, infamous for on-set tantrums, for upstaging other actors—like Ronald Reagan, in one of his few featured scenes in *Santa Fe Trail*. Even when Flynn gave Hollywood its worst public relations black eye in a generation when he went on trial for statutory rape, in 1943, he still stayed a star—starring as an RAF pilot in *Desperate Journey,* playing above Reagan, even though he collapsed twice on set, forcing the picture over budget.

Jane Wyman was also a star. Two months after V-J day she was on the front page of the *Los Angeles Times* B section in a big pinup spread. The accompanying article, by the *Times*' drama editor, lauded her emergence as a great actress, announcing her work in *The Yearling* as an old woman, acting without makeup, wearing burlap.

Ronald Reagan was not a star. He got a photo spread, too, around that time—as a Hollywood househusband: "The Reagans—Ronnie (Dutch), sprout Maureen (Mermy)—have the place to themselves while mom Jane Wyman is on location for MGM's *The Yearling*. And do they keep busy! . . . Parcheesi is Mermy's racket, but Ronnie isn't throwing the game to be acknowledged champ without a struggle. . . . It's a good thing he's at work in *Stallion Road*—the guy would be plumb wore out with a little more of this relaxation."

But *Stallion Road* wouldn't be released for more than a year. When that excruciating wait finally ended, he complained bitterly to Lorraine Wagner that the industry shot itself in the foot by not releasing movies in color (his reactions to his professional misfortunes were frequently to blame them on what he claimed were poor business practices). It was four years since he'd last appeared on a motion picture screen. If he hadn't been auditioning a new identity in which to assert himself, he might have gone just about insane.

THE FLYER SHOWED A GENIE RISING FROM A MUSHROOM CLOUD. THE caption read, "ATOMIC ENERGY—SLAVE OR MASTER?" The event was scheduled for December 12, 1945, and Reagan was to feature alongside Congresswoman Helen Gahagan Douglas and the sentimental liberal radio star Norman Corwin—although, since the ad ended up on Jack Warner's desk first, and one of the sponsors was a leader of the Communist Political Association in Los Angeles, there was some question if Reagan would appear.

"We feel that such a performance on your part would be in violation of the exclusive rights to your services as granted under to us under your employment contract," read the telegram posted to Reagan from Warner Bros.' legal department. Lew Wasserman called Warners executives the next day to reassure them Reagan wouldn't be anywhere near the thing. Reagan went anyway—then fired a broadside at his staunchly Republican boss. "REAGAN DEFENDS ACTOR'S RIGHT TO VOICE AN OPINION," read the headline of Associated Press Hollywood correspondent Bob Thomas's column six weeks later. "I didn't recall that he had been a political thinker," Thomas wrote, "and I asked him if this was a development of the war." Reagan responded: "Before the war I did a lot of talking about politics, but mostly in back rooms. Now that I have seen what war means, I am more determined that my sons won't have to fight a third world war." (At that point he had only one son, Michael, whom he and Wyman adopted in 1945.) He continued: "Some people think an actor should keep his mouth shut. I think that is wrong. An actor should be careful to know that no group is using him for a selfish purpose, but if he sincerely believes in something he should use his voice."

The article also said Jane Wyman was merely "tolerant" of his "new political life." She was quoted complaining that the phone had rung sixteen times with political calls that morning. "Ronnie is a former sports announcer," she said, "and you know how they love to talk."

By the spring his political life was as busy as his screen life was fallow. In March he joined Gregory Peck, Edward G. Robinson, two Democratic congressmen, and the celebrated bass-baritone Paul Robeson on the sponsoring committee of a dinner at the Roosevelt Hotel for the Los Angeles Committee for a Democratic Far Eastern Policy; in April he served as toastmaster for the Americans Veterans Committee's state convention, where the liberal group resolved for United Nations control of atomic energy, the worldwide abolition of forced military conscription, and an end to racially restrictive covenants in housing; in May he joined the executive council of the Hollywood Independent Citizens Committee of the Arts, Sciences and Professions (HICCASP), along with Olivia de Havilland, James Roosevelt, and producer Dore Schary. It had been chartered as a counterweight to the anti–New Deal group the Motion Picture Alliance for the Preservation of American Ideals—which had been formed by, well, people like Reagan's boss, Jack Warner.

Jack Warner wasn't the only concerned party who noticed. Now that human beings had the power to destroy the earth—"stealing God's stuff," as the *New Yorker*'s E. B. White called it—atomic energy's scientist-inventors felt a special responsibility to advocate politically for its control. The new Federation of Atomic Scientists unveiled a book, *One World or None,* at a November 1945 press conference in the Capitol Hill office of Helen Gahagan Douglas, arguing that atomic development "should be in harmony with an international system of control and cooperation and should further provide for scientific freedom and peacetime utilization of atomic energy in the interests of the whole people"—the position advanced at the December 12, 1945, nuclear rally that Jack Warner so desperately did not want Ronald Reagan to attend.

International control of atomic energy, however, was also the policy solution advocated by another American political faction: Communists. In April 1946, it was among the resolutions issued by a "National Committee to Win the Peace" in Washington, D.C. The other resolutions included a demand to remove Herbert Hoover as honorary chairman of an emergency famine relief committee, a call for the new United Nations Security Council to denounce the Spanish fascist Franco, and calls for an end to General MacArthur's "one-man rule of Japan," and for full employment legislation, the extension of Social Security, and the establishment of a national health insurance system. The last paragraph of the Associated Press dispatch on the meeting noted that "five of 20 members of Congress listed as sponsors before the conference was held asked that their names be withdrawn." Cryptic—unless you were reading the tea leaves of America's impending Cold War. For if the above positions were generally congruent with broad liberal opinion, other resolutions at the meeting—denunciation of recent government statements "which appear to be aimed at the embarrassment of the Soviet Union," and a request to the State to Department to "maintain and extend friendly cooperation" with Russia instead—pointed in a more controversial direction.

The Soviet Union had just sacrificed some 20 million of its citizens to vanquish Hitler, in alliance with the United States. In 1943, after, the Germans retreated following the awful siege of Stalingrad, Warner Bros. produced *Mission to Moscow* at President Roosevelt's personal request. It portrayed America's new ambassador to the Soviet Union in his journey from skepticism to enthusiasm for the Communist state. At its gala premiere at Washington's Earle Theater (in the afternoon, to accommodate the wartime blackout), an audience of 4,400 that included cabinet members and senators raised "a burst of applause," the *Washington Post* reported, "that ended only when the theater orchestra drowned it out with the finale." MGM produced *Song of Russia* and *The North Star,* idealized portraits of angelic Russians standing up to barbarian Germans. *Life* devoted its entire March 29 issue to hymning the USSR's glories. ("They live under a system of tight state-controlled information. But probably the attitude to take toward it is not to get too excited about it.") That November some six thousand rallied at Los Angeles's Shrine Auditorium to celebrate the tenth anniversary of normalized U.S.-Soviet relations. The next year Bette Davis cut a birthday cake, with twenty-six candles and inscribed TO OUR GALLANT RUSSIA, with a ceremonial Kazakh sword to honor the twenty-sixth anniversary of the Red Army.

And then, in March 1946, British prime minister Winston Churchill traveled to the small town of Fulton, Missouri, to describe how the lands under Soviet military control following Germany's surrender had fallen behind an "iron curtain" of tyranny—and all of a sudden, with the speed of a swerve in a Communist Party line, the taint of association with the Soviet Union was something all Americans were to avoid on pain of ostracization from decent society or worse.

The problem was discerning where that taint lived.

The history of the Communist Party in the United States was morally complicated: under its Depression-era "Popular Front" strategy, Communists were anodyne bearers of a garden-variety liberalism—while upholding one position that was not anodyne at all: they were the only organized force in white American political life who said black Americans deserved equal rights. In 1940s Hollywood, that hothouse of moral preening, cocktail parties dedicated to the fight against Spanish fascism, to freedom for Chinese sharecroppers, and civil rights, under the sponsorship of the "Communist Political Association" (the party's wartime name), were the places for up-and-coming thespians to see and be seen. "They had not the remotest idea of what Communism was in terms of economic structures of political superstates," *Reader's Digest*'s Communism expert, Eugene Lyons, wrote later. "For nearly all of them, it was an intoxicated state of mind, a glow of inner virtue, and a sort of comradeship in super-charity."

Then peace, and a swerve. Communist leader Earl Browder, who had said that "capitalism and socialism have begun to find their way to peaceful coexistence and collaboration in the same world," was purged; the party reorganized on a Cold War footing and began maliciously infiltrating liberal organizations. It also organized front groups—like the National Committee to Win the Peace. The resolutions at its April 1946 meeting marked that group to those in the know as a Communist front. Which is why five of twenty congressmen sponsoring the meeting dropped out—while the fact that fifteen stayed showed how in flux the situation truly was.

These were complexities to which Ronald Reagan had apparently not given a thought. J. Edgar Hoover, who testified that March that Communism was not a political party but "a condition akin to a disease that spreads like an epidemic, and like an epidemic, quarantine is necessary to keep it from infecting the nation," was also immune to such complexities. His FBI eagerly took the coincidence of positions between liberal idealists and Communist subversives as prima facie evidence of infection, and drew no distinction between groups that seemed genuinely to have begun as Moscow fronts and those, such as the American Veterans Committee, that Communists merely wished to infiltrate. As for HICCASP, an FBI report said, "Every endorsement of public officials made by this organization coincides exactly with that made by the Communist Party of the state."

THE FACT THAT RONALD REAGAN WAS A PRINCIPAL IN ALL THESE groups—and also narrator of *Operation Terror,* a thirteen-part radio series exposing the Ku Klux Klan and sponsored by the Hollywood Writers Mobilization, a Communist front—explained why two FBI agents showed up at Reagan's doorstep one day for the encounter that would change his life forever.

The agents announced themselves at the sprawling modern ranch house he had built for himself and his wife, perched high above Sunset

Boulevard at the bend of a cul-de-sac and an endless curving driveway, with either the ocean or the twinkling valley spread dramatically before any window he cared to peer out of. He remembered serving the FBI agents coffee. "We have some information which might be useful to you," Reagan reported one of them saying, in his memoir *Where's the Rest of Me?* "We thought you might have some information helpful to us."

Reagan then depicted himself introducing a morally complicating factor, a scruple about civil liberties: "Now look, I don't go in for Red-baiting."

Thereupon he depicted the moral complexity melting in the space of a few lines.

G-Man #1: "You served with the Air Corps. You know what spies and saboteurs are."

G-Man #2: "We thought someone the Communists hated as much as they hate you might be willing to help us."

"That got me," he wrote.

"What did they say about me?"

"The exact quotation was: 'What are we going to do about that sonofabitching bastard Reagan?' Will that do for openers?"

He was convinced. From then on he was to be a warrior in a struggle of good versus evil—a battle for the soul of the world.

SOMEWHERE AROUND THIS TIME—THE CHRONOLOGY HAS NEVER BEEN quite clear—Reagan attended a HICCASP board meeting in which all the subtleties of liberal politics in an age of Communist infiltration were aired in a wide-ranging debate. James Roosevelt, the son of the late president, said it was time groups like theirs became more "vigilant against being used by Communist sympathizers." Which, however, meant what? The ranks of such sympathizers had always thinned in the wake of each party-line shift; by the time Earl Browder was purged, there were hardly any Communists left in Hollywood. Wouldn't the attempt to smoke out what few remained turn their group into an ineffectual nest of recrimination? If some random screenwriter agreed that atomic energy should be placed under international control, did that make him fit to be purged? Then so was Albert Einstein—and maybe even Harry Truman, who had said three days after Hiroshima, "We must constitute ourselves trustees of this new force . . . and . . . turn it into the channels of service to mankind."

Reagan rejected the complexity. Alongside Olivia de Havilland, he put a resolution up for a vote at the next meeting: "We reaffirm belief in free enterprise and the democratic system and repudiate Communism as desirable for the United States." (Planning their move, de Havilland and Reagan each pronounced themselves surprised that the other wasn't a secret Communist.) Screenwriters Dalton Trumbo and John Howard Lawson argued against it, because they were Communists. Others, like bandleader Artie Shaw, opposed it on civil liberties grounds. The resolution was voted down. "It was all the proof we needed," Reagan said. "HICCASP had become a Communist front organization, hiding behind a few well-intentioned Hollywood celebrities to give it credibility."

His math did not add up. Lawson and Trumbo represented but one position in an argument that had at least three sides; there were plenty of reasons to vote down the resolution besides some submerged desire for the hammer and sickle to fly over the White House. But the Manichaean logic of Communists and dupes was now how Ronald Reagan thought—and, enraged at having been one of the dupes, he gave the Communists no quarter.

Reagan and de Havilland resigned from HICCASP, but not before Reagan cast himself in a real-life adventure movie: he absconded with the records of the group, and—in a midnight rendezvous at a hamburger stand with his brother, also an FBI informant—claimed to have found in them a plot to deploy an obscure membership regulation to neutralize the power of anti-Communist members; this, Reagan said, was the only reason his resolution could possibly have been voted down.

THAT MANICHAEAN DISPOSITION SOON TURNED OUT TO BE VERY USEFUL to the barons who ruled Hollywood, and who were at that moment badly on the ropes.

Hollywood might be slightly more glamorous. But given its intensely time-sensitive production routines, economically speaking, the dream factory was little different from a fish market (fish rotted by the minute; movie labor costs ballooned by the minute). Which was why Hollywood had something in common with the Brooklyn docks: its unions were controlled by mobbed-up bosses who amassed enormous power by threatening to shut the whole operation down in an instant with the snap of their chubby fingers.

The union that thus controlled Hollywood's dozens of craft locals was the International Alliance of Theatrical Stage Employees, or "IA." It also represented the theater projectionists—everywhere, so a studio that crossed the IA was in danger of losing its entire revenue stream nationwide if the IA's union bosses ordered those projectionists off the job. And one way to cross the IA was to refuse the endless kickbacks, bribes, and featherbedding schemes it demanded. Studio bosses, however, had few problems cooperating, the devil they knew being so useful to them in keeping their workers in line.

In 1941 the IA suffered a setback when its leader, George Browne, and his enforcer, Willie Bioff, an associate of Al Capone's, were sentenced to eight and ten years, respectively, for extortion. Meanwhile, Browne's slightly less corrupt successor, Roy Brewer, fought off an annoyance on his left flank: another labor outfit bidding to represent his workers by promising them actual, honest-to-God integrity—and better wages and hours. The rival organization was called the Conference of Studio Unions (CSU), and its leader was an extraordinary figure. Herbert Sorrell was a former amateur boxer who first got a job painting a movie set in 1925, attended his first union meeting because he heard that the union served illegal beer, and stayed because he loved what unions did at their best—win better lives for regular guys who just wanted to give their kids chances they themselves never got. "We were not out to kill the goose that laid the golden egg," as he put it in settling a 1933 strike, "but we were out to get as many of them as we could."

He also wanted to do something else: prove a union could be run democratically. Bioff offered him $56,000 to stop trying to raid IA locals. No dice; years later, Sorrell told a congressional hearing, "I think you should pass legislation that labor leaders who accept bribes . . . should be shot." And he was hardly less tough than the mobsters who enforced for the IA. He just deployed violence to different ends. When in March 1945 his CSU called a three-day walkout on behalf of set dressers who'd been barred from disaffiliating from the IA, and the IA's president wired its projectionists to stop working so the ruin of an entire industry could be laid at Herb Sorrell's feet, he just laughed. "I have no fear of anybody," he said. "I don't fear the hereafter, and I don't fear no thugs, and I don't fear anybody or anything and I will take mine as it comes. . . . I don't want to be attacked because I will attack back." He won that strike, after thirty-four weeks—and kept on raiding IA jurisdictions. Brewer, meanwhile, tightened his dictatorial grip on his nineteen thousand members and girded for war.

Thus the order of battle: two union federations, one corrupt, the other clean, both prepared for violence, both fighting for the very same prize—the right to represent Hollywood's tens of thousands of production workers. The scene was set for a years-long drama of exceptional complexity—except, of course, to Ronald Reagan, who had looked into Roy Brewer's soul and found him a hero, and into Herb Sorrell's and found a dirty Communist rat.

The CSU's strategy was to charge that workers represented by the IA were doing jobs that rightfully did not belong to them. The American Federation of Labor, called upon to adjudicate the jurisdictional dispute, sent a panel of "Three Wise Men" from the postal workers' union, the barbers' union, and the trainmen's union to referee. Sorrell, meanwhile, called an escalating series of work stoppages through the winter, spring, and summer of 1946. The campaign ended in triumph, with a 25 percent increase in base pay for all production workers—including those represented by the IA—and the first guaranteed full workweek in movie history. It was not enough to endear him to the rival whose monopoly over Hollywood unionism he had broken. Brewer called one of the stoppages leading up to the deal "a last desperate effort to keep Communist control of certain AFL unions in Hollywood." Red-baiting had long been a useful way to destroy enemies in Hollywood—for example, Walt Disney, after Sorrell won a cartoonists' strike against him in 1941, took out a full-page ad in *Variety* braying, "I am positively convinced that Communistic agitation, leadership, and activities have brought about this strike." Shortly after Sorrell's coup in getting a 25 percent raise out of the studios, his enemies—both the studio bosses and the mobbed-up IA—devised an additional way to destroy him.

In September 1946, Americans opened their papers to see extraordinary images: billy clubs, smashed windows, stoned buses, and overturned cars in the place where dreams were made. Ronald Reagan's beloved Hollywood was a war zone. By November, it got even worse: CSU picketers, bearing flyers reading, "Our purpose here is to keep the scabs out and to close the studio down," defied a court ruling keeping them two hundred feet from the gates of Columbia Pictures. Their defiance led to the largest mass arrests in California history. "If it ain't worth going to jail for it ain't worth fighting for!" Herb Sorrell told newsmen as he was led off. His thousands of loyalists cheered—and then, crowded together in the Lincoln Heights lockup, chanted, "We don't want bail, we like this jail!" Los Angeles's overwhelmingly right-wing press knew whom to blame. "RED BID REPORTED," ran the headline above the *Los Angeles Times*' account of the arrests.

Ronald Reagan's political passions had by then found a new channel: the Screen Actors Guild. He showed up in that article addressing a meeting alongside the president of the IA to protest the firebombing of the homes of workers who had crossed the picket lines, allegedly by the CSU, and expressing "gratitude to law enforcement officers for protection given them in their right to work as non-striking union members."

He didn't always quite grasp what unionism was all about—his appearance at a right-to-work meeting demonstrated that. Though at that, SAG was a curious sort of union. Founded in 1933 with a tiny membership of eighty that quickly grew to more than four thousand after the producers formed a cartel among themselves and agreed not to bid competitively for talent, the union impressively pledged itself to help established actors and up-and-comers equally, and signed a pioneering collective bargaining agreement in 1937, a model of union solidarity— but by the end of World War II its leadership was larded with conservative Republicans (George Murphy, the song-and-dance man known as the "Irish Fred Astaire"; Robert Montgomery, who became Reagan's best friend) at a time when the dominant agenda item on the Republican right was destroying the bargaining power of unions.

Reagan rose to the Screen Actors Guild's second vice presidency. In October 1946, the guild voted 2,748 to 509 not to honor the CSU's picket line. The vote was the result of a letter sent to members maintaining that both sides were equally to blame. The CSU called that position "phony impartiality"—claiming that SAG was actually taking the side of management, by coming to the aid of what was effectively a union controlled by the company, not the workers. In public, Reagan aggressively pushed the position that neutrality was the only moral stance. He came to another conclusion privately. It was not that the CSU was equally to blame: it was that they were captive to the Red conspiracy. "The Communist plan for Hollywood was remarkably simple," he wrote in his 1965 memoir. "We had a weekly audience of about 500 million souls. Takeover of this enormous plant and its gradual transformation into a Communist gristmill was a grandiose idea. It would have been a magnificent coup for our enemies. . . . Using the CSU as a vehicle for Communist aims, was a first step of admirable directness." In Ronald Reagan's mind, for a movie actor to show up on set thus made him a frontline hero in the long twilight struggle between freedom and slavery. Honoring the picket line would have made him a stooge of Moscow. Which certainly suggests why he supported neutrality in the strike.

Even if he *himself* had no set to show up on, he showed up instead in Bob Thomas's gossip column: "It looks as though Errol Flynn is set for *Frontiersman*. . . . That's too bad because the role was much wanted by another star who appears to be the least temperamental on the Warner lot—Ronald Reagan. Sometimes temperamental pays off?" Nine days later, he was mentioned in the column again—this time in an item about all the work Jane Wyman was getting: "Says husband Ronald Reagan, her home lot is the only studio that hasn't discovered her."

At least he got to enjoy a real-life role straight out of film noir. One day, he recalled being summoned to a pay phone at a service station.

"'There's a group being formed to deal with you. They're going to fix you so you won't ever act again.'

"I took it as a joke," he wrote. "When I got back to Warner's I found they took it very seriously. The police were waiting with a license to carry a gun. I was fitted with a shoulder holster and a loaded 32 Smith & Wesson."

He stuck to his script even as evidence bulked that it made little sense. A Jesuit priest from Loyola University in Chicago, Father George Dunne, traveled to California to mediate between the IA and CSU. He found the CSU's Herb Sorrell conciliatory. He found the IA's Roy Brewer little more than a criminal thug. Brewer told the priest, "The Conference of Studio Unions was born in destruction and will die in destruction." In January 1947 Father Dunne announced that the CSU "had justice on their side" and that if only the Screen Actors Guild would follow its "moral obligation" to stop going to work, the strike could be over in a day. He recalled in an oral history what happened next: the guild's second vice president, Ronald Reagan, traveled to his Chicago rectory to argue "that Herb Sorrell and the CSU and all these people were Communists, and this was a Communist-led and inspired strike and that I was simply being a dupe for the Communists."

Shortly after Reagan's visit to Chicago, in March 1947, Sorrell was kidnapped by men dressed up as police, beaten, and left to die in the desert—by, a studio labor relations executive later revealed, Chicago gangsters working for Brewer. Reagan still held fast to his conviction that Brewer was unsullied—even after, upon Sorrell's miraculous return, alive, Sorrell once more embraced reconciliation, accepting an arbitration proposal that included major concessions from his union. Los Angeles's conservative diocese newspaper the *Tidings* begged the IA and management to accept, complaining that the producers "have taken a most negative attitude by doing little to settle the dispute . . . with cries of Communism and radicalism."

Their refusal to settle, in fact, began to seem almost inscrutable— until, later that year, a congressman from Pennsylvania named Carroll D. Kearns held extraordinarily detailed hearings on the dispute. One fact that emerged was that Herb Sorrell was *despised* by actual Hollywood Communists, who considered him something like a traitor, and that the producers' own in-house labor relations expert, a right-winger named Pat Casey, said of the CSU leadership, "I do not know of one that I would say was a Communist." ("My God, I have heard

'Communist, Communist, Communist,'" Casey testified in annoyance. "It gets down to where if you do not agree with somebody, you are a Communist.")

Another fact that emerged was that both sides were not equally culpable in this war at all. One day the hearings were rocked by a bombshell: someone introduced leaked minutes of a series of meetings that proved the violence beginning in September 1946 had been deliberately induced by the movie studios and the IA, conspiring to crush the Conference of Studio Unions. The plan had been to unilaterally replace CSU carpenters, building sets in accordance with a compromise arrived at by the "Three Wise Men," with IA carpenters. When the CSU threw up picket lines in response, Teamsters were to truck IA carpenters through the lines. (The Teamster who led the operation was rewarded with a studio executive position.) That, in words quoted from instructions to all studio department heads, would "create an incident." "Assign someone to see no damage is done to the electric generators," ran another part of the instructions; thereupon friendly police, sheriffs, and the district attorney's office would frame the CSU as violent extremists—which is exactly what had happened. In November, six CSU leaders had been charged with criminal conspiracy "to commit acts to pervert and obstruct" the law and "commit assault with a deadly weapon and to commit extortion"—but no charges were issued against the equally violent IA.

The Screen Actors Guild was in on the conspiracy. The same document named a SAG staff member as observing that it was "advisable not to have stars see the picket line broken—but to hold them somewhere until they can enter the studio peacefully."

Reagan probably hadn't been in on the plotting. But shortly after Father Dunne proposed his mediated settlement and a week after Sorrell's kidnapping, Reagan was chosen as interim Screen Actors Guild president. The marquee Hollywood columnist Hedda Hopper recounted that when the old president, hunky Robert Montgomery, informed her he was leaving the office, Montgomery said, "Whatever you do, don't sell my successor short. He's a brilliant, earnest man whose heart and mind are in the right places." She wrote, "Then I almost gasped when he named the fellow as Ronald Reagan." She soon changed her mind, she related: he handled the strike "with courage and intelligence." Hopper, a dyed-in-the-wool conservative who deeply identified with studio management, had reason to think so. In his new role, his greatest passion became blocking impartial arbiters such as the Catholic archdiocese, the

National Labor Relations Board, and an interfaith council of Los Angeles divines from settling the conflict.

Impartial mediation would have allowed the CSU to survive, where the IA and industry sought to crush it. Did Reagan intend this? Was he serving the studio heads' malicious designs? In his testimony to the Kearns Committee, Father Dunne offered a theory: "There is a certain mentality in the leadership of the Screen Actors Guild which is a producer's mentality, rather than a workingman's mentality." He singled out Reagan by name: "His interest as an actor naturally tends, it seems to me, subconsciously to coincide with the producers." Garry Wills, in his book about Reagan, offered another suggestion: that he may have been simply oblivious that his refusal of outside mediation made him the producers' cat's-paw—that he "knew nothing of the plans that had been concerted to break the CSU."

Either way, the result is the same. A very Ronald Reagan result—one strikingly similar to his achievement in another complex dispute, nineteen years earlier. As a freshman at Eureka College he had in just this way reduced the fog of bureaucratic war into a crystal simplicity, claiming his faction's "policy of polite resistance" had united the campus once and for all, purged a villain, and saved the university, bestowed upon all and sundry an "education in human nature and the rights of man to universal education that nothing could erase from our psyches." The gift he provided to his fellow Screen Actors Guild members was similar. Many of them wished to see themselves as liberals, but also just wanted to keep on making movies, not go on strike. What he gave them was a story that turned them into moral innocents instead of scabs. He soon won nomination for a full term as Screen Actors Guild president. He made others feel good.

Except, as ever, those who considered him a fraud and a joke—like a Canadian actor named Alexander Knox, who took the podium at a SAG mass meeting deciding whether to honor the picket line and proceeded to parody its president as a simpleton. "Reagan spoke very fast," Knox later reflected. "He always did, so that he could talk out of both sides of his mouth at once."

MEANWHILE, THERE WAS THAT ACTING CAREER. FATHER DUNNE SAID AT the hearings that it "very clearly would have been injured had he taken the other stand." But that wasn't the case at all. Reagan's career appeared beyond salvation, whatever political stand he did or did not take.

Jack Warner had praised Reagan as "a tower of strength, not only for the actors but for the whole industry" in the strike. It didn't keep Warners from promptly casting Reagan in the worst movie of his career, *That Hagen Girl*, starring Reagan alongside Shirley Temple in her first grown-up role. The newly married Temple, who insisted on being called "Mrs. Agar," looked like a little girl playing dress-up. Reagan played her romantic interest. A *Hollywood Citizen* correspondent visited the set, where the "handsome actor and president of the Screen Actors Guild makes no secret of the fact that he yearns to gallop over movie prairies." The correspondent quoted his complaint, "We are making too many 'parlor stories.' Moviegoers have enough of their own problems today. When they go to see pictures they want some entertainment that will take them out of their own locale and away from their troubles," and then noted, "Ronnie thinks the Western is the answer."

Actually Westerns were Hollywood's most prevalent genre. Though he had an answer to that as well. "'Too often,' he lamented, 'producers will take a story and set it in the outdoors in an attempt to label it a Western. That isn't the way to do it.'

"His suggestion: look into American history, where many unmovie-fied characters with interesting and exciting stories are still hidden. But steer clear of the Civil War, he advised, because there can only be but one ending to such a picture. Even Hollywood can't change that."

And *Hollywood Citizen* reported on his "campaign to escape Warners temporarily to play 'Only the Valiant,' a story of the Indian War which is owned by the Cagneys." But that campaign failed. Nowadays the only place he was starring was behind the podiums.

He skipped his thirty-sixth birthday dinner to give a speech for Truman's housing program; spoke at a fan banquet for baseball stars (the papers identified him as "Ronald Reagan of the movies"—as if readers might not know who he was); emceed the Oscars alongside Jack Benny; helmed a dinner honoring school superintendents; then, still waiting for *Stallion Road* to debut, addressed the convention of the International Association of Y's Men's Clubs. ("As we enjoy the rights and privileges of American citizenship, we must acknowledge a corresponding duty to safeguard those rights to everyone lest they be lost to all . . . and give the bum's rush to the notorious hucksters whenever and wherever they may be found.") And when a Harvard sociologist said the nation was harmed by the "synthetic childless population" and "disintegrated people in Hollywood," it was Reagan, his wife pregnant with their third child, who rose for the defense: "If the professor could be persuaded to leave the cloistered halls where intellectual inbreeding substitutes for the 'synthetic' life of Hollywood, I believe we could show him that the people in the studios, gathered from the cities, towns, and farms, are a pretty good cross section of American life, no worse, no better."

In May 1947 Hedda Hopper published an appreciation of Reagan as a reasonable liberal. "I believe the only logical way to save our country from all extremists," he said, "is to remove conditions that supply fuel for the totalitarian fire. . . . The Reds know that if we can make America a decent living place for all of our people, their cause is lost here." He also said, "I'm not in favor of banning any political party. If we ban the Communists from the polls we set a dangerous precedent. Tomorrow it may be the Democratic or Republican Party that gets the ax. Rather than ban the party, we should force all issues into the open."

These were the standard liberal anti-Communist positions. They were also radically disingenuous. Only one month earlier, Reagan had once more invited two FBI agents into his home. He told them two of his rivals on the SAG board (who were also rivals of each other) "follow the Communist Party line." Then he singled out eight more suspected Communists—including Alexander Knox, the actor who had mocked him at the SAG meeting.

J. Parnell Thomas, the fearsome chair of the House Committee on Un-American Activities, set up shop at the Biltmore Hotel to hold secret hearings on Communist infiltration of Hollywood. That hinge in Hollywood history was followed by yet another hinge in Reagan's own. In June, after plunging into a river to rescue Shirley Temple's character from a suicide attempt, he contracted viral pneumonia. He was resting at Cedars of Lebanon Hospital on June 26 when his wife gave birth three months prematurely—at a hospital three miles away. Hedda Hopper rushed to print to report the child's condition was "satisfactory." But the child, whom the parents named Christine, was dead by the time the column appeared. Reagan would never acknowledge that his wife gave birth. Instead he called it a miscarriage, blaming it on his wife's overwork.

JANE WYMAN *WAS* WORKING HARD, AND EXTRAORDINARILY WELL. FOR *The Yearling* she was nominated for Best Supporting Actress. For her next picture, *Johnny Belinda,* she prepared to play a deaf-mute by studying sign language, learning lip reading, and, not satisfied that she knew what it was like to *feel* deaf, wearing wax earplugs for hours at a time and spending days in isolation, deliberately terrifying herself. "I Broke Myself Down for *Johnny Belinda,*" she wrote in an exceptional article in the *Los Angeles Mirror*—a particular challenge, she said, because there was "nothing groping or uncertain about me. I'm pretty much of a girl who knows her own mind. I've taught myself to make decisions. It's the story of any career woman."

Her husband's acting method, contrastingly, had been recently described by "Hollywood Is My Beat" columnist Sidney Skolsky: "He studies his role by merely sitting down in a comfortable chair and reading and rereading the script until he knows it." Soon after, Dutch attended a preview screening of *That Hagen Girl*. When the audience moaned as he kissed Shirley Temple, he sank down in his chair, then snuck out before the lights went up. (The kiss was cut from the final edit.)

The marriage was falling apart. Jane Wyman was not shy about telling the world she came by these portrayals of lonely women honestly; everyone in Hollywood by then knew that Reagan never shut up, and that Wyman called him "diarrhea mouth." At a dinner party at Dick Powell and June Allyson's house, George Murphy tried to talk him into becoming a Republican. Allyson asked Reagan a question; the answer went on and on and on, until Wyman leaned over and whispered, "Don't ask Ronnie what time it is because he will tell you how a watch is made." Allyson replied, jokingly, "He'll outgrow it." Wyman didn't laugh.

She had also made no secret to friends that Reagan had once responded to one of her periodic melancholy fugues with "We'll have an ideal life if you'll avoid doing one thing: don't think." When *Johnny Belinda* was shot on location in a remote stretch of Mendocino County, just after the death of their infant daughter, she befriended her costar Lew Ayres, an extraordinary figure who had published an open letter in 1942 announcing he was a conscientious objector. (A front-page editorial in the *Hollywood Reporter* begged the public not to blame the motion picture industry for the heresy.) They would disappear for long conversations about the meaning of life, and Hollywood gossip linked them romantically. Reagan promptly visited the set—as if to spy on this coward his true love was choosing over him.

Then, he had to leave. For a crucial appointment beckoned.

The CSU had been crushed. The brass launched the studio on a new project. The Motion Picture Alliance for the Preservation of American Ideals, the coalition of right-wing actors and executives launched in 1944 to combat "the growing impression that the industry is made up of, and dominated by, Communists, radicals, and crackpots," joined forces with the House Un-American Activities Committee to purge the Communists, radicals, and crackpots once and for all. HUAC's chief Hollywood investigator, Allen Smith, who had grown up in Dixon, recommended Reagan be summoned as a "friendly" witness. "He has no fear of anyone and is a nice talker," he reported. "He is of course reticent to testify, because he states that he is a New Deal Liberal, and does not agree with a number of individuals in the Motion Picture Alliance. I believe we straightened him out on a number of differences."

"Hearings Regarding the Communist Infiltration of the Motion Picture Industry" opened in Washington on October 20, 1947, with testimony from the friendly witnesses. The urbane, mustachioed Adolphe Menjou—a far-right ideologue when he wasn't playing well-dressed men-about-town—said that only the "vigilance" of anti-Communists like himself prevented "an enormous amount of sly, subtle, un-American class-struggle propaganda from going into pictures" (though "a communistic actor, even if he were under orders from the head of the studio not to inject communism or un-Americanism or subversion into pictures, could easily subvert that order"—by, say, changing the inflection of his voice). A screenwriter said Communists had mastered the art of introducing a "little drop of cyanide in the picture" that "makes every Senator, every business, every employer a crook and which destroys our beliefs in American free enterprise and free institutions." Writer Ayn Rand had written a guidebook to help producers on the lookout for such surreptitious Communism. (Make sure your pictures "don't smear wealth"; "don't glorify failure"; "don't deify the 'common man.'") At the hearings, she took on *Song of Russia*, that supposedly innocent effort to help defeat Hitler, for daring to depict Soviet citizens who smiled. Ginger Rogers's mother told of how she had forbidden her daughter to act in the film version of Theodore Dreiser's classic novel *Sister Carrie* because it was "open propaganda." Jack Warner held up a picture of John Lawson on the picket line in the 1945 strike—proving, since Lawson was a Communist, that the strike was only "*supposedly* on account of the carpenters and painters." The IA's John Brewer testified of his hope that "with the help of the committee the Communist menace in the motion picture industry may be destroyed, to the end that Hollywood labor may be spared in the future the strife and turmoil of the immediate past"—the same strife and turmoil he himself had deliberately engineered to break a rival union.

It was absurd, but so were the antics on the other side—for instance when Lawson brought a statement to read calling his accusers "stool pigeons, neurotics, publicity-seeking clowns, Gestapo agents, paid informers, and a few ignorant and frightened Hollywood artists."

On October 23, witness Reagan trod a middle ground. He had recently adopted a new technology, contact lenses, but he put them away for the occasion; his horn-rims imparted a more serious air. In his statement he repeated what he had said to Hedda Hopper: he didn't wish "to see any party outlawed on the basis of its political ideology. We have spent a hundred and seventy years in this country on the basis that democracy is strong enough to stand up and fight against the inroads of any ideology." He closed, "I hope we never are prompted by either fear or resentment of Communism into compromising any of our democratic principles in order to fight it." Having delivered a thoughtful, judicious presentation, he was just about the only person to emerge from the sordid proceedings enhanced.

On the other hand, late in July, SAG executive director Jack Dales, almost certainly with Reagan's cooperation, had helped the FBI confirm the identities of fifty-four people whose names it had obtained in an illegal break-in of a Communist Party office. Indeed, Reagan had already dropped the dime on eight suspects himself.

UPON HIS RETURN FROM WASHINGTON, HIS WIFE GREETED HIM AT THE door: "You bore me! Get out!" It was her first categorical insistence upon a divorce. The next week *That Hagen Girl* came out to ghastly notices—one of which regretted Shirley Temple's suicide attempt failed. "Thanks for being frank regarding *That Hagen Girl*, I know the reviews couldn't say much for it, and only did it to accommodate Warner Bros.," he wrote Lorraine Wagner. "They tried others who refused, so they asked me and I said I knew it wouldn't do anything for me, but they were desperate, so you know 'old easy goin' Reagan.'"

Two weeks later, on November 17, a SAG membership meeting passed a resolution decreeing officers had to sign affidavits stipulating that they were not members of the Communist Party—probably in coordination with the studio executives who, six days later, emerged from the Waldorf hotel in Manhattan to announce that "we will not knowingly employ a Communist," and inviting "the Hollywood talent guilds to work with us to eliminate subversives, to protect the innocent, and to safeguard free speech and a free screen wherever they are threatened."

In December, *Johnny Belinda* completed, Wyman traveled to New York City, where she was quoted in a Hollywood column as saying, "There is no use in lying. I am not the happiest girl in the world. It's an accumulation of things that have been coming a long time," though she hoped that when she saw her husband "we can solve our problem." Reagan learned of the quote upon his return from a shopping trip to buy his wife a fabulous Christmas gift. He promptly ran to Hedda Hopper—whose column the next morning reported, "Ronald Reagan declares he merely had tiff with Jane Wyman in answering queries about reports that they are on verge of separation." And what, she'd asked, was he buying his girl for Christmas? "I'm not going to tell you. If I told you, you'd print it and then it wouldn't be a surprise for her. . . . I'm looking forward to a happy life with Jane for as long as we live."

Two weeks later, Old Easy Goin' Reagan earned a new nickname. According to a report by the FBI. "Confidential Informant T-10" told agents of his "firm conviction" that Congress should outlaw the Communist Party and formally designate groups that were Communist fronts, so that members' disloyalty could be legally established. It was the opposite of what he had told HUAC forty days earlier—but consistent with the studio chiefs' request that Congress "enact legislation to assist American industry to rid itself of subversives." One day around that time, he took a long car trip with his former religion professor at Eureka. "He told me of his marriage troubles and of his troubles with Communists at the Guild," the teacher remembered in 1966, when Reagan the gubernatorial candidate was making his bones by fulminating against the wickedness and moral dissolution of the Berkeley student left. But back in 1947 "he told me that there was a group of women at the University of California who were getting men tied into Communism by charm and sex—virtually prostitutes. He told me that like Lincoln if he ever got a chance to crack that, he'd crack it harder than what he's doing now."

DUTCH'S 1948 WAS RUNG IN WITH A TWO-PAGE SPREAD IN *Photoplay*, "Those Fightin' Reagans": "'It's a strange character I'm married to,' Ronnie announced with a wry but unmistakably tender smile, 'But—I love her. . . . Please remember,' he told us, 'that Jane went through a very bad time when, after the strain of waiting for another baby, she lost it. Then, perhaps before she was strong enough, she went into *Johnny Belinda*. . . . Perhaps, too, my seriousness about public affairs has bored Jane,' he added slowly. 'But you must believe me when I say that, less than six weeks before Jane left for New York, we were happy enough for her to tell me, 'I hope it can always be like this between us.' 'I hope so,' Ronnie said, with an earnestness you could reach out and touch. 'Because I believe we belong together.'" In May, Jane filed for divorce on grounds of "extreme mental cruelty." Her husband didn't attend the June dissolution hearing. Readers of the *Los Angeles Times*, however, did. "Despite her lack of interest in his political activities," the paper said, reporting her argument before the bench, "Reagan insisted that she attend meetings with him and that she be present during discussions among his friends. But her own ideas, she complained, 'were never considered important.'"

The following February, Jane Wyman was nominated for the Best Actress Oscar. When she won, her self-possessed and witty speech, the shortest in history, became a Hollywood legend: "I accept this very gratefully for keeping my mouth shut once. I think I'll do it again." It sounded like a dig at her "diarrhea-mouth" ex. Reagan, bitter, cracked, "Maybe I should name *Johnny Belinda* as co-respondent." Decades later, in a rare personal revelation, he recalled to a reporter during a stormy airplane flight (he was afraid of flying), "I tried to go to bed with every starlet in Hollywood and damn near succeeded." One of those starlets later accused him of what would come to be called "date rape"; another, an eighteen-year-old virgin, said he told her she should see a doctor because she couldn't have an orgasm. Sometimes he woke up in one of the bungalows at the legendary Garden of Allah hotel complex on the Sunset Strip not knowing the name of the woman beside him in bed.

No movie roles, let alone in the Westerns he craved. "I was almost on my way to Colorado on location when the studio changed its mind about casting," he wrote in his column in his fan club newsletter of one cowboy role. He did, however, buy a little eight-acre "ranch." "I grab a post hole digger and put up more paddock fences," he wrote, referencing his favorite horse: "It's a job to keep ahead of Tar Baby, who likes to lean on them until something gives." Forlornly, he named the place "Yearling Row"—after the breakthrough movie of his former wife.

At least he had his political obsession to ground him. Most Hollywood liberals had lost interest in politics after the death of FDR; among the stars, Lucille Ball, Robert Ryan, Humphrey Bogart, Lauren Bacall, and Ronald Reagan were almost alone in plumping for the 1948 Democratic ticket. Reagan, on election eve, introduced a new liberal hero, Hubert Humphrey, on a national radio broadcast:

"This is Ronald Reagan speaking to you from Hollywood. You know me as a motion picture actor. But tonight I'm just a citizen, pretty concerned about the election next month, and more than a little impatient about those promises the Republicans made before they got control of Congress a couple of years ago."

He went on to flog the Standard Oil Company for reporting a "net profit of $210 million, *after* taxes, for the first half of '48—an increase in seventy percent in one year": proof, he said, that Republicans were lying in their central election claim: the claim that the postwar epidemic of inflation had been caused by higher wages—not "bigger and bigger profits."

This was boilerplate liberalism, circa 1948. What was extraordinary was the way he found to illustrate the argument. Noting "an Associated Press dispatch I read the other day," he introduced America to one Smith L. Carpenter, who "retired some years ago thinking he had enough money saved so that he could live out his last years without having to worry. But he didn't figure on this Republican inflation which ate up all his savings. So he's gone back to work." He paused for ironic effect: "The reason this is news is Mr. Carpenter is 91 years old."

Here was that soon-to-become trademark skill: illustrating abstract questions of public policy with true heart-tugging stories from genuine folks. Or rather, apparently true. Generations later, when a wondrous technology would let the complete contents of dozens of newspapers be searched in less than a second, the fact could be told. And that fact is that none of these dozens of newspapers ran any Associated Press dispatch about someone named "Smith L. Carpenter," nor anyone else who went to work when he was ninety-one years old because inflation ate up his savings.

One year earlier, Hedda Hopper had written how Reagan "had struck me as being quiet [and] unassuming." Now a profile called him "the spokesman for all movie actors," who "walks around the studio with a portable radio," "reads every book he believes he should read" and "most of the political columns," and habitually shocks tourists "when he walks over and starts chatting." It concluded, in dog-bites-man style, "He is not only an actor, but a politician."

But he still wasn't a movie star. As the emcee who had introduced him on that election eve Democratic radio broadcast said: "Now to Ronald REE-gan in Hollywood." People still didn't know how to pronounce his name.

SOON A SLOW, SUBTLE IDEOLOGICAL SHIFT BEGAN STIRRING IN RONALD Reagan's breast. By 1952, he was campaigning for Dwight Eisenhower—but also for a liberal senatorial candidate. By eight years later, however, he was about as far right as a public figure could be—writing a personal letter to the Republican presidential nominee: "Shouldn't someone tag Mr. Kennedy's 'bold new imaginative program' with its proper age? Under the tousled boyish hair cut it is still old Karl Marx—first launched a century ago. There is nothing new in the idea of a Gov't being Big Brother to us all. Hitler called his 'State Socialism' and way before him it was 'benevolent monarchy.'" Delighted at the spectacle of this Hollywood star calling a centrist Democrat a Commie, Nazi, and monarchist all at once, Richard Nixon issued a command to his staff: "Use him as a speaker wherever possible. He used to be liberal."

The underlying moral logic was the same. He saw good guys. He saw bad guys. Only the identity of the two precisely changed places. How? It was a shift the complexity of which he himself was constitutionally unable to convincingly explain: he said that he hadn't changed—that the Democratic Party had. That made no sense; if anything, the Democratic Party by the time he became a Republican was more conservative than it had been in 1948, when Harry Truman campaigned on a sweeping program of national health insurance. So what had changed? One crucial factor was his views on the subject of taxation—with which the president of the Screen Actors Guild had already begun a lifelong obsession.

His industry became tax-obsessed first. The new Hollywood, like the old one, was built on the manufacture of stars. But now stars manufactured themselves. Once upon a time, in 1932, Clark Gable told *Photoplay*—"smilingly," the picture magazine claimed—"I am paid not to think." Sometime later, when Gable asked for a percentage of the profits of the films in which he starred, a top executive exploded: "He's nobody. We took him from nobody. . . . Who taught him how to walk? We straightened his teeth and capped them into that smile. . . . We taught this dumb cluck how to depict great emotions. And now he wants a piece of the action? Never!" Then came the 1943 California Supreme Court decision in Olivia de Havilland's case, which called traditional studio contracts "indentured servitude"; then, postwar, aggressive Justice Department enforcement against the monopoly practices forbidden by the 1940 Paramount decree; then the labor troubles of 1945–47, eating away at studios' bottom lines. There was, too, the rising medium competing for Americans' entertainment dollars: television. The studios' hand thus weakened, stars making Gable's old demand had considerably more power. This was, ironically, the reason Reagan became SAG president in the first place: Robert Montgomery was one of the first to get a newfangled "profit-sharing deal." That, officially, made Montgomery "management"—and thus disqualified him for union office. This was something his replacement, with far less box-office pull, wouldn't have to worry about.

The new deals made Hollywood stars entrepreneurial, at a time when the Revenue Act of 1941 set the top income tax bracket at 90 percent for every dollar earned above $200,000. So stars started thinking like Republicans: They became tax-obsessed. Indeed, the story Reagan would tell about why he became interested in taxes revolved around that 90 percent top marginal tax rate: he claimed it kept him from adding a new picture to his schedule if it meant getting paid only a dime on the dollar. The story, however, doesn't wash. Reagan was still a contract player, not a freelancer—and still a rather meager contract player at that. In April 1949, when a melodrama of his he thought splendid, called *Night Unto Night,* came out after being held for two years, he confidently refused a loan-out to Columbia for a silly comedy. But *Night Unto Night* got bad reviews. Next *Variety* gave him a good notice ("Reagan is a fellow who has a cheerful way of looking at dames") in *The Girl from Jones Beach*—but the picture was just the sort of fluff he was desperate to avoid. He had done Warners a favor the previous year by filming the war picture *The Hasty Heart* in cold and damp England (the cash-strapped British government had frozen American corporate assets, forcing studios to film more pictures there)—but Warners repaid him by scheduling him in only one picture for the next year.

Early in 1950 a black-tie dinner for his thirty-ninth birthday drew six hundred attendees, including Cecil B. DeMille. Al Jolson sang "Sonny Boy" to the guest of honor. Perhaps buoyed by that, Reagan wrote Jack Warner a letter—addressing him as "Dear Jack" and calling in what he thought was a chit. "You agreed that the script and role were very weak but asked me to do the picture as a personal favor which I gladly did," he wrote of *That Hagen Girl.* "At that time," he pushed, "you encouraged me to bring in a suitable outdoor"—Hollywood jargon for "adventure"—"script which you agreed to buy as a starring vehicle for me." He then noted a rumor that the Western script the studio had purchased on that recommendation had been reassigned to Errol Flynn. He concluded, "I know you too well to ever think you'd break your word. However I am anxious to know something of production plans—starting date etc. in order to better schedule my own plans. Frankly I hope it is soon as I have every confidence in this story."

"Jack" responded through the studio's chief legal counsel: "Maybe it would be a good idea to effect a mutual cancellation of your contract."

Lew Wasserman was able to cobble him a five-picture-a-year-deal at Universal—a second-tier studio that cast him in his most infamous humiliation. Of *Bedtime for Bonzo, Newsweek* opined, "The chimp behaves more credibly than Ronald Reagan." His name was even mispronounced in the trailer. He turned down the sequel, not because of any worries about tax liability, but because he thought the script unrealistic. ("Who could believe a chimp could go to college and play on the football team?" recollected the star of a picture in which the chimp wears glasses, learns table manners, and is adopted as a child by a professor and his wife.) No, this wasn't an actor worried about the tax liability of winning too many roles. In any event, by then a business genius had figured a way out of the 90 percent tax bracket problem. When a studio really wanted a certain actor for a certain role, Lew Wasserman, Reagan's own agent, invented profit-sharing deals that turned the actor into a "corporation," whose stake in a picture could then be taxed at the capital gains rate, a mere 25 percent. But that was only for stars. Wasserman wasn't able to get Reagan any decent pictures at all, on any terms.

The future champion of individualism and entrepreneurship despised the new, more individualistic, entrepreneurial Hollywood. As SAG president, he was obsessed with preserving the factory system: guaranteeing actors "a wage that'll enable them to live during the lay-off periods"; begging the studios in 1950 to re-balloon the number of actors under contract back to more than seven hundred from the current number, 350; arguing in 1952, his last year as SAG president, that by "casting and concentrating on a small group of individuals, who happen to be temporarily 'hot,'" the studios harmed only themselves. (Projecting blame onto the industry for problems he was suffering in his own career was a pattern of his in interviews.) He all but proposed featherbedding make-work for the 5,242 SAG members who made less than $300 a year. (He noted that only 139 members grossed more than $50,000 a year—a point inconsistent with his later argument that the exorbitant top marginal tax rate for those earning over $200,000 was devastating Hollywood.)

The new Hollywood, in fact, was killing him. To keep him working, Wasserman had to search elsewhere within his burgeoning entertainment empire. "REAGAN IN NIGHT CLUB / BUT NOT FROM CHOICE / ACTOR CITES PROBLEMS" reported the newspaper Hollywood Citizen in 1954, announcing his debut as emcee at the Frontier Hotel in Las Vegas, "despite the fact that he is no singer or dancer and could scarcely qualify as a comedian." His costars were an act that specialized in the hardly cutting-edge arts of soft-shoe dancing and barbershop quartet singing. Rounding out this uninspiring evening of entertainment, the Citizen reported, was a "monologue such as he has delivered at countless benefits." Reagan was just grateful for the opportunity—which came, he wrote to Lorraine Wagner on the Frontier's Western-themed stationery, at "about the time when I thought I was going over 'Niagara Falls' in a tub." He also told her the show was "going over real big and the whole thing is really a grand experience." For Ronald Reagan everything always works out in the end, gloriously, even when it does not. His Las Vegas agent described the revue as an "omelet." Having laid that egg, Reagan soon was out of work once again.

This does not sound like a man realistically worried about the tax penalties of taking on extra work. His obsession with the unfairness of the IRS may be better explained by a secret that came out only after his death. A researcher discovered a tax lien against Reagan in the amount of $24,911 (some $200,000 in inflation-adjusted dollars), apparently related to income he had deferred during World War II, when he was pulling down only $280 a month. Who knows what frustrations, during this most frustrating period of his life, lay behind that? What endless phone calls with IRS bureaucrats, what tortured discussions with accountants, what fears that this man for whom appearances counted for everything might be found out? Who knows. If he ever talked about it, no one ever told.

Perhaps he talked about it with Lew Wasserman. Wasserman, though nominally a Democrat, was Hollywood's preeminent tax-hater. Gaming the IRS was at the heart of his business genius. MCA had an "incredibly complicated structure," wrote a biographer, "with ultimately more than two hundred subsidiaries incorporated in many different states as well as abroad." In one dodge, Wasserman figured out that if his clients did all their work outside the country for at least eighteen months, they would receive all their income tax-free; in another, he decorated MCA offices with antiques on which the company claimed depreciations, even while they were gaining in value.

Reagan had always sought older mentors, surrogate fathers; now here was something to more deeply bind him to Wasserman, And he would soon find his animus toward the IRS resonating with a new social circle. That came of a new romantic relationship—the next station in his ideological *Wanderjahr*.

THERE ARE SEVERAL STORIES ABOUT HOW RONALD REAGAN MET AN ACtress, new in town in the fall of 1949, named Nancy Davis. In one version, both attended a dinner party at the home of Dore Schary, whose back her physician stepfather had once fixed. Schary pooh-poohed the seriousness of the Communist threat; Reagan vociferously argued otherwise. Nancy, seated opposite, "kept smiling at him in agreement." In another, Nancy Davis tried to run for the Screen Actors Guild board but was left off the ballot owing to confusion involving another "Nancy Davis" on the membership rolls. In still another story, Davis kept a list of Hollywood's most eligible bachelors whom she wished to woo: actors, lawyers, agents, producers, power players every one—and the Screen Actors Guild president topped the list.

Ronald and Nancy, however, always told still another version. Theirs was a story of rescue.

The story went that a list of Communist sympathizers was published in the *Hollywood Reporter*. "Nancy Davis" was one of them—again, a different Nancy Davis. Director Mervyn LeRoy asked Reagan to meet with her to help clear up the matter. That would have been consistent with Reagan's immersion in a new aspect of film colony culture: the evolving bureaucracy by which accused Communists and sympathizers were ritualistically "cleared" of suspicion. It was a sordid and arbitrary process—for instance, in the case of Alexander Knox, the actor Reagan named to the FBI after Knox mocked him at a SAG mass meeting. Suddenly Knox found himself having to answer fantastic and foundationless charges: that he had attended a meeting at a left-wing bookshop he could not recall entering in his life; that he had protested against the American Nazi Gerald L. K. Smith at a meeting of the Hollywood Independent Citizens Committee of the Arts, Sciences and Professions (he hadn't, though he wondered what was wrong with protesting against a Nazi, and also hadn't belonged to HICCASP); that he had signed a petition asking SAG to review its neutrality policy in the jurisdictional strike (he had, but was baffled as to why that made him a suspected Communist); that he had signed a full-page ad protesting HUAC's investigation (he hadn't). It didn't matter: Knox was unable to make another movie in America until 1967.

Neither Ronald Reagan nor Nancy Davis, however, found the clearance regime sordid. For them it was a prop for a gauzy, romantic fairy tale—like finding the maiden for whom the slipper fit. They met over dinner, where the gentleman agreed to save the damsel from distress. They moved on to the nightclub Ciro's, where they partied into the night. Then, wrote Nancy in her autobiography, "We had dinner the next night and the night after that." They "went together," she wrote, "for about a year."

It was more like two and a half years. And in any event, their story wasn't factual on its face. The mix-up with another "Nancy Davis" believed to be a Red took place not in 1949 but in 1953, when she and Reagan were already married and he was no longer a SAG officer. It was Louella Parsons, not Reagan, who cleared her from the taint. But Nancy Davis had no less a taste for tidying up stories than the man who would become her husband. The truth is that Ronald Reagan *did* rescue Nancy Reagan—who had developed a taste for being rescued since she was a girl.

Her mother, Edith Luckett, had been an itinerant actress whose first husband was a serial failure. They divorced. Edith refused alimony, struggling to raise her daughter alone while she trod the boards up and down the Eastern Seaboard; when that became too much, she left Nancy with her sister's family in Bethesda, Maryland. There Nancy was able to grow up with a double dose of glamour: at Sidwell Friends, the exclusive private school of the Washington elite (though her foster family was poor, and she always had to share a room); and visiting her mother on the road, where she mingled with the likes of Spencer Tracy and the exotic silent film star Alla Nazimova (her godmother), swaddling herself in Edith's dazzling costumes.

In 1927, on a cruise to join a production in England, her mother met a taciturn Chicago professor of medicine, Dr. Loyal Davis, scion of one of the oldest families of Galesburg, Illinois. When Dr. Davis proposed marriage, Edith traveled to Bethesda for a rare visit with her daughter to seek her approval—promising that upon her marriage, she would bring Nancy to live with them in Chicago. Nancy approved. In short order Dr. Davis became a progressively more important figure in Chicago, rising to chief of surgery at Northwestern. Edith landed an easy role on a radio soap opera, contributing to the family's increasingly ample income. Nancy was enrolled in Chicago's toniest high school, Girls Latin. (The caption beneath her photo in the 1939 yearbook read, "Nancy's social perfection is a constant source of amazement. She is invariably becomingly and suitably dressed." In fact she was always afraid her classmates would think she had a weight problem.) Their Lake Shore Drive home became the center of a social whirl: Chicago's towering mayor Ed Kelly was a regular; the legendary Walter Huston was "Uncle Walter"; family friends like Mary Martin, Lillian Gish, and Katharine Hepburn flitted by. Vacations were at the sumptuous Arizona Biltmore.

At age sixteen, Nancy made the rescue legal. She was invited by her biological father, Ken Robbins, and his new wife for a visit. They quarreled; he locked her in a bathroom. Returning home, she asked a retired judge about how she might go about being adopted by her stepfather. She filed the petition herself. Decades later, a reporter confronted her: *Who's Who* said she had been adopted. Her official biography as first lady of California said she "was born in Chicago, the only daughter of Dr. and Mrs. Loyal Davis." She replied, "I don't care what the book

says. He is my father." She repeated herself: "In my mind, he is my father. I have no father except Loyal Davis."

In Chicago, Dr. Davis, whom even his grandchildren would later call
"sir," was infamous for his conservatism. How conservative? A story
about medical interns who prevailed upon the parents of babies they delivered in charity cases on Chicago's black South Side to name their sons
"Loyal" to snub their racist boss sounds apocryphal. The one about
syphilis has more of a ring of truth: Dr. Davis, suspecting that a well-
to-do patient had a tumor, turned the case over to two medical students,
who did a positive test for the venereal disease. They were shocked
when he responded to their presentation of their findings by imperi-
ously pronouncing: "My patients don't have syphilis."

"My patients don't have syphilis": that unbendable will to divide the
world into the virtuous and the wicked, never the twain shall meet—a
family trait. Though at that, once Nancy loosed herself on the wider
world with the ambition to become an actress, a crisis developed: she
found herself on the wrong side of that particular divide. Which was
where the need for her rescue came in.

Nancy Davis majored in drama at Smith College, then struggled to
make it as an actress on Broadway. She did better in her social life. Spencer Tracy suggested Nancy as a date for his widowed friend Clark Gable
when Gable traveled to New York. Gable ended up squiring Nancy
around town for three straight days. "Nancy was one of those girls
whose phone number got handed around a lot," a contemporary recollected. She developed what used to be known as a "reputation."

It is hard to put a polite coloration on what happened next. One of
the men given her number—"She's a nice girl who likes company," he
remembered being told—was the head of casting at MGM. Benny Thau
was fifty-one; she was twenty-eight. Before the evening was out, he invited her to come to Hollywood for a screen test. However, he later expressed severe reservations about her talent: "Stars like Elizabeth Taylor,
she couldn't compete with that. She was attractive, but not what you'd
call beautiful." Nancy Davis appeared to have a guilty conscience about
the coup; she told her mother she earned that screen test after someone
at MGM saw her in a television play.

The screen test was directed by MGM's legendary George Cukor,
and filmed by the studio's best cinematographer, George Folsey; it followed, on Benny Thau's order, three weeks of training from the studio's
drama coach. "All Nancy Davis had to do," an MGM producer later
told a scandal-mongering biographer, "was show up . . . and not up-
chuck on camera." She signed one of those seven-year contracts they

weren't giving out very many of in March 1949. On her studio publicity questionnaire, asked what she would do if not acting, she answered,
"Lord knows!" She said her greatest ambition outside her acting career
was "to have a successful happy marriage." However, the social mores
of the time would make that ambition difficult. She was twenty-eight,
older than the ideal marriageable age. And there were those delicate stories that began to circulate around town, in which she left the offices of
powerful men at odd hours . . .

Then she met a man who lived to rescue, who treated her like a
queen, swaddled her in innocence, and gazed upon her with nothing but
reverence for the rest of their lives.

As their romance blossomed, Ronald Reagan was embarked on a
crusade against Hollywood gossip. One consequence of the softening
of Old Hollywood's autocracies was more autonomy for the fan magazines that once had been all but adjuncts for the studio publicity shops.
In February 1951, emceeing *Photoplay* magazine's annual awards show,
he shocked the assembled luminaries by saying from the podium, "We
as an industry have suffered from irresponsible journalism." The *New
York Times* published an article on the controversy that followed. On a
TV show he argued that the only reason newspapers ever began reporting on movie stars in the first place was as "a circulation gimmick," as if
studio publicists did not exist; then, in the same interview, he said that
"the anxiety of studio press departments for publicity" was the source
of the problem. Thereupon he blamed Hollywood's box-office woes on
media gossip—and concluded with a right-wing fillip: that such gossip
threatened the "rights of a private industry to go on and maintain itself."
Now he was in those fan magazines' sights—those magazines that had
made his career. The editor of *Motion Picture* disemboweled him in an
open letter: "You cited fan magazine stories about your divorce from
Jane Wyman as 'false and irresponsible invasion' of your privacy . . .
you apparently didn't feel the marriage itself was a private affair in
1943 [when] our photographers were permitted to take all the pictures
they wanted of your home, your wife and your family, and in 1941 you
talked freely to our reporter concerning your expected baby, and posed
buying toys, baby powder, and bassinets." Reagan sent an angry several-
page open letter in return. But *Motion Picture* would not publish it.

This was not how Hollywood as he understood it was supposed to
work. Perhaps, with Nancy, order could once more be restored. "They
go as 'steady,'" ran a fan magazine item on the courtship, "as any couple
in Hollywood. . . . For Ronnie, whose last wife was bored by his serious
attention to union matters, etc. Nancy's a good listener."

"REAGAN WILL WED SOCIALITE," was how the nuptials were announced in one news clip. They married on March 3, 1952, in a little private ceremony with William Holden as best man and his wife, Ardis, as matron of honor. It was a nice Hollywood contrivance: as a general rule, the Holdens were not speaking to one another at the time.

NANCY HAD HOPED TO SETTLE DOWN AS A HOUSEWIFE. BUT REAGAN GOT only three pictures in 1952; they had a mortgage on a home overlooking the ocean in the tony suburb of Pacific Palisades, another on the ranch bought the previous summer (350 acres in some accounts, 600 acres in others; it was actually 236), payments on a green Cadillac convertible, child support. They also soon had a new child, Patricia Reagan, born seven and a half months after their nuptials. At that potential scandal, another Hollywood contrivance was generously provided by Louella Parsons: "They were at the horse show Monday night when Nancy was taken directly to the hospital," she columnized. "The baby wasn't due until Christmas." (Actually, Patricia had been conceived before they were married. "My parents have never gone for simple, state-of-the-art lies," she wrote. "They weave bizarre, incredulous tales and stick by them with fierce determination.") So Nancy supplemented the household income by playing in a sci-fi groaner called *Donovan's Brain* and doing ads for Blue Bonnet margarine. ("Mrs. Ronald Reagan, popular wife of the famous movie star, is a winsome socialite of Pacific Palisades, California. . . .")

She did not care for ranch life—though for the sake of the columnists, she made do: "Here Ronnie and his wife, Nancy (Davis), get into blue jeans and tend to the cattle and horses, milk the goats, feed the chicken, and have the time of their lives." That piece, which ran in the *Los Angeles Examiner* at the end of June 1952, was slugged "NICE GUY REAGAN FIGHTS FOR WHAT HE BELIEVES IN" and noted, "His interest in civic and state affairs is so keen, a group of California citizens recently invited him to run for senator. He turned it down with thanks. 'I'm a ham—always was and always will be,' he laughed." It did not note that the citizens were Republicans, and included car dealership magnate Holmes Tuttle, who was at least as conservative as Loyal Davis.

Reagan had just delivered a commencement address at a Disciples of Christ college in Missouri, a curiously nervous performance. "This is a role which, believe me, I approach with more fear than any role I have played," the seasoned podium pro began, before moving on to several disjointed, self-effacing anecdotes and winding up with a series of patriotic bromides—as if what he currently believed was not clear at all, for the first time in his life.

ONE MONTH LATER HE WOULD DELIVER SOMETHING ELSE: A LEGAL DOCument, signed by him in his capacity as union president, granting MCA exclusive right to ignore a crucial Screen Actors Guild rule: a ban on agencies producing TV shows. It was a conflict of interest, because agents had the obligation to get their clients paid as much as possible, and producers had an interest in having them paid the least. But Lew Wasserman saw television as his next gold mine, and he wanted in.

There were 1,126 times more televisions in American homes than there had been in 1946. Studio bosses feared the infernal machines like the plague (for a time Jack Warner banned them as set dressing in Warner Bros. films). Hollywood actors came to fear them, too. "Thousands of hours of entertainment must be available to the television public," the *Saturday Evening Post* reported early in 1952, "and any guess as to where it will come from is as good as another." TV production was almost exclusively done in New York, live, instead of in Los Angeles, where shows were shot on film. If TV shows were filmed, producers were worried that actors would demand payment every time a show was rerun—what was known as a "reuse" payment; producers adamantly refused to even entertain the idea of reuse payments. In Los Angeles, these were perilous times: If actors held the line and continued to demand them, and movies continued to lose market share to TV, Hollywood as an institution might shrivel at an alarming rate.

Within this matrix, Wasserman spied a bonanza business opportunity.

He set up a TV production subsidiary in Los Angeles called Revue— this was, on its face, against SAG rules. Wasserman, however, convinced his favorite client to sell the SAG on the idea of granting MCA a "blanket waiver" of that rule. Wasserman and his lawyer Laurence Beilenson sold the idea to Jack Dales by arguing that the acting game in Los Angeles would die without it—that TV production would stay in New York. But the argument didn't really make sense. For if letting one agency have a blanket waiver, as a monopoly, might open the floodgates to Hollywood TV production, wouldn't it help Los Angeles all the more to let all agencies enjoy the same right?

It made more sense when you considered the sweetener MCA added to the deal: a secret quid pro quo. Revue would give SAG what the studios adamantly refused to grant: reuse fees. How secret was that part of the deal? It may have even been kept from Reagan, who seemed quite in earnest when, asked at a 1962 hearing on MCA's alleged monopoly power, said there was no quid pro quo. At that, a letter from Beilenson to Wasserman recollecting the secret terms—that Revue was willing to sign a contract giving the guild members reuse fees when no one else was willing to do so—was read out. Reagan was asked the question again. He replied, guilelessly, "It's quite conceivable then if he says it in this letter." By that time, Revue was so gigantic that MCA had a direct hand in the production of 45 percent of all network shows.

Maybe Reagan really didn't know that the deal was dirty. Maybe he just convinced himself of his friend and benefactor's incorruptible character. As usual, in those he believed innocent, innocence was all his eyes saw. It was his gift. In any event, he soon would be delivered a gift from Wasserman in return.

THINGS WERE LOOKING UP. IN 1953 HE FINALLY GOT A SCRIPT THAT HE loved—an "outdoor" script. *Prisoner of War* was based on the headlines: POWs held by the enemy in the Korean War had just been repatriated after reportedly ghastly torments and tortures. But some had elected not to come home at all—professing loyalty to the Communist cause. The development brought on great drafts of soul-searching, an anguished national conversation about whether the Communists had mastered the power of "brainwashing"—diabolically rewiring men's entire personalities. This picture had been written with the help of a technical advisor who'd been a North Korean prisoner. It began with our hero, Webb Sloane—Reagan—volunteering to parachute behind the lines to enter a prison camp. There he sees prisoners suffering in excruciating stress positions, confined naked in open holes in the ground, and subjected to cruel psychological manipulation like mock executions. Some respond with selfless heroics. ("Confess to germ warfare or you'll never see your wife again!" says the evil Russian colonel in the blazing white tunic. "PETER REILLY, LIEUTENANT, OC806032," a hero responds every time.) Others thought themselves clever for appearing to cooperate in order to earn favors like drugs for a suffering fellow prisoner. Reagan's Sloane berates a soldier for this. Then, in a twist, he changes sides, pronouncing himself a persuaded "progressive" now. This was a spy's ruse, of course, giving him access to the tools to get word back home about just how diabolical the Communist torture regime truly is.

Here was a key to Reagan's pleasure in the film—its vision of American innocence. *Prisoner of War* implicitly proposed a theory, one set to ease all that anguished national soul-searching: maybe, just maybe, those handful of defecting soldiers, rather than exposing the weakness of America's will, confirmed its strength. Maybe the defectors actually *were* spies, infiltrating the enemy and acting above and beyond the call of duty. Maybe America's will was greater than we had ever dared dream. "The spirit of man can run deep," ran the movie's opening invocation—"far beyond the reach of Communist torture."

That theory, though, didn't help at the box office. *Prisoner of War* came out in the spring of 1954 to lukewarm business. Some reviewers questioned the premise (the *Christian Science Monitor* referred to "atrocities supposed to have been practiced on prisoners"). Others found the execution slapdash and absurd. (Why did the torments never seemed to disturb the actors' perfectly coiffed hair, nor their exquisite physiques?) Reagan was flummoxed. "The picture should have done better," he said disappointedly. Americans had just been presented a portrait of real-life heroism on their screens. And yet they rejected it. Something was wrong. He blamed "the reluctance of extreme liberals to enthuse about anything that upset their illusion about 'agrarian reformers'"—the term of endearment used by those duped that Communists were actually humanitarians.

He was still not a convinced man of the right. In the spring the Army-McCarthy hearings dragged the disapproval ratings of the red-baiting senator from Wisconsin to a record low 45 percent. The nation was now neatly divided between those willing to believe the Communist conspiracy could be present anywhere, capable of subverting anything—and those who found the former group guilty of the same kind of thinking we were supposed to be fighting. That fall Reagan planted his flag with the latter group. "Professional patriots," as he angrily dubbed them, had targeted the United Nations Education, Scientific, and Cultural Organization (UNESCO) as a vector of Communist indoctrination. In Los Angeles, the school superintendent, Dr. Alexander Stoddard, introduced UNESCO study materials into the schools. Stoddard had been the scheduled speaker at a dinner marking the hundredth anniversary of the school system in Schenectady, New York, where the corporation General Electric was based. Then he fell to a heart attack. Reagan, who happened to be in town, was drafted to speak in his place—attributing Stoddard's collapse to "the vicious attacks of the ultra-professional patriotic organizations that can eventually wreck our school system."

He was, however, about to round the final ideological bend—making much the same vicious attacks himself. The development came largely of that gift from Lew Wasserman and MCA.

• • •

THE PRESS RELEASE WENT OUT APRIL 4, 1954, WHILE HE WAS STILL EM-
ceeing his feeble Los Vegas nightclub act: "NEW 'GENERAL ELEC-
TRIC THEATER' SERIES STARTS IN SEPTEMBER WITH
RONALD REAGAN AS HOST." The show was the first major product of Revue, MCA's new TV company, which was enjoying its blanket
waiver to produce the very shows whose talent it represented as agents.
"There was much talk around Hollywood about how Reagan had managed to land this fancy new job, which resurrected his career," Wasserman's biographer wrote. "The connection was hard to miss." Though it
also had to be said that he was a natural for the job. In its first year, before Reagan's arrival, *General Electric Theater* ranked nineteenth in the
Nielsen ratings. Within four months it climbed to tenth, and in the next
year it scored third. It beat its Sunday night competition *Alfred Hitchcock Presents* and *The Ed Sullivan Show* consistently for the duration of
Reagan's run as its host.

What he was hosting was an "anthology" show—one of those 1950s
relics in which a completely different cast of actors each week played
in a completely different mini motion picture, in a bewildering array
of genres: light comedy, Westerns, Hitchcock-style thrillers, miniature
sword-and-sandal epics, family melodramas, slapstick, and more, sometimes starring actors on their way up (James Dean), sometimes those
on their way down (Bette Davis), though more often actors who would
never be much known at all. What held the crazy quilt together was
the host: a "continuing personality on which to hang the production
and advertising of the show," as Reagan described it to an interviewer.
Sometimes he was an actor in the productions, but he was always there
as each episode's introducer, frequently in the same jaunty lean over the
TV lights that featured in his 1937 trailer for *Love Is on the Air,* and projecting that same customary aw-shucks ease—and almost always with a
trademark puffy silk handkerchief protruding from his suit coat.

He starred in GE commercials, too. The short ones. (A shock of
lightning crashing across the screen, punctuating the words rushing
at the viewer: "IN THE HOME . . . ON THE FARM . . . IN RE-
SEARCH . . . IN   ENGINEERING . . . IN   MANUFACTURING
SKILL . . . At General Electric, progress is our most important product!") The long ones, which were a *GE Theater* innovation. Instead of
the standard stretch of thirty- or sixty-second spots dotting the program, each episode featured a sort of halftime intermission, a mini General Electric documentary.

"That was act one of 'Big Break,' starring Johnny Ray with Nancy
Gates," Reagan twinkled in the middle of one show, about a pop singer

who refused to give up his ethnic surname and sing teeny-bopper songs as his record label demanded ("My great grandfather was Pulaski . . . the finest cabinet maker in all Warsaw. . . . I won't change my mind, sir. Not about this"), is fired, then is begged to come back. ("I'll go back. And I'll stick it out. But this time as Johnny Pulaski!")

"Now for a story with a twist, our Progress reporter Don Herbert visits another company, not General Electric—but one in which General Electric is very interested!"

Thereupon the viewer got to tour one of six Junior Achievement companies sponsored by the General Electric Foreman's Association at the twenty-thousand-worker turbine plant in Schenectady, New York: kids capitalizing their own company by selling shares of stock, forming a board of directors and a managerial cadre directing a happy crew manufacturing magazine racks for sale on a veritable production floor. "General Electric employment groups sponsor 68 Junior Achievement chapters in 34 communities. And it's no surprise. General Electric as a company, and its men and women as individuals, have always been interested in building a better America, with and for our young people. For today's youth will bring tomorrow's progress. And at General Electric, progress is our most important product!"

That vignette was a perfect portrait of Ronald Reagan's new corporate benefactor's vision of the world. Few corporations were as obsessed as GE with the problem of corporate image—an image, it was at great pains to establish, of GE as a keystone institution of the American Way. It was a constant target of Progressive Era antitrust enthusiasts when in 1922 a new president named Gerard Swope took over and utterly reorganized the corporation's strategy. Swope now branded its flowing, stylized logo, formerly all but invisible to ordinary consumers, on every product he could—and hired experts in two novel professions, public relations and advertising, to "brand" it in customers' minds as well. An adman from GE's lamp division named Bruce Barton became an articulate propagandist for the new model. "In Barton's theology," a scholar has written, "advertising was a sacred calling primarily concerned with the revelation of the corporate soul." One of Barton's campaigns styled GE (founded by Thomas Edison) as the inventor not just of lightbulbs but of *light:* its employees, he said, were "engaged in the great profession of lighting the world," under a charter from "the beginning of time . . . recorded in the four words, 'Let there be light.'" His colleague, the public relations consultant Edward Bernays, christened the fiftieth anniversary of Edison's 1879 invention "Light's Golden Jubilee." The goal, Barton said, was instilling "electrical consciousness"—a corporate desideratum all the more pressing with the coming of World War II, when GE anticipated the rich prospect of a postwar building boom with ads featuring, for example, a soldier sitting on a park bench with his gal sketching their future home for "when Victory is won": a house, naturally, crowded with the "new comforts, new conveniences, and new economies" of "electrical living."

From the start, GE identified television, which first surpassed radio in ad revenue in 1952, as electrical living's best salesman. GE was an innovative decentralized corporation, with each division and factory managed relatively independently of the others; the TV show was its first "all-company project"—and a pure product of its department of public relations. The show spoke to another Bruce Barton innovation: the notion of a "corporate culture," one that could be sold both internally to its scattered workforce of hundreds of thousands, and externally to millions of consumers. The TV show needed a host who embodied that culture. "We had been very, very definite as to the kind of person we wanted," an executive recalled, "a good, upright kind of person." And when MCA approached GE with Ronald Reagan—the guy whose future agent, in 1937, found him so "likable," "clean-cut," and "all-American"—it approved the casting almost immediately.

He loved the role. Previously a TV-basher in the mold of his erstwhile boss Jack Warner, he now adored the medium for delivering exactly what the newly entrepreneurial world of movie acting could not: job security. As he told the *Hollywood Reporter* in 1955, with a strikingly corporate self-consciousness, "my kind of association with a big business firm not only adds half or better of the economic value of my name, but provides a degree of security entirely foreign to the movie business, which is ruled so much by suicidal fluctuations, fads, and whims." And that self-consciousness—his identification of himself with the fortunes of his corporate sponsor, and the corporate system itself—soon made him even more useful to GE in another role.

Another facet of the self-image GE sought to project to the world was as a steward of America's very well-being. The way those Junior Achievement kids were depicted—niftily and uncomplainingly dividing themselves into an organic hierarchy, owners and managers and workers; frictionlessly coordinating their activities toward economically useful ends, each for the benefit of all; free from any and all resentment—reflected GE's self-image, too. The corporate behemoth saw its 166 plants in nearly thirty-eight states, manufacturing everything from tiny transistors to the nuclear reactors that got Ralph Cordiner on the cover of *Time* in 1959, as miraculously frictionless planes, free from conflict, let alone class conflict—that dreaded notion, beloved of labor unions, that workers and owners just might have interests in contradiction with one another and that their relationship was defined by a contest of wills. Selling that notion of industrial consensus became all the more crucial to GE brass following World War II, after the same 1946 strike wave that convulsed Hollywood shuttered nearly every GE plant in the country, just as the company hoped to flood all those GI starter homes with all the accoutrements of electrical living. The union representing its workers, one of the most radical in the country, won an eighteen-and-a-half-cent raise for production workers—and still they ravened for more.

Almost every GE plant had gone on strike—all except the seven manufacturing subsidiaries managed by a man named Lemuel Boulware, who soon was promoted to be the entire firm's vice president for labor relations. Though Boulware himself requested his title be changed to one that better suited his more visionary understanding of his undertaking: "vice president for public and community relations." An executive with a strong background in marketing, he conceived of his job as far transcending negotiating labor contracts—as, in fact, reshaping the nature of the capitalist firm itself. Quietly, he soon became the most influential American most people have never heard of. More than any other figure before him, he conceptualized a way to promote the sort of right-wing politics traditionally favored by corporate behemoths—low taxes and neutralized union power; unchallenged managerial control and freedom from government regulatory interference; a vision of American power and benevolence backstopped by a conception of the owners of capital as the exemplary citizens of the republic—as a problem in modern marketing. He conceived his most important audience as GE's 250,000 employees, their families, and the communities in which they lived. His goal was to teach them to identify their most intimate interests with the well-being of the company—and their company's with the well-being of the free world itself.

In other words, to turn millions of Americans into right-wing conservatives.

Lemuel Boulware was said by labor experts to understand the mind of the American working class better than any other executive in America. He won that knowledge by means of innovative techniques: surveys; interviews with ministers and voluntary organizations in the communities containing GE's plants; even what marketers would later call "focus groups"—gathering GE toilers before members of his staff of three thousand "job marketers" to test which messages about company benevolence and union malevolence resonated and which ones failed.

The story was sold through slogans: "The Best Balanced Interests of All"; "G.E.—The Initials of a Friend"; "Steady Jobs Through Steady Friends"; "More Sales—More Jobs—More Pay—More Earnings—More Taxes—AND MORE GOOD DONE, TOO!" A constant stream of company-sponsored newspapers and magazines published articles like "How General Electric Keeps Trying to Make Jobs Better" and "What Is Communism? What Is Capitalism? What Is the Difference to You?" and "How Big Are General Electric Profits—Are They Too Big?" (no, that was impossible; if profits were too big, the free market would punish GE when other manufacturers undercut its prices) and "The How and Why of Curbing Inflationary Settlements." (If a contract set wages any higher than what GE's benevolent management, objectively following the dictates of the competitive market, offered at the beginning of contract negotiations, it would only harm workers in the long run when the company was forced by that selfsame market to increase the price of the GE products they bought in the stores and whose profits paid their wages.)

The work drilled down to the most basic conceptions about how society ought to be organized. Every supervisor received a copy of a short book by the right-wing ideologue James Flynn, *The Road Ahead*, which argued that the New Deal was a first step toward a totalitarian nightmare. Every employee received instruction on company time in free-market economics from a specially commissioned textbook by an economics columnist who had once been a radical, Lewis Henry Haney. (Ironically, he had written the socialist economics textbook Ronald Reagan had studied in college.) It advocated repealing the 1937 law that made union organizing a right. It also included the chapter "Seven Ways to Lose Freedom or Save It." (Freedom was always on the brink of extinction.) Managers were also encouraged to convene study groups in their homes. The recommended reading included a free-market primer by the *Wall Street Journal* columnist Henry Hazlitt, called *Economics in One Lesson: The Shortest and Surest Way to Understand Basic Economics* (1946); according to Hazlitt, "economics was haunted by more fallacies than any other study known to man," put forward by political demagogues who "recommend squandering on a national scale as a way to economic salvation." One company publication ran a cartoon version of Austrian economist Friedrich von Hayek's libertarian manifesto *The Road to Serfdom.*

And then, even before *General Electric Theater* debuted on CBS one Sunday night in September 1954, another front in the Boulwarite scheme was opened up: GE's in-house movie star, swooping down on the cities, villages, and burgs containing GE plants, and getting down to the business of his life's work—charming other human beings, making them feel good.

A day might begin at, say, the Skylark Hotel in Hendersonville, North Carolina, a town where GE made outdoor lighting. (The company's expansion into under-unionized Southern states honored a theory of GE's own coinage: valuing a community's "business climate," defined as "an absence of unwarranted strikes and slowdowns," "an adequate supply of people" with "a good work attitude"—and most of all low taxes and prevailing wages.) Then came a series of fifteen-minute talks with general managers and section managers; then tours of four separate parts of the plant—doing his best to meet the eyes of the blurry figures before him (the industrial dust kept him from wearing his contact lenses). Then lunch, meaning separate fifteen-minute back-to-back sessions with hourly and salaried employees; then another factory tour; then a jaunt to the local high school for a preview of the next *GE Theater* episode for employee families; then finally an evening reception at Hendersonville Country Club, where he might avail himself in respectable mixed company of yet one more of his charming gifts: "He was the most inventive man with a dirty joke I've ever known," a GE executive along for the ride marveled. "He could clean up filthy stories and make them fit for an old nun . . . funnier than the original and it was impossible to take offense."

The format, at each gathering, was question-and-answer—which served as cues for favorite colorful (but not too colorful) Hollywood stories. He might show off his shirt, custom sewn by Jimmy Cagney's tailor to make his head look bigger on camera. That might open up to a tale of how Cagney just missed out on the role of Knute Rockne in *Knute Rockne, All American* (Coach Rockne's widow preferred Pat O'Brien). He might call forward his road manager, a former FBI agent named George Dalen, for a knockabout demonstration about how fights were staged for the camera. He might dip a toe, gingerly, in politics, relating that heroic tale about actors thwarting the Communist conspiracy to take over Hollywood—"against tremendous odds while they faced bombing of their homes, overturning of their cars, and burning of the buses that carried them through the picket lines to the lots."

Then the next stop on some yawning plant floor. The women might flock beside him, pressing mash notes into his hand, begging for autographs; the men, watching, glowered ("I bet he's a fag. . . ."). "He would carry on a conversation with the girls just so long," remembered his handler; "then he would leave them and walk over to these fellows. . . . When he left them ten minutes later, they were all slapping him on the back, saying, 'That's the way, Ron!'"

Spouting statistics, he might start in on an obsession: the nation's misperception that movie actors "live in a state of legalized prostitution because of the numerous divorces." That mind of his, always hoovering up statistics, throwing them back in a blizzard: some called it his "photographic memory." Better to say it was a preternatural confidence: details hurled forth with sufficient confidence always sound true—but "facts," in sufficient profusion, whatever their reliability, can serve as fables as well. He said the twenty-six thousand citizens of the movie colony, making up but 1 percent of Los Angeles's population, made 12 percent of its charitable contributions; that 70 percent were married and 68 percent had children and that they led the nation in adoption of children, in church membership, in the absence of crime. And in the solidity of marriage: their divorce rate was 29.9 percent. "So we're asking that you catch up with our high moral standards!" A remarkable claim to make of the homeland of Fatty Arbuckle, Errol Flynn, Lionel Barrymore—and, well, of the recently divorced contract player who kept waking up at the Garden of Allah next to starlets whose names he didn't know.

It opened him up to hecklers: *So why did you divorce Jane Wyman?* *How much are they paying you for this shit?* He learned to put them down with dispatch: *None of your business, buster!* *They haven't got enough to make me put up with you.*

He denied there was anything political about it. ("Actors are citizens and should exert those rights by speaking their minds, but the actor's first duty is to his profession. Hence, you can rest assured that I will never again run for mayor or anything but head man in my own household," he wrote in the November 1955 *Hollywood Reporter*.) But if he happened to change his mind, this was a splendid apprenticeship in retail politics. And soon an ideological apprenticeship as well. He began speaking to community groups. His other road manager, Earl Dunckel, a conservative who liked to debate his companion over politics, recollected how that began. A massive meeting of high school teachers scheduled for the Schenectady armory was on the verge of cancellation when "their speaker came down ill." That led to that speech, reported in national newspapers, in which Reagan castigated the "vicious attacks of the ultra-professional patriotic organizations that can eventually wreck our school system." Dunckel, who had no idea how to write a speech about education and so hadn't wanted to accept the invitation, remembered Reagan coming up with it on his own—and winning a ten-minute standing ovation.

Reagan himself, though, claimed an entirely different genesis for his political speeches under GE's auspices. In his account the transition took place a year later, and his account stuffed his liberalism down the memory hole. He remembered being drafted to speak to a group of employees on the subject of charity—and giving "a speech about the pride of giving and the importance of doing things without waiting for the government to do it for you," and about how "when individuals or private groups were involved in helping the needy none of the contributions were spent on overhead or administrative costs" (a nice fairy tale). "Unlike government relief programs where $2 was often spent on overhead for every $1 that went to needy people." He wrote in a memoir, "As we were driving away from the plant, the man from G.E. said, 'I didn't know you could give speeches.'"

Either way, the company started sending him out as its rhetorical ambassador.

Facing audiences primed by unceasing company propaganda to despise liberal demagogues, he found favor with them by telling tales of corporate heroes doing thankless battle with ceaseless tides of intellectual error, including some in his own beloved movie industry—for instance, tales of the "tremendous harassment" of studios by the IRS via measures like the 20 percent amusement tax and the 90 percent top marginal income tax rate. He spoke against the Justice Department's ban on "so-called block booking that splits up some of the risk in movie making"—block booking being the monopolistic practice of studios of forcing theaters to buy every one of their pictures. In a speech in Youngstown, Ohio, he called that "censorship"—a windup to a peroration about how unless Americans recognized that such injuries against one industry's liberties was an injury to all, they "might be on your doorstep next, and by then it might be too late."

Once more: freedom was always on the verge of extinction; in 1948, the predators were the tax evaders; the prey was the common man. By 1960 the lion and the lamb had switched places: now it was the likes of Standard Oil and Hollywood who were the put-upon martyrs—moral role models, in fact.

One way he found his way to this new set of identifications was psychological: the speaker pulled himself toward his audiences as much as the other way around. "An interesting thing happened," he said of these conclaves of people he might once have judged to be off-putting Babbitts: "No matter where I was, I'd find people from the audience waiting to talk to me after a speech and they'd all say, 'Hey, if you think things are bad in your business, let me tell you what is happening in my business. . . .' I'd listen and they'd cite examples of government interference and snafus and complain how bureaucrats, through overregulation, were telling them how to run their businesses." He adjusted course to better solicit their approbation. This was how he became a hero among the new company he kept.

Another contributing factor: the spokesman was afraid of flying on airplanes. ("I've decided," he wrote to the GE executive who accompanied him during his first two years, Dunckel, decades later, "that I am not going to say I get on planes, I'm just going to say—I wear them.") He was a voracious reader. So the cross-country Super Chief train became his study room. He pored over right-wing fare: William F. Buckley's new biweekly, *National Review* (Reagan was a charter subscriber); *Human Events,* the gut-punching conservative activist newsletter; his old favorite, *Reader's Digest,* more and more given over to horror stories of the H. R. Gross variety about government programs as well-intended sinkholes of waste, fraud, folly, and abuse. He also read books, the sort of books the GE managers read in living-room study groups alongside their wives and neighbors. He called it "a postgraduate course in political science."

One of the books that made an impression on him was Hazlitt's *Economics in One Lesson.* The one lesson, which opened that slim volume as an overture, was only two pages long—though the author said it could also be reduced to a sentence: "The art of economics consists in looking not merely at the immediate but at the longer effect of any policy; it consists of tracing the consequences of that policy not merely for one group but for all groups." The rest was but commentary. For example, in chapter four, Hazlitt wrote of how "taxation for public housing . . . destroys as many jobs in other lines as it creates in housing," in the form of "unbuilt private homes, in unmade washing machines and refrigerators." The Tennessee Valley Authority was Hazlitt's example par excellence of the calamities would-be do-gooders wrought, because of all the "private power plants, the private homes, the typewriters and television sets that were never allowed to come into existence because of the money that was taken from people all over the country to build the photogenic Norris Dam." Beware liberal demagogues bearing gifts. They would bring us an apocalypse that would become evident only when it was too late—but not if patriots sounded the tocsin while they still stood a chance.

And so Ronald Reagan began sounding that tocsin, with the energy of an erupting volcano.

One time, his next GE handler marveled, he did it Mr. Smith–style, before an audience of startled schoolchildren he happened upon after asking for a tour of the Rhode Island state capitol in Providence. His handler remembered the words indelibly:

"If we believe nothing is worth dying for, when did this begin?"

(He waved at the glorious Early Republic edifice before them.)

"Should Moses have told the children of Israel to live in slavery rather than dare the wilderness?

"You and I, my friend, have a rendezvous with destiny," he said soaringly. This was striking: it paraphrased the peroration Franklin Roosevelt had given at his inauguration in June 1936. He concluded, "If we flop, at least our kids could say of us that we justified our brief moment here, 'We did all that could be done.'"

GENERAL ELECTRIC THEATER'S EPISODES ENCODED AN IDEOLOGY IN themselves: its writers devised the most extraordinary conundrums—comic ones, dramatic ones, whichever—each and every time resolving them within the half hour, in perfect expression of that 1950s faith that nothing, anything, need ever remain in friction in the nation God had ordained to benevolently bestride the world.

Then, in mid-story, those commercials. For instance, amid a 1955 episode in which Reagan starred in a melodrama on the Irish civil war, "G.E. Progress Report" correspondent Don Herbert (who'd formerly starred in a show called *Watch Mr. Wizard*) explained to an agog little boy the great strides GE was making on a new technology, "transistors," which might someday produce TVs with flat screens and radios smaller than cigarette packs:

"Where's my Dick Tracy wrist radio?"

"Not so fast! Right now the armed forces have first call on miniaturization developments. It might take ten years before we have them in our homes. But General Electric scientists are always looking for new ways to make living easier and more comfortable."

"And more fun!"

"That's right, Billy. And all that adds up to progress. And at General Electric, progress is our most important product!"

Or the ones that took the viewer, literally, into Ronald and Nancy Reagan's home. This was another facet of the GE corporate culture: the company, in Barton's coinage, as "the headquarters of progress." At the 1939 World's Fair in New York, GE sponsored an "all-electric home" with a "Magic Kitchen that moves, talks, and tells a timely story." Now the Magic Kitchen was in Pacific Palisades, and it starred a handsome movie couple and their cute little kids.

What a historian has called TV's first reality series began in the second season, when his "total electric house," housing "television's first all-electric family," was still under construction. Reagan strolled around the site as his electrical contractor demonstrated how you, the viewer, might wire your property for "full house power." Nancy, in her first screen role since *Donovan's Brain,* broke comically into her husband's technical meanderings to deliver the bottom line for the ladies: "Well I'm glad we have it. Because we're going to have some wonderful electric equipment and we want to have all the entertainment and pleasure and comfort out of that equipment that we can!"

In 1957, the Western *Too Good with a Gun* cross-fades to Don Herbert:

"Tonight we're going visiting at the Ronald Reagans' again, in their new home, to see how their many wonderful electrical servants are helping them, just as they'll help you *live better electrically*!"

Cue Nancy and four-year-old Patti, and the "perfect meal" courtesy of GE's "electrical servants": a toaster oven for the English muffins covered in melted cheese, an automatically timed electric skillet that "makes a tricky dish like soufflé 'easy and safe to make'"—"My electrical appliances do everything!"

(In actuality Nancy didn't cook. Or, as a fan magazine item on their courtship had put it, "Nancy knits Reagan argyle socks, though she doesn't cook for him. Her talent in the kitchen doesn't equal her talent before the cameras, concerning which her boss, Dore Schary says, 'she's a fine actress.'")

Patti, adorably: "What's elesses apolotz?"

"They're all the things around the house that make Mommy's work easier.' . . . One at a time or all together, they make quite a difference in the way we live. That's why every housewife wants them, the latest models with the newest improvements."

Ronnie: "Because she knows that you really begin to live when you live better—"

Patti: "—Eletriffly!"

A market research company studying "impact scores" called *GE Theater* "the leading institutional campaign on television for selling ideas to the public." *TV Guide* called its leading salesman "the ambassador of all things mechanical." A retracting patio canopy roof. A painting of a sailboat that slid to one side to reveal a "projection machine for home movies." Something called a "garbage disposal." A wall cabinet hiding a "high fidelity." (Nancy: "It's almost as if the orchestra were playing right here in the living room"; Ronnie: "There's no trick to it; it's just a matter of starting in easy stages, one item at a time.") "Everything electric but the chair," went Reagan's own joke. Or the one about the guy who watched too much *GE Theater*. "I didn't really need a nuclear submarine," he said. "But I've got one now."

WITHIN A YEAR OF HIS GE DEBUT HE SHARED MASTER-OF-CEREMONY DU-ties with Art Linkletter for the most-watched live television broadcast in history, the grand opening of Disneyland (Reagan introduced Walt Disney). In 1957, when the legendary host of *This Is Your Life,* Ralph Edwards, missed a show for the first time in seventeen years, it was Reagan who filled in for him. He made a triumphant return to deliver the commencement address to Eureka College's Class of 1958. ("This is a land of destiny," he said, "and our forefathers found their way here by some divine system of selective service—gathered here to fulfill a mission to advance man a further step in his climb from the swamps.") That was the year a survey found that Reagan had one of the most recognized names in the country. His corporate Medici had delivered him. In turn, the thrum of corporate life itself came to delight him.

"Reagan Says Business Beats Hollywood at Its Own Game," ran one profile headline. "The Actor in the Gray Flannel Suit," ran another. "Ronald Reagan is one of the few actors in Hollywood who always carries two brief cases," that profile reported. "One of them is jammed with scripts, the other thick with business correspondence and memos." Corporate titans had become his new heroes, his new role models—his new cowboys. They also became his social intimates. That contributed to the ideological transformation, too.

Nancy Reagan had applied herself to an aspiration: to join the ranks of Los Angeles society—the Beverly Hills types with a traditional distaste for sullying their ranks by seeking picture folks out. So Nancy sought them out: sending Patti in 1956 to prekindergarten at the exclusive John Thomas Dye School in Bel Air; telling the proprietress of her favorite Beverly Hills boutique, Amelia Gray, "I'd like to meet some girls out of the picture industry"; charming the ladies she met in said boutiques, such as Betty Adams, scion of one of Los Angeles's first families, and seeking to insinuate her family into their circles—and, soon, famously, succeeding.

Adams hosted a dinner party to introduce "Ronnie and Nancy" to the likes of the Wilsons and the Bloomingdales and the Jorgensens—

Betty Wilson and Bill Wilson, whose father in 1913 founded Pennzoil; Betsy Bloomingdale and Alfred Bloomingdale, president of Diners Club, heir to the department store fortune; Marion Jorgensen and Earle Jorgensen, steel and aluminum magnate. Soon she was prowling the boutiques with the former model and legendary clotheshorse Harriet Deutsch, whose husband, Armand, was grandson of the founder of Sears and reputedly its biggest stockholder. The Reagans began hosting regular barbecues for a tight-knit cadre—"The Group"—of eighteen plutocrats and their society wives, and star couples including the Bill Holdens, the George Burnses, the Jack Bennys. (Benny, for some reason, tabbed Reagan with the nickname "the Governor.")

Maybe it had something to do with his especially close bond with Walter Annenberg, whom Reagan had first met in 1937 when the young publishing heir was running *Screen Guide* and they competed for the same woman. Now with his wife, Lee (Annenberg, like Ronnie, called his wife "Mother"), he owned one of the greatest private art collections in the world, was plumping for Richard Nixon for president as one of the Republican Party's most generous benefactors, and published *TV Guide*—which featured its publisher's dear friends on the cover in November 1958, relaxing in front of a barn with an adorable collie in tow, Ronnie boasting inside about the small profit he made each year in his horse breeding business, reflecting on the secret of *General Electric Theater*'s consistent spot high up the ratings—"keeping the show on an intimate basis where the star is playing to one viewer. There has to be a feeling between the two"—and chuckling about the days when he used to be a liberal: "When you're younger, you have fiery ideas."

He was forty-seven—a conservative now. Given the way he thought about the world, Boulwarism was the perfect conduit: through its sluices, he absorbed a right-wing politics that imagined no necessity for class conflict at all. A perfect conservatism for Ronald Reagan, who hated acknowledging friction—like when he said there need be no conflict in the Hollywood strike, that SAG could simply declare "neutrality" and be done with it; and when he called the blanket waiver he granted MCA a deal that helped everyone in Hollywood. Conflict was always, ever, just something introduced from the outside by alien forces (liberals, Communists), who revealed themselves, in that very act of disturbance, as aliens, enemies to all that was good and true, natural and right. That was how Reagan saw the world. This was how he radiated the aura that made others feel so good.

· · ·

THE TIMING OF HIS IDEOLOGICAL MATURATION WAS PROPITIOUS. BY 1958, the contradictions between the social vision of America's ascendant labor movement—that the individual was best dignified by removing him from the vagaries of market competition—and the vision of corporate barons like GE's—that market competition was precisely what produced individual dignity—seemed to be approaching a pitch near to civil war. Conservatives put antiunion "right to work" initiatives on the ballot in seven states; the AFL-CIO's Committee on Political Education promised its most aggressive electoral drive in history to defeat them. Lemuel Boulware, for his part, convened a historic meeting on a resort island off Florida with like-minded executives from a number of companies to strategize about how they might launch a coordinated national crusade to persuade "vast numbers of other businessmen to rise publicly to defend us when we are under attack," to make producing a healthy "business climate" not just a question for siting General Electric factories, but part of a twilight struggle against the ruinous liberal demagogues in communities everywhere.

For Boulware, moving businessmen into national politics fulfilled an ambition of long standing. "We businessmen are bold and imaginative before commercial competition," as he put it in a widely republished 1949 speech. "We are cowardly and silent in public when confronted with union and other economic and political doctrines contrary to our belief." He was determined they be cowardly no more. "No one," he complained, "seems to be willing to go through the agony of trying to put what we think is right and what we instinctively know is right into language that is intelligible and convincing to the great mass of citizens who at the moment are being lied to by their government and by their unions." Words like these made an enormous impression on his Hollywood ambassador, who was saying almost identical things decades later in speeches as governor to organizations like the National Association of Manufacturers: "It is time for business to start presenting the facts, because the facts are on your side. But, for heaven's sake, don't just repeat them to each other by way of your trade journals. Tell the people, and especially your customers and your employers—and usually they are one and the same—and tell our sons and daughters."

That was in 1972. But he said it first as General Electric's coast-to-coast ambassador from Hollywood. His responsibilities for the company thus grew; the company's relationship with the star became more intimate. More and more, broadcast episodes bore his personal stamp. For the Easter Sunday episode in 1958, for instance, he found a role he told the press was one of the three best he ever had. As the *Miami News* announced it, "Ronald Reagan, personification of the All-American male, gets a reprieve from 'nice guy' roles in the April 6 'General Electric Theater.' He'll play a Skid Row drunk." In the episode, called "No Hiding Place" he played a real-life figure who picks himself out of the gutter and develops a 90 percent success rate saving others from alcoholism. (The script adamantly refused the teachings of his own mother concerning his father, and also the conclusion of Alcoholics Anonymous, that alcohol addiction was a disease. It also eschewed AA's vision of recovery as a complex, fundamentally communal process, the hero preaching instead that addiction was a "a vice . . . acquired as any other vice is acquired," that "you will it on yourself," and that recovery was a simple matter of bootstrapping willpower—enabled, though, by the intervention of the character played by Ronald Reagan, achieving onscreen what he could not achieve as a child: a heroic rescue. It was perhaps the deepest reflection Reagan ever offered the public on his father's affliction.) And, more and more, he was drafted as the company's *ideological* ambassador in the media.

"I have to say," he said in 1958 on the country's most respected syndicated radio interview program (whose host pronounced his name correctly), "from the standpoint of labor, that General Electric has issued quite a challenge. Organized labor had better look around and review their own attitudes, in the face of this very enlightened attitude toward the people who work for them." He plied this ideology now in speaking assignments before civic clubs and for business organizations like the California Fertilizer Association and the National Electrical Contractors Association:

"We can lose our freedom at once by succumbing to Russia or we can lose it gradually by installments—the end result is slavery."

"There can be no moral justification of the progressive tax—an idea hatched in the Communist revolution."

"Get any proposed program accepted, then with the participation of government in the field established, work for expansion, always aiming at the ultimate goal—a government that will someday be Big Brother to us all."

In another speech, this one to GE workers, he spoke of how there were more federal employees "than there are farmers in the U.S."; that taxes ate up 27 percent of a gallon of gas and 34 percent of your phone bill—and that, yet, "we have been told by economists down through the years that if the total tax burden ever reaches 25 percent, we are in danger of undermining our private enterprise system." The litany sounded a hell of a lot better when GE's salaried, pompadoured charmer said it than when it came from some stern-sounding boss.

"UNDERMININE OUR PRIVATE ENTERPRISE SYSTEM." HERE WAS AN IRONY: the high tide of Boulwarism coincided, in the early 1950s and early '60s, with a series of federal indictments of General Electric executives for a conspiracy to fix prices. They had schemed with other electrical manufacturing firms to remove from the exigencies of the marketplace the prices of everything from two-dollar insulators to multimillion-dollar hydroelectric turbines. As a historian of GE explained, the men who ran GE "took a dim view of competition."

In 1960, GE's first strike since 1946 loomed. That same year Reagan earned a promotion. After years of enjoying an informal role in script selection and cast recruitment, he was officially named a producer. Simultaneously, his profile as a political troubador increased. "Boyish of face and gleaming of tooth, Ronald Reagan earned a reputation, among cinemagoers as a pleasant young man in white ducks, whose deepest thought was reserved for the next dance," *Time* magazine explained four months into John F. Kennedy's term, its first mention of Reagan outside the context of acting. "Once an outspoken Democrat, Reagan is now a staunch Republican [and] has developed into a remarkably active spokesman for conservatism." More and more, he devoted his *spare* time to crisscrossing the nation preaching genial hellfire about the nine years America had left before it was all slave or all free, about federal aid to education as a "tool of tyranny," and about welfare recipients as "a faceless mass waiting for a handout." He also volunteered his services to the American Medical Association's Boulware-style lobbying campaign against President Kennedy's plan for government health insurance for the elderly. For what the AMA's strategists labeled "Operation Coffee Cup," Reagan recorded a speech on an LP to be played at housewives' gatherings. In it, he proclaimed that "Medicare" was but an opening wedge for a government takeover of "every area of freedom as we have known in this country." First the federal government would assign where doctors would be allowed to live. Then—who knows? "We are going to spend our sunset years telling our children and our children's children what it was like in America when men were free."

But the company itself grew more cautious about taking on the government as its legal troubles deepened. And it was GE's star propagandist who ended up in the crosshairs. Sometimes Reagan pointed to the Tennessee Valley Authority as the most glaring example available to those seeking to rescue a nation giving up its freedom on the installment plan, just as he'd learned from one of Lem Boulware's favorite books, *Economics in One Lesson*. But the TVA bought its turbines for its massive dams from GE. In his first memoir Reagan describes an awkward conversation with GE's CEO Ralph Cordiner, filled with long pauses, that concluded with Reagan asking, "Mr. Cordiner, what would you say if I said I could make my speech just as effectively without mentioning TVA?" He replied, "Well, it would make my job easier." Reagan dropped TVA from the speech.

At first the company had appeared to be either indifferent to or approving of his extracurricular activities. And with his newfound power he began using *GE Theater* to aggressively evangelize the notion that the Red conspiracy was burrowing within America's institutions as assiduously as it ever had been when he first took up arms against the Communist plot to take over Hollywood. The eighth season opened in September 1961 with Reagan starring as a Russian officer in Soviet-occupied Hungary ordered to break the spirit of a freedom-loving village. His conscience wracked, steely, trembling, Bogart-like, the officer announces his conversion in a melodramatic closing peroration: "In all my life I never knew freedom. Until I saw you lose yours. But you'll win it again. And maybe next time—you'll win it for all of us."

In March 1962 Reagan produced a two-part adaptation of a memoir, *I Was a Spy: The Story of a Brave Housewife*, which told the story a suburban mother, Marion Miller, who in 1950 stumbled into an apparently innocuous meeting of a "Committee for the Protection of the Foreign Born" and discovered it was but a front for what Joseph McCarthy had called that year a "conspiracy on a scale so immense as to dwarf any previous such venture in the history of man." The claim was absurd at the moment McCarthy made it: the American Communist Party that Miller went on to infiltrate on behalf of the FBI had long ago been all but abandoned by the USSR, which had entirely rolled up its espionage networks in America in the wake of the spy scandals of the late 1940s. American Communists were so diminished that soon after, by one estimate, such FBI infiltrators made up 17 percent of the total membership. It was even more absurd in its 1962 incarnation on *GE Theater*. The piece was set in the present, when there were practically no Communists left in America, but that didn't matter; hadn't Hoover said in 1947 that the number of Communists was not relevant, given "the enthusiasm and ironclad discipline under which they operate," their ideology "a condition akin to a disease that spreads like an epidemic"?

To those not inside the far right, "My Dark Days" must have resembled a *Twilight Zone* hijack of a situation comedy starring Donna Reed.

A party leader pays the Millers' home a visit just as their little girl comes out in her nightgown: "Mommy? You said you'd come out and listen to my prayers." "*Prayers?*" the commissar storms, then interrogates the little girl to get her to rat out her parents' ideological deviation.

Next, a comrade is forced to choose between his party membership and his non-Communist girlfriend:

"You can't *live* without love," she implores him.

"I can't quit the party. It would be like cutting out a piece of myself. I'd walk the earth like a ghost for the rest of my life."

He decides, once and for all, in favor of the revolution, and leaves his girlfriend's apartment.

"Jane!! No!!"

She leaps from a window to her death.

"I didn't leave the Democratic Party," Ronald Reagan used to like to say. "The Democratic Party left me." It was another Reagan story that dissolved the more closely it was examined. Once again, the platform JFK ran on in 1960 was well to the right of the one Reagan eagerly boomed out on the radio in 1948. (Kennedy just wanted government health insurance for the aged; Truman wanted it to be universal.) Another major difference, however, between Democrats then and Democrats beginning with Joe McCarthy's fall in the middle of the 1950s, when Reagan was joining up with GE, was that they had largely abandoned the good-versus-evil narrative of an invisible Bolshevik bacillus insinuating itself into a great but complacent nation's bloodstream. Respectable Democrats by Kennedy's day (those, at least, outside the reactionary Deep South) considered that an embarrassing relic of a too-paranoid time.

Ronald Reagan did not. And it is hard to see how Reagan could feel at home in a party that had abandoned a core tenet in his moral vision of the world and his own heroic place in it. Instead, his was now the sort of conservatism associated with the John Birch Society, whose McCarthy-like claim that Dwight D. Eisenhower had been a "conscious agent of the Communist conspiracy" had made that organization a national scandal, denounced by both Democrats and Republicans like Richard Nixon. But Reagan said he could find no "moral justification for repudiating" the Birchers. Indeed, he had adopted many of their nostrums as favorite speech lines. One was "The inescapable truth is that we are at war, and we are losing that war simply because we don't or won't realize we are in it. We have ten years. Not ten years to make up our mind, but ten years to win or lose—by 1970 the world will be all slave or all free." Another was a bogus quote attributed to Nikita Khrushchev:

"You Americans are so gullible. No, you won't accept communism outright. But we'll keep feeding you small doses of socialism until you finally wake up and find you already have communism. We won't have to fight you; we'll so weaken your economy until you fall like overripe fruit into our hands." Reagan gave one speech in 1961 insisting Communists were still "infiltrating all phases of the government." Senator Frank Church of Idaho earnestly wrote to J. Edgar Hoover to ask if he had any information supporting Reagan's charges. Reagan gave another speech to a convention of supermarket executives arguing that the Communist Party, "crawling out from under the rocks," had "ordered once again the infiltration" of the movie industry. This time, it was Hoover himself making the inquiries—once more sending agents to Ronald Reagan's home. He told the G-men he had been misquoted, but that there was still cause for concern—"one can smell a situation once it starts to develop."

And in the spring of 1962, the place he smelled it was in Hollywood's reaction to "My Dark Days."

An FBI document recorded that Reagan was the only producer to show interest in Marion Miller's story; its absurd excesses were surely the reason (the episode's director was so embarrassed by the prayer scene he fought unsuccessfully to have it cut), but Reagan blamed Reds. "On our producing staff the liberal view that communism is only something the 'Right-wingers' dreamed up prevails and they literally resorted to sabotage to pull the punch out of the show," he wrote to Lorraine Wagner. Even worse, someone sabotaged the broadcast. "In one place," he wrote to her, "there was sound but no picture."

Reagan was now a first citizen in the sort of circles that lionized Marion Miller and her husband (who had actually himself, the show did not reveal, been an undercover federal agent since 1939). They showered her with so many testimonials, awards, and patriotic medals that an ad for the next edition of her book called her "the most decorated housewife in the nation." She was one of those "professional patriots" he had tongue-lashed so passionately in 1954. And now, so was he. They shared stages, especially in the McCarthyite petri dish of Orange County, California—for instance, before 17,500 on "youth night" of the Southern California School of Anti-Communism, sponsored by the Australian physician Dr. Fred Schwartz, who preached how the Russians had mastered the techniques of animal husbandry to addle the will of their subject populations. Another man who spoke at the rally was a lawyer—Jane Wyman's divorce lawyer, as it happened—named Loyd Wright, who raised the roof by demanding a "preventive war": issue an ultimatum to the Soviet Union to leave Eastern Europe by a certain date, he proposed; and if it didn't, unleash the nuclear arsenal. "If we have to blow up Moscow, that's too bad."

It was around then that the star's next humiliation unfolded.

BY THE WEEK OF THE BROADCAST OF THE FIRST OF TWO EPISODES OF "MY Dark Days," Reagan learned *General Electric Theater* was in danger of not being renewed for its ninth season. In an interview with the *Boston Globe*'s TV columnist, he blithely chalked it up to vagaries in the executive suites: "CBS is doing all sorts of shuffling of schedules and feels we should move to another day." Instead, it ended up canceled altogether. What was really being discussed in those executive suites? No one ever came to know. There was the story, endlessly recycled, that made of Ronald Reagan a heroic martyr to principle: that he kept on hammering the Tennessee Valley Authority, until his bosses had no choice but to fire him. There is no evidence this was ever the case—not even from Ronald Reagan, who related in *Where's the Rest of Me?* how he obediently began omitting mention of TVA in his speeches the first time that his bosses asked.

A better explanation is Medicare. In June 1961, when Democrats in Congress decided to postpone action on Kennedy's bill because of the volume of angry constituent mail against it, the muckraking columnist Drew Pearson sourced the flood tide directly to Operation Coffee Cup, and claimed that "thanks to a deal with the AMA and the acquiescence of General Electric, Ronald Reagan may be able to out-influence the President of the United States." Reagan wrote an angry letter to Pearson: "I told your representative clearly and categorically that General Electric was not consulted in the matter, did not 'acquiesce' and in short had nothing at all to do with it." It was a very sensitive moment in the history of General Electric's relations with Washington: that summer, the company agreed to pay $7,448,000 in damages to the federal government to settle price-fixing suits.

That same summer, 1962, Loyd Wright ran in a three-way Republican senatorial nomination contest, becoming known as the "John Birch Society" candidate; Reagan served as his campaign chair. Also that summer, according to Reagan, he got a call asking him to limit his talks to commercial pitches for GE products—no politics. Shortly thereafter, he got twenty-four hours' notice that *General Electric Theater* was canceled. An anthology show hosted by Jack Webb, *G.E. True*, began running in its old Sunday night slot that fall, lasting only for one season. But ratings were never Ronald Reagan's problem. Ideology was—or at least the opening episode of *G.E. True* suggested it was: as if in absolution, the story General Electric now presented to the nation was not one of anti-Communist freedom fighters in Hungary nor heroic FBI spies infilitrating the Communist conpsiracy, but a lionization of the left-wing icon Clarence Darrow.

Later, to his daughter Maureen, Reagan told a heroic story about what had happened: a friend had informed him of rumors that the federal government had threatened to cancel its contracts with GE unless he was fired; he checked out the rumor with his boss, who told him that it was true but that the company would not be blackmailed. "'Wait a minute,' dad said back without stopping to think about it," Maureen Reagan wrote in her memoir. "'There are an awful lot of people whose paychecks depend on those contracts. I appreciate your standing up for me, I really do, but I can't abide that.'" He said he offered to quit. However, at the time, he told other stories. He announced that the AFL-CIO "had tagged me as a strident voice of right wing extremism, and under the accepted liberal practice of the end justifying the means, proceeded to issue bulletins long on name-calling and short on truth." He hinted at Communist involvement. He blamed Bobby Kennedy. "Government contracts," he told his teenage son Michael at the dinner table. "This is exactly what I've been out there speaking about. We're on our way to a controlled society. The government is trying to control everything. And Robert Kennedy is behind the attack on me. . . . Because I'm speaking out against the Kennedy Administration and the road they're trying to lead us down."

His wife chimed in: "*Of course* Bobby Kennedy's behind it. It's obvious."

HOWEVER IT HAPPENED, HE NOW HAD LOST A $125,000 SALARY, AND bookings scheduled years into the future. Another professional humiliation. He picked up the occasional commercial, odd jobs like hosting the Rose Bowl Parade, episodes on TV series like *Wagon Train*. Then once more politics saved him.

That fall, he chaired Democrats for Nixon on behalf of Nixon's run for California governor. His anger at his martyrdom fueled him, and vaulted him into conservative movement superstardom—until he was as busy as before. In Long Island, in 1963, Young Americans for Freedom honored him in a rally that drew thirteen thousand people. That summer he began working on his first book. In 1964 he took on working toward Barry Goldwater's presidential nomination practically as a full-time job. The reviews, it turned out, were more spectacular than any he had received in his life: "I think it would have been better if Ronald Reagan had just talked, and Goldwater had just sat there and nodded," one conservative said at the Republican convention that summer in San Francisco. That fall, he picked up host duties for another anthology show, replacing a wizened coot known to the world only as the "Old Ranger." *Death Valley Days* hacked out cheap half-hour Westerns. Syndicated, often running late at night, it was sponsored not by one of America's most majestic corporate citizens but by a brand of soap, Borax.

That meant the image lingering in citizens' minds when he began his political career was of Reagan in Western garb reciting silly sloganeering nonsense about "20-Mule Team Borax"—that, and the image of a sadistic cad smacking around a girl. For he finally landed a meaty roll, his first in decades, in the nifty existentialist crime caper *The Killers*, the very first movie in history produced for broadcast on TV. But it turned out to be far too violent to *show* on TV. It played in theaters instead, where, for the first and last time in his acting career, he played not a rescuer but a bad guy—one whom another bad guy laid flat with a punch. He regretted taking that role for the rest of his life.

And then, on October 27, 1964, with dazzling quickness, the rest of his life began. Barry Goldwater's rich California backers prevailed upon the Goldwater campaign to put on TV the speech Reagan had been giving for years, repurposed for the Republican nominee, to raise money for the flagging presidential campaign. "You and I," he said, "have a rendezvous with destiny. We will preserve for our children, this the last best hope on earth, or we will sentence them to take the first step into a thousand years of darkness." David Broder called it "the most successful national political debut since William Jennings Bryan electrified the 1896 Democratic Convention with the 'Cross of Gold' speech."

He was now a conservative *superstar*. Two years later, he was governor of the nation's largest and richest state. And by 1975, after eight years in office, he was ready to meet his next rendezvous with destiny—ministering to a wounded nation's soul.

CHAPTER EIGHTEEN

Governing

WHEN REAGAN GAVE HIS SPEECH FOR GOLDWATER THE DONATIONS IT brought in erased the deficit of the Goldwater campaign. People started asking their conservative friends, Why wasn't this guy the candidate? And almost before the broadcast was over, Reagan's rich businessmen friends—his "kitchen cabinet"—began putting together an organization to slate him for the 1966 governor's race. He spent six months in 1965 giving speeches around the state, testing the waters; finding them warm, he entered in January with an extraordinary, unprecedented TV show, complete with theme music that sounded like *Leave It to Beaver* and a title graphic (RONALD REAGAN AND A NEED FOR ACTION! over a map of the state). Just as he once did for General Electric, he warmly invited viewers into his home—smiling, be-suited, with one of his trademark pocket silks, again not looking all that different from his first screen appearance leaning jauntily against the camera in a tweed three-piece suit, holding a fedora, in that 1937 trailer for *Love Is on the Air.*

He began, amiably, telling stories from his six-month tour: "I've been on a California street 8,000 feet above sea level, and one below sea level. I've thrown a snowball and watched water-skiers, all in the same day. And I haven't begun to cover the state. Actually I think you could spend a lifetime just seeing and getting to know California...." He picked up a ketchup bottle from a table beside him, like in a TV commercial, with a professional's skill so as to obscure the brand logo, the camera pulling back to show a roaring fire behind him and a leather easy chair to his right: "A ketchup bottle is a pretty commonplace item. But when the secretary of labor and our own state government finished their experiments in reform among farm workers and canceled out the Bracero program, there were twenty-eight million fewer of these manufactured in one plant in Oakland...."

How unlikely was it when this movie-star-cum-pitchman won the nomination that spring against a well-liked pillar of the Republican establishment? So unlikely that a *Washington Star* columnist reported an "air of furtive jubilation at Lassie for Governor headquarters," and *Esquire* said, "The Republican Party isn't bankrupt, or isn't that bankrupt that it has to turn to Liberace for leadership." How unlikely was it that he could survive a general election campaign? Richard Nixon had some thoughts about that. He sent a young aide to take some notes to Reagan for his political coming-out before the National Press Club in Washington. Reagan ignored the advice, and virtually charmed his audience out of their doubts—and after Reagan won the general election, on a platform of singeing student protesters and foregrounding the menace to law and order represented by liberal social programs, Nixon ended up borrowing the themes for his own 1968 campaign. Nixon's presumed student was actually the master.

When Reagan became governor in 1967, the shock for his skeptics was simply this: that the antigovernment supposed incompetent actually governed. "Amazingly enough," *Newsweek* reported upon completion of his first hundred days, the "host of *Death Valley Days* has managed to close one of the widest credibility gaps any politician ever faced." And after he left office in 1975, the postmortems from the guardians of elite discourse were much the same. Elizabeth Drew wrote in the *New Yorker* that "he was a reasonably competent governor of California and that his administration was more progressive than his political rhetoric suggested"; Richard Reeves observed that he had proved himself "passive, moderate, and moderately effective" at providing "big government as usual."

They were not wrong. As governor, Reagan consistently proposed just the sort of conservative policies he had campaigned on—most controversially, immediately upon his ascension, a 10 percent across-the-board cut in the budgets of every state department. And when passage of radical notions like this proved impractical (indiscriminate 10 percent cuts turned out to be a novice's fantasy, given that much of the state budget was hemmed in by federal and state statutes he had no power to change), he changed course, moved on, learned, and adjusted, gladly dropping right-wing orthodoxy when more pragmatic solutions presented themselves. He felt out the status of institutional and popular power for and against his preferred nostrums, playing things by ear. Democrats controlled both houses of the legislature, and in negotiations he took his adversaries seriously, respectfully, and tried to get the best deal he could. He wanted to succeed, to chalk up accomplishments. Indeed, he frustrated conservative purists to such a degree that in 1971 some of them even launched a recall movement, calling him a "discredit to the American spirit, to the West, and to our California heritage."

But Elizabeth Drew and Richard Reeves were not entirely right. Their assessments did not nearly convey the whole story. He was, yes, pragmatic like any successful politician. But the way he did it was different. When he made compromises, he always insisted that they were only tactical and technical—and always, he would say afterward, the fault of someone else: Democrats, generally; liberals, specifically. His rhetorical habit of parsing the world into black-and-white persisted when he became a governing executive. It some ways, it even deepened.

For instance, he had affected horror at a demand from the state legislature in 1971 to make tax collection more efficient by withholding payments automatically from paychecks: "Taxes should hurt," he said, insisting, "My feet are in concrete." He proved able to loosen his feet from that concrete, giving in—then, when the 1972 tax bill he signed brought an unexpected revenue windfall, the $851 million state budgetary surplus it produced became his marquee boast, even though it came largely from reforms in the collection of revenue that he had so adamantly opposed. And the increased money flowing into state coffers also became Exhibit A in proving government was a devouring Gila monster. Indeed, it was the foundational argument for his Proposition 1 tax limitation initiative.

These claims were contradictory. Reagan was opportunistic that way—and rhetorically successful in his opportunism. He proved gifted at jumbling budgetary statistics. "Five years ago our state budget was second in size to the federal government," he said in 1971. (Why shouldn't it be? California was the largest state.) "Today, we are fourth—behind the federal government, New York State, and New York City. Five years ago, there were 102,456 full-time Civil Service employees on the state payroll. When we ended the fiscal year in June there were 101,399, or 1,066 fewer than when we started." It all made his accomplishments sound very . . . Reaganite. What it obscured, though, was that he inherited a $4.6 billion state budget in 1967, and left behind one of $10.2 billion in 1975. And that the average individual Californian's tax burden when he took office was $426, but when he left it was almost double that, $728. But here was the gift: he could claim that this only proved his point—that Sacramento and Washington, whose top-down dictates to states could always be offered as excuses, were intractable puzzle palaces, defying the people's will at ever turn.

When worse came to worst—as when he signed the nation's most liberal abortion law—he might claim an offending passage had been slipped in at the last minute. Excuses were always readily on offer— excuses that ended up making his rhetorical position stronger instead of weaker. Because liberals were furtive and diabolical in ways unsullied innocents could not comprehend.

He framed economy measures, where he achieved them, not just as cost savings, but as shimmering moral advances—for instance his success paring the budget of the state's mental health system. It was, his budget aides suggested, one area where a 10 percent reduction could easily be realized—given that the number of mental patients was already plummeting due to new medical advances like tranquilizing drugs. First in 1967, and then again in 1972, thousands of positions were eliminated from the state's Department of Mental Hygiene. He called that in a 1972 speech a "new approach to the treatment of the mentally ill that has reduced the number of patients sentenced to a hopeless life in our asylums from 16,500 to 7,000"; and who could object to that? Harried, baffled psychiatrists, it turned out, one of whom later recollected how "Reagan with one bold, brilliant stroke abolished mental illness in California," and hospital staffs were required to turn away the most broken people imaginable: "Back to violent alcoholic families. Back to angry spouses . . . to rag-filled grocery carts . . . to sleeping in moldering cars. Back to the community of cocaine-crazed friends and pitiless dealers awaiting them outside the hospital gates." The apparent earlier, salutary decline in mental patients requiring hospitalization, it turned out, had been a mirage—because the ones who were left were the ones unresponsive to the new procedures, and had always required by far the most care. The hospitals themselves had always been understaffed in the first place. The reductions were a plain and simple nightmare. And yet Reagan proved able to blithely deny a problem existed. When a visiting expert from Sweden called a ward in Sonoma County the worst he had seen in several countries, the governor accused the staff there of having "rigged" the poor conditions to sabotage his planned cutbacks. "We lead the nation in the quality of our mental patient care," he simply said, "and we will keep that lead."

To claim a mere mixed success was never enough. Take, for example, the time he set his mind for his second term to reform California's welfare system, which he called "a cancer that is destroying those it should succor and threatening society itself." And it was true the welfare system in California was broken, from whatever ideological position one viewed it. Leftists could point out that benefits had not been raised since 1957—$172 for a family of three when the minimum subsistence income in San Francisco was $271. Conservatives could point out that the number of recipients had exploded from 357,00 in 1963 to 1,566,000 in 1970—an unquestionably unsustainable rate of increase.

But when the process of reforming the system began, the debate soon broke down in a tangle of mutual public recrimination between Reagan and liberals who distrusted his claimed desire to "adequately provide for the truly needy." The impasse was magnanimously broken by his rival, assembly speaker Bob Moretti, who offered to begin negotiations anew even though he held a controlling majority in the legislature. The two sides sat down for two weeks of intense talks, which began each day at 9 A.M. and lasted some nights until after dark. The resulting bill Reagan signed was a genuine compromise product—and, according to an independent analysis published six years later, a genuine success.

The resulting statistics thereafter became a staple of his campaign rhetoric: "When I came into office, California was the welfare capital of the nation. Sixteen percent of all those receiving welfare in the country were in California. The caseload was increasing 40,000 a month. We turned that increase into an 8,000 a month decrease. We returned to the taxpayers $2 billion and we increased grants to the truly needy."

But that this was the product of joint proposals of both Republicans and Democrats—and that the slowed increase in welfare cases was also the fortuitous result of demographic accident (most eligible recipients were already on the rolls by 1971)—was missing from such storytelling. By his account, Democrats had figured merely as wreckers and irritants, moved off the dime only by the fury of an outraged California electorate.

He piled on fantastical claims. One part of the new welfare law, included at his firm insistence, was a pilot program requiring recipients in some counties to work. It failed, most people on welfare lacking the job skills to make them useful to employers, despite the governor's claim that there existed a massive pool of employable lollygaggers. In 1974, the work program's peak year, it was able to enroll only 4,760 out of 182,735 welfare recipients, despite massive investment in staff time and effort from the governor's office. All told, only 0.2 percent of welfare recipients ever received jobs through the program; most were for tasks like raking leaves. And though the program was supposed to decrease the number of people applying for relief, applications for welfare turned out to be greater in counties with the program than those without. In fact, according to a study ordered by Reagan's successor, Governor Brown (a study Reagan cited as authoritative when it came to the parts that suited him politically), the Community Work Experience Program "failed to meet any of its employment objects."

And yet somehow in Ronald Reagan's hands this became a social policy miracle of loaves-and-fishes proportions. On the radio in the middle of 1975 he claimed that "in the 35 counties where it was tried, 25 percent more welfare recipients moved off welfare into jobs than in the state's other 23 counties." Why the statistical discrepancy? Because, he said, "thousands who refused to report were automatically dropped from the welfare rolls and not heard from again"—which didn't explain why there were more welfare case in counties with the program than those without. In fact, what he said made no sense at all.

Governing is not a hero's profession. It is a profession of compromises. Those pesky bureaucrats, always getting in the way with their infernal statistics; those issues whose incommensurate complexities don't allow for Manichaean interpretation; the watchdogs of the press pointing out the contradictions. On the radio, though, when he was telling stories, no such compromises were necessary. Issues could be made to be Manichaean. The statistics were his to superintend. Now the only thing he was accountable for was rhetoric. Gerald Ford, however, enjoyed no such luxury.

RELUCTANTLY, AFTER CLAIMING AROUND THANKSGIVING THAT "OUR country is not in an economic crisis," the president finally admitted it was. "I've got bad news," he said in his State of the Union address, "and I don't expect much, if any applause." His proposal that night for $16 billion in temporary individual and corporate taxes cuts, which he thought of as a pragmatic reversal from his previous call for a tax hike, was dismissed as halfhearted by Democrats in Congress, who responded with a bill cutting taxes permanently by $22.9 billion. His right-wing Treasury secretary William Simon counseled a veto. Another economic advisor, Alan Greenspan, pointed out that a veto would represent Ford's second reversal on basic questions of fiscal policy in only a few months. The press found out about the internal dispute. Successful presidencies manage to contain such palace politics. But regarding the Ford White House, Robert Novak later reflected, "More than any other president, struggles for power were leaked to reporters." This one was resolved in favor of Greenspan—with the president vowing to kill all new spending programs that might add to the deficit. At which he was damned again, this time by the left.

That was nothing compared with the blows from his right. Young Americans for Freedom, calling the tax cut "not enough," announced a mobilization for taxpayers to staple tea bags to their tax returns. Reagan, on the radio in February, said the $52 billion deficit written into Ford's new budget proposal "abandoned his pledge of a balanced budget . . . made little more than four months ago" and required "borrowing on a scale too colossal to comprehend," and also said that the debate in Washington now was not on "whether the federal government must learn to live within its means, but how profligate and irresponsible a government can be without either debauching the currency, squeezing business and consumers out of the money market, and heading toward . . . literal bankruptcy."

And nothing compared to the abuse he now got from the press. The *New Republic*'s John Osborne wrote prior to the State of the Union address, "Gerald Ford is an awfully nice man who isn't up to the presidency." Tom Brokaw of NBC interviewed the president afterward and asked him "a question that isn't easy to phrase, so I will just bore straight ahead with it. As you know, I'm certain, because I have been told that you have commented on this before, but it has been speculated on in print not only in Washington but elsewhere and it crops up in conversations from time to time in this town" (perhaps he was thinking of Lyndon Johnson's oft-repeated bon mot: that Jerry Ford couldn't fart and chew gum at the same time): "the question of whether or not you are intellectually up to the job of being president."

Ford responded by pointing to his college grades—so reporters clamored for the White House to provide his transcripts. Suspicious times, these. Two dozen Republican conservatives soon announced they wouldn't back a primary challenger to the president—"at this time." Though Charles Percy, the liberal Republican senator from Illinois, was making explorations.

In March Ford signed the tax bill, including a $29.2 billion tax cut inserted by the Democrats, calling it the most difficult decision in his life—and had to admit on TV that "the tax cuts in the bill I have just signed and other changes will bring the estimated fiscal year 1976 deficit up to approximately $60 billion," perhaps $100 billion if the "new spending actions which committees of the Congress were already seriously considering" were allowed to prevail.

Damned if he did, damned if he didn't. Reflected a historian, "In what became a familiar pattern, Ford's efforts to unite the country around what he considered reasonable proposals succeeded chiefly in enraging and emboldening his political adversaries. . . . Each time Ford charged course, he looked less like a shrewd pragmatist or a man with the courage to change his mind than a confused flip-flopper." Ronald Reagan would have just blithely denied that he had changed course.

• • •

GOVERNING IN A WORLD GONE MAD:

On January 24, crazed Puerto Rican nationalists bombed a historic tavern in Manhattan's financial district where George Washington had delivered his farewell address to his troops; the Weather Underground staged near-simultaneous blasts at the State Department in Washington, D.C., and an Army induction center in the Oakland federal building. Its communiqué blamed President Ford's request for $522 million in military aid to help South Vietnam stave off a Communist takeover. For his part, Ronald Reagan blamed the terror spree on the dissolving over the past few years of the House Committee on Internal Security, the successor to HUAC; the Internal Security Division of the Justice Department; and the Subversive Activities Control Board—actions taken by Congress, he said, in response to the "howls of complaint from a smorgasbord of Communist sympathizers" like Congressman John Conyers of Michigan, "who has backed causes such as the National Peace Action Committee, which was one of those identified as a Trotskyite front by the very House committee that's being abolished."

In February a slasher roamed the streets of Los Angeles, randomly slitting the throats of victims (but only, curiously, on Wednesdays and weekends). Two radical economists at the Institute of Policy Studies pegged the probability of a 1930s-style depression at 60 percent by 1978, thanks to multinational corporations "beyond the reach of traditional government controls."

On, say, March 15, to take a random day, you could open a paper like the *Milwaukee Journal* and survey a cabinet of horrors just by flipping the pages: a Purdue University coed kidnapped by an assistant professor and held for three weeks "in an apparent experiment to brainwash her into falling in love"; thousands fleeing their riverbank homes after tornadoes across Arkansas and Florida and South Carolina; a former governor of Oklahoma convicted of bribery and extortion; the assassination by police in Saigon (where our embassy still supported hundreds of diplomatic personnel) of a French journalist who had criticized the South Vietnamese government; Rabbi Korff raising money for a cash-strapped Richard Nixon ("He has not been accustomed to economizing"); fresh leads in Pennsylvania in the twelfth month of the manhunt for Patty Hearst and her associates; a hijacking in Ethiopia; a fourteen-year-old from Brooklyn who showed up at a bus station in Omaha, Nebraska, carrying a note reading, "To whom it may concern, I'm Michael's grandmother, and am sending Michael to Boys Town because I don't want him to be here in this awful crime city"; another kidnapped millionaire scion in Italy; a knife-wielding purse-snatcher menacing old women on the streets of Milwaukee—he was only seventeen.

Horrors, of course, drench the news in any decade. By the middle of the 1970s, however, the perception of the density of horrors was so much worse. For instance, the BBC's Alistair Cooke gave a speech as a guest of the House of Representatives in which he declared that "crime and violence in the cities has become greater than at any time since the fifteenth century."

IN WASHINGTON, THE PARANOIA AND DREAD INFECTING THE NATION were finding their institutional expression in the Senate and House investigations of the FBI and CIA. The *New York Times* predicted on February 8 a "Year of Intelligence"—"a thorough and potentially far-reaching review of United States intelligence practices and requirements." Speaking before a friendly House subcommittee on February 20, CIA director William E. Colby begged Congress to move forward in a "sober and responsible manner," said that overmuch criticism "placed American intelligence in danger," and worried that the outcry "raised the question whether secret intelligence operations can be conducted by the United States." Then he acknowledged one of those secret intelligence operations, recently revealed in the news: that among the dissidents on whom the CIA had kept files were four members of Congress who had the temerity to attend antiwar demonstrations.

That was over, he insisted: members of Congress were "not under surveillance." But he added: "active surveillance."

Colby refused to turn over details on his agency budget, customarily hidden within the budgets of the State and Defense departments; he refused to release the CIA's fifty-page report on Seymour Hersh's December 22 exposé; he pleaded that though "there may have been occasions when CIA may have exceeded its proper bounds," any "missteps by CIA were few and far between, have been corrected, and in no way justify the outcry which has been raised."

Eight days later Daniel Schorr, CBS's curmudgeonly attack-dog investigative reporter, broke this news: "President Ford reportedly warned associates that if current investigations go too far, they could uncover several assassinations of foreign officials in which the CIA was involved."

The details, Schorr said, were "closely held." But the best estimates were that three or more such operations took place in the late 1950s or early 1960s. He concluded with a sardonic fillip: "Colby is on the record saying, 'I think that family skeletons are best left where they are—in the closet.' He apparently had some literal skeletons in mind.'"

The claim had taken a labyrinthine course to revelation. It came out of a meeting between President Ford and a group from the *New York Times*—seven top editors and columnists, and publisher Arthur Sulzberger—before the State of the Union. Ford got to work explaining away the embarrassment of offering a tax cut months after proposing a tax increase. Managing editor Abe Rosenthal changed the subject to the Rockefeller Commission, pushing a politer version of the *Times* editors' objection that no real investigation should ever have been entrusted to such a crew of establishment mandarins. Ford came back saying that he had chosen the members precisely for their "responsibility"—because when he became president he had learned things about the CIA to "blacken the name of every President back to Truman," and for the investigators to handle it irresponsibly would "ruin the U.S. image around the world."

Tom Wicker later wrote about what happened next: "At some point in this monologue, Ford had used the word 'assassinations,' and this clearly seemed to be the dark secret in mind." Wicker hadn't been entirely shocked, remembering a sojourn at the LBJ Ranch in January 1964 when Johnson, the new president, as if processing a psychological burden, recalled to a group of reporters his shock upon learning of the CIA's complicity in the coup-murders of Rafael Trujillo of the Dominican Republic and Ngo Dinh Diem of South Vietnam. But 1964, Wicker reflected, had been a "different world." "Then it had not occurred to me that we should print such things; when my colleague Doug Kiker of the *New York Times* and Phil Potter of the *Baltimore Sun* and I later made notes—which I still have—of Johnson's conversation, we carefully entered a cryptic note ('Trujillo and Diem') for that part of it, lest the notes fall into irresponsible hands." Now, however, eleven years later, a reckoning was at hand, and the group had to make an ethical decision on the fly, at a time when the grounds for judgment were shifting beneath their feet. Should they publish?

The group racked their brains over whether the entire session had been demarcated by Ron Nessen, the president's press secretary, as "off the record." Wicker, recalling that Ford had specified at one or two points that they were off the record—but not at this point—offered that he might have leaked out the information on purpose, at least as an investigatory lead. Columnist Wicker was by then a dean of Washington's suspicious circles: author of column after column during the past several years, on Vietnam, on Watergate, on all manner of official abuses, exposing lies, blasting the cult of executive secrecy that enabled the lies, decrying the very longing for national innocence that let hypocritical presidents hiding beneath the cover of "national security" get away with all manner of unpatriotic perfidies in the first place—and seeing suspicion vindicated nearly every time. "By 1975," he remembered, "I thought it intolerable that American government should sponsor such criminal and indefensible acts as political assassinations, and I saw no reason why the *New York Times* should protect Ford against his own disclosures. . . . If the people had a right to know anything, surely they had a right to know murder was being done in their name." His bosses, however, more reticent, asked Nessen whether the remarks had been intended to be off the record. Nessen, aghast, said that of course they had been off the record. At that, Sulzberger scotched further inquiry. The frustrated *Times*men who disagreed leaked word of the debate, which was how word got back to Schorr—who managed to secure an interview with Director Colby.

"Are you people involved in assassinations?" asked Schorr, as coolly as possible.

"Not anymore," replied Colby, explaining that planning assassinations had been banned since 1973.

Schorr asked who'd been the targets prior to then. Colby said, "I can't talk about it." Schorr named the United Nations secretary-general who perished in a 1961 plane crash: "Hammarskjöld?"

"Of course not."

"Lumumba?"—the leftist liberator of the Congo, also killed in 1961.

"I can't go down a list with you. Sorry."

That, as all the Watergate buffs knew who'd read *All the President's Men* (which was just then being knocked off the *New York Times* bestseller list in its thirty-fourth week by Dan Rather's study of the Nixon White House, *The Palace Guard*), was a "non-denial denial." Schorr's producers gave him two minutes on the air to run with the story—a long segment for a piece without any visual component.

Although, at that, it had to be noted that the *Washington Post* had put Schorr's scoop only on page three of the paper. The *Times* buried it on page thirty. *Time* magazine didn't acknowledge it, and put off even mentioning the CIA probes until seventeen days later, a week after Vice President Rockefeller extended his commission's April deadline so it could look into the alleged assassination plots. "We have entered the decade," *Time* quoted Senator Church as saying, "that ends with 1984." *Time* then asked him if the CIA's alleged murders of foreign heads of state could ever be justified. "In the absence of war," he responded, no government agency can be given license to murder. "The President is not a glorified Godfather."

President Ford was soon to begin negotiations with Senator Church about what secret documents his committee would be allowed to access. Ford surely had reason to panic: would he choose the "instincts of openness and candor" to which he pledged his administration the previous August; or the deference to the Cold War cult of executive authority that had defined his thirteen congressional terms—especially now that he was the executive whose authority he would be protecting?

Presently, however, his executive attention was distracted by another intelligence consideration. "The Ford Administration, clearly taken unawares by the turn of events in Vietnam, concentrated yesterday on blaming Congress for the collapse of South Vietnamese resistance in nearly two-thirds of that country," the *Los Angeles Times* reported on March 20. "Privately, intelligence specialists conceded that a major countrywide thrust by Hanoi was not expected this year."

CHAPTER NINETEEN

"Disease, Disease, Disease"

IT ALL HAPPENED SO SHOCKINGLY FAST. AT THE BEGINNING OF THE YEAR the North Vietnamese Communists captured the South Vietnamese province of Phuoc Long on the Cambodian border, seventy-five miles from Saigon. The media called it an isolated fight. But then, early in March, the Communists captured the Central Highlands city of Ban Me Thuot, and South Vietnam's President Thieu began a slow, soiling surrender. First he gave up the northern provinces. Then the entire Central Highlands, cutting his country in two. Instead of the orderly retreat of a disciplined army, "there's a complete lack of communication, a breakdown in the chain of command," an American intelligence officer explained, describing the chaotic rout of this army to which Americans had pledged their lives, their fortune, and their sacred honor. "Colonels aren't following orders. No one cares. It's become every man for himself."

The North Vietnamese politburo had planned the full-on offensive to win the war to take two years. Instead, it was taking a few months. One and a half million refugees poured south to coastal cities they were told were impregnable to the enemy—"from one end of a sinking ship to another," wrote the *New Yorker*'s Jonathan Schell—endless columns of women and children, old men in conical hats, clogging dusty roads to the sea. Along these roads civilians were massacred—not by their ostensible enemy, but by South Vietnamese soldiers, driven by directionless rage. A country, Schell wrote, "tearing itself apart in a frenzy of self-destruction."

Other refugees boarded literal ships—"crowding together," NBC News reported, "without food, without water, starving, dying on the slow voyage south." Children falling overboard, mothers diving after them; people being thrown overboard, by soldiers desperate to flee themselves—scorpions-in-bottle scrambles for scarce resources. Soldiers shed uniforms—but not weapons—and swam desperately for American ships meant to evacuate civilians. They commandeered boats, waging makeshift naval battles against other soldiers. One of these mariners turned out to be the region's military commander, who fought his way to a rescue ship as his former soldiers crashed through the city, firing randomly at passersby.

Vessels arrived at their intended destinations, coastal cities like Qui Nhon, Tuy Hoa, and Nha Trang; desperate passengers discovered that these "safe havens" had already been abandoned to the Communists. Da Nang was the nation's second-largest city, formerly home to the mighty United States air base, once the busiest airport in the world. A great battle was supposedly under way to save the beachside metropolis. Lazy American reporters deployed the usual clichés to describe the fighting: "juggernaut," "blitzkrieg." A skeptical writer, though, quoted a French observer on the scene: "There never was a last battle for Da Nang." Another eyewitness broadened the description: "There is no war." South Vietnam was already lost.

On March 28, South Vietnamese marines clambered aboard the last ship to depart the city, the USS *Pioneer Commander,* and slaughtered twenty-five civilians. All told, there were four thousand passengers aboard—but only a few barrels of water. "One woman's baby had died in her arms while she waited on a barge for four days without water or shelter," read an Associated Press dispatch. "She became hysterical as she came aboard the freighter and leaped overboard."

There were airplanes for the refugees, too. But only three civilians made it aboard the last one to lift off. The rest of the passengers were members of the South Vietnamese 1st Division's Hac Bao, or "Black Panther," unit, who fought their way aboard by opening fire into the waiting crowd. Not every member of the Black Panther unit made it, however, for when the plane landed in Saigon, a mangled body, M-16 rifle still strapped to his shoulder, was found dangling from the fuselage. Others dropped from wheel wells from thousands of feet. Another plane, lifting off south of Ban Me Thuot, was barely able to ascend after a grenade went off under one of the wings. At the South China Sea port of Cam Ranh Bay, amid the Vietnamese marines aiming grenades and rifle fire at both civilians and their very own officers, a helicopter carrying President Ford's personal photographer, part of a White House observational mission, was shot at. He told the *New York Times,* "We decided not to make any more passes over the ship."

THE GRISLY DETAILS FROM THE USS *PIONEER COMMANDER,* THE CHAOTIC last flight out of Da Nang, and other such stories did not run in all too many newspapers, which reserved space for news of, Operation

Babylift, instead. "Their eyes wide with wonder and showing no ill effects from a 25 hour dash across the Pacific from endangered Saigon,
55 Vietnamese orphans have arrived to a new life in the United States,"
ran the front-page article on April 3 in the *Toledo Blade,* complete with
photo of two darling sleeping infants. Americans couldn't get enough
news, either, about the young man who organized Operation Babylift.
Ed Daley, president of World Airways, was "gregarious, an outgoing,
good party guy who will gather up a planeload of friends and fly off to
Europe for a weekend," ran one profile ("TOUGH AIRLINE CHIEF LIKES
CHILDREN; SENDS THOUSANDS TO CIRCUS, SYMPHONY"). On an impulse,
he had flown one of his company's 727s to Da Nang, hoping to help
organize evacuations. He arrived only in time for that last planeload,
the one overrun by the ARVN 1st Division. Throwing punches, crying
"One at a time, one at a time, there's room for everybody"—and then,
his clothes finally ripped to shreds, firing a pistol in the air—Daley was
forced to stand by helplessly as the taxiing plane ran over people on
the runway. Unbowed, he pressed south on to Saigon, confident his
American ingenuity would find a way to redeem the debacle. He had
conceived a plan, and a slogan worthy of an advertising man: Operation
Babylift. "Unable to do anything else in Vietnam," Schell wrote, "the
United States was now making off with planeloads of Vietnamese babies." As freed POWs would redeem the debacle in 1973, rescuing orphans would redeem it now.

And so on April 3, the news was filled with smiling prospective
parents, accounts of Daley's defiance in continuing the operation even
after the Federal Aviation Administration threatened to throw the book
at him, and with testimony about jammed State Department and charity phone lines following the merest rumor of his plans: "We had big
responses from the American public when the Hungarians and Czechs
and Cubans had their crises, but this has been the biggest response in my
thirty years' experience," said a relief specialist from the U.S. Catholic
Conference.

Then, two days later, on April 5, the news was this: "Grim workers
resumed their search today for more bodies of Vietnamese war orphans
killed Friday when a huge U.S. jetliner en route to the United States
crashed in a rice paddy."

The search continued as a special section of *Time* now on the newsstands asked, "Is This What America Has Left?" The *Economist*'s cover,
"The Fading of America," pronounced, "The Indochina rout will now
make every ally of the United States doubt whether it can believe in
the promises of American support." British Petroleum and Gulf final-

ized the sale of their holdings in Kuwait to the government there. The two Western companies had asked a price of $2 billion. They were paid one-fortieth of that. A leader of West Germany's Christian Democrats worried, "If Berlin were attacked tomorrow I am not absolutely certain that the United States would intervene." According to a new poll, only 34 percent of Americans would favor helping West Germany in the event of an invasion, and only 27 percent would want to help Israel.

PRESIDENT FORD, WHATEVER THE FATE OF HIS PERSONAL PHOTOGRA-pher, was still confident the rout could be reversed.

On January 9, Ron Nessen had announced that the president wanted military aid for Vietnam above the $700 million Congress had already authorized for the fiscal year. It was one of the other things that shocked Tom Wicker at the White House meeting between Ford and his *Times* colleagues: the president's brassy conviction that a few hundred million more might just turn this thing around. "Some note in his remarks even suggested to me," he recalled, "the insane possibility of the return of American troops." Only 12 percent of the public in the second week of February thought the United States should send more aid; in mid-March two liberal senators, Republican Charles "Mac" Mathias of Maryland and Democrat Adlai Stevenson III of Illinois, introduced legislation to cut off help to Southeast Asia altogether. Senator Frank Church, for his part, asked, "We have so much blood on our hands out there. Why do we thirst for more?" On March 28 the president sent Army Chief of Staff Fred Weyand to South Vietnam to assess the situation. The conclusions he brought back were simultaneously realistic and fantastical.

Realistic: "The current military situation is critical, and the probability of the survival of South Vietnam as a truncated nation in the southern provinces is marginal at best."

Fantastical: An emergency congressional appropriation of $722 million would be all it would take to save the day.

Nessen announced an April 10 presidential foreign policy speech to a joint session of Congress. In the interim, following a golf date with Bob Hope in Palm Springs and a dinner with Ronald Reagan (who "has been critical of Mr. Ford's policies as President," the *New York Times* explained, "and is being promoted as a possible candidate for President in 1976, even though both he and the President are Republicans and Mr. Ford has announced his intention to seek a Presidential term in his own right"), a reporter at the airport asked Ford what he was doing about the military losses in Southeast Asia. The president "laughed playfully," as the *New Yorker* reported it, "and broke into a run."

How droll: America, the country that ran away.

In a speech to a San Francisco civic organization he deployed the death of the babies to advance what some saw as a message of reconciliation—and others saw as an invitation to civic amnesia: "In this hour of sadness and, I am sure, frustration, let us not dispel our energies with recrimination or assessments of blame. The facts, whatever they may be, will speak for themselves, and historians will have plenty of time to judge later on. What is now essential is that we maintain our balance as a nation and as people and that we maintain our unity as a powerful but peace-loving nation." He added a political fillip, however: "This obviously is not the point in history to dismantle our defenses, nor can we adopt such a naive view of the world that we cripple our vital intelligence agencies."

And that was not a unifying notion at all. Among those who might not agree were the voters of the Academy of Motion Picture Arts and Sciences.

Late in 1974 a director named Peter Davis showed a documentary called *Hearts and Minds* briefly in a Los Angeles theater to qualify it for Academy Award consideration. It opened with an Operation Homecoming parade for POW George Thomas Coker, who told a crowd on the steps of the Linden, New Jersey, city hall about Vietnam, "If it wasn't for the people, it was very pretty. The people there are very backwards and primitive and they make a mess out of everything." General William Westmoreland, commander of U.S. forces, in a comment the director explained had not been spontaneous but had been repeated on three takes, was shown explaining, "The Oriental doesn't put the same high price on life as does a Westerner. Life is plentiful. Life is cheap in the Orient." (Thereupon, the film cut to a sobbing Vietnamese mother being restrained from climbing into the grave atop the coffin of her son.) Daniel Ellsberg was quoted: "We aren't on the wrong side. We are the wrong side." The movie concluded with an interview with an activist from Vietnam Veterans Against the War. "We've all tried very hard to escape what we have learned in Vietnam," he said. "I think Americans have worked extremely hard not to see the criminalities that their officials and their policy-makers exhibited."

A massive thunderstorm raged outside at the Oscar ceremony at the Dorothy Chandler Pavilion on April 8, 1975—where after Sammy Davis Jr.'s musical tribute to Fred Astaire, and Ingrid Bergman's acceptance of the Best Supporting Actress Award for *Murder on the Orient Express,* and Francis Ford Coppola's award for best director (one of six Oscars for *The Godfather: Part II:* "I'm wearing a tuxedo with a bulletproof cummerbund," cohost Bob Hope cracked, "Who knows what will happen if Al Pacino doesn't win"), Lauren Hutton and Danny Thomas opened the envelope and announced that *Hearts and Minds* had won as the year's best documentary.

Producer Bert Schneider took the microphone and said, "It's ironic that we're here at a time just before Vietnam is about to be liberated." Then he read a telegram from the head of the North Vietnamese delegation to the Paris peace talks. It thanked the antiwar movement "for all they have done on behalf of peace.... Greetings of friendship to all American people."

Backstage, Bob Hope was so enraged he tried to push his way past the broadcast's producer to issue an onstage rebuttal. Shirley MacLaine, who had already mocked Sammy Davis from the stage for having endorsed Richard Nixon's reelection, shouted, "Don't you dare." Anguished telegrams from viewers began piling up backstage. One, from a retired Army colonel, read, "WITH 55,000 DEAD YOUNG AMERICANS IN DEFENSE OF FREEDOM AND MILLIONS OF VIETNAMESE FIGHTING FOR FREEDOM ... DEMAND WITHDRAWAL OF AWARD." On the back of that particular wire, Hope madly scribbled something for his cohost Frank Sinatra to read during his next turn on camera—which he did, to a mix of boos and applause: "The Academy is saying we are not responsible for any political utterances on this program and we are sorry that had to take place." Upon which, backstage, the broadcast's third cohost, Shirley MacLaine, berated Sinatra: "You said you were speaking for the Academy. Well, I'm a member of the Academy and you didn't ask me!" Her brother, Warren Beatty, snarled at Sinatra on camera: "Thank you, Frank, you old Republican."

Two nights later, in a haunting, haunted performance full of awkward pauses and applause lines that yielded no applause, the president told Congress that "to build upon our many successes, to repair damage where we find it, to recover our balance, to move ahead as a united people," it should vote $722 million in military assistance for South Vietnam and $250 million for humanitarian and economic aid. (Two Democratic freshmen and Phil Burton walked out.) "Let us put an end to self-inflicted wounds," he said, his Midwestern voice sounding flatter than ever. "Let us remember that our national unity is a most priceless asset. Let us deny our adversaries the satisfaction of using Vietnam to pit Americans against Americans. At this moment, the United States must present to the world a united front."

And then he absorbed the unmistakable fact that the public was already united—against giving Vietnam anything at all. Gallup found that the public opposed humanitarian aid by a margin of 55 percent to 40 percent and military aid by 79 percent to 15. The respondents opposed letting evacuated South Vietnamese live here by 52 percent to 36 percent. Even, apparently, infants: in San Francisco's Presidio district, a warehouse providing temporary housing for the orphans of Operation Babylift (which angry South Vietnamese, Swiss aide workers reported, were now calling "an abduction of children") was under armed military guard after threats to their safety.

The most hawkish Democratic senator, Henry M. "Scoop" Jackson, said he opposed military aid, too, and added, "I don't know of any on the Democratic side who will support it." The Appropriations Committee chair, John McClellan of Arkansas, another hawk, said it would only "prolong the conflict and perhaps postpone the inevitable—a Communist victory, a complete takeover." A Republican dove, Senator Mark Hatfield of Oregon, said, "I am appalled that a man would continue in such a bankrupt policy"—and the most infamous Republican hawk of all, Barry Goldwater, had already announced, a year earlier, "We can scratch South Vietnam. It is imminent that South Vietnam is going to fall into the hands of North Vietnam." You could not reasonably see this as an ideological or partisan choice. But in the future, it would be interpreted by cynical and opportunistic critics as precisely that.

On April 14, the secretaries of state and defense met with Senate leaders to press the case for the appropriations, and to discuss details of the impending likely evacuation of all American personnel from Saigon—and, the president hoped, of thousands of loyal South Vietnamese. Henry Kissinger cited a million as the upward range of the South Vietnamese who would need rescuing, 174,000 as the low number. A mission sent by the Senate Foreign Relations Committee had just returned from Vietnam and reported it might be too late even to safely evacuate Americans. In the private meeting with the secretaries of state and defense, a skeptical Senator Claiborne Pell of Rhode Island said that perhaps the nation of Borneo would welcome refugees: "It has the same latitude, the same climate, and would welcome some anti-Communists."

They were only responding to the will of their constituents. In conservative St. Petersburg, Florida, the newspaper printed readers' responses to a survey. They opposed humanitarian aid 695 to 361 and military aid 1,010 to 65. "I can never understand why our government is always so willing to rush great quantities of materials and equipment to most foreign countries for aid, but when our own people need aid it becomes so hard to come by," one reader wrote.

"When you read what those Vietnamese men did to women and children being rescued, think who would get the food and other aid," wrote another. "If Mr. Ford has millions of dollars to squander on a hopeless cause, he could use it to curb crime . . . here at home."

"Let's stop this once and for all and quit playing on the sympathies of United States citizens."

"It would seem that President Ford has become bereft of his senses. . . . What about the billion dollars' worth of armaments that the South Vietnamese army walked (or ran) away from and which fell into the North Vietnamese's hands?"

Congress voted only the $200 million for humanitarian aid. The House vote against military aid included fifty Republicans. Ford promptly told Congress that it was responsible for the "loss of Vietnam"—not, say, a South Vietnamese army whose officers abandoned their troops to slaughter infant civilians. He claimed that "just a relatively small American commitment" could have met "any military challenges." (He lied. The Pentagon's estimate of what it called an "austere program" to save Saigon had been $1.4 billion at a minimum.) Senators, for their part, saved face by describing how Nixon had gulled them—writing "secret agreements" into the Paris Peace Accords promising future military assistance he had no authority to give.

Two branches of government, hurling recrimination at one another, accusations almost unto treason.

To the west, the capital of Cambodia fell to a fearsome Communist agglomeration known as the Khmer Rouge. This was not bad news, the *Los Angeles Times* editorialized, "for the suffering Cambodians themselves." The *New York Times'* correspondent there, Sydney H. Schanberg, published a reflection amid the collapse noting the "million Cambodians killed or wounded (one seventh of the population), hundreds of thousands of refugees living in shanties, a devastated countryside, children dying of starvation and carpenters turning out a steady stream of coffins made from ammunition crates." It was headlined "INDOCHINA WITHOUT AMERICANS: FOR MOST, A BETTER LIFE." However, within three days, watching the horrors already unfolding under Khmer Rouge rule, Schanberg wrote that he was changing his mind: it was already evident that the Khmer Rouge were beginning a genocide of millions of their countrymen in a lunatic bid to radically engineer an agrarian society without banks, religion, or indeed any modern technology whatsoever, beginning with the purging of intellectuals, businessmen, Buddhists, and foreigners—the establishment of a Communist "Year Zero." "Everyone had felt that when the Communists came and the war finally ended, at least the suffering would largely be over. All of us were wrong."

The North Vietnamese invasion force continued its waltz southward. The *Washington Post* columnist Tom Braden quoted an off-the-record remark of Henry Kissinger that "the United States must carry out some act somewhere in the world which shows its determination to continue to be a world power." On April 21, President Thieu appeared on South Vietnamese TV and resigned his office in a lachrymose, ninety-minute performance, citing Richard Nixon's broken promises of a "full force" if North Vietnam broke the cease-fire. The next day his former government's mighty air base at Bien Hoa, where Bob Hope used to broadcast USO shows at Christmastime, fell to the Communists. The day after that, President Ford told graduates assembled in the Tulane University field house, "Today America can regain the sense of pride that existed before. But it cannot be achieved by refighting a war that is finished as far as America is concerned."

Among those who disagreed—who wished to dwell on Vietnam as a national teachable moment—was a writer in the "Notes and Comments" section of the *New Yorker,* who said, "Our noble commitments, our firm stands, our global responsibilities—how frequently, in recent years, have they served as a cover for self-interest and greed, then as sunglasses against the flames?" And the editors of the liberal weekly the *New Republic,* who observed that this was the week of the two hundredth anniversary of the Battle of Lexington and Concord. "If the Bicentennial helps us focus on the contrast between our idealism and our crimes, so much the better." A contributor in the same issue opined that North Vietnam "is one of the several among the poorest nations in the world that have tried or will try to create a collectivist society, based on principles that are repugnant to us, yet are likely to produce greater welfare and security for its people than any local alternative ever offered, at a cost in freedom that affects [only] a small elite."

And now the revolutionaries would have their chance, in South Vietnam and North Vietnam both—or, as it was soon simply to be known, just "Vietnam."

ON APRIL 28, THE ROCKEFELLER COMMISSION CALLED FORMER CENTRAL Intelligence Agency chief Richard Helms back from his posting as ambassador to Iran to testify about the allegations of CIA assassinations. Eighteen days earlier, President Ford, in his speech asking for Vietnam aid, had said, "The Central Intelligence Agency has been of maximum importance to me. The Central Intelligence Agency and its associated intelligence organizations could be of maximum importance to some of you in this audience who might be President at some later date. I think it would be catastrophic for the Congress or anyone else to destroy the usefulness by dismantling, in effect, our intelligence systems upon which we rest so heavily."

Daniel Schorr confronted Helms on his way out of the hearing room: "Welcome back"

"You cocksucker!" Helms replied. "'Killer Schorr'—that's what they ought to call you!"

The cameras started rolling; Helms was hardly more civil. "I must say, Mr. Schorr, I didn't like what you had to say on some of your broadcasts on the subject. I don't think it was fair, and I don't think it was right. As far as I know, the CIA was never responsible for assassinating any foreign leaders."

Another reporter followed up: had he ever discussed assassinations?

Helms raised his voice: "I don't know whether I've stopped beating my wife, whether you've stopped beating your wife. In government, there are discussions of practically everything under the sun."

"Of assassinations?"

"Of everything."

That same day in Saigon, where the CIA may or may not have assassinated South Vietnamese president Ngo Dinh Diem in 1963, Tan Son Nhut Air Base fell to the Communists. Its fall was hastened by an attack by South Vietnamese troops who, rather than defend the base from their erstwhile enemy, stole a small armada of airplanes themselves.

That was the coup de grâce. The next morning, at six thirty, Secretary of Defense James Schlesinger announced, "The President ordered the final withdrawal of the Americans from Vietnam at approximately 11:00 last night on the advice of the ambassador and subsequent to the closing of Tan Son Nhut making it necessary to go to a helicopter air lift."

The evacuation was dubbed "Operation Frequent Wind"—like a reference to flatulence, like something out of *M*A*S*H*. It was desperate, sordid, unplanned. The American consul general, after all, had been going around town announcing, "Saigon is as sound as the American dollar." (But how sound was that? Inflation was 9.2 percent.) The ambassador's wife resolutely refused to pack.

And Americans, once the film cans were flown back to New York, got to see on TV how it had all gone down.

John Chancellor, opening NBC's evening news broadcast on

April 30: "Good evening. The city of Saigon was renamed today. Victorious Communists who forced the city's surrender said that henceforth the city will be known as 'Ho Chi Minh City.'"

A Soviet-made Vietcong tank was shown crashing through the gate of the presidential palace, a Communist soldier scrambling down the nose, running a National Liberation Front flag across the lawn.

The choppers evacuating Americans maneuvered in zigs and zags, the better to dodge heat-seeking missiles in their seventeen-minute flights to the ships massed in the South China Sea—and to dodge American helicopters commandeered by enemy pilots trying to shoot Americans down. Other helicopters were commandeered by deserters. On the deck of the USS *Blue Ridge* one landed without permission, tangling in the rotor blades of an evacuation chopper. The mightiest nation in the world, unable to control access to its own warships; American authorities finally decided to simply let the deserters board, to class them as refugees. Aboard the *Blue Ridge,* the surplus helicopters were simply pushed overboard, useless military hardware, buried at sea.

The penultimate segment of the previous evenings NBC's newscast had been an editorial from the network's stern house commentator, David Brinkley, broadcast, incongruously, from outdoors:

"The United States did not lose the war since it never really tried to win it, instead trying to help South Vietnam win the war, and finding it would not, or could not; and though the United States did not lose the war, it did lose a great deal. The money, we know about; the inflation, we still live with; the social discords in this country are still to be seen. The other loss we also know about, though we don't talk about it much—"

The camera pulled back, zooming wide, revealing that he was standing in the middle of an endless sea of white tombstones.

"Fifty-six thousand lives, plus about 160,000 seriously wounded, many of whom will never recover. So when some future politician for some reason feels the need to drag this country into a war, he might come to Arlington, and stand maybe right over there somewhere"—he pointed off into the distance, then pulled his hands tight across himself—"to make his announcement and tell what he has in mind. If he can attract public support, speaking from a place like this, then his reasons for starting a war will have to have been good ones."

Then, also incongruously, another editorial followed, from the broadcast's anchor, offering the opposite interpretation. "The American people gave up on Vietnam without telling Vietnam," John Chancellor said, and the image on-screen was a clutch of hip young long-haired men in silken shirts and bell-bottoms, watching TV—as if standing in for a morally dissolute nation that no longer knew how to keep its word. "It didn't dawn on the Vietnamese people that the guarantees were withdrawn until they saw that the United States was not going to help get it back, or even help keep what was left. They did not."

The next night, Brinkley gave another editorial:

"Perhaps in the way the war was ending was explained why it was ending as it did. . . . The North was willing and able to fight. In the South they were desperately trying to abandon their own country. . . ."

And once more John Chancellor from his anchor desk told the opposite story: "During yesterday's Saigon evacuation, a sizable number of South Vietnamese hoped to be rescued from rooftops by American copters, but they weren't. South Vietnamese had hope because they were taught the United States would aid if South Vietnam were in trouble— but the United States did not."

In the *New York Times,* across the entire front page, was the headline: MINH SURRENDERS, VIETCONG IN SAIGON; 1,000 AMERICANS AND 5,500 VIETNAMESE EVACUATED BY COPTERS TO U.S. CARRIERS. Below that, an indelible image: a line of bodies snaking up a ladder to a precipitous shack atop the CIA station chief's residence, the embassy grounds having been commandeered by what Henry Kissinger had once confidently dismissed as a "fourth-rate military power," now far too dangerous for helicopters to lift off from. "Ford Unity Plea," another front-page headline read. But that fantasy could not be sustained even within the confines of a single network newscast. This hell, these scenes out of Hieronymus Bosch, this place people were risking death in order to leave, for which we had sacrificed fifty-six thousand soldiers and half a trillion dollars in national treasure, dividing our nation in half: this is what our investment produced?

SOME OF THE SOUTH VIETNAMESE WHO MADE IT TO THE UNITED STATES were preliminarily resettled at Eglin Air Force Base in the Florida panhandle—in defiance of a hastily assembled petition got up by residents of the base's host city, which was called Niceville. A radio poll that found 80 percent of Niceville's residents didn't want them. The Associated press reported, "Children in one school joked about shooting a few." High school kids spoke in class of plans to organize a "Gook Klux Klan." Students in a twelfth-grade psychology class told their teacher they were worried the refugees would try to convert them to Communism.

"Disease, disease, disease, that's all I've heard," complained a congressman representing another relocation site, the San Diego County Marine base, Camp Pendleton, of the phone calls he was getting. "They think of the Vietnamese as nothing but diseased job seekers." In Arkansas, at Fort Chaffee, which admitted twenty-five thousand refugees, the compound was so well guarded that a radical journalist compared it to the "strategic hamlets" the U.S. military used to build in South Vietnam. A recently returned veteran told him, "I don't like the people personally. I didn't see anything worth saving and I don't now." The protest placards read "GOOKS GO HOME."

In Detroit, a black autoworker told the *New York Times,* "People are losing their cars, houses, jobs. Let them stay there until we do something for people here." In Valparaiso, Indiana, a salesman asked, "How do you know we're not getting the bad guys? You can't say for sure. Nobody can, and Lord knows we've got enough Communist infiltration now." President Ford implored, "We can afford to be generous to refugees" as "a matter of principle." Mayor Daley of Chicago responded, "Charity begins at home." The Seattle City Council voted seven to one against a pro-settlement resolution. California governor Jerry Brown said Congress's refugee bill should be amended with a "jobs for Americans first" pledge. Explained Harvard sociologist David Riesman, "The national mood is poisonous and dangerous and this is one symptom—striking out at helpless refugees whose number is infinitesimal." Though one observer simply didn't see the cruelty of his countrymen before his eyes.

RONALD REAGAN HAD BEEN OBSESSED WITH THE DEBATE OVER AID TO South Vietnam. He heard in it, he said on the radio, "an echo of the hollow tapping of Neville Chamberlain's umbrella on the cobblestones of Munich." He counted dominoes falling: "Japan, the great industrial power capable of modernizing and arming a Communist Asia, has just opened discussions with Hanoi"; "Henry Kissinger returns empty-handed from the Middle East"; "The Sixth fleet may soon find it must withdraw or become a model ship in a bottle." He predicted that a lack of American will to save South Vietnam would "tempt the Soviet Union as it once tempted Hitler and the military rulers of Japan"—ushering in an imminent Communist massacre of innocents (he cited reports of Vietcong soldiers driving over crowds of refugees) behind a liberal "curtain of silence." He predicted purgatory for the "1,300 men still listed as missing in action over there." And, in an interview with the libertarian magazine *Reason,* he repeated his favorite old John Birch Society canard: "You know, Lenin said the Communists will take Eastern Europe, they will organize the hordes of Asia, he said they will then move into Latin America, and he said the United States, the last bastion of capitalism, will fall into their outstretched hands like overripe fruit. . . . [O]ne of these days, under the present policies of the Congress, the United States will stand alone as Lenin envisioned it and face the ultimate from the enemy."

He asked on the radio, of the imminent coming of those Asian hordes: "Will it be said of today's world leaders as it was of the pre–World War II leaders, 'They were better at surviving the catastrophe than they were at preventing it'?"

Then what he feared most came to pass: America denied South Vietnam military aid. America let South Vietnam fall. America cut and ran. It must be a pretty wicked nation, you might think he would have reflected, to countenance an evil like that.

Not at all, Reagan insisted, once it was over. Instead he found a way to see nobility, God's chosen nation doing naught but Christian duty.

He began a broadcast titled "Letters to the Editor": "In these times when so many of us have a tendency to lose faith in ourselves it's good now and then to be reminded of the good-natured, generous spirit that has been an American characteristic as long as there has been an America."

He then recounted a letter he claimed to have seen from an unnamed American missionary in Vietnam to an unidentified publication.

"The reverend described a 20-foot craft adrift in the Gulf of Thailand with no fuel, no food, no water, barely afloat and sinking with its cargo of 82 refugees.

"Towering over it was the aircraft carrier the USS *Midway*. The reference described the *Midway* as tired. It had already deposited some 2,000 refugees on other ships, refugees who had arrived in more than 500 flights. One flight was a light observation plane not designed for carrier landings. The *Midway* had moved up to top speed to enable the pilot to land with an entire family jammed inside the tiny fuselage. There were forty coppers on the deck, brand-new F5E fighters and A37s that had carried people who preferred not to be 'liberated' by the Communists. . . .

"Once onboard they had one question: would they be handed over to an unfriendly government, perhaps to be eventually murdered? The executive officer of the ship told him this would not happen. He said, 'Our job is to keep you as comfortable as possible, heal the sick, and feed you to your hearts' content.' That was the official policy of our nation and therefore of the *Midway*."

He then described a miracle of the loaves and fishes, straight out of the Gospel According to *Reader's Digest*:

"A tiny baby with double pneumonia was cured. People without clothes were given American clothing. Sailors took the old clothing and washed them for their guests. Pretty soon homeless children were being given piggyback rides on the shoulders of American seamen, and Navy T-shirts bearing the *Midway* decal began appearing on the little ones. . . .

"Ads went into the ship's paper asking for toys. Charity begat more charity."

Reagan concluded: "In the dark days right after World War II, when our industrial power and military power were all that stood between a war-ravaged world and a return to the dark ages, Pope Pius XII said, 'America has a genius for great and unselfish deeds. Into the hands of America God has placed the destiny of an afflicted mankind.'

"I think those young men on the *Midway* have reassured God that He hasn't given us more of an assignment than we can handle."

In its years in Southeast Asia, the USS *Midway* had served as a death-dealing juggernaut—a launching pad for air strikes responsible for killing thousands, perhaps millions, of civilians. Listening to Ronald Reagan, you could imagine that its only role had been rescuing widows and orphans. That the *entire war* had been about rescuing widows and orphans. Others told you Vietnam was a crime, a waste—or, at best, something very, very complex. It took Ronald Reagan to explain how simple the whole thing was. Charity begetting more charity: how could it have happened any other way?

HIS COLUMN NOW RAN IN 226 NEWSPAPERS. HE TURNED DOWN DOZENS of speech invitations for every one he accepted. He was now broadcast on 286 stations—laboring mightily to turn his listeners into a dedicated conservative activist army. *"It's time to write your congressman again." "Will Congress do anything about this mess? Well, maybe that's up to you." "You and I should lobby for it. We should demand not only its passage but that the commission be manned by men and women who will determine whether the laws of the marketplace can replace the useless regulations and create real savings for the consumers. Only our indignation voiced out loud will bring this about. . . ."*

He railed against the government bureaucrats who "really rule America," who were "not basically creative," were "low risk takers" and "growing like Topsy"—but so much more dangerous than mere legislators because they made up rules behind closed doors, and "if you break one of those bureaucrat-designed regulations, you're guilty as charged unless you can prove you're innocent." He railed against English teachers replacing grammar drills with "electives like creative writing, filmmaking, mythology, and detective story writing." And the "Alice in Wonderland" world of bureaucracy: "To err is human," he would quip. "It takes a government computer to really louse things up." He told the story of a wife who got a letter informing her that her dead husband could no longer receive Social Security benefits: "Don't tell my husband," she replied. "He'll die of a heart attack." Such tales were good for comic relief. Except when they weren't funny at all. For instance, the "no fewer than five government agencies . . . studying the effects of leaded gasoline" who came up with "no data to verify harm from it," which hadn't kept the EPA from spending $100 million mandating catalytic converters to attenuate the hazardous emissions. But the converters, he said, produced "a substance more harmful to you and me than those emissions they're controlling."

Maybe the stories were true. Maybe they weren't. He had a way of telling a story that made it uncheckable: "An item recently appeared in a national magazine" (which magazine?). "Some years ago a poll was taken" (whose poll?). And the facts went by too fast for innocent radio listeners to check in any event. One time, he sternly lectured against Ahab-like maritime bureaucrats demanding that a tourist paddle wheeler, the *Delta Queen*, be fireproofed according to the law for modern ships. Even though she "has never had a fire." Her owners said that would put them out of business. "No matter, said the bureaucrats in Washington. The *Delta Queen* could not be made an exception." It had had a fire only two and a half years earlier.

But it all sure sounded convincing coming from Reagan. As did his plea that the delivery of first-class mail should be turned over to private companies. And that the government should stop suing the phone company for monopoly: "When government pulls its hand out and lets the law of supply and demand work, that law works naturally," he explained—which was why, he said, a long-distance call used to cost as much as sending 1,376 letters but now cost as much as sending twenty-five.

The tax code should stop being absurd. ("We live in the only country in the world where it takes more sense to figure out your income tax than it does to earn the income.") The politicians calling for gasoline rationing—they now included Melvin Laird, the conservative former Wisconsin congressman who had been Nixon's defense secretary—"have little faith in you and your neighbors. They assume you and your neighbors won't cut back unless a government dictate forces you to." Public employees who went out on strike should be fired outright. And then there was the nightmare of living in a socialist country—like Sweden, "where workers resort to barter." Or France, where "the telephone system is run by the post office." He made them sound no less repressive than China, where it takes "a year to buy a wristwatch." Or Finland, home of the formerly great composer Jean Sibelius. Reagan compared him to Mozart, who thrived artistically to the day he died, because he earned his living in a mercantile society, while the twentieth-century Finn never wrote another note once he was awarded a lifetime government pension.

Some days he thundered forth on geopolitics: the foolishness of recognizing Red China; technical discussions of the SALT II arms control talks ("Now I know that I've thrown a lot of figures at you and they're hard to absorb just hearing them at this one broadcast. You can get a copy by writing to the station"); the crucial strategic importance of the Gulf of Aden, with Somalia and South Yemen "both close to being satellites of the Soviet Union." And to the United Nations' refusal to call Hanoi on its "cruel game of cat and mouse" in denying knowledge of the "1,300 Americans missing in action": he still rode that hobbyhorse, too. He cited "our government's do-nothing approach to the problem," and the Communists' refusal to help "search for our missing men" unless the United States ponied up reconstruction money—

> Well here's one American who's not willing to agree to that kind of deal. It's one thing for a victorious America, generous in victory, to help rebuild a defeated enemy to help strengthen the cause of peace. It's another thing entirely to pay blackmail to a nation that still counts itself as our enemy, and whose word, as we have learned time and again, cannot be trusted. . . . If we have learned nothing else from the Vietnam debacle, we should have learned the Communists only understand strength, and always take advantage of weakness.

Other days he attacked inflation, which was always and only caused by excess government spending (if the Congress would only slash spending, he said, neatly dodging the politics of Watergate and Vietnam, it could easily reverse the polls showing "public confidence in the institutions of government could hardly be lower"). The national debt: if it kept growing "you might need a wheelbarrow to cart your money to the grocery store before long." It all fit together: "As spending for education increased, student test scores have declined," he said in a late February broadcast. "Discipline has deteriorated. In field after field, generous federal spending has caused more problems than it has solved. What an irony! By refusing to cut spending we've contributed to a deterioration of the nation's social fabric at the same time."

He was angry. His volume swelled. His incredulity reached a crescendo:

"It's almost as if we refuse to read the evidence of our senses! Bigger government is not more efficient government. Big government is weak government! Its only strength is its power to bring its weakness, uncertainty, and inefficiency to every corner of American life.

"This is Ronald Reagan. Thanks for listening."

These were things all conservatives said, if not with the same eloquence and aplomb. Here was the thing that made him different: the gift for moral absolutism. Just like that USS *Midway*—not a death-dealing juggernaut but a cornucopia of Christian love. You had to be a liberal to disagree.

He would ask "if you're as fed up as I am with all the prophets of doom who have us living in a sick society, wrapped up in selfish materialism." That was the fault of the liberal media—an institution exercising "both legislative and judicial powers to such an extent that some call them the 'fourth branch of government' . . . prosecutor, judge, and jury, all in one." For instance, he spoke of "any number of stories tucked away in the middle pages of our daily papers, and even more that don't get printed at all, about an America that's all about us every day, a different America than the one that's described by the doom-criers." For an example, he offered "Rocky's Story," which he recorded at the beginning of February. It involved a construction worker traveling with his disabled son. The father discovered after boarding a plane that his wallet was missing. The stewardess began plying the aisles for donations. "The passengers were clapping and cheering." They handed over $426. The dad, according to Reagan, then burst into tears: "I just forgot people were like that."

But they *were* like that. That was just the way Americans—*normal* Americans—did things.

And yet dastardly liberals somehow insistently managed to push stories about how Americans did anything but. Stories implying that liberals were the only moral ones. That *you and I*—a favorite Reagan locution, an intimacy-building formulation borrowed directly from FDR's fireside chats—should somehow feel ashamed. Luckily, here was

Ronald Reagan, melting shame in the warmth of his reassurance. "The trouble with our liberal friends is not that they are ignorant," he liked to say; "it's just that they know so much that isn't so."

On the subject of the plain, simple desire of *you and I* for law and order, for instance. "In the last few years the phrase has become unfashionable. Those who have made it so began looking askance at anyone who used the words. Their arched eyebrows were a reaction to what they had determined was an expression of bigotry. If pressed for an explanation they would inform you that 'law and order' were 'code words' that really meant a call for racial discrimination."

"*Wellll*"—another favored Reaganism, a setup that signaled the debunking to come, frequently followed by "it may surprise you to learn" or "the answer may surprise you," signposting some piece of information that would have been common knowledge were liberal gatekeepers not so skilled in their bamboozling ways—"this inference of bigotry is in itself bigoted. Not only does it impugn without proof the character of the person who uses an appropriate phrase to describe what is all too lacking today, but it casts a slur on an entire racial group"—black Americans, the overwhelming victims of crime, 74 percent of whom according to a "survey done in the nation's capital" wanted tougher action against criminals, compared with 61 percent for whites.

This was like the attempts to shame Americans into boycotting grapes, in support of a strike called by Cesar Chavez's United Farm Workers against Gallo Wine. Reagan would know—"I led the first strike our union was ever forced to call. . . . I figured I ought to give this biographical note so there would be no question about my belief about the right of workers to organize, and to strike if necessary." Next came a blizzard of statistics about how these supposedly noble striking martyrs in fact enjoyed fringe benefits "higher than for any other agricultural workers. . . . So enjoy! Have a grape."

Have a grape. Shaming was just was what liberals did. Don't give in. It was liberals who actually were the selfish people. Their schemes pretended to advance democracy, but were actually a conspiracy to subvert it. Had you noticed, for instance, "in recent years, and without our paying attention"—*our:* that loaded word, the people are being victimized by some alien *them*—"it's become easier and easier to become a registered voter?" That just made it "easier and easier for voting blocs to swing elections even though the bloc doesn't represent a majority."

The inflation *their* profligate spending caused: was it not "the cruelest tax, hitting those hardest who can least afford it"?

Those self-righteous environmentalists, "more concerned about nature than people": "home heating is part of our environment, too!"

Indeed liberals' claim to be the ones who cared about poverty was a slur: "No right-thinking person questions our responsibility to lend our less fortunate neighbors a hand but we cannot ignore any longer the harm we are doing to the very people we are trying to help." Harming the poor was what liberals did. For instance, he explained in a series in April, there was the "so-called 'National Welfare Rights Organization'" (another favored trope: "the so-called 'Watergate climate' of last year"; the "so-called haves and have nots"; "so-called 'blacklisting' of people in Hollywood"). The NWRO's true aim, he said, citing a spokeswoman, was expropriation and chaos: "Everyone in this country has a right to share the wealth. The money has gone into the pockets of the middle class, and if we don't get our share, we're going to disrupt this state, this country, and this capital."

This was a flagrant misquotation. What she had actually said was that "the money has gone into the pockets of the middle-class people and made their pockets that much fatter and we are still poor." But no one was checking. It made people feel good. And, as Gerald Ford's struggles governing an ungovernable nation compounded, it was working.

THREE TIMES AT THE BEGINNING OF MARCH, REAGAN WAS FEATURED ON the network news, in report about his political prospects. In the middle of the month he was on *The Tonight Show* with Johnny Carson. The King of Late Night asked the question on everyone's mind: "There's an election coming up, you're out of politics, but you're speaking, and as I say, you're going around the country; um, can you envision a possibility, say in '76, if the convention, say, was deadlocked—I'm giving you all the theories and so forth—and the conservatives took over—"

Cut to Reagan, modestly grinning from ear to ear, as if incredulous at the prospect.

"—and got control of the electoral process, and they couldn't quite make a decision and they came you and said, 'Governor Reagan'—"

He was all but guffawing now, folding his arms, tucking in his chin, glancing over at old Ed McMahon, and just the easy charm of the physical demurral got warm laughs from the studio audience.

"—we're divided, would you like to go to the White House?"

He responded, to peals of laughter, "Do you remember the answer I gave you about the CIA?"

He continued, "Everyone should hope and pray the people there will do such a good job there won't be any question of that." It was an opening a seasoned interviewer could not but exploit: "Do you think they're doing their job well?" Carson asked. Which was a question even a less skilled demurrer could not but knock out of the park. Reagan said he just wanted to see the president balance a budget. How do you do that? Johnny asked. Reagan answered with a favorite joke: "It's like protecting your virtue. You have to say 'no.'"

And the preponderance of a studio audience who hadn't ever considered they might be conservative, confronted with this charming man they were supposed to deplore, applauded and laughed in delight.

On the newsstands, the cover of the March 24 *Newsweek* featured his face, which the article described as "all crinkly and fluttery-eyed when anybody suggests that there might be anything more to his circuit ride than that." It also said he had "become, at least for a season, the most kinetic single presence in American political life . . . and a long shot challenger to Ford, inside their common party or out, for the Presidency of the United States." It quoted a California conservative as being "disgusted with him for not making the commitment. He's our man, but he just won't come on in." It reported the ecstasy he raised at the closing banquet of that winter's second annual Conservative Political Action Conference at the Mayflower Hotel in Washington. The meeting had been dominated by third-party talk among activists, with Ronald Reagan and George Wallace as their dream ticket. They pointed out that the same late 1974 poll that had found only 18 percent of Americans willing to call themselves Republicans discovered 61 percent thought of themselves as conservatives. Reagan had been introduced, to an immediate standing ovation, by the third-party movement's most prominent mover and shaker, *National Review* publisher William Rusher, as "the next President of the United States." He spoke, and raised the roof again: "You can call it mysticism if you want to, but I have always believed that there was some divine plan that placed this great continent between two oceans to be sought out by those who were possessed of an abiding love of freedom and a special kind of courage." And he addressed Bill Rusher's pet idea—only to shoot it down: "Is it a third party that we need, or is it a new and revitalized second party, raising a banner of no pale pastels, but bold colors which could make it unmistakably clear where we stand on all the issues troubling the people?"

Newsweek quoted a moderate Republican who saw him deliver those same lines on the mashed potato circuit in Illinois. It "went over like gangbusters with our crowd," he said. "I don't even like his philosophy, but I sure liked what he said about the party having one."

He had continued, at CPAC, saying, "Americans are hungry to feel once again a mission of greatness." The disappointed true believers who cornered him in corridors to insist that he be the one to lead that mission received in return the same witty gas as Johnny Carson had. "I got the impression," columnist Vic Gold, Spiro Agnew's former press secretary, reported, "that if the fabled Martian visitor had suddenly pancaked his flying saucer into the meeting hall, popped up and demanded, 'Take me to your leader!' Ronald Reagan would have ducked out the back door." "He's too Hollywood," a California editor pooh-poohed to *Newsweek*'s reporter. "He's waiting for someone to come into his dressing room and tell him he's on."

Reagan or no, third party or not, the message a blind-sided political press came away from in that CPAC conclave was the astonishing depths of revulsion against Ford. Jesse Helms said, "Too often the president's program is so bad that even Republicans have difficulty supporting it"—and proposed a platform convention peopled only by conservatives, independent of the ideologically corrupt Republicans, to draft a "second Declaration of Independence." Another speech cited the deficits projected for Ford's next budget. "The shocked reaction," recorded James Wolcott of the *Village Voice,* "suggested billions of charred babies." CPAC participants had scorned Ford for not controlling his wife, who had declared in her first press conference as first lady that she supported abortion rights, and was now quietly lobbying on behalf of the Equal Rights Amendment. ("Betty Ford's problem," said one woman at CPAC, "is that she's taken Eleanor Roosevelt instead of Pat Nixon for the model of what a First Lady is supposed to be.") Robert Bauman, the conservative congressman from Maryland, listed other betrayals: "amnesty for draft dodgers and deserters . . . relentless pushing of détente . . . the elevation to the high office of Vice President of the single most unacceptable nominee one might contemplate—Nelson Rockefeller!" That got a roar second only to the one granted to Reagan.

It all came as a surprise to the pundits. Here was the most conservative president, in many respects, since Harding: a man who had wanted in 1964 to be Barry Goldwater's running mate, and who had been point man in the 1970 effort to impeach the Supreme Court's most liberal justice, William O. Douglas, allegedly for financial regularities but from Ford's rhetoric seemed more for refusing to rule against pornographers, and for being published in a magazine, *Evergreen Review,* that also published arty nudes (Ford called it "hard-core pornography"). No credit for that on the right, apparently; instead, pundits saw conservative activists behaving as if the ordinary act of governing, which is to say compromising, was offensive in and of itself—almost as if they were policing the membership in a tribe. Alongside a flattering profile was a panel by the *Los Angeles Times*' political cartoonist depicting one pachyderm asking another, "Where do elephants go to die?" Why, "Ronald Reagan's ranch," of course. The imperative incessantly invoked when nonconservative Republicans gathered was "broadening the party." But, *Newsweek*'s startled correspondent reflected, "the right's idea of broadening the party . . . is purifying it." Reagan said so himself: he found in the "almost two-thirds of the citizens who refused to participate" in last year's congressional elections a longing for conservative principles. "And if there are those who cannot subscribe to these principles," he wound up—that was the line that got him his most thunderous ovation—"then let them go their way."

A curious position to take for an alleged aspirant to lead a party commanding the loyalties of only 18 percent of the electorate.

Certainly the White House could not take this seriously. It hadn't bothered to send a representative to the CPAC. The president received a delegation of eight conservative senators led by Senator James A. Mc-Clure of Idaho, leaving them with a noncommittal promise to "maintain communication." Congressional moderates drafted what *Newsweek* called "a blood oath of loyalty to the President and party"; within three days they had the signatures of 113 of 145 GOP congressman and 31 of 38 senators. Ford, who had just hired two joke writers, shortly afterward let loose a zinger: Reagan wasn't too old to be president. His hair was just turning "prematurely orange." Presidential confidant Robert Hartmann assured the media, "Before the leaves fall, we're going to be getting spending bills down here that will have to be vetoed. . . . When he fires about ten bills back, and he's perceived as Horatio at the bridge fighting back against the big spenders, some of the conservatives will moderate their criticism of him."

Then, the Reagan presidential boomlet would be put paid to once and for all.

CHAPTER TWENTY

New Right

FOCUSING ON THE GLITTERING PERSONALITIES, PUNDITS LITTLE NOTICED the right-wing insurgency bubbling barely beneath the surface—what conservatives referred to, like civil rights activists from the 1960s, as "the movement."

Activists in the "pro-life" cause (James Wolcott of the *Village Voice* helpfully explained that the unfamiliar term referred to those fighting against abortion) had been thick on the ground at CPAC. A month before that convention, what *Christianity Today* called "an unexpectedly large turnout" of twenty-five thousand braved the winter chill for the second annual "March for Life," commemorating the Supreme Court's *Roe v. Wade* decision. The previous year's march had drawn only what the AP had estimated as "hundreds." The flagship evangelical magazine, tending toward sympathy with the pro-lifers, indelicately declared, "No longer can they be dismissed as a group of cold-hearted Catholics simply following orders from the Pope." A Catholic senator, James Buckley, and an evangelical one, Mark Hatfield, introduced a resolution the week of the *Roe* anniversary to extend "the right of life—to all human beings including their unborn offspring." Shortly after, Buckley was joined by the very conservative Southern Baptist, Jesse Helms of North Carolina, to propose the same language as part of a constitutional amendment banning abortion.

Another Catholic-evangelical pairing took place in Washington on March 19. Some 2,500 antibusing activists from fourteen states led by Louise Day Hicks, and a massive contingent bused from Kanawha County, West Virginia, marched from the Washington Monument to the Capitol. One of the fundamentalist preachers who'd led the West Virginia fight, Avis Hill, said, "This is the first time the two big struggles, against busing and dirty textbooks, have stood side by side. This is the beginning of a political rebellion. . . . If they can break us in our mountain home, they can break us in the farm towns of Jefferson County. If they can break us in the streets of South Boston, they can break us anywhere." Hicks's colleague Raymond Flynn said "the premises are the same . . . the intrusion of the federal government into what was ordinarily considered a local responsibility." Orated Hicks, "We can never be lambs." The previous day, representatives of both movements met with officials from the White House Domestic Council, who assured them "that President Ford recognizes their protests as an important issue."

Then, on April 7, the bishop for the diocese of the four counties surrounding San Diego, representing some 512,000 Catholics, an activist in the city's nonsectarian Pro-Life League, announced priests would refuse Holy Communion to any Catholic who "admits publicly" to membership in the National Organization for Women or any other group advocating abortion: "The issue at stake is not only what we do to unborn children but what we do to ourselves by permitting them to be killed." He called abortion a "serious moral crime" that "ignores God and his love." NOW proclaimed this year's Mother's Day a "Mother's Day of Outrage"—in response, it said, to the Roman Catholic hierarchy's "attempt to undermine the right of women to control their own bodies." The president of Catholics for Free Choice and the Southern California coordinator for NOW's Human Reproduction Task Force, Jan Gleeson, recently returned from Southeast Asia as an Operation Babylift volunteer, clarified the feminist group's position: "It opposes compulsory pregnancy and reaffirms a woman's right to privacy to control her own body as basic to her spiritual, economic, and social well-being."

"Permitting unborn children to be killed" and "ignoring God and his love," versus "compulsory pregnancy" and "basic spiritual, economic, and social well-being": a showdown loomed between irreconcilables, the passions resembling those in a seventeenth-century European religious war.

That Sunday women and men in NOW buttons picketed all day in front of St. Joseph's Cathedral in downtown San Diego. At the lovely missionary-style parish of St. Brigid (patron saint, ironically, of children whose parents are not married), thirty-five were denied the sacrament at the communion rail, others intercepted as they made their way down the aisle. Fifty "pro-choice" members of Women in Law, a feminist student group at the Catholic University of San Diego, picketed at Immaculate Chapel. In one intimate moment captured in the *New York Times,* a priest asked a would-be communicant if she believed in abortion. She replied, "I believe in the law of our land," and was refused a wafer. Bishop Maher returned from an overseas trip that had included a stop in Saudi Arabia, where he had conferred with Muslim religious leaders, and gave a press conference in which he called his opponents' position "pagan." He pointed to a stack of supportive messages and predicted his decision would spread nationwide. Messages to the *Los Angeles Times*, taking up the entire letters section, were radically divided: "NOW should perhaps establish its own religion with Herod as their God" and "At last there is someone strong enough to protect the needless slaying of innocent life," versus "It is clear that the Catholic hierarchy is getting desperate in its frantic efforts to pass a 'compulsory pregnancy' amendment to the U.S. Constitution" and "NOW is dedicated to the liberation of the human spirit. . . . Is it this freedom of choice-by-conscience that the bishop can't abide?"

In the midst of the controversy Ronald Reagan recorded a broadcast describing his agonies in signing the nation's most liberal abortion law, in 1967. That process had been a debacle. "Faced with an abundance of contradictory and absolutist advice," and polls showing that 72 percent of Californians and 59 percent of California Catholics wanted a liberalized abortion law, a Reagan biographer wrote, "Reagan behaved as if lost at sea." At a news conference two hours before the bill had passed, he complained that its provision granting doctors the right to cite mental health grounds as a medical necessity would make it too easy for abortions to be obtained; then, after signing it into law, he claimed he hadn't even been aware such a mental health "loophole" had existed. On radio, in 1975, he recalled discovering "that neither medicine, law, or theology had ever really found a common ground on the subject. Some believed an unborn child was no more than a growth on the female body and she should be able to remove it as she would her appendix. Others felt a human life existed from the moment a fertilized egg was implanted in the womb."

Now, however, decrying abortion was a marker of belonging in the conservative tribe. And suddenly, he devised a way to realize it had been simple all along: that "there is a quite common acceptance in medical circles that the cell—let's call it the egg—once it has been fertilized is on its way as a human being with individual physical traits and physical characteristics already determined."

And yet he insisted the law he signed in 1967 had been just fine, because "[i]n our Judeo-Christian religion, we recognize the right to take life in defense of our own. Therefore an abortion is justified when it is done in self-defense. My belief is that a woman has the right to protect her own life and health against even her own unborn child. I believe also that just as she has the right to defend herself against rape she should not be made to bear a child resulting from that violation of her person and therefore abortion is an act of self-defense."

No matter that none of that bore any relation to the 1967 law, whose mental health loophole had nothing to do with defense of a mother's life. What was telling about the broadcast was its very existence. The fact that he felt compelled to attempt such gyrations spoke to how important the issue had become. And it spoke, perhaps more than any other sign, to the fact that he was serious about running for president—even more than his public visit to the Annenberg estate in February. Or the trip he made to London in April, when he said the Soviets remained "a serious threat to safeguarding our way of life" and "either we continue the concept that man is a unique human being capable of determining his own destiny, with dignity and God-given inalienable rights, or we admit we are faceless ciphers in a Godless collectivist ant heap." *Pravda,* amused, had reported of the speech that "a dinosaur from the 'cold war' times, by the name of Ronald Reagan, has resurrected and made himself known through bellicose roaring."

He might or might not be aiming at the presidency. But in either case, not everyone was taking him seriously. In the White House, for example, word was that he was considered little more than a joke. The conservative movement wasn't taken seriously, either—even as it grew and grew.

ON MOTHER'S DAY EIGHT HUNDRED PROTESTERS DRESSED IN BLACK WITH red armbands, and carrying signs showing coat hangers dripping in blood, picketed before the Vatican embassy in Washington. The evangelical and Catholic members of Long Beach Voice for the Unborn suspended their twenty-fourth consecutive Sunday picketing the abortionists at Long Beach Memorial Hospital to take up the hospital's invitation to discuss the problem of unwanted pregnancy. The hoped-for meeting of the minds never took off. One eighty-seven-year-old member lambasted the Nineteenth Amendment, granting women the vote; her daughter, agreeing, lambasted the would-be twenty-seventh, the ERA, which she said would establish a federal police force to require women to work outside the home. In San Diego, Anaheim, and Los Angeles, Catholic NOW members staged ceremonies reversing the traditional bell, book, and candle excommunication rite (in Anaheim the "book" was the Constitution and the "bell" was a replica of the Liberty Bell). "At the end," a member of Catholics for the Right to Choose explained, "they snuff out the candle to signify spiritual death. We light the candle to signify life."

Dramatic stuff—though there was no coverage of it on network TV. And new polling by Lou Harris found 54 percent in favor of abortion, at least in the first three months of pregnancy (compared with 38 percent opposed). Pundits didn't find much to say about it, either. The change was registering instead at the level of society's tectonic plates—at the core of America's religious identity.

A certain sort of bland religiosity had expanded enormously in the 1950s. The typical American pursued a faith experience, the sociologist Will Herberg wrote in his influential 1955 book, *Protestant-Catholic-Jew*, "that reassures him about the existential rightness of everything American, his nation, his culture, and himself." President Eisenhower said, "A system of government like ours makes no sense unless founded on a firm faith in religion—and I don't care what it is." Blandness was supposed to be a good thing; it attenuated cultural conflict, smoothed edges, made a diverse nation united and strong.

The denominations expanding the most, in fact, were the blandest of all—the "mainline" ones: Presbyterians, Methodists, Lutherans, the United Church of Christ (a merger of old Congregationalist denominations), and especially the Episcopalian Church, once mocked as the "Republican Party at Prayer," back when Republicanism was understood as the province of stolid moderation—nothing like the people on display that year at the Conservative Political Action Conference, the ones describing abortion as a holocaust and reduced to frenzies of rage at any mention of that bland man Gerald Rudolph Ford. Who was, of course, an Episcopalian.

When church growth plateaued in the 1960s, the conclusion was immediately drawn: congregants fled pews because churches were no longer "relevant." *Relevant:* a very sixties word. It meant that churches did not resemble the world outside their walls—a changing world, a dynamic world, a world of shifting values and softening mores, a tolerant world, a *liberal* world. The churchmen who rose in denominational counsels were the ones who were leaders in liberal, even radical causes. William Sloane Coffin, since 1958 the chaplain at Yale, went on trial for counseling draft resistance in 1967. Portions of the legal defense of Angela Davis, the Afroed American Communist on trial in 1972 for allegedly providing the weapons to black militants who assassinated a judge, were paid for by the United Presbyterian Church of North America. The Catholic Church's Vatican II reforms of the early 1960s brought in their wake by the late 1960s priests who did not just deliver the liturgy in English instead of Latin, facing the congregation rather than the altar, but did so strumming guitars. Others went further: Lutherans in 1970, reform Jews in 1972, and Episcopalians in 1974 started ordaining women as clergy. "EPISCOPAL LEADERSHIP LISTENS TO ITS MEMBERS;

HEADQUARTERS ADMITS CREDIBILITY GAP," read a 1973 headline in the *Los Angeles Times*—the same year Episcopalians recognized civil divorce. In 1975 they rewrote the Book of Common Prayer, one of the literary monuments of Western civilization. One of the changes was a passage endorsing nonmarital sex.

It didn't work. Between 1965 and 1975 all the old gains in membership were reversed: Lutherans by 5 percent, United Methodists by 10 percent, Presbyterians by 7 percent . . . and, most of all, the Episcopalians, who lost 16.7 percent of their membership. One of the auguries in the pulp paperback *Predictions for 1974* was that the Catholic Church would become more liberal "but will continue to lose supporters at a tremendous rate." That one, unlike the prediction that a submarine and a UFO would collide off the Aleutian Islands, turned out to be true.

At that, the churches responded by struggling frenetically to become more relevant. And by 1975, things began getting ridiculous.

That was the year a Palm Sunday "Circus Mass" was held at Holy Trinity in Washington, D.C.: clowns in baggy pants, midgets, an acrobat balanced atop a pole twenty feet above the altar. Later that April, at the First Unitarian Church in Fort Worth, Texas, Pastor William Nichols invited parishioner Diana King to the pulpit. She announced, "I would like to do a sermon using exotic dance, and members of the congregation could join me if they like." She stripped down to only a G-string. Pastor Nichols later told reporters, "I haven't had one complaint. I feel like exotic dancing is a part of life. It fit very well into our service. We are inheritors of the Victorian ethic which I don't accept. She was expressing herself and I think she got that over to the congregation." He also said no one had been aroused—but if anyone had been, that would have been okay, too: "I don't consider the erotic aspect of the dance wrong. After all, that's the way we were conceived." For Mrs. King's part, asked by a reporter "if she thought her nude dance sparked any feelings other than spiritual," she responded, "I don't know what you mean by 'spiritual.' I don't dance to frustrate people. I create a fantasy. I like to turn people on. I really felt good . . . it's affirming nature and love . . . you can't separate body from mind."

It all became easy to mock. A cartoon in the February 28 issue of *Christianity Today* had Jesus rewriting "He that is without sin": "To confront the moral challenge of the complexities and conflicts of our age will require that we resist the temptations of simple answers and resolve instead to be responsive to and responsible for a moral universe that is characterized by both continuity and open-endedness. . . ." John Updike came out that spring with a new novel, *A Month of Sundays*, in which a wayward minister was sent by his bishop to a rest home. It banned "[a]ll traditions, perhaps orthodox, sources of help for emotional and spiritual healing. But the bar opens at noon. . . . Today is Sunday. Though they try to hide this from us, I can count."

Not everyone mocked. Some, simply, left. They didn't want their churches to be "relevant" to the world outside church walls. The reason they went to church in the first place was to *escape* the world outside church walls—a world that liberals had turned into a madhouse. It was like what Ronald Reagan had said on TV in 1964: "They say the world has become too complex for simple answers. They are wrong. There are no easy answers, but there *are* simple answers. We must have the courage to do what we know is morally right." Those were the churches people were turning to now: the ones that didn't doubt what was morally right.

The Holy Roller Church of the Nazarene grew by 8 percent; the hard-core Seventh-Day Adventists grew by 36 percent; the Pentecostal Assemblies of God by 37 percent. The United Methodists suffered a financial crisis because members were no longer interested in sending money to its Board of Missions. They were sending donations, instead, to organizations like the Good News Movement in Wilmore, Kentucky, a "forum for scriptural Christianity within the United Methodist Church," attacking a "radically new secularized philosophy of mission" that sought social change rather than "bringing persons to salvation through a personal relationship with Jesus Christ."

Other such tectonic plates were shifting in Washington.

That spring, a Kanawha-style controversy spread through conservative precincts nationwide. In 1964 the Harvard psychologist Jerome Bruner began writing what was intended as a national social science curriculum for middle schoolers, with support from the Ford Foundation and the National Science Foundation. Bruner reasoned that any subject could be taught in a serious way to children of any age, and that people learned best when "actively and thoughtfully operating on their experiences." What he didn't consider, not at all, was politics.

By 1972 his curriculum, "Man: A Course of Study," or MACOS, was being taught to 400,000 students in 1,700 schools. It sought, said its author, to fight "authoritarian attitudes" instilled by rote instruction. It would inculcate open-minded, scientific attitudes of discovery instead. Little social scientists would, for instance, discuss what made humans human by contrasting films of free-ranging baboons with ethnographic films depicting the traditional practices of the Netsilik Inuit—Eskimo—of the frigid arctic. Then they would be invited to grasp the anthropological concept of cultural relativity by comparing Netsilik cosmology and mythology with that they learned at their parents' knee—"to leave their own specific culture to become critically aware of it and to understand culture as a generic human creation," Bruner wrote.

Kind of like, in that textbook adopted by the Kanawha County School Board, the invitation for children to compare the Greek myth of Androcles and the Lion with the scriptural story of Daniel in the lions' den. And at that, Bruner soon found himself in the lions' den.

The first fires were local. In Quincy, Massachusetts, the protest came from the parent-organizers of South Shore Citizens Against Forced Busing, who alleged their children were being indoctrinated in "unsavory and barbaric Eskimo practices." A Houston parent announced that these included "cannibalism, infanticide, genocide, senilicide . . . stabbing, wife-swapping, animal beating, bloodletting, and mating with all kinds of animals." MACOS defenders pointed out these practices were either from a time before the Netsilik made first contact with the outside world in the 1920s, or from plots in Netsilik *myths.* Course materials made it perfectly clear that present-day Inuit deplored them—just as present-day Jews and Christians deplored, say, all the smiting depicted in the Bible. The point, they said, was to shake students from their complacent notion that theirs was the only legitimate way to view the world—a response heard on the right as but more evidence of the moral turpitude of their secular humanist foes. Then the conflagration became national—as cries were once more heard at the Heritage Foundation in Washington, which found in MACOS another convenient exhibit of the wicked federal bureaucracy's conspiracy to undermine the traditional family.

Quotations from a new volume in Heritage's "Public Policy Studies" series, *Man: A Course of Study—Prototype for Federalized Textbooks?* by Connie Marshner's sister-in-law Susan Marshner, soon began showing up on newspaper editorial pages: that MACOS was "an invasion of privacy of children and their parents"; that students were being manipulated, not into open-ended inquiry, but into the heresy "that there are no moral absolutes." "What this means in practice," interpreted an inventive conservative columnist in the newspaper *Southeast Missourian,* "is that a teacher, for example, may not speak out against cheating if cheating is taking place as a result of an individual 'discovery' process."

The fire spread to Capitol Hill—and threatened to engulf the very concept of federal funding for scientific pedagogy itself. John Conlan, a second-term Republican congressman from Arizona who some evangelicals wanted to run for president, and Olin Teague, the conservative

Texas Democrat who chaired the House Committee on Science and Astronautics, opened hearings on April 9 to "reassert congressional authority over NSF curriculum activities to stop what is shaping up as an insidious attempt to impose particular school courses and approaches to learning on local school districts—using the power and financial resources of the Federal Government to set up a network of educator-lobbyists to control education throughout America." Conlan's constituents, apparently, disagreed: a poll of Phoenix parents found only 8 percent opposed the curriculum. But then maybe they just didn't appreciate, as Conlan thundered from the hearing room dais, that MACOS deployed "cultural shock techniques" to cause kids "to reject the values, beliefs, religions, and national loyalties of their parents and American society generally."

He won. That August, Congress scrapped $9 million from the National Science Foundation budget earmarked for summer workshops for a "variety of recently developed courses for elementary and secondary schools." The following January, Conlan introduced an amendment requiring direct review of *all* NSF curriculum projects. Congressmen didn't know why their phones were ringing off the hook concerning this obscure measure. They didn't know that thousands upon thousands of people whose names happened to repose in a computer data bank, because once upon a time they had donated to Barry Goldwater, or because they had responded to an appeal to send Bibles to Africa or had once subscribed to a conservative magazine, were receiving letters signed by Senator Jesse Helms reading, "Your taxes are being used to pay for grade school courses that teach our children that cannibalism, wife swapping, and the murder of infants and the elderly are acceptable behavior." They just knew that their constituents were concerned. Conlan's radical measure narrowly missed passing the House, by a vote of 196 to 215. A new wellspring of political power had announced itself in Washington.

THE EMERGING CONSERVATIVE INFRASTRUCTURE BEGAN WITH BARRY Goldwater's presidential campaign, which ingathered an army—an army that could lose a battle, suck it up, and then regroup to fight a thousand battles more. The failed Goldwater crusade spawned combat divisions in its wake like the American Conservative Union, a lobbying group that was founded a month after Goldwater's defeat, and now was thriving; it put on the massive CPAC convention each year, alongside the conservative youth group Young Americans for Freedom—which was founded in the wake of the *first* effort to run Barry Goldwater for president, in

1960. These were just two spearheads. Eleven years later, their progeny were rich and variegated.

These progeny included an expanding technology of fund-raising and grassroots communication. In 1961 a young man from Houston named Richard Viguerie, who told reporters his heroes were "the two Macs"—Joe McCarthy and General Douglas MacArthur—took a job as executive director of Young Americans for Freedom. That organization itself began as a bit of a con, something of a front for the ideological ambitions of the grown-ups running *National Review*. The middle-aged man who ran the operation from behind the scenes, Marvin Liebman, was an ideological P. T. Barnum figure, famous on the right for selling the claim that he had amassed a million signatures on petitions opposing the People's Republic of China's entry into the United Nations. (He said they were in a warehouse in New Jersey. No one ever saw the warehouse.) The first thing Liebman told Viguerie was that YAF had two thousand paid members but that in public, he should always claim there were twenty-five thousand. And the first thing that Liebman showed Viguerie was the automated "Robotype" machine used to send out automated fund-raising pitches. Viguerie's eyes widened; he had found his life's calling.

Following Goldwater's defeat, Viguerie went into business for himself. He visited the clerk of the House of Representatives, where the identities of those who donated fifty dollars or more to a presidential campaign were filed. First alone, then with a small army of female temp workers, he started copying down names and addresses in longhand—until a nervous civil servant told him to cease and desist, by which point he had captured thousands of names of the most ardent right-wingers in the nation. Soon, so many unsolicited form letters were being sent over Ronald Reagan's signature that the former governor had to write personal letters to friends apologizing for them. In 1968, Viguerie raised by mail an unheard-of $6 million for George Wallace's presidential run, 76 percent of the campaign's income; in 1970 and 1971 he raised $2.3 million for the antismut group Citizens for Decent Literature (some 84 percent of the money went back into Viguerie's company, though a conservative group that decided to do the same work in-house discovered it could raise funds for fifty cents on the dollar). Then he pulled in $7 million to retire George Wallace's 1972 campaign debt—and his client list grew and grew.

And in May 1975, after trying and failing to buy *Human Events*, Viguerie began publishing *Conservative Digest: A Magazine for the New Majority*, sending out as a subscription premium five thousand copies of

William Rusher's third-party manifesto *The Making of a New Majority Party.* The appeal put the presidency in its sights: "Our country, which badly needs a strong Winston Churchill, is stuck with a weak Gerald Ford." The New Right now had the germ of its own media.

Conservatives also enjoyed an expanding cadre of national newspaper columnists. The latest was Patrick J. Buchanan—appropriately, since one of his jobs in the Nixon White House had been to shame media executives into spasms of contrition for tilting their organs to the left. He had returned to the news briefly the day before Nixon's resignation when it was reported he had written a memo advising the president to burn the White House tapes. A few weeks after that, Alexander Haig begged the new president to honor Buchanan's dear wish to become America's ambassador to South Africa. (Ford did not find that a wise idea.) Instead, in the spring of 1975, his column debuted, syndicated, ironically enough, by the New York Times Company, with a piece on a tax bill just passed by the House. "The redistribution of wealth, downward, is what much of this $21.3 billion worth of 'tax relief' is about," he wrote, complaining that the 4.6 million Americans it dropped from the tax rolls would be "reassigned to that expanding army of citizens who pay nothing in federal income taxes for the broad and widening array of social benefits they enjoy," contributing to "a new class in America, a vast constituency of millions with no interest whatsoever in reducing the power of government, and every incentive to support its continued growth."

That particular argument of Buchanan's was amplified in an unlikely quarter: by a former Trotskyite, more recently an enthusiastic liberal, now writing a column in the *Wall Street Journal* as the public face of a new rightward intellectual tendency. Like many prominent right-leaning intellectuals, Irving Kristol was a Jewish veteran of ideological combat in the lunchroom alcoves at the Depression-era City College of New York, where Stalinists did battle with Trotsykists and honed an ideological fierceness resembling that of public intellectuals in Europe. Bouncing around from publication to publication, he became a liberal increasingly adept at lacerating liberal pieties—for instance, writing in an essay titled "Civil Liberties 1952—A Study in Confusion," that "there is one thing that the American people know about Senator McCarthy: he, like them, is unequivocally anti-Communist. About the spokesmen for American liberalism, they feel they know no such thing." By 1965 he was editing a new magazine, the *Public Interest*, inaugurated in 1965 and financed by a former CIA agent who was now a stockbroker. It specialized in social-science debunkings of Great Society social programs. Its editor was soon on his way to what the democratic socialist Michael Harrington dubbed in 1973 "neoconservatism." And in his May 19, 1975, *Wall Street Journal* column, Kristol published one of neoconservatism's most influential texts. In capital letters, it named, and shamed, what he called capitalism's "New Class": the self-aggrandizing stewards of the welfare state. They were really not much interested in helping people, "but keenly interested in power. Power for what? Well, the power to shape our civilization—a power which, in a capitalist society, is supposed to reside in the free market. This 'new class' wants to see much of the power redistributed to the government, where they will then have a major say in how it is exercised." Then, niftily reversing the traditional understanding that it was rich capitalists whose democratic loyalties were suspicious, Kristol concluded that this "elitist new class" was "hostile to the market precisely because the market is so vulgarly democratic—one dollar, one vote."

Another figure who seemed on his way to becoming a neoconservative was in the news. Daniel Patrick Moynihan was a former Harvard professor who as a Labor Department official under Lyndon Johnson became a lightning rod for criticism by proposing that "the fundamental source of weakness in the Negro community at the present time" was the "tangle of pathologies" inherent in the black family—not, say, a lack of jobs. He became the focus of controversy again as a special assistant in the White House when a 1970 memo he wrote leaked. It argued that a period of "benign neglect" was the best response to racial problems. A blunt, outspoken man, an intellectual: rare in politics. He nonetheless kept rising in the Washington firmament. On May 21, President Ford announced his intention to nominate Moynihan as ambassador to the United Nations—even as a Moynihan essay in a recent issue of *Commentary*, the flagship neoconservative magazine, argued that radical, malevolent Third World elements, resource-rich and puffed up by OPEC's example, were taking over the world body, telling the First World what to do, and that it was "time that the American spokesman came to be feared." A UPI profile explained the stakes: "Moynihan's policy prescription could throw him into direct confrontation with Third World leaders when the UN General Assembly holds a special session next September to consider organizational changes and demand improved economic relationships between rich and poor nations."

On the broader right, more and more "think tanks" emerged to provide intellectual ballast, or in some cases just the appearance of intellectual ballast, to the conservatives on the editorial pages—and on the radio, where Ronald Reagan, who for instance got raw material for his rant about "Polish bisexual frogs" from an outfit called the National Taxpayers Union. Sometimes Reagan promoted the new groups outright—for instance, the Pacific Legal Foundation, a corporate-funded outfit he described to his listeners in June as "a young public interest legal group that has some powerful ax-grinders on the run . . . defending government in one case, and protesting it in another . . . wherever the broader public interest might lie." The bad guys said to be *fighting* the public interest included "hyper environmental groups" opposing the building of a Trident submarine base on Puget Sound, who "seem to conveniently forget that freedom is every bit as fragile and irreplaceable as any given ecological system"; and the EPA bureaucrats he said were trying to create deliberate traffic jams to keep people from using cars; and, naturally, the "so-called 'welfare rights' groups," which served the interests only of grifters like one "Linda Taylor, the champion welfare cheat of all time. She used eighty aliases and fifty addresses to defraud thirteen states of more than half a million dollars."

"It's good to know that you and I are not entirely at the mercy of those special interests who seek to spend our tax money and bend and interpret the laws to their own special points of view!"

The corporate-funded organizations fighting alleged special interests were housed mostly in and around Washington—but also in places like the Hoover Institution at Stanford University. The institution was founded in 1959 by the namesake former president widely considered responsible for the Great Depression with a statement asserting, "The purpose of this institution must be, by its research and publications, to demonstrate the evils of the doctrines of Karl Marx." The institution was featured in a spread in the summer of 1975 in the *Los Angeles Times* noting its $3.5 million annual budget, its handsome new underground building, and that "[i]n recent months the work of Hoover scholars in several domestic fields, among them taxation, government regulation, and healthcare, has been favorably mentioned by Ford administration officials." Its fellows were busy "shuttling back and forth to Washington, testifying before congressional committees and serving as advisors to various federal agencies." Its director, W. Glenn Campbell, was asked about the Stanford faculty members who had tried to shut it down as inconsistent with academic canons of free inquiry. He responded, "If you are asking me if we consider ourselves to be in the liberal academic mainstream, my answer is, 'I hope not because that's disastrous for the country.'"

They were forging new engines for electoral organizing, too. In suburban Rosslyn, Virginia, the four full-time and forty part-time organizers of the National Conservative Political Action Committee (NCPAC) were hard at work raising what would add up to $3 million from conservative donors to build off-the-shelf campaign apparatus for conservative candidates in 1976: press agentry, TV and print ads, campaign consultants, and even campaign managers. The direct mail pitches to raise the funds came from Richard Viguerie's shop. The one on "grade school courses that teach our children that cannibalism," signed by Jesse Helms, the former boss of NCPAC principal Charlie Black, was one of its solicitations; explained executive director Terry Dolan, a former Young Republicans activist, "The shriller you are, the better it is to raise money." Another principle, Roger Stone, former head of the District of Columbia Young Republicans, had been a dirty tricks specialist: he had shown up in the Ervin Committee investigations for hiring a spy who infiltrated the McGovern campaign and reported to Stone; and for sending a two-hundred-dollar donation to the campaign of a liberal Republican running against Nixon in the 1972 New Hampshire primary in the name of the Young Socialist Alliance (he then sent the receipt to Manchester's *Union Leader* so it would report that Nixon's rival was a Red). Dolan later explained to a reporter one of NCPAC's raisons d'être: "We could say whatever we want about an opponent of a Senator Smith and the senator wouldn't have to say anything. A group like ours could lie through its teeth and the candidate it helps stays clean."

Then there was the "Committee for the Survival of a Free Congress," assembled by a Heritage Foundation cofounder from Wisconsin named Paul Weyrich, who from a renovated Capitol Hill carriage house was about to send one hundred thousand letters over Senator James McClure's signature, using Viguerie's mighty mailing lists, appealing for $2 million to defeat a hundred "of the most liberal, anti-business and pro-welfare congressmen," with Bella Abzug and Berkeley's black socialist Ron Dellums topping the list. ("Although the fund-raising letter was written on McClure's U.S. Senate stationery," the AP reported in a June profile on Weyrich's new group, "the senator claimed little knowledge of who the targeted congressmen are or why they were selected.")

Weyrich's money came primarily from a single source: the Coors brewing family of California, whose youngest scion, Joseph, the *Washington Post* reported in a profile, "has been pumping millions of dollars a year into new national organizations with headquarters in the East, designed to push the United States politically to the right." These included Weyrich's Committee for a Free Congress, the Heritage Foundation, the right-wing business groups the National Association of Manufacturers and the National Federation of Independent Businesses, and conservative cells in both chambers of Congress, the House Republican Study Committee, and the Committee of Nine in the Senate—whose "only contributions last year came from the Coors family." (Reagan, for his part, did a favor for Coors with a radio broadcast deploring a federal judicial ruling against one of the company's business practices; one of his political aides in Sacramento, Robert Walker, was now a Coors vice president.) Coors, Weyrich told the *Post,* "Is a man who believes more deeply than anybody I have ever met, except religious monks. When things go wrong that he feels deeply about, he's like a child . . . in sorrow and grief over what's going on, and a frustration over his inability to do anything about it." So he started doing something about it.

Another fledgling ideological force founded by Weyrich got its eighty thousand dollars in seed funding from a rich scion of the old Mellon banking clan. The American Legislative Exchange Council had been a rather sleepy alliance of right-leaning state legislators; its tax status was "501(c)3"—which is to say, a charitable organization whose value as a tax write-off for donors relied on its not getting involved in direct political participation. Of a sudden, its executive director, an Illinois Republican activist named Juanita Barnett, found her group the beneficiary of Richard Mellon Scaife, a Pittsburgh billionaire who'd donated $1 million to Richard Nixon's reelection campaign and whose plaything was the newspaper of a little Pennsylvania town, the *Greensburg Tribune-Review.* Once, when he'd heard one of his reporters celebrating the resignation of Spiro Agnew, he had him fired on the spot. His political ambitions were bigger now. When Barnett asked Weyrich what could possibly make her shell of an organization worth eighty thousand dollars, he responded, basically, that it was worth that much precisely *because* it was a shell of an organization: "Juanita, ALEC is the *only* state legislative organization in the country—of our persuasion—which has a 501(c)3. If they took ALEC to Washington and did a good job, they . . . could go back to Scaife and get Scaife to set up a political Action Committee to finance state legislative campaign races." In other words, ALEC could be a "nonpolitical" Trojan horse for right-wing political activity. It worked: dismissing the meddlesome Juanita Barnett, they set up shop both in Washington and in the rent-free office of a conservative Illinois state representative, whose phone lines they illegally made use of, and began writing model bills for state legislatures, unnoticed by the press until 1978.

Meanwhile, battles were raging for and against the passage of the Equal Rights Amendment to the Constitution. "Equality of rights under the law shall not be denied or abridged by the United States or by any

State on account of sex," ran its apparently anodyne text. The majority of the public supported the idea; respectable moderate Republican women being its main base of support, the Republicans had endorsed it in every one of their party platforms since 1944 and President Eisenhower had asked a joint session of Congress to approve it in 1958. Congress did so, finally, in 1972—at which the movement to achieve the constitutional requirement of approval in two-thirds of state legislatures, thirty-eight to be precise, took off like a rocket, with thirty ratifications by the end 1973.

Then, the progress became like molasses.

Only four more states voted passage by that spring. One reason was a frantic right-wing movement that sprang nearly fully formed from the brow of a single, brilliant, indefatigable middle-aged woman from suburban Alton, Illinois. Phyllis Schlafly had been an accomplished conservative activist since not long after she received her master of business administration degree from Harvard University in 1945. In becoming so accomplished, she mastered a dubious mode of public presentation later adopted to great effect by leaders such as Louise Day Hicks in South Boston and Alice Moore in Kanawha County: just an innocent housewife, went her story, going about her business raising a family like any other, when her sudden shocked discovery of alien impositions on home and hearth by left-wing conspiracists forced her out of her kitchen and into the spotlight as a reluctant warrior for decency. Brochures for Schlafly's 1952 congressional run, in fact, depicted her cooking breakfast in an apron—a housewife identity belied by the fact that she was running for Congress, and held a master's degree from Harvard, but she never let the contradiction detain her. Instead she leveraged it to become perhaps the most effective organizer the right had ever known.

Her signature issue, running for Congress and afterward, had been anti-Communism; her newsletter, the *Phyllis Schlafly Report,* launched in 1967 after the respectable moderate women who so doted on the ERA defeated her for president of the National Federation of Republican Women, bristled with McCarthyite accusations of Communist infiltration in high places. She was riveted by the arcana of geopolitics and nuclear doctrine (here, she obsessively claimed that the strategic preference of Robert McNamara for missiles over bombers was actually a stealth plot to disarm the United States) and was obsessed with the anti-American wickedness of the United Nations; when she thought about the ERA at all, she later said, she considered it "something between innocuous and mildly helpful."

That was then. Now, from the vantage of her brand-new organization the Eagle Forum (because "the eagle is almost the only creature that keeps one mate for a lifetime"), she was convinced that the Equal Rights Amendment was the worst outrage the liberals had yet conceived. She set to work convincing the rest of the world.

The ERA, she argued, would "take away the right of young women to be exempt from the draft." It would "invalidate the state laws that make it the obligation of the husband to support his wife financially." It would "wipe out the right to receive Social Security benefits based on her husband's earnings." It would legalize—nay, encourage—homosexual marriages and adoptions. It would "remake our laws, revise the marriage contract, restructure society, remold our children to conform to liberal values instead of God's values, and replace the image of woman as virtue and mother with the image of prostitute, swinger, and lesbian." It would require the Catholic Church "to admit women to the priesthood and to abandon its single-sex schools . . . or else lose its tax exempt status."

An Illinois state representative who joined the crusade rumbled, "Put it on the heads of your children and your grandchildren and watch and witness the decline of the United States of America, a great country that was founded on the principle of family units. In Colorado, where they have ERA, men want to marry horses. Homosexuals marry homosexuals there. This is what you're talking about with ERA." And, in a charge that seemed to galvanize conservative imaginations most of all, critics insisted it would legally ban the institution of separate restrooms for men and women. As one terrified Florida woman told her state senator, "I do not want to share a public restroom with black or white hippie males."

A powerful nerve had been touched. Phyllis Schlafly was adept at touching nerves. She would claim later that it was her husband, a lawyer, who first helped her appreciate the dangers the ERA foretold. That may or may not be true. But, as with that devastatingly effective husband-and-wife team in the textbook movement who insisted that the media refer to them as the "Mel Gablers," the notion that the antifeminist activist served at the instigation, and pleasure, of the man of the house nicely served the story of the traditional family under siege she was so effectively able to tell: that the barnstorming housewife activist left the home only to *preserve* the home; that traditional bourgeois hierarchies actually preserved liberties and it was the "liberals" who subverted them. It all seemed so maddeningly illogical to her feminist adversaries that they could never contain their rage when they were around her ("I'd like to burn you at the stake!" fumed NOW founder Betty Friedan at a 1973 debate)—which only, of course, helped her cause some more.

By the spring of 1975, however, it all sounded logical enough to the burgeoning armies of the right. For instance, to the antibusing activists of Boston. On April 9, they took over a pro-ERA meeting a Faneuil Hall sponsored by the Governor's Commission on the Status of Women. Elaine Noble, the first openly lesbian state legislator, took the podium; ROAR women drowned her out with the chant "We like men! We like men!"

A genteel feminist lectured ROAR's Pixie Palladino: "You are our guest, and if you don't behave, I'll have to ask you to leave."

"No!" Pixie snarled back at the alien imposition, plainly from Brahmin Wellesley or some such. "You're *our* guests, this is *our* City Hall. No bunch of ladies from the suburbs is going to kick the women of Boston out of their own City Hall."

Spring, 1975: a conservative coming-out. Southern evangelical Protestants and orthodox Catholics, both traditionally Democratic, fighting shoulder to shoulder to protect the "unborn"; an aggressive, expanding "New Right" of conservative politicians, making a run at the very legitimacy of the Republican Party; sophisticated former liberals, "neoconservatives," adding their voice in all the right cosmopolitan precincts; parents agitating against the liberal bureaucrats who were deforming their children with busing and coed bathrooms and secular humanist hokum—a *coalition.*

IT WAS ONE THAT, HOWEVER, THE *NEW YORK TIMES* FOUND EASY TO DISmiss. That summer the newspaper of record did a feature article about textbook fights fanning out nationwide like brooms in the Sorcerer's Apprentice story. It quoted an education publisher: "This thing has spread since the West Virginia outbreak to the point that there is not an educational publisher who has not made at least one minor revision in the face of pressure." But not to fear, the *Times* assured its liberal-minded readers: "The protesters constitute only a few thousand of the millions of parents with children in the nation's public schools"; the organizations coordinating the protest "include the John Birch Society, the Ku Klux Klan . . . and the Heritage Foundation." Yoking the mainstream conservative group that was becoming a constant presence on Capitol Hill to the frightening fringe that burned crosses in the woods made it hard to see this sort of thing as the leading wedge of anything serious at all.

What the *Times* missed was the political undercurrent. This was supposed to be a skeptical age. But the longing for the conservative innocence Ronald Reagan was selling was strong, for those with eyes to see, in all sorts of quarters. Three panels, in the House and the Senate and under the auspices of Vice President Rockefeller, were hard at work behind closed doors investigating epic abuses of public trust by the nation's intelligence agencies. Lillian Hellman, the left-wing playwright, lectured Columbia University graduates in a commencement speech reprinted in the *New York Times:* "You who are graduating today, far more than those who graduated in the sixties, have very possibly lived through the most shocking period in American history . . . you know that government agencies — the CIA, the FBI, the Department of Justice, and God knows what yet hasn't come to light — have spied on innocent people who did nothing more than express their democratic right to say what they thought. You have read that the CIA has not only had a hand in upsetting foreign governments it did not like, it has very possibly been involved in murder, or plots to murder. Murder. We didn't think of ourselves that way once upon a time."

In turn, Rockefeller commission member Ronald Reagan granted absolution on the radio: "Isn't it time to ask if we aren't threatened more by the people the FBI and CIA are watching than we are by the FBI and the CIA?" A House member explained that really, no one cared. "This is not the Watergate investigation. Nobody ever talks to me about it on home trips, and I hear very little about it here."

Cultural undercurrents pointed toward this right-leaning longing for innocence, too. In April, twenty-five red-white-and-blue train cars pulled out of Cameron Station in Alexandria, Virginia, set to streak through all forty-eight continental states in 1976, the bicentennial year for the signing of the Declaration of the Independence. Display cases on the side of some of the Freedom Train's cars featured artifacts of American politics; other cars were entirely encased in transparent material — mobile museum vitrines, displaying the glories of God's chosen nation: a lunar rover, the first horseless carriage to win a transcontinental race, the first typewriter, a Polaroid camera. And a replica of the Liberty Bell, twice the size of the original, donated by the American Legion. Every cent was paid by corporate contributions, General Motors, Kraftco, and Prudential Life Insurance contributing $1 million each. Reagan lionized its private sponsorship as a "miracle in this day of government organized, planned, and managed activity. . . . Where else but in America could this happen? Come to think of it, how many places are left in the world where there is that much freedom to celebrate?"

Early in May, the Columbia University Board of Trustees, which oversaw the selection of Pulitzer Prizes, snubbed its advisory board's selection of Seymour Hersh's blockbuster CIA exposé. Its other selections were anodyne; the trustees "seemed to go out of their way," *Time* observed, "to find relatively noncontroversial subjects." The press, newly emboldened after taking down a president, was supposed to be the headquarters of the new suspicious circles—*The New Muckrakers,* according to the title of a book by the *Washington Post*'s Leonard Downie Jr. Its back cover boomed out: "There is a new kind of American reporter. He does more than record news. He makes history." The book quoted Downie's colleague Bob Woodward: "It's almost a perverse pleasure. I like going out and finding something that is going wrong." But it felt to some as though there had been enough of all that.

As a historian later reflected, Hersh's "early determination to carry the Watergate mentality into the post-Watergate era made his colleagues uncomfortable and even angry"—even, or especially, at the *Washington Post,* which seemed to be shrinking back from its reputation for making history, as if in guilt. The *Post*'s publisher, Katharine Graham, told the Magazine Publishers Association that reporters were becoming "too much a party to events. . . . To see a conspiracy and cover-up in everything is as myopic as to believe that no conspiracies or coverups exist." Its editor Ben Bradlee worried that "these tendencies to develop a social, messianic role for the media, when added to the already feverish drive for the sensationalist story and the scoop, [will] lead to further dispositions that should concern us." And the *Post*'s intelligence beat reporter immediately hit his *Times* counterpart's CIA scoops for a "dearth of hard facts"—even though, in subsequent months, every one of its claims had been vindicated and more. Late in March, Leslie Gelb of the *Times* reflected in the *New Republic* on the reasons for the rest of the media's reluctance to pick up on the CIA story: a history of coziness between the press and the clandestine service "going back to the days of the OSS"; a culture of "long established social relationships"; and even more significantly, a discomfort that the "Stain of Watergate" was "spreading out to the past, to the pre-Nixon years, and to the future. The dream of being able to make Nixon vanish and keep everything else was coming into jeopardy."

And indeed, shortly after that was written, every major media outlet in the nation acceded to a CIA request not to report a story about a failed CIA project to pay $350 million to Howard Hughes to manufacture a salvage vehicle, the Glomar Explorer, for a sunken Soviet submarine. And when the maverick syndicated investigative reporter Jack Anderson *did* finally report the debacle, most outlets reframed it as a heroic triumph—"The Great Submarine Snatch," reported *Time,* taking the opportunity to editorialize that the congressional intelligence investigations could irreparably harm future such missions. When CIA director William Colby came calling, *Esquire*'s William Greider complained, a supposedly "adversarial" press "rolled over on its back to have its tummy rubbed."

A bereft nation had just lost its first war; change was everywhere; and, quietly, Americans were hugging any excuse not to change. The federal government announced a commitment to replace America's outdated, irrational weights and measures—pounds, inches, quart, the "English" system, which even the English didn't use anymore—with the international "metric" standard—kilograms, meters, liters. A leader of the International Brotherhood of Electrical Workers predicted, "There will be massive resistance"—as if some liberal bureaucrat were forcing his kid to be bused to a black school, or learn about Eskimo cannibalism: "What we have here is engineers and scientists trying to make important social and economic change." The June issue of *Texas Monthly*, the magazine for the Lone Star State's hip young professionals, reported in one article on the graduates of the Class of '75, for whom "the romanticism of the Sixties seems to have lost most of its charm, leaving in its place a rush to security." They were returning "to beer and fraternities and sororities. . . . There is also some recognition and perhaps even a dose of respect for, yes, Dad and Mom"—for economic reasons if nothing else: their parents' generation "by and large managed to find and hold jobs." Another article tracked "The New Woman: Returning to Submission." She appeared on the cover, smiling and neatly coiffed, enfolded within a ball and chain. "Will the new trend in male-female roles be the old trends—dominant man, submissive wife, obedient kids?"

January had seen the debut of a TV version of *American Graffiti:* a slapstick sitcom about high school kids in 1950s Milwaukee hanging out at the diner, listening to doo-wop music, zooming around in hot rods (Potsie: "How about seat belts?" Ralph: "What are seat belts?" "It's safety. Pilots wear them. I read about 'em in *Popular Mechanics*")—and, unlike those bothersome real-life teenagers in 1975, not having sex. In the pilot the protagonist, baby-faced, red-haired Richie Cunningham (the same actor who starred as little Opie on *The Andy Griffith Show*) fretted over a date he had coming up. She had a "reputation": "I've just never dated a girl who's gone out with a sailor before." Not to worry: they end up playing chess. The show, called, unsubtly, *Happy Days,* was an enormous hit. It was especially popular among children.

THEN, THREE WEEKS AFTER THE FALL OF SAIGON, CAME THE SAGA OF THE USS *Mayaguez*. A month earlier, Henry Kissinger was quoted as saying that "the United States must carry out some act somewhere in the world which shows its determination to continue to be a world power." Now he and the president would have their chance.

On May 12 a rusty merchant ship called the *Mayaguez* was captured somewhere off the coast of Cambodia, near the island of Koh Tang, having strayed, the new Khmer Rouge government claimed, out of international waters and into its territory. Cambodia being a nation in chaos, communications were sketchy, negotiations difficult. But once upon a time, such dilemmas were not beyond the wit of American officials—for instance in the tiny South American nation of Ecuador, which had seized twenty-three U.S. ships in disputed waters over the previous two decades. Our government had just paid fines to release them, and that had been that.

But South America was not Southeast Asia, and Southeast Asia was the region that had just robbed America of its manhood.

At a National Security Council meeting, the president's most trusted aide, Bob Hartmann, advised, "We should not think of what is the right thing to do, but what the public perceives." Kissinger said it was time to "draw the line." At a meeting the next night, when no one yet knew where the ship's thirty-nine crewmen were or whether they were in actual jeopardy, Kissinger averred, "I think we should seize the island, seize the ship, and hit the mainland . . . people should have the impression that we are potentially trigger happy." The secretary of state had been steeled—armored by nostalgia for a time when U.S. force was an unmitigated good. He had just returned from Independence, Missouri, after visiting with Bess Truman, marinated in all the old Truman legends—not least the one about the thirty-third president's uncomplicated, unapologetic defenses of the atomic bombings of Hiroshima and Nagasaki. "Give 'em hell, Henry!'" a neighbor of the Trumans shouted Kissinger's way.

Back in Washington, at an NSC meeting, someone asked about the new War Powers Act: should Congress be consulted? Ford responded that he would order the strike and deal with the legal implications later.

A Marine landing party stormed the beaches of Koh Tang, as though it were Iwo Jima in 1945—and, meeting heavy resistance, lost fifteen men and eight helicopters. American forces found and boarded the *Mayaguez;* it was abandoned. A Navy pilot spotted white flags waving from a fishing boat—the crew, safe and sound, ready for rescue.

But the White House was not ready to declare victory yet.

"Tell them to bomb the mainland," Kissinger said. "Let's look ferocious." So they did, with B-52s. And by the time it was over, there were forty-nine American military deaths, eighty-two total casualties, eight helicopters destroyed. Thirty hostages "rescued"—though it had never been established that it was the Cambodians' intention to keep them. "They were so nice, really kind," a crew member told reporters. "They fed us first and everything. I hope everybody gets hijacked by them." He should have hoped nobody got rescued by Ford. Later, when documents on the mission were declassified, it emerged that when Ford ordered the bombings, he hadn't known where the men were, and that they might well have ended up as victims of it.

No matter. It had been a *Happy Days* sort of invasion: nostalgic splendor, armed force as cultural platitude. Conservatives loved it. "It was wonderful," Barry Goldwater said. "It shows we've still got balls in this country." Columnist Jeffrey Hart wrote that the "details are irrelevant. It proved that the U.S. government is not paralyzed, and that, in particular, President Ford is capable of acting decisively and with broad support."

But then, most of America loved it, too. Reflected a historian, "The recapture of a single ship was thus said to outweigh and offset the consequences and significance of the defeat of a national government whose independence we had helped to establish and whose integrity we had supported through nearly twenty years of diplomatic, economic, and military aid and for whose sake we had fought a long and costly war." And unlike kerfuffles over abortion and the teaching of Eskimo myths to fifth graders, the putative military triumph made the cover of every newsmagazine. *Newsweek,* the most liberal, called it "a daring show of nerve and steel." *Time*'s cover pictured the president looking resolute, and exulted, "Ford Draws the Line." His approval rating shot up 11 points—the president was finally back up to 50 percent. He started getting standing ovations on his travels. The conservative columnist John Chamberlain predicted that would be it for the Reagan-for-president boom. So did Evans and Novak. Presidential aides put word out to pundits "that Mr. Ford nailed down the Republicans nomination the night he called out the Marines."

And then, for poor old Gerald Ford, it was back to the burdens of governing.

On May 22, the papers reported America was depending more on foreign oil than it was before the 1973 Arab oil embargo. On May 27, sitting at the presidential desk, he went on TV to address the issue. One by one, he ripped sheets from the calendar:

"Now, what did the Congress do in February about energy? Congress did nothing. . . .

"What did the Congress do in March? What did the Congress do in April about energy? Congress did nothing. . . .

"So what has the Congress done in May about energy? Congress did nothing and went home for a 10-day recess. . . ."

But what could *Gerald Ford* do about energy? The statesman-like thing, he insisted: increase prices on purpose. He suggested a new one-dollar-per-barrel fee on foreign crude oil—which might or might not achieve its goal of discouraging consumption of imported fuel, but certainly would make fuel more expensive. He got into the strange technicalities of "old" and "new" domestic oil—the latter subject to price controls, the former not, a complex regulatory workaround left over from the Nixon administration, which had ended up having the perverse effect of creating additional incentives for refiners to import—and explained how he would "decontrol" the new stuff by August. Critics said that this would not just make fuel more expensive but add a new inflationary force to the economy as a whole—which the administration acknowledged was true. Without explanation, he asked for "a windfall profits tax with a plowback provision"—whatever, viewers at home had to be asking themselves, that meant. And there was still the looming threat of another Mideast embargo, which Henry Kissinger was desperately trying to forestall in an international energy conference in Paris. "Indeed," *Time* wrote after the speech, "the Organization of Petroleum Exporting Countries may hike world prices by as much as $2 per barrel in September—a move that would give the American economy a vicious double jolt if Congress and the President let all U.S. price controls die a month earlier."

So much more easy to be Ronald Reagan. Just get rid of all the regulations, he had told *Newsweek* in March. "Then you have competition and the marketplace takes care of itself." As he put it on the radio around the time of Ford's speech, excess government spending was the sole cause of inflation: "It's time for us all to realize that government is not the answer to our economic problems. Government *is* the problem." The messy wages of governance, meanwhile, with all its damned-if-you-do-or-don't dead ends, were solely his rival Gerald Ford's to enjoy.

Four days after his energy speech, Ford landed in Europe for a series of state visits and a meeting with President Anwar Sadat of Egypt on the supremely delicate question of Middle East peace. A rainy morning, a sleepless night, his arthritic football knee acting up and one hand occupied with an enormous umbrella and the other steadying his wife, who was wearing a jaunty angled Barbara Stanwyck–style hat, they strode down the stairs after Air Force One pulled up on a runway in Austria; presently, he thumped down and collapsed in a heap a step above the tarmac. "Thank you for your gracious welcome to Salzburg—and I am sorry that I tumbled in," he joked. Eight hours later, descending a carpeted stairway at the sixteenth-century former residence of Salzburg's archbishops, he tumbled again, this time beside Sadat—who quickly took his arms and helped him down the remaining twenty steps. Six weeks later, the headline from Kincheloe Air Force Base in Michigan read "SLIPS AGAIN": this time, he fell while walking *up* the stairs to Air Force One.

Slips Again: an indelible image to replace the one of the conqueror of Koh Tang Island. His approval rating was back to 45 percent by summer—a summer, once more, of suffusing dread.

CHAPTER TWENTY-ONE

Weimar Summer

IN THE SUMMER OF 1975, JUST LIKE THE WINTER OF 1974, PATRONS WERE waiting in interminable lines to see a scary movie. But this time, unlike those for *The Exorcist*, the lines didn't come to the studio as a surprise. The spur driving people to stand in them wasn't word of mouth but a more novel medium of cinematic promotion: TV commercials—which exploited a masterful score by the composer John Williams, and its creepingly propulsive, suspense-laden riff: *Dah-tum. Dah-tum. Dah-tum dahtum dahtumdahtumdahtum...* And they weren't stretching around urban blocks. The lines were inside air-conditioned suburban shopping malls, which hosted a new sort of theater with half a dozen screens or more, called "multiplexes."

Jaws marked the beginning of an end—the end of a risky, radical period in American moviemaking in which considerable faith was placed in what one critic called "unknown filmmakers and unclassifiable screenplays." Movies made for grown-ups, movies that aspired to *art*. Now, though, America was inching to the right, so was Hollywood: after thirty years of disarray brought on by the Paramount Decree, the collapse of the old factory system of movie production, studios had been tinkering with formulas for manufacturing blockbusters. This latest hit was the movie version of a wildly popular book, like *Love Story*, like *The Godfather*, like *The Exorcist*. And in contrast to the timid way Warners booked *The Exorcist* (fearing a religious picture wouldn't sell; this was supposed to be a skeptical age), *Jaws* opened on hundreds of screens at once, so viewers would know in advance that it was supposed to be an "event."

All the same, this was still the entertainment business. And, in the months and weeks before its June 20 debut, the old Hollywood truism about how it was impossible to predict the success of a new production haunted the director, the producer, the actors: *Nobody knows nothing and anything.* Richard Dreyfuss, the young star, thought the great white shark would be a white elephant, and said so on TV. He was wrong.

June 20, opening day, and the opening shot: beautiful young Chrissie stripping down to her bikini, daring her boyfriend to join her for a playful moonlight dip at a bucolic beachside resort called "Amity." Soothing seaside sounds. A beautiful body, filmed from underneath. *Dah-tum. Dah-dum. Dahtum dahtum dahtumdahtumdahtum . . .*

Screams.

The invisible force, pulling her to her death from below as she prays to God . . .

Just like in *The Exorcist,* terrified audience members shrieked, vomited, jumped from their seats, ran from the theater. The ones who stayed, enraptured, came back to see it again and again.

Jaws became the first movie to gross $100 million. A second ad campaign that fall implored, "SEE IT AGAIN (with your eyes *open*)." By which point the merchandising had taken over: toys, T-shirts, posters, a ride at the Universal Studios theme park—sharks, sharks, sharks, everywhere.

Remember Aristotle, explaining why it is pleasing to be horrified in its theater: he said that tragedy has "pain as its mother," and that displaying that pain, containing it within the safe confines of a theater, in order to thereby reduce it, allowed viewers to "settle down as if they have attained healing"—*catharsis,* in Greek: cleansing, purification, *purgation.*

So what fears was it that *Jaws* purged? What were the pains that were its mother?

Early in the movie, the police chief attempted to shut down the beach; the mayor refused to let him: here was that all too familiar venality of the institutions of authority, too greedy or selfish or incompetent to protect the public, interested only in protecting their prerogatives and power. The picture was shot in the summer of 1974, under the sign of the last days of Watergate—"We used to have these wonderful 'impeach Nixon' parties," Dreyfuss remembered—and on a location across Martha's Vineyard from the Chappaquiddick bridge where, some said, a Kennedy got away with manslaughter of a beautiful young girl or worse. As it came out, the *New York Times* columnist Anthony Lewis collated the latest opinion poll statistics: in ten years the proportion of people who distrusted the government had risen from 22 to 62 percent; the proportion who believed that there were "quite a few" crooks in government had risen from 29 to 45 percent; and 68 percent thought the country's leaders had "consistently lied to the American people—the figure had been 38 percent in 1972.

The film sent out an odd trio to hunt down the shark: in addition to the earnest, thoughtful sheriff there were a mildly hippieish young oceanographer, devoted to cutting-edge technology, and an oddball professional shark hunter, a steely Navy veteran of World War II, from back when America won wars, who relied on intuition, not technology, and harbored Ahab-like tendencies. They agreed about nothing, shared nothing but their rickety vessel (which broke down), distrusted each other and everything else—kind of like America these days. So how could they possibly pull together to vanquish the savage foe?

And then there was the nature of that foe: it was invisible, like dread. Then suddenly it crashed to the surface, savaging helpless innocents, unaware they even had had anything to fear—until the new fear was everywhere, consuming everything.

Which was how it felt to be an American now.

Savage new invisible dangers seemed to lurk around every corner. A new kind of air pollution, sulfur dioxide, a pungent, colorless gas produced by combustion of sulfur-laden fuel oils that combines easily with water vapor and oxygen to form sulfuric acid—"acid rain," supposed to be capable of corroding billboards and maybe even lungs. An official of the Texas Air Control Board said it was already so serious in Corpus Christi "that some hard decisions will have to be made about allowing any further industrial growth there at all." "Killer bees": "Millions of African killer bees with nasty tempers," as UPI described them on June 15, five days before *Jaws* opened, "immune to any kind of geographical or whatever barrier . . . capable of nesting almost anyway . . . headed relentlessly toward the United States." They were the product, allegedly, of a Brazilian beekeeper who in 1957 accidentally released a fierce apian strain brought from Africa, taking over Brazil's native population, science-fiction-style, producing an annual death toll there of three hundred. In an experiment published in *BioScience* magazine, a one-inch by one-inch patch of leather jiggled on a string outside a hive of the "Africanized" bees was stung ninety-two times in five seconds, then the bees "chased the heavily protected experimenter for more than a thousand yards." Then there was butadiene, a hazardous chemical regularly shipped by rail: "Once a car carrying butadiene is punctured, the least spark can cause it to ignite," *Texas Monthly* reported. "That means the railroad tracks had better be in tip-top shape. They aren't."

Dah-tum. Dah-tum. Dahtum dahtum dahtumdahtumdahtum . . .

SIMULTANEOUSLY THAT SUMMER CAME THE NEWS THAT A BELOVED SYMbol of America's long-ago innocence turned out to be not so innocent after all.

It was *Time,* in its June 2 issue, citing "credible sources," that first brought the news: that in 1961 John F. Kennedy and Robert F. Kennedy, enraged at the failure at the Bay of Pigs invasion, "covertly ordered agencies of the U.S. government to find some sure means of deposing Fidel Castro, Cuba's chief of state. Whether or not assassination attempts were authorized by the Kennedys is still unclear.... The CIA did work with two U.S. Mafia leaders, Sam 'Sam the Cigar' Giancana and John 'Handsome John' Roselli, in unsuccessful attempts to kill the Cuban leader." *Time* then drilled down to the scoop's strongest implication: "it tends to knock down the notion that the CIA was operating wildly beyond presidential control in scheming against foreign leaders." It also tended to knock down the notion—"There used to be a President who didn't lie, but he's dead!" as the kindergartner in Long Beach, California, told his teacher the previous year—that once upon a time, America was different; before, that is, sordid old Richard Nixon came along. "The Vanishing American Hero," as a *U.S. News & World Report* cover story put it that summer. *Texas Monthly* countered that fall with a corrective: "Heroes for Post-Watergate America."

Kennedy family retainers rushed into print to defend the dead men's honor. Historian and former Kennedy special assistant Arthur Schlesinger posted a letter to the *New York Times* on June 3 insisting such a thing simply was not possible: "Quite apart from all the other reasons, moral and prudential, that led John and Robert Kennedy to reject the idea of assassinating Castro, it must be remembered that both men were deeply concerned, almost obsessed, with the fate of the Bay of Pigs prisoners. Nothing would have doomed these prisoners more certainly than an American attempt to kill Castro." The next day, in the same paper, William Safire published a column, titled "Nixon Never Did," treating the accusation as settled fact, listing all the sins that rendered President Kennedy morally inferior to *his* former boss, Richard Nixon: *"Nixon never ordered the murder of a fellow chief of state.... Nixon never used the FBI and CIA to spy on political opponents.... Nixon never lied to the people about his health just before an election."*

He concluded, "Of course we would know a great deal more about other things [Kennedy] did if Congress were to spend one-tenth the time and money investigating the previous Administrations that it expended on Nixon's. But that is not to be."

The White House panicked at the news. First, on June 6, Ron Nessen told the press that the Rockefeller Commission report, due the following week, would not discuss assassinations. One reporter, recalling promises of a complete and frank official reckoning, asked if Richard

Nixon had been advising the administration on how to conduct a successful cover-up. For an hour, reporters mercilessly grilled him—until Nessen slammed shut his briefing book and stormed out of the press room. "No Time for Cover-Up," read the *New York Times*' editorial headline: Watergate language. Nessen came to hate the media so much he considered another line of work—though he had himself been an NBC correspondent only ten months earlier. The attorney general found it necessary to assure the nation that "no President may order assassinations"—reassuring, to the suspicious circles, in the same way Richard Nixon assuring the nation he was not a crook was reassuring.

The Rockefeller Commission report dropped on June 10. The *Times* expressed partial satisfaction at the 350-page "trenchant, factual and plain-spoken document." It revealed that the CIA's campaign against domestic dissent, Operation CHAOS, opened files on more than three hundred thousand individuals and organizations, including Martin Luther King's Southern Christian Leadership Conference and the staid establishment Negroes of the Washington Urban League; concluded that the CIA had no role in instigating Watergate, and none in the assassination of President Kennedy—and buried deep within, made the eye-popping revelation that the CIA had tested LSD on people who weren't told of the tests, and that at least one person died in 1953 as a result. But it punted on passing judgment on the "incomplete and extremely sensitive" question of assassinations of foreign leaders. The president promised to pass the assassination files on to the Church Committee, which promised a month of closed-door hearings on the subject. And the reforms it suggested were timorous. The *Times* didn't expect much would come of them. The report also said the CIA had taken steps in 1973 and 1974 that "have gone far to terminate the activities upon which this investigation has focused."

But if the White House thought that would put the CIA story to rest, they were mistaken. Like the great white shark in *Jaws*, the stories kept on crashing to the surface, day after day after day.

Like the fact that the chairman of the House's intelligence inquiry, Lucien Nedzi of Michigan, had been briefed about the CIA's domestic spying, and the possibility it had been involved in assassinations, more than a year earlier and did and said nothing about it—a perfect emblem of precisely the congressional failure of oversight Nedzi's committee had been impaneled to investigate. Another fox guarding the henhouse.

Like the fact, as reported in *Time* the next week, that the *New York Times* had known of the assassination allegations for months but had chosen not to print them. And the news, on June 19, of the suspicious murder of Sam Giancana, the very mafioso reputed to have been the CIA's man in Havana. Five days later, *Time* reported in detail about the agency's bizarre Murder Inc. schemes there: "The medical section of the CIA produced some exotic pills and even 'fixed' a box of fine Havana cigars . . . the pills were turned over to the Mafia. The would-be assassin was to have been paid $150,000 if he succeeded; some earnest money, 'a few thousand dollars,' was turned over to him. Giancana and Roselli expected something more important than money: both were under investigation by the Department of Justice and hoped to escape prosecution." The next week, *Time* reported that in an interview, the man who had been the CIA's general counsel from its 1947 founding through 1973 and "a confidant of one director after another" said Robert F. Kennedy knew all about the plotting by the CIA and "didn't seem very perturbed." ("And what do you do for a living?" the musical political humorist Mark Russell asked, posing as a Church staffer, in his nightclub act, a few nights after Roselli's closed-door testimony. The answer: "I'm a notorious gangster and hit man." "And how long have you worked for the government?")

And then there was the fact that in 1953 a twenty-two-year-old Army biochemist named Frank Olson, an unwitting participant in a CIA study in which his drink was spiked with LSD, jumped out a window to his death. The president publicly invited his outraged family to the Oval Office and apologized for the "inexcusable and unforgivable" incident—perhaps to head off their plans to sue the government for wrongful death. Meanwhile two left-wing congressmen, Bob Kasten and Ron Dellums, claimed evidence of "years-long CIA penetration of the White House itself," without any president's having known. "Vicious nonsense," the CIA director responded—but these days, who knew?

An article by the *Times'* Tad Szulc in *New York* magazine, called "The Politics of Assassination," recorded suspicions that one of the things the Rockefeller Commission was actively covering up was a CIA plot to murder China's premier, Chou En-lai. It noted that the Rockefeller Commission members worked under such intense paranoia they weren't allowed to leave their shoes outside their hotel rooms to be shined lest recording devices be planted inside. Soon after, one of the Democratic heroes of the Judiciary Committee's Watergate investigation, William Hungate, announced he was retiring from Congress in disillusionment. He said "politics has gone from an age of 'Camelot' when all things were possible to the age of 'Watergate' when all things are suspect."

•   •   •

THE GIANCANA NEWS WAS REPORTED IN AN ISSUE OF *TIME* WHOSE COVER
pointed a gun at the reader. It announced an article, at 9,237 words
one of the longest investigations in the magazine's history, documenting a crime wave that was making American streets all but impassable:
eleven murders in Atlanta within seventy-two hours, six by gunfire; a
four-year-old stabbed to death by a teenager seeking the forty cents in
his pocket, outside Detroit; statistics, staggering statistics, including a
20 percent increase in crime over the past twelve months in the supposedly safe suburbs and 21 percent in rural areas—on and on and on, for
page after page. The next month Gallup asked city dwellers what they
thought was America's worst problem. Only 5 percent cited inflation
and 11 percent said unemployment, though both were at their highest levels since shortly after World War II. Twenty-one percent cited
crime—and 75 percent of women said they were afraid to walk near
their homes at night. New Justice Department statistics discovered that
in 1973 one out of four households had endured a robbery, rape, assault,
burglary, larceny, or auto theft—though who knew: Attorney General Edward Levi said a third of all crimes went unreported in official
channels. A sociologist interviewed an old Jewish immigrant woman in
Brooklyn. She said, "I am locked up like the ghettoes of Europe. . . . I
am afraid of people knocking down my door. I am still not free."

Elected officials, too, were going to jail—including, most recently, a
former governor of Oklahoma. The Associated Press reported the findings of two left-wing economists that a combination of multinational
corporations' drive for profit maximization and an inability to control
new ways of rocketing money around the world "could plunge the
nation into a depression comparable to that of the 1930s." In Orange-
burg, South Carolina, a faulty job rigging the explosives was the only
thing that saved the county courthouse—and a church kindergarten
next door—from going up in smithereens: apparently someone was
protesting against civil rights activists who for their part had protested
the police killing of a black youth. What madness couldn't be visited on
America next?

Maybe the bankruptcy of the greatest American city, where middle-
class civil servants were behaving like criminal anarchists.

The lurid images began in May, when hundreds of Hunter College
students took over the office of the dean of students after Mayor Abe
Beame proposed deep cuts in the school's budget. By June, eight thousand New York City municipal workers rallied on the narrow, twisting
downtown streets outside the headquarters of First National City Bank,
accusing the bank of complicity in planned austerity layoffs of thou-

sands of their colleagues. Police threatened a wildcat strike, distributing WELCOME TO FEAR CITY pamphlets with a pirate-style death's head on the cover, advising tourists to stay indoors after dark, skip public transportation, and "until things change, stay away from New York if you possibly can." The feared-for layoffs arrived. On June 28, garbagemen, reacting to the firing of three thousand comrades, staged a one-day walkout. "Wait till the rats come!" they chanted. WELCOME TO STINK CITY, their pamphlets read.

On July 1, five hundred laid-off police officers stationed themselves in blockade formation before the Brooklyn Bridge, let air out of random cars' tires, threatened motorists, and threw cans and bottles at the uniformed fellow cops who were begging them to cease and desist. The next day highway workers blockaded the Henry Hudson Parkway during rush hour. By Independence Day, City Hall and other government buildings came under such frequent siege that cops kept up the crowd-control barriers on a permanent basis—"like part of the city's furniture," a historian wrote. It was summer; it was hot. So when garbage collection began slowing down with the layoffs, New Yorkers started throwing their trash out in the middle of the street, which some people turned into bonfires—right in time for Independence Day, when a journalist in Miami claimed he could convince only one person out of fifty he asked to sign the Declaration of Independence. "Commie junk," one called it. Another threatened to call the cops on him. A third said, "Be careful who you show that kind of anti-government stuff to, buddy." And: "The boss will have to read this before I can let you put it in the shop window. But, politically, I can tell you he don't lean that way. He's a Republican."

HERE WAS ANOTHER OF THOSE *PREDICTIONS FOR 1974:* A "DECLARATION of bankruptcy for New York City"—"the first tangible sign of the collapse of our entire civilization." A year later, that augury looked to be coming true, too.

The roots of the Great New York City Fiscal Crisis lay in recession: the economic downturn of 1974–75 hit the Northeast with a speed and force all out of proportion to the rest of the country. New York had always supported a program of middle-class entitlement unlike anything anywhere else, a sort of socialism in one city: subsidized housing and day-care centers; free college at the world-class City University of New York; free museum admission; nineteen municipal hospitals, many of them world-class; free directory assistance—amenities that seemed only natural for a metropolis transforming itself, in the boom years after

World War II, into the greatest city in the world. "I do not propose," Mayor Robert F. Wagner pronounced in his 1965 budget message, "to permit our fiscal problems to set the limits of our commitments to meet the essential needs of the cities." Neither, indeed, did the city's investment banks, which all but begged the city to keep borrowing money, because municipal bonds paid high interest rates; were exempt from federal, state, and municipal taxes; and seemed to entail negligible risk. It took two to tangle a city in unsustainable debt.

It worked, until it didn't. The city's manufacturing base had declined, and the unemployment rate, under 5 percent in 1970, now hovered above 12 percent. White middle-class New Yorkers, fearing crime, fled to the suburbs. Federal and state aid leveled off; expectations that Richard Nixon's national health insurance bills would relieve the city of its massive outlays for Medicaid came a cropper when Congress voted them down, first in 1971, then in 1974 (conservatives opposed them because they were too generous, liberals because they were not generous enough). Bills came due that this newly atrophied level of revenue simply could not cover: by the days of Nixon's resignation the city's debt was $11 billion, a third of that in short-term notes soon to come due, and more than 11 percent of the city's spending went to interest payments on the debt—to banks suddenly reconsidering their lending practices in a recession. Other tax shelters started looking more attractive to those banks. So did other customers—for instance the same resource-rich Third World nations that so irked Daniel Patrick Moynihan. Banks started asking for some of that loaned money back, and started charging more interest to let New York rent more. In September 1973 the *Wall Street Journal* had reported, "Our cities have by and large weathered their financial crises." Now the greatest city in the world was going broke. Like the energy crisis, this crisis seemed to come out of nowhere.

In December 1974 Mayor Beame made a pilgrimage to Washington, D.C., to meet with treasury secretary William Simon. Beame explained the actions he had already taken to correct the city's fiscal imbalances, including freezing most city hiring and merit pay increases; he then argued that, given that America's most international city had to pay higher interest rates than any municipality in the country, it would be in the national interest for the Treasury Department to loan New York the money it needed by buying its municipal paper directly.

The treasury secretary flipped.

"Mayor," he said, "if we did that the taxpayers would end up financing the campaign promises of every profligate local politician in the country."

There was something very disingenuous in the reaction. Bill Simon had formerly been senior partner in charge of government and municipal bonds at Salomon Brothers, and a member of the investment bank's seven-man executive committee—that is, one of the very people responsible for lending so much money to New York in the first place. In the late 1960s and early 1970s, Simon had even served on a debt advisory committee set up by Beame back when he had been New York's comptroller. If New York had been borrowing beyond its means, William Simon was one of the people personally responsible.

He would later complain that he had been gulled—that the city's "Byzantine accounts" and "tortuous accounting practices" had been willfully devised to forestall just the kind of fiscal reckoning he was now bravely insisting upon. He wrote, "Even the most sophisticated financiers and the Treasury Department itself were totally unprepared" for such disregard of "the basic legal and ethical pact between the city and its debtors." And surely, in City Hall, there was plenty of blame to go around. But other motives, other assumptions, lay beyond Bill Simon's recalcitrance as well. These were ideological.

As he wrote three years later in a book modestly titled *A Time for Truth,* which was published by Reader's Digest Press and which spent some twenty weeks on the bestseller list: "The philosophy that has ruled our nation for over forty years had emerged in large measure from that very city which was America's intellectual headquarters, and inevitably, it was carried to its fullest expression in that city. In the collapse of New York those who choose to understand it could see a terrifying dress rehearsal of the state that lies ahead for this country if it continues to be guided by the same philosophy of government. . . . Nothing has destroyed New York's finances but the liberal political formula. . . . Liberal politics, endlessly glorifying its own 'humanism,' has in fact been annihilating the very conditions for human survival."

He spoke for his class. As a staffer wrote in a memo proposing language for First National City Bank's president to use in discussion with the mayor, this crisis was an opportunity: "many things"—he cited higher subway fares, cutbacks in the city workforce, and budget cuts generally—"can be done even if they are not technically possible." Technically possible, he meant, if interest groups like the municipal unions, the board of education, or municipal hospital administrators were afforded their traditional political deference. Well, they had been deferred to long enough. "The time," the staffer insisted, "is now." Now it was the capitalists' turn to be deferred to. Investment bankers and the mayor's Council of Business and Economic Advisors should "work in concert," he suggested, "to prepare a unified analysis which would clearly demonstrate the absolute inviability of the City if it continued on its present course."

Such language signified another front opening up in the right's political war: the corporate front. During the postwar boom, business had signed on as partners to the New Deal order, which seemed to be delivering an all but permanent broad-based American prosperity. They honored its core intellectual proposition, Keynesianism, which held that a key to building and sustaining prosperity was to harness the power of government to put money into ordinary consumers' pockets. More or less, they acceded to (or at were powerless to stop) the escalating pace of marketplace regulation—which reached its pinnacle under a president from the party of business, Richard Nixon. The *New Republic* called a tax bill he signed in 1969 "far and away the most 'anti-rich' tax reform proposal ever proposed by a Republican President in the 56 years of the existence of the income tax." Much of the new government revenue was spent on new regulatory agencies, like the Environmental Protection Agency, the Occupational Safety and Health Administration, the National Transportation Safety Board, the Consumer Product Safety Commission, and the Mine Safety and Health Administration (created by the most stringent federal mining legislation in U.S. history). In Washington, it felt like liberal lobbies were in the saddle: environmental groups like Friends of the Earth, the Natural Resources Defense Council, and Environmental Action; groups associated with the consumer advocate Ralph Nader; aggressive legal advocates like the Center for Law and Social Policy—with "brilliant young staff members who mistrust or totally disbelieve the attributes of the enterprise system," Barry Goldwater complained in 1974, but who now raced up Capitol Hill to testify before congressional committees and often as not tied up their business adversaries in knots.

It felt endurable when Keynesianism was working. Now, however, it was not. Rates of profit were declining. Labor was more militant than at any time since the 1946–47 strike wave. It was time, the men in their leather-backed chairs and wood-paneled conference rooms began reasoning, to fight back—to create a political opposition, red in tooth and claw, to fight back against liberalism on the national stage.

Lemuel Boulware of General Electric had been saying the same thing for years, of course, going so far as to organize political strategy retreats for executives in all sorts of fields in the late 1950s on Gasparilla Island, off the Florida coast. After the Arab oil shock of 1973–74, he had many more frightened allies. The Conference Board, the venerable publisher of economic indicators like the Consumer Confidence Index, held a series of conclaves through 1974 and 1975 on the social responsibility of business. Discussion soon turned to the question of the *survival* of business, and how "social responsibility" was sabotaging same. One executive worried, "One man, one vote has undermined the power of business in all capitalist countries since World War II." Another complained, "The have-nots are gaining steadily more political power to distribute the wealth downward."

In 1971, a corporate lawyer from Virginia (one of his clients was Philip Morris, and he was frustrated when Congress passed the Public Health Cigarette Smoking Act in 1970), chair of the education committee of the National Chamber of Commerce (whose budget doubled in size between 1974 and 1980), had written a widely circulated memo arguing that "the American economic system is under broad attack." It continued: business had to learn the lesson "that political power is necessary; that such power must be assiduously cultivated; and that when necessary it must be used aggressively and with determination." For instance, "The national television networks should be monitored in the same way that textbooks should be kept under constant surveillance. . . . Efforts should be made to see that the forum-type programs (the Today Show, Meet the Press, etc.) afford at least as much opportunity for supporters of the American system to participate as these programs do for those who attack it."

His memo insisted that advancing pro-free-market politics be "a primary responsibility of corporate management"—"far more than an increased emphasis on 'public relations' or 'government' affairs," but that corporations hire new executive vice presidents whose entire brief was countering "the attack on the enterprise system," with a "budget and staff adequate to the task." Corporate "public affairs" officers— lobbyists—had heretofore worked in Washington mostly to secure companies' advantages against their competitors. He was recommending something more radical: political action to assert the interests of corporate America as a class—a sort of union movement on behalf of capital. "Strength lies in organization, in careful long-range planning and implementation, in consistency of action over an indefinite period of years, in the scale of financing available only through joint effort, and in the political power available only through united action and national organizations." The lawyer, Lewis Powell, was soon appointed by Richard Nixon to the Supreme Court. And what he was recommending had already begun increasing apace. The National Association of Manufacturers had been aggressively lobbying against liberalism for decades, but from New York; in 1972 the group (and its political arm, the Business Industry Political Action Committee, or BIPAC) moved house to Washington, D.C.—because, a spokesman said, "the thing that affects business most today is government."

Two of the most prominent activists in the effort were former Nixon administration officials. Bryce Harlow had been Nixon's appointment secretary, and one of his most trusted confidants—all while on leave from Procter & Gamble's first Washington lobbying shop, which he himself had established in 1961. Now back in harness at P&G, he drafted himself as field general for the kind of organizing Powell proposed. "The danger had suddenly escalated," he recalled, referring to the election of the Watergate Babies in 1974. "We had to prevent business from being rolled up and put in the trash can by that Congress." The other, Charls (sic) Walker, had been a Treasury Department undersecretary. In 1975 he took over a struggling organization that advocated for estate tax recipients and turned it into a turbocharged lobbying shop dedicated to the proposition that the American economy was foundering for a lack of "capital formation"—that business did not have enough money, largely because the government extracted too much from it in taxes, which were then distributed downward to Americans who were not capitalists, destroying the conditions for national prosperity. This argument was precisely the opposite of Keynesianism—but a proposition that proved attractive enough to several formerly Keynesian Fortune 500 corporations that they each contributed two hundred thousand dollars to soon turn Walker's "American Council for Capital Formation" into a Washington juggernaut.

These were the circles in which the present treasury secretary was traveling. And he had no intention of bailing out New York—*ever*. Neither did William Simon intend to let his boss bail out New York—*ever*. Instead, he intended to make an example of it. And what he saw happen next only confirmed him in his judgment.

In December 1974 Mayor Beame ordered large-scale layoffs and cutbacks in municipal employment—and then, following union protests, reversed them. A young lawyer at Bankers Trust reported his accidental discovery that the tax receipts legally required to secure a $260 million note the bank had planned to buy did not exist. In January 1975, the city's comptroller canceled a planned sale of municipal notes; in February, a second sale was canceled. Promptly, the city's Urban Development Corporation became the first major government agency in the United States to go into default since the 1930s. Two weeks later, on March 6, the city offered another note on the market—and didn't receive a single underwriting bid. By May, the city's debt was $12.3 billion, and the word had gone forth from the great investment banks that such debt was unmarketable at just about any interest rate; officials predicted the city would default by June. The mayor made another ill-fated trip to Washington, this time for an audience with the president, Governor Hugh Carey, and representatives from Chase Manhattan, First National City Bank, and Mortgage Guarantee Trust in tow. A federal loan guarantee, Ford told them, would "merely postpone the city's coming to grips with its fiscal problems through needed budget slashing." On May 29, Beame complied, announcing an austerity budget calling for the immediate elimination of more than 12 percent of all city employment—a four-day municipal workweek, reductions in CUNY admissions, and library and health center closures.

He immediately reaped the whirlwind: cops blocking the Brooklyn Bridge; garbageman pledging a pestilence of rats—and no more money forthcoming from banks.

Like the fall of Saigon, it all seemed so sudden. "What was 'sudden,'" thundered back Simon in his 1978 book, "was the traumatic discovery by the financial community that it was being rooked into a Ponzi game." At the time, he was hardly less decorous. "We're going to sell New York to the Shah of Iran," he said to reporters. "It's a hell of an investment."

His voice led a chorus of business conservatives emboldened by the imminent collapse of a great American city to mock the profligacies of an utterly failed liberalism. *Barron's* invoked the news from Cambodia: "All Abe Beame need do is adopt the Khmer solution. That is, order every man, woman, and child out of the city." Christian conservatives, too: "Maybe it would be good for America if New York would go bankrupt," *Christianity Today* opined. "The citizenry might learn some elementary lessons of economics that apply to cities and nations as well as individuals." It was in part, said the young senator from Delaware, Joe Biden, a cultural thing: "Cities are viewed as the seed of corruption and duplicity." His House colleague Richardson Preyer agreed, echoing what he was hearing from his North Carolina constituents: "There is a general negative feeling toward New York. New York has a certain overtone of sinfulness about it."

"New York," *Fortune* magazine reported, "is different. City politicians seldom had to say no to anybody—whether union leaders making extravagant demands or citizens seeking benefits for themselves." Though it in fact was not really all that different. Simon spoke of overpaid, "parasitical" municipal workers, conceptually separate from the "productive population." They drew, he said, "appalling" pensions, though for what it was worth the pension of the average retiring New York City policeman—$9,000—was $3,000 less than a pension in Chicago and less than half that in Los Angeles and San Francisco. City teachers and firemen also earned less than in salary than their counterparts in all of those cities, with a considerably higher cost of living. New York had fewer citizens per capita on public assistance than Philadelphia, Detroit, Milwaukee, and Chicago. (An oft-repeated claim that New York spent the most on welfare in the country ignored the fact that expenses covered elsewhere by state and county governments were borne by city governments in New York State.) Among the private corporations that paid their workers more in pensions than New York City were General Motors and First National City Bank—the financial institution most aggressive in pushing Beame's austerity budget, whose chairman Walter Wriston, municipal labor leaders never tired of pointing out, earned $425,000 a year. Mayor Beame, for his part, never tired of pointing out all the other cities facing similar balance sheet woes— among them Grand Rapids, Michigan, the president's hometown.

On June 10 the state legislature in Albany authorized the Municipal Assistance Corporation ("MAC"), an authority with the power to borrow up to $3 billion in bonds if city default appeared imminent— with the caveat that MAC didn't have to lend money at all if the city did not squeeze its budget according to the specified terms. The man who emerged as MAC's spokesman and most respected member, Felix Rohatyn of the investment bank Lazard Frères, was a Democrat, the son of parents who fled Nazi-occupied France, a recently divorced bachelor, the subject of public fascination and even affection for his "tiny 12-by-15 foot office that looks as if it might have belonged to an accountant of modest means" and his tiny apartment in a residential hotel. A former physics major, he seemed to hold out the promise of a wizardly technical fix: "I look for the basic elements of a problem," he explained in the *Wall Street Journal.* "If you can't get agreement on the nature of the problem, the solution is too difficult."

Alas, the solution to the problem of too little money appeared to rest in the hands of those who held the money. On July 17, a delegation of bankers including Wriston, David Rockefeller of Chase Manhattan, and Donald Regan, who was CEO and chairman of Merrill Lynch and a vice chairman of the New York Stock Exchange, met with Rohatyn and his Municipal Assistance Corporation. Together, they accused MAC of "business as usual"—the Bill Simon line. Rohatyn set up a meeting with the mayor to tell him that the only way to regain the confidence of such investors was to carry out what Rohatyn called "shock impact."

Promptly, MAC and city officials got to work on a financial plan that included four weeks of unpaid furloughs for municipal employees. The next week the Brooklyn Bridge was shut down once more—this time by four thousand doctors, nurses, health workers, and their patients, protesting cuts to the hospital budget.

CAN CAPITALISM SURVIVE? asked *Time* on the cover of its July 14 issue. "The root problem," the editors explained, "is that everybody wants more. Even in prosperous times, the demands of labor for ever higher wages . . . and the less affluent for expanded government services always add up to more than the economy can produce at stable prices. Rather than say no to the demands of any vocal constituency, democratic governments too often find it easier to run huge budget deficits, thus fueling inflation." Though they also quoted seven Nobel laureates in economics, including the legendary Kenneth Arrow, who disagreed, having signed a declaration blaming the economic crisis on corporations that produced "primarily for corporate profit," and demanding that "alternatives to the prevailing Western economic systems must be placed on the agenda at once."

The letters three weeks later were neatly split down the middle, capitalism pro and con—for example, "When farmers are slaughtering calves because it is not profitable to raise them, and when oil companies refuse to drill because it may not be profitable, then we must seriously question whether the system based on the profit motive is meeting the needs of society" (Sanford Stein, Chicago), versus, "Without profit there is no freedom" (Charles T. Clark, Tulsa, Oklahoma).

ANOTHER LETTER IN THAT ISSUE OF *TIME* TARTLY SAVAGED THE PRESIdent for a decision that seemed to have obliterated once and for all whatever political truce he had established with conservatives in the wake of the *Mayaguez* raid. It read, "President Ford's refusal to see Solzhenitsyn [June 21] is the refusal of a midget to see a giant for a very obvious reason. He would have to look up to him."

The arrival of the Nobel Prize winner in literature named Aleksandr Solzhenitsyn in the United States late in June had become a surprise flash point for arguments about the ideological future of the Republican Party. The fifty-seven-year-old Soviet Nobel laureate in literature had turned his 1945 arrest for writing a letter to a friend criticizing Joseph Stalin's conduct of the war ("anti-Soviet propaganda" and "founding a hostile organization"), and his subsequent incarceration in the system of Siberian work camps he memorably dubbed the "Gulag Archipelago," into one of the greatest bodies of writing in twentieth-century Russia.

Soviet authorities had shockingly allowed his first short novel, *One Day in the Life of Ivan Denisovich,* to published in edited form in 1962. Not, however, his staggering nonfiction accomplishment, *The Gulag Archipelago,* as he knew they could not. Fragments of its massive handwritten manuscript, written in secret, were passed from hand to hand over an unfathomably heroic decade-long process of research and composition. It was finally published in the West in 1973, six years after its completion, though not before the KGB seized one of three extant copies at the home of his typist, who promptly hung herself within days of her release by the secret police. In 1971 the KGB had allegedly tried to assassinate Solzhenitsyn. In 1974, the Kremlin expelled him, rendering him a stateless martyr to the endurance of Communist terror, a wandering prophet decrying the mad cruelty of the state that Henry Alfred Kissinger insisted on treating like any other member of the family of nations.

That, at least, was how conservative Republicans and right-leaning Democrats saw it. Back when Henry Kissinger had been practicing it under President Nixon, many of them made their peace with the signature foreign policy known as "détente"—a French word, roughly translated as "relaxation of tensions." Ronald Reagan, for instance, met Brezhnev during his summer 1973 visit to the United States, a moment accompanied by much talk that the Cold War had finally ended. At a lavish pool party for the Soviet leader held at Nixon's Western White House, the California governor exulted over "what I think is the most brilliant accomplishment of any president of this century, and that is the steady progress towards peace and the easing of tensions."

But another definition of détente was "trigger of a gun"—which is what it had come to sound like to Reagan now that the man in charge was Gerald Ford.

"There are some who believe we should grant favors to our adversaries with no strings attached," he said in one of his radio broadcasts. But "Soviet leaders from Lenin to Brezhnev have been realistic, unsentimental bargainers, men highly reluctant to pay for something offered free of charge." And: "'Détente—isn't that what a farmer has with his turkey until Thanksgiving Day?" That was at least more polite than what William Loeb said. The flamboyantly reactionary editor and publisher of the *Union Leader,* the most important newspaper in first-in-the-nation New Hampshire, called Henry Kissinger a "bootlicking supplicant of the Communists."

The fundamental political debate concerned whether relations with other sovereign states should be based in part on how they treated their own citizens. The Nixon-Kissinger position had been: absolutely not.

If that had been the litmus test, there could not have been the historic opening to China. Nor the Strategic Arms Limitation Talks (SALT) Nixon began in 1969, which led in May 1972 to Nixon's signing of an Anti-Ballistic Missile Treaty in Moscow—nor the kind of diplomatic pressure Nixon was able to put on both Communist rivals, China and the Soviet Union, to persuade North Vietnam to negotiate an end to American involvement in Vietnam. It was time to transform the Soviet Union from a "revolutionary" to a "status quo" power, the better to make the world a safe and more stable place, was how Henry Kissinger conceived it—a moral end, he reasoned, in a world armed with enough nuclear warheads to destroy itself.

Now, however, that view was being challenged by a coalition that was not only bipartisan but trans-ideological. In 1973 a liberal Democratic congressman from Minnesota, Donald Fraser, launched hearings that produced a landmark report, *Human Rights in the World Community,* accusing an amoral Nixon of paying for America's supposed diplomatic gains by debasing the most powerful currency America had to offer: its values. "Human rights" was also the rallying cry when Scoop Jackson, a senator so sympathetic to Nixon's foreign policy during his first term that the president had considered him as a potential defense secretary, joined by Democratic congressman Charles Vanik, introduced an amendment to the 1974 Trade Act punishing the Soviet Union for limiting the emigration of Jews. "For if new relations between East and West are to mature into long-term peaceful cooperation there must be progress toward the freer movement of people and ideas between East and West, which is to say progress in the area of human rights and liberty."

The coalition behind Jackson-Vanik included some of the most liberal and most conservative members of Congress. That drove President Ford, who thought he'd acceded to the White House with a mandate to further advance what had once seemed to be Nixon's most popular and uncontroversial achievement—détente—to baffled distraction. Now he wasn't just negotiating with the Soviets. He was negotiating with Scoop Jackson—a puffed-up senator with presidential ambitions—on a piddling *symbol.* But not, apparently, to the House of Representatives, which late in 1974 passed the Jackson-Vanik amendment unanimously. *The Gulag Archipelago* had just wound up an eighteen-week run on the *New York Times* bestseller list. For conservatives, it served a powerfully emotional purpose: it let them believe that Brezhnev's Kremlin, which merely consigned dissidents to mental hospitals, was still identical to Stalin's, which sent them off to rot in sadistic frigid gulags while consigning millions of *kulaks* to die of starvation. It let them dismiss the nuances of diplomatic strategy as sheer moral abdication.

Ford bowed to political pressure and signed the act; the Soviets promptly canceled the entire new trade relationship so carefully negotiated by Nixon and Kissinger in 1972. Kissinger, in a hastily announced press conference, almost sounded like he was complaining about being forced to negotiate for the wrong side. "The Soviet government states that it does not intend to accept a trade status that is discriminatory and subject to political conditions," he said, and promised that the administration "will, of course, continue all available avenues for improvement in relations."

Reagan responded in a broadcast with a cleverly pragmatic argument against the very logical presumptions of détente: because "the Soviets have very little in the way of technology," and "it's unlikely we'd wish to become dependent on them for raw materials when many other sources are available," tough conditions like Jackson-Vanik were in fact the *best* route to improved relations—and, as a bonus, won the moral argument. "The more we focus on internal Soviet repression, and increase our demands in that area, the greater the chance that over the years Soviet society will lose its cruelty and secrecy." He made a similar argument that week with regard to granting diplomatic recognition to Red China: it was part of the détente pattern of an "unending series of one sided concessions," when in "the long run no concession is more important than a relaxation of China's brutal relationship toward its own people."

When Reagan made such arguments on the radio, he sounded uncharacteristically rushed, awkward, outside his zone of comfort. By late April, however, when he spoke to a Republican conclave in Mississippi, the reticence was gone—and the crowd went wild. He continued on to a pharmaceutical industry convention in Boca Raton (for his standard fee: five thousand dollars), to Atlanta for private meetings with Republican politicians, to a lecture on the Georgia Tech campus in which he barked that in refusing to vote through the $720 million aid request for the South Vietnamese military, this Congress had acted "more irresponsibly than any Congress now in our history," and had "blood on their hands." He got a standing ovation—and admitted to a reporter that, yes, these were just the sort of "recriminations" the president had asked Americans to avoid regarding Vietnam. One of his travel companions was columnist Robert Novak—who promptly wrote on May 6 that Reagan, "an enthusiastic détentist so long as Nixon was President," was working so hard he could only be in training for a presidential run.

His martial barks also grew steadily more aggressive that summer. He quoted approvingly the former defense official under Lyndon Johnson, and architect of the Vietnam War, Eugene V. Rostow (who "could be described as liberal but reasonable"), as saying that despite détente-like efforts in American foreign policy since Franklin Roosevelt's time, "There has been no improvement in our relations with the Soviet Union, save in the realms of public relations and wishful thinking," and that the Soviet Union was more dangerous than ever. He added, quoting Senator Jesse Helms, another count to his bill of indictment against détente: the threat to America's "lease in perpetuity" of the Panama Canal, regarding which, "[t]hough he hasn't said anything about it publicly, Secretary of State Henry Kissinger is rumored to be seriously considering plans to make a deal with the Panamanians to mollify" officials there who wanted us to give up the canal. The first step, he reported, had already begun: plans to turn over control of police, fire, and postal services in the Canal Zone to the host government, meaning, he said, Americans could have "all their mail monitored" by the head of Panama's G2 intelligence service, "Lieutenant Colonel"—he paused, struggling with the unfamiliar name—"Manuel Noriega, a man not unfriendly to the Cuban Communists and one very influential in the current Panamanian regime. . . . One can and is forced to ask: Why?

"This is Ronald Reagan. Thanks for listening."

RUSSIA'S SUNKEN-EYED, BEARDED PROPHET ARRIVED ON THESE SHORES just in time for the 199th anniversary of the signing of the Declaration of Independence. Solzhenitsyn asked for an Oval Office meeting. To Ford, the correct response seemed simple enough. The recent humiliations of his negotiating partners in the ongoing SALT II talks needed salving. And it wasn't as if gulags were operational *now,* after all. In less than a month Ford was set to meet with the Soviets during a historic thirty-five-nation summit in Finland—the kind of bold international move that had always sent Richard Nixon's political fortunes into the stratosphere. But an increasingly aggressive cadre of hard-line White House aides—angry, for example, at a recent deal Ford had completed to sell the Soviets wheat on generous terms—argued otherwise. One wrote, "Our refusal to see Solzhenitsyn will come to symbolize a Munich-like deafness in this period." Another, Richard Cheney, wrote a lengthy political memo to his boss, Donald Rumsfeld, Ford's chief of staff: "I can't think of a better way to demonstrate for the American people and for the world that détente . . . does not imply also our approval of their way of life or their authoritarian government." Insulting Solzhenitsyn,

Cheney concluded, would hurt "the President's capacity to deal with the right-wing in America."

But Ford wasn't thinking much about that. He was still dismissing the possibility of a Reagan presidential run. He considered the Russian dissident a "horse's ass." And he didn't like being backed into a corner.

So: no meeting with Solzhenitsyn. But his decision—the details of which were embarrassingly exposed on the Senate floor by Jesse Helms, who reported the Nobelist's anguish that the American people could not realize that World War III was already over and that America had already lost—brought on a firestorm that blindsided him. He tried to reverse himself: a call was placed to invite the Russian to the White House with two hours' notice; Solzhenitsyn loudly and publicly refused. Damned if he did, damned if he didn't.

On July 13 the AFL-CIO held a moving testimonial dinner for the dissident, who told the 2,500 guests, "The Communist ideology is to destroy your society." He said, "The principal argument for the advocates of détente is well known: all of this must be done to avoid a nuclear war. . . . Why should there be a nuclear war if for the last thirty years they have been breaking off as much of the West as they wanted—piece by piece, county after country, and the process keeps going on?" He said the United States should still have troops in Southeast Asia, fighting Communism. Twenty-five hundred eager listeners seemed to agree.

On July 15, the day after Gerald Ford's sixty-second birthday, Ronald Reagan's syndicated column named the president in print for the very first time. He noted that Ron Nessen's latest in a series of constantly shifting rationales for the snubbing of Solzhenitsyn was that presidential meetings must have "substance." "For substance," Reagan stabbed back, "the President has met recently with the Strawberry Queen of West Virginia and the Maid of Cotton."

Détente's symbolic apex was supposed to take place two days later, high up in outer space: the docking between a Soviet Soyuz spacecraft and an American Apollo craft. Technically speaking, it came off without a hitch. The hitches were all political. Jewish Defense League protesters burned a cardboard rocket outside the Soviet mission to the United Nations, chanting, "Dump détente, dump Kissinger, let my people go!" Détente, an all but uncontroversial proposition the day before yesterday, was now politically toxic. So Ford decided to slow talks with Panama over the future disposition of the canal, and to postpone plans to establish formal diplomatic relations with the People's Republic of China until after the 1976 presidential elections.

• • •

REPUBLICAN COUNCILS WERE OBSESSED WITH THE POLL SHOWING THAT only 18 percent of the public identified with the Grand Old Party. Informally, there had been talks about whether to change its tainted name. Another public relations idea was a joke book, *Republican Humor.* Every Republican congressman would be asked to contribute. "Probably some of them won't have anything funny to offer," a staffer observed. What the Grand Old Party settled on instead was three half-hour fund-raising TV specials featuring "everyday Republicans who want to tell why they have stuck with the GOP." The series, coordinated with accompanying lapel buttons for the party faithful to wear to work the next day, was titled *Republicans Are People Too!* The second installment ran on July 1, up against *M*A*S*H* on CBS and a Tuesday Movie of the Week on ABC about a talk radio host who baited a listener into committing suicide. The GOP show's theme, more cheerful, was "Republicans are people who care." It cost $124,000 to produce. It brought in $5,515. The announced third episode never ran.

On July 8, at the height of the Solzhenitsyn debate, the president sat before reporters in the Oval Office and formally announced, "I am a candidate for the Republican nomination for President in 1976," promising to "finish the job I have begun." He announced the "outstanding Americans on whose integrity both my supporters and all others can depend" who would be running his campaign, including the computer magnate David Packard as finance chair, 1964 Goldwater co–campaign manager Dean Burch as head of campaign planning, and Howard "Bo" Callaway, a conservative former Georgia congressman who had been Richard Nixon's secretary of the army, as campaign manager.

Then, on July 16, readers perusing page nineteen of the *New York Times* could learn of a press conference the previous day in a Washington hotel basement from the new "Friends of Ronald Reagan," whose chairman, Nevada senator Paul Laxalt, explained, "The purpose of this committee is to build an organization and raise the money necessary to conduct a viable and effective campaign once Governor Reagan decides to become an active candidate." Laxalt said he hoped that would happen, because even though "all of us, Democrats and Republicans alike, must give him our support lest others in the world receive the impression that America is too weak or immobile to act," the president was a failure. "Mr. Ford's efforts to cope with these problems on a day-to-day basis provide little relief for the vast majority of Americans who yearn for a leader who can communicate a realistic perspective on America's future."

Still, Laxalt would not guarantee Reagan would run. Though he said that if Reagan did, he gave four-to-ten odds he would win.

The *Times,* plainly, disagreed. "A number of Republican professionals," they noted, "said today that the first list of Reagan sponsors reflected some loss of support in recent months, as Mr. Ford's political stock gained and Mr. Reagan remained undecided." Reagan's old radio mentor Congressman H. R. "Charlie" Gross was there, and a former Kentucky governor—but not longtime backers like David Packard, Ford's finance chair; or oilman Henry Salvatori; or California Republican chairman Paul Haerle, Reagan's former appointments secretary, whom the governor had personally elevated to his new job, but who now announced his support for the president. "It is the tradition of our party to support the incumbent," Haerle said in a UPI profile of Reagan that came out that same morning. "I don't happen think anyone, Ronald Reagan, or Jesus Christ reincarnated running against an incumbent who is doing a good job would be a good idea."

A good job: faint praise. But then again, Paul Laxalt said exactly the same thing during his press conference, in the question-and-answer session: "We're not saying President Ford is not doing a good job. But Governor Reagan could do a better job."

There was none of Reagan's rip-roaring anti-détente language of recent weeks, no excoriation of Henry Kissinger, no talk of wicked federal bureaucrats traducing liberty-loving citizens—just vague palaver about how voters "want a change in the direction of government." The whole spectacle, in fact, was anticlimactic. It didn't feel very Reagan-like at all. It left conservative supporters confused. The ones not in the Washington loop wondered who the stocky thirty-five-year-old Ivy League–looking fellow with the flat, round face and imperturbable smile was, constantly by Laxalt's side. The conservatives *in* the Washington loop, however, who knew this longtime Nixon political operative, John Sears, reacted to his presence in two ways. First, they didn't worry: if an operative as serious as John Sears was on board, this meant it was a real presidential campaign. Second, they *worried:* they knew him as a man inordinately proud of his conviction that ideological combat played no necessary role in presidential campaigns. So how could he be running Ronald Reagan's?

The next week the first polling of Republicans on a Reagan-Ford head-to-head matchup came out. Gallup had it as 41 to 20 percent for the president, whose approval rating was a mere 52 percent. Harris had it as 40 to 17 percent. Though given the mess of pottage that was a Republican presidential nomination, did it really matter? The same day as

Paul Laxalt's press conference, Kennedy brother-in-law Sargent Shriver announced his candidacy, making himself one of at least a dozen Democrats lining up for a nomination fight in which victory felt like a golden ticket to the White House. For its June monthly digest, Gallup ranked thirty-four people being talked up for the Democratic nomination according to their name recognition, with Ted Kennedy in the lead with 90 percent and George Wallace second with 88. Frank Church, who'd imagined his ongoing CIA investigation as *his* golden ticket to the front ranks, was in twenty-third place with 24 percent. That put him one spot above the former governor of Georgia; only 23 percent of Democrats were able to recognize the name "Jimmy Carter."

THE PRESIDENT LEFT FOR TEN DAYS OVERSEAS IN LATE JULY. THE *TIMES* sent him off with the headline "Ford Sees 35-Nation Charter as a Gauge on Rights in East Europe"—an index of the new political sensitivity to human rights. The legally nonbinding document to be discussed and perhaps signed in Helsinki would establish that the current boundaries of the nations of Eastern Europe were "inviolable by force"—what the Soviet Union wanted—in exchange for human rights concessions like letting families reunify across national borders—what America wanted. That would mark the first time, Ford was proud to say, that the Communist states that had refused to endorse the 1948 United Nations Universal Declaration of Human Rights acknowledged human rights as a legitimate concern of diplomacy. All that in exchange for a mere formal admission that the map of Europe that had existed since World War II was, well, the map of Europe that had existed since World War II: *something for nothing*, was Ford's triumphant interpretation of what America got out of the Helsinki Accords.

The newly confident conservative foreign policy coalition most strenuously disagreed. The *Wall Street Journal* called it the "new Yalta," the most stinging fighting words a conservative could hurl—Yalta was the site in 1945 where Franklin Roosevelt had supposedly sold out Eastern Europe to the Soviets. Scoop Jackson called it "formal capitulation to Soviet tyranny." Ronald Reagan said, "I am against it, and I think all Americans should be against it." Conservatives also proved unmollified by what happened next: a triumphant tour by Ford of Eastern Europe, throngs cheering an American president wherever he went in what conservatives called the "Captive Nations." In Belgrade, he was even honored with a reception at the city hall—where he landed a blow at the spendthrift liberals running New York by sanctimoniously teaching the Communists a lesson about capitalism: "They don't know how to handle money. All they know how to do is spend it." Came back an aide at New York City Hall, "People in White Houses shouldn't throw stones. At least the City of New York has a balanced budget." He then suggested, "Perhaps Mayor Beame should begin serious talks with the Communist bloc. That appears to be the fastest way to get aid in Washington."

Liberals hated Ford: wasn't that just more reason not to fear a political attack from his right?

The news features on the first anniversary of his presidency flushed out still more professions of hatred for him from liberals. Hubert Humphrey took the occasion to call him "a seventeenth-century physician bleeding his patient in an attempt to cure him." Ralph Nader said he was a "smiling man who makes cruel decisions." That week, Ford surely placated some Southern conservatives when he signed a bill restoring citizenship to General Robert E. Lee.

And maybe some conservatives might have been impressed—if, five days after his return from Europe, he hadn't leaped from the right-wing frying pan right into the right-wing fire, courtesy of his freethinking spouse.

THE INTERVIEW WITH CBS NEWSMAN MORLEY SAFER BROADCAST ON *60 Minutes* on the second Sunday in August wasn't long in turning hot. The first lady volunteered the advice her shrink had been giving her: she was "not taking any time out for Betty." The subject of feminism came up. "I'm not the type that's going to burn my bra," she said, but "nothing could be greater" than passage of the Equal Rights Amendment. *Roe v. Wade* was a "great, great decision." Safer wondered if she thought her kids had tried marijuana. Almost certainly, she answered; these days it was like trying "your first beer or your first cigarette." She also said she thought that the fact that more young people were "living together" wasn't necessarily a bad thing; perhaps it meant the divorce rate would drop.

Safer followed up: "What if Susan Ford came to you and said, 'Mother, I'm having an affair'?"

The first daughter, who that May had held her senior prom in the East Room of the White House, was eighteen years old. The first lady answered, "I wouldn't be surprised. I think she's a perfectly normal human being, like all girls." She explained, however, that she would certainly want to meet the young man to see whether he was "nice or not," and judge whether it was "a worthwhile encounter." (In actual fact Susan Ford had an old-fashioned steady boyfriend who reported in an interview with *Ladies' Home Journal* that Susan opposed women's liberation: "I don't think she'll be a professional woman or anything. I don't think she'll do anything spectacular. She'll be the average mother on the block, always doing a lot for the neighborhood kids. . . . A job is all right if they can do an equal job, but I don't think they can.")

Mrs. Ford had brought up her work with a psychiatrist in her first interview as first lady—and, the following month, indicated that she was a proponent of legal abortion. Back then, White House political handlers rushed her to a maternity ward at a big hospital to be photographed with an adorable babe in arms. This fire would not be so easily contained. It erupted just as another interview, in the women's magazine *McCall's,* was published. In this article, Americans learned that the Fords spurned the White House tradition of separate bedrooms, and Mrs. Ford volunteered that reporters asked her just about everything, except how often she and the leader of the free world had sex. "And if they asked me that I would have told them, 'As often as possible.'" (On *60 Minutes* she elaborated: "I have perfect faith in my husband. But I'm always glad to see him enjoy a pretty girl. And when he stops looking, then I'm going to begin to worry. . . . And he doesn't have time for outside entertainment. Because I keep him busy.")

Mary McGrory, the liberal syndicated columnist, rushed out with a piece headlined in the *Boston Globe* "BETTY FORD'S VIEWS ON SEX FAIL TO STARTLE COUNTRY," confidently pronouncing that the interview merely "indicated she is getting her information from the real world." McGrory reported that by noon Monday the White House press office had fielded only three phone calls on the interview, two taking "[m]ild exception to Mrs. Ford's allowing a total stranger with a microphone to ask her such a question about her 18-year-old daughter. A third objected to the answer." CBS, she said, had received no complaining phone calls at all. And she said that the press office in Vail, Colorado, where the Fords were vacationing, got about a hundred telegrams and phone calls, evenly divided.

She wrote too soon—and too wishfully. Ron Nessen said the president was laughing off the entire thing. Bo Callaway said it wasn't "a major issue in Washington," and that besides, people *liked* the first lady's candor whether they agreed with her or not. For her part, Betty Ford said she'd probably "made a few votes" for her husband. Pulse-taking politicians, and not just conservatives, placed their bets otherwise. Henry Hyde, a Republican congressman from suburban Chicago, compared Betty Ford to Martha Mitchell—the alcoholic, mentally ill wife of the former attorney general who was Washington's gold standard for embarrassing political spouses. A humor columnist, expressing the conventional wisdom, suggested the only thing for Betty to do was resign. ("The networks and women's magazines . . . are making incredible offers to get the First Lady to sit down and openly discuss adultery, drinking, homosexuality and a proposed postal rate hike.") The liberal Hugh Carey, taking a break from negotiations on how to rescue the Big Apple, offered that he wasn't "old-fashioned," but "I do believe in the lyrics of the song Frankie sang so well, 'love and marriage, go together like a horse and carriage.'"

Of course Frank Sinatra had been known to honor that injunction in the breach, rather often. Which was the point McGrory had been making: morally sophisticated people understood that this was how the "real world" worked—nothing simple about it. For others, however, if there were no easy answers, there were simple answers. *Plenty* simple. A Baptist preacher in Charlotte, North Carolina, announced he would be delivering a sermon the following Sunday explaining how the first lady's remarks were "directly contradictory to the teachings of the Bible." Two thousand packed his pews to hear it. Equal Rights Amendment? It was just as Isaiah 3:1–4 prophesied, that "the Lord, the Lord of hosts, doth take away from Jerusalem and from Judah the stay and the staff" if "mighty man, and the man of war, the judge, and the prophet" had his dominion taken from him. Abortion? Premarital sex? I Corinthians, 6:9–10: "Be not deceived: neither fornicators, nor idolaters, nor adulterers, nor effeminate, nor abusers of themselves with mankind . . . shall inherit the kingdom of God." Experimentation with marijuana? The prophet Hosea had something to say about that: "Whoredom and wine and new wine take away the heart."

Twelve North Carolina radio stations picked it up for broadcast. So many callers swamped the Northside Baptist Church's switchboards for printed copies that Pastor Hudson published it as a pamphlet. Soon hundreds of thousands of copies circulated throughout the country.

On August 25 the president stepped into the batter's box to try to knock all the chatter away. Perhaps he had seen the polling from Albert Sindlinger, which Evans and Novak would publicize in their column the next week, finding that in interviews taken on August 24 his approval rating was down to 33.8 percent—whereas it had been 55.3 percent on August 10.

"Betty meant we're deeply concerned about the moral standards" in their family, went his first swing. A whiff.

Strike two: "What Betty was trying to say was that in the closeness of our family we are deeply concerned about the moral standards of how a family is raised. Unfortunately, there has been a misunderstanding. . . ."

One more try: "There are high moral standards in the family, give and take . . ."

But for those drawing their conclusions from Isaiah 3: 1–4, "give and take" within the family and "high moral standards" were precisely opposed notions. So that only dug Gerald Ford deeper in the hole. And he didn't do any better with Pastor Hudson's mortal enemies—as feminists asked what business a husband, even a president, had speaking for his wife in the first place. The messages to the White House, finally tallied up, comprised 10,512 votes in support of the first lady—and 23,308 far more passionate ones opposed. "Your statement on '60 Minutes' cost your husband my vote," ran a typical one—and, said one from the South, "We think this error more serious than anything that President Nixon did."

THE MOST IMPORTANT RESPONSE TO BETTY FORD'S INTERVIEW WAS surely the one that appeared on the front page of the only statewide paper in the home of the nation's first presidential primary, scheduled for February 24, 1976. William Loeb of the Manchester *Union Leader* published one of his trademark front-page editorials. Titled "A DISGRACE TO THE WHITE HOUSE," it opined, "The immorality of Mrs. Ford's remarks is almost exceeded by their utter stupidity. . . . President Ford showed his own lack of guts by saying he had long ago given up commenting on Mrs. Ford's radio interviews. What kind of husband is that? As President of the United States, he should be the moral leader of the nation. . . . It is up to him to take a moral stand. He should repudiate what Mrs. Ford said."

He did not. Nor did he criticize his son Jack, who had indeed smoked marijuana: "I can disagree with what some of our children do," Ford said at a news conference, "but as long as they are honest with us and at least give us an opportunity to express our views, I don't think I should go any further." Jack himself wondered what all the fuss was about: "Everyone in our family is grown up," he said. "We're not under our folks' care any more."

Such family issues felt increasingly political. So when Nancy Reagan seemed to weigh in on the first lady's interview, it felt like a battle line was being drawn. It came at an address to a Republican women's club in the tony Detroit suburb of Grosse Pointe. She said it was the first prepared speech she had ever given. She never mentioned Betty Ford by name, but there wasn't much doubt where she was aiming. "The young people on college campuses and elsewhere are told that to be cool and 'with it,' they should have no 'hang-ups' about sex and premarital living arrangements," she said. "Under the new morality, if they get together for a while and it doesn't work out, they 'split,' as they say. Nothing ventured, nothing gained. Nothing, that is, but the most enriching human experience: the commitment to another human being."

She continued by referencing the latest policy debates over abortion: whether tax money should pay for abortions under Medicaid, and whether underage girls should be able to have abortions without telling their parents. There was no mistaking where Nancy Reagan stood: "our welfare programs making abortions available to under-aged girls regardless of their families' financial situation and without informing the family" were an abomination. Her spokeswoman insisted there were no political implications in her remarks. The ladies of Grosse Point seemed to disagree: "We all came away thinking she would be very worthy of being the First Lady in the White House," one told a reporter.

Maybe she would get the chance. The Ford presidential campaign effort suddenly seemed to be a shambles. Ford interrupted his Vail vacation with political swings into Midwestern and Western states where he vacillated between defending détente and echoing Ronald Reagan. When Reagan's supporters complained about Ford's expenses being paid for by the Republican National Committee, the RNC responded that his travel expenses represented "party building" by the Republicans' "titular leader"—at which a Friends of Ronald Reagan official scouringly questioned whether "Ford is even the titular leader of his party," adding that the Republican treasury "should not become a vehicle for any single candidate in contest for the party's nomination, regardless of any office he may hold."

"Any office he may hold": his perch in the Oval Office was not exactly intimidating the opposition.

Southern Republican state chairmen met in a beach town in North Carolina late in August. Ford campaign lieutenants swooped down on the meeting, lobbying aggressively for loyalty to the president. They heard a mass chorus in return: if the president wanted to dull the Reagan charge, he should drop Nelson Rockefeller from the ticket. Rockefeller then headed South to mend political fences—to "prove to them I don't have horns," he said. In Mobile, Alabama, and Columbia, South Carolina, hat in hand, he all but apologized for the nearly sixteen years of his gubernatorial terms making New York one of the freest-spending states in the union. It didn't work. 'That's all we talked about, replacing Rockefeller," Mississippi chairman Clarke Reed told reporters—and claimed that at least half of his colleagues preferred Reagan, not Ford, as the party's 1976 presidential nominee.

That same week dealt a body blow to Ford's best political bulwark against charges that he was selling out to the Soviets. His hard-line defense secretary, James Schlesinger, had begun making more and more belligerent statements: that "another Korean War" was possible unless America bulked up its post-Vietnam defense posture in Asia; that "Americans must toss off tender sensibilities and set our stomachs," because "the United States might have to make a decision to become the first to introduce atomic weapons." The syndicated columnist Clayton Fritchey pointed out that his tough talk "gives the President some protection from the right wing of his party," and that it was "obvious that the course he is pursuing has the passive, if not the active, approval of the White House." But almost immediately after this column was published, a Pentagon leak revealed that Schlesinger believed his boss had given away the farm in Helsinki.

So much for a coordinated strategy to hold off the right on the foreign policy front.

THE PRESIDENT LEFT FOR A SERIES OF POLITICAL STOPS ON THE WEST Coast. Perhaps the words of three liberal Republican senators who had visited him in the White House—Charles Percy of Illinois, Clifford Case of New Jersey, and Jacob Javits of New York—rang in his ears: they said his attempts to mollify conservatives by aping Reagan on the evils of activist government would be disastrous for the party. If so, he ignored them—telling a fund-raising luncheon in Seattle, "Help me free the free enterprise system." In Portland, Oregon, he attended a "youth Bicentennial rally." He was well received at both. He boarded Air Force One for a stop on Reagan's home turf: Sacramento. To a Chamber of Commerce breakfast, then to the California legislature, he dared venture boasts about the continued success of détente, noting "an important breakthrough we have just made in defusing the time bomb that has been ticking away ominously in the Middle East": Kissinger had just secured a preliminary peace accord between Egypt and Israel. That was well received, too. He reported that 50 percent of Miss Universe contestants, asked on a questionnaire who was "the greatest person in the world today," answered "Henry Kissinger." The audience rocked with appreciative laughter.

He returned to his hotel, then, shortly before 10 A.M. he strode forth for an address to the state legislature at the capitol, across the street.

Skies were clear; a small crowd outside the hotel cheered him on; the sun finally seemed to be shining on Gerald Ford. Crowds lined the restraining ropes snaking through the verdant grounds. The president began shaking hands, confident and smiling.

A blank-faced woman dressed in a dramatic flowing red gown and a bizarre red turban drew a .45-caliber Army Colt automatic from a leg holster.

The leader of the free world flinched, paled; a Secret Service officer grabbed the gun with one hand and this tiny, mousy woman with the other.

She started screaming. "It didn't go off!" she said as she was led away, first in surprise and dismay, then in an apparent attempt at self-exculpation. "Don't worry. It didn't go off, fellows. It didn't go off!"—as if that technicality might free her. She then acted as if the political analysis she confidently shouted into the crowd—which crowd, since it had all happened so fast, hardly realized an assassination had been attempted at all—might explain it all away: "This country is a mess! The man is not your president!"

The president, grimly determined, agents shielding him in every direction, continued on to the capitol building and calmly delivered his speech—which focused, ironically, on "the truly alarming increase in violent crime throughout this country." Meanwhile, journalists got to work identifying the strange small woman in the red turban. Her name, they learned, was Lynette "Squeaky" Fromme, and her guru was none other than Charles Manson.

Americans had retained a death-haunted fascination with this wicked Svengali who somehow insinuated himself inside the minds of a make-shift tribe of young men and women, most from ordinary middle-class suburban backgrounds, and by 1969 turned them into a gang of remorseless killers who fondly hoped their cold-blooded murders of Sharon Tate, Leno and Rosemary LaBianca, and their friends in the Hollywood Hills would foment a national race war. The previous spring, the paperback rights to prosecutor Vincent Bugliosi's bestseller about the case, *Helter Skelter*, sold for an astounding $771,000. Now the lurid fascination was kindled anew.

In 1971, it turned out, Fromme, then twenty-two years old, had been sentenced to ninety days in jail for attempting, by lacing a hamburger with LSD, to keep a witness from testifying in the Tate murder trial. An interview surfaced that she had given in July 1975: "If Nixon's reality wearing a new Ford face continues to run the country against the law, our homes will be bloodier than the Tate-LaBianca houses and My

Lai put together." The Associated Press tracked down her best friend, Sandra Good, "who still bears a deep X scar carved in her forehead in devotion to Manson." Good and Fromme cohabited celibately "as self-avowed 'nuns,'" it was explained. "She's a very, very gentle girl," Good insisted. "That's why all this monstrousness out there hurts her." The "monstrousness," she explained, included "Charlie being locked up, sitting in a cell for five years." (Fromme's trial attorney explained that her goal had been to win Manson a new trial.) And, too, the despoliation of the environment: "Every day," Good said, "we wake up and think, 'How many whales did they kill today?'" She then patiently explained that she and Fromme were members of "a wave of assassins," the "International Peoples' Court of Retribution," "made up of several thousand people throughout the world who love the earth, the children, and their own lives. They have been silently watching executives and chairmen of boards—and their wives—of companies and industries that in any way harm the air, water, earth, and wildlife." Soon after, one of the seventy-five people Good said they'd marked for assassination, a Dow Chemical executive, said that weeks earlier he'd received a threatening phone call from a woman identifying herself as a member of the Charles Manson family.

At her arraignment, Fromme stood up, addressed the judge despite a warning that she might prejudice her chance for a fair trial, and proclaimed, "I want you to order the corps of government engineers to buy up the parks. . . . You have jurisdiction over the redwood trees. The important part is the redwood trees. . . . The gun is pointed, your honor." (She cheerfully addressed the judge as she was led from the courtroom: "I hope I wasn't rude." He assured her she was not.) Another character was introduced in the news: one Harold Eugene Boro, sixty-six, the owner of the gun, a quiet grandfather, divorced for thirty years, who relatives said "never was interested in women or anything," but who nonetheless had become Fromme and Good's "sugar daddy." As for Good, she stood outside their apartment and told reporters that their International Tribunal now marked three thousand people for execution, "if they didn't stop harming the environment and projecting distorted sex images into the media"—though their wives would be "hacked to death" first.

MORE DISTURBANCES.

School was in session—or, in a bewildering array of places around the country, was not in session. Every Chicago school and most New York schools were empty. So were schools in ten separate communities in Rhode Island and thirty-one in Pennsylvania, and in Berkeley and San Jose, California; Wilmington, Delaware; Milan and Brecksville, Ohio; Hoboken, New Jersey; and Lynn and New Bedford, Massachusetts. One municipality that avoided America's unprecedented wave of teacher strikes, however, was Boston. There classes went on as scheduled the first Tuesday after Labor Day—as two hundred young demonstrators in the Charlestown section greeted the second year of court-ordered desegregation by barricading themselves off at the corner of Bunker Hill and Concord streets and stoning police cars.

Gays were on the march—so proclaimed the September 8 cover of *Time,* from which peered a uniformed Air Force officer named Leonard Matlovich declaring, "I am a homosexual." "Similarly jolting," they observed, "have been public announcements of their homosexuality by a variety of people who could be anybody's neighbors." *Redbook,* the ladies' magazine, and syndicated advice columnist Abigail Van Buren said you should have nothing to fear. *Redbook* quoted her response to two worried parents: "Why do you assume that her sexual preference will necessarily 'ruin' her life?"

But the account that ensued in *Time*—"perhaps the most obvious aspect of the male gay subculture is its promiscuity," a "sexual marketplace" of "quick, anonymous and furtive sex in men's rooms of public parks," "prostitutes who are teen-age or younger . . . greatly in demand, particularly by older married men" (a guide to the nation's underage brothels, *Where the Boys Are,* had sold 70,000 copies), and the "orgy rooms" of proliferating bathhouse clubs (one chain had branches in thirty-two cities, like McDonald's)—made it hard for even the most liberal-minded readers to find much tolerance in their hearts for the new developments, or sympathy for a political movement making "headway by using the model of the black civil rights struggle." A psychoanalyst got the last word: "'Anything goes' is a legitimate attitude for consenting adults . . . but for a culture to declare it as a credo is to miss entirely the stake all of us have in the harmony between the sexes and in the family as the irreplaceable necessity of society. This is a society that is increasingly denying its impotence by calling it 'tolerance,' preaching resignation and naming all this 'progress.'"

New York still faced fiscal catastrophe, Felix Rohatyn's Municipal Assistance Corporation having failed to cajole private capital markets into coughing up more loans. Mayor Beame laid off more than eight thousand teachers and school paraprofessionals—and the strike that resulted kept 1,075,000 innocent children from the classroom. Corrections officers briefly blocked the bridges to the jail on Rikers Island; citizens occupied firehouses to keep them from closing. On September 4 the state legislature convened to consider emergency measures. An editorial in that morning's *Wall Street Journal* said the "fiscal agony of New York City has gone so far that the only hope for a responsible and reasonably straightforward resolution is a voluntary bankruptcy." Republicans emboldened by the editorial forced through an Emergency Financial Control Act, which on September 9 all but transformed government in the world's greatest city into an adjunct of a seven-person budget oversight board appointed by largely rural legislators in Albany. It was like what Ronald Reagan now said on the radio. Officials in both parties were talking about siting their national conventions in the city. Reagan said it might be a good idea: "It could be very educational.... New York is an example of what can happen to this entire country if we don't re-chart our course." He was especially offended by the fact that at its public colleges—whose 1,400 professors were also then on strike, with the president of their union beginning to serve a five-month sentence for contempt of court—"not one student, regardless of means, pays a penny in tuition."

The seventh special session of the United Nations General Assembly opened, also in New York. The theme was global economic development. The UN was founded as a majority-European body, but now 70 percent of its membership consisted of Third World states. Those states, emboldened by the success of OPEC's Arab members in unilaterally turning themselves into geostrategic powerhouses by leveraging a commodity that nature happened to have gifted them beneath their sands, had begun playing the natural resource game themselves. Lowly Jamaica, for example, had begun telling America precisely how high it had to jump to access Jamaican bauxite, essential for the manufacture of aluminum. Now these countries' prime ministers and presidents were in Manhattan bearing just such demands, proposing a sweeping reconstruction of the balance of power between have and have-not nations in the institutions of trade. And Daniel Patrick Moynihan, appointed America's UN representative right after insisting it was "time that American spokesmen came to be feared," presented the American response. Which was, pretty much, that the Third World nations would get exactly what they wished—a package of reforms designed to make sure such countries' export programs continued to prosper whatever the fluctuations in demand for their commodities, an effective transfer of billions of dollars of value from the First World to the Third. The Ford administration appeared to have little choice: "at least 75 percent of the holdings of U.S. raw materials located in Third World Nations," according to one estimate, "had been nationalized." Treasury secretary Simon, livid, said of the proposed package, "We are in danger of compromising our basic commitment to the free enterprise system." The *Wall Street Journal* compared such deals to handing over to feckless "international bureaucracies" the power to "balance Mayor Beame's budget."

IN THE SECOND WEEK OF SEPTEMBER, THE ASSOCIATED PRESS REPORTED that telegrams and letters to the White House were running two to one against Betty Ford. A Democratic congressman from Ohio gave a speech on the House floor decrying the fact that twenty-four million-aires paid no federal income tax. And first-in-the-nation New Hampshire treated observers to a sort of referendum on the pressing political question of the moment: moderate Republicanism versus conservative Republicanism, President Gerald Rudolph Ford against Governor Ronald Wilson Reagan.

A bizarre set of circumstances had followed a near tie in the 1974 election to replace a retiring conservative Republican senator from Hampshire: Republican Louis Wyman appeared to be ahead by 355 votes on election night, then Democrat John Durkin demanded a recount that put him ahead by ten votes; the Republican got a second recount that gave him the edge by two votes. Seven months of legal wrangling followed until a new election was called for September 16. President Ford seized on Wyman's campaign as an opportunity. Having defiantly proclaimed following Squeaky Fromme's folly in Sacramento that "no circumstances will preclude me from contacting the American people as I travel from one state to another," he embarked upon an eleven-hour tour of fourteen towns across the lower tier of the state, stopping at several points along the way to make speeches as he perched on the presidential limousine's running board, plunging impromptu into crowds for handshaking sessions, the only evident concession to security a snugger-fitting shirt and two clips from some sort of device above either side of his belt, which reporters guessed must be fastening a bulletproof vest.

It was, the *New York Times'* James Reston wrote, perfectly absurd: "the old crowd-pushing, hand-shaking, good-guy technique is no answer to inflation, unemployment, and the other concerns of the nation, and it is obviously dangerous. For we are living in a troubled and maybe even a demented age." Something else, he wrote in the same column, was also absurd: the political calculation that suggested the necessity of all this campaign-style glad-handing. "The notion that Ronald Reagan can get the Republican presidential nomination," he said, "is patently ridiculous unless you suspect the Republicans of suicidal tendencies."

And yet there was Ronald Reagan, making his own foray into New Hampshire on Louis Wyman's behalf—and, a *Washington Post* columnist taking man-on-the-street soundings of Granite Staters' opinions of the two men discovered, plainly winning by comparison with Ford. A high school teacher on the president: "I have no use for him when he keeps reaching into my pocket." A factory worker: "I hate to turn my back on him, but he doesn't seem to have our interests at heart. Why is he selling wheat to Russians?" An eighty-year-old woman: "I don't believe in that kind of stuff and I never expected to hear it from a First Lady." But the columnist noted, "The universal, high-octane contempt for all politicians somehow stops short of California's former governor. He is perceived as a man of common sense who understands common people, especially New Hampshire retirees who turn purple as they talk of 'all the money Congress voted itself before they sneaked off on vacation,'" and the "white-haired Republican woman" who told the columnist, "he ran that state pretty good, didn't he? He got those people off welfare, didn't he?"

Other columnists reported inside dope. A sitting president was supposed to possess awesome powers to command the allegiance of sitting politicians. But Reagan had already won the state party chairman, its governor—and a crucial fence-sitting former governor, Hugh Gregg, who despised his lunatic far-right governor Meldrim Thomson but gave up on the president after his chief of staff, Donald Rumsfeld, snubbed him, never placing a promised phone call. "The Reagan people were more professional," he said. Evans and Novak learned of a newfangled computer system Reaganites were using in their office that placed Reagan, according to a Republican who still was neutral, "about ten times" ahead of Ford in organization. They also noted that the president "rarely evoked applause" on his twenty stops. They quoted a "distinguished party leader" who said, "Ford had a chance to wrap up this state. He blew it. He absolutely blew it."

Perhaps an upset was conceivable. "Maybe Ford should run against Reagan," a columnist for the *Washington Star* suggested; or maybe he shouldn't be president at all, an editorial in the *New York Times* almost seemed to be saying: "The Ford Administration's economic policies are failing. The economic recovery is sluggish and sputtering . . . inflation is again surging forward." In contrast to the more conservative *Star*, and like its columnist Reston, it rued the role of his conservative challenger in nudging Ford to the right. Fifteen mayors had just begged the president to stave off New York's default, to prevent the shock waves it would send across the entire municipal bond market. West German chancellor Helmut Schmidt warned of the possibility of international economic collapse. "When a multi-billion dollar private corporation is skidding into bankruptcy, alarm arouses the Administration out of do-nothingness," the *Times* opined of Ford's nonresponse. "But when the nation's largest city is in trouble, the Administration adopts the three blind mice as its policy-making model. Indeed, Mr. Ford seems to gloat over New York's distress." They blamed his "new Reaganism"— "budgetary restraint, trickle-down tax proposals, and a hopeful, expect-ant air"—and his "frenetic schedule."

The editorial was published on September 15. The previous day Ford had traveled to Dallas—speaking, of all places, at Love Field, from whence JFK was motorcading when he was shot in 1963. "The nation is not disintegrating," he insisted, "it is going through a period of change." He then ("protected," the Associated Press reported, "by rigid security measures") addressed "prophets of doom and gloom" who said crimi-nals had captured the streets and "the President of the United States is no longer safe greeting citizens in the nation's streets. . . . I've had it with that attitude. I did not take a secret oath of office to preside over the decline and fall of the United States of America." The day before that, police had chased, but did not catch, a man with a gun in the very audi-torium where Ford was to speak in St. Louis.

Next he would head back to California, Reagan's backyard—belying his remonstrances that these were not political appearances. First, though, on September 16, more than two weeks after its original dead-line to submit its report, the Church Committee finally began its first televised hearing. "We will see today the dark side of those activities, where many Americans who were not even *suspected* of crime, were not only spied upon, but they were harassed, they were discredited, and at times endangered," Church thoughtfully intoned in his opening statement—then, in a show carefully scripted for television, a jet-black dart gun was displayed, one designed to deliver a dose of poison derived from a shellfish toxin, untraceable in an autopsy, that could kill a man instantly from one hundred meters away.

Church asked the Central Intelligence Agency's chief William Colby: "Have you brought with you some of those devices which would enable the CIA to use this poison for—"

Colby cut in—"indeed we have"—perhaps to head off the words that Church, angrily, uttered next:

"—for *killing* people?"

Murmurs. Pause. The gun was displayed by a CIA staffer. Church, joking: "Don't point it *at* me!" Laughter. Barry Goldwater, the ranking committee Republican, picked it up, turned it over, and sighted intently down its barrel, providing the picture that showed up in all the papers the next day.

Such chemical agents were supposed to be illegal. An unsigned memo to former director Richard Helms was introduced into evidence, however, written by the director of covert operations and recommending that if Helms wished "to continue this special capability" the unit could stockpile the poisons secretly at a private lab near Baltimore. The poison was indeed retained, and discerned in a vault in downtown Washington—but the committee discovered it would be nearly impossible to retrace the chain of responsibility, because the relevant files had all been destroyed. "I find your testimony rather astounding," Senator Church told the head of the CIA's science and technology branch. Colby, for his part, blamed "reckless insubordination." "The best gloss you can give it," suggested the Republican member from Maryland, Charles "Mac" Mathias, "is that there's always somebody who didn't get the word." A less flattering gloss was suggested by Senator Walter Mondale, Democrat of Minnesota, who cited his "gnawing fear . . . that things are occurring in deliberate contravention and disregard of official orders."

A worse gloss than *that* was that things were occurring *by* official orders—not just in the retention of tiny amounts of deadly toxins, but in all those alleged CIA assassination attempts, too. William Safire, though, sounding as paranoid as any Kennedy assassination conspiracy theorist, said not to count on Senator Church, a presidential aspirant, to look too hard: "Will candidate Church risk his Kennedy support by going after the whole story, or will he again shrink from full disclosure, as he did when the horrors of the Kennedy-CIA secret war on Cuba hove into view? . . . Will television news open up or cover up the [Kennedy] roots of the abuse of federal spying power?"

This debate over responsibility for CIA abuses would haunt the investigations for months to come. It coursed, simultaneously, through popular culture. A new picture, *Three Days of the Condor*, hit screens; it starred Robert Redford as low-level CIA analyst who stumbles upon a high-level plot to seize Arabia's oil fields for the United States—"no match," the *Times'* Vincent Canby concluded, "for stories that have appeared in your local newspaper." Meanwhile, Church's counterpart on the other side of the Capitol, Representative Otis Pike of New York—

tapped to run the House's select committee on intelligence after Lucien Nedzi resigned amid accusations of covering up his previous knowledge of CIA abuses—undertook an equally or even more aggressive inquiry of CIA perfidy. The committee's first report discovered that the General Accounting Office hadn't been allowed to audit the CIA since 1962, that GAO had no idea how much the agency took in or how it was spent, and that only six employees at the Office of Management and Budget, three of them former CIA employees, studied the foreign intelligence budget as a whole. Now, on September 11, they came out with a report alleging basic failures of the CIA in doing what it was supposed to do with all that secret money: deliver intelligence. The day before the 1973 Yom Kippur War broke out, the Pike Committee discovered, the agency had told the president to expect Middle East peace.

A miniature constitutional crisis followed. The White House had tried to block release of that House report—unless, it demanded, four words revealing CIA "sources and methods" (apparently involving broken Egyptian codes) were stricken. Pike roared back. Ideologically moderate but characterologically irreverent, the Long Islander had a bit of the old Sam Ervin spirit in him: he wore flamboyant bow ties, and jealously guarded Congress's prerogatives vis-à-vis the executive branch. The CIA "would simply prefer that we operated in a dictatorship where only one branch of the government has any power over secrecy," he said. "I simply submit to you that that is not the way I read the Constitution of the United States." His colleague Morgan F. Murphy of Illinois, another moderate Democrat, said, "I heard the same argument I heard in defense of President Nixon. He has a right to keep things secret, he has a right not to turn over tapes, and he has a right not to turn over documents. But I thought the Supreme Court settled that matter." Their committee voted six to three to release the report, the four words intact, arguing that the very words in question revealed just the sort of CIA screw-ups it was the committee's job to document. They defiantly subpoenaed more White House documents. The White House refused them. Then the president raised the stakes, sending a Justice Department official up to Capitol Hill to threaten that unless Pike promised not to release more classified information, the committee would get no more documents at all, no officials would testify on classified matters, and previously released classified documents would have to be returned—he was shutting down the investigation. On September 16, at an Oval Office press conference, Ford said that if a private citizen had released the "four words," he would have gone to jail. The *Times* called it "the most serious Constitutional confrontation between the legislative and executive branch since the Watergate scandal." For his part, Watergate-style, Otis Pike threatened to take the president to court.

Two days later, Pike playfully hoisted the president with his own secrecy petard. A White House counsel named Rod Hills, who happened to be the husband of the president's trade representative, left a notebook in Pike's congressional office containing copies of letters marked "Secret Sensitive." So Pike wrote Gerald Ford a letter—and introduced it into the *Congressional Record:* "It is my understanding," he mocked, "that because of an alleged breach of security you would like me to provide you with all secret documents in my possession. I have only one such document. It does in my judgment represent a grave breach of security and I am delighted to be able to present it to you and make a clean breast of the whole affair." He suggested the president deploy the FBI to track down the culprit, and gave a hint as to his identity: "He is the husband of a member of your Cabinet." In conclusion, he twisted the knife: "If he loses it again, it's OK. I have a copy."

That morning, the *New York Times* had editorialized about "The Son of Watergate," arguing that the administration was stonewalling on the CIA investigation: Ford's "real concern," they said, "seems to be to keep the House probers from delving as deeply as they should into the shadowland of intelligence activities." And later that day, Patty Hearst—or "Tania," if you preferred her nom de guerre—on the lam for sixteen months, was finally tracked down and arrested by the FBI, hiding in plain sight in a San Francisco apartment with another Symbionese Liberation Army member. What turned out to be most shocking about her flight from justice was how many otherwise law-abiding citizens had abetted it, apparently seeing shielding a bank robber as a protest against the evils of the American system—including, allegedly, the former athletic director of Oberlin College, who was a housemate of Bill Walton, the young basketball star who for his part had said, when offered $2.5 million to sign with the Portland Trailblazers, "I don't believe in capitalism . . . wealth should be spread around."

At her booking, she was asked her occupation; she responded, "Urban guerrilla. Self-employed." Led from the courtroom, she raised a fist through her handcuffs, smiling broadly. She asked her attorney to relay a message: "Tell everybody that I'm smiling, that I feel free and strong and I send my greetings and love to all the sisters and brothers out there." In her mug shot she looked lovely and glamorous, like a silent-film star. Her mother, when informed of her daughter's apprehension, begged authorities: "She was primarily a kidnap victim. She never went off on anything of her own free will. Please call it a rescue, not a capture." Patty was photographed chatting cordially with her family, dandling a bouquet of yellow roses in her lap. "We laughed and hugged and kissed each other," Mom related. "She said she wanted to come home." The family's lawyer said it had "been as though she lived in a fog, within which she was confused, still unable to distinguish between actuality and fantasy and in a perpetual state of terror."

It had to be said, though, that sixteen months was a long time to be in a fog.

The old debate—Patty Hearst: terrorist or victim?—was revived. Perhaps Patty, like Regan in *The Exorcist,* had suffered some temporary derangement, her very will stolen from her by the demonic energies of the age—"brainwashing," they called it—but now was ready to be returned to the bosom of her family, whole, like Regan at the end of the movie, like it was 1962 all over again. But that conclusion became harder to sustain when news of a jailhouse recording leaked in which Hearst told a childhood friend that she would never accept bail if it meant becoming "a prisoner in my parents' home"—directly contracting the affidavit she had signed saying she disowned her allegiance to her kidnappers and her denunciation of her parents—and that she would soon release a statement proclaiming her "revolutionary feminist" goals. It became harder to sustain, too, when police announced they were checking the loaded .38-caliber pistol seized from Hearst's purse, and another gun they'd found in her closet, to see whether they were connected to the murder of a jailed black radical suspected of squealing.

When a Seattle grocery store was rocked by an explosion, a female caller told a TV station the blast was in retaliation for "the arrest of our SLA brothers and sisters in San Francisco."

In 1963, twice in 1968, Americans learned it was deranged lone assassins we had to be afraid of. Now the deranged assassins belonged to social movements. Crime and social movements seemed almost to merge. That very week a new movie came out in theaters, closely based on a true story, about two gay lovers who rob a bank in Brooklyn to pay for one of them to get a sex-change operation. Everything goes wrong (there is hardly any money in the bank; here was an allegory in itself); a hostage standoff ensues, then a media circus—then the massive crowd of bystanders that gathers in response begins cheering the *bank robbers on,* vilifying the cops. Criminals were being held up by an alienated populace as if they were some new sort of hero. Ronald Reagan, in his first gubernatorial campaign, said of the social chaos of the 1960s that the whole thing started "when the so-called 'free speech' advocates, who in truth have no appreciation for freedom, were allowed to assault and humiliate the symbol of law and order, a police car on the campus. And that was the moment when the ringleaders should have been taken by the scuff of the neck and thrown out of the university once and for all." Now millions of Americans—*Dog Day Afternoon* was a big hit—were delighting in a picture that glamorized thousands of ordinary Americans casually mocking police authority in just the same way. Was Berkeley America now? Could Patty Hearst become a popular hero? The *Chicago Sun-Times* worried she just might: "We cannot help wondering to what extent the spirit of Tania lies dormant, awaiting arousal, in many of the nation's young."

ON SEPTEMBER 21 CAME A REPORT FROM BOB WOODWARD IN THE *Washington Post* that E. Howard Hunt, one of forty-three former Nixon administration officials eventually found guilty of Watergate-related crimes, had been ordered in 1971 by a "senior official" in the White House to assassinate columnist Jack Anderson—via a former CIA physician who would provide poison of "a variety that would leave no trace during a routine medical examination or autopsy." On the twenty-second came another act of violence in retaliation for the arrest of Patty Hearst.

Gerald Ford found his bulletproof vest too warm and confining, even on the cool, crisp San Francisco day when he spoke before two thousand Republicans who paid twenty-five dollars apiece for a fundraiser for the California party. In his speech he attacked Otis Pike by name, promising not to compromise "our intelligence sources and the higher national secrets." (Ronald Reagan, a cosponsor of the event, didn't show, the press reported, as "aides are concerned the joint appearances with Ford might undercut his White House challenge.") Ford did accede, before leaving an interview in the St. Francis Hotel on Knob Hill, to the Secret Service's strenuous request not to wade into the crowd of three thousand lining Powell Street. He just waved to them instead.

He was but a step from his limousine when a squat, homely woman drew a .38-caliber Smith & Wesson revolver and steadied her right wrist like she knew what she was doing.

A single shot ricocheted, grazing a cabdriver. The president crouched down on the floor of his limousine, Secret Service agents and chief of staff Don Rumsfeld shielding his body. A quick-thinking Marine veteran seized the gun before another shot could be fired. Police officers knocked down the assailant, and once more the surreal facts issued forth, if anything more bizarre now than the last time.

Forty-five-year-old Sara Jane Moore had been a suburban country-club mother and certified public accountant when she pulled up stakes after her fifth divorce and alighted on the doorstep of "People in Need," the makeshift charity set up to fulfill the SLA's demand to distribute free groceries to California's poor, the ones upon whom Ronald Reagan had wished botulism. She elbowed her way in as its bookkeeper. "God has sent me," she told the staff. Thereupon, she tried to insinuate herself within the Bay Area's thriving insurrectionist underground. *Time,* in its next issue, profiled that gothic demimonde of at least half a dozen gangs dedicated to "armed struggle against the state," responsible for at least fifty bombings in California so far in 1975, with names like the Tribal Thumb Collective, the New World Liberation Front (responsible for bombings of General Motors, Pacific Gas and Electric, and ITT), the Red Guerrilla Family (they'd bombed an FBI office and PG&E)—and the Weather Underground, whose most infamous fugitive, the ravishing Bernardine Dohrn, was quoted in *Time*'s article as having exulted over the murders by the Manson Family: "Not only did they kill those pigs, they shoved a fork in Tate's stomach and then sat down and ate dinner." ("For the next several days," *Time* quoted a former member as saying, "we all went around giving a sign of three fingers extended. It was to symbolize the fork.") The gangs lived "underground," *Time* explained, many of them collecting food stamps and welfare under phony names, and "their time is largely spent shoplifting food and other necessities, stealing purses, cashing forged checks, searching for new hideouts and plotting." Though they numbered only a few hundred people, they relied on thousands of aboveground sympathizers, with whom they might rendezvous in coffeehouses, bars, or parking lots—or at the spit of land known to Berkeley locals as "Ho Chi Minh Park."

Moore, a radical groupie, had apparently hoped to establish herself as one of their liaisons. Again and again, she was spurned. She was too weird even for them.

She became an FBI and police informant. Then she *told* radicals she was an FBI informant, isolating herself still further. As she kicked around San Francisco and Berkeley, yet more lonely and deranged, increasingly obsessed with Patty Hearst, law enforcement *still* kept her on as a police informant—even as, forty-eight hours before the shooting, she apparently implored police to stop her from doing something she said would horrify them. Then she did it.

Two assassination attempts in nineteen days. Once more the president asserted he wouldn't stop mingling with the public. At least one television network, ABC, took on the policy of prewiring massively expensive live satellite feed setups in every Podunk stop on every presidential itinerary. Treasury secretary Simon testified that the president got some sixteen death threats a day—and that a former mental patient offered a federal undercover agent twenty-five thousand dollars to kill the president. A twenty-two-year-old Michigan man was arrested after telling a police officer he "would kill the president because his mother said he wouldn't do it." Gallup ran a poll asking citizens whether Ford should expose himself to crowds. A near majority, 44 percent, said he should stay in the White House (and, by 67 to 27 percent, respondents said that all firearms should be registered).

Reagan spoke about the assassination attempts on his radio show with typically aphoristic sharpness: "Someone tries to kill the President and the only thing we can suggest is locking up the President." And why, he asked, weren't such lunatics under surveillance or in jail or asylums? Ignoring the fact that police-spy Moore already was under surveillance—and the way his own budget cuts as governor emptied California's mental wards—he blamed "some members of the media, the American Civil Liberties Union, and the Congress . . . hostile to the keeping of files on American citizens even where there's evidence indicating possible danger." He once more rattled off all the McCarthy-era spy bureaucracies liberals had recklessly done away with. He blamed the Church and Pike committees, too, and his own Rockefeller Commission: "What we need is more intelligence gathering and less anti-intelligence hysteria."

Proximately, the week of the second assassination attempt, that hysteria could be taken to refer to Otis Pike taking on Henry Kissinger for refusing to turn over subpoenaed documents, and for ordering his aides not to testify, concerning another intelligence goof-up: the CIA's failure to predict Turkey's destabilizing invasion of Cyprus in 1974. (After CIA director Colby ruled that Pike could have the paperwork anyway, so much of it was redacted the committee voted 10 to 3 to cite Colby for contempt of Congress.) Or to the next phase of Church's televised hearings, on the 1970 "Huston Plan" recommending White House lawbreaking. One of the witnesses was James Jesus Angleton, the CIA's chief of counterintelligence. A senator put it straight to him: "You were specifically asked about shellfish poisons and shellfish toxins. You said, 'It's inconceivable that a secret intelligence arm of the government has to comply with all the overt orders of the government.' Is that an accurate quote or not an accurate quote?" Angleton answered in the most cynical possible way, pulling TV viewers straight into the intelligence world's ugly, extraconstitutional hall of mirrors: "Well if it's accurate, it shouldn't have been said."

Such death-haunted times. On the front pages the CIA news did battle for attention with stories of the pretrial maneuvering of lawyers for Patty Hearst and Sara Jane Moore. In the offices of the Senate Select Committee on Intelligence, visitors, letters, and phone calls flooded in: a woman reporting that the CIA, knowing she had the goods on it, gave her a forced hysterectomy when she was on the operating table for another procedure, to warn her to shut up (she bravely offered the committee her testimony nonetheless); another who said she was ill from the X-rays the CIA had been beaming into her home; a woman who reported telling her lawyer her telephone was bugged, upon which "CIA and FBI agents broke into my home and put me in a straight jacket and took me into this little room at a hospital where they tore off all my clothes and squirted me with cold water." Senator Church's press secretary found himself in a bit of a quandary concerning which lunatics' letters to ignore, and which to pass along to higher-ups; after all, what if someone had called and said, "Tell your senator I have solid evidence that the CIA had a plan to paint Fidel Castro's shoes with a special shoe polish that would make his beard fall out." For, after all, the CIA had actually entertained just such a plan. And he remembered how haughtily he had dismissed the University of Idaho student who swore up and down that the Nixon reelection campaign had hatched a scheme to capture protest leaders at the 1972 Republican convention and hold them prisoner on a boat in the Atlantic Ocean. . . .

Paranoia ran riot—paranoia, seen as a road to redemption. On college campuses, just about any lecturer with a bold new theory about the conspiracists behind the assassination of John F. Kennedy (Mark Lane, author of *Rush to Judgement;* Jim Garrison, the New Orleans district attorney who'd spent years in the late 1960s trying to convince the world the fatal shots could not have come from a single gunman inside the Texas School Book Depository) could draw a standing-room-only crowd—especially if he was implicating the American government itself. The folks who called themselves the "assassination research community" knew from labs they assembled in their garages that the photograph with Lee Harvey Oswald holding the murder weapon in his backyard was fake, and from measurements they took on family trips to Dealey Plaza in Dallas that there could not possibly have been a single shooter. They knew, too, this: that if they simply could expose the lies of the powerful who covered up the veritable regicide, they could bring redemption to a fallen land.

Their worldview had been introduced to the masses back in March, when an enterprisingly frenetic TV host named Geraldo Rivera showed a purloined copy of the live home movie footage of the shooting taken by Dallas dress manufacturer Abraham Zapruder. "That's heavy," the long-haired, thick-mustachioed Rivera pronounced as the audience gasped. His guest pointed out a barely detectable snap of the president's head back and to the left in what knowing "assassinologists" referred to as Frame Z-313—"thus proving," Rivera intoned as if affirming that two plus two equaled four, "that there must have been a marksman firing from somewhere in front of the motorcade, probably at the 'grassy knoll.'" The public was further energized by the murder of Sam Giancana in June—obviously by the CIA, seeking to shut him up. ("They're going to pin the crucification on us next," an agency officer complained.)

The speculation intensified late in August, when it was reported that the FBI had destroyed a letter that Oswald had delivered to the bureau's headquarters in Dallas on November 10, 1963. The speculation was now all but universal. Nearly two-thirds of Americans believed some sort of Kennedy conspiracy theory. A *Washington Post* columnist drew the logical conclusion: "American society has gone buggy on conspiracy theories of late because so many nasty demonstrations of the real thing have turned up." In October, Senator Richard Schweiker of Pennsylvania told a press conference that his intelligence subcommittee had come up with three "very significant leads" about the murder, suggesting that he might open hearings—that Kennedy was killed in a Communist plot, or by a "right-wing conspiracy in the United States," or in a conspiracy by anti-Castro Cubans. Though he declined to speculate on these, he said, "I think the Warren Commission report is like a house of cards. It's going to collapse." In November, a new book by a respected journalist, Robert Sam Anson, *They've Killed the President! The Search for JFK*, proposed the assassination as a joint CIA-mafia project; the first printing was 250,000 copies. A former Los Angeles police official and parttime CIA employee, Hugh McDonald, claimed to have interviewed the real killer, a CIA assassin known as "Saul," who used Oswald's gunfire as cover for his own. Bumper stickers reading "Who Killed Kennedy?" proliferated.

Conspiracies everywhere. Guns everywhere. *Women* with guns everywhere. *Time* quoted Bernardine Dohrn: "Women fighters are frightening apparitions to the enemy and an example for us." One Midwestern paper agreed, calling the "Patty Hearst–Squeaky Fromme–Sara Moore spectacle" but the "latest volcano of nihilism" spewing forth in an America gone mad; a Baptist pastor wrote to the *Washington Star* complaining, "Now the clamor is to get rid of all guns. It is more logical to get rid of all women." It haunted a nation's dreams. At the Miss Universe pageant in Nicaragua, Miss USA pranced onstage in combat fatigues and an automatic rifle prop, simulating an armed robbery. She also said she was not a women's liberationist because she was against "communal toilets."

The Federal Communications Commission, acceding to a well-organized clamor by Christian activists like the Reverend Donald Wildmon's National Federation for Decency, had made that fall's TV season the first to include a mandatory "family hour." *Happy Days* enjoyed its breakthrough season in the ratings by bringing to the foreground a minor character who dressed like James Dean in *Rebel Without a Cause*—only reassuringly domesticated, like a sweet-tempered uncle (when "Fonzie" said a line about how "cool" it was to have a library card, the National Library Association reported registration for cards went up 50 percent). An evangelical group announced the first "Continental Congress on the Family" for St. Louis in October, anticipating three thousand delegates, to "clarify the biblical principles for marriage and family life and . . . relate these to current spiritual and social problems."

It was hard, though, to imagine how these Augean stables might be cleaned. "In a rather short time we can expect to see Christians put in decision dilemmas in which their scriptural beliefs run strongly counter to the general will of the people," one of the organizers reflected. In wicked Gotham, a rumor circulated about a new genre of pornography popular among a wealthy underground "select clientele": "Snuff Porn—The Actress Is Actually Murdered," reported the *New York Post*. *New York Times* columnist William Shannon wrote, "There are fleeting moments when the public scene recalls the Weimar republic of 1932–33. In this American phantasmagoria, an empty-faced girl in a scarlet cloak and a clown's hat points a gun . . . the unemployed mill about . . . the largest city is about to go bankrupt . . . a feckless President, another wooden titan, drones stolidly . . . exorcists, astrologers, and strange oriental gurus wander through . . . the screens, large and small, pulsate with violence and pornography . . . the godfathers last tango with clockwork orange in deep throat . . . women in pants bawl lustily while anguished youths try to be gay . . . a motherly woman raises her gun and fires . . . screams . . .

"Underlying all this is a new spirit of nihilism, a radical disbelief in any rational, objective basis for ethical norms or for orderly political change."

CHAPTER TWENTY-TWO

The Nation's Soul

PRESIDENT FORD'S APPROVAL RATING WAS 46 PERCENT. THE *NEW YORK Times* reported on October 5 that his presidential campaign "has encountered some serious internal difficulties, and a new political director has been brought in to get things on track" (and that "Gov. Ronald Reagan of California, who is not yet an announced candidate, is ahead in terms of organization in several of the most important states"). The next day Ford spoke on TV from the Oval Office. He announced "a crossroads in our history": "whether we shall continue in the direction of recent years—the path toward bigger government, higher taxes, and higher inflation—or whether we shall now take a new direction, bringing to a halt the enormous growth of government, restoring our prosperity, and allowing each of you a greater voice in your own future." The nation's economic problems "bear a label: 'Made in Washington, D.C.'"—where "America's vitality and prosperity have been drained away. It is here that one big spending program after another has been piled on the federal pyramid, taking a larger share of your personal income and creating record budget deficits and inflation." He then proposed a permanent $28 billion income tax cut, the biggest in history, to "get the government off your back and out of your pocket," and a cap of $395 billion in spending in the coming year—"a cut of $28 billion below what we will spend if we just stand still and let the train run over us."

It just sounded like another fiscal swerve, given his previous admission that the tax bill he had reluctantly signed in March would balloon the deficit by as much as $100 million. Damned if he did, damned if he didn't.

Two days later, the fiscal focus returned to New York City. Treasury secretary Simon testified before a Senate panel that the damage from a bond default would be "negligible." Of the bailout package Congress was discussing, Simon urged "that the financial terms of assistance be so punitive, the overall experience so painful, that no city, no political subdivision, would ever be tempted to go down the same road again." The

New York Post's headline was SIMON ON U.S. AID: MAKE CITY SUFFER. A paper in far-off Atlanta said, SIMON THROWS NEW YORK TO THE WOLVES.

Felix Rohatyn, working so hard just maintaining a day-to-day cash flow for the city that he ignored a fire drill in his office building, responded that if the city defaulted, "we'd probably have to bring the troops home from Germany to keep order." Governor Carey told the same congressional committee the choice was between "federal money and federal troops." He asked for $5 billion in loan guarantees to avoid "the most costly mistake in the history of this nation," an "economic Pearl Harbor." Unmoved, Senator Edward Brooke of Massachusetts, a Republican liberal, responded that if the state needed more money it should just increase taxes.

Ronald Reagan responded, too. He wrote in his newspaper column that "Carey's comments reflect New York parochialism. . . . Tell an audience in Ohio or Texas (or almost anywhere else outside of New York) that you don't think the federal government should be in a rush to bail out New York, and they erupt with wild applause." (He neglected to note that most of his audiences on his speaking tours were either business groups or conservative Republicans. To one of them, he said, "I include in my prayers every day that the federal government will not bail out New York.") He ticked off the grounds for disgust: "too-powerful union leaders and news media, timid elected officials, wild spending, dirty streets, pornography, and a general decline in civility." He added, with Simon, that if aid came it should have "so many strings attached that a generation may pass before any New York City politician gets up the nerve to tell his constituents that the moon is really made of green cheese."

That was turning out to be the winning argument. The next week *Time* put on its cover a caricature of Abe Beame holding a beggar's cup. It quoted Simon's predecessor, Arthur Burns, as saying that in the event of a bailout, "self-reliance in our country, which has been diminishing, will be dealt another blow. . . . The free enterprise system involves a certain degree of risk, and we should let that risk be taken and the consequences as well." As if the city were a poorly managed haberdashery, and its economic ruin bore no consequences at all for the rest of the country.

The nation gorged on such images: New Yorkers as greedy hedonists (the *Economist*: "Rich, chic, thriftless, insufferably superior, overeducated"); New York as a nest of iniquity, New York as open sewer, New York as a heroin addict. (If you have a daughter who's a junkie, said Ron Nessen, who seemed to take particular glee in abusing the city, "you don't just give her $100 a day to support her habit. You make her go cold turkey.") An article in *Texas Monthly*, reviewing a "balance sheet of fiscal sins too numerous to detail," included this Reaganite embellishment: "Welfare recipients in the Waldorf." New Yorkers even heaped abuse on themselves. *New York*, the magazine the hip set preferred, didn't target the Sunbelt rubes at *Texas Monthly* for mockery. Instead, it reran *Texas Monthly*'s article without comment. And one of its staff contributors, Ken Auletta, wrote of how when William F. Buckley Jr., in his quixotic campaign for mayor in 1965, warned "New York must discontinue its present borrowing policies and learn to live within its income before it goes bankrupt . . . one would have thought Buckley had proposed to drop the atom bomb on Israel." But Auletta said Buckley was right: "We have conducted a noble experiment in local socialism and income redistribution, one clear result of which has been to redistribute much of our tax base and many jobs out of the city."

New York had been considered a house organ for the rich, chic, thriftless, insufferably superior, overeducated liberals. Now here it was embracing neoconservatism. Another ideological watershed had been quietly passed. Meanwhile, another ideological watershed had *not* been passed. The distinguished editor of *Congressional Quarterly* wrote how, despite warnings that the new, overwhelmingly Democratic Congress would be a puppet of the labor movement, liberalism there was hard to find. The House failed to override Ford's veto on a public jobs bill the AFL-CIO desperately wanted and the Senate killed a $9 billion bill for economic relief introduced by the liberal Walter Mondale despite a massive lobbying effort by labor. Labor now could count on only thirty votes in the upper body, where it used to have at least thirty-eight. "The freshman Democrat today is likely to be an upper-income type," a labor lobbyist said. "I think a lot of them are more concerned with inflation than with unemployment." Both parties were now leaning more to the right. Gary Hart had said his Watergate Babies were "not a bunch of little Hubert Humphreys." Apparently, he was right.

REAGAN HAD MADE HIS OWN CONTRIBUTION TO THE FISCAL DEBATE ON September 26 in a speech to the Chicago Executives Club, called "Let the People Rule." He began by quoting Jefferson: "A wise and frugal government which shall restrain men from injuring one another, shall leave them otherwise free to regulate their own pursuits of industry and improvement, and shall not take from the mouth of labor the bread it has earned: This is the sum of good government." Reagan said that it was the expansion of government at all levels to 37 percent of gross national product that "has created all our economic problems." He then argued that "nothing less than a systematic transfer of authority and resources to the states," including welfare, education, housing programs, food stamps, Medicare, and Medicaid—"a program of creative federalism for America's third century"—would "reduce the outlay of the federal government by more than $90 billion. . . . With such a savings, it would be possible to balance the federal budget, make an initial $5 billion payment on national debt, and cut the federal personal income tax burden of every American by an average of twenty-three percent."

No one paid much attention. No one paid much attention, either, when Reagan said almost precisely the same thing to the New York Conservative Party a few weeks later; or to the simultaneous announcement that his daily radio show was moving to the Mutual Network, which might beam it over 1,300 stations instead of its current 310; or to the news that Reagan would announce around Thanksgiving that he would become a formal candidate for the White House. Gallup was reporting that Ford was 23 points ahead of him among Republicans. Gallup had also recently discovered that, presented with the option of "Candidate A," who "says we should cut government spending on social programs and try harder to balance the U.S. budget," or "Candidate B," who "says the government should spend more money to create employment and spur public buying," Mr. B won by 46 to 42 percent (though A won by 46 to 38 in the South). Some old friends called Reagan in California to warn that he was at risk "of becoming the Harold Stassen of 1976." (Stassen, who became known as the "boy wonder" of politics when he was elected governor of Minnesota in 1939, had run for the Republican presidential nomination six times since, each run more ineffectual than the last.)

Horse-pickers paid more attention to "Big John" Connally, the former JFK naval secretary and LBJ confidant who had switched to the Republican Party during his tenure as Nixon's treasury secretary. Nixon had hoped Connally would succeed him as president. He was one of those perennial Washington power players upon whose prospects Georgetown's villagers never tired of speculating—even now that he had been only narrowly acquitted for his role in the milk industry's bribery scandal. He had announced the formation of an outfit, Vital Issues for America, that would sponsor an extensive speaking tour. Opportunistically predicting a "horse race" between Ford and Reagan in the primaries, he said he even might just run as a favorite son in Texas. And his recent trial? "As a matter a fact," he told reporters, "it helped me. The jury said, 'Not guilty.' How does that hurt you?"

On the Republican left, Senator Mac Mathias grumbled from the podium of the National Press Club that "President Ford's fascination with a very real threat on his right is limiting debate among Republicans." He said he might run in a primary or two, as well—because a conservative nominee would render Republicans "the Whigs of 1976." There was talk, too, that the Senate's "Wednesday Club," a weekly whiskey-klatch of liberal Republicans, would seek to counter the party's Reagan-driven drift to the right by sponsoring a run by one of their fellow travelers, with speculation centering on Howard Baker, who was considered especially electable.

So now Washington's gossipmongers were off to the races speculating about a potential quadruple-barrel challenge to poor Gerald Ford—when they weren't mocking Ford's latest ridiculous physical mishap: a collision on October 14 between the presidential limousine and the car of a teenager in Hartford, Connecticut, who complained that he was the one who had the right of way (local police had neglected to block off the intersection). Or when they weren't reciting routines from a hilarious new TV variety program, *NBC's Saturday Night*—soon renamed *Saturday Night Live*—whose standout new talent, a young comedian whose unlikely name was the same as that of a Washington suburb, opened the first episode's mock newscast, "Weekend Update," on October 11, datelined Washington:

"At a press conference Thursday night, President Ford blew his nose. Alert Secret Service agents seized his handkerchief and wrestled it to the ground.

"And yesterday, in Washington, President Ford bumped his head three times getting into his helicopter. The CIA immediately denied reports that it had deliberately lowered the top of the doorway.

"And Ford was on the campaign trail announcing in Detroit that he has written his own campaign slogan. The slogan? 'If he's so dumb, how come he's president?'"

Chevy Chase's next joke: "The Post Office announced today that it is going to issue a stamp commemorating prostitution in the United States. It's a ten-cent stamp, but if you lick it, it's a quarter." The conservative medium whose three networks usually converged in a safe middlebrow banality had never seen irreverence like this.

The second week, Chase, who considered Ford a cruel man who "never gave a shit about people," was if anything crueler: "President Ford's regular weekly accident took place this week in Hartford, Connecticut, where Ford's Lincoln was hit by a Buick. Alert Secret Service agents seized the Buick and wrestled it to the ground. No one was injured in the accident, but when the President got out to see what had happened, he tore his jacket sleeve on the car bumper, bumped his head, and stuck his thumb in his eye. Alert Secret Service agents immediately seized the thumb and wrestled it to the ground. . . . Concerning the collision, New Orleans district attorney Jim Garrison says he will immediately launch an investigation into the 'second car theory.'" The studio audience applauded boisterously.

The next week, Weekend Update's "top story" was the president's stubborn cold: "White House physicians say that, after a mild cold of that sort, it will take the President a few days to recover his motor skills fully, citing the period after his last cold when he tied his shoe to his hair blower and inadvertently pardoned Richard Nixon."

Then he turned to another joke: the former governor of California. "Starting a speaking tour this week . . . Reagan spoke out against marijuana, abortion, the Equal Rights Amendment, busing, and gun control legislation. When asked what he was for, Reagan replied, quote, 'hair dye.'"

Although the nation's new jester did not find Ronald Reagan nearly as pathetic as the hapless Leader of the Free World. Chase ended the segment "quoting" Reagan as saying that, like the Democratic right-wing populist former governor of Georgia, George Wallace, who had been crippled in a 1972 assassination attempt and was also angling his way toward a presidential announcement, he would be campaigning in a wheelchair: "It's not for the sympathy I would get. It just makes the race more fair."

FORD SOON FACED A NEW SET OF INTELLIGENCE CONTROVERSIES. FIRST Frank Church turned his hearings to political abuses by the Internal Revenue Service (among the thousands of dangerous extremists who allegedly had been politically singled out for audits were Joseph Alsop, James Brown, Nobel Prize–winning scientist Linus Pauling, and two United States senators). Then, hard upon new reports that the CIA had recruited Christian missionaries in defiance of an Eisenhower-era directive outlawing the practice, he revealed to Americans that Big Brother had also been opening their mail—more than 215,000 pieces in New York City alone between 1953 and 1973, including one, in 1968, from presidential candidate Richard Nixon to his speechwriter Ray Price.

Richard Helms, called back from Iran to testify, admitted it all was illegal. He then reintroduced Americans to a concept from the Watergate days: "plausible deniability." Conceding that he had signed a report in 1970 to Richard Nixon announcing such practices were to be discontinued, he admitted they had continued nonetheless, without the president's knowledge. "Because," he explained, "you've got to protect the President from the dirty stuff."

Over on the House side of the Capitol, feisty Bella Abzug of New York, eyeing a run against Senator James Buckley in 1976, publicized two government surveillance projects, code-named "SHAMROCK" and "MINARET," run by a government bureau that was so secret most Americans didn't even know it existed. "With a reputed budget of some $1.2 billion and a manpower roster far greater than the CIA," the Associated Press explained, the National Security Agency had been "established in 1952 with a charter that is still classified as top secret." (Its initials, the joke went, stood for "No Such Agency.") It had also, Abzug revealed, been monitoring both the phone calls and the telegrams of American citizens for decades. President Ford had persuaded Church not to hold hearings on the matter. Abzug proceeded on her own. At first, when she subpoenaed the private-sector executives responsible for going along with the programs, the White House tried to prevent their testimony by claiming that each participating private company was "an agent of the United States." When they did appear, they admitted their companies had voluntarily been turning over records and cables to the government at the end of every single day for more than forty years. The NSA said the programs had been discontinued. Abzug claimed they still survived, but under different names. At that, Church changed his mind: the contempt for the law here was so flagrant, he decided, he would initiate NSA hearings, too.

Conservative members of his committee issued defiant shrieks: "People's right to know should be subordinated to the people's right to be secure," said Senator John Tower. It would "adversely affect our intelligence-gathering capability," said Barry Goldwater. Church replied that this didn't matter if the government was breaking the law. He called the NSA's director to testify before Congress for the first time in history. Appearing in uniform, Lieutenant General Lew Allen Jr. obediently disclosed that his agency's spying on Americans was far vaster than what had even been revealed to the Rockefeller Commission. He admitted that it was, technically, illegal, and had been carried out without specific approval from any president. But he declined to explain how it worked. He added that thanks to such surveillance, "We are aware that a major terrorist attack in the United States was prevented." He refused to give further details on that, either—as if daring the senators to object.

• • •

THE PRESIDENT COULD COMFORT HIMSELF WITH THE THOUGHT THAT few were paying attention. Back in August, Rockefeller Commission member Ronald Reagan had informed his listeners, "My own reaction after months of testimony and discussion during the investigation of the CIA is 'much ado about—if not nothing, at least very little'": just "instances of some wrongdoing with regard to keyhole peeking," long since corrected by the agency itself. He claimed his commission's most important finding—that more Soviet spies than ever were living and working in America—had been buried. Instead "the media seized upon whatever misdeeds we found and played them up, possibly to confirm the earlier charges and possibly because they thought they made for exciting drama."

That fall he acquired a surprising ally in the argument: Senator William J. Fulbright, whose devastating 1966 hearings against the Vietnam War were so subversive to the Establishment's amour propre that CBS cut away to a rerun of *The Andy Griffith Show* rather than continue live coverage. Now Fulbright published an article in the *Columbia Journalism Review*. He allowed that recent revelations about the CIA might be true. "But I have come to feel of late that these are not the kind of truths we need most right now; these truths which must injure if not kill a nation." What was needed was "restored stability and confidence." What the press required was "voluntary restraint" to reaffirm the "social contract." What the public most certainly did not need was the media's present "inquisition psychology."

In truth, though, the media were proving not very inquisitive at all. The *Washington Post*'s William Greider wrote in *Esquire* about the scanty coverage of the intelligence hearings, especially after the blanket coverage of Watergate, "There is a strong wish all over town, a palpable feeling that it would be nice if somehow this genie could be put back in the bottle . . . a nostalgic longing for the easy consensual atmosphere which once existed among the contending elements in Washington." He noted how "the press essentially tugs back and forth at itself, alternatively pushing the adrenal instincts unleashed by Watergate, the rabid distrust bred by a decade of out-front official lies, and then abruptly playing the cozy lapdog." And October, apparently, was a lapdog month.

Abzug's revelations received hardly any coverage. General Allen's testimony was buried in back pages (in the *Louisville Courier Journal* it was trumped by news of a religious community of 177 in Arkansas whose members pulled their children out of school to await the second coming of Christ). A stunning colloquy between Senator Walter Mon-

dale, the liberal Democrat from Minnesota, and NSA deputy director
Benson Buffham—

> **Mondale:** "Were you concerned about its legality?"
> **Buffham:** "Legality?"
> **Mondale:** "Whether it was legal."
> **Buffham:** "In what sense? Whether that would have been a legal
>   thing to do?"
> **Mondale:** "Yes."
> **Buffham:** "That particular aspect didn't enter into the discussion."

—was not quoted anywhere at all, even by the *New York Times,* whose
article on the NSA hearing ran on page eighty-one. As for the president,
he followed the recommendation of Donald Rumsfeld and Dick Cheney
and closed down further inquiry into the NSA by extending executive
privilege to the officials and telecommunications executives involved.
This institutionalization of what had been a novel, and exceptionally
controversial, legal doctrine in a brand-new presidential administration
got no coverage, either.

A lot had changed since those English-muffin days when he said in
his inaugural speech, "In all my public and private acts as your president, I expect to follow my instincts of openness and candor with full
confidence that honesty is always the best policy in the end." Indeed,
Ford had recently established a top-level White House working group,
including Kissinger, Schlesinger, Rumsfeld, the CIA's budget director,
and one of Ford's top legal counsels, to meet every single day and manage public relations to push back against the intelligence investigations.
Perhaps that work explained why the investigating committees were so
effectively rocked back on their heels by the next turn in the story.

Glamorous, globe-trotting Henry Kissinger had weathered his own
Watergate storm—for bugging reporters and his own staffers—and
remained the punditocracy's beau ideal. He was fresh from his latest
triumph in "shuttle diplomacy," securing a preliminary peace frame-
work between Israel and Egypt, when the indefatigable Otis Pike had
the temerity to demand from him a memo by a State Department staffer
named Thomas Boyatt that had apparently criticized the CIA's poor
intelligence regarding the crisis in Cyprus, where the U.S. ambassador,
Rodger Paul Davies, had been machine-gunned to death the previous
August. The Pike Committee's chief counsel soon received a thundering
phone call from the *Times'* James Reston: "What the hell are you guys
doing down there? Are you reviving McCarthyism?"

This, it turned out, was the administration's public relations line—Pike was running a "McCarthyite inquisition," as State Department official Lawrence Eagleburger said in his testimony before the committee. An editorial called "Pike's Pique" noted that by calling "junior staff officers to testify under oath about what recommendations they made to the policy officials," the congressman was reintroducing the practices that "almost wrecked the U.S. Foreign Service during the McCarthy period." Then, since Kissinger forbade such junior staffers to testify, the Church Committee voted to subpoena Kissinger himself—and the *Times'* editorialists called that "neo-McCarthyism," too. Kissinger decided to testify before the Pike Committee the day after General Allen of the NSA, on October 30, though on his own terms: he summarized what he said was the thrust of Boyatt memo, still withholding the actual document from evidence—just the sort of Stennis-style compromise that, when Richard Nixon had proposed it during the crisis of October 1973, had sent *tout* Washington up in arms.

Ron Dellums, the socialist from Berkeley, who had once set up an exhibit of American war crimes in Vietnam outside his congressional office, took his turn to question Kissinger. Dellums cited Kissinger's perch atop the shadowy "40 Committee," which reviewed every covert U.S. intelligence operation; his overlapping jobs as national security advisor and secretary of state; and "testimony that you have participated in directing operations which were not fully discussed, analyzed, or evaluated by those authorized to do so"—and which had been "purposefully hidden." He noted, "You have been involved in wiretaps of employees," and thundered, "You now refuse information to Congress on a rather specious basis."

Convinced he had the Establishment's darling in his sights, Dellums moved in for the kill.

"Frankly, Mr. Secretary," he said, "and I mean this very seriously . . . the method of your operation . . . may indeed be contrary to the law."

Kissinger paused with a comedian's art. He smiled: "Except for that, there is nothing wrong with my operation?" The hearing room erupted in laughter.

That was the clip that ran on the evening newscasts: a witty man humiliating a dour one. A quip had been all it took to turn the allegedly "McCarthyite" inquisition aside. Maybe people had had enough of inquisitions: suffering, the *Washington Post* had recently suggested—after My Lai, after Cambodia, after Watergate, after the year without Christmas lights, after Patty Hearst and all the rest—"a kind of deadening of moral nerve-ends, a near inability to be surprised, let alone disturbed."

The new president took office promising "In all my public and private acts as your president, I expect to follow my instincts of openness and candor with full confidence that honesty is always the best policy in the end. My fellow Americans, our long national nightmare is over"—and also the words recorded on this pin (above). At first the media could not get enough of this kind man and his easygoing family. At his first state dinner he danced joyously to "Bad, Bad Leroy Brown" with his wife, Betty, the candid former professional dancer who in her first interview as First Lady revealed she saw a psychiatrist.

September 23, 1974   75 cents

Newsweek

How Sick is Nixon?

As American as apple pie.

Paramount Pictures Presents
AN ALAN J. PAKULA PRODUCTION
WARREN BEATTY
THE PARALLAX VIEW

Co-starring
HUME CRONYN · WILLIAM DANIELS and **PAULA PRENTISS**
Director of Photography GORDON WILLIS · Music Scored by MICHAEL SMALL
Executive Producer GABRIEL KATZKA · Screenplay by DAVID GILER and LORENZO SEMPLE, Jr.
Produced and Directed by ALAN J. PAKULA · PANAVISION® TECHNICOLOR® A Paramount Picture

THE PARALLAX VIEW

The honeymoon ended early. On his thirty-first day in office, Ford, citing the need for national unity, and quoting Scripture and Abraham Lincoln, announced a "full, free, and absolute pardon unto Richard Nixon." His approval ratings plummeted. The slate was not to be wiped clean of a nation's dreads and divisions— as seen by the suspicion generated when Nixon's doctor claimed he was too sick to testify in the cover-up trials of his aides ("How Sick Is Nixon?"), and paranoia-drenched films like, from the left, *The Parallax View* and, from the right, *Death Wish*.

The school year began violently. In Kanawha County, West Virginia, an emerging new right, led by the new Washington think tank the Heritage Foundation, joined a movement to protest "secular humanist" textbooks that escalated to the dynamiting of the school-board building.

In Boston, scene of this rally, a federal judge's desegregation order led to running battles between South Boston toughs and the police.

Reagan emerged as the conservative alternative to Ford—but first he had to become a conservative. That happened in Hollywood. He arrived in 1937 a "hemophiliac, bleeding heart liberal," with the world as his oyster—landing a leading role in his very first picture, *Love Is on the Air.*

[48]
His career soon flatlined, then picked up again with the backing of columnist Louella Parsons, as he established an image in the fan magazines as a family man. (Here he is with wife Jane Wyman and their first child, Maureen.) But World War II set him back profoundly. He was stuck stateside making training films at "Fort Wacky" while other stars became heroes in the war, and younger, more fashionable actors like Van Johnson (who didn't serve because of a car accident and was linked romantically to Jane Wyman) passed him by.

49

Those Fightin' Reagans

Three times before they have said goodbye. Is this the last round for Ronnie and his Jane?

BY GLADYS HALL

His wife passed him by, too. Once a mere "starlet," she emerged after the war as a top dramatic player, to her husband's consternation. Their marriage fell apart after she won a Best Actress Oscar for playing a deaf-mute rape victim. Reagan quipped bitterly, "Maybe I should name *Johnny Belinda* as a co-respondent" in their divorce suit.

IT WAS just before Christmas in New York. Jane Wyman paced the length and breadth of her hotel suite, awaiting a call from La Guardia Airport. The telephone rang, as it had rung half a dozen times that morning. An official voice said, "Sorry, Mrs. Reagan, planes still grounded—ceiling zero."

"Call me again." Jane's voice was urgent. "I'll stand by. Keep calling."

Her pacing was resumed together with her vigils at the windows that framed a city blanketed in fog. Back and forth again went little Miss Button-nose (so pet-named by her husband) awaiting the wanted word from La Guardia that she could plane back to Hollywood—back to Ronnie?

Yet only the night before, Jane had told a friend, "We're through, we're finished, and it's all my fault." Three times before, Jane has said goodbye to her marriage, 'then reconciled.

Is this the last round in the marriage ring that has encircled the fighting Reagans for ten sometimes stormy but all the time, we believe, in-love years?

That Ronnie is still deeply in love with Jane is very evident. In fact, he says so. When reached in Hollywood, and faced with Jane's latest verdict on their marriage, "It's a strange character I'm married to," Ronnie announced with a wry but unmistakably tender smile, "But—I love her."

That Jane is still deeply in love with Ronnie (or why her frantic eagerness to get back to where he was?) is, in our opinion, also very evident. "We're through, we're finished," she says. But somehow we do not take this too seriously. Words can be so many little masks to cover up the heart.

"They were blissfully happy together," a close friend says of them, "until the war came."

Yet it was during the war that they adopted a son who, in addition to their own little Maureen, is a bond between them—a bond they surely would not have sought, being responsible citizens, if there had not been peace between them.

What are the counts against them? What, in a word, goes? Is it that Jane (Continued on page 91)

He had by then found a more dependable outlet for his energies: politics. He served both as a liberal activist, joining several groups later named as Communist fronts, and as president of the Screen Actors Guild, where he effectively took the side of management in a bitter jurisdictional strike by technical workers. Reagan, whom the FBI had turned into an informant, insisted they were in league with Communists. (Here, testifying at the House Committee on un-American Activities' hearings on alleged Communist infiltration of Hollywood.)

As a performer he was suffering mostly humiliations: sharing a screen kiss with Shirley Temple in her first adult role; starring alongside a chimpanzee in *Bedtime for Bonzo*; and, when his agent Lew Wasserman couldn't find him any film roles at all, in a corny Las Vegas revue that closed soon after it opened.

[52]

THEATER
RONALD REAGAN

He was saved by a corporation in the market for a "good, upright kind of person." Hosting the new *General Electric Theater,* part of his job was making publicity tours of their hundreds of production facilities scattered throughout the nation, where he learned important political skills.

[53]

55

G.E.'s pioneering public relations and labor relations executive Lemuel Boulware influenced Reagan's shift to the right. Boulware had G.E. personnel study right-wing authors like Henry Hazlitt, from whom Reagan learned to think of big government programs, such as the Tennessee Valley Authority, as impositions upon the public. Another contributing factor was his second marriage, to Nancy Davis—thanks both to the influence of her stepfather, Dr. Loyal Davis, a prominent Chicago conservative, and of the Southern California industrialists and their wives with whom Nancy aggressively sought to socialize. Soon, concurrent with his rightward traverse, Reagan became better known as a political spokesman than an actor—leading to his 1962 firing by G.E. and culminating in his run for California governor in 1966, which he announced on a TV show redolent of his introductions to *G.E. Theater* episodes. (He wielded a ketchup bottle to illustrate jobs lost due to, he asserted, foolish government policies.)

As Reagan's gubernatorial term ended, 1975 dawned as the year of the "Watergate Babies," new young members of Congress, many in their first political office, who snatched the People's House from old men seen as symbols of its corrupt ossification—such as Wilbur Mills, who lost his seat after a scandal with the stripper Fanne Foxe, the "Argentinian Firecracker."

At the dilapidated California statehouse (which warned visitors to enter at their own risk), Reagan turned over the reins to the Zen Buddhist Jerry Brown. But fresh faces were not able to restore trust in institutions at a time when, as a columnist put it, the best political outcome people expected was that described by Albert Camus: "not to be cured but to live with one's ailments."

In the spring came the Hieronymus Bosch images from South Vietnam, as the government America had supported fell to the Communists. Thousands of refugees clambered aboard ships built not to accommodate passengers at all; this craft, the *Pioneer Commander*, was commandeered by escaping South Vietnamese marines who massacred twenty-five civilians and forced the U.S. crew to barricade themselves in the cabin. The country upon which Americans had invested billions of dollars and some 58,000 soldiers' lives was "tearing itself apart in a frenzy of self-destruction," as one journalist described it, and Americans themselves could hardly escape safely, as this famous image of Americans climbing atop the roof of the CIA station chief's residence to board an escape helicopter attests.

60

Americans preferred the Madonna and Child images of "Operation Babylift," the sentimental rescue of Vietnamese orphans. The Vietnamese themselves considered it the "abduction of children." Secretary of State Henry Kissinger, meanwhile, insisted "the United States must carry out some act somewhere in the world which shows its determination to continue to be a world power"— so two weeks after Saigon fell Ford had forces storm a beach off Cambodia, unleashing B-52 bombing sallies to "rescue" the crew of a captured merchant ship, who were actually already safe. That led to the deaths of forty-nine Americans, but the absurd operation was celebrated as a triumph by a nation longing for patriotic reassurance. Below: *Newsweek*'s fantastical cover, which resembled Soviet propaganda.

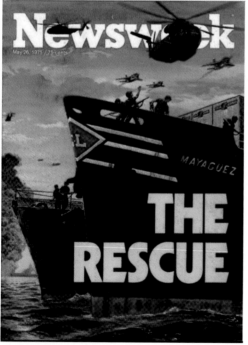

64

Send in a teabag with your taxes

SAN DIEGO, Calif. (AP) — The conservative Young Americans for Freedom are urging taxpayers to staple teabags to their income tax forms to protest against high taxes.

YAF's Gary Kreep told a news conference President Ford's tax proposals are "not enough" and warned that elected officials will face a hostile voting public unless they lower government spending and reduce taxes significantly.

Kreep said the teabag campaign would continue through April 15, when state and federal income taxes are due.

America's political culture was moving rightward, much more than the pundits noticed. President Ford suffered politically for not seeing the towering Soviet dissident Aleksandr Solzhenitsyn when he visited in July. Solzhenitsyn spoke instead to thunderous applause from 2,500 at an AFL-CIO testimonial dinner, arguing that America should stay in Vietnam. Young Americans for Freedom protested high taxes, despite the fact that President Ford had cut them. The Equal Rights Amendment—supported by Gerald and Betty, opposed by Ronald and Nancy—needed ratification from only four more states to join the Constitution. But in November of 1975 anti-ERA forces won shocking upsets in New Jersey and New York, where the successful campaigners dubbed it the "Common Toilet" law.

65

[66]

A *New York Times* columnist reflected in October, "There are fleeting moments when the public scene recalls the Weimar republic of 1932–33." There was the opening of televised hearings by the Church and Pike Committees investigating the FBI and the CIA. Church had already established that the CIA had a hand in attempting to assassinate foreign leaders. Here, he displays a dart gun designed to kill from 100 meters using a toxin—untraceable in any autopsy—that was legally supposed to have been destroyed but was not because the CIA director of covert operations wished "to continue this special capability."

[67]

[68]

September saw two assassination attempts against Gerald Ford, one by a follower of Charles Manson, Lynette "Squeaky" Fromme, here being led away crying she shouldn't be arrested because "the gun didn't go off," and another by a housewife sympathizer of the Symbionese Liberation Army. Patty Hearst was caught, and the *Chicago Sun-Times* editorialized, "We cannot help wondering to what extent the spirit of Tania lies dormant, awaiting arousal, in many of the nation's young." Here, the Secret Service surround Reagan with their bodies after an apparent attempt on his life by a twenty-year-old who had demanded Squeaky Fromme be freed.

69

New York was nearly broke. President Ford refused a federal bailout. Garbage workers struck, promising to turn New York into "Stink City." In some neighborhoods, citizens made bonfires of the trash that piled up in the street. Ford's right-wing treasury secretary later wrote in a bestselling book that this was the "terrifying dress rehearsal of the state that lies ahead for this country if it continues to be guided by the same philosophy of government"— liberalism.

Gerald Ford, a former football star and an expert skier, was America's most physically accomplished president. But after he slipped down the steps of the presidential plane on a 1975 visit to Salzburg—the first of a series of mishaps that included bumping his head on the door of his helicopter, a limousine collision with a teenager's Buick, and a televised tumble on the ski slopes at Vail—the president's supposedly uncontrollable body, mocked every weekend on *Saturday Night Live*, served as a stand-in for a *body politic* out of control. Not the most promising image to take into a primary fight against the graceful Ronald Reagan—who, after his first tour of New Hampshire, shocked pundits by pulling ahead of Ford in the polls.

On the Democratic side, Jimmy Carter, the determinately homespun, even hokey, candidate of "anti-politics"—his symbol was the humble peanut; his signature line, "I am not a lawyer . . . I'm not from Washington . . . I've never been part of the federal government," brought down the house; his beer-swillin', gas-station-owning brother Billy (above, left) became a sort of national mascot; his campaign headquarters was this modest train depot in his hometown of Plains, Georgia, pop. 600—was nominated at the convention in New York. "I hate to get corny at this late date in a cynical life," columnist Mike Royko wrote, "but the arrival of Jimmy Carter at the affectionate, emotional bedlam of Madison Square Garden . . . was one very memorable experience."

74

[75]

Ronald Reagan left for the Republican convention—the "Shootout at Kansas City"—with a decent chance he might win.

The close convention was bedlam. Betty Ford had become reviled among Reagan fans after a *60 Minutes* interview in which she praised *Roe v. Wade,* the ERA, compared smoking marijuana to "trying your first cigarette," and said if her daughter was having an affair, she would only want to know whether the fellow was "nice or not." In her own *60 Minutes* profile, Nancy Reagan supported the death penalty, reviled marijuana, and said of abortion, "I can't get over the point of it being that you're killing somebody." They went to war for the public's affections in Kansas City in what *Time* called "The Battle of the Queens"—much to the consternation of convention chairman Bob Dole, whose job it was to shut down the hooting and hollering that broke out any time either of them appeared in the convention hall. Here, Betty dances "the Bump" at a reception at the convention with popular singer Tony Orlando.

[76]

[77]

And then after Ronald Reagan lost, he won. Called up to the podium for an apparently spontaneous address after Ford's acceptance speech, he spoke of a time capsule that might foretell whether humanity had been able to avoid a nuclear Armageddon, drinking in the crowd's spellbound, almost religious awe. The *New Yorker*'s correspondent called it his greatest speech in a career of great speeches—though noting elegiacally, "This is probably the end of Reagan's political career."

• • •

NEW YORKERS WERE SURPRISED AND DISTURBED.

In the middle of the month, after trustees of the teachers' union pension fund refused a City Hall plea to help out by buying city bonds, lawyers drew up a bankruptcy petition ("The City of New York is unable to pay its debts or obligations as they mature"). Governor Carey announced an austerity plan he said went "to the limits of what we can apply to the city in terms of economies." President Ford considered backtracking on the question of a bailout. Top advisors proposed he sign a package of loans for the city working its way through Congress. "Hell, no!" Donald Rumsfeld bellowed back at a cabinet meeting. He spoke for the mood of the room.

On October 29, at high noon, the president made a luncheon address at the National Press Club carried, unlike the Pike and Church committee proceedings, live on all three networks. He described the latest eleventh-hour stopgap to keep New York solvent, passed the previous week in Albany. He outlined Mayor Beame's argument that "unless the federal government intervenes, New York City within a short time will no longer be able to pay its bills." And he responded with William Simon's and Ronald Reagan's arguments: it was all New York City's fault, for giving away candy it could not afford. And he wouldn't stand for it.

"I can tell you, and tell you now, that I am prepared to veto any bill that has as its purpose a federal bailout of New York City to prevent default. . . . If they can scare the whole country into providing that alternative . . . it would promise immediate rewards and eventual rescue to every other city that follows the tragic example of our largest city." He proposed bankruptcy proceedings in federal court instead. "Other cities," he concluded, "other states, as well as the federal government, are not immune to the insidious disease from which New York City is suffering. This sickness is brought on by years and years of higher spending, higher deficits, more inflation, and more borrowing to pay for higher spending, higher deficits, and so on, and so on, and so on. It is a progressive disease, and there is no painless cure. . . . If we go on spending more than we have, providing more benefits and services than we can pay for, then a day of reckoning will come to Washington and the whole country just as it has to New York." And when "that day of reckoning comes, who will bail out the United States of America?"

In the editorial offices of the *New York Daily News* the talk was of how the press conference reminded them of a line in the 1950 George Cukor screwball comedy, *Born Yesterday:* "Would you do me a favor, Harry?" deadpans Judy Holliday. "What?" replies Broderick Crawford.

"Drop dead!" Someone scrawled a headline, as a joke. Someone else looked it over: "Holy Christ, yes! Put it in the paper."

Next morning. FORD TO CITY: DROP DEAD. It was accompanied by a photograph in which the formerly amiable butterer of English muffins appeared to be sneering.

It was the day before Halloween—and open season on New York. *Newsweek*'s cover starred Abe Beame, swaddled like a baby, Gerald Ford spanking him over his knee. *Newsweek* quoted Lester Maddox, the racist Atlanta restaurateur elected governor of Georgia in 1966 after having run blacks off his property with an ax handle, now an authority on municipal finance: "The thing I don't like about New York is the tendency to reward bums and penalize hard work." *Newsweek* columnist Milton Friedman, the conservative economist, wrote that the city shared an "instinct for self-destruction matched only by its exaggerated sense of self-importance." Theodore White, who in his "Making of the President" series used to present the expansion of the liberal state as self-evidently wise, wrote in *New York* magazine, "New York City has now reached the point where it is entirely incapable of self-government," and called the city's political pressure groups "a giant Soviet."

On this subject, the president was in sync with the mood of the nation. And yet somehow at exactly the same time it became open season on *him*.

Halloween fell on a Friday. On Saturday, news broke that the Ford campaign's finance chair, David Packard, had resigned. Having set a goal in July to raise $10 million by the time of the Republican convention, with a little more than two-thirds of that time to go he had found only $600,000. The *New York Times* observed, "Mr. Packard's resignation served to underscore the difficulty Mr. Ford appeared to have in getting his campaign under way—an unusual problem for an incumbent president." Then, that Sunday, in Florida (site of the third presidential primary), at a dinner honoring the visiting president of Egypt, the tuxedo-clad president toasted "the people of Israel."

In Washington, gossip circulated about extraordinary doings in the White House. On Monday night, all became plain. The president appeared in the East Room, with the entire White House press corps and the network cameras assembled before him, and revealed the biggest cabinet shakeup in the history of the Republic.

"Good evening. I have several announcements to make tonight":

At the Department of Defense, Donald Rumsfeld for James Schlesinger. At the National Security Council, Brent Scowcroft for Henry Kissinger. Dick Cheney to replace Donald Rumsfeld as chief of staff, Elliot Richardson for Rogers Morton at Commerce. At CIA, George H. W. Bush for William Colby (later believed to have been fired for being too cooperative with Congress's investigation of his agency)— on and on it went, like clowns stumbling out of a tiny car at the circus. Or maybe, Washington hands thought, more like something out of *The Godfather.* Someone thought to call the interlocking set of simultaneous bureaucratic assassinations the "Halloween Massacre."

News of another bureaucratic assassination—or had it been a suicide?—had broken earlier in the day. For months the blood feud between the vice president and the conservative Republicans who despised him had transfixed the Georgetown villagers. In spring came rumors that Rockefeller might be dropped from the 1976 ticket. Then the president's pal Mel Laird floated the idea of an "open convention" to choose the next running mate. If this was bait for Reagan fans, they gladly rose to it: in June a conclave of conservative senators said the idea "would be in the best interests of the Republican Party and the nation." In July reporters grilled campaign manager Bo Callaway about why there were no pictures of Rockefeller at Ford-for-President headquarters. He admitted, "A lot of Reagan people are not supporters of Rockefeller, and I want it clear to them that we want their support whether they support Rockefeller or not." Jacob Javits, the liberal Republican senator, then warned that dumping Rockefeller would "endanger the President's support from the whole centrist bloc in the country."

In the fall, to shore up Rockefeller's political position, the president announced the vice president would appear before a series of public forums. Rockefeller landed in Tampa for the first one back on Wednesday, October 29. To the reporters badgering him on the tarmac, he claimed "I honestly don't know" what the president would say in that evening's address on New York's fiscal situation, adding, "I have been totally supportive of President Ford's position"—which was rich, given that barely two weeks earlier he had said a federal failure to bail out the city would be a "catastrophe."

Then that Monday morning the White House released a letter from Rockefeller to his boss announcing, "After much thought, I have decided further that I do not wish my name to enter into your consideration for the upcoming Republican Vice Presidential nominee." The *Times* quoted an unnamed White House official who said "that Mr. Rockefeller had been unable to make his peace with the right wing of the Republican Party. He was, therefore, regarded as a liability by the President Ford Committee." Mac Mathias said it proved Ford had become "a captive of the Reagan right."

• • •

ROCKEFELLER HAD WITHDRAWN FROM THE POLITICAL FIELD. AND BY THE
end of the night, the man whose Washington ascent he had sponsored,
Henry Kissinger, had lost his perch atop the National Security Council,
which had given him daily access to the president in the Oval Office.

The speculation immediately began: Was the Halloween Massacre
about placating the right? But if so, why had Ford cashiered conservatives' favorite cabinet officer, James Schlesinger? And what to make of
the fact that the president's *new* national security advisor, Brent Scowcroft, was a trusted Kissinger deputy—"replacing Kissinger with Kissinger," as one senator put it?

In the East Room, the reporters' grilling commenced, *sans* mercy.
First question: had Rockefeller "sacrificed himself on your political
behalf, and have you in any way urged him to do so?" The president
dissembled, convolutedly: "The decision by the Vice President was a
decision on his own."

And then, when another reporter soon asked the same question, he
repeated the same thing, as if he had rehearsed it. And then, a few questions after *that*, when asked what reasons Rockefeller gave for his decision, Ford said Rockefeller's letter, which in fact said virtually nothing,
"speaks for itself."

Someone asked if the reason was New York City. Ford responded,
"Our differences over the handling of New York City are minimal"—
then, like a mynah bird, repeated, "I think the letter speaks for itself."

RON NESSEN KEPT A SIGN UP IN HIS OFFICE: "WATERGATE IS HARDER TO
wash away than the spray of a skunk." It helped explain one thing Gerald Ford was trying to accomplish with his bureaucratic coup, getting
rid of Nixon holdovers. That backfired. The "Halloween Massacre"
moniker recalled another shocking weekend firing—the Saturday Night
Massacre. Jules Witcover called the press conference "worthy of Nixon
at his most trapped mien" and said the president had just burned away
"one of his few strengths—personal warmth and integrity." Ford had
hoped to finally establish an image as his own man—an accidental
president no more. That backfired, too. A reporter had asked, "How do
you make a high-level personnel shift of this kind, such a fast shift? Did
you do this largely on your own." Ford responded, "I did it totally on
my own." He was protesting too much—as the lead article in the next
morning's *Washington Post*, syndicated nationwide, made embarrassingly plain:

WASHINGTON—White House chief of staff Donald H. Rumsfeld, considered the master maneuverer of the Ford Administration, was widely credited Monday for being the silent architect of the President's dramatic cabinet shakeup.

The soft-spoken, hard-driving former Illinois congressman emerged as the big winner of the Byzantine battle for power that went on behind the closed doors of the supposedly open Ford administration.

Not only did Rumsfeld wind up with an important cabinet post and equal access with Henry Kissinger to President Ford. He also left behind him in the White House as chief of staff his deputy, Richard Cheney, who is considered both highly capable and totally loyal to Rumsfeld. . . .

Rumsfeld left no fingerprints on any of his internal recommendations that helped produce the shakeup within the White House.

He was not even around Sunday when Mr. Ford fired Secretary of Defense James R. Schlesinger and Central Intelligence Agency Director William E. Colby. Instead, Rumsfeld took a rare day off and went to the Washington Redskins–Dallas Cowboys football game. . . .

He also presumably made himself available for the vice presidential vacancy that was created by the withdrawal of Nelson Rockefeller from the 1976 ticket.

There weren't supposed to have been any "silent architects" in Gerald Ford's ultratransparent White House. Nor any "Byzantine" battles for power. And yet here, on the front page of the *Washington Post,* the nation's next secretary of defense, a man most people outside Washington wouldn't recognize, whose qualifications to be defense secretary as Ford described them at his press conference ("a person who is experienced in the field of foreign policy and who served in the Department of Defense as a naval aviator") sounded conspicuously thin, was depicted as the power behind the throne.

Moderates were not placated: the piece also quoted highly placed sources who said that Kissinger was incensed by the changes. Another facet of the political mess was that rumors soon surfaced insisting that Rockefeller had not jumped but had been pushed. But even that didn't placate the conservatives: "I am not appeased," was Ronald Reagan's response. Meanwhile, at his own press conference, Rockefeller was badgered by questions about whether *he'd* run for president in 1976.

Time noted that though he sounded angry, Reagan "could only feel helped by President's Ford's clumsy handling of the Cabinet shake ups and his diminished credibility." It cited a Gallup poll taken before the massacre that had Ford ahead among Republicans 58 to 36 percent—and an NBC poll taken afterward that gave it to Reagan, 44 to 43 percent.

"MR. PRESIDENT," FORD HAD BEEN ASKED IN THE EAST ROOM, "HOW worried are you about Ronald Reagan?" He answered that he was not. It was just about the only nakedly honest thing he said that night.

Reagan, Ford told confidants, was a lightweight. Barry Goldwater himself told Ford's staffers there was no way Reagan could win in big states. Ford could be cheered that his campaign had righted itself somewhat. His finance chairman had failed, yes; Bo Callaway was gaffe-prone; but the campaign had meanwhile poached two impressive technicians from the enemy camp: the pioneering political consultant Stuart Spencer, who had fashioned Reagan into a credible gubernatorial challenger in 1966, and F. Clifton White, an unsung conservative hero who had wired the insurgent movement that delivered the Republican nomination to Barry Goldwater in 1964.

Supreme Court justice William O. Douglas, an old adversary, was about to retire, so soon Ford would get to display the mighty power of his office by picking a lifetime replacement. Ford's wife, it turned out, was not a liability. In fact it seemed to be just the opposite. A new Harris poll revealed that 64 percent supported and only 23 percent opposed what she said about her daughter's theoretical affair. Seventy percent liked her views on the Equal Rights Amendment. All in all, Lou Harris wrote, "Betty Ford has become one of the most popular wives of a President to occupy the White House." Whatever the wages of Halloween, Ford was confident; he was, after all, an incumbent president—still careening around the country for personal appearances even in the face of testimony from the Treasury secretary that he had faced 320 death threats in twenty days that fall alone.

But in a suspicious age, as compared with the past, the advantages of incumbency broke differently.

In October 1974, haunted by testimony from the Ervin Committee's green table about suitcases filled with cash, negotiable securities, and checks laundered through Mexican banks, Congress passed, and Ford signed, amendments to the Federal Election Campaign Act that had the potential to revolutionize the way elections were financed. Among these measures was a $1,000 limit on what any one individual could contribute to a campaign, a cap on primary spending and general election spending of $10 million for each major party's presidential candidate, strict standards of campaign disclosure, and the public provision of up to $5 million in "matching funds" for any candidate for federal office who raised at least $5,000 in contributions of $250 or under in each of twenty states. It provided for a new agency, the Federal Election Commission, to adjudicate these and other rules. It all was one reason the Reagan political team was keeping its man from announcing an official candidacy until as late as possible before the New Hampshire primary, set for February 24: that way, the disgusted editorialists of the *Boston Globe* pointed out, Reagan could conduct "a national campaign, in the guise of operating a business, for almost a year before he announced," evading "every reporting regulation for political organizations."

That didn't prevent Friends of Ronald Reagan, the organization officially purporting not to be a presidential campaign, from now making an aggressive play for strict scrutiny of the president by the new FEC. The Republican National Committee was paying for the president's travels, money that would be reimbursed by the new system's matching funds. The Reagan exploratory committee said its not-candidate should get the same deal—because there was no reason to assume the president was actually even "the titular leader of his party." The FEC announced it would rule on that challenge by the end of November.

And then there was the Ford campaign organization's other liability: the candidate himself.

On November 7 he headed off to Massachusetts; there was a primary there March 2, and New Hampshire was just over the border. On the tarmac at Westover Air Force Base, he announced he would enter every primary in the nation. That caught his campaign strategists by horrified surprise, considering how Nixon's pledge to campaign in every state doomed him in 1960: it took careful strategic targeting to win a marathon national election. He then tripped over a wheelchair. Or so it at least appeared to some. A Secret Service agent, conversely, presumed his lurch tarmac-ward had been effectuated by an excited little boy's American flag, which the agent brutishly wrested from the kid's hand; it looked like a scene from one of Chevy Chase's Weekend Updates.

Then, speaking before New England business leaders, Ford defensively addressed critics of his personnel shifts: "I want to be absolutely sure these domestic political potshots are not 'heard 'round the world.' . . . The temptation to political adversaries to take advantage of any apparent weakness, disunity, and decision could become irresistible. . . . Weakness invites war. . . . Without a clear consensus among the 214 million Americans . . . the ability of a President to carry out his constitutional duties would be dangerously diminished." The *Globe* editorialized with distaste, "His confusion between his personal political fortunes and the well-being of the nation was disturbingly reminiscent of Richard Nixon."

It was a Friday—which meant *Saturday Night Live* was on the next night. This time, after a week's hiatus, opening the show, Chevy Chase upped the satirical stakes by *playing* the president. Onscreen: the familiar presidential podium, a pitcher of water, two glasses. Chase entering, tuxedo-clad, to "Hail to the Chief," bumping into the flag, dropping his papers, fumblingly scooping them up:

"My fellow Americans, ladies and gentlemen, members of the press, and my immediate family. First, may I thank you all for being here. And I am in my immediate family.

"First, may I thank you all for being here"—Absent-mindedly, the Nutty President repeated himself—"and I am in my immediate family."

He announced the show's host: "Harvey" Cosell.

He poured water into one of the glasses. Then drank from another, empty glass.

One awkward pause, one pratfall, one head-banging fall to the podium ("Whoop! No problem! Okay! No problem! Sorry! No problem!"), and one more sip from the empty water glass later:

"I know a fella who is going to enter the New Hampshire, Massachusetts, Florida, and every other primary! And I *know* he is going to win! And if he has *any* other competition, right up to the end of 1976—"

(He thumped once more to the floor. "Uh-oh! No problem! No problem!")

"And if I *don't* win, I will *continue* to run, even if there are none! And now for my second announcement—"

He made the announcement from the floor, after tripping over two folding chairs:

"Live from New York! It's Saturday night!"

It wasn't fair. Every public figure constantly on TV sometimes stumbles. It wasn't the president's fault that a car hit his limousine, or that it was raining that spring in Austria when he had been gentlemanly enough to concentrate on his wife's safety instead of his own; or that he was hobbled from knee surgery in 1972. In fact, he was the most physically accomplished man to have ever held the office: a triple letterman in football, basketball, and track in high school; an all-American center on the gridiron at the University of Michigan, passing up offers to join the Green Bay Packers and Detroit Lions in order to go to law school; an expert skier whom far-younger Secret Service men had a hard time keeping up with at Vail (his excuse that "every skier takes a fall once in a while" didn't help when, in December 1975, the TV cameras caught him collapsing in a heap). No one had thought to consider him clumsy when he acceded to the office the previous August. In fact, back then, the comedian Rich Little, who'd risen to stardom on the back of his Nixon impression, complained he was having a hard time finding anything funny to imitate about Gerald Ford at all. "The trouble is that the President is not visual: he has no distinct mannerisms."

Comedians didn't worry about that now.

Some new President Ford jokes:

The only thing between Nelson Rockefeller and the presidency is a banana peel.

Why won't Ford help New York in the fiscal crisis? He was once trapped there for six hours on an escalator.

Why won't Ford be throwing out the first pitch on Opening Day? The Secret Service is worried he'll be beaned in the head.

Woody Allen, by way of Patty Hearst: "It's possible it was all a result of my brainwashing but I was then brought into a room where President Gerald Ford shook my hand and asked me if I would follow him around the country and take a shot at him now and then, being careful to miss. He said it would give him a chance to act bravely and could serve as a distraction from genuine issues, which he felt unequipped to deal with."

And just in time for Chevy Chase's onslaught that November, the first book about Ford as president came out. It was called *A Ford, Not a Lincoln,* and in it, Richard Reeves described him as "slow, plodding, pedestrian, unimaginative," "inarticulate," and "ignorant"—though you didn't have to take Reeves's word for it. He also quoted the president's Grand Rapids pastor: "Gerald Ford is a normal, decent, God-fearing man, but you can say that about a lot of people."

THERE IS A MEDIEVAL POLITICAL MAXIM THAT "THE KING HAS TWO BODies." A "body natural," that is to say—the real one that he carts around day to day, like any ordinary mortal—and a "body politic"—his symbolic presence as head of state. A president also has two bodies. The symbolic one glows on the TV screen, emanating a two-hundred-year-old nation's authority, of the safe, solid power of the free world, tangible evidence of the continued smooth functioning of a superpower. Now that America's power seemed neither safe nor solid, however, the continuity of its institutions was no longer guaranteed, and the president's two bodies collapsed one into the other—and his corporeal self was cast as a fourth member of the Three Stooges, to star in an allegory about a nation that no longer worked.

The evidence accumulated apace. In Pennsylvania, on October 21, the state secretary of heath had announced the discovery of a mysterious new disease, "pantosomatitis," said to be contagious, chronic, extremely painful, and fatal in 2.5 to 3 percent of cases; involving dozens of widely varying symptoms; and spreading up and down the East Coast. The news understandably transfixed the nation. Then, ten days later, the Associated Press reported that the researchers the physician claimed helped him make the discovery had never worked with him and that no medical publication or writer had been able to verify it actually existed.

On October 23, Mike Royko wrote of meeting a lawyer at a party and asking him what kind of law he practiced: "'I fix,' he said," and Royko wasn't sure he'd heard him correctly. "'You fix cases?' I asked. 'Judges?' He nodded. When he saw the look of surprise on my face he looked amused. And he said that if I quoted him by name, he would naturally deny it and sue the pants off me." His new friend said he didn't even know how to file a lawsuit or appear in a courtroom: "He has done nothing but fix." Royko thought he'd seen it all in twenty years as a hard-drinking Chicago newsman. But this brazenness was a new one on him.

It was an appropriate moment for Gallup, on October 30, to release its latest poll on public trust: Sixty-eight percent thought the country's leaders "consistently lied to the American people"; in 1972 that figure had been but 38 percent. And Americans hadn't even heard yet of the Halloween Massacre. Nor of the claim, in a story that broke four days later, that defense contractor Martin Marietta kept a hunting lodge where it plied Pentagon officials with prostitutes.

That was nothing compared with the story that broke on November 19. In 1964, a little more than a month before Martin Luther King was set to travel to Stockholm to accept the Nobel Peace Prize, the FBI sent him a package of unspecified material meant to blackmail him, accompanied by an anonymous letter. A Church Committee counsel read it aloud at an open hearing: "You know you are a complete fraud a great liability to all of us negroes. The American public will know you for what you are, an evil abnormal beast. King, there is one thing left to do. You [know] what it is. You are done. There is but one way out for you. You better take it before your filthy, abnormal, fraudulent self is bared to the nation . . . you have just 34 days." Part of a seven-year FBI campaign of harassment against King, the letter was an attempt to spur the civil rights leader to suicide. Another letter that was entered into evidence, from deputy FBI director William C. Sullivan to J. Edgar Hoover and dated a little less than two years earlier, revealed the motive. It proposed "taking him completely off his pedestal." "This can be done and will be done. Obviously, confusion will reign . . . the Negroes will be left without a national leader."

The news set off a flurry of morbid speculation. Royko, reflecting on a presumed kook who insisted the FBI had rubbed out Martin Luther King in 1968, remembered back when he could have dismissed that as ridiculous; now, "all I could say was, 'I don't know.'" Coretta Scott King, the great man's widow, called for an investigation of just that charge, and even the *New York Times* observed that given the kind of things the Church Committee was turning up, "the very least once can wonder, considering the late FBI director J. Edgar Hoover's feelings about Dr. King, is whether he could have put his agency's whole heart into the investigation of the assassination." The *Saginaw News* editorialized that though such speculation was "chilling," it was "hardly more chilling than testimony already a matter of record concerning alleged spy network involvement with organized crime in the field of international assassinations."

That fact was confirmed as far more than mere speculation on November 20, when the Church Committee, once more over strenuous White House objections, released a 346-page report titled *Alleged Assassination Plots Involving Foreign Leaders*. It established that the CIA had tried to off Fidel Castro eight times, had supplied weapons to the plotters against the Dominican Republic's Rafael Trujillo (the plotters succeeded, though not with the CIA's weapons), and had encouraged but not directly intervened in the assassinations of three more, including Ngo Diem Dinh in November 1963—the same South Vietnamese president whom America (and the CIA) had financed and backed for almost a decade prior. It also reported that the CIA helped a group that kidnapped a Chilean general who stood in the way of their attempt to overthrow Salvador Allende.

That morning a spokesman for the Justice Department announced that it was weighing whether to bring criminal charges against those involved in the assassination plots the report described. That night, Daniel Schorr said on the CBS news, "It seems, according to this report, to be true (as ex-director Richard Helms has said) that the CIA never *assassinated* any foreign leaders. It seems also to be true that it wasn't for want of trying." Editorials the next morning called the revelations "shocking and disturbing," "revolting," "inexcusable by any standards of international morality and diplomatic expediency." Moral government, insisted the *New York Times,* "is not the impractical dream of naive do-gooders. It is the only inherent strength of a self-governing nation."

But if that were so, it was hard to see how Church's report might help heal the wound. In fact, it only compounded the nation's enervated confusion, complicating a debate that had rumbled across the entire season of inquiry: Who, exactly, was supposed to be blamed? And if no one knew whom to blame, how could the crisis be fixed?

Frank Church's own contribution was not always helpful. Some derided him as a stuffy, pompous moralist, an orator above all—"Frank Sunday School," they called him, or sometimes, even better, "Frank Cathedral." When he was fourteen years old, in 1939, a letter he wrote urging isolationism was printed on the front page of a Boise newspaper. He then served with honor as an intelligence officer in World War II, earning a Bronze Star; then, at twenty-three, he survived what his doctors thought was fatal cancer. Nine years later, in 1956, "the boy wonder from Idaho" was elected to the Senate—where he displayed courage proper to someone who had cheated death.

But not always. For he was also a *senator,* possessed of the bland passion for compromise then native to that tribe. And, at that, a presidential aspirant—possessed by the omnidirectional imperative to placate the myriad factions and personalities of that most fractured of political tribes, the Democratic Party. A successful Democratic presidential nominee also had to defer to the memory of that party's beloved martyred Hero in Chief; all that certainly helped explain the certain curious willful resistance Church displayed in following his own evidence where it frequently led. He had imagined, when he took on this inquiry as his own, that it would help put the final nails in the coffin for the legacy of Richard M. Nixon. He hardly knew how to respond when so many of the most frightening discoveries pointed instead to the administration of John F. Kennedy—at whose 1960 convention he had delivered a striking keynote speech.

In July he gave a press conference in which he used a memorable phrase: *rogue elephant.* He said there was a "very real possibility" that the Central Intelligence Agency conceived and attempted assassinations on its own, without the knowledge of anyone outside the agency—that the CIA "may have been behaving like a rogue elephant on a rampage." It proved a comforting notion to an establishment longing for innocence. It was abetted by the intelligence community's very manner of operation—the layers of plausible denial baked into the CIA cake. On the first day of the public hearings in September, for instance, Senator Mondale had suggested that "things are occurring in deliberate contravention and disregard of official orders." But he quickly grew exasperated asking low-level agents just who had approved their actions, and hearing in response: "Well, I don't know—you'll have to ask someone higher up." The same pattern repeated itself up and up and up the chain of command. "[T]hey all said the same thing," he later reflected; "none of them knew who had authorized anything. The process was clearly designed for fog—to hide responsibility and prevent anyone from ever being called to account." He compared affixing ultimate responsibility to nailing Jell-O to a wall. Very soon, however, he arrived at the famous conclusion President Harry Truman displayed on his desk: The Buck Stops Here. With the Presidents of the United States. And, in any event, by October 30, when Henry Kissinger testified, surely to protect his own skin, that every covert action undertaken by the American intelligence community was personally approved by the president, the "rogue elephant" theory would have seemed to be largely refuted.

But that didn't keep Senator Church from writing in his November 20 assassination report, "Even after our long investigation, it is unclear whether the conflicting and inconclusive state of the evidence is due to the system of plausible denial or whether there were, in fact, serious shortcomings in the system of authorization"—this despite his own report reaching, to take one example, a "reasonable inference" that President Eisenhower had authorized the coup against President Patrice Lumumba of the Congo in 1960.

And so, for those few scattered Americans seriously following the intelligence investigations, a fundamental and fundamentally disturbing question lingered: Were our presidents lawless and wicked? Or just bumbling nobodies, Gerald Fords, every last one of them—dumb, ignorant pawns of secret police agencies?

To ask the question was to stare into an abyss. So Senator Church papered over the abyss.

He appended a three-paragraph epilogue to the committee report—and found it so important he read it aloud to reporters: "The committee does not believe that the acts which it has examined represent the real American character. . . . They do not reflect the ideals which have given the people of this country and of the world hope for a better, fuller, fairer life. We regard the assassination plots as aberrations." (He did not note that the "aberrations" spanned two decades and four presidential administrations.) "The United States," he continued, "must not adopt the tactics of the enemy." He concluded, "Despite our distaste for what we have seen, we have great faith in this country. The story is sad, but this country has the strength to hear the story and to learn from it. We must remain a people who confront our mistakes and resolve not to repeat them. If we do not, we will decline, but if we do, our future will be worthy of the best of our past."

The *Washington Post* singled out that epilogue for applause: "To believe otherwise is to assault the basic process of consensus and correction by which a democratic society must proceed." The *Milwaukee Journal* ran it on the front page, under the headline "MORAL FOR U.S." As instructive was the number of newspapers that ran nothing at all about the Church Committee assassination report on their front pages. Like the *Tri-City Herald* of Dubuque, Iowa, and environs, where it was trumped by news of butter prices, the political progress of the Communist Party in Portugal, a government effort to regulate unsafe Christmas lights, and the question of whether the Ford campaign would get equal time when stations showed Ronald Reagan movies—as well as the story "Blind Bow Hunter Bags Deer."

Mary McGrory, downplaying Church's pulling of punches, and contradicting her colleagues on the *Post* editorial page, wrote in a column titled "Sen. Church's Topic: The Nation's Soul" that "if this country is ready to face the facts about itself Church could become our next president."

Or, if the nation's soul tended otherwise, the presidency might go to someone who preferred stories of patriotic reassurance.

CHAPTER TWENTY-THREE

"Has the Gallup Poll Gone Bananas?"

RONALD REAGAN HAD ALWAYS SAID, WHEN ASKED IF HE WAS RUNNING FOR president, that a man does not seek the office; the office seeks him. A rescuer, after all, does not ask to rescue. He must be summoned.

When Ronald Reagan flew on commercial flights he always sat in the first row. That way he could greet passengers as they boarded. One day he was flying between Los Angeles and San Francisco. A woman threw her arms around him and said, "Oh, Governor, you've got to run for president!"

"Well," he said, turning to Michael Deaver, dead serious, "I guess I'd better do it."

Yes: he had been summoned. That was early in 1975. He had likely been running in his mind ever since. On November 20, one week before Thanksgiving Thursday, and the day the seal of the United States Senate was affixed to the conclusion that America's secret spy agency plotted the murder of leaders of sovereign states, he made it official.

PUBLICLY HE HAD KEPT HIS OWN COUNSEL IN ALL THOSE INTERVENING months; Ronald Reagan could be quite disciplined politically when he put his mind to it. It was spring before he told a meeting of supporters that he was disillusioned enough with Jerry Ford to run. The White House sent emissaries to hint that he might make a nice running mate for Ford, then offered him a job as commerce secretary; they failed to dissuade him. The conservatives pining for a third political party asked him to become their candidate; but any temptations Reagan felt in that directions were scotched when Holmes Tuttle, first among equals in his "kitchen cabinet" of wealthy backers, told him he wouldn't see another penny if that was what he decided. Late in April, at Reagan's home in Pacific Palisades, *National Review* publisher and third-party enthusiast William Rusher presented Reagan with a copy of his new book, *The Making of the New Majority,* and tried one more time:

"The GOP won't nominate you in 1976," Rusher said.

"Well, now, that remains to be seen," Reagan responded.

He was ready to fight for the Republican nomination. On the day of the fall of Saigon, columnist Robert Novak flew with him in a small private prop plane from a triumphant appearance in Mississippi to his next speech, in Florida, before a pharmaceutical convention (for the standard five-thousand-dollar fee). Something was different about Reagan, Novak decided. In their previous encounters it was almost as if the old trouper was reading from a script. Perhaps it was the frightening thunderstorm rattling the plane. But now he behaved entirely differently. He favored Novak with some of the jokes that his staff forbade him to tell in public, ones literally learned at his late mother's knee. (Nelle Reagan was proud of her comic accents, and her son had studied well: "His Jewish dialect was hilarious," Novak recollected.) He told tales out of school about Hollywood executives, about the dark years after his marriage broke up. ("I tried to go to bed with every starlet in Hollywood, and I damn near succeeded.")

Then, another triumph before the pharmaceutical executives. Then, a backroom conclave with Republican pols in Atlanta. Then, a speech to the students of Georgia Tech (he said the Democratic Congress had "blood on its hands" for losing Vietnam—an implicit thumb in the eye of a president who had just implored the nation to avoid "recrimination or assessments of blame"). Then he took on détente: "If the Communists get the prestige and material aid they need without having to change any of their own policies, the seeds of future conflict will be continually nourished, ready to sprout anew with little or no warning." Novak promptly filed a column under his and his partner Rowland Evans's byline to run May 2: "A determined eight-hour sleeper with regular daytime rest periods as governor"—a rarity among politicians, who are generally a manic lot—"Reagan steadily lost sleep thought interminable days of speaking and handshaking, aggravated by slow, small private planes. . . . Most startling to longtime Reagan watchers, he did not even complain. . . . Having convinced himself Mr. Ford is not up to the presidency, Reagan must also convince himself he could stand a frantic national campaign."

His aides lined up a national campaign organization, while the candidate who said he was running for nothing stockpiled income and national attention. They devised a strategy: primaries, not party caucuses—an outside game. And they devised an outsider's rhetorical stance—but not *too much* of an outsider's stance, lest anyone powerful become personally offended. It would be a run, not against Gerald

Ford or even Congress or Democrats, but something grander, a post-Watergate crusade against "the 'buddy system' in Washington."

Writers visited his office in Los Angeles that summer; it featured a desk he brought over from the governor's mansion and was crowded with toy elephants and political mementoes, such as a slab of concrete with a pair of shoes embedded therein (a gift from newsmen reminding him of the time he had said "my feet are in concrete" on the subject of state income tax withholding, and then had reversed himself). Family snapshots, pictures of Ronald Reagan with Dwight D. Eisenhower in golf togs, Ronald Reagan with the pope, Ronald Reagan with Billy Graham, lined the walls—but not, as one columnist noticed, any of Ronald Reagan with Richard Nixon or Gerald Ford. Books, too, including one sitting out on the desk: Lawrence Welk's autobiography, *Ah-One! Ah-Two!*

(A Reagan flack assured the columnist who recorded this "that the books in the room did not necessarily reflect Reagan's reading tastes, that he was sent dozens of volumes by admirers.")

All evidence suggested an organization gearing up for a serious and sustained national campaign. And yet, as late as September, a memo crossed President Ford's desk arguing that the governor was not going to run. The White House simply refused to gear up for a serious fight. Richard Nixon had just told Ford's advisor Jerry Jones that Reagan was a "lightweight." Internal political memorandums referred to the grassroots organization Reagan's people were carefully cultivating around the country as "right-wing nuts."

In October, Reagan disappeared from the radio. In his place were greatest-hits reruns. (One was "The Superintendent's Dilemma," an allegory in verse about a forlorn educator rendered superfluous by power-mad bureaucrats. Another poem was "The Incredible Bread Machine," a libertarian loaves-and-fishes miracle tale of a man who invents a cheaper way to manufacture bread, becomes wealthy by ending world hunger, then is punished out of existence by a vindictive state; later in the year it was made into a movie with an introduction by treasury secretary Simon.) Julie Nixon substituted as host one week. (She promoted "National Employ the Handicapped Week" and excoriated college students supposedly flocking onto the welfare rolls.) And on November 17 Reagan was on the covers of *Newsweek* ("Can He Stop Ford?") and *Time* ("The Star Shakes Up the Party"). In *Time*'s article, a "former close adviser" was quoted: "I never ever saw him initiate an order on his own. . . . That's what made Reagan so easy for us to program. . . . If he becomes President, it is a terribly important question—who's running the country?"

Then, the big day arrived.

HE DID NOT HAVE HIS FAMILY BY HIS SIDE. THAT WAS A POLITICAL DECIsion. Adult children—his adopted son, Michael, just married the previous week, was thirty-two; daughter Maureen was thirty-four; Patti was twenty-three; Ron was seventeen—would only point up that in February, Ronald Reagan would be eligible for Social Security. The presence of Maureen and Michael—identified, invariably, as "the adopted son and the daughter of Ronald Reagan and Jane Wyman"—would remind voters that he would be the first president who had been divorced. Reagan was supposed to be the embodiment of wholesome family values; the Fords were supposed to be the embodiment of 1970s moral dissolution. Best not to complicate things.

Jack Ford, twenty-three, had just admitted publicly that he had smoked marijuana, and his brother Steve, nineteen, who had just changed his major from range science to animal science at the University of Utah, told reporters, "Right now, I'm against legalizing marijuana, although sometimes I'm for it and sometimes I'm against it." It made for a contrast to Patti Davis—she changed her name to her mother's in college so as to avoid any association with her father, then dropped out—who smoked marijuana, too. In fact the vociferously antidrug governor's daughter did rather more than that: when she had asked her parents to pay for psychotherapy, they refused, so she starting buying the stuff by the pound and selling it to pay for the treatment herself. She certainly never publicly talked about drugs, however. "I had been taught to keep secrets, to keep our image intact for the world," she wrote in a memoir. "Under our family's definition of 'loyalty,' the public should never see that under a carefully preserved surface was a group of people who knew how to inflict wounds, and then convincingly say those wounds never existed."

Maureen Reagan described the lesson of her upbringing as "Be nice to people, but don't tell them anything, because your parents make good copy." However, like her mother, Jane Wyman, who displayed her marriage's dirty laundry in newspapers, she honored the principle in the breach. Nine days before her father's candidacy was announced she told reporters, "I am the most vociferous of all his detractors in our family regarding his candidacy. It is for reasons all personal and very selfish. They come after eight years of having to make phone calls to arrange appointments to speak to my own father." Compare the Fords. As son Steve explained to reporters: "Everyone in our family is grown up. We're not under our folks' care anymore." They did what they wanted, unashamed to tell the world, and with their parents' implicit blessing, too. It was hard to imagine them having to make an appointment to speak to Dad.

Contrast that to the family of the family-values candidate: four kids, seven marriages, zero college degrees, several expulsions from boarding school, two contemplated suicide attempts. Once, Patti had been studying at Northwestern when her father intervened to have a black man arrested with whom she liked to share friendly banter. She was so humiliated she considered suicide—she "touched the blade to my wrist and felt how easy it would be." After she transferred to USC, her young brother showed up once on her doorstep, a sixteen-year-old runaway, sick of his mother hassling him to cut his hair and spying on him using the house's intercoms (she used them as a dedicated surveillance system: better living, electrically). The last straw had been when she searched his room (she found, naturally, a bag of marijuana). Patti soon returned him back home. She feared her mother was about to report her to the authorities for kidnapping. Once, her father asked an acquaintance, referring to this daughter of his, "Do you think a child can be born evil?"

Their memoirs are filled with images of abandonment, distance, cruelty, dispossession, silence. "I spent so much time alone during my early high school years," wrote Maureen of the prep schools she shuttled between, one all the way across the country, "that I began to wonder if I would ever fit in anywhere." Michael, adopted by Jane Wyman and Ronald Reagan in 1945, was sexually abused by a camp counselor when he was seven and lived every day in fear that the nude photos his victimizer took would surface, or that the world would learn that he was a "bastard." He was afraid to tell his parents about it. Patti put forward outright horror stories. Her mother would scream at her in public as passersby stared, and one time locked her in a sweltering car. She beat Patti almost daily, and her father refused to believe it—though Patti said once there had been a witness: Holmes Tuttle, his political benefactor, whose only response, after pulling Nancy off her daughter, was to have said, "Don't ever do that in front of me again." Nancy also popped pills, blaming Patti, whose physician grandfather once handed her a thick manila folder. "This is a medical report on your mother," he said. "Her condition is very serious. Emotions can kill someone, you know. And if you don't start behaving, we could lose her."

When her half brother Michael was fourteen and she was seven, he came to live, on weekends when he wasn't in boarding school, in their

Pacific Palisades house, so perfect and pristine that Patti feared to play in it. He had to sleep on the couch. He was thrilled when construction finally began, more than a year later, on a new room—"the symbol of my acceptance in the family," he thought, until he learned it was for little Ron's live-in nurse instead, and he was to sleep on the nurse's old daybed in the playroom.

It was around then, in 1960, after dropping out of college, that Maureen began living with a married police officer twelve years her senior. (Her father confirmed this when he asked the FBI, as a favor, to investigate.) In 1961 she married the cop, who beat her; in 1962, they divorced. The next year, at Michael's high school graduation the commencement speaker was his father. Afterward Reagan made the rounds of students for introductions. He stopped before one, stuck out his hand: "My name is Ronald Reagan. What's yours?" His son, anxious every day of his life about whether his adoptive father truly accepted him, took off his mortarboard and responded, "Remember me? I'm your son Mike."

That happened with all his children, all the time: "I frequently had to remind him that I was his child," Patti wrote. "[I]t seemed sometimes to slip his mind. Often I'd come into a room and he'd look up from his notecards as though he wasn't sure who I was. Ron would race up to him, small and brimming with a child's enthusiasm, and I'd see the same bewildered look in my father's eyes." It confused her when, shortly after her twelfth birthday, she saw his famous 1964 address for Barry Goldwater on TV, the one in which he intoned: "We must preserve for our children this, the last best hope on earth, or we'll sentence them to take the last step into a thousand years of darkness." She thought, *What about his children?*

Michael matriculated at Arizona State University, where he raised hell with a kid named Joe Bonanno Jr., son of the capo of the Bonanno crime family, on whom an FBI investigation was closing in. (At that, J. Edgar Hoover did another favor for Reagan, who was about to begin running for governor—Hoover hoped to enlist Governor Reagan's aid in firing system president Clark Kerr. The FBI informed Reagan about his son's association, even though that may have compromised the investigation of Joe Bonanno Sr.) Michael flunked out, began working as a fry cook, was fired, worked on the docks in Los Angeles, became a professional motorboat racer, got married—then his pregnant wife left him, and a district attorney told him he would be sent to jail unless he agreed to grant her a divorce and pay back child support. Patti, meanwhile, opened up to her father about how her mother had constantly beaten her when she was a child. "What the hell is it with you?" Patti remembers him responding. "Why do you make these things up about your mother? She is the most loving, caring person in the world, and you've caused her nothing but unhappiness."

She met a member of the rock band the Eagles, made love with him that very day in the open air, and told her mother she would be traveling with the band to Europe. The mother about whom so many sordid rumors once circulated snapped, "Well, you're going to have a separate hotel room, aren't you?"

Not likely. Soon Patti moved into the rock star's house, and her father, who used to wake up in bungalows at the Garden of Allah not knowing the name of the girl sleeping next to him, roared into the phone, "This is just immoral, what you're doing. Living together without the benefit of marriage is a sin in the eyes of God. He tells us this in the Bible." (He didn't, the insolent daughter insisted. "The disciples wrote the Bible." "No, they didn't. God wrote it." She thought this "the most aggravating aspect of discussing anything with my father. He has this ability to make statements that are so far outside the parameters of logic that they leave you speechless.") They stopped speaking, though she did receive a letter that November: "I'm sorry you didn't choose to come to the family meeting the other night when I told everyone I'd decided to run for President." But she had never been informed of the meeting.

In her memoir she remembered her parents' odd behavior when John F. Kennedy died and tearful parents came to pick up tearful children from school: "I wished desperately for my mother's face to soften, to crumble—to share in the anguish that was all around us. When the car doors closed around us and the sound of my crying was magnified by the small space we now shared, she turned to me and said, 'All right, Patti. I think that's enough now.'" That night, November 22, 1963, a dinner party with the Robert Taylors, Alfred Bloomingdales, and Holmes Tuttles went on as planned, convivially. The event apparently made so little impression on the future president that his candidacy announcement had originally been planned for November 22, 1975—until his savvy press secretary, Lyn Nofziger, pointed out that this was the anniversary of Kennedy's assassination. So they made it two days earlier instead.

ON THE AFTERNOON OF NOVEMBER 19, RONALD REAGAN CALLED THE White House.

"Well, Mr. President," he said, "I am going to make an announcement and I want to tell you about it ahead of time. I am going to run for President. I trust we can have a good contest, and I hope it won't be divisive."

"I'm sorry you're getting into this. I believe I've done a good job, and that I can be elected. Regardless of your good intentions, your bid is bound to be divisive."

"I don't think it will harm the party."

"Well, I think it will," the President of the United States responded— and hung up.

The night of November 19, Reagan took questions from an audience of one thousand New Hampshirites for almost an hour. He was asked about Charles Percy's remark that he suffered from "simplistic thinking," that a "Reagan nomination and the crushing defeat likely to follow could signal the beginning of the end of our party as an effective force in American political life," that he was "far out of the centrist stream," and that if the president "wins the nomination by out-Reaganing Reagan, it will cost him the election." Reagan answered, "You know, sometimes I think moderation should be taken in moderation." That had the audience in stitches. Seventy-five percent of its members lined up for almost an hour to shake his hand. Jules Witcover saw him "taking not only the person's hand in his, but his or her eyes with his own, holding the contact until the other person's glance fell away." He wrote, "Anyone who saw him at the Sheraton-Wayfarer Hotel in Bedford, New Hampshire, that night had to be convinced that Jerry Ford was going to have his hands full with Reagan."

The next morning, you could flip open your *New York Times* and read in Scotty Reston's column, "The astonishing thing is that this amusing but frivolous Reagan fantasy is taken so seriously by the news media and particularly by the President. It makes a lot of news, but it doesn't make much sense."

THE "AMUSING BUT FRIVOLOUS FANTASY" BEGAN WITH A SPEECH, though one female admirer's fantasy began before that, when she intercepted the candidate on the way to the podium for a quick encounter. "If only everybody could meet him one-on-one and see those incredibly blue eyes," she reported. "No wonder he didn't like to wear his glasses."

It was 9:30 A.M., at the National Press Club on Fourteenth and F, three blocks from the White House; he wore a purple plaid suit his staff abhorred and a pinstripe shirt and polka-dot tie and a folded white silk puffing up extravagantly out of his pocket—this had become his trademark back when he introduced *General Electric Theater* on TV. "I have called this press conference to announce that I am a candidate for the presidency and to ask for the support of all Americans who share my belief that our nation needs to embark on a new, constructive course," he said. Perhaps with the previous night's conversation with the president in mind, he added, "I believe my candidacy will be healthy for my nation and the party."

He didn't refer to his opponent. That, the news reports would conveniently mention, honored his "11th Commandment"—*Thou shalt not speak ill of another Republican*—coined by the chairman of the GOP in California in 1966, and loudly taken up by Reagan during his gubernatorial primary run that year against the liberal former mayor of San Francisco. It had been one of the most enduringly effective snow jobs in the history of electoral politics: the party chairman, an obstetrician from Orange County named Gaylord Parkinson, was simultaneously on the payroll of the Reagan campaign, which had arrived at the strategic calculation that a campaign focused on personalities would disadvantage Reagan.

All three networks went live. Reagan took the high road of policy: "In just a few years, three vital measures of economic decay—unemployment, inflation, and interest rates—have more than doubled, at times reaching ten percent and even more. Government at all levels now absorbs more than forty-four percent of our personal income. It has become more intrusive, more meddlesome, and less effective."

Gerald Ford had been saying precisely the same things in *his* speeches—he had, after all, precisely six weeks earlier, flayed "the enormous growth of government" that was draining away America's "vitality and prosperity" and that bore the label "Made in Washington." But, well, there was an inconvenient fact: Ford had *lived* in Washington, D.C., since 1948, when he was elected to the first of his thirteen terms in Congress, making friends, making deals, making himself, Reagan now thundered like Professor Harold Hill, *part of the problem,* "right here in Washington, D.C. Our nation's capital has become the seat of a buddy system that functions for its own benefit—increasingly insensitive to the needs of the American worker, who supports it with his taxes. Today, it is difficult to find leaders who are independent of the forces that have brought us our problems—the Congress, the bureaucracy, the lobbyists, big business and big labor. . . .

"I don't believe for one moment that four more years of business as usual in Washington is the answer to our problems, and I don't believe the American people believe it, either."

Then there was foreign policy. A week earlier the president had received a memo from his pollster Robert Teeter: "'Détente' is a particularly unpopular idea with most Republican primary voters. . . . We ought to stop using the word whenever possible." The president decided to oblige him—too late to keep Ronald Reagan from rubbing the dread seven letters in his face nonetheless: "A decade ago we had military superiority. Today we are in danger of being surpassed by a nation that has never made any effort to hide its hostility to everything we stand for. Through détente we have sought peace with our adversaries. We should continue to do so but must make it plain that we expect a stronger indication that they also seek a lasting peace with us."

He concluded with a sparkle in his eye. "We, as a people, aren't happy if we are not moving forward," he said. "We must offer progress instead of stagnation, truth instead of promises, hope and faith instead of defeatism and despair. Then, I am sure, the people will make those decisions which will restore confidence in our way of life and release that energy that *is* the American people."

Then he took reporters' questions. He was asked about the FBI's investigation of Martin Luther King, reported in that morning's papers. He said he had not read the morning papers.

GERALD FORD MUST HAVE BEEN BEREFT. HE HAD GIVEN ALL HIS ADULT life to his party. Loyalty—"unbending, undying, unthinking loyalty to the Republican Party," Richard Reeves labeled it—had been his calling card: voting with President Nixon at the second-highest rate of all members of Congress; announcing, after a select, secret briefing on Nixon's secret bombing of Cambodia, that Nixon had not been "false or deceptive" in claiming he'd never violated that country's neutrality; helping scotch Wright Patman's Watergate inquiry in the House. "Team player" was his highest term of praise. And now, here was his reward: another member of his team was charging into battle against him. Punishing him for doing what he'd been called against his inclination (he had hoped, in 1974, to retire) to do: *govern*.

Screw the eleventh commandment. Came a statement from his campaign organization, the "President Ford Committee": "Despite how well Ronald Reagan does or does not do in the early primaries, the simple political fact is that he cannot defeat any candidate the Democrats put up. Reagan's constituency is much too narrow, even within the Republican Party. . . . While not unmindful of his ability, he does not have the critical national and international experience that President Ford has gained through 25 years of public service. . . . We want a united party going into the General Election. Any motion against unity is counterproductive and damaging to our prospects next November."

In the West Wing the chatter was about how Reagan had embarrassed himself. Ron Nessen's memo on the press coverage cited stuff like, "The trouble with Reagan, of course, is that his positions on the major issues are cunningly phrased nonsense" (the liberal *Chicago Daily News*); and "The Reagan challenge to Mr. Ford comes from the right, the radical right, which cherishes notions that often are too simple, too negative, and too risky . . . if Mr. Ford falters or swings too far right, we would welcome the candidacies of others speaking for the Republican mainstream" (the *Baltimore Sun*); and "His image is largely that of the role-playing actor . . . ill-equipped for the real world beyond the footlights" (from conservative columnist James J. Kilpatrick, who misspelled "Regan's" name). A staffer who actually attended the Press Club, however—Ford's close personal aide Jerry Jones—concluded that "we are in for a real battle." He thought Reagan "had his answers down pat" and "handled the questioners with a sense of candor, humor, and calm." Ford's savvy young director of communications, David Gergen, was pretty impressed with him, too.

REAGAN HIT THE ROAD. THE METHOD DEVISED BY THE PROS IN THE CAM-paign organization—christened "Citizens for Reagan," a name drawn from Reagan's 1966 campaign theme of running as a "citizen politician"—aped Nixon's in 1968: a very small number of events, timed for maximal exposure on each night's evening news, the applause lines in each speech carefully indicated in text handouts dispensed to reporters each morning. A striking number of his campaign staff bore the Watergate taint: Lyn Nofziger, his longtime Sacramento press aide, who'd been responsible for the Nixon White House's project to harass the Long Island paper *Newsday* after it ran an investigation of Nixon's buddy Bebe Rebozo; Roger Stone, CREEP national youth director, who'd posted a fake check to the *Manchester Union Leader* to try to frame a rival of Nixon's in 1972 for ties to revolutionary socialists; Kenneth Reitz, who in 1973 lost his job supervising congressional campaigns for the Republican National Committee when it was discovered he'd helped spy on Edmund Muskie for the Committee to Re-elect the President, and was now Reagan's coordinator for the California primary. But no one seemed to notice.

The first stop was Miami. The site was a Ramada Inn, near the airport (a Nixon campaign trick: that way the national TV reporters could ship their tape to New York in time for the evenings newscasts), in a ballroom not unlike the one in which Bobby Kennedy was speaking seven years earlier just before he was shot.

He began with a question: "If the trumpet gives an uncertain sound, who shall prepare himself for battle?" Then he quoted Franklin Delano Roosevelt, who, he said, after embarking "on a course that made bold use of the government to ease the pain of those times," was "soon moved to sound a warning": *"We have built new instruments of public power in the hands of the people's government . . . but in the hands of political puppets of an economic aristocracy, such power would provide shackles for the liberties of our people."* Reagan said, "Unfortunately, that warning went unheeded. Today, there is an economic aristocracy, born of government's growing interference in our lives." A rather brazen interpretation, given that the speech he quoted, FDR's annual message to Congress in January 1936, had actually been referring to "financial and industrial groups" who in their "domination of government" and "entrenched greed" do "not want to return to that individualism of which they prate" but seek only "power for themselves, enslavement for the public."

The press, though, wouldn't have much time to reflect on the contradictions. Reagan finished his speech and began shaking hands—and a twenty-year-old man pulled out what turned out to be a toy .45-caliber pistol and was wrestled to the ground by three Secret Service agents. He had already threatened the lives of the president, vice president, and Governor Reagan on the demand that "Squeaky" Fromme be freed.

Reagan did not appear shaken. He never stopped smiling as he was led away. The Secret Service's local special agent in charge, citing the already enormous Democratic presidential field—it included Indiana senator Birch Bayh, Texas senator Lloyd Bentsen, former Georgia governor Jimmy Carter, Oklahoma senator Fred Harris, North Carolina governor Terry Sanford, former Peace Corps director Sargent Shriver, Arizona congressman Morris Udall, Pennsylvania governor Milton Shapp, George Wallace, "and more candidates on the way"—predicted it "would only get worse." It was almost now a rite of passage. "[I]f he didn't feel like a candidate before," a Reagan aide told CBS, "he does now."

On each day's schedule was an extended press conference. At the one in Miami, he was asked how the incident would affect his support for gun rights. He had entered that debate aggressively on the radio the previous summer. Barely four years earlier there had been all but a consensus that cheap handguns—"Saturday night specials"—had to be removed from city streets; when a bill was introduced in Congress in 1971 to ban them, the National Rifle Association announced, "We are for it 100 percent." The 1972 Republican platform promised to "intensify efforts to prevent criminal access to all weapons, including special emphasis on cheap, readily-obtainable handguns." But since then a civil war had broken out within both the NRA and the Republican Party. One faction within the NRA, formerly an anodyne organization for sportsmen, saw any attempt to restrict any gun as an expression of the Communist line; its adherents mailed glowing reports of vigilante heroics to the NRA magazine *American Rifleman* for its "Armed Citizen" column. The other faction, which controlled the national office in Washington, published a *Fact Book on Firearms Control* endorsing such "reasonable regulation" as "a waiting period between purchases and delivery," strict record keeping for manufacturers and retailers, controls on "all machine guns," and limits placed upon those "wishing to carry a concealed firearm." But it was the former group that took control of the NRA's new lobbying arm, the Institute for Legal Action. Its lobbyist, a fearsome former border control agent named Harlon Carter, called "the so-called Saturday night specials . . . a girl's best friend. They're small enough to fit into a woman's purse or be at her bedside at home." He boasted of killing the very anti–Saturday night special bill the NRA had been instrumental in introducing—and announced that henceforth, the organization would oppose any law aimed at "inanimate objects instead of the evildoer."

That was Ronald Reagan's sort of language. In 1967 he had signed one of the nation's strongest gun control laws, after armed Black Panthers stormed into the California legislature on a lobbying mission of their own. But in June 1975, as Gallup reported 67 percent of Americans favored "the registration of all firearms," Ford's attorney general, Edward Levi, proposed a new law tightening access to guns in high-crime urban areas, Reagan thundered on the radio: "Now that's funny. It seems to me that the best way to deter murderers and thieves is to arm law-abiding folk and not to disarm them. . . . As news story after news story shows, if the victim is armed, he has a chance—a better chance by far than if he isn't armed. Nobody knows in fact how many crimes are *not* committed because criminals know a certain store owner has a gun—and will use it." He said the attorney general "should encourage homeowners and business people to purchase them and use them properly. . . . After all, guns don't make criminals. It's criminals who make use of guns. They're the ones who should be punished—not the law-abiding citizen who seeks to defend himself."

So had he now changed his mind? Not at all, he replied in Miami: it "would be naive and foolish to simply disarm the citizen." Reagan was not trimming his sails to win support. That was one reason he *inspired* so much support.

That, and his passionately creative visions of innocence. As at his next stop, in North Carolina, which held a crucial primary on March 23.

In this Southern state he chose to launch into a homily on racial reconciliation: "When the first bombs were dropped on Pearl Harbor there was great segregation in the military forces," he explained. "In World War II, this was corrected." This was news to the more historically minded reporters, who knew the armed forces had integrated only under an executive order from Harry Truman, in 1948, three years after the war ended—and that segregation ended in the rest of society only after concerted protest and civil disobedience. In the press conference that followed he was asked whether he had approved of Martin Luther King's civil disobedience tactics.

No, he responded: "There can never be any justification for breaking the law."

Someone followed up: then how could blacks have ever gained their civil rights in places like North Carolina?

That pressed a button, activating a core component of the man's amour propre: "I am just incapable of prejudice," as he had said in 1966 during his debut on *Meet the Press,* and many times since. Raised by a Protestant mother who married his Catholic father in an anti-Catholic age; having played side by side with black boys; having been raised in a church that preached racial brotherhood, his mother having taken in released prisoners, black and white, to convalesce in the family sewing room—how could he be racist? He just disliked civil rights laws. He'd said the 1964 act outlawing discrimination in public accommodations was "a bad piece of legislation," an unwarranted intrusion of federal power into the lives of individuals.

He had many stories about his racial enlightenment. There was the time he wanted to see *The Birth of a Nation,* D. W. Griffith's pro–Ku Klux Klan blockbuster. "My brother and I were the only kids not to see it," he would say, reciting his father's words: "The Klan's the Klan, and a sheet's a sheet, and any man who wears one over his head is a bum. And I want no more words on the subject." And the time his father was working as a traveling salesman and the desk clerk at the only hotel in a small town proudly informed him that the place didn't serve Jews; Jack announced they wouldn't be serving this Catholic, either, and slept a winter's night in his car. There was the time when a visiting team could find no hotel to stay in, for the team had two black players, who were welcomed into the Reagan home instead. It was precisely such magnanimous gestures on the part of individual whites that could solve any lingering racial problem; and, since Americans were magnanimous, it *would* solve the problem.

"There must be no lack of equal opportunity, no inequality before the law," he said in the televised opening speech of his 1966 gubernatorial campaign. But: "There is a limit to what can be accomplished by laws and regulations, and I seriously question whether anything additional is needed in that line." That year, in Washington, a new civil rights law banning housing discrimination was being debated; in Chicago, marching through the city's white bungalow belt in favor of the principle, Martin Luther King was jeered by swastika-wielding protesters, and knives and rocks were thrown at his head. That did not change his mind. The next year Reagan, returning to his alma mater to dedicate a new library, asked Eureka students rhetorically, "Are the problems of the urban ghetto the result of selfishness on our part, of indifference to suffering?" The answer to him seemed plain: "No people in all the history of mankind have shaped so wisely its material circumstances." Speaking again at Eureka in 1973 he marveled at those who claimed America was still marred by racism: hadn't Los Angeles just elected a Negro mayor? In 1968, when a black questioner asked him why she never saw blacks at Republican events, he politely but forcefully replied that it wasn't Republicans who were racist but the supposedly liberal Democrats, "a party that had betrayed them. . . . The Negro has delivered himself to those who have no other intention than to create a Federal plantation and ignore him." The *Washington Post* reported, "Reagan handled the situation so smoothly that some of the newsmen aboard his chartered 727 suggested, half-seriously, that the Reagan organization had set up the incident." It was part of his liturgy of absolution.

He had not always handled such questions so smoothly. He almost never lost his temper in public. He did once, however, during his 1966 gubernatorial primary campaign. A delegate at the National Negro Republican Assembly in Santa Monica said, "It grieves me when a leading Republican candidate says the Civil Rights Act is a bad piece of legislation." Reagan then shocked the assembly by slamming down his note cards and shouting, "I resent the implication that there is any bigotry in my nature. Don't anyone ever imply I lack integrity. I will not stand silent and let anyone imply that—in this or any other group." He slammed his fist into his palm, muttered something, and walked out of the room.

He knew better than to blow up again. Now he just told the stories. In Charlotte on the second day of his presidential campaign the story he told was about "where I think the first change began. . . . I have often stated publicly that the great tragedy was then that we didn't even know that we had a racial problem. It wasn't even recognized. But our generation, and I take great pride in this, were the ones who first of all recognized and then began doing something about it."

Reportorial ears pricked up: *this* was going to be something.

"I have called attention to the fact that when I was a sports announcer, broadcasting major-league baseball, most Americans had forgotten that at the time the opening lines of the official baseball guide read, 'Baseball is a game for Caucasian gentlemen,' and in organized baseball no one but Caucasians were allowed. Well, there were many of us when I was broadcasting, sportswriters, sportscasters, myself included, [who] began editorializing about what a ridiculous thing this was and why it should be changed. And one day it was changed."

And indeed, he *had* called attention to that, in 1967, in a televised debate with Robert Kennedy, when he told the same story about baseball. In the interim, if anyone had bothered to point out to him that there was no line in the official baseball guide asserting that "baseball is a game for Caucasian gentlemen," or had pointed out to him that he stopped broadcasting baseball in 1937 and the sport wasn't integrated until 1947, the intervention clearly didn't take. He was still telling the story in the White House nine years later.

The next question was a routine one—and so was his answer. Someone asked what he thought about Senator Percy's claim that Reagan's lack of moderation would tank the Republican Party. A non sequitur quip followed: "If you're lying on the operating table and the man is standing there with a scalpel in his hand"—*smile*—"I'd like to know he has more than a moderately successful record." That introduced a list of statistics: that he'd hired more minorities than any previous governor; reduced the population of mental hospitals from 26,500 to 7,000 "by adequately funding county mental health clinics"; cut welfare rolls by 400,000 while "boosting aid to the genuinely needy." Punch line: "Maybe Senator Percy will tell me what is immoderate about those things that we did."

Then he was off to raise the roof at his next campaign speech.

On the plane back to Los Angeles he acknowledged what had become by then a cliché: "There's no question Goldwater tried to tell us some things that maybe eleven years ago we weren't ready to hear. We still were wrapped in the New Deal syndrome of believing that government could do all of these things for us. I insist Barry Goldwater never was defeated on the basis of his philosophy. The opposition, aided and abetted by Republican opponents in the primaries—which makes me so strong in my Eleventh Commandment belief—created a straw man, and what the people really voted against was a false image of a dangerous radical."

The *New York Times* disagreed, but then, it would. Columnist William Shannon, surveying Pat Buchanan's new book, *Conservative Votes, Liberal Victories* (published, as it happened, by Quadrangle/ The New York Times Book Company), that Sunday in the book review section, said George Wallace's primary victories "may have been only protest votes of transient import. . . . Senator Goldwater, after all, was crushed at the polls when he presented the Conservative message straightforwardly."

RONALD REAGAN WAS NOT SENATOR GOLDWATER—A HYPOTHESIS, AS IT happened, that one now could scrutinize scientifically.

The Federal Communications Commission had ruled that showing Reagan's movies on TV triggered the equal-time provision—the Ford campaign would get an equivalent amount of free screen time for balance. It happened just as the new Federal Election Commission ruled that the RNC could pay for Gerald Ford's travels, but not Ronald Reagan's: advantage Ford. Chevy Chase had a bonanza that weekend. First he parodied Ford's reversal on a New York City bailout. (Chase mocked Ford: "Let me be clear. . . . As President, I will change my mind whenever I want." Then he answered a glass of water instead of the red phone.) Chase next aimed at the Church Committee's report on the assassination of foreign leaders. ("Commented Ford upon reading the report, quote, 'Boy, I'm sure glad I'm not foreign.'") Then, on the FCC decision, a groaner about how the wheelchair-bound George Wallace would get to show a minute of *Ironsides* for each minute of a Ronald Reagan flick. But Reagan's line on the subject was funnier than Chevy Chase. "Somebody must have goofed," he said, "because I've made some movies that, if they put them on television, *I'd* demand equal time."

Another outcome of the equal-time rule was that Barry Goldwater filled in for Reagan on his radio show. He said the same sorts of things Reagan did—ponderously, technically, and charmlessly.

On the campaign plane, Jules Witcover asked Reagan point-blank how he could possibly succeed when his positions on things like Social Security were the same ones that caused the 1964 nominee to be cut down at the knees. Reagan returned, "The funny thing is in the speech I made about him which was so well-received, I said some of the same things." He then described, with a refreshingly rare frankness, how he accomplished this—how his rhetoric succeeded where Goldwater's did not.

"I've always believed that you say the qualifier first. If you say, 'Now, let's make it plain: the first priority must be that no one who is depending on that for their non-earning years should have it taken away from him, or have it endangered. It is endangered today by the shape that it is in.' So you then can go on and say, 'Now, the program is out of balance. Down the line someplace, can come a very great tragedy of finding the cupboard is bare. Before that happens, let's fix Social Security.'"

Or, on the subject of welfare: "'Now, I am not suggesting that we stop welfare tomorrow. *So, having qualified with that,* let me say, I just have faith in the American people that, if through some set of circumstances welfare disappeared tomorrow, no one would miss a meal. The people in this country, in every community all over, would get together and form emergency committees, and take up the slack. Those are the kind of people they are.'"

Maybe they were. Maybe they weren't. Be that as it may, Americans seemed to like to hear it. In a Gallup poll taken the day his first tour ended, Reagan had gone from trailing Gerald Ford by 23 points among Republicans to a 40 to 32 percent lead, an unprecedented one-month jump. Independent voters said they preferred the former actor over the president by 27 percent to 25. "Ronald Reagan more popular than the President? Has the Gallup Poll gone bananas?" the *Pittsburgh News'* political columnist wondered. "Are the Republicans once again prepared to self-destruct by nominating another Barry Goldwater? . . . And have those 11,324 Democratic presidential candidates trained their sights on the wrong man?"

CIVILIZATION CONTINUED ITS COLLAPSE.

Tom Wicker complained that "no one in Congress or the executive branch has even begun to face" the philosophical and institutional consequences of the Church Committee's and Pike Committee's revelations. Pike tried to cite Henry Kissinger for contempt of Congress and was blocked at every turn. A citation, he complained in an open letter to colleagues, would not "cause the earth to tremble nor the sun to stop in its tracks. No one is seeking to place Mr. Kissinger in jail, and the worst that can happen to him is that he might have to provide the documents subpoenaed to Congress"—and if that be "McCarthyism," "then the State Department has arrogated unto itself total non-accountability."

His conservative Democratic colleague George Mahon of Texas promptly posted a letter of apology to the White House "for the continual confrontation between Congress and the executive branch" that was "tearing our country apart."

Meg Greenfield in *Newsweek* wondered why, even as the Church Committee's assassination report if anything exceeded all fears, "the bomb proved something of a dud." She decided it was "the anesthetizing effect of years of revelation and shock. . . . Washington, by virtue of a seemingly unending flow of such disclosures in the past couple of years, has managed to perform a . . . nationwide lobotomy of the public." On December 8, the *Times'* editorialists all but absolved the preceding president of Watergate: "By the time Richard Nixon became President, the practiced seaminess had become so entrenched that the deception of Watergate flowed with alarming naturalness." Meanwhile, on the other side of the op-ed page, William Safire, in a column headlined "Orchestrating Outrage," concluded, "History will show the Nixon Administration not as the one that invented abuse of power, but the one that gloriously if unwittingly served the cause of individual liberty by the clumsy way it tried to continue the abuses of Kennedy and Johnson."

Like clockwork a new outrage emerged to be ignored. Back at the end of April, as Saigon fell, NBC's David Brinkley had editorialized in his stern grandfatherly way that "now, for the first time since Hitler invaded Poland, there is no war anywhere in the world. . . . Since Hitler it has become a major industry, with huge amounts of the people's money being spent to pay for wars already fought, paying either in money or inflation or both, and spent on hiring armies and buying hardware for some war that may come, or be contrived. Numerous national leaders, including some of ours, have turned to the military in times of stress in the hopes of quick and spectacular solutions. Well, now, after several spectacular failures, people might hope their politicians will be less quick to reach for their guns." Not so fast, Mr. Brinkley: hardly eight months later the CIA director confirmed that the agency was aiding one of three sides in a complex civil war in the oil-rich African nation of Angola.

The political context was fraught. The previous summer, Congress voted to withdraw arms aid to Turkey, following its invasion of Cyprus, the first real test of the War Powers Act of 1974 forbidding military action without congressional authorization. Simultaneously, a "Carnation Revolution" broke out in Portugal, overthrowing the fascist Portuguese dictatorship (it began with a bloodless coup by military officers and ended in a popular uprising in which grateful citizens stuck carnations into the barrels of government soldiers' guns; Reagan called it the work of "leftist street hoodlums"). Portugal promptly divested itself of its colonies, including Angola, where, that December, Soviet-backed guerrillas were on the verge of seizing power. That was the final straw, for the American right, against Gerald Ford and his timorous doctrine of détente. William Rusher's column predicted the arrival of thousands of Soviet-equipped Cubans, "spearheading and stiffening a drive by local Communist forces to take over all of Angola. . . . If they succeed, Communism will have reached the eastern shore of the Atlantic on a front nearly a thousand miles long." He concluded, "That rumble you hear isn't dominoes falling. It's the roof caving in." James J. Kilpatrick wrote that a land "almost as large as Britain, France, and Spain combined" would be within a month "for all practical purposes . . . a virtual satellite of the Soviet Union." He concluded, "It might have been possible for the Central Intelligence Agency to avert this calamity—but the CIA has been crippled by a moralizing Senate."

Not so crippled, it turned out. The CIA was already funneling arms and advice to a faction called UNITA, whose cynical and ideologically flexible leader, Jonas Savimbi, had only recently called himself a Maoist, but now declared himself an acolyte of American-style capitalism. Outgoing CIA director Colby defended the decision before the House Intelligence Committee: "If you see the Soviet Union deliberately trying to expand its power, is it more prudent for the United States to take some modest action or do nothing?" He also reminded the committee that this was legal because paramilitary operations were eliminated from the War Powers Act. Senator Dick Clark, a liberal Democrat from Iowa, pointed out that such "modest" CIA action was exactly how the Vietnam debacle began. And the Church Committee had just released its final report on U.S actions in Chile, concluding, "Eight million dollars was spent, covertly, in the three years between 1970 and the military coup in September 1973, with over three million dollars expended in fiscal 1972 alone." Clark introduced legislation to cut off military aid and covert action in Angola. His colleague Clifford Case of New Jersey, the ranking Republican on the Foreign Relations Committee, complained, "I don't think we can just *pull out* of Angola"—which is what the Foreign Relations Committee had said about Vietnam, too.

Anthony Lewis advanced the theory, marveling at his own cynicism, that the leak of CIA involvement had come straight from the top—that the Oval Office hoped Congress would react by cutting off aid, allowing the administration to ask the red-baiting question "Who lost Angola?" in an election year. He pointed out that government officials had been admitting "it made no difference to us which nationalist faction won the internal struggle" ("What the hell is Angola?" asked one senator), and yet we intervened in favor of one faction. "What the world sees as self-inflicted wounds may look to the authors like a way of electing Gerald Ford and keeping Henry Kissinger in office," he wrote, by running against "a Democratic Congress that he can imply is soft on Communism, loose with secrets, and ready to retreat from American greatness. That line is especially useful for competing with Ronald Reagan."

Why not? Ford was once more ensnared in the embarrassments of governance, and, politically, at the worst possible time. He returned from a state visit to China, which could not endear him to conservatives but didn't impress the sophisticates, either. ("C'mon Hank, you can tell me!" an Oliphant cartoon syndicated by the *Washington Star* was captioned. "What *were* all those secret discussions about?") Congress moved to extend his temporary tax cut, but not, as he had demanded, alongside accompanying spending cuts to pay for it. He vetoed the bill and the House was not able to override it, but the *Times* called it a defeat for him nonetheless, because "public displeasure about the quality of political leadership will probably be reinforced." Congress adjourned "leaving Mr. Ford the solitary embarrassment of signing legislation that does not give him what he wants"—and which conservatives judged as yet one more liberal sellout. Meanwhile the FEC ruled that Ford's travels paid for by the Republican National Committee were party building, not campaigning, so they need not be counted against his spending limit. A conference of Southern Republicans opened in Houston. Ford decided not to show up—he showed up instead in news pictures falling on his ass while skiing in Vail—and reinforced the snub by sending in his stead Nelson Rockefeller, who insulted the participants: "You got me out, you sons of bitches," he reportedly said; "now get off your asses and help the President." Reagan appeared in Houston and, unsurprisingly, raised the roof.

THAT SUNDAY'S *60 MINUTES*, THE CBS "NEWSMAGAZINE" THAT HAD helped induct millions of middle Americans into the ranks of the suspicious circles with its hard-hitting investigative journalism, and had become that fall the first news show to vault to the top of the network ratings after it moved to a new time slot at 7 P.M. on Sundays, featured a Ralph Nader–style exposé of a factory in Virginia owned by a company called Allied Chemical. Its product, a pesticide called Kepone, was alleged to cause brain damage in its workers. Heartbreakingly, the camera lingered on one tremulous victim who, for an excruciating forty-five seconds, tried and failed to drive in a bolt with a screwdriver. Then *60 Minutes'* new reporter, former White House correspondent Dan Rather, moved in for what would become his trademark on *60 Minutes* (though the style was already familiar to viewers who remembered when the young newsman stood up at a televised news conference in March 1974 in Houston and embarrassed Richard Nixon with the toughest question of his presidency). In the office of the company's director of agricultural research, a man named William Moore, Rather pulled out a sheaf of books—"studies sponsored by Allied Chemical":

"Are you familiar with these materials? This—"

"No."

"Never seen those?"

"Never seen them."

"Right in the summary, very top: 'The characteristic effect of this compound is the development of DDT-like tremors, the severity of which depends upon dosage level and duration of exposure.' Quote, unquote—from the first sentence of the summary. You don't know about this?"

"No, no."

But Mr. Moore, Rather revealed, was the author of that very study.

The suspicious circles were still thrusting. There came next, however, another, very different sort of segment the producers of *60 Minutes* favored: the fluffy celebrity profile. The subject, however, was a politician—one who, in contrast to the story just told, used to say things on the radio like "Right now business is regulated in America by government more than it is in any other country in the world." And that the federal Occupational Safety and Health Administration's goal seemed to be to "make a worker completely safe by taking away his job." And who in speeches to business conventions spoke of the nation's preeminent consumer advocate as "Little Sir Ralph who has become a folk hero taking whacks at you with his wooden sword," his minions "attempting to take from you the prerogatives of management without accepting any of the responsibilities that drive you on occasion to a Miltown." (Miltown was a popular tranquilizer; Nancy Reagan took it.)

But *60 Minutes* didn't get into any of that. Instead, after a title card that presented the handsome sixty-four-year-old in a white cowboy hat cocked just so, a jeep rumbled from over the horizon, out of the mountains and into the pale prairie light, filmed heroically from below just the way John Ford shot John Wayne, as Mike Wallace's pleasant voice-over intoned:

"Mr. Right. That's how Nancy Reagan feels about her husband. Apparently it's also about how millions of Republicans feel about Nancy Reagan's husband. For the Gallup poll released just two days ago has him leading the President for the Republican nomination by a full eight points. . . . But while the pundits and the pollsters have been turning Reagan inside out, *60 Minutes* elected to spend some time with Ronald and Nancy Reagan at home in California."

It had always been Ronald Reagan's remarkable gift—ever aware of the gaze of others, reflecting on it, adjusting himself to it, inviting it—to model himself in his mind's eye according to how he presented himself physically to others, adjusting himself to be seen as he wished others to see him, almost as if *he* were the one guiding the cameras that captured his image. Now, as Gerald Ford stumbled, it was how his team managed to reintroduce him to the nation, on the nation's top-rated news show: as an avuncular cowboy naturalist—just folks.

Reagan, from the driver's seat: "Well, we're coming now to what's called Bald Mountain, matter of fact it's on the map."

Wallace, sitting beside him: "Here you are in your six hundred, seven hundred acres at the top of the most beautiful part of California, horses, family. What in the world would persuade you? You've got it made."

"Yeah."

"You've worked hard, you've saved money, you've got a family."

"I don't know, someone said life begins when you begin to serve. Maybe if there's a feeling that you can be of service, then you feel you have to do it."

He was now a rich man, Mike Wallace explained, "but none of his possessions mean as much to him"—the ex-governor in the Western garb was pictured calling to a horse—"as the ranch he bought last year. 'Rancho Cielo,' he calls it. Ranch of Heaven. One senses this is something he and Nancy had yearned for."

(Not quite; Nancy didn't care for any ranch. And at that, when he rode horses he hadn't previously dressed like a cowboy; he rode English style, wearing jodhpurs and boots.)

"Mrs. Reagan, do I understand you met this fellow because you were a subscriber to the *Daily Worker*?"

"There wasn't, but there was a Nancy Davis who was—"

She relayed a version of the dubious story of how they met, interrupted by a bark—"That's our dog Wallace. Hates the Communists just like his mommy and daddy!" Then came a scene from the one movie where they acted together, *Hellcats of the Navy,* two lovebirds walking off into the sunset—and then that cut away to the same shot, only in real life.

Ronnie: "For all the years we've been married it's been *we*, not you and I. It would be inconceivable to me to go my way without her."

Nancy in red sweater and silver-and-turquoise belt, testifying to her husband's cruel victimization at the hands of the press:

"Whenever anyone would say something about Ronnie that I thought was unkind, cruel, or unjust, untrue, I'd go in and I'd take a long bath and carry out imaginary conversations in which—*I*—*was*—*just*—*marvelous*. I'd say all those things you'd hope you'd have a chance to say, and nobody could talk back to you, and I was tremendous! And by the time I was done with the bath, I was OK!"

(That week, *People* magazine featured a "Chinese face reader" expounding on people in the news, including Nancy, "a poised patrician-born"—the article said—"size 6 who often makes best-dressed lists": *"Look at the indirect focus of her eyes; they do not match her expression. She doesn't care about what others feel and may not be open about her own feelings. Perhaps she is fearful she will be found out. . . . She is a vital person and will remain active into old age. But she is out for herself."*)

Wallace read aloud from a new book called *The Power Lovers*, on political marriages: "'Why, my joy is being Mrs. Ronald Reagan.'" (Wallace sounded smug, Nancy looked like she was about to sigh in frustration—*this again . . .*) "'My life began with Ronnie'—and people chuckle."

Unembarrassed, she replied, "Well, they chuckle. But—it did." She smiled defiantly, eyebrows raised.

A public-policy discussion:

"The death penalty?" "I'm in favor of the death penalty." (*Why?*) "Because I think it saves lives. I think people are alive today because of the death penalty." She smiled.

"Abortion?" "I, I can't get over the point of it being that you're killing somebody." She still was smiling. "I can't get beyond that."

"Marijuana. Marijuana seems to be a fact of life," Nancy said softly, ruefully—"unfortunately." "You would obviously not legalize it." "No, I would not be in favor of legalizing it." "We were talking to Maureen, your stepdaughter, and we asked if she could imagine Ronnie and Nancy Reagan sitting there of a summer's night or whenever smoking a joint together." Nancy laughed heartily. "That," Wallace said, "was her reaction to it."

The candidate was lobbed a few softballs: "Governor, some people call you a button-pusher. They're scared to have you in the White House. You wanted to win in Vietnam, you're against détente and the Chinese. You're a hard-liner. You frighten some people." Soothingly, he responded, now in a tan sport coat and shirt and brown tie, with red-woods wallpaper in the background: "*Welllll,* let me explain. I'm not a hard-liner. Anyone in my generation who's lived through four wars and been part of one of them can't be for anything but peace." And: "The greatest immorality is to ask young men to fight or die for my country if it's not a cause we are willing to win."

Some light political chitchat: George Wallace. Ted Kennedy. Hubert Humphrey, being talked up by pundits as the Democrats' best '76 hope. "Can you beat him?" "Well, I'd sure give it a good country try!"

The "sour" public mood, "corruption at the top . . . pursuit of hedonism, rising crime rates, a lower faith in many of our institutions. How come?" *Easy:* "When you take away from people any sense of responsibility, or any feeling that they have any part in the decisions, or any part in the control, then people do begin to drift and go their own way, I suppose. What's happened to our people is that they have a feeling that government is beyond them, that they cannot influence it."

"Tell me the last time we had a leader we had a good deal of faith in."

"Franklin Delano Roosevelt. He took his case to the people. When the New Deal started he was faced with a Congress that wouldn't go along. He went over their heads with the fireside chats. . . . And he enlightened the people. . . . The greatest leader is not one who does the greatest things. He is the one who gets the people to do the greatest things. And that's what is lacking now."

At home with the Ronald Reagans, as poor Gerald Ford governed and stumbled, stumbled and governed.

"I don't think the system has failed, or that the system has failed us. But I think a great many people have failed the system." Cut back to that jeep for one more ride into the sunset. The ticking *60 Minutes* clock. As, the next day, one more nail was driven into Camelot's coffin, and the Church Committee finally generated a story that riveted the nation.

ON MONDAY A PRETTY FORTY-ONE-YEAR-OLD NAMED JUDITH CAMPBELL Exner, her tanned face obscured behind large saucer-shaped sunglasses, stepped up to press conference microphones in San Diego: "My relationship with Jack Kennedy was of a close, personal nature and did not involve conspiratorial shenanigans of any kind," she said. "We never discussed politics or international affairs. To me, he was Jack Kennedy and not the President."

And why were political or international affairs relevant to the discussion? Because, it turned out, Exner, described on newswires as "a comely brunette woman with a hazy past," *also* had a "relationship" with the two mobsters who had helped the CIA try to assassinate Fidel Castro—but those, too, she avowed, were "of a personal nature and were no way related to or affected by my relationship with Jack Kennedy, nor did I discuss either of them with the other."

The story of the gangsters' moll and the president had begun with an oblique footnote on page 129 of the Church Committee assassination report: "Evidence before the committee indicates that a close friend of President Kennedy had frequent contact with the President from the end of 1960 through mid 1962. FBI reports and testimony indicate that the President's friend was also a close friend of John Roselli and Sam Giancana and saw them often during this same period.... White House telephone logs show seventy instances of phone contact between the White House and the President's friend whose testimony confirms frequent phone contact with the President himself. Both the President's friend and Roselli testified that the friend did not know about either the assassination operation or the wire tap case. Giancana was killed before he was available for questioning." That the "close friend" may have been a *close friend* emerged from a staff leak published by two reporters from the Scripps-Howard chain a month earlier. Then, three days before Exner's press conference, *New York Times* columnist William Safire, charging a cover-up by a Church Committee "plumbers' operation," introduced J. Edgar Hoover into the question. He had, Safire reported, met with JFK one March day in 1962, immediately before the Exner-Kennedy calls stopped—which raised what Safire called "substantive questions," such as "Did the Mafia figures encourage the girl's White House relationship, and if so, to what end?" And "Why did Mr. Hoover check with the CIA and then tell a Las Vegas sheriff to stop prosecuting Giancana for wiretapping an unfaithful girlfriend—right after his luncheon showdown with President Kennedy." And whether "the Mafia, by silencing Giancana forever, has clamped down the lid from its end." And whether Hoover had used this leverage to blackmail the Kennedys into wiretapping Martin Luther King.

Or whether the secret of JFK's assassination lurked beneath: "Too many coincidences... When the President winds up murdered by a supporter of Castro, target of the aborted CIA assassination plot, the matter is worth a thorough public examination."

Exner said she called her press conference to close off just such "lurid speculation." Not likely. A reporter delicately asked if she had ever met Kennedy's wife; Exner replied that she hadn't. A less decorous newsman came straight out with it: "Did you ever go to bed with

John Fitzgerald Kennedy?" Exner responded, "That's in the personal arena"—her lawyer adding that he had her full testimony, transcribed and documented, stored in a secure area, "to be released at a proper time and in a proper manner."

Once more Kennedy family retainers popped out of the woodwork to proclaim incredulity. "I think there's a campaign to give it to the Kennedys," said JFK's personal secretary Kenny O'Donnell, who claimed that there were "no secret passages" in the presidential appointment book he kept, and that "there is not much in his life after 1957 that I didn't know about." "Even Jacqueline Kennedy didn't have lunch twenty times with the President," he added of claims of sixteen to twenty White House visits by Exner—perhaps revealing more than he intended. Senator Church called claims that his committee had covered up the story for partisan reasons "preposterous"—details irrelevant to the investigation had been withheld by unanimous agreement of committee senators, and if there had been evidence that the president's liaison had been brokered by the mafia, "we would have included it in the report." Exner wouldn't name the friend who introduced her to Kennedy and then to Giancana, though speculation centered on Frank Sinatra, who came out with an eleven-word statement to the press: "Hell hath no fury like a hustler with a literary agent."

Safire assiduously fueled the fire. Richard Nixon had been last seen in public print running from a *St. Louis Post-Dispatch* reporter who stalked him at the eighteenth hole at his retreat in San Clemente for a two-part profile ("Nixon Believes His Memoirs Will Vindicate Him") depicting a pale, pathetic man pocked with liver spots, begging Rabbi Korff to raise funds to keep him solvent, and playing golf for eight hours straight every day except when an errant shot frustrated him and he quit after seven. Only in the columns of the former PR flack Safire was he still a great man—or at least, no less great than his Democratic forebears, who were actually much, much worse. It had been Safire's project since joining the *Times*. Like J. J. Hunsecker, the scabrous scribe played by Burt Lancaster in *Sweet Smell of Success,* in his op-ed page essays he took advantage of a columnists' license to introduce literary techniques that would have gotten a reporter fired had he tried them in the news pages—insinuating questions, dubious "coincidences," morbid speculation, guilt by association, character assassination—to establish, as he put it on December 8, "the greatest cover-up of all . . . the suppression of truth about Democratic precedents to Watergate, on the grounds that it might ameliorate the hatred being focused on Richard Nixon." On December 22, in his first column after the Exner press conference, he trumpeted "murder and attempted murder at the highest level that spans fifteen years": Castro, Kennedy, and now Sam Giancana, "who presumably encouraged one of his girls to nourish a White House–Mafia liaison . . . the dead body of Sam Giancana lies across Frank Church's path to the Presidency." For these ambitions, Safire claimed, Church had closed the books on a murder most foul, threatening perjury and warning of lie detector tests to staffers who wouldn't get with the program. *But.* "Senator Church cannot slam the lid of Pandora's box back down now that he has glimpsed the evil that lurks therein."

The luridness was only beginning. Though at least with Exner the claim could be reasonably made that a matter of public interest was at stake. Then came Fiddle and Faddle:

"When Judith Campbell Exner said last week that she had 'a close personal' relationship with Jack Kennedy she was only confirming what had long been a matter of open and widespread speculation." Speculate no more, said *Time* magazine in the issue that appeared on newsstands the day before Christmas. There was the time the thirty-fifth president startled the British prime minister and foreign minister by confiding that "if he went too long without a woman, he suffered severe headaches." Jayne Mansfield claimed an affair with Kennedy lasting three years and "[t]here is little doubt that Marilyn Monroe also had a sexual relationship with the President" (they met—the claim was sourced to a Hollywood gossip writer—at the Carlyle Hotel, the Beverly Hills Hotel, Peter Lawford's house in Santa Monica, the White House, "and even in the Kennedy private plane, the Caroline"). There were also airline stewardesses. And, during the 1960 Democratic National Convention, after claiming he was off to meet with his father, there was a "diplomat's wife he had known for some time." And a "smashing brunette" sent over as a gift by a newsman ("I got your message—both of them"). The woman who suffered the interruption of "[t]wo top foreign affairs advisers with a batch of secret cables." ("Never bothering to close the door, Kennedy cooled down, read the dispatches, and made his decision before he returned to his friend.") And last but not least, "two women who displayed few secretarial skills but worked on his staff" and were described by British dramatist Jonathan Miller as looking "like unused tennis balls—they had the fuzz still on them" and were "assigned quarters near the President and were code-named 'Fiddle' and 'Faddle' by the Secret Service."

Then there were the tales *Time* repeated from a book by the former White House kennel keeper—"impossible to verify"—that "Jack would sometimes lounge naked around the White House swimming pool when

Jackie was away, and women would arrive, undress, and join him," and that once "Jackie allegedly found a woman's undergarment tucked into a pillow slip. She is supposed to have said calmly to Jack: 'Would you please shop around and see who these belong to? They're not my size.'" A reader wrote in that the article showed how it was "possible to assassinate someone twice."

ON DECEMBER 21, IN VIENNA, SIX MILITANTS FROM THE "ARM OF THE Arab Revolution" group forced their way into a meeting of OPEC leaders, issued a communiqué demanding a "total liberation war" against Israel, took sixty hostages, and killed three, before, the next day, releasing their surviving charges in Tripoli. Now, it appeared, the people by whose command flowed the lifeblood of entire global economy, petroleum, were at the mercy of a terrorist known as "Carlos the Jackal." The next week, in New York, terrorists took advantage of peak holiday travel to explode a bomb, equivalent to twenty-five sticks of dynamite, that they had hidden in a coin locker—collapsing the floor and ceiling, hurling shrapnel from the metal lockers that pierced through flesh and left body parts scattered throughout the main baggage claim area at La Guardia Airport. Fourteen people were killed. No one ever claimed responsibility. No perpetrator was ever found. "Terrorism," FBI director Clarence Kelley said, "is, indeed, the ultimate evil in our society. And no one can consider himself immune from terrorist acts." Most shockingly of all, "some otherwise law-abiding people provide moral and material support to terrorists, apparently for idealistic reasons"— like the people who had gladly kept Patty Hearst, whose trial was set to begin in two weeks, from justice in her fourteen months on the lam.

La Guardia was the eighty-ninth bombing in the United States attributable to terrorist activity in 1975, compared with forty-five in 1974 and twenty-four in 1973. What would 1976 bring?

CHAPTER TWENTY-FOUR

Negatives Are Positives

AT CHRISTMASTIME IN 1897, AN EIGHT-YEAR-OLD GIRL FROM NEW YORK wrote to a newspaper editor, "Some of my little friends say there is no Santa Claus.... Please tell me the truth; is there a Santa Claus." The editor responded for the ages: "Yes, Virginia, there is a Santa Claus."

At Christmastime in 1975, two girls asked the same question of a columnist, Alan MacLeese, at the *Flint Journal* in Michigan. He wrote back, "No, Gretchen and Stacy, there is no such man."

America was trying to celebrate. It really was. At the Waldorf-Astoria in New York, 1976 was rung in with Guy Lombardo's orchestra leading a sing-along of "Happy Birthday, America"; in Philadelphia, it was rung in with the midnight ride of the Liberty Bell from Independence Hall to a large building where it would welcome tourists all during the nation's Bicentennial year; the next morning, in Pasadena, California, Kate Smith offered her famous rendition of "God Bless America" as grand marshal of the Rose Bowl Parade. But streetside revelers who opened their copies of the *Los Angeles Times* during a lull in the proceedings could read the offering that morning of columnist Robert J. Donovan: "The inescapable commentary of fading 1975 and its several predecessors is that, combined, they are sending the country into bicentennial 1976 in such a state of disillusion and moral confusion that no one is sure how best to celebrate the nation's 200th birthday."

In Cleveland, the *Plain Dealer* editorialized that "1975 was at least something of an improvement over 1974," though whether 1976 might be an improvement over that was "a mystery." Under the dark penumbra of Watergate; the revelations about that womanizer and would-be assassin of Castro, John F. Kennedy (who according to the new book *The Search for JFK* had been a terrible naval commander to boot, who did not "save his crew" after a Japanese warship rammed his PT boat, instead his negligence having been responsible for the sinking itself); the wave of bombings and kidnappings in America and around the world—and who was to say, the *Plain Dealer* mused, that mad terrorists might not soon have nukes—"as the New Year arrives it sometimes seems as if modern government is helpless." The Census Bureau came out with a new report on marriage: it was on the way out, with the number of people between 25 and 34 years old who had never been married increasing by half since 1970. One-parent families were skyrocketing too, from 1.6 to 7.2 million. The journalist Elizabeth Drew, in her weekly "Journal" column in the *New Yorker,* wrote, of the nation's two-hundredth birthday, "we don't seem to know how to celebrate it. There is a vague feeling that the merchandisers have already made off with the occasion, and that the orators will bore us to death . . . there is also an uneasiness about celebrating. Our history began so grandly, and it doesn't seem so grand anymore."

Her catalogue of horrors included Watergate, of course. ("We had had a kind of faith that we would never elect a really bad man as President.") And inflation. And the "threat of widespread food shortages; the continuing energy problem; the threatening scarcity of other natural resources." And the "continuing social and economic plight of the country's black people; the crisis of the cities; the increasing number of ecological problems." And "the excesses, at home and abroad, of our secret intelligence-gathering agencies." She also interviewed Senator Adlai Stevenson III of Illinois, who added capitalism itself to the list of society's failures: "The institutions of free enterprise," he told the *New Yorker,* "are not equal to the realities of the new era: cartels, fixed prices, commodity shortages."

A PRESS RELEASE ANNOUNCED ONE CELEBRATION: "ONE HUNDRED YEARS ago, an enterprising and forward-looking New York publisher, Mrs. Charles F. Deihm, had an idea, to create a depository of materials gathered at the time of the United States Centennial celebration that could be unveiled 100 years later." The unveiling took place in January in a lobby of the U.S. Capitol. "Happy birthday, America!" Congresswoman Lindy Boggs cried from the ceremonial dais; members of Congress's Joint Committee on Arrangements for the Commemoration of the Bicentennial sat arrayed beside her. The House and Senate chaplains said prayers; Senator Mark Hatfield of Oregon, representing Vice President Rockefeller, president of the Senate, presented the official Bicentennial flag—it featured a red-white-and-blue star with modishly rounded corners—to House Speaker Carl Albert and said there were already eight thousand of them flying around the country. Carl Albert said, "We meet today under very inspiring circumstances."

And thereupon, with fanfare, the double doors to the elegant black-lacquered safe, reposing patiently in a Capitol storeroom lo these last hundred years, fanned open. But these ended up opening only to another set of locked doors, so all they could access was a written message: "It is the wish of Mrs. Deihm that this safe may remain closed until July 4, 1976."

Crushingly appropriate, that anticlimax. It seemed like nothing worked in America anymore. People's lives were not working; the previous November, Ann Landers received a letter from a young couple who asked the columnist to poll her readership to ask if having a child would be worth it—"Were the rewards enough to make up for the grief?" The letters poured in, and on January 23, she tallied up the score: 70 percent told her *no*. Wrote a forty-year-old with young twins, "I was an attractive, fulfilled career woman before I had these kids. Now I'm an overly exhausted nervous wreck." Said a seventy-year-old mother of five, "Not one of our children has given us any pleasure. God knows we did our best, but we were failures as parents, and they are failures as people."

Failures as people: millions of Americans felt that this description fit them to a T. Seeking a solution, any solution, they eagerly forked over their cash to any huckster who promised release, the quicker and more effortlessly the better: therapies like "bioenergetics" ("The Revolutionary Therapy That Uses the Language of the Body to Heal the Problems of the Mind"); Primal Scream (which held that when patients shrieked in a therapist's office, childhood trauma could be reexperienced, then released; John Lennon and James Earl Jones were fans); or Transcendental Meditation, which promised that deliverance could come if you merely closed your eyes and chanted a mantra (the "TM" organization sold personal mantras, each supposedly "unique," to hundreds of thousands of devotees). Or "religions" like the Church Universal and Triumphant, or the Reverend Sun Myung Moon's Unification Church, or "Scientology"—this last one invented by a science fiction writer, reportedly on a bet. Devotees paid cash to be "audited" by practitioners who claimed the power—if, naturally, you paid for enough sessions—to remove "trauma patterns" accreted over the 75 million years that had passed since Xenu, tyrant of the Galactic Confederacy, deposited billions of people on earth next to volcanoes and detonated hydrogen bombs inside those volcanos, thus scattering harming "body thetans" to attach to the souls of the living, which once unlatched allowed practitioners to cross the "bridge to total freedom" and "unlimited creativity." Another religion, the story had it, promised "perfect knowledge"—though its adherents' public meeting was held up several hours because none of them knew how to run the movie projector. Gallup reported that six million Americans had tried TM, five million had twisted themselves into yoga poses, and two million had sampled some sort of Oriental religion.

And hundreds of thousands of Americans in eleven cities had plunked down $250 for the privilege being screamed at as "assholes."

"est"—*Erhard Seminars Training*, named after the only-in-America hustler who invented it, Werner Erhard, originally Jack Rosenberg, a former used-car and encyclopedia salesman who had tried and failed to join the Marines (this was not incidental) at the age of seventeen, and experienced a spiritual rebirth one morning while driving across the Golden Gate Bridge ("I realized that I knew nothing. . . . In the next instant—after I realized that I knew nothing—I realized that I knew everything")—promised "to transform one's ability to experience living so that the situations one had been trying to change or had been putting up with, clear up just in the process of life itself," all that in just sixty hours, courtesy of a for-profit corporation whose president had been general manager of the Coca-Cola Bottling Company of California and a former member of the Harvard Business School faculty.

A journalist decided to go through the process and write a book about it. He described showing up at 9 A.M. with 239 others at a Howard Johnson's conference room in Boston for the first of four all-day sessions over two successive weekends, and at the start being forced to leave his watch at the door. He sat down in a hard-backed chair—the organizers made sure these chairs were uncomfortable—and heard the rules he would have to agree to in order to stay. They were read out in a mechanical drone: no food or drink (the meal break came at nine at night); no talking; no taking notes, chewing gum, reading, sitting next to someone you knew, or making any trips to the bathroom (the bathroom break came after twelve hours); don't discuss what happens in est training with anyone other than est graduates. Over those sixty hours everything would be controlled, right down to how acolytes were to hold the microphone. ("Stand up. Extend your arms. Now make a fist with your left hand around your right thumb. Now with your left thumb extended outward . . .")

"Keep your ass in the room . . . follow the instructions, and take what you get. . . . The reasons why our lives don't work, the reason why you're assholes, is that you don't keep your agreements! . . . You assholes keep your agreements with me and your lives will work. Is everybody clear on that now?"

The trainer invited questions. The acolytes, careful to extend their left thumbs outward, asked some. A woman said she'd been studying Buddhism for seven years, and that if she believed in anything, it was the Buddha. . . .

"Buddha is dogshit until you experience being the Buddha!"

(He added, "You women would be a lot happier if you realized that you get paid to clean the house and cook dinner.")

He asked who thought they knew why their arms moved when they raised their hands.

"The muscles contract," someone returned.

"They do, huh? What makes them contract?"

"They receive stimulus from the brain," someone offered.

"Wait a minute," proposed the trainer, who went only by the name "Brendan." "How do you know you have a brain?"

There was a pause, and someone named Richard, confident he'd figured out the game, stood up and answered, "Because that's the way we came into the universe."

"What universe?! You people don't know anything, do you? *Do you?"*

Richard returned to his seat.

A man with "Steve" written on his name tag raised his hand: "I don't see any blacks. I don't see any Chicanos. I don't see—"

"Brendan" cut him off: "My answer to you, Steve, is that anyone can take this training. And you know something, Steve? You're the one who hates niggers."

A pert young woman objected: "It's not necessary to use that kind of language."

He imitated her, mocking: *"Oh, it isn't necessary to use that kind of language.* I got that, Mary, so you can wipe that sexy little smile off your face." He addressed his congregation: "I want you to notice Mary's act: press her buttons and she smiles." He addressed her: "You've been smiling all your life, Mary, and where has it gotten you? Right here!"

Mary whimpered; Brendan responded.

"Press another button and Mary starts to cry. Press another button and she screws. . . . Mary, you ain't nothin' but a little China doll. Do you get that? Thank you, Mary, you can sit down. . . .

"I was only using Mary as an example. There isn't one person in here that I couldn't manipulate as easily as I manipulated Mary."

He snarled, "It ain't gonna get no better in here. It's going to get a lot worse, and if you have any notions about not keeping your agreements, remember that you haven't got what you came here for, and I do. I've already got your two hundred and fifty bucks. It's going to get so bad in here that the only thing that's going to keep you in your seats is your money. Is that clear?"

On the second day came the "truth process." Laying his charges down on the floor, the trainer, after a guided meditation leading them to the painful emotions and problems they were there to try to resolve, would command them to "take our fingers off the repress button," and the journalist described the moans and groans that followed as "like listening to a secret sound track of Dante's *Inferno*—as if someone had plugged an audio hookup into the purgatorial paintings of Hieronymus Bosch." (The staff kept bright silver barf bags on hand, just in case.) Next came the "danger process," though he was not allowed to write about that—perhaps because it sounded legally actionable: a participant was ordered to the stage to stand straight as a ramrod, then one of a special team of "confronters" stood nose to nose with the frightened trainee, staring menacingly into his eyes, as another shouted insults; a separate team of "body catchers" caught these trainees when their legs invariably gave out from the strain. Then, at the conclusion of the second day, all would lie on the floor again, this time to imagine each was terrified of everyone else, then that they were all terrified of *everyone* and *everything* in the world; and more Hieronymus Bosch screaming ensued.

For those who came back the next weekend—most did; they had invested $250, after all—there came a tedious lecture, which went on as long as ten hours, in which the trainer expounded (*"I'll tell you everything I know about life"*) on the est theory of the mind as a perfectly plastic machine that could manifest anything it deemed true and obliterate anything that it deemed false, because nothing, really, was real:

"The opposite of reality is the experience of illusion. And what happens when we look at our experience and tell the truth about it? It disappears. . . . So when you experience the truth, you know it's nothing but an illusion!"

A skeptic asked, "So how did all this stuff get here?" He was answered, "It never did." Naturally.

Amid delighted laughter and shrieks of epiphany, the trainer—this one was named "Rod"—asked for a show of hands of those who had "gotten it." Those who did not raise their hands were confronted one more time: "I don't get it," one might say. "Good," he would hear in return. "There's nothing to get. So you get it." At which he might decide, triumphantly—he had paid $250 for this, after all—"I get it! So 'getting it' is whatever you get," and, yes, the trainer would literally respond like this: "If that's what you got."

The journalist, whose name was Robert Hargrove, concluded, "The est training is a process in which you are literally driven right out of your mind, and there is nothing you can do about it except resist." And boy, was he grateful. "Most would be able to walk out of that same room the following weekend and be able to say, 'I am the cause of my own experience' and mean it. . . . They have spent their whole lives playing the victim, but somehow in the process of the training, that attitude and the darkness that was in their faces would disappear." He wrote that he "realized that in my whole life I've never before seen people for what they are." And that he now enjoyed experiencing "a semipermanent state of meditation in which I began to notice more things" and in which he became "more conscious in more and more areas of my life . . . accompanied by the physical sensation that someone was lifting an enormous rock off the top of my head." And that "the value my wife and I got out of it would have made it a knockdown bargain at twice the price." Even the Howard Johnson's cigarette-burned and coffee-stained rug transfixed him: "How many saints and sadhus had attained enlightenment on a snowcapped mountain or a river bank or in a coconut grove and had become so attached to the 'spirit of the place' that they forgot that the experience was within them?" As Hargrove wrote in the preface to *est: Making Life Work*—one of at least five books from major paperback houses extolling est that year—*est: Four Days to Make Your Life Work; The est Experience; est: the Movement and the Man; The Book of est* (except, oops, "this is a book, and the est experience cannot result from reading any book")—"est was like a laser; it took all the light in the rainbow and condensed it into a single beam." Because, "At the moment that you 'get' the training, you know what the *self* really is."

But how did it work? Don't ask, Hargrove insisted. The attempt would forge but one more illusion. "It's like a photograph of an ice-cream cone. If you try to describe its flavor in terms of the form, data, or processes with which it is made, it is not likely that you will be understood. The only way to experience the satisfaction of eating an ice cream cone is to eat one."

Some derided est as a crypto-fascist cult of personality. Others thought it was a CIA front designed to drain Americans of their will to make political change, by convincing them that social problems were all in their heads. But est's evangelists included, in addition to John Denver and Jerry Rubin, such respectable figures as Buzz Aldrin, the second man to walk on the moon, and Watergate's John Dean. Not everyone among the 100,000 who had already taken est (there was a waiting list of 12,000) agreed that it helped them. But as two social scientists discovered when they researched a book published two years later, called *Snapping,* on America's "epidemic of sudden personality change," it was hard to find anyone who would say est hadn't helped him. For as all good con men knew, no one wants to admit to having been conned.

They found one person harmed by the program who was willing to talk, a middle-aged, college-educated divorcée desperate for meaning now that her kids had grown—a description she shared with Sara Jane Moore, whose preferred route to redemption had led her to the attempted assassination of Gerald Ford. The woman they interviewed tried TM and saw "glimpses of what it would be like to live on a different level"—until that rosy glow faded, and she discovered "encounter groups" and learned for the first time "what it was like to be close with another woman"—until that wore off and she tried est, which she almost abandoned after the first weekend produced shooting pains in her legs: "If I hadn't paid two hundred dollars I wouldn't have gone back." After the second weekend, though, she believed herself to have been cured of her arthritis, and was left in a state of ecstasy that lasted the week—until she suffered a dissociative breakdown, her first experience of mental illness in her life, then a manic episode in which, first, she couldn't stop dancing, and then began babbling in a made-up language until she ended up in a mental hospital for the first of two stints. The first scientific study of est confirmed that several such cases had presented themselves to hospital psychiatric wards. When *Snapping*'s authors found her she was "was still anxious—and still searching. . . . 'I've been experiencing some discomfort and tension in my body and I've been waking up with feelings of anger,'" she said. But she would not give up. Next she was going to try acupuncture.

Maybe, just maybe, *that* would work. Or maybe it would not. Maybe she could read one of the offerings from the *Psychology Today* Book Club: *How to Be Your Own Best Friend; How to Be Awake and Alive; The You That Could Be; You Are Not Alone; Creative Coping; Getting It Together; New Mind, New Body.* A blunt fact of the Bicentennial year: this bottomless supply of Americans for whom the basic institutions of society had failed so badly that they longed to become different people entirely. Which made it a hell of a time for a nationwide birthday party.

MAYBE IT WOULD BE EASIER TO CELEBRATE, SOME SILENT POLITICAL force seemed to dictate, if people could only forget what they had learned about their nation over the past two years. Like what they had learned about the CIA. So it was that the first big news story of 1976 did not concern the excesses of secret intelligence. It concerned the alleged excesses of those seeking to contain such intelligence.

Inside the Company: CIA Diary, the memoir of spy-turned-radical Philip Agee, had come out in the United States in July despite government attempts to suppress it. In the book a twelve-year veteran of the agency working South and Central America chronicled his growing realization "that millions of people all over the world had been killed or had their lives destroyed by the C.I.A. and the institutions it supports"—as when he was ordered to fabricate out of whole cloth a report "establishing" Communist infiltration of the Uruguayan government. He turned the document over to a police chief, then heard screams of torture coming from the next room, from one of the supposed infiltrators he'd named in his report—the dawn of his apostasy. At the end of the story he explained that he "wrote it as a contribution to socialist revolution." A handy appendix revealed the CIA's hand in as many front groups as he could recollect, complete with proper names; an analyst thus concluded in the agency's classified review of the book that he was the CIA's "first real defector in the classic sense of the word."

By the end of 1975, from his hideout in Communist Cuba, Agee had joined a movement. Anti-CIA activists, including the novelist Norman Mailer, published a magazine, *counterspy,* and Agee wrote in the winter issue, "The most effective and important systematic effort to counter the CIA that can be undertaken right now [is] the identification, exposure, and neutralization of its people working abroad." One of the people Agee's article thus identified was Richard Welch, whom he fingered as the station chief in Lima, Peru.

By then, however, Welch was not the station chief in Lima. He was the station chief in Athens—where, two days before Christmas, he was ambushed and assassinated by masked men outside his home.

Agee's article was apparently merely coincidental to the attack—and in Athens, Welch's cover had already, independently, been blown (as, in fact, it had been in Lima), not least because he lived in a house whose CIA identity was a matter of public knowledge (an Athens newspaper had already identified him as the station chief along with publishing his address and phone number). The work being done by the House and Senate select committees on intelligence had even less to do with it. No matter. Just as Richard Nixon had exploited the POWs—"to restore the military to its proper position"—a complex story was cynically distorted into a crystalline patriotic allegory. Immediately, presidential press secretary Ron Nessen insinuated that the intelligence committees' carelessness was responsible for the tragedy. The plane bearing Welch's coffin was timed to touch down at Andrews Air Force Base for live coverage on the morning news, and was greeted by an Air Force honor guard. (Just like Nixon used to do, President Ford had the plane circle for fifteen minutes to get the timing just right.) *Time* had already eulogized Welch as a "scholar, wit, athlete, spy"—a regular James Bond.

"Never before," Daniel Schorr announced on the CBS news on December 30, "had a fallen secret agent come home as such a public hero," and it was only the beginning. Over the protests of the Veterans of Foreign Wars, Welch's burial broke military protocol by taking place at Arlington Cemetery, starring more honor guards, dozens of flags, the flower of the American defense establishment, and the very same horse-drawn caisson used for the interment of President Kennedy. President Ford escorted the veiled widow at the funeral. Conservative senators demanded congressional investigations; Frank Church's conservative Idaho colleague James McClure toured the state to lecture Church's constituents, saying that such murders were just what happened when liberals get control of congressional investigations. Hundreds of telegrams and letters—some consisting of the single word "Murderer!"—flooded across his transom from angry citizens alert to the administration's insinuations that it all must have been the congressional investigators' fault. A supposedly adversarial press piled on, too, especially the *Washington Post*. In 1974 it brought down a president; now it ran thirteen stories in the week after Welch's death following the administration line, and an editorial labeling the death "[t]he entirely predictable result of the disclosure tactics chosen by certain American critics of the agency." Wrote the *Post*'s admirably independent ombudsman, Charles Seib, "The press was used to publicize what in its broad effect was an attack on itself."

Church, thrown on the defensive, called for criminal sanctions against those who identified secret agents. And it all happened just as the committees were drawing up their final reports and recommendations regarding intelligence reform—terrified, now, that further disclosure of *any* secret would discredit the entirety of their work.

That was no accident. It was an orchestrated campaign—one taking advantage, not of the committees' recklessness (in fact they were remarkably free from leaks) but of their very deliberateness, the months of quiet investigation and backroom executive sessions that provided an opening for White House propaganda to utterly blindside these earnest tribunes of reform. A high-ranking CIA official named David Atlee Phillips, who had specialized in propaganda, quit the agency to organize retirees into an apparently independent lobby. Though they were in the shadowlands of espionage, nothing could be so straightforward. They actually worked in harness with a president who used words like "crippling" and "dismantling" in his every reference to the intelligence investigations. And by the time the White House began all but dancing on Richard Welch's grave, Phillips's six-hundred-member Association of Retired Intelligence Officers was ready to wave the bloody shirt on the president's behalf—in speeches, letters to the editor, and canned op-eds from a forty-eight-page guide, all pressing the message that the expansion of the suspicious circles into the sacred precincts of intelligence was putting the nation's heroes in danger. Hardly three weeks after Welch's death, the momentum for reining in the intelligence community was at all but a standstill—just as planned. "REVAMPING THE CIA: EASIER SAID THAN DONE," as the *New York Times* headlined on January 18. And so, after one more turn of the screw, it would turn out to be.

SENATOR CHURCH HAD HOPED BY THEN TO BE OTHERWISE OCCUPIED. IT was the presidential primary season. This spook-chasing that he had hoped would become his royal road to front-runner status had proved interminable: his committee had missed the first deadline—September 1, 1975—before the public hearings had even begun; it now looked as though the final report would not be out before spring, and so he hadn't been able to prepare a presidential campaign at all. Now he just hoped to enter sometime early in spring in a late-breaking swoop, win a few primaries, and present himself as the consensus rescuer should the convention in New York City descend into unmanageable rancor. That didn't seem at all unlikely, given that by then there were nine Democratic candidates prowling New Hampshire, and eleven who on January 2 drew the first matching checks from the federal Treasury—but not a clear front-runner in the bunch.

First, however, would come Iowa, a new historical development: it became important only in 1972, when George McGovern's campaign realized that a victory in this small, unrepresentative state's January precinct caucuses—an event merely preliminary to the state convention that actually selected delegates, 47 out of the convention total of 3,008—could be held up as a signal that their man was the season's front-runner, giving them momentum going into the much more firmly established primary in the Granite State. And so now, the political sages watched the Hawkeye State like hawks—for instance, eight days before the January 19 precinct caucuses, when Senator Birch Bayh of Indiana won a straw poll in Sioux City with the help of the state's established labor unions, which pundits said put him ahead.

That, however, was pretty much the last that was heard of Birch Bayh in 1976. Which said a hell of a lot about 1976.

On paper, no one looked better than Bayh. Young and handsome, but also experienced and accomplished, the blue-eyed forty-eight-year-old third-term liberal was elected to the Indiana house of representatives at age twenty-four and moved up to become the youngest speaker of the house in state history. In the U.S. Senate he became a star on the Judiciary Committee, where he shepherded two constitutional amendments to passage, a record (the twenty-fifth, establishing an orderly process of presidential succession, and the twenty-sixth, enfranchising eighteen-year-olds); passed a landmark law opening up interscholastic athletic competition to women; and won two straight historic fights against President Nixon's attempts to put Southern segregationists on the Supreme Court (and thus raced to the top of Nixon's Enemies List). He'd explored a presidential run in 1972, which seasoned him; since then he'd been laboring mightily on the Equal Rights Amendment, a measure enormously popular with the Democratic base.

But he also lived in Washington. Which was Gomorrah. And worked in the United States Capitol—which was where mountebanks and blackguard lawyers held court.

The last three elected presidents—JFK, LBJ, and Nixon—had all once been senators, and it had once been the conventional wisdom that the next several presidents were likely to be former senators, too. That was then. Now Birch Bayh was forced to make a virtue of necessity. His dimpled face, set plain against a stark bare backdrop, stared straight into the camera in his TV commercial:

"To listen to the other candidates, none of them are politicians. Even the ones who've held public office say they're not politicians. Well, I'm Birch Bayh—and I'm a politician. It took a good politician to stop Nixon's plan to pack the Supreme Court. And it's going to take a good politician to break up the big oil companies and get jobs for unemployed workers and hold food prices in line. The question isn't whether you're a politician, but what kind of politician makes a good president."

Following the fashion, he promised "moral leadership." His most prominent endorser—though traditional endorsements were unfashionable, too, this year—was Watergate prosecutor Archie Cox, who said, "Trust in government is not to be had for the asking, nor is it gained by the politics of image. It begins with the trust that those who govern repose in people. Only a man of character can restore that confidence. Only a man of openness and courage can bring us together."

Which was all well and good. But senators are forced to take stands, or are at least forced to appear to take stands—they leave paper trails. Bayh would have preferred to avoid one on, say, an ideological mine-field like abortion. But as chairman of the Senate judiciary subcommittee on constitutional amendments, overseeing hearings the previous fall on the proposed "human life" amendment, he came under vituperative criticism from women's groups who claimed he was giving more time to "pro-life" than "pro-choice" forces—like the four Catholic cardinals who, in one heavily publicized session, testified that abortions should be illegal even to save the life of the mother. "The life of a woman, they argued," according to Hearst columnist Marianne Means, "is not as important as the life of a fetus, which might turn out to be a male." After the subcommittee voted not to let the amendment proceed, pro-lifers— "There is no special interest lobby as well-organized, as single minded, or as vicious to its opponents as the anti-abortion activists," Means wrote—accused the Catholic senator, who had never declared himself publicly one way or the other on the issue, of tanking it on purpose. He soon found himself barraged by seven thousand letters from angry constituents on both sides—this just on the eve of entering the race, which he did too late, given the new campaign finance laws limiting individual donors to one thousand dollars, advantaging those who'd been plugging away the longest.

And so, a week after finishing a distant third in the New Hampshire primary, this onetime logical front-runner permanently suspended his campaign.

A GOVERNOR WHO HAD BEEN OUT OF OFFICE SEVERAL YEARS SEEMED TO be in a more propitious position—for instance, for avoiding those ideological minefields.

On New Year's Day, Jimmy Carter arrived for his latest visit to Iowa in a blizzard and windchill of forty-five below zero, suffering from an intestinal bug. His personal aide stepped off the plane in Des Moines having left his coat in Atlanta, where it was 103 degrees. They made their way to an event in the basement of the Holy Spirit Church in the little town of Creston. After his speech, Carter was asked by a concerned churchwoman about a recent interview he had given to a Catholic publication in which he said he personally considered abortion "morally wrong," but also opposed a constitutional amendment to ban it, but *did* support a "national statute" of some sort. In Creston, a reporter heard him tell the woman, speaking "even more softly than usual," that "under certain circumstances" he would support a state abortion ban like the one passed in his native Georgia, even though that had been struck down by the U.S. Supreme Court. He then issued a clarifying statement insisting that he had "had a very consistent position on abortion for several years," encompassing his personal opposition, his opposition to both the proposed constitutional amendment banning all abortions and another that would give states the right to ban it themselves, and endorsing more wider availability "of contraception devices for those who believe in their use" and of "[b]etter adoption procedures to minimize abortion." Which was even more confusing. It was then that the comedian Pat Paulsen began telling the joke about how officials wanted to put Jimmy Carter on Mount Rushmore. "But they didn't have room for two faces."

But voters, apparently, did not agree. "Ambiguous though it was," Evans and Novak soon were reporting, "Carter's reply gave pro-life forces more than they get from other major Democratic contenders here," and "also explains the growing outrage among Carter's famous opponents here over the little peanut farmer from Plains, Georgia, out-sharking them by winning anti-abortion liberals." Leave the jokes to the cynics. In Iowa, Jimmy Carter—always *Jimmy* Carter, never *James*—was playing beautifully. He was just the sort of antipolitician in whom people clearly longed to believe. The reasons seemed far more spiritual than political—and were revealed far better by the dreamscape of popular culture than by the mundane world of polls or public policy.

There was a curious little movie that came out the previous summer, the summer of *Jaws*, which cineasts adored but the public avoided. Brilliant, yes, but difficult: a sort of scattered, discursive allegory for a national mood buried a bit too far beneath the surface of the national consciousness to make it a simple thing to explain. The picture, called *Nashville*, was directed by Robert Altman. It began with the perambulations of a sound truck for presidential candidate Hal Philip Walker, blaring aphorisms, folksy but vague:

"I'm often confronted with the statement, 'I don't want to get mixed up in politics. . . . I can't do anything about it anyway.' We *can* do something about it"—

(In the background, a billboard reading "The Bank," dilapidated, like American capitalism itself.)

"When you pay more for an automobile than it cost Columbus to take his entire voyage to the New World"—

And from there, a random, unmotivated cut to an apparently entirely unrelated scene—Altman's method throughout the whole film. A country star named Haven Hamilton (a haven and a Founding Father) is recording a soppy Bicentennial anthem, somehow simultaneously brashly jingoistic and apologetic—more or less like the nation it was celebrating, these days: "We must be doing something right to last two hundred years."

Cue melodramatic timpani roll.

A pretty female BBC reporter is on the scene, kicked out of the studio, finding her way to another in which a white singer played by Lily Tomlin is recording a song with a black gospel choir. Cut back to Haven Hamilton, berating a hippie musician for his long hair. Another country star, Barbara Jean, receives a hero's welcome at the Nashville airport. The sound truck happens by: "When the government begins to ask the citizens to swallow the camel, it's time to do some accounting." Comes a hip young stud on a Harley-Davidson, played by Jeff Goldblum. A drill team in blue sequins and batons. A waifish hippie, played by Shelley Duvall. A rock band. A soldier. (He's asked, "Did you kill anybody this week?") A black man. A good ol' boy campaign manager.

"Congress is run by lawyers . . . and you wonder what's wrong with Congress."

"I don't vote for anybody for president."

A huge pileup on the expressway, all these random, unrelated people suddenly thrown together in the same space, the same situation, wandering randomly, wandering like the pilgrims in Chaucer's Canterbury Tales or the animals leaving Noah's Ark, but wandering toward which destination, or surviving what flood, it was never made clear. A mysterious man with a violin case, popping up in scene after scene. A bluegrass band playing at a bar; a John F. Kennedy poster, people waving a Confederate flag. A song floated throughout the soundtrack: "It don't worry me. . . . "

In a voice-over, the real-life newsman Howard K. Smith narrates Hal Philip Walker's unlikely story. He gave a commencement address that made him a national sensation—with bromides like "Have you stood on a high and windy hill and heard the acorns drop and roll? Have you walked along the valley beside the brook, walked alone and remembered? Does Christmas smell like oranges to you?"—then won three presidential primaries in a row, and was about to win a fourth, here in Tennessee.

Two and a half hours pass onscreen. This motley assemblage unites once more, apparently by chance, at a rally for Walker at the curious replica of the Greek Parthenon that Nashville ("the Athens of the South") built for the 1897 World's Fair: the red-white-and-blue bunting everywhere, the brass bands, the glad-handers, patriotic songs, masses of security men looking around nervously—and the man with the violin case. The viewer knows how this ends. A flag ripples. Shots ring out.

Haven Hamilton takes control: "Y'all take it easy now. This isn't Dallas, it's Nashville. They can't do this to us here in Nashville! Let's show them what we're made of. Come on, everybody, sing! Somebody, sing!" And they, all of them, gospel choir, rock band, country band, sing: "*It don't worry me. . . .*" The camera pulls back to take in the entire scene, a rippling flag, a Walker for President sign, then up to the heavens, longingly.

Nashville: you could pick through the various runes and try to make them signify something coherent, but the incoherence felt like *the point*—but an incoherence, be that as it is may, that is *shared.* That somehow ends with this shambling, variegated community *redeemed,* as one. Like a nation—our nation, our confused, ambivalent, longing nation, looking for meaning in the Bicentennial year, looking for meaning, finding none, but insisting on meaning nonetheless. *All in it together.*

And maybe that redemption could come from the old bloody South: Sam Ervin's South, Howard Baker's South—the South of the men who redeemed the nation from the wicked Nixon.

The presidential candidate was never pictured. What he looked like was entirely left to the viewer's imagination. Nor was his proposed "replacement," what it actually might consist of in practical political terms, ever described. Both were left as absences—voids into which voters could project their very desire.

Maybe he looked like James Earl Carter.

HE WAS BORN IN A TOWN OF 550 SOULS, PLAINS, GEORGIA, IN 1924, A FEW miles south of the cemetery that housed the first Carter to settle those parts, born in 1798. "My life on the farm during the Great Depression more nearly resembled farm life of fully 2,000 years ago than farm life today," his campaign memoir proclaimed: bricks heated on a fire to keep people warm at night and only the breezes to keep them cool; an outdoor privy and a hand pump for water, heated on the woodstove when it came time for the luxury of a warm bath; hand-cranked clippers to cut the hair of both humans and mules. An extraordinary, demanding, hardworking, conservative, civic-minded father—first director of the local Rural Electrification Administration office, when "Jimmy" turned thirteen; an extraordinarily brave, independent-minded mother, a nurse (actually more of a community doctor) who defiantly insisted on treating black people the same way she treated whites and was famous or infamous as the most liberal woman in the county.

The farm was the center of a civilization—"Mr. Earl's" civilization. Crops to grow, harvest, and market; livestock to raise—but also meat to cure, sugar to grind into juice and boil into syrup, timber to hew, lard to render. There was a blacksmith shop; a tannery; a general store with staples and products of the Carters' own manufacture: stuffed sausage, sweet milk separated into its component parts, butter, pickled pig's feet, wool blankets. The store was the lifeline for the twenty-five black families whose wage labor drove the machine, and who had a little village of their own, called Archery, with their own African Methodist Episcopal church, and whose children played on terms of equality alongside Jimmy and his brother Billy and sisters Gloria and Ruth— except for certain social conventions that had to be hewed to, and never questioned. ("We never went to the same church or school. . . . We did not sit together on the two-car diesel train that could be flagged down in Archery.") They all worked together on terms of equality, too, starting at 4 A.M., when the whole community was awoken by the clang of the bell. The mules had to be rounded up by lantern light; "cotton had to be picked by hand; peanuts were pulled out from the ground, the dirt shaken off them, and then stacked on poles to dry; the whole round of work that lasted until sundown. Later in the year the corn leaves were pulled, the fodder tied into little bundles and stuck on top of the corn stalk to dry." Autumn meant harvesting corn and velvet beans ("the stinging fuzz made this one of the most difficult of all farm jobs"). Winter meant slaughtering hogs and cutting cane and felling and stacking timber—"and then the annual cycle would repeat itself." But he still had enough energy, starting when he was but five years old, to regularly walk two miles down the railroad tracks to sell boiled peanuts on his own in the streets of Plains. Twice a year, a medicine show came to visit, but that's not where he spent his newfound riches. The boy his father nicknamed "Hotshot" bought five bales of cotton when he was nine years old and kept it in his father's storehouses until the price rose from five to eighteen cents; out of the proceeds he bought five houses and collected $16.50 a month from the tenants in rent until he left home for the U.S. Naval Academy. (He'd been so ambitious to go to school in Annapolis that he'd rolled his feet on Coca-Cola bottles for hours every week when he read that flat arches disqualified applicants.)

Perhaps it was the intricate, self-sufficient complexity of this miniature world into which his father initiated him that gave Carter his preternatural confidence. It had been more than three years earlier when he told his mother he intended to run for president. "President of what?" she earnestly responded.

She was not alone. "Jimmy who?" was the question in Washington; the first time Carter traveled to Iowa the only people who showed up for a reception scheduled at a Des Moines hotel were the candidate, his longtime press secretary Jody Powell, their local organizer—and just three Iowans. They had ordered enough food to serve two hundred. At least, Carter later joked to journalist Martin Schram, the embarrassment was easy to contain: "There weren't any newspeople there to cover the event." Although it had to be said that this was in February 1975—far, far earlier than any other candidate had bothered to campaign in Iowa before, even George McGovern, who also had made it his strategy to try to get the press to report "surprise" strong showings in Iowa and New Hampshire as momentum to catapult him into later contests.

Carter had, by then, a national profile of sorts, at least among political junkies. The day after his failed bid for the Democratic nomination for governor in 1966 he announced his campaign for 1970, exhibiting the indefatigable energy for which he would become known. He claimed to have made approximately 1.5 speeches per day in the intervening four years and to have shaken six hundred thousand hands, or half the voting population of Georgia. He prevailed; his January 1971 inaugural speech—"I say to you quite frankly the time for racial discrimination is over"—got his face on the May 31, 1971, cover of *Time* ("Dixie Whistles a Different Tune"). In his campaign book he wrote with surprising frankness about his experience, as a mere second-year governor, of meeting the 1972 Democratic presidential prospects, and Nelson Rockefeller, and Richard Nixon, and Spiro Agnew. He wasn't impressed. He began "to realize that the president is just a human being. . . . I lost my feeling of awe about presidents." That summer he joined the movement to stop George McGovern, and delivered a nominating speech for Scoop Jackson at the convention; that November, his aide and confidant Hamilton Jordan wrote a ninety-page strategy memo on how he might *become* president, and another aide moved to Washington, D.C., to open a Carter beachhead. Carter traveled to Latin America, then Europe and Israel, and joined David Rockefeller's Trilateral Commission, a sort of study club for the internationalist foreign policy elite, mingling with the likes of cofounder Zbigniew Brzezinski, a foreign policy mandarin under Kennedy and Johnson with whom he established a rapport. He started showing up in the news, picking fights with Richard Nixon (Nixon was "conspiring with major oil companies to increase bottle gas prices by as much as 410 percent"). And he began hogging the TV networks' cameras so adamantly—he made himself conspicuously present at every milestone in Hank Aaron's home-run chase, and even made a cameo on the game show *What's My Line* (no one knew who he was)— that a Nixon-loving letter writer to the *Atlanta Constitution* referred to him as "the carping-peanut-brain self-serving public image builder, Jimmy Carter."

And, while doing so, he was folksy. Always, he was folksy.

He hit the road for the DNC as chairman of its congressional campaign effort in 1974. "It scared us in the beginning, not being from Washington," the staffer he traveled with that year later related to Richard Reeves, in one of the many where-did-Jimmy-Carter-come-from profiles that began appearing week in and week out. "But in most of the campaigns we concentrated on, we were dealing with non-incumbents, and almost all of them benefitted from being able to joke about Washington or take some licks against what was happening there"—and Carter's staffers were among the first to realize that Watergate might make it an *advantage* not to be an incumbent, for the first time in political history.

Just to make sure, though, they commissioned a poll. Its central question was "People say a member of Congress should be preferred as a presidential candidate because of broad foreign policy experience. Others say a governor should be preferred because of experience running things. Which make sense to you?" "Governor" won, by a ratio of three to two. Carter began, too, his practice of staying in ordinary citizens' homes; the Carter camp didn't know anyone else and was on a shoestring. But necessity soon became a virtue: it was folksy, and useful for establishing a national network of volunteers. Ted Sorensen, who had been JFK's speechwriter and was now a Carter supporter, pointed out: "How can you vote against someone that slept on your couch?"

The notion of a savior from Dixie was in the political air, too—especially one without the racist baggage of George Corley Wallace. The Democrats' first "mini-convention" in November 1974, in Kansas City (where, in keeping with the nation's new longing for nostalgic innocence, the delegates made constant pilgrimages to the Harry Truman Library), was noisy with Southern drawls trying to affect a presidential air: Lloyd Bentsen of Texas, Dale Bumpers of Arkansas, Terry Sanford of North Carolina, George Wallace, Robert Byrd.

But only one of them, who had officially announced his presidential campaign way back in December 1974, was already establishing his beachhead in Iowa.

The standard tactic was to persuade the biggest name you could find to head your statewide organizations. But this was impossible when your national name recognition was only 2 percent. Virtue of necessity: having any well-known figurehead would only pigeonhole the candidate with the ideology of that person. So Carter's staff put together a twenty-member "Iowa Carter for President Steering Committee" instead, a geographical and ideological smorgasbord—which automatically granted them twenty well-dispersed field offices. It also provided a plethora of local knowledge—for instance, that Democrats in the Sioux City area might appreciate the gesture, for his campaign's opening banquet, of honoring a nearly blind old woman named Marie Jahn, who thirty-eight years earlier had become the first female officeholder in the state, in her little town of Le Mars, population 8,895. The event, on February 26, 1975, was the first of Carter's unprecedented twenty-one campaign visits to the state—the first of many times perhaps (for the event was too far below the radar for any record of it to have been preserved) in which he drawled winsomely that, since his assets were already listed in his campaign literature, he would instead note his liabilities:

"I'm not a lawyer." (A good laugh line.)

"I'm not from Washington." (That one was even better.)

"I'm not a member of Congress." (Bull's-eye.)

"I've *never* been part of the national government." That line, a reporter, said "drew so much laughter that he couldn't continue.

The post-Watergate riffs came easily, a product of biography. There was his first run for elected office, for state senator, in 1962, as an independent against a corrupt courthouse machine. The fraud against him was blatant and extravagant: votes by dead men recorded; entire precincts that supposedly voted in alphabetical order; stuffed—overstuffed—ballot boxes. (One district of 333 voters recorded 431 votes; voters who watched their ballots torn up in front of them were threatened with death should they report what they saw.) The review board ruling upon his challenge did not even hear witnesses. With no small courage, Carter appealed. He won. His longing for political service was like something evangelical. (When his pastor asked him why in the world he wanted to enter a profession so sordid as politics, he retorted, "How would you like to be the pastor of a church with eighty thousand members?") The gospel of good government would be his ministry: he was the only legislator to read every bill, and his proudest accomplishments as governor (he spoke of these as if he'd cured a dread disease) were technocratic feats like reducing the number of state departments and agencies from three hundred to twenty and, he said, cutting administrative costs in half.

A technocrat, yes, but one who got to the statehouse telling stories like a populist: "My chief opponent"—Carl Sanders, a pillar of the Georgia political establishment whom his campaign labeled "Cufflink Carl"—"got almost all the endorsements," Carter later recollected. "We made an issue of the big shots standing between him and the people, and eventually almost every endorsement (which he avidly sought) cost him votes in some fashion or another."

His presidential campaign autobiography, *Why Not the Best*, was published by a Christian press. (On the back cover: "Other Inspiring Broadman Books . . . *Modern Stories of Inspiration*, Compiled by Bill Stephens. True stories of people who have encountered God.") He liked to quote a line from a favorite sermon: "If you were arrested for being a Christian, would there be enough evidence to convict you?" He also liked to dwell on a word that almost never appeared in political speeches: *love*. How we needed "to bind our people together to work in harmony and love one another." How federal employees should begin each workweek with "their hearts full of love." How we needed a government "as filled with love as are the American people." His Iowa state chair, Tom Whitney, related how he chose this dark horse: "we spent two hours talking about Christ. For a moment we shared a concept and a thought process that we both believe is a fundamental need in our society. Which was the concept of love—love thy neighbor. We explored the 'I am Third' process in which God is first, family and friends second, and I am third. This nation needs a totally loving president."

Carter made personal contact his campaign's fetish. Driving between Ames, Iowa, and Marshalltown, he happened upon a farm. He stopped. The proprietor, named Fred McClain, was not home. Carter took a piece of campaign stationery, wrote out a note, and stuck it in the front door: he was sorry he had missed him. And Mr. McClain had a "beautiful farm." It was signed, "Jimmy."

A physics professor at Iowa State, Charles Hammer, a Democratic chairman for his congressional district who had worked for the antiwar liberals Eugene McCarthy and George McGovern, had been impressed watching "Jimmy" field tough questions at a town meeting. He got a call: "This is Jimmy Carter. I'd like you to be on the state campaign committee." Hammer said he would have to think about it. The governor gave the professor a phone number, a date, and a time to call him back. The professor called him at the appointed time to announce he'd decided to take him up on the offer. He expected a campaign office on the other end of the line, but Mrs. Carter answered the phone instead. At their Plains, Georgia, home. He was shocked, though not as shocked as when Rosalynn Carter said, "Hello, Charles. How's Hazel"—his wife. And that "Rosalynn"—first names only—had recalled Hazel telling her she had a brother in Michigan, and asked for her brother's address so Jimmy could write him a note. "He always sent handwritten notes," another Carter watcher marveled. "He wrote them to anyone. He'd get all the names at the meeting and he'd go to Powell, who usually followed his boss around, noting names and addresses of people Carter met at gatherings. And he'd write them."

In the normal course of modern politics, in a time when more and more politicians sold themselves via the cold, impersonal media of direct mail and TV, this stuff was about as strange as est. But it worked: not, of course, merely on the objects of this unusual attention, but on the reporters who wrote about how it was unprecedented.

There was an annual Jefferson-Jackson fund-raising dinner in Des Moines, held in October, attended by thousands of Iowa Democrats. "We figured," Jody Powell later recollected, "that somebody'd take a straw poll or something like that." And indeed, the *Des Moines Register* did, though no campaign had ever thought to make anything out of it before. The Carter machine, though, already humming, decided to make this a test of its organization. The other candidates showed up, caring only to polish their after-dinner speeches. Only Carter showed up with an entire armada. In the parking lot volunteers did "visibility" work, chanting and singing Carter songs, holding up Carter signs. Inside his steering committee worked the aisles like convention floor whips. Their candidate got 23 percent of the votes; Hubert Humphrey was second, but with only 12 percent; Bayh was third with 10; other supposedly marquee candidates—Sargent Shriver; Congressman Morris "Mo" Udall of Arizona; Fred Harris, a former liberal senator from Oklahoma who had served as chairman of the Democratic Committee—brought up the rear. Jody Powell, meanwhile, had casually tipped off reporters: "the *Register* had a poll that was worth looking at." The *New York Times* bit—and ran the following headline the next morning: "CARTER APPEARS TO HOLD A SOLID LEAD IN IOWA AS THE CAMPAIGN'S FIRST TEST APPROACHES." Birch Bayh had finally entered the race only three days earlier; George Wallace would not enter for another two weeks. "Sometimes," an aide told a reporter just around them, "I think we're the only people trying to win this nomination."

Seven weeks later Carter was profiled in the *New York Times Magazine*—"Peanut Farmer for President." The article was packaged on the cover with a drawing of Carter as a country boy in straw hat and overalls, and inside, with a portrait of the candidate as a smiling seven-year-old boy, another of him playing barefoot, a steely one of him as an Annapolis midshipman, and one captioned, "Peanut farmer, 1975" (he wasn't really a peanut farmer; he owned a peanut warehousing business). The writer was a novelist named Patrick Anderson, who had ghostwritten Jeb Magruder's new memoir, *An American Life*. He had asked to profile Carter after the editors had proposed to him Daniel Patrick Moynihan or Nelson Rockefeller. He described the Georgian as "a soft-spoken, thoughtful, likable man, an introspective man who enjoys the songs of Bob Dylan, the poems of Dylan Thomas, and the writing of James Agee, William Faulkner, John McPhee, and Reinhold Niebuhr," and who "stubbornly defied segregation in his hometown of Plains."

The piece was reported out of Florida, another key early state where Carter's organizing had been early and intense. Anderson followed him pressing flesh at a resort town, charming locals with a joke at President Ford's expense that reporters could soon recite by heart, about how *he* would respond when asked how he would feel if his daughter had a premarital affair: "I told him that Mrs. Carter and I would be deeply hurt and shocked and disappointed . . . because our daughter is only seven years old." Anderson went on to puff Carter as a kind of ideological Superman: a get-tough conservative (pledging "all-out economic" war in the event of another oil embargo before he would let America be "brought to her knees again"), a compassionate liberal, and an organizational genius, who, forced to agree not to fire any employees to get his reorganization bill passed, still managed to reduce the state's payroll "from an annual increase of 14 to 2 percent."

Most of all, he depicted a soothing counterimage to the dreaded George C. Wallace, that toxic perennial of presidential campaign seasons going back all the way to 1964. Wallace's moment in the national spotlight began the same year Carter entered the Georgia state legislature, when Wallace proclaimed in his 1963 inaugural address, "segregation now, segregation tomorrow, segregation forever," then "stood in the schoolhouse door" to keep the University of Alabama from being integrated. Each of the three times he subsequently ran for president he softened his image more; however, each time that only terrified liberals some more: maybe this was the year he'd prove palatable enough to the masses to *win*, and the demonic energies released in places like South Boston and Kanawha County, West Virginia, would ride roughshod over the nation. Wallace entered this year's race on Veterans Day, November 11. He was making his biggest stand in Florida. And it was in Florida, the *New York Times Magazine* reported, that Carter handled a "tanned, ponytailed, fortyish, and mad as hell" woman at a campaign event with near-heroic aplomb. "What are you gonna do about those welfare cases who don't want to work?" she demanded. "The ones who've already bankrupted New York City and Detroit and Washington, D.C?"

"I'm glad you asked that," said Carter, the very soul of reason. "I think the first thing we have to do is to separate those who can work from those who can't."

"They don't want to work," the lady protested. "I've talked to people on welfare who *enjoy* it!"

"Well, the statistics show that only about 10 percent of the people on welfare are able to work," Carter said. "The rest are children or mothers or handicapped or . . ."

"I don't believe that," the blonde cried.

"Well, perhaps you'd better believe your statistics and I'll believe mine," Carter said, and began to outline his finely canted position on welfare, which was that the system should be simplified, that some sort of national minimum income should be provided, that able-bodied recipients should be offered training jobs—and be denied benefits if they refuse a job—and that those welfare recipients who can't work should be treated with compassion and respect.

"But they don't want to work!" the blonde persisted, as people began to shush her and mutter that she was drunk. Carter patiently soldiered on, reasonably, liberally—but, somehow, also conservatively, too. He spoke both of his compassion for those on welfare, and of his insistence on putting them to work, for example in one of 136 day-care centers for the mentally retarded that were staffed by welfare mothers. Anderson, the *Times* reporter: "Down at my end of the bar, I scribbled in my notebook: 'Good—stubborn—stuck to his guns.' But at the same time I was wondering if any man could hope to defeat George Wallace in Florida advocating 'compassion and respect' for welfare recipients."

Anderson clearly hoped Carter would defeat Wallace. He went on to describe Carter's other heroic acts of racial reconciliation: his repeated stands for racial integration in Plains, even upon pain of a boycott of his business; his insistence on running in 1970 as a "pro–civil rights" candidate (though Anderson noted that "many conservatives seemingly chose to disbelieve him, or to see him as a lesser evil to the known 'liberalism' of Sanders"). Anderson later noted that some among "the Eastern liberals for whom reading the Sunday *New York Times* is a religious experience" told him that it was his article that turned them on to Carter.

The article went on, eloquently, about the soul of the Southerner's "Replacement Party"–style appeal: "Carter's pitch is more idealistic than ideological. He says that America is drifting, that people are ashamed of their government, and that all he wants is to see America with a government 'as idealistic, as decent, as competent, as compassionate, as good as its people.' He closes almost every speech by saying earnestly that he would never tell a lie or duck an issue just to be president—a piety that makes some journalists groan aloud, but that apparently impresses many listeners."

One of those impressed listeners, it turned out, was the reporter, Patrick Anderson, who soon joined the Carter campaign as a speechwriter.

Another Carter panegyric, in what one of Carter's anguished competitors, Mo Udall, called the "incredible flow of press starting with that silly poll in Iowa," appeared on January 16 on page A1 of the *Washington Post*. It introduced the political class to some members of his homespun family: his mother, Lillian, "a remarkable woman of broad interests who went to India as a Peace Corps volunteer nurse 10 years ago, at age 67"; his steely wife, Rosalynn, daughter of a mechanic father and a mother who still worked at the post office, and who some said wanted the presidency worse than he did.

But the *Post* also dwelled on that preternatural confidence. It reported him working for zoning laws in Plains to control commercial development and souvenir sales for "when I am president," his conversations with reporters about "my inaugural address," and programs planned for "the first year of my administration." It noted, too, a certain contempt for the very calling he had chosen for his lifework. It quoted one of his former supporters in the state legislature: "Jimmy never learned the three guiding rules of politics—reward your friends, punish your enemies, and then make up with your enemies." Another critic, who insisted on anonymity, called him abrasive, unfeeling, ruthless— "and totally egocentric." And another: "Politicians don't like him because he doesn't like them."

Ah, but that was the point: all the usual résumé lines that boosted candidates in every previous campaign in history—experienced, connections, institutionally savvy—could only hurt you in the first presidential election after Watergate.

An interviewer asked Carter how he had hit on these themes, so unusual for a presidential campaign in any other year: trust, integrity, openness, *love*. He replied, "All Democratic candidates—congressional, governors—have available to us polls showing broad thematic studies. The polls showed us the post-Vietnam feeling, the feeling of exclusion, the embarrassment at lower ethical standards, at Washington. Those were available."

This was an interesting answer. It spoke to the man's arrogance: *everyone had access to this information, but I was the only one with the wit to listen*. The candid moment also revealed a snag in the very story line: what does sincerity mean if it is chosen as deliberate strategy?

And besides, the other candidates *had* listened to such poll messages.

It was the zeitgeist; how could they avoid it? There was Birch Bayh's "moral leadership" pledge (and a biographical film in which he sifted a lump of dirt: "I come off a farm in a little place called Shirkieville . . ."). There was George Wallace, whose entire national political appeal had always been built on projecting a homespun, anti-Washington image. When Frank Church finally got his candidacy on line he featured slogans like "For Old-Fashioned Honesty: Church for President," and "In 1976 vote for the man who saved us from 1984." Fred Harris, a former liberal senator from Oklahoma who had served as chairman of the Democratic National Committee, would apologize to crowds for having been "part of the mess"—and told friends, "I spent five lousy years kissing their asses in Washington before I figured out it didn't mean anything." Mo Udall foregrounded his upbringing in a town with but ninety-three souls, and his campaign materials pushed his "integrity"— so much so that at a fortnightly on-the-record breakfast for Washington bureau chiefs, columnists, and reporters one of them asked, "Are you prick enough to be president?" The eight-term congressman, whose memoir was titled *Too Funny to Be President,* responded with a joke whose punch line involved the candidate riding a horse in a parade. The owner insisted it was a mare but the politician said it must be a stallion: "I can distinctly remember riding through the streets and hearing people say, look at the prick on that big white horse."

Political pricks on big white horses were in such bad odor in 1976 that, as one political handicapper put it, "this year, negatives are positives." And for now, Jimmy Carter was playing that game the best of them all. The thirty-five thousand Democratic activists raised their hands in their precinct caucuses on January 19, the same day that Gerald Ford delivered his second State of the Union address. "Uncommitted" won: who wanted to commit to a *politician?* But among those willing to stake themselves on one, it was James Earl Carter who prevailed. The next morning he was featured on the *Today* show, the *CBS Morning News,* and *Good Morning America.* That night, Walter Cronkite said Iowans had spoken, "and for the Democrats, what they said was Jimmy Carter."

Yet how much that could possibly mean for the long haul was up in the air. When William Safire ran his New Year's Day "1976 Office Pool" column, question three read, "The Democratic ticket will be (a) Jackson-Brown (b) Bayh-Carey (c) Humphrey-Carter (d) Kennedy-Bentsen"—four senators being almost the only choices on offer. Antipolitics sounded all well and good. But how could someone running against Washington win the support it took among the powerful to *get* to Washington?

CHAPTER TWENTY-FIVE

"Not the Candidate of Kooks"

TWELVE MONTHS EARLIER, THE PRESIDENT ORATED BEFORE THE JOINT session of Congress, "The state of the union is not good." Indubitably, that still was the case. But this was an election year. And the Bicentennial year. Surely different rhetoric was called for. And so in this year's State of the Union speech it arrived: "In man's long, upward march from savagery and slavery, throughout the nearly 2,000 years of the Christian calendar, the nearly 6,000 years of Jewish reckoning, there have been many deep, terrifying valleys," but also one example that "shines forth of a people uniting to produce abundance and to share the good life fairly and with freedom. One union holds out the promise of justice and opportunity for every citizen. That union is the United States of America."

He said, "In the recent past," Americans "sometimes forgot the sound principles that guided us throughout our history. . . . We thought we could transform the country through massive national programs. . . . Too often they only made things worse." And so he proposed transferring $10 billion from the federal government down to the states so they could take more control of administering the Medicaid program themselves; matching every dollar in slowed growth in the federal budget with a dollar in tax cuts; a tightening of welfare eligibility and "long-overdue reform of the scandal-riddled food stamp program"; more funds for federal prisons and longer sentences for drug offenders; a defense budget increase; a cap on the pay for federal workers. He proposed a bill for catastrophic health coverage for seniors but said we "cannot realistically afford federally dictated national health insurance." The controlling trope was "common sense," and "new realism" was the headline phrase.

He was fighting for his political life against Ronald Reagan. More and more, he sounded like Ronald Reagan.

And in New Hampshire, his campaign strategists had arrived at a deviously brilliant strategy: that Reagan the antitax crusader was going to raise their taxes.

New Hampshire was a haven of antitax absolutists. It had no state income tax and no state sales tax—and all gubernatorial candidates had to sign a pledge never to propose if they wanted to live to see another political day. That was courtesy of William Loeb, publisher of the only newspaper with a statewide reach, the *Manchester Union-Leader,* a Reagan booster and passionate foe of the man he called in his front-page editorials "Jerry the Jerk."

Reagan had spent December at his ranch, resting and, his campaign staff said, "studying the issues." He arrived in the Granite State on January 2 with a clever gimmick borrowed from Richard Nixon's campaign in 1968: "citizens' press conferences," which let ordinary voters question the candidate, thus giving the appearance of post-Watergate transparency, while at the same time excluding experienced reporters from pressing him, thus actually limiting it. Handicappers were giving Reagan an edge to win the February 24 primary in the most conservative state in the union outside the South. The citizens, however, did not cooperate— once the Ford staffers sprang their clever trap.

It came of Reagan's ignored speech to the Chicago Executives Club back in September, in which he argued that "a systematic transfer of authority and resources to the states" would save the federal government $90 billion. Campaign chiefs Bo Callaway and Stuart Spencer circulated a memo to reporters pointing out that for states to administer such programs they'd need to fund such administration, too. The memo included a column criticizing the speech by, of all people, Pat Buchanan. And it laid out back-of-the-envelope calculations that in a place like New Hampshire this would require $13 million in new revenue—and itemized how many libraries, fire trucks, sidewalks, and police equipment would have to be scrapped to raise the funds. Barring, of course—as Spencer said in a press conference in the state capital just prior to the landing of Reagan's chartered 727—"the specter of new and higher taxes as the price of Reagan's folly." Soon that was all anyone in New Hampshire wanted to discuss.

"The people of New Hampshire, I understand, are worried that I have some devious plot to impose the sales or income tax on them," Reagan immediately was forced to respond before the Moultonborough, New Hampshire, Lions Club. "Believe me, I have no such intention and I don't think there is any danger that New Hampshire is getting one." Lyn Nofziger said, "We're not backing away from the concept at all.

We think this is a good Republican approach." Another key spokesman, Governor Meldrim Thomson, promptly contradicted that: "I think that's probably a program which he will be thinking of taking a second thought on."

The Associated Press: "In three days of campaigning in New Hampshire . . . Reagan was bombarded at each stop with questions on his plan to cut the federal budget by turning over responsibility for most federal welfare and social service programs to the states. . . . Reagan has avoided saying specifically how the states would be expected to fund the programs." An editorial from the *Nashua Telegraph:* "The man who wants Republicans in New Hampshire to turn their backs on President Ford ought to answer specifically the welter of questions his $90 billion panacea has provoked. . . . [A] scheme that would require Congress to rewrite or undo 40 years of laws and that would require each of the state governments to cope with the trauma of writing new laws and enacting new or increased taxes . . . never will be simple—10,000 press agents shouting to the contrary notwithstanding." They pointed to his promise that nothing in the plan required new state taxes, and savaged his campaign's signature gimmick. "Since Mr. Reagan is protected in his 'citizen press conferences' from follow-up questions, that supposedly settles that. That settles nothing. We don't give a hoot about Mr. Reagan's sweet intentions; we want to know about the bitter consequences of his scheme." Bo Callaway got a nice pop in the media saying Reagan wanted to "throw old people in the snow"; Mary McGrory pivoted off that to write, "It could be that the people of New Hampshire are as flinty as their reputation and would endorse the idea of throwing old people out in the snow and be glad that Ronald Reagan had made cold-heartedness respectable." And so at that, after eleven days of floundering that resulted in the national press deploying Reagan's words to insult the electorate of New Hampshire itself, he took it all back: "I guess I made a mistake in the speech I made in Chicago last September," he said in Illinois, which was voting next after Florida, and claimed he had devised a technical fix that preserved the heart of the proposal while cushioning states from the financial consequences; how it would do this, though, he could not quite explain. At that his Illinois communications director reversed the reversal and said, "I think he's sorry he ever alluded to the $90 billion figure at all."

Disarray: precisely why this attack was so clever. It neutralized Reagan's biggest strength—his reputation as a tax cutter—and engaged his biggest weakness: explaining complicated ideas on the fly, setting up a story line that Reagan was lazy and stupid and couldn't lead without guidance from unseen hands. A poll of Republican state chairmen found 90 percent of the respondents worried about the "Reagan problem," that he had "simplistic approaches," "no depth in federal government administration," and "no experience in foreign affairs."

THE REAGAN CAMPAIGN WAS A CHICKEN WITH ITS HEAD CUT OFF, BUT Ford had problems of his own. He had won the conservative New Hampshire senator Norris Cotton to his side, a Pyrrhic victory: Cotton told the press that he preferred Reagan's ideology, and that Ford had "a bad organization." A Supreme Court decision validated California's unique "winner-take-all" primary system, which meant whichever candidate won 51 percent or more when the Golden State voted in June— Ronald Reagan, almost certainly—would harvest 167 delegates out of the 1,130 needed to nominate. On January 24 the columnist George Will reported that Mac Mathias, "a member of the GOP's embattled Corregidor Garrison of liberals," bored with "what he calls 'the Ford-Reagan monologue,'" was still thinking of making the race. President Ford swooped down upon New Hampshire in Air Force One to dazzle the locals, but, as Reagan's twenty-eight-year-old campaign aide David Keene observed to a reporter, kidding on the square, "Every time Ford flies out for another speech, we gain two percent in the polls."

Then there was the headache of managing the foreign policy of a global power during a political campaign, a damned-if-he-did-damned-if-he-didn't conundrum if there ever was one.

On January 15 it was announced that Henry Kissinger would soon jet off to Moscow to resume the next Strategic Arms Limitation Talks ("SALT II"), one week after the Harris poll found that Americans, by 44 to 25 percent, preferred Reagan's hard line on the Soviets over détente, and nine days before Evans and Novak commented that the new, conservative secretary of defense, Donald Rumsfeld, still had enough muscle with the White House to kill SALT II altogether. "We must not face a future in which we can no longer help our friends, such as Angola, even in limited and carefully controlled ways," Ford had said in the State of the Union address, something executives in less suspicious times, when presidents managed foreign policy on their own, would never need mention. But now Congress was debating whether to permanently kill aid to the MPLA, our faction in the African nation's civil war. Kissinger told Ford, "We're living in a nihilistic nightmare."

Another thing Ford made sure to touch upon in his State of the Union address was "[t]he crippling of our foreign intelligence services," which he claimed "increases the danger of American involvement in direct armed conflict. Our adversaries are encouraged to attempt new adventures . . . the United States stands blindfolded and hobbled."

In case rhetoric wasn't enough to do the trick, nor the public ceremonies surrounding the death of the CIA's Richard Welch, the day after the State of the Union message, and two days after the *Times*' article "Revamping the CIA: Easier Said Than Done," another opportunity presented itself to discredit Congress's intelligence investigations and hobble serious CIA reform once and for all. Daniel Schorr of CBS began reporting choice bits from a leaked copy of the final report of Otis Pike's House Select Committee on Intelligence, which report was scheduled for publication at the end of January. So did the *New York Times:* stuff like how an Italian neofascist general got paid $800,000 for services rendered to the CIA, stuff which had nothing to do with violating national security but everything to do with exposing agency incompetence and immorality. Be that as it may. Following so close on Philip Agee's call to out CIA agents and the death of Richard Welch, the very fact of "unauthorized leaks" provided the opening. Ron Nessen said they raised "serious questions about how classified material can be handled by Congress when national security is at stake." The CIA said genial, bow-tied Otis Pike might soon be responsible for the blood of more dead CIA agents. An intimidated liberal Democratic congressman begged Pike to find out who had passed on copies to the press. Pike replied, "What do you recommend, precisely? Lie detector tests to members of Congress?"

Maybe. The report, drafted by an Ervin Committee veteran, was, for a government document, a literary masterpiece, and hard-hitting as hell. It opened with seventy pages savaging the Ford administration's lack of cooperation with Congress's work, and continued, more aggressively than Pike's public hearings—which had been plenty aggressive themselves, far more so than Senator Church's—by documenting the CIA's wasteful spending (where it could figure out *what* it spent), its bald failures at prediction, its abuses of civil liberties, and its blanket indifference that any of this might pose a problem. The report singled out Henry Kissinger for his "passion for secrecy" and statements "at variance with facts"; it detailed a number of failed covert actions—not naming countries, but with plenty of identifying details to make things obvious enough for those who cared to infer. For instance, how the Nixon administration encouraged the Kurdish minority in Iraq to revolt, then abandoned these Kurds when the shah of Iran objected. "Even in the context of covert action," it concluded concerning *that* one, "ours was a cynical exercise."

And something about all this seemed to spook cowed congressmen—who soon were voting to neuter themselves.

The House Rules Committee approved, by nine votes to seven, a measure to suppress publication of the report unless President Ford approved its contents. The full House debated whether to accept or reject the recommendation. Those against argued that the "classification" system itself violated the canons of checks and balances that were supposed to be the foundation of the republic. A moderate Republican from Colorado pointed out that the executive branch was desperate to serve as judge and jury in the very case in which it was the plaintiff. The report definitively established that the CIA had committed "despicable, detestable acts," but "we are being castigated by those who perpetrate the acts and classify them." Pike made a demystifying point: that each of these things called "secrets," hemmed around with such sacralizing foofaraw and talked about as if they were blatant instructions to our enemies on how to defeat us, "is a fact or opinion to which some bureaucrat has applied a rubber stamp." A Democrat from suburban Chicago drove home the bottom line: "If we are not a coequal branch of this government, if we are not equal to the President and the Supreme Court, then let the CIA write this report; let the President write this report; and we ought to fold our tent and go home."

To no avail. On January 29, the full House, led by conservatives, voted by a ratio of two to one to suppress the very report it had authorized and which took a year of work and several hundred thousand dollars to produce.

It all was too much for Daniel Schorr. He took his copy to his bosses at CBS: "We owe it to history to publish it," he said. They disagreed. He went to a nonprofit organization called the Reporters Committee for Freedom of the Press to see if it could find a publishing house that might be interested, with the proceeds perhaps going to its group. It could not. Finally the alternative weekly the *Village Voice* agreed to publish the report, in a massive special issue, and since the Reporters Committee now controlled the document, the *Voice* made a contribution to the group. This set off a fierce backlash among the polite guardians of journalistic decorum; the *New York Times* editorialized that by "making the report available for cash," Daniel Schorr was guilty of "selling secrets." On ABC, anchor Sam Donaldson said, "There are those that argue that in an open society like ours nothing should be concealed from the public. Depending on who espouses it, that position is either cynical, or naive." He said "mature and rational citizens" understood this—but not, apparently, Daniel Schorr. Nor Schorr's bosses at CBS News, who suspended him, though local affiliates begged CBS brass to fire him.

The House Ethics Committee opened an investigation into who leaked the document to Schorr, who never coughed up his source; the committee ended up spending $350,000, interviewing four hundred witnesses, and coming up with, yes, one leaker, Democratic congressman Les Aspin of Wisconsin—but he had leaked it to the *CIA*, not the press, as a political favor. In desultory fashion, Congress went on to debate intelligence reform through spring. But the version it settled upon was the weakest possible: two standing House and Senate select committees to exercise the same sort of lukewarm oversight as preceded the investigations, with no reform of the CIA's charter.

It never became any kind of campaign issue; in public opinion polls slightly more citizens disapproved than approved of the Pike and Church committees, and a majority feared they'd harmed national security. Pike gave an interview that spring to the *New Republic.* He told interviewer Oriana Fallaci, "It took this investigation to convince me that I had always been told lies, to make me realize that I was tired of being told lies." And he explained why he thought the intelligence scandals hadn't achieved the public concern of Watergate—why the "Year of Intelligence" had failed. "Oh, they think it is better not to know. There are too many things that embarrass Americans in that report. You see, this country went through an awful trauma with Watergate. But, even then, all they were asked to believe was that their President had been a bad person. In this new situation they are asked much more; they are asked to believe that their country has been evil. And nobody wants to believe that." The CIA itself believed it had beaten the investigators: "Where is the legislation, the great piece of legislation, that was going to come out of the Church Committee hearings?" Richard Helms asked. "I haven't seen it." The radical journalist I. F. Stone even argued in the April 1, 1976, *New York Review of Books* that Helms and Company must have been the ones to leak the Pike Report to Daniel Schorr, the better to provoke the backlash against them. Schorr published a postmortem for the Year of Intelligence: "You peel off Watergate and you find the Plumbers and the Ellsberg break-in. Peel off the Plumbers and you find the 1970 Huston plan. . . . But what would you find if you peeled off another layer and had a close look at that secret world from which these things had been launched?"

Alas, no one cared much. Otis Pike had hoped to ride his inquiry to the Senate. So much for that. Lucy, the psychiatrist from *Peanuts,* explained why: "It used to be that a person could live isolated from the world's problems. Then it got to be that we all knew everything that was going on. The problem now is that we know everything about everything except what's going on. That's why you feel nervous.... Five cents, please!"

SUSPICIOUS TIMES. OR MAYBE NOT. AMERICA COULDN'T DECIDE. CAME the news on the last Wednesday in January that all major presidential candidates had released their medical records, the world apparently needing to know, for instance, about President Ford's hemorrhoid surgery and Senator Church's single testicle and Mo Udall's glass eye (a Washington joke suggested a Church/Udall ticket with the slogan "Keep your eye on the ball"). The next day, the House voted 323 to 99 against allowing any further money in the Defense Appropriations Bill to be spent in Angola. Ford replied, "They've lost their guts ... and I think they'll learn to regret [it]." The *Times*' Anthony Lewis said his "phrasing had the delicacy of Joe McCarthy." The day after that, the Supreme Court dialed back the major reforms the congressional culture of suspicion had wrought: the 1974 campaign finance law banning the buying off of political candidates. Giving money to a presidential candidate, the justices now said, was the same thing as speech.

Buckley v. Valeo said that Congress could, if it wished, rewrite the law to enforce the $1,000 limit on individual contributions—but only for candidates voluntarily accepting matching funds (as both Reagan and Ford had done, receiving their first federal welfare checks, as it were, on January 2, Reagan for $100,000 and Ford for $342,422). Until Congress rewrote the law, no matching funds could be disbursed. One of the conservatives who welcomed the news—in addition to Senator James Buckley, the plaintiff in the suit—was Irving Kristol, the neoconservative columnist. Before the year was out he published an impassioned essay in the *New York Times Magazine* called "Post-Watergate Morality: Too Good for Our Own Good?: The Reforms Aimed at Solving Today's Problems Are Likely to Constitute the Problems of Tomorrow," arguing that the kind of suspicion that produced the new campaign finance law was ruining the country. "Let me emphasize—in our post-Watergate atmosphere I had better emphasize—that I personally think bribery is a bad thing," he wrote. But the "spasmodic self-abuse" now in evidence, the "self-righteous moralism" and "vigilante-like passions with which the news media track down every sort of misdemeanor committed by officials," could only have baleful unintended consequences. It was the most coherent intellectual case so far for the Reaganite idea that suspicious circles were a very bad thing.

An unintended consequence of *Buckley v. Valeo* was that it advantaged conservatives. For it contained a loophole: independent groups could spend whatever they wanted, on behalf of whomever they wanted, as long as they didn't coordinate it with candidates who accepted matching funds. Groups, that is to say, like the New Right letterhead organizations braying about Eskimo cannibalism and the Nazi regime of genderless restrooms to be ushered in by the ERA. The more ideological the candidates were, the more this brave new campaign finance world would advantage them—and by the same token it would disadvantage moderates like Gerald Ford.

The surprise bonus didn't come a moment too soon. Those on the Reagan team were worried about an old problem: their candidate being dismissed as an extremist. They rejoiced when Governor Meldrim Thomson, the lunatic who wanted to issue nuclear weapons to the National Guard, surprised them by not asking to chair the campaign. They had managed to recruit instead New Hampshire's moderate Republican boss Hugh Gregg. "In getting Hugh Gregg," a Reagan manager said, "we were trying to establish we were not the candidate of the kooks." But the media, which had all but ignored him as a potential national force the previous year, were working overtime to establish that very proposition now that he was a presidential contender.

Call it the "*Bedtime for Bonzo* Problem." Garry Wills wrote in his newspaper column, "Reagan thinks he is being unfairly treated by the press, and he is probably right. It is unfair to expect accuracy or depth from him." Mike Royko referred to his "TV-anchorman face." The February *Harper's* featured "The Candidate from Disneyland," labeling him "Nixon without the savvy or self-pity, another pious boyhood pauper in whom God has confided the friendship of suntanned millionaires. Ronald Duck. That he should be regarded as a serious candidate for President is a shame and embarrassment for the country at large to swallow." More earnestly—and less dismissibly—Elizabeth Drew reported from the campaign plane, "Reagan is a dim figure. There is so much that we don't know about him. What is he doing with these public relations people as his key advisors? How does his own mind work? Is he a contrived figure? One cannot shake the idea that this is Ronald Reagan the movie actor. . . . His 'speeches' are actually sets of four-by-six-inch cards on which he has written paragraphs and anecdotes with a felt-tipped pen, and which he shuffles to give slight variations. His fund of knowledge seems to be made up largely of clippings—stories and polls he has come across that will make good material." But texts like these revealed more about their authors than they did about the candidate and his political prospects.

The media had said the same thing in 1966, when he won the Republican nomination for governor—and the "joke" had won the election nonetheless, as much because of their condescension as despite it. Reagan had learned what Nixon taught, that being despised by the patronizing Eastern Establishment swells, who pontificated knowingly about the "country at large," was nothing but a recommendation to the middle-class, middle-American "silent majority" who felt patronized by the same people themselves. He wasn't a "dim figure" to them. They knew, because they had listened to his radio broadcasts and read the proliferating numbers of conservative movement newspaper columnists from which he so frequently drew his material. Apparently you had to be a *New Yorker* writer not to understand what he was all about.

And you apparently had to be a *Washington Star* reporter not to know about another frequent Reagan reference from his broadcasts over the previous year—which, a February 9 feature in the *Star* reported, had "hit a nerve" with his New Hampshire audiences. The piece began:

WASHINGTON, Feb. 14—Few people realize it, but Linda Taylor, a 47-year-old Chicago welfare recipient, has became a major campaign issue in the New Hampshire Republican Primary.

Former Gov. Ronald Reagan of California has referred to her at nearly every stop, using her as part of his "citizens' press conference" format.

"There's a woman in Chicago," the Republican candidate said recently to an audience in Gilford, N.H., during his free-swinging attack on welfare abuses. "She has 80 names, 30 addresses, 12 Social Security cards, and is collecting veterans' benefits on four non-existing deceased husbands." He added:

"And she's collecting Social Security on her cards. She's got Medicaid, getting food stamps, and she is collecting welfare under each of her names. Her tax-free cash income alone is over $150,000."

Neither that reporter nor the *New York Times* editors who reprinted his piece on February 15 seemed to know that Taylor had been the subject of scores of stories in the *Chicago Tribune* and other major newspapers since 1974 (indeed, the *Times* reported on her in December 1974); the *Trib* even had nickname for her, the "Welfare Queen." The *Washington Star* went on to patiently debunk the claim: she was being prosecuted for $8,000 in welfare fraud, not $150,000, though the prosecutor allowed that she may have made off with a greater amount. (The *Star* didn't point out that Reagan had no evidence to suggest her scams were typical, that using Taylor to cast aspersions on welfare as such was like citing the exploits of a notorious bank robber in order to argue we shouldn't have banks.)

The *Star* article went on to debunk other Reagan claims: "We lopped 400,000 off the welfare roles" (it was 232,070). In New York, "If you are a slum dweller, you can get an apartment with 11-foot ceilings, with a 20-foot balcony, a swimming pool and gymnasium, laundry room, and the rent begins at $113.20" (92 out of a total of 656 units in Taino Towers were six-bedroom apartments for large families; these had a high ceiling over only the kitchen and living room "to allow a space configuration that saves what would otherwise be wasted corridor space," and they went for around $450 a month; the pool, gym, and laundry room served 200,000 neighborhood residents). Social Security was "$2.5 trillion out of balance" (the chief actuary for the Social Security Administration explained that was only true "if the nation stopped producing new workers"). "No other country in the world puts so many taxes on business." ("According to tax experts, comparative taxation is a very difficult subject because it can be compared so many different ways.")

The same day there were also would-be embarrassing revelations about Reagan in the *Boston Globe* ("OIL, GAS DONATIONS FLOWING TO REAGAN") and the Scripps-Howard newspapers, which revived the story that he paid no taxes in 1971, after Ford released his own federal ($106,000 paid on an income of $250,000) and Michigan state ($9,123) tax returns. Neither made much of an impact. How could a guy who sounded as warmly populist as this—"I believe that the President of the United States is what Harry Truman called him: he is the people's lobbyist in Washington . . . the only one there who was elected for all the people," responsible for "taking problems over the heads of the Congress to the people"—be a money-lusting plutocrat?

The $90 million brouhaha having died down, he next faced a brouhaha over Social Security. Having promised in a Florida appearance to reverse the policy of denying benefits to retirees making more than $2,700, he was asked how in the world the country could afford it. He said the only reason we couldn't was that the Social Security funds "are not invested, as they could be invested, in the industrial might of America"—in the stock market, where they should be. Ford said that this was "back door socialism" and threatened the existence of Social Security itself. Reagan gave back as good as he got: "It is unconscionable," he said at a senior citizens' home in Manchester, "for whatever political purpose, for someone to frighten people who are dependent on Social Security into believing that something may interrupt their payments." He, on the other hand, was working to *preserve* their payments: "If Social Security were an insurance company, they'd be put in jail by now. . . . Government is not the answer to the problem; government *is* the problem."

He was now eligible for Social Security himself, having turned sixty-five on February 6; if he was elected there would be only one president who had been older—William Henry Harrison, who lasted a month in office before croaking. It did not show. The *Globe* described the "old Gipper" campaigning tirelessly, hatless and coatless, taking questions from all comers for upwards of an hour, "while the reporters and photographers slowly turned gray with fatigue and cold." (His handlers might have wanted him to play down his age, but he wasn't having any of it, telling crowds outside a fire station of the time he dreamed of becoming a fireman—"back when horses were still pulling the engines.")

Ford arrived to a modest turnout on a clear day at the Manchester airport for his first election outside Michigan in his life, and his first competitive campaign since the early 1950s. The stylistic contrast was striking: Ford looked stolid, plodding, square (his face, literally, looked square); his voice sounded simultaneously flat and forced, too slow then suddenly too fast, as if he had glue in his mouth. The ideological contrast, meanwhile, he deliberately obscured. The elite's media culture might still be liberal. ABC News, for instance, ran a rueful Valentine's Day report decrying "rampant nationalism" at the Winter Olympics in Innsbruck, Austria: a poignant narration of the games' decline from the original goal of the revived modern Olympics as not "just a place for people to win medals, nor certainly a place to demonstrate the superiority of one political system over another," but rather "a festival of life and sport," to something where "the sporting links between athletes from five continents seemed distressingly absent." Athletes and coaches skipped the recital of the Olympic oath, Peter Jennings ruefully intoned; American fans "seem to see hockey as an extension of the Cold War on ice." Republican primary voters in New Hampshire were different.

So, standing behind a podium bedecked with the presidential seal, Ford offered Reaganite utterances that the U.S. government couldn't have built a Model T for less than fifty thousand dollars. He added boasts that the unemployment rate had dropped from 8.3 to 7.8 percent, and demagogic promises to keep open the Portsmouth Naval Shipyard and widen coastal fishing boundaries—then said that "anybody to the right of me, Democrat or Republican, can't win a national election." He sent surrogates to dole out the tough stuff. Henry Kissinger said negotiations with China and the USSR were "too delicate, too important for world peace to be used for simply partisan sloganeering." A team including San Diego mayor Pete Wilson; treasury secretary William Simon; John Tower, the conservative senator; and Elliot Richardson, the Watergate hero, now commerce secretary, fanned out through New Hampshire for Ford. Wilson called Reagan "the worst governor in the history of the state." Richardson said the prospect of a Reagan presidency terrified him, and called his supporters "right-wing ultra conservatives." Reagan responded niftily to that: "I'm a little surprised by this statement about my so-called extremism," he said with a smile. "It does come rather strange because [Ford] tried on two different occasions to persuade me to accept any of several cabinet positions in his administration, and he did appoint me subsequently to his CIA investigating commission."

A reporter followed up: to dissuade you from running? "No," he chuckled. "I just thought he recognized my executive ability." An embarrassed Ford campaign was forced to confirm that what Reagan said about the cabinet offers was true.

The Granite State endured an infestation of hecklers. They came from an outfit called the People's Bicentennial Commission, whose chairman, Jeremy Rifkin, said "corporate America has conceived a Bicentennial plan to manipulate the mass psychology of an entire nation back into conformity with its vision of what American life should be," and whose sympathizer Douglas Dowd, a professor at Cornell, published a widely circulated Marxist interpretation of American economic history titled *The Twisted Dream*. "Now," Reagan had explained on the radio the previous October, "this group should not be confused with the official American Revolution Bicentennial Committee, though just to fuzz things up a bit the People's Bicentennial Commission did manage to squeeze some federal grant money out of some gullible bureaucrats to foster its effort to prove that the American Revolution was in reality a kissing cousin to Marxism and Leninism."

Ford handled them well enough. At the University of New Hampshire, before 3,500 people, a student in an ape suit, representing Ronald Reagan's most famous costar—not Bette Davis—asked the president a leading question about the abuses of big business. Ford, unruffled, said he couldn't understand one of the words, got him to repeat it, then answered the question. Reagan, though, veritably thrived in their presence—approaching them before they had a chance to approach him. "Don't let me get away with it," he told them. "Check me out. Don't let yourself be the sucker generation. Check out both sides of an issue. Don't let anyone indoctrinate you in or out of the question." Then he gave his side. He quoted Rifkin equating America's eighteenth-century revolutionaries with Mao, Lenin, Che. "Do you agree with that?"

Students at Dartmouth cheered.

"I'm disappointed. I don't associate those Americans with the genocide and the dungeon states created by Lenin and the others."

"He's good," said someone who was supposed to be protesting against him, admiringly.

Not that he stopped saying what some might consider to be kooky things—for instance, accusing the National Education Association, the teachers' union, of working for a "federal educational system" like the one he said had been a "road to disaster" once upon a time, in Germany: "They changed their academic system to suit the rule of the dictator who was in charge at that time. . . . Where they had a national school system . . . when [he] said burn the books, they burned the books." Or, speaking to a "ranch breakfast" at a Holiday Inn ballroom in Kankakee, Illinois, on February 13, "I happen to believe there was a divine plan in the settling of this land between the oceans." Even the skeptical Elizabeth Drew had to admit how good he sounded doing it. "He comes across as a pleasant man who understands why people are angry. . . . He talks to people's grievances, but he doesn't seem mean," she wrote; his was "a respectful mad, a decent American fedupness. . . . It is the same list that George Wallace and Spiro Agnew attacked. . . . But Reagan comes across as doing it in a much nicer way."

Ford, tacking right once more with an announcement that he'd newly support the death penalty for some crimes, suffered his usual blight of bad luck. His vice president humiliated him by announcing he would not rule out running himself if Ford were defeated in a few primaries. (Reagan came back with another nice quip: "If he chooses to run that's fine, but they've got twenty-seven candidates on the other side tied for last.") The man who made Ford president, Richard Nixon, humiliated him by reemerging in the news with the announcement from San Clemente that he would be making a return trip to China, just before the New Hampshire vote. (William Loeb ran a front-page editorial: LET THE RED CHINESE KEEP HIM.) In the week before the balloting, polls had them neck-and-neck. Mel Thomson went on *Meet the Press* and said Reagan would win the New Hampshire primary by 5 points. A Ford supporter said, "If people are apathetic and don't vote, Reagan wins because those goddamned Reagan people will vote no matter what."

"MR. GELINAS, I AM DICK DENNY FROM ATLANTA, GEORGIA, AND I AM here on behalf of my friend Jimmy Carter."

Of the twenty-seven Democrats tied for last place in New Hampshire—well, there were only nine, but who was counting—once more it was Carter who defined the terrain, and once more that was the product of sedulous organization. Since April he'd had a cadre of political guerrilla warriors living and working out of a drafty, tumble-down house in Manchester—"Camp Carter." That fall, they established the "Peanut Brigade," Hamilton Jordan's revision of a program from the 1970 governor's race in which natives of Carter's Sumter County fanned out across Georgia carrying scrolls with testimonials to their man's character and integrity. Gone national, the cadre brought some ninety-eight from the Peach State to the Granite State in a Southern Air-ways charter, ages fifteen to seventy-eight, including an air-conditioning contractor, a history professor, a grandmother of six, the retired dean of Georgia Southern College (he smoked a cigar), the wife of Lieutenant Governor Zell Miller, a rehabilitated drug addict, and Starlett Macken-dree, proprietor of Possum's Poke & Tote Shop in Albany, Georgia. Not to mention a complement from Carter's colorful family: Aunt Sissy, Cousin Hugh—and Ruth Carter Stapleton, the candidate's sister, proprietor of a faith-healing ministry, who in a story soon to become famous led her brother to a "born again" experience during a walk in the woods after his crushing 1966 loss in his first gubernatorial race. They arrived in New Hampshire on February 4 to subzero weather and three feet of snow, which made for splendid pictures on that evening's news when many threw snowballs for the first time in their lives.

The next morning, bundled up in boots and gloves and "'long Johns,' or thermal underwear"—as their Boswell, Harold Isaacs, de-scribed the novel garment in a 1977 book—they headed out, baffled by New England street numbers, 100 on one side of the street and 1700 on the other. They aimed to reach forty thousand voters—one-third of the state's Democrats—and reached a third of their goal in the first three days alone.

A retired college dean said: "We've got a mighty good man running for President from our state."

A housewife, teeth chattering so hard she could barely speak, was invited in for a cup of hot coffee and told by her host, "Bless your heart, we don't even go out in this weather ourselves."

Roy Wood, from Roswell, Georgia, won a vote from a little old lady who thought he was the plumber she'd called and who was so em-barrassed she invited him in for Greek wine: "They know we believe in him," he said of what the other outmatched campaigns derided as "peanut crackin' storm troopers" and "a group of carpetbaggers telling

New Hampshire to vote," and evidence—these opponents wished—that Carter didn't have enough local support to staff a campaign.

The Georgians returned home, and sent their own handwritten notes: to those they had met ("I liked your cute dog"; "I hope your boy is feeling better"), and those they had not ("Tim and Judy, Jimmy Carter did a great job straightening out Georgia," ran suggested language in the *Jimmy Carter Presidential Campaign—New Hampshire Campaign Manual* binder, in the section marked "Postcard Plan"; "I think he could do the same thing in Washington. I hope you'll support him on February 24")—six thousand letters in all.

Meanwhile, in the same way as with Reagan, now that Carter was plainly a serious contender the suspicious circles were taking a very hard look—and finding some very hard facts. In the *Village Voice* on February 9, the radical press critic Alexander Cockburn, in "The Truth About Jimmy Carter," tore apart his image as a post-Wallace racial reconciliationist. Cockburn printed a letter to a Southern woman, Mrs. Lena Dempsey, from the previous summer, in which Carter averred, "I have never had anything but the highest praise for Governor Wallace." And: "I think that you will find that Senator Jackson"—whose campaign strategy was to pick off Wallace's supporters by aping his antibusing stand—"and I are in close agreement on most issues." As to why he didn't support Wallace's presidential bid in 1972 as she wished, he told Mrs. Dempsey, "There are times when two men working toward the same end can accomplish more. I think you will find Governor Wallace understands this"—cynical stuff from a candidate whose commercials had him earnestly intoning, "I'll never tell a lie. I'll never avoid a controversial issue. . . . Watch television, listen to the radio. If I ever do any of those things, don't support me."

"Jimmy Carter's Pathetic Lies," which appeared a few days later in the March issue of *Harper's,* was considerably harsher.

There, journalist Steve Brill quoted the Georgia state archivist as saying the governor's staff "only sent me the speeches they wanted me to include"—not including, for example, a tribute delivered in 1970 for "George Wallace Appreciation Day" in Red Level, Georgia. In the piece, 1970 was a key year, the year of which Patrick Anderson gushed in the *New York Times Magazine* that Carter had run as a "pro–civil rights" candidate, even if "many conservatives seemingly chose to disbelieve him." They disbelieved him, Brill established, because Carter's campaign was fundamentally dishonest on the subject. A leaflet had circulated then, showing his opponent Carl Sanders getting champagne dumped on him by two black members of the Atlanta Hawks basketball team, of which Sanders was part owner. Carter denied any knowledge of the item. But Brill quoted a public relations man who worked for Carter's adman, Jerry Rafshoon, one of his closest friends and advisors: "We distributed the leaflet. It was prepared by Bill Pope, who was then Carter's press secretary. It was part of an operation we called 'the stink tank.'" He also reported that the Carter campaign financed and produced the radio commercials of a third candidate, a black lawyer, to dilute Sanders's support among blacks. And that his claim to have opened day-care centers for the retarded staffed by welfare mothers was bogus. ("There is no program," the deputy director of the state mental health division said. "No one has been taken off welfare and put in any mental health job.") He debunked Carter's claim to have produced a $116 million surplus in the budget (the state auditor told Brill the surplus had been $91 million when Carter came into office and $43 million when he left) and quoted Carter as deriding détente, like Ronald Reagan, and as supporting the death penalty, opposing the New York City bailout, and calling for the abolition of the corporate income tax.

Brill then cited the civil rights hero and Georgia state senator Julian Bond: "Jimmy Carter wouldn't be my first choice for president or even my fifth. The reason he gets such good press is that whenever the rest of the country thinks of Georgia, they think of Lester Maddox." Brill quoted the prominent New York liberal William vanden Heuvel, a confidant of the late Bobby Kennedy, who touted Carter as "someone who has stood with us on the right side in every fight that's been important to us over the last two decades." He quoted that in order to record his incredulity: why were so many liberals embracing Carter as though he was one of them?

It spoke to another of Carter's political gifts: being all things to all people. The *New York Times* recorded him in colloquy with a voter who wanted to know if he was a liberal, a conservative, or a centrist. He replied, "I don't like to categorize, I don't see myself as liberal or conservative or the like. I'm a farmer, you know. Now, you ask most farmers whether they are liberal or conservative, and they often say conservative. The same with businessmen. And I'm a businessman, too."

(He added, just in case he'd offended someone, "But that isn't to say all businessmen and farmers are conservative.")

It played off a favorite riff of his. As he wrote in his campaign autobiography, "I am a Southerner and an American. I am a farmer, an engineer, a father and husband, a Christian, a politician and former governor, a planner, a businessman, a nuclear physicist, a Naval officer, a canoeist, and, among other things, a lover of Bob Dylan's songs and

Dylan Thomas's poetry." But that all wasn't quite true, either: he was a warehouseman for other farmers, not really a farmer himself; not a nuclear physicist but a former member of Admiral Hyman Rickover's nuclear submarine corps who'd done a little bit of graduate work in engineering. In that autobiography he referred to what Northerners called the "Civil War" as the "War Between the States," a term that pandered to Southerners; asked by a young woman who his running mate might be, he replied, "I won't give you a name, but I'll tell you the qualities she'll have." To a group of schoolgirls who asked for his position on the Equal Rights Amendment, he said, through what would soon become his famous megawatt grin: "I can answer that in three words. I'm for it." The girls cheered; the candidate, complimented by a sympathetic reporter for his liberality, frowned and said: "Half those people probably oppose the ERA."

The anticynical cynic. And, as Steve Brill had documented, someone who got away with lies.

The consensus was that it couldn't last long. "He's trapped now that he's up front," observed the New Hampshire house's majority leader, chairman of the flailing Birch Bayh campaign. "He can't have it both ways if he wants to win. He's got to start answering the tough ones." But he did not. And still he kept winning recruits—among voters, and just as important, among the reporters who watched him do it with awe. He was all things to them, too.

Patrick Anderson, the *Times* writer, watched Carter give his standard speech to a Kiwanis meeting. Carter observed how Americans were "deeply wounded" by Vietnam, Watergate, inflation, recession. Then he would ask two questions: Could government be made to work again? And could it become a source of pride again? He answered them with the story of the time his towering naval commander, Admiral Rickover, interviewed him for the job as a nuclear submariner. The great man asked the young man if he had always done his best at the Naval Academy.

"I wanted to say yes. But I thought of all the times I'd read a novel or listened to classical records when I should have been studying. So I had to say, 'No sir, I didn't.'" The commander, the candidate told the Kiwanis crowd, answered him with a bark: "Why not the best?"

Wrote Anderson: "That, Carter concluded—and by then the room was hushed—was the question America must ask itself in 1976: *Why not the best?* ... It was corny and self-serving, but it worked. The Kiwanians leaped to their feet, applauding. I too was moved. Perhaps all of us, cynical novelists and Kiwanians alike, sometimes wish we had always been our best. Carter had touched his audience not with 'issues' but by tapping into emotions that were universal."

They yearned to believe. Reporters yearned to believe, too—like another *Village Voice* writer, the acerbic critic James Wolcott, who fell for Carter while watching him hang out in Atlanta with Bob Dylan's former backing group, the Band. ("Carter's association with Rickover quickly surfaced in all early campaign conversations with what he considered the 'conservative' press," Spiro Agnew's former press secretary, Vic Gold, now a columnist for the *Washingtonian,* soon observed. "Whenever, however, talking to younger, non-Establishment members of the media, he spoke of his admiration for Bob Dylan, Gregg Allman.") Wolcott tried on a hipper-than-thou cynicism at the top of his copy— "The media are ready to accept Carter's emergence as the presidential symbol of Southern enlightenment"—then dropped it, embarrassed by his own knowing New York ways. Carter had told the story, a familiar one, of the little room next to the governor's executive office where he would repair to pray during difficult moments. "I spent more time on my knees as a governor than all the rest of my life," Wolcott recorded Carter saying, then wrote, "I started to laugh, then looked around at the faces beaming approval and bit my lip." Manhattan rock-and-roll hipsters, too, yearned to believe. Wolcott concluded, referring to the club where a new genre called "punk rock" was just then emerging from the Bowery grime, "Could a CBGB neo-classicist like myself conceivably vote for Jimmy Carter? A tentative 10-4."

It was working. All of it was working. So Carter kept burbling Sunday school bromides, dropping Dylan references, biblical references, Rickover references, Reinhold Niebuhr references (the political editor of the *Atlanta Journal* said of his former governor, "He'll quote some obscure philosopher you never heard of quicker than a cat can scratch")—and, above all, straddling issues. On amnesty for draft evaders. (The journalist Martin Schram wrote of his position, "It is not an answer; it is an art form—carefully constructed so as to diffuse the emotions of the subject and come up with something for everyone. The shorthand of it is that he starts out by saying he is against amnesty, but he winds up saying he is for pardon. And he tells interviewers, when asked, that he thinks there is a difference, even though Webster's defines 'amnesty' as a 'general pardon.'" Schram quoted that answer. It went on for well over a hundred words—with lots and lots of ellipses.) Some sort of straddle on desegregation (it was wonderful; but "forced busing" was wrong). And on Angola, where on February 9 Soviet- and Cuban-backed forces took Huambo, formerly New Lisbon, capital of the forces backed by the United States. Mo Udall, point-blank, said, "President Ford and Secretary Kissinger want another Vietnam in Angola." Carter, all over the place, said that he was against military intervention "except in a clear-cut case of national defense," but that he didn't know what to do about Angola because the administration was keeping so much secret: nothing to offend anybody in that.

Udall was one of four liberals running seriously in New Hampshire. No wonder left field was so crowded: Warren Miller of the University of Michigan, one of the country's top political scientists, proclaimed the scientific conclusion: "Both parties would be wise to move their ideological centers of gravity in a liberal, left-of-center direction," given the emergence of a massive young "new left" coalition sure to soon form a more dominant force than the New Deal coalition Roosevelt crafted in the 1930s. And so there was Bayh (asked about Angola, he paused sadly, looked down, and said, "I don't know why we never learn," and mused about whether we had been "on the wrong side" in places like Vietnam). Sargent Shriver, former director of the War on Poverty and the Peace Corps, the husband of Kennedy's sister Eunice, tried, earnestly and ineffectually, to steal Carter's march ("decent and honest and truthful and fair—that represents what the American people are"). Fred Harris, a portly, booming populist whose motto was "The Issue Is Privilege," and who said the trouble with the War on Poverty was "that you can't really do something about poverty unless you're going to do something about the distribution of wealth and power." Milton Shapp, the Jewish governor of Pennsylvania and the only announced candidate not to qualify for matching funds, who handicappers thought was gunning for the vice presidential spot.

The talk everywhere was of drafting Hubert Humphrey, an old familiar name, as prophylactic against the anxieties of a new, unfamiliar time; people still talked up Ted Kennedy despite his repeated avowals, going back two years, that he wouldn't run. George Wallace was concentrating on Florida; Scoop Jackson, who was talked up as a frontrunner through much of 1975, and whose distinct calling cards were his Wallace-like loathing of busing and his Reagan-like passion for taking on the Soviets, had decided to give New Hampshire a pass, too.

That left only one candidate chasing through the snow to monopolize the devotion of every New Hampshire Democrat who was not in the market for a liberal. And guess which candidate was ahead?

IT WAS DAMNED HARD WORK. UDALL'S SCHEDULE FOR A SINGLE DAY LATE in January included twenty-three events in seven cities in two states, from six in the morning to nine fifteen at night. Walter Mondale, the Minnesota senator who distinguished himself on the Church Committee, asked why he'd dropped consideration of a bid way back in 1974, had said, "I found I did not have the overwhelming desire to be president which is essential to the kind of campaign that is required. . . . For one thing, I have no desire to spend the next two years sleeping in a different Holiday Inn every night." At least eight men at this point, Republican and Democrat, apparently still did have that overwhelming desire. The question, however, was how many, beyond the cadres of reporters who did it for a living, even cared.

"A DISENCHANTED ELECTORATE MAY STAY HOME IN DROVES," the *New York Times*' Christopher Lydon reported early in February: "In ivory towers and the back rooms of numerous campaign headquarters, distrust and disillusionment are found to be the essential attributes of the American citizenry in this Bicentennial year." He quoted one pollster, Peter Hart, who said that "the only majority we find is a cynical majority," and another who said that only 36 percent who voted in 1974 thought their votes "made a difference." Candidates like Carter, of course, built this insight into their very campaign plans. But Lydon quipped, "A practical question about such strategies is whether voters are alienated now from 'alienation campaigns.'" Fred Dutton, advisor to the presidential campaigns of Bobby Kennedy and George McGovern, noted how "people talk about 'somebody catching fire' in the primaries, but I say it will be a very small firecracker"—a nice Bicentennial image. "If people could have their way, they'd leave the presidency vacant for four years." Walter Dean Burnham, then of the Massachusetts Institute of Technology, explained why: "The gap between beliefs and actions, between traditional values and the way the system is organized, keeps growing. All the major components of society are in crisis."

As the newsmagazines began collecting portraits of the candidates for possible New Hampshire covers, evidence for that insight abounded. One Bicentennial letter to the editor: "Having been born and raised in Milwaukee, I have always been proud to call it my home. Now—after having been mugged, having had my home burglarized . . . I leave Milwaukee with no regrets." Another, from the *Baltimore Sun:* "Women cannot walk the streets in broad daylight or at night without the absolute fear of rape." From small-town Portsmouth, Ohio: "The people aren't safe anymore, which is what our own city is getting like. It isn't safe to walk the streets in broad daylight anymore." Three of General Electric's most experienced nuclear engineers quit publicly on February 2, proclaiming that atomic power—"a technological monster, and it is not clear who, if anyone, is in control," one called it in his resignation letter—ought to be banned. A few weeks later a plant safety coordinator at the Nuclear Regulatory Commission quit, saying his recommendations had been ignored and his bosses were evading their responsibility "by not telling the public and power licensing boards all the facts we know." In New York, an opportunistic B-movie distributor purchased an unreleased horror movie called *The Slaughter*, added an unrelated scene purporting to show the movie's director murdering two female crew members, and retitled it *Snuff*. Feminist protesters, ignoring the film critics who spotted a poorly produced hoax, claimed "the bodies of the two women were found sometime after the film was made." For who knew what nihilistic depravities weren't possible in this day and age?

More barbarities: The right-wing radio and TV evangelist Billy James Hargis denied true reports (the product of a "godless, left-wing pagan press") that he'd engaged in bisexual affairs with students at his American Christian College. The latest scandal from the days of Camelot pealed forth—that JFK had allegedly smoked pot with a prostitute. (According to a story in the *National Enquirer*, "at first JFK didn't seem to feel anything but then he began to laugh and told her: 'We're having a White House conference on narcotics here in two weeks.'" Two joints later, he told her, "No more, suppose the Russians did something now?") Although at that, it might not be long before prostitution was not illegal at all: in Philadelphia, 266 delegates to the American Bar Association's convention came within two votes of recommending the removal of all criminal penalties for exchanging sex for money.

New York magazine ran the first-person account of an officer in New York's 41st Police Precinct in the Bronx, the most violent in the city—"Fort Apache," the cops called it, a wasteland of buildings burned out by their owners for the insurance money, of junkies, of decent families barely holding on to their sanity. One thug fells another using, of all things, a bow and arrow—and then, when he's arrested, the perp's friends and family attack the precinct house with a hail of bricks. The cops have to barricade themselves inside. On another day a citizen stumbles through the front door shouting for help: "They threw my son off the roof. He's stuck between two buildings."

News was that the world as we know it might be ending, but that was an evergreen 1970s story; the latest twist was the suggestion by a deputy director of the National Agricultural Laboratory that global food supplies would soon be so scarce it was high time for folks to develop a taste for "locusts, termites, and other insects." "As the population explosion continues," Dean F. Gamble told the American Association for the Advancement of Science, "it may be impossible to continue to ignore these unexploited food resources." That article ran, in one newspaper, next to two pieces on developments in the latest financial scandal: multinational corporations including Exxon, Lockheed, Gulf, Northrop, and United Brands had admitted to funneling huge amounts of cash to foreign officials in exchange for their nations' business. The oil company Tenneco admitted to making payments "that may have been illegal to candidates and local officials in at least ten states." In Japan, a right-wing lobbyist was alleged to have been paid $7 million to promote sales of one company's aircraft; the same company was said to have bribed Italian cabinet ministers to get them to buy its F-104s and Hercules C-130s. The *Financial Times* of London complained about the bribery complaints: "Without it, business simply would not get done!"

Then there was Patty Hearst's trial for armed robbery—and the outbreak of terrorism that ensued.

The trial had opened January 15 in San Francisco with jury selection, the nation once more riveted by the bizarre tale (it had been impossible to find jurors who weren't familiar with the case). The argument for the defense, led by celebrity lawyer F. Lee Bailey, was "brainwashing": Bailey endeavored to convince these twelve citizens, including a retired Air Force colonel, an airline stewardess, a housewife, and a self-employed potter, that Patty, a woman living a "most ordinary life," had been so abused by her captors, so terrified that her safety was linked to theirs, that, his psychiatric witnesses would demonstrate, they had drained her of her free will, rendering her a virtual child—a "prisoner of war for twenty months," just like the Korean War POWs whom Chinese mind-control experts had convinced to defect from the United States. (This was now popularly known as the "Stockholm syndrome," after a 1973 case in which a hostage in a robbery at the Sveriges Kreditbank in Sweden had an affair with one of her captors and proclaimed all of them "very nice.") The prosecution said it was absurd to call a woman a victim who had posed with the machine gun with which she helped rob a bank, who had avidly proclaimed herself a revolutionary even after her arrest, who had taken one of the gang members for a lover. *Time* called it "The Battle over Patty's Brain," and interviewed the nation's beloved, heroic experts on the psychological effects of captivity—Vietnam War POWs—to pass judgment. They were withering: "If you were weak and really screwed up beforehand, you might go over," said a retired Air Force colonel held captive for seven and a half years.

It was announced that Patty would testify on February 13, and that she would reiterate her defense lawyer's horrifying story: her kidnapping by an armed gang; her confinement, blindfolded, in a narrow closet, which the supposed revolutionary hero Field Marshal Cinque would visit in order to sexually assault her. And then, in anticipation of that testimony, on February 12, a terrorist's time bomb went off at the famous Hearst Castle in San Simeon, California, causing $1 million in damage to priceless art and just missing fifty-three visitors touring the mansion, which was now a state park. There would be many more bombings, a group called the New World Liberation Front soon promised—unless a quarter of a million dollars was put into a defense fund for two of Patty's former Symbionese Liberation Army comrades who were still proud revolutionaries.

The bombing was meant to intimidate a traitor to the revolution. The revolutionaries were dead serious. In direct examination by F. Lee Bailey, Hearst explained why she had never tried to escape: because she had been convinced the FBI would assassinate her, then blame it on the SLA to make them unpalatable to the masses. Bailey asked her why, after one of her comrades had been apprehended for shoplifting at a sporting goods store, she had opened fire with a semiautomatic rifle. Because, she said, she had been told how under "codes of war," she herself would be killed if she had not.

The next week, on February 18, as the Peanut Brigade made their second, homestretch trip to New Hampshire amid mounds of snow twenty feet high, the prosecution team, led by a Nixon appointee and former Young Republicans president, began cross-examination with a surprise tactic: inquiring about the defendant's pre-capture reading list. Black revolutionary George Jackson's *Blood in My Eye.* A novel by a black feminist, Rita Mae Brown's *Rubyfruit Jungle* (she admitted it "impressed" her). One book on the Wobblies, another on guerrilla movements in Latin America; sociologist G. William Domhoff's *Who Rules America?* "So in essence," a prosecuting attorney asked, "you were—would it be a fair statement to say—quite interested in revolution, social change?"

She admitted that, yes, "I was interested in social changes."

The judge, in a controversial decision, had allowed a text she had narrated about her confinement—the "Tania Diaries," as they become known—into evidence. It included statements like "I believe that the term 'brainwashing' has meaning only when one is referring to the process which begins in the school system and is continued via the controlled media. . . . Like someone said in a letter to the *Berkeley Barb,* I've been brainwashed for twenty years, but it only took the SLA six weeks to straighten her out." The prosecutors grilled her about that—

and pointed out, for instance, that though she had given a detailed description of the SLA apartment, she had never mentioned any closet. They asked about the year she had spent on the lam; on that particular subject, she took the Fifth Amendment forty-two times.

The next week the defense and the prosecution both called expert psychiatric witnesses. One of the defense's witnesses cited the Air Force's "survival, evasion, resistance, and escape" (SERE) training, which caused such controversy when it had been revealed in the press in 1973: mock POW exercises in which, the psychiatrist explained, formerly tough trainees frequently developed "an uncommon terrible fear . . . out of all proportion to what the reality of their situation was," and henceforth became as obedient as children—comparing that to Hearst's reasons for not trying to escape and her desperate need for her captors' approval. ("Did I do right?" she'd asked in the speeding getaway van after she'd opened her semiautomatic on civilians, he pointed out.) He referred to the dissociation suffered by Nazi concentration camp survivors, who couldn't even remember the cruel things they'd done to survive, and the case of Jozsef Cardinal Mindszenty, who while under confinement by Communists in Hungary was tortured until he confessed to absurd crimes like planning a third world war.

The defense psychiatrists, in other words, offered up what was essentially a left-wing view of the self—as plastic, protean, moldable—and of human beings as the product of their environment, *not quite* responsible for their individual decisions and acts.

A prosecution psychiatrist, conversely, said Hearst had been an antiestablishment hellion all along—telling a nun to "go to hell," described by her boyfriend as possessing an "[u]nparalleled . . . capacity for sarcasm." Another said: "I think this was all *in* her. In a sense she was a member of the SLA in spirit, without knowing it, for a long, long time." They argued that she was *one of them:* not Patty Hearst, girl-victim, but "Tania," under the revolutionary nom de guerre she had chosen. Or at least a left-wing sympathizer. And wasn't that evidence enough?

This was a right-wing view, a Reaganite conception: good guys and bad guys. And that was the view that was generally being embraced in the court of public opinion—where, if the Patty Hearst trial was taking shape as a proxy war on the meaning of the 1960s and what it had done to our children, the prosecution was winning. The *Arizona Republic* (motto: "Where the Spirit of the Lord Is, There Is Liberty") editorialized that in the world according F. Lee Bailey, "Any felon could claim that psychological conditions in his home during childhood spawned criminal acts. A thief could claim that his family's pressure on him to acquire more belongings promoted stealing. The possibilities would be endless." The *Detroit Free Press* said an acquittal would rationalize any criminality committed by "the poor, or mistreated, or culturally deprived." The *Baltimore Sun* claimed the very "concept of responsibility that forms the core of criminal law was at stake," and a student wrote a letter to the *Denver Post* saying the stakes were even higher: if Patty went free, "It would show others that the United States is getting weaker while the underworld parties are getting stronger."

Expect more Patty Hearsts, the argument seemed to go: unless the nation got with the way Ronald Reagan saw the world.

ON FEBRUARY 21, REAGAN ARRIVED IN NEW HAMPSHIRE FOR ONE LAST visit, with the actors Lloyd Nolan and Jimmy Stewart in tow—and baffled and frustrated his managers by ordering his campaign plane to Illinois, where he made a nostalgic tour of his birthplace in Tampico, which housed an honorary Reagan for President national headquarters. (A *New York Times* reporter came up to Peter Hannaford: "Where's the manger, upstairs or down?") In the receiving line a local planted a wet kiss on his wife. ("He was hustled off by outraged aides while she searched for a Kleenex," a historian recorded. "And that part of Illinois was declared terra non grata on future trips." Reagan did not return until 1992.) The entourage made its way to the grammar school where he attended third grade, his classmates now reassembled for a photograph ("they all looked about twenty years older than Reagan"), then a big rally at Tampico High School (which he hadn't attended). "Oh my, such memories here," he said. "You could get bathed in a warm bath of nostalgia."

In front of his honorary national headquarters, he presented himself to the crowd balanced between two parked cars some thirty inches apart, one foot perched on each bumper, an extraordinarily graceful act, the long, lithe lines of his body stretched taut, the face of the aide behind him wrinkled with concern—but his own face radiating joy. Gerald Ford spent the days leading up to the balloting with far less grace. There was one of his campaign chairmen, Senator Norris Cotton, introducing a speech by Ronald Reagan, calling him "my kind of fellow." Then the thirty-seventh president of the United States, Richard Milhous Nixon, monopolized the front pages by landing in China, a development Ford had been sufficiently desperate to prevent that he considered impounding the plane the Chinese sent out to fetch him, as payment for confiscated American property from the revolution; he decided against it for fear it would be discovered and draw him even closer to the disgraced president in the public mind. Senator Richard Schweiker from Pennsylvania, a strong Ford supporter, said Nixon had timed his trip deliberately, to sabotage Ford and open the field for his friend John Connally.

On Election Day in New Hampshire, as a jury in San Francisco heard testimony that Patty Hearst had used marijuana and LSD, Ronald Reagan was in Illinois taking one more occasion to minimize Nixon's alleged sins. Asked if he would offer Nixon a cabinet post, he said he wouldn't be able to answer "until history itself . . . tells us more about the situation that saw his resignation . . . unless history gives us a different perspective on Watergate than the one we have now." He then said the investigations of the CIA were "one of the most irresponsible things that a Congress of the United State has ever done."

At midnight on February 24, the Californian was 1,500 votes ahead—too close for the papers to declare a winner, which they were able to do only the next day: 49.4 percent for Ford. 48 percent for Reagan—a difference of 1,587 votes. And though Reagan's chairman, Mel Thomson, had badly botched the expectations game with his prediction of a victory by 5 points, and though he leaked a poll that Evans and Novak reported that predicted him winning by 8, the very idea of coming within 1.5 percentage points of a president—Lyndon Johnson had won New Hampshire by 7.7 points over Eugene McCarthy in 1968, and was shocked enough to soon abdicate his reelection bid—was earth-shattering. Journalists watched "a senior White House official get wobbly from long swigs from a tumbler kept full of a dark amber liquid." Might Gerald Ford become the first incumbent president to be denied his party's nomination in a competitive race since Chester Alan Arthur in 1884? It now seemed like a possibility.

Another thing that was not supposed to be possible in these modern times: "Carter should understand," Vic Gold had written, "that no ex-Governor of Georgia can become a Presidential nominee, even if there weren't a nonrecognition factor to overcome. No. He can't because he is going up against a prejudice bigger than one John F. Kennedy faced in 1960. Much bigger, more complex: if Jesus Christ Himself returned to proclaim Roman Catholicism the Truth Faith, Christianity could survive; but if He spoke His parables in a Georgia accent, St. Patrick's would convert to a mosque within a week."

Think again. Sargent Shriver, brother-in-law of a sainted Democratic martyr: 8.7 percent. Fred Harris, senator and former Democratic National Committee chairman: 11.4. Birch Bayh, Mo Udall, congressmen and onetime projected front-runners, 16.2 and 23.9 percent, respectively. "Jimmy Who?": 29.4 percent, something like a landslide—although whether it was possible to count something as a landslide in this age of apathy was an open question. Only 32.5 percent of the Granite State's voting population voted, way down from 1972 and 1968, despite hard-fought contests in both parties, the sort reporters called, on instinct, "closely watched."

CHAPTER TWENTY-SIX

Born Again

GEORGE WALLACE WAS BESIDE HIMSELF.

"That little room where he said he spent all his time on his knees — that's where he made that little agreement with me that I wouldn't run delegates against his precinct delegates in Georgia, and he said he would support me provided I got three hundred or more delegates, and we shook hands." He was sitting with Elizabeth Drew, who did the best she could to capture his every Alabaman inflection for the *New Yorker*'s readers. From a bed next to his wheelchair, Wallace was waving a pile of yellowed news clippings dating back to 1972, ones he had preserved all these years, with that same smoldering resentment and righteous contempt that when unleashed from behind a podium made him one of the most powerful orators in the history of American politics.

He read a quote from Carter, a month before the 1972 Democratic convention, saying he could support a Humphrey-Wallace ticket. "And now he says, 'I never supported Wallace and I never would.'"

He railed about how he got three hundred delegates, the number Carter set as a threshold for supporting him — then how Carter turned around and gave the nominating speech for Scoop Jackson instead. "Maybe someday he'd like to take a polygraph test on that."

She asked him if his losses were hard. "His voice was soft as he replied. 'Oh, no, honey,' he said. 'Nothing's that tough. After you've been shot five times and suffered the loss of walking, what's a loss?' He paused, and then he continued, '[N]ot being able to walk. But I'm living. I thought I was going to die as soon I was hit. So losing a campaign — my goodness, that's not your life.'"

Though *Wallace* probably could not pass a polygraph test on that. Politics, power, was what he lived for. Reporters wondered whether his handlers, who loved him like a brother, didn't keep him campaigning in order to keep him alive. Wallace, after saying politics didn't matter when you've almost met your maker, kept railing about Carter. He imitated Carter: "I will never lie to you; I will never *misleeeeeeeed* you." He complained, "He can go out and shake hands and get on television. I can't do that. He was my friend when I was popular. He said he was for me when he thought I'd die. . . . Those other fellows criticize me, but they didn't use me." He repeated himself: "He talks about spending all that time on his *kneeeeees*. Well, I'm going to church tomorrow, but I don't go around talking about my religion."

She wrote, "Twice, he asked me to get him a glass of water. He apologized for asking for my help."

Drew got up to leave. He bleated out after her: "He *yuuuuused* me when I was popular. Look out for phonies, honey."

THE INTERVIEW HAD COME AFTER A CRUCIAL PRIMARY SHOWDOWN, IN Florida. The liberals, making the same calculation, stayed out, overestimating Wallace, underestimating Carter, glad to watch one of them knock the other out in that curiously half-Southern state, and hoping for both of them to rough up the third contestant in the race, Scoop Jackson, who was bidding for a strong show of support from the faction that made up a lion's share of the *other* half of Florida's unusual electorate—transplanted Jewish retirees.

But they were fighting another year's battles. They did not grasp that Wallace was now just a political vestige, and a pathetic one at that. Reporter Martin Schram looked in on a Wallace rally in a Vero Beach high school gym, all the old accoutrements still in place: Billy Grammer and his Grand Ole Opry Band to warm up the crowd; the red-white-and-blue bunting (Carter's campaign was done up all in green: fresh start, grass roots, the greening of America, *love*); the same focused rage, now aimed at his Georgia nemesis ("I'm tired of all this *high*-pocrisy. . . . I'm not the one who says, 'I'm a Southerner but I'm a *different kind* of Southerner.' What kind of Southerner does he *mean*? I think all Southerners are good"). The same raps on professors "totin' briefcases around and writin' things for one another," against "rip-off artists on welfare," and "[j]udges in the federal system" who "pay more attention to those who shoot you than those of you who got shot." He said the other candidates were ganging up on him—that is, ganging up on *you:* "They just don't like me stirring up the middle class so they can't control you."

But this year, the red meat earned him more pity than rebel yells. "Poor fella," a voter said when the candidate was wheeled behind the short, lead-reinforced lectern. "Look what it's like for him now."

When Wallace won the Florida primary in 1972, front-runner Edmund Muskie said it "reveal[ed] to a greater extent than I had imagined some of the worst instincts of which human beings are capable." Then the assassination attempt at the Laurel, Maryland, shopping center—the *crack, crack, crack, crack, crack* by a madman from Milwaukee imagining that a grand heroic act might finally win him the attention of pretty girls. Then the bedside vigils, tense moments near death, operation after operation (he still won primaries in Maryland and Michigan, both states in which white suburban voters were terrified that some federal judge might soon force their children to go to school with black kids); his pallid, ghostly appearance behind a specially designed podium at the Democratic convention in Miami Beach, a less frightening Wallace, a more domesticated Wallace—a Wallace, many of his listeners realized that day, whom maybe they could learn to live with.

More and more Northern Democrats began taking a new look at the former outcast, wondering whether the story he was telling might be adapted to their purpose as well—a rehabilitation that began in earnest with a joint appearance by Wallace and Ted Kennedy at a fairground in Decatur, Alabama, on July 4, 1973, for a "Spirit of America" rally, one DNC chairman Robert Strauss described as a "love fest." It was a story, people now began to reason, that was not really about race, or at least not only about race: his exhortations against "pointy-headed bureaucrats who couldn't park their bicycle straight" and "the pseudo-intellectual government, where a select, elite group have written guidelines in bureaus and court decisions, have spoken from some pulpits, some college campuses, some newspaper offices, looking down their noses at the average man on the street," just might speak best to the ruddy small-*d* democratic faith that honored the best in America.

Wallace himself began talking about the bad old days as if it had all been some massive misunderstanding: "I was for segregation because it was the law," he said in a 1974 interview. "Well, it's not the law anymore." That year his gubernatorial campaign courted black voters. ("Sure, I look like a white man. But my heart is as black as anyone's here," he said in an infamous stumble, which could hardly disturb any of his supporters: it only proved he wasn't a "pseudo-intellectual.") By the middle of 1975 there was talk that he might well capture the Democratic nomination. And that violence around the edges—his talk, in 1968, about how a protester who lay down in front of *his* limousine wouldn't live to see another day (that one always got thunderous applause); or, eight years later, the time a Peanut Brigadier at a hardware store in Okaloosa County in the Dixified Florida panhandle was told, "Young lady, you shouldn't be here. This is Wallace Country and you might be in danger"—well, maybe that could be ignored too. "Every one of them is talking about the things that I talked about in '72, aren't they?" George Wallace asked Elizabeth Drew. "I was talking about welfare; I was talking about foreign aid; I was talking about national defense; I was talking about tax reform," he explained. "I wanted to show that people of my region were in the mainstream of American political thought." More and more, it seemed he was right.

Memories, however, were long; when he spoke to the Arkansas legislature, for example (he said that "the people of Arkansas and Alabama speak the language the great majority wanted to hear politicians speak for so long"), the black members boycotted the chamber. Tom Wicker had compared the new rapprochement between Wallace and the liberals to the one that ended Reconstruction in 1876, when President Rutherford B. Hayes withdrew federal troops from the South and "the nation entered a 75-year period in which it tacitly permitted lily-white politics and social institutions in a quarter of the states." Long memories— indeed some going back to 1876 and before—were precisely what created the space that Jimmy Carter so ably filled: all the ruddy democratic faith and Southern gentility, with none of the snarling, slave plantation, fascist overtones. Like the time when a little lady from the Peanut Brigade showed up in the Okaloosa hardware store. Smiling, in a sweet soft Southern voice, she replied to the man warning about her safety because this was "Wallace country" that if he were a Wallace man in Carter country, he wouldn't be in danger at all.

The Alabaman grasped it best himself. "All of them done stole my water," he carped to a *Washington Post* reporter. "They're drinking out of my dipper." He'd already won. Which was why he would lose. Jimmy Carter certainly thought so. When *he* walked into a café and was told, "There ain't no need coming in here, this is Wallace Country," he replied with that famous wide grin: "OK, good deal, wouldn't want it to be unanimous."

FIRST, ON MARCH 6, CAME MASSACHUSETTS—WHERE ADS IN THE BOSTON papers featured photographs of Senator Henry "Scoop" Jackson and the big, blunt pronouncement, "I AM AGAINST BUSING." Massachusetts was where Jackson chose to make his stand. Like Wallace, he thought Jimmy Carter was a meretricious phony. Like Wallace, he was determined to crush him.

Scoop Jackson was one of those politicians who seemed to have been around forever. A four-term senator from Washington State, and before that a seven-term representative, he'd been mentioned for the vice presidency in 1960; then Kennedy made him chairman of the Democratic National Committee. In 1970 he won reelection with 84 percent of the vote, more than any other Northern senator received—and, there being few senators who didn't look in the mirror and imagine a presidential prospect staring back at him, he naturally made a bid for the 1972 nomination, as the voice for those Democrats, as he put it, who didn't want "to make abortion, gay liberation, and the legalization of marijuana the primary issues of the country." He failed badly, accomplishing little save spreading poison against the eventual nominee George McGovern. But he was back in the headlines in 1973, calling energy executives before his Senate committee, browbeating them as profiteers, calling for the nationalization of their companies, accusing Nixon of caring more about their profits than the price of gasoline at the pump. It was the sort of muscular old economic populism that Gary Hart was talking about when he derided those who "clung to the Roosevelt model long after it had ceased to relate to reality."

Yes, Scoop Jackson was boring: a "black hole of charisma," one political journalist called him, and during one dreary summer in Washington the humorist Mark Russell joked it was "so boring that the kids sit around in circles and get high on Scoop Jackson speeches."

Since then, though, he'd had speech coaching, he'd had surgery to perk up his drooping eyelids, he cut out starches, he grew out his hair a little bit. His handlers tried to recruit Warren Beatty to support the campaign. His economic populism was, well, popular. And in a Democratic Party whose younger lights were racing to the left on lifestyle issues, a square like him filled a rather large niche. Besides, asked Richard Reeves at the end of 1973 in a *New York* magazine cover story called "The Dawn of an Old Era: The Inevitability of Scoop Jackson," if not Scoop in 1976, who else?

It didn't look so inevitable now. But maybe if he could make something happen in Massachusetts, he could become the default for the increasing number of Democrats who thought that weird Carter guy was a creep.

One of his old-fashioned notions was that, "détente" notwithstanding, the Soviet Union was as dangerously threatening as ever. (One of Daniel Schorr's biggest scoops from the Pike Report was the revelation that Jackson secretly helped the CIA evade the investigation.) But that didn't play in the one state that George McGovern won. That left busing—and in Boston, buses were still rolling under police escort. Boston's Hyde Park High closed because of racial violence in January; a hundred kids threw bottles and rocks and set fires and smashed police-cruiser windshields near the Bunker Hill Monument in February. Scoop Jackson loudly insisted that neither his proposed constitutional amendment to stop busing, nor antibusing protest itself, had anything to do with racial animus. "I think the people of this state aren't racist," he said at his opening campaign event in Beantown. "They're good, decent Americans. The people of Massachusetts resent that if you're opposed to forced busing, you're labeled a racist." He also insisted he wasn't campaigning to take votes away from George Wallace—who was not bothering to be polite about it. The Alabaman just traipsed through South Boston in 1976, announcing, "They said busing, and I said no." A columnist who watched him say it at Lithuanian Hall reported what happened next: "Cries of 'up, up' erupted. . . . They leaped to their feet, shaking their fists, some of them. George Wallace leaned back and drank in the pandemonium. He could have taken them anywhere he wanted."

Jackson gained an inside track in Massachusetts by striking hard and smart against Jimmy Carter's arrogance, which had grown overwhelming. At Faneuil Hall, during a week when his face was on the cover of *Time* and *Newsweek,* Carter promised that all the criticism being aimed at him by the other candidates wouldn't hurt him. "But I'm afraid it might hurt this country." Carter's team had decided to throw all they had into Massachusetts, extending their ad buys on Boston TV stations from the New Hampshire campaign through the Massachusetts voting a week later. A twenty-nine-year-old on the Carter team named Greg Schneiders wrote a memo warning that if the campaign peaked that early it would only give any "stop Carter" movement among an angry Washington, D.C., establishment more time to gel. He proved to be a lone voice. Everyone else was convinced that three wins in a row, in the farm belt, a New England state, and then one of the biggest industrial states in the country—and then, the next week, in the Southern state of Florida— would all put the finishing touches on the race.

And at that, a disciplined candidate grew sloppy.

The day before the New Hampshire primary, he was asked at a televised League of Women Voters forum for details about how he would change the tax code, which he liked to call a "disgrace." For instance, would he end the home mortgage interest deduction? Yes, Carter answered, that "would be among those I would like to do away with."

The other candidates attacked—none more aggressively than Jackson. He put up TV commercials saying this inexperienced outsider who understood nothing about the federal government had proposed an idea that meant "American homeowners will have to pay $6 billion more in taxes." He told reporters, "He'd better do some homework before he comes up with fuzzy ideas."

The old politics had struck back. Jackson upset the Massachusetts field with 23 percent of the vote. The liberal Udall came in second with 18, and Wallace came in third with 17 (though he scored 68 and 61 percent respectively in South Boston's two wards). Jimmy Carter, with 14 percent, finished fourth; none of the other liberals—Harris, Shriver, Shapp, and Bayh (who announced he was suspending his campaign)—got more than 10 percent. Commentators started talking about a "Jackson juggernaut"—and wondered whether last year's invincible newcomer wasn't just a flash in the pan and all those acres of newsprint spent anatomizing and extolling "antipolitics" and the "revolt against Washington" weren't so much useless bird-cage liner now that the longest-serving legislator in the race, the unashamed champion of big-government federal programs, the Cold Warrior, had prevailed. Maybe, just maybe, nothing in the Democratic Party had truly changed. Certainly the victor thought so: "We put together the grand old coalition that elected Roosevelt, Truman, Kennedy, and Lyndon Johnson"—ignoring the fact of the plain anti–civil rights undertone of his appeal.

JIMMY CARTER DIDN'T IGNORE IT. HE LET HIS BITTERNESS SHOW: "IF I have to win by appealing to an emotional, negative issue, that has connotations of racism, I don't want to win that kind of race." Reporters asked him if he was calling Scoop Jackson a racist, and he flipped out: *"I didn't say Senator Jackson was a racist."* Thereafter, though, he upped the ante, saying in Florida the week before the balloting, "To build a campaign in a state like Massachusetts on an issue that's already divided the people, already created disharmony, sometimes even bloodshed, which is obviously a very emotional issue which has racial connotations, this is a wrong thing." His campaign, in fact, had been startled to learn that in the black Boston neighborhood of Roxbury, he had come in first. They actually couldn't quite believe their good fortune. A smart campaigner, he adapted, pressing an unexpected advantage: ducking into Illinois, which voted on March 16, and which he was now building up as "my most important state in the nation," and speaking at the Monument of Faith Evangelistic Church in a converted synagogue on Chicago's black South Side:

"We worked in the same fields, we fished in the same creek bed, went swimming in the same swimming hole, played with the same steel rails, homemade toys. We got on the train, me and my black playmates, we didn't sit together. My black playmates—I couldn't understand why—went to the back."

Taking on the slow, rhythmic cadences of a preacher, he spoke of unveiling Martin Luther King's portrait in the state capitol in 1974 alongside his widow, Coretta Scott King, and his father Martin Luther "Daddy" King, "and we sang together 'We Shall Overcome.'" He said, "You don't see any rich people in prison," and spoke of Jack Kennedy, who offered solidarity to Coretta when her husband was in an Atlanta jail: "We all feel like we're outsiders." His listeners' attentions was riveted. Then in Rockford he told a press conference that he thought détente was splendid—but "I would be very much tougher in the future in our negotiations with the Soviet Union." At a UAW hall, he spoke of "my intimate relationship with the working people of this country" and said "I know what it means to work for a living." In a president "I think we need somebody who understands what it means to work." Those were the populist Fred Harris's lines—although Harris would soon no longer deliver them: within three weeks, Harris's campaign's telephones were cut off. Maybe being all things to all people could *work*.

In Florida Carter bid for a key part of Jackson's constituency. He put on a yarmulke and spoke at synagogues and at Jewish centers in Miami, trumpeting a colloquy he'd enjoyed in Israel with Golda Meir. It wasn't quite as effective. He looked, Martin Schram wrote, like "Jimmy, chief of the Mouseketeers," and sounded like "grits at a seder." He did better recruiting many of the leaders of the country's most liberal unions—the UAW, the Machinists, the Communications Workers—playing to their eagerness to head off Wallace's dark appeal to their members. Co-opting Wallace's old slogan, Carter said to working-class audiences, "Let's not send them a message. Let's send them a president."

Jackson set up squads to prowl the condominiums that house Jewish retirees, and campaigned with Daniel Patrick Moynihan, the near neoconservative who'd resigned from his position at the United Nations ("a sad day for America," Jackson's statement had noted), eager to help save the Democratic Party from itself: "Look at what American liberalism has done!" Moynihan cried to a friend. "It's pushed Boston so far that it's voting for George Wallace! John Kennedy's city!" Mo Udall trumpeted his second-place Massachusetts finish, saying that it anointed him as the leading "progressive"—"progressive centrist," actually. Reporters asked if that was different from being a "liberal." He said it most certainly was—but how, exactly, he was not able to explain. Then he admitted it was mostly an exercise in public relations—"People relate better to 'progressive.' 'Liberal' is equated in some places with too much spending, softness on welfare and on crime, and some of the social issues such as abortion and amnesty"—which didn't help; two weeks later, he was still being asked to explain. "I haven't changed a single program," he complained in Oshkosh, Wisconsin. "Progressive is an honorable label and I've been using it lately." He was now the field's front-runner in semantics. "My campaign began to lose momentum," he wrote in *Too Funny to Be President,* "and soon we were bogged down like a dinosaur in a tar pit."

The talk around Washington was that Frank Church would soon enter, and maybe California governor Jerry Brown, too. They had read the tea leaves in the latest polls, which now suggested that on March 9 in Florida, the old politics—George Wallace's politics, Scoop Jackson's politics—would in fact get crushed.

Primary night in Florida. Some two dozen Carter relatives gathered at a hotel in Atlanta, cameras everywhere. Peanut Brigadiers who'd fanned out for a "Battle of Jacksonville," where they made 70,000 voter contacts and passed out 100,000 pieces of literature in a city with a large proportion of the voters undecided between Wallace and Carter, chewed fingernails. No one, actually, could quite predict anything in a state where some 200,000 new voters had moved in since 1972. The candidate certainly still seemed testy: "Do you want to stop talking so I can give you my answer or do you want to go ahead and ask a second question as well?" he snapped at one reporter. "I'll be glad to repeat myself again—or else you can play your tape back to yourself," he yowled at another.

He needn't worry: Carter, 35 percent. Wallace, 32 percent. Jackson, 22 percent.

Jimmy Carter had been born again. He was the front-runner once more.

ON THE REPUBLICAN SIDE, A NEW DEVELOPMENT. RONALD REAGAN HAD been reticent about taking the fight to Gerald Ford on foreign policy; his campaign manager, John Sears, had been whispering in his ear that too much criticism of détente could only offend the Republican establishment and cripple him in the general election. His standard speech of thirty-five minutes had thirty seconds on the subject, calling détente a "one-way street," or saying the only thing it availed America was "the right to sell Pepsi-Cola in Siberia." It always won a thunderclap of applause. His opening speech had but a line on the subject. ("A decade ago we had military superiority. Today we are in danger of being surpassed by a nation that has never made any effort to hide its hostility to everything we stand for.") He even, the night before the New Hampshire primary, wondered in a befuddled tone whether Congress hadn't done the right thing by banning aid for Angola, for all he knew, given the "mystery" surrounding the issue. Perhaps it was a patriotic thing. How did it serve the battle for civilization against the forces of evil to too harshly second-guess a commander in chief?

Now, not *Nancy* Reagan. David Keene once explained to the couple his plan to compromise to win some delegates at a state convention. He apologized for his lack of political aggressiveness: "We have to do it, though personally, I'd rather sail in and kick the shit out of 'em." Nancy promptly reared up with gleaming eyes: "Now *that* is the kind of talk I like to hear."

Her husband meanwhile had said at a Concord, New Hampshire, press conference, after losing that primary, that he "couldn't be more pleased" with the state results—why, if you counted the Democratic write-in votes (which didn't count), it had been a virtual tie! And he pointed reporters to a hand-lettered sign on his chartered 727, which read "Air Force One—'77." Everything always worked out in the end, gloriously

His handlers, less optimistic, were dumbfounded by what had happened on election night in New Hampshire. Their whole strategy had been built on a quick win there, a quick win in Florida, a quick win in Illinois—and a quick concession from unelected, unloved President Ford. John Sears had a mantra: "Politics is motion." Now they had none. In a predawn, booze-soaked meeting after New Hampshire's election night, they contemplated their internal poll, which Meldrim Thomson had oafishly leaked to the media, showing Reagan going into the voting 8 points ahead—and a poll, which they prayed no one saw, showing that their previous lead in Florida had been wiped away. They prevailed upon their candidate: it was time to take the knife to their opponent at his most vulnerable point, and at Reagan's strongest point. That was foreign policy. That was the dreaded doctrine of "détente."

They had a poll from January showing that 44 percent of *all* Americans preferred Reagan's hard line on the Soviets, compared with 25 percent who liked Ford's. (A majority agreed that Reagan "would be unafraid to stand up to the Russians, and that is right.") They reminded him how cutting the president and the surrogates had been in the homestretch. They implored him: just make it about the State Department; you don't have to mention Jerry Ford by name. Maybe they reminded him of a line he liked to drop in on the apparently obscure subject of the Panama Canal Zone.

Negotiations to reform the 1904 treaty that turned the ten-mile-wide strip surrounding the canal into a nearly sovereign entity of the United States in perpetuity had been ongoing since the administration of Dwight D. Eisenhower. The treaty was an ugly thing, a relic of a more imperialist, less suspicious, age: it was a gift to the United States from the rebels who established the Republic of Panama by breaking away from the nation of Colombia with the aid of the gunboat USS *Nashville* and a convenient shutdown of the U.S.-owned Panamanian Railway, which kept Colombia's army from Panama City. Then came the heroic work of building a modern eleventh wonder of the world—a tale, stripped of the military bullying and backhanded chicanery, told to generations of rapt American schoolboys in textbooks that proclaimed, for example, "American pluck and luck conquered all. . . . The grand dream was realized. In 1913 the waters of the Atlantic and the Pacific were united."

But to the poor put-upon Panamanians, the "Zone"—"as much a part of the United States as is Omaha, Nebraska," the travel writer John Gunther observed—was a nightmare of colonialist humiliation. So they fought back: in 1913, when Panamanian police shot three unarmed U.S. marines; in 1947, after America sought to make permanent its supposedly temporary wartime military bases in defiance of the unanimous vote of the National Assembly; in 1958, when students defiantly planted their nation's flag at fifty points inside the Zone, and 1959, when they burned Americans' cars; and then, finally, in the 1964 riots that left four Americans and twenty-four Panamanians dead. By the end of 1964 Lyndon Johnson announced plans for an "entirely new treaty" that would "recognize the sovereignty of Panama" over the Zone. And by the presidency of Richard Nixon, Henry Kissinger was warning, "It will turn into a Vietnam-type situation" unless the Panamanians get some concessions. In February 1974, the State Department announced new negotiating principles "that will guarantee continued effective operation of the Canal while meeting Panama's legitimate aspirations," including greater input from Panama into the canal's administration, a greater share of the canal's profits—and, most significant, an eventual, if theoretical, end to America's control of the canal "in perpetuity."

And at that, conservatives went berserk.

Strom Thurmond of South Carolina introduced a resolution for "continued undiluted United States sovereignty over the United States–owned Canal Zone on the Isthmus of Panama." It included an imperishable comment: "We own it. We bought it. It's ours." Ronald Reagan, for one, was sold. In a May 1975 radio broadcast he quoted Senator Jesse Helms, who said, "I have received reliable information, that Dr. Kissinger has approved plans to turn over effective control of police and fire protection and postal services in the Canal Zone of the Republic of Panama." Reagan then argued that this meant America would soon be help-less to fight back against the next civil disturbance, and that Americans would have their mail opened by the fearsome head of the state security service, "Lieutenant Colonel"—he paused, struggling to pronounce the unfamiliar name—"Manuel Noriega, a man not unfriendly to the Cuban Communists." He concluded in tones of the John Birch Society—which soon began distributing bumper strikers reading DON'T GIVE PANAMA OUR CANAL: GIVE THEM KISSINGER INSTEAD!—"One can and is forced to ask: Why?"

On Memorial Day he tied "our seeming willingness to give away the Panama Canal" to the same liberal fecklessness that produced Tru-man's stalemate in Korea, Kennedy's betrayal at the Bay of Pigs, and now our humiliating retreat in Vietnam. He asked, "Have we stopped to think that young Americans have seldom if ever in their lives seen America act as a great nation?" (Apparently the civil rights movement didn't count.) He told the Veterans of Foreign Wars at their annual con-vention in August that "that nation exists only because of us"; that the current government of Omar Torrijos was "Marxist" (he was actually an anti-Communist authoritarian, one of the reasons American presidents had trusted him in negotiations); and that under our benign protec-tion "Panama has the highest standard of living in Central America." That fall, George Wallace joined in, angrily confronting Kissinger at a governors' conference. A conservative issue was born. In a speech in Bicentennial-happy Philadelphia a month before his official entry into the presidential campaign, Reagan tried on Helms's line: "I think we'd be damn fools to turn over the Panama Canal. We built it. We paid for it. It's ours." It fit like a glove: the *Philadelphia Inquirer* said he then re-ceived "thunderous applause."

Ford and Kissinger had desperately hoped to keep the issue out of the presidential campaign. Barry Goldwater, who had come out for call-ing out the Marines during the 1964 crisis over flying the U.S. flag, now said a new treaty was desperately needed because the canal was all but indefensible against guerrilla sabotage—and accused Reagan of "gross factual errors" and "a surprisingly dangerous state of mind." Reagan ignored his old friend.

He'd given a hard-hitting foreign policy speech in New Hampshire on February 10, but the audience was a bunch of prep school boys at Phillips Exeter Academy, and the address had fallen flat. This time, the new rhetorical strategy was tried at a stadium: on February 27 at a spring-training ball field in Winter Park, Florida, idled by a major-league labor dispute. The climax went:

"State Department actions for several years now have suggested that they are intimidated by the propaganda of Panama's military dictator, Fidel Castro's good friend, Gen. Omar Torrijos. Our State Department apparently believes the hints regularly dispensed by the leftist Torrijos regime that the canal will be sabotaged if we don't hand it over. Our government has maintained a mouse-like silence as criticisms of the giveaway have increased. . . . I don't understand how the State Department can suggest we pay blackmail to this dictator, for blackmail is what it is. When it comes to the Canal, we bought it, we paid for it, it's ours, and we should tell Torrijos and company that we are going to keep it."

The crowd went wild.

David Keene, in charge of organizing Florida for Reagan, was surprised: People weren't reading about Panama in the newspapers. So why were they reacting like this? Ronald Reagan understood. "The issue I sense," he told Kevin Phillips, "is, 'The empire is in decline.' . . . The Establishment doesn't want to raise it." His listeners remembered those shameful images of the evacuation of Saigon, that line of bodies snaking up the ladder to that shack atop the CIA station chief's home. God's chosen nation, with its tail between its legs. They remembered those Panamanian riots from 1964, and now Panama was being rewarded for rioting—just like those ungrateful Negroes in those Northern cities they had left behind to retire in Florida: they had rioted, and then got more civil rights bills and social programs. ("Rioting for rent supplements," a congressman had called it back in the 1960s.) And now Jerry Ford was ready to let it happen again. Damn right they cheered. We bought it. We paid for it. It's ours.

Evans and Novak had described his previous rhetoric in Florida as "wrapped in cotton wadding with scarcely a glint of a sharp edge." Now he wielded a dagger. To a woman who asked, "Will you help New York please?" he answered, "Well, I won't saw it off." And at a March 4 press conference in Orlando he said, "All I can see is what other nations the world over see: the collapse of the American will and the retreat of American power. There is little doubt in my mind that the Soviet Union will not stop taking advantage of détente until it sees that the American people have elected a new President and appointed a new Secretary of State." That made news—news that a Republican presidential administration might *not* star Henry Kissinger any longer. He said, "Last year and this, the Soviet Union, using Castro's mercenaries, intervened decisively in the Angolan civil war and routed pro-Western forces. Yet Ford and Kissinger continue to tell us that we must not let that interfere with détente." He continued, "Despite Mr. Ford's evident"—ouch!—

"decency, honor, and patriotism, he has shown neither the vision nor leadership necessary to halt and reverse the diplomatic and military decline of the United States." So it was high time for Ford to announce, "We are getting out of détente. . . . I believe in the peace of which Mr. Ford speaks—as much as any man. But in places such as Angola, Cambodia, and Vietnam, the peace they have come to know is the peace of the grave."

That same morning left-leaning Mozambique closed its border with Rhodesia, a white-ruled anti-Communist power, and Kissinger testified before the House International Relations Committee, warning, if that was the word, that Cuba should act "with great circumspection" in southern Africa. Compared to that, Reagan's dagger thrust that "under Kissinger and Ford this nation has become number two in military power in a world where it is dangerous—if not fatal—to be second best" sounded swell to Florida's retirees.

IT WAS NOT ENOUGH IN FLORIDA TO WIN. IN FACT, REAGAN LOST BY A wider margin there than in New Hampshire. He also lost that week in Vermont (Ford 84 percent, Reagan 15), and Massachusetts (Ford 61, Reagan 34, with twenty-seven delegates for Ford and fifteen for Reagan; a *Boston Globe* exit poll found he'd done well only among "conservative" and "very conservative" voters), two states where he hadn't campaigned. Florida, in fact, was his fifth loss in a row—though he still managed to respond, the next day, "I cannot tell you how delighted I am. The incumbent in these first couple of primaries has thrown the whole load at us; he has shot all the big artillery there is, used everything in the incumbency he can, and we are still possessing almost half the Republican vote."

The Florida loss had been in the cards. His campaign chairman was an overweight, oafish car dealer who told reporters things like "If I was going to give the world an enema, I'd insert the nozzle in Washington." Stuart Spencer, who'd helped run Reagan's 1966 campaign but was now working for Ford's, was not surprised by his former client's string of losses: "He's lazy, that's all," Spencer told Vic Gold. "I think his energy level is going to be a problem. Low blood sugar. I think that's why he likes those jelly beans. . . . Sure, aides can brief him. But if a guy's deep, he's deep. If he's shallow, he's shallow."

The president's campaign machine, on the other hand, was finally humming. Dick Cheney, his tough chief of staff, was riding herd—hiring twenty-four new staffers in ten days and opening a phone office that reached four hundred thousand voters. The candidate toughened up his Cold War rhetoric, blunting Reagan's: he said he would have nothing to do with "international outlaw" Fidel Castro—this scuttled plans to begin normalizing relations with Cuba—and claimed "détente was only a word that was coined" and he would no longer use it. His actual policy, he said, was "peace through strength."

He made the remarks on Castro while swearing in 1,161 new citizens from Cuba. Noted a reporter, "Ronald Reagan brings a political campaign to town. Gerald Ford brings the White House." And so Ford dangled a Treasury Department job before the former president of the Florida Conservative Union. He also announced so much pork for Florida, Reagan told his audiences, that "when he [Ford] arrived in their town 'the band won't know whether to play 'Hail to the Chief' or 'Santa Claus Is Coming to Town.'" A free tape of Betty Ford urging everyone to vote was sent to every radio station in Florida. The first lady's press secretary denied this was dirty pool; it was only, she said, a "public service announcement."

Reagan went on *Meet the Press* and downplayed expectations for the next primary, in Illinois, saying he'd be happy with only 40 percent—in the state where he'd been born and spent his youth, and which John Sears's original campaign plan had pegged as Ford's Waterloo. Fighting a cold, and, reportedly, depression, he leveled the nasty swipe that the Chinese invited Nixon back to China because they did not have faith in Gerald Ford, and that having Ford on the ballot in November would mean "having to defend a part of the past which Republicans would like to be left to history." He backtracked in the face of a flurry of questions from reporters who wanted to know if that meant he held Ford responsible for Watergate.

The genial optimist was uncharacteristically desperate. His campaign had a $688,000 deficit; Ford's had a $1.15 million surplus. Citizens for Reagan filed a complaint with the FEC, maintaining that since Kissinger was "using his high office for the express purposes of a campaign platform to promote the Ford candidacy," his trips should be charged as a campaign expenditure. Reagan's aide Don Totten, in remarks the *New York Times* reported had been approved in advance by the campaign press secretary, said Ford's strategy was "actual buying of the votes by outright bribery." Reagan, asked if he agreed, said only that he would not have used the same words—and also said on the campaign trail that Ford's deputies were "lying through their teeth" when they said Reagan had expected victory in New Hampshire (they weren't).

It got the president's back up—he was suddenly filled with a gust of fighting spirit. The *Times* quoted an aide who spoke for the mood of the campaign concerning Reagan: that it was time to "crush him"—once and for all.

And, in Illinois on March 16, crush him Ford did, with 58.9 percent of the vote. Reagan responded in a statement from California, "We appear to have met our goal with something over 40 percent of the vote. I have never been under any illusion that our grassroots campaign could successfully buck both the Illinois Republican organization and the promises being issued so bountifully by the White House. . . . I look forward to the North Carolina primary next week."

That was his rebuff to fellow Republicans who were telling him that it was now time for him to quit.

THE DAY BEFORE THE ILLINOIS BALLOTING, AND EIGHT DAYS BEFORE North Carolina's, the Reagan campaign 727, scheduled for Raleigh, North Carolina, sat idling for hours on the tarmac in Los Angeles. The staffers were waiting while volunteers in Washington emptied envelopes and counted checks to see if they had enough to pay for the flight. They made plans to start taking commercial flights. The day before Illinois, Frank Reynolds of ABC said, "The odds against him are very long now and because he is not a dreamer, Ronald Reagan must know he is on the edge of defeat." The *Times* quoted Ford supporters like Senator Charles Percy patting his opponent condescendingly on the head: "Ronald Reagan has sharpened up the Ford organization. His campaign has helped us. It would have been a very poor organization . . . without the Reagan challenge." The *New Yorker*'s Elizabeth Drew wrote, "the problem with suggestions that Reagan quit is that they overlook the fact that to quit would leave him without a role." As the *New York Times* reported, "The Californian argued that he still had a 50–50 chance of nomination—an assessment even his staff made no attempt to defend."

It was around then that the candidate walked in on a meeting between his wife and Lyn Nofziger. She thought her husband was beginning to look "foolish." She was in the middle of pleading with his old confidant to talk him into dropping out.

Reagan had had quite enough of talk like that. On the nineteenth, reporters waved a press release from the National Conference of Republican Mayors announcing their telegram to him begging him to step aside, which brought on a rare break in the old trouper's composure: "For heaven's sake, fellas, let's not be naive. That pressure to quit the race is being engineered from the same place that engineered pressure for me not to run in the first place—The White House! I'm not getting out! I'm not going to pay any attention to them now when they suggest that I should quit. Why doesn't *he* quit?"

Someone then asked him again: why don't you quit? There followed several seconds of awkward silence, before Ronald Reagan walked away.

Besides, he knew something that Chuck Percy, ABC News, the *New Yorker,* the *New York Times,* and even the President of the United States did not know: a new conservative-movement political machine was humming just beneath the Establishment's radar in North Carolina, ready to rewire what people thought they knew about how American politics worked.

THE CULTURAL CONDITIONS FOR A CONSERVATIVE ELECTORAL UPSURGE that March were propitious. The POWs were back in the news: on the fourth, Admiral James Stockdale became the seventh captive awarded the Medal of Honor (those seven were nearly 3 percent of the war's total recipients)—and the first in the history of the award to win it for a suicide attempt. The citation read, "He deliberately inflicted a near-mortal wound to his person in order to convince his captors of his willingness to give up his life rather than capitulate." That instantiated the Reaganite narrative that these stout-hearted men all but single-handedly proved the nobility of America's resistance to Communism in Vietnam—that "we walked out of Hanoi as winners." (Perhaps sensitive to the political implications, President Ford folded a campaign slogan into his East Room presentation of the medal to Stockdale and three other Vietnam vets: "As we celebrate our Bicentennial Year, we take satisfaction in our power to preserve peace through strength.")

Bicentennial observations were becoming ubiquitous that unexpectedly balmy spring: the Freedom Train, rolling through burg after burg with its display cases of American Revolutionary artifacts and technological marvels, and also a "Freedom Wagon Train" that covered twenty miles a day and stopped each night in a different "Bicentennial town" for a performance by the Penn State University Show Troupe. There were Bicentennial quarters, Bicentennial flags—and, each night on CBS, a "Bicentennial minute," in which a different celebrity backed by sonorous brass and snapping snares, narrated the heroic self-sacrifices of America's original patriots, ending with a version of Walter Cronkite's famous sign-off, "And that's the way it was," adding, "two hundred years ago today."

Patriotism: a splendid spur to nostalgic right-wing reveries—as was, that March, the continuing wave of terrorism that accompanied Patty

Hearst's trial. Two days after the Florida primary, part of a defective bomb exploded at a Hearst family retreat near Redding, California; the New World Liberation Front claimed responsibility. Three days later the *Chicago Tribune* published the first in a horrifying series, "WEATHER UNDERGROUND HAS 'BLUEPRINT FOR TERROR,'" claiming to have evidence that it all was part of a coordinated conspiracy that would only grow:

> SAN FRANCISCO—Members of the radical Weather Underground have masterminded a wave of violence throughout the country by secretly organizing small bands of terrorists operating under a variety of names, the *Chicago Tribune* has learned. This previously undisclosed blueprint for terror has been pieced together in the last two weeks by federal investigators and police in San Francisco, where the Patricia Hearst trial has focused new attention on these far-flung radical activities. . . .
>
> The picture emerged from a detailed study of thousands of internal documents seized here in raids in recent weeks and from inside knowledge provided by at least two admitted terrorists who have turned informants. . . .
>
> Investigators noted that the emergence of the Weather group as the rallying force in the underground world of terrorism fits into a program espoused by the group five years ago. The program was adopted from a similar one used by South American guerillas and calls for a cadre of nine persons to fan out across the country and organize other nine-person cells. These cells would operate under different names, and eventually send their members out to form new cells. The process would continue until a national network of terrorists was built. "Bombings in New York, Chicago, Los Angeles, Seattle, and the San Francisco Bay area during the past year is evidence that these cells are in existence," one investigator said.

The next day the Associated Press reported that the FBI and Secret Service were investigating the testimony of an undercover informant that a "commando-style assassination team" from the San Francisco Bay area was planning attempts on Reagan's and Ford's lives at the Republican convention in Kansas City, "designed to throw the convention into complete chaos." The *Chicago Tribune*'s report contributed this detail: "From the intelligence we have been able to gather, the terror groups want to move their emphasis from bombings to other violent acts in the urban guerrilla handbook, like assassinations and kidnappings."

Another conservative strand came from New York, where "pro-life" activists took advantage of the federal campaign finance law to make sure television viewers in every last primary state knew that abortion was the most hideous sort of cold-blooded murder, through free TV commercials for a "Human Life" constitutional amendment. The trick, pulled together by the New York State Right to Life Party, was to invent a dummy presidential campaign. The candidate, named Ellen McCormack, was a Long Island housewife who wrote a column syndicated to Catholic newspapers called "Who Speaks for the Unborn?" All that these activists needed to do to haul in $100,000 in matching funds for her was to raise at least $5,000 in each of twenty states by February 1976, and prove "viability" by getting her name on some primary ballots. They got her listed in fifteen states—and were certified by the FEC as passing the funding threshold on February 18. The National Abortion Rights Action League filed suit against the scheme on technical grounds—some newspaper ads soliciting funds didn't say anything about a presidential campaign, just "YOU CAN FIGHT ABORTION and SAVE BABIES' LIVES by helping sponsor PRO-LIFE TV ADS"—and lost. The commercials went on the air during the game show *Name That Tune*. A loophole in the campaign finance law meant that every taxpayer in the United States had become a de facto antiabortion activist.

In the Tar Heel State, a barely noticed right-wing infrastructure worked to bring those waters to a primary-day boil. A columnist chasing Reagan up and down the Florida Gulf Coast had asked Lyn Nofziger if this was the end of the road. The rumpled, cynical, fast-talking, hard-drinking press secretary looked uncharacteristically sincere: "Wait 'til North Carolina."

WHAT WAS ABOUT TO HAPPEN IN NORTH CAROLINA WAS IN PART A RESULT of that loophole in the new campaign finance law: the fact that independent groups could spend money without limit to help a political campaign, even a political campaign that accepted federal matching funds, so long as they did not coordinate their activities with that campaign. This would apply to an independent group like, say, the American Conservative Union. The ACU's chairman since 1971 was a perfervid ideological warrior named M. Stanton Evans. He was a Joseph McCarthy devotee, was the author of Young Americans for Freedom's 1960 manifesto the "Sharon Statement," and had only recently retired at the ripe old age of forty as editor of the *Indianapolis News*. Evans prevailed upon the ACU's board to commit huge resources to the presidential race. The

ACU had begun, tentatively, with Illinois. It was in North Carolina that the organization went, as the poker players say, all in. It spent tens of thousands of dollars on newspaper and radio ads alone. Read in Evans's mellifluous voice, the radio ads presented a bill of indictment: *"Gerald Ford appointed Nelson Rockefeller. . . ."* It ran almost a thousand times.

And it came partly from the work of a senator unlike any other the world's greatest deliberate body had ever seen—the first pure electoral product of America's nascent new right.

Jesse Alexander Helms Jr. was born in the typical Southern small town of Monroe, North Carolina, in 1921, the year a progressive new governor took office in the South's most liberal state promising a "war for righteousness with the reactionary and unprogressive forces of our state." Helms's father—"Mr. Jesse"—was both the town's police chief and its fire chief. His family was made up of Baptist teetotalers—who didn't just hate liquor, the joke went, but hated the farmer who grew the corn that made the liquor. When he became a politician he liked to invoke his fondest childhood memory in speeches: "The honks and shrieks of the town band . . . the chilled lemonade—a nickel a glass . . . horses . . . prancing and snorting . . . both of the town's highly polished fire engines with a multitude of ecstatic youngsters perched atop them; the town's single police car—three sirens in a row in a sort of discordant symphony. . . . In the burning noontime sun, men and women—and little boys and girls, too—stood reverently as a prayer of thanksgiving was offered for the liberty and freedom which were God's gift to America. Nobody doubted it." He was describing the town's annual Independence Day parade—in a time, now, when *everybody* seemed to doubt it.

But if his vision of the world was almost militantly old-fashioned, the things that made Jesse Helms *Jesse Helms* were resolutely, ruthlessly modern. He was a master of electronic media and electronic public relations techniques. A high school newspaperman who said in his senior yearbook that his life's ambition was to be a columnist, he dropped out of tiny Wingate Junior College when he got a job reading proofs at the *Raleigh News & Observer*—then was recruited by the more conservative afternoon *Raleigh Times* as assistant city editor at the age of twenty. He discovered a passion for PR during wartime Navy basic training—and, when he was sent back to North Carolina as a recruiter, the joys of the radio microphone. By 1948 he was news director at a tiny but ambitious radio station, WRAL—where he put his editorial thumb on the scales for the U.S. Senate campaign of a McCarthyite reactionary named Willis Smith, who defeated the incumbent, the enlightened former president of the University of North Carolina, with the help, to take one example, of a handbill depicting the incumbent's wife alone with a black man, looking a little bit as if they were dancing. The advertising manager of the *News & Observer* told a Helms biographer that he'd seen the WRAL news director scissoring several other people out of the picture.

He went to Washington as Smith's executive assistant—and then, tiring of that, took a job as spokesman and lobbyist for the North Carolina Bankers Association, which had the advantage of providing him with a platform for his political views, in a full-page column in monthly trade magazine he edited. Those views were ahead of their time. Other Dixie ideologues, in the wake of *Brown v. Board of Education*, were talking about keeping unelected Yankee judges away from their public schools. Helms, a devotee of the Austrian libertarian economist Ludwig von Mises, instead argued that if they did away with public schools *altogether*, "[p]olitical sociologists would forever be unable to dictate terms and procedures to the people of America regarding our schools. . . . Unless our Negro citizens submit more easily than we predict they will, North Carolina does not have the simple choice between segregated schools and integrated schools. Our only choice is between instead public schools and free-choice private schools." His column, in the *Tarheel Banker*, was modestly titled "By Jesse Helms."

These views made him a Tarheel household name when, in 1960, WRAL got a license to open a TV station (slogan: "The miracle of America is the free enterprise system") and Helms was made news director. At the end of every newscast, he recited one of his own editorials, which were rebroadcast every morning and on the radio over the seventy or so stations of his boss's "Tobacco Network." His broadcast demeanor was almost deliberately bland—akin to his owlish horn rims and shapeless, old-fashioned suits, like those of a small-town banker, bought off the rack at a conservative Raleigh haberdashery. Aides once advised him to spruce up his image. Wisely, he did not let them prevail. In 1972 the celebrity ran for the Senate. He always wore American flag and Mason pins on his lapel, and a POW bracelet around his wrist. His slogan was "Elect Jesse Helms—He's one of us." (His opponent, who had an ethnic name—Galifianakis, as in "McGovern-Galifianakis cut and run" policies in Vietnam, and "McGovern-Galifianakis welfare giveaways"—was not one of us.) In his campaign he pledged to "[r]esist with all the strength I can muster the destructive tactics of the Teddy Kennedys, the Hubert Humphreys, the Muskies and McGoverns—and all the rest of the wrecking crew now dominating the United States Senate." He had in mind some destructive tactics of his own.

He won, though Helms the supposed budget hawk went into debt to do it—which turned out to be a very good thing. To retire the debt, his political deputy Tom Ellis, a California native who had transferred from Dartmouth College to North Carolina and fell in love with the "Southern way of life" and Southern slash-and-burn politics—regarding which he had the zeal of the convert—turned to Richard Viguerie, the master of ideological direct mail and interlocking political committees. Thus Helms became the New Right hustlers' second most useful name, behind Reagan's, for signing fund-raising appeals. That created a set of debts, which were paid back to Helms in fund-raising and publicity favors, and these helped Ellis begin to build a direct mail empire of his own, on his boss's behalf. Soon, Helms's "Congressional Club" and its satellites dwarfed the budgets of North Carolina's Republican and Democratic parties.

It worked, to take an example from the 1980s, like this. All the names on the Congressional Club's long mailing lists received a missive including a picture of a beautiful young family with two little girls, taken from their Christmas card. In the letter the senator recollected waiting for a flight in an airport in Alaska:

"The three-year-old was sitting on her mother's lap and the five-year-old was perched on the arm of the chair. The mother was reading a story. . . . I moved over and introduced myself." He played, he said, a silly little game with them that he liked to play with his grandchildren. Then the family's flight number—007—was called. That was the flight number, as all the readers would recognize, of a plane to Korea the Soviets accidentally shot down.

Not accidentally, right-wing conspiracists like Helms insisted. The letter concluded, "It was difficult to express the shock and horror and anger that I felt, and still feel, about the Soviet Union's wanton, deliberate, premeditated, callous, and cruel destruction of 269 innocent people—including those two little girls." It demanded "a renewed understanding of Communist brutality." Luckily, he was ready to help—if he could stay in Washington. "Can you help once more with a special significant contribution? Without your help, our work cannot continue. Jesse Helms."

Complaints flowed in, including one from the family, who had never authorized the use of their image or story. Helms and Ellis ignored them. More important was the money that arrived in a torrent. And that the message—Senator Helms stands up to the Communists— came through. Meanwhile, another message-building component of the Helms machine clanked along—on the floor of the Senate. Inspired by the tactics of a reactionary Democrat from Alabama named James Allen, the new senator, ninety-fifth in seniority, learned to offer numerous un-related amendments to big bills that needed to pass, sometimes a dozen amendments or more, each requiring a certain amount of debate, to le-verage one-man filibusters against ideas conservatives didn't like—such as the federal juvenile delinquency program (he was the only senator to vote against it); antipollution devices in cars (he attracted two support-ers for that); reauthorization of the Voting Rights Act; and, of course, legal abortion—"the human holocaust with no parallel in history," he would say, noting several cities where there were supposedly more abor-tions than births, adding, "Washington, D.C., is one of them."

He sometimes introduced bills of his own—for instance, to strip the courts of the authority to rule on the constitutionality of school prayer. It didn't matter how many times it failed, or by how many votes. A bi-ographer wrote that each "was like another WRAL editorial, drawn up to make a point. . . . He was reaching out to a national constituency, to frustrated Americans among whom his hard-line tactics stood for cour-age and leadership rather than obstruction and obfuscation." He liked to say, "I know nothing about being a politician."

Ironically, such tactics, and his status as a conservative hero second only to Reagan by 1976, would not have been possible without the insti-tutional reforms put in place by the Watergate Babies, which were sup-posed to be liberal. As a Democratic colleague explained (though Helms hardly considered liberals his "colleagues"), "The consequences of his being a pariah don't matter as much as they used to. The leadership can't discipline a senator as it once did. In the old days, you couldn't get a vote if the leadership didn't want to have one. Now it's gone the other way. . . . People are coming to realize the only way to deal with him is not to afford him the usual courtesies, to recognize that he's fighting trench warfare and they have to fight it in the same way. He and his people drag you down in the gutter to fight them . . . it's wreaking havoc on the institution."

What Helms was doing in the Senate, and what Tom Ellis did with his banks of computers, fueled one another, upending every old model for building senatorial power—patiently, cordially, honoring the vener-able maxim (beloved by gracious Southern solons like his senior Tarheel colleague Sam Ervin) "Fight today, friends tomorrow." Instead, he was a McLuhanite politician: the medium was the message. Observed a frus-trated Democratic senator, "with these interlocking political committees of his," Helms "works not so much within the Senate as outside. Often the whole purpose of his programming a vote is politics, so then he can use it with a press release or by mailing off thousands of letters by pushing a button on a computer." Organizing by building a mailing list favors a politics of melodrama, never the give-and-take between the myriad interests groups that make up partisan, let alone bipartisan, coalitions. It makes the political party a mere vehicle of convenience—indeed, Helms had been a registered Democrat until 1970, and had been one of the leading advocates for a third, conservative, party following Nixon's resignation. As a fellow Republican put it, "It's frustrating, often impossible to get serious business done. You might be working on a foreign aid bill or a change in the debt limit and all of a sudden you find you're voting on school prayer or abortion. Helms is no respecter of the institution. He uses the Senate for his own ends, his own causes, and they are not the same as the goals of the country."

It was, however, splendid for flushing out angry anti-Establishment right-wing voters in a Southern state for a presidential primary.

When Gerald Ford announced, late in 1975, that his campaign chairman in the state would be the moderate governor, James Holshouser—Helms's one rival for primacy in North Carolina Republican politics—Helms decided to turn his mighty machine to defeating the president. Ellis confronted John Sears—whom he respected for his expertise, and despised for his indifference to conservative ideology—and demanded complete control of the Reagan campaign, right down to the candidate's schedule, as the condition for Jesse Helms's help. Sears gave in. (Why not? Sears might have reasoned. He hadn't drawn a paycheck since February.) Helms's cast of characters would eventually become household names, at least among political junkies. Nobody had heard of them then. A twenty-two-year-old, born in Havana, named Alex Castellanos. A young Jewish conservative named Arthur Finkelstein, who'd engineered James Buckley's Senate win on the New York Conservative Party line in 1970. And Ellis himself—one of the most influential strategists in American electoral politics. Quietly, he'd been engineering efforts to get Democrats to reregister as Republicans to vote against the liberal turncoat Gerald Ford, and get young people to register for the first time, but that would become evident only later.

The Dixie boys opened up the thinking of what had turned into a stodgy campaign, for instance on the matter of the original source of their candidate's celebrity. Citizens for Reagan had polls indicating that foregrounding Reagan's Hollywood past didn't hurt him—it helped him. But Sears had directed the campaign to avoid any intimation of Hollywood glamour. Instead he commissioned a series of commercials that were deliberately unglamorous: poorly lit, poorly photographed footage of the candidate at citizen press conferences, in the cinema verité style then fashionable among politicians hoping to prove their antipolitical cred. But then, most politicians hoping to prove their anti-Establishment cred weren't Ronald Reagan. Antipolitics wasn't the only thing popular that spring: so was Reagan-style nostalgia. James Brolin and Jill Clayburgh were in theaters reenacting one of classic Hollywood's most storied romances in *Gable and Lombard* (Lombard was killed in a plane crash while publicizing World War II Liberty Bonds); F. Scott Fitzgerald's inside-Hollywood novel *The Last Tycoon* was in production at Paramount. Ellis ash-canned the cinema verité—and brought in Jimmy Stewart, who'd just finished an old-fashioned Western with John Wayne, *The Shootist,* to stump beside Reagan each and every day in the campaign's final week. Paul Laxalt, the original Senate booster of Reagan's presidential campaign, persuaded him to toss his note cards and trust his instincts instead. ("What kind of foreign policy is it when a little tinhorn dictator in Panama says he is going to start guerrilla warfare against us unless we give him the Panama Canal?") Reagan told Nancy that going a whole day speaking without his notes made him feel alive. Laxalt thought he looked like a little kid: he was flying.

The candidate had an idea: another bit, as it were, of nostalgia—one of those five-, fifteen-, or thirty-minute, look-at-the-camera-and-talk speeches that had been the staple of political TV until they were superseded by the slick thirty-second spot. He had been begging his campaign managers to do one—like what he had done in 1964 for Barry Goldwater, the one David Broder called "the most successful national political debut since William Jennings Bryan electrified the 1896 Democratic Convention with the 'Cross of Gold' speech." The answer always came back: "Gov, that stuff worked for you back in 1964, but this is different." Years later, Lyn Nofziger had to laugh: "Everybody wants to do something their own way with Ronald Reagan. And the best way is just to let him talk. Nobody ever figures it out. Each time, you have to go through this whole hassle."

Ellis loved the idea of a just-the-issues conservative appeal. This time the hassle involved Sears, who apparently emerged from his idleness to put his foot down against the ridiculous idea. Reagan's chief of staff Mike Deaver and press secretary Nofziger pressed him to give it a shot (perhaps they pointed out it might raise enough money to pay Sears's back salary). They had the film in hand—a thirty-minute shoot they'd done for the homestretch in Florida after a TV station donated the time to both candidates. They would only have to edit out the palm trees.

And that is indeed what they did.

One reviewer—Elizabeth Drew—found it "rather poor. Reagan jumped from subject to subject, just as he had in his early speeches, when he shuffled his four-by-six cards; he talked too fast about too many things, from energy to Social Security to the Panama Canal." But *New Yorker* writers did not have a vote in North Carolina Republican primaries. The ones who did have votes responded to the message that Gerald Ford was surreptitiously giving away the might of God's chosen nation, for free, to a Marxist tinhorn dictator in Panama—just like Franklin Roosevelt had given away Eastern Europe at Yalta—like people hearing the Holy Word.

The money started pouring in—literally too fast to count. Instead the campaign in Washington established a line of revolving credit with a bank that let them estimate the take by weighing the dozens of bags of cash and checks lying around. Meanwhile, underneath the radar, the gears in Ellis's machine continued to clank. A flyer akin to the one Helms scissored in 1950 depicting the opponent's wife dancing with a black man suddenly began appearing: it reprinted an article in which Ford said the black Republican senator from Massachusetts, Edward Brooke, "should be considered" for the vice presidency. (Reagan got to have it both ways on that one, loudly denouncing it to the press while benefiting from the race-baiting, too.) Meanwhile, all year, an enthusiastic young Congressional Club staffer had been visiting county courthouses to forage through whatever back rooms and attics held the lists of Republican primary records. He pulled together a roll of eighty thousand names, an accomplishment never attempted before—almost half the number of votes cast and about eighty thousand more names than the Ford organization had—to receive literature and get-out-the-vote phone calls.

Meanwhile the President of the United States coasted. One of his only two days in the state in the month of March even entered the crowded annals of Gerald Ford humor: a rousing speech to a Future Homemakers of America convention concluding, "I say—and it is with *emphasis* and *conviction*—that homemaking is good for America. I say that homemaking is not out of date and I reject strongly such accusations."

The president had read the Reagan campaign's reviews in the papers—

William F. Buckley's column, Monday, March 22: "Ronald Reagan, it would appear, has lost his fight for the presidential nomination."

James J. Kirkpatrick, Tuesday, March 23: "His role in the '76 campaign is just about played out."

—so why strain himself?

And on that very Tuesday, one of those balmy, sunny days that always favor incumbents over insurgents, North Carolina voted.

The Reagan gang was in La Crosse, Wisconsin, where the vote was to take place in two weeks. ABC's Frank Reynolds asked two listless handlers who were going through the motions, working for a nearly dead compaign, if they'd heard the results. They hadn't. Why pay attention to another defeat?

"Well, I have, and your man is winning."

They were gobsmacked. They hadn't quite believed it would work. The idled regular campaign had all but packed it in. Now, they learned they'd beaten the president of the United States by 52.4 to 46 percent—the first time a sitting president had been defeated in a primary in which he had actively campaigned.

Ronald Reagan, too, had been born again.

CHAPTER TWENTY-SEVEN

"Always Shuck the Tamale"

"BORN AGAIN." THE PHRASE WAS A NEW ONE IN THE LEXICON THAT PO-litical season. It was the title of a new memoir by former prisoner 23226 at Maxwell Federal Prison camp. "In one sense, I had lost everything," Chuck Colson wrote. "But in another sense I had found everything, all that really matters: a personal relationship with the living God. My life had been dramatically transformed by Jesus Christ." Then there was Jimmy Carter. Desolate after his loss in the 1966 governor's race, the story ran, he took a walk in the woods with his sister, Ruth Carter Stapleton, the one who operated a faith-healing ministry. "I had a per-sonal spiritual experience that is difficult to explain to people who have never had such an experience," he said in an Associated Press article that appeared in May; he accepted Christ as his personal savior, and that day his life began anew. He explained, "Many of the newsmen who asked about this have never had this experience. Some of them are downright cynical about it. I think it worries some of them." The article was called "Carter's Convictions Mystify News Media."

Those convictions had only recently been relatively private. They first surfaced on the campaign trail during a small fund-raiser in a home in Winston-Salem, North Carolina, when he told donors, "I recognized for the first time that I lacked something very precious—a complete commitment to Christ, a presence of the Holy Spirit in my life in a more profound and personal way. And since then I've had an inner peace and inner conviction and assurance that transformed my life for the better." He assured them, "I don't think I'm ordained by God to be President." He added that the "only prayer that I've ever had concerning the elec-tion is that I do the right thing. And if I win or lose, my religious faith won't be shaken." He elaborated the next day at a press conference: "It was not a profound stroke of miracle. It wasn't a voice of God from heaven. It was not anything of that kind. It wasn't mysterious. It might have been the same kind of experience as millions of people have who do become Christians in a deeply personal way."

Just about simultaneously, on the cover of *New York* magazine, Richard Reeves published "Carter's Secret: Understanding America's Spiritual Crisis." He quoted a *New Republic* columnist: "My impression is that audiences yearn to believe Jimmy Carter. They're looking for something. It is his manner and tone." Carter attributed some of his power to pull in voters to his experience pulling in souls: after his born-again experience, Reeves reported, Carter traveled to New York City as a Baptist missionary. He wrote, "No doubt Jimmy Carter knows what he is doing when he refers constantly and reverently to 'my daddy' and 'my mamma.'" Reeves concluded that maybe this "highly sophisticated 51-year-old man sounding like the thinking man's Billy Sunday" understood "something the rest of us don't." Observed *New York* magazine's editors in a preface, "What liberals perceive as a political crisis in the country may in fact be a crisis of the spirit . . . and Jimmy Carter has figured that out."

Other scribes started investigating. The *Washington Post*'s Myra MacPherson looked into the beliefs of his sister. Her column, headlined "Devout 'Minister' Healing the Wounds of the 'Inner Child'"—note the distancing quotation marks—described what Ruth Stapleton Carter called her "ministry of inner healing," in which she "takes her patients back to their childhood then conducts them on a trip of faith and imagination, traveling through their troubled childhood, but this time traveling with Jesus." She reported Ruth's recollection of the dialogue on Jimmy's walk in the woods with her: "You and I are both Baptists, but what is it that you have and that I haven't got?" he was supposed to have asked, and she replied, "Jimmy, through my hurt and pain it finally got so bad off I had to forget everything I was. What it amounts to in religious terms is total commitment. I belong to Jesus. Everything I am." She then said she guided her brother through a mental inventory of what he had to be willing to give up if he wished for a total commitment to Christ: money, friends, family—even political ambition. She said he then "put his face in his hands and cried like a baby."

The candidate denied that particular detail, and others. And in pious North Carolina, where he hoped to finish off George Wallace once and for all, he began telling the story on his own. He would say, like a convert to Werner Erhard's est, "I didn't get any sense of accomplishment when I achieved success and I felt like my religious beliefs were shallow and just a matter of self-pride." But now that he was born again, he felt otherwise.

To these hard-bitten ink-stained wretches—those from the North, who wrote about evangelical faith, a historian observed, "as if it were as alien to American culture as a Balinese cockfight," and those from the South, who'd seen all too many hustling piety-peddlers who, as they used to say about old Senator Estes Kefauver of Tennessee, "ran around the woods with his Bible in one hand and his pecker in another"—this all was just a little bit much. To intellectual sophisticates, it was like a visitation from another planet. Perhaps they had read a widely reported recent study by the religious historian James Hitchcock, who predicted that soon American society would have an "unbelieving popular majority." "Christians must accept being a definite minority for the time being," Hitchcock told a reporter.

The scholar was well wide of the mark. That February, two thousand delegates packed the combined convention of the National Religious Broadcasters and the National Association of Evangelicals. For the first time, a president addressed them—"The faith of our Fathers is living still in America today," Gerald Ford said—and so did the Christian conservative congressman John Conlan, wrapped up in a knock-down, drag-out primary for Senate in Arizona, where he campaigned against fellow conservative Sam Steiger by asking voters if they wanted "a Jew from New York telling Arizona what to do." Conlan said his goal as a politician was to make this a "Christian nation." In a profile of Chuck Colson in the *New York Times Magazine,* Garry Wills reported estimates that the evangelical movement encompassed some 67 million Americans—40 million of voting age, or about a quarter of the electorate. No wonder President Ford, one of whose public liaisons in the White House, Ted Mars, proclaimed, "We believe our nation must come back to God or else," stopped by the evangelicals' convention to say hello.

One evangelical broadcaster, Oral Roberts, reached seven million viewers a week on 349 local and satellite stations. Another, Pat Robertson, had his own satellite network. A third, Jerry Falwell, proprietor of *The Old-Time Gospel Hour,* was touring around the country with a group of fresh-faced, dancing, singing youngsters for Bicentennial "I Love America" rallies. "There's no question about it," he'd say on TV. "This nation was intended to be a Christian nation by our founding fathers." Reagan, for his part, was part of the flock of the muscular evangelical Donn Moomaw, a former football all-American at UCLA, who assured fellow evangelicals of his most famous parishioner's "alive faith."

Christian popular culture exploded. Twenty thousand gathered in a pasture outside Disney World for a three-day rock-concert-style "Jesus '76" rally starring Robertson, Conlan, Pat Boone, and Hal Lindsey, who swooped down to the stage from the sky in helicopters, like at Woodstock—then, in Mercer, Pennsylvania, the same show drew seventy thousand, more than half of whom camped out on the site. Christian couples devoured Beverly and Tim LaHaye's *The Act of Marriage: The Beauty of Sexual Love,* which explained of the clitoris that God "placed it there for your enjoyment," and excoriated the husband "who told his frustrated wife, 'Nice girls aren't supposed to climax.' Today's wife knows better." The *Los Angeles Times,* that May, reported on a theological debate within the evangelical community over the inerrancy of the Bible as if it were a contest between the Rams and the Jets. Two wealthy Los Angeles men printed 2.5 million copies of the 1910 tract *The Fundamentals* and sent it, reportedly, to every pastor, evangelist, missionary, and church worker in the country. Ten other rich Christians pledged $25,000 each to launch a "Third Century Index"—a rating of congressmen on a 1–100 scale, like the ones published by the AFL-CIO and the liberal Americans for Democratic Action. Their spokesman, Rus Walton—a principal in Barry Goldwater's 1964 presidential campaign— explained, 'The vision is to rebuild the foundations of the Republic as it was when first founded—a 'Christian Republic.'"

The conversion of Reagan's former archenemy Eldridge Cleaver, the Black Panther leader, to conservative Christianity would soon be in the papers. "I'd like to caution people that the simple things we've been taught from childhood in the end are the most profound," Cleaver said. Enough ordinary Americans agreed that when two private citizens petitioned the Federal Communications Commission complaining of the way "back-to-the-Bible fundamentalism" was monopolizing the portions of the AM and FM bands reserved for educational programming, and a rumor ensued that the FCC sought to ban religious broadcasting, the federal agency was flooded with fifty thousand letters of complaint.

I FOUND IT, the bumper stickers distributed by the Campus Crusade for Christ proclaimed. Jimmy Carter had found it, too. "I'm not afraid to see my life ended," he told Bill Moyers on the latter's PBS program later that spring. "I don't have any fear at all of death. I feel like I'm doing the best I can, and if I get elected President, I'll have a chance to magnify my own influence maybe in a beneficial way. If I don't get elected President, I'll go back to Plains."

Moyers asked: did he have any doubts about himself, about God, about life?

"I can't think of any."

. . .

IT SOUNDED GOOD TO VOTERS—THE SORT FLOCKING TO EST, TO EVAN-gelicalism, to something, anything, to anchor a firm sense of meaning in their lives. The fact remained, though, that for the guardians of the permanent Washington establishment—who were, Reeves wrote, in a "small panic" over Carter, whom one of the Washington press corps, the *Times'* James Reston, called "Wee Jimmy"—it was just one more thing that made James Earl Carter sound so *weird*.

The people *around him* were weird, come to think of it—Hamilton Jordan, who almost always wore a denim jacket, and stuck with boots even when he had to wear a suit; Jody Powell, who looked like a boy; Charles Kirbo, to whom Carter was personally closest, and who a po-litical correspondent for *New York* thought "sounds like a gorilla"; Jerry Rafshoon, who sat on desks and tables instead of chairs, and was quite the player in the ad game ... in Atlanta, Georgia, where Carter had inscrutably chosen to base his campaign, surrounded by this tight little group. "How can he be nominated?" asked Ambassador Averell Harriman, the eighty-five-year-old emperor of the Georgetown cocktail circuit. "I don't know him, and neither do any of my friends." Another insider, a journalist, said, "Carter can't be President. He doesn't know his way around this city."

It was around then, with a man they considered a weirdo unques-tionably ahead in the Democratic race, that this cozy little D.C. village of friends began to talk up one of their own: former senator, former vice president, former three-time presidential candidate, and onetime nomi-nee Hubert Horatio Humphrey. Surely he could be nominated without having to enter him in all these meddlesome primaries—just like in 1968. If "old Hubert" was picked, one of his friends explained, possibly not quite joking, "most people at the Federal City Club wouldn't have to change a name on their rolodexes." It was widely presumed the AFL-CIO was planning to endorse him and was just holding out for the right signal from him. He certainly seemed interested; the day after the North Carolina primary he sat with reporters for an on-the-record conversa-tion for an hour—and made a veiled swipe at Carter: "Running against Washington won't be a winner in November," he said. "It's essentially an attack on the federal programs, and that's an attack on the poor, the blacks, the minorities and the cities. It's a disguised new form of racism, a disguised new form of conservatism."

Humphrey was the grand old man of Democratic politics. But the old man's very intimacy with the tragedies and triumphs of Democratic presidencies past was precisely what made him disgusting to the bright-eyed tribunes of antipolitics—like the *Village Voice*'s James Wolcott, who wrote, "As far as I'm concerned, any party which again—again!—selects Hubert Vietnam Humphrey to carry its banner deserves the fiery fate which befalls a zeppelin piloted by George C. Scott," star recently of *The Hindenburg*.

The possibility that the old standby might any day answer the Democratic Establishment's draft threw a spanner in the works of every other candidate's strategy. So it was that Carter, the day before the Illinois primary, made a pilgrimage to the nation's capital to pay obeisance to that Establishment, at a dinner with Clark Clifford, the mandarin who in 1973 had decorously suggested Richard Nixon resign the presidency in favor of a bipartisan "government of national unity"; Katharine Graham, the publisher of her family's newspaper the *Washington Post;* and Gaylord Nelson of Wisconsin, Humphrey's biggest booster in the Senate. Carter also gave a second extended interview to Elizabeth Drew. The first time, he had been short and snappish. This time he was solicitous and welcoming.

Then he jetted off to New York—the better to be surrounded by network cameras as he took in the news of his victory in Illinois.

HE HAD GOOD REASON TO START MAKING NICER WITH THE PRESS: THE reporters were on to him. The new narrative was no longer "Jimmy Who?" It was: Jimmy the Hustler, who had mastered the old bunkum artist's motto that if you can fake sincerity, you've got it made. Elizabeth Drew's interview with George Wallace ("He talks about spending all that time on his *kneeeeees*") ran in the *New Yorker.* The *New York Times Magazine* ran Joseph Lelyveld's profile of Jerry Rafshoon, in which the adman promoted himself as the man behind the curtain, prompting the wizard, through the long months of 1975, to speak not from the heart, but purely on the basis of audience response. ("We used to say that's a C performance or that's a B performance or that's an A performance," Rafshoon recalled of the candidate who was supposed never to be performing at all. "We knew instinctively in our minds what made an A and what made a B.")

If you can fake sincerity, you've got it made. If you can project humility brashly, you've got it made. People wanted to believe.

He now had two new opponents. On March 12, California governor Jerry Brown said he soon would enter the presidential race. Carter, traveling in California, responded by announcing he would enter every primary in the nation, no matter who contested him. On March 18, Frank Church finally announced his presidential campaign. He did so just as his work investigating the CIA returned to the news, when Richard Nixon released his answers to a set of questions from the Church Committee over his administration's role in overthrowing Salvador Allende in Chile. Nixon wrote, newspapers reported, that whatever he might or might not have done, he was only continuing Kennedy's and Johnson's policies, and concluded, "I realize it is in vogue to rail against covert activities and clandestine operations," but "the pendulum has swung too far." Church responded in his pious way, acknowledging that his committee had indeed uncovered abuses by Johnson and Kennedy in South America, but that the resulting lesson was not that "illegal actions were justified," but that "once government officials start believing they have the power to act secretly and outside the law we have started down a long slippery slope which culminates in Watergate."

The Democratic race turned south. North Carolina voted on the twenty-third; South Carolina held Democratic precinct caucuses throughout the month. In these states Carter campaigned like Wallace always did—with a country band, which performed "Dixie." That provided the excuse for reporters to pummel him on the inconsistencies in his claim never to have courted Wallace as a political ally in that now-infamous little room off the governor's office in Atlanta. He responded testily: "I didn't care whether he came into Georgia to campaign or not. I never promised him anything." They homed in on his vagueness on the issues—which Carter then turned around, martyrlike, as an unfair attack on him by the Yankee Establishment press: "I don't feel intimidated. I won't be pressured into making rash statements." Interviewers also asked him about a campaign photograph that seemed to play up his resemblance to John F. Kennedy. His handlers claimed never to have noticed such a resemblance at all.

He won North Carolina with 53.6 percent to Wallace's 34.75 percent. Also-rans were dropping like flies: Sargent Shriver suspended his campaign on the twenty-second; Fred Harris's telephones were cut off on the twenty-fourth. The assaults affected the Carter juggernaut hardly a whit.

THE HEADLINE IN THE *MILWAUKEE SENTINEL*'S FIRST EDITION ON APRIL 7 WAS "CARTER UPSET BY UDALL"—followed, in the next edition, after a nail-biting few hours, a headline in the final edition reading "CARTER EDGES OUT UDALL." (When it started looking close, Carter shrewdly made sure aides ran out and got a first edition showing Udall had won, so he could hold it up for photographers just in case it turned out Udall hadn't.) Ford won in Wisconsin by a healthy 11 percentage points because Reagan had canceled his appearances there to prepare for a national TV address. The speech's drafters were adding another count in the anti-détente indictment: as reported by Evans and Novak, Henry Kissinger's close aide Helmut Sonnenfeldt had told a London meeting of U.S. ambassadors that "it must be our policy to strive for an evolution that makes the relationship between the Eastern Europeans and the Soviet Union an organic one," and that an "inorganic, unnatural relationship [that tries to divide Russia and Eastern Europe] is a far greater danger to world peace than the conflict between East and West"—a doctrine, Reagan thundered, "that slaves should accept their fate."

Meanwhile, evidence mounted that the victory on January 20, 1977, might be Pyrrhic—that whoever the next president was, he'd be remembered by history as the captain of a capsizing ship.

Patty Hearst was convicted of armed robbery on Monday, March 21; the *Winston-Salem Journal* worried about a proliferation of an "ever-growing number of Patricia-Hearst-like personalities in this country," due to the decline in "the transmission of ethics from generation to generation."

Was the end of the line coming for America's world dominance? Henry Kissinger apparently thought so. Boomed Reagan in that nationally televised foreign policy speech: "Now we must ask if someone is giving away our own freedom." Which someone? Guess who. "Dr. Kissinger is quoted as saying that he thinks of the United States as Athens and the Soviet Union as Sparta. 'The day of the United States is past and today is the day of the Soviet Union.' And he added, 'My job as Secretary of State is to negotiate the most acceptable second-best position possible."

Reagan didn't cite a source. But a campaign spokesman confirmed it came from a new memoir by Admiral Elmo "Bud" Zumwalt, who was running for the Senate as a Democrat from Virginia. Kissinger's top aide, Lawrence Eagleburger, replied, "He did not say that. It is pure invention and totally irresponsible." Another spokesman said the words were "completely contrary to United States foreign policy"; the White House released a ten-page point-by-point refutation. But plenty of people had heard Kissinger say similar things before. Reagan said, "I will stand by everything I said." A historian later discovered a memo in which Zumwalt transcribed a call he received on March 26 in which an unidentified voice told him, "You should know that on at least two occasions recently Kissinger has said to [Soviet ambassador Anatoly] Dobrynin 'an accident should happen to Admiral Zumwalt.'"

Here was one of the nation's most distinguished retired military officers, convinced he was being set up for a hit by the secretary of state: all kinds of Americans were paranoid these days. Readers that month were snapping up Irving Wallace's new thriller *The R Document,* which had already been sold to the movies. It was set on the eve of the ratification of the Thirty-fifth Amendment, which suspended the Bill of Rights during an epidemic of violent crime and served as cover for the evil FBI director's plan to assassinate the president and set up concentration camps. Nature continued her revenge: on April 17 at Cincinnati's Riverfront Stadium a swarm of five thousand to ten thousand bees hovered over the on-deck circle, then took up residence in the San Francisco Giants' dugout, forcing a thirty-five-minute delay of the game. That was followed soon after by a panic over African clawed frogs—exotic pets imported from South Africa, which bred beyond control and took over the waterways around Riverside, California, exterminating the native fish population. Then came the killer bees, once more: after they swarmed a bus driver in Rio de Janeiro, running him off the road and into another bus, the House passed a bill regulating the importation of honeybee semen into the United States.

What times. What a country. One entrant on the nonfiction side of the *New York Times* bestseller list was called *Winning Through Intimidation.* It fought it out for the top spot with a book that made the fly-on-the-Oval-Office-wall case that Nixon had come closer to meltdown in August 1974 than even the most paranoid dared imagine.

The most melodramatic scene in Carl Bernstein and Bob Woodward's *The Final Days* became a subject for a classic *Saturday Night Live* sketch: Henry Kissinger (played by John Belushi) visits a sozzled Nixon (Dan Aykroyd) in the Lincoln sitting room, whining self-pityingly, "Will history treat me more kindly than my contemporaries?" He breaks into sobs, begging Kissinger to get down on his knees and join him in prayer. Aykroyd: "Don't you *want* to pray, you Christ killer?" Belushi: "I don't vant to get into zat again, Mr. President. Excuse me, I've got to go warn the Strategic Air Command to ignore all presidential orders." That referenced two of the book's other mind-blowing revelations: that Kissinger found Nixon a raging anti-Semite, and that Secretary of Defense James Schlesinger ordered military commanders to ignore Nixon's orders as the presidency slipped through his fingers. Still another was that Kissinger considered Nixon ragingly stupid: "Don't ever write anything more complicated than a *Reader's Digest* article for Nixon," he supposedly instructed his aides.

It also depicted a president on the verge of suicide. "You fellows in your business," he was depicted telling Alexander Haig, "you have a way of handling problems like this. Somebody leaves a pistol in the drawer. I don't have a pistol"—"as if," Woodward and Bernstein wrote, "he were half asking to be given one." Haig was reported to have passed on orders to keep the president away from pills. His son-in-law Edward Cox said Nixon stalked the White House halls at night, "talking to pictures of former Presidents." (Aykroyd to a painting of Kennedy: "Having sex with women within these very walls! That never happened when Dick Nixon was in the White House!" Another of the book's revelations was that Pat and Dick hadn't had sex in fourteen years.) Showing up at noon meetings so drunk that treasury secretary Simon thought he was acting like a "windup doll." Pat spending all day in bed, drunk (he'd promised her in 1962, after all, that he'd never run for office again).

The book was a sensation, outselling *All the President's Men* two to one. The initial printing of two hundred thousand was the largest in Simon & Schuster's history but proved to be not nearly large enough: one bookstore reported selling a hundred copies a day. In the popular culture, it became known, simply, as "the Book." The paperback rights sold for a record $1.55 million.

It was also ferociously controversial—as Woodward and Bernstein knew it would be. They had kept the manuscript under lock and key. The authors broke journalistic precedent by not naming sources or including any footnotes for the reported dialogue, and many of the principals denied having said the words attributed to them. The book also reported the supposed inner thoughts of the characters. Ford's former press secretary Jerry terHorst called it "fictionalized journalism." Typical letters to the editor to *Newsweek,* which ran prepublication excerpts: "I am completely repulsed. . . . They are gossipy little men," and, "You two can be compared to Judas as you sold the heart and soul of a man for a few pieces of silver. May God forgive you for the sorrow you have caused Mr. Nixon and his family." The affair might well have damaged its authors' reputations irrevocably—were those authors not enjoying the roseate glow that accompanied the debut of the actual fictionalization of their journalism on the silver screen, starring Robert Redford as Bob Woodward and Dustin Hoffman as Carl Bernstein.

All the President's Men had its Washington premiere at the Kennedy Center before 1,100 people, where the all-star Hollywood-and-D.C. crowd had weathered the ferocious scramble for twenty-five-dollar tickets for the surreal experience of watching Howard Hunt and his Cubans commit burglary onscreen just down the street from where it actually happened. It provided a sort of synthesis of genres then dominating theaters: disaster movies, like George C. Scott's *The Hindenburg,* which were actually otherwise frequently optimistic and heartening, with Americans from all walks of life pulling together to save the day; nostalgic romps (one of them, *Midway,* an unlikely hit, was about the days when America won its wars); and horrifying world-turned-upside-down depictions of America gone mad, like the new picture *Taxi Driver,* in which a deranged former marine plying his trade down Manhattan's filth-strewn streets tries to assassinate a presidential candidate, in part to impress a preteen prostitute, in part to get back at a woman repulsed when he took her to a pornographic movie on a date (he somehow in all the confusion ends up celebrated as a national hero for saving the candidate's life). On March 29, another such portrait of America gone mad, *One Flew Over the Cuckoo's Nest,* became only the second picture to win all five major Academy Awards (Best Picture, Actor in Lead Role, Actress in Lead Role, Director, and Screenplay) since *It Happened One Night* in 1934.

All the President's Men was nostalgic in its way, too: it was basically a police procedural, in which the two indefatigable, mismatched detectives patiently assembled clues to a world in moral chaos, resolved into order against all the odds. In the last shot the bad guys were depicted as being squarely nailed dead to rights, as ever-more-definitive newspaper copy was clacked out on Woodward's or Bernstein's typewriter. It was a colossal hit—the vehicle by which millions of Americans finally figured out what Watergate had truly been about. The picture even made the cover of *Time* magazine.

Watergate was everywhere that presidential primary season, still. Book after book: Jimmy Breslin's bestseller *How the Good Guys Finally Won;* Jeb Magruder's and Chuck Colson's memoirs and soon one from Maureen "Mo" Dean; Theodore White's *Breach of Faith. Texas Monthly* began its ongoing series, "Heroes for Post-Watergate America." Panasonic ran full-page magazine ads proposing, "How to make sure the candidate of your choice lives up to his word. . . . It's easy. With Panasonic portable cassette tape recorders. All with built-in condenser microphones. So you can record your candidate, just about anywhere his promises take him." A satirical faux documentary, *The Faking of the President,* debuted. It depicted Ron Ziegler dressed as a Nazi, Nixon stealing flowers from the grave of FDR's terrier Fala to place beside Checkers's headstone, and Nixon tearfully confessing. At its premiere in Salt Lake City, during a Mormon convention, the overflow crowd rioted twenty minutes into the screening, tearing up seats, breaking a glass showcase, and overturning a car and setting it on fire.

One place the ongoing fascination with Watergate couldn't have been too popular was the White House. On March 21 the *New York Times* profiled Ford campaign headquarters. The article began with a young volunteer suggesting the office needed a paper shredder to reduce the volume of trash. "'Oh, gee, I don't think so,' Peter F. Kaye, the campaign spokesman, remembers having replied, with an equanimity that hid a shuddering awareness of how inappropriate the recommendation was. The swift burial of the paper shredder idea was one illustration of an unwritten rule at Mr. Ford's campaign headquarters: Don't CREEP." The previous week Ford campaign manager Bo Callaway had been placed on temporary leave, then left the campaign altogether, after the *Denver Post* and NBC carried a report charging him with using his position as secretary of the army to discuss with U.S. Forest Service representatives the expansion of a Colorado ski resort he partly owned. (Nothing came of the charges, but such was the culture of suspicion that the Ford campaign erred on the side of caution.) The next day brought Evans and Novak's scoop on the "Sonnenfeldt Doctrine." On April 6, as Wisconsin went to the polls, the president announced a cabinet-level committee investigating the overseas corporate bribery scandal. Three days later, backfilling the damage from the Sonnenfeldt revelations and Zumwalt's quotes from Henry Kissinger, he opened his campaign for the May 1 primary showdown in Texas John Wayne–style, at the Alamo, pledging, "All of our courage, all of our skill in battle will profit us very, very little if we fail to maintain the unsurpassed military strength which this dangerous world demands of us."

Then he accepted a snack—a tamale—before the cameras, not knowing that before you bit into one you were supposed to strip off the cornleaf husk. That was the lead story the next day. Poor Jerry Ford.

THE NEXT BIG DEMOCRATIC PRIMARY WAS IN PENNSYLVANIA ON APRIL 27; the Republicans were not contesting it. The Supreme Court's *Buckley* opinion had cut off the flow of more than a million dollars in federal matching funds owed the candidates until Congress passed and the president signed a new campaign finance law. On April 22 all of the candidates except the president filed suit on First Amendment grounds arguing that the cutoff violated the First Amendment rights of citizens who'd checked the box on their tax returns to contribute to the federal election fund. The cutoff had already almost finished Morris Udall— about whom the campaign reporters had penned the ditty "Second Place Mo" after his third second-place finish, in Wisconsin, and who in Pennsylvania cut back his television ad expenditures from $150,000 to $85,000 and chopped his radio commercials altogether. The Gallup poll had Carter and the noncandidate Humphrey tied at 31 percent nationwide among Democrats, with Wallace at 13, Scoop Jackson at 6, and Udall at 5. "Where I can get known, I do well," Udall told reporters, desperately, shaking hands at a Fisher body plant in Pittsburgh.

Scoop Jackson had high hopes for the Keystone State, where the old-line union locals that favored both Jackson and Humphrey were powerful. He had won the New York primary handily on April 6—though the effect was severely attenuated by the fact that he'd predicted "a landslide," and that the media interpreted it as an endorsement of the politics of Hubert Humphrey. (Second Place Mo had finished ... second.) Humphrey, Jackson, Udall, and Carter had shared the stage in New York City at a conference of mayors just before the primary there, and Humphrey had stolen the show. Pennsylvania was shaping up as a battle for the "lunch-bucket" voters: those white ethnic building-trade and factory workers who had proved so susceptible to right-wing populist appeals—like the guy who starred in a Nixon campaign commercial in 1972, sitting high up on a construction girder eating his lunch, listening with grave concern as the voice-over instructed him how George McGovern's economic plans "would make forty-seven percent of the people in the United States eligible for welfare" and stick him with the bill. And the voters that same year who had given George Wallace his overwhelming primary victories in Michigan and Maryland that year over the issue of forced busing.

Jimmy Carter, for his part, changed his commercials. Hearing from pollsters that undecided voters found him vague on the issues, his team had an announcer tack introductions onto the existing spots—things like, "Jimmy Carter on the *issue* of health care," and "Jimmy Carter on the *issue* of unemployment"—and then a conclusion in which the same voice said, "If you think about this *critical issue* the way Jimmy Carter does, then vote for him."

Then Carter, tied with a candidate who wasn't even running for president, made his play for the lunch-bucket voters and ended up with the first serious gaffe of his campaign.

It came just before the voting in Wisconsin, and just as a new poll came out that had him ahead of Ford in a head-to-head matchup. He was quoted, deep within a New York *Daily News* story on April 2 concerning government policies to finance construction of low-income housing in middle-class neighborhoods, as saying: "I see nothing wrong with ethnic purity being maintained. I would not force racial integration on a neighborhood by government action. But I would not permit discrimination against a family moving into the neighborhood." A CBS reporter asked him, "What did you mean by ethnic purity?" He answered, "I have nothing against a community that's made up of people who are Polish, Czechoslovakians, French-Canadians, or blacks who are trying to maintain the ethnic purity of their neighborhood. This is a natural inclination on the part of people. . . . I don't think government ought to deliberately break down an ethnically oriented community deliberately by interjecting into it a member of another race. To me, this is contrary to the best interests of the community." Asked to clarify by reporters in Indiana, which voted on May 4, Carter was convoluted: "I'm not trying to say I want to maintain with any kind of government interference the ethnic purity of neighborhoods. What I say is the government ought not to take as a major purpose the intrusion of alien groups into a neighborhood, simply to establish that intrusion."

It was the words "ethnic purity" upon which the critics pounced. They threatened to blunt a key component of his appeal. Carter had a favorite story he liked to tell for black audiences—and white ones who were proud of their own racial enlightenment. It involved the time Joe Louis, the "Brown Bomber," fought Max Schmeling, Hitler's champion, for the heavyweight title in 1938. The twenty-five black families of Archery, Georgia, asked his father, "Mr. Earl," if they could listen to the fight, and he agreed—setting the radio on the windowsill, outside which the congregation gathered. Louis prevailed in a single round. The black listeners made not a sound—saving their whoops and hollers until they were over the railroad tracks and almost out of earshot. Jimmy Carter, went the message, understood segregation. He understood the damage it did to communities, to human decency, to men's souls—segregator and segregated both. As an adult, he had taken serious personal and professional risks to fight to end it. But now, as the Democratic front-runner, a surprise favorite of black voters, he was on the record saying something that sounded like it had come from the mouth of a Klansman.

Seventeen members of the Congressional Black Caucus denounced him, including Andrew Young of Georgia, one of his leading supporters. Scoop Jackson weighed in on ABC's *Issues and Answers*: "It raises the question of his judgment." It was an opportunistic move, for Jackson had the machine of the racist mayor Frank Rizzo organizing for him in Philadelphia. Jackson asked, "Do we want a man as president who has to go around apologizing for the things he has said?" (Jackson's campaign ally Rizzo, on the other hand, had said the previous year during his reelection campaign, "I'm going to make Attila the Hun look like a faggot.") Lester Maddox, who had beaten Carter for governor in 1966 and was famous for chasing blacks off his property with an ax handle after passage of the Civil Rights Act, said he welcomed "the new segregationist term" and offered to lend Carter an ax handle.

Carter made a half apology at a news conference on April 8 in Philadelphia: "I do want to apologize to all those who have been concerned about the unfortunate use of the term 'ethnic purity,'" he said. "I would make sure that anyone who wanted to move into a neighborhood would have the right to do it." He added, though, that he stood behind the general thought. As he put it in a second apology, "I should have said something like 'ethnic personality,'" but he still opposed the "arbitrary use of federal force" to change the ethnic character of neighborhoods.

Here was the signature Carter straddle. As Udall complained, "That add-on is characteristic of his approach. On an amazing number of issues Jimmy meets himself going through that revolving door." But the same straddle was made by the president—who responded to a question about Carter's gaffe by saying that "an ethnic heritage is a great treasure," and adding, "I don't think that federal action should be used to destroy that ethnic treasure." Ford also wondered "whether that remark will have any impact on the support that he has heretofore gotten in the black communities of the various states." Carter cleverly responded to *that* by elevating himself to the status of Ford's presumptive opponent: "I am happy to have aroused the interest and the opposition of the President. . . . I guess now he's joined the 'Stop Carter' movement. But what he should know from me is that I am going to stop him in November."

On the defensive? Not so much. Instead he displayed another signature political skill: turning adversity into advantage. At a press conference in Philadelphia, he held up a newspaper with the headline "STOP-CARTER ALLIANCE IS FORMED." He replied, "I'm not going to yield anything to the political bosses. . . . I am letting the voters know that I belong to them. . . . I have never predicated my campaign on endorsements." He then traveled to Detroit (Michigan's primary was on May 18), speaking next to the city's black mayor, Coleman Young—who had endorsed him. And then before thousands in Atlanta at a rally with Daddy King, who had endorsed him, too, assuring the audience, "I love him and believe in him." Meanwhile, the Associated Press story about Carter's serial apologies appeared in many papers beside another AP piece about how the federal government's welfare costs increased 21.4 percent in a single year, adding to the rolls 266,000 families, 11.3 million individuals, and running up a $24.8 billion bill all told.

You might be a voter panicked to think that hordes of black welfare recipients might soon crowd you out of a neighborhood whose, um, "ethnic personality" you cherished. Or you might be one who revered Martin Luther King. Either way, if you were a Pennsylvanian, you might well have voted for James Earl Carter. His victory there was called on TV "overwhelming" within three hours after the polls closed. He got twice as many delegates as Scoop.

Two days later, Jackson announced he wouldn't be campaigning in Indiana—it looked like the end of the road. It was also the deadline for entering the New Jersey primary, held on June 8. This was the last chance to enter a primary for the year, and a poll in New Jersey showed the Minnesotan ahead of the Georgian by forty-six points. Humphrey had asked the chairman of the state's Democratic Party to gather signatures to get him on the ballot. At a news conference on April 11 he said, "If I'm a candidate I'll win. Make no mistake about that . . . should my party need me at the convention, I would consider it an honor to serve the party. . . . I'm ready." But on April 29 Humphrey stepped up to the press conference microphones for a statement so eagerly anticipated that the networks cut into the soap operas to broadcast it. It was anticlimactic: "I shall not seek it; I shall not compete for it; I shall not search for it; I shall not scramble for it," he said of the possibility he might actively campaign for the presidency. "One thing I don't need at my stage of life is to be ridiculous." He joked that he hadn't thought about a "brokered convention"—one in which no candidate got a majority on the first ballot, and bosses began horse-trading the delegates they controlled in exchange for favors; the Democrats hadn't had one since 1952—"since eleven A.M."

But he also said, not joking: "I'm around."

GERALD FORD WAS IN HOUSTON SAYING CARTER "HAS NOT DEALT WITH the hard decisions of the Oval Office"—as if Carter were already the nominee. Texas, for the Republicans, was shaping up as slash-and-burn. Ronald Reagan had not dealt with the hard decisions of the Oval Office, either. And Gerald Ford did not intend to let Texans forget it.

For his part, Reagan had to turn up the volume. Bereft of matching funds, he was still practically broke. He had pulled out of Wisconsin two weeks before the April 6 primary, claiming he was preparing for his March 31 televised speech. But he had actually stopped traveling to save money, which banks would no longer loan him—fearing repercussions from the White House, John Sears claimed, though it's just as likely would-be creditors just feared they would never get their money back. Reagan made only one trip in the two weeks before April 6, slaying them at a party fund-raiser in Virginia (he revised a favorite old story about the man who got read a letter informing him he would no longer be getting Social Security payments because he was dead, this time around adding that a sympathetic bureaucrat who learned about the mistake sent him seven hundred dollars for "funeral expenses" to tide him over). And in fact that March 31 broadcast almost hadn't come about at all. First, the networks wouldn't sell him the time. Then, when NBC changed its mind, the campaign didn't have the money—until a conservative banker from Houston came through with an emergency $100,000 loan.

Privation, though, and the president's insults—and receptive foot-stomping Texan audiences—turned out to concentrate Reagan's mind beautifully. Ford hadn't even opened his campaign at the Alamo when Reagan claimed he'd seen a transcript of some obscure testimony from the State Department's negotiator in Panama, Ambassador-at-Large Ellsworth Bunker, to the Panama Canal Subcommittee of the House Merchant Marine and Fisheries Committee, which Reagan said laid out the administration's intention to "give away" the canal. He would say that the Panama Canal Zone was "sovereign U.S. territory, every bit the same as Alaska and all the states that were carved from the Louisiana Purchase."

He would say it, and the Texas foot-stomping would commence; it was something to behold.

Even though it was not true.

The 1904 treaty granted the United States not sovereignty but "rights, power, and authority" there "as if it were the sovereign of the territory," a crucial distinction: if a baby was born to a foreigner in Alaska or Louisiana, that child would be an American citizen, certainly not the case for Panamanians who gave birth in the Zone.

Tell that, though, to a foot-stomping Texan. You might get stomped upon yourself.

It had to be excruciating for Jerry Ford. But running against Ronald Reagan for anything must have been excruciating for those who wished to honor truth. There was that tourist paddle wheeler the *Delta Queen*, ordered by meddlesome Washington bureaucrats to be fire-proofed, when it had "never had a fire," though she had actually caught fire shortly before he said this. Or the time, at a 1975 roundtable at the conservative think tank the American Enterprise Institute, when he said that the Food and Drug Administration was killing Americans: "I think something more than 40,000 tuberculars alone have died in this country who conceivably could have been saved by a drug that has been widely used the past few years through Europe." In fact the drug, rifampin, had been on the market since 1971—and the FDA had approved it even before the manufacturer submitted the application. And the number of people who died of tuberculosis was less than 28,000 in the decade when he spoke. As it happened, this contradicted what Reagan said on the radio that summer in a rant against socialist medicine. He quoted Teddy Kennedy as saying that medical costs were increasing while quality was declining. Reagan said, "He's talking about the country in which . . . tuberculosis, typhoid fever, and many other diseases have disappeared in our lifetime."

He had a favorite bowdlerization of a quote from Thomas Jefferson: "The American people won't make a mistake if they're given all the facts." Surely Gerald Ford wished that this were actually so. Didn't Mark Twain once say something about how a lie can travel halfway around the world before the truth has time to lace up its shoes?

In Texas, the lies wore cowboy boots. Reagan would say, "We should end those negotiations and tell them we bought it, we paid for it, we built it, and we intend to keep it," and the stomping would start up anew. The "we built it" part was a new addition, playing to generations of heroic schoolboy tales about beating back the swamps and jungles in the interest of progress, but that wasn't quite accurate, either: Panamanians and other contract laborers were the ones who overwhelmingly wielded the tools. Although at that, Ford was telling a half-truth about Panama, too: that America "will never give up its right to the canal." But the testimony to the Fisheries Committee flushed out by Reagan had Ambassador Bunker admitting that his negotiating directive was to offer to yield the Canal Zone "after a period of time" and the canal itself "over a longer period of time." And on April 16, after Reagan pounded him in Texas for three days straight on the subject, the president admitted that, yes, negotiations could lead to eventual Panamanian control, but only after another "thirty to fifty years." But that failure to write a new treaty could lead to further rioting in Panama and perhaps elsewhere in Latin American—which, of course, only played into Reagan's charge that Ford was letting America be pushed around by tinhorn dictators.

Damned if he did, damned if he didn't.

Late in March the Ford campaign had defied a letter from a Reagan campaign lawyer to the FEC charging that since the secretary of state was "using his high office for the express purpose of a campaign platform to promote the Ford candidacy," Kissinger's travels should be charged against Ford's campaign spending limit. And the campaign staff sent Kissinger to Dallas for a series of speeches to answer Reagan. Kissinger said America and Russia were in a position of "rough equilibrium" on nuclear arms, and that "nothing we could have done would have prevented it," and "nothing we can do now will make it disappear"—not exactly stirring stuff. Then Ford's own new campaign manager, Rogers Morton, predicted, without warning his boss, that Kissinger would soon be fired. The president was forced in an April 13 press conference to affirm that "Secretary Kissinger has been one of the finest, if not the finest, Secretary of State this country has ever had"— not the sort of thing that played well in Texas.

On April 17, Ford's press secretary, Ron Nessen, the first to come to the job from TV instead of print media, did something the White House thought frightfully clever, in order to dispel the president's klutz image: Nessen hosted *Saturday Night Live*. After members of the "Dead String Quartet" opened the show by keeling over, Nessen's monologue nearly had the audience doing the same; after Dan Aykroyd's pitch for the Super Bass-o-Matic '76 (a blender: "Wow," exclaimed Laraine Newman, drinking down a blended beverage, "that's terrific bass!"), Nessen fell flat playing beside Chevy Chase as the president and a stuffed dog depicting the presidential pooch Liberty. After John Belushi played a lieutenant colonel puffing a joint as an inducement to recruiting today's counterculture youth, and a video cameo from the real-life Gerald Ford appropriating Chevy Chase's tagline ("Good evening, I'm Gerald Ford, and you're not"), Nessen sat embarrassed through a Weekend Update gag in which the pronunciation-impaired Miss Emily Litella (Gilda Radner) railed against "all this fuss I've been hearing about the 1976 presidential erection." At one point he was booed. The exercise was a bomb—not least in Texas, where marijuana-scented parodies of America's military honor were not exactly appreciated.

On April 20, Washingtonians who had been waiting for an official endorsement of Ford from John Connally, still Texas's most towering political figure, were shocked when the former treasury secretary, who knew a political dead fish when he saw one, stabbed the President of the United States in the back. He would endorse neither man, and hinted he might launch a third-party run. Reagan took the gloves off. Ford had signed a bill that made moves toward allowing U.S. companies to crack the embargo against the Republic of Vietnam, and opened the door to diplomatic recognition—Reagan's opening to reintroduce the Vietnam MIA card. No matter that a delegation led by the conservative Mississippi Democrat Gillespie "Sonny" Montgomery, chairman of the House Select Committee on Missing Persons in Southeast Asia, had traveled to Vietnam and concluded that the notion of MIAs still in Vietnam was a myth, manufactured by the Chinese to keep their rival from diplomatic recognition by the United States. Reagan remained adamant. "If there is to be any recognition," he boomed on April 20 in a shopping center in Macon, Georgia, which voted on May 4 along with Indiana, "let it be discussed only after they have kept their pledge to give a full accounting of our men still listed as missing in action." He also charged that Ford's "attorney general is promoting a seven-point measure which is gun control and will take guns away from law-abiding citizens."

The next day's Evans and Novak column spied in Reagan's rhetoric a new electoral strategy: since Texas was an "open" primary state, where citizens could choose to vote in either party's primary, Reagan was pushing hard on the sort of cultural resentments that once drove Democrats to George Wallace. He put on a TV commercial written by Arthur Finkelstein starring a Fort Worth voter named Rollie Millirons, who said, "I've always been a Democrat. As much as I hate to admit it, George Wallace can't be nominated. So for the first time in my life I'm gonna vote in the Republican primary. I'm gonna vote for Ronald Reagan." Flyers featured a drawing of an elephant—"I'm for Reagan!"—and a donkey—"Me too!" Evans and Novak made a sartorial observation from a Reagan rally to suggest that it was working: "The remarkable gathering of over 3,000 lacked the sleek, chic look of Texas Republicans and seemed much more like a typical Wallace rally—women in house dresses, sport-shirted men, lots of American flags. If the virtual collapse of Wallace's candidacy is sending right-wing populist Democrats across party lines to Reagan, President Ford is in deepening trouble here."

More conservative movement money came in: a total of $778,000 from a mailing in North Carolina, $110,000 in "independent expenditures" from the ACU's Conservative Victory Fund, $24,000 from a former high school government teacher for ads that instructed Democrats to "call your local newspaper" to learn how they could register as Republicans to vote for Reagan; so many calls swamped the *Waco News-Tribune* that the paper ran instructions on its front page to ease the strain on its switchboard. And Ronald Reagan was now defining the political playing field. Ford intensified his language against Hanoi: "Under no circumstances do we contemplate recognizing North Vietnam." His press secretary was forced to defend the president against charges that he was manipulating Congress to stall a new campaign finance bill to renew matching funds, in order to "starve out" Reagan. As Pat Buchanan wrote, "The liberal wing of the Republican Party is a spectator now. It lacked the numbers to advance its own candidate, or the will to save its own champion, the Vice President. The civil war in the GOP is between conservatives—militant and moderate."

THE SORTS OF STORIES THAT MADE THE SUSPICIOUS CIRCLES NOD SMUGLY crowded the news. For instance, from San Diego, the story of a mentally retarded Marine private beaten by other recruits for some forty-five minutes on the orders of their drill sergeant as the victim cried, "God, make them stop"—until he was finally silenced by his death. And, from the small town of Grangeville, Idaho, the city council that considered a proposal to outlaw the wearing of handguns within city limits after a posse of armed citizens confronted the county prosecutor demanding his resignation. Thirty of them, armed to the teeth, visited the council chamber as the measure was being debated. One said the Second Amendment right was "just like any other muscle in your body. If you don't exercise it regularly it goes away. I only exercised my inalienable right. I'm glad I did it because I can see that this right is in danger." They then presented a letter announcing, "We will resist with all lawful means your tyrannical act which attempts to abrogate the Second Amendment to the U.S. Constitution.... If anyone should be disarmed it should be the government, not us." Retailers testified that the gun-toters were scaring off their customers. To no avail: the ordinance failed.

Time featured the nation's "Porno Plague," an "open, aggressive, $2-billion-a-year, crime-ridden growth enterprise," flourishing now that "most of the traditional barriers to porn are now down," and reported a demonstration of 1,200 marchers, including two hundred schoolchildren, in front of "Show World," the sexual supermarket on New York's Forty-second Street that introduced live sex shows, a forty-four-second peep for only a quarter. And in Boston, the ongoing busing crisis—and the anger of white construction workers over affirmative action—once again turned violent. Early in April, one hundred fifty antibusing youth confronted a black man in a three-piece suit, attorney Theodore Landsmark, executive director of the association of black contractors agitating for more city contracts, with the most convenient weapon they could get their hands on: a large American flag, with which one of them appeared to run Landsmark through as if with a spear. The mayor, stunned, watched the scene from his office up above. The picture of the attack appeared the next day on the front page of the *Boston Globe.*

Landsmark appeared at a press conference with his entire face crisscrossed by white bandages, excoriating city officials, like school committee member Louise Day Hicks, who "incite and encourage" racist violence. In the *Globe* the president of the South Boston High School and Home Association, James M. Kelly, said that the attack was "retaliation" for "black crime." Two Saturdays later, on April 24, liberal religious leaders, the mayor, and senators Brooke and Kennedy led a "Procession Against Violence" of about fifty thousand people through the city—though few blacks and fewer antibusing whites showed up. "Teach us, O God, that the voice of violence speaks not for democracy but for the devil of fascism," a rabbi prayed. The march was followed by bomb threats and stone throwing.

But, simultaneously with all that, came another development that helped define the political playing field. Call it patriotism chic—another edge for Ronald Reagan. It was a journeyman outfielder for the Chicago Cubs who came to the rescue, the afternoon after that Boston violence. Some knucklehead ran onto dead center of the playing field at Dodger Stadium with his eleven-year-old son, set down an American flag, doused it with lighter fluid, and struggled to strike a match. All of a sudden the center fielder dashed into the frame, swooped down and grabbed up the flag, and deposited it safely in the dugout as police arrested the intruders. RICK MONDAY . . . YOU MADE A GREAT PLAY, the scoreboard spelled out when he came to bat in the next half inning.

UPI sent out a feature by its sports editor:

"Rick Monday isn't one of those super-patriots. He's just an ordinary guy. Ordinary in the sense he doesn't get up on a soapbox making speeches but still appreciates all the opportunities this country offers over so many others.

"The action he took when he saw the flag about to be burned may signal the beginning of some kind of turnaround in the general pattern of our behavior.

"Maybe we're getting back to that point where it once was fashionable for everyone to respect not only his country and his flag but also himself, and if it turns out that somebody like Rick Monday had to be the one to show the way then I say hooray for him. . . .

"In that regard, I seem to be noticing an increasing number of people, including some like Muhammad Ali who were critical of this country in the past, suddenly rediscovering many of its advantages. These advantages were here all the time but somehow were overlooked in all the babble and confusion."

The accompanying photograph showed Monday accepting a peck on the cheek from "Miss Illinois Teenager" Mary Lou Valkenberg during Rick Monday Day ceremonies at Wrigley Field. "I'd like to thank the American public, which typifies what the American flag means," he said, the echo booming like in the climactic scene of *Pride of the Yankees.* "God bless America!" More such ceremonies followed. America had a new national hero, who said into one of the microphones stuck in his face, "If you're going to burn the flag, don't do it around me. I've been to too many veterans' hospitals and seen too many broken bodies of guys who tried to protect it."

THE PRESIDENT LANDED IN TEXAS ON TUESDAY, FOUR DAYS BEFORE THE May 4 primary, bearing signs reminding voters who had the power to deliver the pork: PRESIDENT FORD, '76. His secretary of state, however, landed in Africa—hat in hand. Part of his agenda for his unprecedented two-week trip to the continent was to represent the United States at a conclave between First World and Third World nations, the latter still swaggering after the 1973 Arab oil embargo—and the American colossus's humiliation in Vietnam. Kissinger hoped to put a finger in the dike against developing nations' radical schemes to form cartels intended to advantage sellers over buyers of crucial commodities like bauxite. A political cartoon mocked the notion of mighty Henry Kissinger as humble supplicant. He wore safari gear and a pith helmet. He shook the hand of a handsome, dark-skinned potentate in a suit, who greeted him, "Dr. Kissinger, I presume." The political timing was terrible. Texas cowboys didn't care for secretaries of state on safari.

Another goal was to unveil a new diplomatic stance toward the landlocked southern African nation named after the British colonialist Cecil Rhodes—a country ruled by whites who were outnumbered by native blacks by a factor of twenty-three. "Time is running out for Rhodesia's white rulers," Kissinger said as he stepped off his silver-and-blue jet. "The future of Africa must be shaped by Africans." On April 28 he announced as official U.S. policy "unrelenting U.S. opposition" and "massive discouragement" toward anything standing in the way of a peaceful transfer of power to the black majority. Warning that violent civil war was imminent between the white government and black militants who'd been waging a guerrilla war against it since the country ceased being a British colony in 1965, he advised Americans to leave the country for their own safety. He also said the administration would work for repeal of the "Byrd Amendment," a law that directed the State Department to ignore a United Nations embargo against the purchase of Rhodesia's number-one export, chromium—a crucial ingredient in the manufacture of stainless steel.

The next day, back in the United States, as Hubert Humphrey decided not to enter the New Jersey primary and a bomb blast injured

twenty-two at a courthouse in Boston and police weighed the seriousness of further threats against two state office buildings, the John F.
Kennedy Federal Building, the Statler Hilton hotel, several banks, and
the police precinct investigating the courthouse blast, the Reagan team
spied in Henry Kissinger's African peregrinations another opportunity
for an offensive. "Rhodesia, primarily, and South Africa, secondarily,"
UPI explained, "are favorite causes of right-wing Republicans and
major U.S. industrial firms." The generous interpretation of this was
that conservatives pragmatically judged these maligned but pro-Western
nations as important strategic bulwarks against the spread of Communism. (The world's only other exporter of chromium happened to be
the Soviet Union.) The ungenerous interpretation was that they thought
black Africans lacked the capacity to govern themselves. Leave it to the
silver-tongued Reagan to devise a rhetoric that made holding off on
black rule sound humanitarian, an anti- rather than a pro-imperialist
imperative.

Reagan made the argument the day before the primary, in San Antonio, to three thousand, just outside the Alamo fortress. "We seem to
be embarking on a policy of dictating to the people of southern Africa
and running the risk of increased violence and bloodshed in an area
already beset by tremendous antagonism and difficulties," he said. His
claim was that what Kissinger called a necessity to ratchet down civil
war was in fact instigating civil war. "The people of Rhodesia—black
and white—have never been our enemies. They fought with us in World
War II against Hitler and in the Pacific. If they show a creative attitude
that can lead to a peaceful settlement, ourselves and others should avoid
rhetoric or actions that could trigger chaos or violence. They have special problems which require time to solve. We're not going to cure the
ills of the world overnight. The great issue of racial justice is as vital here
at home as it is in Africa, and it would be well to make sure our own
house is in order before we fly off to other lands to attempt to dictate
policies to them."

We shall overcome.

Then came a low blow. He said of Kissinger, "What is more incredible is his announcement that our citizens in Rhodesia will not be protected by the United States government and that U.S. citizens residing
in Rhodesia will be advised to get out. This has to be a first—the United
States government proclaiming officially that its citizens must go unpro-
tected in a foreign land."

Then he was off to speak at the Houston Music Theater, also before
three thousand people, who gave him two standing ovations, the first

after he promised to "put God back in the classrooms," the second after he pledged to "never allow American soldiers to die in a no-win war."

He had already said, in Georgia, of the Kissinger-Ford Rhodesia policy, "I'm afraid we are going to have a massacre." Now Kissinger was livid. This was the real world he was dealing with: one of trade-offs, compromises, negotiation, intelligence assessments—such as the ones that, apparently, suggested the white government wasn't long for this world, and that it was time to get on the side of the winners if America wanted to preserve a flow of cheap chrome for the future, and preserve stability in a newly vital strategic region. What the hell, Kissinger plainly thought, did Ronald Reagan know? (Or: what the hell did Kissinger's old rival James Schlesinger, the right-wing former defense secretary now advising Reagan, know?) Ford gave Kissinger leave to vent spleen, on the record (previously, his attacks on Reagan had come through the media via an unnamed "senior American diplomat"). He did so on a plane to Monrovia, saying that Reagan's warnings of a "massacre" were "totally irresponsible," that "all states bordering Rhodesia have declared that the armed struggle has already started and as far as we can see, it has started. There is danger of outside intervention that would intensify it. I tried to develop a program that puts emphasis on negotiation and put a timetable on it as the only hope for avoiding massacre."

Not the kind of language conservative Texans liked to hear. President Ford, apparently, knew it. Damned if he did, damned if he didn't. At a speech in Dallas on Thursday, April 29, he bragged he would win—despite the fact that the day before, his audience ignored him in Lubbock (until he introduced his supporter, Dallas Cowboys coach Tom Landry), and half his audience had walked out of his next speech, in Houston, before the scheduled Q&A. By April 30, however, the boasting was dropped—though the attacks picked up. "When it comes to the life and death decisions of our national security the decisions must be the right one. There are no retakes in the Oval Office." (Reagan, asked by the *Dallas Morning News* what he would think if he was asked by Ford to be vice president, answered, "*Welllll,* maybe he would like to have a Vice President that makes retakes and who is irresponsible.") The President Ford Committee was also spending four times more money than Citizens for Reagan, almost a stunning million dollars, to no avail; every time Reagan mentioned Panama, a historian noted, "voters would inundate Ford's campaign offices with phone calls wanting to know why the President was giving it away."

The next night the president spoke at the White House Correspondents Dinner, where a president's job was to let his hair down and tell jokes. Ford told his just as the polls closed in Texas: "I have a great many friends in Texas, but we won't know exactly how many for an hour." "I totally agree with Reagan about Panama"—he put on a garish Panama hat—"I bought it, I paid for it, I own it, and I'm going to keep it." And: "I learned two things in Texas: Never underestimate your opponent. And always shuck the tamale."

Then he learned how few friends he had in Texas. He lost, 33 to 66 percent. Reagan garnered all ninety-six of the state's Republican delegates. That was almost 9 percent of what he needed for the nomination—the Republicans' delegate formula happening to tilt toward the conservative South and Southwest. It was the worst election defeat ever suffered by a sitting president.

THE FORD CAMPAIGN LEARNED SOMETHING ELSE, SOMETHING THE STAFF should have figured out much earlier. Republican turnout in, for instance, El Paso, had doubled since the last election. An unsigned Ford campaign memo written shortly after the Texas landslide pondered the mystery: "The unexpected Reagan success in certain caucus states— New Mexico, Kansas, Colorado—seems puzzling. Turnout is very high, the people coming to vote or to the caucuses are unknown and have not been involved in the Republican political system before; they vote overwhelmingly for Reagan."

It continued, "A clear pattern is emerging; these turnouts now do not seem accidental but appear to be the result of skillful organization by extreme right wing political groups in the Reagan camp." (How right-wing? One questioner at a presidential rally asked, "Do you plan to continue to lead this country to full socialism?") They were "operating almost invisibly through direct mail and voter turnout efforts conducted by . . . a loose coalition of right-wing political committees set up by or in conjunction with Richard Vigurie's [sic] political direct mail firm. Others have been funded either by a wealthy sponsor (Joe Coors) or by a special interest group like the NRA. . . . They have been raising money for many years, and have extensive mailing lists made up of people interested in these issues."

The memo named some of the groups: George Wallace's old American Independence Party ("Vigurie [sic] conducted the Wallace fund raising operation and owns this mailing list"), the National Conservative Political Action Committee, the National Right to Work Committee, the American Medical Association's PAC, the NRA, the ACU, the Committee for the Survival of a Free Congress, the Heritage Foundation. It noted, "Many of the members of these groups are not loyal Republicans or Democrats. They are alienated from both parties because neither takes a sympathetic view toward their issues. Particularly those groups controlled by Vigurie [*sic*] hold a 'rule or ruin' attitude toward the GOP." It named frightening stakes for Gerald Ford: "Being well funded, they can afford to conduct independent advertising campaigns on behalf of Reagan. Such expenditures are not chargeable to Reagan's campaign"—meaning effectively that Reagan could still earn matching funds even if his supporters spent an *infinite* amount of money, whatever caps were designated by the campaign finance law.

And it adumbrated their brave new political methodology: "They can target an effective direct mail campaign based on response to fund raising mail using outrageous literature designed to motivate people interested in a right-wing cause. . . . In a state where the GOP vote is traditionally small such an effort can be devastating. In caucus states where few people attend the county caucuses such an effort can control the state conventions."

It was striking that the scales fell from Republican establishment eyes only then—that in the middle of 1976 a top staffer in an incumbent president's campaign didn't even know how to spell "Richard Viguerie." But the Reagan hands still flying commercial instead of charter, who hadn't been sure they would win Texas at all, were a little taken aback by their right-wing infrastructure's sudden full flowering in the field of presidential politics, too. It had been sudden, this brave new political world coming into bloom, this bastard child of the 1974 Campaign Finance Reform Act. Five hundred and sixteen political action committees were registered with the FEC in 1974; by the end of 1976 there were 1,116 Though not all, of course, were conservative, the most aggressive ones were: Paul Weyrich's Committee for the Survival of a Free Congress raised $1.7 million in 1976. All told that year "New Right" PACs—excluding preexisting conservative groups, who'd raised but $250,000 for congressional races in 1972—raised $5.6 million.

The memo concluded, with the key words underlined: "We are in real danger of being out-organized by a small number of highly motivated *right wing nuts.*"

But they were also in danger of being outmotivated by voters who were not that nutty at all. William Safire published a smart postmortem on Texas. He pointed out that Henry Kissinger's speeches for Ford in Dallas "gave a boost to the *Reagan* forces"—as did his attack on Reagan from overseas.

In words that applied to Jimmy Carter's successes, too, he said, "The campaign centers on who can best appeal to our pride rather than our guilt. Who can assert America's moral strength and affirm our greatness?" Not Henry Kissinger: "In Texas, relinquishing the Panama Canal was a vivid symbol of the 'one-way street' to national decline, and this cannot be dismissed as mere cowboy kookies." It was not what the pundits had seen coming, Reagan's "kind of pushy patriotism, by jingo, a reaction to Vietnam-Watergate that the self-flagellators did not expect." But Gerald Ford had better pay attention, the Florida paper advised him: stop condescending to Reagan. "Instead, make the case for what you're doing to regenerate our national will. You can't shuck your diplomatic tamale now—that would be a sign of weakness—but you can start making your own case."

Especially after what happened right after Texas. Speaking to ten thousand in the coliseum at Fort Wayne, Indiana, the president desperately waved the recent words of Barry Goldwater in the air: the 1964 nominee said he supported Ford on Panama "and I think Reagan would too if he knew more about it." He said in a TV interview that "Governor Reagan has taken many, too many simplistic statements and indicated in one way or another he might take a rash action."

Then, on Tuesday, May 4, Indiana, Georgia, and Alabama went to the polls—and gave the rash Reagan 51, 68, and 71 percent respectively. In Indiana Reagan had scored a last-minute 10-point turnaround. The delegate count was now reportedly 381 to 372 for Reagan. The AP's political commentator Walter Mears wrote, "Reagan's victories put the President's political future in jeopardy." Evans and Novak wrote that it "opens the distinct possibility that Gerald R. Ford may not win the Republican nomination." Rogers Morton, asked how he planned to respond, answered with a gaffe: "I'm not going to rearrange the furniture on the *Titanic*!"

The next week was Nebraska. Barry Goldwater wrote a letter of advice to Ford: "You are the President. Do not stupe [*sic*] to arguing with another candidate." Another candidate, he suggested, for whom he had hearty contempt: "Reagan's trick, as you know is to have a whole handful of cards and he shuffles out whatever comes out to be ten minutes of speaking." (So Ford's speeches, the 1964 nominee suggested, should be equally "punchy.") He also betrayed contempt for Reagan's supporters—Goldwater supporters, once upon a time: "You are not going to get the Reagan vote. These are the same people who got me the nomination and they will never swerve." Instead he should concentrate on "middle America. They have never had it so good"—though who knows where Goldwater got that argument. The latest unemployment rate was 9 percent.

But Reagan won Nebraska 51 to 49. Which was even worse for Ford than a mere loss. This was Reagan's first victory in a state that did not allow Democrats to vote for Republicans—destroying Ford's argument that Reagan's victories were owed only to Wallace Democrats crossing over to vote Republican. Counting a Ford win that same day in West Virginia, the score over the first eleven days including the "May Day Massacre" was 282 delegates for Ronald Reagan, and 27 for the President of the United States.

He showed up in caricature on the cover of that week's *Time* wearing a "WIN" button alongside Reagan in a schoolboy's goofy helicopter beanie. The issue included an interview with Reagan, who went after the Democrats' Georgian heir apparent like it was a general election—though a Republican general election candidate hadn't sounded like this since Barry Goldwater in 1964: "He's for the Humphrey-Hawkins bill"—Senator Humphrey and Watts Congressman Augustus F. Hawkins's legislation to require the Federal Reserve to implement monetary policy with full employment (defined originally as a 2 percent unemployment rate) as its target—and if 2 percent or less unemployment did not result, for the government to directly provide jobs.

"If ever there was a design for fascism, that's it. Fascism was really the basis for the New Deal. It was Mussolini's success in Italy, with his government-directed economy, that led the early New Dealers to say, 'But Mussolini keeps the trains running on time.' The Humphrey-Hawkins bill calls for the same kind of planned economy, and that would mark the end of the free marketplace in this country."

CHAPTER TWENTY-EIGHT

They Yearned to Believe

THE CHURCH COMMITTEE'S FINAL REPORT HAD BEEN RELEASED THE morning of the Pennsylvania primary, April 27, full of stunning revelations about the CIA and FBI dressed in short, sharp prose: "unsavory and vicious tactics have been employed—including anonymous attempts to break up marriages, disrupt meetings, ostracize persons from their professions, and provoke target groups into rivalries that might result in deaths"; "many Americans and domestic groups have been subjected to investigation who were not suspected of criminal activity"; "the intelligence agencies have regularly collected information about personal and political activities irrelevant to any legitimate government interest." But even that was not biting enough for three Democratic members, Phil Hart, Walter Mondale, and Gary Hart, who called the report "diluted," its "most important implications either lost or obscured in vague language."

Once more, not too many people cared. The *New York Times* was about the only paper to quote the part about "unsavory and vicious tactics." None, apparently, quoted the report's conclusion that "the Constitution has been violated in secret and the power of the executive branch has gone unchecked, unchallenged." A quote from the former head of the FBI's domestic surveillance division—"Never once did I hear anybody, including myself, raise the question: 'Is this course of action which we have agreed upon lawful, is it legal, is it ethical or moral?'"—went virtually unnoticed. The report also printed in full a once-top-secret 1954 document by World War II air ace General Jimmy Doolittle describing the CIA's expanded mission: "long-standing American concepts of 'fair play' must be reconsidered. We must . . . learn to subvert, sabotage, and destroy our enemies by more clever, more sophisticated, and more effective methods than those used against us. It may become necessary that the American people be made acquainted with, understand, and support this fundamentally repugnant philosophy." But the American people did not formally make the acquaintance of that philosophy, not in 1954, or 1976—for few if any papers quoted the Doolittle Report, either.

As Otis Pike said, "they think it is better not to know."

Frank Church had finally entered the presidential race. "To those who say it's too late," he said in the tiny town of Idaho City (tinier than Plains, Georgia!), where he grew up, "I reply that it's never too late— nor are the odds ever too great—to try. In that spirit the West was won, and in that spirit, I announce my candidacy for the Presidency of the United States." But when he entered Nebraska's May 11 primary it was easy for the media to dismiss him; newspapers and networks weren't even sending reporters into the state, so sure were they of another Carter win.

Carter won Texas and Indiana on May 4, both handily (in Indiana he got 68 percent), and made the covers of *Time* and *Newsweek* as the presumptive nominee. Washington sages started watching Old Man Daley, seeing if the Chicago mayor was ready to move in with an endorsement, the traditional sign that in the party of Jefferson and Jackson the fat lady had sung. He was not ready yet—though he did say the combo of Carter and Adlai Stevenson III, the senator his machine was responsible for electing, would make an "outstanding" ticket.

Then, a bombshell. Carter had hired a brilliant young speechwriter named Bob Shrum. Nine days into his employment—and the day after the Pennsylvania primary—Shrum resigned. He made his resignation letter public. He said he'd joined the campaign because he thought Carter had "found the idiom to reach across the deep divisions of our time." He said he quit because Carter was "manipulative and deceitful." He gave examples: Of a plan to help coal miners suffering from black lung disease, Carter had allegedly said, "It would offend the operators. And why should I do this for Arnold Miller"—the head of the union— "if he won't come and endorse me? . . . I don't think the benefits should be automatic. They chose to be miners." And of the Israeli-Palestinian crisis, "I don't want any more statements on the Middle East or Lebanon. Jackson has all the Jews anyway." And though Carter pledged, on the campaign trail, a 5 to 7 percent cut in Pentagon spending, Shrum claimed he privately said he might favor "a substantial increase in the defense budget."

Shrum addressed Carter in his letter: "You say you wish to keep your options open. Within reason, that is understandable. But an election is the only option the people have. After carefully reflecting on what I have seen and heard here, I don't know what you would do as president." Shrum told Mary McGrory, one of those who warned he would never work in Washington again, "But he lies, and nobody will say it. I can't excuse myself from saying something because I tell myself that it wouldn't make any difference. Too many people did that during the Vietnam War." Carter, wounded, responded, "I don't feel inclined to comment on this young man's statement."

But Carter added, he "obviously wrote the letter for the news media. . . . I'm not a liar and I don't make statements in private contrary to those I make in public."

Which, however, was a lie. And contrary to what he said in private.

Came the results from Nebraska: Frank Church, 38.4 percent; Jimmy Carter, 37.62 percent. Hardly mentioning his recent career as a scourge of the national security establishment, presenting himself, Elizabeth Drew observed, "as a good, safe, traditional Democrat, a responsible senator," Church won by hitting a sweet spot: not too liberal, not too conservative—and not Jimmy Carter. That same day Carter barely won Connecticut, edging out the persistent Second Place Mo by little more than 2 points.

Carter traveled once more in Washington. After long claiming his run had nothing to do with endorsements, he was now hunting endorsements—and got them: Senator Thomas Eagleton and a number of other prominent Missourians; eighteen House freshmen. He met with George Meany; he ducked into New York and reportedly won over former Jackson supporter Abe Beame of New York. The message was that it was time to get aboard the winning bandwagon before it was too late, though bandwagoneers came bearing demands of their own. "His health insurance speech," like his recent embrace of the Humphrey-Hawkins Bill," Elizabeth Drew wrote, "brought him into the orbit of the Democratic Party's interest group politics. The speech was worked out in negotiations with the United Auto Workers."

Carter responded to the bad news out of Nebraska while attending a party in Washington, D.C. Smiling grimly, he said, "I can't win 'em all." The farmer was wearing black tie, which pointed up a curious dynamic. An antipolitician is hardly an antipolitician once he starts winning and works to close the deal by sewing up the Establishment. People start saying things like what Birch Bayh said while endorsing him in Indiana on the eve of a landslide—oily things: "While I was an active candidate for the presidency I expressed concern about Governor Carter's position on several important national issues. Subsequent personal conversations have convinced me that Governor Carter and I share a deep common concern on most issues facing our nation." Soon such praising with faint damns started rolling in from the power-hungry—as in the following uninspiring endorsement from a congressional freshman: "The complete politician is someone who can be his own man and still have everybody like him. That's the epitome of the politician. Carter appears to be his own man and still have all kinds of groups liking him."

At times like this the front-runner began to look like the same old scum on the pond. A new fresh breeze can then whip through the pines.

JERRY BROWN STARTED CAMPAIGNING IN MARYLAND WITH THE SUPPORT of the Democratic machine (Governor Marvin Mandel there despised the Georgian front-runner). "Where is the real Jimmy Carter?" Brown asked. "There's that smile, but who's the person behind it?" Udall hit him on the same score in Michigan: Mo's cartoon ads showed Carter as two-faced, and pointed out that in 1971, as governor in a conservative state, he'd called for withdrawal from Vietnam—but only because we weren't doing enough there to win (Ronald Reagan's position); the next year he urged Democratic governors not to make a political issue of Vietnam after he'd made it one himself as a hawk; and in 1975 Carter had supported Ford's call for last-minute assistance to the Saigon government. "So who is Jimmy Carter? What does he really believe?"

These two "M" states, Michigan and Maryland, were interesting. George Wallace had won both in 1972, while still in the hospital after his assassination attempt. Michigan was one of those open primary states, where racial reactionaries in both parties might crowd to the polls for Ronald Reagan—as they had four years earlier for Wallace. In fact Reagan might win *more* of them than Wallace. From time to time since 1972, the *New York Times* had been checking in with a "typical" blue-collar Michigan voter named Dewey Burton and his family. Burton was typical in that he'd been an avid union man and Democratic voter in 1968, and a Wallace supporter in 1972—and he now supported Ronald Reagan. He liked him because he was like Wallace, just "without the shadow of racism behind him." Reagan also benefited from the *Nashville*-style "Replacement Party" mood, as he himself noted: "The results of the last several primaries—in both parties—reveal a great desire on the part of the people for a change, an end to politics as usual."

What it all meant was that the state that returned Gerald Ford to Congress eight times since 1948 might reject Ford in its primary in 1976—at a stand-or-fall moment in his presidential campaign. Reported the *Times*, "The Nebraska defeat transforms Mr. Ford's political condition from serious to critical. If he loses in Michigan next week, it may become terminal." One former congressman and Ford delegate said that if he lost in Michigan, "The President should withdraw as a candidate."

The newspaper of record cited another "unfavorable omen for Mr. Ford": Michigan was one of the few non-Southern or non-Western states left to select their delegates. Most of the upcoming primaries were in conservative states where Reagan could run up the score: places like Arizona, Tennessee, Louisiana, and his native California. The *New York Times* now reported that Reagan was ahead in the delegate count 476 to 333, with about 1,400 left to select (he was behind 40 to 54 percent in Gallup's popularity poll, but political parties are not quite democracies). London bookies now gave Reagan seven-to-four odds to win—whereas they had been ten to one against Reagan but a month earlier. Commentators started using words like "crucial" and "critical" and "last chance" to describe the incumbent's campaign.

Ford decided a change was in order: he would be nice now— "presidential." Why vote for him? "Because," he answered his own question for the Economic Club of Detroit, "I've done a good job. Because I've turned a lot of things around and we're going in the right direction. Because I want a mandate from Michigan and the American people to finish the job." (Reagan told the same group of wealthy executives that "the automobile and the men and women who make it are under constant attack from . . . elitists, some of whom feel guilty because Americans have built such a prosperous nation, and some of whom seem obsessed with the need to substitute government control in place of individual decision making.") But Ford also did something nasty: when the new campaign finance bill that would free up frozen matching funds finally hit his desk on May 5, he waited five days to sign it.

The two candidates split the voting on May 11. Ford won West Virginia. Maybe his kowtowing to the antitextbook militants in 1974 had helped. Reagan won Nebraska—despite radio commercials by Barry Goldwater for Gerald Ford in which the conservative hero said, "I know Ronald Reagan's public statements concerning the Panama Canal contained gross factual errors. . . . He has clearly represented himself in an irresponsible manner on an issue which could affect the nation's security." Polls had put Ford way ahead just weeks earlier. As for Goldwater, he soon was fielding messages so angry that he told his friend Sally Quinn of the *Washington Post*, "I didn't realize Western Union would send telegrams like that."

Ford waited several more days to appoint commissioners to the newly reconstituted FEC who could sign off on releasing matching funds, at a time when the Reagan campaign was $1.2 million in debt. His campaign began putting pressure on Reagan through the press to release his tax return; Reagan refused. That led to more press reports about how his investment in that cattle tax shelter in 1970 helped him pay no state income tax, and a *New York Times* report that he probably hadn't paid federal tax that year either. (The campaign responded that he had paid "at least" several hundred dollars.) And Ford directed the governor of Michigan, William Milliken, to get nasty on the campaign's behalf. Milliken promptly said Michigan was where "box office diplomacy [and] the celluloid candidacy of Ronald Reagan would be exposed."

It was desperation—as were his Reaganward policy feints: putting off signing a nuclear treaty with the Soviet Union years in the making; ordering his attorney general to find an "appropriate" dispute through which to challenge busing in the Supreme Court. It was hard to stay nice when your twenty-seven-year political career might be nearing the precipice, and your stressed-out advisors were attacking each other in the press in increasingly rancorous terms.

Soon, on the stump, the candidate of calm started losing his cool, too.

Ford had embarked upon an old-fashioned whistle-stop tour through the Wolverine State. On Saturday, May 15, he boasted from the platform on the train's caboose of the improved economy. "Yeah?" a heckler responded. "You blew it."

Grumpy old Ford: "We blew it in the right direction, young man, and if you'd go out and look for a job you'd find out."

Ford's boorish reply was seized upon by Carter at a mall in the Michigan town of Livonia: "Twelve and a half percent of the people in the workforce in Michigan are unemployed and for the President to insinuate that anybody in this country can find [a job] shows he's been in Washington too long . . . and shows he's been out of touch with what's going on in this country." Carter gave it to Reagan, too, for "refusing to let people know that . . . he paid zero taxes on a very large income." He ignored his Democratic rivals. He was "absolutely" sure, he told reporters, he'd win the nomination.

Hubris. He was shocked to be beaten in Maryland 49 to 37 percent by Jerry Brown. He edged out Udall in Michigan by a nose. Energized stop-Carter forces jammed the phone lines of Congressman Paul Simon of Illinois, thought to be the one brokering a convention usurpation on behalf of Humphrey. Touts also pressed Ted Kennedy for his response. "There are some who will not believe until someone else is nominated," wrote Elizabeth Drew, "that Kennedy will not run."

Meanwhile, Gerald Ford was safe, for now: he won Maryland 58 to 42 and Michigan 65 to 43. The Republican race, cliché-minded reporters now wrote, was a "seesaw battle."

• • •

ALL EYES WERE ON JERRY BROWN. IT WAS TIME FOR A NEW INSURGENT—
an antipolitician for those for whom Jimmy Carter had never been
nearly antipolitical enough. For folks who thought Carter too rigid on
the issues. Weird, weird Jerry Brown.

He explained, in an article on Reagan's taxes, why he did not claim
deductions on his own return: "It doesn't turn me on."

An interviewer asked him why he didn't talk about his gubernatorial
accomplishments before audiences: "That's not part of my process."

He said, "My attitude is that you want to liberate people to find
themselves and find space to live and explore life."

And: "I don't have answers. I have questions."

"It's a commitment to a process that will have to be filled in."

"Just to stay where we are may take some pretty profound changes."

Edmund G. "Jerry" Brown Jr. was the son of a very conventional,
Irish Catholic, ward-heeler style of Democratic politician, Pat Brown,
who rode to glory by doing what all successful Democratic politicians
did during the postwar economic boom: he built. A $1.99 billion aque-
duct system to deliver water to Southern California. A thousand more
miles of freeways. Seven new public university campuses. He built the
ladder upon which California's middle class had climbed. Then he was
undone by the shocking challenge of Ronald Reagan in 1966. His fourth
child, born in 1938, observed his father's political fall from a rather odd
place: a Jesuit seminary, where he spent three and a half years, one of
them entirely silent. He had since identified with the fashionable religion of Zen Buddhism.

When Junior became governor, in 1975, he did not build. He cut
spending for education. He stopped providing free briefcases for state
bureaucrats. He lobbied against his own pay raise. He gave janitors the
exact same pay raise as judges. His state-of-the-state address lasted seven
minutes. Like the young Colorado governor Richard Lamm, elected for
fighting Denver's Winter Olympics bid, or Mayor Tom Bradley in Los
Angeles, who made a campaign promise *not* to build new highways or
homes, Jerry Brown fetishized *limits*—much to traditional liberals' chagrin. "He was Pat Brown's son, and everyone figured that Jerry Brown's
election meant that the faucets would start flowing again," a prominent
Democratic pol related to a journalist. "Well, everyone was wrong."
Liberal groups and unions bitterly joked about wanting their campaign
donations back. *Was* he even a liberal? Answered Jerry Brown, "I am
not restrained by the metaphors and mythologies associated with the
term."

It made him stunningly popular. By the end of 1975, only 7 percent of the state's residents rated his performance as "poor."

He had come up through the civil rights and antiwar movements, the first politician of national stature to do so. He served as a member of the University of California Board of Regents, then as state attorney general, and was the basis for the character played by Robert Redford in the 1972 movie *The Candidate*. ("What do we do now?" the Candidate asks at the end of the picture, blankly, after he wins.) He won the governor's mansion at the youthful age of thirty-six—well, actually, he bypassed the new governor's mansion, which had been built for Reagan by his friends for $8.4 million in 2013 dollars, in favor of a modest bachelor apartment, where he slept on a mattress on the floor and kept a copy of Aristotle on the coffee table. He ate in health food restaurants. He refused the gubernatorial chauffeured limousine—he drove himself in a 1967 Plymouth sedan. He quoted *Small Is Beautiful,* and the radical social philosopher and designer Buckminster Fuller: "We are on a very small Spaceship Earth, and we've got to respect the limits." He did things like appointing antiwar POW Edison Miller to the Orange County Board of Supervisors; Miller was the one who'd turned his back on his fellow marines upon his return to Camp Pendleton. ("I will try my best to have every veteran in the state of Oklahoma vote against Jerry Brown for anything," responded another POW, who headed the Naval ROTC at the University of Oklahoma. "I will take off my uniform to do that.") One of his handpicked candidates to be a presidential convention delegate was Elaine Brown, a Black Panther leader. Mike Royko called him "Governor Moonbeam." *Doonesbury* once featured a character who traveled to California to work for him. But before he got there, he had to brush up on the governor's California-speak. He asked an expert how one might translate a passage of Blake: "The moon like a flower in heaven's high bower, with silent delight, sits and smiles on the night." The answer: "OH, WOW, LOOK AT THE MOON."

California loved him. Now the nation would meet him.

His April 28 trip to Maryland to campaign was his first travel outside California since he'd been elected a year and a half earlier. As he toured a waste management facility, he turned to reporters: "What is the inner meaning of this? Why are we here? What are we doing?" He toured a Westinghouse plant, shook hands, told a worker, "I hope you'll vote for me." The reply: "I will." A double take: "You will? But you don't know anything about me." A reporter asked him who his favorite political philosopher was. He answered, "Thomas Hooker." Another inquired who Thomas Hooker was. The answer: "I'm just being facetious. He's the only obscure name I could remember from political science class." His TV commercials had him antipolitically saying that a president "comes in the morning, leaves at night. . . . He is just a human being like everybody else. There's no magic, there's no genius."

Nevertheless, beneath his blathering political anti-blather many of his views turned out to be shockingly conventional, and he had always been strikingly shrewd about the uses of power. Shaking hands while running for governor, he'd say, "Hello, I'm Jerry Brown. I'm Pat Brown's son, and I'm running for governor. I hope you'll vote for me." He boasted in speeches of a bill he was about to sign providing for stricter safety regulations for the construction of nuclear plants—but took no position on a proposition on California ballots that year to limit such construction. He said he wouldn't cut the defense budget.

He was also disarmingly honest—quite the calling card, in 1976.

In both parties May 25 would be a crucial test; Idaho, Nevada, and Oregon; and Tennessee, Arkansas, and Kentucky, two sort-of regional primaries. In Oregon, Elizabeth Drew sat down for a conversation with Jerry Brown, although, she wrote, "One does not hold a conversation with Brown—one holds a symposium with him." She asked him about his attraction to Zen Buddhism. He replied, "I pick things up from a variety of sources. Zen stresses living in the moment. So do the Jesuits, so does monastic living—living in the present moment, don't worry about tomorrow. Divine Providence will take care of it. Be in the present moment. *Age quod agis*—that's a Jesuit motto. Do whatever you're doing. That could be Zen as well as Jesuit." He was asked how "living for the moment" squared with the task of planning the governing of the nation's largest state. He replied by describing his philosophy as "creative non-action": "Many possibilities can be in your mind. You try to think ahead, but you can't recognize the multiplicity of possibilities. You can't control events and you can't predict them."

Wow. Look at the moon.

She came away convinced Brown was running for president because he was bored with being governor. (He was easily bored; he once called being governor "a pain in the ass.") She recorded him, on the campaign trail, making fun of political conventions and political language (which, of course, he had grown up with), and even making fun of the voters to their faces: "As Bend goes . . . so goes Oregon, and so goes the country," he goofed in front of an audience in . . . Bend. (Not Carter. He'd added to his usual litany—that he'd been a farmer, an engineer, and a businessman—that he had "substantial timber holdings," timber, of course, being a major export of Oregon.)

In Bend, Brown was applauded uproariously for pointing up the bill he had signed two days earlier to give a 10 percent tax deduction to homeowners who installed solar panels, and his measure to reduce the amount of water that toilets use when they flush, and for cutting the highway department from 16,000 to 13,500 employees.

His audience also liked this:

"We have fiscal limits, we have ecological limits, we even have human limits . . . too much over-promising, too much overselling . . . the human species is not going to make it unless we can figure out another way. . . . How long is it going to take before we blow this whole planet up?"

AND OREGON LOVED IT. HE WAS SO IN DEMAND, AND SO WILLING TO hold symposia with voters, that he started showing up hours late for appearances. Voters just patiently waited for him to arrive, then stood listening, rapt. (Drew reflected, "It is a cool night in Coos Bay, and the crowd is paying close attention to this young man who tells it that the world may blow up.") *Doonesbury* soon depicted his fans offering the following campaign chant: "Hey, ho! Go with the flow!" And imagined this dialogue:

"But if you admit to not having the answer to any of the problems facing the nation, why should anyone vote of your for President?"

"I believe I am the best qualified to wing it."

But winning Oregon would be a challenge for Brown: his name wasn't on the ballot. That became one of his jokes: look for the blank spot on the ballot. "That doesn't represent my mind—it's not blank. But it's open. . . . There's a certain amount of Zen emptiness." His campaign storefronts bustled with volunteers—just like Jimmy Carter's once had. Jimmy Carter, who no longer looked like an insurgent at all. The week before Oregon voted, the story dominating the coverage of Carter's campaign was his response back in 1971 when William "Rusty" Calley had been convicted for mass murder at the Vietnam village of My Lai. Carter had declared "American Fighting Man's Day" and recommended all Georgians drive with their headlights on to "honor the flag as Rusty had done." Now he denied ever having said it: just another politician.

NATIONWIDE, MORE CHAOS, MORE EMBARRASSMENT, MORE MORAL COR-rosion. An even worse cheating scandal was revealed at the U.S. Military Academy at West Point, the largest in its 174-year history. (The student body responded by voting to reduce the penalty for cheating.) A front-page report in the *Philadelphia Inquirer* stated, "An alarming amount of nuclear fuel has disappeared from the nation's nuclear power plants— more than enough for terrorist fanatics to build atomic bombs capable of killing thousands. Embarrassed nuclear officials admit they don't know how much is missing, or where it has gone. But angry experts told the *Inquirer* that enough plutonium and uranium has vanished to build an entire arsenal of nuclear weapons." (An MIT physicist said, "America is sitting on a nuclear time bomb. The fuse is getting shorter all the time." Paul Ehrlich was quoted: "Any determined person or group with some intelligence can build a bomb. . . . At one plant it was possible to enter a room containing raw material for bombs merely by pulling off flimsy metal louvers covering vent holes in a wall.") A conference at the State University of New York in Brockport on cheating in sports concluded it was being engaged in "not only by individual athletes, but also by whole teams, by coaches, managers, owners, and even judges."

Sports was the subject of a popular Hollywood farce that came out on April 22. The plot of *The Bad News Bears* was a traditionally uplifting one—that familiar old Capraesque story about the sad sacks banding together and beating the swells through sheer democratic pluck. But it was conveyed with a crudeness unimaginable onscreen before Watergate. A drunken lout played by Walter Matthau is recruited to coach a Little League team. One player, a budding black nationalist, calls him "honky." He recruits a tomboy with a vicious curveball, played by Tatum O'Neal, but he has to bribe her to lure her away from her lucrative hustle of selling phony maps to the homes of the Hollywood stars. ("I know it says a buck twenty-five on the map but it's really two dollars because of inflation.") A teammate greets her: "Jews, spics, niggers, and now a girl?" Matthau teaches her how to throw illegal spitballs. A kid trips a base runner—no criticism from the coach; likewise when another surreptitiously hits a competitor in the genitals. O'Neal tries to recruit to the team a juvenile delinquent, who is preoccupied with his own hustle—air hockey, a dollar a game. She has to go on a date with him when she loses, inspiring the following dialogue:

Matthau: "Eleven-year-old girls don't go on dates!"

O'Neal: "Blow it out your bunghole. I know an eleven-year-old girl who's already on the pill."

These eleven-year-olds also swear like sailors, wear Budweiser shirts, and drink the beers their alcoholic coach hands out. The bad guy is a city councilman who cynically keeps pictures of JFK, RFK, and Martin Luther King on his office wall, the better to cover up his Nixon-like scams. The Bears make it to the championship, where Matthau advises a player to cheat. ("Get hit in the arm or the leg. Don't make it obvious.") He won't take his girl pitcher out of the game even at the risk of injury to her arm. The last line of the picture, when the team wins second place, is "Hey Yankees—you can take your apology and your trophy and shove it up your ass!"

And this was a *kids'* movie.

Another gag sent up something else unsavory: the nation's birthday party. The Bears' uniforms were sponsored by "Chico's Bail Bonds"— slogan, "Let Freedom Ring"; logo, the Liberty Bell. Just like real life, where the Bicentennial was taking shape with all the class of a holiday mattress sale. The suspicious circles derided it as the "buycentennial." The Bicentennial Wagon Train was sponsored by Holiday Inn, Mayflower Moving, and Gulf Oil. Each of CBS's "Bicentennial Minutes" ended with a commercial for Shell Oil; as it happened, Bicentennial sponsors Gulf and Shell were both wrapped up in bribery scandals. All told, some 250 corporations sponsored official programs of the American Revolution Bicentennial Commission, whose chairman was a Hollywood producer, to the tune of $38.9 million.

More prosaically, you could buy Bicentennial garbage cans, a Bicentennial "commemorative LP" with the story of the nation's founding as read by radio host Paul Harvey ("Ideal gift for every occasion in '76! . . . *HAND LETTERING • HANDSOME ILLUSTRATIONS • QUALITY PAPER • ELEGANT GOLD EMBOSSING*"); phony Bicentennial parchments with a scriptural affirmation of God's hand in America's future (2 Chronicles 7:14: "If my people, which are called by my name, shall humble themselves, and pray, and seek my face, and turn from their wicked ways; then will I hear from heaven, and will forgive their sin, *and* will heal their land"); Bicentennial medallions; Bicentennial whoopee cushions, garbage cans, toilet seats—even, thanks to one intrepid entrepreneur, a Bicentennial casket. "News accounts pointed out that cheap Bicentennial trinkets were often made in overseas factories," a historian noticed—even the ones from the companies that kicked back a fee to the official Bicentennial Commission, and so got to feature the official logo on their product. Among those who probably didn't go through the trouble were the guy who opened a Bicentennial massage parlor, the "Uncle Sam's" chain of discos (they had a drink called the Firecracker), and the car dealership in San Jose that sponsored a man who was attempting to break the record for "pole sitting," and who planned to descend on July 4.

And all to celebrate—what? Our glorious cities? A May 18 headline in the *Los Angeles Times:* "TWO SLAIN GUARDING CHURCH." The article

was about how at the ornate Our Lady of Guadalupe, in a neighborhood of intensifying drug- and gang-related violence, a mother of
three who'd joined a nightly anti-vandalism patrol and a forty-three-
year-old maintenance worker were shot down by gang members. Government by the people, of the people, and for the people? "CLOSED
SESSION ROMANCE ON THE HILL: REP. WAYNE HAYS' $14,000-A-YEAR
CLERK SAYS SHE'S HIS MISTRESS," read the *Washington Post* lead headline
on May 23. Hays, sixty-four, who'd married another secretary back
in Ohio five weeks earlier, was that creepy chair of the House Buildings and Grounds Committee—"the meanest man in Congress"—who
survived the threat of losing his chairmanship in 1975 by engineering a
congressional pay raise. The twenty-seven-year-old in question, Elizabeth Ray, pictured on the front page of the *Post* in a low-cut swimsuit,
was quoted as saying, "I can't type, I can't file, I can't even answer the
phone. . . . Supposedly, I'm on the oversight committee. But I call it the
Out of Sight Committee." In Washington, people talked of hardly anything else. Betty Ford, candid as ever, said that since Hays was not married at the time of the affair he should not be judged harshly.

Would-be Woodwards and Bernsteins went off on mistress hunts.
One unfortunate victim was a congressman, Allan T. Howe, who
showed up in a Salt Lake City police blotter for soliciting a prostitute,
then withdrew from his reelection run even though there wasn't any evidence he was guilty. Wrote Tom Wicker, "If Howe's case had occurred
anytime except at the height of the Wayne Hays scandal, the Utah congressman would have been front page news nowhere outside the *Deseret
News.*" As it was, he became more evidence of the thoroughgoing rot in
the political class. In 1970, there had been sixty-three indictments of of-
ficeholders by federal grand juries. In 1976, there were 337.

THE CHURCH COMMITTEE BEGAN RELEASING SUPPLEMENTARY REPORTS,
which for some reason now caught the attention of the evening news,
forcing replies from the directors of the CIA and FBI—the latter, Clarence Kelley, finally acknowledging abuses by his predecessor J. Edgar
Hoover, such as the attempt to make Martin Luther King commit
suicide. Then came the voting in Oregon on May 25. The Democrats'
results were a surprise. Carter did not win, nor Brown; Frank Church
did. He also won the same day in his home state, Idaho (where Carter,
bringing his all-things-to-all-people shtick to a new low, told voters he
felt a deep kinship with them because he too raised a crop that grew
underground). "I hope here in Oregon," Church had said in an appeal
for votes, "that those Democrats who have been supporting Jackson

and Humphrey and Udall will unite together behind my candidacy." He argued, "I just don't believe that the White House is the proper place for on-the-job training." He denounced "the politics of style." And since he was the only candidate saying such things, he monopolized the votes of those who agreed. He now was three-for-three—a contender.

Carter, meanwhile, won in Kentucky, Tennessee, and Arkansas—but those states had been virtually uncontested. He just wasn't "closing," as the salesmen say. Once more in Washington the stop-Carter forces—now known as "ABC," or "Anyone But Carter," after 1972's version, ABM, "Anyone But McGovern"—stirred. "Holding for Hubert," read buttons some Democratic politicians wore.

ON MAY 21 RONALD REAGAN WON ROOF-SHAKING ACCLAIM FROM 3,500 at a Christian college in Chattanooga by proclaiming, "Never again should this country send its young men to die in a war unless the country is totally committed to winning it as quickly as possible." But Tennessee was also home to the Tennessee Valley Authority, and when the press asked him in Nashville what he thought about the TVA, he responded with what he had learned from reading Henry Hazlitt's *Economics in One Lesson* under Lemuel Boulware's tutelage in the 1950s—the same answer that cost Barry Goldwater the Volunteer State in 1964. He said, "I still believe in free enterprise, and the government doesn't have any place in it." Reporters pressed, asking him if that meant he would sell to private interests the extensive network of dams that had brought electricity to the impoverished rural masses. "We'd have to look at it," he replied.

Ford won Oregon. That was expected. Reagan won Arkansas, Nevada, and Idaho—and that was expected, too. The shock was in Tennessee, an open primary full of Wallace Democrats. But even conservatives loved the TVA in the Volunteer State. Which was why Ford won Tennessee—an astonishing boost. Despite this, as Elizabeth Drew noted, "That the race between the President and Ronald Reagan has got to this point" was in itself "astonishing."

The melodrama was only just beginning. Much more than the Democrats, Republicans picked many of their delegates in convention and caucuses. Winning these kinds of proceedings—a dark art that often involved manipulations of parliamentary procedure and backroom cajoling almost unto blackmail—had been a specialty for the generation of young conservatives who'd been protégés of a man named F. Clifton White. In the 1940s and 1950s, he had assembled within the Young Republicans National Federation a cabal that became known as the

"Syndicate," and made it the spine of the stealth organization that seized the Republican Party from the bottom up in the early 1960s to grab the nomination for Goldwater.

Ironically, White himself was now working for Ford. His disciples, though, were hard at work for Reagan, plucking delegates one by one from the grip of Republican machines in states that pundits had believed were all but in the bag for the incumbent. On May 8, they won ten of seventeen delegates chosen in Wyoming's GOP state convention and eighteen in Oklahoma. The next Saturday they won nine more in Louisiana. A scouting trip to Missouri by John Sears and David Keane revealed slim pickings for the Show Me State's June 11 convention—but they dispatched Morton Blackwell and Don Devine, two former Young Republican hands and were now professional conservative activists, and who got to work organizing there. "There is a developing trend for people we had counted on in caucus states to move to an uncommitted posture," one worried Ford official told the *New York Times*.

Another worrisome trend for Ford: in states like New Jersey, with its sixty-seven delegates to be chosen in a June 8 primary, Reagan forces decided not to waste resources in the face of a liberal Republican establishment. So low-level Republican officials and just plain ordinary folks took matters into their own hands—the better to save civilization from the infidels. "A vote for Ford is a vote for Kissinger and I'm not going to let the Republican Party sell our country down the river or down the Panama Canal either," a Mrs. Eleanor Day Wimill told the reporters who came calling on her little basement organization. This cadre was made up of small businessmen, retirees, housewives, and college students. Their leader was a phone installer. They had little money, only enthusiasm—and the lethargy of the Ford campaign. One Ford supporter in New Jersey, the former congressman Charles Sandman, said he preferred Nelson Rockefeller. Rockefeller, for his part, did not say no when asked if he might ever become a candidate. Instead he was vague: "I don't see that scenario." He added that Ford's moves to the right were "very dangerous" for the general election.

Reagan's forces grew arrogant. At a rally in Ohio a helicopter trailed the banner, "REAGAN FOR PRESIDENT, FORD FOR VICE PRESIDENT." The candidate began speaking of a "probable" first-ballot win. For his part Ford spoke more and more about his admiration of Harry Truman— who'd declined to run for reelection in 1952 rather than face a humiliating loss. "Some observers," the *New York Times* reported, "said they sensed that Mr. Ford's emotion might bespeak an awareness that his Presidency could be of a brief duration." The president zoomed ahead by about a hundred convention votes the last week in May when 119 of 154 New York delegates officially pledged for Ford. But no one knew what would happen to all those delegates nationwide that Ford *thought* had pledged for him, but which now seemed so very, very soft. The answer might come on June 8—when contests in California, Ohio, and New Jersey would select a third of the delegates needed to nominate.

IT WAS THE SAME ON THE DEMOCRATIC SIDE—WHERE JIMMY CARTER WAS struggling, and straddling, to close the sale. Elizabeth Drew did further damage to his "sincerity" image by deconstructing the calculation behind it: "The small-town, rural image was debated long and hard. The prevailing feeling was that although most people didn't have anything similar in their own lives, it had appealing overtones of roots, stability, things to which even people in cities would be drawn. . . . The decision to situate the Carter campaign headquarters in Atlanta instead of Washington, another much debated one, was based not just on logistics— the fact that Carter and his staff lived in Atlanta, the availability of volunteers—but also on image . . . of being not-of-Washington. . . . Even the role of the peanut"—the campaign's charming symbol—"was discussed. Some argued that it should be played down, because it might seem a little corny. But then it was found that the peanut had a sort of humble quality, and this became convenient to a campaign in which, as an aide put it, smiling, 'humility was not our long suit.'"

Straddling was his long suit. In San Francisco he said he both supported biblical teachings against homosexuality (he mentioned Leviticus 20:13, which reads, "If a man also lie with mankind, as he lieth with a woman, both of them have committed an abomination: they shall surely be put to death, their blood shall be upon them") *and* would sign a bill protecting gay rights. He said, "I will pick my Cabinet on the basis of merit, not politics," and that others were "horse-trading for the highest office of the world—I've not done that." Yet he also began embracing an idea he had heretofore rejected, the Kennedy-Corman universal heath insurance bill, beloved of the labor leaders he was courting. He said both that he would never give up control of the Panama Canal *and* that he would renegotiate the treaty (but Panamanians made America giving up control of the canal their condition for negotiating).

But the deconstructions were not having an effect. Carter spoke to the Ohio AFL-CIO convention in Cincinnati and said his was "the one campaign that speaks to and for the average hardworking, taxpaying American." He said, "My critics don't want to stop Carter. They want to stop the reforms I'm committed to. They want to stop the people of this country from regaining control of their government. They want to preserve the status quo, to preserve politics as usual, to maintain at all costs their own entrenched, unresponsive, bankrupt, irresponsible, political power." Then he quoted Bob Dylan. The next day a CBS/*New York Times* poll showed he was the only Democratic contender running ahead of President Ford.

He spoke to the California state legislature (a sign by the door warned visitors to enter at their own risk because the building was not structurally sound), saying, "If I had to sum up in one word what this campaign is all about, that word would be 'faith.'" A cover article appeared in *Rolling Stone* by the magazine's drug-addled gonzo literary superhero Hunter S. Thompson; it was more than fifteen thousand words long. He wrote that "on the 200th anniversary of what used to be called 'The American Dream,' we are going to have our noses rubbed, day after day—on the tube and in the headlines—in this mess we have made for ourselves"—but that Jimmy Carter just might point the way out. Thompson wrote of a 1974 Law Day speech by Carter in Georgia he happened to stumble into, and called it "the heaviest and most eloquent thing I have ever heard from the mouth of a politician." The article was called "Jimmy Carter and the Great Leap of Faith." People yearned to believe.

Carter traveled to Los Angeles to speak at the dedication of a new wing of Martin Luther King Hospital in Watts. He launched into a preacherly rhythm:

> *I see an America poised not only on the brink of a new century but at the dawn of a new era of honest, compassionate, responsive government.*
>
> *I see an American government that has turned away from scandals and corruption and official cynicism and finally become as decent as its people.*
>
> *I see an America with a tax system that does not steal from the poor and give to the rich.*
>
> *I see an America with a job for every man and woman who can work, and a decent standard of living for those who cannot.*
>
> *I see an America in which my child and your child and every child receives an education second to none in the world.*
>
> *I see an American government that does not spy on its citizens or harass its citizens, but respects your dignity and your privacy and your right to be let alone.*
>
> *I see an American foreign policy that is firm and consistent*

and generous, and that once again is a beacon for the hopes of the world. . . .

I see an America in which Martin Luther King's dream is our national dream.

I see an American on the move again, united, its wounds healed, its head high, a diverse and vital nation, moving into its third century with confidence and competence and compassion, an America that lives up the majesty of its Constitution and the simple decency of its people.

This is the America that I see and that I am committed to as I run for President.

I ask for your help.

You will always have mine.

The speech was titled "The Power of Love." The campaign bought five minutes on all three networks to run a commercial based on its themes. The *New York Times'* Charles Mohr called it "one of the most moving speeches on the racial dilemma heard in a long time," and reported, "An almost physical wave of love seemed to pass from the black listeners to Mr. Carter"—"ethnic purity" be damned.

That was June 1. On June 4, the Associated Press revealed that only 20 percent of Carter's backers knew his positions on the issues. But they yearned to believe.

The next day, Hubert Humphrey said he was still considering accepting a convention draft, and would make his ultimate decision on June 18. Frank Church was surging—then, when he was on the bus to his next event in Ohio, he received news that the Teton Dam, whose construction he had controversially backed, had been breached. He told the press that "a wall of water fifteen feet high is heading toward Idaho Falls," and broke off his campaign. Governor Brown might be a fascinating fellow—but no: it was simply too late. Mathematically, it was now unlikely Carter would fall below the majority threshold a draft would require. Mayor Daley said that if Carter won Ohio he would be the nominee. Carter began speaking of his nomination campaign in the past tense: "I think a lot of people have become more aware of the presence of peanuts in the country this year. I think that the image of a peanut, which is a crop that I grow, being kind of small and insignificant but cumulatively being very important to the American people, is one that fairly accurately mirrors the kind of campaign that we've run." For its June 8 issue the *National Enquirer* dug up a quote about a 1969 incident in which he'd said, "One thing's for sure, I'll never make fun of people who say they've seen unidentified objects in the sky. If I become President, I'll make every piece of information this country has about UFO sightings available to the public and the scientists."

As goes the *National Enquirer,* so goes the nation?

ELIZABETH DREW VISITED A TYPICAL REAGAN CAMPAIGN RALLY THE SUN-day before the Ohio, New Jersey, and California elections, in a high school auditorium in "one of the more conservative sections of the conservative city"—Cincinnati, her hometown. Ford would almost certainly win a landslide in New Jersey. Reagan would almost certainly win a landslide in California. What happened in Ohio, the classic presidential bellwether state—where Reagan's campaign had set a modest expectation of ten of ninety-seven delegates up for grabs—might just determine whether the Republicans would see their first brokered convention since 1948.

The auditorium was draped in red, white, and blue. ("Ford's decor usually consists of blue-and-white President Ford banners.") The star entered; the crowd erupted. A supporting cast warmed them up as the man of the hour stood by at the ready: Ken Curtis, the man who played Festus in *Gunsmoke* ("I am speaking up for Governor Reagan because I am a concerned American"); the Hollywood superstar introduced as "General Jimmy Stewart," who, in his best aw-shucks Mr. Smith tones, spoke of Reagan's ability to reach all sorts of people—"I know in the acting racket this is one of the things you're supposed to be able to do. . . . There are all sort of tricks." Ronald Reagan, though, was *for real.*

The man of the hour took the podium; another roar. He told a favorite joke, about how the government was like a baby ("an alimentary canal with a big appetite at one end and no sense of responsibility at the other"). He laid into his opponent, who "has spent most of his adult life as a member of the Washington establishment"—"Eleventh Commandment" be damned. He said he would create a budget surplus—then turn the money back over to the people. "It's never been done!" he quoted a government official as having told him. "*Wellll,* they've never had an actor up there before!"—and the audience roared. (Nancy, "who has perfected the adoring gaze," looked up at him—adoringly.) He offered a favorite homily about federal waste—a supposed sociology study backed by $249,000 in federal money "to find out it's better to be young, rich, and healthy than old, poor, and sick." He spoke of all the things he'd done for education and health as California governor, "and he sounds almost like a disciple of the Great Society," Drew said. Then, both speaker and audience indifferent to the contradiction, he said government "does its best for us when it does nothing." The crowd went wild.

Then it was foreign policy time, and the crowd was launched into the stratosphere.

"I don't believe the United States can afford to give up something that belongs to us because we've been threatened with trouble from a dictator. . . .

"Détente has become a one-way street." (When, an Agence France-Presse reporter asked plaintively, "has *zees* become a dirty French word?")

He said, "It's time to give the schools back to the states and the local districts, where they belong."

An aide nudged Elizabeth Drew and told her to be ready for what was about to happen next: the biggest applause line of every single speech:

"And who knows? If we can get Washington out of the classroom, maybe we can get God back in."

At that, the *New Yorker*'s political correspondent apologized to her readers for having told them only months earlier that running for president was something Reagan the radio personality was doing only to burnish his marketing potential. This was a "real challenge to the President. . . . This year has taught us not to underestimate him."

WHERE IT DID NOT UNDERESTIMATE HIM, THE EASTERN ESTABLISHMENT Press insulted him.

May 31, the *Washington Post*, from Los Angeles, reported: "Reagan, who last week received the Father of the Year award in a ceremony here, will miss the high school graduation of his 17-year-old son, Ronald Prescott, in order to campaign in Ohio." The next day it corrected this: "The *Washington Post* incorrectly reported the campaign schedule of Ronald Reagan in yesterday's paper. Reagan will attend the high school graduation of his son this Friday and also attended a Los Angeles Republican dinner before leaving Saturday to campaign in Ohio." Perhaps to mitigate the damage to his family-friendly image, a spot was filmed for the California primary with daughter Maureen, sitting on the floor with a family scrapbook.

President Ford had some new commercials of his own. He had recently retained the Madison Avenue wizard who for Ty-D-Bol launched the little man sailing across a toilet tank, for Wisk invented "ring around the collar," and who bid to make Schaefer the brew of preference for alcoholics—"Schaefer is the one beer to have when you're having more than one." To that august body of work he now added an imperishable ad for the Leader of the Free World:

> *"Ellie! Are you working for President Ford?"*
> *"Only about twenty-six hours a day!"*
> (The two friends pass a supermarket.)
> *"Notice anything about these fruit prices lately?"*
> *"Well, they don't seem to be going up the way they used to."*
> *"President Ford has cut inflation in half."*
> *"In half? Wow!"*

(The *New York Times*, for the benefit of sophisticates who boasted of not owning a television set, helpfully explained that the line was delivered "in the astonished tones TV housewives use when they discover that their brand of paper towels doesn't absorb water nearly so rapidly as a friend's.")

"It's just that I hate to think where we'd be without him."

Comes the male voice-over: "President Ford is leading us back to prosperity. Stay with him. He knows the way."

The Ford campaign also added this commercial, in heavy rotation in California. It sent Ronald Reagan ballistic:

> *If you've been waiting for this presidential campaign to become a little clearer so that you can make a choice—it's happened. Last Wednesday Ronald Reagan said he would send American troops to Rhodesia. Thursday he clarified that. He said they could be observers or advisors. What does he think happened in Vietnam? Or was Governor Reagan playing with words?*
>
> *When you vote on Tuesday remember—Governor Reagan couldn't start a war. President Reagan could.*

The record of what he had actually said about Rhodesia, in a press conference at the Sacramento Press Club, was vague. Reagan called the ad a "smear" and an "absolute distortion of the facts." "The words poured out of him in angry, snapping tones," said the *New York Times*. It raised the vituperation between the two men to the proverbial fever pitch. On *Face the Nation* the Sunday before the three big primaries, Ford said Reagan's opposition to the Panama negotiations could lead to "guerrilla war," and pointed Republicans to "the tragedy of 1964" should Reagan be nominated. Reagan all but called his opponent a liar: "Leadership today, I believe, calls for going to the American people and telling them the truth." Ford sent his wife out to be interviewed by columnist Helen Thomas—who learned that "Betty Ford feels almost as strongly against forced busing as her husband." Reagan said he might not vote for Ford if the latter ended up the nominee. John Wayne introduced Reagan in Newport Beach, California—and, asked by NBC why he was supporting him, answered, "Because Jerry Ford is too fucking dumb to be president."

Next, as if on cue, it sounded like Jerry Ford was impersonating Chevy Chase instead of the other way around.

> WASHINGTON (AP)—Six-foot-tall President Ford may have to get a helicopter with a higher doorway.
>
> He lightly bumped his head again Sunday as he was getting aboard on the South Lawn for the start of a campaign trip to New Jersey and Ohio.
>
> The incident happened as the President was trying to turn and wave good-bye.

Then he motorcaded through the Buckeye State. In Middletown, where they made stainless steel, he announced he was limiting imports of the stuff. In Dayton, he announced he was ordering $36 million in new construction at the city's Wright-Patterson Air Force Base. Garry Trudeau in *Doonesbury*, for his part, presented a bemused Democratic candidate: "I believe that Mr. Ford has reacted desperately to the Reagan challenge. Especially in the use of the patronage prerogatives of his office!" "Governor, are you referring to Nebraska's new submarine base?"

IT WORKED IN OHIO, WHERE FORD PREVAILED 55 TO 45, WITH REAGAN picking up only six delegates. But in California the Reagan landslide was even greater than expected, 65 to 35. Stu Spencer speculated that Ford's Rhodesia commercial had backfired, costing the president 8 points. The Republican race was still on.

On election night Reagan's adopted and biological children appeared onstage together for the first time, on a set made up to look like a train to the Republican National Convention in Kansas City. Wrote Michael Reagan in his memoir, "I was so proud to be on that stage with my father that I didn't want the moment to end. If only some of the love those people had for Dad would somehow find its way to me, my problems would be solved. Please love me too, I thought."

Jerry Brown (a rare childless bachelor in politics) won a landslide in California, too. "Every state I've gone into, Jimmy Carter's lost," Jerry

Brown said. "So I will go forward. . . . The Democratic contest is still on." It wasn't. Carter had 1,514 delegates, nine more than he needed to be nominated on the first ballot. Brown added, "The American people have begun to question what Carter is saying, if he's saying anything at all." They hadn't. Gallup's postprimary poll found voters favoring him over Ford 53 to 39 and over Reagan 58 to 35.

Insider Washington was a different story. George McGovern called Jimmy Carter "a dangerous man." Bob Shrum called him "not human." Joseph Kraft called him "a pig in a poke" and Evans and Novak noticed his "streak of vindictiveness" and "implacable hostility to any opposition." But outside Washington, the people had spoken. They yearned to believe. And so the leaders followed. Hubert Humphrey took himself out of the race. George Wallace said, "He's entitled to the nomination. . . . We've got to overlook many things. He'll make a fine candidate." Mayor Daley said that "the ballgame is over." Scoop Jackson, Ted Kennedy, Robert Byrd, and Lloyd Bentsen all announced their support. The nominee-apparent announced a speaking tour staking out his foreign policy, finally—having said all spring that he would offer specifics on world affairs only after he had won.

BICENTENNIAL NEWS: ON JUNE 1 IN NEW YORK, HUNDREDS OF GLASSY-eyed Moonies, after knocking on doors for weeks, plastering the Bronx with slick posters in which their True Father raised his arm in a distinctly Hitlerian salute, managed to help half-fill Yankee Stadium for a five-hour "Bicentennial God Bless America" rally. Outside, a pamphlet war raged: Jews for Jesus and "Jews for Judaism"; feuding Evangelical denominations; Hare Krishna and the followers of Guru Ji; National Citizens Engaged in Reuniting Families Inc. (A member of that anticult group said of Moon's Unification Church, "They took our children, and we want to get them back." Another parent of a Moonie, however, disagreed. She told a reporter she was glad her twenty-six-year-old daughter had finally found something "genuine.") Inside the ballpark high winds scattered red, white, and blue balloons and after a summer squall nearly ripped down the giant REV. SUN MYUNG MOON, PRINCIPLE SPEAKER banner that hung between the upper and lower decks. Fireworks and a marching band ushered Rev. Moon to an outfield podium. He had just bought the forty-one-floor New Yorker Hotel, across the street from Madison Square Garden, as the church's "World Mission Center" and faced a $1.8 million lawsuit for holding a nineteen-year-old in involuntary servitude and violating federal labor laws for his unpaid army of evangelists. He held forth in Korean as his chief deputy,

Bo Hi Pak, a former colonel in the South Korean army, cried out in simultaneous translation:

> There are critics who say, "Why is Reverend Moon so involved
> in America's Bicentennial? It is none of his business." Ladies and
> gentlemen, if there is illness in your home, do you not need a doctor
> from outside? If your home catches on fire, do you not need fire-
> fighters from outside? God has sent me to America in the role of a
> doctor, in the role of a firefighter.

(Moonies applauded in creepy unison. Others booed and streamed
for the exits.)

> In the 1950s America seemed to be the hope of the world. The
> symbol of America was the city of New York. Today, however, the
> world has lost faith in America, and New York has become a jungle
> of immorality and depravity, a city transformed under the attack of
> evil.

(His point was conveniently illustrated by marauding bands of
teenagers, exploding firecrackers, throwing smoke bombs, and hurtling
refuse from the upper deck.)

In Boston that same week, someone set fire to the gift shop of the
tourist replica of the ship from the Boston Tea Party; two days later, a
bomb rocked Plymouth Rock. An anonymous call to the papers from
something called the "Defense League" said the attacks were responses
to Attorney General Levi's decision not to intervene in Supreme Court
appeals of Judge Garrity's desegregation decision, and that more bombs
would follow unless forced busing was immediately stopped.

Boston had lost the competition to be seat of the nation's Bicentennial festivities to Philadelphia, whose mayor, Frank Rizzo, faced
a corruption-driven recall drive and was described by a writer in the
Catholic magazine *Commonweal* as a "racist whose very existence
should be a national embarrassment." Rizzo told the hometown *Inquirer* that the city had become "a target for attempts at disruption and
violence by a substantial coalition of leftist radicals" who intend "to
come here in the thousands" to disrupt "the rights of the majority who
are going here to enjoy themselves with their family." He asked for fifteen thousand federal troops.

A Washington, D.C., police official testified to the Senate internal
security subcommittee, "A variety of groups, most of them basically

Marxist-Leninist and some openly terrorist, have discussed plans to disrupt the Bicentennial . . . commanded by the Prairie Fire Organizing Committee, a support organization for the Weather Underground."

At West Point, the entire junior class was barred from summer break as a result of the cheating investigation. In Phoenix, on June 2, a forty-seven-year-old investigative reporter for the *Arizona Republic,* a father of seven, was murdered while pursuing a tip in a corporate corruption investigation when he turned the key in his car's ignition and a bomb planted in the floorboard exploded. In Miami, on June 4, $3 million in smuggled cocaine was found on Colombia's 203-foot three-masted entrant in the festive "Tall Ships" race to Newport, Rhode Island ("COCAINE FOUND ON BICENTENNIAL SHIP"). The United Nations World Food Council, meeting in Rome, released a report predicting a "world food disaster by 1985."

America's incoming ambassador to Lebanon, Francis E. Meloy Jr., on his way to present his credentials to the country's president, was kidnapped with one of the embassy's economic counselors by the Popular Front for the Liberation of Palestine while crossing the division between Beirut's Christian and Muslim sectors. Their bullet-riddled bodies were found on a beach shortly thereafter. Meloy was the second U.S. ambassador to be killed by terrorists in the line of duty during Gerald Ford's tenure, after Rodger Paul Davies in Cyprus.

Six fully rigged vessels collided with one another at the start of the Tall Ships race in Bermuda. And on the lighter side, Harry Reasoner gave an editorial on *ABC News.* With distaste, he noted the half-kidding remark of a friend that all these primaries were great for the moral health of America: "Several hundred of the best reporters in the country have been following the candidates around. This keeps them from other investigations, so if anything bad is going on, maybe at least we don't know about it, which is nice for a change." Happy birthday, America!

FORD AND REAGAN BOTH DROPPED IN ON THE MISSOURI REPUBLICAN Party's weekend convention. Thirty of the state's delegates had already been chosen in balloting by congressional district, fifteen for Ford, twelve for Reagan, three uncommitted. Nineteen would be chosen here in Springfield. Most, the conventional wisdom had augured, would be going to Ford: the handsome young governor, Christopher "Kit" Bond, and his attorney general, John Danforth, had it wired. At the podium at the Shrine Mosque, both officials told the delegates they couldn't be reelected on a ticket headed by Ronald Reagan. Bond pointed out the new Gallup poll showing Ford as the better candidate against Carter.

Then, on Friday June 11, the President of the United States all but put some 1,400 Missouri Republicans to sleep with his flat Midwestern drone. In the same spot on the next day, the former governor of California electrified them.

And behind the scenes Morton Blackwell and Don Devine got to work.

Ford forces had made a motion to de-credential Reagan delegates on technical grounds; that was a typical feint at contested political conventions. And frequently—for instance, at the Democratic conclave in Miami Beach that nominated George McGovern in 1972—a melodrama would ensue over the question of whether the rules should be interpreted to allow challenged delegates to vote on the disposition of their own case. This was a political tradition.

In the Republican Party, however, there was another tradition: conservatives, practiced in the arts of martyrdom, half out of a sincere sense of cultural grievance and half in poker-style bluffing, whiningly accuse wicked "liberal" party grandees—"[t]he New York kingmakers' establishment," with their "America Last foreign policy," as Phyllis Schlafly put it in her 1964 classic of the genre, *A Choice, Not an Echo*—of fraud and theft when challenged conservative delegates are not allowed to vote on their own case (or when challenged delegates *are* allowed to vote on their own case, if it is conservatives doing the challenging). And this time, such whining worked.

Blackwell and Devine read out the bill of grievance at a news conference. "Thou Shalt Not Steal" signs they passed out dotted the floor, for the benefit of news cameras, during convention sessions They put together a mock "newsletter" decrying all manner of sins by Ford forces, taping their draft to the door of the Ford offices and threatening to release it to the papers the next day unless the Ford campaign buckled. Which, after a dramatic night of negotiations, they did. Reagan emerged with eighteen delegates—it would have been nineteen had the governor's wife not broken out in tears at the podium, begging the delegates to let her husband participate in the convention in Kansas City.

It was the first state convention after the primaries closed. The Reagan forces scored a coup—a "humiliating rebuff," according to Evans and Novak. The Reagan forces had apparently worked those columnists over, too: they accused Fordites of trying "to frighten grass-roots conservative diehards into ignoring their hearts and following their appointed president." The *Washington Post* published an estimate that Reagan was now but seventy-one delegates behind, 958 to 887, with 259 uncommitted or yet to be decided. "Our Next President (Pick One)," read the *Time* cover on newsstands that Monday. It quoted the Ford hand James A. Baker III, a Texas attorney who'd gotten into politics to help his friend George H. W. Bush, and whom *Time* called "Fred" Baker: "These Reagan people don't care: they're absolutely ruthless. Our people just aren't used to this uncompromising hardball stuff."

And in a letter signed "Dutch" to his dear friend Lorraine Wagner, the former fan club president, Reagan wrote about how the Ford people had "shamelessly railroaded" delegates at the previous weekend's conventions in Arkansas and Kansas. "Then came Missouri and we were ready. . . . It's a battle now for each single delegate so we'll go after the undecided or the shaky committed. If you know of any let us know."

THE NEXT WEEKEND IN IOWA, FORD WON NINETEEN DELEGATES AND REA-gan won seventeen—but the president's aides had hoped to do much better. (The Ford campaign had canceled on the Iowans after the assassination of the ambassador in Lebanon—and released pictures showing a commander in chief poring over military-looking maps.) In Washington State it was Reagan, thirty-one to seven; in a congressional district convention in Colorado he picked up three; in a Texas meeting to pick at-large delegates he scooped up four more.

David Broder talked about maps on Monday in the *Washington Post*. He detailed how Reagan was now down by only fifty-five delegates, 997 to 942, and said that the two camps were converging—despite psychological gamesmanship by both sides to bluff the highest number they could credibly get away with. He estimated that Ford might be no more than twenty-five votes ahead, or even a little bit behind, when state conventions ended July 17. "In either case," he concluded, "the balance of power will lie with the bloc of uncommitted delegates now numbering 159."

Time was impressed by the smooth-running Reagan machine, doing its job F. Clifton White–style: "For months Reagan's men burrowed into the bedrock, taking control of the local parties at the ward and precinct level. Where Ford built his organization from the top down, Reagan built from the bottom up." The magazine quoted Betty Ford sniping at her husband's staff: "They just sit back complacently, thinking that the President would be nominated, that it was some sort of shoo-in." Her husband was barely less hard on himself in an interview with Hugh Sidey: "I'm the first to admit that I'm not an accomplished speaker. My own speechmaking ability from a text is not first class. . . . I have developed a bad reputation both as to speeches and presentation." Elizabeth Drew found a Ford-friendly congressman who said, "Ford is so inept that we'd have been better off if Nixon had burned the tapes on the back lawn." Reagan's speeches at the state conventions now stressed electability—"Look at the record in California, where I was elected in a state where Democrats outnumber Republicans almost two to one and I won the governorship by nearly a million-vote margin"—and stole a line from the president's old argument: *Ford* was the regional candidate, a minority taste of the Northeast, and Reagan was the national one.

The national headlines were crazy, as usual. On June 22, the news was that all 50,000 employees of the state of Massachusetts were going out on strike and that seventy miles of Long Island beaches were closed when the tide brought in a gagging plague of sewage. On June 24, the front page of the *Washington Post* included the following stories:

"The Senate intelligence committee said yesterday that senior officials of both the CIA and the FBI covered up crucial information in the course of investigating President Kennedy's assassination."

"Anthony (Tony Pro) Provenzano, a central figure in the investigation of former Teamster union President James R. Hoffa's disappearance, has been indicted on charges involving the 1961 kidnaping and murder of a New Jersey Teamsters official."

"A 19-year-old Wheaton [Illinois] woman, charged with murder in the beating death of her infant son last April, has told psychiatrists and investigators that she was trying to rid the baby of a demon that had possessed him."

"The United States vetoed Angola's application for U.N. membership today because of the 'continuing presence and apparent influence of Cuban troops' in the West African nation."

That same day, Dr. Maurice Sage, president of the Jewish National Fund of America, was about to present Betty Ford with the gift of a ceremonial Bible when he collapsed of a heart attack. As Secret Service agents sought to revive him, the first lady, cool and calm, took the podium to lead the crowd in a silent prayer. Reporters began noticing the button showing up on the lapels of Republican liberals at the state conventions: "Elect Betty's Husband."

The evangelicals at *Christianity Today* responded cruelly. They had recently run an interview with Reagan affirming his evangelical bona fides. "There's been a wave of humanism and hedonism in the land. However, I am optimistic because I sense in this land a great revolution against this," he said. "I think there is a hunger in this land for spiritual revival, a return to a belief in moral absolutes—the same morals upon which the nation was founded. . . . When you go out across the country and meet the people you can't help but pray and remind God of Second

Chronicles 7:14, because the people of this country are not beyond redemption. They are good people and believe this nation has a destiny
yet unfilled."

He also said, "There is a widespread but false interpretation in
many areas that separation of church and state means separation from
God. . . . I don't think He ever should have been expelled." Of pornography he said, "You can make immorality legal but you cannot make it
moral." Of the Bible, he affirmed, "I have never had any doubt about
it being of divine origin. . . . How can you write off the prophesies in
the Old Testament that hundreds of years before the birth of Christ
predicted every single facet of his life, his death, and that he was the
Messiah?" Concerning abortion—no ambiguity: "I think it comes down
to one simple answer: you cannot interrupt a pregnancy without taking
a human life." And he asserted, "I have had an experience that could be
described as 'born again.'" The editors captioned the article "Promising
Candidate." Those same editors did not feel so generous toward Ford—
whose son was an evangelical seminarian. After the first lady's call to
prayer for God to preserve Dr. Sage's life, they deadpanned that he "was
pronounced dead at a nearby hospital a short time later."

On the weekend of June 26, Reagan took only ten of forty-two delegates at the convention of Minnesota's Republican Party (which in a fit
of post-Watergate embarrassment had changed its name to "Independent Republican Party"). But Reagan swept all but one of the available
delegates in New Mexico, Idaho—and Montana, where party officials
had tried to make a truce between the two warring factions by dividing the delegation equally. But as a Ford supporter told the *Washington
Post,* the Reagan team "insisted upon a political bloodbath."

On June 27 the Popular Front for the Liberation of Palestine hijacked an Air France plane bound to Paris from Tel Aviv, forcing a landing at the airport in Entebbe, Uganda, where the hijackers divided the
passengers into Jewish and non-Jewish groups, letting the non-Jews go
free, like Nazis filling a boxcar for Auschwitz. A twenty-seven-year-old
launched his balloon *The Spirit of '76* from New Jersey in an attempt
to become the first man to float over the Atlantic. He abandoned the
deflating craft, broke three ribs, and was retrieved by the Soviet ship
Dekabrist.

Reagan's advisors announced a series of television broadcasts to
"reposition him on the issues," the *Washington Star* reported, "to make
it easier for voters to identify with his conservative ideology. Where he
has spoken in the past of the 'free enterprise system' he will now stress
'jobs.'" "There will be an effort to moderate the image," John Sears told

Elizabeth Drew. "We'll start repositioning for the fall." On July 1 Joseph Kraft reported a leak that Ford had changed his mind and was considering Reagan for his running mate. James Reston approved, partly: "In fact the Vice Presidency, if it weren't for the possibility of its leading to the Presidency, is almost perfect for Ronald Reagan: decorative, theatrical, and not too much work." Reagan did not approve of the idea himself. He said, "Only the lead horse gets a change of view." He was adamant: the notion of an "ideologically balanced" ticket was a political abomination.

On the front page on July 2, Woodward and Bernstein turned their investigatory attention to the Republican miasma, confronting a senator from Wyoming, Cliff Hansen, with evidence that he had promised seven delegates to Ford in exchange for measures to enhance his state's oil and gas revenue. He denied it. Then, under the investigative reporters' cross-examination, he cracked. "Well, maybe I did. Okay, I did. Goddamn you." On July 3, Ron Nessen dissolved the story in an acid bath of cleverness, asking reporters why, if Ford were trading delegates for oil industry favors, he had signed an energy bill that kept him from winning in Texas.

Then, on July 4, the president embarked on a busy day of travel, to culminate with an appearance on the deck of the carrier USS *Nashville* to watch the Tall Ships sail into New York Harbor, accompanied by seven special guests—all uncommitted delegates.

CHAPTER TWENTY-NINE

Bicentennial

IF YOU AWOKE ON INDEPENDENCE DAY AND FLIPPED OPEN YOUR PAPER to the Sunday funnies—and you happened to be a member of the suspicious circles—*Doonesbury* provided a comforting dose of cynicism. A plantation slave hears the bells over the horizon and asks, "Hey! Is that freedom I hear ringing?!" His master reads him something from the morning newspaper: "... *that all men are created equal, that they are endowed by their creator with certain unalienable rights.... Life, liberty, and the pursuit of happiness!*" The slave asks, "That mean what I think it does?" The master answers, "Probably not, Sammy." The slave concludes, "You mean Jefferson sold us out?"

The previous evening, in Philadelphia, Frank Rizzo had hissed out a warning: "I hope and pray that nothing happens, but know this—a lot of people are coming to this town who are bent on violence." Amtrak closed luggage lockers in stations along the Northeast Corridor, a precaution against those who might use them to hide bombs. The People's Bicentennial Commission promised two hundred thousand marchers on Washington to declare "Independence from Big Business."

There was plenty, then, for skeptics to feast upon when America celebrated its two hundredth birthday party on July 4, 1976. But the skeptics turned out to be lonely. Everyone else just forgot their fears and had fun. They heeded John Adams, who said when the Declaration of Independence was signed in 1776, "It ought to be solemnized with pomp and parade, with shows, games, sports, guns, bells, bonfires, and illuminations from one end of this continent to the other from this time forward forever more." And so it was—beginning where light first reached the North American continent, high atop Mars Hills Mountain in Maine, when NBC and CBS began sixteen hours of live coverage with the raising of the Bicentennial flag to the accompaniment of a fifty-gun salute.

Came next a riot of parades and picnics. Kids in their crepe-paper-draped bikes and red wagons. Clanging fire trucks, clambakes, rodeos. Sack races, ox roasts, barbecues—*nostalgia,* which a grateful

nation drank in like so much ice-cold lemonade. America the beautiful. Land of the free, home of the brave. My country 'tis of thee. This
land is your land. And it all felt very, very good. Yes: people yearned to
believe—suspicious circles be damned.

THE PRESIDENT BEGAN HIS LONG WEEKEND ON THURSDAY, DEDICATING
the new National Air and Space Museum on the National Mall in
Washington, D.C. ("Confined within these walls and windows are the
products of American men and women whose imagination and determination could not be confined.") He led a ceremony that unveiled a
continuous seventy-six-hour display of the nation's official copies of the
Declaration of Independence and Constitution. He went by helicopter
to Valley Forge, Pennsylvania, where two thousand pilgrims in two
hundred covered wagons from all fifty states camped out in anticipation. There, he signed a bill establishing as a national park the sacred
site where General Washington's Continental Army camped out over
the frigid winter of 1777–78—then signed a scroll of 22 million names
of Americans pledging to rededicate themselves to the principles of the
Declaration of Independence. "Our Bicentennial is the 'happy birthday'
of all fifty states," he said, clambering with boyish glee up to the seat of
the covered wagon representing his home state, Michigan.

He was next ferried to Philadelphia, where at precisely 2 P.M. he
tolled the Centennial Bell thirteen times (the Liberty Bell was too
fragile)—one of thousands pealing nationwide, from church towers
and town halls and front yards at the exact instant the Declaration was
said to have been announced. Then he gave the first of his six speeches
that day. ("The world may or may not follow, but we lead because our
whole history says we must.") Queen Elizabeth II stood by his side
(she caused a stir by touching the Liberty Bell). A visiting boys choir
from Paris sang. The "Mummers" of South Philadelphia's Italian neighborhoods, famous for their gaily costumed New Year's parade antics
for seventy-five years, delighted children. A 49,000-pound cake was
displayed—though an even bigger cake in Baltimore helped celebrate
the flag at Fort McHenry that inspired "The Star-Spangled Banner."

Goofy, delirious fun: for America's sacred days, no massed displays
of military weaponry like in those other, less idealistic nations. "A Super
Bowl of superlatives," a columnist in Columbus, Ohio, called it: "the
biggest, the loudest, the best and the brightest; a blur of extravaganzas
months in anticipation." The sixty-square-foot cherry pie on display
in the aptly named town of George, Washington. That world-record-
setting pole-sitter, descending from his perch to delighted cheers in San

Jose, California. (Had it been conceived to boost the sales of a car dealership? No one cared.) A goofball arrived in the City of Brotherly Love after pushing a watermelon all the way from Georgia. In Hawaii the telescope at Mauna Kea Observatory focused light from a star precisely two hundred light-years away onto a sensor that triggered a switch that transmitted the current that relit the lantern of one-if-by-land Old North Church in Boston, as the USS *Constitution* boomed its guns for the first time in a century in a twenty-one-gun salute. A woman in Peoria, Illinois, shouted to a reporter over the blare of a passing parade, "It makes you want to believe in the country!"

An estimated ten thousand immigrants took the oath of citizenship—7,141 in Miami alone. In Lake City, Pennsylvania, a 2,300-citizen town near Lake Erie, workers threw the switch on a landing pad for flying saucers—approved by the federal Bicentennial Administration for listing in the official Bicentennial program—encircled by a red, a white, and a blue ring of light. "We thought if there actually were UFOs, we might as well give them a place to land," said the project's director. "This thing is bringing the whole town together. And isn't that what the Bicentennial is all about?"

The presidential helicopter alighted atop the USS *Nashville* in New York Harbor. Millions massed on both sides of the Hudson, two hundred thousand people in Weehawken, New Jersey, alone. "We don't know if those antique railings can hold and frankly we anticipate fatalities," the mayor warned. But everything turned out fine. They witnessed the magical parade of 224 Tall Ships and thousands of small boats, in the city where the Democrats would hold their nominating convention in a week; then the president was off to Washington, D.C., to review an eighteen-float "Pageant of Freedom" depicting the nation's history in eight twenty-five-year tableaux, culminating with the 1969 moon shot (though Los Angeles's parade, which lasted eight hours, was bigger).

Suddenly the nation's capital was not a seat of wickedness and dissolution. It was lawns honeycombed with happy families, museums bursting with awestruck tourists—and, after darkness fell, the "damnedest fireworks display the world has ever seen," in the words of the chairman of the convening group, Happy Birthday, U.S.A., whose day job was president of the Giant supermarket chain. People watched from picnic blankets, from hotel rooms, from town-house rooftops in Georgetown, from cars stalled in a massive Bicentennial traffic snarl that somehow seemed to agitate drivers not at all—900,000 happy revelers oohing and aahing over twenty thousand rockets and thirty-three tons of explosives, controlled by a sixteen-mile matrix of electrical wires.

And the president saw it was good. He bade his countrymen good night from the Oval Office: "In its first two centuries the nation has not been able to right every wrong, to correct every injustice, or to reach every worthy goal. But for two hundred years we have tried, and we will continue to strive to make the lives of individual men and women in this country and on this earth better lives—more hopeful and happy, more prosperous and peaceful, more fulfilling and more free. This is our common dedication and it will be our common glory as we enter the third century of the American adventure." Before his own head hit the pillow, he would later recollect, he declared a personal victory: "Well, Jerry," he told himself, "I guess we've healed America."

YOU COULD MOCK.

You could laugh at Mayor Rizzo because his city got half as many tourists as expected because he had scared all the rest away. You could point out that Philadelphia's original Bicentennial plans for a World's Fair had been scrapped years earlier, organizers explaining that "national and international hard times" made it impractical. You could laugh at the fact that the lasers during the D.C. fireworks show that were supposed to spell out "Happy Birthday America 1776–1976" did not quite work on cue. You could laugh at Reverend Sun Myung Moon, who'd marched his zombies across the Mall in revolutionary costume, then allegedly gathered them at midnight at the Washington Monument, where they poured their blood into a vat and prayed for True Father's "success in America." You could point out the Bronx cheers the president would have earned if he had had the guts to actually *set foot* in Manhattan—CITY TO FORD: DROP DEAD—instead of hiding on an aircraft carrier watching the ships go by. (One of them, it was reported, the four-masted barkentine from Chile, had been used as a torture chamber by General Pinochet.) You could point out superciliously that many of Philadelphia's Mummers only a dozen years earlier had pranced about in blackface.

You could point out that the nation being celebrated was more and more one of cynics and smart-asses, the gross and the uncouth (like the broad in the halter top from a home movie of the parade in Minersville, Pennsylvania, who looked into the camera from amid the shirtless and hot-pants-wearing throng, smirked, and threw up a two-handed middle-finger salute). Or that the estimated $400 million spent on the parties, including $51.8 million in federal funds for the American Revolutionary Bicentennial Commission, could have been spent more patriotically by actually making America a better place.

You could celebrate Boston University's curmudgeonly president, John Silber, who gave a grumpy address called "Counterfeits of Democracy" at Faneuil Hall: "Increasingly, we confuse the pursuit of happiness, guaranteed by the Declaration of Independence, with the pursuit of pleasure."

You could point out—like *Doonesbury* in the Sunday morning paper and Jesse Jackson calling for blacks to boycott and the Native American group in Portland, Oregon, who said their invitation to join the Bicentennial Wagon Train was like Jews being invited to a party for Adolf Hitler—that the American dream did not include all Americans' dreams.

You could point out, as media voices did during Operation Homecoming in 1973, that the whole thing served the malign ideological purpose of dissuading a nation from a desperately needed reckoning with the sins of its past.

You could dismiss the whole thing as infantilizing: "birthday parties," after all, were for children.

And some people did. But the vast, vast majority did not. Indeed, wrote Elizabeth Drew, "the children understood better that this was a special evening"—the *New Yorker* implying that they were the ones who had it right.

The day after, it was almost hard to remember that the keynote of the preparations had been ambivalence and embarrassment—the ambivalence of a nation where only eight months earlier, 68 percent of citizens had told Gallup pollsters that the government consistently lied. (George Gallup wrote, "If this persists, it is within the realm of possibility that the United States will in the near future experience its greatest crisis of confidence since 1933.") Indeed when Oberlin, Ohio, was chosen as a stop on the Bicentennial Wagon Train the local newspaper's editors confessed nothing but apprehension. They reported, "The Bicentennial [has] not really caught on here or across the nation." In a special Bicentennial edition of the paper in April, they reflected that the celebration had been "conceived more out of obligation than desire . . . the nation as a whole is not much in the mood for a birthday party. With a choice of red, white and blue decorations, the dominant tone seems to be blue."

Then, the day arrived, and those same editors changed their mind.

"Our apprehensions were unfounded," they wrote. "America truly does have a heritage to celebrate this year and the wagon train made part of that heritage come to life for us." And lots of people agreed. Card-carrying, charter members of the suspicious circles tried on the sort of simple patriotism associated with followers of Ronald Reagan, some for the first time—and discovered they liked it. And for the many who had liked it already, the reaction was sheer unadulterated relief that they could tune those suspicious circles out.

Dread proved unfounded:

There were no fatalities in Weehawken.

Only about five thousand protesters showed up in Washington.

The National Safety Council said that highway casualties had been "normal."

And, lo, there were no terrorist attacks.

And dread suddenly became passé. *Time*: "[T]he best part of it was that its supreme characteristics were good will, good humor and, after a long night of paralyzing self-doubt, good feelings about the U.S. . . . Only five year ago, in protest against the U.S.'s involvement in Indochina, the flag was being burned, burlesqued, and spat upon. Today many of the self same Americans who chose then to disown their flag are hoisting it high." And *Newsweek:* "It's nice that we're promoting our country for a change rather than putting it down." And, of course, the president: "After two centuries there is still something wonderful about being an American," he said while turning immigrants into citizens at Monticello. "If we cannot quite express it we know what it is. You know what it is or you would not be here."

There turned out to be something so exuberantly spontaneous about the way people felt their way through the festivities—like the riders of a subway car in tense, violent Boston who broke out in a rendition of "Happy Birthday, America," and the revelers who found themselves dancing—"spontaneously and jubilantly," Elizabeth Drew observed— when Arthur Fiedler's Boston Pops ripped into a boisterous "Stars and Stripes Forever." And the throngs who surprised themselves by applauding the most famous lines when a lecturer in Revolutionary costume read out the Declaration on the National Archives steps.

IF THE KEYNOTE OF THE PREPARATIONS WAS AMBIVALENCE, THE WORD that dominated the post hoc reflections was *surprise.*

An AP special correspondent ("Nation's Hunger to Feel Good Erupts in Fever of Patriotism") exulted at how the day "turned out to be a big, warm surprise party. . . . The grim clichés of more than a decade—'the American malaise,' 'the sick society'—were scarcely heard in the land, praise God." Blacks were "less reproachful," Indians less "militant," the distaff sex "paused in her march to full equality" (a good thing!), the young were becoming "less critical."

Elizabeth Drew: "The feeling of the day sort of crept up on many of us, took us by surprise. There was a spirit to it that could not have been anticipated. For those of us who had been in despair about this Bicentennial Fourth of July, who feared the worst, the surprise was a very pleasing one . . . a lot of us have become so jaded that it is hard to believe that anything is real. But the politicians and the salesmen did not destroy the day—they became almost irrelevant. The celebrating seemed genuine. . . . the feelings came up on us when we least expected them."

A Toledo resident who journeyed to New York: "We're all so jaded, but we were able to savor each one of the ships. . . . It's real exciting because all these countries have gotten together to celebrate the Bicentennial with us."

The *Birmingham News:* "America turned a corner on a self-induced illness of the spirit and stretched its psyche in a burst of national joy and celebration."

Self-induced: throw a big party, and the illness was gone.

ONE OF THE FEW DISSENTS CAME FROM AN UNUSUAL SOURCE. A REMARKable thing had taken place while Americans enjoyed their birthday party. For days a hundred Israeli commandos had been drilling painstakingly for "Operation Thunderbolt," using a precise replica of Entebbe's airport terminal; the model was based on intelligence gained from construction workers and interviews with released hostages. Late on Bicentennial eve, transport planes ferried the commandos 2,500 miles to Entebbe, Uganda; to avoid radar detection they were never more than a hundred feet above the sea and the land. On July 4 they set down with their planes' cargo bays already opened, disgorging jeeps that they then drove to the terminal, dropping two Ugandan sentries with silenced pistols. They overpowered the Palestinian kidnappers and their Ugandan security force, then scooped up the hostages and loaded them into the rescue planes under enemy fire. Simultaneously three more cargo planes unloaded the armored personnel carriers whose forces disabled eleven Ugandan MiGs that might have pursued the rescued hostages as they winged their way to freedom. The whole thing took but an hour and a half—102 hostages rescued, only three killed. The Israelis lost only one commando.

Almost immediately some half-dozen Hollywood companies vied for rights to tell the story. And a former Hollywood hand named Reagan voiced a certain disappointment. He said, "This is what Americans used to do."

THE GOOD FEELINGS LINGERED INTO THE DEMOCRATIC CONVENTION A week later in New York City. Gotham, said Jules Witcover, "left its customary cauldron of ill temper, rudeness, and freneticism in an uncommon mood of cordiality. Cab drivers who on other occasions not only refused to stop for rush-hour passengers but also tossed epithets as they sped by now became ambassadors of good will. Waitresses, elevator operators, hotel clerks, shopkeepers were uncharacteristically courteous. Police put off their snarling and helped conventioneers find their way around."

The city, he said, seemed eager "to live down its reputation." So did the Democratic Party—that cantankerous conglomeration H. L. Mencken once called "gangs of mutual enemies in a precarious state of symbiosis." Platform drafters finished their work at the Mayflower Hotel a day early, having produced a document as ideologically nondisputatious as the man who would run on it. Feminist forces led by Bella Abzug who had come in demanding 50 percent of delegate slots for women at the 1980 convention came away, satisfied, with a deal promising the party would merely "promote" gender equality and that a President Carter would press for the ERA. Forces led by Jerry Brown's state treasurer, Sam Brown, who had organized the Vietnam Moratorium demonstration in 1969, when some two million Americans stayed home from work or school on the same day to protest the war, came in demanding the endorsement of a "full and complete pardon" for all those in "legal or financial jeopardy" for evading the draft or deserting the military, and came away satisfied with an amendment merely promising pardon consideration on a case-by-case basis. (They also got a symbolic concession: a speech from the convention platform by the wheelchair-bound Vietnam veteran Ron Kovic, author of a forthcoming memoir, *Born on the Fourth of July*.) "You have to give up a bit," Sam Brown the former antiwar firebrand said, "in order to take control of the presidency."

"The idea that the Democrats, if they behaved, might actually inhabit the White House once again," Witcover wrote, had "mellowed that usually fractious party." So had their mellow nominee-apparent—and, perhaps, the mild springlike breezes that transformed the customarily sweltering city into what the journalists phoning in their copy invariably called a "lovefest." The party chairman, the glad-handing Texan Robert Strauss, was asked if the convention would be "dull." He answered, smiling, "It can't get too dull for me."

There had been storm clouds over the horizon. In the middle of June, Carter decamped for a relaxing trip to Sea Island, Georgia. He wore an Allman Brothers Band T-shirt while fishing, reporters noticed. In Georgia, the red-hot Southern rockers, whose singer Gregg Allman was married to Cher, "have the force of religion," the *Village Voice's* James Wolcott explained. Their label was Macon-based Capricorn Records. Carter had been friends with its CEO, Phil Walden, since 1973 when the governor called on him to talk about boosting the state's entertainment industry. Carter then signed a law tightening protection of record companies from the scourge of bootleg cassette tapes. Walden promised a series of fund-raising concerts starring the Allmans, Wet Willie, the Marshall Tucker Band, and the Charlie Daniels Band to help put him in the White House—a nice solution to get around the FEC's thousand-dollar contribution limit. But rock stars enjoyed certain recreational activities hazardous to the reputation of Baptist presidential candidates. A federal grand jury was considering drug charges against a number of those in the Capricorn Records orbit; then came the news that the Allmans' former road manager had been convicted for conspiracy and drug distribution, partly on Greg Allman's testimony offered under immunity. Suspicions lingered that Capricorn was more or less a front for a drug ring.

But nothing whatsoever ended up being made of it in the presidential campaign. The drug connections of the powerful were no longer really news.

Drugs, in fact, were everywhere, and hardly anywhere controversial. The editors of *Consumer Reports* had published *Licit & Illicit Drugs: The Consumers Union Report on Narcotics, Stimulants, Depressants, Inhalants, Hallucinogens and Marijuana—Including Caffeine, Nicotine, and Alcohol,* weighing in at 623 pages, treating substances illegal under federal law no differently from their ratings of toasters or the new Chrysler LeBaron (Section VI: "Inhalants, Solvents, Glue-Sniffing"). In 1975 a new magazine had been inaugurated, *Marijuana Monthly*—"a publication," its prospectus read, "dealing with marijuana's growing impact upon society. We present the facts, the fiction, the humor and the opinion about marijuana and the lifestyle of its users." *High Times,* which began publication a year earlier, had been intended as a single-issue parody of *Playboy* (complete with a centerfold picture of a high-grade cannabis specimen). It was selling 550,000 copies a month by 1975. *Saturday Night Live* made plain every week that bingeing on pot was just what your ordinary mildly antiauthoritarian hip young professional was *supposed* to do. (One Chevy Chase gag noted the FBI was warning of a shipment of "killer dope" infiltrating New York. "In an effort to aid the FBI in its investigation, Weekend Update is undertaking its own analysis of the marijuana sent to us anonymously by any viewers who may be worried. Simply place a small sample of the suspected cannabis in an envelope and send it immediately to: Chevy Chase, Apartment 12, 827 West 81st Street, New York City 10053.")

Carter had promised to end federal penalties for possession of less than an ounce of pot, eleven states having already decriminalized the stuff. President Ford was asked by a student on the campaign trail in New Hampshire if he agreed. His reply: "Until there is a higher degree of unanimity among the scientific world that marijuana is not harmful to the individual, I do not think we should decriminalize marijuana." But that seemed like only a matter of time. As for cocaine—"not, strictly speaking, an addictive drug," *New York* magazine reported late in 1973—in 1977 Eric Clapton and Jackson Browne both recorded celebratory songs on the subject; Clapton's eventually charted at No. 30.

In the summer of 1976 the Associated Press reported that one of Carter's nephews, William Carter Spann, was serving ten to life in Vacaville, California, for two armed robberies in San Francisco. The name never made the news again. It seemed no one cared about Jimmy Carter's vagrant relations, nor his stoned rock-and-roll friends—except, perhaps, those young voters for whom the latter was a recommendation, and who joined the lovefest along with everyone else.

YOU COULD SEE IT IN THE VERITABLE STREET FESTIVAL OUT IN FRONT OF the Americana Hotel, where the Carter forces were headquartered: announcements stenciled on the pavement and volunteers passing out leaflets like carnival barkers, Italian ice and pretzels vended by colorful characters in carts and balloons and Bicentennial Big Apple T-shirts and Carter buttons and that wacky fellow in the Uncle Sam costume who always seems to show up at national conventions. Carter strode out upon a makeshift sidewalk dais, more relaxed than ever—"it looks like his more natural smile," a journalist wrote—with his wife and their darling eight-year-old Amy, trying out jokes, teasing the throng by hinting that he might just shock the world by revealing his running mate right then and there, promising that he would never, ever tell New York to drop dead. He ended with the patriotic affirmation that "we still live in the greatest nation on earth."

Former candidates exuded love, too: Mo Udall, affirming, "Now we're here to help Jimmy Carter celebrate his victory"; Jerry Brown, the last holdout, calling Carter "our nominee." High-minded delegates toured the exhibit at the Whitney, "Two Hundred Years of American Scripture"; the proverbial curtain opened at Madison Square Garden

Monday evening, July 12, on a set that featured a white picket fence, and red-white-and-blue bunting meant to call forth nostalgic recollections of the last time the Democrats met at Madison Square Garden, in 1924.

The first keynote speaker was John Glenn, now a senator, formerly an astronaut—an old-fashioned sort of hero. ("Doubts? Fears? Lagging confidence? Well, no wonder. With all that has befallen us, a lesser nation might well have collapsed.") The second keynoter was a new-fashioned sort of hero: Barbara Jordan, star of the House Judiciary Committee impeachment hearings two years earlier, who if anything topped her patriotic oration of 1974 ("My faith in the Constitution is *whole,* it is *complete,* it is *total*"). She was took the stage to the strains of "Deep in the Heart of Texas," and the standing ovation lasted two minutes, roaring right on through the chairman's frustrated gavel bangs ("*Ladies and gentlemen! . . . You're neither ladies nor are you gentlemen!*"), and then she was introduced, and the ovation lasted for another sixty seconds after that.

"It was 144 years ago," her deep voice rumbled, "that members of the Democratic Party first met in convention to select a presidential candidate." (She smiled, anticipating the delight at what she was about to say.)

"Since that time Democrats have continued to convene once every four years and draft the party platform and nominate presidential candidate. Our meeting this week is a continuation of that tradition.

"But there is something *different* about tonight, there is something *special* about tonight. What is different, what is special? I, Barbara Jordan, am a keynote speaker!"

Another thirty-second standing ovation.

She concluded, some twenty minutes later:

"We cannot improve on the system of government handed down to us by the founders of the republic. There is no way to improve upon that, but what we can do is to find new ways to implement that system and realize our destiny.

"Now, I began this speech by commenting to you on the uniqueness of a Barbara Jordan making a keynote address. Well, I am going to close my speech by quoting a Republican president. . . . *'As I would not be a slave, so I would not be a master'*—

More roars interrupted her.

"*'This expresses my idea of democracy. Whatever differs from this, to the extent of the difference is no democracy.'*"

Quoting Lincoln, she got another standing ovation, wave after wave after wave. It all felt very, very good.

• • •

THE NEXT NIGHT, ON GERALD FORD'S SIXTY-THIRD BIRTHDAY, BASTILLE Day, the speakers included George S. McGovern: "Eight years ago some Democrats had doubts about Hubert Humphrey. And they gave us Nixon's first four years of war and domestic strife. Four years ago, some Democrats had doubts about me—and we got Nixon again. To repeat that sort of folly would be unconscionable." Then Hubert H. Humphrey: "The patriots of 1776 believed, and this party has always believed, that a democratic government must be an active force for the betterment of human life. But there are new Tories abroad in the land. And their words are newly fashionable. They appeal to cynicism. They cater to the people's mistrust of their own institutions. . . . They tell us our afflictions will be healed if we but leave them alone—if we seek private gain rather than public good. . . . There was no room for the Tories in Philadelphia in 1776. And I say there is no room for them in New York in 1976 or in Washington in 1977." Young Michael Dukakis of Massachusetts also spoke, and the first black mayor of Los Angeles, Tom Bradley, and George Wallace, Coretta Scott King, Mayor Daley, Frank Church, and Admiral Zumwalt—*unity.*

The next night was the ceremony of nomination. One of the heroes of Watergate, Peter Rodino, put in Jimmy Carter's name. Another Watergate hero, Archibald Cox, nominated Mo Udall, who said, "As I leave this convention hall, I'm going to have one of those green buttons that dogged me all over America. . . . And tomorrow morning I'm enlisting as a soldier in the Carter campaign." Then Cesar Chavez nominated Jerry Brown.

A televised image: Jimmy Carter in shirtsleeves, fiddling with the back of his hotel room's TV—*just folks.*

The roll call of states; Ohio put him over the top.

On TV: Amy and Carter's grandson Jason clambered onto the candidate's lap, and his wife Rosalynn down in the convention hall said into a reporter's microphone, "I miss Jimmy not being here with me," and Jerry Brown was recognized on the convention floor: "I don't think it's going to be done in a hundred days or a thousand days. It's going to be a long, difficult struggle to live within our environment, and work together and bring about justice. I think Jimmy Carter can do that; he's proved it to you, he's proved it to me, and I just want to be able to announce that the California delegation votes two hundred and seventy-eight votes to Mr. Carter and we're on our way to bring this country back to the Democratic column."

A ceremonial committee was named from the rostrum to bring the news to Jimmy Carter that, some five hundred days since announcing his candidacy, he was the Democratic nominee, with 2,468 of 2,925 votes. Democrats went off to bed, six of them very nervously: Frank Church, John Glenn, Walter Mondale, Adlai Stevenson, Henry Jackson, and Edmund Muskie, who all got calls from Carter's personal aide Greg Schneiders that they were under consideration to become Carter's running mate, and would receive a call between 8:30 and 9 A.M. with his final decision.

THE ASSOCIATED PRESS PULLED TOGETHER A MORE OR LESS VERBATIM transcript of a call Thursday morning to one of the also-rans:

"Hello?"

"Ed?"

"I just called to tell you I selected someone else."

It spoke to the awesome discipline of the Carter campaign: determined that there not be a leak, he didn't even tell the losers who the winner was. And when the winner got *his* call—"Would you like to run with me?"—he was beseeched to tell not a single soul. Not even the printing plant knew: instructed to produce six green-and-white designs for campaign posters, each with a different running mate's face, the staff there got the call to run off the sheets with Walter Mondale's face only that morning.

The selection process had also been awesomely disciplined—for Jimmy Carter, there were to be no last-minute fiascoes like George McGovern's when he had to abandon his running mate, Thomas Eagleton, after the press learned that Eagleton had undergone electroshock treatment for depression. Having sealed the nomination more than a month earlier, Carter had more time to mull over his decision than any other Democratic nonincumbent in history—and the campaign had been planning for the decision since April, when Hamilton Jordan devised a literal point scale to weigh the possibilities (zero to fifteen for "ability"; zero to fifteen for "integrity"; zero to ten for "acceptance") and graded every last Democratic senator and governor and a clutch of representatives and mayors, too. Those with fewer than twenty-seven points were culled from the pool. Only then were those left considered on factors like political philosophy.

A June 2 memo from Hamilton Jordan reminded Carter this was the first decision "of presidential magnitude you will make," and made the argument that an anti-Establishment presidential candidate had to choose an Establishment running mate: "The best politics is to select a person who is accurately perceived by the American people as being qualified and able to serve as President if that becomes necessary." A new kind of balanced ticket was called for in the age of antipolitics.

Twenty possible candidates were interviewed by aide Charles Kirbo—some not really possibilities, but the bluff put Carter on good terms with the candidates' various political patrons. Hamilton Jordan made an adman's sort of contribution: "reflecting the Carter campaign's propensity for thinking in terms of the words that convey impressions," Elizabeth Drew later learned, "Jordan listed the finalists and the words that he thought attached to their names."

Carter began calling candidates to Plains, Georgia, upon his return from his fishing trip in July. He'd found Muskie too stiff, and was worried about his temper. Senate colleagues reportedly told Carter that Frank Church, who polled best, had handled the CIA investigation poorly and was a weak senator, and Carter worried about their compatibility. (Church himself, who badly wanted the job, would later maintain that the CIA had sabotaged him by spreading a rumor about KGB infiltration of his staff.) But Carter hit it off with Walter "Fritz" Mondale, whom he'd met only twice before, in 1974 when the Minnesota senator dropped in on him in Atlanta, and earlier in 1976 on Capitol Hill. Carter liked that Mondale was a favorite with reporters, was popular with labor and liberals, and was a protégé of Hubert Humphrey, which gave Mondale points with the Establishment. A nice, safe, straddling choice.

Carter walked into the Georgian Ballroom at the Americana Hotel with his wife an hour and a half after telling Mondale the news, mentioning nothing about point scales or advertising semiotics. Carter announced he'd chosen Mondale for his "comprehension and compassion for people who need the services of government most," and that he was someone who'd shown "sound judgment in times of difficulty," and had "the trust of a wide range of Democrats. . . . I feel completely compatible with Senator Mondale. . . . It is a very sure feeling that I have about that point."

He was asked if he was worried about whether Mondale was up for a tough campaign, given that he'd dropped out of the presidential running in 1974. He answered that Mondale had dropped out because "he knew that he could not win"—which was not true, and a strange thing to say about a running mate in any event. Mondale entered with his wife, Joan, and one of the things he was asked about was how he prepared to be interviewed by Carter. He answered, "The first thing I did was to read the most remarkable book ever written, called *Why Not the Best?* I found every word absolutely magnificent."

It was so different from the kind of joke Jimmy Carter would ever make that reporters had to wonder about this vaunted "compatibility" Carter was supposedly so sure about.

Carter moved on to his next event, speaking beside Jerry Brown in a ballroom at the Hilton. Brown introduced him with evident lack of enthusiasm. Carter said of Brown, "we've grown to be close friends"—which was not even close to true. Then he rhetorically insulted his vanquished foe: "There's no limits on us. Material limits, yes. Governmental limits, yes. But I'm not ready to recognize that there's a limit to hope, to freedom, to individuality."

Then it was time for Madison Square Garden, where all was celebration.

A GIANT RED-WHITE-AND-BLUE BEACH BALL BOINGED FESTIVELY FROM one cheering delegation to the next. A section of the gallery flashed cards reading, TEXAS LOVES NEW YORK. Others broke out into singing. The banners flanking the rostrum read, "FOR AMERICA'S THIRD CENTURY, WHY NOT THE BEST." Mondale made his maiden speech, a post-Watergate jeremiad. The line that got the biggest applause of the night: "Roosevelt said that the presidency is preeminently a place of moral leadership. But we have just lived the *Worst, Political, Scandal,* in American history"—*stab, stab, stab,* went his finger with each word—"and are now led by a President who pardoned the person who did it."

He concluded, "The year of our two hundredth birthday, the year of the election of Jimmy Carter, will go down as one of the greatest years of public reform in American history." The standing ovation was so enthusiastic that Robert Strauss had to beg for order.

The lights went down; a movie screen was lowered: Jimmy Carter in jeans, in a peanut field; Jimmy Carter in a suit, speaking noble words. Jimmy Carter rendered in cartoon form—or at least Jimmy Carter's teeth: "Jimmy!" Rosalynn calls out from the dark. "Cut it out and go to sleep!" Uproarious laughter.

Strauss introduced "the next President of the United States." Carter's smile was at least that glowing as he walked forth in an unprecedented way: from the rear, through the delegate floor, working his way through the crowd, shaking hands, shouting greetings—a man of the people. A man of love.

He bolted up the stairs. He planted himself on the rostrum, family by his side:

"My name is Jimmy Carter, and I'm running for President!"

Roars.

It was an even funnier joke than the glow-in-the-dark teeth. That was the line he'd said a thousand times before, in Iowa, in New Hampshire, in primaries across the fruited plain. *I'm running for president:* "President of what?" his mother had asked when he told him that more than three years before. No one was asking that now.

He made a kind of Democratic inside joke: it was a pleasure "to see that our Bicentennial celebration and our Bicentennial convention has been one of decorum and order without any fights or free-for-alls. Among Democrats that can only happen once every two hundred years." He was interrupted by applause for the fifth time—and it was only his fifth sentence.

He promised that 1976 could be "a year of inspiration and hope," a year "when we give the government of this country back to the *people* of this country," the year of a "new mood in America." He said, "This has been a long and personal campaign—a humbling experience, reminding us that ultimate political influence rests not with power-brokers, but with the people."

He spoke of his memories of himself as a farm boy; hailed the great Democrats who came before him; and said, "Our country has lived through a time of torment. It is now a time for healing. We want to have faith again. We want to be proud again. We just want the truth again. It is time for the people to run the government, and not the other way around!" He spoke of America's "mistakes": "the tragedy of Vietnam and Cambodia, the disgrace of Watergate and the embarrassment of the CIA revelations"—all of which could have been avoided if only "our government had simply reflected the sound judgment and the good common sense and the high moral character of the American people."

And they interrupted him with acclaim for the twenty-fifth time. He built up momentum:

"It's time for our government leaders to respect the law no less than the humblest citizen"—he was interrupted with lusty cheers in the middle of the sentence—"so that we can end once and for all a double standard of justice. I see no reason—*I see no reason!*—why big-shot crooks should go free and the poor ones go to jail."

That got a standing ovation.

"We have an America that, in Bob Dylan's phrase, is busy being born—not busy dying!

"We can have an American government that has turned away from scandal and corruption and official cynicism and is once again as decent and as competent as its people. . . .

"As I've said many times before, we can have an American President who does not govern with negativism and fear of the future, but with vigor and vision and aggressive leadership—a President who's not isolated from the people, but who *feels your pain* and shares your dreams and takes his strength and his wisdom and his courage from you. . . . And once again, as brothers and sisters, our hearts will swell with pride to call ourselves Americans."

The official record noted the fifty-fifth ovation of the speech. And then the emotion crescendoed yet more.

ROBERT STRAUSS TOOK TO THE PODIUM AND CALLED UP ALL THE OPPO-nents who were opponents no more, Udall and Jackson and Bayh and Shapp and Church and Brown and Wallace and Shriver—then, "with all the subtlety of a nuclear explosive," Witcover wrote, called up still more dignitaries: New York's mayor and New Orleans's mayor, the governors of New Jersey and Arizona, all the vice presidential runners-up, "literally dozens of the party's second- and third-string luminaries to the platform," by now "like a drinker who has to have one more, and another, and one more after that."

And then he called up Daddy King—the father of the civil rights martyr.

The hall had already begun to empty. Now people rushed back to their seats. The stout old preacher said, "I would like very much that we would cease walking, talking. In fact, not a word be uttered, unless that word is uttered to God."

He preached: "Surely the Lord is in this place. Surely the Lord sent Jimmy Carter to come on out and bring America back where she belongs."

He beseeched his congregation to fall to its knees: "It's time for prayer."

And America's Democrats, assembled at the big Baptist church called Madison Square Garden, bowed their heads, and some indeed fell to their knees. He bent over double, he raised his fists to the heavens, he preached some more: "I've been doing this sixty-odd years, I have had my trials, my tribulations, my ups and downs, my losses, but I'm determined I'm not going to let nothing get me down!" He thundered: "I'm going on and see what the *end* is going to be to all of this! This Lord *blesssss* you! And *keeeep* you! The Lord makes His face to *shine* upon you, and be *gracious* unto you. The Lord lifts up the light of his *countenance* upon *you*!—and gives *you*!—peace. *Noooooooow!* And *alllllllways*!"

The convention orchestra struck up "We Shall Overcome," and an audience that had become a congregation sang along with tears streaking down their faces. Then raised up once more in the biggest standing ovation yet. They believed. "If there were differences remaining in the Democratic Party, they were laid aside in this one emotional wave that swept over all reservations," Jules Witcover wrote. Another professional curmudgeon, Mike Royko of Chicago, believed, too. "I hate to get corny at this late date in a cynical life, but the arrival of Jimmy Carter at the affectionate, emotional bedlam of Madison Square Garden, staged as it all may have been, was one very memorable experience," he began his syndicated column. "This was a guy who, less than two years ago, was almost considered some kind of kook. An unknown Southern local politician, a peanut-picker, a man with virtually no power base, setting out almost like a traveling salesman with a dream to be President of the United States.

"Now he was walking into the convention hall of his party's national convention to get the nomination, and the delegates, including most established powers, were on their feet cheering their heads off. Some were even crying. . . .

"We've grown used to politicians appealing to our baser instincts. . . . But here comes this guy who dusts off an old word like love, and he managed to persuade the most cantankerous group of individuals in the country—the Democratic Party—to practically fall into each other's arms. . . . It was the cornball American dream come true, and it was something to see and remember. . . . I hope he can be believed. We don't need any more highly skillful liars. We've already been pushed to the brink of a national nervous breakdown by that. We deserve a break."

Harris polled the American people to see what they thought. They wanted Carter over Ford by 66 percent to 27, Carter over Reagan 68 to 26—the greatest postconvention margin ever. Which meant that Republicans and independents believed, too.

CHAPTER THIRTY

"You're in the Catbird Seat"

JIMMY CARTER HAD SAID IN HIS ACCEPTANCE SPEECH, "WITH THIS KIND of a united Democratic Party, we are ready and eager to take on the Republicans, whichever Republican Party they decide to send against us in November." Which was no more clear in the middle of July than it had been in the middle of June. "Republican professionals," *Newsweek* reported, feared "a nasty summer, a bloody convention—and a party split so badly that only a shotgun pairing of Ford and Reagan on the same ticket could heal it." But Ronald Reagan had categorically ruled out running on the same ticket with Ford. So there was no healing to be had.

The name of the game was now the 150 or so "uncommitted" delegates—and the game was so heartily silly that when a political cartoon depicted Marine One hovering over a remote country store, one woman explaining to another, "That must be President Ford again . . . Merle's an uncommitted delegate, you know," it hardly felt like a joke at all. One obscure Republican official from Suffolk County, New York, emerged from a ten-minute audience announcing that the Leader of the Free World had agreed to take a closer look at the problems of his local sewage district. And when the queen of England arrived at the White House for a sumptuous state dinner, the gentleman the president chose to seat next to her was Clarke Reed, chairman of the largest uncommitted delegation—Mississippi's, with thirty convention votes. The joke went around that another uncommitted delegate, from New Jersey, had received the same invitation from the president. He paused, then asked: "What's on the menu?"

Ford was hardly governing. He was campaigning, like a ward heeler—one voter at a time. A crew of uncommitteds would be ushered into the Cabinet Room or the East Room or the Blue Room or even the State Dining Room. The chairs would be set up as at a press conference. The president would mingle informally for a half an hour, then stand behind a podium for ten minutes relating his accomplishments, then open the floor to questions—tough questions: about his pardon of Nixon;

about his views on abortion, on offshore oil drilling or the closing of a military base in a delegate's backyard. The ritual went on for as long as it took, for an hour or sometimes more.

Before any delegate got to that point he'd already been well massaged on the phone—an intricate strategic operation that involved consulting an elaborate binder, updated daily, in which each delegate's ideology, employment, spouse's name and children's names and ages, hobbies, what issues the delegate cared about ("upset about federal regulation of independent dairy producers," read the entry for a delegate named Charles N. Dodd, which also noted that he should be addressed as "Chuck"), religion . . . and, most crucially, the names of the Republican officials most likely to hold sway over his loyalties. Constant follow-up babysitting calls—*What do you need? What do you want?*—came next, exquisitely calculated to stop just shy of feeling like *pressure*.

Reagan, lacking a state dining room or Marine helicopter, did the same work in hotel suites, deploying his own special secret weapon: charm. Whenever Ford or Reagan moved a single delegate—after a conclave with Reagan at the Penn-Harris Motor Inn in Harrisburg, a twenty-one-year-old college student and former Ford-leaner named James Stein "emerged from the meeting . . . to announce that he was now 'unleaned'"—it was news in the *Washington Post* or the *New York Times.*

The final round of state conventions had come the weekend of July 9. On July 6, Reagan had rented a half hour on ABC. His speech projected the confidence of a general-election candidate. Mentioning neither Ford nor Kissinger, he called for a "New Coalition" of Republicans and right-leaning Democrats and Independents. He thrust a dagger at Jimmy Carter: "You can't get to the heart of an issue by being vague about it. I'm not asking you to help me because I say, 'Trust me, don't ask questions, and everything will be fine.' I ask you to trust yourself. Trust your own knowledge of what's happening in America." (Then, aiming at the Catholic swing vote, he repeated one of his favorite quotations—from Pope Pius XII: "The American people have a genius for great and unselfish deeds. Into the hands of America, God has placed the destiny of an afflicted mankind.")

One thousand one hundred thirty delegates were needed for the nomination. The *New York Times* said Ford had 1,067 committed to him and Reagan had 1,043. On Friday Ford pulled in twelve in Nebraska, four went for Reagan, and two emerged uncommitted. The president gave a surprise press conference in which he said his earlier statements that Reagan was not qualified to be president should be considered "political license" and that now "I exclude nobody." (The *Times:* "FORD NOW FINDS REAGAN QUALIFIED TO BE PRESIDENT.") On July 10 Evans and Novak reported, "President Ford's fractious campaign is lurching toward his increasingly probable nomination in an atmosphere contaminated by recriminations, backstabbing, and personal power plays which have brought the campaign to the brink of anarchy." Then that night Reagan emerged with fifteen of sixteen at-large delegates from Colorado. It had been ugly: the pro-Ford convention chairman slashed his hand across his throat to have Reagan's microphone cut after he exceeded a supposed ten-minute time limit; then the president's son Jack was allowed to go on for sixteen minutes.

The *Washington Post* said the score was now Ford 1,052, Reagan 995.

ALL EYES TURNED SOUTH—FIRST TO PLAINS, GEORGIA, POPULATION SIX hundred, where another sort of joyous summer political festival was under way. At the tiny town's quaint little railroad depot, which Carter folks had shrewdly turned into his symbolic national campaign headquarters, Fritz and his pal Jimmy gave an impromptu press conference filled with humor and good cheer. The Georgian was challenged by a reporter who wondered if the Minnesotan was willing to undergo a grueling campaign, having given up on the idea in 1974. Carter responded earnestly, "There is no doubt in my mind that he would be willing"— and then a reporter interrupted by recalling Mondale's quip upon quitting that he didn't want to "spend the rest of my life in Holiday Inns." Carter looked over at his running mate, smiled, and handed him the microphone. Mondale, after pausing with fine comic timing: "I've checked and found they've all been redecorated. They're marvelous places to stay and I've thought it over and that's where I'd like to be."

The press corps cooed at eight-year-old Amy and her cute cat, Misty Malarky Ying Yang. The reporters challenged the Secret Service to a softball game. The Democratic nominee pitched for each team; Ralph Nader, the scourge of corporate America, umpired, wearing a suit and tie despite the stifling heat. A *boom* sounded in the distance. Secret Service agents rushed to the source: the gas station owned by Jimmy's little brother Billy, where a spark from a vending machine had set off a three-thousand-gallon oil truck. How refreshing it must have been to witness an explosion not caused by the New World Liberation Front or the Red Guerrilla Family or the Weather Underground. It took but ten minutes for the tiny Plains fire department to contain the blaze; afterward, Billy handed out free beer. A reporter asked what his first thought had been when he heard the blast. He answered, "What was in that damn cash register. Saturday is a big day."

Billy—"Cast Iron," according to the family nickname, for the stomach that seemed to withstand any abuse, especially from the beers he poured down his gullet one after the other after the other—was a star attraction. Reporters flocked to his Amoco station—one of only two places in town to buy beer. He had run for alderman, the story went, won, and made his first political act voting himself a liquor license; the only other filling station in town was owned by teetotalers. ("Billy gets the drinkers and the Williams boys get the Baptists," Mayor A. L. Blanton explained.) There Billy held court on a wooden crate, chewing the fat with good ol' boys, just like he did even when the likes of Clark Clifford weren't blowing through town. He told reporters, "I got a mamma who joined the Peace Corps and went to India when she was sixty-eight. I got one sister who's a holy-roller preacher. I got another sister who wears a helmet and rides a motorcycle. And I got a brother who thinks he's going to be president. So that makes me the only sane person in the family."

He told Mike Royko how he'd liked New York (seventy-four Carter relatives attended the convention: Dogpatch at Madison Square Garden). "I went to this big party that *Rollin' Stone* magazine threw, and there were all kinds of celebrities there, I guess. They took my picture and the *Washington Post* put it in the paper. I told the editor I'm gonna sue him. He put me in the society page instead of where I belong. Haw! I belong in the police news. . . . Anyway, I met this nice fella and he took me to lunch today. Turns out he's president of the Atlantic Richfield Oil Company."

The Billy Carter fad was of a piece with a new facet of the national mood. People called it "Redneck Chic." The Allman Brothers and Billy Carter. The hard-stompin' boogie of ZZ Top, whose Worldwide Texas Tour opened that spring and packed auditoriums and stadiums across the country for the next eighteen months, and included onstage some 260 speakers, 130 lights, a longhorn steer, a bison, two vultures, a veritable garden of cacti, and two very live rattlesnakes. And citizens band radios—especially citizens band radios: "that Japanese toy, the trucker's joy," as the country song put it.

Millions of Americans who did not own eighteen-wheelers and who did not have to evade the highway patrol were snapping up CBs, participating vicariously in the culture of America's new cowboys, the over-the-road independent truckers celebrated in the hit country song

"Convoy" (five million copies sold, and soon to be a major motion picture). *Time* magazine ran a feature on CBs in May ("Jimmy's Breakthrough" was on the cover) and its users' "cryptic, demotic jargon," which "threatens to outdate any dictionary of American slang within months": "double-nickel" (the national speed limit of 55 mph), "smokey bears" (cops), "Tricky Dick's" (San Clemente, California). Snoopy had a CB radio. So did Betty Ford. Her handle was "First Momma." "People in our kind of society, torn from our roots, want to relate," the Columbia University sociologist Amitai Etzioni explained. "With a CB, you can have a personal contact with the turn of a dial."

That was what Plains was about, too—and the way Georgia, the state where Jimmy Carter's predecessor became governor by running black customers off his restaurant's property with a pistol, had suddenly become *cool.* Looking in on Jimmy's hometown, America could partake of a sort of Dixie Disneyland. The news shows couldn't get enough of it: all the elements in the Democrats' once-fractious coalition ambling along its sunbaked streets—or street, really; Plains pretty much had only one, where every other store, Mondale later remembered, was "a Carter worm shop or a Carter peanut warehouse." This, in between appointments to supplicate the potential next Leader of the Free World for a cabinet post or brief him on the situation in the Middle East—or, in the case of Ralph Nader, recommend he read the antibusiness tracts *Taming the Giant Corporation* and *America, Inc.* to understand the corporate establishment resistance he would be up against.

Another establishment—that of the Democratic Party—swallowed hard when *New York* magazine reported that month that Charles Kirbo, one of Carter's right-hand men, had once asked, "Who's this fella Califano? He called me and said he wants to help." Joseph Califano, one of Lyndon Baines Johnson's closest White House aides, former general counsel to the Democratic National Committee, was one of the most powerful Democratic attorneys in Washington. *Who are these bozos who want to run our town and don't even know who Joseph Califano is?* In Plains, though, that fence was mended when Carter named Califano his "special adviser on family matters." He also went hard against Jerry Ford, in a press conference, on the steps of Plains High School, following the Senate's passage of a new special prosecutor bill: "Had I been president," he said, "I would not have pardoned President Nixon until after the trial had been completed in order to let all the facts relating to his crimes be known."

Then he started traveling. On July 22 he lunched with business leaders at "21" in Manhattan. (Billy Carter had dined there during the convention; denied entrance because he wasn't wearing a tie, he borrowed the one the maître d' was wearing.) "One week after he attacked the 'political and economic elite' in his acceptance speech," Elizabeth Drew reported, he "told the businessmen that he would not come up with his tax-reform proposals until he had been in office a year . . . and he was negative or opaque about changing certain existing tax benefits for business." It made for quite a contrast to his rhetoric on the Democratic primary trail, during which he promised on each and every stop to completely overhaul a tax system he called "a disgrace to the human race." Ten-four on that, good buddy.

THE *WASHINGTON POST* RAN A BIG FRONT-PAGE BANNER HEADLINE ON July 19: "REAGAN CAMP: AIR OF RESIGNATION." It began, "Ronald Reagan has returned to his ranch from the last Republican state convention, with some of his top aides and supporters acknowledging privately that he may have reached the end of the Presidential political trail." The reporter, Lou Cannon, who'd been building trust with Reagan since he covered him from the beginning of his first term in Sacramento, found the Californian "subdued." Reagan told him, "I think my candidacy has been worthwhile." Cannon called these "the words of a seemingly defeated candidate who was going back to his ranch content, believing that he had done his best even if that best proved not to be quite enough for victory."

The *Post* also reported the day's estimated delegate tally: 1,093 for Ford and 1,030 for Reagan, with 136 uncommitted. But *Time* had it much closer, 1,104 to 1,090. And the *Post* soon climbed down from its claim after Senator Laxalt railed at the capital's paper of record like a reanimated political ghost of Ron Ziegler: "What we are seeing on the part of the *Washington Post* . . . is an effort to psych out Ronald Reagan's delegates, potential delegates, and supporters. It won't work. They are not about to be fooled into forfeiting that chance by liberals in the media who are fearful that Reagan will win." The next *Post* headline was "REAGAN CAMP CLAIMS ENOUGH DELEGATES TO WIN." But Ford strategists claimed sixteen new delegates had moved to their camp, with Ford announcing from the North Lawn of the White House, "We're getting very close right now to the magic number." Reagan forces then announced six more delegates, and said the new ones Ford was claiming had been counted in his column already. There were now more delegates being counted by both sides than would be present at the convention; the psychological gamesmanship had become absurd.

• • •

WHAT MATTERED MOST NOW WAS MISSISSIPPI, WHERE IT APPEARED SOME sixty souls would have it in their power to decide the fate of their party.

The Mississippi delegation would have thirty votes in Kansas City but sixty *voters*—thirty regular delegates and thirty alternates, each of their choices counting for one-half of a vote. But it was yet more complicated. The rules of the Mississippi Republican Party stipulated that it voted at the conventions as a bloc: either thirty votes for Reagan, or thirty votes for Ford. The requirement that the choice of a majority of a delegation would control the vote of the entire delegation was called a "unit rule." Unit rules were supposed to be illegal under the bylaws of the national party. But the Magnolia State had traditionally been allowed an exception. Meanwhile, Mississippi's bylaws *also* allowed the unit rule to be set aside if a majority of the delegates and alternates chose to do so. A complicated business. But Republicanism in Mississippi was a complicated thing.

For most of a century, by most white people south of the Mason-Dixon Line, the Republican Party was viewed as little more than the political wing of the Union army—the marauding band that looted plantations, burned fields from Atlanta to the sea, and turned freed slaves into an occupying political army. The ruling Bourbons in states like Mississippi—especially Mississippi—indoctrinated the white population, rich and poor, to believe that a strong Republican Party, if allowed to flourish in the South, would court "niggers" as its shock troops: a bloc vote to revive the "Black Republican" tyranny of the Reconstruction era. So it was that to vote Republican in the South, where the secret ballot hardly existed, was to risk violence at worst and social ostracization at best. Indeed, preventing a viable Republican Party was one of the purposes for which the Ku Klux Klan was formed.

After Reconstruction, Southern Republican organizations were shells, "post office parties" that existed merely for the purpose of choosing delegations to Republican conventions. These Southern Republican delegations served a crucial ideological purpose within a Republican Party that prided itself on its racial tolerance, because the delegations were mostly African-American—"black and tan," as they were known. The organizations weren't real parties. For thirty-six years, indeed, Mississippi's black Republican chairman didn't even live in Mississippi.

That ended abruptly in 1964, when a Democratic president from the South signed his landmark civil rights bill and the Republicans nominated a senator, Barry Goldwater, who opposed it. Mississippi voted 87 percent for Goldwater in 1964—only three months after FBI agents pulled the rotting corpses of three Northern civil rights workers—James

Chaney, Michael Schwerner, and Andrew Goodman—out from beneath the earthen dam where they'd been buried by Klansmen with the cooperation of local law enforcement. The state's all-white Democratic Party ran Mississippi as a racist terror-state—but after the national Democratic Party betrayed them, conservatives chose, as Barry Goldwater once put it, to "go hunting where the ducks are." Republicans recruited segregationists to their side with the argument that their party shared the Southern view that the federal government was a tyranny. Mississippi's Republican platform read, "We feel segregation of the races is absolutely essential to harmonious racial relations and the continued progress of both races in the State of Mississippi."

Desegregation, when it finally started coming, was a moderating influence. The Republican candidate for governor in 1967, Rubel Phillips, said he hoped blacks would "become productive citizens and be taken off the welfare rolls," which counted as moderation when compared with incumbent John Bell Williams's favorite quip on the stump: "N.A.A.C.P. stands for 'Niggers, Apes, Alligators, Coons, and Possums.'" Governor Reagan made a campaign commercial for Phillips; his daughter Maureen campaigned for him across the state. He got only 29.7 percent of the vote, but in 1972, Mississippi sent two Republicans to the House of Representatives, Trent Lott and Thad Cochran. Soon the state party chairman, a dynamic, garrulous, and ambitious operative named Clarke Reed, was saying, "The race issue is dead. The GOP won't rely on demagoguery to win elections . . . there are other issues that are more important."

By then Republicans in Washington, and conservatives in Mississippi be they Republican or Democrat (like the incumbent Senator James Eastland, whose reelection Nixon secretly backed in 1972), were fighting for exactly the same things, in the same way. Like keeping the federal tax exemptions for the private schools that sprang up, often housed in churches, in direct proportion to the federal government's aggressiveness in enforcing *Brown v. Board of Education*. (There were 17 non-Catholic private schools in Mississippi in the 1963–64 school year and 155 in 1970, with each of their 42,000 students enjoying a $185 state subsidy that typically covered half or more of the tuition.) Or fighting busing with the supposedly color-blind rhetoric of "neighborhood schools" and "quality education"—which was exactly what Gerald Ford said when he talked about busing, too.

That convergence, though, now had a political consequence, which threatened to cleave the Mississippi Republican Party in two.

The state party had decided to try to build for its future by handing out alternate spots to up-and-coming young Mississippi professionals. They were the type of people least in touch with folk traditions of the Republican right—such as an instinctive revulsion regarding arrogant Northeasterners. They were also more distant from the political folk traditions of the Southland—the anguished martyr complexes, the obsession with not being disrespected by the Yankee swells. Unlike the ideological dead-enders, veterans of the Goldwater campaign, they didn't see much difference between Reagan and Ford—and, other things being equal, they were more inclined to side with the establishment than with the insurgency as the best course for their own personal and professional advancement. The upshot was that the Mississippi convention delegation, the tipping point for the entire contest, was for all practical purposes tied between Reagan and Ford supporters.

Reaganites had not seen the problem coming. Clarke Reed was believed by Reagan's strategists to be a solid conservative. Mississippi was the most conservative state in the union. So the matter was thought settled: Mississippi would go for Reagan. "Don't worry about Clarke," went David Keene's refrain, every time a concerned Reaganite asked him what resources they were pouring into Mississippi. And indeed Ford might not have contested the state at all, were the race not so precariously close. But Reed turned out to be worth worrying about. His conservatism and his Southern patriotism appeared to be diluted by his lust to be a national Republican power broker—the guy national reporters called up for quotes. (He gave good quote, his Delta drawl dipping into the argot of a Greenwich Village hipster. Of a fellow political operative: "Man, this cat is good." Of Ford attacking Reagan on the campaign trail: "It turns me off bad.")

The Ford team played to Reed's vanity—calls from Dick Cheney, from Secretary of Agriculture Earl Butz, from Bill Simon, from Barry Goldwater; that invitation to sit next to the queen of England at a state dinner. They thought he might be easy to shake. For though Reed thought himself a master of Byzantine political power plays, they believed he would be easy to manipulate. He tried to hold his cards close to his chest, bluffing a strong hand—even while, behind his back, Ford operatives called his delegation one by one on the phone and worked an old political trick: *"I've got thirty votes committed to the president, and we just need yours to put him over. Yours will be the thirty-first. You can give the president the nomination."* In that way they won what they thought were commitments from twenty-seven of the sixty Mississippians who would be traveling to Kansas City. The conservative in charge of Reagan's operation in Mississippi, whose name was Billy Mounger, was outraged, claiming Reed must be running some sort of con. "You can't trust Clarke Reed," the administrative assistant to Representative Trent Lott, a Reagan backer, had told Reagan's campaign managers back in January. "He's a slippery, no-good son of a bitch." But Reed himself was just as livid to learn that his delegates, still supposed to be uncommitted, were declaring willy-nilly for Ford.

It was a mess. It came to a head at a final delegate caucus in Jackson on Sunday, July 25, just as the contest was becoming so close that the courting of undecided delegates entered you-can't-make-this-stuff-up territory. A delegate from Oakville, Missouri, named Marlene Zinzel told the press what it had been like when the phone rang at the beauty parlor while she was having her hair set, and it was the President of the United States on the other end: "I could not believe it. I can hardly remember it. He told me he could win over Carter. He asked me if I would consider him and I said that I would." A Rochester, New York, delegate told the press, "I hope they're sending Air Force One for me because I won't settle for anything else." A New York delegate named Vito Battista told David Broder he would have been warmer for Ford had he been served Italian food in the White House. Ford won over an uncommitted delegate from Cherokee County, South Carolina, after his complaint about the cancellation of his small business loan earned him a personal letter of concern from the president and an hour-long phone call from the commerce secretary. Another uncommitted delegate was reported to have offered his vote if Reagan would arrange for $250,000 in new business for his law firm.

And in Jackson, Harry Dent of South Carolina made the argument for Ford at Mississippi's delegate caucus. Dent was the White House's Southern liaison and as Strom Thurmond's top political deputy the man most responsible for ensuring Nixon's nomination in 1968. Dent was a Southern patriot—of the new, Republican breed. In the small Southern town that produced him, his great-uncle John "the Baptist" Prickett edited the newspaper. One upon a time, back in the days when South Carolina didn't celebrate Independence Day because it was a "Yankee holiday," an outraged reader called Prickett a "Republican S.O.B." Prickett, who of course like every other white man in the Palmetto State was a Democrat, laid him flat with a punch. The baffled reader, upon recovering, asked what was the matter with calling him an S.O.B. "But you called me a *Republican* S.O.B.," Prickett answered.

In Jackson, Dent made an argument that played to the old familiar wounded Southern regional pride. Dent had been with Thurmond when he made the historic switch from Democrat to Republican to back Barry

Goldwater in 1964 after Lyndon Johnson signed the Civil Rights Act. After Nixon won the nomination in 1968, Dent ran Nixon's "Thurmond Speaks for Nixon-Agnew" committee to keep Southerners from voting for George Wallace. Then he went to work in the White House, given the job of assuring Dixie power brokers that Nixon wouldn't do anything to disturb the "Southern way of life." He stayed in the job under Ford. Now he said the same thing in 1976 for Ford that he'd said in 1968 for Nixon, when a late-inning candidacy by Ronald Reagan had threatened Nixon's hold on that convention's Southern delegation. The argument was that a president who owed his victory to the South would eat out of Southerners' hands.

"Now my good friend Clarke is probably a little peeved with us because we've been down here trying to lobby you good folks," he said, oozing South Carolina charm.

"But I told Clarke that you can't dress sixty beautiful women up in bikinis and put them on Broadway and not expect Gerald Ford and Ronald Reagan to turn their heads and look at 'em. . . .

"Friends, we're looking at you. My goodness, you're in the catbird seat if I've ever seen it. You know it took the whole South to do that in '68 in the convention. Now it's coming down just to Mississippi. Mississippi's got a chance to strike a real blow for the South."

He drove home the argument retailing a Redneck Chic of his own—with a hint of anti-Semitic code. New York's Republican state chairman, a Rockefeller protégé and Ford partisan, was Richard "Rosie" Rosenbaum. "It's a question of whether Clarke's gonna be the kingmaker or Rosie Rosenbaum's gonna be the kingmaker," Dent drawled. "That is, New York or Mississippi. Don't let us down, friends. I'm not talking about Ford. I'm talking about the South. I'm in this thing because I'm for the South, and I feel what's good for the South is good for the country and good for the Republican Party."

Dent almost, but not quite, prevailed. The meeting adjourned still uncommitted, delegates and alternates from each side shrieking at one another about sellouts and quislings and dirty deals, with neither campaign having any idea whether the thirty-one votes it needed would ever be forthcoming.

And so Reagan's John Sears finally decided on another strategy for the uncommitted-delegate quest: a Hail Mary pass.

ELIZABETH DREW WAS ABLE TO CONNECT BY PHONE WITH A VERY BUSY Clarke Reed, who claimed his delegation was now leaning toward Reagan, but that "the only way we could abandon our neutrality up until the convention is if we had certain commitments. What Ford needs now is to show that he's going to pick a running mate that will be compatible with his philosophy. The split ticket is a nightmare and a horror. With the so-called balanced ticket between a liberal and a conservative, you vote for a conservative and if he dies you get a liberal."

It hardly would have occurred to him to make the same public demand to Ronald Reagan, whose public pronuncions on the idea of picking a liberal running mate were quite as strong as Reed's own: "I don't believe in the old tradition of picking someone at the opposite end of the political spectrum because he can get some votes that you can't get himself," Reagan would say, "because that's being false with the people who vote for you and your philosophy." Then came John Sears's surprise.

Sears had brilliantly stewarded Ronald Reagan's run from near impossibility to a dead heat. But when Robert Novak interviewed him in the middle of July, the columnist observed that it looked like he was now at the end of the road: Novak didn't see any math that let Reagan win. Sears responded by hinting that he had an ace hidden away in an unexpected place: the three big Northeastern states—New York, New Jersey, and Pennsylvania—where Reagan had claimed only 33 of 324 delegates so far.

Sears had that trademark saying: politics is motion. When your campaign sets the terms of the debate, you are winning. When your opponent has to catch up with one of your moves, he is losing. What Sears had decided, without consulting the candidate at all, was that he could put this race back into motion by picking a liberal running mate for Reagan from a Northeastern state—and force Gerald Ford to respond.

Which running mate? It almost didn't matter. The thing was to get the press to report that the race was back on. It was the only way to snatch victory from the jaws of defeat.

Sears explained the selection process to a reporter after it was all over. "We took all the Republican senators and governors," he said, "and that didn't take very long. When you ruled out those who were too old, in our party you didn't have too much left." In Senator Paul Laxalt's accounting the process sounded even more limited: "So we sort of backed into the situation. When you looked at the people who realistically fit into that slot, it was damned thin. Schweiker's name kept popping up."

Richard Schweiker—not to be confused with Lowell Weicker—was the fifty-year-old son of a tiling contractor from Norristown, Pennsylvania, who joined the family business after college, getting involved in Republican politics on the side. He was elected to the House of Representatives in 1960, representing a Republican district that included the swanky Philadelphia Main Line, after defeating a conservative primary opponent. His issues included civil rights, expanding Social Security, and establishing federal rent subsidies for the poor. In 1968 he defeated an incumbent to rise to the Senate, where he became a leading Republican critic of the Vietnam War and opposed Nixon's nomination of two conservative Southerners to the Supreme Court. He won an 89 percent rating from the lefties at Americans for Democratic Action. He had shaggy hair, longish for a senator, and sideburns. He was best known recently—though not all that well known—for his service on the Church Committee, where he called the CIA a "shadow government."

Schweiker was also obsessed with flushing out what he called "the failures of the U.S. intelligence establishment in their investigation of President Kennedy's assassination, and their coverup to the Warren commission"—an obsession he shared with much of the American left. Though he harbored a few ideological idiosyncrasies (he sponsored a bill to bring Bible reading back into public schools; he hated abortion and he opposed mandatory busing; he was against gun control), he was by most measures a liberal, even an "ultraliberal," as Evans and Novak pegged him. He was also a Ford supporter. In February he had charged Richard Nixon with attempting to sabotage Ford's election by traveling to China just before the New Hampshire primary, and just two months earlier he had proudly endorsed a resolution adopted by eighty-nine of Pennsylvania's ninety-eight-member delegation—the convention's third largest—supporting Ford's renomination.

Reagan had sent Sears forth to find a running mate with only the following instructions: someone who would help unite the party, someone he could trust and work with, someone whose ethical record wouldn't embarrass him, and someone who wasn't a member of the "Washington buddy system." Schweiker, Sears decided, was close enough.

Sears called the senator on July 16 and set up a meeting. There Schweiker learned he was the campaign's first choice—which didn't shock him as much as learning that the plan was to announce the pick long before the convention opened, on August 16. This was an unprecedented notion—the heart of Sears's motion-making surprise. The idea was to back Ford into a political corner by forcing him to announce his *own* pick, perchance to shake loose some conservative delegates if Ford picked a liberal, and some liberal delegates if he picked a conservative. (The presumption was that Reagan's delegates were too loyal to budge, no matter what.) Schweiker was also surprised to learn that

Reagan didn't even know about this meeting. "They explained," Jules Witcover wrote, "that while the last word would be Reagan's, 'they had every reason to believe he would accept it,' having requested their recommendation."

Schweiker told them he would think about it. That took only a day. On the twenty-third, Sears unveiled the pick to his boss, gingerly: he first made the case to Reagan for a liberal, in the abstract, mentioning the name of the particular liberal only after a half hour. "There is a fellow in the Senate with a pretty liberal voting record," he said, "but he's against gun control, he's a big man in the Captive Nations movement, and he's against abortion, and basically on all the emotional issues he's got a pretty defendable record. And he's absolutely clean." Robert Novak later wrote that he was almost certain Reagan had never heard of Dick Schweiker before. And it didn't seem to detain him that picking Schweiker went back on his every pledge not to pick an ideologically balanced ticket. "Reagan's first question," Witcover reported in his book about the 1976 election, which came out the next year, "was not about any aspect of the political strategy, or about what kind of man or political creature Dick Schweiker was, but instead, 'Do you think he'd do it?'"

Yes, Sears answered, he would. "Reagan seemed pleased."

The next morning, a Friday, the two men were ushered together into a room in Reagan's house in Pacific Palisades. Schweiker had to be coached before going in not to call him "*Ree*-gan." *Ray*-gan's first big question to him was whether he would support his positions on the campaign trail and in the White House. Schweiker responded, "As long as I'm on the plane on the takeoff, I'll be the first one out defending it after the crash." He set only one condition: that he be allowed to say his piece on any policy disagreements, after which he promised to fall into line whether he agreed with Reagan or not. Reagan was pleased to hear it. Three and a half hours into their conversation came the word: "I've made a decision, senator, and I'd like you to be my running mate"—and then they talked for two and a half hours more.

So why would Ronald Reagan pick as a running mate a veritable stranger whose ideology by Reagan's own words rendered him "false with the people who vote for" him? Surely because he wanted to win, and John Sears, who had gotten him this far, had told him this was what it would take to get there. But: then he had to rationalize this to himself—as a moral act, as a noble act, as an act consistent with what *Ronald Reagan* would do. And how did Ronald Reagan manage to do that? The same way he rationalized everything that did not accord with the world as he preferred it exist: he cast himself as hero. He told Schweiker at one point in their conversation, "I have a strong feeling that I'm looking at myself some years ago."

He would *convert* Richard Schweiker from liberal to conservative. After all, he had converted so many others. It was his gift; it was his grace. Everything would work out in the end, gloriously.

SUNDAY NIGHT. REAGAN CALLED HIS MOST IMPORTANT SUPPORTERS. JESSE Helms got the call at 9:05: he made a note of it, he later told Robert Novak, "to record for posterity the exact time I received the shock of my life." David Keene called some lesser lights, like Governor Jim Edwards of South Carolina, whom he asked to come to Washington the next day, without telling him what he wanted to talk about. Edwards showed up with bells on. Then he was told about Dick Schweiker—and, according to Keene, "sort of looked at his watch and said, 'Well, if I hurry I think I can get back to South Carolina.'"

Reagan gave the press conference in California: "Since I now feel that the people and the delegates have a right to know in advance of the convention who a nominee's vice presidential choice would be, I am today departing from tradition and announcing my selection." He described the man who had just said he would follow any position Reagan wanted, no matter if he disagreed, as "a man of independent thought and action." He described a man who'd been in Congress for more than fifteen years as *not* "a captive of what I call the 'Washington buddy system.'" Then he claimed they shared the "same basic values." He rushed off without taking questions.

Schweiker, who was listed in a binder at Ford headquarters as a "C"—committed Ford delegate—then appeared in a Senate caucus room crowded with cameras, trailed by John Sears, his well-scrubbed family, and a grimly loyal Jesse Helms ("You won't believe how really conservative he is," Reagan told him). He announced that his new boss "in one fell swoop has united the Republican Party for November by bringing together the conservative and moderate wings of our party. It instantly gives our party across-the-board appeal." He conceded his selection would "blow the minds of some people." He claimed that "up until now" the Ford campaign probably had the delegate edge (this contradicted what the man behind him, Sears, had been telling the media)—but not anymore. He took questions. Concerning his position on the Panama Canal, he hemmed and hawed—then finally admitted he had no position on the Panama Canal at all. He also said, "We make no apologies. We think it's the only way to win in November."

The reviews rolled in.

Howard Phillips of the Conservative Caucus said Reagan had just "betrayed the trust of those who look to him for leadership."

Congressman John Ashbrook of Ohio, who had run a quixotic campaign from the right against Richard Nixon in New Hampshire in 1972, publicly called it "the dumbest thing I've ever heard of." (Privately he had told the Reagan aide who called him with the news, "Reagan can plumb fuck himself," then hung up.)

Steve Symms of Idaho, who had braved Republican cloakroom taunts as one of the few Reagan delegates in the House, said, "I thought it was a practical joke." Days later, he said, "I'm still sick."

Clarke Reed told a reporter, "I've had it. I've said I'm ready to jump, but I'm trying to keep my people in mind."

Governor Meldrim Thomson of New Hampshire said that Reagan had "abandoned the conservative cause and scuttled his own political principles," and that he would not make his planned seconding speech at the convention, so as not to "assist in selling this opportunistic team to the Republican delegates." And that he'd prefer "someone like Jesse Helms." George Will called it "slapstick." The *New Yorker* noted that only a week earlier Reagan been deriding Carter's pick of Walter Mondale as too liberal even though Mondale had a 93 percent rating from the AFL-CIO's Committee on Political Education—but Schweiker's was 100 percent, and he had received labor's eighth-biggest political donation in 1974. CBS News ran a clip of Reagan saying, "I don't believe in the old tradition of picking someone at the opposite end of the political spectrum." The newscast next featured an outraged conservative who said that "the reason Reagan chose Schweiker was because Mondale was already taken."

But still, it worked, after a fashion. CBS's previous plan for that evening's newscast was for Walter Cronkite to announce that Ford had clinched the nomination. That might have ended things then and there. The Schweiker pick really had rescued Reagan. The question was how long the rescue would last.

HARRY DENT LEARNED THE NEWS FROM DICK CHENEY. HE PROMPTLY RE-leased a statement calling it the "most colossal political boner of the century." Then he sent to Reagan delegates a memo on Schweiker's record in voting for things like a bill to break up the oil companies. Keene made a breakneck canvass of the Northeastern states, and found no leakage from Ford to Reagan whatsoever. Ford's man James Baker was worried that they'd lose perhaps four votes in Pennsylvania—but was optimistic that the pick would firm up the support of other delegates whose loyalty to Ford they'd feared had been weak.

The next day John Connally—who conservatives like Pat Buchanan had thought would be the perfect running mate for Reagan—stood in the White House driveway and proclaimed his endorsement of Ford. (Ford dodged on whether he thought Connally would make a good vice president.) Important conservatives—Jesse Helms, Governor Edwards of South Carolina, the editors of *Human Events* (finding "not a scintilla of evidence" that Reagan had "yielded to liberalism or relinquished any conservative principles"), Young Americans for Freedom, even John Ashbrook—swallowed their doubts and said they still were for Reagan. Utah's twenty Reagan delegates announced themselves "pacified," too. But the man everyone was watching was the mercurial Mississippian Clarke Reed—and he now announced his "personal endorsement" of Ford.

"This kind of vice president," Reed said, was "too big a price to pay for the nomination." The Ford people at first presumed that this meant they had Mississippi, and perhaps the nomination, wrapped up. They found they had another thing coming. Reed had so squandered the trust of his delegates that he couldn't bring them along: too many loved Reagan too much. Ford made ready to travel to Jackson, his campaign announcing he was considering a "large and growing list" of at least a dozen running mates, though he would name only one—Connally. Two days later the White House announced the president would send out 4,518 letters to delegates, alternate delegates, RNC members, and Republican congressmen, senators, and governors asking them to list their preferred running mates, in order of preference.

Schweiker claimed he'd persuaded six Pennsylvania delegates to switch from Ford to Reagan and moved "in excess of thirteen" Ford delegates into the uncommitted ranks—though he declined to name a single one. The Keystone State's delegation caravanned to Washington to be wooed, first in the Senate caucus room by Schweiker, then in the White House by Ford. Elizabeth Drew took the political temperature of the caucus room: "If there is a Reagan supporter in the room, I can't find him." One of Schweiker's best political friends told Drew how aghast he was that Schweiker hadn't consulted a single political ally before making his decision. Another told her, "I was absolutely stunned." The state's senior senator, Minority Leader Hugh Scott, opened the meeting reading Schweiker's letter of resignation as a delegate; he couldn't very well serve, given that his vote was pledged to Gerald Ford. Then his junior colleague entered.

Schweiker looked shell-shocked. He had entered the political big leagues now. But he hadn't counted the costs. "He stands in a corner on the right, like a schoolboy who has been bad, and reads a statement," Drew reported. She found it "more like a confession," or "an apologia," than a political appeal: he spoke of "trials and tribulations," "shocks and tremors," and then, apologetically, said he'd made the choice because it was "probably the only way that the Republican Party could be re-united, not become extinct." The audience applauded only politely. The Associated Press reported, "Three delegates who had said they were un-committed now say they are for Ford."

Schweiker recovered in a visit to West Virginia, earning a standing ovation and winning over an uncommitted delegate.

The AP's tally was 1,104 to 1,023, with 132 uncommitted—and Mis-sissippi still up in the air. "Anyone who tells you he knows who the Re-publican nominee will be in Kansas City is really dancing in the dark," one columnist wrote. "The contest, despite claims from both the Ford and Reagan camps, is still unsettled."

HALF THE NATION'S COAL MINERS WERE OUT IN A WILDCAT STRIKE across six states. More than $100 million in tax loopholes had been se-cretly slipped into a tax reform bill with nary a hearing or vote, includ-ing a tax credit to the Mobil Oil Corporation specifically forbidden by a law the president had signed the previous year. Ted Kennedy com-plained. Robert Dole huffed back, "You have impugned the integrity of the committee and some of us don't like it!"

Secret Service agents shot to death a thirty-year-old taxi driver and decorated Vietnam veteran named Chester F. Plummer after he scaled the White House fence bearing a three-foot length of pipe, making it sixty feet onto the Executive Mansion's grounds while the president was reading in his private quarters. ("He was just a quiet guy," the detective investigating for the District of Columbia police reported after inter-views with friends, family, neighbors. "He never made threats.") It was the fifth incursion onto the White House lawn during Ford's presidency.

The Associated Press wire brought news of a raid by the Boston vice squad of a new "Freedom Expression Church," which served free beer and screened the movie *Deep Throat* and whose slogan announced, "Ask and you shall receive whatever you desire. Free." ("I don't see what all the fuss is about," the pastor said. "We're just a group of people helping other people.") Two young women sitting in an Oldsmobile in the Bronx were set upon by a man who would turn out to be named David Berkowitz, who shot both with a .44-caliber pistol, killing one.

Twenty-six children and their bus driver simply vanished in Chow-chilla, California; for twenty-four hours, the only thing found was an empty bus. (It turned out to be a mass kidnaping: a ransom note demanding $5 million turned up, then the victims escaped, then three bored rich kids were caught and arrested for the crime. "None of the three showed any reaction when attorneys entered not-guilty pleas," the news reported.) Ninety-four cadets were expelled in the West Point cheating scandal. Jimmy Carter raised eyebrows in his first general election campaign tour, to New Hampshire, for two reasons: first, for not waiting for the traditional Democratic presidential kickoff Labor Day rally in Cadillac Square in Detroit—was this a snub to the AFL-CIO?—and second, for referring to the "Nixon-Ford administration"—an opening-round low blow, pundits said.

Robert Vesco, the crooked financier who became infamous during Watergate for delivering suitcases containing hundreds of thousands of dollars in cash to the Nixon campaign, renounced his U.S. citizenship and turned up in Italy.

Ford's choice of a new White House science advisor revived the controversy over "Man: A Course of Study," because H. Guyford Stever had been head of the National Science Foundation, whose grants to the MACOS curriculum Representative Conlan now called a "new height in science porno literature." CIA documents were released in response to a Freedom of Information Act request concerning the agency's history of experimentation with drugs from 1953 to 1967, as part of the program code-named "MKULTRA"; a 1953 memo revealed that the CIA was considering getting enough LSD to produce 100 million experimental doses; a 1963 report said the research was "considered by many authorities in medicine and related fields to be professionally unethical"—leading to the inspiring conclusion, "Public disclosure of some aspects of MKULTRA activity could induce serious adverse reaction in U.S. public opinion." A January 1975 "Memorandum for the Record," signed simply "CIA Officer," said, "Over my stated objection, the MKULTRA files were destroyed by order of the Director, Central Intelligence—Mr. Helms—shortly before his departure from office."

Members of the American Legion, returning home from a huge convention in Philadelphia, began developing pneumonia and fevers upwards of 107 degrees; by the first week in August the media began reporting that twenty-two victims had died and 131 were in the hospital, an extraordinary mortality rate; no lab tests could identify the cause. The notion of a devastating epidemic that could strike without warning and kill thousands was very much in the air. There had been the false "pantosomatitis" of the previous year. Then, in February 1976, just to show that not all such fears turn out to be hoaxes, the H1N1 virus— "swine flu"— killed an army recruit at Fort Dix, its first victim since 1919 (when it killed more Americans than died on the World War I battlefields). By March, two dozen top scientists met with the president to discuss the unprecedented immunization of every single American man, woman, and child. The Centers for Disease Control sent twenty epidemiologists across the country to study the medical records, around the clock, of at least ten thousand Legionnaires who might have been ex- posed to the mystery Philadelphia illness, or could have imported it into the city. "What it's going to do," the head of the Pennsylvania virology lab undertaking some of the work said on the news, eyes cast nervously to one side, "God only knows."

No, President Ford: the nation had not been healed.

Ford landed in Jackson on July 30 for a five-hour meeting with Mississippi delegates. He emerged telling reporters, "They had a lot of good hard questions, but I think I answered them all." He couldn't say, though, if he changed any minds. Ron Nessen said that the team already had enough delegates to win on the first ballot, but that the president "wants to go into the convention not with just a bare ma- jority." Reagan would speak to the delegates on August 4. Schweiker went to South Carolina "to show them I don't have horns"—and said that he would support Reagan positions, including antilabor positions, that he disagreed with a few weeks earlier because "I am now changing constituencies."

Schweiker's and Reagan's plane landed in Mississippi, though an- other politician's did not. The twin-engine plane containing Jerry Lit- ton, a millionaire Democratic congressman from Missouri, and his entire family crashed en route to the victory party in Kansas City for his just-won Senate nomination while the teletypes were still clicking away with election returns; the four Littons and two others were killed. Hard to be a politician—all those bumpy flights on small planes. Hard to be a politician—explaining yourself when you had hardly a leg to stand on.

Schweiker told the delegates that, yes, he had indeed once supported Ted Kennedy's national health-care bill and the Humphrey-Hawkins full-employment bill, but no longer—because, he said, according to an arch Elizabeth Drew, "Ronald Reagan had told him about this wonder- ful thing called free enterprise which could deal with those problems." He said he knew and respected the South, having gone to Georgia Mili- tary Academy. "My father and grandfather were Baptists. . . . And I do not grow peanuts!"

Mississippians were not moved. Reagan spoke to each delegate personally to shoot down a rumor that he would accept a spot on Gerald Ford's ticket. They were not all that moved by that, either. It was no longer a big deal to get a meeting with a presidential candidate. Looking uncharacteristically fidgety in a cream-colored summer suit at the press conference, Reagan claimed that "he [Schweiker] and I are identical in our views on national defense, on détente—we even agree on the Panama Canal." (He craned his neck, as if to see if anyone out there was buying it.) "I *don't* think I went opposite to compatibility with my philosophy!"

The running mates made a last-ditch visit to Philadelphia. They emerged, emitting undignified whines: Reagan said his Pennsylvania delegates had been subjected to "a horrendous amount of heavy-handed pressure to renege." (But, oops, the *Washington Post* interviewed two of those Pennsylvania delegates formerly for Reagan who said that there had been no pressure.) Schweiker said the only reason Reagan fans in the delegation weren't making commitments was that "they don't want to be pressured like ping-pong balls." He claimed that thirty Pennsylvania Ford delegates would soon switch to them. The state party chairman, once a dear friend of his, responded, "He has lost credibility with people who think most highly of him."

Reagan now claimed 1,140 delegates. Ford now claimed 1,135. That added up to 2,275 votes; only 2,258 delegates would be voting in Kansas City. Was Ford in the lead? Probably. But this thing was still up for grabs.

CHAPTER THIRTY-ONE

"Don't Let Satan Have His Way—Stop the ERA"

IT WAS A STUNNING POLITICAL ACHIEVEMENT.

Ever since early in 1973, when Ronald Reagan announced he wouldn't be running for a third term as governor, features about his possible presidential run became a nice little evergreen assignment for political reporters; badgering potential presidential aspirants was just something political reporters were supposed to do, even if none of them took this particular one seriously. A Reagan nomination was akin to a second Goldwater nomination—suicide for a party already quite nearly on its deathbed.

The low ebb had come in June 1974, when Rowland Evans and Robert Novak quoted those anguished, despairing Reagan hands in Sacramento who dearly wished to work someday under Reagan in the White House but feared that the day would never come unless Reagan made "a polite but clear break with President Nixon." The political necessity seemed self-evident: at the time the columnists wrote, Richard Nixon's approval rating was only 25 percent. But Reagan's break with him never came.

In fact, when Reagan deigned to discuss Watergate at all—which he frequently simply refused to do, insisting he didn't find the issue particularly important—he continued to say precisely the opposite of what just about every other prominent politician said. During season after season of anxious soul-searching about what Watergate said about America, he answered that it said nothing at all—except that the nation harbored a whole lot of spoilsports who just didn't understand what America was truly about. *"Into the hands of America, God has placed the destiny of an afflicted mankind. . . ."*

It was the same way with Vietnam. Let the liberal editorialists at the *New Republic* write, when the fall of Saigon coincided with the two-hundredth anniversary of Lexington and Concord, "If the Bicentennial helps us focus on the contrast between our idealism and our crimes, so much the better." Reagan blithely told another story: not that the

Vietnam War revealed an America that suddenly knew sin, but that it helped reveal once more that America was a nation that redeemed everything it touched. It showed in his description of what he said was the work of the USS *Midway* that same spring. (*"A tiny baby with double pneumonia was cured. People without clothes were given American clothing. ..."*) And when he so doted upon the returned POWs (*"We walked out of Hanoi as winners."*)

And so on, and so forth. Energy problems, economic problems, inflation: they revealed nothing essential about America, certainly nothing about what others chose to call its "decline"—though they said a lot, he insisted, about America's federal government, which he spoke of almost as an imposition *upon* America. "It's time for us all to realize that government is not the answer to our economic problems. Government *is* the problem," he said in May 1975 in one of his syndicated radio broadcasts, this one on how "money spent by government doesn't have the multiplier effect of money spent in the private sector. In fact government spending is a *drag* on the economy and slows economic recovery."

Though Gerald Ford liked to say that sort of thing, too.

It puzzled his political contemporaries: why had the prediction that Reagan would have to distance himself from Richard Nixon and Watergate in order to thrive proved so wrong?

And another puzzlement: how had the race between Reagan and Ford managed to get this far?

A weary Ford campaign aide had recently told a reporter, "Reagan and Ford basically believe the same things." And that was true. "[B]ut they project different styles." And that was even more true. Gerald Ford shared something with the suspicious circles: he liked the idea of national modesty. He embodied modesty, *was* modesty: "A Ford, not a Lincoln," as he'd said in introducing himself to the nation upon becoming vice president in 1973. When a political scientist interviewed his admirers, their favorite word for him was "solid":

"He's solid, not hot air."

"He's a solid citizen with the right instincts."

"Solid in character, not flashy or phony ... consistent and predictable."

"He's down-to-earth."

Ronald Reagan was not down-to-earth. Nor, he insisted, was the nation about which, and to which, he addressed his panegyrics. Instead, it was celestial.

Here was what Evans and Novak had not understood. America had not yet become *Reagan's* America. Not yet. Reagan's America would embrace an almost official cult of optimism—the belief that America could do no wrong. Or, to put it another way, that if America did it, it was by definition *not* wrong. That would come later. But signs were already pointing in that direction.

Certainly they had been there in the Bicentennial celebration, when Americans surprised themselves in their simple patriotic joy—as if Watergate, as if Vietnam, had never even happened; as if the nation's economy had never in fact been held hostage by Arab oil sheikhs; as if the Church and Pike committees had never revealed the nation's security agencies as cold-blooded outlaws.

And here is what Evans and Novak *had not understood*: that Reagan's refusal to wax morose about Watergate was not an impediment to his political appeal. It was central to his political appeal.

At the beginning of 1973, the editor of *Intellectual Digest* explained on the *Today* show what was different about the time when the POWs went off to war and the time when they returned: "For the first time Americans have had at least a partial loss in the fundamental belief in ourselves. We've always believed we were the new men, the new people, the new society. The 'last best hope on earth,' in Lincoln's terms. For the first time, we've really begun to doubt it."

And *here* was an answer to the Ford aide who was so frustrated that this campaign even had to be fought, even more frustrated that it had become so *close*. Every time a major distinction emerged between the two candidates, the nub was what kind of nation America *was*. The Panama Canal issue, for example. Ford's argument was, fundamentally, that the world's rules must apply to America as well, that the way America had all but annexed the sovereignty of another nation was an embarrassing and dangerous relic of another time. Reagan's riposte: the world's rules did not apply to America at all—for into the hands of America God has placed the destiny of an afflicted mankind.

Don't doubt. Blithe optimism in the face of what others called chaos had always marked his uniqueness—at least since, around the time of his tenth birthday, he began mastering the art of turning the chaotic and confusing doubts of his childhood into a simple and stout-hearted certainty. It marked, too, what made others feel so good in his presence—and what drove still others, those suspicious circles for whom doubt was the soul of civic wisdom, to annoyed bafflement at his success.

And now it was what had brought him to the brink of the Republican presidential nomination—if his campaign could just game this convention right.

• • •

FIRST CAME A WEEK OF PRELIMINARIES: CREDENTIALS COMMITTEE MEET-
ings and Rules Committee meetings and Platform Committee meetings
that were supposed to be interminable and boring, especially when an
incumbent president was up for renomination. Not this year—the first
since 1952 when the identity of the Republican Party's nominee was
genuinely in doubt.

Close presidential nominating conventions could be extraordinarily
dramatic. Smoke-filled hotel rooms, hot asphalt parking lots, convention
hall back corridors could become like unto the alleys and cul-de-sacs of
a casbah—you could disappear in the intrigue. The key to these dramas
was always a single elegant, but portentous, fact: in order to be nominated as a party's presidential candidate, you needed a majority of the
votes of the party's convention delegates. Come just one vote shy of that
majority—even if you had vastly more than any other contender—and
the balloting went into a second, or third, or fourth roll call, as many as
it took to get to a majority. During that interval after the first roll call,
everything could come up for grabs; an also-ran could become a front-
runner in an instant, if only the right bargains were struck.

Even the possibility of a less-than-certain first-ballot majority could
throw the situation suddenly into disarray. In 1968, for example, at the
very last moment, when Richard Nixon's nomination was supposed
to be all but assured, both Nelson Rockefeller and Ronald Reagan
launched campaigns that were not really even campaigns. The two
sides were practically in cahoots—in the hope that denying Nixon his
first-ballot win would show him up as a "loser" who'd surrendered the
confidence of his party, thereby "tipping the football," which Rocky
and Reagan forces each believed they both thereafter might catch and
so emerge with the big prize. It had come much closer to happening
than anyone had realized at the time, until Senator Strom Thurmond of
South Carolina, who preferred Reagan, cut a deal in which Nixon promised him a veto on his running mate choice, and if he became president,
special consideration to keep Southern schools segregated and South
Carolina textile mills freer from foreign competition and the Supreme
Court conservative.

This time the possibility that the vote would extend past the first
ballot was much more probable, perhaps even likely. A South Carolina
undecided named Sherry Martschink became a celebrity for switching
once, twice, and then again—making the *New York Times* for consulting her former dentist (now better known as South Carolina governor
James Edwards) on the subject. ("He told me if I didn't vote for Reagan he'd quit pulling my teeth and start knocking them out. But he

was only kidding.") "At the moment I'm a lot more worried about the possibility of chaos than I am about who the nominee will be," one Republican state chairman said. And as July became August, and news about individual uncommitted delegates breaking this way and that, according to one observer, was "greeted by the media with the fanfare usually reserved for visiting heads of state," whispers of which wild card might usher in the chaos that might break the convention Reagan's way sounded everywhere.

There was the question of "Trojan horse" delegates. State laws bound a little less than half the delegates—943 of them—to vote the way they were assigned by primary results, but only on the *first* ballot. Within many of those state delegations, Ford delegates, given the job as a perk for loyal party service, were actually Reagan partisans. That could give Reagan a boost of forty or fifty or, according to one reliable estimate, seventy-five extra votes, well more than it would take to put him over the top in even the most Ford-friendly estimates, if the nominating went into a second ballot. And yet more intriguingly than that, Reagan's campaign chairman Paul Laxalt hinted that some of these delegates might be willing to break the law, voting by conscience on the *first* ballot. Why not? How many divisions did a convention parliamentarian have? A meeting in Kansas City, Missouri, after all, had no apparatus to enforce a law binding in, say, North Carolina—a state where all but two of Ford's twenty-five delegates were actually hungry for Reagan.

And though touts thought that designating Schweiker might have scotched this possibility—"Nobody's going to break the law for Reagan now," one potential Trojan horse told *Time*—the mischievous Laxalt had also floated a yet slyer possibility, which also happened to be legal: Trojan horses could *abstain* on the first ballot, denying Ford his victory, persuading delegates rendered emotionally vulnerable in the heat of the moment—these things moved fast—that Ford was a loser, and thus open the floodgates for Reagan once and for all.

Then there was the possibility of credential fights—like in the case of a New Jersey man named Joseph Yglesias, who replaced a delegate who'd died a month earlier. The replacement decided for Reagan, because, he said, "Mr. Ford failed to show concern about the loss of jobs at a Bayonne military base"—but Ford forces said that the method of Yglesias's selection had violated party procedures, and that the seat properly belonged to one Maria Scalia. Despite a previous accord not to press credential challenges, John Sears promised on August 8 to "go all the way with Joe"—and who knew how many others. The early strength Dwight D. Eisenhower and George McGovern had displayed in credential challenges, after all, was what had broken the back of *their* opponents in contested conventions in 1952 and 1972.

Or maybe the fight would be over the platform—where Sears could leverage nonnegotiable ideological differences between Reagan and Ford into a resounding victory for Reagan's positions. There was the Equal Rights Amendment, at a crucial hinge point in 1976: only four more states had to ratify it for "Equality of rights under the law shall not be denied or abridged by the United States or by any State on account of sex" to be enshrined in the Constitution. But in shocking referenda results the previous November, both New York and New Jersey had voted against ratification. Gerald Ford was for the ERA (as was Betty Ford), and Ronald Reagan was against it (as was Nancy Reagan). And there was abortion. Ronald Reagan was for the "Human Life Amendment" to the Constitution, banning abortion outright. But in a February interview with Walter Cronkite leading up to the New Hampshire primary, Ford had staked out what he called the "moderate" position, that "each individual state should decide what it wished to do." And then there was pesky Henry Kissinger, from whom Ford staunchly refused to distance himself, and whom Reaganites considered Beelzebub. Maybe some amendment could be whipped, forcing the president to twist in the wind around *that*.

Meanwhile, impassioned Reaganites impelled by state laws to vote for the president in the first ballot could vote any way they wanted on *procedural* questions—so, even if all the media estimates had Ford ahead by several dozen votes for the nomination roll call, John Sears estimated he enjoyed a twenty-vote advantage on procedural votes. Call such a vote at just the right time, on just the right question—one that, say, could be spun beforehand as a high-minded, commonsense reform, and afterward as a resounding political defeat for the president—and the president's aura of inevitability could be broken. (Ford, after all, didn't *have* impassioned supporters. "He lacks the ability to inspire people," one Ford delegate told a visiting political scientist. Opined another: "I wish he were more forceful and charismatic.") And once that aura was broken—well, then the nomination would fall like overripe fruit into Reagan's hands. Everyone wanted to get on the right side of the man who might soon be the most powerful man in the free world.

A PLATFORM FIGHT SEEMED THE SMARTEST PLAY. WHATEVER FORD'S DELegate lead, this was, by any measure, a predominantly right-wing gathering. In one survey 63 percent of the delegates called themselves "conservatives," up 10 percent from 1972, with the number who called themselves "liberals" dropping from 12 percent to 6. That was in part a function of a new rightward tilt in the nation's electorate—but it was also due to a historical quirk. States that voted Republican in the previous presidential election got bonus delegates for the next convention—so that in 1964, when Goldwater won only six states, five of them in the Deep South and the sixth his native Arizona, those states were further advantaged in a delegate formula that already favored states with small, generally rural—hence conservative—populations. In 1971 the progressive Republican organization the Ripon Society sued on the grounds that such imbalance was unconstitutionally antidemocratic. (Conservatives, in turn, called *the lawsuit* antidemocratic—an attempt to win through the judiciary what couldn't be won through grassroots political effort.) The suit made it all the way to the Supreme Court—which ruled that such things were up to the parties to decide. So the question was put to debate at the Republican convention in Miami Beach in 1972—and reformers, led by the moderate congressman William Steiger, lost in a floor vote, 910 to 434. (Nixon, who liked the rules as they were, did everything he could to fix the vote, including tapping the Ripon operatives' phones.) The upshot was that the eight biggest states, with 49 percent of the population, had only 37 percent of delegate votes—and these were Ford-leaning states, mostly. Put ERA, abortion, or détente up for a vote and you could stage a story line about a party abandoning the nonelected incumbent. *Presto!* A runaway convention. For many Reagan devotees streaming into Kansas City, this strategy seemed obvious.

But not, apparently, to John Sears. Practically every time a microphone was placed before him, when he wasn't gaming delegate numbers he was telling the press that he would be avoiding any strategy for victory that would unleash the sort of ideologically driven emotionalism that would divide the party for the general election. That, after all, was what had happened in 1964—and look how well the Republican nominee had done then.

But John Sears, he of the recruitment of Richard Schweiker, was a sneaky cat. Elizabeth Drew noted his "flat, round, moon face" and "light, mysterious—sphinx-like—smile"; he seemed, she said, "imperturbable. He moves slowly, talks slowly, and never appears rattled." He never told anyone what he had up his sleeve, even those close to him in the Reagan campaign; he never committed strategies to paper. He had, she said, "the other side thoroughly spooked. When they talk about him, they nervously cite his maxim 'politics is motion.' And they await his next move."

And no one saw coming the *next* wild card Sears ended up playing, least of all the Ford camp, who were left flat-footed.

MONDAY, AUGUST 9, WAS THE OPENING OF THE WEEK FOR THE RULES, Platform, and Credentials committee meetings. It was also the second anniversary of Richard Nixon's helicopter ride to oblivion. Writers noted the connection when they described the trailers the campaigns were setting up in the convention parking lot: extensive temporary networks of secret communications lines to the delegations and leaders and whips on the convention floor: phones, television monitors, walkie-talkies—not unlike the listening post across the street from the Watergate used to monitor the Democratic National Committee, revealed when those Cubans were arrested that summer night in 1972. The lines were guarded by security cameras and swept daily for bugs. Because the Ford campaign's phone lines had to pass beneath the Reagan trailer, they were encased in steel to guard against possible taps.

You could also preview the fight to come on the lapels of the committee members trickling into the city: "BETTY'S HUSBAND FOR PRESIDENT"—something to bait the conservatives with the "GIVE 'EM HELMS" badges, for whom the first lady remained the nadir of America's moral dissolution. Posters bearing Reagan's face: "HE'LL BEAT CARTER"—something to bait Ford supporters by calling their man a loser. President Ford looking stern on *his* posters—a deliberate choice, a strategic swerve from the guy-next-door English muffin image. And one button in which the two contenders faced off Western-style, brandishing pistols: "Shootout at Kansas City." Which captured the soul of the gathering right there.

Reagan forces drew first blood, at a preliminary meeting of a key platform subcommittee. Before the full platform committee the previous day, a Saturday, Joseph Coors, the Colorado brewer and New Right donor, moved to let each subcommittee select its own chairman; that motion passed 43 to 39. So for head of the Subcommittee on Human Rights and Responsibilities the Reaganites were able to jettison the moderate governor of Iowa, Robert D. Ray, impaneling instead Charles Pickering, a conservative state senator set to take over the chairmanship of the Mississippi Republican Party in 1977. The victory came because Ford delegates had better things to do on a Sunday night, perhaps sampling Kansas City barbecue. "The right-wingers always come early and stay late," Ford's spokesman Peter Kaye, frustrated, told the *Washington Post*. The pundits read the tea leaves and saw a platform fight on the horizon—because Human Rights and Responsibilities was where hot-button issues like abortion, the ERA, busing, and gun control would be decided.

AT A MEETING OF THE REPUBLICAN PARTY'S RULES COMMITTEE IN THE ballroom of the grand old Continental Hotel at Eleventh and Baltimore—this committee was separate from the convention's Rules Committee; such things could be confusing—John Sears rose to speak. The expectation was that he would oppose the Ford campaign's proposed "justice amendment," which would bind delegates to follow all state laws, keeping designated Ford delegates from voting for Reagan on the first ballot. The cagey Sears defied that expectation. Instead he proposed to add to the convention's Rule 16—of which subsection (a) said the nomination had to have majority support from at least five delegations and (b) said, among other banalities, that nominating and seconding speeches had to be limited to fifteen minutes—a subsection (c), which would say: "All persons seeking to be nominated for President under Sections (a) and (b) above shall announce to the convention and file with its Secretary a declaration stating whom he or she will recommend to the convention as the Vice Presidential nominee. This declaration shall be filed with the Secretary of the convention by 9:00 A.M. on the day on which the nomination for President is held."

Sounded boring. It was actually explosive. It had been the prerogative of presidential nominees since time immemorial to present the vice presidential pick *after* the nomination—present it, in other words, as a fait accompli, for the convention to rubber-stamp. Now Sears was saying Ford must do what Reagan did: name his running mate in advance, subject to convention debate.

Sears made an earnest, high-minded pitch for what soon became known to every political junkie in America by the shorthand "16-C." And there was an earnest argument to be made. The issue of presidential succession had been far from academic since John F. Kennedy's assassination. At the joint session of Congress in which the new president pledged to fulfill Kennedy's legacy, before Johnson had time to nominate a new vice president, the second and third in line in presidential succession, the House speaker and president pro tem of the Senate, looked so old and frail sitting behind him that they inspired a movement for a Twenty-fifth Amendment to the Constitution, clarifying rules for presidential succession, which passed in 1967. As for the running mates picked at conventions, the one chosen by Barry Goldwater was such a nonentity he inspired nothing but jokes: "Here's a riddle / It's a killer / Who the hell is William Miller?" Same with Spiro Agnew, Nixon's pick in 1968—"Sparrow who?" someone asked at the announcement press conference. And everyone remembered what had happened to poor George McGovern: his selection process was so hasty and incompetent that the campaign never knew Thomas Eagleton had undergone electro-shock treatment for depression. According to Sears's argument, the re-sponsibility for choosing the man a heartbeat away from the presidency should be subject to the cool, deliberate vetting of an august body such as the one assembled before him—not a choice made in haste, via who knew what backroom quid pro quo. Delegates, he said, had a "right to know" what sort of ticket they were picking when they cast their con-vention votes. "I think most people worry about the vice presidency and the way that it's done simply because they wonder if someone isn't being paid off after the fact."

The savvy knew that he was spouting nonsense: that this was a po-litical move, through and through. That once Sears's team whipped both enough disciplined Reagan (and Reagan Trojan horse) delegates, and enough naive reform-minded Ford delegates, into voting for 16-C, the vote would be spun into a narrative in which the Reagan forces were in control of the convention—and Ford's soft supporters might stam-pede to Reagan. And even if the stampede didn't begin then, it might after Ford suffered the same political awkwardness Reagan had with his choice of Schweiker: losing conservatives if he picked a moderate, losing moderates if he picked a conservative. This was not a "right to know" but a "misery loves company rule," complained one Ford supporter— the "right to save a campaign manager amendment," said another.

Be that as it may. Ford's side, for now, had no way to respond but with jokes.

The party Rules Committee, stacked with Ford stalwarts, easily voted the measure down. But that was only the first step. On Saturday, the convention rules committee could get to vote on 16-C, dragging the controversy out nicely. A Ford spokesman promptly announced that the president would announce his pick in the "traditional" way—which played nicely into Sears's hands. *Why didn't Ford trust this Republican convention?* The *New Yorker* asked Sears if he had any more surprises in store. The smiling Sphinx responded: "I really don't know what sur-prises you. There will be other things that will be newsworthy. It is our feeling here that this probably stands to be the most exciting convention that our party has ever held."

. . .

THIS WAS CORRECT, BUT NOT ONLY FOR REASONS HE WOULD HAVE PRE-
ferred. Things soon got more interesting when a mutiny developed on
Sears's right flank.

A Sphinx who offered too-clever-by-half procedural strategies out
of one side of his mouth and insisted he wanted a united convention
out of the other was not to the New Right's taste at all. Pat Buchanan,
with his usual aphoristic intelligence, explained the New Right's way
of thinking in a May column in *Human Events*. "Ford is a conservative," he allowed; but his was "a conservatism marked by wariness of
conflict, resistance to change, and an abiding ambition to conserve the
status quo.... It is a don't-rock-the-boat conservatism exemplified ...
by what Mr. Ford calls the politics of cooperation, conciliation, compromise, and consensus"—but thank God, Buchanan exulted, Reagan was
there to lead the army of "Republicans who believe that conflict, not
compromise, is the essence of politics."

Jesse Helms articulated another facet of the right's maximalist mind-
set on the Senate floor earlier in August. His colleagues had been mocking him for his loyalty to Reagan. William F. Buckley described what
happened next in his newspaper column: "His eyes passed over the great
chamber and he mused that this probably was the most concentrated
group of successful politicians in the United States." (Recall that *politician* was a term of abuse for Helms; "I know nothing about being a politician," was one of his favorite maxims.) "He then told his colleagues
that several of them ('You know who you are') had confided in him in
recent months that they would prefer Reagan over Ford as president,
but that they couldn't, for political reasons, make that known." Buckley
concluded, "If everybody in and around government and the Republican party who is privately for Reagan had made known that preference,
Reagan could have picked John Wayne as his running mate."

This political faith of a Bill Buckley, a Jesse Helms, a Pat Buchanan—
and the hundreds of Reagan delegates who thought the same way—was
announced in one of Barry Goldwater's 1964 campaign slogans: "In
your heart you know he's right." The faith was that millions of Americans, both ordinary citizens and politicians, were actually bone-deep
conservatives, but were intimidated out of acting on conviction by the
malign hegemony of the all-powerful liberals. And the only way to flush
out the Trojan horses—across the nation generally, and, this week, in
Kansas City—was to deploy another Goldwater slogan: give them "a
choice, not an echo."

You did things, in other words, like forcing platform fights. Not nuanced procedural schemes.

But such fights were precisely what Sears's strategy was designed to avoid. He reasoned that Ford would find it all too easy to water down the proposed conservative language, or just swallow, say, an anti-ERA or antiabortion plank, then run the other way in the general election, rendering the conservatives' imagined "showdown" more akin to punching a pillow—and making Reagan look politically weaker than he actually was. Whereas 16-C was elegantly designed to make him look stronger.

Helms wasn't having a bit of it. His planning for Kansas City had begun in July, shortly before Schweiker was chosen, when he called warriors of like mind to a meeting in Atlanta, where they began drafting twenty-two planks upon which to make their stand. They covered the waterfront: against gun control; for "sovereignty" over the Panama Canal Zone; for "superiority," not parity, in nuclear arms; for trade with Rhodesia's white minority government, whatever the United Nations said; a fight to the death for the anti-Communist Chinese government-in-exile in Taiwan; for constitutional amendments to ban abortion and forced busing and to require a balanced budget—and for throwing "détente" onto the ash heap of history. Four key Sears aides were there, too, nodding politely, each side adhering to a principle articulated by Michael Corleone in *The Godfather: Part II*: "Keep your friends close and your enemies closer."

Helms made his next move the Sunday before committee week, the same day Sears was introducing the 16-C fight. Helms invited fifty conservative delegates and alternates for some serious backroom plotting because the actual planks that the Reagan high command had apparently signed off on were offensively pallid. (The one on Panama read merely, "In no events will the U.S. surrender fundamental interests." The one on Taiwan said only, "We shall not remain indifferent to assuring the future security of Taiwan.")

They called their strategy "purposeful conflict on substantive issues." Helms insisted they were working "independent of Reagan and not taking orders from anyone." Insider pundits greeted that claim skeptically. Wrote columnist Charles Bartlett (sufficiently an insider to have once set up young Jacqueline Bouvier on a blind date with Senator John F. Kennedy), "Although a delusion is being floated that he is acting on his own, this has to be a Helms-Reagan strategy, because the two have taken the long, winding road together." He described the scheme as "raising a series of nerve-tingling, party-splitting issues which will oblige the President to take positions on which a majority of the uncommitted delegates may not be willing to follow him." He called that "burning down the house to roast the wienie," concluding: "A nomination secured through the success of a divisive pull to the right will be no great prize," serving only as "a reminder that Helms belongs to that rabid band of committed conservatives who stop just short of conceding that they are willing to kill the party if they can't control it."

Like most Washington insiders, Bartlett was unaware that without Helms's stealth New Right machine, Reagan would have never won his come-from-behind victory there—and never would have made it this far. To pundits, the Helms forces were merely stupid—"incredibly," one wrote, "many of them did not comprehend the very simple politics in 16-C. They took it simply as a reform of the system, the kind of thing 'liberals' proposed, and turned their noses up at it." And, yes, this view had evidence to recommend it. Plenty of conservatives preferred gut feelings to math: 86 percent of Reagan delegates told a pollster that if he were the nominee he would defeat Jimmy Carter in the fall; the Gallup poll, with more objectivity, gave it to Carter, 64 to 28. They were the sort of ideologues who spied conspiracies everywhere. One told a visiting political scientist that at Helsinki, "a Republican president voted people into absolute slavery." Another, unable to believe a nice man like Ford could conceive such wickedness on his own, said, "If I were a political cartoonist, I would draw a two-headed Edgar Bergen with Kissinger and Rockefeller as the heads, and Ford as Charlie McCarthy."

But politics is about more than mathematics. It is also a matter of *will*. Polite Georgetown insiders didn't like to admit this. Sometimes they willfully ignored it—moderates could be as oblivious to evidence that didn't confirm their biases as any conspiracy-mongering extremist. Rabid partisans beat moderates all the time, precisely by dint of the very passion that sometimes blinds them.

And in any event, the extremists were too powerful for the official Reagan campaign to ignore.

Sears dispatched six of his top men to meet with them, Reagan intimates including Edwin Meese and Martin Anderson, and the Houston banker who had all but single-handedly saved the campaign back in May with a $100,000 unsecured loan. The Helms bitter-enders appeared unimpressed. They emerged, Helms floating word that it might make sense to give delegates a *third* first-ballot option for the presidential nomination: Senator James Buckley of New York.

This was some Sears-style cleverness of their own: Reagan delegates could defect to Buckley, signaling their frustration with the Reagan campaign while simultaneously denying Ford the nomination on the first ballot, forcing the Reagan campaign to capitulate to the "true" conservatives by the time of the second ballot, perhaps by dropping Schweiker. ("I think it's a distinct possibility," Helms said.) The New York senator, for his part, claiming he'd been approached by representatives of both candidates (though he was able to name only Reaganites), said he would not "slam the door." The Californian was asked about the news by the UPI for the papers published August 11: "All Ronald Reagan could utter was a puzzled, surprised 'Gosh,'" the article reported. Maybe these half-cocked insurrectionists were crazy enough to try a Buckley bid for real—who knew? "The possible entry of New York's conservative Senator James Buckley into the Presidential race has added to the confusion and the infighting already underway. With the nomination still undecided, the jockeying for position becomes more complex every day."

And so the insurrectionists prepared to march into a subcommittee meeting helmed by Charlie Pickering to force confrontations on the "hot-button" issues—busing, abortion, the ERA, gun control—to flatten the opposition with an ideological artillery barrage. Not that sneaky sissy stuff favored by John Sears.

AN UNLIKELY SOUND—SHRIEKING BABIES—FILLED THE TOO-SMALL, TOO-hot hotel meeting room. Some of the squalls came from infants, cradled by pro-life activist mothers, many of whom were wrestling toddlers with their free hand. Others were recorded, and issued from the portable speakers other activists carried into the room. Some of those carrying neither infants nor loudspeakers held pictures of bloody fetuses. Others shouted insults at their sworn adversaries, who made up another cadre of ideological warriors who'd come to Kansas City eager to provide the Helmsites just the showdown they'd been itching for: the feminists of the Republican Women's Task Force.

The Republican Women's Task Force grew out of the 1972 convention, where Republican women had won a (watered-down, unenforceable) rule that the party should "take positive action to achieve the broadest possible participation in party affairs" by racial, ethic, and religious minorities, and that "each state shall endeavor to have equal representation of men and women in its delegation to the Republican National Convention." That year, 30 percent of the delegates had been women. As 1976 dawned, they thought they might have a better chance with Ford—an ERA supporter, he of the feminist wife, with a decent record appointing female officials like Secretary of Housing and Urban Development Carla Hills and the RNC chairman, Mary Louise Smith. Surely it would be a piece of cake to keep the party's historic endorsement of the Equal Rights Amendment in the platform, perhaps with even strengthened language. As for abortion, their demand was a simple one: keep the divisive issue out of the platform altogether—hard to disagree with that.

History, feminists were confident, was on their side. The progress, really, was staggering. Married women had as a matter of course been denied bank accounts and credit cards; in 1974 the Equal Credit Opportunity Act made that illegal. In some states, mostly in the South, women were omitted from jury duty; the Supreme Court banned that in 1975. In California, the entire estate of a deceased man was taxed, the taxes to be paid by the widow, even though under community property laws, half the estate belonged to the spouse; soon that was gone, too. In 1967 the first woman entered the Boston Marathon—and the race organizer chased after her and tried to pull the number off her jersey. She had to complete the race (time: three hours, seven minutes, twenty-nine seconds) surrounded by a protective cordon. But in 1976 the first woman entered astronaut training. That January *Time* had declared "American Women" as its, um, Man of the Year. "Feminism has transcended the feminist movement," the editors wrote. "In 1975 the women's drive penetrated every layer of society, matured beyond ideology to a new status of general—and sometimes unconscious—acceptance."

But not in Kansas City, where only 31.5 percent of the delegates were women.

Republican feminists had already been disappointed by Ford on abortion. In the heat of the New Hampshire primary, in that interview with Walter Cronkite on CBS, Ford had staked out what he called his "moderate position": abjuring a "Human Life" constitutional amendment, but averring that since *Roe v. Wade* had gone "too far," "each individual state should decide what it wished to do." The press, back then, had been surprised he'd chosen to address the matter at all; the *Washington Post* said the issue had "got somewhat overblown and out of hand." If so, it got more overblown that next day, when Betty Ford released a statement, "I am glad to see that abortion has been taken out of the backwoods and put into the hospital where it belongs." The *Boston Globe* responded, "President Ford would be a better man and a better leader if he paid more heed to his wife, Betty, who is consistently demonstrating that she has more sense, honesty, and moral courage than the man she married." However, what the liberal editorialists judged as plain, uncontroversial evidence of "sense, honesty, and moral courage" was in fact but a pole in what was becoming one of the most scarifying debates to emerge in American politics in a generation—a position that tens of millions of *other* Americans, conservative ones, believed to be inherently sense*less, dis*honest, *im*moral, cowardly, or all of the above. Liberals tend to get into the biggest political trouble when they presume that a reform is an inevitable concomitant of progress. This is when they are most unprepared for the blinding backlash that invariably ensues.

As, indeed, had been happening with the Equal Rights Amendment, too. It had passed in thirty-four of the thirty-eight states required for it to be put in the Constitution for all time. But the setbacks in New Jersey and New York the previous November had been brutal. Its champions in the Empire State had campaigned with the slogan "All *people* are created equal," printed on red-white-and-blue Bicentennial-style buttons. The slogan "didn't work very well," the campaign's leader admitted to a scholar. "Our natural constituency wasn't turned on by it, and the average person on the street didn't understand what we were getting at." The opposition, organized into a coalition with the hair-on-fire moniker "Wake Up New York," did much better with leaflets calling ERA the "Common Toilet" law. A local Fair Campaign Practices Commission in Rochester unanimously ruled that the leaflet was unfair; experts agreed ERA would mandate nothing of the sort; the coalition continued using it anyway, calling the FCPC a "kangaroo court." They told the story, too, of a mining camp in Montana, which had a state ERA, where women were forced to use the same restrooms as men; the pro-ERA forces then pointed out that the mining camp in question in fact did not even have female employees. Wake Up New York still kept making the same claims—and won, in November 1975, with 57 percent of the vote.

And so, the following summer, the Republican Women's Task Force booked rooms across the Missouri River in Kansas, in protest against the Show Me State's failure to ratify the ERA. They dropped a rules challenge to delegations with too few women when advised it might threaten Ford's nomination. But they rebuffed warnings that an abortion fight would embarrass the president. "We believed the party must take a stand for abortion rights," one of their leaders, a Republican activist named Tanya Melich, wrote later. "If the Republican Party was going to give up on women's freedom, there had to at least be a fight."

The language the subcommittee debated proposed "to restore protection of the right to life of unborn children," without specifying state or federal action, and criticized a recent Supreme Court decision allowing minor children to obtain abortions without parental consent under some circumstances. It was introduced by Robert Dole, who had barely won back his seat in the Watergate backlash election of 1974 against a pro-choice obstetrician. He believed his slim margin of victory had come from his strong right-to-life stance and the energy antiabortion warriors had poured into his campaign.

He was eager to cement those political gains for himself. But his language was not nearly far right enough for the forces led by Helms: dodging the question of federal action, and a constitutional amendment, it was just the sort of Ford straddle they despised. (The Democrats went with an only slightly less anodyne statement: "We fully recognize the religious and ethical nature of the concerns which many Americans have on the subject of abortion. We feel, however, that it is undesirable to attempt to amend the U.S. Constitution to overturn the Supreme Court decision in this area.") The conservatives in the room were out of step with the convention as a whole, which was if anything to the left of the Republican Women's Task Force's position to drop abortion from the platform altogether: a survey of 449 randomly selected convention delegates found that a majority of 60 to 32 percent agreed it was "the right of a woman to decide whether to have an abortion"; even 48 percent of Reagan supporters agreed.

But when you believed a society gone mad was sanctioning genocide, math like that didn't matter much.

The debate began. Witnesses addressed a fifteen-member subcommittee stacked by Ford's team in consultation with Reagan's, with only three pro-choice but nine pro-life members—the apparent calculation being that a more even representation would heighten the confrontation. That calculation proved wrong. Private security guards prowled the corridors outside; inside, photographers and reporters and TV cameramen jostled for space with pro-lifers shouting about the "mass murderers and baby-killers" on the other side. "The more epithets they shouted at us, the happier they seemed," Melich wrote. "Our testimony was thoughtful and reasonable"—though her opponents surely judged it brainless and insane. The vote was called: ten to one for Dole's antiabortion language.

A discussion on the ERA language, which supported efforts for equality for women but didn't specifically mention the constitutional amendment—a starting place already to the right of any previous Republican platform since 1940—was gaveled forth. Opponents' signs read, "DON'T LET SATAN HAVE HIS WAY—STOP THE ERA," "ABORT ERA," and "MY DAUGHTERS HAVE THE RIGHT TO BE HOMEMAKERS—DON'T LET THE ERA TAKE IT AWAY," and referenced the perversions of nature like homosexual marriage that would surely follow its passage. A pro-ERA subcommittee member pronounced himself baffled: "It is a basic guarantee of women's rights—there is no basis in it for abortion or homosexual marriages." The vote deadlocked, seven to seven—a shock to the feminists, given that Ford forces whipped in favor of it. The subcommittee then voted ten to three to endorse voluntary prayer in the schools. Another subcommittee approved Ford's preferred language that America would not give up rights over any area of Panama "necessary for the protection of security of the U.S. and the entire Western Hemisphere." The Associated Press reported that this particular vote "gave Ford a narrow edge in the first major convention confrontation"—because, AP said, "It was on the foreign policy planks that Ford strategists said they had to engage in a test of strength with the Reagan forces rather than commit the party to positions contradicting the policies pursued by Ford and Secretary of State Henry A. Kissinger. . . . On domestic issues such as abortion and school busing, the Ford and Reagan positions were close enough in principle that the President's manager felt he had plenty of room for agreement."

On CBS, Eric Sevareid predicted that the Republican Party would go the way of the Whigs if the "revival tent across the road where the orthodox could kneel and touch the remnant of their true cross"— the Reagan campaign, headquartered at the Alameda Plaza Hotel— prevailed. The question remained, though: Which Reagan campaign? The ERA and abortion fights would go next to the full Platform Committee—but so would some of the twenty-two Helms planks, filed as minority reports, which the *Washington Post* reported might receive forty-five out of the 106 Platform Committee votes. The Platform Committee held its opening debate, on gun control, where "Reagan supporters"—the Associated Press didn't specify which ones; perhaps it didn't even know—"defeated an attempt to water down a plank putting the Republicans on record in opposition to all forms of gun control." The 16-C fight, Sears's ace in the hole against Ford's first-ballot nomination, would soon go on to the full Rules Committee—but without buy-in from those selfsame Helms devotees.

It was only halfway through preconvention week, and the intrigue had hardly begun.

ON THURSDAY THE PRESIDENT NAMED NAMES. AMONG THE RUNNING mates he was considering, the White House announced, were senators Bill Brock of Tennessee, Jim Buckley of New York, and John Connally, all conservatives—and Lowell Weicker, the liberal senator who'd been among Nixon's most relentless pursuers on the Ervin Committee; Edward Brooke, the liberal senator who happened to be black; and Mark Hatfield, the liberal senator who'd been the Senate's second most aggressive Vietnam dove, behind George McGovern. The list also included William Ruckelshaus and Howard Baker, two ideological moderates who were also Watergate heroes, at a time when the Reagan position—that Watergate was a liberal witch hunt—was becoming more and more conservatives' standby position. Clarke Reed, chief of the still-uncommitted Mississippi delegation, suddenly used this list as an opportunity to save face with his conservative brethren—who were flooding him with letters and telegrams and phone calls calling him a traitor or a quisling or worse—and announced that, since the president was "considering several possible running mates to the left of the mainstream of the Republican Party," he was reconsidering his previously pledged loyalty to Ford.

He had already, at the meeting of the party Rules Committee, threatened to break with the Ford campaign and vote for 16-C when the convention's Rules Committee met Saturday—in other words, vote with the Reagan side to force Ford to name his running mate early.

Saturday came.

On TV: a riot of colorful confetti-and-balloon-laden ceremonies; "Youth for Reagan" sending off their hero in Los Angeles, then boarding their own buses for Kansas City (back on the radio in October, Reagan would exaggerate their sacrifice as a "forty-eight-hour" bus ride); Richard Schweiker and his wife arrived to enthusiastic crowds at the Kansas City airport. Rockefeller and his wife, Happy, touched down to talk from Rockefeller's aides, humiliating to the president, that Rockefeller might still make a great running mate. Then he spoke before the full Platform Committee: "Americans must see events in their true light and not permit emotionalism to substitute for moral judgement."

Behind closed doors: breakfast deep within the Ford high command in the Crown Center Hotel, the most powerful men in the Republican Party surrounding Clarke Reed and warning him of dire consequences if he crossed them at the Rules Committee meeting that afternoon.

Reed assured them, "I'll be all right on 16-C . . . I'm not going to flip. They ain't gonna get me."

Came the afternoon Rules Committee meeting. Rarely had a boring backroom meeting on convention procedures been so closely watched. John Sears worked his hustle, arguing that his was simply a common-sense reform: "Trust the delegates. . . . All it does is put the delegates and the people in the candidates' confidence before it is the irrevocable choice of the party." A Reagan delegate recalled, "People were all around us, these little Hitler Gestapo guys with walkie-talkies. They'd radio back to command headquarters about who did not vote properly."

The question was called, the proposed rule failing by a vote of fifty-nine to forty—the gestapo guys apparently prevailing. A naive Ford aide, one of his top men, told the *Washington Post,* "We're out of the procedural minefield now"—ignorant that things were unfolding just as Sears planned: losers of full-committee votes had the opportunity to file minority reports to bring the question before the entire convention if they received but 25 percent of a full committee's 106 members. Which meant a floor fight, live on prime-time TV. Which had been Sears's plan all along.

And Clarke Reed? He'd flipped. He voted with Reagan.

He excused himself by saying that, since Ford won decisively, they hadn't needed his vote anyway. He was working every side of the street. And it was still only beginning. Both sides fanned out their deputies to hostelries across the Missouri River valley, getting their ducks in a row for a vote scheduled for the Tuesday evening of the convention on an obscure little procedural question that might well decide who became the next President of the United States.

THAT SAME SATURDAY AFTERNOON THE FEMINISTS WERE GETTING THEIR ducks in a row on abortion. Their point woman was the Platform Committee's only feminist officeholder. Millicent Fenwick was brash, spicy, a Katharine Hepburn character come to life: after her doctor warned her against cigarettes, she started smoking a pipe. She was a former fashion model who'd become a New Jersey congresswoman at age sixty-four. Wayne Hays once threatened to keep her staff from getting paid "if that woman doesn't sit down and keep quiet." A male colleague, in a debate on the ERA, addressed her on the House floor: "I just don't like this amendment. I've always thought of women as kissable, cuddly and smelling good." She replied, "That's the way I feel about men, too. I only hope for your sake that you haven't been disappointed as often as I have."

Her job that Saturday was leading the debate to try to ensure that the issue upon which they believed the very liberty of women to control their own lives hinged was *not* mentioned in the Republican Party's 1976 platform. But "in another hot room," Tanya Melich wrote, "again filled with a profusion of television cameras and right-to-life and pro-choice partisans, and a surfeit of security guards," Fenwick failed. The vote was twenty-six to sixty-five—one shy of the twenty-seven needed to bring a minority report for a floor debate recommending that the platform not mention abortion.

The members of the Republican Women's Task Force thought they could get twenty-seven signatures, though, for a minority report recommending the following plank: *"There is no wide public consensus on this issue. It is felt by some to be a moral issue and by others to be an issue of personal choice, but most agree it should not be in a political party platform. . . . [W]e think that the Republican party platform, like those of years past, should not attempt to commit its candidates and officers, as well as members, as though this were a traditional political issue."* They had forty hours to file the signatures. They decided on stealth—if the Ford campaign found out, it might put a stop to the potential disruption. But stealth wasn't hard to achieve, since the press was preoccupied with the 16-C soap opera. Armed with lists of Platform Committee members and their addresses at hotels across the city and its environs, they bodied forth, located their quarry, and found little resistance: "Glad you're doing this, thank God someone's concerned." "This is right." "What's gotten into Ford?" Two of their signatories were doctors. Several more were doctors' wives. Four were pledged to Ronald Reagan. They reached one sleeping delegate at his airport hotel an hour away at midnight; he signed in his pajamas. "They represented," Melich remembered, "every section of the nation but one. It was as though we were reliving the Civil War. No one from the South or the Border States was represented, except Faye Chiles of Tennessee, and Tennessee had been on the Union side."

The same regional balance of forces had marked the full Platform Committee's earlier vote on ERA—fifty-one to forty-seven to keep it, a squeaker. Then John Sears asked Phyllis Schlafly to forgo the attempt to win her own minority report for a floor fight. More politically disciplined than Jesse Helms, she acceded. "I consider it immensely more important that Reagan be nominated. If Reagan is nominated, the platform is irrelevant because Reagan is against ERA and Mrs. Reagan is against ERA. If Reagan is nominated, we've won."

GERALD FORD HAD REACHED A SIMILAR CONCLUSION: ALMOST ANY IN-sult on the platform could be swallowed, if it advanced his nomination. Coincidentally, Sears was backtracking a bit on his strategy not to confront Ford frontally on ideology. He feared a genuine mutiny on his right flank if he did not throw the Helmsian fire-breathers a bone. "We were asking our troops to fight battles that were important, but were not the kind of battles they came to Kansas City to fight," his conservative deputy David Keene told Jules Witcover in an after-action review. "You had to give them something to keep the blood warm in their veins."

There also was the problem of the vote count on Rule 16-C: he wasn't confident he could win, or win decisively enough to deal Ford a true setback. So he devised one more strategy, to kill two birds with one stone: confront Ford with the one platform insult he *couldn't* swallow. Not the ERA, not abortion, not budgetary politics. But détente, Henry Kissinger, Panama, Aleksandr Solzhenitsyn, Helsinki—the president's prerogative to make foreign policy, which happened to be what Jesse Helms cared about most, the soft underbelly where Ford's political manhood could *really* be poked. Surely he'd rise to *that* bait. There would be a rip-roaring debate on the convention floor: true drama, Reagan's vision versus Ford's. A debate Reagan had the votes to win, and one that Ford, because suitable foreign policy language was so important to him that his proxies kept the Platform Committee debate on the subject going until 3 A.M., wouldn't dare duck.

And so, as Witcover described it, Reagan's most trusted strategists, Ed Meese, Martin Anderson, and Peter Hannaford, joined Sears in "drafting a comprehensive foreign policy plank," to be filed as a minority report, "that was compatible with Reagan's position and party policy, but that would *have* to be contested by the Ford camp. The language had to make the challenge unmistakable, yet it had to be deftly worded so that it did not too crassly repudiate the incumbent Republican President."

Richard Schweiker alighted in ABC's suite and sat down for its Sunday interview show *Issues as Answers,* claiming hidden delegates, now as many as fifty from Pennsylvania alone. No one trusted him. Garry Wills noticed even Reagan distancing himself from him by consistently mispronouncing his name. Evans and Novak had reported, "Whereas poisonous erosion of Reagan strength in the South can be blamed on Schweiker, he cannot take credit for modest Reagan advances in the Northeast." He also starred in the Sunday morning papers:

> WASHINGTON (AP)—Senator S. Schweiker, R-Pa., was a top congressional participant in a Nixon-era program set up to help find government jobs for friends of the White House, and members of Congress, government documents reveal. . . . Civil Service Commission investigators found the purposes of the unit was to assure "that timely and responsible action would be taken on referrals received from members of Congress and administration officials." Records of the special unit show that it received 134 referrals of job applicants from Schweiker. . . . Only the Nixon White House personnel office had more.

But the report had no apparent impact. No one seemed to care about Richard Schweiker one way or another. It was like a Greek tragedy about the fate that befalls bearers of vaulting ambition.

Ronald Reagan arrived in Kansas City, met by the usual delirious throngs. He said, "We come here with our heads high and our hearts full. We're going to come here and do what we have to do." He argued that he'd done delegates the honor of giving them three weeks to learn about his running-mate selection, where Ford would give them but half a day. Then, three hours hence, an incredible development: the president arrived.

Air Force One landed. The president ambled down the steps with the first lady and his photogenic children in tow (Reagan had only three kids present; Patti abstained), taking in the gaze of all three networks' live cameras, acting as if this was not an unprecedented sign of weakness: incumbent presidents were supposed to arrive at political conventions the day of the nomination, brashly confident, not sullying their office by politicking like ward bosses. A reporter said Ford looked as humble as a pilgrim. He worked the delegates' hotels, trailing clouds of Secret Service men bearing plastic stanchions to cordon off aisles for him to walk through. A man wearing a giant Styrofoam Snoopy head showed up wherever the stanchions did—the *Peanuts* character was running for president, sponsored by Dolly Madison cakes, and his handlers were keen to get him in a photograph with Gerald Ford, who was busy re-wooing delegates supposedly already committed to him but now threatening to withhold their support unless he chose a running mate congenial to them: indignity upon indignity.

Reagan glad-handed at various delegations, too—then repaired to his headquarters at the Alameda Plaza Hotel, where he lunched with Joseph Coors, Jesse Helms, and a dozen other conservative movement leaders. Then he glad-handed some more. It was only at a late-night meeting alongside his wife, Nancy, that Reagan was finally apprised by Sears of the details of the strategy by which his nomination could be won: the 16-C debate and vote, then the foreign policy plank debate and vote before the whole convention on Tuesday night, the day before the final balloting. "Two rolls of the dice to take the whole pot" is how an old ink-stained wretch from the campaign planes, where they knew a thing or two about gambling, described it.

The *Washington Post* went to press with the observation, "The spectacle of a President enduring such blatant pressure tactics from the party rank and file is mind-boggling to anyone who recalls the manner in which Mr. Ford's two most immediate predecessors, Lyndon B. Johnson and Richard M. Nixon, lorded over their party convention."

Dawn broke Monday on a metaphoric shoot-out in Kansas City.

CHAPTER THIRTY-TWO

The End?

"THE CITY OF FOUNTAINS," THE TOUR-BUS DRIVERS INSTRUCTED THEIR passengers to call Kansas City—more fountains than any city but Rome, went the civic boast. Like the one in front of Ronald Reagan's massive Spanish-themed headquarters hotel, the Alameda, which featured a frolicking naked woman. "The men have the look of successful business and new-car franchises, their women the aura of beauty-parlor habit and the bridge table," Jules Witcover wrote. They were welcomed at hot buffets with cold shrimp at receptions where busboys frantically popped stems into disposable plastic wineglasses, in hotel banquet rooms with the letters *G* and *O* and *P* hewn out of giant blocks of ice. Kansas City's hotels were putting on the dog: it was the first national political convention held there since 1928.

Hotels, and motels: there being not nearly enough fancy hostelries downtown to accommodate the thirty thousand visitors, delegations were stashed as far as an hour down the freeway. Pennsylvania's chairman told *Time* his place near the airport was "like getting stuck in the middle of a cornfield—you can't walk to a bar or get a suit pressed." The manager threatened to cancel his entire delegation's reservations until the chairman apologized; the place had *four* bars, and valet service, too.

Two hundred Texans, a hundred delegates and a hundred alternates, all pledged by law to Reagan on the first, second, and third ballots and in their hearts until hell itself froze over, were in a motel half an hour away. *Texas Monthly* sent a sardonic reporter to report on the home-state delegation for an article that ran under the title "Republicans Are People Too":

"A man wearing an authentic Nazi helmet and who has a red terry cloth T-Shirt draped over his beer gut blows a charge on a bugle, a sound that slices right through the glee club's gloomy rendition of 'Climb Every Mountain.'

"'Yeah, *Ree*-gan,' he yells. 'The neksht preshident—*Ree*-gan!'"

(The alcohol flowed freely in a thousand hospitality suites.)

Downtown, the hustlers vying for attention included animal rights crusaders who'd erected a four-foot-high display of color pictures of foxes chewing their own bloody legs off to escape traps, to compete with the bloody pictures of aborted fetuses; "Jesus Freaks"; venders of elephant trinkets, Ford masks, Rockefeller masks, Reagan masks, four-foot-long drinking straws, the sort of silly hats delegates wear to get their faces on TV; a man dressed as Abraham Lincoln with what a reporter thought was "something frightful and unstoppable in his eyes"— assassin eyes.

Celebrities, trailing boom microphones: for Ford, Cary Grant, Sonny Bono, and Tony Orlando, spotted doing the "Bump" with Betty Ford; for Reagan, Pat Boone, and—"Oh, look! That's Efrem Zimbalist Jr. Oh, God, he's so *beautiful*!" John Dean, looking tanned and relaxed, was fawned over everywhere like a movie star. *Rolling Stone* had sent him. A reporter called that "a benevolent act of genius: they have provided the only evidence at this convention that Nixon ever existed."

The city's anemic red-light district was festooned with red, white, and blue bunting; several of the smut peddlers featured dancers in elephant costume in their windows. For nostalgia's sake, Alf Landon, Kansas's own eighty-nine-year-old former presidential candidate, was wheeled out, photographed riding his horse at his Topeka farm, regaling reporters: "There are some intelligent people in Washington, but there are more of 'em in Kansas." (Of Jimmy Carter: "Do you know anyone who has figured him out?" Of Gerald Ford: "He did exactly the right thing [pardoning Nixon]. It had nothing to do with Nixon personally.")

Political rumors, thicker than in an Oriental bazaar: the latest was that with Jim Buckley having removed his name from consideration, under pressure from the New York State Republican Party (which he couldn't afford to cross, as he would be facing a reelection fight against the winner of September's Democratic primary between the neocon-leaning Daniel Patrick Moynihan and the hard-left Bella Abzug), Jesse Helms would be placed in nomination instead. Rumors abounded about filthy hippie hordes set to descend on the city from up in the hills. ("They're all behind the monument," a cabdriver told a visitor, passing the city's World War I memorial. "You can't see 'em from here.")

Political billboards, mostly Gerald Ford's: the official campaign photo, PRESIDENT FORD, the one where he didn't smile.

Political street-corner sign-bearers: TRANSCEND GUTLESS PLACATER WITH REAGAN.

Monday afternoon, they all streamed in the ninety-degree heat to Kansas City's striking (some said bizarre) new Kemper Arena, designed by architect Helmut Jahn with all the trusses on the outside to keep the views unobstructed on the inside. In classic 1970s fashion, what was supposed to be a stirring sight, a fifty-foot-tall, 1,500-pound inflated elephant set to soar high above the arena, drooped flaccidly in the parking lot, its stomach accidentally punctured by its rigging. Inside, in air-conditioned splendor, delegates enjoyed unobstructed views, at the convention's only daytime session, of spectacles like the Tennessee congressman offering his dramatic reading of the lyrics of the Johnny Cash song "Ragged Old Flag," the presentation of a ceremonial gavel to the local industrialist after whom the arena was named, the interminable reading out of roll calls and rules, speech after speech by obscurities like the chairmen of the National Black Republican Council and the Republican National Hispanic Assembly and the chairman of the College Republican National Committee—a kid named Karl Rove, who said students' "allegiance will be won only by the intelligence and soundness of our issues and the quality of our candidates."

Peaceful so far.

Then the evening session. "I know you will all share my enthusiasm and pleasure over this next announcement," said RNC chairman Mary Smith. "Princess Pale Moon, the beautiful Cherokee Indian, who sang the National Anthem, will entertain us once again. She will sing the brand-new patriotic selection, which was written by Will Rose. This is the first time that this selection has ever been heard in public. If you will watch carefully, you will find that Princess Pale Moon will interpret the lyrics with beautiful Indian dance movements."

Texans, down on the floor in matching red-white-and-blue cowboy hats, were fidgety, waiting for something to happen. "I want to skin Dan Rather," their chairman, Ray Barnhart, told *Texas Monthly*'s reporter (who backhandedly complimented him for his "unqualifiedly handsome face and a patina of good breeding") about something the CBS newsmen had said about their delegation being ready to give up on Reagan. "You know one of the problems with a thing like this is all of a sudden you hear a rumor and—zoom!—it's a reality." Perhaps the person in his delegation who started the spontaneous demonstration for Reagan overheard him, and decided to prove Dan Rather wrong. The delegation revived an old ritual conservatives had begun at the 1964 convention— the conservative Woodstock, some called it. The Texans on the convention floor turned to the Texans clustered together up above them in the arena's raked seating—the gallery—and cried "Viva!"

The gallery answered back: "Olé!"

Directly between them, as it happened, were the Ford family's box seats. And it was at precisely that moment that Betty Ford—accompanied by her son Jack, the one who had tried marijuana, and her son Steve, the one who was studying stockyard management, and who wore a cowboy hat—appeared at one of the openings into the arena. Every Ford supporter in the house applauded. But Betty didn't make her move to the family box behind the boisterous Texas delegation; instead she milked the reaction. Maureen Reagan, a sharp political operative herself, saw what was happening: the convention managers had held the Fords' arrival for the moment when they could dampen the first show of enthusiasm for Reagan. Michael Reagan was about to escort his stepmother down to their seats. Maureen held them back, got the attention of the California delegation, signaled madly with her arms—and got them restarted on another round of "Viva!" and "Olé!" with the Texans all the way on the other side of the arena. She recorded the political triumph in her memoirs: "Thinking this signaled Nancy's arrival, Betty Ford made her entrance. We quieted the crowd as best we could and allowed the Ford delegates to cheer Betty's arrival. She seemed thrilled, thinking she had cut short the welcome intended for Nancy," and sat down in the family box.

Then Maureen had her mother walk in.

The reception was staggering. The band, as it had been instructed to do when Nancy Reagan arrived, struck up "California, Here I Come," chorus after chorus. *Time*, which hadn't even noticed Betty's entrance ("Nancy made the first move"; the band had goofed, and gave Betty no welcoming song), called her "a stunning study in red." And the Reaganites could not get enough.

Mary Smith: "Ladies and gentlemen, may we please have your help, please, so that we can go on with our agenda."

More earsplitting din.

"We love the enthusiasm. We appreciate your spirit. Will you please come to order!"

But there was no order.

"May I have your help please!"

Finally, after fifteen minutes, the noise began to die down. "I can look up from the back row of the Texas delegation," the *Monthly*'s reporter wrote, "and see the underside of Betty Ford's chin"; she looked "calm, regal, arrogant." Then, sheathed in an aquamarine dress, Betty swept her arms high to the crowd. But the response from her supporters could not silence the Reagan throngs. She had been upstaged.

The convention script that night had been written to maximize comity. But there was none. The governor of Illinois charged that Reagan supporters had literally tried to purchase the votes of two Illinois Ford delegates. One of them said, no, it was the Ford campaign that offered cash to a congressional campaign he was managing. The FBI opened an investigation.

Old rivals spoke: Nelson Rockefeller, joking about his sixteen years trying and failing to get the Republican nomination; Barry Goldwater, who'd denied him in 1964, hailing "two of the best candidates ever to come before a convention," calling upon the crowd "to pick one, and then . . . work, work, work to elect him" over "Mr. Carter and his warped idea of what this country is about." But when Rockefeller began, a journalist said, "the convention's enthusiasm pull[ed] back like a tide." The public address system failed for a moment; Rockefeller later fumed that Dick Cheney must have pulled the plug. As for Goldwater, as he made his way to the podium, slowly, on crutches from a knee infection (he hadn't even wanted to show up), the word "sellout!" rang out in the great hall. Afterward, in an interview, he sounded like Dr. Frankenstein surveying the work of his monster. His former supporters now working for Reagan, he said, were "some of the most vicious people I have ever known. If you waver an inch they call and write and say you're a dirty s.o.b."

Extremism in defense of liberty: now a vice.

Goldwater was gulping bourbon. He told his interviewer, "Reagan has become one of those people, the really ideological ones who won't change."

THE MISSISSIPPI DELEGATION, STILL UNCOMMITTED, STILL THE KEYSTONE of either side's victory, would still be a thirty-vote bloc—unless they voted to undo their unit rule, which was a possibility, too. Reagan operatives reminding him of his conservatism, and Ford operatives reminding him of their pledge to him, trailed Clarke Reed like shadows, wheedling him, humoring him, threatening him. Reporters trailed him, too—at first to his evident delight, and then, as the pressure closed in, to his growing discomfort. Monday morning at the Muehlebach Hotel, Truman's Midwestern White House and the convention headquarters hotel, while shopping in the men's clothing store, Reed had told one journalist he was taking a "good, hard look at 16-C" as a means of pressuring Ford to name a conservative running mate. Someone relayed to Ford's Southern chief, Harry Dent: "Better watch Clarke, he's flipping." Charlie Pickering, the conservative who was to succeed Reed as state chairman, announced his switch from Reagan to uncommitted—though Pickering, smarter than Reed, did it as a maneuver to move *other* uncommitted Mississippians to Reagan. Then Reed said he might have "overreacted" when he endorsed the president. Dent gathered his Ford allies within the Mississippi delegation in a room at their hotel, the Ramada East, preaching to them like a black Baptist, half humorous, half serious as a heart attack, saying any of them who liked Ronald Reagan—which was most of them—had better hold fast against 16-C if they wanted to see Reagan live another day in Republican politics: his only hope now was to be named as Ford's running mate, which would be impossible if Ford had to name a running mate while the contest was still going on. He was bluffing; Ford had zero intention of tapping Reagan. Intrigue upon intrigue.

Mike Wallace shoved a microphone into Reed's face on the floor early Monday afternoon. Ford's Mississippi floor whip, Jack Lee, in a red baseball cap (Ford state whips wore red caps so they could easily be identified at a distance during the fast-moving chaos of a contested vote; "floating" whips, who moved between delegations, wore yellow), thought he overheard Reed say he planned to vote for 16-C on the floor the next night—maybe even (hard to tell; convention floors were noisy) *lead* the fight for the Reagan amendment. Lee pushed a button on an electronic console: a code red that went straight to the Ford trailer. Harry Dent ambushed Reed later in his room at the Ramada East Hotel.

"Clarke, my goodness, what in the world you doing to us!"

"Whattaya mean, whattaya mean, cat?"

"You just told Mike Wallace on CBS you gonna lead the fight and deliver thirty votes for Rule 16-C."

Reed, overwhelmed by the pressure, flopped, exhausted, onto his bed. "Oh my God! What can I do? What can I do?" (He was getting some pretty nasty letters from Ronald Reagan fans, calling him a scumbag and worse; maybe that had something to do with it.)

What he could do, Dent firmly advised him, was honor his pledge to the man in possession of the nation's nuclear codes.

"I gotta get out of this! I gotta get out of this!" answered poor Clarke Reed, his rather pathetic attempt to cast himself as the Mark Hanna of the 1976 Republican Party plainly reaching the end of the line.

Back in the arena, under the red Mississippi standard, Dent and Reagan's leader in the delegation, Billy Mounger, were toe-to-toe, throwing hot words at one another, Dent arguing that the delegation was so divided they should hold a formal caucus to vote on its will. Other key players joined the scrum; like iron filings drawn to a magnet, reporters pulled toward them to listen in. The Magnolia State Republicans' twenty-nine-year-old executive director, Haley Barbour, belted out the names of Mississippi's eighty-two counties in backward alphabetical order, Yazoo to Adams, to safeguard the privacy of the deliberations. It didn't work; the screaming was too loud. Mounger to Dent: "You're not a member of this delegation! We don't want a vote!" Dent to Mounger: "I know why you don't want a vote! We've got the votes and you don't!"

Princess Pale Moon made beautiful Indian dance movements. Four Mississippi Republican leaders and a White House official from South Carolina found a dark warren behind some bunting to crouch beneath and continue deliberating to find some mutually agreeable procedure to determine the fate of the delegation to determine the fate of the convention to determine whether it would be Ronald Reagan or Gerald Ford to face Jimmy Carter in the fall. Pat Boone, meanwhile, worked over a black female minister, Jean Long of Gulfport, Mississippi, who'd declared for Ford after visiting with him on July 30. The Christian conservative crooner persuaded her to visit Reagan's suite. There, Reagan turned her around. After which, according to Ford's daily diary preserved at the National Archives, she heard out the president once more. Recorded Jules Witcover, "Nobody knew whose nose count was right by now."

The gavel sounded, closing the first evening's session. At that, the Texas contingent joined forces with Reagan's twenty-nine delegates in the Michigan delegation and charged through a Ford cocktail party in a sunken pit of the Crown Center Hotel lobby chanting, "We want Reagan! We want Reagan!" with hands outstretched in the "hook 'em horns" gesture, encircling the traitors, who joined the battle themselves:

"Ford can win! Ford can win!"

"We're against Ford! We're against Ford!"

Grown men and women. The custodians of a major American political party. "The pandemonium," *Texas Monthly* reported, "is total."

TUESDAY MORNING. ALL OVER THE TRAFFIC-JAMMED TOWN, EACH SIDE was tearing down and ripping up the other's posters. Two teams of young supporters, "Youth for Reagan" and "The Presidentials," like homecoming football game rivals, lined the driveways of both campaigns' headquarters hotels, cheering and booing and beaming and glowering at motorcades accompanied by police cruisers in the ninety-degree heat.

Open the papers: "REAGAN DELEGATES TURN ON THEIR MAN" was the headline of a UPI article about conservative opposition to 16-C. Conservatives were unimpressed with the argument of Mary McGrory that "John Sears had saved Reagan the fate of being labeled another Goldwater," who "won the nomination in 1964 with the help of right-wing fanatics and hit-men." A conservative spokesman was quoted, though whether he meant Sears or Sears's candidate went unspecified: "He can go to hell.... In the bottom half of the ninth inning here they come with a Mickey Mouse proposal."

Jack Anderson reported on the doings of Richard Nixon: "His memoirs, according to sources who have been in touch with him, will reassert the President's right to steal and wiretap and rig court cases in the national interest." And of Spiro Agnew, who'd raised thousands in donations from conservatives including Joseph Coors, William Rusher, John Wayne, and Ronald Reagan for a nonprofit, "according to associates, to assert his views and assail his enemies. He is particularly eager, the associates say, to renew his assaults upon the press." A *New York Times* feature alerted the nation to the importance of one Phyllis Schlafly, "who introduces herself as a lawyer's wife from Alton, Ill., and the mother of six, a correct but incomplete description.... A blonde with deep blue eyes, a figure that can still be called willowy, and a winning smile," she was also author of "two book-length tracts, *Kissinger on the Couch*"—actually more than ordinary book length; it was 846 pages—"and, hot off the presses, *Ambush at Vladivostok*."

The *Times* also profiled one of her adversaries, Elisabeth "Betsy" Griffin of the Republican Women's Task Force. "Tall and blond and—to repeat an adjective because once again it applies—glamorous," Griffin was quoted as mocking Schlafly's claim that ERA was an attack on "homemakers": "I know perfectly well that Phyllis Schlafly has domestic help to scrub her kitchen floors. I scrub my own kitchen floors. Some day we can compare dishpan hands." It continued, "Miss Griffin, who is married to John Deardourff, a political consultant who specializes in moderate Republicans, made it a point to bring her wedding ring, which she doesn't normally wear." (The *Times* didn't mention Griffin's profession: she was headmistress of a prestigious private school.)

"Do you hate men?" a delegate asked her.

"Can't you tell I'm pregnant?" she replied. "I have a lovely husband who supports the Equal Rights Amendment."

But this fight was just one of the sideshows. Turn on the TV, and the *Today* show starred the only delegates who now seemed to matter—the ones from Mississippi who were uncommitted. They were talking about the only issue that seemed to matter. "The energy, in these pre-16-C hours, is intense," *Texas Monthly*'s man observed. "You can sense the desperation with which the caucus drives off intimations of defeat." Ray Barnhart: "I'm reminded that according to all the experts Ronald Reagan didn't have a chance. Well, I'm afraid that some of our pollsters along with some of our politicians just don't understand people."

Maybe so. Strategists on both sides had been agonizing over whether to lobby Mississippi to dissolve its unit rule. First the president's man James Baker decided a split vote would advantage Ford; then he changed his mind and decided to go for the all-or-nothing bloc. "How many other Clarke Reeds might there be out there," a historian later imagined him thinking, "telling him one thing and doing another?"

The two sides agreed that the crucial delegates would gather for a 3 P.M. caucus at their hotel, to vote first on the unit rule, and then on 16-C. The media assembled, noses veritably pressed behind one of those banquet room sliding doors. A limousine pulled up. John Connally, a true larger-than-life personage—*Texas Monthly*'s reporter said you could feel the force of his handshakes ten feet away; "your digits are empathetically crushed"—stepped out. Ford's trial balloon of him as a running mate had deflated when nine Ford delegates from Maine threatened to abstain on the first ballot if the Watergate-tainted Texan's name was put forward. "From my point of view John Connally represents the power politics of the Sixties," said Maine congressman William Cohen, one of the impeachers on the Judiciary Committee. "I think it's an era that has gone by." He pointed to an infamous March 23, 1971, Nixon tape—Connally had briefed the president about exactly what dairy lobbyists were demanding in exchange for a political donation—as something "the American people would no longer tolerate." Garry Wills, though, had a great riff in his newspaper column: "He is the only candidate," he said, referencing Connally's miraculous acquittal in that milk-bribery case, "who can prove he is not a crook—after all, the jury said he was not." And the man himself never seemed to recognize there was anything to be ashamed of. *Texas Monthly*'s reporter said, "He looks like a man who is confidently awaiting a time when the presidency itself will be conferred by natural selection."

Upon his arrival at Mississippi's motel, Connally was pulled into the room of Haley Barbour. Connally emerged, but not into the caucus to ply the delegates for Ford as expected; Charlie Pickering, the Reagan man pretending to be uncommitted, observed that and showed no emotion; Dent, observing *Pickering,* was heard by a reporter saying with apparent elation to Connally, "Governor, that means we got the vote." There were four or more layers of possible poker bluffs to decipher here—whether Connally was sent away because his presence would hurt Ford, because Mississippians had grown resentful at heavy-handed White House tactics, or whether Connally was sent away to make it *appear* his presence would hurt Ford, because Barbour was for Reagan; whether Pickering was showing a poker face; whether Dent was sincerely expressing his confidence or making it appear to a powerful man that he was confident—and, beneath all the intrigue, who knew?

Harry Dent entered the conference room, apparently to make the case for Ford.

Reagan showed up and entered the conference room.

Haley Barbour left the room. "They voted?" Dent asked him. "How did they vote?"

They had voted to keep the unit rule and, by three votes with one abstention, to vote their delegation as a bloc *against* 16-C—for, by inference, Gerald Ford. The word flashed across Kansas City that it just might be over, and the stampede to Ford could begin. Coincidentally, CBS News reported that for the first time since it had begun counting, Ford was over the top with 1,132 "firm or committed" delegates. The Reaganites at the Ramada streamed to the hotel pool, where they had hoped to enjoy a victory party. The cases of beer had been sent over with the compliments of conservative benefactor Joseph Coors. They flipped them open and drowned their sorrows before the evening's full-convention debates and votes over the platform and the rules.

IT WASN'T OVER, NOT NECESSARILY. BY THE SAME MONDAY DEADLINE that the feminist abortion supporters had also been racing to meet, the Reagan campaign filed its anti-Kissinger minority report, a plank to be tacked on to the platform's existing language and titled "Morality in Foreign Policy." It began—

"The goal of Republican foreign policy is the achievement of liberty under law and a just and lasting peace in the world. The principles by which we act to achieve peace and to protect the interests of the United States must merit the restored confidence of our people. We recognize and commend that great beacon of human courage and morality, Alexander Solzhenitsyn, for his compelling message that we must face the world with no illusions about the nature of tyranny. Ours will be a foreign policy that keeps this in mind."

—and that couldn't have been a more frontal attack against the president who had so conspicuously refused to meet with Solzhenitsyn during his summer 1975 visit to the United States. It continued, "Ours will be a foreign policy which recognizes that in international negotiations we must make no undue concessions; that in pursuing détente we must not grant unilateral favors with only the hope of getting future favors in return."

—and that could almost have been a transcription of one of Ronald Reagan's 1975 radio broadcasts. It excoriated the Helsinki Accords (which "take from those who do not have freedom the hope of one day gaining it") and eviscerated "secret agreements, hidden from our people," which not only referenced the Panama Canal negotiations but harked back to the most macabre horror of right-wing folklore: the 1945 negotiations at Yalta in which an enfeebled Franklin D. Roosevelt, with Soviet agent Alger Hiss supposedly whispering advice into his ear, sold out Eastern Europe to the Reds. It concluded, more in the sonorities of a manifesto than in the half-loaf bureaucratese of a conventional party platform, "Honestly, openly, and with firm conviction, we shall go forward as a united people to forge a lasting peace in the world based on our deep belief in the rights of man, the rule of law, and guidance by the hand of God."

It wasn't as bad as it could be—Sears had seen to that—so it "wasn't an outright sock in the jaw." Thirty conservative leaders had signed their names to a text that explicitly mentioned Panama and Taiwan but those references mysteriously disappeared by the time it was filed with the convention secretary. Nonetheless, Ford was furious. Henry Kissinger, his political mentor Nelson Rockefeller, and his acolyte Brent Scowcroft were even more furious. Giving in to Jesse Helms on, say, gun control ("We support the right of citizens to keep and bear arms. We oppose federal registration of firearms. Mandatory sentences for crimes committed with a lethal weapon are the only effective solution to this problem"), even though Ford wanted regulation of Saturday night specials, was one thing. Telling the commander in chief how to deal with the Soviets was another.

And so, two showdowns between Ford and Reagan on the Tuesday night schedule of the shoot-out in Kansas City. First 16-C. And then "Morality in Foreign Policy."

THE TV SHOW BEGAN WITH A KEYNOTE SPEECH BY JOHN CONNALLY. IT was Churchillian, patriotic—and full of confident proclamations that America's problems were all the fault of the Democratic Party he'd belonged to just two years before: "through its absolute domination of the Congress, which has relentlessly stoked the fires of inflation" and "built the federal bureaucracy ever larger and larger and directed the agents of that bureaucracy to penetrate ever deeper and deeper into the conduct of all of this nation's private affairs and personal lives," it "has unleashed upon the American people the curse and abomination of government which today careens about, so clearly out of effective control," and dared "seek to elect a veto-proof Congress."

He concluded: "I would hope that when the record of our service is finally written . . . up to the very end we resisted with every fiber of our being the oppressive hand of an all-powerful central and dominating government" (strange: as treasury secretary he'd been the architect of the biggest increase in government power since World War II, Nixon's wage and price controls); "and up to that very end we had an abiding faith in an Almighty God and that there is more good than evil in man." And, thus fired up, Reagan partisans began another braying demonstration.

"*Viva!*"

"*Olé!*"

"*Viva!*"

"*Olé!*"

Texas Monthly: "'Aren't these conventions fun?' a delegate named Donald Turman from Victoria asks me. 'I feel like it's a small guy who doesn't make a lot of money against the establishment rich. That's the way I look at it, man'"—he shifted focus, standing on his chair: 'Hooooooooo-WOOOOOOOO!'—then turned back to his interviewer: 'Wheee! It sure wears you out, though.'"

Robert Dole, on the podium: "Ladies and gentlemen, we would like to take the official photograph of the convention."

He thumped his gavel, to no avail.

"Ladies and gentlemen, would you please take your seats"—he surveyed the dizzy madness before him—"or take *anybody's* seat. Thank you very much. We are about to take an official photograph. In 1972 that was the most exciting part of our convention! So if you will please take your seats. Thank you very much."

Nothing.

"Will the delegates and alternates in the balcony and on the floor please be seated? Thank you very much. Your special attention is needed at this time. Will the delegates and alternates please be seated? Will our guests in the balcony please let us proceed?"

Nope. The two sides were shouting chants at each other, the Reagan forces blowing long plastic horns they'd brought with them, and which the *New York Times* thought sounded "uncannily reminiscent of the ululations of Arab women." Some had cowbells. Reagan operatives with green baseball caps and earphones and walkie-talkies were spotted, coordinating the din. Dole tried again: "I remember in 1972 in Miami, when I was chairman of the Republican Party, the most exciting event was taking the official photograph. But I can see from this audience and from the enthusiasm here that you may have other things in mind. . . . If all of the alternates and delegates would look toward the CBS anchor booth on the right, and if you can refrain from moving or speaking for thirty seconds, you may set a record and you may also receive a photograph. . . ."

And, finally, they did: one more 1970s family picture of forced grins occluding seething resentment and rage; or maybe they didn't. The *Official Report of the Proceedings of the Thirty-First Republican National Convention* did not include an official photograph of the floor.

IT WAS TIME; THE MOMENT HAD COME. ("WE ARE ABOUT TO PROCEED with very historic business," implored Senator Dole, once more begging the delegates to return to their seats. "I wouldn't want you to miss this.") A delegate from Missouri, U.S. representative Thomas B. Curtis, introduced the 16-C amendment for the Reagan campaign. He read out its dry, legalistic language ("No delegate or alternate to the convention shall be bound by any commitment of any kind, public or private, to support any presidential candidate who does not file such a declaration. . . ."), and suddenly the din rose again. "I would only ask that you listen to me for about thirty seconds," Bob Dole cried—but this was not to be. Betty Ford entered the building, and the Ford supporters went wild.

Then, moments later, Nancy Reagan entered. The band struck up "California, Here I Come." She made her way up to the family box, a glass aerie at the far end of the hall more than two hundred feet from the stage, and the cacophony grew and grew—bigger than Betty's. Nancy was winning.

Then the first lady pulled a virtual ace from her evening gown sleeve.

A certain song was sounding in the background, courtesy of the house band: "Tie a Yellow Ribbon Round the Ole Oak Tree," the best-selling record of 1973. Its singer was the vaguely Latino, mustachioed Tony Orlando, who starred every Wednesday night on CBS on his own slightly racy variety show (beginning the next month it would open with a five-minute monologue by George Carlin)—a Ford supporter. Presently Orlando himself appeared, and pulled Betty into the aisle, and they delighted (about half) the crowd with a spirited dance.

Time called it "The Contest of the Queens": "a battle in red and aqua, a regal contest between the strikingly handsome, radiantly smiling wives of the Presidential candidates at either end of the convention hall." *Time* interviewed Betty, whom it declared the winner, and who insulted Ronald Reagan: "He is a good speaker, he comes across well on TV—after all, that was his trade.... Jerry Ford is not fluff; he knows the meat-and-potatoes part." Betty insulted Nancy Reagan, too: "I just think that when Nancy met Ronnie, that was it as far as her own life was concerned. She just fell apart at the seams." And she gave her political analysis: "Personally, I think it should have been uncontested. Jerry has done such a good job in the past two years. The fight is very bad, very bad for the parties; it has built up animosities." Indeed. *Time* also interviewed Nancy, who gave as good as she got: "It was just Ron and a handful of staff against the tremendous power of the other side." ("Though her smoothly modulated voice never wavered, her hurt came through.") "I've never known the White House to be used by either party the way it was in this campaign. The White House stands for something. I don't think it should be concerned about uncommitted delegates." And, in fine family form, she denied she'd even noticed the Tuesday night fuss: "I'm nearsighted. I couldn't see the other end of the hall."

The dance routine had been choreographed, of course—planned for the moment of maximal political import, the 16-C debate. Bill Carruthers, the Ford campaign's audiovisual coordinator (or as NBC called him, Ford's "cosmetic advance man"; he'd been in charge of things in the previous administration like making sure Nixon didn't look "jowly"), and George Murphy, the former senator and movie musical song-and-dance man, came up with the idea after the first lady's humiliation the previous night; the band was to treat Nancy's arrival as its cue to launch into "Tie a Yellow Ribbon." Vic Gold of the *Washingtonian*, whose sources within the world of political public relations were unmatched, explained how "the media was measuring crowd enthusiasm for the wives in gauging crowd enthusiasm for Ford-Reagan delegate strength." So "Carruthers and Murphy called in show business reinforcements." They did their job well. *Newsweek* was among the outlets who described the Orlando gambol as "spontaneous." Knowing his side had been licked, Ray Barnhart, the chief delegate from Texas—who'd led the stampede of the previous evening's Gerald Ford hotel-lobby cocktail party—told reporters, "I thought it was in very bad taste."

REPRESENTATIVE CURTIS HAD TO READ THROUGH THE AMENDMENT again; no one could possibly have heard it the first time around. He finished and yielded the microphone to a testy Bob Dole: "I would ask that the aisles be cleared! . . . Will the sergeant at arms please cooperate, or will the media please cooperate? . . . All those in the aisle on my right, all those in the aisle on my left, we want to get on with this very important business. . . . The delegates have a right to be heard. . . . Would the sergeant at arms please clear the aisles? We will have order before we proceed!" He rapped his gavel like a demonic woodpecker.

There was next to be a half hour of debate over 16-C. The two sides alternated speeches of two minutes, each choosing ordinary delegates to deliver its message. The Reagan side spoke against type in the civic abstractions of reformers like Common Cause: "a binding, moral commitment to the principles of openness, full disclosure, and complete trust in the American people"; "tell us who is on the team before asking us to join it"; "Haven't we had enough backroom decisions for the vice presidency?" Ford delegates spoke of "the political mistake of naming Senator Schweiker" and "desperation and blatant political opportunism" and the "wedge of division in our party" it would produce. Passions were absurdly high. A Reagan precinct worker from California finished up to such barking enthusiasm that Dole appeared to be scared: "Those on both sides have a right to be heard. . . . Everyone who walks up here is nervous to begin with. Don't frighten us any more." Sherry Martschink, the delegate from South Carolina who became a national celebrity for her quips about former dentist Governor James Edwards, began a labored metaphor about changing the rules in the middle of a game of checkers, and was vociferously booed. A Ford delegate from Arkansas said that because 16-C would exclude Reagan from vice presidential consideration, it "disenfranchises me and disenfranchises you"— and the Reaganite outburst that followed the ugly word *disenfranchise* was so unceasing that Dole said he worried 16-C's deadline for naming a running mate would come (at nine the next morning) before the roll call on it concluded—

He paused, looking out at a commotion on the floor.

"Will the sergeant at arms please try to clear the aisle on the right one more time, and will the delegates from New York please be seated?"

He conferred with someone.

"There is something wrong with the telephone. They can't hear the phone ringing."

They couldn't hear the telephone connected to the Ford command trailer because it had been ripped out of the floor.

The vice president of the United States had spotted a Mormon preacher from Utah who'd invaded the space of the New York delegation and was bearing a "Reagan Country" sign. "With an adolescent grin on his face," said *Texas Monthly*, Rockefeller snatched the offending sign from the minister's hands.

Conservatives recognized that adolescent grin. It was the same simpering expression Rockefeller had worn in 1964, speaking from the convention podium in San Francisco about the "radical well-financed minority" taking over the Republican Party—when he was booed, and the crowd started chanting "We want Barry!" He simpered arrogantly then, too, muttering, "That's right, that's right"—relishing the opportunity to display just how uncivil the right-wing opposition truly was. However, this time the incivility started with him. It proceeded to escalate. The Utah Reagan leader, Douglas Bischoff, chased after Rockefeller to retrieve his placard. He and New York GOP chairman Rosie Rosenbaum scuffled. Rockefeller claimed to have overheard someone say "if he didn't get that sign back he was going to rip out the phone"—and, presently, the white phone connecting the New York delegation to the Ford command trailer in the parking lot was indeed ripped out while the chairman held the receiver to his ear, surrounded by a crush of reporters attempting to overhear him.

"I want that man arrested!" Rosenbaum yelled as Bischoff attempted unsuccessfully to scuttle down an aisle ahead of the Secret Service agents, who apprehended him for questioning beneath the stands. "He ripped my phone out. That's what Reagan people are like."

Rockefeller held up the severed phone for the cameras, sweat breaking through his dress shirt. He then gave the sign back to a Reagan delegate—after ripping it in half.

The American flag on the stage fell over.

New York and North Carolina delegates, whose standards were next to one another on the floor, issued catcalls at one another, waving fists, making threats.

Dole, at the podium, was livid. He admonished the crowd, then America's richest man directly like he was a naughty schoolboy: "Ladies and gentlemen—Mr. Vice President!—ladies and gentlemen, delegates, please take your seats." "The usual aplomb of the Vice President of the United States," Ray Barnhart sneered, standing next to a microphone, ready to announce a hundred Texas votes for 16-C. When Rockefeller exited the floor, Secret Service agents had to surround him. New York delegates chanted angrily; "We want a phone! We want a phone!"

Just about the only person who was calm through the entire thing was Ronald Reagan. He watched it on television in his hotel suite, dissolving in laughter. Then, he saw a televised image of himself on television watching it on television—*that doesn't look good*—and his smile disappeared.

A PANIC SHOT THROUGH THE FORD SKYBOX: JIM BAKER HANDED HARRY Dent a copy of the *Birmingham News* with the headline, "Ford Would Write Off the Cotton South," which was apparently circulating through the Mississippi delegation they thought they'd sewn up.

This was the sort of lightning-fast development that made conventions *really* interesting—that historians wrote about decades later, like when a mysterious "voice from the sewers" in Chicago in 1940 cried, "We want Roosevelt! We want Roosevelt!" and started the demonstration that stilled political doubts about whether Franklin Roosevelt should be nominated for an unprecedented third term. Mississippi Reagan partisans Pickering and Mounger brandished the paper, demanding a new caucus to dissolve the unit rule, which might just pry lose enough votes for Reagan to go over the top on 16-C, with the votes of thirty-one of sixty delegates plus alternates. But media hound Clarke Reed, the only one who could call a poll of the caucus, was detained in an interview with NBC, and Harry Dent, thinking fast, and *moving* fast—a close convention was about not only commanding time but mastering space—was able to dash up to where Mississippi's thirty alternates were, those ambitious young professionals recruited by Reed who ended up being overwhelmingly for Ford, and told them not to budge from their seats. Ford quickly got on the horn and claimed to Reed that he'd be campaigning long and hard in Jimmy Carter's home region. Harry Dent managed to spin the call for a poll of the caucus as such a dastardly dirty trick, that one of the last uncommitted Mississippi delegates unpinned a Ford badge from Dent's lapel and—"That does it!"—pinned it on his own.

So the last 16-C fire was doused—at the price of a pledge that the Republican Party would remain enthralled by the "Cotton South."

Debate time expired. The Idaho chairman was recognized and called for the vote. It was alphabetical, Ford having tried and failed in a rules challenge to get states called randomly. That was because Alabama, Alaska, Arizona, Arkansas, California, and Colorado were all Reagan-heavy states. And that meant the suspense continued, as Reagan rocketed ahead.

But the alphabet only forestalled the inevitable. "For the benefit of the cameras," the *Texas Monthly*'s man wrote, Barnhart and his deputies keeping track of the 16-C roll call tally sheets "manage tight, cheerless smiles." Texas was called—"one hundred principled votes for 'aye'!"—

and the faces beneath silly Reagan hats rallied briefly; then conservative Wyoming, which surprised everyone by giving eight of its seventeen votes for Ford. (Dick Cheney, Ford's chief of staff and de facto campaign manager, had invited his home-state delegation to the state dinner for Queen Elizabeth.) Florida, which had abstained, voted thirty-eight to twenty-eight for the president's position, and that put the vote over the top.

The process, which was supposed to take an hour or so at most on the schedule, was over. The convention rules were adopted unanimously. There were a few more desultory speeches, and then the meeting moved to the question of the platform—at more than an hour past midnight Central Standard Time.

"THE FIRST ABORTION DEBATE AT A NATIONAL POLITICAL CONVENTION started at 1:15 a.m.," the feminist Republican activist Tanya Melich later recounted. "Just as the Ford campaign wished." What kind of citizen would be moved to warm feelings about Republicans—or the Republican whose position on abortion was that it should be left to the states—by language like "Are we in this nation to follow the path of Nazi Germany and consign people to death because they are too expensive to let them live?"

That was Representative Robert Bauman of Maryland. Another pro-lifer during the twelve minutes allotted to debate complained of the feminists' proposed language, "It gives the husband no say-so." Another, the Republican whip in the California state assembly, called the fetus a "pre-born baby" (novel language), claimed "at eight to nine weeks, the baby can squint, swallow, and clench its fist"—you could almost picture the cute little guy in his crib—and quoted Albert Schweitzer: "Evil consists in destroying life, doing it injury, and hindering its development."

Their side, Melich recollected, arguing for an amendment committing the party to neutrality, spoke "in jackhammer spurts." Hers, she lamented, was "civilized and tentative and deadly dull." She agonized: "All that work to get to this? Were the moderates, as our critics said, constitutionally unable to be passionate about anything?"

Millicent Fenwick tried to get recognition to call a roll-call vote on the question; the feminists wanted their adversaries on the record on national television. But that could be politically embarrassing for the president. The rules allowed a roll call by written request, which Fenwick sought recognition to present. But Arizona congressman John Rhodes, who had spelled Dole as chairman, said time had expired, and wouldn't call on her. "A phalanx of people surrounded him," Melich wrote, "and several strong-armed men blocked our page from giving him Fenwick's note." Rhodes called a voice vote; Melich thought she heard her side's "ayes" as having been overwhelming. Not the chair, though. The language of the platform draft would stand: It called for "public dialogue on abortion"—but also endorsed a "constitutional amendment to restore protection of the right to life for unborn children."

However, that was a development of interest mostly to history. Once more the abortion fight got little coverage. Either outcome of it would have had no bearing on the question that mattered most: who would the Republicans nominate? And despite the 16-C outcome, the Reagan camp nurtured hope for the big prize. Their "Morality in Foreign Policy" plank was up for debate next. Gerald Ford would surely never allow his darling Henry Kissinger to be humiliated like this. And *that*, surely, would be their dagger. That was obvious enough when no one in Kansas City spotted "Henry the K" at any of the glamorous cocktail parties upon which the nation's most unlikely sex symbol so doted. He was under "political house arrest," people said. Ford knew how politically toxic Kissinger remained for the vast majority of Republicans, so he was damned if he did, damned if he didn't: Lose the debate for a Reaganite plank, and surely many delegates would stampede for Reagan in tomorrow's nomination roll call. Win the debate—well, even then, that would just show how committed to détente's sellout of America the accidental president truly was.

This could get interesting. The people who'd managed to stick around through these early A.M. hours, on TV and in Kemper Arena, were at least guaranteed one more good fight.

But in the Ford skybox, the chief of staff was making an aggressive argument.

Richard Bruce Cheney of Casper, Wyoming, had begun his Washington career in 1969 at the age of twenty-eight interning in the office of moderate congressman William Steiger from Wisconsin, having dropped out of a doctoral program in political science at the university in Madison. In the Nixon White House he apprenticed himself to another moderate, Donald Rumsfeld, who headed Nixon's Office of Economic Opportunity; Cheney then followed Rumsfeld to the Ford White House, first as chief of staff, then (after Rumsfeld engineered the "Halloween Massacre") as secretary of defense. Cheney's defining passion in Ford's White House was his rage at Congress's Watergate-era reassertion of power against the executive branch and the national security state. One of his ideas had been to been to appoint Robert Bork, the former acting attorney general who'd fired Archibald Cox, as the new CIA director ("a strong team player," Rumsfeld called him). Another was to burglarize Seymour Hersh's apartment for his exposés on the CIA. He'd also been the most aggressive advocate for a White House meeting with Solzhenitsyn. Like his mentor Rumsfeld he was a masterful bureaucratic infighter, which was how, after taking Rumsfeld's place as chief of staff in the Halloween Massacre, he had managed to also insinuate himself now, in effect, as Ford's campaign manager. From that perch he argued to the candidate that the platforms didn't mean anything; he should just swallow the "Morality in Foreign Policy" plank because if he fought it the nomination might slip out of his grasp.

Cheney's arguments, in other words, were tactical, though Cheney's goals, surely, were also ideological. If Rumsfeld had moved right only gradually (under Nixon he'd recommended unilateral withdrawal from Vietnam), his student Cheney had been a right-winger all along. He loved the plank in itself.

Ford yielded to Cheney's argument. They called no witnesses in opposition to the Reagan amendment. Voice vote; the *ayes* had it. Which was how, by the time weary delegates were finally able to go to bed, in addition to becoming the first American party to go on the record against abortion they were now the first to revile détente. Jim Lake, Reagan's press secretary, later reflected that they should have made its language stronger—"an outright sock in the jaw." James Baker said that would have been the right play: make it two words, "fire Kissinger," and the football just might have been tipped.

IT DID NOT. WEDNESDAY, A DAY FOR HEADLINES LIKE "EVENT DEGENER-ates to Chaos" (the *Milwaukee Sentinel*), and also for faits accomplis. Grassroots Reagan activists refused to believe it. One group tried to drum up an eleventh-hour firing of John Sears in favor of Lyn Nofziger. After what their Boswell called "a tearful locker room scene . . . that lasted until 4 A.M.," a cohort of Texans made a pilgrimage to the governor's suite in order to ask him to dump Schweiker. One of the emissaries reported, "Governor Reagan came out and before we could even get started, he shut us down real quick. 'If you could . . . guarantee me the nomination, I still wouldn't do it.' And that made us all feel really small for even attempting it." *Wall Street Journal* writer Jude Wanniski plied Peter Hannaford with his "Two Santa Clauses" theory—that if a Republican president radically lowered taxes, economic growth would somehow magically skyrocket, and Democrats who opposed lowering taxes would become villains and be voted out of office—and said that

Jack Kemp, the New York congressman and former pro football player whom he'd turned into a supporter of the idea, would switch from Ford to Reagan if the Californian backed massive tax cuts, too. Hannaford looked at Wanniski as if he was crazy, and walked away.

And there was one fait not yet accompli, thanks to the failure of 16-C: who would be Gerald Ford's running mate? That morning the *New York Times* reported the speculation was down to William Ruckelshaus and Howard Baker, two names to remove the sting from Jimmy Carter's "Nixon-Ford administration" thrusts. Then word emerged that Baker's wife, Joy, had been hospitalized for alcoholism, and this, according to the prejudices of the day, removed him from consideration. Touts were still floating the names of liberals, but one of them, William Warren Scranton, had taken over the stop-Goldwater baton from Nelson Rockefeller and was just about equally despised. Pick wrong, and angry conservatives could abandon Ford in droves for the general election; he wasn't going to take chances. His deputies were negotiating with their all-but-vanquished foes about a postnomination meeting between the two principals.

The *Texas Monthly*'s reporter headed up in the hills behind the war memorial, where it was said the hippies were camping. He found "kids skinny dipping in the fountains and running naked in the grass. Teenage girls are guzzling bottles of Coronado wine and singing 'Cocaine don't make me lazy.'" He approached a fellow, who, too wary to talk, suggested he introduce himself to "Marijuana Mike, who is something of a leader. . . . Marijuana Mike has only one tooth, a long festering stalactite occasionally visible in the cave-like darkness of his empty mouth." Mike told the reporter—after a detour for a joint—"We are now on the grounds some four hundred non-delegates to the un-convention for the election of Nobody."

The reporter looked around: five or six tents, clusters gathered around cooking fires, "thirty non-delegates at most."

Marijuana Mike told him that if enough people voted for "Nobody" the election would deadlock, throwing it into the Electoral College. The reporter asked him what good that would do: "'Oh, man.' He turns away in disgust and mutters something about a kangaroo and a carcinogenic civilization."

The dregs of the 1960s: nothing much for worried Republican matrons to fear.

The nominating convention session began. Signs: ROCKY DON'T STEAL THIS SIGN; SEND FORD TO HELSINKI, SEND REAGAN TO WASHING-

TON; PRESIDENT REAGAN '77. The Texans added kazoos to their arsenals. "I'm very, very hopeful," an alternate from Fort Worth said. "I'm just hoping for Reagan to pull it out." A delegate told the *Texas Monthly* reporter, against all evident reality, "It's going to be close." Another alternate, from Waco, told the reporter, like one of the hippies up in the hills, "Right now, right now I just feel there's an inherent goodness and goodwill in the world."

The first speaker, Governor Arch Moore of West Virginia, finished— and the chairman had to complain, "May we have order, please? There will be time for tooting of horns and other noisemakers later on, but this is not the time. We have important business to conduct."

The next speaker, a Michigan congressman—then the chairman: "Ladies and gentlemen, will you *please* take your seats? Time for demonstrations has not yet arrived. We still have business to perform."

Not likely. The next speaker, Jacob Javits, was among the figures most hated by the right. This time the interruption began almost immediately, drowning him out. The band had taken to playing "God Bless America" between speakers, sheer patriotic reverence having some effect in goading the noisy and noisome conservatives to surcease. This time the musicians had to start the song during Javits's oration—and it didn't have any effect. A Sousa march: nothing. So the Ford family was cued for an entrance, to the strains of the University of Michigan fight song, "The Victors." "One way to overcome noise," Jules Witcover explained, "is with more noise." But the impromptu Reagan demonstrators were proving unstoppable. So the band threw them a bone, pealing forth with "California, Here I Come"—as with overtired children, maybe one last spurt of hyperactivity would work.

Nope. One more "God Bless America," but hundreds of razzing kazoos swarmed over the song. This noise to no political purpose was starting to scare people: 1964 again.

Another Sousa march, another "Victors." Nancy entered, to another "California, Here I Come," as Javits tried to break through, with liberal bromides about "human vicissitudes and human catastrophes" and how "headlines don't cry the tears of individual hurt and individual need" and "real people with real problems."

Two more rounds of "God Bless America." Fans of the incumbent waved their arms, crying "Ford! Ford! Ford!" Elizabeth Drew of the *New Yorker* struggled with herself, dropping objectivity, outing herself—"we"—as a partisan, an enemy of passion itself: "We tend to think this is OK because we think Ford is OK, safe. But what are the real distinctions among political emotions? Some of the most menacing political figures in the history of the world have used stadiums and bands to whip up their followers."

John Rhodes had had it, too, hurling the ultimate insult: "May we please quit acting like a Democratic convention?" At which, finally, business proceeded. A ceremonial roll call, then Paul Laxalt took the microphone, a year and a month after unveiling "Friends of Ronald Reagan" to a nonplused crowd of skeptical journalists at the National Press Club (an event that had made only page nineteen of the *New York Times*), to place into nomination "the finest Republican candidate that has hit a Republican convention in recent years: Ronald Reagan!"

EVERY FOUR YEARS THE PARTIES PUBLISH A BOUND VOLUME OF THE OF-ficial proceedings of their national conventions, with every utterance made from the podium transcribed. Dreary, somnolent volumes that convey only the most austere sense of what these silly, cacophonous fiestas are actually like; exclamation points never make it into these records, and only the barest indications are offered about anything that happens that isn't what someone says into the microphone on the stage. In *Official Report of the Proceedings of the Thirty-First Republican National Convention Held in Kansas City, Missouri, August 16, 17, 18, 19, 1976*, for example, after Laxalt's speech for Reagan, the following words appeared, in parentheses: "(A great demonstration followed this speech, lasting approximately thirty minutes.)"

Some scenes not captured by those bare words:

A middle-aged man with glasses, wearing a Reagan boater, observed by Mary McGrory standing "precariously with a leg on each arm of his chair in the gallery, holding a huge flag in one hand and a Reagan poster in the other. For the entire, ear-splitting forty-four minutes, he kept his position." (She reflected, "Nobody would have done that for Gerald Ford.")

The band, gamely trying to keep up with the crowd's energy, playing "California, Here I Come" and "Dixie" (Reagan was favored over Ford in the Southern delegations by a ratio of four to one) and "The Pennsylvania Polka" for Richard Schweiker. And then "Dixie" again—this song always "inspiring fresh frenzies," *Texas Monthly* observed.

Those infernal blue plastic horns, four feet long, droning away. Whenever the energy started to flag, the Texans began to cry *Viva!* and California answered back *Olé!*

Viva!

Olé!

Viva!
Olé!
Viva!
Olé!
Viva!

Patti Davis was at home in Topanga, California, watching on TV, seeing "Ron, Michael, and Maureen in the box with my mother and Betsy Bloomingdale, their hairdresser Julius, and Jerry Zipkin," a real estate heir whose 1995 obituary described him as "a celebrated fixture on the international social scene for almost half a century. . . . He traveled widely with many female friends, and lunched with one or more on most days of the week, usually at Le Cirque or Mortimer's." Patti read her mother's face: "She knew my father had lost; she was angry, upset, and determined not to slink away unnoticed."

A young woman in one of the galleries waggling a hand-lettered sign, unceasingly, reading (*sic*) "CLARK REED IS ARNOLD BENEDICT." The taunts against Reed from Southerners grew so vicious that he had to slink off the floor, fearing violence.

Ford supporters in the balcony threw trash at the delegates from Texas.

John Rhodes let the energy ride for twenty minutes. Anxious Ford deputies, fretting that the madness would knock the president's nomination off prime time, cued the band to begin more rounds of "God Bless America" in a desperate attempt to cauterize the enthusiasm. Then, at thirty minutes, Rhodes began to glower. Reagan himself asked one of his staffers to make the demonstration stop. But his deputy answered back that there was nothing anyone could do to make it stop.

And then Rhodes tried something that might.

"Fellow delegates, I am about to introduce to you a very distinguished citizen from the state of North Carolina to second the nomination of the Honorable Ronald Reagan for President of the United States."

It still didn't work. Rhodes continued his admonishments as Jesse Helms stood next to him at the podium. Rhodes handed the gavel to Helms; maybe that would prove he wasn't trying to sabotage Reagan. The band quieted, the lights went down—and still: nothing. Helms finally spoke. (Evans and Novak's review: "He seemed for a while to be nominating Alexander Solzhenitsyn.") But the convention was still out of control. Then, Mary McGrory observed a little cruelly, "The unexpected appearance of a black woman, Gloria Toote of New York, as a seconder, quieted them down." So did the nineteen seconding speeches for Gerald Ford, which began at twenty minutes before midnight. The candidate of boredom. The candidate of calm. He got 1,187 votes on the roll call to 1,070 for Reagan; West Virginia put him over the top at 1:25 A.M. When the chairman moved to make it unanimous, Ray Barnhart of Texas, the guy who'd called Betty Ford's dance with Tony Orlando "bad taste," fought his way to the floor microphone and shouted, "No! No! No! No! No!"

A reporter made it down to Reagan headquarters, where staffers were packing boxes. A woman intoned into a pay phone: "Are you *sure* he wouldn't take the vice presidency? Can't we draft him? Are you *sure*?" Another told a friend, "This has been my life since October. I'd have done anything for him."

GERALD FORD ANNOUNCED HIS RUNNING MATE THE NEXT MORNING AT the Century Ballroom of the Crown Center Hotel. "I'm really thrilled with the opportunity of having Bob Dole as my running mate," he said. "Bob Dole will help to heal any divisiveness within the party." Ford looked tired. Perhaps Dole would perk things up. He was a slasher. *Time* printed some examples of his arch wit. (After Nixon offered to campaign for him in 1974: "I haven't invited him to stump for me, but I wouldn't mind if Nixon flew over the state.") And Dole was a conservative, which was why Gerald Ford chose him—so Ronald Reagan would sign off on him. Dole himself had half-expected to be picked by Reagan, and had even sent feelers to Lyn Nofziger regarding the job. He later described himself as having been "Schweikered." Later, sources revealed that Ford had wanted Ruckelshaus. But Reagan didn't want him—and that was that.

They had met during the previous night at 1:30 A.M., the winner, by prearrangement, calling upon the loser. A stipulation of the Reagan camp was that Ford not ask him to run. He had sent a handwritten note to the California delegation: "There is no circumstance whatsoever under which I would accept the nomination for Vice President. That is absolutely final." Claire Schweiker, the senator's wife, had tearfully told him, "Oh, Governor, I'm so sorry." Reagan embraced her: "Claire, you really shouldn't be upset about the outcome because it wasn't part of God's plan." He told his son Mike, "God chooses his own time." Then he went to meet with Ford, who shared his short list with him, and Reagan spoke highly of Ford. Reagan emerged and told his son, "He didn't ask me." However, when Jim Baker was his White House chief of staff in 1982, Reagan told him that he would have taken the running mate spot if Ford had offered it. God might choose his own time, but Ronald

Reagan always had a taste for being called to a rescue. And it's always nice to be asked.

The Reagans walked into a gathering of some two hundred staffers and supporters, he in a dark blue suit, she in white knit—"the entrance of royalty," Elizabeth Drew thought. Most of his audience was crying. Billy Mounger said he'd never cried so hard in his life. Even Nancy was crying (embarrassed, she turned her back to the cameras). Reagan opened, as usual, with a joke: "Backstage politics is like looking at civilization with its pants down." He acknowledged their tears: "Sure, there's disappointment in what happened, but the cause—the cause goes on."

Reagan, too, was fighting back tears.

"It's just one battle in a long war, and it will go on as long as we all wage it. . . . The cause is still there." He quoted his favorite English ballad, from Dryden: "Though I am wounded, I am not slain; I shall rise and fight again." He promised he and Nancy "are not just going to go back and sit in a rocking chair and say, 'That's all for us'"—and neither should you: "Don't give up on your ideals. Don't get cynical. Look at yourself and realize all you were willing to do, and realize there are millions of Americans out there who feel as you do—who want it to be the shining city on the hill."

To his right, past the American flag, tears rolled down the cheek of a young man wearing a checked shirt. Reagan's voice caught, and he turned away, blinking back tears; his speech was finished. He had mentioned neither Gerald Ford, the upcoming fall campaign, nor the need for Republican unity.

A GIANT PAINTING OF GERALD FORD HUNG FROM THE CEILING FOR THE last session. A reporter thought it "depicted Ford's smile as a primate's sneer." The roll call of the states yielded 1,921 votes for Bob Dole and 338 for others, including Reagan, William F. Buckley, John Sears, William Simon, Reagan's young conservative staffer David Keene—and forty-one for Jesse Helms, whose name was officially placed in nomination by Bob Bauman. The move recalled a signal moment in conservative history. Barry Goldwater's name had been placed in nomination in 1960, allowing the Arizonan to give a speech refusing the honor, making a call to arms, and offering a promissory note—"Let's grow up, conservatives. If we want to take this party back, and I think we can someday, let's get back to work"—that was redeemed four years later in 1964. Bauman cited it: "Barry Goldwater stood at the rostrum in Chicago, and I, as a young member of the staff from the Maryland delegation, heard him tell me, 'Grow up conservative.'" Bauman continued, "We have grown up. The fight here was between two groups of conservatives. And the conservatives will win this year in November."

This wasn't a bad argument, given the convention just past, which had ratified a pro-life, anti-détente, pro-gun, antibusing, pro-school-prayer platform, and had created the conditions that made nominating a liberal vice presidential candidate politically impossible. And now it was a convention in which Senator Jesse Helms had a prime-time televised speaking spot, and he was milking it for all it was worth:

> What we do here . . . can be the prelude to a sort of spiritual rebirth across this land. The American people believe in God, and now is the time for us to show it.
>
> The American people are worried about the forces in our society that seem to be tearing down the moral fabric of our nation, particularly as it is centered around the family, and they see government as threatening the moral order, and they are concerned about the secularization of education as though God didn't matter in the classroom. They are worried about the textbooks and the federal government's manipulation of the curriculum.
>
> In other words, our platform, the one we adopted here this week, speaks to the concerns of the American people. . . . It is our covenant, it is our pledge, and we must live up to it."

The New Right had arrived. This wasn't Gerald Ford's show.

Cary Grant gave a tribute to Betty ("What is a party without remarkable women?"), who got the kind of ovation her husband never could. ("Thank you. And, Mr. Grant, I accept your nomination. After all, what woman could turn down Mr. Cary Grant?") A film showed the president looking presidential. (One shot had his back to the camera just like a famous image of JFK.) Ronald and Nancy Reagan stepped up to their skybox to hear Ford's acceptance speech and to receive one more uncontrollable demonstration. It had been a matter of resentment for the Reagan family that they were stuck behind glass, way up in the rafters, afraid it would make them look regal. Leave it to Dutch to figure out a way to make it a stage. He stood on his seat, so that his shoulders were above the top of the partition, and waved down to the crowd from up there. Elizabeth Drew recorded that the sound once more "[f]eeds on itself and grows, and then, after a while, the band plays 'God Bless America' and Ronald Reagan . . . and his wife stand and join the audience in singing the song that is intended to silence the cheers for him." Edwin Newman on NBC said that "were it not for Irving Berlin, this convention might go on forever." John Chancellor said, "This is not a late-night movie, it only seems like one. The plot involves an accidental President who fought for his life in a very hard campaign against a former movie actor. The President is a kind of plodder."

For the plodder's acceptance speech, made in an old-fashioned banker's three-piece suit, the podium was switched out for one bearing the presidential seal:

"I am honored by your nomination, and I accept it with pride, with gratitude, and with a total will to win a great victory for the American people. We concede not a single state. . . . We concede not a single vote. . . . America is at peace. . . . This nation is sound; this nation is secure; this nation is on the march to full economic recovery and a better quality of life for *all* Americans."

He challenged Jimmy Carter to debate—this was newsworthy; there hadn't been a presidential debate since the first one, between Nixon and Kennedy in 1960—and the crowd cheered him: "We want Ford! We want Ford!"

He said, "After the scrimmages of the past few months, it really feels good to have Ron Reagan on the same side of the line." (Reagan waved, then clasped both hands above his head.)

Ford turned to the subject of August 9, 1974, when "I placed my hand on the Bible, which Betty held, and took the same constitutional oath that was administered to George Washington. I had faith in our people, our institutions, and in myself. 'My fellow Americans,' I said, 'our long national nightmare is over.' It was an hour in our history that troubled our minds and tore at our hearts. Anger and hatred had risen to dangerous levels, dividing friends and families. The polarization of our political order had aroused unworthy passions of reprisal and revenge. Our governmental system was closer to stalemate than at any time since Abraham Lincoln took the same oath of office. Our economy was in the throes of runaway inflation, taking us headlong into the worst recession since Franklin D. Roosevelt took the same oath."

He spoke, then, of a marble fireplace in the White House carved with a prayer written by John Adams. "It concludes, 'May none but honest and wise men rule under this roof.' Since I have resided in that historic house, I have tried to live by that prayer."

The president was able to boast of genuine recovery: inflation cut in half, payrolls and profits and production and purchases up. "This year more men and women have jobs than ever before in the history of the United States." He boasted, that, after "a decade of Congresses had shortchanged our global defenses"—Democratic Congresses, he need not say—"and threatened our strategic posture . . . [t]he whole world watched and wondered where America was going. Did we in our domestic turmoil have the will, the stamina, and the unity to stand up for freedom?"

Take that, Ronald Reagan: America did. "Look at the record since August, two years ago. Today America is at peace and seeks peace for all nations. . . . The world now respects America's policy of peace through strength. The United States is again the confident leader of the free world."

Yes: "Two years ago people's confidence in their highest officials, to whom they had overwhelmingly entrusted power, had twice been shattered. Losing faith in the word of their elected leaders, Americans lost some of their own faith in themselves." And this: "From the start my administration has been open, candid, forthright." Even this Republican audience wasn't buying that, however; it got the least noise of any of his applause lines. They liked this: "Whether in the nation's capital or the state capital or city hall, private morality and public trust must go together." And they liked this implicit dig at his Democratic opponent, he of the jack-o'-lantern grin—"My record is one of specifics, not smiles"—even more.

Ford said, nodding at détente, "We will build a safer and saner world through patient negotiations and dependable arms agreements which reduce the danger of conflict and horror of thermonuclear war. While I am President, we will not return to a collision course that could reduce civilization to ashes."

He concluded: "I have no fear for the future of this great country." And he invoked the words of Lincoln: "As we go forward together, I promise you once more what I promised before: to uphold the Constitution, to do what is right as God gives me to see the right, and to do the very best I can for America. God help me, I won't let you down."

And the reviews said it was just about the best speech he'd ever given.

Jerry and Betty, arm in arm, acknowledged the cheers. Rockefeller and Robert and Elizabeth Dole, too, though more awkwardly. The band boomed "Marching Along Together."

Then Ford surprised the gathering.

By one account, Reagan was busy signing autographs in the mezzanine when an aide told him that Ford was beckoning him to the rostrum. The fact that few saw it coming was vouchsafed by the fact that Michael and Maureen Reagan had already left Kemper Arena and returned to the Alameda Plaza Hotel for another planned family dinner; Lyn Nofziger

hadn't bothered to go to the arena that night at all. Gerald Ford looked skyward, waved his arm in an ingathering gesture, and asked for "my good friend, Ron Reagan, to come down and bring Nancy." (A wire reporter called that "a friendship that was one day old." Reagan had told the *New York Times* in an interview that morning that Ford had won only because of manipulation in "the machine states," blamed "party bossism," and said, "There's no place in America for some of the things we saw happen to us.")

Reagan responded with an embarrassed grin. He pursed his lips, stood, and blew a little kiss as Nancy raised her left hand in acknowledgment. He smiled shyly, reluctance written in every gesture. The "We want Reagan!" chants were, if possible, louder than any that had come before. Again and again, he lowered his palms as a signal for his adorers to sit down, or raised a finger to his lips in a *Shhhh,* but the chant became "Speech! Speech!" Michael Reagan said the din "seemed to last an hour. The pianist must have played 'California, Here I Come' a dozen times." ABC's Frank Reynolds, who'd grown close to the Reagans covering the campaign, was in tears.

Next, one of the party's most universally respected old men, Bryce Harlow, a White House hand going back to Eisenhower, took the podium from Ford to beg for Reagan's presence. Clearly now there was no way he could refuse. Nancy Reagan recollected for a documentary camera that Reagan's words to her when he finally made his way out of the box were "I haven't the foggiest idea of what I'm going to say!" Which is to say, it was a surprise to everyone, an improvisation, this spectacle of Ford granting Reagan this opportunity to speak. Elizabeth Drew reported in authoritative tones: "The President's aides were reluctant to have him do so, in order to make sure that Reagan did not cause the President to suffer by contrast." And as Mr. and Mrs. Reagan finally completed the long odyssey from skybox to stage, the cheers indeed seemed so much louder than the ones that had come before for Ford.

Reagan took his place behind the speaker's stand with the presidential seal affixed; now his face was all radiance, the president behind him, Betty in yellow to his left, and Nancy in a white sweater-dress trimmed in black, gazing adoringly up at him.

And after the polite pleasantries ("Ladies and gentlemen—I am going to say 'fellow Republicans' here, but those of you who are watching from a distance, all of those millions of Democrats and independents who I know are looking for a cause around which to rally and which I believe we can give them . . ."), he bragged about the party platform: "There are cynics who say that a party platform is something that no one bothers to read and it doesn't often amount to much. Whether it is different this time than it has ever been before, I believe the Republican Party has a platform that is a banner of bold, unmistakable colors with no pastel shades."

It echoed something he'd said in early 1975 at the Conservative Political Action Conference, the one that had rung with calls for a third party with Reagan at its head—*"Is it a third party we need, or is it a new and revitalized second party, raising a banner of no pale pastels, but bold colors which could make it unmistakably clear where we stand on all the issues troubling the people?"* That got a massive ovation. And since that no-pale-pastels platform was more his, some said, than Ford's, it sounded like some kind of declaration of victory—a declaration that it was *he,* and his minions, who had delivered the nation this newly revitalized Republican Party.

He said it revealed "to the American people the difference between this platform and the platform of the opposing party, which is nothing but a revamp, and a reissue, and a running of a late, late show of the thing that we've been hearing from them for the last forty years." And his audience once more exploded.

Then he launched into a story. It was lovely—amazing, really. Even more amazing given all the evidence that he was apparently spinning this all out on the fly:

I had an assignment the other day. Someone asked me to write a letter for a time capsule that is going to be opened in Los Angeles a hundred years from now, on our Tricentennial.

It sounded like an easy assignment. They suggested I write something about the problems and issues of the day. And I said I could do so. Riding down the coast in an automobile, looking at the blue Pacific on one side and the Santa Ynez Mountains on the other, and I couldn't help but wonder if it was going to be that beautiful a hundred years from now as it was on that summer day.

Then, as I tried to write—let your own minds turn to that task: you're going to write for people a hundred years from now who know all about us, we know nothing about them; we don't know what kind of a world they'll be living in.

And suddenly I thought to myself as I wrote of the problems: they'll be the domestic problems of which the President spoke here tonight; the challenges confronting us—the erosion of freedom that has taken place under Democrat rule in this country; the invasion of private rights; the controls and restrictions on the vitality of the great free economy that we enjoy. These are our challenges that we must meet.

And then again there is that challenge of which he spoke, that we live in a world in which the great powers have poised and aimed at each other horrible missiles of destruction—

One of the network broadcasts cut to a shot from the floor, and a man with his mouth hanging a little bit open, as if in religious awe. The gathering at long last was all silent—a *congregation*, like Madison Square Garden when Daddy King preached.

—nuclear weapons that can in a matter of minutes arrive in each other's country and destroy, virtually, the civilized world we live in. And suddenly it dawned on me—

(A woman clasping her hands, as if in prayer. A young blond woman, arms folded, looking soulfully down to the ground, another looking up, as if scanning the sky.)

—those who would read this letter a hundred years from now will know whether those missiles were fired. They will know whether we met our challenge.

His words took on a cadence like the Gettysburg Address (*"The world will little note, nor long remember what we say here. . . ."*):

Whether they had the freedom that we have known up until now will depend on what we do here.

Will they look back with appreciation and say, thank God for those people in 1976 who headed off that loss of freedom, who kept us now a hundred years later free, who kept our world from nuclear destruction? And if we fail, they probably won't get to read the letter at all because it spoke of individual freedom and they won't be allowed to talk of that or read it.

(A line of delegates holding hands, gauzy-eyed, like people in church.)

This is our challenge. And this is why we are here in this hall tonight. Better than we've ever done before, we've got to quit talking to each other and about each other and go out and communicate to the world that we may be fewer in numbers than we've ever been, but we carry the message they've been waiting for.

We must go forth from here united, determined that what a great general said a few years ago was true: there is no substitute for victory.

Then began an enormous ovation. "Mr. President," he started saying—then stopped. Some thought he was about to address nice things directly to Mr. President; others that he was about to make clear that "there is no substitute for victory" had been intended, aggressively, *toward* Mr. President. In any event he knew to leave well enough alone. Delegates were standing on their chairs, waving Reagan placards, openly weeping. Nobody noticed anyone weeping when Gerald Ford spoke.

The two men faced each other, clasped hands—you could just overhear Ford saying, "Great job"—then they faced the audience, arms raised together. Reagan worked the line of dignitaries behind him—Nelson Rockefeller reached for Reagan's hand and said a single word: "Beautiful"—as the band struck up a brassy "The Victors," as if this were Gerald Ford's moment, which it most decidedly was not. A camera cut to two women holding a yellow hand-lettered sign—maybe hand-lettered during the speech: MR PRESIDENT USA NEEDS REAGAN SEC OF STATE. And of fists pumping enthusiastically beneath blue FORD AND DOLE signs, the official ones provided for delegates beneath their chairs. Another improvised banner: THANKS GOV & NANCY REAGAN. Reporters scrawling: Elizabeth Drew wrote that Reagan spoke "more effectively than I ever before heard him speak." She spoke for the consensus of reporters—awed at how Reagan could pull together such inspiring remarks on the fly.

Posterity, for the most part, chose to record just how spontaneous those remarks were. A historian who published a book on Reagan's 1976 campaign and gave an entire chapter to the time-capsule speech, for instance, recorded that "Reagan was utterly content to watch the proceedings with Nancy, sign a few autographs, and savor the rousing reception he had received earlier. . . . [A] very intoxicated RNC aide had come to Reagan's skybox and asked Mike Deaver to please ask Reagan once again to reconsider the invitation to speak to the convention. But the aide was summarily dismissed." Then Reagan changed his mind at the last minute, and decided to speak.

It made for a very good story.

• • •

VIC GOLD, THE POLITICAL PUBLIC RELATIONS EXPERT, A SARDONIC DE-bunker, the guy who knew all the backstage magicians and lived to expose their bags of tricks, wrote in a book he published the next year, *PR as in President,* about the meeting that took place between Reagan and Ford the Monday evening of the convention, where the governor accepted the president's invitation to speak to the convention that Thursday night. Which is to say the speech was never spontaneous at all. "Carruthers' problem"—Bill Carruthers, the Ford campaign's stage-management wizard—"was where to fit the Reagan speech into his closing night ceremonies."

Gold noted:

> Carruthers and the other members of the President's PR team envied the dramatic success that Bob Strauss and Jimmy Carter achieved following Carter's acceptance speech at Madison Square Garden. The Democrats had first brought all elements of their party to the platform in an audiovisual smorgasbord of milling unity. Then followed "Daddy" King's moving benediction, to bring the convention to a final ovation. Contrary to traditional PR wisdom which dictates, *Never risk topping your candidate*, King's prayer-speech enhanced rather than detracted from Carter's acceptance. Carruthers wanted a similar all-factions smorgasbord for his closing night platform, with network cameras focused on a Republican Party unified behind Jerry Ford. Carruthers' solution was a stroke in unorthodox convention scheduling. He decided to cast Reagan as the "Daddy" King of the Republican convention.

Gold also noted a nerve-racking glitch, one that spoke to how stealthily the plan went down: John Rhodes, not in on the secret, called for Reagan to come to the podium *before* Ford's speech, during the demonstration that erupted at his entrance. Reagan stalled, telling an interviewer, "This isn't my night. It's the President's night," and managed to refuse. (Vic Gold: "Thank God, Carruthers is thinking, that at least we've got a losing candidate who knows how to follow a script.")

Ronald Reagan's gift: If a camera was present, he was aware of it—aware, always, of the gaze of others, reflecting it, adjusting himself to it, inviting it. Modeling himself, in his mind's eye, according to how he presented himself physically to others. Adjusting himself to be seen as he wished others to see him. Simultaneously maintaining an image as a VIP and an ordinary guy, always making others feel good in his presence—his most exquisitely cultivated skill. His wife, too: with iron political discipline, she preserved the secret forevermore. No one noticed Gold's book; or if they did, they didn't care. Teflon.

Once, in 1966, when Reagan was running for the Republican gubernatorial nomination, his opponent, George Christopher, the highly favored candidate of the party establishment, thought he'd devised a clinching campaign strategy. Reagan was harvesting voters by the bushelful going up and down the state decrying the student strikes to change the rules at Berkeley. But what about Reagan's rank hypocrisy? So Christopher related Reagan's days as "a student at Eureka College, Illinois . . . leading a student uprising against the rules of his own college." And what of Reagan the stout anti-Communist? Pressed Christopher, "Did he jointly sponsor protest on U.S. atomic policies with the chairman of the Communist Party in Los Angeles"—indeed he had— "and how long did this association last?"

A fat lot of good that did. Reagan flicked the charges away by huffing about how his candidate was breaking the California Republican Party's unofficial "Eleventh Commandment," *Thou shalt not speak ill of another Republican*—which had been of course been promulgated by a party chairman who was secretly on the payroll of Reagan's campaign.

People want to believe. Ronald Reagan was able to make people believe.

Though not enough, apparently. Theatrics might have gotten him this far. But this was the end of the road: he could not travel any further. There were still certain political facts of life no amount of political hocus-pocus could obscure. "At sixty-five years of age," the *New York Times* noted, he was "too old to consider seriously another run at the Presidency."

Acknowledgments

AMERICA HAS EXPERIENCED QUITE THE WILD RIDE SINCE MY AGENT AND I completed the agreement to write this book, in the week after Lehman Brothers declared bankruptcy, and America began its most dramatic economic collapse since the Great Depression. Its author has experienced a quite a ride, too. A profound period of personal transition and growth accompanied the gestation of this volume. So first off, I want to thank the extraordinary friends who stood by my side, inspiriting me, teaching me, listening to me, succoring me. They include, in no particular order (I swear), Allison Xantha Miller; Jared Sagoff; Karl Fogel (whose expert editorial ministrations defrenzified the manuscript by a welcome 11.83 percent); Elizabeth Prince (who graciously worked through her contempt for the book's protagonist to take on editorial tasks); Barrie Cole; Margarita, Simon, Eryk, and Maia Cygielska; Jade Netanya; Steven, Renée, and Iris Klein; Jennifer Timmons; Jason Vest; Leon Pasker, Harry Osoff; Karen Underhill, Elijah Underhill-Miller, and Rick Meller; Lucy Knight; Ethan Porter; the late Aaron Swartz; Laura Schaeffer; Tom Geoghegan; Lew and Joanne Koch; Victor, Isabella, and Victoria Harbison; Micah Uetricht; Neil Landers; Aaron Lav and Heather Blair; and J. Robert Parks. And I thank Roberta Walker for bringing yet more meaning to my life, and reminding me of the infinite gifts of literacy. I thank Kath Duffy and Lisa Meyerson for their support and for their critical readings of parts of the manuscript, too.

I'd be nowhere without the writers and scholars upon which my work is all but parasitic. The research and analysis of Michael Allen, H. Bruce Franklin, Mary Hershberger, and especially Craig Howe undergird my account of Operation Homecoming, which serves as this opera's overture. Jeanine Basinger and Thomas Schatz taught me what I needed to know to place Ronald Reagan in his Hollywood context. Kathleen Geier helped with that and much more besides. Thomas W. Evans and Timothy Raphael gave me Reagan at GE, and Mark Inabinett taught me about the Golden Age of Sports.

Speaking of early Reagan biography, Anne Edwards's is the best—
and her public-spiritedness in depositing her research materials at the
UCLA Library made my own hack at the subject much, much richer.
The shared obsession of the late Paul Cowan and the late Tony Lukas—
dedicatees of my last book—with the warfare of America's tribes on the
left and right once more informed my project's foundation. It was built
out thanks to the crucial contributions of Ronald P. Formisano (on the
Boston busing crisis), William Graebner (on Patty Hearst), Kathryn
Olmsted (on the Church and Pike committee investigations), and Carol
Mason (on the Kanawha County textbook war). I was fortunate to meet
Monica Schneider and get hold of her Oberlin University bachelor's
thesis, because it forms the core of the book's insights on the Bicentennial celebration; ditto for Sam Black's bachelor's thesis of the New
York City fiscal crisis. (Kids today!) Elizabeth Drew's careful real-time
chronicle of the political events of 1976 saved me 4.38 months of labor.
Craig Shirley's book on Reagan's 1976 campaign saved me 3.76 months;
and once more I couldn't have completed the marathon without the
benefit of Jules Witcover's contemporary reporting.

That's the first string—those without whom the project's core con-
ceptions would not exist. Others on whom I relied include Howard
Bryant, the late Clifford Doerksen, John Dean, Jefferson Cowie, Flo
Conway and Jim Siegelman, Robert M. Collins, Adam Clymer, Rob-
ert A. Hargrove, Yanek Mieczkhowski, Joshua B. Freeman, David
Frum, Vic Gold, David Greenberg, John Gorenfeld, Ernest B. Fer-
guson, Philip Jenkins, Andreas Killen, Stanley Kutler, Laura Kalman,
J. Hoberman, Nina Silber, John B. Judis, David Farber, Christopher
Capozzola, Kim Phillips-Fein, Karen R. Merrill, Tanya Melich, Allen
J. Matusow, Louis P. Masur, William Martin, Jane Mansbridge, Edward
D. Berkowitz, Peter Carroll, James Mann, Geoffrey Kabaservice, Bob
Colacello, Natasha Zaretsky, Lou Cannon, Jesse Walker, Ron Reagan,
Tom Edsall, Marc Eliot, Seth Rosenfeld, Richard Reeves, Jonathan
Schell, Julian E. Zelizer, William Shawcross, Whitney Strub, Karen
Staller, Judith Stein, Connie Bruck, Dennis McDougal, the late Tom
Wicker, Norman E. Wymbs, Alicia C. Shepard, and Bill Boyarsky—and
Martin Anderson, Kiron K. Skinner, and Annelise Anderson, valuable
archivist of the public record. Thanks, also, to William Staudenmeier
and Junius Rodriguez of Eureka College for their guidance both at, and
about, Reagan's alma mater.

I am a political animal, and once more Heather "Digby" Parton and
her blog Hullabaloo fed my heroin-like habit of tacking between past
and present in order to make sense of our strange United States. Thanks,

too, to her partners in crime-fighting, Howie Klein, John Amato, and David Neiwert; and also Josh Marshall's crew at Talking Points Memo; and Corey Robin and Ta-Nahesi Coates, the two writers I read online whenever I crave inspiration. And my lively and cherished community of Facebook friends came to the crowdsourcing rescue when I needed, say, stories about what it was like to watch the Watergate hearings on TV, or see *The Exorcist* for the first time.

I thank Matthew Sawh for his research assistance. And, wow, that Doug Grant. Somewhere along the way some college kid started sending me nagging email: *Mr. Perlstein, can I be your research assistant?* "No money for that sort of thing," said I. *No, I'm not looking for a job, I just love history, and I want to help you out.* That went on, and on, for months. Finally I had the good fortune to assent to his insistent entreaties. How much better did that decision end up making this book? By 15.03 percent. I suspect that Doug, astonishingly, knows more 1970s political history than I do. I became used to his drumbeat of questions— like "Do you have all the chaos in Kansas City at the 76 GOP convention? where Rockefeller broke in half a Reagan delegate's sign?" I didn't. Thanks to Doug, though, I do now, and so do you (pages 784–85)—not to mention dozens of other amazing details that he seemed to turn up almost weekly. Thank you, Doug.

Moshe Marvit, David Glenn, Howard Park, and Ryan Hayes all generously and thoughtfully passed on items from their personal collections—DVDs of Ronald Reagan on *General Electric Theater*, rare and ancient books, kitschy detritus from political campaigns past—that helped add texture to my research. David's gift of Richard Vander Veen's self-published memoir was especially useful.

I praise, collectively, my community in Hyde Park, Chicago, especially its political activists; and the proprietors who kindly provided me office space with the daily rental of a single cup of joe, first at the late, lamented Third World Cafe on Fifty-third and Kimbark, then at Cafe 53 on Fifty-third and Kenwood (I'll give some praise to my friends at Dolce Casa in Ravenswood, too); and the Seminary Co-op bookstore for sponsoring my monthly interview series with Chicago authors and activists and for helping launch this project into the marketplace; and the gang at Freehling Pots and Pans; and, for their wise counsel and love, my friends Jane Averill and Tom Panelas, Liz Goldwyn, Teresa Kilbane, Joe and Betty Check, Larry Boyle, and especially Vicky Stein.

I thank the scholars who invited me to their campuses and arranged the honoraria that helped me sustain the project; I thank *Rolling Stone* for providing a home for my journalism in 2012; and I especially thank the *Nation*, and Richard Kim and Katrina vanden Heuvel, for giving me such freedom and support all through 2013 and beyond to do journalism and tell people what I thought they should think about history. I thank Kath Duffy for her helpful manuscript comments as well. I thank my wise, kind, savvy agent, Tina Bennett (and her able assistant Svetlana Katz), and I thank Jonathan Karp for the extraordinary grant of trust he gifted me with at the beginning and end of this process. I'm grateful, too, for his team at Simon & Schuster, including Cary Goldstein, Larry Hughes, and Nicholas Greene.

I thank Judy Cohn, because I love her, and she loves me.

I thank my family: mom Sandi, brother Ben, sister Linda, and brother Steve. (Steve, I should probably return those 1970s *Doonesbury* books I stole from you in the middle of the 1980s. Forgive me, but I couldn't have found my vocation without them.) We lost my father, Jerry Perlstein, in September 2013. This book is dedicated to him.

A Note on Sources

THE PLEASURE OF WRITING AND READING RECENT HISTORY HAS DEEP-
ened these last several years, now that we all carry computers in our
pockets and pocketbooks and on our laps that allow us to sate our
skepticism about whether a claim is true or a source really said what
an author said it said or even to watch an event or listen to the events
that exist on the page only as a word picture—be it Evel Knievel trying
and failing to rocket over the Snake River Canyon or Gerald Ford, that
very same day, proclaiming a "full, free, and absolute pardon unto Richard Nixon for all offenses against the United States which he, Richard
Nixon, has committed, or may have committed or taken part in." The
Internet has, paradoxically, made source documentation simultaneously
less and more useful: less useful, in that the customary dozens of pages
of source notes that burden the end pages of a book like this become
mostly superfluous—and make the book more expensive to produce
and purchase; and more useful in that the chance to actually *follow up*
on those sources, either to check them or to delve deeper into the subject, no longer requires arduous trips to libraries or archives. Oh, and
there's this: they no longer require the historian to make nearly so many
such trips, either. When I wanted to know about the telegrams of protest
that piled up backstage at the Oscar ceremony in 1975 after the producer of a scouring anti–Vietnam War documentary paid tribute to the
North Vietnamese, it took but a few moments of googling to stumble
upon the page on the Library of Congress website that reproduced
them—hip-pocket history, a net gain for the republic of letters if there
ever was one.

That is why my publishers and I have decided to put the source
notes for the book online, with clickable URLs whenever possible. Perhaps 80 percent of the newspaper articles quoted herein were found, and
remain findable, via Google's project of scanning dozens of newspapers
and making them fully searchable and browsable—try it yourself: go to
http://news.google.com/newspapers and type in, say, "Children in one

school joked about shooting a few"; and while you're there, hell, type in the name of your grandfather the opera singer and see what kind of reviews he got for his 1947 debut in *La Traviata*. Those with access to a university library with Proquest Historical Newspapers can delve even deeper, into papers like the *New York Times* and the *Washington Post*.

And though Google's book search isn't as useful when it comes to reading books (Google likes to drop out one of every ten pages or so for copyright purposes), it's a great way to confirm citations, so you can do that here, too. Same for several archives; Gerald Ford's presidential library, for instance, has an excellent collection of source documents. There are limits, however: to reconstruct the story of the return of the Vietnam War POWs and to document Ronald Reagan's relative absence from the national political discussion in 1973–74, I spent a dazzling week at the Vanderbilt Television News Archive, where I'd spend half my life if I could. It's the closest thing we mortals will ever get to being inside a time machine: every single second of every single network newscast is fully accessible on a computer screen within seconds, just like it was YouTube. And although the catalogue is available and searchable online, the actual videos are not, because the networks consider them intellectual property, not what they actually are: part of our nation's historical patrimony. So I link to the archive's record of the relevant newscasts, though to actually watch them requires a trip to Nashville, which I heartily recommend.

Find and explore my source notes at rickperlstein.net.

Index

About Rick Perlstein

Rick Perlstein is the author of *Nixonland: The Rise of a President and the Fracturing of America*, a *New York Times* bestseller picked as one of the best nonfiction books of the year by more than a dozen publications, and *Before the Storm: Barry Goldwater and the Unmaking of the American Consensus*, which won the 2001 *Los Angeles Times* Book Award for history and appeared on the best books of the year lists of the *New York Times*, the *Washington Post*, and *Chicago Tribune*. His essays and book reviews have been published in the *New York Times*, the *Washington Post*, the *Nation*, the *Village Voice*, and the *New Republic*, among others. He has received a National Endowment for the Humanities grant for independent scholars. He lives in Chicago.

Photo Credits

1. CORBIS
2. CORBIS
3. CORBIS
4. Courtesy of Ronald Reagan Presidential Library and Museum
5. Courtesy of Ronald Reagan Presidential Library and Museum
6. Courtesy of Ronald Reagan Presidential Library and Museum
7. Courtesy of Ronald Reagan Presidential Library and Museum
8. CORBIS
9. CORBIS
10. United Feature Syndicate
11. Used with permission of the Conrad Estate
12. Author's collection
13. CORBIS
14. CORBIS
15. CORBIS
16. CORBIS
17. Getty
18. Published by Grosset & Dunlop, now an imprint of Penguin Group (USA)
19. CORBIS
20. CORBIS
21. CORBIS
22. CORBIS
23. Courtesy of *Newsweek*
24. CORBIS
25. CORBIS
26. Getty
27. Getty
28. Published by Berkley Books, an imprint of Penguin Group (USA)
29. CORBIS
30. CORBIS
31. Associated Press
32. Courtesy of the *Los Angeles Times*
33. Award Books

34. Time/Life Star Vista
35. Courtesy of Ronald Reagan Presidential Library and Museum
36. CORBIS
37. National Citizens Committee for Fairness to the Presidency
38. CORBIS
39. Getty
40. Author's collection
41. Getty
42. Getty
43. Courtesy of *Newsweek*
44. Courtesy of Paramount Pictures
45. Courtesy of Charleston Newspapers
46. Getty
47. Licensed by: Warner Bros. Entertainment Inc. All Rights Reserved.
48. CORBIS
49. *Photoplay*
50. Courtesy of Ronald Reagan Presidential Library and Museum
51. Courtesy of Ronald Reagan Presidential Library and Museum and Las Vegas News Bureau
52. Courtesy of Ronald Reagan Presidential Library and Museum
53. Courtesy of Ronald Reagan Presidential Library and Museum
54. *Fortune* magazine
55. Courtesy of Ronald Reagan Presidential Library and Museum
56. Courtesy of Conelrad.com
57. CORBIS
58. CORBIS
59. CORBIS
60. CORBIS
61. Getty
62. Courtesy of *Newsweek*
63. CORBIS
64. Associated Press
65. CORBIS
66. Associated Press
67. Getty
68. CORBIS
69. Getty
70. Getty
71. CORBIS
72. CORBIS
73. CORBIS
74. CORBIS
75. CORBIS
76. CORBIS
77. Getty